BUSINESS LAW

ELEVENTH EDITION

Henry R. Cheeseman
Professor Emeritus
Marshall School of Business
University of Southern California

Pearson

Please contact https://support.pearson.com/getsupport/s/ with any queries on this content

Cover Image by Chinaface/E+/Getty Images

Library of Congress Cataloging-in-Publication Data
Names: Cheeseman, Henry R, author.
Title: Business law / Henry R. Cheeseman, Professor Emeritus, Marshall School of Business, University of Southern California.
Description: Eleventh edition. | New York, NY : Pearson, [2022] | Includes bibliographical references and index. |
Summary: "Business law is an evolving outgrowth of its environment, and the legal environment keeps changing. This new edition of Business Law emphasizes coverage of online law, e-commerce, and information technology as key parts of the legal environment. In addition, this book covers social, ethical, and global issues that are important to the study of business law"— Provided by publisher.
Identifiers: LCCN 2020039917 (print) | LCCN 2020039918 (ebook) | ISBN 9780136828075 (hardcover) | ISBN 0136828078 |
ISBN 9780136994619 (ebook)
Subjects: LCSH: Commercial law—United States. | Business enterprises—Law and legislation—United States. | LCGFT: Casebooks (Law)
Classification: LCC KF889 .C433 2022 (print) | LCC KF889 (ebook) | DDC 346.7307—dc23
LC record available at https://lccn.loc.gov/2020039917
LC ebook record available at https://lccn.loc.gov/2020039918

1 2020

Pearson

ISBN-10: 0-13-682807-8
ISBN-13: 978-0-13-682807-5

To my wife, Jin,
and our twins,
Ziva and Xavier

BRIEF CONTENTS

CONTENTS

PREFACE

New to the Eleventh Edition

This eleventh edition of *Business Law* is a significant revision of Professor Cheeseman's business law and legal environment text that includes many new cases and features, as well as new text and examples.

New U.S. Supreme Court Cases

More than 10 new U.S. Supreme Court cases, including:

- Chapter 2: *Bristol-Myers Squibb Company v. Superior Court of California* (Under the Due Process Clause, California lacked personal jurisdiction over nonresident plaintiffs.)
- Chapter 3: *Ernst & Young LLC v. Morris* (The U.S. Supreme Court held that an arbitration agreement that provided for individualized one-on-one arbitration, and with a collective class, was enforceable.)
- Chapter 4: *Tennessee Wine and Spirits Retailers Association v. Thomas* (A state law that required a two-year state residency to obtain a retail liquor store license unduly burdened interstate commerce in violation of the Commerce Clause.)
- Chapter 4: *Iancu v. Brunetti* (A federal law that prohibits the registration of trademarks that consist of or comprise "immoral or scandalous matter" violates the Free Speech Clause of the First Amendment to the U.S. Constitution.)
- Chapter 7: *WesternGeco LLC v. ION Geophysical Corporation* (A company that engaged in patent infringement and sold the infringing technology was liable for lost profits suffered by the patent holder.)
- Chapter 8: *Collins v. Virginia* (The Fourth Amendment to the U.S. Constitution was violated when a police officer conducted a warrantless search of the curtilage of a house.)
- Chapter 32: *Janus v. American Federation of State, County, and Municipal Employees, Council 31* (Public-sector labor union agency-shop arrangements violate the First Amendment to the U.S. Constitution.)
- Chapter 33: *Bostock v. Clayton County, Georgia* (The U.S. Supreme Court held that Title VII

Information Technology

CASE 7.1 U.S. SUPREME COURT CASE Patent Infringement

WesternGeco LLC v. ION Geophysical Corporation

138 S.Ct. 2129 (2018)
Supreme Court of the United States

"The Patent Act gives patent owners a civil action for infringement."
—Clarence Thomas, Justice

Facts

Petitioner WesternGeco LLC owns four patents relating to a system that it developed for surveying the ocean floor. WesternGeco does not sell its technology or license it to competitors. Instead, it uses the technology itself, performing surveys for oil and gas companies. ION Geophysical Corporation, a U.S.-based company, used WesternGeco's public patent information and began manufacturing and selling competing systems to foreign companies, which in turn sold the systems in the U.S. in direct competition with WesternGeco. The foreign companies made millions of dollars in profits from such sales. WesternGeco sued ION for patent infringement. The jury found ION liable for patent infringement and ordered ION to pay $12.5 million in damages as a royalty payment to WesternGeco. The jury also assessed $93 million against ION for the profits lost by WesternGeco because of foreign company sales of ION's infringing technology. The U.S. court of appeals held that ION was not liable for the foreign company sales. WesternGeco appealed to the U.S. Supreme Court.

Issue

Can WesternGeco recover damages from ION for profits WesternGeco lost because of foreign company sales of ION's infringing technology?

CASE 33.1 U.S. SUPREME COURT CASE Homosexual and Transgender Discrimination

Bostock v. Clayton County, Georgia

140 S.Ct. 1731, 2020 U.S. Lexis 3252 (2020)
Supreme Court of the United States

"An individual's homosexuality or transgender status is not relevant to employment decisions."
—Neil Gorsuch, Justice

Facts

The U.S. Supreme Court consolidated three cases that started in the same way: an employer fired a long-time employee shortly after the employee revealed that he or she is homosexual or transgender—and allegedly for no reason other than the employee's homosexuality or transgender status. Each employee brought suit under Title VII alleging unlawful discrimination on the basis of sex. The three cases are:

Issue

Does Title VII prohibit employment discrimination against homosexual and transgender individuals?

Language of the U.S. Supreme Court

Today, we must decide whether an employer can fire someone simply for being homosexual or transgender. The answer is clear. An employer who fires an individual for being homosexual or transgender fires that person for traits or actions it would not have questioned in members of a different sex. Sex plays a necessary and undisguisable role in the decision, exactly what Title VII forbids.

of the Civil Rights Act of 1964 prohibits employment discrimination against homosexual and transgender individuals.)

- Chapter 46: *Ohio v. American Express Company* (Merchant fees charged by American Express to retailers who accept Amex credit cards are not an unreasonable restraint of trade.)

New State and Federal Court Cases

More than 30 new state and federal court cases, including:

- Chapter 3: *Casey v. McDonald's Corporation* (Summary judgment was granted to McDonald's when the restaurant was sued for damages by a patron who was injured by another patron during a fight at the restaurant.)

CASE 5.3 ***STATE COURT CASE Negligence***

Reckis v. Johnson & Johnson

28 N.E.3d 445, 471 Mass. 272 (2015)
Supreme Judicial Court of Massachusetts

"We cannot say that the jury's award is greatly disproportionate to Samantha's grave injuries."

—Margot Botsford, Justice

Facts

When seven-year-old Samantha Reckis had a fever and sinus congestion, her father, Richard, purchased a bottle of Children's Motrin, which is a brand of ibuprofen manufactured by a division of Johnson & Johnson. It is an anti-inflammatory drug used to the afternoon. That night Samantha had a fever and congestion, so Richard gave her a second dose of Children's Motrin.

The next morning Samantha woke with redness and a rash on her chest and neck, and a sore throat; she had the same fever and congestion as she had the night before. Richard gave her a third dose of Children's Motrin. Throughout the day, Samantha had a fever, nasal congestion, crusty eyes, cracked lips, and a rash. Samantha's mother, Lisa, gave Samantha a

- Chapter 5: *Reckis v. Johnson & Johnson* (Producer of Children's Motrin pain reliever was ordered to pay $50 million in damages to a child who suffered severe permanent injuries because the company negligently failed to warn of potential of life-threatening disease.)
- Chapter 5: *Stevens v. MTR Gaming Group, Inc.* (Casino and manufacturer of gaming machines is not liable for damages to a patron with a gambling addiction who lost substantial money at the casino.)
- Chapter 6: *Ford Motor Company v. Trejo* (Ford Motor Company is liable for product liability to the spouse of man killed in a rollover accident because an SUV's roof was defectively designed and did not withstand crushing during a rollover accident.)
- Chapter 7: *Disney Enterprises, Inc. v. VidAngel, Inc.* (Disney and other movie and film studios were granted an injunction that enjoined a third party from streaming edited versions of their copyrighted works.)
- Chapter 9: *McKee v. Isle of Capri Casinos, Inc.* (Due to an error in a casino slot machine, the screen showed that a gambler had won $41,797,550.16 when in fact she had won $1.85. The casino did not have to pay the greater amount because its digital contract, which the gambler had not read, stated "Malfunctions Void All Pays and Plays.")
- Chapter 12: *Langlois v. NOVA River Runners, Inc.* (A release of liability clause in a river-rafting contract signed by a husband was enforceable and prevented his spouse from recovering damages for his accidental death while river rafting.)
- Chapter 18: *Erie Insurance Company v. Amazon.com, Inc.* (Amazon.com is not a seller of the goods that it distributes for third-party sellers on its online website.)
- Chapter 21: *Sorchaga v. Ride Auto, LLC* (An "as is" warranty disclaimer is not enforceable where the seller has made fraudulent statements to induce a purchaser to buy a product.)

CASE 18.1 ***FEDERAL COURT CASE Seller***

Erie Insurance Company v. Amazon.com, Inc.

925 F.3d 135 (2019)
United States Court of Appeals for the Fourth Circuit

"When Amazon sells its own goods on its website, it has the responsibility of a seller, just as any other retailer would have."

—Paul Niemeyer, Circuit Judge

Facts

Trung Cao purchased online an LED headlamp used for cycling, camping, and hiking and gave it as a gift to his friends, Minh and Anh Nguyen. Both Cao and the Nguyens lived in Maryland. Cao purchased the headlamp on **Amazon.com**'s website, which stated that the headlamp was "sold by: Dream Light" and "fulfilled by: Amazon." Cao paid by credit card. Amathat Amazon was liable as a seller of the headlamp. Amazon argued that it was not the seller but that Dream Light was the seller. The U.S. district court held that Amazon was not the seller of the headlamp and therefore was not liable. Erie appealed.

Issue

Was Amazon the seller of the headlamp?

Language of the Court

The ordinary meaning of a seller is one that offers property for sale, with sale defined as the transfer of ownership of and title to property of

- Chapter 40: *Salazar v. McDonald's Corporation* (McDonald's, as the franchisor, was not a joint employer with a franchisee and was therefore not liable for the franchisee's violation of overtime pay and wage laws.)
- Chapter 51: *Yung v. Grant Thornton, LLP* (Accountants were found liable for committing fraud on a client, and the client was awarded $80 million in punitive damages.)
- Chapter 54: *Devengoechea v. Bolivarian Republic of Venezuela* (Commercial activity exception to sovereign immunity applied and permitted a lawsuit against a foreign government to proceed in U.S. district court.)

New Special Features on Ethics

More than 10 new special features covering ethics, including:

- Chapter 1: **Ethics:** *Apple Agrees to Pay $500 Million to Settle Consumer Fraud Lawsuit*
- Chapter 8: **Ethics:** *Billion-Dollar Ponzi Scheme Collapses*
- Chapter 30: **Ethics:** *Are U.S. Retailers Liable for Unsafe Working Conditions of Suppliers Located in Foreign Countries?*
- Chapter 39: **Ethics:** *Coca-Cola Shareholder Resolution on Sugar and Public Health*
- Chapter 42: **Ethics:** *France Fines Apple for Secretly Slowing Down Older iPhones*
- Chapter 44: **Ethics:** *Regulation of Tobacco Products and Electronic Nicotine Delivery Systems*
- Chapter 44: **Ethics:** *False Product Claims and Fake Reviews on Amazon*
- Chapter 46: **Ethics:** *Tech Companies Settle Lawsuit for Agreeing Not to Solicit Each Other's Employees*

Ethics

Apple Agrees to Pay $500 Million to Settle Consumer Fraud Lawsuit

It is impossible to discuss business and business law without also discussing business ethics. Many decisions made by businesses, managers, and employees have an ethical component. Their duty is not only to act legally but also to act ethically. Sometimes companies are caught acting unethically. Consider the following case involving Apple Inc.

Apple is the developer, designer, and distributor of many

Once Apple's actions were uncovered, dozens of class action lawsuits were filed against the company, alleging that Apple engaged in fraudulent conduct intended to sell more new iPhones. Apple denied any wrongdoing. The lawsuits were consolidated into one lawsuit heard by a U.S. district court located in California. Evidence was developed over a two-year period. Before the case went to trial, however, Apple agreed to a settlement.

New Features on Information Technology, Critical Legal Thinking, and Contemporary Environment

More than 10 new special features covering critical legal thinking, information technology, and contemporary environment, including:

- Chapter 3: **Information Technology**: *Facebook Settles Algorithmic Discrimination Lawsuits*
- Chapter 5: **Information Technology**: *Apple Not Liable for Accident Caused by Driver's Texting*
- Chapter 11: **Critical Legal Thinking:** *Doctrine of Promissory Estoppel Requires a Subcontractor to Honor Its Bid*
- Chapter 21: **Information Technology**: *Warranty Disclaimers in Social Media Software Licenses*

Information Technology

Facebook Settles Algorithmic Discrimination Lawsuits

The social media giant Facebook has a vast trove of personal and demographic data on its users that attracts companies to post advertisements on Facebook. Facebook's system and algorithms permit data mining that allows advertisers to micro-target any desired group of Facebook users. However, federal civil rights acts prohibit discrimination in employment, housing, and granting of credit based on race, ethnicity, sex, age, disabilities, and other protected classes.

against Facebook alleging that it engaged in discrimination in violation of federal antidiscrimination laws.

Facebook originally denied liability. However, after discovery of further evidence, Facebook reached an agreement to settle the civil rights lawsuits brought against it. Pursuant to the agreement, Facebook must create a separate portal for advertisements in the areas of employment, housing, and credit on Facebook, Instagram, and Messenger, and can no longer

- Chapter 44: **Contemporary Environment**: *Bioengineered Food Disclosure Law*
- Chapter 44: **Contemporary Environment**: *Nutrition Facts Label*

New and Revised Text

New text and material have been added throughout this book that discuss recent laws and modern issues, including:

- **United States–Mexico–Canada Agreement (USMCA)** A new regional trade agreement that reduces tariffs and regulatory restrictions on goods and services sold or transferred among the United States, Mexico, and Canada. The USMCA replaces the North American Free Trade Agreement (NAFTA)
- **Foreign Investment Risk Review Modernization Act (FIRRMA)** A new federal statute that prohibits the acquisition by foreign governments and agencies of critical U.S. technologies and infrastructure, personal private data, or sensitively located real estate, and prohibits U.S.-origin technology transfers.

> ### United States–Mexico–Canada Agreement (USMCA)
>
> **54.5 Describe the United States–Mexico–Canada Agreement (USMCA) and the relevant provisions of the treaty.**
>
> In 1994, the United States, Mexico, and Canada entered into the **North American Free Trade Agreement (NAFTA)**, a trade treaty between the three countries. Although often referred to as a "free trade" pact, NAFTA was primarily a managed trade agreement that eliminated some duties, tariffs, and barriers to trade, but also permitted duties, tariffs, and trade restrictions on protected goods and services.
>
> Beginning in 2018, at the instigation of the United States, the three countries entered into negotiations to replace NAFTA. In 2020, the three countries ratified the **United States–Mexico–Canada Agreement (USMCA)**, a new trade treaty between the member nations. The USMCA replaces NAFTA. The trade zone brings
>
> United States–Mexico–Canada Agreement (USMCA)

- **FDA Enforcement Policy onCartridge-Based lectronic Nicotine Delivery Systems (ENDS)** A Food and Drug Administration (FDA) policy that eliminates the sale of most flavored cartridge-based electronic nicotine delivery systems (ENDS) and regulates the marketing and sale of these products
- **Music Modernization Act (MMA)** A new federal statute that modernizes copyright law regarding digital streaming and downloading of music and provides a method for licensing music.
- **Clarifying Lawful Overseas Use of Data Act (CLOUD Act)** A new federal statute that establishes rules for how tech companies must respond to warrants issued by law enforcement agencies.
- **Telephone Robocall Abuse Criminal Enforcement and Deterrence Act (TRACED ACT)** A new federal statute that provides protections against illegal robocalls, spam calls and texts, and malicious caller ID spoofing.
- **Securities and Exchange Commission (SEC) Guidelines** New guidelines issued by the SEC that state that initial coin offerings (ICO) and security token offerings (STO) are subject to federal securities laws.
- **First Step Act** A new federal statute that reforms federal sentencing laws and promotes rehabilitation rather than just punishment of certain convicted criminals.

In addition, the text has been significantly revised in many areas, including electronic contracts, cybercrime, securities law, consumer protection, ethics, business organizations (partnerships, limited liability companies, and corporations), immigration law, and other subjects.

Bringing Business Law to Life

Students and graduates are guided and protected by law and legal principles every day of their lives. These laws and legal principles are based on common sense. They are not mysterious or hidden, or difficult to understand. In fact, they are very straightforward. The results reached by the application of legal principles are quite predictable and understandable.

You are the benefactors of centuries of laws developed to meet the needs of society and business. Just think of the rights you have: freedom to enter into contracts; freedom of speech, assembly, and religion; protections afforded by consumer protection and environmental laws, laws that protect employees from discrimination in the workplace, and laws you should know if you are starting a business. The law keeps pace with society and technological innovation. You will study laws developed for the Information Age and that apply to your digital world.

Business law is not difficult. Should you study the material in this text? Yes. Is it difficult to learn the concepts and laws in this text? No. At the end of every semester I always have students say to me that they were originally apprehensive about taking their business law or legal environment course, but in the end found that the material was easy to understand and extremely useful to their personal life and future in business.

To help you learn the concepts, the text is extremely readable. Cases throughout demonstrate how the law is applied to people like you and to situations similar to those in which you will be involved. Hundreds of definitions and summaries are placed throughout the text. This text, and its examples and Pedagogical features, make the rules and concepts of law come to life.

Solving Learning and Teaching Challenges

Pedagogical Features of the Textbook

In addition to a clearly written text, the book contains several major Pedagogical features that enhance a student's learning experience, including:

- **Examples** Examples are placed throughout the chapters of the text to demonstrate the application of legal concepts and rules to the real world. These examples work exceptionally well to clarify the concepts and issues studied in this course. There's no guessing at what a legal term means or how it applies; an example immediately shows you. More than 1,000 examples are presented in this text.
- **Definitions** A running glossary of definitions of the terms and concepts discussed in the text are presented in each chapter. These definitions allow students to review key concepts as they read the chapter or subsequently when they review a chapter or study for exams. Definitions are available when you need them; that is, when you are reading a chapter. More than 1,600 definitions appear in the margins of this book.
- **Concept Summaries** Concept Summaries are conveniently placed throughout the chapters of this book. These features summarize important concepts and laws immediately after they have been presented in a chapter. These summaries appear within the chapters, thus supporting your learning of the course materials. Concept Summaries help reinforce a student's mastery of the material.
- **End-of-Chapter Case Questions** Multiple case questions appear at the end of each chapter that set forth the facts of actual lawsuits. These are not hypothetical cases, but real-life situations and disputes that persons like yourself have encountered. These cases may be used during class discussions, assigned for group or class presentation, or designated as individual or collaborative writing assignments. There are more than 300 case questions in this text.

These and other features of the text, as well as exceptional student resources that accompany the text, combine to provide students with a valuable educational experience.

Critical Legal Thinking

Interest Rates of Over 1,000 Percent per Year on Consumer Loans Found Unconscionable

"We conclude that the interest rates in this case are substantively unconscionable."

—Edward Chavez, Justice

B&B Investment Group, Inc. marketed high-cost signature loans of $50 to $300 from offices located in New Mexico. B&B targeted the working poor, most of whom were less educated and financially unsophisticated individuals who were usually under or near the poverty level. Most borrowers did not have a bank account, or if they did, it was to receive government assistance deposits. The loans were for one year, on which B&B charged annual percentage interest rates ranging from 1,147 to 1,500 percent. B&B employees were instructed to describe loan costs as $1.00 or $1.50 per day, which was itself usually only half of what the loan cost daily, and to never disclose the annual percentage rate (APR).

If borrowers failed to make required loan payments, B&B would have their wages garnished so that their employers were required to make the loan payments out of the borrower's paycheck. Based on the terms of the loans, borrowers were liable for B&B's costs on collecting the debt, including attorney fees. Nonpayment of loans destroyed the credit ratings of the borrowers who missed loan payments.

The attorney general for the state of New Mexico sued B&B for unconscionable trade practices. The Supreme Court of New Mexico held that the small-principal, high-interest-rate signature loans made by B&B were unconscionable. The court stated, "We conclude that the interest rates in this case are substantively unconscionable. We hold it is grossly unreasonable and against public policy to offer installment loans at 1,147 to 1,500 percent interest."

The Supreme Court of New Mexico ordered B&B to refund all money collected on the loans that exceeded 15 percent of the loan principal and to refund any fees and penalties it collected from the borrowers. The court also issued an injunction against B&B's engaging in unfair practices in the future. *State of New Mexico v. B&B Investment Group, Inc.*, 329 P.3d 658, 2014 N.M. Lexis 230 (Supreme Court of New Mexico, 2014)

Critical Legal Thinking Questions

The general rule is "A contract is a contract is a contract" that will be enforced according to its terms. Why did the courts adopt the equity doctrine of unconscionable contract that deviates from the legal rule? In addition, the court could have voided the loan contracts entirely and let the borrowers keep the money B&B loaned to them. Do you think that the court should have imposed this penalty?

Developing Skills for Your Career

If you have not yet decided on a major, you may be thinking that this course is not relevant to you. Let me assure you it is. Whether or not you plan a career in business, the lessons you learn in this course will help you in business and in your life in many ways. Moreover, it is through the aggregate of your educational experience that you will have the opportunity to develop many of the skills that employers have identified as critical to success in the workplace. In this course, and specifically in this text, you will have the opportunity to develop your critical thinking skills and practice these skills by analyzing the legal principles, cases, and examples provided throughout this text.

For more information and resources, visit www.pearson.com.

Acknowledgments

When I first began writing this book, I was a solitary figure, researching cases online and in the law library and writing text on the computer and by hand at my desk. As time passed, others entered upon the scene—copyeditors, developmental editors, reviewers, and production personnel—and touched the project and made it better. Although my name appears on the cover of this book, it is no longer mine alone. I humbly thank the following persons for their contributions to this project.

The Exceptional Pearson Professionals

I appreciate the ideas, encouragement, effort, and decisions of the management team at Pearson: Lynn Huddon, Manager, Content Strategy; Melissa Feimer, Managing Content Producer; Krista Mastroianni, Product Manager; and Lacey Vitetta, Director, Content Strategy.

I'd also like to thank Kathryn Brightney, Content Analyst, for her many contributions to this book, and Kristin Jobe, Associate Managing Editor, Integra Software Services, for her outstanding management of the copyediting and proofreading of this revision.

And a special thanks to Sugandh Juneja, and Bhanuprakash Sherla, Content Producers, for their excellent work on producing the book. It was a delight working with such professionals.

I would especially like to thank the professionals of the sales staff of Pearson Education, Inc., particularly all the knowledgeable sales representatives.

Personal Acknowledgments

My Family

I would like to dedicate this book to my wife, Jin, and our twins, Ziva and Xavier.

My Relatives

I thank my parents—Henry B. and Florence, deceased—who had a profound effect on me and my ability to be a professor and writer. I also thank other members of my family, particularly my brother Gregory—with whom a special bond exists as twins—and the rest of my family, including my sister Marcia, deceased; Gregory's wife, Lana; my nephew Gregory and his wife, Karen; my niece Nicky and her husband Jerry; and my great nieces Addison, Lauren, and Shelby.

Students

I'd like to acknowledge the students at the University of Southern California (USC) and the students at other colleges and universities in the United States and around the world. Their spirit, energy, and joy are contagious. I loved teaching my students (and, as important, my students teaching me). At the end of each semester, I was sad that the students I had come to know were moving on. But each new semester brought another group of students who were a joy to teach. And thus, the cycle continued.

Colleagues

I would like to thank Kerry Fields, my colleague who teaches business, international, real estate, and employment law courses at the University of Southern California, who is a superb professor and a wonderful friend. I also thank Kevin Fields, my colleague who teaches business, corporation, and real estate law courses at the University of Southern California, who is an excellent professor and also a close friend.

Business Law Professors

I would also like to thank the professors who teach business law, legal environment of business, and other law-related courses at undergraduate and MBA programs at colleges and universities in the United States and around the world for their dedication to the discipline. Their experience in the law and teaching ability make them some of the greatest professors on any college or university campus.

Richard Bennett, Three Rivers Community College
Howard Davidoff, Brooklyn College
Jeffrey Herron, Middlesex County College
Natasha Maddox, Maysville Community and Technical College
Jeremy Pittman, Coahoma Community College
Lauren Ross, California State University, Northridge
Lori Sandman, Embry–Riddle Aeronautical University
Kurt Saunders, California State University, Northridge
James Shepherd, Lakes Region Community College
Arlena Sullivan, Jones County Junior College
Joe Welker, College of Western Idaho

Author's Personal Statement

While writing the preface and acknowledgments, I have thought about the thousands of hours I have spent researching, writing, and preparing this manuscript. I've loved every minute, and the knowledge gained has been sufficient reward for the endeavor. I hope this book and its supplementary materials will serve you as well as they have served me.

With joy and sadness,
emptiness and fullness,
honor and humility,
I surrender the fruits of this labor

Henry R. Cheeseman

ABOUT THE AUTHOR

Henry R. Cheeseman is professor emeritus of the Marshall School of Business of the University of Southern California (USC), Los Angeles, California.

Professor Cheeseman earned a bachelor's degree in finance from Marquette University, both a master's in business administration (MBA) and a master's in business taxation (MBT) from the University of Southern California, a juris doctor (JD) degree from the University of California at Los Angeles (UCLA) School of Law, a master's degree with an emphasis on law and economics from the University of Chicago, and a master's in law (LLM) degree in financial institutions law from Boston University.

Professor Cheeseman was director of the Legal Studies in Business Program at the University of Southern California. He taught business law, legal environment, and ethics courses in both the MBA and undergraduate programs of the Marshall School of Business. At the MBA level, he developed and taught courses on corporate governance, securities regulation, mergers and acquisitions, and bankruptcy law. At the undergraduate level, he taught courses on business law, the legal environment of business, ethics, business organizations, cyberlaw, and intellectual property.

Professor Cheeseman received the Golden Apple Teaching Award on many occasions by being voted by the students as the best professor at the Marshall School of Business. He was named a fellow of the Center for Excellence in Teaching at the University of Southern California by the dean of the Marshall School of Business. The USC's Torch and Tassel Chapter of the Mortar Board, a national senior honor society, tapped Professor Cheeseman for recognition of his leadership, commitment, and excellence in teaching.

Professor Cheeseman writes leading business law and legal environment textbooks that are published by Pearson Education, Inc. These textbooks include *Business Law, Contemporary Business Law*, and *Legal Environment of Business*.

To the Students

Contemporary students have different needs than previous generations. Having existed in an information technology world for your entire lives, you think, learn, and process information in different ways than prior generations. This new eleventh edition of *Business Law* and its student support materials have been designed especially for your needs.

As you embark on your study of the law, you will learn that this course presents the "real world"—that is, real legal disputes involving real people like you. The course also offers you an opportunity to develop critical thinking skills that will serve you in addressing legal and other issues that you may encounter. And lastly, learning the subject matter of this course will help you make more informed and confident decisions in your business and personal life.

Each semester your youth, enthusiasm, and questions motivate your professor's teaching. Every time you open your minds to look at an issue from a new perspective or critically question something, they receive a wonderful reward for the work they do. I remind myself of this every time I write and revise *Business Law*. My goal is to present business law in a way that will spur you to ask "how" and "why" as you study this course material in a classroom or online setting.

Business law is an evolving outgrowth of its environment and keeps changing to meet the demands of the modern world. This new eleventh edition of *Business Law* emphasizes coverage of digital law, information technology, and e-commerce as key parts of the legal environment. In addition, this book covers social and ethical issues that are important to the study of law.

It is my wish that my commitment to these goals shines through in this labor of love, and I hope you have as much pleasure in using this book as I have had in creating it for you.

Henry R. Cheeseman

PART

I

Legal Environment, Judicial System, Dispute Resolution, and Constitutional Law

Henry R. Cheeseman

CHAPTER

1 Legal Heritage and the Information Age

Henry R. Cheeseman

U.S. CAPITOL, WASHINGTON DC

The U.S. Congress, which is a bicameral system made up of the U.S. Senate and the U.S. House of Representatives, creates federal law by enacting statutes. Each state has two senators and is allocated a certain number of representatives based on population. The U.S. Senate and U.S. House of Representatives are based in the Capitol building.

Learning Objectives

After studying this chapter, you should be able to:

1.1 Define *law*.

1.2 Describe the flexibility of the law.

1.3 List and describe the schools of judicial thought.

1.4 Learn the history and development of American law.

1.5 List and describe the sources of law in the United States.

1.6 Describe the doctrine of *stare decisis*.

1.7 Describe how existing laws are being applied to the digital environment and how new laws are being enacted that specifically address issues of the information age.

1.8 Learn what critical legal thinking is and how to apply it to analyzing legal cases.

1.9 Learn how the material, cases, and lessons of this book will apply to your future career.

> *"Where there is no law, there is no freedom."*
>
> —*John Locke (1632–1704)*
> *Second Treatise of Government, Sec. 57*

Introduction to Legal Heritage and the Information Age

In the words of Judge Learned Hand, "Without law we cannot live; only with it can we insure the future which by right is ours. The best of men's hopes are enmeshed in its success."[1] Every society makes and enforces laws that govern the conduct of the individuals, businesses, and other organizations that function within it.

Although the law of the United States is based primarily on English common law, other legal systems, such as Spanish and French civil law, also influence it. The sources of law in this country are the U.S. Constitution, state constitutions, federal and state statutes, ordinances, administrative agency rules and regulations, executive orders, and judicial decisions by federal and state courts.

Human beings do not ever make laws; it is the accidents and catastrophes of all kinds happening in every conceivable way that make law for us.

Plato (427–347 BCE)
Laws IV, 709

Businesses that are organized in the United States are subject to its laws. They are also subject to the laws of other countries in which they operate. Businesses organized in other countries must obey the laws of the United States when doing business here. In addition, businesspeople owe a duty to act ethically in the conduct of their affairs, and businesses owe a responsibility not to harm society.

This chapter discusses the nature and definition of law, theories about the development of law, the history and sources of law in the United States, and the application of the law to the information age.

What Is Law?

1.1 Define *law*.

The law consists of rules that regulate the conduct of individuals, businesses, and other organizations in society. It is intended to protect persons and their property against unwanted interference from others. In other words, the law forbids persons from engaging in certain undesirable activities. Consider the following passage:

> *Hardly anyone living in a civilized society has not at some time been told to do something or to refrain from doing something, because there is a law requiring it, or because it is against the law. What do we mean when we say such things?*
>
> *At the end of the 18th century, Immanuel Kant wrote of the question "What is law?" that it "may be said to be about as embarrassing to the jurist as the well-known question 'What is truth?' is to the logician."*[2]

A lawyer without history or literature is a mechanic, a mere working mason: if he possesses some knowledge of these, he may venture to call himself an architect.

Sir Walter Scott
Guy Mannering, Ch. 37 (1815)

Definition of *Law*

The concept of **law** is broad. Although it is difficult to state a precise definition, *Black's Law Dictionary* gives one that is sufficient for this text:

> *Law, in its generic sense, is a body of rules of action or conduct prescribed by controlling authority, and having binding legal force. That which must be obeyed and followed by citizens subject to sanctions or legal consequences is a law.*[3]

law
That which must be obeyed and followed by citizens, subject to sanctions or legal consequences; a body of rules of action or conduct prescribed by controlling authority and having binding legal force.

The following feature discusses the functions of the law.

Contemporary Environment

Functions of the Law

The law is often described by the function it serves in a society. The primary *functions* served by the law in this country are the following:

1. Keeping the peace

   Example Some laws make certain activities crimes.
2. Shaping moral standards

   Example Some laws discourage drug and alcohol abuse.
3. Promoting social justice

   Example Some laws prohibit discrimination in employment.
4. Maintaining the status quo

   Example Some laws prevent the forceful overthrow of the government.
5. Facilitating orderly change

   Example Laws are enacted only after considerable study, debate, and public input.
6. Facilitating planning

   Example Well-designed commercial laws allow businesses to plan their activities, allocate their productive resources, and assess the risks they take.
7. Providing a basis for compromise

   Example Laws allow for the settlement of cases prior to trial. Approximately 95 percent of all lawsuits are settled in this manner.
8. Maximizing individual freedom

   Example The rights of freedom of speech, religion, and association are granted by the First Amendment to the U.S. Constitution.

CONCEPT SUMMARY

FUNCTIONS OF THE LAW

1. Keep the peace	5. Facilitate orderly change
2. Shape moral standards	6. Facilitate planning
3. Promote social justice	7. Provide a basis for compromise
4. Maintain the status quo	8. Maximize individual freedom

Fairness of the Law

The law, in its majestic equality, forbids the rich as well as the poor to sleep under bridges.

Anatole France (1844–1924)

The U.S. legal system is one of the most comprehensive, fair, and democratic systems of law ever developed and enforced. Nevertheless, some misuses and oversights of our legal system—including abuses of discretion and mistakes by judges and juries, unequal applications of the law, and procedural mishaps—allow some guilty parties to go unpunished.

Example In *Standefer v. United States,*[4] Chief Justice Warren Burger of the U.S. Supreme Court stated, "This case does no more than manifest the simple, if discomforting, reality that different juries may reach different results under any criminal statute. That is one of the consequences we accept under our jury system."

Flexibility of the Law

1.2 Describe the flexibility of the law.

United States law evolves and changes along with the norms of society, technology, and the growth and expansion of commerce in the United States and the world. The following quote by Judge Jerome Frank discusses the value of the adaptability of law:

> *The law always has been, is now, and will ever continue to be, largely vague and variable. And how could this be otherwise? The law deals with human relations in their most complicated aspects. The whole confused, shifting helter-skelter of life parades before it—more confused than ever, in our kaleidoscopic age.*
>
> *The constant development of unprecedented problems requires a legal system capable of fluidity and pliancy. Our society would be straightjacketed were not the courts, with the able assistance of the lawyers, constantly overhauling the law and adapting it to the realities of ever-changing social, industrial, and political conditions; although changes cannot be made lightly, yet rules of law must be more or less impermanent, experimental and therefore not nicely calculable.*
>
> *Much of the uncertainty of law is not an unfortunate accident; it is of immense social value.*[5]

A landmark U.S. Supreme Court case—*Brown v. Board of Education*—is discussed in the following feature. This case shows the flexibility of the law because the U.S. Supreme Court overturned a past decision of the Court.

Law must be stable and yet it cannot stand still.

Roscoe Pound
Interpretations of Legal History (1923)

Critical Legal Thinking

Are there any benefits for the law being "vague and variable"? Are bright-line tests possible for the law? Explain the statement, "Much of the uncertainty of law is not an unfortunate accident; it is of immense social value."

Critical Legal Thinking

Brown v. Board of Education

"We conclude that in the field of public education the doctrine of 'separate but equal' has no place."

—Earl Warren, Chief Justice

Slavery was abolished by the Thirteenth Amendment to the Constitution in 1865. The Fourteenth Amendment, added to the Constitution in 1868, contains the Equal Protection Clause, which provides that no state shall "deny to any person within its jurisdiction the equal protection of the laws." The original intent of this amendment was to guarantee equality to freed African Americans. But equality was denied to African Americans for a century. This included discrimination in housing, transportation, education, jobs, service at restaurants, and other activities.

In 1896, the U.S. Supreme Court decided the case *Plessy v. Ferguson*.[6] In that case, the state of Louisiana had a law that provided for separate but equal accommodations for African American and White railway passengers. The Supreme Court held that the "separate but equal" state law did not violate the Equal Protection Clause of the Fourteenth Amendment. The "separate but equal" doctrine was then applied to all areas of life, including public education.

It was not until 1954 that the U.S. Supreme Court decided a case that challenged the "separate but equal" doctrine as it applied to public elementary and high schools. In ***Brown v. Board of Education***, a unanimous Supreme Court, in an opinion written by Chief Justice Earl Warren, reversed prior precedent and held that the separate but equal doctrine violated the Equal Protection Clause of the Fourteenth Amendment to the Constitution. In its opinion, the Court stated,

> *Today, education is perhaps the most important function of state and local governments. We conclude that in the field of public education the doctrine of "separate but equal" has no place. Separate educational facilities are inherently unequal.*

After *Brown v. Board of Education* was decided, it took court orders as well as U.S. army enforcement to integrate many of the public schools in this country. *Brown v. Board of Education*, 347 U.S. 483, 74 S.Ct. 686, 1954 U.S. Lexis 2094 (Supreme Court of the United States, 1954).

Critical Legal Thinking Questions

It has been said that the U.S. Constitution is a "living document"—that is, one that can adapt to changing times. Do you think this is a good policy? Or should the U.S. Constitution be interpreted narrowly and literally, as originally written?

OLD ORANGE COUNTY COURTHOUSE, SANTA ANA, CALIFORNIA

Courts hear and decide civil and criminal cases. Court decisions are based on what the law says and what the evidence proves. Courts also protect individuals from abusive government action.

Henry R. Cheeseman

Schools of Jurisprudential Thought

1.3 List and describe the schools of judicial thought.

jurisprudence
The philosophy or science of law.

The philosophy or science of the law is referred to as **jurisprudence**. There are several different philosophies about how the law developed, ranging from the classical natural theory to modern theories of law and economics and critical legal studies. Classical legal philosophies are discussed in the following paragraphs.

Natural Law School

The **Natural Law School** of jurisprudence postulates that the law is based on what is "correct." Natural law philosophers emphasize a **moral theory of law**—that is, law should be based on morality and ethics. Natural law is "discovered" by humans through the use of reason and choosing between good and evil.

Examples Documents such as the U.S. Constitution, the Magna Carta, and the United Nations Charter reflect this theory.

Historical School

WEB EXERCISE
Go to **www.loc.gov/exhibits/brown/brown-brown.html** and read information about the U.S. Supreme Court's decision in *Brown v. Board of Education*.

The **Historical School** of jurisprudence believes that the law is an aggregate of social traditions and customs that have developed over the centuries. It believes that changes in the norms of society will gradually be reflected in the law. To these legal philosophers, the law is an evolutionary process.

Example Historical legal scholars look to past legal decisions (precedent) to solve contemporary problems.

Analytical School

The **Analytical School** of jurisprudence maintains that the law is shaped by logic. Analytical philosophers believe that results are reached by applying principles of logic to the specific facts of a case. The emphasis is on the logic of the result rather than on how the result is reached.

Example When a bill is introduced in the U.S. House of Representatives or U.S. Senate, Democrat, Republican, third-party, and independent members often must reach a compromise for a law to be enacted.

Sociological School

The **Sociological School** of jurisprudence asserts that the law is a means of achieving and advancing certain sociological goals. The followers of this philosophy, known as *realists*, believe that the purpose of law is to shape social behavior. Sociological philosophers are unlikely to adhere to past law as precedent.

The law is not a series of calculating machines where definitions and answers come tumbling out when the right levers are pushed.
William O. Douglas
Dissent, A Safeguard of Democracy (1948)

Examples Laws that make discrimination in employment illegal and laws that impose penalties for drunk driving reflect this theory.

Command School

The philosophers of the **Command School** of jurisprudence believe that the law is a set of rules developed, communicated, and enforced by the ruling party rather than a reflection of the society's morality, history, logic, or sociology. This school maintains that law changes when the ruling class changes.

Example During certain military conflicts, such as World War II and the Vietnam War, the federal government has enacted draft laws that require men of a certain age to serve in the military if they meet certain physical and other requirements.

Critical Legal Studies School

The **Critical Legal Studies School** proposes that legal rules are unnecessary and are used as an obstacle by the powerful to maintain the status quo. Critical legal theorists argue that legal disputes should be solved by applying arbitrary rules that are based on broad notions of what is "fair" in each circumstance. Under this theory, subjective decision making by judges would be permitted.

A kingdom founded on injustice never lasts.
Lucius Annaeus Seneca
(4 BCE–65 ACE)

Example This school postulates that many sexual assault laws make it difficult to litigate and prosecute sexual assault cases because the laws were drafted without factoring in the impact on victims of the experience of sexual assault. Therefore, says this school, judges should have broad discretion to decide whether a sexual assault has occured.

Law and Economics School

The **Law and Economics School** believes that promoting market efficiency should be the central goal of legal decision making. This school is also called the **Chicago School**, named after the University of Chicago, where it was first developed.

Example Proponents of the law and economics theory suggest that the federal government's policy of subsidizing housing—by a law that permits a portion of interest paid on mortgage loans to be deducted from an individual borrower's federal income taxes and laws that created government-sponsored enterprises (Fannie Mae and Freddie Mac) that purchase low-rate interest mortgages made by banks and other lending institutions—provide incentives so that too many homes are built. If these laws did not exist, then the free market would determine the exact number of homes that should be built.

CONCEPT SUMMARY

SCHOOLS OF JURISPRUDENTIAL THOUGHT

School	Philosophy
Natural Law	Postulates that law is based on what is "correct." It emphasizes a moral theory of law—that is, law should be based on morality and ethics.
Historical	Believes that law is an aggregate of social traditions and customs.
Analytical	Maintains that law is shaped by logic.
Sociological	Asserts that the law is a means of achieving and advancing certain sociological goals.
Command	Believes that the law is a set of rules developed, communicated, and enforced by the ruling party.
Critical Legal Studies	Maintains that legal rules are unnecessary and that legal disputes should be solved by applying arbitrary rules based on fairness.
Law and Economics	Believes that promoting market efficiency should be the central concern of legal decision making.

History of American Law

1.4 Learn the history and development of American law.

When the American colonies were first settled, the English system of law was generally adopted as the system of jurisprudence. This was the foundation from which American judges developed a common law in America.

English common law
Law developed by judges who issue their opinions when deciding a case. The principles announced in these cases became precedent for later judges deciding similar cases.

English Common Law

English common law was law developed by judges who issued their opinions when deciding cases. The principles announced in these cases became

PALACE OF WESTMINSTER, LONDON, ENGLAND
The court system of England consists of trial courts that hear criminal and civil cases and appellate courts. The House of Lords, in London, is the supreme court of appeal. The legal profession of England is divided into two groups: solicitors and barristers. Solicitors are lawyers who have direct contact with clients and handle legal matters for clients other than appearing in court. Barristers are engaged to appear in court on behalf of a client.

stoyanh/Shutterstock

precedent for later judges deciding similar cases. The English common law can be divided into cases decided by the *law courts, equity courts*, and *merchant courts*.

Law Courts Prior to the Norman Conquest of England in 1066, each locality in England was subject to local laws, as established by the lord or chieftain in control of a local area. There was no countrywide system of law. After 1066, William the Conqueror and his successors to the throne of England began to replace the various local laws with one uniform system of law. To accomplish this, the king or queen appointed loyal followers as judges in all local areas. These judges were charged with administering the law in a uniform manner, in courts that were called **law courts**. Law at that time tended to emphasize the form (legal procedure) over the substance (merit) of a case. The only relief available at law courts was a monetary award for damages.

Chancery (Equity) Courts Because of some unfair results and limited remedies available in the law courts, a second set of courts—the **Court of Chancery** (or **equity court**)—was established. These courts were under the authority of the lord chancellor. Persons who believed that the decision of a law court was unfair or believed that the law court could not grant an appropriate remedy could seek relief in the Court of Chancery. Rather than emphasize legal procedure, the chancery court inquired into the merits of the case. The chancellor's remedies were called *equitable remedies* because they were shaped to fit each situation. Equitable orders and remedies of the Court of Chancery took precedence over the legal decisions and remedies of the law courts.

Merchant Courts As trade developed during the Middle Ages, merchants who traveled about England and Europe developed certain rules to solve their commercial disputes. These rules, known as the "law of merchants," or the **Law Merchant**, were based on common trade practices and usage. Eventually, a separate set of courts was established to administer these rules. This court was called the **Merchant Court**. In the early 1900s, the Merchant Court was absorbed into the regular law court system of England.

The following feature discusses the adoption of English common law in the United States.

Landmark Law

Adoption of English Common Law in America

All the states—except Louisiana—of the United States of America base their legal systems primarily on the English common law. In the United States, the law, equity, and merchant courts have been merged. Thus, most U.S. courts permit the aggrieved party to seek both legal and equitable orders and remedies.

The importance of **common law** to the American legal system is described in the following excerpt from Justice Douglas's opinion in the 1841 case *Penny v. Little*:

> *The common law is a beautiful system, containing the wisdom and experiences of ages. Like the people it ruled and protected, it was simple and crude in its infancy and became enlarged, improved, and polished as the nation advanced in civilization, virtue, and intelligence. Adapting itself to the conditions and circumstances of the people and relying upon them for its administration, it necessarily improved as the condition of the people was elevated. The inhabitants of this country always claimed the common law as their birthright, and at an early period established it as the basis of their jurisprudence.*[7]

Currently, the law of the United States (Anglo-American law) is a combination of law created by the judicial system and by congressional legislation.

The following feature discusses the development of the civil law system in Europe.

Global Law

Civil Law System of France and Germany

One of the major legal systems that developed in the world in addition to the Anglo-American common law system is the **Romano-Germanic civil law system**. This legal system, which is commonly called the **civil law**, dates to 450 BCE, when Rome adopted the Twelve Tables, a code of laws governing Roman society. A compilation of Roman law, called the *Corpus Juris Civilis* ("Body of Civil Law"), was completed in CE 534. Later, two national codes—the **French Civil Code of 1804 (the Napoleonic Code)** and the **German Civil Code of 1896**—became models for countries that adopted civil codes.

In contrast to the Anglo-American law, in which laws are created by the judicial system as well as by congressional legislation, the civil code and parliamentary statutes are the sole sources of the law in most civil law countries. Thus, the adjudication of a case is simply the application of the code or the statutes to a particular set of facts. In some civil law countries, court decisions do not have the force of law.

Many countries in Europe still follow the civil law system.

Sources of Law in the United States

1.5 List and describe the sources of law in the United States.

In the more than 200 years since the founding of the United States and the adoption of the English common law, the lawmakers of this country have developed a substantial body of law. The *sources of modern law* in the United States are discussed in the paragraphs that follow.

Constitutions

Constitution of the United States of America
The supreme law of the United States.

The **Constitution of the United States of America** is the *supreme law of the land.* This means that any law—whether federal, state, or local—that conflicts with the U.S. Constitution is unconstitutional and therefore unenforceable.

The principles enumerated in the U.S. Constitution are extremely broad because the framers of the Constitution intended them to be applied to evolving social, technological, and economic conditions. The U.S. Constitution is often referred to as a "living document" because it is so adaptable.

The U.S. Constitution established the structure of the federal government. It created three branches of government and gave them the following powers:

- The **legislative branch (Congress)** has the power to make (enact) the law.
- The **executive branch (president)** has the power to enforce the law.
- The **judicial branch (courts)** has the power to interpret and determine the validity of the law.

Powers not given to the federal government by the Constitution are reserved for the states. States also have their own constitutions. **State constitutions** are often patterned after the U.S. Constitution, although many are more detailed. State constitutions establish the legislative, executive, and judicial branches of state government and establish the powers of each branch. Provisions of state constitutions are valid unless they conflict with the U.S. Constitution or any valid federal law.

Treaties

treaty
A compact made between two or more nations.

The U.S. Constitution provides that the president, with the advice and consent of two-thirds of the Senate, may enter into **treaties** with foreign governments. Treaties become part of the supreme law of the land. With increasing international economic relations among nations, treaties will become an even more important source of law that will affect business in the future.

Federal Statutes

Statutes are written laws that establish certain courses of conduct that covered parties must adhere to. The U.S. Congress is empowered by the Commerce Clause and other provisions of the U.S. Constitution to enact **federal statutes** to regulate foreign and interstate commerce.

statute
Written law enacted by the legislative branch of the federal and state governments that establishes certain courses of conduct that covered parties must adhere to.

Examples The federal Clean Water Act regulates the quality of water and restricts water pollution. The federal Securities Act of 1933 regulates the issuance of securities. The federal National Labor Relations Act establishes the right of employees to form and join labor organizations.

Federal statutes are organized by topic into **code books**. This is often referred to as **codified law**. Federal statutes can be found in these hardcopy books and online.

The following feature describes how a bill becomes law.

Contemporary Environment

How a Bill Becomes Law

The **U.S. Congress** is composed of two chambers, the **U.S. House of Representatives** and the **U.S. Senate**. Thousands of **bills** are introduced in the U.S. Congress each year, but only a small percentage of them become law. The process of legislation at the federal level is as follows:

1. A member of the U.S. House of Representatives or U.S. Senate introduces a bill in his or her **chamber**. The bill is assigned a number: "H.R. [number]#" for House bills and "S [number]#" for Senate bills. All bills for raising revenue must originate in the U.S. House of Representatives.
2. The bill is referred to the appropriate **committee** for review and study. The committee can do the following: (1) reject the bill; (2) report it to the full chamber for vote; (3) simply not act on it, in which case the bill is said to have died in committee—many bills meet this fate; or (4) send the bill to a **subcommittee** for further study. A subcommittee can let the bill die or report it back to the full committee.
3. Bills that receive the vote of a committee are reported to the full chamber, where they are debated and voted on. If the bill receives a majority vote of the chamber, it is sent to the other chamber, where the previously outlined process is followed. If the second chamber makes no changes in the original bill, the bill is reported for vote by that chamber. If the second chamber makes significant changes to the bill, a **conference committee** that is made up of members of both chambers will try to reconcile the differences. If a compromise version is agreed to by the conference committee, the bill is reported for vote.
4. A bill that is reported to a full chamber must receive the majority vote of the chamber, and if it receives this vote, it is forwarded to the other chamber. If a majority of the second chamber approves the bill, it is then sent to the president's desk.
5. If the president signs a bill, it becomes law. If the president takes no action for 10 days, the bill automatically becomes law. If the president vetoes the bill, the bill can be passed into law if two-thirds of the members of the House and two-thirds of the members of the Senate vote to override the veto and approve the bill. Many bills that are vetoed by the president do not obtain the necessary two-thirds vote to override the veto.

Because of this detailed and political legislative process, few of the many bills that are submitted by members of the U.S. House of Representatives or U.S. Senate become law.

State Statutes

State legislatures enact **state statutes**. Such statutes are placed in code books. State statutes can be accessed in these hardcopy code books or online.

Critical Legal Thinking
Why is the process of the U.S. Congress enacting statutes so complex? What checks and balances are built into the system before a bill can become law?

Examples The state of Florida has enacted the Lake Okeechobee Protection Act to protect Lake Okeechobee and the northern Everglades ecosystem. The Nevada Corporations Code outlines how to form and operate a Nevada corporation. The Texas Natural Resources Code regulates oil, gas, mining, geothermal, and other natural resources in the state.

Ordinances

State legislatures often delegate lawmaking authority to local government bodies, including cities and municipalities, counties, school districts, and water districts. These governmental units are empowered to adopt **ordinances**. Ordinances are also codified.

ordinance
Law enacted by local government bodies, such as cities and municipalities, counties, school districts, and water districts.

Examples Mackinac Island, Michigan, a city of 19th-century Victorian-style houses and buildings, has enacted ordinances that keep the island car free, keep out fast-food chains, and require buildings to adhere to era-specific aesthetic standards. Other examples of city ordinances include zoning laws, building codes, and sign restrictions.

Executive Orders

The executive branch of government, which includes the president of the United States and state governors, is empowered to issue **executive orders**. This power is derived from express delegation from the legislative branch and is implied from the U.S. Constitution and state constitutions.

executive order
An order issued by a member of the executive branch of the government.

Example In response to North Korea's pursuit of nuclear and missile programs, the launching of ballistic missiles in the area of Japan and other countries, cyber-attacks on U.S. government and other computer systems, and engaging in other actions that are detrimental to the interests of the United States and constitute a threat to national security, the president issued executive orders freezing the assets of the government of North Korea and the Workers' Party of Korea located in the United States, and prohibiting U.S. companies and individuals from selling or transferring products and services to the government of North Korea and parties associated with the government of North Korea that relate to energy, metal, graphite, mining, coal, transportation, financial services, software, and any other products and services that would benefit the nuclear and missile program of the government of North Korea.

WHITE HOUSE, WASHINGTON DC
The White House is located at 1600 Pennsylvania Avenue, Washington DC. The White House is the principal residence and office of the president of the United States of America.

Henry R. Cheeseman

Regulations and Orders of Administrative Agencies

The legislative and executive branches of federal and state governments are empowered to establish **administrative agencies** to enforce and interpret statutes enacted by Congress and state legislatures. Many of these agencies regulate business.

administrative agencies
Agencies (such as the Securities and Exchange Commission and the Federal Trade Commission) that the legislative and executive branches of federal and state governments are empowered to establish.

Examples Congress has created the Securities and Exchange Commission (SEC) to enforce federal securities laws and the Federal Trade Commission (FTC) to enforce consumer protection statutes.

Congress or the state legislatures usually empower these agencies to adopt **administrative rules and regulations** to interpret the statutes that the agency is authorized to enforce. These rules and regulations have the force of law. Administrative agencies usually have the power to hear and decide disputes. Their decisions are called **orders**. Because of their power, administrative agencies are often informally referred to as the "fourth branch of government."

Judicial Decisions

When deciding individual lawsuits, federal and state courts issue **judicial decisions**. In these written opinions, a judge or justice usually explains the legal reasoning used to decide the case. These opinions often include interpretations of statutes, ordinances, and administrative regulations and the announcement of legal principles used to decide the case. Many court decisions are reported by electronic research services such as Lexis, on the internet, and in books.

judicial decision
A decision about an individual lawsuit issued by a federal or state court.

Priority of Law in the United States

As mentioned previously, the U.S. Constitution and treaties take precedence over all other laws in the United States. Federal statutes take precedence over federal regulations. Valid federal law takes precedence over any conflicting state or local law. State constitutions rank as the highest state law. State statutes take precedence over state regulations. Valid state law takes precedence over local laws.

CONCEPT SUMMARY

SOURCES OF LAW IN THE UNITED STATES

Source of Law	Description
Constitutions	The U.S. Constitution establishes the federal government and enumerates its powers. Powers not given to the federal government are reserved to the states. State constitutions establish state governments and enumerate their powers.
Treaties	The president, with the advice and consent of two-thirds of the Senate, may enter into treaties with foreign countries.
Codified law: statutes and ordinances	Statutes are enacted by Congress and state legislatures. Ordinances are enacted by municipalities and local government bodies. They establish courses of conduct that covered parties must follow.
Executive orders	Issued by the president and governors of states. Executive orders regulate the conduct of covered parties.

(continued)

Source of Law	Description
Regulations and orders of administrative agencies	Administrative agencies are created by the legislative and executive branches of government. They may adopt rules and regulations that regulate the conduct of covered parties as well as issue orders.
Judicial decisions	Courts decide controversies. In doing so, a court issues an opinion that states the decision of the court and the rationale used in reaching that decision.

Doctrine of *Stare Decisis*

1.6 Describe the doctrine of *stare decisis*.

precedent
A rule of law established in a court decision. Lower courts must follow the precedent established by higher courts.

Based on common law tradition, past court decisions become **precedent** for deciding future cases. Lower courts must follow the precedent established by higher courts. That is why all federal and state courts in the United States must follow the precedents established by U.S. Supreme Court decisions.

The courts of one jurisdiction are not bound by the precedents established by the courts of another jurisdiction, although they may look to each other for guidance.

Example State courts of one state are not required to follow the legal precedents established by the courts of another state.

stare decisis
Latin for "to stand by the decision." Adherence to precedent.

Adherence to precedent is called the doctrine of ***stare decisis*** ("to stand by the decision"). The doctrine of *stare decisis* promotes uniformity of law within a jurisdiction, makes the court system more efficient, and makes the law more predictable for individuals and businesses.

Critical Legal Thinking
Why was the doctrine of *stare decisis* developed? What would be the consequences if the doctrine of *stare decisis* was not followed?

The doctrine of *stare decisis* is discussed in the following excerpt from Justice Musmanno's decision in *Flagiello v. Pennsylvania*:

> *Without* stare decisis, *there would be no stability in our system of jurisprudence.* Stare decisis *channels the law. It erects lighthouses and flies the signal of safety. The ships of jurisprudence must follow that well-defined channel which, over the years, has been proved to be secure and worthy.*[8]

A court may later change or reverse its legal reasoning if a new case is presented to it and change is warranted. The U.S. Supreme Court has stated, "Overruling precedent is never a small matter. What we can decide, we can undecide. But *stare decisis* teaches that we should exercise that authority sparingly."[9]

Law in the Information Age

1.7 Describe how existing laws are being applied to the digital environment and how new laws are being enacted that specifically address issues of the information age.

Even when laws have been written down, they ought not always to remain unaltered.
Aristotle (384–322 BCE)

In a span of about three decades, computers and other electronic devices have revolutionized society. Computers, once primarily used by businesses, have permeated the everyday lives of most people outside work as well. In addition, many other electronic devices are commonly in use, such as smartphones, tablets, televisions, digital cameras, and electronic game devices. In addition to the digital devices, technology has brought new ways of communicating, such as email and texting, as well as the use of social networks.

The information age arrived before new laws were written that were unique and specific to this environment. Courts have applied existing laws to the new digital and technological environment by requiring interpretations and applications. In addition, new laws have been written that apply specifically to this new digital and information technology environment. The U.S. Congress has led the way, enacting many new federal statutes to regulate the new environment.

The application of existing laws to the digital and technology environment and new laws that have been enacted that specifically address legal issues of the information age are discussed throughout this text.

The following feature discusses business ethics.

Ethics

Apple Agrees to Pay $500 Million to Settle Consumer Fraud Lawsuit

It is impossible to discuss business and business law without also discussing business ethics. Many decisions made by businesses, managers, and employees have an ethical component. Their duty is not only to act legally but also to act ethically. Sometimes companies are caught acting unethically. Consider the following case involving Apple Inc.

Apple is the developer, designer, and distributor of many forms of digital technology, including the ubiquitous iPhone. In 2007 Apple released its first version of the iPhone, which has subsequently gone through almost annual iterations. Some users move on to the next version immediately, while other users continue using older versions of the phones as long as they work for their purposes.

Apple continually provides software updates for prior models. Most users think that these updates make their phones work more efficiently, and in most cases they probably do. However, in some updates Apple secretly included software that actually made the phone's performance slower and the phone harder to use. Apple did not reveal this fact to consumers, tricking many users into believing that their older phones were simply slowing down from age. As a result, many people gave up their older iPhones and bought new iPhones.

Once Apple's actions were uncovered, dozens of class action lawsuits were filed against the company, alleging that Apple engaged in fraudulent conduct intended to sell more new iPhones. Apple denied any wrongdoing. The lawsuits were consolidated into one lawsuit heard by a U.S. district court located in California. Evidence was developed over a two-year period. Before the case went to trial, however, Apple agreed to a settlement.

In 2020, Apple agreed to pay at minimum $325 million and at maximum $500 million to users of iPhones who had their phones secretly slowed down. Lead plaintiffs received $1,500 each, and those that gave evidence received $3,500 each. All other class members received about $25 each. Apple agreed to pay the plaintiffs' lawyers $90 million. Apple now notifies iPhone users of software updates that would cause an adverse effect on performance, offering users the choice to opt out of such updates.

Ethics Questions

What reason would Apple have not to tell consumers that it was slowing down older iPhones when the users installed software updates? Was there any legitimate reason not to make this fact public? Do you think that the settlement amount was fair?

Critical Legal Thinking

1.8 Learn what critical legal thinking is and how to apply it to analyzing legal cases.

The U.S. Supreme Court, which is composed of nine justices, often issues nonunanimous decisions. Why? It is because each justice has analyzed the facts of a case and the legal issue presented, applied critical legal thinking to reason through the case, and come up with his or her own conclusion. The key is that each justice applied critical thinking in reaching his or her conclusion.

Critical thinking is important to all subjects taken by college and university students, no matter what their major or what course is taken. But critical thinking in law courses—referred to as *critical legal thinking*—is of significance because in the law there is not always a bright-line answer; in fact, there seldom is. This is where the famous "gray area" of the law appears. Thus, critical thinking becomes especially important in solving legal disputes.

Defining *Critical Legal Thinking*

Critical Legal Thinking
A method of thinking that consists of investigating, analyzing, evaluating, and interpreting information to solve a legal issue or case.

What is critical legal thinking? **Critical legal thinking** consists of investigating, analyzing, evaluating, and interpreting information to solve simple or complex legal issues or cases. Critical legal thinking requires intellectually disciplined thinking. This requires a person to recognize and identify problems, engage in logical inquiry and reasoning, evaluate information and appraise evidence, consider alternative perspectives, question assumptions, identify unjustified inferences and irrelevant information, evaluate opposing positions and arguments, and assess one's own thinking and conclusions.

Your professors have a deep understanding of critical legal thinking that they have developed during years of study in law school, in teaching and scholarship, and often in private practice or government employment as well. Over the course of the semester, they will impart to you not only knowledge of the law but also a unique and intelligent way of thinking through and solving complex problems. Critical legal thinking can serve 21st-century students and leaders.

Socratic Method

Socratic method
A process that consists of a series of questions and answers and a give-and-take inquiry and debate between a professor and students.

"Education is the kindling of a flame, not the filling of a vessel."
Socrates (469–399 BCE)

In class, many law professors use the **Socratic method** when discussing a case. The Socratic method consists of the professor asking students questions about a case or legal issue to stimulate critical thinking by the students. This process consists of a series of questions and answers and a give-and-take inquiry and debate between a professor and the students. The Socratic method stimulates class discussions. Good teachers recognize and focus on the questions and activities that stimulate the mind. The Socratic method of questioning is named after the Greek philosopher Socrates.

IRAC Method

IRAC method
A method used to examine a law case. *IRAC* is an acronym that stands for *issue, rule, application*, and *conclusion*.

Legal cases are usually examined using the following critical legal thinking method. First, the *facts* of the case must be investigated and understood. Next, the *legal issue* that is to be answered must be identified and succinctly stated. Then, the *law* that is to be applied to the case must be identified, read, and understood. Once the facts, law, and legal issue have been stated, critical thinking must be used in applying the law to the facts of the case. This requires that the decision maker—whether a judge, juror, or student—*analyze*, examine, evaluate, interpret, and apply the law to the facts of the case. Last, the critical legal thinker must reach a *conclusion* and state his or her judgment. In the study of law, this process is often referred to as the **IRAC method** (an acronym that stands for **issue, rule, application**, and **conclusion**) as outlined in the following:

I = What is the legal *issue* in the case?
R = What is the *rule* (law) of the case?
A = What is the court's *application* and its rationale?
C = What was the *conclusion* or outcome of the case?

This text—whether in its print or electronic version—offers students ample opportunities to develop and apply critical legal thinking. The text contains real-world cases in which actual disputing parties have become embroiled. The law cases are real, the parties are real, and the decisions reached by juries and judges are real. Some cases are easier to decide than others, but all provide a unique set of facts that require critical legal thinking to solve.

Developing Skills for Your Career

1.9 Learn how the material, cases, and lessons of this book will apply to your future career.

If you are not pursuing a profession in law, you may think this text is irrelevant to your future career. Let me assure you that that is not the case. Whatever career path you follow, you will be able to take the lessons from this text and develop career skills that are useful, regardless of the future job you will hold. Communication, critical thinking, collaboration, knowledge application and analysis, business ethics and social responsibility, and information technology application are key to a successful career today, and this text will help you develop many of these employment skills.

Court cases presented throughout the text will develop your critical legal thinking skills as you are asked to apply what you have learned to situations similar to those that you may encounter during your career. Some cases push beyond legal thinking, and into the question of ethical thinking. As you pick apart complex cases and legal issues, you will develop your analytical thinking skills.

Class discussion, homework, and other content will develop your written and oral communication skills through meaningful discussion and assignments, honing your ability to communicate effectively.

This book, its content, cases, special features, critical thinking questions, and other material and assignments will well prepare you to solve actual business issues that you will encounter during your future career.

Key Terms and Concepts

Administrative agencies (13)
Administrative rules and regulations (13)
Analytical School (7)
Bills (11)
Brown v. Board of Education (5)
Chamber (11)
Civil law (10)
Code book (11)
Codified law (11)
Command School (7)
Committee (11)
Common law (9)
Conference committee (11)
Constitution of the United States of America (10)
Court of Chancery (equity court) (9)
Critical Legal Studies School (7)
Critical legal thinking (16)
English common law (8)
Executive branch (president) (10)
Executive order (12)
Federal statute (11)
French Civil Code of 1804 (the Napoleonic Code) (10)
German Civil Code of 1896 (10)
Historical School (6)
IRAC method (16)
Judicial branch (courts) (10)
Judicial decision (13)
Jurisprudence (6)
Law (3)
Law and Economics School (Chicago School) (7)
Law courts (9)
Law Merchant (9)
Legislative branch (Congress) (10)
Merchant Court (9)
Moral theory of law (6)
Natural Law School (6)
Order (13)
Ordinance (12)
Precedent (14)
Romano-Germanic civil law system (10)
Sociological School (7)
Socratic method (16)
Stare decisis (14)
State constitution (10)
State statute (11)
Statute (11)
Subcommittee (11)
Treaty (10)
U.S. Congress (11)
U.S. House of Representatives (11)
U.S. Senate (11)

Critical Legal Thinking Cases

1.1 School of Jurisprudential Thought The legislature of the state of Texas enacted the Top Ten Percent Law, which guarantees college admission to students who graduate from a Texas high school in the top 10 percent of their class. Those students may choose to attend any of the public universities in the state, including the University of Texas at Austin (University). The University admits approximately 25 percent of an incoming class from applicants who do not qualify for admission under the 10 percent rule. These students are admitted based on a combination of their Academic Index (AI), which is calculated by combining an applicant's SAT score and academic performance in high school, and Personal Achievement Index (PAI), which is a holistic review of the applicant's essays, leadership and work experience, extracurricular activities, community service, and other special characteristics. Race is given weight as a factor within the PAI. The University states that it includes race as a factor in admissions so that it can create a diverse student body.

Petitioner Abigail Fisher applied for admission to the University's freshman class. She was not in the top 10 percent of her high school class, but qualified to be evaluated for admission through the holistic review. Fisher's application was rejected by the University. Fisher, who is white, filed suit, alleging that the University's consideration of race as part of its holistic review process disadvantaged her and other white applicants in violation of the Equal Protection Clause of the U.S. Constitution.

The U.S. district court entered judgment in the University's favor. The U.S. court of appeals affirmed, determining that the holistic admission standard of the University conformed to the Equal Protection Clause. Fisher appealed to the U.S. Supreme Court. Is the race-conscious admissions program at the University of Texas lawful under the Equal Protection Clause? What school of jurisprudential thought do you think a holistic admissions policy promotes? *Fisher v. University of Texas at Austin*, 136 S.Ct. 2198, 2016 U.S. Lexis 4059 (Supreme Court of the United States, 2016)

1.2 Fairness of the Law In 1909, the state legislature of Illinois enacted a statute called the Woman's 10-Hour Law. The law prohibited women who were employed in factories and other manufacturing facilities from working more than 10 hours per day. The law did not apply to men. W. C. Ritchie & Co., an employer, brought a lawsuit that challenged the statute as being unconstitutional, in violation of the equal protection clause of the Illinois constitution. In upholding the statute, the Illinois Supreme Court stated,

> *It is known to all men (and what we know as men we cannot profess to be ignorant of as judges) that woman's physical structure and the performance of maternal functions place her at a great disadvantage in the battle of life; that while a man can work for more than 10 hours a day without injury to himself, a woman, especially when the burdens of motherhood are upon her, cannot; that while a man can work standing upon his feet for more than 10 hours a day, day after day, without injury to himself, a woman cannot; and that to require a woman to stand upon her feet for more than 10 hours in any one day and perform severe manual labor while thus standing, day after day, has the effect to impair her health, and that as weakly and sickly women cannot be mothers of vigorous children.*
>
> *We think the general consensus of opinion, not only in this country but in the civilized countries of Europe, is, that a working day of not more than 10 hours for women is justified for the following reasons: (1) the physical organization of women, (2) her maternal function, (3) the rearing and education of children, (4) the maintenance of the home; and these conditions are, so far, matters of general knowledge that the courts will take judicial cognizance of their existence.*
>
> *Surrounded as women are by changing conditions of society, and the evolution of employment which environs them, we agree fully with what is said by the Supreme Court of Washington in the Buchanan case; "law is, or ought to be, a progressive science."*

Is the statute fair? Would the statute be lawful today? Should the law be a "progressive science"? *W. C. Ritchie & Co. v. Wayman, Attorney for Cook County, Illinois*, 91 N.E. 695, 1910 Ill. Lexis 1958 (Supreme Court of Illinois)

Ethics Cases

1.3 Ethics Case When the Constitution was ratified by the original colonies in 1788, it delegated to the federal government the exclusive power to regulate commerce with Native American tribes. During the next 100 years, as the colonists migrated westward, the federal government entered into many treaties with Native American nations. One such treaty was with the Ojibwe Indians in 1837, whereby the Ojibwe sold land located in the Minnesota territory to the United States. The treaty provided, "The privilege of hunting, fishing, and gathering wild rice, upon the lands, the rivers and the lakes included in the territory ceded, is guaranteed to the Indians." The state of Minnesota was admitted into the Union in 1858.

In 1990, the Mille Lacs Band of the Ojibwe tribe sued the state of Minnesota, seeking declaratory judgment that they retained the hunting, fishing, and gathering rights provided in the 1837 treaty and an injunction to prevent Minnesota from interfering with those rights. The state of Minnesota argued that when Minnesota entered the Union in 1858, those rights were extinguished. Are the hunting, fishing, and gathering rights guaranteed to the Ojibwe in the 1837 treaty still valid and enforceable? Did the state of Minnesota act ethically when it asserted that the Ojibwe's hunting, fishing, and gathering rights no longer were valid? *Minnesota v. Mille Lacs Band of Chippewa Indians*, 526 U.S. 172, 119 S.Ct. 1187, 1999 U.S. Lexis 2190 (Supreme Court of the United States)

1.4 Ethics Case In 1975, after the war in Vietnam, the U.S. government discontinued draft registration for men in this country. In 1980, after the Soviet Union invaded Afghanistan, President Jimmy Carter asked Congress for funds to reactivate draft registration. President Carter suggested that both men and women be required to register. Congress allocated funds only for the registration of men. Several men who were subject to draft registration brought a lawsuit that challenged the law as being unconstitutional, in violation of the Equal Protection Clause of the U.S. Constitution. The U.S. Supreme Court upheld the constitutionality of the draft registration law, reasoning as follows:

> *The question of registering women for the draft not only received considerable national attention and was the subject of wide-ranging public debate, but also was extensively considered by Congress in hearings, floor debate, and in committee. The foregoing clearly establishes that the decision to exempt women from registration was not the "accidental by-product of a traditional way of thinking about women."*
>
> *This is not a case of Congress arbitrarily choosing to burden one of two similarly situated groups, such as would be the case with an all-black or all-white, or an all-Catholic or all-Lutheran, or an all-Republican or all-Democratic registration. Men and women are simply not similarly situated for purposes of a draft or registration for a draft.*

Justice Marshall dissented, stating,

> *The Court today places its imprimatur on one of the most potent remaining public expressions of "ancient canards about the proper role of women." It upholds a statute that requires males but not females to register for the draft, and which thereby categorically excludes women from a fundamental civil obligation. I dissent.*

What arguments did the U.S. Supreme Court assert to justify requiring men, but not women, to register for the draft? Is the law, as determined by the U.S. Supreme Court, fair? Do you agree with the dissent? *Rostker, Director of Selective Service v. Goldberg*, 453 U.S. 57, 101 S.Ct. 2646, 1981 U.S. Lexis 126 (Supreme Court of the United States)

Notes

1. *The Spirit of Liberty*, 3rd ed. (New York, NY: Alfred A. Knopf, 1960).
2. "Introduction," in *The Nature of Law: Readings in Legal Philosophy*, M. P. Golding (New York, NY: Random House, 1966).
3. Henry Campbell Black. *Black's Law Dictionary*, 5th ed. (St. Paul, Minnesota: West).
4. 447 U.S. 10, 100 S.Ct. 1999, 1980 U.S. Lexis 127 (Supreme Court of the United States).
5. Jerome Frank. *Law and the Modern Mind* (New York: Brentano's, 1930).
6. 163 U.S. 537, 16 S.Ct. 1138, 1896 U.S. Lexis 3390 (Supreme Court of the United States, 1896).
7. 4 Ill. 301, 1841 Ill. Lexis 98 (Ill.).
8. Flagiello, Appellant, v. Pennsylvania Hospital 417 Pa. 486, 208 A.2d 193, 1965 Pa. Lexis 442 (Supreme Court of Pennsylvania).
9. 135 S.Ct. 2401, 2015 U.S. Lexis 4067 (Supreme Court of the United States, 2015).

CHAPTER

2 Courts and Jurisdiction

Henry R. Cheeseman

SUPREME COURT OF THE UNITED STATES, WASHINGTON DC

The highest court in the land is the Supreme Court of the United States, located in Washington DC. The U.S. Supreme Court decides the most important constitutional law cases and other important issues it deems ripe for review and decision. The Supreme Court's unanimous and majority decisions are precedent for all the other courts in the country.

Learning Objectives

After studying this chapter, you should be able to:

2.1 Describe state court systems.

2.2 Describe the federal court system.

2.3 Describe the U.S. Supreme Court and the types of cases it decides.

2.4 Explain the jurisdiction of federal courts and compare it with the jurisdiction of state courts.

2.5 Define *standing to sue, jurisdiction*, and *venue*.

2.6 Explain how jurisdiction is applied to digital commerce.

> *"I was never ruined but twice; once when I lost a lawsuit, and once when I won one."*
>
> —*Voltaire (1694–1778)*

Introduction to Courts, Jurisdiction, and Administrative Law

There are two major court systems in the United States: (1) the federal court system and (2) the court systems of the 50 states, Washington DC (District of Columbia), and territories of the United States. Each of these systems has jurisdiction to hear different types of lawsuits.

This chapter discusses state court systems, the federal court system, and the jurisdiction of courts to hear and decide cases.

The glorious uncertainty of law.

Thomas Wilbraham
A toast at a dinner of judges and counsel at Serjeants' Inn Hall, 1756

State Court Systems

2.1 Describe state court systems.

Each state, Washington DC, and each territory of the United States has its own separate court system (hereafter collectively referred to as **state courts**). State courts resolve more than 95 percent of the lawsuits brought in this country. Most state court systems include the following: *limited-jurisdiction trial courts, general-jurisdiction trial courts, intermediate appellate courts,* and a *highest state court.*

Limited-Jurisdiction Trial Courts

State **limited-jurisdiction trial courts**, which are sometimes referred to as **inferior trial courts**, hear matters of a specialized or limited nature.

limited-jurisdiction trial court (inferior trial court)
A court that hears matters of a specialized or limited nature.

Examples Traffic courts, juvenile courts, justice-of-the-peace courts, probate courts, family law courts, and courts that hear misdemeanor criminal law cases are limited-jurisdiction courts in many states.

Because limited-jurisdiction courts are trial courts, evidence can be introduced and testimony can be given. Most limited-jurisdiction courts keep records of their proceedings. A decision of such a court can usually be appealed to a general-jurisdiction court or an appellate court.

Many states have also created **small claims courts** to hear civil cases involving small dollar amounts (e.g., $5,000, $10,000). Generally, the parties must appear individually and cannot have lawyers represent them. The decisions of small claims courts are often appealable to general-jurisdiction trial courts or appellate courts.

WEB EXERCISE
Use **www.google.com** or another internet search engine and find out whether your state has a small claims court. If so, what is the dollar-amount limit for cases to qualify for small claims court?

General-Jurisdiction Trial Courts

Every state has a **general-jurisdiction trial court**. These courts are often referred to as **courts of record** because the testimony and evidence at trial are recorded and stored for future reference. These courts hear cases that are not within the jurisdiction of limited-jurisdiction trial courts, such as felonies or civil cases involving more than a certain dollar amount.

general-jurisdiction trial court (court of record)
A court that hears cases of a general nature that is not within the jurisdiction of limited-jurisdiction trial courts. Testimony and evidence at trial are recorded and stored for future reference.

Some states divide their general-jurisdiction courts into two divisions, one for criminal cases and the other for civil cases. Evidence and testimony are given at general-jurisdiction trial courts. The decisions handed down by these courts are appealable to an intermediate appellate court or the state supreme court, depending on the circumstances.

BANDERA COUNTY COURTHOUSE, BANDERA, TEXAS
This is a county courthouse of the state of Texas.

Witold Skrypczak/Alamy Stock Photo

Intermediate Appellate Courts

intermediate appellate court (appellate court or court of appeals)
A court that hears appeals from trial courts.

In many states, **intermediate appellate courts** (also called **appellate courts** or **courts of appeals**) hear appeals from trial courts. They review the trial court record to determine whether there have been any errors at trial that would require reversal or modification of the trial court's decision. Thus, an appellate court reviews either pertinent parts or the whole trial court record from the lower court. No new evidence or testimony is permitted.

The parties usually file legal *briefs* with the appellate court stating the law and facts that support their positions. Appellate courts usually grant a brief oral hearing to the parties. Appellate court decisions are appealable to the state's highest court. In sparsely populated states that do not have an intermediate appellate court, trial court decisions can be appealed directly to the state's highest court.

Highest State Court

highest state court
The highest court in a state court system; it hears appeals from intermediate appellate state courts and certain trial courts.

Each state has a **highest state court** in its court system. Many states call this highest court the **state supreme court**. Some states use other names for their highest courts. The function of a state's highest court is to hear appeals from intermediate appellate state courts and certain trial courts. No new evidence or testimony is heard. The parties usually submit pertinent parts of or the entire lower court record for review. The parties also submit legal briefs to the court and are usually granted a brief oral hearing. Decisions of highest state courts are final unless a question of law is involved that is appealable to the U.S. Supreme Court.

Exhibit 2.1 portrays a typical state court system. Exhibit 2.2 lists the websites for the court systems of the 50 states, the District of Columbia, and territories associated with the United States.

Exhibit 2.1 TYPICAL STATE COURT SYSTEM

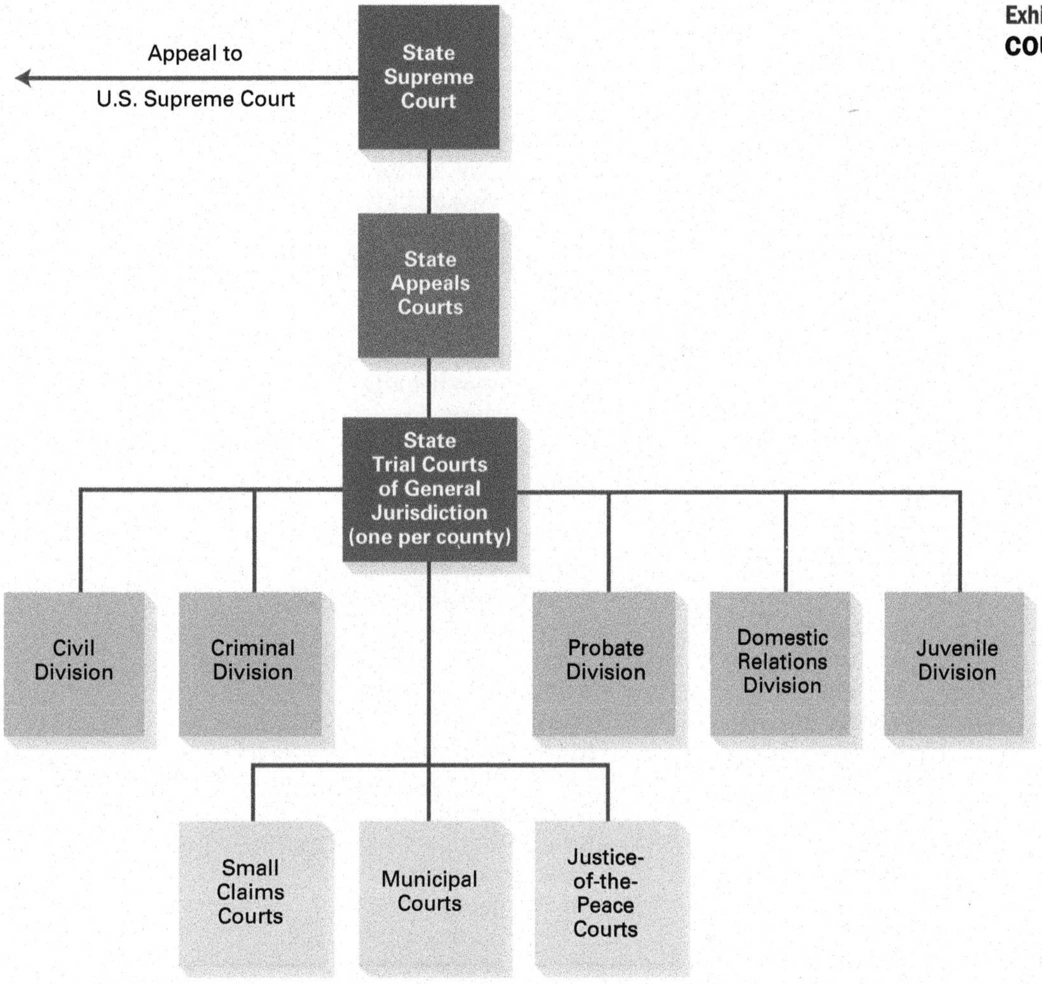

The following feature discusses special business courts.

Business Environment

Delaware Courts Specialize in Business Disputes

In most states, business and commercial disputes are heard by the same courts that hear and decide criminal, landlord–tenant, matrimonial, medical malpractice, and other non-business-related cases. One major exception to this standard has been the state of Delaware, where a special chancery court hears and decides business litigation.

The **Delaware Court of Chancery**, which decides cases involving corporate governance, fiduciary duties of corporate officers and directors, mergers and acquisitions, and other business issues, has earned a reputation for its expertise in handling and deciding corporate matters. Perhaps the existence of this special court and a corporation code that tends to favor corporate management are the primary reasons that more than 50 percent of the corporations listed on the New York Stock Exchange (NYSE) and the NASDAQ stock exchange are incorporated in Delaware.

Businesses tend to favor special commercial courts because the judges in these courts have the expertise to decide complex business lawsuits. The courts are also expected to be more efficient in deciding business-related cases, thus saving time and money for the parties. Other states are also establishing courts that specialize in commercial matters.

Exhibit 2.2 WEBSITES FOR STATE, DISTRICT OF COLUMBIA, AND TERRITORY COURT SYSTEMS

State, District, or Territory	Website
Alabama	judicial.alabama.gov
Alaska	courts.alaska.gov
Arizona	https://www.azcourts.gov
Arkansas	https://www.arcourts.gov
California	www.courts.ca.gov
Colorado	https://www.courts.state.co.us
Connecticut	https://www.jud.ct.gov
Delaware	https://courts.delaware.gov
District of Columbia	https://www.dccourts.gov
Florida	https://www.flcourts.org
Georgia	georgiacourts.gov
Guam	www.guamcourts.org
Hawaii	https://www.courts.state.hi.us
Idaho	https://isc.idaho.gov
Illinois	www.illinoiscourts.gov
Indiana	https://www.in.gov/judiciary/
Iowa	https://www.iowacourts.gov
Kansas	www.kscourts.org
Kentucky	https://courts.ky.gov/Pages/default.aspx
Louisiana	www.lasc.org
Maine	https://www.courts.maine.gov
Maryland	https://www.courts.state.md.us
Massachusetts	https://www.mass.gov/orgs/massachusetts-court-system
Michigan	https://courts.michigan.gov/Pages/default.aspx
Minnesota	www.mncourts.gov
Mississippi	https://courts.ms.gov
Missouri	https://www.courts.mo.gov
Montana	https://courts.mt.gov
Nebraska	https://supremecourt.nebraska.gov
Nevada	https://nvcourts.gov
New Hampshire	https://www.courts.state.nh.us
New Jersey	https://www.njcourts.gov
New Mexico	https://www.nmcourts.gov
New York	www.courts.state.ny.us
North Carolina	https://www.nccourts.gov
North Dakota	https://www.ndcourts.gov
Northern Mariana Islands	www.nmijudiciary.com
Ohio	www.sconet.state.oh.us
Oklahoma	www.oscn.net/oscn/schome/
Oregon	https://www.courts.oregon.gov/Pages/default.aspx
Pennsylvania	www.pacourts.us
Puerto Rico	www.ramajudicial.pr
Rhode Island	https://www.courts.ri.gov/Pages/default.aspx
South Carolina	https://www.sccourts.org
South Dakota	www.ujs.sd.gov
Tennessee	www.tsc.state.tn.us
Texas	www.courts.state.tx.us
Utah	https://www.utcourts.gov/index.html
Vermont	www.vermontjudiciary.org
Virginia	www.courts.state.va.us
Virgin Islands	www.visuperiorcourt.org
Washington	www.courts.wa.gov
West Virginia	www.courtswv.gov
Wisconsin	https://www.wicourts.gov
Wyoming	https://www.courts.state.wy.us

Federal Court System

2.2 Describe the federal court system.

Article III of the U.S. Constitution provides that the federal government's judicial power is vested in one "Supreme Court." This court is the U.S. Supreme Court. Article III authorizes Congress to establish "inferior" federal courts. Pursuant to its Article III power, Congress has established the U.S. district courts, the U.S. courts of appeals, and the U.S. bankruptcy courts. Pursuant to other authority in the Constitution, the U.S. Congress has established other federal courts. Federal judges of the U.S. Supreme Court, U.S. courts of appeals, and U.S. district courts are appointed for life by the president, with the advice and consent of the Senate. Judges of other courts are not appointed for life but are appointed for various periods of time (e.g., bankruptcy court judges are appointed for 14-year terms).

It is, emphatically, the province and duty of the judicial department, to say what the law is.

Marbury v. Madison
5 U.S. 137 (1803)
John Marshall, Chief Justice
Supreme Court of the United States

Special Federal Courts

The **special federal courts** established by Congress have limited jurisdiction. They include the following:

special federal courts
Federal courts that hear matters of specialized or limited jurisdiction.

- **U.S. Tax Court.** The **U.S. Tax Court** hears cases that involve federal tax laws. Website: https://www.ustaxcourt.gov.
- **U.S. Court of Federal Claims.** The **U.S. Court of Federal Claims** hears cases brought against the United States. Website: www.uscfc.uscourts.gov.
- **U.S. Court of International Trade.** The **U.S. Court of International Trade** hears civil cases arising out of customs and international trade laws of the United States. Website: https://www.cit.uscourts.gov.
- **U.S. Bankruptcy Court**. The **U.S. Bankruptcy Court** hears cases that involve federal bankruptcy laws. Website: https://www.uscourts.gov/services-forms/bankruptcy.
- **U.S. Court of Appeals for the Armed Forces.** The **U.S. Court of Appeals for the Armed Forces** exercises appellate jurisdiction over members of the armed services. Website: https://www.armfor.uscourts.gov.
- **U.S. Court of Appeals for Veterans Claims.** The **U.S. Court of Appeals for Veterans Claims** exercises jurisdiction over decisions of the Department of Veterans Affairs. Website: www.uscourts.cavc.gov.

The following feature discusses a controversial court of the federal court system.

WEB EXERCISE
Go to the website of the FISA court at **www.fisc.uscourts.gov**. Read the description of the court.

Contemporary Environment

Foreign Intelligence Surveillance Court

In 1978, Congress created the **U.S. Foreign Intelligence Surveillance Court (FISA court)**, located in Washington DC. The 11 judges of the FISA court are appointed by the chief justice of the United States.

The FISA court hears requests by federal law enforcement agencies, such as the Federal Bureau of Investigation (FBI) and National Security Agency (NSA), for warrants, called **FISA warrants**, to conduct physical searches and electronic surveillance of Americans or foreigners in the United States who are deemed a threat to national security. The application for a surveillance warrant is heard by one of the judges who sit on the court. It is rare for an application for a warrant to be rejected by the FISA court.

The FISA court is a "secret court" because its hearings are not open to the public and its decisions are classified. The court rarely releases documents, and when it does, the documents are usually highly redacted; that is, certain sensitive information is either removed or obscured before release. FISA court website: https://www.fisc.uscourts.gov.

If the FISA court denies a government application for a FISA warrant, the government may appeal the decision to the **U.S. Foreign Intelligence Surveillance Court of Review (FISCR)**. FISCR website: https://www.fisc.uscourts.gov/FISCR.

U.S. DISTRICT COURT, LAS VEGAS, NEVADA
This is the Lloyd D. George United States District Court for the District of Nevada, in Las Vegas, Nevada. This is a federal trial court. This federal trial court, along with the other U.S. district courts located throughout the country, hears and decides lawsuits concerning matters over which it has jurisdiction.

Henry R. Cheeseman

U.S. District Courts

U.S. district courts
The federal court system's trial courts of general jurisdiction.

The **U.S. district courts** are the federal court system's trial courts of *general jurisdiction*. There are 94 U.S. district courts. There is at least one federal district court in each state and the District of Columbia, and heavily populated states and geographically large states have more than one district court.

Examples California, New York, and Texas each have four U.S. district courts.

The geographical area served by each court is referred to as a **district**. The federal district courts are empowered to impanel juries, receive evidence, hear testimony, and decide cases. Most federal cases originate in federal district courts.

U.S. territorial courts are federal trial courts located on Guam, the Northern Mariana Islands, and the U.S. Virgin Islands. These courts have jurisdiction similar to U.S. district courts.

U.S. Courts of Appeals

U.S. courts of appeals
The federal court system's intermediate appellate courts.

The **U.S. courts of appeals** are the federal court system's intermediate appellate courts. There are 13 circuits in the federal court system. The first 12 are geographical. Eleven are designated by numbers, as the "First Circuit," "Second Circuit," "Third Circuit," and so on. The geographical area served by each court is referred to as a **circuit**. A 12th circuit court, located in Washington DC, is called the **U.S. District of Columbia Circuit**.

U.S. Court of Appeals for the Federal Circuit
A U.S. court of appeals in Washington DC that has special appellate jurisdiction to review the decisions of the Court of Federal Claims, the Patent and Trademark Office, and the Court of International Trade.

Congress created a 13th court of appeals in 1982. It is called the **U.S. Court of Appeals for the Federal Circuit**, located in Washington DC. This court has special appellate jurisdiction to review the decisions of the Court of Federal Claims, the Patent and Trademark Office, and the Court of International Trade. It was created to provide uniformity in the application of federal law in certain areas, particularly patent law.

As appellate courts, each of these courts hears appeals from the district courts located in its circuit as well as from certain special courts and federal administrative agencies. An appellate court reviews the record of the lower court or

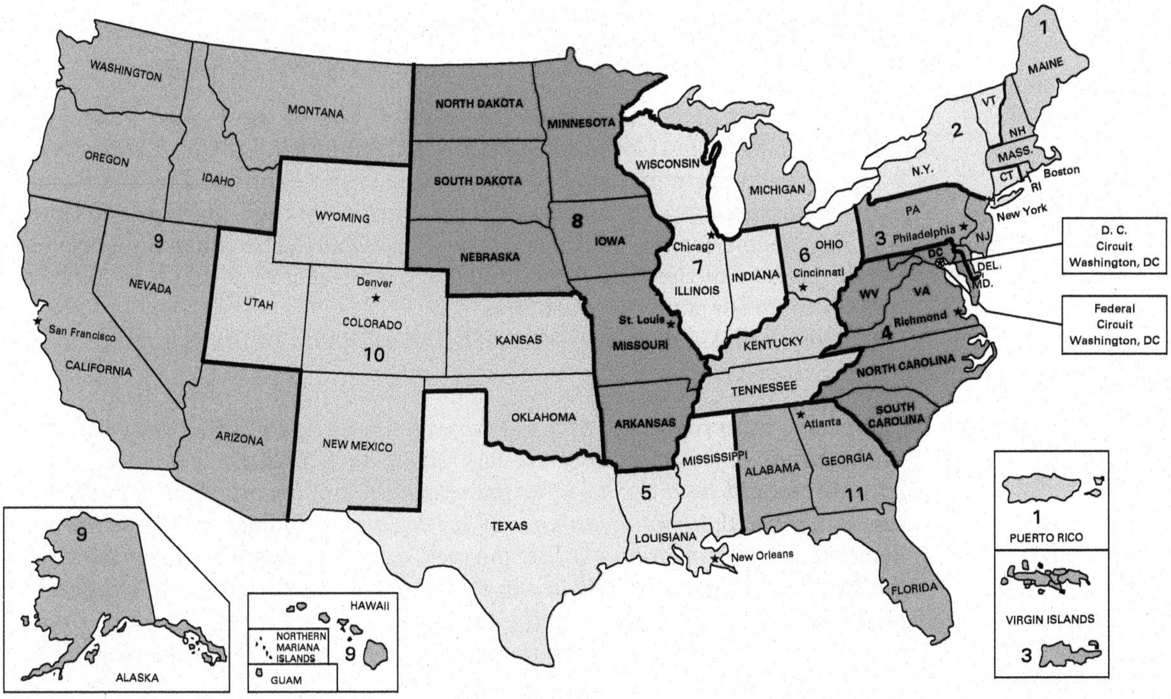

Exhibit 2.3 MAP OF THE FEDERAL CIRCUIT COURTS

administrative agency proceedings to determine whether there has been any error that would warrant reversal or modification of the lower court decision. No new evidence or testimony is heard. The parties file legal briefs with the court and are given a short oral hearing. The number of judges of various U.S. courts of appeals ranges from approximately 6 to 30. Appeals are usually heard by a three-judge panel. After a decision is rendered by the three-judge panel, a petitioner can request an ***en banc* review** by the full appeals court.

Exhibit 2.3 shows a map of the 13 federal circuit courts of appeals. Exhibit 2.4 lists the websites of the 13 U.S. courts of appeals.

Exhibit 2.4 WEBSITES FOR THE FEDERAL COURTS OF APPEALS

U. S. Court of Appeals	Main Office	Website
First Circuit	Boston, Massachusetts	www.ca1.uscourts.gov
Second Circuit	New York, New York	www.ca2.uscourts.gov
Third Circuit	Philadelphia, Pennsylvania	www.ca3.uscourts.gov
Fourth Circuit	Richmond, Virginia	www.ca4.uscourts.gov
Fifth Circuit	New Orleans, Louisiana	www.ca5.uscourts.gov
Sixth Circuit	Cincinnati, Ohio	www.ca6.uscourts.gov
Seventh Circuit	Chicago, Illinois	www.ca7.uscourts.gov
Eighth Circuit	St. Paul, Minnesota	www.ca8.uscourts.gov
Ninth Circuit	San Francisco, California	www.ca9.uscourts.gov
Tenth Circuit	Denver, Colorado	www.ca10.uscourts.gov
Eleventh Circuit	Atlanta, Georgia	www.ca11.uscourts.gov
District of Columbia	Washington DC	www.dcd.uscourts.gov
Court of Appeals for the Federal Circuit	Washington DC	www.cafc.uscourts.gov

Supreme Court of the United States

2.3 Describe the U.S. Supreme Court and the types of cases it decides.

Supreme Court of the United States (U.S. Supreme Court)
The highest court in the United States, located in Washington DC. The Supreme Court was created by Article III of the U.S. Constitution.

The highest court in the land is the **Supreme Court of the United States**, also called the **U.S. Supreme Court**, located in Washington DC. The Court is composed of 9 justices who are nominated by the president and confirmed by the Senate. The president appoints one justice as the **chief justice of the U.S. Supreme Court**, who is responsible for the administration of the Court. The other 8 justices are **associate justices of the U.S. Supreme Court**. The website of the U.S. Supreme Court is http://www.supremecourt.gov.

Following is Alexis de Tocqueville's 1840 description of the Supreme Court's role in U.S. society:

> *The peace, the prosperity, and the very existence of the Union are vested in the hands of the justices of the Supreme Court. Without them, the Constitution would be a dead letter: the executive appeals to them for assistance against the encroachments of the legislative power; the legislature demands their protection against the assaults of the executive; they defend the Union from the disobedience of the states, the states from the exaggerated claims of the Union; the public interest against private interests, and the conservative spirit of stability against the fickleness of the democracy.*[1]

The following feature discusses the process of choosing a U.S. Supreme Court justice.

WEB EXERCISE
Go to the website **www.supremecourt.gov/about/biographies.aspx**. Who are the current members of the Supreme Court? Who is the chief justice? Pick a justice and read his or her biography.

Critical Legal Thinking
Is the U.S. Supreme Court apolitical? Explain the difference between a policy-oriented Supreme Court and an original constructionist Supreme Court. Why are U.S. Supreme Court justices appointed for life?

Contemporary Environment

Process of Nominating and Confirming a U.S. Supreme Court Justice

To strike a balance of power between the executive and legislative branches of government, Article II, Section 2, of the U.S. Constitution gives the president the power to appoint Supreme Court justices "with the advice and consent of the Senate." This means that the majority of senators must approve the president's nominee for that nominee to become a justice of the U.S. Supreme Court.

With the advice of senators and others, the president selects a candidate and nominates that person for the U.S. Supreme Court. The U.S. Senate Judiciary Committee holds a hearing on the nominee. The committee examines records concerning the nominee and holds a hearing where witnesses are heard from and the nominee is subjected to questioning by committee members. The committee votes and sends its recommendation to the full Senate, where the Senate conducts a debate on the merits of the nominee. When the debate ends, the Senate votes on the nomination. The nominee is confirmed if a majority of the senators present and voting vote for confirmation. If there is a tie vote, the vice president, who presides over the Senate, casts the deciding vote. Many recent Senate hearings on nominees have been somewhat contentious.

President George W. Bush, a Republican, while in office from 2001 to 2009, placed two justices on the Supreme Court, Chief Justice John G. Roberts Jr. and Associate Justice Samuel A. Alito Jr. Both justices were confirmed by the U.S. Senate.

President Barack Obama, a Democrat, while in office from 2009 to 2017, placed two justices on the Supreme Court, Associate Justice Sonia Sotomayor and Associate Justice Elena Kagan. Justice Sotomayor is the first Hispanic person to be a justice of the Supreme Court.

President Donald Trump, a Republican, nominated Neil Gorsuch, Brett Kavanaugh, and Amy Coney Barrett as associate justices of the Supreme Court. Each was confirmed by the U.S. Senate.

A president who is elected to one or two four-year terms in office may have the opportunity to nominate justices to the U.S. Supreme Court who, if confirmed, may serve many years after the president leaves office.

Jurisdiction of the U.S. Supreme Court

The Supreme Court, which is an appellate court, hears appeals from federal circuit courts of appeals and, under certain circumstances, from federal district courts, special federal courts, and the highest state courts. No new evidence or testimony is heard. As with other appellate courts, the lower court record is reviewed to

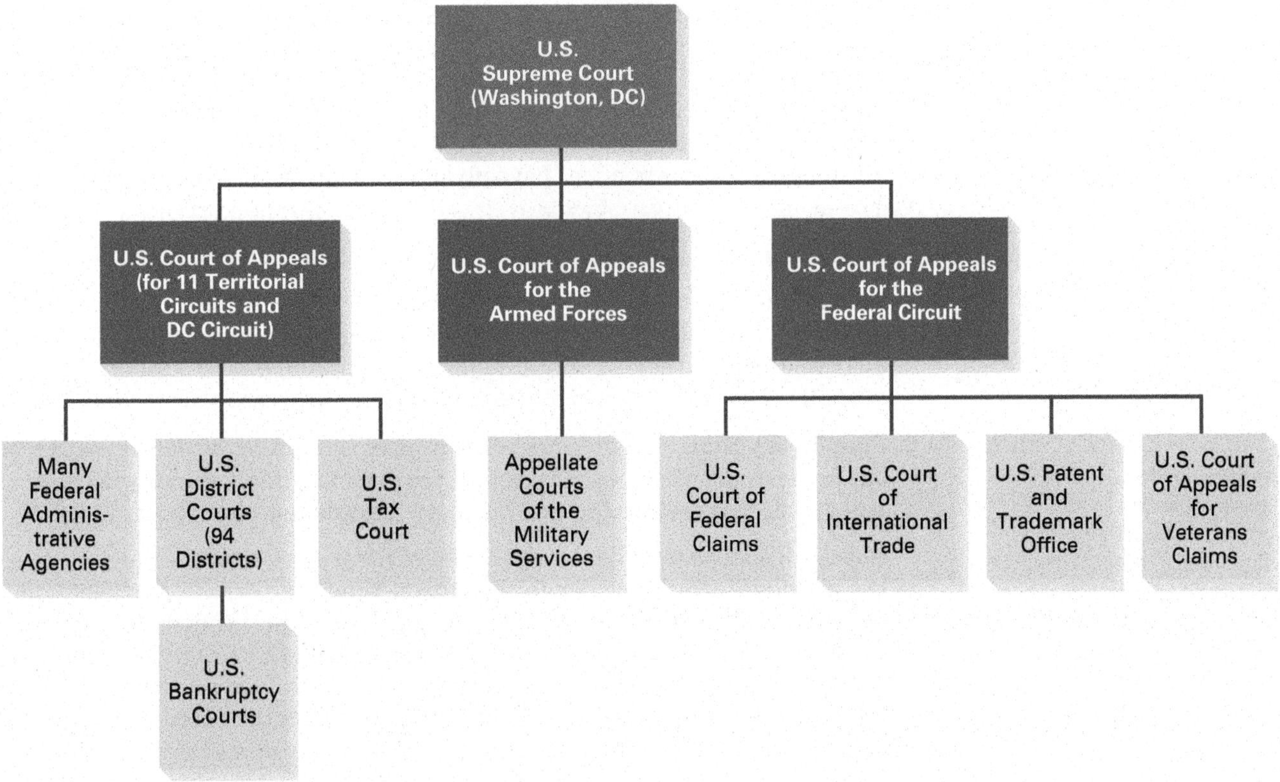

Exhibit 2.5 FEDERAL COURT SYSTEM

determine whether there has been an error that warrants a reversal or modification of the decision. Legal briefs are filed, and the parties are granted a brief oral hearing. The Supreme Court's decision is final.

The federal court system is illustrated in Exhibit 2.5.

Decisions of the U.S. Supreme Court

The U.S. Constitution gives Congress the authority to establish rules for the appellate review of cases by the Supreme Court, except in the rare case in which mandatory review is required. Congress has given the Supreme Court discretion to decide what cases it will hear.

A petitioner must file a **petition for certiorari**, asking the Supreme Court to hear the case. If the Court decides to review a case, it issues a **writ of certiorari**. Because the Court issues only about 100 opinions each year, writs are usually granted only in cases involving constitutional and other important issues.

petition for certiorari
A petition asking the Supreme Court to hear a case.

writ of certiorari
An official notice that the Supreme Court will review a case.

Each justice of the Supreme Court, including the chief justice, has an equal vote. The Supreme Court can issue several types of decisions:

1. **Unanimous decision.** If all the justices voting agree as to the outcome and reasoning used to decide a case, it is a **unanimous decision**. Unanimous decisions are precedent for later cases.

   Example If all 9 justices hear a case and all 9 agree to the outcome (e.g., the petitioner wins) and the reason why (e.g., the Equal Protection Clause of the U.S. Constitution had been violated), it is a unanimous decision. This unanimous decision becomes precedent for later cases.

2. **Majority decision.** If a majority of the justices agree as to the outcome and reasoning used to decide a case, it is a **majority decision**. Majority decisions are precedent for later cases. A majority decision occurs if 5, 6, 7, or 8 justices vote for the same outcome for the same reason.

unanimous decision
A decision of the court in which all of the justices agree as to the outcome and reasoning used to decide a case. The decision becomes precedent.

majority decision
A decision of the court in which a majority of the justices agree as to the outcome and reasoning used to decide a case. The decision becomes precedent.

Example If all 9 justices hear a case and 5 of them agree as to the outcome (e.g., the petitioner wins) and these 5 justices agree to the same reason why (e.g., the Equal Protection Clause of the U.S. Constitution has been violated), it is a majority opinion. The majority opinion becomes precedent for later cases and has the same force of law as a unanimous decision. The votes of the remaining 4 justices for the respondent have no legal effect whatsoever.

A majority decision can also be reached if fewer than 9 justices hear and rule in the case and a majority agree to the outcome and reason for the outcome.

Example In some cases a justice will recuse him- or herself—not take part in deciding a case—because the justice has a conflict of interest. If that leaves 8 justices, then the majority of those justices, either 5, 6, or 7, can create precedent if the majority agrees to the outcome and the reason for the outcome.

plurality decision
A decision of the court in which a majority of the justices agree as to the outcome of a case but not as to the reasoning for reaching the outcome. A plurality decision settles the case but is not precedent for later cases.

3. **Plurality decision.** If a majority of the justices agree as to the outcome of a case but not as to the reasoning for reaching the outcome, it is a **plurality decision**. A plurality decision settles the case but is not precedent for later cases.

   Example If all 9 justices hear a case and 5 of them agree as to the outcome (e.g., the petitioner wins) but not to the reason why (e.g., 3 base their vote on a violation of the Equal Protection Clause and 2 base their vote on a violation of the Due Process Clause of the U.S. Constitution), it is a plurality decision. Five justices have agreed to the same outcome, but those 5 have not agreed for the same reason. The petitioner wins his or her case, but the decision is not precedent for later cases. The votes of the remaining 4 justices for the respondent have no legal effect whatsoever.

4. **Tie Decision.** Sometimes the Supreme Court sits without all 9 justices being present. This could happen because of illness, conflict of interest, or a justice not having been confirmed to fill a vacant seat on the Court. If there is a **tie decision**, the lower court decision is affirmed. Such votes are not precedent for later cases.

   Example A petitioner wins his or her case at the U.S. court of appeals. At the Supreme Court, only 8 justices hear the case. Four justices vote for the petitioner, and 4 justices vote for the respondent. This is a tie vote. The petitioner remains the winner because he or she won at the court of appeals. This decision of the Supreme Court sets no precedent for later cases.

A justice who agrees with the outcome of a case but not the reason proffered by other justices can issue a **concurring opinion** that sets forth his or her reasons for deciding the case. A justice who does not agree with a decision can file a **dissenting opinion** that sets forth the reasons for his or her dissent.

The following feature discusses the process for having a case heard by the U.S. Supreme Court.

Contemporary Environment

"I'll Take You to the U.S. Supreme Court!"

Having a case heard by the U.S. Supreme Court is rare. Each year, approximately 10,000 petitioners ask the Supreme Court to hear their cases. In recent years, the Supreme Court has accepted fewer than 100 of these cases for full review each term.

The 9 Supreme Court justices meet once a week to discuss what cases merit review. The votes of 4 justices are necessary to grant an appeal and schedule an oral argument before the Court; this is called the **rule of four**. The decision and written opinions by the justices are usually issued many months later.

What does it take to win a review by the Supreme Court? The U.S. Supreme Court usually decides to hear cases involving major constitutional questions, such as freedom of speech, freedom of religion, equal protection, and due process. The Supreme Court also hears many cases involving the interpretation of federal statutes enacted by Congress. The Court rarely decides day-to-day legal issues such as breach of contract, tort liability, or corporation law unless they involve more important constitutional or federal law questions.

Jurisdiction of Federal and State Courts

2.4 Explain the jurisdiction of federal courts and compare it with the jurisdiction of state courts.

Article III, Section 2, of the U.S. Constitution sets forth the jurisdiction of federal courts. Federal courts have *limited jurisdiction* to hear cases involving a *federal question* or *diversity of citizenship*. Each of these topics is discussed in the following paragraphs.

Federal Question

The federal courts have subject matter jurisdiction to hear cases involving "federal questions." **Federal question cases** are cases arising under the U.S. Constitution, treaties, and federal statutes and regulations. There is no dollar-amount limit on federal question cases that can be brought in federal court.

federal question case
A case arising under the U.S. Constitution, treaties, or federal statutes and regulations.

Example A defendant is sued by a plaintiff for engaging in insider trading, in violation of the Securities Exchange Act of 1934, which is a federal statute. This lawsuit involves a federal question, a federal statute, and therefore qualifies to be brought in federal court.

Diversity of Citizenship

A case may be brought in federal court even though it involves a nonfederal subject matter question, which would usually be heard by state, Washington DC, or territory courts, if there is diversity of citizenship. **Diversity of citizenship** occurs if a lawsuit involves (1) citizens of different states or (2) a citizen of a state and a citizen or subject of a foreign country.

diversity of citizenship
A means for bringing a lawsuit in federal court that involves a nonfederal question if the parties are (1) citizens of different states or (2) a citizen of a state and a citizen or subject of a foreign country.

If there is diversity of citizenship, the plaintiff may bring the case in either state or federal court. If a plaintiff brings a diversity of citizenship case in federal court, it remains there. If the plaintiff brings a diversity of citizenship case in state court, it will remain there unless the defendant removes the case to federal court. Federal courts must apply the relevant state law to diversity of citizenship cases.

The original reason for providing diversity of citizenship jurisdiction to federal courts was to prevent state court bias against nonresidents, although this reason has been questioned as irrelevant in modern times. The federal court must apply the appropriate state's law in deciding the case. The dollar amount of the controversy must exceed the sum or value of $75,000. If this requirement is not met, the action must be brought in the appropriate state, Washington DC, or territory court.

Example Johann, a resident of the state of Idaho, is driving his automobile in Idaho when he negligently hits an automobile driven by Micaela, a resident of the state of New York. Micaela is injured in the accident. There is no federal question involved in this case; it is an automobile accident that involves state negligence law. However, there is diversity of citizenship in this case because the parties are residents of different states. Therefore, Micaela can sue Johann, bring her case in federal court in Idaho, and, if she does, the case will remain in federal court. If she brings the case in Idaho state court, the case will remain in Idaho state court unless Johann has the case removed to federal court. If this case is heard by a federal court, the court must apply Idaho law to the case.

Critical Legal Thinking
What was the original reason for the doctrine of diversity of citizenship? Do you think that this reason is valid today?

A corporation is considered to be a citizen of the state in which it is incorporated and the state in which its principal place of business, such as its headquarters, is located. Thus, if a plaintiff who is a resident of one of these states sues the corporation in the same state, there is no diversity of citizenship, and the case will be heard in state court. However, if a plaintiff who is a resident of one state sues the corporation in any state in which the corporation is not a citizen, there is diversity of citizenship; the case will be heard in a U.S. district court if the plaintiff brings the case in federal court or if the corporate defendant moves the case to federal court should the plaintiff have brought the case in state court. A corporation could be incorporated and have its principal place of business in one state, therefore making it a citizen of only one state.

Example Game Company, Inc. is incorporated in Delaware and has its principal place of business in California. Therefore, it is considered a resident of these two states. If an employee of Game Company negligently causes an automobile accident in Iowa in which Adan, a resident of Iowa, is injured, there is diversity of citizenship. Adan can bring a lawsuit against Game Company in Iowa state court, where the company can defend the case, or have the case removed to a federal court in Iowa. Adan could have originally brought the case in federal court in Iowa, where the case would be heard.

Federal courts have **exclusive jurisdiction** to hear cases involving federal crimes, antitrust, bankruptcy, patent and copyright, lawsuits against the United States, and most admiralty cases. State courts cannot hear these cases.

CONCEPT SUMMARY
JURISDICTION OF FEDERAL COURTS

Type of Jurisdiction	Description
Federal question	Cases arising under the U.S. Constitution, treaties, and federal statutes and regulations. There is no dollar-amount limit for federal question cases that can be brought in federal court.
Diversity of citizenship	Cases between citizens of different states or between a citizen of a state and a citizen or subject of a foreign country. Federal courts must apply the appropriate state law in such cases. The controversy must exceed the dollar limit of $75,000 for the federal court to hear the case.

Jurisdiction of State Courts

State courts and the courts of Washington DC and the territories of the United States have jurisdiction to hear cases that federal courts do not have jurisdiction to hear. These usually involve laws of states, Washington DC, territories, and local governments (e.g., cities and counties).

Examples Cases involving real estate, corporations, partnerships, limited liability companies, contracts, sales and lease contracts, and negotiable instruments are usually state law subject matters.

State courts have **concurrent jurisdiction** with federal courts to hear cases involving diversity of citizenship and federal questions over which federal courts do not have exclusive jurisdiction. If a case involving concurrent jurisdiction is brought by a plaintiff in federal court, the case remains in federal court. If the plaintiff brings a case involving concurrent jurisdiction in state court, the defendant can either let the case be decided by the state court or remove the case to federal court. If a case does not qualify to be brought in federal court, it must be brought in the appropriate state court.

Full Faith and Credit Clause
A clause in the U.S. Constitution that states that a judgment of a court of one state must be given "full faith and credit" by courts of another state.

Full Faith and Credit Clause

Under the **Full Faith and Credit Clause** of the U.S. Constitution (Article IV, Section 1), a judgment of a court of one state must be given "full faith and credit" by the courts of another state.

Example A plaintiff wins a monetary judgment against a defendant in California court. The defendant owns property in Ohio. If the defendant refuses to pay the judgment, the plaintiff can file a lawsuit in Ohio to enforce the California judgment and collect against the defendant's property in Ohio.

In the following case, the U.S. Supreme Court applied the Full Faith and Credit Clause.

CASE 2.1 *U.S. SUPREME COURT CASE Full Faith and Credit Clause*

V.L. v. E.L.

136 S.Ct. 1017, 2016 U.S. Lexis 1653 (2016)
Supreme Court of the United States

"With respect to judgments, the full faith and credit obligation is exacting."
—Per Curiam

Facts

V.L. and E.L. are two women who were in a relationship from approximately 1995 to 2011. Through assisted reproductive technology, E.L. gave birth to a child named S.L. in 2002 and twins named N.L. and H.L. in 2004. After the children were born, E.L. and V.L. raised them as joint parents. E.L. and V.L. decided to give legal parental status to V.L. by having her adopt the children. A Georgia court entered a final judgment of adoption making V.L. a legal parent of the children that she and E.L. had raised together since birth.

E.L. and V.L. ended their relationship in 2011, while living in Alabama, and V.L. moved out of the house that the couple had shared. V.L. filed a petition in a circuit court of Alabama alleging that E.L. had denied her access to the children and interfered with her ability to exercise parental rights. V.L. asked the Alabama court to register the Georgia adoption judgment and award her some measure of custody or visitation rights. The Georgia circuit court entered a judgment awarding V.L. scheduled visitation with the children. The Alabama Supreme Court reversed, holding that Alabama did not have to enforce the Georgia adoption judgment. V.L. appealed to the U.S. Supreme Court.

Issue

Does the Full Faith and Credit Clause require Alabama to enforce Georgia's adoption judgment?

Language of the U.S. Supreme Court

The Constitution provides that "Full Faith and Credit shall be given in each state to the public Acts, Records, and judicial Proceedings of every other State." That Clause requires each State to recognize and give effect to valid judgments rendered by the courts of its sister states. With respect to judgments, the full faith and credit obligation is exacting. A final judgment in one State, if rendered by a court with adjudicatory authority over the subject matter and persons governed by the judgment, qualifies for recognition throughout the land. It follows that the Alabama Supreme Court erred in refusing to grant that judgment full faith and credit.

Decision

The U.S. Supreme Court reversed the decision of the Alabama Supreme Court and remanded the case for further proceedings consistent with its opinion.

Critical Legal Thinking Questions

What does the Full Faith and Credit Clause provide? What would be the consequences if there were no Full Faith and Credit Clause in the Constitution?

Standing to Sue, Jurisdiction, and Venue

2.5 Define *standing to sue*, *jurisdiction*, and *venue*.

Not every court has the authority to hear all types of cases. First, to bring a lawsuit in a court, the plaintiff must have *standing to sue*. In addition, the court must have *personal jurisdiction* or other jurisdiction to hear the case, and the case must be brought in the proper *venue*. These topics are discussed in the following paragraphs.

Standing to Sue

standing to sue
Having some stake in the outcome of a lawsuit.

To bring a lawsuit, a plaintiff must have **standing to sue**. This means the plaintiff must have some stake in the outcome of the lawsuit.

Example Linda's friend Jon is injured in an accident caused by Emily. Jon refuses to sue. Linda cannot sue Emily on Jon's behalf because she does not have an interest in the result of the case.

A few states now permit investors to invest money in a lawsuit for a percentage return of any award of judgment. Courts hear and decide actual disputes involving specific controversies. Hypothetical questions will not be heard, and trivial lawsuits will be dismissed.

In Personam Jurisdiction

***in personam* jurisdiction (personal jurisdiction)**
Jurisdiction over the parties to a lawsuit.

A court's jurisdiction over a person is called ***in personam* jurisdiction**, or **personal jurisdiction.** A plaintiff, by filing a lawsuit with a court, gives the court *in personam* jurisdiction over him- or herself. The court must also have *in personam* jurisdiction over the defendant. Jurisdiction over a defendant is obtained in one of the following two ways:

general jurisdiction (all-purpose jurisdiction)
The jurisdiction in which a defendant can be sued regardless of where the underlying action prompting the lawsuit occurred.

- **General jurisdiction.** **General jurisdiction** means the jurisdiction in which a defendant can be sued regardless of where the underlying action prompting the lawsuit occurred. For an individual defendant, this is the state where the individual resides. For a corporation, this is the state in which the corporation is incorporated and the state in which it has its headquarters. General jurisdiction is referred to as **all-purpose jurisdiction.**

  Example Nokomis is a resident of North Dakota. Nokomis causes an automobile accident in Michigan that injures Jacinto. Jacinto, the injured plaintiff, can sue Nokomis in North Dakota because Nokomis is a resident of North Dakota and the courts of North Dakota have general jurisdiction over her. Jacinto cannot sue Nokomis in Wisconsin because Wisconsin has no jurisdiction over her.

specific jurisdiction (case-specific jurisdiction)
The jurisdiction in which a defendant can be sued because of the defendant's contacts with that jurisdiction.

- **Specific jurisdiction.** **Specific jurisdiction** means that a jurisdiction has personal jurisdiction to hear the case because of the defendant's contacts with that jurisdiction. Specific jurisdiction is referred to a **case-specific jurisdiction.**

  Example In the prior example, Jacinto, the injured plaintiff, can sue Nokomis in Michigan because that is where the accident occurred.

Service of Process

service of process
A summons being served on a defendant to obtain personal jurisdiction over him or her.

The Due Process clauses in the U.S. Constitution prohibit courts from exercising personal jurisdiction over a defendant unless the defendant has proper notice of the court's proceedings. Thus, a defendant must be notified that he or she is being sued and the court in which the lawsuit is being brought. This is usually accomplished by having a court summons and copy of the plaintiff's complaint formally served on the defendant. This is called **service of process.** Service of process is usually accomplished by having the summons and complaint given directly to the defendant. Personal service must be performed by an adult who is not a party to the lawsuit. Most often, a professional process server is hired to serve defendants.

If personal service is not possible, alternative forms of notice, such as serving persons at the defendant's residence or business, and mailing or emailing of the summons and complaint or publication of a notice in a newspaper, may be permitted. A corporation is subject to personal jurisdiction in the state in which it is incorporated and at its principal office.

A party who disputes the jurisdiction of a court can make a *special appearance* in that court to argue against imposition of jurisdiction. Service of process is not permitted during such an appearance.

Long-Arm Statute

In most states, a state court can obtain jurisdiction in a civil lawsuit over persons and businesses located in another state or country through the state's **long-arm statute**. These statutes extend a state's jurisdiction to nonresidents who are not served a summons within the state. The nonresident defendant in the civil lawsuit must have had some **minimum contact** with the state such that the maintenance of that lawsuit in that state does not offend traditional notions of *fair play* and *substantial justice*.

long-arm statute
A statute that extends a state's jurisdiction to nonresidents who were not served a summons within the state.

Following is the landmark U.S. Supreme Court case that established the minimum contacts standard.

Critical Legal Thinking

International Shoe Company v. State of Washington

"... have certain minimum contacts with [the state] such that the maintenance of that suit does not offend traditional notions of fair play and substantial justice."

—Harlan Stone, Chief Justice

How far can a state go to require a person or business to defend him-, her-, or itself in a court of law in that state? That question was presented to the Supreme Court of the United States in the landmark case ***International Shoe Company v. State of Washington***.

The International Shoe Company was a Delaware corporation that had its principal place of business in St. Louis, Missouri. In the state of Washington, the company's sales representative did not have a specific office but sold the shoes door-to-door and sometimes at temporary locations.

The state of Washington assessed an unemployment tax on International Shoe. International Shoe made a special appearance in the Washington court to argue that it did not do sufficient business in Washington to warrant having to pay unemployment taxes in that state. Eventually, International Shoe appealed its case to the U.S. Supreme Court. In its decision, the U.S. Supreme Court stated,

Due process requires only that in order to subject a defendant to a judgment in personam, if he be not present within the territory of the forum, he have certain minimum contacts with it such that the maintenance of that suit does not offend traditional notions of fair play and substantial justice.

Applying this standard, the U.S. Supreme Court held that International Shoe was subject to the lawsuit in Washington. Thus, the famous "minimum contacts" test and "traditional notions of fair play and substantial justice" establish when a state may require a person or business to appear in its courtrooms. Obviously, this is not a bright-line test, so battles of *in personam* jurisdiction abound to this day. *International Shoe Company v. State of Washington,* 326 U.S. 310, 66 S.Ct. 154, 1945 U.S. Lexis 1447 (Supreme Court of the United States, 1945)

Critical Legal Thinking Questions

Is it difficult determining when a party has had the minimum contacts with a state? How does one determine what constitutes "traditional notions of fair play and substantial justice"?

The exercise of long-arm jurisdiction is generally permitted over nonresidents who have (1) committed torts within the state (e.g., caused an automobile accident in the state), (2) entered into a contract either in the state or that affects the state (and allegedly breached the contract), or (3) transacted other business in the state that allegedly caused injury to another person.

In the following case, the U.S. Supreme Court had to decide whether a state had jurisdiction to hear and decide certain cases.

CASE 2.2 *U.S. SUPREME COURT CASE Jurisdiction*

Bristol-Myers Squibb Company v. Superior Court of California

137 S.Ct. 1773 (2017)
Supreme Court of the United States

"What is needed—and what is missing here—is a connection between the forum and the specific claims at issue."

—Samuel Alito, Justice

Facts

Bristol-Myers Squibb Company (BMS), a large pharmaceutical company, is incorporated in Delaware and headquartered in New York, and it maintains substantial operations in both New York and New Jersey. One of the pharmaceuticals that BMS manufactures and sells is Plavix, a prescription drug that thins the blood and inhibits blood clotting. BMS did not develop Plavix in California, and did not manufacture, label, package, or work on regulatory approval of the product in California. But BMS does sell Plavix in California.

A group of plaintiffs—consisting of 86 California residents and 592 nonresidents from 33 other states—filed eight complaints in California court, alleging that Plavix had damaged their health. All the complaints allege claims under California law, including products liability, negligent misrepresentation, and misleading advertising claims. The nonresident plaintiffs did not allege that they obtained Plavix through California physicians or any other California source, nor did they claim that they were injured by Plavix or were treated for their injuries in California. Asserting lack of personal jurisdiction, BMS moved to squash the nonresidents' claims. The California Supreme Court held that California had jurisdiction to hear both resident and nonresident claims. BMS appealed to the U.S. Supreme Court, alleging that under the Due Process Clause of the Fourteenth Amendment to the U.S. Constitution, California lacked personal jurisdiction to hear the nonresident cases.

Issue

Does California's exercise of jurisdiction over the nonresident plaintiffs violate the Due Process Clause?

Language of the U.S. Supreme Court

In order for a state court to exercise specific jurisdiction, the suit must arise out of or relate to the defendant's contacts with the forum. The State Supreme Court found that specific jurisdiction was present without identifying any adequate link between the state and the nonresidents' claims. The nonresidents were not prescribed Plavix in California, did not purchase Plavix in California, did not ingest Plavix in California, and were not injured by Plavix in California. The mere fact that other plaintiffs were prescribed, obtained, and ingested Plavix in California—and allegedly sustained the same injuries as did the nonresidents—does not allow the State to assert specific jurisdiction over the nonresidents' claims. What is needed—and what is missing here—is a connection between the forum and the specific claims at issue. It follows that California courts cannot claim specific jurisdiction.

Decision

The U.S. Supreme Court held that under the Due Process Clause, California does not have personal jurisdiction to hear the nonresidents' cases against BMS.

Ethics Questions

Can California residents sue BMS in California court? Can the nonresidents of California sue BMS elsewhere? Why might the nonresidents have preferred to sue BMS in California instead of their home states?

In Rem Jurisdiction

***in rem* jurisdiction**
Jurisdiction to hear a case because of jurisdiction over the property of the lawsuit.

A court may have jurisdiction to hear and decide a case because it has jurisdiction over the property of the lawsuit. This is called ***in rem* jurisdiction** ("jurisdiction over the thing"). *In rem* jurisdiction often is used to decide disputes over the ownership of real estate located within the state. This is so even if one or more of the disputing parties live in another state or states.

Example One party, a resident of New York, claims ownership of a piece of real estate located in Michigan. Another party, a resident of Wisconsin, claims ownership to the same piece of property. A Michigan court has *in rem* jurisdiction to decide the dispute because the real property is located in Michigan.

Quasi in Rem Jurisdiction

Sometimes, a plaintiff who obtains a judgment against a defendant in one state will try to collect the judgment by attaching property of the defendant that is located in another state. The plaintiff can bring a court action in the state in which the property is located to recover the judgment. This is permitted under ***quasi in rem* jurisdiction**, or **attachment jurisdiction**.

***quasi in rem* jurisdiction (attachment jurisdiction)**
Jurisdiction that allows a plaintiff who obtains a judgment in one state to try to collect the judgment by attaching the defendant's property located in another state.

Example A motorist, who resides and is driving in New Mexico, causes an automobile accident that injures Darius. Darius sues the defendant in New Mexico and recovers a judgment of $1 million. The defendant owns no property in New Mexico but does own property in Florida. Darius, under *quasi in rem* jurisdiction, can bring a legal action in Florida to recover the defendant's property located there.

CONCEPT SUMMARY

IN PERSONAM, *IN REM*, AND *QUASI IN REM* JURISDICTION

Type of Jurisdiction	Description
In personam jurisdiction	A court has jurisdiction over the parties to the lawsuit. The plaintiff submits to the jurisdiction of the court by filing the lawsuit there. Personal jurisdiction is obtained over the defendant through *service of process* to that person.
In rem jurisdiction	A court has jurisdiction to hear and decide a case because it has jurisdiction over the property at issue in the lawsuit (e.g., real property located in the state).
Quasi in rem jurisdiction	A plaintiff who obtains a judgment against a defendant in one state may utilize the court system of another state to attach property of the defendant that is located in the second state.

Venue

Venue is concerned with the geographical location of the court where a lawsuit is commenced. Each state has a trial court system with individual trial courts located throughout the state. Most states have a trial court located in each county. Each state has at least one U.S. district court, or more, which are the trial courts of the federal government. Venue determines the locale of the state court (county) or federal court (district) that will hear the case.

venue
The geographical location of the state court (county) or federal court (district) that will hear a law case.

Venue is usually the trial court of the appropriate court system that is located closest to where a substantial amount of the events giving rise to the lawsuit occurred. Evidence and witnesses are often available near this location. Other factors, such as the residence of the parties, may be considered when determining venue. A case can be brought in only one venue.

Example Prentice, a resident of the state of Michigan, commits a felony crime in Los Angeles County, California. The California trial court system has jurisdiction to hear the case. Each county in the state of California has a trial court. The state trial court located in the county of Los Angeles is the proper venue because the crime was committed in Los Angeles, the witnesses are probably from the area, and so on. Although Prentice is a resident of Michigan, the state of Michigan is not the proper jurisdiction or venue for this case.

Occasionally, pretrial publicity may prejudice jurors located in the proper venue. In such cases, a **change of venue** may be requested so that a more impartial jury can be found. Changes of venue, however, are rare.

The courts generally frown on **forum shopping** (i.e., looking for a favorable court without a valid reason).

Forum-Selection and Choice-of-Law Clauses

One issue that often comes up when parties from different states or countries have a legal dispute is which jurisdiction's court will be used. Also, sometimes there is a dispute as to which jurisdiction's laws apply to a case. When the parties have not agreed in advance, courts must make the decision about which court has jurisdiction and what law applies. This situation causes ambiguity, and resolving it will cost the parties time and money.

Therefore, parties sometimes agree in their contract as to what state's courts, what federal court, or what country's court will have jurisdiction to hear a legal dispute should one arise. Such clauses in contracts are called **forum-selection clauses** or **choice-of-forum clauses**. Of course, the selected court must have jurisdiction to hear the case.

forum-selection clause (choice-of-forum clause)
A contract provision that designates a certain court to hear any dispute concerning nonperformance of the contract.

choice-of-law clause
A contract provision that designates a certain state's or country's law that will be applied in any dispute concerning nonperformance of the contract.

In addition to agreeing to a forum, the parties also often agree in contracts as to what state's law or country's law will apply in resolving a dispute. These clauses are called **choice-of-law clauses**. The selected law may be of a jurisdiction that does not have jurisdiction to hear the case.

Example Export Company, located in Shanghai, China, enters into a contract with Import Company, located in San Francisco, California, United States, whereby Export Company agrees to deliver designated goods to Import Company. In their contract, the parties agree that, if there is a dispute, the Superior Court of California, located in San Francisco, will hear the case and that the United Nations Convention on Contracts for the International Sale of Goods (CISG) will be the contract law that will be applied in resolving the dispute.

In the following case, the court had to decide whether to enforce a forum-selection clause.

Case 2.3 *FEDERAL COURT CASE Forum-Selection Clause*

Carter's of New Bedford, Inc. v. Nike, Inc.

790 F.3d 289, 2015 U.S. App. Lexis 10692 (2015)
United States Court of Appeals for the First Circuit

"The district court determined that Carter's did not meet its burden to show that the forum-selection clause would deprive Carter's of its day in court."

—Juan Torruella, Circuit Judge

Facts

Nike, Inc. is a worldwide seller of shoes, apparel, and other items carrying the Nike brand. Nike's headquarters is in Beaverton, Oregon. Carter's of New Bedford, Inc. is a family-owned retail clothing and footwear business that operates two stores in Massachusetts. Carter's has sold Nike products for 28 years. The agreement between Nike and Carter's is contained in the invoices that Nike provides to Carter's, which are agreed to by both parties. The invoice agreements include a forum-selection clause that requires any claims that Carter's has with Nike to be brought in Oregon, not Massachusetts. When Nike notified Carter's that it was terminating the parties' business relationship, Carter's sued Nike in Massachusetts court alleging that Nike breached its agreement with Carter's. Nike argued that any claim Carter's has against Nike must be brought in Oregon pursuant to the forum-selection clause and moved to have Carter's Massachusetts lawsuit dismissed. The U.S. district court dismissed the lawsuit. Carter's appealed.

Issue

Is the forum-selection clause enforceable?

Language of the Court

The district court determined that Carter's did not meet its burden to show that the forum-selection clause would deprive Carter's of its day in court. Carter's argues that it should not be required to finance a cross country legal battle against an international behemoth and that it would face extreme hardship if forced to go to Oregon. Carter's fails to persuade this court that enforcement of the forum-selection clause would make it practically impossible for it to litigate in Oregon.

Decision

The U.S. court of appeals affirmed the district court's decision that enforced the forum-selection clause and dismissed Carter's Massachusetts lawsuit against Nike.

Critical Legal Thinking Questions

Do you think small retailers like Carter's will sue Nike in Oregon? Why or why not? Did Nike act ethically in enforcing the forum-selection clause against Carter's?

Jurisdiction in Digital Commerce

2.6 Explain how jurisdiction is applied to digital commerce.

Obtaining personal jurisdiction over a defendant in another state has always been difficult for courts. Today, with the advent of the internet and the ability of persons and businesses to reach millions of people in other states electronically, particularly through websites, modern issues arise as to whether courts have jurisdiction in cyberspace. For example, if a person in one state uses the website of an internet seller located in another state, can the user sue the internet seller in his or her state under that state's long-arm statute?

One seminal case that addressed jurisdiction in cyberspace was ***Zippo Manufacturing Company v. Zippo Dot Com, Inc.***[2] Zippo Manufacturing Company (Zippo) manufactures a well-known line of tobacco lighters in Bradford, Pennsylvania, and sells them worldwide. Zippo Dot Com, Inc. (Dot Com), which was a California corporation with its principal place of business and its servers located in Sunnyvale, California, operated an internet website that transmitted information and sexually explicit material to its subscribers.

Zippo Manufacturing Company v. Zippo Dot Com, Inc. An important case that established a test for determining when a court has jurisdiction over the owner or operator of an interactive, semi-interactive, or passive website.

Three thousand Dot Com paying subscribers, of 140,000 subscribers worldwide, were located in Pennsylvania. Zippo sued Dot Com in U.S. district court in Pennsylvania for trademark infringement. Dot Com defended, alleging that it was not subject to personal jurisdiction in Pennsylvania because the "minimum contacts" and "traditional notions of fair play and substantial justice" standards were not met and therefore did not permit Pennsylvania to assert jurisdiction over it. In addressing jurisdiction, the court created a "sliding scale" in order to measure the nature and quality of the commercial activity effectuated in a forum state through a website:

At one end of the spectrum are situations where a defendant clearly does business over the internet. If the defendant enters into contracts with residents of a foreign jurisdiction that involve the knowing and repeated transmission of computer files over the internet, personal jurisdiction is proper. At the opposite end are situations where a defendant has simply posted information on an internet website which is accessible to users in foreign jurisdictions. A passive website that does little more than make information available to those who are interested in it is not grounds for the exercise of personal jurisdiction. The middle ground is occupied by interactive websites where a user can exchange information with the host computer. In these cases, the exercise of jurisdiction is determined by examining the level of interactivity and commercial nature of the exchange of information that occurs on the website.

In applying this standard, the court found that the case involved doing business over the internet. The court held that Dot Com was subject to personal jurisdiction under the Pennsylvania long-arm statute and ordered Dot Com to defend itself in Pennsylvania.

The following feature discusses a state court's jurisdiction over an internet eBay seller.

Information Technology

Jurisdiction Over an Internet eBay Seller

"Internet forums such as eBay expand the seller's market literally to the world ..."
—Doug Combs, Justice

Odil Ostonakulov, a resident of Tennessee, operates Motorcars of Nashville, Inc. (MNI), a Tennessee corporation. The company sells used automobiles to residents of 50 states on eBay, averaging 12–35 cars for sale every day on eBay. Samantha Guffey, a resident of Oklahoma, was the winning bidder on a used Volvo automobile listed by MNI on eBay. In addition to Guffey, MNI made sales of vehicles to other residents of Oklahoma. After receiving the automobile, Guffey determined that the automobile was not in the condition advertised and sued Ostonakulov and MNI in Oklahoma court alleging that the defendants had engaged in fraud. The defendants filed a motion with the Oklahoma court to have the case dismissed, alleging that Oklahoma lacked personal jurisdiction over the defendants because they did not possess minimum contacts with Oklahoma to be subject to Oklahoma's long-arm statute. The trial court dismissed the lawsuit, finding that Oklahoma lacked personal jurisdiction over the defendants. Guffey appealed.

The Supreme Court of Oklahoma held that Oklahoma possessed personal jurisdiction over the Tennessee individual and corporation which operated a commercial enterprise that sold an automobile on eBay to an Oklahoma resident. The court stated, "Internet forums such as eBay expand the seller's market literally to the world and sellers know that, and avail themselves of the benefits of this greatly expanded marketplace. Sellers cannot expect to avail themselves of the benefits of the internet-created world market that they purposely exploit and profit from without accepting the concomitant legal responsibilities that such an expanded market may bring with it." The court ordered the defendants to stand trial in Oklahoma. *Guffey v. Ostonakulov*, 321 P.3d 971 (Supreme Court of Oklahoma, 2014)

Critical Legal Thinking Questions

Is the test of minimum contacts easy to apply? Would Oklahoma have had personal jurisdiction over an individual from another state who sold his or her used private vehicle on eBay to an Oklahoma purchaser?

The following feature compares the legal systems of Japan and the United States.

Global Law

Judicial System of Japan

Businesses often complain that there are too many lawyers and there is too much litigation in the United States. There are currently more than 1 million lawyers and approximately 20 million civil lawsuits filed per year in this country. On the other hand, in Japan, a country with about 40 percent of the population of the United States, there are approximately 25,000 lawyers and much less litigation.

Much of the difference is cultural: Japan nurtures the attitude that confrontation should be avoided, and the Japanese bias against courtroom solutions is strong. Thus, companies often avoid battle in court and instead opt for private arbitration of many of their disputes.

Other differences are built into the legal system itself. Plaintiffs usually must pay their lawyers a large up-front fee to represent them. Plaintiffs must pay a filing fee with the court, which is based on amount claimed rather than a flat fee. And contingency fees are not available in many cases.

Henry R. Cheeseman

JAPAN

Key Terms and Concepts

In rem jurisdiction (36)
Intermediate appellate court (appellate court or court of appeals) (22)
International Shoe Company v. State of Washington (35)
Limited-jurisdiction trial court (inferior trial court) (21)
Long-arm statute (35)
Majority decision (29)
Minimum contact (35)
Petition for certiorari (29)
Plurality decision (30)
Quasi in rem jurisdiction (attachment jurisdiction) (37)
Rule of four (30)
Service of process (34)
Small claims court (21)
Special federal courts (25)
Specific jurisdiction (case-specific jurisdiction) (34)
Standing to sue (34)
State courts (21)
State supreme court (22)
Supreme Court of the United States (U.S. Supreme Court) (28)
Tie decision (30)
Unanimous decision (29)
U.S. Bankruptcy Court (25)
U.S. courts of appeals (26)
U.S. Court of Appeals for the Armed Forces (25)
U.S. Court of Appeals for the Federal Circuit (26)
U.S. Court of Appeals for Veterans Claims (25)
U.S. Court of Federal Claims (25)
U.S. Court of International Trade (25)
U.S. district courts (26)
U.S. District of Columbia Circuit (26)
U.S. Foreign Intelligence Surveillance Court (FISA court) (25)
U.S. Foreign Intelligence Surveillance Court of Review (FISCR) (25)
U.S. Tax Court (25)
U.S. territorial courts (26)
Venue (37)
Writ of certiorari (29)
Zippo Manufacturing Company v. Zippo Dot Com, Inc. (39)

Critical Legal Thinking Cases

2.1 Personal Jurisdiction Richtone Design Group LLC (Richtone) is a New York limited liability company (LLC) that owns the copyright to the Pilates Teacher Training Manual and licenses fitness instructors to teach Pilates exercise programs. Live Siri Art, Inc. is a California corporation owned by Siri Galliano. Richtone learned that Live Siri Art and Galliano were selling the Pilates manual over a website for profit without permission. They sold several copies of the manual to New York residents, making only about $1,000 in sales in New York from 2000 to 2012. Defendants have no office, property, or bank accounts in New York. Richtone brought a copyright infringement lawsuit against Live Siri Art and Galliano in U.S. district court in New York, alleging that the defendants were subject to personal jurisdiction in New York based on New York's long-arm statute. The defendants Live Siri Art and Galliano defended, alleging that they were not subject to suit in New York because they were residents of California, that they did not have the requisite minimum contacts with New York to be subject to suit in that state, and that to make them defend the lawsuit in New York violated their due process rights. The defendants made a motion to dismiss the New York lawsuit based on lack of personal jurisdiction. Are the defendants subject to lawsuit in New York? *Richtone Design Group, LLC v. Live Art, Inc.*, 2013 U.S. Dist. Lexis 157781 (United States District Court for the Southern District of New York, 2013)

2.2 Service of Process Facebook, Inc. filed a complaint in the U.S. district court against numerous defendants alleging that the named defendants engaged in trademark infringement, cybersquatting, and false designation of origin. Facebook seeks to enjoin the defendants from engaging in typosquatting schemes whereby the defendants register internet domain names that are confusingly similar to facebook.com (e.g., facebock.com); potential users of Facebook's website who enter a typographical error are diverted to the typesquatter's website, which is designed to look strikingly similar in appearance to Facebook's website, to trick users into thinking that they are using Facebook's website. Facebook served the defendants except 14, who Facebook has not been able to serve personally, by mail, or by telephone. Facebook made a motion to the U.S. district court to be permitted to serve these defendants by sending an email notice to the defendants' websites. May Facebook use alternative service of process by sending email notices to the defendants' websites? *Facebook, Inc. v. Banana Ads LLC*, 2013 U.S. Dist. Lexis 65834 (United States District Court for the Northern District of California, 2013)

2.3 Standing to Sue Four friends, John Bertram, Matt Norden, Scott Olson, and Tony Harvey, all residents of Ohio, traveled to the Upper Peninsula of Michigan to go snowmobiling. On their first day of snowmobiling, after going about 135 miles, the lead snowmobiler, Olson, came to a stop sign on the snowmobile trail where it intersected a private driveway. As Olson approached the sign, he gave the customary hand signal and stopped his snowmobile. Harvey, second in line, was going too fast to stop, so Olson pulled his snowmobile to the right side of the private driveway. Harvey, to avoid hitting Olson, pulled his snowmobile to the left and went over a 5- or 6-foot snow embankment. Bertram, third in line, going about 30 miles per hour, slammed on his brake, turned 45 degrees, and slammed into Olson's snowmobile.

Bertram was thrown from his snowmobile. Norden, fourth in line, could not stop, and his snowmobile hit Bertram's leg, breaking it in several places. Bertram had to undergo surgery to repair the broken bones.

Bertram filed a lawsuit against Olson, Harvey, and Norden in a trial court in Ohio, claiming that each of his friends was liable to him for their negligent snowmobile operation. A Michigan statute specifically stated that snowmobilers assumed the risks associated with snowmobiling. Ohio law did not contain an assumption of the risk rule regarding snowmobiling. The three defendants made a motion for summary judgment. Does Michigan or Ohio law apply to this case? *Bertram v. Norden, et al.*, 823 N.E.2d 478, 2004 Ohio App. Lexis 550 (Court of Appeals of Ohio, 2004)

2.4 Long-Arm Statute Casino Queen, Inc. operates a gambling and hotel establishment in East St. Louis, Illinois. Casino Queen's location places it within a large metropolitan area composed of East St. Louis, Illinois, and St. Louis, Missouri, and several other cities in both Illinois and Missouri. Casino Queen advertises through print, radio, and television media in Missouri. Mark Myers is a resident of St. Louis County, Missouri. Myers went to Casino Queen to gamble and won $17,500. He cashed out his winnings and took a cab to Missouri. Two individuals who saw him cash out his winnings at the casino followed Myers in a cab to Missouri, where they beat him and robbed him of his winnings. Myers sued Casino Queen in a Missouri court, alleging that the casino was negligent in not providing Myers warnings of such illegal activities and protecting him from such activities. Casino Queen, an Illinois corporation, made a motion to have the lawsuit dismissed by the Missouri court, alleging that the Missouri court did not have personal jurisdiction over the Illinois casino. Myers argued that Missouri's long-arm statute gave it personal jurisdiction over Casino Queen. Does the Missouri court have personal jurisdiction over the Illinois casino based on Missouri's long-arm statute? *Myers v. Casino Queen, Inc.*, 689 F.3d 904, 2012 U.S. App. Lexis 17543 (United States Court of Appeals for the Eighth Circuit, 2012)

2.5 Standing to Sue McDonald's Corporation owns, operates, and franchises fast-food restaurants. Over the years, McDonald's ran promotional games such as Monopoly Game at McDonald's, Who Wants to Be a Millionaire, and other games where high-value prizes, including vehicles and cash up to $1 million, could be won. A person could win by collecting certain games pieces distributed by McDonald's. McDonald's employed Simon Marketing, Inc. (Simon) to operate the promotional games. An investigation by the Federal Bureau of Investigation (FBI) uncovered a criminal ring led by Jerome Jacobson, director of security at Simon, whereby he embezzled game pieces and diverted them to "winners" who collected more than $20 million in high-value prizes. After being caught, Jacobson and other members of the ring entered guilty pleas in connection with the conspiracy.

The Burger King Corporation, a competitor of McDonald's, owns, operates, and franchises fast-food restaurants. One franchisee is Phoenix of Broward, Inc. (Phoenix), which operates a Burger King restaurant in Fort Lauderdale, Florida. Phoenix brought a class action lawsuit in U.S. District Court on behalf of Burger King franchises against McDonald's, alleging that McDonald's engaged in false advertising in violation of the federal Lanham Act when it advertised that players had an equal chance of winning high-value prizes when in fact they did not because of the Jacobson's criminal conspiracy. Phoenix alleged that it suffered injuries of lost sales because of McDonald's false advertising claims. McDonald's filed a motion to dismiss Phoenix's lawsuit, asserting that Phoenix had no standing to sue. Did plaintiff Phoenix have standing to sue McDonald's? *Phoenix of Broward, Inc. v. McDonald's Corporation*, 441 F.Supp.2d 1241, 2006 U.S. Dist. Lexis 55112 (United States District Court for the Northern District of Georgia, 2006)

2.6 U.S. Supreme Court Decision Two brothers were shot and killed in their Houston home. The police found shotgun shells at the scene of the crime. Witness testimony led the police to consider Genovevo Salinas to be a person of interest. Police found Salinas at his home, where he agreed to turn over his shotgun for ballistics testing and accompanied the officers to the police station for questioning. The interview with the police was custodial: It lasted approximately 1 hour, and Salinas was not read his *Miranda* rights. For most of the interview, Salinas answered the officers' questions. However, when asked whether his shotgun would match the shells recovered at the scene of the murder, Salinas declined to answer and remained silent. The police let Salinas go. Eventually, after more evidence was obtained, the government brought murder charges against Salinas. At trial, over Salinas's objection, the police witnesses testified that when Salinas was asked whether the shotgun shells found at the scene would match Salinas's shotgun, he grew silent and refused to answer that question. The jury found Salinas guilty, and he received a 20-year sentence. Salinas appealed, alleging that the evidence that he remained silent when asked the question regarding his shotgun and the shells at the scene of crime should not have been admitted at trial. His appeal reached the U.S. Supreme Court.

Three justices wrote the Court's opinion, two justices concurred, and four dissented. What kind of decision is this U.S. Supreme Court decision? Does this decision establish precedent? *Salinas v. Texas*, 133 S.Ct. 2174, 2012 U.S. Lexis 4697 (Supreme Court of the United States, 2012)

Ethics Cases

2.7 Ethics Case Chanel, Inc. is a corporate entity duly organized under the laws of the state of New York, with its principal place of business in New York City. Chanel is engaged in the business of manufacturing and distributing throughout the world various luxury goods, including handbags, wallets, and numerous other products under the federally registered trademark "Chanel" and monogram marks. Chanel filed a lawsuit in the U.S. district court in Maryland against defendant Ladawn Banks, a resident of Florida. Chanel alleged that Banks owned and operated the fully interactive website www.lovenamebrands.com, through which she sold handbags and wallets bearing counterfeit trademarks identical to the registered Chanel marks. The goods at issue in this case were sold over the internet to a resident of Maryland. The court had to address the issue of whether Maryland had personal jurisdiction under its long-arm statute over the Florida defendant Banks. Does the Maryland court have personal jurisdiction over the Florida defendant? Did defendant Banks act ethically in this case? *Chanel, Inc. v. Banks*, 2010 U.S. Dist. Lexis 135374 (United States District Court for Maryland, 2010)

2.8 Ethics Case Hertz Corporation is incorporated in the state of Delaware and has its headquarters in the state of New Jersey. Melinda Friend, a California citizen, sued the Hertz Corporation in California state court seeking damages for Hertz's alleged violation of California's wage and hour laws. Hertz filed notice to move the case from state court to U.S. district court, a federal court, asserting diversity of citizenship between the parties. Friend argued that because Hertz operated more than 270 rental car locations and had more than 2,000 employees in California, it was a citizen of California; thus diversity of citizenship did not apply and the case could not be moved to federal court but should be decided by a California state court. Is Hertz Corporation a citizen of California and subject to suit in state court? Was it ethical for Hertz to deny citizenship in California when it had such a large presence in California with its 270 rental car locations and more than 2,000 employees there? *Hertz Corporation v. Friend*, 559 U.S. 77, 130 S.Ct. 1181, 2010 U.S. Lexis 1897 (Supreme Court of the United States, 2010)

Notes

1. Alexis de Tocqueville, Book I, Chapter 8, *Democracy in America*. 1835. Liberty Fund, Inc.
2. *Zippo Manufacturing Company v. Zippo Dot Com, Inc.* 952 F.Supp. 1119 (U.S. District Court, Western District of Pennsylvania).

CHAPTER 3

Judicial, Alternative, and E-Dispute Resolution

OLD COURTHOUSE, ST. LOUIS, MISSOURI

This is the old state courthouse located in St. Louis, Missouri. It is now part of Gateway Arch National Park. More than 75 million lawsuits are brought in state and federal courts annually. More than 95 percent of the cases are settled, and the rest go to trial. Of the cases decided by trial courts, fewer than 5 percent are appealed.

Henry R. Cheeseman

Learning Objectives

After studying this chapter, you should be able to:

- **3.1** Describe how attorneys are compensated.
- **3.2** Describe the pretrial litigation process.
- **3.3** Define *complaint*, *summons*, and *answer* and describe the pleading process.
- **3.4** Define *class action* and describe the requirements for bringing a class action lawsuit.
- **3.5** Describe the discovery process and the various methods of discovery.
- **3.6** Describe e-discovery and how electronic evidence can be used at a legal proceeding.
- **3.7** Contrast the different types of pretrial motions.
- **3.8** Describe the goals and procedures of a settlement conference.
- **3.9** Describe the trial process.
- **3.10** Explain how electronic technology is being used in courts and legal proceedings.
- **3.11** Describe the appellate process and the possible results of an appeal.
- **3.12** Explain the use of arbitration and other methods of alternative dispute resolution.
- **3.13** Describe forms of e-dispute resolution.

"*We're the jury, dread our fury!*"

—William S. Gilbert, *Trial by Jury (1875)*

Introduction to Judicial, Alternative, and E-Dispute Resolution

Pieces of evidence, each by itself insufficient, may together constitute a significant whole and justify by their combined effect a conclusion.

Lord Wright
Grant v. Australian Knitting Mills, Ltd. (1936)

The process of bringing, maintaining, and defending a lawsuit is called *litigation*. It is also called *judicial dispute resolution* because courts are used to decide the case. Litigation is a difficult, time-consuming, and costly process that must comply with complex procedural rules. Although it is not required, most parties employ a lawyer to represent them when they are involved in a lawsuit.

Several forms of *nonjudicial dispute resolution* have been developed in response to the expense and difficulty of bringing a lawsuit. These methods, collectively called *alternative dispute resolution*, are being used more and more often to resolve contract and commercial disputes.

The computer, the internet, and electronic devices are now heavily used when resolving legal disputes. Many courts either allow or mandate that documents be submitted to the court electronically. Lawyers often correspond with each other, hold depositions, and do various other tasks using electronic means. In addition, electronic arbitration and mediation is often used to resolve legal disputes. The resolution of legal disputes using electronic means is often referred to as *e-dispute resolution*.

This chapter discusses the judicial litigation process, alternative dispute resolution, and e-dispute resolution.

Attorney Representation

3.1 Describe how attorneys are compensated.

Trial by jury is as essential to secure the liberty of the people as any one of the pre-existent rights of nature.
James Madison
Former president of the United States

Speech in Congress Proposing Constitutional Amendments (1789)

Most parties to a legal transaction or a civil lawsuit or arbitration employ attorneys to represent them. Each party will hire their own lawyer. Some lawyers practice as sole practitioners. Others practice law with law firms. In such a case, the fee agreement is often between the client and the law firm. Law firms range in size from two-partner law firms to law firms with hundreds of lawyers and offices worldwide.

Lawyers most often charge an *hourly rate* for their services. The fee charged reflects the attorney's experience, cost of operations, and the location of his or her practice. Attorneys in small towns and rural areas tend to charge around \$100 to \$200 per hour. In metropolitan areas fees usually range from \$200 to \$500 per hour. Lawyers in more specialized areas, such as mergers, patent law, and securities law, will charge even higher rates. Attorneys often require a client to pay a **retainer**, that is, a specified dollar amount deposited by the client before the lawyer proceeds, which is placed in a trust account. The lawyer's fees are taken from the trust account as he or she provides hourly services. Often, the retainer must be replenished as attorneys' fees are billed against the retainer. Fees are also charged for paralegals who work on the case, for expenses such as copying documents, filing fees with the court, fees for expert witnesses, and other fees associated with the case or legal transaction.

Where a legal matter is straightforward and well defined, attorneys often charge a *flat fee*. This fee arrangement is often used to draft wills and trusts, form small corporations and limited liability companies, file simple bankruptcy proceedings, settle uncontested divorces, and the like.

contingency fee
A fee arrangement with a client whereby a lawyer receives a percentage of the amount recovered by winning or settling a lawsuit. If the lawyer does not win or settle the case in the client's favor, the lawyer receives nothing.

In certain types of cases, attorneys work on a **contingency-fee** basis. Under a contingency-fee arrangement, the lawyer receives a percentage of the amount recovered by winning or settling a case. Contingency fees normally range from 20 to 50 percent of the award or settlement, with the average being about 35 to

40 percent. Expenses for expert witnesses and the like are deducted from the gross amount recovered. The client receives the remainder after attorney fees and expenses have been deducted. If the lawyer does not win or settle the case in the client's favor, the lawyer receives nothing. Contingency-fee arrangements are often used in automobile accident lawsuits, medical malpractice claims, product liability lawsuits, and other personal injury lawsuits.

In criminal cases, the government is represented by a prosecutor who most likely is a government employee. Some governments employ private attorneys to act as prosecutors. A defendant in a criminal case can hire his or her own attorney. If the defendant cannot afford an attorney, the government will provide an attorney to represent the defendant free of charge. This attorney is usually a government attorney, although some governments hire private attorneys to act as defense attorneys in criminal cases.

Pretrial Litigation Process

3.2 Describe the pretrial litigation process.

The bringing, maintaining, and defending of a lawsuit is generally referred to as the *litigation process*, or **litigation**. The pretrial litigation process can be divided into the following major phases: *pleadings, discovery, pretrial motions*, and *settlement conference*. Each of these phases is discussed in the sections that follow.

litigation
The process of bringing, maintaining, and defending a lawsuit.

Pleadings

3.3 Define *complaint, summons*, and *answer* and describe the pleading process.

The paperwork that is filed with the court to initiate and respond to a lawsuit is referred to as the **pleadings**. The major pleadings are the *complaint*, the *answer*, the *cross-complaint*, and the *reply*.

pleadings
The paperwork that is filed with the court to initiate and respond to a lawsuit.

Complaint and Summons

To initiate a lawsuit, the party who is suing (the **plaintiff**) must file a **complaint** in the proper court. The complaint names the parties to the lawsuit, alleges the ultimate facts and law violated, and contains a "prayer for relief" for a remedy to be awarded by the court. The complaint can be as long as necessary, depending on the case's complexity. A sample complaint appears in Exhibit 3.1.

Once a complaint has been filed with the court, the court issues a summons. A **summons** is a court order directing the defendant to appear in court and answer the complaint. The complaint and summons are served on the defendant. This is called **service of process**. Usually this is accomplished by a sheriff, another government official, or a private process server personally serving the complaint and summons on the defendant. If personal service has been tried and is unsuccessful, the court may permit alternative forms of service, such as by fax, by mailing the complaint to the last known address of the defendant, or by email.

plaintiff
The party who files a complaint.

complaint
The document a plaintiff files with the court and serves on the defendant to initiate a lawsuit.

summons
A court order that directs the defendant to appear in court and answer the complaint.

Answer

The party who is being sued (the **defendant**) must file an **answer** to the plaintiff's complaint. The defendant's answer is filed with the court and served on the plaintiff. In the answer, the defendant admits or denies the allegations contained in the plaintiff's complaint. A judgment is entered against a defendant who admits all of the allegations in the complaint. The case proceeds if the defendant denies all or some of the allegations.

If the defendant does not answer the complaint, a **default judgment** is entered against him or her. A default judgment establishes the defendant's liability. The plaintiff then has only to prove damages.

defendant
The party who files an answer.

answer
The defendant's written response to a plaintiff's complaint that is filed with the court and served on the plaintiff.

Exhibit 3.1 SAMPLE COMPLAINT

In the United States District Court for the District of Idaho

John Doe
Plaintiff

v.

Jane Roe

Defendant

Civil No. 2-1001

COMPLAINT

The plaintiff, by and through his attorney, alleges:

1. The plaintiff is a resident of the State of Idaho, the defendant is a resident of the State of Washington, and there is diversity of citizenship between the parties.
2. The amount in controversy exceeds the sum of $75,000, exclusive of interest and costs.
3. On January 10, 2020, plaintiff was exercising reasonable care while walking across the intersection of Sun Valley Road and Main Street, Ketchum, Idaho when defendant negligently drove her car through a red light at the intersection and struck plaintiff.
4. As a result of the defendant's negligence, plaintiff has incurred medical expenses of $104,000 and suffered severe physical injury and mental distress.

WHEREFORE, plaintiff claims judgment in the amount of $1,000,000 interest at the maximum legal rate, and costs of this action.

By ____________________
Edward Lawson
Attorney for Plaintiff
100 Main Street
Ketchum, Idaho

In addition to answering the complaint, a defendant's answer can assert **affirmative defenses**.

Examples If a complaint alleges that the plaintiff was personally injured by the defendant, the defendant's answer could state that he or she acted in self-defense. Another affirmative defense would be an assertion that the plaintiff's lawsuit is barred because the *statute of limitations* (time within which to bring the lawsuit) has expired.

cross-complaint
A document filed by the defendant against the plaintiff to seek damages or some other remedy.

reply
A document filed by the original plaintiff to answer the defendant's cross-complaint.

Cross-Complaint and Reply

A defendant who believes that he or she has been injured by the plaintiff can file a **cross-complaint** against the plaintiff in addition to an answer. In the cross-complaint, the defendant (now the **cross-complainant**) sues the plaintiff (now the **cross-defendant**) for damages or some other remedy. The original plaintiff must file a **reply** (answer) to the cross-complaint. The reply, which can include affirmative defenses, must be filed with the court and served on the original defendant.

CONCEPT SUMMARY
PLEADINGS

Type of Pleading	Description
Complaint	A document filed by a plaintiff with a court and served with a *summons* on the defendant. It sets forth the basis of the lawsuit.
Answer	A document filed by a defendant with a court and served on the plaintiff. It usually denies most allegations of the complaint.
Cross-complaint and reply	A *cross-complaint* is the document that is filed and served by a defendant if he or she countersues the plaintiff. The defendant is the *cross-complainant* and the plaintiff is the *cross-defendant*. The cross-defendant must file and serve a *reply* (answer).

Intervention and Consolidation

If other persons have an interest in a lawsuit, they may *intervene* and become parties to the lawsuit. This is called **intervention**.

intervention
The act of others to join as parties to an existing lawsuit.

Example A bank that has made a secured loan on a piece of real estate can intervene in a lawsuit between parties who are litigating ownership of the property.

If several plaintiffs have filed separate lawsuits stemming from the same fact situation against the same defendant, the court can *consolidate* the cases into one case if doing so would not cause undue prejudice to the parties. This process is called **consolidation**.

consolidation
The act of a court to combine two or more separate lawsuits into one lawsuit.

Example If a commercial airplane crashes, killing and injuring many people, the court could consolidate all the lawsuits against the defendant airline. This is because the deaths and injuries all relate to the same fact situation.

Statute of Limitations

A **statute of limitations** establishes the period during which a plaintiff must bring a lawsuit against a defendant. If a lawsuit is not filed within this time, the plaintiff loses the right to sue. A statute of limitations begins to "run" at the time the plaintiff first has the right to sue the defendant (e.g., when the accident happens, the breach of contract occurs, or the crime is committed). Federal and state governments have established statutes of limitations for each type of lawsuit. Statutes of limitations vary considerably by jurisdiction and by the type of case.

statute of limitations
A statute that establishes the period during which a plaintiff must bring a lawsuit against a defendant.

For civil lawsuits, such as for automobile accidents and other forms of negligence, breach of contract claims, and other noncriminal cases, the statute of limitations is usually between one and four years.

Example The state of Idaho has a two-year statute of limitations for personal injury actions. On July 1, 2022, Otis negligently causes an automobile accident in Sun Valley, Idaho, in which Cha-Yen is injured. Cha-Yen has until July 1, 2024, to bring a negligence lawsuit against Otis. If she waits longer than that, she loses her right to sue him.

WEB EXERCISE
Go to **resources.lawinfo.com/criminal-defense/criminal-statute-limitations-time-limits.html** and find the statute of limitations for crimes committed in your state.

Criminal cases involving serious felonies, such as assault, robbery, burglary, and the like, have statutes of limitations usually from 5 to 20 years. Misdemeanors have shorter statutes of limitations, usually six months to 5 years.

Example The state of Rhode Island has a 10-year statute of limitations for larceny, bribery, embezzlement, and extortion. On July 1, 2021, James embezzles $100,000 from his employer. If the embezzlement is discovered before July 1, 2031, the state may prosecute James for the crime. If the embezzlement is not discovered until after that date, the state can no longer prosecute James for the crime.

In many states, serious crimes such as murder, sexual crimes against minors, kidnapping, arson, rape, and other violent crimes have no statute of limitations.

The following feature discusses the cost–benefit analysis of a lawsuit.

Contemporary Environment

Cost–Benefit Analysis of a Lawsuit

The choice of whether to bring or defend a lawsuit, or to settle a lawsuit, should be analyzed like any other business decision. This includes performing a **cost–benefit analysis** of the lawsuit. For the plaintiff, it may be wise not to sue. For the defendant and the plaintiff, it may be wise to settle the case. The following factors should be considered in deciding whether to bring or settle a lawsuit:

(continued)

- The probability of winning or losing
- The amount of money to be won or lost
- Lawyers' fees and other costs of litigation
- Loss of time by managers and other personnel
- The long-term effects on the relationship and reputation of the parties
- The amount of prejudgment interest provided by law
- The aggravation and psychological costs associated with a lawsuit
- The unpredictability of the legal system and the possibility of error
- Other factors peculiar to the parties and lawsuit

Class Action

3.4 Define *class action* and describe the requirements for bringing a class action lawsuit.

class action
A lawsuit where a group of plaintiffs with common claims collectively bring a lawsuit against a defendant.

If certain requirements are met, a lawsuit can be brought as a **class action**. A class action occurs when a group of plaintiffs collectively bring a lawsuit against a defendant. Usually, one or several named plaintiffs file a lawsuit against a defendant on behalf of her-, him-, or themselves and other similarly situated allegedly aggrieved parties.

To maintain a class action lawsuit, a class must be *certified* by the appropriate federal or state court. A class can be certified if the legal and factual claims of all the parties are common, it is impracticable for individual claimants to bring multiple lawsuits against the defendant, the claims and defenses are typical for the plaintiffs and the defendant, and the representative parties will adequately protect the interests of the class. A class will not be certified if there is not sufficient commonality among the plaintiffs' claims or if the court otherwise finds that a class action is not suitable to the facts of the case.

Critical Legal Thinking
What is the purpose of a class action lawsuit? Would some plaintiffs be denied redress for grievances if class action lawsuits were not permitted?

Example Three individual employees of Walmart, Inc. brought a class action lawsuit in U.S. district court against Walmart alleging that it systematically engaged in sex discrimination against women in violation of federal employment law. The U.S. district court certified the class and the U.S. court of appeals affirmed the class certification. However, the U.S. Supreme Court refused to grant certification because the class would consist of more than 1.5 million claimants spread over more than 3,400 stores in a multitude of different jobs involving thousands of supervisors over varying time periods. The U.S. Supreme Court stated, "Walmart is entitled to individualized determinations of each employee's eligibility for back pay."[1]

If a court certifies a class, notice of the class action must be sent, published, or broadcast to class members. Class members have the right to opt out of the class action and pursue their own legal process against the defendant. If a class action lawsuit is won or a settlement is obtained from the defendant, the members of the class share the proceeds as determined by the court.

Class Action Fairness Act (CAFA)
A federal statute that requires certain class action lawsuits to be brought in or transferred to federal courts.

Attorneys are often more likely to represent a class of plaintiffs with aggregate monetary claims than an individual plaintiff with a small claim. Class action lawsuits increase court efficiency and lower the costs of litigation. Class actions are usually disfavored by defendants.

The following feature discusses a federal law that applies to class action lawsuits.

Business Environment

Class Action Fairness Act

Businesses are the usual defendants in class action lawsuits. Businesses believed that many large class action lawsuits were brought by law firms that shopped for the best state court system and the best court location within that system to file the class action lawsuit. The plaintiffs were seeking locations where juries were more likely to hold for the plaintiffs and award large damage amounts.

Businesses lobbied the U.S. Congress, which enacted the **Class Action Fairness Act (CAFA)**.[2] The act gives federal courts jurisdiction to hear many class action lawsuits that would otherwise be heard by state courts. The act is designed to reduce plaintiffs' forum shopping for sympathetic state courts and to give federal courts jurisdiction to hear large class action lawsuits.

The act provides that class actions where the amount in controversy totals $5 million or more, there are more than 100 class members, and the class members are residents in multiple states, must be brought in federal court. Federal courts have jurisdiction to hear and decide class action lawsuits that involve a federal law.

The act protects class members from abusive settlements by permitting federal courts to rule on the reasonableness of **coupon settlements** where plaintiffs are offered coupons to purchase the defendant's merchandise instead of being paid cash. The act also permits the federal court to determine the reasonableness of attorney's fees in such settlements.

Discovery

3.5 Describe the discovery process and the various methods of discovery.

The legal process provides for a detailed pretrial procedure called **discovery**. During discovery, each party engages in various activities to discover facts of the case from the other party and witnesses prior to trial. Discovery serves several functions, including preventing surprises, allowing parties to prepare thoroughly for trial, preserving evidence, saving court time, and promoting the settlement of cases. The major forms of discovery are discussed in the following paragraphs.

discovery
A legal process during which each party engages in various activities to discover facts of the case from the other party and witnesses prior to trial.

Deposition

A **deposition** is oral testimony given by a party or witness prior to trial. The person giving a deposition is called the **deponent**. A *party* to the lawsuit must give a deposition if called on by the other party to do so. The deposition of a *witness* can be given voluntarily or pursuant to a subpoena (court order). The deponent can be required to bring documents to the deposition. Most depositions are taken at the office of one of the attorneys.

The deponent is placed under oath and then asked questions orally by one or both of the attorneys. The questions and answers are recorded in written form by a court reporter. Depositions can also be video-recorded. The deponent is given an opportunity to correct his or her answers prior to signing the deposition. Depositions are used to preserve evidence (e.g., if the deponent dies, is ill, or is not otherwise available at trial) and to impeach testimony given by witnesses at trial. Remote witness depositions are sometimes permitted.

deposition
Oral testimony given by a party or witness prior to trial. The testimony is given under oath and is transcribed.

deponent
A party who gives his or her deposition.

Interrogatories

Interrogatories are written questions submitted by one party to a lawsuit to another party. The questions can be very detailed. In addition, certain documents might be attached to the answers. A party is required to answer interrogatories in writing within a specified time period (e.g., 60 to 90 days). An attorney usually helps with the preparation of the answers. The answers are signed under oath.

interrogatories
Written questions submitted by one party to another party. The questions must be answered in writing within a stipulated time.

Production of Documents

Often, particularly in complex business cases, a substantial portion of a lawsuit may be based on information contained in documents (e.g., memorandums, correspondence, and company records). One party to a lawsuit may request that the other party produce all documents that are relevant to the case prior to trial. This is called **production of documents**. If the documents sought are too voluminous to be moved or are in permanent storage or if their movement would disrupt the ongoing business of the party that is to produce them, the requesting party may be required to examine the documents at the other party's premises.

production of documents
A request by one party to another party to produce all documents relevant to the case prior to the trial.

Physical or Mental Examination

physical or mental examination
A court-ordered examination of a party to a lawsuit before trial to determine the extent of the alleged injuries.

In cases that concern the physical or mental condition of a party, a court can order the party to submit to certain **physical or mental examinations** to determine the extent of the alleged injuries. This would occur, for example, where the plaintiff has been injured in an accident and is seeking damages for physical injury and mental distress.

The following feature discusses the nondisclosure of evidence.

Ethics

Nondisclosure of Evidence by Walmart

"Rather, any prejudice that the jury may have harbored was due to Walmart's initial refusal to produce evidence of or admit the evidence of the grease spill."
—Nancy Rice, Justice

Holly Averyt, a commercial truck driver, slipped in grease while making a delivery to Walmart store number 980 in Greeley, Colorado. Averyt ruptured a disc in her spine and injured her shoulder and neck. These injuries left her unable to perform many daily functions. Averyt sued Walmart Stores, Inc., alleging claims of negligence and premises liability. Averyt's attorney sought evidence from Walmart documenting the grease spill, but Walmart denied the existence of the grease spill and did not turn over documents to Averyt. At trial, Averyt's attorney introduced a memorandum produced by the City of Greeley that documented the grease spill and the cleanup of the spill.

The next day, Walmart informed the court that it had located an assistant manager who remembered the grease spill and disclosed documents that confirmed the existence of the spill, including documents from three companies that were involved in cleaning up the spill. Walmart ceased to deny the existence of the grease spill but instead asserted that it had exercised reasonable care to clean up the spill. The jury found in Averyt's favor and the court awarded her $11 million in damages.

On appeal, the Colorado Supreme Court upheld Walmart's liability and the award of damages. The court stated, "Any prejudice that the jury may have harbored was due to Walmart's initial refusal to produce evidence of or admit the evidence of the grease spill. We do not find that the jury's award was the result of unfair prejudice." *Averyt v. Walmart Stores, Inc.*, 265 P.3d 456, 2011 Colo. Lexis 857 (Supreme Court of Colorado, 2011)

Ethics Questions
Do you think that Walmart willfully did not disclose the evidence of the grease spill? Do you believe that the jury considered Walmart's conduct when it reached its verdict?

E-Discovery

3.6 Describe e-discovery and how electronic evidence can be used at a legal proceeding.

electronic discovery (e-discovery)
A process whereby relevant electronic documents are discovered, exchanged, collected, preserved, and processed during a lawsuit.

In today's paperless world, most business documents and much personal information are stored in electronic format rather than in printed form. This information is stored on computers, external hard drives, smartphones, cloud platforms, or other digital devices. In many lawsuits, the discovery of electronic data is critical. **Electronic discovery**, or **e-discovery**, is the process whereby relevant electronic documents are discovered, exchanged, collected, preserved, and processed during a lawsuit.

Relevant **electronically stored information (ESI)** must be produced by the parties in litigation and arbitration proceedings. Discoverable ESI includes electronic documents, emails, voice mail messages, instant messages, text messages, e-calendars, cloud storage, phone records, electronic data stored on handheld devices, pdfs of key files, PowerPoint slides, graphics, photographs, spreadsheets, audio and visual files, social media posts, website captures, metadata, and other digital information.

A party must produce ESI as it is kept in the usual course of business, or organize and label it to correspond to the categories in a discovery request. If the discovery request does not specify the form for producing ESI, then a party must produce it in a form in which it is ordinarily maintained.

Anyone who is a party to litigation, or reasonably anticipates being a party, has a duty to preserve relevant ESI that may be useful to an adversary. Parties may object to the production of ESI. The objections must be stated with specificity, and the court will decide the merits of the objection. In some instances, experts in computer forensics are necessary to recover misplaced, altered, or hidden electronic documents.

States have enacted laws that require the discovery and production of ESI in state court proceedings.

The following feature discusses whether information stored on cellphones can be discovered as evidence in a lawsuit.

Information Technology

Cellphone Texts Are Discoverable Evidence in an Automobile Accident Case

"Petitioner considers the inspection an improper fishing expedition in a digital ocean."
—Timothy Osterhaus, Justice

A vehicle driven by Tabitha Antico collided with a truck owned by Sindt Trucking, Inc. Antico was killed in the accident. The personal representative of Antico brought a civil wrongful death action against Sindt Trucking. The company denied liability, alleging that Antico was either solely or partially at fault for the accident because she was distracted by texting or otherwise using her cellphone while driving. Testimony from two witnesses and responding troopers indicated that Antico had been utilizing her cellphone at the time of the accident.

Sindt made a motion to the trial court to permit an expert to inspect Antico's cellphone's data, including text messages, internet website access history, and other use of Antico's cellphone on the day of the accident. The plaintiff countered that the discovery would violate Antico's privacy rights. The trial court approved the discovery of the cellphone data, limiting the discovery to the nine-hour period preceding and including the time of the accident.

The court of appeal affirmed the trial court's ruling permitting inspection of the cellphone for a nine-hour period on the day of the accident. The court stated, "Petitioner considers the inspection an improper fishing expedition in a digital ocean. Contrary to petitioner's argument, privacy rights do not completely foreclose the prospect of discovery of data stored on electronic devices." *Antico v. Sindt Trucking, Inc.*, 148 So.3d 163, 2014 Fla. App. Lexis 16746 (District Court of Appeal of Florida, 2014)

Critical Legal Thinking Questions

Do you think that many people use their cellphones while driving? Have you ever texted anyone while you were driving a vehicle?

The following feature discusses whether photographs posted on social media are discoverable evidence.

Information Technology

Social Media Postings and Photographs Are Discoverable Evidence

"There is no better portrayal of what an individual's life was like than those photographs the individual has chosen to share through social media."
—Robert Gross, Judge

Maria Nucci claimed that when she was in a store owned by Target Corporation, she slipped and fell on a foreign substance on the floor of the store. Nucci sued Target to recover damages for her alleged injuries. Nucci claimed that she was seriously injured, experiences pain from the injury, suffers emotional pain and suffering, and suffers permanent and continuing injuries. After the incident, Target obtained surveillance videos that showed Nucci carrying heavy bags, jugs of water, and doing other physical acts that refute her claim of serious personal injury.

Target served Nucci with a Request for Production of Electronic Media to obtain photographs of her from her social media accounts for the two years prior to the date of the incident to the present. The trial court issued an order compelling discovery of the photographs from Nucci's social media sites. In upholding the order, the court of appeals stated, "The information sought, photographs of Nucci posted on

(continued)

Nucci's social media sites, is highly relevant. If a photograph is worth a thousand words, there is no better portrayal of what an individual's life was like than those photographs the individual has chosen to share through social media." *Nucci v. Target Corporation*, 162 So.3d 146, 2015 Fla. App. Lexis 153 (District Court of Appeal of Florida, 2015)

Critical Legal Thinking Questions

Can your life be traced through the photographs you post on social media sites? Do you think that the disclosure of the photographs from Nucci's social media sites will help or damage her case?

CONCEPT SUMMARY

DISCOVERY

Type	Description
Deposition	Oral testimony given by a *deponent*, either a party or witness. Depositions are transcribed.
Interrogatories	Written questions submitted by one party to the other party of a lawsuit. They must be answered within a specified period of time.
Production of documents	Copies of all relevant documents obtained by a party to a lawsuit from another party upon order of the court.
Physical or mental examination	Court-ordered examination of a party where injuries are alleged that could be verified or disputed by such examination.

Pretrial Motions

3.7 Contrast the different types of pretrial motions.

pretrial motion
A motion a party can make to try to dispose of all or part of a lawsuit prior to trial.

Parties to a lawsuit can make several **pretrial motions** to try to resolve or dispose of all or part of a lawsuit prior to trial. The two pretrial motions are *motion for judgment on the pleadings* and *motion for summary judgment*.

Motion for Judgment on the Pleadings

motion for judgment on the pleadings
A motion that alleges that if all the facts presented in the pleadings are taken as true, the party making the motion would win the lawsuit when the proper law is applied to these asserted facts.

A **motion for judgment on the pleadings** can be made by either party once the pleadings are complete. This motion alleges that if all the facts presented in the pleadings are true, the party making the motion would win the lawsuit when the proper law is applied to these facts. In deciding this motion, the judge cannot consider any facts outside the pleadings.

Example A plaintiff files a complaint alleging that the defendant breached an oral contract and allegedly owes the plaintiff damages. If the state's statute of limitations requires that a lawsuit be brought within two years from the date that an oral contract was breached and the pleadings show that the lawsuit has been filed after the two-year period has expired, the defendant can make a motion to have the plaintiff's lawsuit dismissed based on the facts alleged in the pleadings.

Motion for Summary Judgment

motion for summary judgment
A motion that asserts that there are no factual disputes to be decided by the jury and that the judge can apply the proper law to the undisputed facts and decide the case without a jury. These motions are supported by affidavits, documents, and deposition testimony.

The trier of fact (i.e., the jury or, if there is no jury, the judge) determines factual issues. A **motion for summary judgment** asserts that there are no factual disputes to be decided by the jury and that the judge should apply the relevant law to the undisputed facts and decide the case. Thus, the case can be decided before trial by a judge who reaches a conclusion and issues a summary judgment in the moving party's favor. Motions for summary judgment, which can be made by either party, are supported by evidence outside the pleadings. Affidavits from the parties and witnesses, documents (e.g., a written contract between the parties), depositions, and so on are common forms of evidence.

If, after examining the evidence, the court finds no factual dispute, it can decide the issue or issues raised in the summary judgment motion. It may then dispense with the entire case or with part of the case. If the judge finds that a factual dispute exists, the motion will be denied, and the case will go to trial.

The following case involves a motion for summary judgment.

CASE 3.1 *FEDERAL COURT CASE Summary Judgment*

Casey v. McDonald's Corporation

880 F.3d 564 (2018)

United States Court of Appeals for the District of Columbia

"Under District of Columbia law, a tort-law plaintiff in a negligence case must show that the defendant violated a national standard of care."

—Brett Kavanaugh, Circuit Judge

Facts

After a Friday night of bar hopping, two groups of men began an altercation by exchanging words at a McDonald's restaurant in Washington DC. Jason Ward was in one group, and Patrick Casey was in the other. The men eventually ended up just outside the restaurant, on the sidewalk. At that point, Ward punched Casey. Casey fell to the ground and hit his head on the sidewalk. Casey was taken to a local hospital, where he died.

The parents of the victim sued McDonald's Corporation for negligence. The Caseys contended that McDonald's acted negligently in three ways: (1) McDonald's failed to have a security guard on duty, (2) no McDonald's employee called 911, and (3) McDonald's failed to properly train its employees to prevent or to break up a fight. The U.S. district court granted summary judgment to McDonald's, finding that there was no evidence that McDonald's acted negligently. The Caseys appealed.

Issue

Should the court have granted summary judgment to McDonald's?

Language of the Court

Under District of Columbia law, a tort-law plaintiff in a negligence case must show that the defendant violated a national standard of care. The Caseys' expert witness noted that security guards can help maintain a safe environment and intervene in fights. But that truism alone does not establish a standard of care for tort cases. The Caseys allege that McDonald's employees should have called 911 at some point during the altercation. That alone does not establish a standard of care. It also bears mention that the physical altercation did not escalate until the men were outside of McDonald's on the sidewalk. The Caseys allege that McDonald's failed to properly train its employees on how to handle drunk and unruly patrons, and to stop these kinds of altercations. That argument fails because the Caseys have not provided any evidence suggesting a standard of care that requires fast-food restaurant employees to break up or prevent fights between drunk patrons (potentially endangering the employees' own lives by doing so).

Decision

The U.S. court of appeals affirmed the district court's grant of summary judgment to McDonald's.

Critical Legal Thinking Questions

What purpose is served by permitting courts to grant summary judgment instead of allowing cases to go to trial and be decided by a jury? Do you think that McDonald's should have been granted summary judgment in this case?

Settlement Conference

3.8 Describe the goals and procedures of a settlement conference.

Federal court rules and most state court rules permit the court to direct the attorneys or parties to appear before the court for a **settlement conference**, or **pretrial hearing**. One of the major purposes of such hearings is to facilitate the settlement

settlement agreement
An agreement voluntarily entered into by the parties to a lawsuit whereby they agree to settle their dispute.

Critical Legal Thinking

Why are so many cases settled before trial? What would be the consequences if most cases actually went to trial?

of a case. Pretrial conferences are often held informally in the judge's chambers. If a settlement is reached, the parties will execute a **settlement agreement** that sets forth the terms of their settlement. Many parties settle their case prior to the settlement conference, often before or after discovery. More than 95 percent of all cases are settled before they go to trial.

The following feature discusses a settlement of multiple discrimination lawsuits brought against Facebook.

Information Technology

Facebook Settles Algorithmic Discrimination Lawsuits

The social media giant Facebook has a vast trove of personal and demographic data on its users that attracts companies to post advertisements on Facebook. Facebook's system and algorithms permit data mining that allows advertisers to micro-target any desired group of Facebook users. However, federal civil rights acts prohibit discrimination in employment, housing, and granting of credit based on race, ethnicity, sex, age, disabilities, and other protected classes.

Many advertisers of job openings, sale or rental of housing, and offers of credit paid Facebook to post advertisements that targeted audiences identified by race, gender, age, disabilities, or other protected classes. For example, many housing and credit advertisements excluded minority users of Facebook. Many job openings targeted younger age groups and were not sent to older Facebook users, while other advertisements were aimed at users of a specific gender. Even some of Facebook's own employment advertisements screened out older users. The use of data mining to sell online discriminatory advertising is referred to as **algorithmic discrimination** or **Weblining**.

After extensive investigation, which included placing dummy ads to test whether Facebook's system only delivered the ads to certain Facebook users and not to others, several civil rights and housing organizations brought lawsuits against Facebook alleging that it engaged in discrimination in violation of federal antidiscrimination laws.

Facebook originally denied liability. However, after discovery of further evidence, Facebook reached an agreement to settle the civil rights lawsuits brought against it. Pursuant to the agreement, Facebook must create a separate portal for advertisements in the areas of employment, housing, and credit on Facebook, Instagram, and Messenger, and can no longer permit advertisers to target users by race, ethnicity, gender, age, disabilities, or other protected class if the advertisement is related to employment, housing, or credit. Facebook must stop using membership in Facebook "groups" when creating audiences for advertisers, and targeting based on ZIP codes or a geographic area that is less than a 15-mile radius is not allowed. Facebook is subject to monitoring by civil rights organizations for three years. The settlement, however, does not require Facebook to admit liability for violating antidiscrimination laws. If Facebook had not settled the cases and instead had lost in court, it could have faced significant liability.

Advertisements related to products or services other than employment, housing, and credit are not affected by the settlement. For example, a professional baseball team could place an advertisement to sell clothing and memorabilia to Facebook users identified as being interested in the team.

Trial

3.9 Describe the trial process.

Pursuant to the Seventh Amendment to the U.S. Constitution, a party to a civil action at law is guaranteed the right to a **jury trial** in a case in federal court.[3] Most of the state constitutions contain a similar guarantee for state court actions. If either party requests a jury, the trial will be by jury. If both parties waive their right to a jury, the trial will occur without a jury. The judge sits as the **trier of fact** in nonjury trials. At the time of trial, each party usually submits to the judge a **trial brief** that contains legal support for its side of the case.

trier of fact
The jury in a jury trial; the judge when there is not a jury trial.

A trial can last less than one day to many months, depending on the type and complexity of the case. A typical trial is divided into stages. The stages of a trial are discussed in the following paragraphs.

Jury Selection

voir dire
The process whereby the judge and attorneys ask prospective jurors questions to determine whether they would be biased in their decisions.

The pool of potential jurors is usually selected from voter or automobile registration lists. Individuals are selected to hear specific cases through a process called ***voir*** *dire* ("to speak the truth"). Lawyers for each party and the judge can ask prospective jurors questions to determine whether they would be biased in their decisions. Individuals who are determined to be biased are prohibited from serving as a juror.

Most state and federal courts permit each party a specified number of **peremptory challenges**, also called **peremptory strikes**. This permits each party to remove a potential juror without showing that the juror is biased. Peremptory challenges allow each side to contribute to the configuration of the jury. These strikes cannot be used to remove jurors based on race, ethnicity, or gender.

peremptory challenge (peremptory strike)
A rule that permits each party to a lawsuit to dismiss a limited number of proposed jurors from becoming jurors without having to show that the dismissed individuals were biased.

Example In federal courts each party is entitled to six peremptory challenges in civil cases. In federal criminal trials the plaintiff is allowed six challenges and the defendant is allowed 10 challenges.

Federal courts and most state courts require a 12-person jury in criminal cases. Juries in civil cases are usually 6 to 12 jurors, depending on the jurisdiction. Several *alternative jurors* are also usually selected to replace jurors who cannot complete the trial because of death, illness, later discovered bias, or other reason. Once the appropriate number of jurors is selected they are **impanelled** to hear the case and are sworn in. A jury can be **sequestered** (i.e., separated from family and so on) in important cases.

WEB EXERCISE
Go to **https://digitalcommons.law.scu.edu/historical/1627/** to view a copy of a complaint filed in a U.S. district court. Read the first four pages of the complaint.

Opening Statements

Each party's attorney is allowed to make an **opening statement** to the jury at the beginning of a trial. During opening statements, an attorney usually summarizes the main factual and legal issues of the case and describes why he or she believes the client's position is valid. The information given in this statement is not considered as evidence.

The Plaintiff's Case

A plaintiff bears the **burden of proof** to persuade the trier of fact of the merits of his or her case. This is called the **plaintiff's case**. The plaintiff's attorney calls witnesses to give testimony. After a witness has been sworn in, the plaintiff's attorney examines (i.e., questions) the witness. This is called **direct examination**. Documents and other evidence can be introduced through each witness. After the plaintiff's attorney has completed his or her questions, the defendant's attorney can question the witness. This is called **cross-examination**. The defendant's attorney can ask questions only about the subjects that were brought up during the direct examination. After the defendant's attorney completes his or her questions, the plaintiff's attorney can ask questions of the witness. This is called **re-direct examination**.

The Defendant's Case

The **defendant's case** proceeds after the plaintiff has concluded his or her case. The defendant's case must (1) rebut the plaintiff's evidence, (2) prove any affirmative defenses asserted by the defendant, and (3) prove any allegations contained in the defendant's cross-complaint. The defendant's witnesses are examined by the defendant's attorney. The plaintiff's attorney can cross-examine each witness. This is followed by re-direct examination by the defendant and re-cross-examination by the plaintiff.

Rebuttal and Rejoinder

After the defendant's attorney has finished calling witnesses, the plaintiff's attorney can call witnesses and put forth evidence to rebut the defendant's case. This is called a **rebuttal**. The defendant's attorney can call additional witnesses and introduce other evidence to counter the rebuttal. This is called the **rejoinder**.

Closing Arguments

After the presentation of the evidence each party's attorney is permitted to make a **closing argument**, also called a **closing statement**, to the jury. Each attorney tries to convince the jury to render a verdict for his or her client by pointing out the strengths in the client's case and the weaknesses in the other side's case. Information given by the attorneys in their closing statements is not evidence.

Jury Instructions, Deliberation, and Verdict

jury instructions (charges)
Instructions that the judge gives to the jury that inform the jurors of the law to be applied in the case.

Once the closing arguments are completed, the judge reads **jury instructions** (or **charges**) to the jury. These instructions inform the jury about what law to apply when they decide the case.

Example In a criminal trial, the judge reads the jury the statutory definition of the crime charged (e.g., first-degree murder). In an unintentional automobile accident case, the judge reads the jury the legal definition of *negligence*.

After the judge reads the jury instructions, the jury retires to the jury room to consider the evidence and attempt to reach a decision. This is called **jury deliberation**, and it can take from a few minutes to many weeks. After deliberation, the jury reaches a **verdict**. In civil cases, the jury assesses damages against the defendant if they have held in favor of the plaintiff. In criminal cases, if the jury finds the defendant guilty, the jury may assess penalties on the defendant in some jurisdictions or cases.

Entry of Judgment

judgment
The official decision of the court.

After the jury has returned its verdict, in most cases the judge enters a **judgment** to the successful party, based on the verdict. This is the official decision of the court.

The court may overturn the verdict, however, if it finds bias or jury misconduct. This is called a **judgment notwithstanding the verdict** (or **judgment n.o.v.** or **j.n.o.v.**).

In a civil case, the judge may reduce the amount of monetary damages awarded by the jury if he or she finds the jury to have been biased, emotional, or inflamed. This is called **remittitur**.

The trial court usually issues a **written memorandum** that sets forth the reasons for the judgment. This memorandum, together with the trial transcript and evidence introduced at trial, constitutes the permanent **record** of the trial court proceeding.

In the following case, the court had to decide whether to overturn a jury's verdict.

CASE 3.2 *FEDERAL COURT CASE Jury Verdict*

Stults v. International Flavors & Fragrances, Inc.

815 F.3d 409 (2016)
United States Court of Appeals for the Eighth Circuit

"Where conflicting inferences reasonably can be drawn from the evidence, it is the role of the jury, not the court, to determine which inference shall be drawn."

—William Riley, Chief Judge

Facts

David Stults consumed one to three bags of microwave popcorn each day for approximately 20 years. He practiced a ritual of slowly opening the freshly popped bag as he breathed the aroma in through his nose. Stults was later diagnosed with the lung disease bronchiolitis obliterans. Stults sued International Flavors & Fragrances, Inc. (IFF), a maker of microwave popcorn that he ate, to recover damages for his injury, alleging that his disease was caused by inhaling diacetyl, the chemical used to give popcorn its buttery flavor. IFF asserted that Stults's disease was caused by a rheumatoid autoimmune condition unrelated to diacetyl exposure.

One of Stults's expert witnesses, Dr. David Egilman, testified that Stults's bronchiolitis obliterans was caused by his inhalation of microwave popcorn fumes containing diacetyl. Dr. Allen Parmet, an occupational medicine expert, testified that diacetyl was "the most probable cause" of Stults's condition.

One of IFF's expert witnesses, Dr. Paul Wolters, testified that he did not believe diacetyl was the culprit. Another of IFF's expert witnesses, Dr. Coreen Robbins, an industrial hygienist, testified that "consumer exposure to diacetyl from popping microwave popcorn is insignificant." Dr. Richard Switzer, Stults's primary-care physician, testified that he had no opinion as to whether Stults's diacetyl exposure caused his bronchiolitis obliterans. And Stults's rheumatologist, Dr. Aaron Eggebeen, testified, "Whether or not the diacetyl has anything to do with it, I'm not sure how to judge that."

After hearing the evidence, the jury found in favor of IFF. Stults requested that the U.S. district court disregard the jury's verdict and find in his favor as a matter of law or that the court grant a new trial. The district court denied Stults's motions. Stults appealed.

Issue

Should the jury's verdict be overturned?

Language of the Court

It is the province of the jury to decide which experts are more credible and persuasive. A jury's credibility determinations are well-nigh unreviewable because the jury is in the best position to assess the credibility of witnesses and resolve inconsistent testimony. We conclude the district court did not abuse its discretion because Stults failed to show the outcome is against the great weight of the evidence so as to constitute a miscarriage of justice necessitating a new trial. Where conflicting inferences reasonably can be drawn from the evidence, it is the role of the jury, not the court, to determine which inference shall be drawn.

Decision

The U.S. court of appeals affirmed the decision of the U.S. district court.

Critical Legal Thinking Questions

What are the duties of a jury? What are the duties of the judge? Do you think it is difficult for a jury to weigh conflicting evidence and reach a decision?

E-Courts and Information Technology

3.10 Explain how electronic technology is being used in courts and legal proceedings.

Electronic technology has transformed how lawyers and courts operate. The law profession has automated most processes in offering legal services to clients. Most lawyers have websites so that interested parties can read about the law firm, its members, and the law firm's expertise.

Relevant documents of the law firm and clients are scanned into computers and storage devices. This eliminates the need for storing documents in paper filing systems and boxes that was the norm prior to modern information technology. Digitized documents can be retrieved when required.

How many a dispute could have been deflated into a single paragraph if the disputants had dared to define their terms.
Aristotle (384–322 BCE)

The internet, email, texting, and other digital technologies allow lawyers and clients to easily communicate with one another. Documents may be transmitted as attachments to emails. Lawyers may also easily communicate with lawyers who represent opposing parties to litigation, as well as with judges. The availability of video conferencing and teleconferencing eliminate time-consuming meetings that were previously required prior to electronic technology. Much travel time and waiting time is eliminated. Social media is used by lawyers to communicate, collaborate, and network with one another.

Contracts, legal forms, and other information are stored and are electronically accessible for review and editing. When drafting documents for clients, lawyers often access stored documents and forms. Lawyers can then use these electronic documents as a basis to create new documents that fit the specific needs of a client. Wills, trusts, contracts, legal pleadings, and many other documents are prepared this way.

There are several digital research services that offer access to most court cases decided by federal trial and appellate courts, and decisions of the U.S. Supreme Court. Most cases decided by state appeals and supreme courts are also available electronically. Lawyers can conduct legal research using these services to prepare memoranda and legal briefs that are filed with courts.

electronic filing (e-filing)
The electronic filing of pleadings, briefs, and other documents with the court.

electronic court (e-court or virtual court)
A court that either mandates or permits the electronic filing of pleadings, briefs, and other documents related to a lawsuit.

Most courts provide for **electronic filing—e-filing**—of pleadings, briefs, and other documents related to a lawsuit. The federal judiciary provides a case management and electronic case files system that allows case documents to be filed with federal courts. Most states also provide for the electronic filing of documents. In some courts, e-filing of pleadings and other documents is mandatory. High technology courts are often referred to as **electronic courts**, **e-courts**, or **virtual courts**.

Lawyers often use video and electronic display of evidence in the courtroom. Courts sometimes permit remote testimony during trial. Annotation monitors are available in some courts that allow witnesses to mark an exhibit with notations that will be electronically preserved for later viewing. Use of evidence cameras allows for the instantaneous conversion of a paper document or physical exhibit to an electronic image for display on courtroom monitors. Search engines allow lawyers to find documents, evidence, and depositions quickly during trial.

Artificial intelligence (AI) programs are now available to analyze contracts and other documents and automate the editing process. AI will enhance the provision of legal services and the operation of courts.

Appeal

3.11 Describe the appellate process and the possible results of an appeal.

appeal
The act of asking an appellate court to overturn a decision after the trial court's final judgment has been entered.

appellant (petitioner)
The appealing party in an appeal.

appellee (respondent)
The responding party in an appeal.

In a civil case, either party can **appeal** the trial court's decision once a **final judgment** is entered. Only the defendant can appeal in a criminal case. The appeal is made to the appropriate appellate court. A **notice of appeal** must be filed by a party within a prescribed time after judgment is entered (usually within 60 or 90 days).

The appealing party is called the **appellant**, or **petitioner**. The responding party is called the **appellee**, or **respondent**. The appellant is often required to post bond (e.g., one and one-half times the judgment) on appeal.

The parties may designate all or relevant portions of the trial record to be submitted to the appellate court for review. The appellant's attorney usually must file an **opening brief** with the court that sets forth legal research and other information to support his or her contentions on appeal. The appellee can file a **responding brief** that answers the appellant's contentions. Appellate courts usually permit a brief oral argument at which each party's attorney is heard.

An appellate court will reverse a lower court decision if it finds an **error of law** in the record.

Courts of appeals should be constantly alert to the trial judge's first-hand knowledge of witnesses, testimony, and issues; in other words, appellate courts should give due consideration to the first-instance decision maker's "feel" for the overall case.

Justice Ruth Bader Ginsburg
Weisgram v. Marley Company
528 U.S. 440, 120 S.Ct. 1011, 2000 U.S. Lexis 1011 (2000)

Examples Errors of law occur if prejudicial evidence was admitted at trial when it should have been excluded, prejudicial evidence was admitted that was obtained through an unconstitutional search and seizure, the jury was instructed improperly by the judge, and the like.

An appellate court will not reverse a **finding of fact** made by a jury, or made by a judge if there is no jury, unless such finding is unsupported by the evidence or is contradicted by the evidence. Very few trial court decisions are reversed because most findings of fact are supported by the evidence. On rare occasions, an appellate court will overturn a jury verdict if the appellate court cannot, from the record of the trial court, find sufficient evidence to support the trier of fact's findings.

Alternative Dispute Resolution

3.12 Explain the use of arbitration and other methods of alternative dispute resolution.

The use of the court system to resolve business and other disputes can take years and cost thousands or even millions of dollars in legal fees and expenses. In commercial litigation, the normal business operations of the parties are often disrupted. To avoid or reduce these problems, businesses and individuals are increasingly turning to methods of **nonjudicial dispute resolution** where disputes are resolved outside the court judicial system. This is often referred to as **alternative dispute resolution (ADR)**. The most common form of ADR is *arbitration*. Other forms of ADR are *negotiation, mediation, mini-trial, fact-finding*, and using a *judicial referee*.

alternative dispute resolution (ADR)
Methods of resolving disputes other than litigation.

Negotiation

The simplest form of alternative dispute resolution is engaging in negotiations between the parties to try to settle a dispute. **Negotiation** is a procedure whereby the parties to a legal dispute engage in discussions to try to reach a voluntary settlement of their dispute. Negotiation may take place before a lawsuit is filed, after a lawsuit is filed, or before other forms of alternative dispute resolution are used.

negotiation
A procedure whereby the parties to a dispute engage in discussions and bargaining to try to reach a voluntary settlement of their dispute.

In a negotiation, the parties, who are often represented by attorneys, negotiate with each other to try to reach an agreeable solution to their dispute. During negotiation proceedings, the parties usually make offers and counteroffers to one another. The parties or their attorneys also may provide information to the other side in order to assist the other side in reaching an amicable settlement.

Many courts require that the parties to a lawsuit engage in settlement discussions prior to trial to try to negotiate a settlement of the case. In these instances, the judge must be assured that a settlement of the case is not possible before permitting the case to go to trial. Judges may convince the parties to engage in further negotiations if they determine that the parties are not too far apart in the negotiation of a settlement.

If a settlement of a dispute is reached through negotiation, a settlement agreement is drafted that contains the terms of the agreement. Each side must sign the settlement agreement for it to be effective. The settlement agreement is usually submitted to the court, and the case will be dismissed based on the execution of the settlement agreement.

Arbitration

In **arbitration**, the parties choose an impartial third party to hear and decide the dispute. This neutral party is called the **arbitrator**. Arbitrators are usually members of the American Arbitration Association (AAA) or another arbitration association. Labor union agreements, franchise agreements, leases, employment contracts, and other commercial contracts often contain **arbitration clauses** that require disputes arising out of the contract to be submitted to arbitration. If there is no arbitration clause, the parties can enter into a **submission agreement** whereby they agree to submit a dispute to arbitration after the dispute arises.

arbitration
A form of alternative dispute resolution in which the parties choose an impartial third party to hear and decide the dispute.

arbitration clause
A clause in a contract that requires disputes arising out of the contract to be submitted to arbitration.

Congress enacted the *Federal Arbitration Act* to promote the arbitration of disputes. Many states have adopted the **Uniform Arbitration Act**, which promotes

Federal Arbitration Act (FAA)
A federal statute that provides for the enforcement of most arbitration agreements.

the arbitration of disputes at the state level. Many federal and state courts have instituted programs to refer legal disputes to arbitration or another form of ADR.

ADR services are usually provided by private organizations or individuals who qualify to hear and decide certain disputes. A landmark federal arbitration statute is discussed in the following feature.

Landmark Law

Federal Arbitration Act

The **Federal Arbitration Act (FAA)**[4] was enacted in 1925 to reverse long-standing judicial hostility to arbitration agreements. The FAA provides that arbitration agreements involving commerce are valid, irrevocable, and enforceable contracts, unless some grounds exist at law or equity (e.g., fraud or duress) to revoke them. The FAA permits one party to obtain a court order to compel arbitration if the other party has failed or refused to comply with an arbitration agreement.

Since the FAA's enactment, the courts have wrestled with the problem of which types of disputes should be arbitrated. Breach of contract is subject to arbitration if there is a valid arbitration agreement. In addition, the U.S. Supreme Court has enforced arbitration agreements that call for the resolution of disputes arising under federal statutes. The Supreme Court has stated, "By agreeing to arbitrate a statutory claim, a party does not forgo the substantive rights afforded by the statute, it only submits to their resolution in an arbitral, rather than a judicial, forum."[5]

Arbitration Procedure

WEB EXERCISE
Go to the website of the American Arbitration Association (AAA) at **www.adr.org/arbitration** and read the information on arbitration.

An arbitration agreement often describes the specific procedures that must be followed for a case to proceed to and through arbitration. If one party seeks to enforce an arbitration clause, that party must give notice to the other party. The parties then select an arbitration association or arbitrator, as provided in the agreement. The parties usually agree on the date, time, and place of the arbitration (e.g., at the arbitrator's office or some other agreed-on location).

At the arbitration, the parties can call witnesses to give testimony and introduce evidence to support their case and refute the other side's case. Rules similar to those followed by federal courts are usually followed at an arbitration hearing. Each party often pays a filing fee and other fees for the arbitration. Sometimes the agreement provides that one party will pay all the costs of the arbitration. Arbitrators are paid by the hour, day, or other agreed-on method of compensation.

After an arbitration hearing is complete, the arbitrator reaches a decision and issues an award. The parties often agree in advance to be bound by the arbitrator's decision and remedy. This is called **binding arbitration**. In this situation, the decision and award of the arbitrator cannot be appealed to the courts. If the arbitration is not binding, the decision and award of the arbitrator can be appealed to the courts. This is called **nonbinding arbitration**. Courts usually give great deference to an arbitrator's decision and award.

If an arbitrator has rendered a decision and an award but a party refuses to abide by the arbitrator's decision, the other party may file an action in court to have the arbitrator's decision enforced.

Critical Legal Thinking
What are the benefits and detriments of arbitration versus a lawsuit? Are you currently subject to any arbitration agreements?

Class actions allow many complainants to join to sue a defendant whom they believe has harmed them under similar circumstances. To curtail the use of class actions in arbitration, many companies place **class action waivers** in their arbitration agreements. This prevents defendants subject to the class action waiver from joining together to pursue a single defendant in an arbitration proceeding. The U.S. Supreme Court has held that class action waivers in arbitration agreements are legal.[6]

In the following case, the U.S. Supreme Court determined whether an arbitration agreement was enforceable.

CASE 3.3 ***U.S. SUPREME COURT CASE Arbitration Agreement***

Ernst & Young LLP v. Morris

138 S.Ct. 1612 (2018)
Supreme Court of the United States

"Arbitration agreements like those before us must be enforced as written."

—Neil Gorsuch, Justice

Facts

Ernst & Young LLP, an accounting firm, and one of its junior accountants, Stephen Morris, entered into an employment agreement that provided that they would arbitrate any dispute that might arise between them. The agreement specified individual arbitration, not collective arbitration with a class of employees. After his employment ended, Morris brought a class action lawsuit in federal court alleging that Ernst & Young had violated the federal Fair Labor Standards Act by not paying him and others overtime pay. Ernst & Young made a motion to compel arbitration individually with Morris. The U.S. district court granted the motion, but the U.S. court of appeals reversed the judgment. Ernst & Young appealed to the U.S. Supreme Court.

Issue

Should employees and employers be allowed to agree that any disputes between them will be resolved through one-on-one arbitration?

Language of the U.S. Supreme Court

In the Federal Arbitration Act, Congress has instructed federal courts to enforce arbitration agreements according to their terms—including terms providing for individualized proceedings. Congress adopted the Arbitration Act in 1925 in response to a perception that the courts were unduly hostile to arbitration. Congress directed the courts to abandon their hostility and instead treat arbitration agreements as valid, irrevocable, and enforceable. The Arbitration Act requires courts rigorously to enforce arbitration agreements according to their terms, including terms that specify with whom the parties choose to arbitrate their disputes and the rules under which that arbitration will be conducted. Arbitration agreements like those before us must be enforced as written.

Decision

The U.S. Supreme Court held that arbitration agreements that provide for individualized proceedings are enforceable.

Critical Legal Thinking Questions

Why do plaintiffs try to have their cases heard in court rather than through arbitration? Why would the plaintiff in this case want the case tried as a class action rather than on an individual basis with his employer?

Mediation

Mediation is a form of negotiation in which a neutral third party assists the disputing parties in reaching a settlement of their dispute. The neutral third party is called a **mediator**. The mediator is usually a person who is an expert of the area of the dispute or a lawyer or retired judge. The mediator is selected by the parties as provided in their agreement or as otherwise agreed by the parties. Unlike an arbitrator, however, a mediator does not issue a decision or an award.

mediation
A form of alternative dispute resolution in which the parties use a mediator to try to reach a settlement of their dispute.

A mediator's role is to assist the parties in reaching a settlement. The mediator usually acts as an intermediary between the parties. In many cases, the mediator meets with the two parties at an agreed-on location, often the mediator's office or one of the offices of the parties. The mediator then meets with both parties, usually separately, to discuss each side of the case.

After discussing the facts of the case with both sides, the mediator will encourage settlement of the dispute and transmit settlement offers from one side to the other. In doing so, the mediator points out the strengths and weaknesses of each party's case and gives an opinion to each side about why they should decrease or increase their settlement offers.

If the parties agree to a settlement, a settlement agreement is drafted that expresses their agreement. Execution of the settlement agreement ends the dispute. The parties, of course, must perform their duties under the settlement agreement. If an agreement is not reached, the parties may proceed to a judicial resolution of their case.

Example Parties to a divorce action often use mediation to try to help resolve the issues involved in the divorce, including property settlement, payment of alimony and child support, custody of children, and visitation rights.

E-Dispute Resolution

3.13 Describe forms of e-dispute resolution.

Electronic technologies have made it possible to settle disputes online. This is referred to as **electronic dispute resolution**, or **e-dispute resolution**. Many ADR providers offer electronic arbitration, or e-arbitration, services. Most of these services allow a party to a legal dispute to register the dispute with the service and then notify the other party by email of the registration of the dispute. The parties may be represented by attorneys if they so choose.

electronic dispute resolution (e-dispute resolution)
Use of online alternative dispute resolution services to resolve a dispute.

Most online arbitration, called **electronic arbitration** or **e-arbitration**, requires the registering party to submit an amount that the party is willing to accept or pay to the other party in the online arbitration. The other party is afforded the opportunity to accept the offer. If that party accepts the offer, a settlement has been reached. However, the other party may return a counteroffer. The process continues until a settlement is reached or one or both parties remove themselves from the online ADR process.

electronic arbitration (e-arbitration)
The arbitration of a dispute using online arbitration services.

Several websites offer online mediation, called **electronic mediation** or **e-mediation**. In an online mediation, the parties use their video-enabled devices to sign on to the website. A chat room is assigned to each party and the mediator, and another is set aside for both parties and the mediator. The individual chat rooms are used for private conversations with the online mediator, and the other chat room is for conversations between both parties and the mediator.

electronic mediation (e-mediation)
The mediation of a dispute using online mediation services.

Online arbitration and online mediation services charge fees, but the fees are reasonable. In an online arbitration or online mediation, a settlement can be reached rather quickly, without paying substantial lawyers' fees and court costs. The parties also act through a more objective online process rather than meet face-to-face or negotiate over the telephone, either of which could involve verbal arguments.

If a legal dispute is not settled using e-arbitration or e-mediation, the parties may pursue their case in the courts.

Key Terms and Concepts

Affirmative defense (48)
Algorithmic discrimination (Weblining) (56)
Alternative dispute resolution (ADR) (61)
Answer (47)
Appeal (60)
Appellant (petitioner) (60)
Appellee (respondent) (60)
Arbitration (61)
Arbitration clause (61)
Arbitrator (61)
Binding arbitration (62)
Burden of proof (57)
Class action (50)
Class Action Fairness Act (CAFA) (50)
Class action waiver (62)
Closing argument (closing statement) (58)
Complaint (47)
Consolidation (49)
Contingency fee (46)
Cost–benefit analysis (49)
Coupon settlement (51)
Cross-complainant (48)
Cross-complaint (48)
Cross-defendant (48)
Cross-examination (57)
Default judgment (47)
Defendant (57)
Defendant's case (57)
Deponent (51)
Deposition (51)
Direct examination (57)
Discovery (51)
Electronic arbitration (e-arbitration) (64)
Electronic court (e-court or virtual court) (60)
Electronic discovery (e-discovery) (52)
Electronic dispute resolution (e-dispute resolution) (64)
Electronic filing (e-filing) (60)
Electronic mediation (e-mediation) (64)
Electronically stored information (ESI) (52)
Error of law (60)
Federal Arbitration Act (FAA) (62)
Final judgment (60)
Finding of fact (60)
Impanel (57)
Interrogatories (51)
Intervention (49)
Judgment (58)
Judgment notwithstanding the verdict (judgment n.o.v. or j.n.o.v.) (58)
Jury deliberation (58)
Jury instructions (charges) (58)
Jury trial (56)
Litigation (47)
Mediation (63)
Mediator (63)
Motion for judgment on the pleadings (54)
Motion for summary judgment (54)
Negotiation (61)
Nonbinding arbitration (62)
Nonjudicial dispute resolution (61)
Notice of appeal (60)
Opening brief (60)
Opening statement (57)
Peremptory challenge (peremptory strike) (57)
Physical or mental examination (52)
Plaintiff (47)
Plaintiff's case (57)
Pleadings (47)
Pretrial motions (54)
Production of documents (51)
Rebuttal (57)
Record (58)
Re-direct examination (57)
Rejoinder (57)
Remittitur (58)
Reply (48)
Responding brief (60)
Retainer (46)
Sequester (57)
Service of process (47)
Settlement agreement (56)
Settlement conference (pretrial hearing) (55)
Statute of limitations (49)
Submission agreement (61)
Summons (47)
Trial brief (56)
Trier of fact (56)
Uniform Arbitration Act (61)
Verdict (58)
Voir dire (56)
Written memorandum (58)

Critical Legal Thinking Cases

3.1 Contingency Fee Five-year-old Cole Goesel was injured when a toy robot shattered and punctured the lens of his right eye. Cole's parents retained the law firm of Williams, Bax & Saltxman, P.C., to sue the manufacturer and distributor on Cole's behalf. The retainer agreement was a contingency-fee contract that stipulated the law firm would receive one-third of any gross judgment or settlement and the Goesels would be responsible for litigation expenses if the case was won or was settled. The contingency-fee agreement provided that in the event of no recovery the Goesels were not responsible for paying attorney's fees or expenses and the law firm would receive nothing.

The case included extensive discovery and the retention of multiple expert witnesses. After nearly four years of contentious litigation, the parties settled on the eve of trial. The defendants agreed to pay $687,500. Under the contingency-fee arrangement, the law firm's one-third of the gross settlement was $229,166, and litigation expenses totaled $172,949, leaving the Goesels with $285,384, or roughly 42 percent of the total recovery. The U.S. district court judge found that the contingency-fee agreement was not fair or reasonable and refused to approve the settlement unless litigation expenses were deducted off the top and one-third of the net settlement was allocated to the law firm. The law firm appealed. Is the contingency-fee agreement enforceable as written? *Goesel v. Boley International (H.K.) Ltd.*, 806 F.3d 414, 2015 U.S. App. Lexis 19353 (United States Court of Appeals for the Seventh Circuit, 2015)

3.2 Service of Process Jon Sommervold purchased a remote-controlled toy watercraft from the Walmart store located in Aberdeen, South Dakota. The plaintiff sued Walmart, Inc. for alleged defective design and failure to warn that arose out of the trauma he suffered when the toy watercraft exploded when he was handling it. Nine days before the three-year statute of limitations was to run out on the plaintiff's claim, the plaintiff had a process server serve his complaint and summons against Walmart. The process server served the complaint and summons on Josh Hehn, a Walmart assistant manager in charge of the apparel department at Walmart's Aberdeen, South Dakota, store. The assistant manager and the manager of the store were physically available at the store at the time of service. South Dakota law requires that service of process be made on the president, officer, director, or registered agent of a defendant corporation. Walmart had designated a registered agent, whose name was publicly available at a state government office as required by law, to accept service of process for South Dakota lawsuits. Walmart challenged the plaintiff's service of process on an assistant manager at a Walmart store rather than on its resident agent, asserting that the plaintiff's service violated South Dakota's statute for service of process against corporations. The three-year statute of limitations on Sommervold's claim had run out before Walmart's challenge to the legality of the service of process was heard by the court. Has the plaintiff properly served defendant Walmart? *Sommervold v. Walmart, Inc.*, 709 F.3d 1234, 2013 U.S. App. Lexis 4972 (United States Court of Appeals for the Eighth Circuit, 2013)

3.3 Summary Judgment Sandra Primrose, who was 73 years old, was shopping in a Walmart store owned and operated by Walmart Stores, Inc. She picked up a watermelon from a large display stand and as she took several steps around the display to reach her shopping cart, she tripped over a corner of the display. Primrose sustained a concussion and other serious injuries from the accident. Primrose sued Walmart for negligence to recover damages, alleging that Walmart "created a trap," causing her to fall. Evidence showed that the watermelon display had been used for more than four years without incident, and photographs showed that the four corners of the display were visibly marked with "Watch Step" warning signs. Walmart noted that the area in question was open and obvious. Walmart, alleging that no material facts were in dispute, made a motion for summary judgment, which plaintiff Primrose objected to. Should Walmart be granted summary judgment? *Primrose v. Walmart, Inc.*, 127 So.3d 13, 2013 La. App. Lexis 1985 (Court of Appeals of Louisiana, 2013)

3.4 Class Action Tyson Foods, Inc. is a major food processor that operates a pork processing plant in Storm Lake, Iowa. The company's employees slaughter and trim hogs and prepare the meat for shipment. It is dangerous and grueling work that requires employees to wear certain protective gear. Tyson paid these employees for the 40 hours they worked each week but did not pay them for time spent donning and doffing the protective equipment.

The Fair Labor Standards Act (FLSA) is a federal statute that requires employers to pay overtime pay of one and one-half times regular pay to employees for time worked that exceeds 40 hours in a week. The affected employees filed a class action lawsuit in U.S. district court alleging that Tyson violated the overtime pay requirements of the FLSA by not paying them overtime pay for the time spent donning and doffing protective gear. Tyson argued that the class should not be certified and that the plaintiffs' only recourse is to bring individual lawsuits against Tyson. Should the class be certified? *Tyson Foods, Inc. v. Bouaphakeo*, 136 S.Ct. 1036, 2016 U.S. Lexis 2134 (Supreme Court of the United States, 2016)

3.5 Arbitration Eddie Howard and Shane D. Schneider worked as employees of Nitro-Lift Technologies, L.L.C. Howard and Schneider entered into a noncompetition agreement with Nitro-Lift whereby they agreed that they would not work for a competitor of Nitro-Lift's for a stated period of time after they left Nitro-Lift's employment. The agreement contained an arbitration clause wherein the parties agreed to submit any contract dispute to arbitration. When Howard and Schneider quit their jobs and began working for Nitro-Lift's competitors, Nitro-Lift served the two men with a demand for arbitration to enforce the noncompetition agreement. Howard and Schneider filed a lawsuit in Oklahoma state court asking the court to declare the noncompetition agreement null and void. The supreme court of Oklahoma held that the state court and not an arbitrator should hear and decide the dispute. Defendant Nitro-Lift appealed to the U.S. Supreme Court. Is the contract dispute between the plaintiffs and defendant subject to arbitration? *Nitro-Lift Technologies, L.L.C. v. Howard,* 568 U.S. 17, 133 S.Ct. 500, 2012 U.S. Lexis 8897 (Supreme Court of the United States, 2012)

3.6 Arbitration Kindred Nursing Centers Limited Partnership operates nursing homes and rehabilitation centers. Olive Clark was a resident at the Kindred nursing home called Winchester Centre. Janis Clark was the daughter of Olive Clark. Olive had previously signed a power of attorney that named Janis her attorney-in-fact that gave Janis "full power to transact, handle, and dispose of all matters affecting me/or my estate in any possible way," including the power to "draw, make, and sign in my name any and all contracts, deeds, and agreements."

When Olive moved into the Winchester Centre, Janis completed the necessary paperwork. The contract that Janis signed with Kindred provided "any and all claims or controversies arising out of or in any way relating to the Resident's stay at the Facility" would be resolved through "binding arbitration" rather than a lawsuit. One year later, Olive died. Janis sued Kindred in Kentucky state court, alleging that Kindred's substandard care caused

Olive's death. Kindred made a motion to dismiss the case, arguing that the arbitration agreement prohibited Janis from bringing the dispute in court. Is an arbitration agreement enforceable? *Kindred Nursing Centers Limited Partnership v. Clark*, 137 S.Ct. 1421, 2017 U.S. Lexis 2948 (Supreme Court of the United States, 2017)

Ethics Cases

3.7 Ethics Case During the month of February, Elijah Murphy drove to a McDonald's restaurant in New Carlisle, Ohio, and parked his vehicle in the parking area. The front of his vehicle faced a 4-inch-high, 30-inch-long concrete median that divided the parking area from the restaurant's drive-through lane. The median was covered with snow that had been plowed from the drive-through lane and the parking area. On leaving the restaurant, Murphy walked across the drive-through lane and the median. As he stepped down from the median onto the pavement next to his vehicle, Murphy slipped on the icy pavement and fell. Murphy's left foot ended up underneath the front wheel of the pickup truck parked next to his vehicle. Murphy suffered severe ankle dislocation that required surgery. Murphy sued McDonald's to recover damages for negligence. After several depositions were taken, McDonald's moved for summary judgment, alleging that no genuine issue of material fact existed that needed to be decided by a jury. McDonald's asserted that since no factual issues remained, the court could apply the law to the case and grant summary judgment to McDonald's. Is there a genuine issue of material fact that would deny a grant of summary judgment? *Murphy v. McDonald's Restaurants of Ohio*, 2010 Ohio App. Lexis 402 (Court of Appeals of Ohio, 2010)

3.8 Ethics Case Starbucks Corporation operates a national chain of upscale coffee houses, including outlets in Massachusetts. Employees are divided into four subcategories: store managers, assistant managers, shift supervisors, and baristas. Baristas are frontline employees who serve food and beverages to customers, are paid wages for hours worked, and have no management responsibilities. Starbucks stores maintain tip containers in which customers may deposit tips. The accumulated tips are distributed weekly to baristas and shift supervisors within the store in proportion to the number of hours worked that week by each individual.

The Massachusetts Tips Act, applicable to the restaurant industry, stipulates that wait-staff employees shall not be required to share tips with anyone who is not a wait-staff employee. Starbucks baristas filed a class action lawsuit against Starbucks on behalf of all Starbucks baristas who worked in Massachusetts, alleging that Starbucks's policy of permitting shift supervisors to share in pooled tips violated the Massachusetts Tips Act. The plaintiffs alleged that their class consists of baristas who worked during an identified class period of six years. Starbucks challenged the certification of the class. Can the case be properly certified as class action? Did Starbucks act ethically in this case? *Matamoros v. Starbucks Corporation*, 699 F.3d 129, 2012 U.S. App. Lexis 23185 (United States Court of Appeals for the First Circuit, 2012)

Notes

1. *Walmart Stores, Inc. v. Dukes*, 564 U.S. 338, 131 S.Ct. 2541, 2011 U.S. Lexis 4567 (Supreme Court of the United States, 2011).
2. 28 U.S.C. Sections 1332(d), 1453, and 1711—1715.
3. There is no right to a jury trial for actions in equity (e.g., injunctions, specific performance).
4. 9 U.S.C. Section 1 et seq.
5. *Gilmer v. Interstate/Johnson Lane Corporation*, 500 U.S. 20, 111 S.Ct. 1647, 1991 U.S. Lexis 2529 (Supreme Court of the United States, 1991).
6. *AT&T Mobility LLC v. Concepcion*, 563 U.S. 333, 131 S.Ct. 1740, 2011 U.S. Lexis 3367 (Supreme Court of the United States, 2011).

CHAPTER

4 Constitutional Law for Business and E-Commerce

Henry R. Cheeseman

SUPREME COURT OF THE UNITED STATES, WASHINGTON DC

This photograph is of the interior of the Supreme Court of the United States. During court sessions, the chief justice sits in the middle chair, while the eight associate justices sit in designated chairs on each side of the chief justice as determined by tenure on the Court.

Learning Objectives

After studying this chapter, you should be able to:

4.1 Describe the U.S. Constitution and the concepts of federalism and separation of powers.

4.2 Define and apply the Supremacy Clause of the U.S. Constitution.

4.3 Explain the Commerce Clause and the federal government's authority to regulate interstate and foreign commerce.

4.4 Describe how the Commerce Clause is applied to e-commerce.

4.5 Describe the Bill of Rights and the process for amending the U.S. Constitution.

4.6 Explain how freedom of speech is protected by the First Amendment.

4.7 Explain how freedom of religion is protected and how the government may not promote religion.

4.8 Explain the equal protection doctrine and how it protects persons from unequal treatment by the government.

4.9 Describe the Due Process Clause and substantive and procedural due process.

4.10 Explain how the government can take private property but must pay just compensation for the taking.

4.11 Explain how the privileges and immunities doctrine protects citizens from unfavorable treatment by the government.

> *"We the People of the United States, in Order to form a more perfect Union, establish Justice, insure domestic Tranquility, provide for the common defense, promote the general Welfare, and secure the Blessings of Liberty to ourselves and our Posterity, do ordain and establish this Constitution for the United States of America."*
>
> —*Preamble to the Constitution of the United States of America (ratified 1788)*

Introduction to Constitutional Law for Business and E-Commerce

Prior to the American Revolution, each of the 13 original colonies operated as a separate sovereignty under the rule of Great Britain. In September 1774, representatives of the colonies met as a Continental Congress. In 1776, the colonies declared independence from England, and the American Revolution ensued. The **Declaration of Independence** was the document that declared the American colonies' independence from Great Britain.

This chapter examines the major provisions of the U.S. Constitution and the amendments that have been added to the Constitution. Of particular importance, this chapter discusses how these provisions affect the operations of business in this country. The Constitution, with amendments, is set forth as Appendix A to this text.

The nation's armour of defence against the passions of men is the Constitution. Take that away, and the nation goes down into the field of its conflicts like a warrior without armour.

Henry Ward Beecher
Proverbs from Plymouth Pulpit, 1887

WEB EXERCISE
Go to **www.ushistory.org/declaration/document/index.htm** for the text of the Declaration of Independence. Read the first two paragraphs of the Declaration of Independence.

Constitution of the United States of America

4.1 Describe the U.S. Constitution and the concepts of federalism and separation of powers.

In 1777, the Continental Congress formed a **federal government** and adopted the **Articles of Confederation**. The Articles of Confederation, which was ratified in 1781, created a federal Congress composed of representatives of the 13 colonies. The Articles of Confederation was a particularly weak document that gave limited power to the newly created federal government. It did not provide Congress with the power to levy and collect taxes, regulate commerce with foreign countries, or regulate interstate commerce.

A **Constitutional Convention** was convened in Philadelphia in May 1787. The primary purpose of the convention was to strengthen the federal government. After substantial debate, the delegates agreed to a new **U.S. Constitution**. The Constitution was approved by Congress in September 1787. Ratification of the Constitution by the colonies was completed in 1788. During the period 1788–1790, individual colonies converted to state governments. Amendments, including the Bill of Rights, have been added to the Constitution.

U.S. Constitution
The fundamental law of the United States of America. It was ratified by the states in 1788.

The U.S. Constitution, as amended, serves two major functions:

1. It creates the three branches of the federal government (i.e., the legislative, executive, and judicial branches) and allocates powers to these branches.
2. It protects individual rights by limiting the government's ability to restrict those rights.

The Constitution itself provides that it may be amended to address social and economic changes. Some important constitutional concepts are discussed in the following paragraphs.

Federalism and Delegated Powers

federalism
The U.S. form of government in which the federal government and the 50 state governments share powers.

enumerated powers
Express powers delegated to the federal government by the states.

Article I, Section 8 of the U.S. Constitution
The part of the U.S. Constitution that lists express powers granted to the U.S. Congress.

Necessary and Proper Clause (elastic clause)
A clause of the U.S. Constitution that grants the U.S. Congress the power to make federal laws that are necessary and proper to implement its express powers.

Our country's form of government is referred to as **federalism**, which means that the federal government and the 50 state governments share powers.

When the states ratified the Constitution, they *delegated* certain express powers—called **enumerated powers**—to the federal government. **Article I, Section 8** of the Constitution grants Congress the power to declare war, raise and support an army and navy, coin money, collect taxes, pay debts, borrow money, regulate commerce with foreign nations and among the states, create courts inferior to the Supreme Court, establish rules for naturalization, establish post offices, punish felonies on the high seas, and other powers. Other articles and some amendments to the Constitution grant additional powers to Congress.

The last paragraph of Article 8 grants Congress the power to enact federal laws which are necessary and proper to implement its express powers. This is called the **Necessary and Proper Clause**, also referred to as the **elastic clause**. This clause, which is one of the most important clauses in the Constitution, has been used to significantly expand the role of the federal government.

Examples Pursuant to the express power to regulate commerce among the states, Congress has enacted transportation laws, securities laws, antidiscrimination laws, labor laws, environmental laws, consumer protection laws, antitrust laws, and many other laws.

Any powers that are not specifically delegated to the federal government by the Constitution are reserved to the state governments. These are called **reserved powers**. State governments are empowered to enact laws that govern state-related matters.

Examples State governments enact partnership and corporation laws, family law, property law, and educational law.

Native American nations exercise limited powers. They often provide education, social and health programs, land development and improvements, and first-responder services.

Henry R. Cheeseman

CONSTITUTION OF THE UNITED STATES OF AMERICA
The U.S. Constitution was adopted in 1787 and was subsequently ratified by each state in the name of "the people." Ratification by the required number of states was completed on June 21, 1788. In 1790, Rhode Island became the last of the original 13 states to ratify the Constitution. The U.S. Constitution establishes the federal government and delegates certain powers to the federal government.

Doctrine of Separation of Powers

As mentioned previously, the federal government is divided into three branches:

1. **Article I: Legislative branch.** **Article I of the U.S. Constitution** establishes the **legislative branch** of the federal government. The legislative branch is responsible for making federal law. This branch is **bicameral**; that is, it consists of the U.S. Senate and the U.S. House of Representatives. Collectively, they are referred to as the **U.S. Congress**, or simply **Congress**.[1] Each state has two senators in the **U.S. Senate**. The number of representatives to the **U.S. House of Representatives** is determined according to the population of each state. The current number of representatives is determined by the most recent national census.
2. **Article II: Executive branch.** **Article II of the U.S. Constitution** establishes the **executive branch** of the federal government by providing for the election of the president and vice president. The president is not elected by popular vote, but instead is selected by the **Electoral College**, whose representatives are appointed by state delegations.[2] The executive branch is responsible for enforcing federal law.
3. **Article III: Judicial branch.** **Article III of the U.S. Constitution** establishes the **judicial branch** of the federal government by establishing the U.S. Supreme Court and providing for the creation of other federal courts by Congress.[3] The judicial branch of the government is responsible for interpreting the U.S. Constitution and federal law.

The following feature discusses checks and balances established by the U.S. Constitution.

legislative branch
The part of the U.S. government that makes federal laws. It is known as Congress (the Senate and the House of Representatives).

executive branch
The part of the U.S. government that enforces the federal law; it consists of the president and vice president.

judicial branch
The part of the U.S. government that interprets the law. It consists of the Supreme Court and other federal courts.

checks and balances
A system built into the U.S. Constitution to prevent any one of the three branches of the government from becoming too powerful.

Critical Legal Thinking

Checks and Balances

Certain **checks and balances** are built into the U.S. Constitution to ensure that no one branch of the federal government becomes too powerful. Following are several of these major checks and balances.

- The *judicial* branch has authority to examine the acts of the other two branches of government and determine whether those acts are constitutional.[4]
- The *executive* branch can enter into treaties with foreign governments only with the advice and consent of the Senate.
- The *legislative* branch is authorized to create federal courts and determine their jurisdiction and to enact statutes that change judicially made law.
- To solve the power issue between states with large populations and those with small populations, a *compromise* was reached whereby the number of representatives from a state is based on population while each state has two senators no matter how large or small its population.
- Within the *legislative branch* a bill only becomes law if the majority of the members of the Senate and the House who vote approve the identical final bill.
- The president has *veto power* over bills passed by Congress. If a bill has been vetoed by the president, the bill goes back to Congress, where a vote of two-thirds of both the Senate and the House of Representatives is required to override the president's veto.
- The president nominates individuals to be federal judges but a majority vote of the U.S. Senate is required to *confirm* the nominee as a federal judge.
- A president can be removed from office following impeachment and conviction for treason, bribery, or other crimes. The process starts in the House of Representatives, which can approve articles of impeachment by a majority vote. The Senate tries the case, where a two-thirds vote is required for conviction. If convicted, the president is removed from office.

Critical Legal Thinking Questions
Why are checks and balances built into the U.S. Constitution? Several alternative proposals that were debated at the Constitutional Convention were to have a one-branch (unicameral) legislature, to have the chief executive serve for life, and to have the number of senators and representatives be based on the population of the states. What would have been the effect if any of these proposals had been adopted?

CONCEPT SUMMARY

BASIC CONSTITUTIONAL CONCEPTS

Concept	Description
Federalism	The Constitution created the federal government. The federal government, the 50 state governments, and Washington DC share powers in this country.
Delegated powers	When the states ratified the Constitution, they delegated certain powers to the federal government. These are called *enumerated powers*.
Reserved powers	Those powers not granted to the federal government by the Constitution are reserved to the state governments.
Separation of powers	Each branch of the federal government has separate powers. These powers are the following: a. Legislative branch—power to make the law. b. Executive branch—power to enforce the law. c. Judicial branch—power to interpret the law.
Checks and balances	Certain checks and balances are built into the Constitution to ensure that no one branch of the federal government becomes too powerful.

Supremacy Clause

4.2 Define and apply the Supremacy Clause of the U.S. Constitution.

Supremacy Clause
A clause of the U.S. Constitution that establishes the U.S. Constitution and federal treaties, laws, and regulations as the supreme law of the land.

preemption doctrine
A doctrine stating that federal law takes precedence over state or local law.

The **Supremacy Clause** establishes that the U.S. Constitution and federal treaties, laws, and regulations are the supreme law of the land.[5] State and local laws that conflict with valid federal law are unconstitutional. The concept of federal law taking precedence over state or local law is commonly called the **preemption doctrine**.

Congress may expressly provide that a particular federal statute *exclusively* regulates a specific area or activity. No state or local law regulating the area or activity is valid if there is such a statute. Often, though, federal statutes do not expressly provide for exclusive jurisdiction. In these instances, state and local governments have *concurrent jurisdiction* to regulate the area or activity. However, any state or local law that "directly and substantially" conflicts with valid federal law is preempted under the Supremacy Clause.

The following U.S. Supreme Court case involves the Supremacy Clause.

CASE 4.1 U.S. SUPREME COURT CASE Supremacy Clause

Mutual Pharmaceutical Company, Inc. v. Bartlett

133 S.Ct. 2466, 2013 U.S. Lexis 4702 (2013)
Supreme Court of the United States

"Sympathy for respondent does not relieve us of the responsibility of following the law."

—Samuel Alito, Justice

Facts

The Food and Drug Administration (FDA), a federal government agency, approved the use of a nonsteroidal anti-inflammatory pain reliever called sulindac. Federal law requires that sellers of sulindac use exact federally required wording on the drug's label warning of the side effects of the drug. This required label does not provide for warning of the possible side effect of toxic epidermal necrolysis that may result from use of sulindac.

Karen L. Bartlett was prescribed sulindac manufactured by Mutual Pharmaceutical Company, Inc. (Mutual). After use of the drug, Bartlett suffered toxic epidermal necrolysis which resulted in horrific injuries requiring six months of a medically induced coma, 12 surgeries, and tube feeding for one year. She is now severely disfigured, has physical disabilities, and is nearly blind.

Bartlett sued Mutual in U.S. district court for violating a broader New Hampshire labeling law for failing to warn her against the possible side effect of toxic epidermal necrolysis. The jury awarded Bartlett $21 million in damages, and the U.S. court of appeals affirmed the award. Mutual appealed to the U.S. Supreme Court, asserting that the federal labeling law preempted New Hampshire law under the Supremacy Clause.

Issue

Does the federal drug labeling law preempt the state drug labeling law?

Language of the U.S. Supreme Court

Under the Supremacy Clause, state laws that require a private party to violate federal law are preempted and, thus, are "without effect." In the instant case, it was impossible for Mutual to comply with both its state-law duty to strengthen the warnings on sulindac's label and its federal-law duty not to alter sulindac's label. Accordingly, the state law is preempted. Sympathy for respondent does not relieve us of the responsibility of following the law.

Decision

The U.S. Supreme Court held that federal drug labeling law preempted New Hampshire's stricter labeling law under the Supremacy Clause of the U.S. Constitution. The Supreme Court reversed the U.S. court of appeals decision.

Critical Legal Thinking Questions

What is the public policy purpose for having the Supremacy Clause? Do you think that pharmaceutical companies supported the passage of the federal drug labeling statute?

Commerce Clause

4.3 Explain the Commerce Clause and the federal government's authority to regulate interstate and foreign commerce.

The **Commerce Clause** of the U.S. Constitution grants Congress the power "to regulate commerce with foreign nations, and among the several states, and with Indian tribes."[6] Because this clause authorizes the federal government to regulate commerce, it has a greater impact on business than any other provision in the Constitution. Among other things, this clause is intended to foster the development of a national market and free trade among the states.

The U.S. Constitution grants the federal government the power to regulate three types of commerce:

1. Commerce with Native American tribes
2. Foreign commerce
3. Interstate commerce

Each of these is discussed in the following paragraphs.

Critical Legal Thinking

Why was the Supremacy Clause added to the U.S. Constitution? What would be the result if there were no Supremacy Clause?

Commerce Clause
A clause of the U.S. Constitution that grants Congress the power "to regulate commerce with foreign nations, and among the several states, and with Indian tribes."

Commerce with Native Americans

Before Europeans arrived in North, South, and Central America the land had been occupied for thousands of years by native inhabitants. There were many different Native American tribes, each having its own independent and self-governing system of laws.

When the United States was first founded more than 200 years ago, it consisted of the original 13 colonies, all located in the east, primarily on the Atlantic Ocean. After fighting the American Revolution and winning their independence from Great Britain, the states ratified the U.S. Constitution, which came into force in 1788. In the Constitution the states delegated to the federal government the authority to regulate commerce with the Native American tribes, in both the original 13 states and the territory that was to eventually become part of the United States of America.

Under its Commerce Clause powers, the federal government entered into treaties with many Native American nations. Most tribes, in the face of white settlers' encroachment on their land and federal government pressure, sold their lands to the federal government, usually for very insufficient compensation. The federal government obtained many treaties through unscrupulous means, cheating the Native Americans out of their land. These tribes were then relocated to other, smaller pieces of land called *reservations*, often outside their typical tribal lands. The federal government eventually broke many of the treaties.

Once Native Americans came under U.S. authority, they lost much of their political power. Most tribes were allowed to keep their own governments but were placed under the protection of the U.S. government. In general, the United States treats Native Americans as belonging to separate nations with limited sovereignty.

Indian Gaming Regulatory Act In the late 1980s, the federal government authorized Native American tribes to operate gaming facilities. Congress passed the **Indian Gaming Regulatory Act**,[7] a federal statute that establishes the requirements for conducting casino gambling and other gaming activities on tribal land. This act allows Native Americans to negotiate with the states for gaming compacts and ensures that the states do so in good faith. If a state fails to do so, the tribe can bring suit in federal court, forcing the state to comply. Today, casinos operated by Native Americans can be found in many states. Profits from the casinos have become an important source of income for members of certain tribes.

Let our last sleep be in the graves of our native land!
Osceola (1804–1838)

Foreign Commerce

Foreign Commerce Clause
The Commerce Clause grants the federal government the authority to regulate foreign commerce.

The Commerce Clause of the U.S. Constitution gives the federal government the *exclusive power* to regulate commerce with foreign nations. This is referred to as the **Foreign Commerce Clause**. Direct and indirect regulation of foreign commerce by state or local governments that *unduly burdens* foreign commerce violates the Foreign Commerce Clause and is therefore unconstitutional.

Examples The federal government could enact a law that forbids another country from doing business in the United States if that country engages in activities that are not condoned by the United States. A state, however, could not enact a law that forbids a foreign country from doing business in that state if that country engages in activities that are not condoned by that state.

Example Suppose the Michigan state legislature enacts a law that imposes a 100 percent state tax on any automobile, SUV, or other vehicle sold in Michigan that does not have at least 50 percent of its parts made in the United States, but does not impose the same tax on vehicles sold in Michigan that do have 50 percent or more of their parts made in the United States. The Michigan state tax violates the Foreign Commerce Clause and is therefore unconstitutional and void. However, the federal government could enact this tax.

Interstate Commerce

interstate commerce
Commerce that moves between states or that affects commerce between states.

The Commerce Clause gives the federal government the authority to regulate **interstate commerce**. Originally, the courts interpreted this clause to mean that the federal government could regulate only commerce that moved *in* interstate commerce, that is, commerce that is conducted across state borders. The modern interpretation, however, allows the federal government to regulate activities that *affect* interstate commerce.

Under the **effects on interstate commerce test** the regulated activity does not itself have to be in interstate commerce. Thus, any local (*intrastate*) activity that has an effect on interstate commerce is subject to federal regulation. Theoretically, this test subjects a substantial amount of business activity in the United States to federal regulation.

Example In the famous case ***Wickard, Secretary of Agriculture v. Filburn***,[8] a federal statute limited the amount of wheat that a farmer could plant and harvest for home consumption. Filburn, a farmer, violated the law. The U.S. Supreme Court upheld the federal statute on the grounds that it involved interstate commerce because the statute was designed to prevent nationwide surpluses and shortages of wheat. The Court reasoned that wheat grown for home consumption would affect the supply of wheat available in interstate commerce.

The American Constitution is, so far as I can see, the most wonderful work ever struck off at a given time by the brain and purpose of man.

William Ewart Gladstone
Kin Beyond Sea (1878)

State Police Power

The states did not delegate all power to regulate business to the federal government. They retained the power to regulate **intrastate commerce** and much of the interstate commerce that occurs within their borders. This is commonly referred to as states' **police power**.

Police power permits states (and, by delegation, local governments) to enact laws to protect or promote the *public health, safety, morals, and general welfare*. This includes the authority to enact laws that regulate the conduct of business.

police power
Power that permits state and local governments to enact laws to protect or promote the public health, safety, morals, and general welfare.

Example State real property laws, personal property laws, and state environmental laws are enacted under state police power.

Dormant Commerce Clause

If the federal government has chosen not to regulate an area of interstate commerce that it has the power to regulate under its Commerce Clause powers, this area of commerce is subject to what is referred to as the **Dormant Commerce Clause**. A state, under its police power, can enact laws to regulate that area of commerce. However, if a state enacts laws to regulate commerce that the federal government has the power to regulate but has chosen not to regulate, the Dormant Commerce Clause prohibits the state's regulation from **unduly burdening interstate commerce**.

Dormant Commerce Clause
A situation in which the federal government has the Commerce Clause power to regulate an area of commerce but has chosen not to regulate that area of commerce.

Example The federal government, under its interstate commerce powers, could, if it wanted to, regulate corporations. However, the federal government has chosen not to. Thus, states regulate corporations. Assume that one state's corporation code permits only corporations from that state but from no other state to conduct business in that state. That state's law would unduly burden interstate commerce and would be unconstitutional.

unduly burdening interstate commerce
A concept that says states may enact laws that protect or promote the public health, safety, morals, and general welfare as long as the laws do not unduly burden interstate commerce.

The following U.S. Supreme Court case involves the Commerce Clause.

CASE 4.2 *U.S. SUPREME COURT CASE Commerce Clause*

Tennessee Wine and Spirits Retailers Association v. Thomas

139 S.Ct. 2449 (2019)
Supreme Court of the United States

"Removing state trade barriers was a principal reason for the adoption of the Constitution."

—Samuel Alito, Justice

Facts

Tennessee, like many other states, requires producers, wholesalers, and retailers of alcoholic beverages to qualify for and obtain an appropriate license from the state. Tennessee requires that a person who wants to obtain a license to operate a retail liquor store in the state demonstrate that he or she has been a resident of the state for two years. Several out-of-state residents applied for licenses to operate retail liquor stores in Tennessee. The Tennessee Wine and

(continued)

Spirits Retailers Association (Association)—a trade association of in-state liquor stores—threatened to sue the state if it granted these licenses. Tennessee filed a declaratory judgment action in U.S. district court asking the court to determine whether its two-year residency requirement was constitutional. The U.S. district court held that the law discriminated against out-of-state parties in violation of the Dormant Commerce Clause. The U.S. court of appeals affirmed. The Association appealed to the U.S. Supreme Court.

Issue

Does Tennessee's two-year residency requirement to obtain a retail liquor store license unduly burden interstate commerce in violation of the Dormant Commerce Clause?

Language of the U.S. Supreme Court

We have long held that the Commerce Clause prohibits state laws that unduly restrict interstate Commerce. This aspect of the Commerce Clause prevents the States from adopting protectionist measures and thus preserves a national market for goods and services. Removing state trade barriers was a principal reason for the adoption of the Constitution. The Commerce Clause by its own force restricts state regulation of interstate commerce. The Commerce Clause prevents states from discriminating against the citizens and products of other States. The predominate effect of the two-year residency requirement is simply to protect the Association's members from out-of-state competition. We therefore hold that this provision violates the Commerce Clause.

Decision

The U.S. Supreme Court held that Tennessee's two-year residency requirement to obtain a retail liquor store license unduly burdens interstate commerce and violates the Dormant Commerce Clause.

Critical Legal Thinking Questions

Wat are the main purposes of the Commerce Clause? What is the Dormant Commerce Clause? Why did Tennessee adopt the two-year residency requirement to obtain a retail liquor store license?

E-Commerce and the Constitution

4.4 Describe how the Commerce Clause is applied to e-commerce.

Critical Legal Thinking

Can the law keep up with the changes brought by e-commerce and digital devices? Are new laws required to apply to the digital environment?

The advent of the internet has caused a revolution in how commerce is conducted. The internet and other computer networks permit parties to obtain website domain names and conduct business electronically. This is usually referred to as **electronic commerce** or **e-commerce**. Some businesses that conduct e-commerce over the internet do not have any physical location, whereas many brick-and-mortar businesses augment their traditional sales with e-commerce sales. Currently, a significant portion of the sales of goods, licensing of intellectual property, and sales of services are accomplished through e-commerce. Because e-commerce is commerce, it is subject to the Commerce Clause of the U.S. Constitution.

The following feature discusses a U.S. Supreme Court case that applies the Commerce Clause to e-commerce.

Information Technology

E-Commerce and the Commerce Clause

"State bans on interstate direct shipping represent the single largest regulatory barrier to expanded e-commerce."
—Anthony Kennedy, Justice

In this information age, federal and state governments have had to grapple with how to regulate the internet and e-commerce. State laws that unduly burden interstate e-commerce are unconstitutional. Consider the following case.

Michigan law permits in-state wineries to sell wine directly to consumers, including by mail, internet, and other means of sale. Michigan law prohibits out-of-state wineries from selling wine directly to Michigan consumers, including over the internet. Michigan requires out-of-state wineries to sell their wine to Michigan wholesalers, who then sell the wine to Michigan retailers, who then sell the wine to Michigan consumers.

Domaine Alfred, a small winery located in San Luis Obispo, California, and several other out-of-state wineries that were prohibited from selling wine directly to Michigan consumers sued Michigan. The plaintiff wineries alleged that the Michigan law caused an undue burden on interstate e-commerce in violation of the Commerce Clause of the U.S. Constitution.

The U.S. Supreme Court held that the Michigan state law that discriminated against out-of-state wineries in favor of in-state wineries caused an undue burden on interstate e-commerce, in violation of the Commerce Clause of the U.S. Constitution. The U.S. Supreme Court stated, "State bans on interstate direct shipping represent the single largest regulatory barrier to expanded e-commerce." *Granholm, Governor of Michigan v. Heald*, 544 U.S. 460, 125 S.Ct. 1885, 2005 U.S. Lexis 4174 (Supreme Court of the United States, 2005)

Critical Legal Thinking Questions

What does the doctrine of undue burden on interstate commerce accomplish? Should the government be allowed to treat internet sales differently than in-store sales?

Bill of Rights and Other Amendments to the U.S. Constitution

4.5 Describe the Bill of Rights and the process for amending the U.S. Constitution.

The U.S. Constitution provides that it may be amended. Currently, there are 27 **amendments to the U.S. Constitution.**

In 1791, the 10 amendments that are commonly referred to as the **Bill of Rights** were ratified by the states and became part of the U.S. Constitution. The Bill of Rights guarantees certain fundamental rights and protects these rights from intrusive government action.

Bill of Rights
The first 10 amendments to the Constitution, which were added to the U.S. Constitution in 1791.

Examples Fundamental rights guaranteed in the **First Amendment** include *freedom of speech, freedom to assemble, freedom of the press*, and *freedom of religion*. Most of these rights have also been found applicable to so-called artificial persons (i.e., corporations).

In addition to the Bill of Rights, 17 other amendments have been added to the Constitution. These amendments cover a variety of issues.

Pgiam/iStock Unreleased/Getty Images

FREEDOM OF SPEECH
This plaque on the steps of the Lincoln Memorial in Washington DC marks the spot where the Reverend Dr. Martin Luther King, Jr. gave his famous "I Have a Dream" speech to civil rights marchers on August 28, 1963.

I disapprove of what you say, but I will defend to the death your right to say it.

Voltaire (1694–1778)

Examples The additional 17 amendments to the Constitution have abolished slavery, prohibited discrimination, authorized the federal income tax, given women the right to vote, and specifically recognized that persons 18 years of age and older have the right to vote.

Originally, the Bill of Rights limited intrusive action by the *federal government* only. Intrusive actions by state and local governments were not limited until the *Due Process Clause of the Fourteenth Amendment* was added to the Constitution in 1868. The Supreme Court has applied the **incorporation doctrine** and held that most of the fundamental guarantees contained in the Bill of Rights are applicable to *state and local government* action. The amendments to the Constitution that are most applicable to business are discussed in the sections that follow.

Freedom of Speech

4.6 Explain how freedom of speech is protected by the First Amendment.

freedom of speech
The right to engage in oral, written, and symbolic speech protected by the First Amendment.

One of the most honored freedoms guaranteed by the Bill of Rights is the **freedom of speech** of the First Amendment. Many other constitutional freedoms would be meaningless without it. The First Amendment's Freedom of Speech Clause protects speech only, not conduct. The U.S. Supreme Court places speech into three categories: (1) *fully protected*, (2) *limited protected*, and (3) *unprotected speech*. These types of speech are discussed in the following paragraphs.

Fully Protected Speech

fully protected speech
Speech that cannot be prohibited or regulated by the government.

Fully protected speech is speech that the government cannot prohibit or regulate. The government cannot prohibit or regulate the content of fully protected speech.

Example Political speech is an example of fully protected speech. Thus, the government could not enact a law that forbids citizens from criticizing the current president.

The First Amendment protects oral, written, and symbolic speech.

Example Burning the American flag in protest of a federal government military action is protected symbolic speech.

The following U.S. Supreme Court case involves freedom of speech.

CASE 4.3 *U.S. SUPREME COURT CASE Freedom of Speech*

Iancu v. Brunetti

139 S.Ct. 2294 (2019)
Supreme Court of the United States

"The government may not discriminate against speech based on the ideas or opinion it conveys."

—Elena Kagan, Justice

Facts

Eric Brunetti is an artist and entrepreneur who founded a clothing line using the brand name FUCT. According to Brunetti the name is pronounced as four letters, one after the other: F-U-C-T. However, most people read the letters as one word, which is the past participle form of a well-known word of profanity. When Brunetti tried to register the name as a trademark at the U.S. Patent and Trademark Office (PTO), the PTO examining attorney and the PTO's Trademark Trial and Appeal Board refused to register the mark FUCT. In doing so, they relied on a provision of the Lanham Trademark Act, a federal statute, that prohibits the registration of a mark that consists of or comprises "immoral or scandalous matter." On appeal, the U.S. court of appeals held that the immoral and scandalous matter section of the Lanham Act violated the Free Speech Clause of the First Amendment. The case was appealed to the U.S. Supreme Court.

Issue

Does the "immoral and scandalous matter" provision of the Lanham Act violate the Free Speech Clause of the First Amendment?

Language of the U.S. Supreme Court

The government may not discriminate against speech based on the ideas or opinion it conveys. The criteria for federal trademark registration must be viewpoint-neutral to survive Free Speech Clause review. So, the key question becomes: Is the "immoral and scandalous" criterion in the Lanham Act viewpoint-neutral or viewpoint-based? It is viewpoint-based. The Lanham Act permits registration of marks that champion society's sense of rectitude and morality, but not marks that denigrate those concepts. A law disfavoring "ideas that offend" discriminates based on viewpoint, in violation of the First Amendment. The immoral and scandalous bar is substantially overbroad. There are a great many immoral and scandalous ideas in the world (even more than there are swear-words), and the Lanham Act covers them all. It therefore violates the First Amendment.

Decision

The U.S. Supreme Court held that the immoral and scandalous matter prohibition of the Lanham Act violates the Free Speech Clause of the First Amendment.

The Court's decision today will beget unfortunate results. The government will have no statutory basis to refuse registering marks containing the most vulgar, profane, or obscene words and images imaginable.
—Sonia Sotomayor, Justice, concurring in part and dissenting in part

Critical Legal Thinking Questions

Do you think that everyone agrees as to what constitutes "immoral or scandalous matter"? Will there be a rush to register vulgar, profane, or obscene words and images as trademarks?

Limited Protected Speech

The Supreme Court has held that certain types of speech have only *limited protection* under the First Amendment. The government cannot forbid this type of speech, but it can subject this speech to *time, place, and manner restrictions*. Two major forms of **limited protected speech** are *offensive speech* and *commercial speech*.

limited protected speech Speech that the government may not prohibit but that is subject to time, place, and manner restrictions.

Offensive speech is speech that offends many members of society. (It is not the same as obscene speech, however.) The Supreme Court has held that the content of offensive speech may not be forbidden but that it may be restricted by the government under time, place, and manner restrictions.

offensive speech Speech that is offensive to many members of society. It is subject to time, place, and manner restrictions.

Example The Federal Communications Commission (FCC) is a federal administrative agency that regulates radio, television, and cable stations. Under its powers, the FCC has regulated the use of offensive language on television by limiting such language to time periods when children would be unlikely to be watching (e.g., late at night).

Commercial speech, such as advertising, was once considered unprotected by the First Amendment. Today, because of U.S. Supreme Court decisions, however, the content of commercial speech is protected but is also subject to time, place, and manner restrictions.

commercial speech Speech used by businesses, such as advertisers. It is subject to time, place, and manner restrictions.

Example In *Virginia State Board of Pharmacy v. Virginia Citizens Consumer Council, Inc.*,[9] the U.S. Supreme Court held that a state statute that prohibited a pharmacist from advertising the price of prescription drugs was unconstitutional because it violated the Freedom of Speech Clause. The U.S. Supreme Court held that this was commercial speech that was protected by the First Amendment.

Example A city can prohibit billboards along its highways for safety and aesthetic reasons if other forms of advertising (e.g., print media) are available. This is a lawful place restriction.

Unprotected Speech

unprotected speech
Speech that is not protected by the First Amendment and may be forbidden by the government.

The U.S. Supreme Court has held that certain speech is **unprotected speech** that is not protected by the First Amendment and may be forbidden totally by the government. The Supreme Court has held that the following types of speech are unprotected speech:

1. **Dangerous speech**

   Example Yelling "fire" in a crowded theater when there is no fire is not protected speech.

Critical Legal Thinking
Why does the U.S. Supreme Court designate some speech as being not protected by the First Amendment? Do you think that these exceptions are warranted?

2. **Fighting words that are likely to provoke a hostile or violent response from an average person**[10]

   Example Walking up to a person and intentionally calling that person names because of race or ethnicity would not be protected speech if it would likely cause the person being called the names to respond in a hostile manner.

3. **Speech that incites the violent or revolutionary overthrow of the government** However, the mere abstract teaching of the morality and consequences of such action is protected.[11]
4. **Defamatory language**[12]

   Example Committing libel or slander by writing or telling untrue statements about another person or committing product disparagement or trade libel by writing or telling untrue statements about a company's products or services is not protected speech, and the injured party may bring a civil lawsuit to recover damages.

5. **Child pornography**[13]

   Example Selling material depicting children engaged in sexual activity is unprotected speech.

obscene speech
Speech that (1) appeals to the prurient interest, (2) depicts sexual conduct in a patently offensive way, and (3) lacks serious literary, artistic, political, or scientific value.

6. **Obscene speech**[14] If speech is considered **obscene speech**, it has no protection under the Freedom of Speech Clause of the First Amendment and can be banned by the government.

   Examples Movies, videos, music, and other forms of speech that are obscene are unprotected speech.

The definition of *obscenity* has plagued the courts. The definition of *obscene speech* is quite subjective. One Supreme Court justice stated, "I know it when I see it."[15] In ***Miller v. California***, the U.S. Supreme Court determined that speech is obscene when:

1. The average person, applying contemporary community standards, would find that the work, taken as a whole, appeals to the *prurient interest*.
2. The work depicts or describes, in a patently offensive way, sexual conduct specifically defined by the applicable state law.
3. The work, taken as a whole, lacks serious literary, artistic, political, or scientific value.[16]

States are free to define what constitutes obscene speech. Movie theaters, magazine publishers, and so on are often subject to challenges that the materials they display or sell are obscene and therefore not protected by the First Amendment. Over the years, the content of material that has been found to be obscene has shifted to a more liberal view as the general norms of society have become more liberal. Today, fewer obscenity cases are brought than was true in the past.

In the following feature, the U.S. Supreme Court applied the Free Speech Clause to video games.

Information Technology

Free Speech and Video Games

"And whatever the challenges of applying the Constitution to ever-advancing technology, the basic principles of freedom of speech and the press do not vary when a new and different medium for communication appears."
—Antonin Scalia, Justice

Video games are played by millions of youth and adults. Some of the games contain violent content. The state of California enacted a state statute that prohibits the sale or rental of "violent video games" to minors. The act covers games in which the range of options available to a player includes killing, maiming, dismembering, or sexually assaulting an image of a human being. Violation of the act is punishable by a civil fine of up to $1,000.

Members of the video game and software industries challenged the enforcement of the act, alleging that the state law violated their constitutional free speech rights. The U.S. Supreme Court held that the California act violated the Free Speech Clause of the First Amendment to the U.S. Constitution. The Supreme Court stated:

> *Whatever the challenges of applying the Constitution to ever-advancing technology, the basic principles of freedom of speech and the press do not vary when a new and different medium for communication appears. Certainly, the books we give children to read—or read to them when they are younger—contain no shortage of gore. As her just deserts for trying to poison Snow White, the wicked queen is made to dance in red hot slippers. Cinderella's evil stepsisters have their eyes pecked out by doves. And Hansel and Gretel (children!) kill their captor by baking her in an oven.*

The U.S. Supreme Court held that California had singled out the purveyors of video games for disfavored treatment—at least when compared to booksellers, cartoonists, and movie producers—and has given no persuasive reason why. *Brown, Governor of California v. Entertainment Merchants Association*, 564 U.S. 786, 131 S.Ct. 2729, 2011 U.S. Lexis 4802 (Supreme Court of the United States, 2011)

Critical Legal Thinking Questions

Should violent video games be regulated by the government? What about the nature of video games might have made California think it could legally justify singling them out from other kinds of media for regulation?

Freedom of Religion

4.7 Explain how freedom of religion is protected and how the government may not promote religion.

Freedom of religion is a key concept addressed by the First Amendment. The First Amendment contains two separate religion clauses: the *Establishment Clause* and the *Free Exercise Clause*. These two clauses are discussed in the following paragraphs.

Establishment Clause

The U.S. Constitution requires federal, state, and local governments to be neutral toward religion. The **Establishment Clause** prohibits the government from either establishing a government-sponsored religion or promoting one religion over another. Thus, it guarantees that there will be no state-sponsored religion.

Establishment Clause
A clause of the First Amendment that prohibits the government from either establishing a state religion or promoting one religion over another.

Example The U.S. Supreme Court ruled that an Alabama statute that authorized a one-minute period of silence in school for "meditation or voluntary prayer" was invalid.[17] The Court held that the statute endorsed religion.

However, government action or assistance that implicates religion may be held not to violate the Establishment Clause if the challenged action (1) has a secular purpose; (2) has a principal or primary effect that neither advances nor inhibits religion; and (3) does not foster an excessive government entanglement with religion.

Example States that provide government busing or purchase secular textbooks for students of public schools may also provide busing and purchase secular textbooks for students who attend religious schools.

The following case involves the Establishment Clause.

CASE 4.4 U.S. SUPREME COURT CASE Establishment Clause

The American Legion v. American Humanist Association

139 S.Ct. 2067 (2019)
Supreme Court of the United States

"Even if the original purpose of a monument was infused with religion, the passage of time may obscure that sentiment."

—Samuel Alito, Justice

Facts

In 1925, the residents of Prince George's County, Maryland, along with the American Legion, a military veterans' organization, erected a war memorial to honor the persons of the community who had given their lives in the First World War, later known as World War I. It is a 32-foot-tall Latin cross that sits on a large pedestal. The American Legion's emblem is displayed at its center. The pedestal features a 9- by 2.5-foot bronze plaque explaining that the monument is "Dedicated to the heroes of Prince George's County, Maryland, who lost their lives in the Great War for the liberty of the world." The plaque lists the names of 49 local men, both black and white, who died in the war. The memorial is called the Bladensburg Peace Cross (Cross).

The Cross is currently located on public property that is maintained by the Maryland-National Capital Park and Planning Commission (Commission), a government entity. Since its dedication, the Cross has served as the site of patriotic events honoring veterans, including gatherings on Veterans Day, Memorial Day, and Independence Day. Over the years, memorials honoring the veterans of the Revolutionary War, War of 1812, World War II, Korean War, and a memorial for September 11, 2001, have been added to the surrounding area, which is now known as Veterans Memorial Park.

Eighty-nine years after the dedication of the Cross, several individuals who are atheists, and the American Humanist Society, an atheist organization (collectively, AHS), filed a lawsuit in U.S. district court claiming that they are offended by the sight of the Cross on public land and that its presence there violates the Establishment Clause of the First Amendment. The American Legion intervened to protect the Cross. The plaintiffs demanded that the court order either the alteration of the Cross, chopping off the arms of the Cross so that it would not look like a cross, or the removal of the Cross. The district court found that a reasonable observer aware of the Cross's history, setting, and secular elements would not view the Cross as having the effect of impermissibly endorsing religion, and therefore it did not violate the Establishment Clause. The district court granted summary judgment to the Commission and the American Legion. The U.S. court of appeals reversed, finding that a reasonable observer would view the Commission's maintenance of the Cross on public property as an endorsement of Christianity. The court of appeals decided that the best option was the amputation of the arms of the Cross so that it would no longer look like a cross. The Commission and the American Legion appealed to the U.S. Supreme Court.

Issue

Does the presence of the Bladensburg Peace Cross on public property and its maintenance by a public entity violate the Establishment Clause?

Language of the U.S. Supreme Court

Even if the original purpose of a monument was infused with religion, the passage of time may obscure that sentiment. A community may preserve such monuments, symbols, and practices for the sake of their historical significance or their place in a common cultural heritage. Just as the purpose for maintaining a monument, symbol, or practice may evolve, the message conveyed may change over time. With sufficient time, religiously expressive monuments, symbols, and practices can become embedded features of a community's landscape and identity. The community may come to value them without necessarily embracing their religious roots.

Retaining established, religiously expressive monuments, symbols, and practices is quite different from erecting or adopting new ones. The passage of time gives rise to a strong presumption of constitutionality. A monument may express many purposes and convey many different messages, both secular and religious. We conclude that the Bladensburg Cross does not violate the Establishment Clause. The Cross does not offend the Constitution.

Decision

The U.S. Supreme Court held that the Bladensburg Cross did not violate the Establishment Clause and reversed the decision of the U.S. court of appeals.

Critical Legal Thinking Questions

Should the Establishment Clause be applied literally to abolish all implications of the government with religion? Should a secular purpose exception be permitted? Do new religious monuments, symbols, or practices qualify for the secular purpose exception?

Free Exercise Clause

The **Free Exercise Clause** prohibits the government from interfering with the free exercise of religion in the United States. Generally, this clause prevents the government from enacting laws that either prohibit or inhibit individuals from participating in or practicing their chosen religions.

Free Exercise Clause
A clause of the First Amendment that prohibits the government from interfering with the free exercise of religion in the United States.

Examples Federal, state, or local governments cannot enact a law that prohibits all religions. The government cannot enact a law that prohibits churches, synagogues, mosques, or temples. The government cannot prohibit religious practitioners from celebrating their major holidays and high holy days.

Example In *Church of Lukumi Babalu Aye, Inc. v. City of Hialeah, Florida*[18] the U.S. Supreme Court held that a city ordinance that prohibited ritual sacrifices of chickens during church service violated the Free Exercise Clause and that such sacrifices should be allowed.

Of course, the right to be free from government intervention in the practice of religion is not absolute.

Example Human sacrifices are unlawful and are not protected by the First Amendment.

CONCEPT SUMMARY

FREEDOM OF RELIGION

Clause	Description
Establishment Clause	Prohibits the government from establishing a government-sponsored religion and from promoting one religion over other religions.
Free Exercise Clause	Prohibits the government from enacting laws that either prohibit or inhibit individuals from participating in or practicing their chosen religions.

Equal Protection

4.8 Explain the equal protection doctrine and how it protects persons from unequal treatment by the government.

The **Fourteenth Amendment** was added to the U.S. Constitution in 1868. Its original purpose was to guarantee equal rights to all persons after the Civil War. The **Equal Protection Clause** of the Fourteenth Amendment provides that a state cannot "deny to any person within its jurisdiction the equal protection of the laws." Although this clause expressly applies to state and local government action, the Supreme Court has held that it also applies to federal government action.

Fourteenth Amendment
An amendment added to the U.S. Constitution in 1868 that contains the Due Process, Equal Protection, and Privileges and Immunities clauses.

This clause prohibits state, local, and federal governments from enacting laws that classify and treat "similarly situated" persons differently. Artificial persons, such as corporations, are also protected. Note that this clause is designed to prohibit invidious discrimination: It does not make the classification of individuals unlawful per se.

Equal Protection Clause
A clause that provides that a state cannot "deny to any person within its jurisdiction the equal protection of the laws."

Standards of Review

The Supreme Court, over years of making decisions involving the Equal Protection Clause, has held that the government can treat people or businesses differently from one another if the government has sufficient justification for doing so. The Supreme Court has adopted three different standards of review for deciding whether the government's different treatment of people or businesses violates or does not violate the Equal Protection Clause:

1. **Strict scrutiny test.** Any government activity or regulation that classifies persons based on a **suspect class** (e.g., *race, national origin, religion*, or *citizenship*) or involves **fundamental rights** (e.g., *voting rights, access to courts*) is reviewed for lawfulness using a **strict scrutiny test**. This means that the government must have an exceptionally important reason for treating persons differently because of their race or suspect class status in order for such unequal treatment to be lawful. Under this standard, many government classifications of persons based on race are found to be unconstitutional. Others are found lawful.

   strict scrutiny test
   A test that is applied to determine the constitutionality of classifications by the government that are based on a suspect class (e.g., race, national origin, religion, citizenship) or a fundamental right (e.g., voting rights, access to courts).

   Example A government rule that permits persons of one race but not of another race to receive government benefits such as Medicaid would violate this test.

2. **Intermediate scrutiny test.** The lawfulness of government classifications based on a **protected class** other than a suspect class or a fundamental right, such as a classification based on *gender*, is examined using an **intermediate scrutiny test**. This means that the government must have an important reason for treating persons differently because of their sex or protected class status in order for such unequal treatment to be lawful. Applying this standard, many government classifications of persons based on sex are found to be unconstitutional. Under this standard, the courts must determine whether the government classification is "reasonably related" to a legitimate government purpose.

   intermediate scrutiny test
   A test that is applied to determine the constitutionality of classifications by the government that are based on a protected class other than a suspect class or a fundamental right (e.g., gender).

   Example The federal government's requirement that men (upon reaching the age of 18) must register for a military draft but that women do not have to register for the draft has been held to be constitutional by the U.S. Supreme Court.[19]

3. **Rational basis test.** The lawfulness of all government classifications that do not involve a suspect class, a fundamental right, or a protected class is examined using a **rational basis test**. Under this test, a law must be rationally related to a legitimate government interest to be found constitutional. Government distinctions based on *age* are examined using this test. Most government regulation of business is found to be lawful applying this test.

   rational basis test
   A test that is applied to determine the constitutionality of classifications by the government that do not involve a suspect class, a fundamental right, or a protected class (e.g., age, government regulation).

   Example Providing government subsidies to farmers but not to those in other occupations is permissible.

   Example The federal government's Social Security program, which pays benefits to older members of society but not to younger members of society, is lawful. The reason is that older members of society have earned this right during their lifetimes.

Due Process

4.9 Describe the Due Process Clause and substantive and procedural due process.

Due Process Clause
A clause that provides that no person shall be deprived of "life, liberty, or property" without due process of the law.

The Fifth and Fourteenth Amendments to the U.S. Constitution contain a **Due Process Clause**. These clauses provide that no person shall be deprived of "life, liberty, or property" without due process of the law. The Due Process Clause of the Fifth Amendment applies to federal government action; that of the Fourteenth Amendment applies to state and local government action. It is important to understand that the government is not prohibited from taking a person's life, liberty, or property. However, the government must follow due process to do so.

In the following case, the U.S. Supreme Court held that same-sex partners have the right to marry.

CASE 4.5 *U.S. SUPREME COURT CASE Due Process and Equal Protection Clauses*

Obergefell v. Hodges

135 S.Ct. 2584, 2015 U.S. Lexis 4250 (2015)
Supreme Court of the United States

"Petitioners ask for equal dignity in the eyes of the law. The Constitution grants them that right."

—Anthony Kennedy, Justice

Facts

Michigan, Kentucky, Ohio, and Tennessee defined marriage as a union between one man and one woman. State officials enforced these laws and refused to marry same-sex couples. Ohio, Tennessee, and Kentucky refused to recognize same-sex marriages performed in states that permit same-sex marriage. Petitioners—same-sex couples—challenged these state laws in U.S. district courts. Each district court ruled in the petitioners' favor. The U.S. Court of Appeals for the Sixth Circuit consolidated the cases and reversed the judgments of the district courts. The U.S. Supreme Court granted certiorari to hear the petitioners' appeal. The petitioners alleged that the challenged state laws violated their liberty as guaranteed by the Due Process Clause of the Fourteenth Amendment and also violated the Equal Protection Clause of the Fourteenth Amendment.

Issue

Do the challenged state laws that do not permit or recognize same-sex marriages violate the Due Process Clause and Equal Protection Clause of the Fourteenth Amendment to the U.S. Constitution?

Language of the U.S. Supreme Court

Under the Due Process Clause of the Fourteenth Amendment, no State shall "deprive any person of life, liberty, or property, without due process of law." This analysis compels the conclusion that same-sex couples may exercise the right to marry. The right to marry thus dignifies couples who wish to define themselves by their commitment to each other. Same-sex couples have the same right as opposite-sex couples to enjoy intimate association.

The right of same-sex couples to marry that is part of the liberty promised by the Fourteenth Amendment is derived, too, from that Amendment's guarantee of the equal protection of the laws. It is now clear that the challenged laws burden the liberty of same-sex couples, and it must be further acknowledged that they abridge central precepts of equality. The Court now holds that same-sex couples may exercise the fundamental right to marry.

Decision

The U.S. Supreme Court held that state laws that prohibit same-sex marriage or that do not recognize valid same-sex marriages are unconstitutional. The Supreme Court reversed the judgment of the Court of Appeals for the Sixth Circuit.

Critical Legal Thinking Questions

What is the policy underlying the Due Process Clause? How did it apply in this case? What is the policy underlying the Equal Protection Clause? How did it apply in this case? How important is the Supreme Court's decision?

There are two categories of due process: *substantive* and *procedural*.

Substantive Due Process

The **substantive due process** category of due process requires that government statutes, ordinances, regulations, and other laws be clear on their face and not overly broad in scope. The test of whether substantive due process is met is whether a "reasonable person" could understand the law to be able to comply with it. Laws that do not meet this test are declared *void for vagueness*.

substantive due process
A category of due process that requires government statutes, ordinances, regulations, or other laws be clear on their face and not overly broad in scope.

LINCOLN MEMORIAL, WASHINGTON DC

The United States has had many blemishes on its citizen's constitutional rights. Women did not get the right to vote until the Nineteenth Amendment was added to the U.S. Constitution in 1920. During World War II, Japanese Americans were involuntarily placed in camps. During the McCarthy hearings of the 1950s, citizens who were communists or associated with communists were blacklisted from their occupations, most notably in the film industry. Prohibitions against interracial marriage were not made illegal until 1967.[20] *And it was not until the mid-1960s that equal opportunity laws outlawed discrimination in the workplace based on race and gender.*

Example A city ordinance making it illegal for persons to wear "clothes of the opposite sex" would be held unconstitutional as void for vagueness because a reasonable person could not clearly determine whether his or her conduct violates the law.

Most government laws, although often written in "legalese," are considered not to violate substantive due process.

Procedural Due Process

procedural due process
A category of due process that requires that the government give a person proper notice and hearing of the legal action before that person is deprived of his or her life, liberty, or property.

The **procedural due process** form of due process requires that the government give a person proper *notice* and *hearing* of legal action before that person is deprived of his or her life, liberty, or property.

Example If the federal government or a state government brings a criminal lawsuit against a defendant for the alleged commission of a crime, the government must notify the person of its intent (by charging the defendant with a crime) and provide the defendant with a proper hearing (a trial).

Government Taking of Property

4.10 Explain how the government can take private property but must pay just compensation for the taking.

Takings Clause
A clause that allows the government to take property for public use.

Just Compensation Clause
A clause that requires the government to compensate a property owner when the government takes the owner's property.

At times, governments may need to acquire private property to be used for governmental purposes. The **Takings Clause** of the Fifth Amendment to the U.S. Constitution provides the government with this power. Private property can only be taken for *public use*. The **Just Compensation Clause** of the Fifth Amendment to the U.S. Constitution requires the government to compensate the property owner when it takes private property.

Examples The government may use its Takings Clause power to acquire private property on which to build a new school or a firehouse, or to construct a road or freeway. The government must pay just compensation for the private property it acquires.

Privileges and Immunities

4.11 Explain how the privileges and immunities doctrine protects citizens from unfavorable treatment by the government.

The purpose of the U.S. Constitution is to promote nationalism. If the states were permitted to enact laws that favored their residents over out-of-state residents, the concept of nationalism would be defeated.

Article IV of the Constitution contains the **Privileges and Immunities Clause**, which provides that "The Citizens of each State shall be entitled to all Privileges and Immunities of Citizens in the several states." The Fourteenth Amendment contains the **Privileges or Immunities Clause**, which provides that "No State shall make or enforce any law that shall abridge the privileges or immunities of the citizens of the United States." These two provisions are sometimes collectively referred to as the **privileges and immunities clauses**.

privileges and immunities clauses
Constitutional provisions that prohibit states from enacting laws that unduly discriminate in favor of their residents.

Collectively, the clauses prohibit states from enacting laws that unduly discriminate in favor of their residents. Note that the clauses apply only to citizens; they do not protect corporations or aliens.

Example A state cannot enact a law that prevents residents of other states from owning property or businesses in that state.

Example Residents of one state have the right to travel freely to other states.

Courts have held that certain types of discrimination that favor state residents over nonresidents are lawful.

Examples State universities are permitted to charge out-of-state residents higher tuition than in-state residents. States are also permitted to charge higher fees to nonresidents for hunting and fishing licenses.

The Constitution of the United States is not a mere lawyers' document: It is a vehicle of life, and its spirit is always the spirit of the age.

Woodrow Wilson
Former president of the United States
Constitutional Government in the United States (1908)

Key Terms and Concepts

Critical Legal Thinking Cases

4.1 Establishment Clause Beginning in 1864, coins and currency of the United States have been imprinted with the national motto "In God We Trust." Individuals who are atheists and several atheist organizations, who definitely do not trust in God, sued the United States and officials of the U.S. Mint, Treasury, and Bureau of Engraving and Printing (collectively, "the Government"), alleging that the motto is purely religious, is an explicit endorsement of Christianity and monotheism, and therefore violates the Establishment Clause of the U.S. Constitution. Plaintiffs sought a permanent injunction barring the Government from minting coins or printing currency with the phrase "In God We Trust." The Government filed a motion to dismiss the plaintiffs' case, asserting that printing the motto "In God We Trust" on coins and currency does not violate the Establishment Clause because it derives from and serves historical purposes. Does inscribing the motto "In God We Trust" on U.S. coins and currency violate the Establishment Clause? *New Doe Child #1 v. United States*, 901 F.3d 1015 (United States Court of Appeals for the Eighth Circuit, 2018)

4.2 Free Speech North Carolina enacted a criminal statute that makes it a felony for a registered sex offender to access social networking websites, such as Facebook, where the sex offender knows that the site permits minor children to become members, or to create or maintain personal web pages. The statute permits sex offenders to use commercial transaction websites such as Amazon.com. North Carolina has prosecuted more than 1,000 individuals for violating the statute.

When Lester Gerard Packingham was a 21-year-old college student he had sex with a 13-year-old girl. He pleaded guilty to taking indecent liberties with a child. Packingham was required to register as a sex offender—a status that can endure for 30 years or more. Eight years after his conviction, while Packingham resided in North Carolina, he began posting messages on Facebook. He did not contact a minor or engage in any illicit act on the internet. North Carolina indicted Packingham for the crime of using social media in violation of state law. At trial, Packingham asserted that the North Carolina law violated his First Amendment free speech rights. Does the North Carolina statute that prohibits registered sex offenders from using social media websites violate the Free Speech Clause of the First Amendment? *Packingham v. North Carolina*, 137 S.Ct. 1730, 2017 U.S. Lexis 3871 (Supreme Court of the United States, 2017)

4.3 Equal Protection Clause Greensburg Community School Corporation is a public school located in Greensburg, Indiana. The school includes a junior high school and a high school. The school has a policy that boys who want to play on the school's basketball teams must keep their hair cut short. No such similar rule applies to girls who play on the girls' basketball teams. A.H., a male student, qualified to play on the high school basketball team but was not permitted to do so because he had long hair and refused to cut it. A.H.'s parent sued the school, alleging sex discrimination in violation of the Equal Protection Clause of the Fourteenth Amendment to the U.S. Constitution. Does the school's haircut policy constitute sex discrimination in violation of the Equal Protection Clause? *Hayden v. Greensburg Community School Corporation*, 743 F.3d 569 (United States Court of Appeals for the Seventh Circuit, 2014)

4.4 Due Process The Federal Communications Commission (FCC) is a federal administrative agency that regulates television and radio. The FCC is authorized to restrict indecent material on television during the hours of 6:00 a.m. to 10:00 p.m. In 2001, the FCC issued guidelines stating that material that dwelled on or repeated at length offensive descriptions or depictions violated federal communications laws. In both the 2002 and 2003 Billboard Music Awards program televised live by Fox Television Stations, Inc. (Fox), a person used the f-word once in each broadcast. In 2003, an episode of *NYPD Blue,* a regular television show broadcast by ABC Television Network (ABC), showed the nude buttocks of an adult woman for approximately seven seconds as she entered a shower.

In 2004, the FCC issued guidelines that stipulated that fleeting expletives and momentary nudity on television was a violation of federal communications law. The FCC applied the 2004 guidelines retroactively and issued orders finding that both Fox and ABC violated communications law by showing fleeting expletives and momentary nudity on television in 2002 and 2003. The FCC assessed a $1.24 million penalty on ABC. Fox and ABC challenged the orders, alleging that there had been a violation of the Fifth Amendment's Due Process Clause because they had not been notified prior to the events occurring that fleeting expletives and momentary nudity violated communications law. Did the FCC violate the Fifth Amendment's due process rights of Fox and ABC? *Federal Communications Commission v. Fox Television Stations, Inc.*, 567 U.S. 239, 132 S.Ct. 2307, 2012 U.S. Lexis 4661 (Supreme Court of the United States, 2012)

4.5 Commerce Clause State departments of motor vehicles (DMVs) register automobiles and issue driver's licenses. State DMVs require automobile owners and drivers to provide personal information—including a person's name, address, telephone number, vehicle description, Social Security number, medical information, and a photograph—as a condition for registering an automobile or obtaining a driver's license. Many states' DMVs sold this personal information to individuals, advertisers, and businesses. These sales generated significant revenues for the states.

After receiving thousands of complaints from individuals whose personal information had been sold, the U.S. Congress enacted the Driver's Privacy Protection Act of 1994 (DPPA). This federal statute prohibits a state from selling the personal information of a person unless the state obtains that person's affirmative consent to do so. South Carolina sued the United States, alleging that the federal government violated the Commerce Clause by adopting the DPPA. Was the Driver's Privacy Protection Act properly enacted by the federal government pursuant to its Commerce Clause power? *Reno, Attorney General of the United States v. Condon, Attorney General of South Carolina*, 528 U.S. 141, 120 S.Ct. 666, 2000 U.S. Lexis 503 (Supreme Court of the United States, 2000)

4.6 **Free Speech** Fred Phelps founded the Westboro Baptist Church in Topeka, Kansas. The church's congregation believes that God hates and punishes the United States. The church frequently communicates its views by picketing at military funerals.

Lance Corporal Matthew Snyder, a member of the U.S. Marines, was killed in Iraq in the line of duty. Lance Corporal Snyder's father, Albert Snyder, selected the Catholic Church in the Snyders' hometown of Westminster, Maryland, as the site for his son's funeral. Phelps traveled to Maryland with six other Westboro Baptist parishioners to picket at Lance Corporal Snyder's funeral service. The Westboro congregation members picketed while standing on public land adjacent to a public street approximately 1,000 feet from the church. They carried placards that read "God Hates the USA/Thank God for 9/11," "America Is Doomed," "Thank God for Dead Soldiers," and "You're Going to Hell." The picketers sang hymns and recited Bible verses. The funeral procession passed within 200 to 300 feet of the picket site.

Albert Snyder filed a lawsuit against Phelps and the Westboro Baptist Church ("Westboro") in U.S. district court. Snyder alleged intentional infliction of emotional distress and other state law tort claims. Westboro argued that their speech was protected by the First Amendment. The jury found for Snyder and held Westboro liable for $2.9 million in compensatory damages and $8 million in punitive damages. The U.S. district court remitted the punitive damages to $2.1 million. The U.S. court of appeals held that the First Amendment protected Westboro's speech and reversed the judgment. Snyder appealed to the U.S. Supreme Court. Does the Free Speech Clause of the First Amendment shield church members from tort liability for their picketing speech at funerals? *Snyder v. Phelps*, 562 U.S. 443, 131 S.Ct. 1207, 2011 U.S. Lexis 1903 (Supreme Court of the United States, 2011)

Ethics Cases

4.7 **Ethics Case** Vaccines are biological preparations usually containing an agent that resembles a disease-causing microorganism, which is often administered by needle and which improves immunity to a particular disease. Vaccines are subject to federal premarket approval of the federal Food and Drug Administration (FDA). The elimination of communicable diseases through vaccination was one of the greatest achievements of public health in the twentieth century. However, harm caused by side effects to some individuals led to a massive increase in vaccine-related tort litigation against the manufacturers of vaccines. One group of manufacturers that was subject to such lawsuits was those who made the vaccine against diphtheria, tetanus, and pertussis (DTP). Because of the lawsuits, two of the three domestic manufacturers of DTP withdrew from the market. In response, the U.S. Congress enacted the National Childhood Vaccine Injury Act of 1986 (NCVIA). One of the provisions of the act stated,

> *No vaccine manufacturer shall be liable in a civil action for damages arising from a vaccine-related injury or death associated with the administration of a vaccine after October 1, 1988, if the injury or death resulted from side effects that were unavoidable even though the vaccine was properly prepared and was accompanied by proper directions and warnings.*

When Hanna Bruesewitz was one year old, her pediatrician administered doses of DTP vaccine that was manufactured by Lederle Laboratories (later purchased by Wyeth LLC). Hanna immediately started to experience seizures, and has suffered seizures since being vaccinated. Hanna's parents filed a lawsuit against Lederle alleging that the company was liable for strict liability and negligent design of the vaccine. The U.S. district court granted Wyeth summary judgment, holding that Bruesewitz's causes of action were preempted by the NCVIA. The U.S. court of appeals affirmed the judgment. Bruesewitz appealed to the U.S. Supreme Court. Does the preemption provision in the federal NCVIA bar state law design-defect product liability claims against vaccine manufacturers? Is it ethical for vaccine manufacturers to be absolved from liability by federal law? What is the public policy underlying the federal law? *Bruesewitz v.*

Wyeth LLC, 562 U.S. 223, 131 S.Ct. 1068, 2011 U.S. Lexis 1085 (Supreme Court of the United States, 2011)

4.8 Ethics Case Raisin Committee, a federal government entity of the U.S. Department of Agriculture, enforces a reserve requirement that requires growers of raisins to annually turn over a percentage of their crop to the U.S. government, free of charge. The percentage is determined each year by the government and usually ranges from 30 percent to 50 percent. The government acquires title to those raisins and sells them to exporters, federal agencies, or foreign governments, or donates them to charitable organizations.

Melvin and Laura Horne, who are raisin growers, refused to set aside any raisins for the government. The government assessed a fine of $480,000 against the Hornes, which was the market value of withheld raisins, as well as a civil fine of $200,000 for disobeying the government's order. The Hornes sued in U.S. district court, alleging that the government's actions constituted an unconscionable taking of their personal property in violation of the Fifth Amendment to the U.S. Constitution. Does the government's action constitute a taking of personal property under the Takings Clause of the Fifth Amendment that requires the payment of just compensation? Did the government act ethically in taking the raisins without paying for them? *Horne v. Department of Agriculture*, 135 S.Ct. 2419, 2015 U.S. Lexis 4064 (Supreme Court of the United States, 2015)

Notes

1. To be elected to Congress, an individual must be a U.S. citizen, either naturally born or granted citizenship. To serve in the Senate, a person must be 30 years of age or older. To serve in the House of Representatives, a person must be 25 years of age or older.
2. To be president, a person must be 35 years of age or older and a natural-born citizen of the United States. According to the Twenty-Second Amendment to the Constitution, a person can serve only two full terms as president.
3. Federal court judges and justices are appointed by the president, with the consent of the Senate.
4. The principle that the U.S. Supreme Court is the final arbiter of the U.S. Constitution evolved from *Marbury v. Madison*, 1 Cranch 137, 5 U.S. 137, 1803 U.S. Lexis 352 (Supreme Court of the United States, 1803). In that case, the Supreme Court held that a judiciary statute enacted by Congress was unconstitutional.
5. Article VI, Section 2.
6. Article I, Section 8, clause 3.
7. 25 U.S.C. Sections 2701–2721.
8. 317 U.S. 111, 63 S.Ct. 82, 1942 U.S. Lexis 1046 (Supreme Court of the United States).
9. 425 U.S. 748, 96 S.Ct. 1817, 1976 U.S. Lexis 55 (Supreme Court of the United States).
10. *Chaplinsky v. New Hampshire*, 315 U.S. 568, 62 S.Ct. 766, 1942 U.S. Lexis 851 (Supreme Court of the United States).
11. *Brandenburg v. Ohio*, 395 U.S. 444, 89 S.Ct. 1827, 1969 U.S. Lexis 1367 (Supreme Court of the United States).
12. *Beauharnais v. Illinois*, 343 U.S. 250, 72 S.Ct. 725, 1952 U.S. Lexis 2799 (Supreme Court of the United States).
13. *New York v. Ferber*, 458 U.S. 747, 102 S.Ct. 334, 1982 U.S. Lexis 12 (Supreme Court of the United States).
14. *Roth v. United States*, 354 U.S. 476, 77 S.Ct. 1304, 1957 U.S. Lexis 587 (Supreme Court of the United States).
15. Justice Stewart in *Jacobellis v. Ohio*, 378 U.S. 184, 84 S.Ct. 1676, 1964 U.S. Lexis 822 (Supreme Court of the United States).
16. 413 U.S. 15, 93 S.Ct. 2607, 1973 U.S. Lexis 149 (Supreme Court of the United States).
17. *Wallace v. Jaffree*, 472 U.S. 38, 105 S.Ct. 2479, 1985 U.S. Lexis 91 (Supreme Court of the United States).
18. 508 U.S. 520, 113 S.Ct. 2217, 1993 U.S. Lexis 4022 (Supreme Court of the United States).
19. *Rostker v. Goldberg*, 453 U.S. 57, 101 S.Ct. 2646, 1981 U.S. Lexis 126 (Supreme Court of the United States).
20. *Loving v. Virginia*, 388 U.S. 1, 87 S.Ct. 1817, 1967 U.S. Lexis 1082 (Supreme Court of the United States).

PART

II

Torts, Crimes, and Intellectual Property

Henry R. Cheeseman

CHAPTER

5 Intentional Torts and Negligence

AUTOMOBILE ACCIDENT

Motor vehicle accidents are a primary cause of injury and death in the United States. Most accidents are the result of negligence. Each year, over 6 million motor vehicle accidents occur that result in over 4 million injuries that require medical treatment and approximately 40,000 fatalities of passenger car and truck occupants, pedestrians, motorcyclists, and bicyclists. Thus, more than 100 people die every day in motor vehicle accidents in this country. Drunk drivers cause one-third of the fatalities.

Dmitry Kalinovsky/123RF

Learning Objectives

After studying this chapter, you should be able to:

5.1 List and describe intentional torts.

5.2 Explain the elements necessary to prove negligence.

5.3 List and describe special negligence doctrines.

5.4 Describe the defenses that can be raised against a claim of negligence.

5.5 Describe the difference between *contributory negligence*, *comparative negligence*, and *partial comparative negligence*.

5.6 Define and apply the doctrine of strict liability.

> *"Negligence is not actionable unless it involves the invasion of a legally protected interest, the violation of a right. Proof of negligence in the air, so to speak, will not do."*
>
> — *Chief Judge Benjamin Cardozo*
> *Palsgraf v. Long Island Railroad Co. 248 N.Y. 339, 162 N.E. 99, 128 N.Y. Lexis 1269 (1928)*

Introduction to Intentional Torts and Negligence

Tort is the French word for "a wrong." The law provides remedies to persons and businesses that are injured by the tortious actions of others. Under tort law, an injured party can bring a *civil lawsuit* to seek compensation for a wrong done to the party or to the party's property. Many torts have their origin in common law. The courts and legislatures have extended tort law to reflect changes in modern society. Most torts are either intentional torts or unintentional torts such as negligence. These are based on the concept of fault. In many jurisdictions, the law recognizes the doctrine of *strict liability*. Under this doctrine, in certain circumstances, defendants may be held liable without fault.

tort
A wrong. There are three categories of torts: (1) intentional torts, (2) unintentional torts (negligence), and (3) strict liability.

Tort damages are monetary damages that are sought from the offending party. They are intended to compensate the injured party for the injury suffered. Such injury may consist of past and future medical expenses, loss of wages, pain and suffering, mental distress, and other damages caused by the defendant's tortious conduct. If the victim of a tort dies, his or her beneficiaries can bring a *wrongful death action* to recover damages from the defendant.

> *Thoughts much too deep for tears subdue the Court.*
> *When I assumpsit bring, and God-like waive a tort.*
>
> J. L. Adolphus
> *The Circuiteers (1885)*

This chapter discusses intentional torts, negligence, special tort doctrines, and the doctrine of strict liability.

Intentional Torts

5.1 List and describe intentional torts.

The law protects a person from unauthorized touching, restraint, or other contact. In addition, the law protects a person's reputation and privacy. Violations of these rights are actionable as torts. **Intentional torts** against persons are discussed in the paragraphs that follow.

intentional tort
A category of torts that requires that the defendant possessed the intent to do the act that caused the plaintiff's injuries.

Assault

Assault is (1) the threat of immediate harm or offensive contact or (2) any action that arouses reasonable apprehension of imminent harm. Actual physical contact is unnecessary. Threats of future harm are not actionable.

assault
(1) The threat of immediate harm or offensive contact or (2) any action that arouses reasonable apprehension of imminent harm. Actual physical contact is unnecessary.

Example Suppose a 6-foot, 5-inch, 250-pound person makes a fist and threatens to punch a 5-foot, 100-pound person. If the threatened person is afraid that he or she will be physically harmed, that person can sue the threatening person to recover damages for the assault.

Battery

Battery is unauthorized and harmful or offensive physical contact with another person that causes injury. Basically, the interest protected here is each person's reasonable sense of dignity and safety. Direct physical contact, such as intentionally hitting someone with a fist, is battery.

battery
Unauthorized and harmful or offensive direct or indirect physical contact with another person that causes injury.

Indirect physical contact between the victim and the perpetrator is also battery, as long as injury results.

Examples Throwing a rock, shooting an arrow or a bullet, knocking off a hat, pulling a chair out from under someone, and poisoning a drink are all instances of actionable battery. The victim need not be aware of the harmful or offensive contact (e.g., it may take place while the victim is asleep).

Assault and battery often occur together, although they do not have to (e.g., the perpetrator hits the victim on the back of the head without any warning).

transferred intent doctrine
Under this doctrine, the law transfers the perpetrator's intent from the target to the actual victim of the act.

Transferred Intent Doctrine Sometimes a person acts with the intent to injure one person but injures another. The **transferred intent doctrine** applies to such situations. Under this doctrine, the law transfers the perpetrator's intent from the target to the actual victim of the act. The victim can then sue the defendant.

False Imprisonment

false imprisonment
The intentional confinement or restraint of another person without authority or justification and without that person's consent.

The intentional confinement or restraint of another person without authority or justification and without that person's consent constitutes **false imprisonment**. The victim may be restrained or confined by physical force, barriers, threats of physical harm, or the perpetrator's false assertion of legal authority (i.e., false arrest). A threat of future harm or moral pressure is not considered false imprisonment. The false imprisonment must be complete.

Examples A person who locks the doors in a house or automobile and does not let another person leave is liable for false imprisonment. Merely locking one door to a building when other exits are not locked is not false imprisonment. However, a person is not obliged to risk danger or an affront to his or her dignity by attempting to escape.

Shoplifting and Merchant Protection Statutes

merchant protection statutes (shopkeeper's privilege)
Statutes that allow merchants to stop, detain, and investigate suspected shoplifters without being held liable for false imprisonment if (1) there are reasonable grounds for the suspicion, (2) suspects are detained for only a reasonable time, and (3) investigations are conducted in a reasonable manner.

Shoplifting causes substantial losses to retail and other merchants each year. Suspected shoplifters are often stopped by the store employees, and their suspected shoplifting is investigated. These stops sometimes lead to the merchant being sued for false imprisonment because the merchant detained the suspect.

Almost all states have enacted **merchant protection statutes**, also known as the **shopkeeper's privilege**. These statutes allow merchants to stop, detain, and investigate suspected shoplifters without being held liable for false imprisonment if:

1. There are *reasonable grounds* for the suspicion.
2. Suspects are detained for only a *reasonable time*.
3. Investigations are conducted in a *reasonable manner*.

Proving these elements is sometimes difficult. The following case applies the merchant protection statute.

CASE 5.1 *STATE COURT CASE False Imprisonment*

Walmart Stores, Inc. v. Cockrell

61 S.W.3d 774, 2001 Tex. App. Lexis 7992 (2001)
Court of Appeals of Texas

"He made me feel like I was scum. That I had no say-so in the matter, that just made me feel like a little kid on the block, like the bully beating the kid up."

—Karl Cockrell

Facts

Karl Cockrell and his parents went to a store owned by Walmart Stores, Inc. Cockrell stayed for about five minutes and decided to leave. As he was going out the front door, Raymond Navarro, a Walmart loss-prevention officer, stopped him and requested that Cockrell follow him to the manager's office. Once in the office, Navarro told Cockrell to pull his pants down. Cockrell put his hands between his shorts and underwear, shook them and nothing fell out. Next, Navarro told him to take off his shirt. Cockrell raised his shirt, revealing a large bandage that covered a surgical wound on the right side of his abdomen. Cockrell had recently had a liver transplant. Navarro asked him to take off the bandage, despite Cockrell's explanation that the bandage maintained a sterile environment around his surgical wound. On Navarro's insistence, Cockrell took down the bandage, revealing the wound. Navarro let Cockrell go. Cockrell sued Walmart to recover damages for false imprisonment. Walmart defended, alleging that the shopkeeper's privilege protected the store from liability. The trial court found in favor of Cockrell and awarded him $300,000 for his mental anguish. Walmart appealed.

Issue

Does the shopkeeper's privilege protect Walmart from liability under the circumstances of the case?

Language of the Court

Navarro claimed he had reasons to suspect Cockrell of shoplifting. He said that Cockrell was acting suspiciously, because he saw him in the women's department standing very close to a rack of clothes and looking around. We conclude that a rational jury could have found that Navarro did not "reasonably believe" a theft had occurred and therefore lacked authority to detain Cockrell. Navarro's search was unreasonable in scope, because he had no probable cause to believe that Cockrell had hidden any merchandise under the bandage. Removal of the bandage compromised the sterile environment surrounding the wound.

Decision

The court of appeals upheld the trial court's finding that Walmart had falsely imprisoned Cockrell and had not proved the shopkeeper's privilege. The court of appeals upheld the trial court's judgment that awarded Cockrell $300,000 for mental anguish.

Critical Legal Thinking Questions

Did Navarro, the Walmart employee, act responsibly in this case? Did Walmart act ethically in denying liability in this case?

Misappropriation of the Right to Publicity

Each person has the exclusive legal right to control and profit from the commercial use of his or her name and identity during his or her lifetime. This is a valuable right, particularly to well-known persons such as sports figures and movie stars. Any attempt by another person to appropriate a living person's name or identity for commercial purposes is actionable. The wrongdoer is liable for the tort of **misappropriation of the right to publicity** (also called the **tort of appropriation**).

In such cases, the plaintiff can (1) recover the unauthorized profits made by the offending party and (2) obtain an injunction preventing further unauthorized use of his or her name or identity. Many states provide that the right to publicity survives a person's death and may be enforced by the deceased's heirs.

misappropriation of the right to publicity (tort of appropriation)
An attempt by another person to appropriate a living person's name or identity for commercial purposes.

Example Antonio is a famous movie star. If an advertising agency places Antonio's likeness (e.g., photo) on a billboard advertising a product without Antonio's permission, it has engaged in the tort of misappropriation of the right to publicity. Antonio could sue and recover the profits made by the offending party as well as obtain an injunction to prevent unauthorized use of his likeness by the offending party.

Invasion of the Right to Privacy

The law recognizes each person's right to live his or her life without being subjected to unwarranted and undesired publicity. A violation of this right constitutes the tort of **invasion of the right to privacy**. If a fact is public information,

invasion of the right to privacy
The unwarranted and undesired publicity of a private fact about a person. The fact does not have to be untrue.

there is no claim to privacy. However, a fact that was once public (e.g., the commission of a crime) may become private after the passage of time.

Examples Taking a photograph of someone in a compromising position without authorization to do so, and reading someone else's mail, email, or texts without authorization to do so are examples of invasion of the right to privacy.

Placing someone in a "false light" constitutes an invasion of privacy.

Example Sending an objectionable telegram to a third party and signing another's name would place the purported sender in a false light in the eyes of the receiver.

Defamation of Character

A person's reputation is a valuable asset. Therefore, every person is protected from false statements made by others during his or her lifetime. This protection ends upon a person's death. The tort of **defamation of character** requires a plaintiff to prove that:

defamation of character
False statement(s) made by one person about another. In court, the plaintiff must prove that (1) the defendant made an untrue statement of fact about the plaintiff and (2) the statement was intentionally or accidentally published to a third party.

1. The defendant made an *untrue statement of fact* about the plaintiff.
2. The statement was intentionally or accidentally *published* to a third party. In this context, *publication* simply means that a third person heard or saw the untrue statement. It does not require appearance in newspapers, magazines, or books.

A false statement that appears in writing or other fixed medium is **libel**. An oral defamatory statement is **slander**.

libel
A false statement that appears in a letter, newspaper, magazine, book, photograph, movie, DVD, video game, and so on.

slander
Oral defamation of character.

Examples False statements that appear in a letter, newspaper, magazine, book, photograph, and the like are libel. If a person verbally makes an untrue statement of fact about another person to a third person, such oral statement constitutes slander. Most courts hold that defamatory statements in radio and television broadcasts, DVDs, video games, blogs, and the like are considered libel because of the permanency of the media.

The publication of an untrue statement of fact is not the same as the publication of an *opinion*. The publication of opinions is usually not actionable. Because defamation is defined as an untrue statement of fact, truth is an absolute defense to a charge of defamation.

Examples The statement "My lawyer is lousy" is an opinion and is not defamation. The statement "My lawyer has been disbarred from the practice of law," when the lawyer has not been disbarred, is an untrue statement of fact and is actionable as defamation.

Great cases like hard cases make bad law.

Oliver Wendell Holmes, Jr.
Northern Securities Co. v. United States
193 U.S. 197, 24 S.Ct. 436, 1904 U.S. Lexis 933 (1904)
Supreme Court of the United States

Public Figures as Plaintiffs In ***New York Times Co. v. Sullivan***,[1] the U.S. Supreme Court held that *public officials* cannot recover for defamation unless they can prove that the defendant acted with "actual malice." Actual malice means that the defendant made the false statement knowingly or with reckless disregard of its falsity. This requirement has since been extended to **public figure** plaintiffs such as movie stars, sports personalities, and other celebrities.

Disparagement

Business firms rely on their reputation and the quality of their products and services to attract and keep customers. That is why state unfair-competition laws protect businesses from disparaging statements made by competitors or others. A disparaging statement is an untrue statement made by one person or business about the products, services, property, or reputation of another business.

To prove **disparagement**, which is also called **trade libel, product disparagement**, and **slander of title**, the plaintiff must show that the defendant (1) made an untrue statement about the plaintiff's products, services, property, or business reputation; (2) published that untrue statement to a third party; (3) knew the statement was not true; and (4) made the statement maliciously (i.e., with intent to injure the plaintiff).

disparagement
False statements about a competitor's products, services, property, or business reputation.

Critical Legal Thinking

Should defendants that lose cases and plaintiffs that do not win cases have to pay the other side's legal expenses? What would be the consequences of such a rule?

Example If a competitor of John Deere tractors told a prospective customer that "John Deere tractors often break down" when in fact they rarely do, that would be product disparagement.

The following ethics feature discusses fraud.

Ethics

Intentional Misrepresentation (Fraud)

One of the most pervasive business torts is **intentional misrepresentation**. This tort is also known as **fraudulent misrepresentation** or **fraud** or **deceit**. It occurs when a wrongdoer deceives another person out of money, property, or something else of value. A person who has been injured by intentional misrepresentation can recover damages from the wrongdoer. Four elements are required to find fraud:

1. The wrongdoer made a false representation of a material fact.
2. The wrongdoer had knowledge that the representation was false and intended to deceive the innocent party.
3. The innocent party justifiably relied on the misrepresentation.
4. The innocent party was injured.

Item 2, which is called ***scienter***, refers to intentional conduct. It also includes situations in which the wrongdoer recklessly disregards the truth in making a representation that is false. Intent or recklessness can be inferred from the circumstances.

Example Mattias, a person claiming to be a minerals expert, convinces 100 people to invest $10,000 each with him so that he can purchase, on their behalf, a gold mine he claims is located in the state of North Dakota. Mattias shows the prospective investors photographs of a gold mine to substantiate his story. The investors give Mattias their money. There is no gold mine. Instead, Mattias runs off with the investors' money. Mattias intended to steal the money from the investors. This is an example of fraud: (1) Mattias made a false representation of fact (there was no gold mine, and he did not intend to invest their money to purchase the gold mine), (2) Mattias knew that his statements were false and intended to steal the investors' money, (3) the investors relied on Mattias's statements, and (4) the investors were injured by losing their money.

Ethics Questions
What are the necessary elements to prove fraud? Do persons who commit fraud know that their conduct is unethical? In many instances of fraud, do you think that victims should have figured out that they were being defrauded?

Intentional Infliction of Emotional Distress

In some situations, a victim may suffer mental or emotional distress without first being physically harmed. The *Restatement (Second) of Torts* provides that a person whose *extreme and outrageous* conduct intentionally or recklessly causes severe emotional distress to another is liable for that emotional distress.[2] This is called the tort of **intentional infliction of emotional distress**, or the **tort of outrage**.

The plaintiff must prove that the defendant's conduct was "so outrageous in character and so extreme in degree as to go beyond all possible bounds of decency, and to be regarded as atrocious and utterly intolerable in a civilized society."[3] The tort does not require any publication to a third party or physical contact between the plaintiff and defendant.

An indignity, an annoyance, rough language, or an occasional inconsiderate or unkind act does not constitute outrageous behavior. However, repeated annoyances or harassment coupled with threats are considered outrageous.

The mental distress suffered by the plaintiff must be severe. Many states require that this mental distress be manifested by some form of physical injury,

He that's cheated twice by the same man, is an accomplice with the Cheater.

Thomas Fuller
Gnomologia (1732)

intentional misrepresentation (fraud or deceit)
The intentional defrauding of a person out of money, property, or something else of value.

intentional infliction of emotional distress (tort of outrage)
A tort that says a person whose extreme and outrageous conduct intentionally or recklessly causes severe emotional distress to another person is liable for that emotional distress.

discomfort, or illness, such as nausea, ulcers, headaches, or miscarriage. This requirement is intended to prevent false claims. Some states have abandoned this requirement.

Examples Shame, humiliation, embarrassment, anger, fear, and worry constitute severe mental distress.

Malicious Prosecution

malicious prosecution
A lawsuit in which the original defendant sues the original plaintiff. In the second lawsuit, the defendant becomes the plaintiff and vice versa.

Businesses and individuals often believe they have a reason to sue someone to recover damages or other remedies. If the plaintiff has a legitimate reason to bring the lawsuit and does so but the plaintiff does not win the lawsuit, he or she does not have to worry about being sued by the person whom he or she sued. But a losing plaintiff does have to worry about being sued by the defendant in a second lawsuit for **malicious prosecution** if certain elements are met. In a lawsuit for malicious prosecution, the original defendant sues the original plaintiff. In this second lawsuit, which is a *civil* action for damages, the original defendant is the plaintiff and the original plaintiff is the defendant. To succeed in a malicious prosecution lawsuit, the courts require the plaintiff to prove all of the following:

1. The plaintiff in the original lawsuit (now the defendant) instituted or was responsible for instituting the original lawsuit.
2. There was no *probable cause* for the first lawsuit (i.e., it was a frivolous lawsuit).
3. The plaintiff in the original action brought it with *malice*. (Caution: This is a very difficult element to prove.)
4. The original lawsuit was terminated in favor of the original defendant (now the plaintiff).
5. The current plaintiff suffered injury as a result of the original lawsuit.

The courts do not look favorably on malicious prosecution lawsuits because they feel that such lawsuits inhibit the original plaintiff's incentive to sue.

Example One student actor wins a part in a play over another student actor. To get back at the winning student, the rejected student files a lawsuit against the winning student, alleging intentional infliction of emotional distress, defamation, and negligence. The lawsuit is unfounded, but the winning student must defend the lawsuit. The jury returns a verdict exonerating the defendant. The defendant now can sue the plaintiff for malicious prosecution and has a very good chance of winning the lawsuit.

Unintentional Torts (Negligence)

5.2 Explain the elements necessary to prove negligence.

unintentional tort (negligence)
A doctrine that says a person is liable for harm that is the foreseeable consequence of his or her actions.

Under the doctrine of **unintentional tort**, commonly referred to as **ordinary negligence** or **negligence**, a person is liable for harm that is the *foreseeable consequence* of his or her actions. *Negligence* is defined as "the omission to do something which a reasonable man would do, or doing something which a prudent and reasonable man would not do."[4]

To be successful in a negligence lawsuit, the plaintiff must prove that (1) the defendant owed a *duty of care* to the plaintiff, (2) the defendant *breached* this duty of care, (3) the plaintiff suffered *injury*, (4) the defendant's negligent act was the *actual cause* of plaintiff's injury, and (5) the defendant's negligent act was the *proximate cause* of the plaintiff's injuries. Each of these elements is discussed in the paragraphs that follow.

1. Duty of Care

To determine whether a defendant is liable for negligence, it must first be ascertained whether the defendant owed a **duty of care** to the plaintiff. *Duty of care* refers to the obligation people owe each other—that is, the duty not to cause any unreasonable harm or risk of harm.

duty of care
The obligation people owe each other not to cause any unreasonable harm or risk of harm.

Examples Each person owes a duty to drive his or her car carefully, not to push or shove on escalators, not to leave skateboards on the sidewalk, and the like. Businesses owe a duty to make safe products, not to cause accidents, and so on.

The courts decide whether a duty of care is owed in specific cases by applying a **reasonable person standard**. Under this test, the courts attempt to determine how an *objective, careful, and conscientious person would have acted in the same circumstances* and then measure the defendant's conduct against that standard. The defendant's subjective intent ("I did not mean to do it") is immaterial in assessing liability. Certain impairments do not affect the reasonable person standard.

reasonable person standard
A test used to determine whether a defendant owes a duty of care. This test measures the defendant's conduct against how an objective, careful, and conscientious person would have acted in the same circumstances.

Defendants with a particular expertise or competence are measured against a **reasonable professional standard**. Applying this test, the courts attempt to determine how an objective, careful, and conscientious equivalent professional would have acted in the same circumstances and then measure the defendant professional's conduct against that standard.

No court has ever given, nor do we think ever can give, a definition of what constitutes a reasonable or an average man.

Lord Goddard C.J.R.
Regina v. McCarthy, 2 Q.B. 105 (1954)

Examples A brain surgeon is measured against a reasonable brain surgeon standard. A general practitioner doctor who is the only doctor who serves a small community is measured against a reasonable small-town general practitioner standard.

In the following negligence lawsuit, the court had to decide whether the defendants owed a duty to a plaintiff.

CASE 5.2 *STATE COURT CASE Duty*

Stevens v. MTR Gaming Group, Inc.

788 S.E.2d 59, 237 W.Va. 531 (2016)
Supreme Court of Appeals of West Virginia

"In short, no action for negligence will lie without a duty broken."

—Brent Benjamin, Justice

Facts

MTR Gaming Group, Inc. (MTR) operates a casino in Chester, West Virginia, in which it has installed video lottery terminals manufactured by International Gaming Technology, Inc. (IGT). For a period of approximately five years, Scott Stevens regularly patronized the casino and used the video lottery terminals. Scott, who embezzled over $7 million from his employer, spent this money and his family's savings, his retirement account, and his children's college funds playing at the casino's video lottery terminals. After gambling away the last of his money, Scott took his own life.

Stacy Stevens, Scott's widow, brought a lawsuit against MTR and IGT for negligence. She alleged that during the course of his patronage, Scott developed a medical condition known as "gambling disorder." Stacy asserts that the video lottery terminals played by Scott employed features that deceptively cause gamblers to play longer, more quickly, and more intensively. The casino is alleged to have facilitated compulsive behavior with marketing ploys such as offering complimentary food and lodging. Stacy contends that MTR breached its duty of care to Scott by failing to deny him access to the casino in light of his psychological infirmities, and that IGT should have programmed its terminals to permit players to

(continued)

lock themselves out after having expended a certain amount of time or money.

Issue

Did MTR and IGT owe a duty to prevent Scott Stevens's compulsive gambling?

Language of the Court

The threshold question in all actions in negligence is whether a duty was owed. In short, no action for negligence will lie without a duty broken. The court expressed a broader concern that, moreover, the imposition of such a duty would, in effect, have no limit. For example, plaintiff's theory would impose a duty on shopping malls and credit-card companies to identify and exclude compulsive shoppers. We hold that no duty of care exists on the part of manufacturers of video lottery terminals, or the casinos in which the terminals are located, to protect users from compulsively gambling.

Decision

The court held that defendants MTR and IGT were not negligent.

Critical Legal Thinking Questions

Do you think that the defendants were negligent? What would be the consequences if the defendants were found liable for negligence?

2. Breach of the Duty of Care

breach of the duty of care
A failure to exercise care or to act as a reasonable person would act.

Negligence is the omission to do something which a reasonable man would do, or doing something which a prudent and reasonable man would not do.

B. Alderson
Blyth v. Birmingham Waterworks Co. 11 Ex. Ch. 781 (1856)

Once a court finds that the defendant owed the plaintiff a duty of care, it must determine whether the defendant breached that duty. A **breach of the duty of care** is the failure to exercise care. In other words, it is the failure to act as a reasonable person would act. A breach of this duty may consist of an action.

Example Throwing a lit match on the ground in the forest and causing a fire is a breach of a duty of care.

A breach of duty may also consist of a failure to act when there is a duty to act.

Example A firefighter who refuses to put out a fire when her safety is not at stake breaches her duty of care for failing to act when she has a duty to act.

The following ethics feature discusses a classic case involving the issue of negligence.

Ethics

Ouch! McDonald's Coffee Is Too Hot!

Stella Liebeck, a 79-year-old resident of Albuquerque, New Mexico, visited a drive-through window of a McDonald's restaurant with her grandson Chris. Her grandson, the driver of the vehicle, placed the order for breakfast. When breakfast came at the drive-through window, Chris handed a hot cup of coffee to Stella. Chris pulled over so that Stella could put cream and sugar in her coffee. Stella took the lid off the coffee cup that she held in her lap and hot coffee spilled on her, causing third-degree burns on her legs, thighs, groin, and buttocks. Stella was driven to the emergency room and was hospitalized for seven days. She required medical treatment and later returned to the hospital to have skin grafts. She suffered permanent scars from the incident.

Stella's medical costs were $11,000. Stella asked McDonald's to pay her $20,000 to settle the case, but McDonald's offered only $800. Stella refused this settlement and sued McDonald's in court for negligence for selling coffee that was too hot and for failing to warn her of the danger of the hot coffee it served. At trial, McDonald's denied that it had been negligent and asserted that Stella's own negligence—opening a hot coffee cup over her lap—had caused her injuries. The jury heard the following evidence:

- McDonald's enforces a quality-control rule that requires its restaurants and franchises to serve coffee at 180 to 190 degrees Fahrenheit.
- Third-degree burns occur on skin in just two to five seconds when coffee is served at 185 degrees.
- McDonald's coffee temperature was 20 degrees hotter than coffee served by competing restaurant chains.

- McDonald's coffee temperature was approximately 40 to 50 degrees hotter than normal house-brewed coffee.
- McDonald's had received more than 700 prior complaints of people who had been scalded by McDonald's coffee.
- McDonald's did not place a warning on its coffee cups to alert patrons that the coffee it served was exceptionally hot.

Based on this evidence, the jury concluded that McDonald's acted recklessly and awarded Stella $200,000 in compensatory damages, which was then reduced by $40,000 because of her own negligence, and $2.7 million in punitive damages. The trial court judge reduced the amount of punitive damages to $480,000, which was three times the amount of compensatory damages. McDonald's now places a warning on its coffee cups that its coffee is hot. *Liebeck v. McDonald's Restaurants, P.T.S., Inc.* (New Mexico District Court, Bernalillo County, New Mexico, 1994)

Ethics Questions

Do you think that McDonald's properly warned Stella Liebeck of the dangers of drinking McDonald's hot coffee? Do you think McDonald's acted ethically in offering Stella an $800 settlement? Was the award of punitive damages justified in this case? Why or why not?

3. Injury to Plaintiff

Even though a defendant's negligent act may have breached a duty of care owed to the plaintiff, this breach is not actionable unless the plaintiff suffers **injury** or injury to his or her property. That is, the plaintiff must have suffered some injury before he or she can recover any damages. The damages recoverable depend on the effect of the injury on the plaintiff's life or profession.

injury
A plaintiff's personal injury or damage to his or her property that enables him or her to recover monetary damages for the defendant's negligence.

Examples Suppose that a person injures her hand when subway doors malfunction. The subway operator is found negligent. If the injured person is a star professional basketball player who makes $8 million per year with an expected seven years of good playing time left, but can no longer play basketball because of the injury, this plaintiff can recover multiple millions of dollars because she can no longer play professional basketball. However, if the injured person is a college professor with 15 years until retirement who is making only one-fortieth per year of what the basketball player makes, and may still be able to continue working, she can recover for her injuries but not as much as the basketball player can recover.

The following case is an example of a finding of negligence and the award of damages.

CASE 5.3 *STATE COURT CASE Negligence*

Reckis v. Johnson & Johnson

28 N.E.3d 445, 471 Mass. 272 (2015)
Supreme Judicial Court of Massachusetts

"We cannot say that the jury's award is greatly disproportionate to Samantha's grave injuries."

—Margot Botsford, Justice

Facts

When seven-year-old Samantha Reckis had a fever and sinus congestion, her father, Richard, purchased a bottle of Children's Motrin, which is a brand of ibuprofen manufactured by a division of Johnson & Johnson. It is an anti-inflammatory drug used to treat minor aches and pains as well as fever. The bottle was packaged inside a box, with an identical warning on the outside of the box and on the bottle. Richard read the warnings on each, and administered a dose of Children's Motrin to Samantha in the afternoon. That night Samantha had a fever and congestion, so Richard gave her a second dose of Children's Motrin.

The next morning Samantha woke with redness and a rash on her chest and neck, and a sore throat; she had the same fever and congestion as she had the night before. Richard gave her a third dose of Children's Motrin. Throughout the day, Samantha had a fever, nasal congestion, crusty eyes, cracked lips, and a rash. Samantha's mother, Lisa, gave Samantha a dose of Children's Motrin that evening after reading the warning label on the bottle.

The warning section of the Children's Motrin label contained an allergy alert that read: "Ibuprofen may cause a severe allergic reaction which may include hives, facial swelling, asthma (wheezing) and shock." The label did not mention the possibility of skin reddening, rash, or blisters, or the onset of the life-threatening disease called toxic epidermal necrolysis (TEN).

When Samantha woke up the next morning, most of her body was covered in blisters. She could not open her eyes or mouth, and her lips were bleeding. Lisa and Richard took Samantha to Shriners Hospital for Children (Shriners) in Boston, where doctors diagnosed Samantha with TEN and informed Lisa and Richard that Samantha had a minuscule chance of surviving through the night.

Samantha was put into a medically induced coma to ease her pain for approximately one month, and was hospitalized for the next six months. During her hospitalization, Samantha's TEN affected 95 percent of her body's surface. She suffered heart and liver failure. She suffered a stroke followed shortly thereafter by an aneurysm. She also suffered a cranial hemorrhage that caused seizures, and she underwent brain surgery. While in the hospital, she had only 20 percent of her lung capacity. Around the time of her release from the hospital, Samantha weighed approximately 35 pounds. After being released from Shriners Hospital, Samantha had to eat through a feeding tube for two years, and she required oxygen assistance at night for two years as well. Samantha has had more than 12 eye surgeries. Samantha cannot live on her own and will always need to be taken care of.

During the acute stage of Samantha's TEN and in the years that followed, her parents devoted themselves to caring for Samantha's many needs. They stayed with her throughout her hospitalization. They suffered significant distress in monitoring the progression of Samantha's disease and were often told during Samantha's hospitalization that she probably would not survive. In all, Lisa and Richard have not been able to watch Samantha enjoy a normal childhood as a result of the numerous, significant, and constant challenges of her health.

Samantha's parents brought a lawsuit on her behalf against Johnson & Johnson, which alleged that the company was negligent by failing to warn of the potential lethal side effects of Children's Motrin. The lawsuit sought to recover damages for Samantha for her past and future injuries. The parents also sued Johnson & Johnson for loss of consortium for their emotional distress. The jury found that Johnson & Johnson negligently failed to provide proper warnings in connection with Children's Motrin, which caused harm to Samantha. The jury awarded Samantha $50 million in compensatory damages, and awarded $6.5 million each to Lisa and Richard for loss of consortium. Johnson & Johnson appealed.

Issue

Did the evidence support the finding of negligence and the award of damages?

Language of the Court

The plaintiff's trial counsel stated explicitly to the jury in his closing argument that the warning should have mentioned the possibility that redness, rash, or blisters could lead to a life-threatening disease. The jury awarded a total of $50 million in compensatory damages to Samantha as a general award of damages. The jury was instructed on pain and suffering, future medical expenses, and the loss of future earning capacity as categories of damages. We cannot say that the jury's award is greatly disproportionate to Samantha's grave injuries. We decline to disturb the jury's awards to Lisa and Richard.

Decision

The Supreme Judicial Court of Massachusetts affirmed the trial court's findings of negligence by Johnson & Johnson and the award of damages.

Critical Legal Thinking Questions

Were the elements of negligence proven in this case? Do you believe that the amount of damages awarded in this case was warranted?

4. Actual Cause

actual cause (causation in fact)
The actual cause of negligence. A person who commits a negligent act is not liable unless actual cause can be proven.

A defendant's negligent act must be the **actual cause** (also called **causation in fact**) of the plaintiff's injuries. The test is this: "But for" the defendant's conduct, would the accident have happened? If the defendant's act caused the plaintiff's injuries, there is causation in fact.

Examples Suppose a corporation negligently pollutes the plaintiff's drinking water. The plaintiff dies of a heart attack unrelated to the polluted water. Although the corporation has acted negligently, it is not liable for the plaintiff's death. There was a negligent act and an injury, but there was no cause-and-effect relationship between them. If, instead, the plaintiff had died from the polluted drinking water, there would have been causation in fact, and the polluting corporation would have been liable.

If two (or more) persons are liable for negligently causing the plaintiff's injuries, both (or all) can be held liable to the plaintiff if each of their acts is a substantial factor in causing the plaintiff's injuries.

5. Proximate Cause

Under the law, a negligent party is not necessarily liable for all damages set in motion by his or her negligent act. Based on public policy, the law establishes a point along the damage chain after which the negligent party is no longer responsible for the consequences of his or her actions. This limitation on liability is referred to as **proximate cause** (also called **legal cause**). The general test of proximate cause is *foreseeability*. A negligent party who is found to be the actual cause—but not the proximate cause—of the plaintiff's injuries is not liable to the plaintiff. Situations are examined on a case-by-case basis.

proximate cause (legal cause)
A point along a chain of events caused by a negligent party after which this party is no longer legally responsible for the consequences of his or her actions.

In the landmark case ***Palsgraf v. The Long Island Railroad Company***, where proximate cause was not found, Justice Benjamin Cardozo famously said, "Negligence is not actionable unless it involves the invasion of a legally protected interest, the violation of a right. Proof of negligence in the air, so to speak, will not do."[5]

Example A person is walking on a public sidewalk. When he finishes smoking a cigarette, which is still lit, he negligently tosses it and it lands close to a house. The cigarette causes a fire that burns the house down. In this instance, the smoker is the proximate cause of the damage because it is reasonably foreseeable that his action could burn down the house. If the fire jumps and burns down the adjacent house, the smoker is still the proximate cause. If the third house in the row burns, he is probably still the proximate cause. However, if the fire spreads and burns down 100 houses before it is put out (the smoker is the *actual cause* of the damage under the "but for" test), the smoker would not be the *proximate cause* of burning the 100th house because it would not be reasonably foreseeable that his action of throwing a lit cigarette would burn down so many houses. Where does one draw the line of liability? At the fourth house? The 20th house? The 40th house? This decision is left up to the jury.

In the following feature, a court had to decide whether proximate cause had been proven.

Information Technology

Apple Not Liable for Accident Caused by Driver's Texting

Ashley Kubiak was driving her pickup truck when she received a text message on her iPhone. Kubiak looked down to read the text, after which she turned her attention back to the road. At that point it was too late to avoid colliding with a vehicle carrying two adults and a child. The adults died, while the child survived but was rendered paraplegic. Representatives of the victims of the accident sued Apple, the producer of the iPhone, for negligence. The plaintiffs alleged that the receipt of a text message triggers in the recipient an unconscious and automatic compulsion to engage in texting behavior, and that Apple was negligent in not warning users of this behavior.

The U.S. district court granted Apple's motion to dismiss, and the U.S. court of appeals affirmed. The court of appeals stated: "Negligence requires a showing of proximate cause. Proximate cause means that the defendant's act or omission was a substantial factor in bringing about the injury which would not otherwise have occurred. No authority indicates to us that courts, contemplating reasonable persons and ordinary minds, would recognize a person's induced responses to her phone as a substantial factor in her tortious acts and therefore hold the phone's manufacturer responsible." *Meador v. Apple, Incorporated*, 911 F.3d 260 (United States Court of Appeals for the Fifth Circuit, 2018)

CONCEPT SUMMARY

ELEMENTS OF NEGLIGENCE

1. The defendant owed a *duty of care* to the plaintiff.
2. The defendant *breached this duty*.
3. The plaintiff suffered *injury*.
4. The defendant's negligent act was the *actual cause* (or *causation in fact*) of the plaintiff's injuries.
5. The defendant's negligent act was the *proximate cause* (or *legal cause*) of the plaintiff's injuries. The defendant is liable only for the *foreseeable* consequences of his or her negligent act.

Special Negligence Doctrines

5.3 List and describe special negligence doctrines.

The courts have developed many *special negligence doctrines*. The most important of these are discussed in the paragraphs that follow.

Professional Malpractice

Professionals, such as doctors, lawyers, architects, accountants, and others, owe a duty of ordinary care in providing their services. This duty is known as the *reasonable professional standard*. A professional who breaches this duty of care is liable for the injury his or her negligence causes. This liability is commonly referred to as **professional malpractice**.

professional malpractice
The liability of a professional who breaches his or her duty of ordinary care.

Examples A doctor who accidently leaves a medical instrument in a patient after an operation has been completed is liable for *medical malpractice*. A lawyer who fails to file a document with the court on time, thus causing the client's case to be dismissed, is liable for *legal malpractice*.

Negligent Infliction of Emotional Distress

Some jurisdictions have extended the tort of emotional distress to include the **negligent infliction of emotional distress**. Here, a person who is not physically injured by the defendant's negligence suffers emotional distress because of the defendant's action and can recover damages from the defendant for emotional distress.

negligent infliction of emotional distress
A tort that permits a person to recover for emotional distress caused by the defendant's negligent conduct.

The most common example of negligent infliction of emotional distress involves bystanders who witness the injury or death of a relative that is caused by another's negligent conduct. Under this tort, the bystander, even though not physically injured personally, may be able to recover damages against the negligent party for his or her own mental suffering. Many states require that the following elements are proved in bystander cases:

1. A close relative was killed or injured by the defendant.
2. The plaintiff suffered severe emotional distress.
3. The plaintiff's mental distress resulted from a sensory and contemporaneous observance of the accident.

Some states require that the plaintiff's mental distress be manifested by some physical injury; other states have eliminated this requirement.

WEB EXERCISE
Use **www.google.com** and find out whether your state has a duty to rescue law. If so, who does it apply to and under what circumstances?

Example A father is walking his young daughter to school when a driver of an automobile negligently runs off the road and onto the sidewalk, hitting the girl but not her father. Suppose that the young daughter dies from her injuries. The father suffers severe emotional distress by seeing his daughter die and manifests his distress by suffering physically. The father can recover damages for negligent infliction of emotional distress for the severe distress he suffered by seeing his daughter die.

The following feature describes duty to rescue laws.

Contemporary Environment

Duty to Rescue Laws

Under common law, there generally is no duty to assist or rescue a person who is in peril. However, some states have adopted **duty to rescue laws** that, under certain circumstances, impose a duty on a person to assist or rescue another person who is in peril. A duty to rescue may be imposed if there is a special relationship between the parties. For example, most states require parents to rescue their minor children, and spouses to rescue their spouses. Some states require persons to rescue other persons that they have put in danger. If a duty to rescue exists, the rescuer is obligated to render reasonable assistance, though they need not endanger themselves in conducting a rescue.

Many states have enacted **duty to notify laws** that require persons who see that someone is in peril to make an emergency 911 call so that proper authorities, such as law enforcement, the fire department, or medical personnel may respond to the scene.

Negligence *Per Se*

Statutes often establish duties owed by one person to another. The violation of a statute that proximately causes an injury is **negligence *per se***. The plaintiff in such an action must prove that (1) a statute existed, (2) the statute was enacted to prevent the type of injury suffered, and (3) the plaintiff was within a class of persons meant to be protected by the statute.

negligence *per se*
A tort in which the violation of a statute or an ordinance constitutes the breach of the duty of care.

Example Most cities have an ordinance that places the responsibility for fixing public sidewalks in residential areas on the homeowners whose homes front the sidewalks. A homeowner is liable if he or she fails to repair a damaged sidewalk in front of his or her home if a pedestrian trips and is injured because of the unrepaired sidewalk. The injured party does not have to prove that the homeowner owed the duty because the statute establishes that.

Res Ipsa Loquitur

If a defendant is in control of a situation in which a plaintiff has been injured and has superior knowledge of the circumstances surrounding the injury, the plaintiff might have difficulty proving the defendant's negligence. In such a situation, the law applies the doctrine of ***res ipsa loquitur*** (Latin for "the thing speaks for itself"). This doctrine raises a presumption of negligence and switches the burden to the defendant to prove that he or she was not negligent. *Res ipsa loquitur* applies in cases where the following conditions are met:

1. The defendant had exclusive control of the instrumentality or situation that caused the plaintiff's injury.
2. The injury would not have occurred ordinarily but for someone's negligence.

res ipsa loquitur
A tort in which the presumption of negligence arises because (1) the defendant was in exclusive control of the situation and (2) the plaintiff would not have suffered injury but for someone's negligence. The burden switches to the defendant to prove that he or she was not negligent.

Examples Haeran goes in for major surgery and is given anesthesia to put her to sleep during the operation. Sometime after the operation, it is discovered that a surgical instrument was left in Haeran, and she suffers severe injury because of this. Haeran has no way to identify which doctor or nurse carelessly left the instrument. In this case, the court can apply the doctrine of *res ipsa loquitur* and place the presumption of negligence on the defendants. Any defendant who can prove that he or she did not leave the instrument in Haeran escapes liability; any defendant who does not disprove his or her negligence is liable. Other typical *res ipsa loquitur* cases involve commercial airplane crashes, falling elevators, and the like.

Gross Negligence

gross negligence
A doctrine that says a person is liable for harm that is caused by his or her willful misconduct or reckless behavior. Punitive damages may be assessed.

Critical Legal Thinking
How does gross negligence differ from ordinary negligence? What is the advantage for a plaintiff to try to prove gross negligence rather than ordinary negligence?

A person can be liable for injury and damage caused by their **gross negligence**. Gross negligence is extreme when compared with ordinary negligence. Gross negligence has often been defined as either a want of even scant care or an extreme departure from the ordinary standard of conduct. In most jurisdictions, gross negligence requires a finding that the defendant engaged in willful misconduct or reckless behavior. People who engage in wanton and reckless conduct usually have no intent to cause harm to others. However, they perform an act that they know or should have known is so unreasonable and dangerous that it is likely to cause harm. Because the definition of gross negligence is vague, a claim for gross negligence is often difficult to prove. The determination of whether a party's conduct is ordinary negligence or gross negligence depends on the unique circumstances of the case.

A person who injures someone by his or her gross negligence is liable for compensatory damages suffered by the injured party, including actual losses such as medical costs as well as for pain and suffering. If gross negligence is found, *punitive damages* may also be awarded.

Example If an automobile driver runs a stop sign by mistake and hits another car, causing injury to its occupants, the driver is liable for ordinary negligence. If that driver had been drinking alcohol before running the stop sign and his alcohol levels are well above the legal limit, the driver would be found liable for gross negligence because of his reckless disregard for the safety of others, which is caused by his excessive drinking and then driving.

attractive nuisance doctrine
A tort rule that imposes liability on a landowner to children who have been attracted onto the landowner's property by an attractive nuisance and who are killed or injured on the property.

Attractive Nuisance Doctrine

The **attractive nuisance doctrine** is a special tort rule that imposes liability on a landowner to children who have trespassed onto his or her property with the intent to play on the attractive nuisance and are killed or injured while doing so. The underlying reason for this doctrine is that children, due to their youth, do not understand the potential risk associated with the hazard. To find the landowner liable to the child, the attraction must pose an unreasonable risk of death or serious bodily harm.

Good Samaritan laws
Statutes that relieve medical professionals from liability for ordinary negligence when they stop and render aid to victims in emergency situations.

Critical Legal Thinking
What is the purpose of relieving medical personnel from liability for ordinary negligence when rendering aid? Do persons who do not qualify for protection under the Good Samaritan law run a risk of liability if they choose to render aid?

Examples Attractive nuisances include machinery, abandoned refrigerators and freezers, junk yards, open pits, and unguarded pools.

The landowner owes a duty to remove the dangerous condition or take steps to prevent children from reaching the dangerous object.

Example Homeowners owe a duty to place a fence and locked gate around a swimming pool in their yard.

The following feature describes Good Samaritan laws.

Critical Legal Thinking

Good Samaritan Laws

In the past, liability exposure made many doctors, nurses, and other medical professionals reluctant to stop and render aid to victims in emergency situations, such as highway accidents. Almost all states have enacted **Good Samaritan laws** that relieve medical professionals from liability for injury caused by their ordinary negligence in such circumstances.

Good Samaritan laws protect medical professionals only from liability for their *ordinary negligence*, not for injuries caused by their gross negligence or reckless or intentional conduct. Most Good Samaritan laws protect licensed doctors, nurses, and laypersons certified in cardiopulmonary resuscitation (CPR).

Laypersons not trained in CPR are not generally protected by Good Samaritan statutes—that is, they are liable for injuries caused by their ordinary negligence in rendering aid.

Example Sam is injured in an automobile accident and is unconscious in his automobile alongside the road. Dr. Pamela Heathcoat, who is driving by the scene of the accident, stops, pulls Sam from the burning wreckage, and administers first aid. In doing so, Pamela negligently breaks Sam's shoulder. If Pamela's negligence is *ordinary negligence*, she is not liable to Sam because the Good Samaritan law protects her from liability; if Pamela was *grossly negligent* or *reckless* in administering aid to Sam, she is liable to him for the injuries she caused. It is a question of fact for the jury to decide whether a doctor's conduct was ordinary negligence or gross negligence or recklessness.

Example If, in the prior example, Pamela was not a doctor or otherwise protected by the Good Samaritan law, she would be liable for any injuries caused to Sam by her *ordinary negligence* (or gross negligence or recklessness) while rendering aid to Sam.

Critical Legal Thinking Questions
What is the public policy underlying Good Samaritan laws? Should ordinary citizens be held liable for ordinary negligence caused while rendering aid to an injured person?

Defenses Against Negligence

5.4 Describe the defenses that can be raised against a claim of negligence.

A defendant in a negligence lawsuit may raise several defenses to the imposition of liability. These defenses are discussed in the following paragraphs.

Superseding or Intervening Event

Under negligence, a person is liable only for foreseeable events. Therefore, an original negligent party can raise a **superseding event** or an **intervening event** as a defense to liability.

superseding event (intervening event)
An event for which a defendant is not responsible. The defendant is not liable for injuries caused by the superseding or intervening event.

Example Assume that an avid golfer negligently hits a spectator with a golf ball, knocking the spectator unconscious. While lying on the ground, waiting for an ambulance to come, the spectator is struck by a bolt of lightning and killed. The golfer is liable for the injuries caused by the golf ball. He is not liable for the death of the spectator, however, because the lightning bolt was an unforeseen intervening event.

Assumption of the Risk

If a plaintiff knows of and voluntarily enters into or participates in a risky activity that results in injury, the law recognizes that the plaintiff assumed, or took on, the risk involved. Thus, the defendant can raise the defense of **assumption of the risk** against the plaintiff. This defense assumes that the plaintiff (1) had knowledge of the specific risk and (2) voluntarily assumed that risk. Assumption of the risk is often applied to injuries incurred while participating in sporting activities.

assumption of the risk
A defense that a defendant can use against a plaintiff who knowingly and voluntarily enters into or participates in a risky activity that results in injury.

Example A race-car driver assumes the risk of being injured or killed in a crash.

Some states have enacted statutes that apply the doctrine of assumption of the risk to participation in certain sports and recreational activities. The case on the following page involves such a statute.

Contributory and Comparative Negligence

5.5 Describe the difference between *contributory negligence*, *comparative negligence*, and *partial comparative negligence*.

Sometimes a plaintiff is partially liable for causing his own injuries. In such cases, the law usually penalizes the plaintiff for his negligence. States have adopted one of three doctrines to apply where a plaintiff is partially at fault: *contributory negligence*, *comparative negligence*, and *partial comparative negligence*. These doctrines are discussed in the following paragraphs.

CASE 5.4 *FEDERAL COURT CASE Assumption of the Risk*

Roberts v. Jackson Hole Mountain Resort Corporation

884 F.3d 967 (2018)
United States Court of Appeals for the Tenth Circuit

"The Wyoming Recreation Safety Act codifies the common-law concept of primary assumption of the risk."

—David Ebel, Circuit Judge

Facts

The Jackson Hole Ski Resort, which is located in Wyoming, is operated by the Jackson Hole Mountain Resort Corporation (JHMR). The resort has groomed ski hills that most skiers use, and has ungroomed, natural state terrain (called off-piste) ski areas for more adventuresome skiers. Saratoga Bowl is an off-piste area dotted with trees, rocks, and swaths of open, often-untouched snow that weaves throughout natural obstacles. Michael Roberts, an experienced skier and ski instructor from California, and four friends visited Jackson Hole and choose to ski Saratoga Bowl. Partway down, Roberts skied over a rock and tumbled into a crevice between two large boulders. The ski patrol was called, and Roberts was taken to the hospital. As a result of his fall, Roberts fractured his pelvis, broke seven ribs, lacerated his liver, punctured a lung, and incurred various other injuries. Roberts sued JHMR for negligence. Wyoming has enacted the Wyoming Recreation Safety Act (WRSA), a state statute which provides that:

> *Any person who takes part in any sport or recreational opportunity assumes the inherent risks in that sport or recreational opportunity, whether those risks are known or unknown, and is legally responsible for any and all damage, injury or death that results from the inherent risks in that sport or recreational opportunity.*

The U.S. district court held that the statute barred Roberts's claim and granted summary judgment to JHMR. Roberts appealed.

Issue

Did the WRSA bar Roberts's claim of negligence?

Language of the Court

> *The Wyoming Recreation Safety Act codifies the common-law concept of primary assumption of the risk. Roberts was not directed to Saratoga Bowl by an employee offering statements about its safety; in fact, advanced skiers in search of fresh untracked and unconsolidated powder are attracted to off-piste terrain such as Saratoga Bowl because it is ungroomed, untamed, and provides the types of natural obstacles that distinguish such runs from those frequented by less talented skiers. Boulders and the gaps of widely varying dimensions between them, at times exposed to the elements and at others lightly covered in fresh snow, are an inherent risk of skiing an off-piste run such as Saratoga Bowl.*

Decision

The U.S. court of appeals affirmed the district court's grant of summary judgment to the defendant.

Critical Legal Thinking Questions

What is the public policy underlying the doctrine of assumption of the risk? Why do states enact statutes to codify the doctrine of assumption of the risk?

Contributory Negligence

contributory negligence
A doctrine that says that a plaintiff who is partially at fault for his or her own injury cannot recover against the negligent defendant.

Some states apply the doctrine of **contributory negligence**, which holds that a plaintiff who is partially at fault for his or her own injury cannot recover against the negligent defendant.

Example Suppose a driver who is driving over the speed limit negligently hits and injures a pedestrian who is jaywalking against a red "Don't Walk" sign. Suppose the jury finds that the driver is 80 percent responsible for the accident and that the jaywalker is 20 percent responsible. The pedestrian suffered $100,000 in injuries. Under the doctrine of contributory negligence, the pedestrian cannot recover any damages from the driver.

Comparative Negligence

Many states have replaced the doctrine of contributory negligence with the doctrine of **comparative negligence**, also called **comparative fault**. Under this doctrine, damages are apportioned according to fault.

comparative negligence (comparative fault)
A doctrine under which damages are apportioned according to fault.

Example When the comparative negligence rule is applied to the previous example in which the pedestrian suffered $100,000 of injuries the result is much fairer. The plaintiff-pedestrian, who was 20 percent at fault for causing his own injuries, can recover 80 percent of his damages (or $80,000) from the negligent defendant-driver.

Critical Legal Thinking

What are the differences between contributory negligence, comparative negligence, and partial comparative negligence? Which rule do you think is the fairest rule?

WEB EXERCISE

Use **www.google.com** and find out whether your state follows the contributory negligence, comparative negligence, or partial comparative negligence standard.

Partial Comparative Negligence

Several states have adopted **partial comparative negligence**, also called **modified comparative negligence**, which provides that a plaintiff must be less than 50 percent responsible for causing his or her own injuries to recover under comparative negligence; otherwise, contributory negligence applies.

Example Suppose a commercial truck collides with an automobile. The driver of the automobile suffers $100,000 in injuries while the driver of the truck suffers no injuries. If the driver of the commercial truck is 51 percent responsible for causing the accident and the driver of the automobile is 49 percent responsible, then the injured automobile driver may recover $51,000 from the driver of the commercial truck. If, however, the driver of the truck is 49 percent liable for causing the accident and the driver of the automobile is found to be 51 percent responsible, then the owner of the automobile recovers nothing for her injuries.

The majority of states have adopted the doctrine of comparative negligence.

Strict Liability

5.6 Define and apply the doctrine of strict liability.

Strict liability, another category of torts, is *liability without fault*. That is, a participant in a covered activity will be held liable for any injuries caused by the activity, even if he or she was not negligent. This doctrine holds that (1) there are certain activities that can place the public at risk of injury even if reasonable care is taken and that (2) the public should have some means of compensation if such injury occurs. Strict liability is imposed for **abnormally dangerous activities** that cause injury or death.

strict liability
A tort doctrine that imposes liability without fault on a person who engages in an abnormally dangerous activity that causes injury or death to another person.

Activities such as crop dusting, blasting, fumigation, burning of fields, storage of explosives, and the keeping of animals and pets are usually considered activities to which strict liability applies.

Example Emera has owned a dog for years. The dog has shown no dangerous propensities and has never bitten anyone. Emera goes out of town on a business trip and has her neighbor take care of the dog while she is gone. While Emera is gone, the neighbor, while walking the dog, lets the dog off of her leash to play with a child who has asked to play with the dog. When the child hits the dog in the eye, the dog bites the child, injuring the child. Here, Emera is strictly liable for the injuries caused by her dog even though she has committed no negligence herself.

Key Terms and Concepts

Abnormally dangerous activities (109)
Actual cause (causation in fact) (102)
Assault (93)
Assumption of the risk (107)
Attractive nuisance doctrine (106)
Battery (93)
Breach of the duty of care (100)
Comparative negligence (comparative fault) (109)
Contributory negligence (108)
Defamation of character (96)
Disparagement (trade libel, product disparagement, or slander of title) (97)
Duty of care (99)
Duty to notify laws (105)
Duty to rescue laws (105)
False imprisonment (94)
Good Samaritan laws (106)
Gross negligence (106)
Injury (101)
Intentional infliction of emotional distress (tort of outrage) (97)
Intentional misrepresentation (fraudulent misrepresentation or fraud or deceit) (97)
Intentional tort (93)
Invasion of the right to privacy (95)
Libel (96)
Malicious prosecution (98)
Merchant protection statute (shopkeeper's privilege) (94)
Misappropriation of the right to publicity (tort of appropriation) (95)
Negligence (unintentional tort or ordinary negligence) (98)
Negligence *per se* (105)
Negligent infliction of emotional distress (104)
New York Times Co. v. Sullivan (96)
Ordinary negligence (unintentional tort or negligence) (98)
Palsgraf v. The Long Island Railroad Company (103)
Partial comparative negligence (modified comparative negligence) (109)
Professional malpractice (104)
Proximate cause (legal cause) (103)
Public figure (96)
Reasonable person standard (99)
Reasonable professional standard (99)
Res ipsa loquitur (105)
Scienter (97)
Slander (96)
Strict liability (109)
Superseding event (intervening event) (107)
Tort (93)
Transferred intent doctrine (94)
Unintentional tort (ordinary negligence or negligence) (98)

Critical Legal Thinking Cases

5.1 Assumption of the Risk Greater Gulf State Fair, Inc. operated the Gulf State Fair in Mobile County, Alabama. One of the events at the fair was a mechanical bull ride, and participants paid money to ride the mechanical bull, a ride where the rider sits on a motorized device shaped like a real bull that simulates a real bull ride as the mechanical bull turns, twists, and bucks. The challenge is to stay on the bull and not be thrown off it. A large banner above the ride reads "Rolling Thunder."

John Lilya and a friend watched a rider being thrown from the mechanical bull. Lilya also watched as his friend paid and rode the bull and was also thrown off. Lilya then paid the $5 admission charge and boarded the mechanical bull. He was immediately thrown off onto a soft pad underneath the bull. Lilya reboarded the bull for a second ride. The bull ride began again and became progressively faster, spinning and bucking to the left and right until Lilya fell off the bull. On the fall, Lilya landed on his head and shoulders and suffered a fractured neck. Lilya sued Gulf State Fair to recover damages for his severe injuries. Was riding the mechanical bull an open and obvious danger for which Lilya had voluntarily assumed the risk? *Lilya v. The Greater Gulf State Fair, Inc.*, 855 So.2d 1049, 2003 Ala. Lexis 57 (Supreme Court of Alabama, 2003)

5.2 Gross Negligence Toys "R" Us, a toy retailer, purchased Banzai Falls In-Ground Pool Slides from a vendor in China. Each slide was made of a tent-like fabric with a rubber-coated sliding surface and was sold with an electric unit to inflate it. The slide was intended to be installed adjacent to an in-ground swimming pool so that a person using the slide may descend the slide ramp into the pool. Sarah Letsky purchased a Banzai Pool Slide from Toys "R" Us using the internet. She and her husband installed the slide beside the swimming pool at their home.

One day the Letskys had family and friends over, including Robin and Michael Aleo. Robin, who weighed 140 pounds, climbed to the top of the slide and descended head first. The bottom part of the slide collapsed, and Robin's head struck the pool ledge through the fabric of the slide. Robin died from the accident. The slide had not been tested to ensure that it complied with federal safety standards that required pool slides to be capable of supporting up to 350 pounds and be safe for head-first sliding. Michael, Robin's husband, sued Toys "R" Us to recover damages for gross negligence. Is Toys "R" Us liable for gross negligence? *Aleo v. SLB Toys USA, Inc.*, 995 N.E.2d 740, 2013 Mass. Lexis 709 (Supreme Judicial Court of Massachusetts, 2013)

5.3 Proximate Cause Michael Carneal was a 14-year-old freshman student in high school in Paducah, Kentucky. Carneal regularly played violent interactive video and computer games that involve the player shooting virtual opponents with computer guns and other weapons. Carneal also watched violent video-recorded movies and internet sites. Carneal took a .22-caliber pistol and five shotguns into the lobby of his high school and shot several of his fellow students, killing three and wounding many others. The three students killed were Jessica James, Kayce Steger, and Nicole Hadley.

The parents of the three dead children sued the producers and distributors of the violent video games and movies that Carneal had watched prior to the shooting. The parents sued to recover damages for wrongful death, alleging that the defendants were negligent in producing and distributing such games and movies to Carneal. The defendants responded by asserting that they were not the proximate cause of Carneal's school shooting, and that they were therefore not liable to the plaintiffs for the damage caused by Carneal's actions. Were the producers and distributors of the video games and movies the proximate cause of the death of the victims of Carneal's actions? *James v. Meow Media, Inc.*, 300 F.3d 683, 2002 U.S. App. Lexis 16185 (United States Court of Appeals for the Sixth Circuit, 2002)

5.4 Disparagement Zagat Survey, LLC, publishes the famous Zagat series of dining, travel, and leisure guides for different cities and locations. The Zagat restaurant guides lists and ranks each reviewed restaurant from 0 to 30 for categories such as food, décor, and service. These ratings are calculated from surveys of customers of the restaurants, and the Zagat guide often quotes anonymous consumer comments. Lucky Cheng's is a restaurant owned by Themed Restaurants, Inc., that is located in Manhattan, New York. The *Zagat Survey of New York City Restaurants* rated the food at Lucky Cheng's as 9 and rated the décor and service as 15. The Zagat guide then stated: "God knows 'you don't go for the food' at this East Village Asian-Eclectic." Themed Restaurants sued Zagat for disparagement. Zagat defended, arguing that the ratings and comments about Lucky Cheng's restaurant that appeared in the Zagat guide were opinions and not statements of fact and were, therefore, not actionable as disparagement. Were the statements made in Zagat's restaurant guide statements of fact or statements of opinion? Is Zagat liable for disparagement? *Themed Restaurants, Inc., Doing Business as Lucky Cheng's v. Zagat Survey, LLC*, 801 N.Y.S.2d 38, 2005 N.Y. App. Div. Lexis 9275 (Supreme Court of New York, Appellate Division, 2005)

5.5 Negligence Mark Jones was a firefighter for the city of Seattle, Washington. He was assigned to the Station 33 firehouse, where he remained on duty for long shifts, including staying overnight. Jones slept in quarters on the second floor of the firehouse. One of the common features of many firehouses, including the one Jones worked in, is the pole hole in the second floor with a pole leading to the first floor. When called to action, firefighters slide down the pole to reach the first floor and their firefighting equipment and vehicles to quickly respond to emergencies. One night, around 3:00 a.m., Jones fell 15 feet through the fire station's pole hole. Jones told a responding medic that he had awoken to use the bathroom, which was next to the pole hole. Jones sustained serious physical and cognitive impairments because of his fall. Because of his permanent impaired mental and physical injuries, Jones's sister Meg was appointed his guardian. Meg, on behalf of Jones, sued the city of Seattle for injuries caused to Jones by the accident, alleging that the city was negligent in failing to block accidental access to the pole hole. Is the city of Seattle liable for negligence? If so, what damages should be awarded? *Jones v. City of Seattle, Washington*, 314 P.3d 380, 2013 Wash. Lexis 955 (Supreme Court of Washington, 2013)

5.6 Negligence One morning, after working at night, Tim Clancy was driving a Chevrolet S-10 pickup truck on State Road 231. Clancy fell asleep at the wheel of the truck. Robert and Dianna Goad, husband and wife, were riding separate motorcycles on the other side of the road. Clancy's truck crossed the center line of the road and collided with Dianna's motorcycle. The collision immediately severed Dianna's leg above the knee, and she was thrown from her motorcycle into a water-filled ditch at the side of the road. Clancy was awakened by the sound of the impact, and the truck veered into the ditch as well. Robert stopped his motorcycle, ran back to the scene of the accident, and held Dianna's head out of the water-filled ditch. Clancy called 911, and when the paramedics arrived, Dianna was taken to the hospital. Dianna remained in a coma for two weeks. Her leg had to be amputated. In addition, Dianna suffered from a fractured pelvic bone, a fractured left elbow, and a lacerated spleen, which had to be removed. Dianna endured multiple skin graft procedures. At the time of the trial, Dianna had undergone seven surgeries, she had taken more than 6,800 pills, and her medical expenses totaled more than $368,000. Furthermore, Dianna's medical expenses and challenges continue and are expected to continue indefinitely. In addition, Dianna has been fitted with a C-leg, a computerized prosthetic leg. A C-leg needs to be replaced every three to five years, at full cost. Dianna sued Clancy to recover damages based on his negligence. Had Clancy been negligent? If so, what amount of damages should be awarded to Dianna? *Clancy v. Goad*, 858 N.E.2d 653, 2006 Ind. App. Lexis 2576 (Court of Appeals of Indiana, 2006)

Ethics Cases

5.7 Ethics The Houston Astros professional baseball team is owned and operated by Houston McLane Company, LLC. Shirley and Richard Martinez, along with five young children they were caring for, attended a Houston Astros baseball game at a baseball stadium in Houston. Their seats were in the bleachers behind the right field wall, which is an area where a fly ball hit during the game would be a home run. The baseball stadium contains more than 40,000 seats, of which about 5,000 seats located behind home plate are shielded by a protective screen. The rest of the seats, including those in the right field bleachers where the Martinezes sat, were open and did not have a protective screen.

Prior to the game the teams were practicing on the field, including taking batting practice. When Shirley Martinez was walking on the steps near her seats carrying a young child, she heard someone yell a warning that a fly ball was coming toward her. She shielded the child with her arms and was struck in the face by the ball. She suffered an orbital fracture and corneal laceration. Martinez sued the owner of the Houston Astros professional baseball team to recover damages for negligence. Houston asserted in defense that Martinez had assumed the risk of getting hit by flying baseballs and it was therefore not liable for negligence. Is the defendant baseball team owner liable for negligence? Was it ethical for the baseball team owner not to pay Martinez for her injuries? *Martinez v. Houston McLane Company, LLC*, 414 S.W.3d 219 (Court of Appeals of Texas, 2013)

5.8 Ethics Case Shortly after 2:00 A.M. one summer night, 12-year-old Denise Colbert and several friends took a motor-boat out on Lake Tapps in Washington. Denise had been drinking. Skier's Choice, Inc. had manufactured the Moomba brand boat they were using. Denise and several of her friends jumped off the boat into the water and held onto the boat's rear platform as the boat drove slowly toward shore. When the boat was about 200 yards from shore, Denise and Lindsay Lynam began swimming to shore. Sometime between 3:00 and 3:30 A.M., Lindsay noticed that Denise had disappeared beneath the water's surface. The friends called 911 and began searching for Denise. One of the friends called Denise's father, Jay Colbert, and told him that Denise had fallen off the boat and they could not find her.

Police and other rescuers arrived around 3:45 A.M., and Mr. Colbert arrived sometime thereafter. Mr. Colbert went to a friend's dock, where he could watch the rescuers search for Denise. The rescuers searched with boats, spotlights, and divers. Sometime after 6:00 A.M., the rescuers found Denise's body. About 10 minutes later, Mr. Colbert saw the rescuers, about 100 yards away, pull a body out of the water and onto a boat. The rescuers wrapped the body in a blanket and placed the body in an ambulance while Mr. Colbert looked on. The medical examiner reported the cause of Denise's death as drowning. The examiner noted two other significant conditions: high levels of carbon monoxide and ethanol toxicity that would come from a boat's engine.

Thereafter, Mr. Colbert saw a psychologist, who later testified that Mr. Colbert was suffering from severe emotional distress caused by the death of his daughter. Mr. Colbert sued Skier's Choice, Inc., the manufacturer of the boat, to recover damages under the doctrine of negligent infliction of emotional distress. The trial court dismissed Mr. Colbert's claim. Mr. Colbert appealed. Is the defendant liable to Mr. Colbert under the legal theory of negligent infliction of emotional distress in this case? Did the defendant act ethically by denying liability in this case? *Colbert v. Moomba Sports, Inc. and Skier's Choice, Inc.*, 135 P.3d 485, 2006 Wash. App. Lexis 975 (Court of Appeals of Washington, 2006)

Notes

1. 376 U.S. 254, 84 S.Ct. 710, 1964 U.S. Lexis 1655 (Supreme Court of the United States, 1964).
2. *Restatement (Second) of Torts*, Section 46.
3. *Restatement (Second) of Torts*, Section 46, Comment d.
4. Justice B. Anderson, *Blyth v. Birmingham Waterworks Co.*, 11 Ex. Ch. 781, 784 (Court of Exchequer, 1856).
5. *Palsgraf v. The Long Island Railroad Company*, 248 N.Y. 339, 162 N.E. 99, 1928 N.Y. Lexis 1269 (Court of Appeals of New York, 1928).

CHAPTER 6

Product and Strict Liability

FOOTBALL FIELD
Football helmets and other sports equipment are usually designed to be as safe as possible. However, many manufacturers have discontinued making football helmets because of the exposure to product liability lawsuits.

Henry R. Cheeseman

Learning Objectives

After studying this chapter, you should be able to:

6.1 Describe how a defendant is liable for negligently producing a product.

6.2 Describe how a defendant is liable for misrepresenting the quality of a product.

6.3 Define the doctrine of *strict liability*.

6.4 List the types of product defects upon which a strict liability lawsuit may be based.

6.5 Describe defects in manufacture.

6.6 Describe defects in design.

6.7 Describe defects of failure to warn.

6.8 Describe defects in packaging.

6.9 Describe other defects upon which a strict liability action may be brought.

6.10 List and describe the defenses that may be raised against a product liability claim.

> *"A manufacturer is strictly liable in tort when an article he places on the market, knowing that it is to be used without inspection for defects, proves to have a defect that causes injury to a human being."*
>
> —*Roger Traynor, Justice*
> *Greenman v. Yuba Power Products, Inc.* 59 Cal.2d 57, 27 Cal.Rptr. 697, 1963 Cal. Lexis 140 (1963)

Introduction to Product and Strict Liability

Nobody has a more sacred obligation to obey the law than those who make the law.
Sophocles (496–406 BCE)

product liability
The liability of manufacturers, sellers, and others for the injuries caused by defective products.

If a product defect causes injury or death to purchasers, lessees, users, or bystanders, the injured party or the heirs of a deceased person may bring legal actions and recover damages under certain tort doctrines. These tort doctrines include negligence, misrepresentation, and the modern theory of strict liability. The liability of manufacturers, sellers, lessors, and others for injuries caused by defective products is commonly referred to as **product liability**.

The doctrine of strict liability imposes liability on defendants without showing fault. Under the doctrine of strict liability, a plaintiff may also recover punitive damages if the defendant's conduct has been reckless or intentional.

The various tort principles that permit injured parties to recover damages caused by defective products are discussed in this chapter.

Product Liability: Negligence

6.1 Describe how a defendant is liable for negligently producing a product.

negligence
A tort related to defective products in which the defendant has breached a duty of due care and caused harm to the plaintiff. Also called *unintentional tort* or *ordinary negligence*.

Often, the plaintiff who brings a product liability action relies on the traditional tort theory of **negligence**, also called **unintentional tort** or **ordinary negligence**. Negligence requires the defendant to be *at fault* for causing the plaintiff's injuries. To be successful, the plaintiff must prove that the defendant breached a duty of due care to the plaintiff and thereby caused the plaintiff's injuries. In other words, the plaintiff must prove that the defendant was at fault for causing his or her injuries.

Failure to exercise due care includes failure to assemble a product carefully, negligent product design, negligent inspection or testing of a product, negligent packaging, failure to warn of the dangerous propensities of a product, and so forth. It is important to note that in a negligence lawsuit only a party who was actually negligent is liable to the plaintiff.

Example Assume that the purchaser of a motorcycle is injured in an accident. The accident occurred because a screw was missing from the motorcycle. How does the buyer prove who was negligent? Was it the manufacturer, which left out the screw during the assembly of the motorcycle? Was it the retailer, who negligently failed to discover the missing screw while preparing the motorcycle for sale? Was it the mechanic, who failed to replace the screw after repairing the motorcycle? To be successful, the plaintiff must prove that the defendant breached a duty of due care to the plaintiff and thereby caused the plaintiff's injuries. In other words, the plaintiff must prove that the defendant was at fault for causing his or her injuries. Negligence remains a viable, yet sometimes difficult, theory on which to base a product liability action.

In the following case, the court found a defendant liable for a product defect.

CASE 6.1 *FEDERAL COURT CASE Product Liability*

Bilenky v. Ryobi Technologies, Inc.

115 F.Supp.3d 661, 2015 U.S. Dist. Lexis 83564 (2015)
United States District Court for the Eastern District of Virginia

"There is nothing in the laws of the United States that requires a jury to leave its common sense in the public corridors of the courthouse when it gathers to deliberate."

—Raymond Jackson, District Judge

Facts

Frank Wright purchased a lawn tractor at Home Depot, Inc. that was branded with the name "Ryobi." When Frank Wright was operating the Ryobi lawn tractor it caught on fire. His wife testified that she heard a very loud noise and looked outside and saw her husband and the lawn tractor consumed in flames. Mr. Wright later died from injuries he suffered from the fire. The administrator of Wright's estate sued Ryobi to recover damages for negligence for selling a defective product. The jury found that a defective fuel tank system caused the fuel-fed fire that killed Wright. The jury held Ryobi liable and awarded the plaintiff $2.5 million. Ryobi made a motion to the U.S. district court for judgment as a matter of law.

Issue

Is Ryobi liable for negligence for selling a defective lawn tractor to Wright?

Language of the Court

Specifically, Plaintiff argues that it's common sense—if you put your name on a product you bear the responsibility for that product if it harms a consumer. Not only is it common sense, but it's a valid legal principle. This jury was presented with evidence that Mr. Wright purchased a tractor with the word "Ryobi" printed on its side. The Court finds that the jury was presented with legally sufficient evidence to support a negligence finding against Ryobi Technologies, Inc.

Decision

The U.S. district court upheld the jury's finding that Ryobi was negligent in placing a defective product in the marketplace. The court upheld the jury's award of damages of $2.5 million.

Critical Legal Thinking Questions

Is a company liable for a defect in a product that bears its brand name even though it did not manufacture the product? Did Ryobi act ethically in denying liability?

Product Liability: Misrepresentation

6.2 Describe how a defendant is liable for misrepresenting the quality of a product.

A buyer or lessee who is injured because a seller or lessor fraudulently misrepresented the quality of a product can sue the seller for the tort of **intentional misrepresentation**, also called **fraudulent misrepresentation** or **fraud** or **deceit**. Recovery is limited to persons who were injured because they relied on the misrepresentation.

Intentional misrepresentation occurs when a seller or lessor either (1) affirmatively misrepresents the quality of a product or (2) conceals a defect in it. Because most reputable manufacturers, sellers, and lessors do not intentionally misrepresent the quality of their products, fraud is not often used as the basis for product liability actions.

intentional misrepresentation
A tort in which a seller or lessor fraudulently misrepresents the quality of a product and a buyer is injured thereby. Also called *fraudulent misrepresentation* or *fraud* or *deceit*.

Product Liability: Strict Liability

6.3 Define the doctrine of *strict liability*.

In the landmark case ***Greenman v. Yuba Power Products, Inc.***,[1] the California Supreme Court adopted the doctrine of **strict liability** in tort as a basis for product

strict liability
A tort doctrine that makes manufacturers, distributors, wholesalers, retailers, and others in the chain of distribution of a defective product liable for the damages caused by the defect, *regardless of fault*.

liability actions. Most states have now adopted this doctrine as a basis for product liability actions. The doctrine of strict liability removes many of the difficulties for the plaintiff associated with other theories of product liability. This section examines the special features of the doctrine of strict liability.

The following feature discusses the doctrine of strict liability.

Critical Legal Thinking

Strict Liability—Liability Without Fault

Unlike negligence, strict liability does not require the injured person to prove that the defendant breached a duty of care. Strict liability is **liability without fault**. A seller or lessor can be found strictly liable even though he or she has exercised all possible care in the preparation and sale or lease of the product. The doctrine of strict liability applies to sellers and lessors of products who are engaged in the business of selling and leasing products. Strict liability may not be disclaimed.

All parties in the **chain of distribution** of a defective product are strictly liable for the injuries caused by that product. Thus, all manufacturers, distributors, wholesalers, retailers, lessors, and subcomponent manufacturers may be sued and assessed liability under the doctrine of strict liability in tort.

The doctrine of strict liability is based on public policy. First, the injured party will have more parties from whom to recover damages for injuries. This is particularly important if the negligent party is out of business or does not have the money to pay the judgment. Second, lawmakers presume that sellers and lessors will insure against the risk of a strict liability lawsuit and spread the cost to their consumers by raising the price of their products. Third, parties in the chain of distribution may be more careful about the products they distribute.

Example Suppose a subcomponent tire manufacturer produces a defective tire and sells it to a truck manufacturer. The truck manufacturer places the defective tire on one of its new-model trucks. The truck is sold to a retail car dealership. Ultimately, the car dealership sells the truck to a buyer. Neither the truck manufacturer nor the car dealership could have determined that the tire was defective. The defective tire causes an accident in which the buyer is injured. All the parties in the tire's chain of distribution can be sued by the injured party; in this case, the liable parties are the subcomponent tire manufacturer, the truck manufacturer, and the car dealership.

A defendant who has not been negligent but who is made to pay a strict liability judgment can bring a separate action against the negligent party in the chain of distribution to recover losses.

Critical Legal Thinking Questions

What is the doctrine of strict liability? Why do states recognize this doctrine? Should sellers and lessors of products who did not make the product be held liable for injuries caused by a product produced by a manufacturer?

---

chain of distribution
All manufacturers, distributors, wholesalers, retailers, lessors, and subcomponent manufacturers involved in a transaction.

Strict liability applies only to products, not to services. In hybrid transactions that involve both services and products, the dominant element of the transaction dictates whether strict liability applies.

Example In a medical operation that requires a doctor to insert an electronic pacemaker to help a patient's heart pump blood regularly, the surgical operation would be the dominant element and the provision of the pacemaker would not be the dominant element. Therefore, the doctor would not be liable for strict liability if the pacemaker is defective and fails, causing injury to the patient. However, the manufacturer and seller of the defective pacemaker (a product) would be strictly liable.

Critical Legal Thinking Questions
What is the public policy for holding parties in the chain of distribution of a product strictly liable *without fault*? What can sellers and lessors of products do to protect against liability for some other party's negligence?

Strict liability does not apply to casual sales and transactions by nonmerchants. Thus, a person who sells a defective product to a neighbor in a casual sale is not strictly liable if the product causes injury.

Exhibit 6.1 compares the doctrines of negligence and strict liability.

Parties Who Can Recover for Strict Liability

Because strict liability is a tort doctrine, **privity of contract** between the plaintiff and the defendant is not required. In other words, the doctrine applies even if the injured party had no contractual relations with the defendant. Thus,

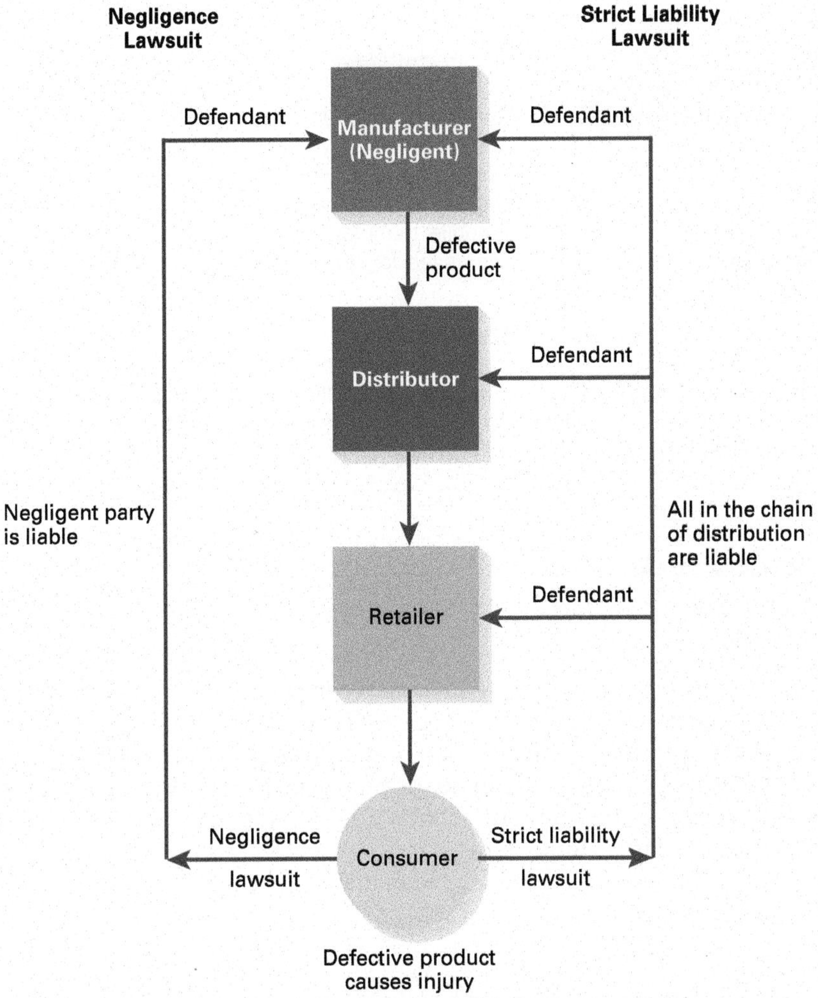

Exhibit 6.1 NEGLIGENCE AND STRICT LIABILITY COMPARED

manufacturers, distributors, sellers, and lessors of a defective product are liable to the consumer who purchased the product and any user of the product. Users include the purchaser or lessee, family members, guests, employees, customers, and persons who passively enjoy the benefits of the product (e.g., passengers in automobiles).

The manufacturer, distributor, seller, and lessor of a defective product are also liable to third-party bystanders injured by the defective product. The courts have stated that bystanders who are injured by a defective product should be entitled to the same protection as consumers or users. Bystanders and nonusers do not have the opportunity to inspect products for defects that have caused their injury.

Damages Recoverable for Strict Liability

The damages recoverable in a strict liability action vary by jurisdiction. Damages for personal injuries are recoverable in all jurisdictions that have adopted the doctrine of strict liability, although some jurisdictions limit the dollar amount of the award. Property damage is recoverable in most jurisdictions, but economic loss (e.g., lost income) is recoverable in only a few jurisdictions.

The following feature discusses punitive damages.

Ethics

Punitive Damages

In product liability cases, a court can award **punitive damages** if it finds that the defendant's conduct was committed with intent or with reckless disregard for human life. Punitive damages are meant to punish the defendant and to send a message to the defendant (and other companies) that such behavior will not be tolerated.

Example An automobile manufacturer realizes that one of its vehicle models has a defect in the braking mechanism. If the automobile manufacturer does not notify the owners of this type of vehicle of the defect and someone is injured because of the defect, the manufacturer will be liable for compensatory damages for the injuries caused to the injured party. The automobile manufacturer will most likely be assessed punitive damages for its callous disregard for the safety of the public.

Ethics Questions

What are punitive damages? When are punitive damages awarded in a product liability case? Do you think that the imposition of punitive damages has a deterrent effect on illegal and unethical conduct by business?

punitive damages
Monetary damages that are awarded to punish a defendant who either intentionally or recklessly injured the plaintiff.

product defect
Something wrong, inadequate, or improper in the manufacture, design, packaging, warning, or instructions about a product.

Product Defects

6.4 List the types of product defects upon which a strict liability lawsuit may be based.

To recover for strict liability, the injured party must show that the product that caused the injury was somehow *defective*. (Remember that the injured party does not have to prove who caused the product to become defective.) A **product defect** is something wrong, inadequate, or improper in the manufacture, design, packaging, warning, or instructions about a product. Plaintiffs can allege multiple product defects in one lawsuit.

A product can be found to be defective in many ways. The most common types of product defects are:

- Defect in manufacture
- Defect in design
- Failure to warn
- Defect in packaging
- Failure to provide adequate instructions

The feature on the following page discusses the risk–utility test and consumer expectation test that are used in evaluating whether a product is defective.

The types of defects subject to strict liability are discussed in the following sections.

Defect in Manufacture

6.5 Describe defects in manufacture.

defect in manufacture
A defect that occurs when a manufacturer fails to (1) assemble a product properly, (2) test a product properly, or (3) check the quality of the product adequately.

A **defect in manufacture** occurs when the manufacturer fails to (1) assemble a product properly, (2) test a product properly, or (3) check the quality of a product adequately.

Example American Ladder Company designs, manufactures, and sells ladders. While manufacturing a ladder, a worker at the company fails to insert one of the screws that would support one of the steps of the ladder. The ladder is sold to Weingard Distributor, a wholesaler, which sells it to Reynolds Hardware Store, which ultimately sells the ladder to Heather, a consumer. When Heather is on the ladder painting her house, the step of the ladder breaks because of the missing screw, and Heather falls and is injured. The missing screw is an example of a defect in manufacture. Under the doctrine of strict liability, American Ladder Company, Weingard Distributor, and Reynolds Hardware Store are liable for Heather's injury.

WEB EXERCISE
Use **www.google.com** and check to see whether your state uses the risk–utility test or consumer expectation test for strict liability lawsuits.

Contemporary Environment

Risk–Utility Test and Consumer Expectation Test

In evaluating whether a product's design, warnings, packaging, or instructions are defective, a court may apply either of the following tests, depending on the state:

1. **Risk–utility test.** In determining whether a defect exists, the **risk–utility test** requires the court to consider the gravity of the danger posed by the design or warning, the likelihood that injury will occur, the social utility of the product, the availability and cost of producing a safer alternative design that remains functional and reasonably priced, the ability of the user to avoid injury by careful use of the product, and other factors. The risk–utility test is basically a cost-benefit analysis that assesses a product's risk versus its utility. The risk–utility test usually requires a plaintiff to present proof of a feasible alternative design or warning.
2. **Consumer expectation test.** In determining whether a defect exists, the **consumer expectation test** requires the plaintiff to demonstrate that the product is more dangerous than a reasonable consumer would expect. This test asks whether a consumer would reasonably appreciate a product's danger and its potential to cause injury. Basically, the test asks a jury to determine whether the product's design or warning works as safely as a reasonable consumer would expect.

Approximately two-thirds of the states use the risk–utility test in strict liability lawsuits involving defect in design, failure to warn, defect in packaging, and failure to provide adequate instructions claims. The remaining states use the consumer expectation test for these cases. The consumer expectation test is used to establish whether a product has a manufacturing defect.

Defect in Design

6.6 Describe defects in design.

A **defect in design** can support a strict liability action. A defect in design occurs when a product is designed incorrectly and could have reasonably been designed to be safer. In design defect cases, often all of the same product line will contain the defect. In this case, not just one item has a defect, but all products bearing the same design are defective and can cause injury.

defect in design
A defect that occurs when a product is designed improperly.

Example All of the vehicles of a certain make and model of an electric automobile have the same defectively designed one-pedal driving system.

Many design defects that have supported strict liability awards include consumer products such as home appliances, personal care products, furniture, tools, automobiles and other vehicles, electronic devices, and such.

Example An action-figure doll for children is designed, manufactured, and sold to consumers. However, the toy is defective because it has breakable parts that can be swallowed by children, which can cause injury. This is a design defect because *all* the toys of this figure are improperly designed with the breakable parts. Children who are injured by the breakable parts can recover damages for their injuries. Here, all the parties in the chain of distribution—the manufacturer of the defective toy, and the distributors, wholesalers, and retailers who sold the toy—are strictly liable.

WEB EXERCISE
Go to website of the U.S. Consumer Product Safety Commission at **www.cpsc.gov/Recalls**. Read the information about the first five items on the list that have been recalled.

In the following case, the court applied the consumer expectation test in finding a design defect.

Crashworthiness Doctrine

Often, when an automobile is involved in an accident, the driver or passengers are not injured by the blow itself. Instead, they are injured when their bodies strike something inside their own automobile (e.g., the dashboard or the steering wheel). This is commonly referred to as the "second collision." The courts have held that automobile manufacturers are under a duty to design automobiles to take into account the possibility of this second collision. This is called the **crashworthiness doctrine**.

crashworthiness doctrine
A doctrine that says that automobile manufacturers are under a duty to design automobiles so that they take into account the possibility of harm from a person's body striking something inside the automobile in the case of a car accident.

CASE 6.2 *STATE COURT CASE Defect in Design*

Ford Motor Company v. Trejo

402 P.3d 649 (2017)
Supreme Court of Nevada

"In Nevada, claims of design defect are governed by the consumer-expectation test."

—Lidia Stiglich, Justice

Facts

Teresa Trejo, a resident of Las Vegas, was driving a Ford Excursion SUV with a trailer attached. Her husband, Rafael Trejo, was seated in the passenger seat. While driving on the highway, Trejo attempted to change lanes to make room for merging traffic. When the trailer attached to the Excursion started to fishtail, Trejo swerved, and the Excursion rolled over 1.5 to 2.5 times, then came to rest upside down. A couple driving by assisted Rafael from the vehicle, but his injuries were severe, and emergency services pronounced him dead at the scene.

Teresa Trejo sued Ford Motor Company for strict liability, alleging that the roof of the Excursion was not properly designed to withstand rollover accidents. Ford's internal guidelines required that a vehicle weighing 8,500 pounds have a roof strength-to-weight ratio of 1.725 pounds. Although the gross vehicle weight of the Excursion was 8,600 pounds, thus exceeding the 8,500-pound threshold, the strength-to-weight ratio of the Excursion was only 1.25 pounds. At trial, Ford conceded that it did not perform any physical roof-crush tests on the Excursion. Further, Trejo produced evidence that Ford could have reinforced the roof of the Excursion for an additional $70 in production costs.

The court instructed the jury that the consumer expectation standard applied to strict liability cases. The jury found that the roof of the Ford Excursion was defective in design and awarded Trejo $4.5 million in damages. Ford appealed.

Issue

Was the roof of the Ford Excursion SUV defectively designed?

Language of the Court

In Nevada, claims of design defect are governed by the consumer expectation test. Defective products are more dangerous than would be contemplated by the ordinary user having the ordinary knowledge available in the community. Trejo presented sufficient evidence for a jury to conclude that the level of protection actually provided by the roof in a rollover accident was less than would be expected by a reasonable consumer. Trejo also presented evidence sufficient to demonstrate that Rafael Trejo's death was caused by this defect.

Decision

The Supreme Court of Nevada affirmed the trial court's finding that there was a defect in design of the roof of the Ford Excursion.

Critical Legal Thinking Questions

What is the consumer expectation test? Is this a fair standard for determining whether a product is defective?

Example Failure of an automobile manufacturer to design an automobile to protect occupants from foreseeable dangers caused by a second collision when the automobile is involved in an accident subjects the manufacturer and car dealer who sold the vehicle to strict liability.

Failure to Warn

6.7 Describe defects of failure to warn.

Certain products are inherently dangerous and cannot be made any safer and still accomplish the purpose for which they are designed. Many such products have risks and side effects caused by their use. Manufacturers and sellers owe a duty to warn consumers and users about the dangers of using these products. A proper and conspicuous warning placed on the product insulates the manufacturer and others in the chain of distribution from strict liability. **Failure to warn** of these dangerous propensities is a defect that supports a strict liability action.

failure to warn
A defect that occurs when a manufacturer does not place a warning on the packaging of products that could cause injury if the danger is unknown to potential consumers.

Example Prescription medicine must contain warnings of its *side effects*. That way, a person can make an informed decision whether to use the medicine or not. If a manufacturer produces a prescription medicine but fails to warn about its known side effects, any person who uses the medicine and suffers from the side effects can sue and recover damages based on failure to warn.

The following case involves the issue of failure to warn.

CASE 6.3 *FEDERAL COURT CASE Failure to Warn*

Williams v. Manitowoc Cranes, L.L.C.

898 F.3d 607 (2018)
United States Court of Appeals for the Fifth Circuit

"There is no bright-line rule for whether a warning is adequate."
—Don Willett, Circuit Judge

Facts

John Williams Jr. worked as a crane operator at VT Halter Marine shipyard in Pascagoula, Mississippi. John typically operated a Manitowoc Model 16000 Series crawler crane, which crawls along tracks and can lift hundreds of tons of weight. The Model 16000 has a counterweight tray on its rear; the tray holds a stack of large steel counterweights. Each counterweight is roughly 7 feet wide, 8 feet long, and 9.5 inches tall, and weighs 18,000 pounds.

One day, John operated a Manitowoc Model 16000 in a tandem lift, which involved two cranes moving a bow section of a ship toward the hull of another ship under construction. Unexpectedly, the cranes began to separate from one another, and the other crane pulled John's crane forward, causing the tracks on John's crane to rise up. John stayed in the operator's cab and attempted to control the load, but within three minutes, the crane had toppled. As John's crane tipped over, the nine-ton counterweights stacked in the rear of the crane began to rain down, striking the operator's cab. The collision propelled John from the cab to the ground—an eight-foot, head-first fall onto concrete. John survived, but his physical and mental capacities were permanently impaired.

Wanda Williams, John's spouse, brought suit in U.S. district court against the crane manufacturer, Manitowoc Cranes, for product liability, alleging that Manitowoc failed to warn crane operators that when the Model 16000 crane tips over, the large weights stacked in the rear of the crane can slide forward and strike the operator's cab. The jury found Manitowoc liable for failure to warn and awarded the Williamses $2.8 million in economic damages and $600,000 in non-economic damages. Manitowoc appealed.

Issue

Is Manitowoc liable for failure to warn?

Language of the Court

There is no bright-line rule for whether a warning is adequate. The inadequacy dispute here centers on whether Manitowoc needed to warn operators about the specific hazard that counterweights could fall during a tip-over. Manitowoc never warned operators that unsecured counterweights could slide forward during a tip-over, striking the cab and potentially injuring the operator. Manitowoc knew about this risk yet said nothing. The jury had an adequate basis for finding Manitowoc's warning inadequate. Here, it took over three minutes for the crane to topple, which likely would have given John adequate time to leave the cab, walk down the catwalk, and descend the crane's stairs. We conclude the jury had an adequate basis for finding that an alternative warning could have communicated valuable additional information about the falling counterweight danger, allowing John to avoid injury.

Decision

The U.S. court of appeals upheld the district court's finding of failure to warn.

Critical Legal Thinking Questions

Do you think that the defendant needed to warn of the dangers of sliding counterweights, or was this danger obvious? If there is no bright-line rule for adequate warning, how did the court reach its decision?

Defect in Packaging

6.8 Describe defects in packaging.

Manufacturers owe a duty to design and provide safe packages for their products. This duty requires manufacturers to provide packages and containers that are tamperproof or that clearly indicate whether they have been tampered with. Certain manufacturers, such as drug manufacturers, owe a duty to place their products in containers that cannot be opened by children. A manufacturer's failure to meet this duty—a **defect in packaging**—subjects the manufacturer and others in the chain of distribution of the product to strict liability.

defect in packaging
A defect that occurs when a product has been placed in packaging that is insufficiently tamperproof.

Example A manufacturer that fails to place some form of tamperproof seal or identification on its product that notifies consumers if the product has been tampered with prior to sale is liable if a consumer is injured because the product has been tampered with by a third person (e.g., by poison placed in food items) before the item was sold to an innocent consumer who cannot determine if the product has been tampered with.

Other Defects

6.9 Describe other defects upon which a strict liability action may be brought.

Sellers are responsible for providing adequate instructions for the safe assembly and use of the products they sell. **Failure to provide adequate instructions** for the safe assembly and use of a product is a defect that subjects the manufacturer and others in the chain of distribution to strict liability.

failure to provide adequate instructions
A defect that occurs when a manufacturer does not provide detailed directions for safe assembly and use of a product.

Example A mother goes to a retailer and buys her 4-year-old daughter Lia a tricycle that has been manufactured by Bicycle Corporation. The tricycle comes in a box with many parts that need to be assembled. The instructions for assembly are vague and hard to follow. The mother puts together the tricycle, using these instructions. The first time Lia uses the tricycle, a pedal becomes loose and Lia's tricycle goes into the street, where she is hit and injured by an automobile. In this case, the Mother could sue Bicycle Corporation and the retailer on behalf of Lia for strict liability to recover damages for failing to provide adequate instructions.

Other defects that support a finding of product liability based on strict liability include inadequate testing of products, inadequate selection of component parts or materials, and improper certification of the safety of a product. The concept of "defect" is an expanding area of the law.

Defenses to Product Liability

6.10 List and describe the defenses that may be raised against a product liability claim.

Defendant manufacturers and sellers in negligence and strict liability actions may raise certain defenses to the imposition of liability. Some of the most common defenses are:

- **Generally known danger**. Certain products are inherently dangerous and are known to the general population to be so. Manufacturers and sellers are not strictly liable for failing to warn of a **generally known danger**.

  Example Because it is a known fact that guns shoot bullets, manufacturers and sellers of guns do not have to place a warning on the barrel of a gun warning of this generally known danger.

- **Government contractor defense**. Defense and other contractors that manufacture products to government specifications are not usually liable if such a product causes injury. This is called the **government contractor defense**.

generally known danger
A defense that acknowledges that certain products are inherently dangerous and are known to the general population to be so.

government contractor defense
A defense that provides that contractors that manufacture products to government specifications are not usually liable if such a product causes injury.

Example A manufacturer that produces a weapon to U.S. Army specifications is not liable if the weapon is defective and causes injury.

- **Abnormal misuse**. A manufacturer or seller is relieved of product liability if the plaintiff has been injured by an **abnormal misuse** of a product. This is a blatant misuse of a product that the manufacturer or seller did not intend, expect, or anticipate.

  Example A manufacturer or seller of a power lawn mower is not liable if a consumer lifts the power lawn mower on its side to cut a hedge and is injured when the lawn mower falls and cuts him.

  However, if a misuse of a product is **reasonably foreseeable misuse** and could easily and reasonably be designed to be prevented, then a manufacturer will not be absolved from liability caused by this preventable danger.

  Example Legal speed limits on highways and freeways in the United States usually vary from 55 mph to 75 mph. However, it is reasonably foreseeable that drivers often violate these laws and reach speeds exceeding 100 mph. A tire manufacturer must design its tires to be safe at these higher speeds.

abnormal misuse
A defense that relieves a seller of product liability if the user *abnormally* misused a product.

- **Supervening event**. The manufacturer or seller is not liable if a product is materially altered or modified after it leaves the seller's possession and the alteration or modification causes an injury. Such alteration or modification is called a **supervening event**.

  Example A seller is not liable if a consumer purchases a truck and then replaces the tires with large off-road tires that cause the truck to roll over, injuring the driver or another person.

supervening event
An alteration or a modification of a product by a party in the chain of distribution that absolves all prior sellers from strict liability.

- **Assumption of the risk**. The doctrine of **assumption of the risk** can be asserted as a defense to a product liability action. For this defense to apply, the defendant must prove that (1) the plaintiff knew and appreciated the risk and that (2) the plaintiff voluntarily assumed the risk.

  Example A prescription drug manufacturer warns of the dangerous side effects of taking a prescription drug. A user is injured by a disclosed side effect. The user assumed the disclosed risk and therefore the manufacturer is not liable for product liability.

The following case illustrates a claim of abnormal misuse of a product.

CASE 6.4 *STATE COURT CASE Misuse of a Product*

Campbell Hausfeld/Scott Fetzer Company v. Johnson

109 N.E.3d 953 (2018)
Supreme Court of Indiana

"We hold that misuse is a complete defense."
—Steven David, Justice

Facts

Campbell Hausfeld/Scott Fetzer Company designs and sells power tools to consumers. Paul Johnson purchased a Campbell Hausfeld mini air die grinder, which is an eight-inch, handheld, air-powered tool intended for grinding, polishing, deburring, and smoothing sharp surfaces. Different attachments can be used with the grinder. The grinder comes with warnings and instructions, including (1) an instruction to wear safety glasses, (2) a warning not to use a cut-off disc attachment unless a safety guard is in place, and (3) a warning not to use attachments rated below 25,000 RPM, which is the rating of the grinder. The product packaging and manual contain these warnings.

(continued)

Johnson decided to help install new headlights on a friend's truck, which required him to use a cut-off disc to cut openings to accommodate larger headlights. While cutting the openings, Johnson wore his prescription glasses but did not wear safety glasses; he used a cut-off disc without putting a safety guard in place; and he used an attachment that was rated 19,000 RPM, which did not meet the required minimum of 25,000 RPM. While Johnson was using the grinder, the cut-off disc came apart and a piece struck him on the left side of his face, breaking his eyeglasses and causing serious injury to his face and eye. Johnson ultimately lost his left eye. Johnson sued Campbell Hausfeld for product liability, alleging that the grinder was defectively designed and that the company failed to warn him of the possible dangers. The company asserted that Johnson's misuse of the grinder was an abnormal misuse and a complete defense to liability. The trial court found that Johnson had misused the grinder and granted summary judgment to Campbell Hausfeld. Johnson appealed.

Issue

Was Johnson's misuse of the grinder a complete defense against liability?

Language of the Court

We hold that misuse is a complete defense. Johnson's injuries could have been avoided had he followed the instructions, and Campbell Hausfeld could not reasonably expect that a consumer would misuse the grinder in three distinct ways. The instructions on the grinder warn users to use attachments rated for a minimum of 25,000 RPM, and Johnson disregarded this warning as the cut-off disc he used was rated for 19,000 RPM. Had Johnson used a guard and safety glasses, his injuries would have been avoided. His multiple failures to follow the grinder's instructions were the cause of his injuries, and taken together, could not reasonably be expected by a seller.

Decision

The Supreme Court of Indiana affirmed the trial court's grant of summary judgment to Campbell Hausfeld.

Critical Legal Thinking Questions

Should misuse of a product be a defense to liability? Do you think that the finding of misuse was appropriate in this case?

Statute of Limitations

Most states have a **statute of limitations** that requires an injured person to bring an action within a certain number of years from the time that he or she was injured by a defective product. If the plaintiff does not bring the lawsuit in the allotted time, he or she loses the right to sue.

statute of repose
A statute that limits the seller's liability to a certain number of years from the date when the product was first sold.

Example Assume that a state statute of limitations for strict liability is two years. The plaintiff is injured by a defective product on May 1, 2021. The plaintiff must sue the defendant by May 1, 2023. After that date, the plaintiff loses his right to sue the defendant.

The following feature discusses statutes of repose.

Business Environment

Statute of Repose

Manufacturers, sellers, and lessors of products have long complained that they should not be held liable for injuries that occur from the use of their products many years after the product was first sold or leased. In response to these complaints, many states have enacted a **statute of repose**, which limits a manufacturer's, seller's, and lessor's liability to a certain number of years from the date when the product was first sold. The period of repose varies from state to state.

Example Assume that a state's statute of repose for product liability is seven years. If a party purchases or leases a product on May 1, 2021, the statute of repose expires May 1, 2028. If an individual is injured from the use of the product following that date, the manufacturer, seller, and lessor are relieved of liability.

CONCEPT SUMMARY

STATUTE OF LIMITATIONS AND STATUTE OF REPOSE

Statute	Begins to Run
Statute of limitations	When the plaintiff suffers injury
Statute of repose	When the product is first sold

Plaintiff Partially at Fault

Sometimes a person who is injured by a defective product is negligent and contributes to his or her own injuries. States have adopted one of three doctrines to apply where a plaintiff is partially at fault in a product liability action: *contributory negligence, comparative negligence*, and *partial comparative negligence*. These doctrines are discussed in the following paragraphs.

Contributory Negligence

Under the doctrine of **contributory negligence**, a party who is partially at fault for causing her own injuries is barred from recovering damages from the defendant in a product liability action.

contributory negligence
A defense that says that a person who is injured by a defective product but has been negligent and has contributed to his or her own injuries cannot recover from the defendant.

Example An automobile manufacturer produces a car with a design defect, and a consumer purchases the car from an automobile dealer. The consumer is injured in an automobile accident in which the defect is found to be 75 percent responsible for the accident, and the consumer's negligent driving is found to be 25 percent responsible. Under the doctrine of contributory negligence, the plaintiff cannot recover damages from the defendant.

Comparative Negligence

Many states apply the doctrine of **comparative negligence**, also known as **comparative fault**, to product liability actions. Under this doctrine, where a plaintiff has been partially responsible for causing his own injuries, liability is assessed *proportionately* to the degree of fault of each party. Under this doctrine, damages are apportioned according to fault.

comparative negligence (comparative fault)
A doctrine that applies to strict liability actions that says a plaintiff who is contributorily negligent for his or her injuries is responsible for a proportional share of the damages.

Example An automobile manufacturer produces a car with a failure to warn defect, and a consumer purchases the car from an automobile dealer. The consumer is injured in an automobile accident in which the defect is found to be 75 percent responsible for the accident, and the consumer's negligent driving is found to be 25 percent responsible. The plaintiff suffers $1 million worth of injuries. Under the doctrine of comparative negligence, the plaintiff would recover $750,000 from the defendants (75 percent of $1 million).

Partial Comparative Negligence

Several states have adopted **partial comparative negligence**, also called **modified comparative negligence**, which provides that if a plaintiff is less than 50 percent responsible for causing her own injuries, the plaintiff may recover damages under the doctrine of comparative negligence; if the plaintiff is 50 percent or more responsible for causing her injuries, then the doctrine of contributory negligence applies, and the plaintiff recovers nothing.

The following feature applies the doctrine of comparative negligence.

Critical Legal Thinking

Comparative Fault Doctrine

E-Z-GO, a division of Textron, Inc., makes various utility vehicles, including the ST 350 Workhorse, which is derived from E-Z-GO's ubiquitous golf-cart designs but is intended for use in other contexts, such as farming and ranching. A key is used to turn on the Workhorse's electrical system, but the key does not start the engine; pushing the accelerator floor pedal turns on the engine and propels the vehicle. The floor pedal also contains a parking brake, which is engaged by pressing down on the pedal, which shuts off the engine and stops the vehicle in place, allowing the driver to leave the vehicle. To restart the vehicle, the operator presses the floor pedal to (1) turn on the engine; (2) release the parking brake; and (3) accelerate the vehicle.

Gini and Robert Nester owned and used a Workhorse on their Texas ranch. One afternoon, Gini set out on the Workhorse to feed and move a group of cattle; she had a 50-pound bag of cattle feed on the Workhorse's floorboard. Once Gini reached a gate, she applied the parking brake and exited the vehicle. The cattle knocked the feed bag onto the accelerator, causing the Workhorse to run over Gini. She was pinned to the ground and unable to move or call for help; her husband found her four hours later. The injury fractured vertebrae in Gini's neck, rendering her quadriplegic and in need of constant care.

The Nesters sued Textron in U.S. district court, alleging that the pedal system was defectively designed. The jury found that placing the accelerator and parking brake on the same pedal was a design defect that created an unreasonable risk of unintended acceleration. The jury awarded $15 million, finding that Textron was 50 percent at fault and that Gini was negligent and was 50 percent at fault. Applying the doctrine of comparative negligence, the Nesters were awarded one-half of the damages.

On appeal, the U.S. court of appeals upheld the finding of design defect, the award of damages, and the apportioning of damages pursuant to the doctrine of comparative fault. *Nester v. Textron, Incorporated*, 888 F.3d 151 (United States Court of Appeals for the Fifth Circuit, 2018)

Critical Legal Thinking Questions

What does the doctrine of comparative fault provide? Do you think that it reaches a fair result? Which of the following doctrines do you prefer: contributory negligence, comparative negligence, or partial comparative negligence?

CONCEPT SUMMARY

CONTRIBUTORY NEGLIGENCE AND COMPARATIVE FAULT

Doctrine	Description
Contributory negligence	A person who is partially responsible for causing his or her own injuries may not recover anything from the manufacturer or seller of a defective product.
Comparative negligence	A person who is partially responsible for causing his or her own injuries is responsible for a proportional share of the damages. The manufacturer or seller of the defective product is responsible for the remainder of the plaintiff's damages.
Partial comparative negligence	A person who is less than 50 percent responsible for causing his or her own injuries may recover damages under the doctrine of comparative negligence; if a person is 50 percent or more responsible for causing his or her own injuries, then the doctrine of contributory negligence applies, and the plaintiff recovers nothing.

Key Terms and Concepts

Abnormal misuse (123)
Assumption of the risk (123)
Chain of distribution (116)
Comparative negligence (comparative fault) (125)
Consumer expectation test (119)
Contributory negligence (125)
Crashworthiness doctrine (119)
Defect in design (119)
Defect in manufacture (118)
Defect in packaging (122)
Failure to provide adequate instructions (122)
Failure to warn (121)
Generally known danger (122)
Government contractor defense (122)
Greenman v. Yuba Power Products, Inc (115)
Intentional misrepresentation (fraudulent misrepresentation or fraud or deceit) (115)
Liability without fault (116)
Negligence (unintentional tort or ordinary negligence) (114)
Partial comparative negligence (modified comparative negligence) (125)
Privity of contract (116)
Product defect (118)
Product liability (114)
Punitive damages (118)
Reasonably foreseeable misuse (123)
Risk–utility test (119)
Statute of limitations (124)
Statute of repose (124)
Strict liability (115)
Supervening event (123)

Critical Legal Thinking Cases

6.1 Defect in Design Victoria Berridge, Robert Cook, Robert Walsh, and the pilot, Scott Cowan, boarded a Twin Otter airplane for a skydiving expedition. Shortly after takeoff, the right engine failed and the airplane crashed. All four persons aboard the airplane died because of the crash. Plaintiffs, the decedents' parents, filed a strict liability lawsuit for wrongful death against Doncasters, Inc., a company that manufactured the blades used in the turbine engines of the airplane. Plaintiffs introduced evidence at trial that showed that the blades manufactured by Doncasters were defective because the aluminide coating and base metal alloy used in the blades made the blades unsafe for use in the airplane's engine. Plaintiffs' expert witnesses testified that the coating used by Doncasters was prone to cracking and that the base metal alloy had low oxidation resistance, both of which made Doncasters' blades defective. Other evidence showed that the blades had never passed a required 150-hour endurance test before they were installed. The parents sought compensatory damages for each of the deceased parties as well as punitive damages against Doncasters. Is Doncasters, Inc. strictly liable for the death of the deceased parties of the airplane crash because of a defect in design of the blades used in the engine of the crashed airplane? Is Doncasters liable for punitive damages? *Delacroix v. Doncasters, Inc.*, 407 S.W.3d 13, 2013 Mo. App. Lexis 567 (Missouri Court of Appeals, 2013)

6.2 Defect in Manufacture Western Manufacturing, Incorporated manufactures a mobile pump for the commercial application of stucco to buildings. The pump consists of a diesel engine, a mixer for the stucco, a batch hopper, a pumping mechanism, and a hose, all mounted on a two-wheel trailer that can be hitched to a truck. The pump pulls slurry from the hopper into a thick 250-foot-long rubber hose for application. The slurry is made with cement and water in the mixer and then added to the hopper. A fitting lock attaches the hose in place. Dorel Roman is a stucco subcontractor. About 15 minutes after one of Roman's workers had started using the pump to spray stucco on a building, the high-pressure hose dislodged and struck Roman, who was 20 feet from the hose, causing severe injuries to Roman's legs. Roman sued Western for strict liability to recover damages for his injuries. Roman alleged that the mobile pump contained a defect in construction when it was produced by Western that caused the hose to dislodge, thus causing Roman's injuries. Roman introduced expert witnesses who testified that the pump had been improperly manufactured by Western and that there was a defect in manufacture. Is Western Manufacturing strictly liable for Roman's injuries based on a defect in manufacture? *Roman v. Western Manufacturing, Incorporated*, 691 F.3d 686, 2012 U.S. App. Lexis 17353 (United States Court of Appeals for the Fifth Circuit, 2012)

6.3 Design Defect Dwayne Maddox and his wife, Amanda, were driving home on a highway in their Nissan Pathfinder SUV. Dwayne, who was driving the vehicle, weighed 170 pounds, and Amanda, who was sitting in the passenger seat, weighed 240 pounds. Amanda had previously had a gastric bypass surgery to help control her weight. Both were wearing their seat belts. Another driver, Edward Sapp, who was greatly intoxicated, drove his vehicle on the wrong side of the highway and collided head-on with Maddoxes' SUV. Sapp died at the scene. Dwayne exited the SUV and suffered a shattered right heel. Amanda, however, was trapped inside the front passenger seat, and rescuers needed to extricate her from the vehicle with hydraulic equipment. Amanda was transported to a medical center. Amanda's seat belt did not properly protect her and her abdomen ruptured at the site of a prior gastric bypass surgery. Amanda's injuries were extensive. She suffered fractures of her sternum, several ribs, vertebrae, and hip. Amanda was hospitalized for 139 days, had 75 surgical procedures, was unable to eat food for seven months, and was medically required to keep an open abdominal wound—with her internal organs visible—during part of the time she was hospitalized. Amanda sued Nissan Motor Company, Ltd., the company that manufactured the Nissan Pathfinder SUV that she and her husband were in at the time of the accident, to recover damages for strict liability based on an alleged defect in design of the seat belt restraint system of the SUV. Amanda alleged that Nissan designed its seat belt restraint system to protect persons weighing approximately 171 pounds, that the restraint system was not properly designed to protect a person of her weight, and that Nissan should be found strictly liable for a design defect for not designing its seat belt restraint system to safely protect persons of her weight. Is Nissan strictly liable for failing to design a seat belt restraint system to safely protect heavier persons in vehicle collisions? *Nissan Motor Company, Ltd. v. Maddox*, 486 S.W.3d 838 (Supreme Court of Kentucky, 2016)

6.4 **Supervening Event** Cincinnati Incorporated (Cincinnati) manufactures a hydraulic press brake, a machine tool commonly used to shape sheet metal. The tool consists of a hydraulic ram that presses the metal, and a die onto which the metal is pressed. The operator feeds sheet metal between the die and the ram, and the ram descends to bend the sheet metal. The press is operated by a foot pedal, known as a footswitch. As originally sold by Cincinnati, the press was equipped with a footswitch that had a front flap, or gate, to prevent accidental depression. The operator had to lift the gate with his or her foot to access the enclosed pedal. The press also came equipped with two footswitches, each of which had to be depressed simultaneously by two different operators in order to trigger the ram. When the press was first sold by Cincinnati to a company named Steelgard, this safety equipment was in place. The press was sold several times to other companies before Ventaire, Inc. acquired it 20 years after it was manufactured. Sometime between the press's original sale and its sale to Ventaire, the original footswitches were removed and replaced with footswitches that did not have a gate. In addition, one of the footswitches had been disabled so that the press could be operated with a single footswitch unprotected by any gate. The press still contained the original conspicuous signs that warned the operator not to place his or her hands in the press and that his or her fingers or hands could be crushed if he or she did so.

While Derek Braswell, an employee of Ventaire, was operating the press, he reached into the die area of the press with his right hand to remove a jammed piece of metal. While doing so, he accidentally stepped on the footswitch, triggering the ram's descent and crushing his right arm, which was later amputated. Braswell filed a strict liability lawsuit against Cincinnati to recover damages for his injuries, alleging that Cincinnati's press was designed defectively. In its defense, Cincinnati asserted that the press was designed properly and equipped with safety features when it was first sold, which would have prevented this type of accident, and that the removal and disabling of the safety features was a supervening event such that it is not responsible for Braswell's injuries. Is Cincinnati liable in strict liability for a design defect? *Braswell v. Cincinnati Incorporated*, 731 F.3d 1081, 2013 U.S. App. Lexis 19451 (United States Court of Appeals for the Tenth Circuit, 2013)

6.5 **Design Defect** Intex Recreation designed and sold the Sno-Tube II. This snow tube is ridden by a user down snow-covered hills and can reach a speed of 30 miles per hour. The snow tube has no steering device, and therefore a rider may end up spinning and going down a hill backwards. Dan Falkner bought a Sno-Tube II and went sledding with it. During Falkner's second run down the hill the tube rotated backward. A group of parents, including Tom Higgins, stood near the bottom of the hill. When Higgins saw 7-year-old Kyle Potter in the path of Falkner's speeding snow tube he ran and grabbed Potter to save him from harm, but while doing so the snow tube hit Higgins and threw him into the air. Higgins landed on his forehead, which snapped his head back, severed his spinal cord, and left him quadriplegic. Higgins sued Intex for strict liability based on the alleged design defect of the Sno-Tube. Evidence was introduced at trial that showed that the Sno-Tube had no guiding mechanism or steering device to keep it from rotating while going downhill and that Intex could have put ridges on the bottom of the snow tube, which would have prevented it from rotating. Was the Sno-Tube II defectively designed? *Higgins v. Intex Recreation Corporation*, 99 P.3d 421, 2004 Wash. Lexis 2424 (Court of Appeals of Washington, 2004)

6.6 **Failure to Warn** Joe and Loretta Franks purchased a pool liner from McMasker Enterprises, Inc. to use on their aboveground pool frame, which was 33 feet long, 18 feet wide, and 4 feet deep. The pool liner was manufactured by Hoffinger Industries, Inc. Joe built a deck around the pool at the level of the pool frame. The Franks attached to the pool the warning label provided by Hoffinger, which read "Caution—no diving—shallow water." The warning label was .75 inches wide and 5 inches long. Leesa Bunch, age 11, was using the

Franks' outdoor pool and dove into the pool. Bunch hit her head on the bottom of the pool and was rendered a quadriplegic by injuries sustained during the dive. Bunch sued Hoffinger for strict liability for failure to adequately warn her of the danger of diving into the pool. Evidence at trial against Hoffinger proved that during the past 17 years there had been 47 prior instances of persons becoming quadriplegic after diving into Hoffinger pools. Was there a defect of failure to warn? *Bunch v. Hoffinger Industries, Inc.*, 123 Cal.App.4th 1278, 20 Cal.Rptr.3rd 780, 2004 Cal. App. Lexis 1869 (Court of Appeal of California, 2004)

Ethics Cases

6.7 Ethics Case The minor victim, referred to simply as "CAP," sustained serious burns when he was 3 years old. CAP had just returned to his mother's home after an overnight visit with his father, Thor Polley. CAP found a cigarette lighter on the floor of his father's truck, and he took the lighter with him when he returned to his mother's home. After arriving to his mother's home, CAP lit the lighter, and his shirt caught on fire, and he was burned from the waist up. CAP was taken to the hospital, where he received treatment for second- and third-degree burns to his face and chest and underwent several skin graft surgeries. A black BIC cigarette lighter was found at the scene of the fire and delivered to Police Chief John Brady. The lighter was admitted into evidence at trial, where Chief Brady testified that the lighter was worn and that the legally required child safety guard had been removed from the lighter before it was taken into evidence. CAP's father, Thor, acknowledged that he usually bought BIC lighters and customarily removed the child safety guards from his lighters to make them easier to use.

The conservator for CAP sued BIC USA, Inc., the manufacturer of the lighter, to recover damages for the injuries suffered by CAP. BIC defended, alleging that the BIC lighter was not defective, and that a supervening event, namely, that someone had removed the child safety guard from the lighter, was the cause of CAP's injuries. In closing arguments to the jury, BIC's lawyer Edward H. Stopher made the following remarks: "Thor Polley made an intentional adult choice to disable that lighter. And by his testimony, he disabled it because he said it made it easier to light. It is undisputed that no one can make a foolproof lighter. No one, based on the evidence that we have heard, can make a Thor-proof lighter." Was the lighter defective, or was there a supervening event that discharged the claim of liability against BIC? Did BIC act ethically in denying liability? Did the plaintiff act ethically by suing BIC? *Cummins v. BIC USA, Inc.*, 727 F.3d 506, 2013 U.S. App. Lexis 16800 (United States Court of Appeals for the Sixth Circuit, 2013)

6.8 Ethics Case Genie Industries, Inc. manufactures and sells aerial lifts that are used to raise a worker on a platform to reach ceilings of tall buildings or other high places. One of these lifts is the AWP-40S, which is lightweight, portable, and designed for indoor work. It can pass through ordinary doorways and can be used in tight spaces. Before elevating the platform, operators must stabilize the machine by attaching four removable outriggers, one to each of the four corners of the base. The outriggers increase the lift's footprint and its stability, preventing it from tipping over. Four green lights signal the proper deployment of the outriggers. Several signs on the lift warn users not to release the lift's outriggers while it is in use. One sign, located at eye level on the machine, displays an image of a man pushing the lift while elevated, and states "DANGER: Tip-over hazard. Attempting to move the machine with platform raised will tip the machine over and cause death or serious injury." A similar warning appears in the lift's operating manual. The lift's design complies with federal Occupational Safety and Health Administration safety standards.

Gulf Coast Electric was hired by a church in Beaumont, Texas, to run electrical cables in the ceilings of the church. James Boggin and Walter Matak, Gulf Coast employees, used an AWP-40S to do the work. Matak stood on the platform of the AWP-40S to lay the cable in the ceiling. At first, each time the employees needed to reposition the lift to reach a different area, they lowered the platform, and Matak stepped down. Then they raised the outriggers, rolled the lift to another location, and redeployed the outriggers. Matak would step back onto the platform, the platform would be raised, and he would continue the work.

However, after some time, the employees decided to move the machine with Matak on the platform when the lift was extended to its full 40-foot height. After they raised two of the outriggers a few inches, the machine tipped over and crashed to the floor. Matak died of massive head injuries. Matak's survivors brought a civil wrongful death action against Genie Industries to recover damages, alleging that the AWP-40S was defectively designed. Was the Genie AWP-40S defectively designed? Did the plaintiffs act ethically in suing Genie Industries? *Genie Industries, Inc. v. Matak*, 462 S.W.3d 1, 2015 Tex. Lexis 437 (Supreme Court of Texas, 2015)

Notes

1. 59 Cal.2d 57, 377 P.2d 897, 27 Cal. Rptr. 697, 1963 Cal. Lexis 140 (Supreme Court of California).

CHAPTER

7

Intellectual Property and Information Technology

Maksim Kabakou/Shutterstock

INTELLECTUAL PROPERTY
The owners of copyrighted material such as books, movies, CDs, DVDs, and video games; the owners of trademarks such as McDonald's Corporation and Starbucks Corporation; the creators of patents such as Microsoft Corporation and Intel Corporation; the owners of trade secrets such as the Coca-Cola Corporation; and the owners of other intellectual property lose substantial revenues caused by the sale of knockoffs of their intellectual property. Computers and software programs have helped increase cyber-piracy of intellectual property. Intellectual property is protected by a variety of civil and criminal laws.

Learning Objectives

After studying this chapter, you should be able to:

7.1 Define *intellectual property* and list the types of intellectual property.

7.2 Define *trade secret* and describe the misappropriation of a trade secret.

7.3 Describe how an invention can be patented and the penalties for patent infringement.

7.4 Describe the items that can be copyrighted and describe the penalties for copyright infringement.

7.5 Define *trademark* and *service mark* and describe the penalties for trademark infringement.

7.6 Define *dilution* and describe the forms of dilution of a trademark.

“The Congress shall have the power . . . to promote the Progress of Science and useful Arts, by securing for limited Times to Authors and Inventors the exclusive Right to their respective Writings and Discoveries.”

—Article 1, Section 8, Clause 8 of the U.S. Constitution

Introduction to Intellectual Property and Information Technology

The U.S. economy is based on the freedom of ownership of property. In addition to real estate and personal property, *intellectual property rights* have value to both businesses and individuals. This is particularly the case in the modern era of the information age, computers, and the internet.

Federal law provides protections for intellectual property rights, such as trade secrets, patents, copyrights, and trademarks. Certain federal statutes provide for either civil damages or criminal penalties or both to be assessed against infringers of patents, copyrights, and trademarks. Federal and state law impose civil damages or criminal penalties or both against persons who misappropriate trade secrets.

And he that invents a machine augments the power of a man and the well-being of mankind.

Henry Ward Beecher
Proverbs from Plymouth Pulpit (1887)

This chapter discusses trade secrets, patents, copyrights, and trademarks and how to protect them from infringement, misappropriation, and cyber-piracy.

Intellectual Property

7.1 Define *intellectual property* and list the types of intellectual property.

intellectual property
Patents, copyrights, trademarks, and trade secrets. Federal and state laws protect intellectual property rights from misappropriation and infringement.

Intellectual property is a term that describes property that is developed through an intellectual and creative process. Intellectual property falls into a category of property known as *intangible rights*, which are not tangible physical objects.

Most persons are familiar with the fact that intellectual property includes trade secrets, patents, copyrights, and trademarks. For trade secrets, think of Coca-Cola Company’s secret recipe for making Coca-Cola. For patents, think of Microsoft’s patents on its operating system. Microsoft has obtained more than 10,000 patents. For copyrights, think of music, movies, books, and video games. Nike’s slogan “Just Do It” and Swoosh logo and McDonald’s Big Mac and “I’m lovin’ it” are recognizable trademarks. Patents, trademarks, and copyrights give their owners or holders monopoly rights for specified periods of time. Trade secrets remain valuable if they are not easily discovered.

Intellectual property is of significant value to companies in the United States and globally as well. Over one-half of the value of large companies in the United States is related to their intangible property rights. Some industries are intellectual property–intensive, such as the music and movie industries. Other industries that are not intellectual property–intensive, such as the automobile and food industries, are still highly dependent on their intellectual property rights.

Where a new invention promises to be useful, it ought to be tried.

Thomas Jefferson
(1743–1826) Third President of the United States

Because of their intangible nature, intellectual property rights are more subject to misappropriation than is tangible property. It is almost impossible to steal real estate, and it is often difficult to steal tangible property, such as equipment, furniture, and other personal property. However, intellectual property rights are much easier to misappropriate. Think of illegally downloaded copyrighted music, movies, and video games, and fake designer purses. In addition, computers and cyber-piracy make it easier to steal many forms of intellectual property. The misappropriation of intellectual property rights is one of the major threats to companies today.

Trade Secret

7.2 Define *trade secret* and describe the misappropriation of a trade secret.

Many businesses are successful because their **trade secrets** set them apart from their competitors. Trade secrets may be product formulas, patterns, designs, compilations of data, software algorithms, source codes, customer lists, supplier lists, ingredients, proprietary information, manufacturing processes, or other business secrets. Many trade secrets do not qualify to be—or simply are not—patented, copyrighted, or trademarked. Most states have adopted the **Uniform Trade Secrets Act** to give statutory protection to trade secrets.

trade secret
A product formula, pattern, design, compilation of data, customer list, or other business secret.

State laws allow the owner of a trade secret to bring a civil lawsuit for *misappropriation* against anyone who steals a trade secret. For the lawsuit to be actionable, the defendant must have obtained the trade secret through unlawful means, such as theft, bribery, or industrial espionage. No tort has occurred if there is no misappropriation.

More than 80 percent of trade secrets that are misappropriated are taken by employees and departing employees or business partners. Competitors often target another company's trade secrets. Trade secret theft is also global, with foreign companies and foreign governments using economic espionage and cyberattacks to steal trade secrets. Because most business documents are stored electronically, including trade secrets, they can easily be misappropriated by sending emails with attached information, copying information to flash drives and other portable storage devices, stealing information using smartphones, placing information in the cloud, and using other means of electronic theft.

The owner of a trade secret is obliged to take all reasonable precautions to prevent that secret from being discovered by others. If the owner fails to take such actions, the secret is no longer subject to protection under state unfair competition laws. Precautions to protect a trade secret may include fencing in buildings, placing locks on doors, hiring security guards, and the like.

Companies must also put in place cybersecurity protections to prevent the electronic theft of trade secrets, including monitoring email, preventing the use of portable or mobile devices in the workplace, installing systems to detect the use of portable storage devices, limiting access to trade secrets to certain management levels or persons with designated responsibilities, requiring the use of special passwords to access trade secret information, installing enhanced encryption to protect trade secrets, and such.

WEB EXERCISE
Use **www.google.com** to see whether you can find the purported secret recipe for original Coca-Cola posted on someone's website.

Example Trade secrets include KFC's recipe of 11 herbs and spices for the batter used on the Colonel's Original Recipe Kentucky Fried Chicken, McDonald's Big Mac special sauce, Bush's Baked Beans, and Twinkies; Google's search algorithm; and the formula for the lubricant WD-40.

Reverse Engineering

A competitor can lawfully discover a trade secret by **reverse engineering** (i.e., taking apart and examining a rival's product or re-creating a secret recipe). A competitor or other party who has reverse engineered a trade secret can use the trade secret but not the trademarked name used by the original creator of the trade secret.

Example An inventor invents a new formula for a perfume. The inventor decides not to get a patent for her new formula (because patent protection is good for only 20 years). Instead, the inventor chooses to try to protect it as a trade secret, which gives her protection for as long as she can successfully keep it a secret. Another party purchases the perfume, chemically analyzes it, and discovers the formula. The trade secret has been reverse engineered, and the second party may begin producing a perfume using the inventor's formula.

Misappropriation of a Trade Secret

Defend Trade Secrets Act (DTSA)
A federal statute that allows an owner of a trade secret to bring a civil lawsuit in federal court against a defendant for the misappropriation of a trade secret.

The owner of a trade secret can bring a *civil lawsuit* under state law against anyone who has misappropriated a trade secret through unlawful means, such as theft, bribery, industrial espionage, or electronic theft. Generally, a successful plaintiff in a **misappropriation of a trade secret** action can (1) recover the *profits* made by the offender from the use of the trade secret, (2) recover for *damages*, and (3) obtain an *injunction* prohibiting the offender from divulging or using the trade secret.

Prior to 2016, the owner of a trade secret could only use state law to sue for the misappropriation of a trade secret. The following feature discusses a federal law designed to protect trade secrets.

Information Technology

Defend Trade Secrets Act

In 2016, the U.S. government enacted the **Defend Trade Secrets Act (DTSA).**[1] The DTSA is a federal statute that allows an owner of a trade secret to bring a civil lawsuit in federal court against a defendant for the misappropriation of a trade secret. Thus, the DTSA creates a federal remedy for trade secret theft. Under the DTSA, a lawsuit must be brought within three years from the date the misappropriation is discovered or should have been discovered.

The DTSA provides extensive remedies for the misappropriation of trade secrets. The trade secret owner may recover as compensatory damages its actual loss plus any unjust enrichment obtained by the defendant from the use of the misappropriated secret. In the alternative, and where appropriate, the trade secret owner may recover a reasonable royalty for the unauthorized use of its trade secrets. If the misappropriation is willful or malicious, the trade secret owner may recover exemplary damages of not more than double the compensatory damages, as well as attorney's fees incurred in bringing the case. A federal court can issue an injunction to prevent threatened or further misappropriation of trade secrets.

The DTSA contains a unique provision that allows trade secret owners to seek, on an ex parte basis (i.e., without telling defendants), an order to seize allegedly stolen trade secret items in the defendant's possession. An *ex parte seizure order* may be issued by a federal court if the trade secret owner shows that it will suffer immediate and irreparable injury if a seizure order is not issued, the owner is likely to succeed on the merits at trial, and the party against whom the seizure is requested would destroy, move, hide, or make such matter inaccessible to the court if they were given notice.

The DTSA does not preempt existing state trade secret laws. Thus, a plaintiff has the option to pursue federal or state remedies, or to bring a state law claim alongside a federal claim.

Economic Espionage Act

Economic Espionage Act
A federal statute that makes it a crime for any person to convert a trade secret for his or her own or another's benefit, knowing or intending to cause injury to the owners of the trade secret.

Congress enacted the federal **Economic Espionage Act (EEA)**,[2] which makes it a federal *crime* to steal another's trade secrets. Under the EEA, it is a federal crime for any person to convert a trade secret to his or her benefit or for the benefit of others, knowing or intending that the act would cause injury to the owner of the trade secret. The definition of *trade secret* under the EEA is very broad and parallels the definition used under the civil laws of misappropriating a trade secret.

One of the major reasons for the passage of the EEA was to address the ease of stealing trade secrets through computer espionage and use of the internet. Confidential information can be downloaded onto a flash drive, placed in a pocket, and taken from the legal owner. Computer hackers can hack into a company's computers and steal customer lists, databases, formulas, and other trade secrets. The EEA is a very important weapon in addressing computer and internet espionage and penalizing those who commit it.

The EEA provides severe criminal penalties, including imposing prison sentences on individuals and assessing fines on individuals and organizations. The prison term for individuals and the criminal fines for organizations can be increased if the theft of a trade secret was made to benefit a foreign government.

Critical Legal Thinking Questions

Why did the founders of the United States place protections for inventors and writers in Article I of the U.S. Constitution? Have these protections become even more important in the current digital age?

Patent

7.3 Describe how an invention can be patented and the penalties for patent infringement.

When drafting the Constitution of the United States of America, the founders provided for protection of the work of inventors and writers. Article I, Section 8, of the Constitution provides, "The Congress shall have Power . . . To promote the Progress of Science and useful Arts, by securing for limited Times to Authors and Inventors the exclusive Right to their respective Writings and Discoveries." Pursuant to the express authority granted in the U.S. Constitution, Congress enacted the **Federal Patent Statute** of 1952 to provide for obtaining and protecting patents.[3]

Federal Patent Statute
A federal statute that establishes the requirements for obtaining a patent and protects patented inventions from infringement.

A **patent** is a grant by the federal government to the inventor of an invention for the exclusive right to use, sell, or license the invention for a limited amount of time.

patent
A grant by the federal government to the inventor of an invention for the exclusive right to use, sell, or license the invention for a limited amount of time.

Patent law is intended to provide an incentive for inventors to invent and make their inventions public and to protect patented inventions from infringement. Federal patent law is exclusive; there are no state patent laws. Applications for patents must be filed with the **U.S. Patent and Trademark Office (PTO)** in Washington DC. The PTO grants more than 300,000 patents each year.

U.S. Court of Appeals for the Federal Circuit

The **U.S. Court of Appeals for the Federal Circuit** in Washington DC was created in 1982. This is a special federal appeals court that hears appeals from the Patent Trial and Appeal Board of the U.S. Patent and Trademark Office and U.S. district courts concerning patent issues. This court of appeals was created to promote uniformity in patent law.

U.S. Court of Appeals for the Federal Circuit
A special federal appeals court that hears appeals from the Patent Trial and Appeal Board and U.S. district courts concerning patent issues.

Patent Application

To obtain a patent, a **patent application** must be filed with the PTO in Washington DC. The PTO provides for the online submission of patent applications and supporting documents through its EFS-Web system. A patent application must contain a written description of the invention. Patent applications are complicated. Therefore, an inventor should hire a patent attorney to assist in obtaining a patent for an invention.

The PTO must decide whether to grant a patent within three years from the date of filing a patent application. For the payment of approximately $5,000 inventors can move their patent application to the top of the list of other patent applications for review by the PTO and receive an answer within one year. The PTO can grant priority to patent applications for products, processes, or technologies that are important to the national economy or national competitiveness.

An inventor may file a **provisional application** with the PTO. This provisional right gives inventors three months to prepare and file a final and complete patent application.

provisional application
An application that an inventor may file with the PTO to obtain three months to prepare a final patent application.

Third parties may file a pre-issuance challenge to a pending patent application asserting that the sought-after patent is not patentable because it appeared in **prior art**. This could be a reference, description, or event in the past that demonstrates that the invention in question is not new. There is also a nine-month period after the issuance of a patent for a third party to seek post-grant review of a patent by submitting prior art references and other information that assert that the patent holder's claim is not patentable.

The patent system added the fuel of interest to the fire of genius.

Abraham Lincoln
(1809–1865) Sixteenth
President of the United States

The **Patent Trial and Appeal Board (PTAB)**, a section within the PTO, reviews adverse decisions by patent examiners, reviews reexaminations, conducts

Exhibit 7.1 PATENT APPLICATION FOR THE FACEBOOK SOCIAL NETWORKING SYSTEM

Source: United States Patent and Trademark Office

Systems and Methods for Social Mapping

Abstract

A system, method, and computer program for social mapping is provided. Data about a plurality of social network members is received. A first member of the plurality of social network members is allowed to identify a second member of the plurality of social network members with whom the first member wishes to establish a relationship. The data is then sent to the second member about the first member based on the identification. Input from the second member is received in response to the data. The relationship between the first member and the second member is confirmed based on the input in order to map the first member to the second member.

post-grant reviews, and conducts other patent challenge proceedings. By permitting pre-issuance and post-grant challenges within the PTO, the law attempts to have disputes resolved within the PTO before reaching the litigation stage.

Patent Number

If a patent is granted, the invention is assigned a **patent number**. Patent holders usually affix the word *patent* or *pat.* and the patent number on the patented article. A patent holder may mark an item "Patent" or "Pat" and direct a party to a freely accessible web address that identifies the product covered by the patent number. If a patent application is filed but a patent has not yet been issued, the applicant usually places the words **patent pending** on the article.

Exhibit 7.1 shows the abstract from the patent application for the Facebook social networking system (U.S. Patent 20070192299).

Subject Matter That Can Be Patented

utility patent
A patent that protects the functionality of the invention.

Most patents are **utility patents**; that is, they protect the functionality of the item. The term *patent* is commonly used in place of the words *utility patent*. Only certain subject matter can be patented. Federal patent law recognizes categories of innovation that can be patented, including:

- Machines (e.g., mechanical device, something with moving parts or circuitry)
- Processes (e.g., new way to manufacture glue)
- Article of manufacture (e.g., new tool)
- Compositions of matter (e.g., chemical pharmaceutical)
- Improvements to existing machines, processes, manufacture, or compositions of matter
- Asexually reproduced plants (e.g., newly developed plant breeds)
- Living material invented by a person (e.g., genetically modified organisms)

Laws of nature, abstract ideas, naturally occurring substances, mathematical formulas, and scientific principles cannot be patented. The Leahy-Smith America Invents Act (AIA) of 2011 prohibits any claim encompassing a human organism from being patented (e.g., human clone).

Example Einstein's theory of relativity ($E = mc^2$) cannot be patented.

For centuries, most patents involved tangible inventions and machines, such as the telephone and the light bulb. Next, chemical and polymer inventions were patented. Then biotechnology patents were granted. More recently, subject matter involving the computer, internet, and e-commerce has been added to what can be patented.

Requirements for Obtaining a Patent

To be patented, an invention must be (1) *novel*, (2) *useful*, and (3) *nonobvious*. An invention must meet all three of these requirements. If an invention is found not to meet any one of these requirements, it cannot be patented:

1. **Novel**. An invention is **novel** if it is new and has not been invented and used in the past. If an invention has been used in "prior art," it is not novel and cannot be patented.

   Example College and professional football games are often shown on television. It is often difficult, however, for a viewer to tell how far the offensive team must go to get a first down and keep possession of the football. Inventors invented a system whereby a colored line is digitally drawn across the football field at the distance that a team must go to obtain a first down. This invention qualified for a patent because it was novel.

2. **Useful**. An invention is **useful** if it has some practical purpose. If an invention has only theoretical benefit and no useful purpose, it cannot be patented.

   Example A cardboard or heavy paper sleeve that can be placed over the outside of a paper coffee cup so that the cup will not be too hot to hold serves a useful purpose. Many coffee shops use these sleeves. The sleeve serves a useful purpose and therefore qualifies to be patented.

3. **Nonobvious**. If an invention is **nonobvious**, it qualifies for a patent; if it is obvious, then it does not qualify for a patent.

   Example An applicant filed for and was granted a patent for a peanut butter and jelly sandwich with the crust removed from the bread. A court later rejected the patent for the sandwich as being obvious.

CONCEPT SUMMARY

REQUIREMENTS FOR OBTAINING A PATENT

1. **Novel**. An invention is novel if it is new and has not been invented and used in the past. If an invention has been used in "prior art," it is not novel and cannot be patented.
2. **Useful**. An invention is useful if it has some practical purpose. If an invention has only theoretical benefit and no useful purpose, it cannot be patented.
3. **Nonobvious**. If an invention is nonobvious, it qualifies for a patent; if it is obvious, then it does not qualify for a patent.

Patent Period

In 2011, Congress passed the **Leahy-Smith America Invents Act (AIA).**[4] The act stipulates a **first-to-file rule** for determining the priority of a patent. This means that the first party to file a patent on an invention receives the patent even though some other party was the first to invent the invention. Previously, the United States followed the **first-to-invent rule**, whereby the party that first invented the invention was awarded the patent even if another party had previously filed for and received the patent. The adoption of the first-to-file rule is a major change in U.S. patent law.

Leahy-Smith America Invents Act (AIA)
A federal statute that significantly amended federal patent law.

Utility patents for inventions are valid for 20 years. The patent term begins to run from the date the patent application is filed.

After the patent period runs out, the invention or design enters the **public domain**, which means that anyone can produce and sell the invention without paying the prior patent holder.

Example On January 12, 2022, an inventor invents a formula for a new prescription drug. On March 1, 2022, the inventor files for and is eventually granted a 20-year patent for this invention. Twenty years after the filing of the patent application, on March 1, 2042, the patent expires. The next day, the patent enters the public domain, and anyone can use the formula to produce the same prescription drug.

Patent Infringement

patent infringement
Unauthorized use of another's patent. A patent holder may recover damages and other remedies against a patent infringer.

Patent holders own exclusive rights to use and exploit their patents. **Patent infringement** occurs when someone makes unauthorized use of another's patent. Patent infringement claims must be brought in the U.S. district court that has jurisdiction to hear the case. Patent decisions of the U.S. district courts can be appealed to the U.S. Court of Appeals for the Federal Circuit.

In a suit for patent infringement, a successful plaintiff can recover (1) money damages equal to a reasonable royalty rate on the sale of the infringed articles, (2) other damages caused by the infringement (e.g., loss of customers), (3) an order requiring the destruction of the infringing article, and (4) an injunction preventing the infringer from such action in the future. The court has the discretion to award up to treble damages if the infringement was intentional. It costs between several hundred thousand dollars and several million dollars to bring an infringement case to trial.

The following U.S. Supreme Court decision involves the issue of patent infringement.

Information Technology

CASE 7.1 *U.S. SUPREME COURT CASE Patent Infringement*

WesternGeco LLC v. ION Geophysical Corporation

138 S.Ct. 2129 (2018)
Supreme Court of the United States

"The Patent Act gives patent owners a civil action for infringement."

—Clarence Thomas, Justice

Facts

Petitioner WesternGeco LLC owns four patents relating to a system that it developed for surveying the ocean floor. WesternGeco does not sell its technology or license it to competitors. Instead, it uses the technology itself, performing surveys for oil and gas companies. ION Geophysical Corporation, a U.S.-based company, used WesternGeco's public patent information and began manufacturing and selling competing systems to foreign companies, which in turn sold the systems in the U.S. in direct competition with WesternGeco. The foreign companies made millions of dollars in profits from such sales. WesternGeco sued ION for patent infringement. The jury found ION liable for patent infringement and ordered ION to pay $12.5 million in damages as a royalty payment to WesternGeco. The jury also assessed $93 million against ION for the profits lost by WesternGeco because of foreign company sales of ION's infringing technology. The U.S. court of appeals held that ION was not liable for the foreign company sales. WesternGeco appealed to the U.S. Supreme Court.

Issue

Can WesternGeco recover damages from ION for profits WesternGeco lost because of foreign company sales of ION's infringing technology?

Language of the U.S. Supreme Court

The Patent Act gives patent owners a civil action for infringement. A company shall be liable as an infringer if it supplies certain components of a patented invention in or from the United States with the intent that they will be combined outside of the United States in a manner that would infringe the patent if such combination occurred in the United States. The conduct in this case that is relevant clearly occurred in the United States, as it was ION's domestic act of supplying the components that infringed WesternGeco's patents.

Decision

The U.S. Supreme Court held that ION had engaged in patent infringement and was liable to WesternGeco for damages, including the lost profits suffered by WesternGeco because of the foreign company sales that used ION's infringing technology. The Supreme Court reversed the decision of the court of appeals.

Critical Legal Thinking Questions

Is it easy for a party to find patent information? Is any stealth, or misappropriation of a trade secret, necessary? Do you think that ION should have been held liable for the profits made by the foreign company sales?

Design Patent

In addition to utility patents, a party can obtain a design patent. A **design patent** is a patent that may be obtained for the ornamental nonfunctional design of an item. A design patent protects the appearance of an item and not the function or internal mechanical operation of the item. A design patent is valid for 14 years.

design patent
A patent that may be obtained for the ornamental nonfunctional design of an item.

Example The designs for jewelry, automobiles, furniture, shoes, bottles, the shape of smartphones, and computer icons (such as emojis) are examples of design patents.

Example The original curvy Coca-Cola bottle is a classic design patent that was patented in 1915, Patent No. 48,160. The Statue of Liberty is one of the most famous design patents. It was patented in the United States by Frédéric Auguste Bartholdi, of France, in 1879, Patent No. 11,023.

Copyright

7.4 Describe the items that can be copyrighted and describe the penalties for copyright infringement.

Article I, Section 8, of the Constitution of the United States of America authorizes Congress to enact statutes to protect the works of writers for limited times.

Pursuant to this authority, Congress has enacted copyright statutes that establish the requirement for obtaining a copyright. **Copyright** is a legal right that gives the author of qualifying subject matter who meets other requirements established by copyright law the exclusive right to publish, produce, sell, license, and distribute the work.

copyright
A legal right that gives the author of qualifying subject matter, who meets other requirements established by copyright law, the exclusive right to publish, produce, sell, license, and distribute the work.

The **Copyright Revision Act** of 1976, as amended, currently governs copyright law.[5] The act establishes the requirements for obtaining a copyright and protects copyrighted works from infringement. Federal copyright law is exclusive; there are no state copyright laws. Federal copyright law protects the work of authors and other creative persons from the unauthorized use of their copyrighted materials and provides a financial incentive for authors to write, thereby increasing the number of creative works available in society. Copyrights can be sold or licensed to others, whose rights are then protected by copyright law.

Copyright Revision Act
A federal statute that (1) establishes the requirements for obtaining a copyright and (2) protects copyrighted works from infringement.

Tangible Writing

Only **tangible writings**—writings that can be physically seen—are subject to copyright registration and protection. The term *writing* has been broadly defined.

The law in respect to literature ought to remain upon the same footing as that which regards the profits of mechanical inventions and chemical discoveries.
William Wordsworth
Letter (1838)

Example Books, e-books, periodicals, and newspapers; musical compositions, manuscripts, screenplays, and graphic designs; plays, motion pictures, and radio and television productions; websites, video and electronic games, smartphone apps, online media, blogs, and virtual reality applications; computer programs and software; lectures, sermons, addresses, and poems; maps; works of art, including paintings, drawings, jewelry, glassware, tapestry, lithographs, and sculptural works; architectural drawings and models; photographs, including digital photographs, prints, slides, and filmstrips; greeting cards and picture postcards; photoplays, including feature films, cartoons, newsreels, travelogues, and training films; and sound recordings published in the form of CDs and digital files qualify for copyright protection.

Registration of Copyrights

To be protected under federal copyright law, a work must be the original work of the author. A copyright is automatically granted the moment a work is created and fixed in tangible form.

Example When a student writes a term paper for her class, she owns a copyright to her work.

Berne Convention
An international copyright treaty.

In 1989, the United States signed the **Berne Convention**, an international copyright treaty. This law eliminated the need to place the symbol © or the word *copyright* or *copr.* on a copyrighted work. However, it is still advisable to place the copyright notice ©, the year of publication, and the author's name on many copyrighted works because it notifies the world that the work is protected by a copyright, identifies the owner of the copyright, and shows the year of its publication. This helps eliminate a defendant's claim of innocent copyright.

Example Copyright © 2022 Henry Richard Cheeseman; Copyright 2022 Henry Richard Cheeseman; and © 2022 Henry Richard Cheeseman.

Published and unpublished works may be registered with the **U.S. Copyright Office** in Washington DC. Registration of a copyright is permissive and voluntary and can be effectuated at any time during the term of the copyright. Copyright registration creates a public record of the copyrighted work. A **copyright registration certificate** is issued to the copyright holder. Registration permits a holder to obtain statutory damages for copyright infringement, which may be greater than actual damages, and attorney's fees.

Copyright Period

The **Copyright Term Extension Act** of 1998 extended copyright protection for works published in the United States after January 1, 1978:[6]

1. Individuals are granted copyright protection for their lifetime plus 70 years.
2. Copyrights owned by businesses, which are usually works for hire created by employees in the course of their employment or works that are specifically commissioned by a business, are protected for the shorter of either:
   a. 120 years from the year of creation, or
   b. 95 years from the year of first publication

Works created prior to January 1, 1978, are subject to varying copyright periods as set by federal copyright law.

A copyright work enters the public domain on January 1 of the year following the year of expiration. For copyright purposes, January 1 of each year is referred to as "public domain day."

Example If Brianna Young writes and publishes a novel in 2020, and she lives until April 1, 2060, her heirs will own the copyright until the end of the day on December 31, 2130. On January 1, 2131, the work enters the public domain.

Example In 2016, the song "Happy Birthday to You" entered the public domain; on January 1, 2021, F. Scott Fitzgerald's novel *The Great Gatsby* entered the public domain; and on January 1, 2022, Ernest Hemingway's novel *The Sun Also Rises* entered the public domain.

WEB EXERCISE
Use **www.google.com** and check to see what famous books and films enter the public domain on January 1 of next year.

After a work enters the public domain, anyone can publish or produce the work without paying the prior copyright holder. In addition to publishing or producing the original work, the works may also be used in different media. For example, novels may be made into movies, plays, musicals, children's books, digital games, board games, and the like.

Social Media Platforms

When a person signs up to use a social media platform, such as Facebook or YouTube, the user owns the copyright to the photographs and other content that they post. However, the user is bound by the company's "Terms and Conditions of Use," which often grant the social media platform a license to use posted photographs and other posted content.

CONCEPT SUMMARY
COPYRIGHT PERIOD

Type of Holder	Copyright Period
Individual	Life of the author plus 70 years beyond the author's life
Business	The shorter of either 95 years from the year of first publication or 120 years from the year of creation

Civil Copyright Law: Copyright Infringement

Copyright infringement occurs when a party copies a substantial and material part of the plaintiff's copyrighted work without permission. The copying does not have to be either word for word or the entire work.

copyright infringement
An infringement that occurs when a party copies a substantial and material part of a plaintiff's copyrighted work without permission. A copyright holder may recover damages and other remedies against the infringer.

Example Copyright infringement includes the following: downloading music and other digital files from pirate sites (web or FTP) or peer-to-peer systems, whether or not such services charge a fee; printing and selling copies of a book without permission; making unauthorized copies of copyrighted CDs, DVDs, or video games and selling or giving them to others; downloading licensed software from non-authorized websites; copying software programs without permission of the copyright holder and using them or selling them to others; and using a popular song as background to your own video posted on YouTube.

A plaintiff can bring a civil action against the alleged infringer and, if successful, recover (1) the profit made by the defendant from the copyright infringement, (2) damages suffered by the plaintiff, (3) an order requiring the impoundment and destruction of the infringing works, and (4) an injunction preventing the defendant from infringing in the future. The court, at its discretion, can award statutory damages for willful infringement in lieu of actual damages.

In the following case, the court had to decide whether copyright infringement had occurred.

Critical Legal Thinking Questions

Has copyright infringement become endemic? Is illegal downloading of copyrighted music, movies, and video games "stealing"? Can copyright law and enforcement keep up with digital piracy?

Information Technology

CASE 7.2 *FEDERAL COURT CASE Copyright Infringement*

Disney Enterprises, Inc. v. VidAngel, Inc.

869 F.3d 848 (2017)
United States Court of Appeals for the Ninth Circuit

"Copyright owners have the exclusive right to reproduce the copyrighted work in copies, or to authorize another to do so."

—Andrew Hurwitz, Circuit Judge

Facts

Disney Enterprises, Lucasfilm Limited, Twentieth Century Fox Film Corporation, and Warner Brothers Entertainment (the Studios) produce and distribute copyrighted motion pictures and television shows. The Studios distribute and license these works for public dissemination through several distribution channels: (1) movie theaters; (2) sale or rental of physical discs in DVD, Blu-ray, and other formats; (3) sale of digital downloads through online services, such as iTunes or Amazon Video; (4) on-demand rental for short-term viewing through cable and satellite television or internet video-on-demand platforms, such as iTunes or Google Play; and (5) subscription-on-demand streaming online outlets, such as Netflix, Hulu, HBO GO, and cable television. Digital distribution provides a large source of revenue for the Studios. The Studios employ encryption technology to protect against unauthorized access to and copying of their works.

VidAngel, Inc. operates an online streaming service that removes objectionable content from movies and televisions shows. To do this, VidAngel purchases physical discs containing copyrighted movies and television shows and then decrypts the discs and "rips" a digital copy to a computer. After decryption, VidAngel converts the files to a live-streaming format, edits them, and breaks them into segments that can be tagged with over 80 categories of inappropriate content. Once the segments are tagged, they are encrypted and stored on cloud servers. VidAngel streams filtered versions of the works to customers at rates of $1 to $2 per movie or television episode per night. VidAngel offers thousands of edited movies and television episodes on its service.

The Studios sued VidAngel for copyright infringement. The U.S. district court issued a preliminary injunction enjoining VidAngel from copying and streaming, transmitting, or otherwise publicly performing or displaying any of the Studios' copyrighted works. VidAngel appealed.

Issue

Should VidAngel be enjoined from streaming altered versions of the Studios' movies and television programs?

Language of the Court

> *Copyright owners have the exclusive right to reproduce the copyrighted work in copies, or to authorize another to do so. The district court found that VidAngel's service simply omits portions that viewers find objectionable, and transmits them for the same intrinsic entertainment value as the originals. Star Wars is still Star Wars, even without Princess Leia's bikini scene. VidAngel's service does not require removing a crucial plot element—it requires the use of only one filter, which can be an audio filter temporarily silencing a portion of a scene without removing imagery, or skipping a gratuitous scene. The district court had substantial evidence before it that VidAngel's service undermines the value of the Studios' copyrighted works.*

Decision

The U.S. court of appeals upheld the district court's injunction against VidAngel.

Critical Legal Thinking Questions

Do you think that the defendant engaged in copyright infringement? What do you think the defendant's motive was for creating the filtered versions of the Studios' copyrighted works?

Fair Use Doctrine

A copyright holder's right in a work is not absolute. The law permits certain limited unauthorized use of copyrighted materials under the **fair use doctrine**. The following uses are protected under this doctrine: (1) quotation of the copyrighted work for review or criticism or in a scholarly or technical work, (2) use in a parody or satire, (3) brief quotation in a news report, (4) reproduction by a teacher or student of a small part of the work to illustrate a lesson, (5) incidental reproduction of a work in a newsreel or broadcast of an event being reported, and (6) reproduction of a work in a legislative or judicial proceeding. The copyright holder cannot recover for copyright infringement where fair use is found.

fair use doctrine
A doctrine that permits certain limited use of a copyright by someone other than the copyright holder without the permission of the copyright holder.

Example A student is assigned to write a paper in class about a certain subject. The student conducts research and writes her paper. In her paper, she uses two paragraphs from a copyrighted book and places these paragraphs in quotation marks and properly cites the source and author in a footnote. This is fair use for academic purposes. However, if the student copies and uses three pages from the book, this would not be fair use and would constitute copyright infringement whether she cites the author and his or her work in a footnote or not.

Example A comedy television show that performs parodies and satires on famous celebrities is an example of *parody fair use*.

The following feature discusses a federal copyright law that specifically applies to digital downloading and streaming of music.

Music Modernization Act (MMA)
A federal statute that provides for the creation of a music database and permits digital services to obtain a blanket license to stream and or permit the downloading of the music.

Information Technology

Music Modernization Act

In 2018, the U.S. government enacted the **Music Modernization Act (MMA)**.[7] The MMA is a federal statute that is designed to keep pace with technological developments regarding the way users receive music, such as by digital streaming and downloading, through satellite and internet radio, and via cable TV music services. The MMA only applies to the music industry and does not apply to other copyrighted works such as books, periodicals, or newspapers. The MMA is effective as of January 1, 2021.

Prior to the enactment of the MMA, digital services licensed and paid for music on a song-by-song basis, which was a complicated process. The MMA changes all that. Under the MMA, the Register of Copyrights has designated the Mechanical Licensing Collective (MLC), a quasi-administrative entity, to create and maintain a database of all musical compositions, their owners, and the percentage of ownership, if applicable. The board of directors of the MLC is composed of music publishers and songwriters. The cost of creating and maintaining the music database is paid for by the digital and streaming services.

Digital services can purchase a *blanket license* from the MLC and acquire the music of the database to stream or provide for downloading. The single license will cover all songs streamed in the United States, whether domestic or foreign in origin. There is no opt-out provision. The digital licensor makes one payment to the MLC, which then distributes royalties to the appropriate registered parties. Royalties for each musical work are set by the MLC using open-market rates. To receive royalty payments, composers, songwriters, and other copyright holders must register their ownership interests in musical compositions with the MLC.

Under this system, digital licensees who purchase a blanket license from the MLC will be protected from lawsuits by composers, songwriters, and others holding an ownership interest in music compositions. In return, copyright holders will be more assured of receiving royalty payments without reverting to legal action.

The MMA permits digital services and copyright holders of music to enter into individual direct licenses outside of the procedure established by the MMA. In such cases, the MLC plays no role in the licensing of the music or the collection of royalties.

The MMA brings pre-1972 sound recordings, which had previously been subject to state laws, into the federal copyright system. The MMA preempts state laws and establishes federal copyright periods for pre-1972 music. Now, when pre-1972 sound recordings are downloaded or streamed during the applicable copyright periods, royalties will be distributed by the MLC.

Most of the MMA applies only to the digital delivery of music. However, a section of the MMA establishes how music producers will be paid royalties for public performances of their music. The sale of physical CDs and vinyl recordings is not covered by the MMA.

Henry R. Cheeseman

FBI Warning
The Federal Bureau of Investigation (FBI), a federal government agency, is authorized to investigate violations of copyright law. An FBI warning concerning copyright infringement usually appears at the beginning of feature movies and on DVDs, CDs, and games sold in the United States. The FBI warning was developed to deter illegal piracy and increase awareness of the criminal penalties associated with piracy.

Criminal Copyright Law: No Electronic Theft Act

No Electronic Theft Act (NET Act)
A federal statute that makes it a crime for a person to infringe willfully on a copyright.

In 1997, Congress enacted the **No Electronic Theft Act (NET Act)**, a federal statute that *criminalizes* certain copyright infringement.[8] The NET Act prohibits any person from willfully infringing a copyright for commercial advantage or financial gain or by reproduction or distribution even without commercial advantage or financial gain, including by electronic means. Thus, the NET Act makes it a federal crime to reproduce, share, or distribute copyrighted electronic works, including movies, songs, software programs, and video games.

Digital Millennium Copyright Act (DMCA)
A federal statute that prohibits unauthorized access to copyrighted digital works by circumventing encryption technology or the manufacture and distribution of technologies designed for the purpose of circumventing encryption protection of digital works.

Example Violations of the NET Act include distributing copyrighted works without permission of the copyright holder over the internet, uploading such works to a website, and posting information about the availability of such uploaded electronic works.

Criminal penalties for violating the act include imprisonment and fines. The creation of the NET Act adds a new law that the federal government can use to attack criminal copyright infringement and curb digital piracy.

The following feature discusses a federal law designed to protect digital copyright material.

Information Technology

Digital Millennium Copyright Act

The internet makes it easier than ever before for people to copy and distribute copyrighted works illegally. To combat this, software and entertainment companies have developed digital wrappers and **encryption technology** to protect their copyrighted works from unauthorized access. Not to be outdone, software pirates have devised ways to crack these wrappers and protection devices.

Software and entertainment companies lobbied Congress to enact federal legislation to make the cracking of their wrappers and selling of technology to do so illegal. In response, Congress enacted the **Digital Millennium Copyright Act (DMCA)**,[9] a federal statute that does the following:

- Prohibits unauthorized access to copyrighted *digital works* by circumventing the wrapper or encryption technology that protects the intellectual property

Digital Millennium Copyright Act

- Prohibits the manufacture and distribution of technologies, products, or services primarily designed for the purpose of circumventing wrappers or encryption technology protecting digital works

Congress granted exceptions to DMCA liability to (1) software developers to achieve compatibility of their software with the protected work; (2) federal, state, and local law enforcement agencies conducting criminal investigations; (3) parents who are protecting children from pornography or other harmful materials available on the internet; (4) internet users who are identifying and disabling cookies and other identification devices that invade their personal privacy rights; and (5) nonprofit libraries, educational institutions, and archives that access a protected work to determine whether to acquire the work.

The DMCA imposes civil and criminal penalties.

Trademark

7.5 Define *trademark* and *service mark* and describe the penalties for trademark infringement.

Businesses often develop company names, as well as advertising slogans, symbols, and commercial logos, to promote the sale of their goods and services. Companies such as Apple, Nike, Microsoft, Louis Vuitton, McDonald's, and Starbucks spend millions of dollars annually promoting their names, slogans, symbols, and logos to gain market recognition from consumers. The U.S. Congress has enacted trademark laws to provide legal protection for these names, slogans, and logos.

A **mark** is any trade name, symbol, word, logo, design, or device used to identify and distinguish goods of a manufacturer or seller or services of a provider from those of other manufacturers, sellers, or providers.

mark
Any trade name, symbol, word, logo, design, or device used to identify and distinguish goods of a manufacturer or seller or services of a provider from those of other manufacturers, sellers, or providers.

In 1946, Congress enacted the **Lanham (Trademark) Act**,[10] commonly referred to as the **Lanham Act**, to provide federal protection to trademarks, service marks, and other marks. This act, as amended, is intended to (1) protect the owner's investment and goodwill in a mark and (2) prevent consumers from being confused about the origin of goods and services.

Lanham (Trademark) Act
A federal statute that (1) establishes the requirements for obtaining a federal mark and (2) protects marks from infringement.

Registration of a Mark

Marks can be registered with the U.S. Patent and Trademark Office (PTO) in Washington DC. A registrant must file an application with the PTO wherein the registrant designates the name, symbol, slogan, or logo that he or she is requesting to be registered. Registrants must either prove that they have used the intended mark in commerce (e.g., used the mark in the sale of goods or services) or state that they intend to use the mark in commerce within six months from the filing of the application. In the latter case, if the proposed mark is not used in commerce within this six-month period, the applicant loses the right to register the mark. However, the applicant may file for a six-month extension to use the mark in commerce, which is often granted by the PTO.

The PTO requires that trademark applications be filed electronically using its **Trademark Electronic Application System (TEAS)**. A party other than the registrant can submit an *opposition* to a proposed registration of a mark.

WEB EXERCISE
Go to the website **https://www.google.com/permissions/trademark/trademark-list.html** to view a list of Google, LLC's trademarks and service marks.

The PTO registers a mark if it determines that the mark does not infringe any existing marks, the applicant has paid the registration fee (approximately $400), and other requirements for registering the mark have been met.

Once the PTO has issued a registration of the mark, the owner is entitled to use the registered mark symbol ® with a registered trademark or service mark. The symbol ® is used to designate marks that have been registered with the PTO. The use of the symbol ® is not mandatory, although it is wise to use the symbol to put others on notice that the trademark or service mark is registered with the PTO.

®
A symbol that is used to designate marks that have been registered with the U.S. Patent and Trademark Office.

Once a mark is registered, it is given nationwide effect, serves as constructive notice that the mark is the registrant's personal property, and provides that federal lawsuits may be brought to protect the mark. The original registration of a mark is valid for 10 years, and it can be renewed for an unlimited number of 10-year periods.

While the application is pending with the PTO, the registrant cannot use the symbol ®. However, during the application period, a registrant can use the symbol **TM** for goods or **SM** for services to alert the public to the registrant's legal claim.

TM
A symbol that designates an owner's legal claim to an unregistered mark that is associated with a product.

SM
A symbol that designates an owner's legal claim to an unregistered mark that is associated with a service.

A party who sells goods and services using brand names is not required to register these names as marks with the PTO. A party who has not registered a mark with the PTO can claim common law trademark rights under state law in brand names of businesses, products, and services that they are using in commerce. However, instead of the national protection provided to marks registered with the PTO, common law trademark protection provides rights only within the borders of one state, and then only within the geographical area of the state where the name is used. Lawsuits involving common law trademark claims are decided by state courts. Common law trademarks are not listed in the PTO's online data bases, and do not have the right to use the federal registration symbol ®. A party claiming common law trademark rights in a product or service brand name can use the symbols TM and SM, respectively.

A party may file for the *cancellation* of a previously registered mark if the party believes that the registrant did not meet the requirements for being issued the mark or if a mark has been abandoned.

CONCEPT SUMMARY

MEANING OF SYMBOLS USED IN ASSOCIATION WITH MARKS

Symbol	Meaning
TM	Unregistered mark used with goods
SM	Unregistered mark used with services
®	Registered mark

Types of Marks

The word *mark* collectively refers to *trademarks, service marks, certification marks*, and *collective membership marks* that are registered with the PTO.

trademark
A distinctive mark, symbol, name, word, motto, or device that identifies the goods of a particular business.

- **Trademark.** A **trademark** is a distinctive mark, symbol, name, word, motto, or device that identifies the *goods* of a business.

  Example *Tesla* (Tesla Motors, Inc.), *Coca-Cola* (The Coca-Cola Company), *Big Mac* (McDonald's Corporation), *iPhone* (Apple Inc.), *Levi's* (Levi Strauss & Co.), *Harley* (Harley-Davidson Motor Company), *The Ultimate Driving Machine* (BMW AG), *LV* (Louis Vuitton Malletier), *F-150* (Ford Motor Company), and *A Diamond Is Forever* (DeBeers UL Ltd.) are trademarks.

service mark
A mark that distinguishes the services of the holder from those of its competitors.

- **Service mark.** A **service mark** is used to distinguish the *services* of the holder from those of its competitors.

  Example *WW* (Weight Watchers International, Inc.), *Like a Good Neighbor, State Farm Is There* (State Farm Mutual Automobile Insurance Company), *Apple Store* (Apple, Inc.), *FedEx* (FedEx Corporation), *What's in Your Wallet?* (Capital One Financial Corporation), *Fly the Friendly Skies* (United Airlines, Inc.), and *Citi* (Citigroup, Inc.) are service marks.

certification mark
A mark that certifies that a seller of a product or service has met certain geographical location requirements, quality standards, material standards, or mode of manufacturing standards established by the owner of the mark.

- **Certification mark.** A **certification mark** is a mark usually owned by a nonprofit cooperative or association. The owner of the mark establishes certain geographical location requirements, quality standards, material standards, or mode of manufacturing standards that must be met by a seller of products or services to use the certification mark. If a seller meets these requirements, the seller applies to the cooperative or association to use the mark on its products or in connection with the sale of services. The owner of the certification mark usually licenses sellers who meet the requirements to use the mark. A party does not have to be a member of the organization to use the mark.

Example A *UL* mark certifies that products meet safety standards set by Underwriters Laboratories, Inc. The *Good Housekeeping Seal of Approval* certifies that products meet certain quality specifications set by *Good Housekeeping* magazine (Good Housekeeping Research Institute). Other certification marks are *Certified Maine Lobster*, which indicates lobster or lobster products originating in the coastal waters of the state of Maine (Maine Lobster Promotion Council); *100% Napa Valley*, which is associated with grape wine from the Napa Valley, California (Napa Valley Vintners Association); and *Grown in Idaho*, which indicates potatoes grown in the state of Idaho (State of Idaho Potato Commission).

- **Collective membership mark.** A **collective membership mark** is owned by an organization (such as an association) whose members use it to identify themselves with a level of quality or accuracy or other characteristics set by the organization. Only members of the association or organization can use the mark. A collective membership mark identifies membership in an organization but does not identify goods or services.

collective membership mark
A mark that indicates that a person has met the standards set by an organization and is a member of that organization.

Example *CPA* is used to indicate that someone is a member of the Society of Certified Public Accountants, *Teamster* is used to indicate that a person is a member of The International Brotherhood of Teamsters (IBT) labor union, and *Realtor* is used to indicate that a person is a member of the National Association of Realtors.

Some companies use the same name as both a registered trademark and a registered service mark because they sell goods and provide services.

Example *Amazon* designates online shopping services and branded products like the Kindle e-reader. *McDonald's* designates dining services and specific products. *Starbucks* designates food services and branded coffee beans and other products.

WEB EXERCISE
Go to **https://www.apple.com/legal/intellectual-property/trademark/appletmlist.html** and view the trademarks and service marks of Apple, Inc.

Certain marks cannot be registered. They include (1) the flag or coat of arms of the United States, any state, municipality, or foreign nation; (2) geographical names standing alone (e.g., "South"); (3) surnames standing alone (note that a surname can be registered if it is accompanied by a picture or fanciful name, such as *Smith Brothers Cough Drops*); and (4) any mark that resembles a mark already registered with the federal PTO.

CONCEPT SUMMARY
TYPES OF MARKS

1. **Trademark.** A distinctive mark, symbol, name, word, motto, or device that identifies the *goods* of a business.
2. **Service mark.** A mark used to distinguish the *services* of the holder from those of its competitors.
3. **Certification mark.** A mark that establishes certain geographical location requirements, quality standards, material standards, or mode of manufacturing standards that must be met by a seller of products or services to use the certification mark.
4. **Collective membership mark.** A mark owned by an organization whose members use it to identify themselves with a level of quality or accuracy or other characteristics set by the organization.

Distinctiveness or Secondary Meaning

distinctive
Being unique and fabricated.

secondary meaning
A brand name that has evolved from an ordinary term.

To qualify for federal protection, a mark must either (1) be **distinctive** or (2) have acquired a **secondary meaning**:

- **Distinctive.** A distinctive mark would be a word or design that is unique. It therefore qualifies as a mark. The words of the mark must not be ordinary words or symbols.

  Example Words such a *Xerox* (Xerox Corporation), *Acura* (Honda Motor Corporation), *Google* (Google, Inc.), *Exxon* (Exxon Mobil Corporation), and *Pinkberry* (Pinkberry, Inc.) are distinctive words and therefore qualify as marks.

- **Secondary meaning.** Ordinary words or symbols that have taken on a secondary meaning can qualify as marks. These are words or symbols that have an established meaning but have acquired a secondary meaning that is attached to a product or service.

  Example *Just Do It* (Nike Corporation), *I'm lovin' it* (McDonald's Corporation), *Think different* (Apple Inc.), and *The Ultimate Driving Machine* (BMW of North America, LLC) are ordinary words that have taken on a secondary meaning when used to designate the products or services of the owners of the marks.

Words that are descriptive but have no secondary meaning cannot be trademarked.

Example Subway was denied a trademark for the word "Footlong" because other vendors had been using the term long before Subway. Harley-Davidson was denied a trademark for the sound of its revving engine because other manufacturers produced motorcycle engines that sounded the same. Walmart tried to claim the yellow smiley face as a trademark but was denied because others had used the design for decades before Walmart filed for the trademark.

Trademark Infringement

trademark infringement
Unauthorized use of another's mark. The holder may recover damages and other remedies from the infringer.

The owner of a mark can sue a third party for the unauthorized use of the mark. To succeed in a **trademark infringement** case, the owner must prove that (1) the defendant infringed the plaintiff's mark by using it in an unauthorized manner and (2) such use is likely to cause confusion, mistake, or deception of the public as to the origin of the goods or services.

A successful plaintiff can recover (1) the profits made by the infringer through the unauthorized use of the mark, (2) damages caused to the plaintiff's business and reputation, (3) an order requiring the defendant to destroy all goods containing the unauthorized mark, and (4) an injunction preventing the defendant from such infringement in the future. The court has discretion to award up to treble damages where intentional infringement is found.

Critical Legal Thinking Questions

More than 5 percent of global trade is composed of illegal knockoffs of clothing, handbags, toys, pharmaceuticals, and other products. Can such counterfeiting be curtailed successfully?

Example The most common examples of trademark infringement occur when counterfeiters sell fake "knockoff" goods sporting famous brand names to the public. Luxury consumer goods, including purses, handbags, jewelry, shoes, clothing, watches, and other high-end fashion apparel are easy to duplicate. Brands such as Louis Vuitton, Gucci, Prada, Coach, Hermes, Cartier, Bespoke, Tiffany, Rolex, Patek Philippe, and Van Cleef & Arpels are luxury goods that are commonly counterfeited by trademark infringers. The trademark holder can sue the seller for trademark infringement, but the high number of infringers makes this a difficult task.

Abandonment of a Mark

For a holder to keep a trademark or service mark, the mark must be used in commerce. If a holder of a mark fails to use or continue to use a mark in commerce, the holder runs the risk of being found to have abandoned the mark. Nonuse in commerce for three consecutive years is evidence of **abandonment of a mark**. If a mark is abandoned, the PTO can cancel the mark. If a mark is determined to have been abandoned, it enters the public domain and can be used and registered as the mark of another party.

Generic Names

If a word, name, or slogan is *generic* it cannot be registered as a trademark. If a word is not generic, it can be trademarked.

Example The word *secret* cannot be trademarked because it is a generic name or word. However, the brand name *Victoria's Secret* is permitted to be trademarked because it is not a generic name.

Once a company has been granted a trademark or service mark, it usually uses the mark as a brand name to promote its goods or services. Obviously, the owner of the mark wants to promote its brand so that consumers and users will easily recognize the brand name.

However, sometimes a company may be *too* successful in promoting a mark, and at some point the public begins to use the brand name as a common name to denote the type of product or service being sold rather than as the trademark or service mark of the individual seller. A trademark that becomes a common term for a product line or type of service is called a **generic name**. Once a trademark becomes a generic name, the term loses its protection under federal trademark law.

generic name
A term for a mark that has become a common term for a product line or type of service and therefore has lost its trademark protection.

Example Sailboards are boards that have sails mounted on them that people use to ride on water. There were many manufacturers and sellers of sailboards. However, the most successful manufacturer of these sailboards used the trademarked brand name Windsurfer. However, the word *windsurfer* was used so often by the public for all brands of sailboards that the trademarked name Windsurfer was found to be a generic name, and its trademark was canceled.

Exhibit 7.2 lists names that at one time were trademarked but lost trademark protection because the trademarked names became overused and generic.

The following feature discusses whether a trademarked name has become a generic name.

Exhibit 7.2 GENERIC NAMES

The following once-trademarked names have been so overused to designate an entire class of products that they have been found to be generic and have lost their trademark status.

Windsurfer	Frisbee
Laser	Trampoline
Escalator	Cornflakes
Kerosene	Yo-yo
Aspirin	Raisin bran
Thermos	Tollhouse cookies
Linoleum	Nylon
Cellophane	Zipper

Information Technology

"Google" Trademark Is Not a Generic Name

"Over time the holder of a valid trademark may become a victim of genericide."

—Richard Tallman, Circuit Judge

Chris Gillespie registered 763 domain names that included the word "Google." Each of these domain names paired the word "google" with some other term identifying a specific brand, product, or person—for example, "googledisney.com" and "googlebarackobama.com." Google, Inc. objected to these registrations and filed a complaint with the National Arbitration Forum (NAF), which has authority to decide domain name disputes. Google claimed that the domain names were confusingly similar to its GOOGLE trademark. The NAF agreed and transferred the domain names to Google.

Gillespie sued in U.S. district court seeking cancellation of the GOOGLE trademark, alleging that the GOOGLE trademark had become generic. Gillespie alleged that the word "google" is primarily understood as a generic term universally used to describe the act of internet searching using all search engines. The U.S. district court held that the trademark GOOGLE was not generic and granted summary judgment to Google. The U.S. court of appeals agreed. The court of appeals stated, "Over time the holder of a valid trademark may become a victim of genericide when the public appropriates a trademark and uses it as a generic name for particular types of goods or services irrespective of its source." However, the court held that the trademark word GOOGLE had not reached this stage. The court of appeals affirmed the grant of summary judgment to Google. *Elliot v. Google, Inc.*, 860 F.3d 1151 (United States Court of Appeals for the Ninth Circuit, 2017)

CONCEPT SUMMARY

TYPES OF INTELLECTUAL PROPERTY PROTECTED BY FEDERAL LAW

Type	Subject Matter	Term
Trade secret	Trade secret (e.g., product formulas, patterns, designs, compilations of data, software algorithms, source codes, customer and supplier lists, and ingredients).	Unlimited
	Owner must take reasonable precautions to prevent the secret from being discovered.	
	Reverse engineering: Trade secret status is lost if another party lawfully discovers the secret.	
Patent	Inventions (e.g., machines, processes, compositions of matter, designs for articles of manufacture, and improvements to existing machines and processes).	Patents on articles of manufacture and processes: 20 years; design patents: 14 years.
	Invention must be novel, useful, and nonobvious.	
	Public use doctrine: Patent is not granted if the invention was used in public for more than one year prior to the filing of the patent application.	
Copyright	Tangible writings (e.g., books, magazines, newspapers, lectures, operas, plays, screenplays, musical compositions, maps, works of art, lithographs, photographs, postcards, greeting cards, motion pictures, newsreels, sound recordings, computer programs, video games, and mask works fixed to semiconductor chips).	Individual holder: life of author plus 70 years. Corporate holder: the shorter of either 120 years from the year of creation or 95 years from the year of first publication.
	Writing must be the original work of the author.	

Type	Subject Matter	Term
	Fair use doctrine: Permits the use of copyrighted material without consent for limited uses (e.g., scholarly work, parody or satire, and brief quotation in news reports).	
Trademark	Marks (e.g., name, symbol, word, logo, or device). Marks include trademarks, service marks, certification marks, and collective marks. Mark must be distinctive or have acquired a secondary meaning. *Generic name*: A mark that becomes a common term for a product line or type of service loses its protection under federal trademark law.	Original registration: 10 years. Renewal registration: unlimited number of renewals for 10-year terms.

Dilution

7.6 Define *dilution* and describe the forms of dilution of a trademark.

Many companies that own trademarks spend millions of dollars each year advertising and promoting the quality of the goods and services sold under their names. Many of these become household names that are recognized by millions of consumers, such as Coca-Cola, McDonald's, Microsoft, and Nike.

Traditional trademark law protected these marks where an infringer used the mark and confused consumers as to the source of the goods or services. For example, if a knockoff company sold athletic shoes and apparel under the name Nike, there would be trademark infringement because there would be confusion as to the source of the goods.

Often, however, a party uses a name similar to or close to but not exactly identical to a holder's trademark name and sells other goods or services or misuses the name. Because there was no direct competition, the trademark owner often could not win a trademark infringement case.

To address this problem, Congress enacted the **Federal Trademark Dilution Act (FTDA)** of 1995 to protect famous marks from **dilution.**[11] The FTDA provides that owners of marks have a valuable property right in their marks that should not be *diluted, blurred, tarnished*, or *eroded* in any way by another.

Federal Trademark Dilution Act (FTDA)
A federal statute that protects famous marks from dilution, erosion, blurring, or tarnishing.

Dilution is broadly defined as the lessening of the capacity of a famous mark to identify and distinguish its holder's goods and services, regardless of the presence or absence of competition between the owner of the mark and the other party. The two most common forms of dilution are blurring and tarnishment:

- **Blurring** occurs where a party uses another party's famous mark to designate a product or service in another market so that the unique significance of the famous mark is weakened.

  Example Rolex skateboards or eBay toiletries are examples of blurring.

- **Tarnishment** occurs where a famous mark is linked to products of inferior quality or is portrayed in an unflattering, immoral, or reprehensible context likely to evoke negative beliefs about the mark's owner.

  Example Using the mark Gucci on a deck of playing cards depicting inappropriate graphics is an example of tarnishment.

Trademark Dilution Revision Act
A federal statute that states that a plaintiff must only show that there is a *likelihood of dilution* to prevail in a dilution lawsuit against a defendant.

Congress revised the FTDA when it enacted the **Trademark Dilution Revision Act** of 2006.[12] The act provides that a dilution plaintiff does not need to show that it has suffered actual harm to prevail in its dilution lawsuit but instead only needs to show that there would be the *likelihood of dilution*. The FTDA, as amended, has three fundamental requirements that the holder of the senior mark must prove:

1. Its mark is famous.
2. The use by the other party is commercial.
3. The use by the other party causes *a likelihood of dilution* of the distinctive quality of the mark.

The following case involves the dilution of a famous mark.

Information Technology

CASE 7.3 *FEDERAL COURT CASE Dilution of a Trademark*

V Secret Catalogue, Inc. and Victoria's Secret Stores, Inc. v. Moseley

605 F.3d 382, 2010 U.S. App. Lexis 10150 (2010)
United States Court of Appeals for the Sixth Circuit

"The phrase 'likely to cause dilution' used in the new statute significantly changes the meaning of the law from 'causes actual harm' under the preexisting law."

—Gilbert Merritt, Circuit Judge

Facts

Victoria's Secret is a successful worldwide retailer of women's lingerie, clothing, and beauty products that owns the famous trademark "Victoria's Secret." A small store in Elizabethtown, Kentucky, owned and operated by Victor and Cathy Moseley, used the business names "Victor's Secret" and "Victor's Little Secret." The store sold adult videos, novelties, sex toys, and racy lingerie. Victoria's Secret sued the Moseleys, alleging a violation of the Federal Trademark Dilution Act of 1995. The case eventually was decided by the U.S. Supreme Court in favor of the Moseleys when the Court found that there was no showing of *actual dilution* by the junior marks, as required by the statute. The U.S. Congress overturned the Supreme Court's decision by enacting the Trademark Dilution Revision Act of 2006, which requires the easier showing of a *likelihood of dilution* of the senior mark. On remand, the U.S. district court applied the new likelihood of dilution test, found a presumption of tarnishment of the Victoria's Secret mark that the Moseleys failed to rebut, and held against the Moseleys. The Moseleys appealed to the U.S. court of appeals.

Issue

Is there tarnishment of the Victoria's Secret senior mark by the Moseleys' use of the junior marks Victor's Secret and Victor's Little Secret?

Language of the Court

The phrase "likely to cause dilution" used in the new statute significantly changes the meaning of the law from "causes actual harm" under the preexisting law. In the present case, the Moseleys have had two opportunities in the District Court to offer evidence that there is no real probability of tarnishment and have not done so. The defendants have given us no basis to reverse the judgment of the District Court.

Decision

The U.S. court of appeals affirmed the U.S. district court's judgment in favor of Victoria's Secret.

Critical Legal Thinking Questions

Do you think the Moseleys were trading off the famous Victoria's Secret name? Do you think that the Moseleys had a legitimate claim to their business names because the husband's name was Victor?

The following feature discusses international treaties that protect intellectual property rights.

Global Law

International Protection of Intellectual Property

There are many multilateral and bilateral treaties that protect intellectual property rights internationally. Several of these are discussed in the following paragraphs.

Patents. The *Paris Convention for the Protection of Industrial Property (Paris Convention)* requires contracting countries to provide the same patent protection to other countries as it provides to its own nationals. The *Patent Cooperation Treaty (PCT)* provides a standard application format for the uniform filing of patent applications for contracting countries. Under the PCT, a patent applicant may file its patent application with its national patent office or with an international patent bureau located in Geneva, Switzerland.

Copyrights. The *Berne Convention for the Protection for Literary and Artistic Works (Berne Convention)* provides authors, musicians, painters, and other creators of intellectual property to control how their works are used, by whom, and under what terms. The *World Intellectual Property Organization Copyright Treaty (WIPO Copyright Treaty)* is a special agreement that protects the works and rights of authors in the digital environment.

Trademarks. The Paris Convention provides similar protections for trademarks and other marks as it does for patents. The *Protocol Relating to the Madrid Agreement Concerning the International Registration of Marks (Madrid Protocol)* provides an international system for registering marks. The *Nice Agreement Concerning the International Classification of Goods and Services for the Purpose of the Registration of Marks (Nice Agreement)* establishes the international classification of goods and services for the purpose of registering trademarks and service marks.

TRIPS. The *Agreement on Trade-Related Aspects of Intellectual Property Rights (TRIPS)* protects patents, copyrights, trademarks, and other intellectual property rights internationally. Members of the World Trade Organization (WTO) are subject to the provisions of TRIPS.

The United States is a signatory to all of the above treaties. The U.S. also has unilateral intellectual property protection treaties with many individual countries. The enforcement of intellectual property treaties is difficult.

Key Terms and Concepts

© (140)
® (145)
Abandonment of a mark (149)
Berne Convention (140)
Blurring (151)
Certification mark (146)
Collective membership mark (147)
Copyright (139)
Copyright infringement (141)
Copyright registration certificate (140)
Copyright Revision Act (139)
Copyright Term Extension Act (140)
Defend Trade Secrets Act (DTSA) (134)
Design patent (139)
Digital Millennium Copyright Act (DMCA) (144)
Dilution (151)
Distinctive (148)
Economic Espionage Act (EEA) (134)
Encryption technology (144)
Fair use doctrine (143)
Federal Patent Statute (135)
Federal Trademark Dilution Act (FTDA) (151)
First-to-file rule (137)
First-to-invent rule (137)
Generic name (149)
Intellectual property (132)
Lanham (Trademark) Act (Lanham Act) (145)
Leahy-Smith America Invents Act (AIA) (137)
Mark (145)
Misappropriation of a trade secret (134)
Music Modernization Act (MMA) (143)
No Electronic Theft Act (NET Act) (144)
Nonobvious (137)
Novel (137)
Patent (135)
Patent application (135)
Patent infringement (138)
Patent number (136)
Patent pending (136)
Patent Trial and Appeal Board (PTAB) (135)
Prior art (135)
Provisional application (135)
Public domain (138)
Reverse engineering (133)
Secondary meaning (148)
Service mark (146)
SM (146)
Tangible writings (139)
Tarnishment (151)
TM (146)
Trade secret (133)
Trademark (146)
Trademark Dilution Revision Act (151)
Trademark Electronic Application System (TEAS) (145)
Trademark infringement (148)
Uniform Trade Secrets Act (133)
U.S. Copyright Office (140)
U.S. Court of Appeals for the Federal Circuit (135)
U.S. Patent and Trademark Office (PTO) (135)
Useful (137)
Utility patent (136)

Critical Legal Thinking Cases

7.1 Patent Bernard Bilski and Rand Warsaw filed a patent application with the U.S. Patent and Trademark Office (PTO). The application sought patent protection for a claimed invention that explains how buyers and sellers of commodities in the energy market can hedge against the risk of price changes. The key claims are claims 1 and 4. Claim 1 describes a series of steps instructing how to hedge risk. Claim 4 puts the concept articulated in claim 1 into a simple mathematical formula. The remaining claims describe how claims 1 and 4 can be applied to allow energy suppliers and consumers to minimize the risks resulting from fluctuations in market demand for energy. The PTO rejected the patent application, holding that it merely manipulates an abstract idea and solves a purely mathematical problem. Bilski and Warsaw brought their case to the U.S. Supreme Court, arguing that their claimed invention deserved a patent. Is the claimed invention patentable? *Bilski v. Kappos, Director, Patent and Trademark Office*, 561 U.S. 593, 130 S.Ct. 3218, 2010 U.S. Lexis 5521 (Supreme Court of the United States, 2010)

7.2 Trademark Zura Kazhiloti sold jewelry bearing the luxury brand names "Cartier" and "Van Cleef & Arpels" to jewelry stores. The retailers then sold the jewelry through their brick-and-mortar stores, through websites, and through the internet auction site eBay. The jewelry was high-quality counterfeits, however, that Kazhiloti sold at high prices and from which he made hundreds of thousands of dollars in revenues. Each piece of fake Cartier jewelry bore the Cartier stylized "C" design trademark and other Cartier design trademarks. Each piece of fake Van Cleef & Arpels jewelry bore the Van Cleef & Arpels or "VCA" design trademark and other Van Cleef & Arpels design trademarks. The counterfeit jewelry used stones of inferior quality and cuts and inferior chains and clasps compared to the authentic pieces. The counterfeits also contained serial numbers similar to those used by Cartier and Van Cleef & Arpels. Kazhiloti supplied fake certificates of authenticity with each piece of jewelry. Eventually, Kazhiloti's scheme was uncovered. In total, 24 pieces of counterfeit Cartier and 83 pieces of counterfeit Van Cleef & Arpels jewelry were purchased or seized from the jewelry stores. Cartier International AG and Van Cleef & Arpels S.A. sued Kazhiloti for trademark infringement. The plaintiffs sought a permanent injunction against Kazhiloti engaging in such activity and to recover monetary damages. Kazhiloti asserted his Fifth Amendment constitutional right against self-incrimination and refused to speak to authorities or produce any documents. Is Kazhiloti liable for trademark infringement? *Cartier International A.G. and Van Cleef & Arpels S.A. v. Kazhiloti*, 2013 U.S. Dist. Lexis 145278 (United States District Court for the District of New Jersey, 2013)

7.3 Copyright Norton's Country Corner (Norton's) is a cowboy bar located in Queen Creek, Arizona. The bar is owned by McDade & Sons, Inc., which is owned 100 percent by Nancy McDade, its sole officer and director. Live bands play country-and-western music at Norton's during the week. Certain copyright owners of music have authorized Broadcast Music, Inc. (BMI) to license the use of their copyrighted songs to broadcasters and to owners of concert halls, restaurants, and nightclubs for live performances of the copyrighted music. BMI often attends public performances of music to determine whether any copyrighted songs it is authorized to license are being performed without such license.

One night, a BMI representative attended a live band performance at Norton's and recorded the songs played by the band that night. The audio recording showed that 13 copyrighted songs that BMI was authorized to license were played by the band at Norton's without the required license and without paying a copyright fee to BMI. BMI sued McDade & Sons, Inc. and Nancy McDade in U.S. district court for copyright infringement. The defendants argued they had not committed copyright infringement and that copyright law did not apply to owners of small establishments. Are the defendants liable for copyright infringement? *Broadcast Music, Inc. v. McDade & Sons, Inc.*, 928 F.Supp.2d 1120, 2013 U.S. Dist. Lexis 30211 (United States District Court for Arizona, 2013)

7.4 Trademark Kraft Foods Group Brands, LLC (Kraft) is a well-known manufacturer of food products sold in more than 15,000 grocery stores located throughout the United States. Many of its packaged cheeses that are sold in outlets are available under Kraft's trademarked "Cracker Barrel" label. Kraft has been selling cheeses in grocery stores under the Cracker Barrel trademark for more than 50 years. Cracker Barrel Old Country Store, Inc. (CBOCS) operates a well-known chain of more than 600 low-price restaurants. On learning that CBOCS planned to sell a variety of food products in grocery stores under the logo "Cracker Barrel Old Country Store," Kraft filed a lawsuit for trademark infringement. Kraft argues that consumers will be confused by the similarity of the names and alleges that it will be hurt financially. Kraft filed for an injunction to prevent CBOCS from selling products containing the "Cracker Barrel" name in grocery stores. Will CBOCS's use of the Cracker Barrel name on the food products it proposes to sell in grocery stores infringe on Kraft's Cracker Barrel trademark? *Kraft Foods Group Brands LLC v. Cracker Barrel Old Country Store, Inc.*, 735 F.3d 735, 2013 U.S. App. Lexis 23124 (United States Court of Appeals for the Seventh Circuit, 2013)

7.5 Copyright Varsity Brands, Inc. (Varsity) designs, makes, and sells cheerleading uniforms. Varsity has obtained more than 200 U.S. copyright registrations for two-dimensional designs that can be placed on the surface of its uniforms. Star Athletica, LLC (Star) also markets and sells cheerleading uniforms. Varsity sued Star for infringing on several of its copyrighted designs. Federal copyright law protects pictorial, graphic, and sculptural features of the design of useful articles, but does not protect useful articles themselves. The U.S. district court granted summary judgment to Star, finding that Varsity's designs were not separate from the useful object, the cheerleading uniform. The U.S. court of appeals reversed in favor of Varsity, finding that Varsity's designs were separate from and capable of existing independently of the utilitarian aspects of the cheerleading uniforms, and therefore qualified for copyright protection. Star appealed to the U.S. Supreme Court. Are Varsity's designs and graphics on its cheerleading uniforms protected by copyright law? *Star Athletica, LLC v. Varsity Brands, Inc.*, 137 S.Ct. 1002, 2017 U.S. Lexis 2026 (Supreme Court of the United States, 2017)

7.6 Fair Use Dodger Productions, Inc. produced a stage musical called *Jersey Boys*. The musical is a historical dramatization about the American rock 'n' roll singing group the Four Seasons and contains hit songs of the group. *The Ed Sullivan Show* was a weekly television show that highlighted many singing groups. One night the Four Seasons appeared and sang on *The Ed Sullivan Show*. At the end of the first act of *Jersey Boys*, a seven-second clip is shown on a screen hanging over the middle of the stage of the Four Seasons television appearance on *The Ed Sullivan Show*. SOFA Entertainment, Inc. (SOFA) owns copyrights to *The Ed Sullivan Show*, including the appearance of the Four Seasons. SOFA sued Dodger Productions for copyright infringement. Dodger Productions asserted the defense of fair use. Does the doctrine of fair use protect Dodger Productions from the charge of copyright infringement? *SOFA Entertainment, Inc. v. Dodger Productions, Inc.*, 709 F.3d 1273, 2013 U.S. App. Lexis 4830 (United States Court of Appeals for the Ninth Circuit, 2013)

Ethics Cases

7.7 Ethics Case Intel Corporation is a large company that distributes its entire line of products and services under the registered trademark and service mark INTEL. The company also owns numerous marks that incorporate its INTEL marks as a permanent component, such as the marks INTEL INSIDE, INTEL SPEEDSTEP, INTEL XEON, and INTEL NETMERGE. Intelsys Software, LLC, which is owned by another party, develops software applications for network utilities and wireless applications. Intelsys uses the mark Intelsys Software and maintains a website at **www.intelsys.com**. Intel Corporation brought an action in U.S. district court against Intelsys Software, LLC, alleging that Intelsys infringed on Intel's trademarks and service marks, in violation of the Lanham Act. Intel filed a motion for judgment and a permanent injunction against Intelsys's use of the mark INTEL in any of its company, product, or service names. Is there trademark infringement that warrants the issuance of a permanent injunction against Intelsys? Did Intelsys act ethically in this case? *Intel Corporation v. Intelsys Software, LLC*, 2009 U.S. Dist. Lexis 14761 (United States District Court for the Northern District of California, 2009)

7.8 Ethics Case Apple, Inc. released its first-generation iPhone in 2007. The iPhone is a smartphone, a cellphone with a broad range of functions based on advanced computing capability, large storage capacity, and internet connectivity. Apple obviously secured utility patents on the functionality of its smartphones. Apple also secured the following design patents for the iPhone: (1) D618,677 patent, covering a black rectangular front face with rounded corners; (2) D593,087 patent, covering a rectangular front face with rounded corners and a raised rim; and (3) D604,305 patent, covering a grid of colorful icons on a black screen. After Apple released its iPhone, Samsung Electric Co., Ltd. (Samsung) manufactured and sold a series of smartphones that resembled the iPhone in design. Apple sued Samsung, alleging that various Samsung smartphones infringed on Apple's design patents. Did Samsung infringe on Apple's design patents? Did Samsung act ethically in this case? *Samsung Electronics Co., Ltd. v. Apple, Inc.*, 137 S.Ct. 429, 2016 U.S. Lexis 7419 (Supreme Court of the United States, 2016)

Notes

1. 18 U.S.C. Section 1836 et seq.
2. 18 U.S.C. Sections 1831–1839.
3. 35 U.S.C. Section 10 et seq.
4. Public Law 112–129.
5. 17 U.S.C. Section 101 et seq.
6. Public Law 105–298.
7. Public Law 115–264.
8. Public Law 105–147.
9. 17 U.S.C. Section 1201.
10. 15 U.S.C. Section 1114 et seq.
11. 15 U.S.C. Section 1125.
12. Public Law No. 109–312, 15 U.S.C. Section 1125(c).

CHAPTER

8 Criminal Law and Cybercrime

Henry R. Cheeseman

STATUE OF AUTHORITY OF LAW, U.S. SUPREME COURT, WASHINGTON DC

In the United States, suspected criminals are given many rights by the U.S. Constitution and state constitutions. Parties in the United States are free from unreasonable searches and seizures of evidence, and any evidence obtained illegally is considered tainted evidence and cannot be used in court. People who are suspected of a criminal act may assert their right of privilege against self-incrimination and may choose not to testify at any pretrial proceedings or at trial. In addition, if convicted of a crime, the criminal is free from cruel and unusual punishment.

Learning Objectives

After studying this chapter, you should be able to:

8.1 Define *crime* and describe the essential elements of a crime.

8.2 Describe criminal procedure, including arrest, indictment, and arraignment.

8.3 Describe a criminal trial and the standard of proof that must be met to find a person guilty of a crime.

8.4 Describe common crimes such as murder, robbery, and larceny.

8.5 Identify and describe business and white-collar crimes.

8.6 List and describe cybercrimes.

8.7 Explain the Fourth Amendment protection from unreasonable search and seizure.

8.8 Explain the Fifth Amendment privilege against self-incrimination and other privileges recognized in criminal matters.

8.9 Explain the protections provided by the Double Jeopardy Clause, the right to a public jury trial, the right to counsel, and protection against cruel and unusual punishment.

> *"It is better that ten guilty persons escape than that one innocent suffer."*
>
> —*Sir William Blackstone*
> *Commentaries on the Law of England (1765)*

Introduction to Criminal Law and Cybercrime

For members of society to coexist peacefully and for commerce to flourish, people and their property must be protected from injury by other members of society. Federal, state, and local governments' **criminal law** is intended to afford this protection by providing an incentive for persons to act reasonably in society and imposing penalties on persons who violate the law.

There can be no equal justice where the kind of trial a man gets depends on the amount of money he has.

Justice Hugo Black
Griffin v. Illinois 351 U.S. 12, 76 S.Ct. 585, 1956 U.S. Lexis 1059 Supreme Court of the United States (1956)

The United States has one of the most advanced and humane criminal law systems in the world. It differs from other criminal law systems in several respects. Under many other countries' legal systems, a person accused of a crime is presumed guilty unless the person can prove he or she is not. A person charged with a crime in the United States is **presumed innocent until proven guilty**. The **burden of proof** in a criminal trial is on the government to prove that the accused is guilty of the crime charged. Further, the accused must be found guilty **beyond a reasonable doubt**. Conviction requires a unanimous jury vote. A person charged with a crime in the United States is also provided with substantial constitutional safeguards during the criminal justice process.

Many crimes are referred to as *white-collar crimes* because they are most often committed by business managers and employees. These crimes include fraud, bribery, and other such crimes. In addition, in the information age, many *cybercrimes* are committed using computers and the internet.

This chapter discusses criminal procedure, crimes, business and white-collar crimes, cybercrimes, and constitutional safeguards afforded criminal defendants.

The jury, passing on the prisoner's life,
May, in the sworn twelve, have a thief or two
Guiltier than him they try.

William Shakespeare
Measure for Measure (1604)

Definition of a Crime

8.1 Define *crime* and describe the essential elements of a crime.

A **crime** is defined as any act done by an individual in violation of those duties that he or she owes to society and for the breach of which the law provides that the wrongdoer shall make amends to the public. Many activities have been considered crimes through the ages, whereas other crimes are of more recent origin.

crime
A violation of a statute for which the government imposes a punishment.

Penal Codes

Statutes are the primary source of criminal law. Most states have adopted comprehensive **penal codes** that define in detail the activities considered to be crimes within their jurisdictions and the penalties that will be imposed for their commission. A comprehensive federal criminal code defines federal crimes.[1]

penal code
A collection of criminal statutes.

Example Each state has a criminal penal code that lists and defines the activities that are illegal in that state. These crimes include first-degree murder, burglary, robbery, arson, rape, and other crimes.

Parties to a Criminal Action

The **government** is the governing body of a nation, state, county, or city. In a criminal lawsuit, the government (not a private party) is the **plaintiff**. In most criminal actions, either the federal government or a state or territorial government is the plaintiff. The government is represented by a lawyer called the **prosecutor** or **prosecuting attorney**. The accused, which is usually an

Law cannot persuade where it cannot punish.

Thomas Fuller
Gnomologia (1732)

individual or a business, is the **defendant**. The accused is represented by a **defense attorney**. Sometimes the accused will hire a private attorney to represent them if they can afford to do so. If the accused cannot afford a private defense lawyer, the government will provide one free of charge, or for a nominal fee if the accused can afford to pay such fee. This government defense attorney is often called a **public defender**.

Criminal Penalties

The penalty for committing a crime may consist of the imposition of a fine, imprisonment, both, or some other form of punishment (e.g., probation). Generally, imprisonment is imposed to (1) incapacitate the criminal so he or she will not harm others in society, (2) provide a means to rehabilitate the criminal, (3) deter others from similar conduct, and (4) inhibit personal retribution by the victim.

Federal law imposes mandatory minimum sentences for serious and violent crimes, including certain drug offenses, use of guns in drug trafficking or crimes of violence, and convictions for child pornography, as well as for repeat offenders. Many states have also enacted minimum mandatory sentences for certain crimes and repeat offenders. Instead of a fixed mandatory sentence, many jurisdictions provide a sentencing range for the commission of different crimes, and court may impose a sentence within that range.

Example If a state establishes a sentencing range of three to eight years for armed robbery, a judge may sentence a person who is convicted of armed robbery to a period of time in jail that is within this range.

Defendants may receive less than the stipulated mandatory sentence based on their cooperation with the government. Mandatory sentencing does not apply if the criminal defendant and the government enter into a plea agreement that imposes an agreed-upon sentence. In some jurisdictions, judges are given discretion to impose less than the mandatory sentences under certain circumstances.

The following feature discusses a statute that reforms federal criminal law.

Contemporary Environment

First Step Act

In 2018, the federal government enacted the **Formerly Incarcerated Reenter Society Transformed Safely Transitioning Every Person Act**, commonly referred to as the **First Step Act**.[2] The goals of the act are to reform sentencing laws, steer federal prisons toward rehabilitation rather than just punishment, reduce recidivism, and provide nonviolent offenders the opportunity to reenter society as productive citizens. The act increases the time inmates can cut off their prison sentences for good behavior; allows inmates who participate in vocational and rehabilitative programs to be released early and serve the remainder of their sentences in halfway houses or under house arrest; requires that prisoners be placed within 500 driving miles from their family when possible, helping to maintain bonds with loved ones while the prisoner is incarcerated; expands compassionate release for terminally ill and elderly inmates; and reduces mandatory minimum sentences for nonviolent drug offenses from life to 25 years for third drug offenses, and from 25 years to 15 years for second drug offenses.

The act provides for the release of some prisoners who received harsh sentences for some drug offenses and gives judges more discretion to deviate from the mandatory minimum sentences when sentencing for nonviolent drug offenses; bans the practice of putting juveniles in solitary confinement; provides women in prison with adequate hygiene items, free of charge, and improves conditions for all prisoners; gives the U.S. Congress more oversight powers regarding federal prisons; and imposes auditing and reporting requirements to assess whether the provisions of the act are being properly administered. The act only affects persons incarcerated in federal prisons. Some states have enacted similar reform laws, and more states are expected to follow.

Classification of Crimes

Crimes are classified from serious to minor. A crime is usually classified as one of the following:

- **Felony. Felonies** are the most serious kinds of crimes. Felonies include crimes that are ***mala in se***—that is, inherently evil. Felonies are usually punishable by imprisonment. In some jurisdictions, certain felonies (e.g., first-degree murder) are punishable by death. Federal law[3] and some state laws require mandatory sentencing for specified crimes. Many statutes define different degrees of crimes (e.g., first-, second-, and third-degree murder). Each degree earns different penalties. Serious violations of regulatory statutes are also felonies.

  Example Most crimes against persons (e.g., murder, rape) and certain business-related crimes (e.g., embezzlement, bribery) are felonies in most jurisdictions.

felony
The most serious type of crime; an inherently evil crime. Most crimes against persons and some business-related crimes are felonies.

- **Misdemeanor. Misdemeanors** are less serious than felonies. They are crimes ***mala prohibita***; that is, they are not inherently evil but are prohibited by society. Misdemeanors carry lesser penalties than felonies. They are usually punishable by fines and/or imprisonment for one year or less.

  Example Many crimes committed against property, such as robbery, burglary, and less serious violations of regulatory statutes, are classified as misdemeanors in most jurisdictions.

misdemeanor
A crime that is less serious than a felony; a crime that is not inherently evil but is prohibited by society. Many crimes against property are misdemeanors.

- **Violation. Violations** are the least serious of crimes. These crimes are generally punishable by fines. Occasionally, one day or a few days of imprisonment is imposed.

  Example Crimes such as traffic offenses and jaywalking are usually classified as violations.

violation
A crime that is neither a felony nor a misdemeanor that is usually punishable by a fine.

CONCEPT SUMMARY
CLASSIFICATION OF CRIMES

Classification	Description
Felony	The most serious kinds of crimes. They are *mala in se* (inherently evil) and are usually punishable by imprisonment.
Misdemeanor	Crimes that are less serious than felonies. They are *mala prohibita* (prohibited by society) and are usually punishable by fine and/or imprisonment for less than one year.
Violation	Crimes that are neither felonies nor misdemeanors. Violations are generally punishable by a fine.

General Intent and Specific Crimes

Most crimes require **criminal intent** to be proven before the accused can be found guilty of the defined crime. Two elements must be proven for a person to be found guilty of an **intent crime**: (1) criminal act (*actus reus*) and (2) criminal intent (*mens rea*).

intent crime
A crime that requires the defendant to be found guilty of committing a criminal act (*actus reus*) with criminal intent (*mens rea*).

1. **Criminal act (*actus reus*).** The defendant must have performed the prohibited act. The actual performance of the criminal act is called the ***actus reus* (guilty act)**. Sometimes, the omission of an act can constitute the requisite *actus reus*.

   Example Killing someone without legal justification constitutes a criminal act (*actus reus*) because the law forbids persons from killing one another. If a taxpayer who is under a legal duty to file income tax returns and to pay

actus reus
"Guilty act"—the actual performance of a criminal act.

income taxes that are due the government fails to do so, there is the requisite criminal act (*actus reus*). A person who commits auto theft has engaged in a criminal act.

2. **Criminal intent** (*mens rea*). To be found guilty of an intent crime, the accused must be found to have possessed the requisite state of mind when the act was performed. This is called ***mens rea*** **(evil intent)**. Juries may infer a defendant's intent from the facts and circumstances of the case. Many jurisdictions have defined intent crimes as either *general intent* crimes or *specific intent* crimes:

mens rea
"Evil intent"—the possession of the requisite state of mind to commit a prohibited act.

   a. **Specific intent crime.** A **specific intent crime** requires that the perpetrator intended to achieve a specific result from his or her illegal act.

specific intent crime
A crime that requires that the perpetrator intended to achieve a specific result from his or her illegal act.

   Example Premeditated murder is a specific intent crime because the perpetrator intends a specific result, the death of the victim. Arson, forgery, and fraud are other examples of specific intent crimes.

   b. **General intent crime.** A **general intent crime** requires that the perpetrator either knew or should have known that his or her actions would lead to harmful results. The government does not have to prove that the accused intended the precise harm that resulted from his or her actions.

general intent crime
A crime that requires that the perpetrator either knew or should have known that his or her actions would lead to harmful results.

   Example Assault and battery are usually considered general intent crimes because the perpetrator intends to commit the crime but does not know the actual result of the crime in advance.

Individual criminal statutes state whether the crime requires a showing of specific or general intent. Some jurisdictions have eliminated the distinction between specific and general crimes.

Merely thinking about committing a crime is not a crime because no action has been taken. Thus, merely thinking about killing someone or evading taxes and not actually doing so is not a crime.

CONCEPT SUMMARY

ELEMENTS OF AN INTENT CRIME

Element	Description
Actus reus	Guilty act
Mens rea	Evil intent

Nonintent Crimes

Most states have enacted laws that define certain unintended conduct as a crime. These are called **nonintent crimes**. Nonintent crimes are often imposed for reckless or grossly negligent conduct that causes injury to another person.

nonintent crime
A crime that imposes criminal liability for reckless or grossly negligent conduct that causes death or injury to another person.

Example The crime of manslaughter only requires that a person acted with recklessness or gross negligence when someone is killed or injured. A speeding automobile driver who kills a pedestrian may not have intended to kill the victim, but will be found guilty of the nonintent crime of manslaughter.

Strict Liability Crimes

In certain circumstances, the commission of a prohibited act is the crime. The government does not have to prove that the defendant acted with intent or was reckless or grossly negligent, but only that a specified law has been violated. These are called **strict liability crimes**.

strict liability crime
A crime that imposes criminal liability for the commission of a prohibited act without requiring proof of intent, recklessness, or grossly negligent conduct.

Example Drunk driving laws provide that a person who is driving with a blood alcohol level above a stipulated level is guilty of the crime of drunk driving. The state does not have to prove that the driver knew that his or her blood alcohol level exceeded the lawful limit.

Example Many state statutory rape laws provide that an adult is guilty of the crime of statutory rape if the adult has sex with a minor who is under a specified age. The state does not have to prove that the defendant knew that the other person was a minor.

The following feature discusses how criminal acts may also be the basis for civil tort actions by an injured victim or a deceased victim's relatives.

Contemporary Environment

Criminal Acts as the Basis for Tort Actions

An injured victim of a crime or the relatives of a deceased victim of a crime may bring a **civil action** against a wrongdoer who has caused injury or death during the commission of a criminal act. Civil lawsuits are separate from the government's criminal action against the wrongdoer. In a civil lawsuit, the plaintiff usually wants to recover monetary damages from the wrongdoer.

Example A person commits the crime of battery and physically injures the victim. In this case, the government can prosecute the perpetrator for the crime of battery. In addition, the victim may sue the perpetrator in a civil lawsuit to recover monetary damages for the injuries the victim suffers because of the attack.

In many cases, a person injured by a criminal act does not sue the criminal to recover civil damages because the criminal is often **judgment proof**—that is, the criminal does not have the money to pay a civil judgment.

Criminal and civil law differ in the following ways:

Issue	Civil Law	Criminal Law
Party who brings the action	The plaintiff	The government
Trial by jury	Yes, except actions for equity	Yes
Burden of proof	Preponderance of the evidence	Beyond a reasonable doubt
Jury vote	Judgment for plaintiff requires specific jury vote (e.g., 9 of 12 jurors)	Conviction requires unanimous jury vote
Sanctions and penalties	Monetary damages and equitable remedies (e.g., injunction, specific performance)	Imprisonment, capital punishment, fine, probation

Criminal Procedure

8.2 Describe criminal procedure, including arrest, indictment, and arraignment.

The procedure for initiating and maintaining a criminal action is quite detailed. It includes both pretrial procedures and the actual trial.

Critical Legal Thinking Questions

Compare a criminal case with a civil case. Why is there such a difference in the burden of proof? Why is there a difference in the required jury vote?

Arrest

Before the police can **arrest** a person for the commission of a crime, they usually must obtain an **arrest warrant** based on a showing of probable cause. The police go before a judge and present the evidence they have for arresting the suspect. If the judge finds that there is *probable cause* to issue the warrant, he or she will

arrest warrant
A document for a person's detainment, based on a showing of probable cause that the person committed a crime.

do so. The police will then use the arrest warrant to arrest the suspect. **Probable cause** is defined as the substantial likelihood that a person either committed or is about to commit a crime.

probable cause
Probability of the substantial likelihood that a person either committed or is about to commit a crime.

Example The police obtain information from a reliable informant about the criminal activity of an individual, further investigate the situation, and arrive at the conclusion that the individual who is the target of their investigation is involved in the illegal selling of drugs. The police can take this evidence, place it before a judge, and request that the judge issue an arrest warrant. If the judge believes there is probable cause, the judge will issue an arrest warrant. The police can then arrest the suspect pursuant to the arrest warrant.

warrantless arrest
An arrest that is made without obtaining an arrest warrant. The arrest must be based on probable cause and a showing that it was not feasible to obtain an arrest warrant.

An arrest can be made without obtaining an arrest warrant if there is no time to obtain one or it is otherwise not feasible to obtain a warrant prior to the arrest. **Warrantless arrests** must be based on probable cause.

Example The police can make a warrantless arrest if they arrive during the commission of a crime, when a person is fleeing from the scene of a crime, or when it is likely that evidence will be destroyed.

WEB EXERCISE
Go to **www.fbi.gov** and click on "Most Wanted" and then "Ten Most Wanted Fugitives." Who is the number-one fugitive listed, and what crime is he or she wanted for?

Example In *Atwater v. Lago Vista, Texas*,[4] the U.S. Supreme Court held that a police officer may make a warrantless arrest pursuant to a minor criminal offense.

Booking

After a person is arrested, he or she is taken to the police station to be booked. **Booking** is the administrative procedure for recording an arrest, which includes fingerprinting the suspect, taking a photograph of the suspect (often called a "mug shot"), and so on. A DNA sample may be taken from a suspect as part of the booking process for serious offenses.

Bail and Bail Bonds

bail
An amount of money established by a court that a person who has been arrested may post with the court in order to be released from custody, usually jail, pending the trial of his or her case.

When a person is arrested and charged with a crime, a **bail** amount is often set by the court, usually during the suspect's first appearance in court. If bail is set, the suspect can post bail by paying the court the amount of the bail and then be released pending trial. However, if the suspect does not post bail, he or she may be kept in jail for some period of time, and often until the date of trial. Often, in instances of very serious criminal charges, no bail will be set, and the suspect will remain in prison until and during the criminal trial.

bail bond
An instrument that is purchased from a bail bonds person by a person who has been arrested and ordered to post a bond with the court in order to be released from custody, usually jail, pending the trial of his or her case. The bail bonds persons submits the bail bond to the court in substitution for the bail that the arrested person would be required to post.

If bail has been set and the suspect cannot afford to pay the bail or does not wish to pay the amount of the bail, the suspect can pay a bail bond agent to post a **bail bond** with the court so that the suspect can be released until trial. Bail bond agents usually charge a fee of 10 percent or more of the bail amount to post a bail bond. The bail bond guarantees the court that the bail bond agent will pay the amount of the bail if the suspect does not show up for trial. The bail bond agent keeps the fee paid by the purchaser of the bond whether or not the suspect shows up for trial. If the suspect does not show up for trial, the bail bond agent must pay the amount of the bond to the court. In such cases, the bail bond agent will attempt to recover the bail amount from the person who paid for the bail bond, including foreclosing on any collateral given by that person.

In some cases, usually for less serious charges and if the suspect is not a flight risk, the court will grant a suspect's release pending trial based on his or her own **recognizance (OR)**. No bail money need be paid to the court, and no bond is necessary. The suspect promises to return for future court proceedings.

Indictment or Information Statement

An accused person must be formally charged with a crime before being brought to trial. This is usually done through an indictment issued by a grand jury or an information statement issued by an attorney of the government or a magistrate judge.

Evidence of serious felonies (e.g., murder, battery, rape, arson, aggravated assault with a deadly weapon, fraud) is usually presented to a **grand jury**. Most grand juries are composed of between 6 and 24 citizens who are charged with evaluating the evidence presented by the government. Grand jurors sit for a fixed time, such as one year. If the grand jury determines that there is probable cause to hold the accused for trial, it issues an **indictment**. Note that the grand jury does not determine guilt or punishment. If an indictment is issued, the accused will be held for later trial. In states that do not provide for grand juries, courts hold preliminary hearings, at which time a judge will decide if there is probable cause to issue an indictment against the accused.

indictment
The charge of having committed a crime (usually a felony), based on the judgment of a grand jury.

Evidence of misdemeanors (e.g., trespassing, shoplifting, public intoxication, stalking) is examined by a prosecutor. If the prosecutor finds that there is enough evidence to hold the accused for trial, an **information statement** will be issued charging the accused with the crime. In some jurisdictions, the evidence of misdemeanors is presented to a magistrate judge who decides whether there is probable cause for issuing an information statement charging the accused with the crime.

The case against the accused is dismissed if neither an indictment nor an information statement is issued.

A **magistrate judge** who often oversees the first appearance of a criminal defendant sets bail, issues search warrants and arrest warrants, holds preliminary proceedings, and assists in other administrative duties of the court.

Arraignment

If an indictment or information statement is issued, the accused is brought before a court for an **arraignment** proceeding during which the accused is (1) informed of the charges and (2) asked to enter a **plea**. The accused may plead **guilty** or **not guilty**.

arraignment
A hearing during which the accused is brought before a court and is (1) informed of the charges and (2) asked to enter a plea.

Example Peter has been arrested for the crime of automobile theft. At the arraignment, Peter is asked how he pleads. Peter replies, "Not guilty." Peter has pleaded not guilty rather than guilty. Most accused people plead not guilty at their arraignment.

Nolo Contendere A party may enter a plea of ***nolo contendere*** whereby the accused agrees to the imposition of a penalty but does not admit guilt. The government has the option of accepting a *nolo contendere* plea or requiring the defendant to plead guilty or not guilty. If the government agrees to accept the *nolo contendere* plea, the accused and the government usually enter into a plea bargain whereby the accused agrees to the imposition of a penalty but does not admit guilt. A *nolo contendere* plea cannot be used as evidence of liability against the accused at a subsequent civil trial. Corporate defendants often enter this plea.

Example The government brings charges against a corporation for criminally violating environmental pollution laws. The government and the corporation enter into an agreement whereby the corporation pleads *nolo contendere* and agrees to pay a fine of $5 million but does not plead guilty to the violation.

The following feature discusses plea bargain agreements that are used in many criminal cases.

Critical Legal Thinking Questions

Why does the government offer plea bargains rather than go to trial? Is there any reason why an innocent person may agree to a plea bargain of criminal charges?

Ethics

Plea Bargain Agreements in Criminal Cases

Sometimes the accused and the government enter **plea bargain** negotiations prior to trial with the intent of avoiding a trial. If an agreement is reached, the government and the accused execute a **plea bargain agreement** that sets forth the terms of their agreement.

Example An accused is charged with first-degree murder, which, if proven, carries a penalty of life in prison. The government and the accused engage in plea bargaining, and an agreement is reached whereby the accused agrees to plead guilty to the crime of second-degree murder, which carries a maximum penalty of 20 years in jail. Therefore, a trial is avoided.

The government engages in plea bargaining to save costs, avoid the risks of a trial, and prevent further overcrowding of the prisons. In return, the government agrees to impose a lesser penalty or sentence on the accused than might have been obtained had the case gone to trial and the accused been found guilty. The accused often agrees to a plea bargain to avoid the risks of trial, where, if found guilty, he or she would be subject to a greater penalty than the penalty imposed by the plea bargain agreed to with the government. Approximately 95 percent of criminal cases are plea bargained and do not go to trial. Of those that go to trial, the government wins a conviction in approximately 75 percent.

Ethics Questions
Why does the government enter into so many plea bargain agreements? Why do defendants agree to plea bargain agreements? Is it ethical for the government not to prosecute a defendant for the crime committed?

---

plea bargain agreement
An agreement in which the accused admits to a lesser crime than charged. In return, the government agrees to impose a lesser sentence than might have been obtained had the case gone to trial.

Criminal Trial

8.3 Describe a criminal trial and the standard of proof that must be met to find a person guilty of a crime.

At a criminal trial, all jurors must *unanimously* agree before the accused is found *guilty* of the crime charged. If even one juror disagrees (i.e., has reasonable doubt) about the guilt of the accused, the accused cannot be found guilty of the crime charged. If all the jurors agree that the accused did not commit the crime, the accused is found *not guilty* of the crime charged. After trial, the following rules apply:

- If the defendant is found guilty, he or she may appeal.
- If the defendant is found not guilty, the government cannot appeal.
- If the jury cannot come to a **unanimous decision** about the defendant's guilt one way or the other, the jury is considered a **hung jury**. In this situation, the government may choose to retry the case before a new judge and jury.

hung jury
A jury that cannot come to a unanimous decision about the defendant's guilt. In the case of a hung jury, the government may choose to retry the case.

Example A defendant is tried for the crime of murder. A 12-person jury hears the case. If 10 jurors find the defendant guilty but two jurors find the defendant not guilty, then there is a hung jury. The government may retry the defendant and often does so with such a vote. However, if the vote had been four jurors voting guilty and eight jurors voting not guilty, it is highly unlikely the government would retry the case.

Common Crimes

8.4 Describe common crimes such as murder, robbery, and larceny.

Many **common crimes** are committed against persons and property. Some of the most important common crimes against persons and property are discussed in the following paragraphs.

Murder

murder
The unlawful killing of a human being by another person without justification.

Murder is defined as the unlawful killing of a human being by another person without justification. In most states, there are several degrees of murder—usually defined as *first-degree murder, second-degree murder, voluntary manslaughter,* and *involuntary manslaughter.*

1. **First-degree murder**. **First-degree murder** is the intentional unlawful killing of a human being by another person with premeditation, malice aforethought, and willful act. When a person can be executed for committing the murder, it is referred to as **capital murder**.

   Example A person purchases a weapon for the purpose of killing someone, lies in wait to kill that person, and then carries out the murder.

first-degree murder
The intentional unlawful killing of a human being by another person with premeditation, malice aforethought, and willful act.

2. **Second-degree murder**. **Second-degree murder** is the intentional unlawful killing of a human being by another person that is not premeditated or planned in advance. Second-degree murder involves some deliberation but not long-term planning.

   Example Two persons who are at a bar get into an unplanned fight, and one of the combatants kills the other.

second-degree murder
The intentional unlawful killing of a human being by another person that is not premeditated or planned in advance.

3. **Voluntary manslaughter**. **Voluntary manslaughter** is the intentional unlawful killing of a human being by another person that is not premeditated or planned in advance and that is committed under circumstances that would cause a person to become emotionally upset. Some states refer to this crime as *third-degree murder*.

   Example A spouse comes home unexpectedly, finds the other spouse committing an act of infidelity, and in the heat of passion "snaps" and kills the spouse, the lover, or both.

voluntary manslaughter
The intentional unlawful killing of a human being by another person that is not premeditated or planned in advance and that is committed under circumstances that would cause a reasonable person to become emotionally disturbed.

4. **Involuntary manslaughter**. **Involuntary manslaughter** is the unintentional unlawful killing of a human being by another person that is caused from a reckless or negligent act. Some states refer to this crime as *negligent homicide*.

   Example A drunk driver unintentionally causes another person's death.

involuntary manslaughter
The unintentional unlawful killing of a human being by another person that is caused from a reckless or negligent act.

The first three crimes are intent crimes. The fourth is a nonintent crime. The penalties assessed against persons found to have committed these crimes differ by state.

Felony Murder Rule Sometimes a murder is committed during the commission of another crime even though the perpetrator did not originally intend to commit murder. Most states hold the perpetrator liable for the crime of murder in addition to the other crime. This is called the **felony murder rule**. The intent to commit the murder is inferred from the intent to commit the other crime. Many states also hold accomplices liable under this doctrine.

The criminal is to go free because the constable has blundered.

Chief Judge Benjamin Cardozo
People v. Defore
242 N.Y. 13, 150 N.E. 585, 1926 N.Y. Lexis 956 (1926)

Robbery

In common law, **robbery** is defined as the taking of personal property from another person or business using fear or force. Robbery with a deadly weapon is generally considered aggravated robbery (or armed robbery) and carries a harsher penalty.

Example If a person threatens to shoot another person with a gun unless the victim gives up her purse, this constitutes the crime of robbery. If a person picks a wallet from someone's pocket, it is not robbery because there has been no use of force or fear. This is a theft.

robbery
The taking of personal property from another person by the use of fear or force.

Burglary

In common law, **burglary** is defined as "breaking and entering a dwelling at night" with the intent to commit a felony. Modern penal codes have broadened this

burglary
The taking of personal property from another's home, office, or commercial or other type of building.

definition to include daytime thefts from homes, offices, commercial buildings, and other buildings. In addition, the "breaking-in" element has been abandoned by most modern definitions of burglary. Thus, unauthorized entering of a building through an unlocked door is sufficient. Aggravated burglary (or armed burglary) carries stiffer penalties.

Example Harold breaks into Sibyl's home and steals jewelry and other items. Harold is guilty of the crime of burglary because he entered a dwelling and committed theft.

Larceny

larceny
The taking of another's personal property other than from his or her person or building.

In common law, **larceny** is defined as the wrongful and fraudulent taking of another person's personal property that is not robbery or burglary. Most personal property—including tangible property, trade secrets, computer programs, and other business property—is subject to larceny. Neither the use of force nor the entry of a building is required. Some states distinguish between grand larceny and petit larceny. This distinction depends on the value of the property taken.

Example Stealing automobiles and stealing satellite radios from automobiles are considered larcenies.

Theft

Some states have dropped the distinction among the crimes of robbery, burglary, and larceny. Instead, these states group these crimes under the general crime of **theft**. Most of these states distinguish between grand theft and petit theft. The distinction depends on the value of the property taken, an amount that varies from one state to the next.

Receiving Stolen Property

receiving stolen property
A crime that involves (1) knowingly receiving stolen property and (2) intending to deprive the rightful owner of that property.

A person commits the crime of **receiving stolen property** if he or she (1) knowingly receives stolen property and (2) intends to deprive the rightful owner of that property. Knowledge and intent can be inferred from the circumstances. The stolen property can be any tangible property (e.g., personal property, money, negotiable instruments, and stock certificates).

Example David is walking down the street and is approached by a man who offers to sell David a Rolex watch "at a bargain price." David looks at the 20 Rolex watches that the man displays, chooses one that would normally sell in a retail store for $1,000, and pays $200 for it. It is an authentic Rolex watch. David is guilty of the crime of receiving stolen property because it could easily be proven by circumstantial evidence that he had knowledge that the watch was stolen property.

Arson

arson
The willful or malicious burning of a building.

In common law, **arson** is defined as the malicious or willful burning of the dwelling of another person. Modern penal codes have expanded this definition to include the burning of all types of private, commercial, and public buildings.

Example An owner of a motel burns down the motel to collect fire insurance proceeds. The owner is guilty of the crime of arson. In this case, the insurance company does not have to pay the proceeds of any insurance policy on the burned property to the arsonist-owner. On the other hand, if a third-party arsonist burned down the motel without the knowledge or assistance of the owner, the third party is the arsonist, and the owner is entitled to recover the proceeds of any fire insurance he had on the property.

Business and White-Collar Crimes

8.5 Identify and describe business and white-collar crimes.

Certain types of crimes are prone to being committed by businesspeople. These crimes are often referred to as **white-collar crimes**. Such crimes usually involve cunning and deceit rather than physical force. Many of the most important white-collar crimes are discussed in the paragraphs that follow.

white-collar crime
Crimes that are often committed by businesspeople.

Forgery

The crime of **forgery** occurs if a written document is fraudulently made or altered and that change affects the legal liability of another person. Counterfeiting, falsifying public records, and materially altering legal documents are examples of forgery.

forgery
The fraudulent making or alteration of a written document that affects the legal liability of another person.

Example Signing another person's signature to a check or changing the amount of a check without the owner's permission is forgery.

Note that signing another person's signature without intent to defraud is not forgery.

Example Forgery has not been committed if one spouse signs the other spouse's payroll check for deposit in a joint checking or savings account at the bank.

Embezzlement

The crime of **embezzlement** is the fraudulent conversion of property by a person to whom that property was entrusted. Typically, embezzlement is committed by an employer's employees, agents, or representatives (e.g., accountants, lawyers, trust officers, treasurers). Embezzlers often try to cover their tracks by preparing false books, records, or entries.

The key element here is that the stolen property was *entrusted* to the embezzler. This differs from robbery, burglary, and larceny, where property is taken by someone not entrusted with the property.

embezzlement
The fraudulent conversion of property by a person to whom that property was entrusted.

Example A bank entrusts a teller to take deposits from its customers and deposit them into the customers' accounts at the bank. Instead, the bank teller absconds with the money. This is embezzlement. A lawyer who steals money from a trust fund that has been entrusted to him or her to administer commits the crime of embezzlement.

Bribery

Bribery is one of the most prevalent forms of white-collar crime. A bribe can be money, property, favors, or anything else of value. The crime of commercial bribery entails the payment of bribes to private persons and businesses. This type of bribe is often referred to as a **kickback**, or **payoff**. Intent is a necessary element of this crime. The offeror of a bribe commits the crime of bribery when the bribe is tendered. The offeree is guilty of the crime of bribery when he or she accepts the bribe. The offeror can be found liable for the crime of bribery even if the person to whom the bribe is offered rejects the bribe.

bribery
A crime in which one person gives another person money, property, favors, or anything else of value for a favor in return. A bribe is often referred to as a *payoff* or *kickback*.

Example Harriet Landers is the purchasing agent for the ABC Corporation and is in charge of purchasing equipment to be used by the corporation. Neal Brown, the sales representative of a company that makes equipment that can be used by the ABC Corporation, offers to pay her a 10 percent kickback if she buys equipment from him. She accepts the bribe and orders the equipment. Both parties are guilty of bribery.

Modern penal codes also make it a crime to bribe public officials.

Example If a real estate developer who is constructing an apartment building offers to pay the building inspector to overlook a building code violation, this is bribery.

Extortion

extortion
A threat to expose something about another person unless that other person gives money or property; often referred to as *blackmail*.

The crime of **extortion** involves the obtaining of property from another, with his or her consent, induced by wrongful use of actual or threatened force, violence, or fear. Extortion occurs when a person threatens to expose something about another person unless that other person gives money or property. The truth or falsity of the information is immaterial. Extortion of private persons is commonly referred to as **blackmail**. Extortion of public officials is called **extortion under color of official right**.

Example A person knows that an executive who works for a company has been engaged in a physical altercation with another person. The person who knows this information threatens the executive that he will disclose this fact to the company unless the executive pays him money. The person who makes the threat of exposure has committed the crime of extortion even though the fact he or she threatens to divulge is true.

Criminal Fraud

criminal fraud (false pretenses or deceit)
A crime that involves obtaining title to property through deception or trickery.

Criminal fraud, also known as **false pretenses** or **deceit**, is an act whereby a perpetrator makes a misrepresentation that causes a detriment to someone who acts upon the false statement. The elements of criminal fraud are that (1) the perpetrator makes a misrepresentation of a material fact; (2) the perpetrator knows that the alleged fact is false; (3) the misrepresentation is made with the intent to defraud; (4) the victim justifiably relies on the misrepresentation; and (5) the victim suffers actual loss from the reliance. It is the use of intentional deception for monetary or personal gain.

There are some frauds so well conducted that it would be stupidity not to be deceived by them.

C. C. Colton
Lacon, Volume 1 (1820)

Example Types of fraud include bank, insurance, telemarketing, check, Medicare and other health care, and bankruptcy fraud; securities and investment fraud; credit card and debit card fraud; and fake charities fraud as well as identity theft and forgery.

Fraud is often committed using computers, the internet, email, social media, and other digital means.

Example A hacker mimics a reputable company (e.g., Amazon, eBay, PayPal), redirecting computer users to another website where they enter their credit card or other financial information. The criminal then uses this information to make personal purchases. This is the crime of web misdirection.

Mail Fraud, Wire Fraud, and Electronic Communications Fraud

Federal law prohibits the use of mail (U.S. Postal Service, Federal Express, UPS, or other private or commercial carrier) to defraud another person. This crime is called **mail fraud.**[5] Mail fraud requires that a suspect uses a scheme to defraud another person in which mail or other covered means of delivery is used.

Federal law prohibits the use of wires (e.g., telephone, radio, television, fax machine) to defraud another person. This crime is called **wire fraud.**[6] Federal law also prohibits the use of electronic communication devices and systems (e.g., computer, email, internet, social media messaging, cellphone, smart tablet) to defraud another person.

The government often includes these crimes in a criminal charge against a defendant who is charged with committing another crime but who also used the mail, wires, or electronic means to further the crime. Sometimes the government prosecutes a suspect under these statutes if there is insufficient evidence to prove the real crime that the criminal was attempting to commit, or if the target of the fraud did not act upon attempted fraud.

Example If a scammer telephones a mass number of people in a telemarketing scheme to obtain personal information (e.g., Social Security numbers, credit card information, bank account information), this is wire fraud.

Persons convicted of mail or wire fraud are subject to imprisonment and the imposition of monetary fines.

In the following feature, the court had to address the issue of securities fraud.

Ethics

Billion-Dollar Ponzi Scheme Collapses

"One of the most egregious frauds ever presented to a trial jury in federal court."

—David Hittner, District Judge

Robert Allen Stanford, a Texas businessman, operated several investment companies, including an offshore bank on the island of Antigua in the Caribbean. Stanford established a family of companies in Houston, Texas, including Stanford International Bank, Ltd. Stanford was a citizen of both the United States and Antigua.

Stanford operated his businesses by selling certificates of deposit (CDs) to investors with promises of above-market rates of return, touting the investments as being safer than U.S. government bank accounts. Over the course of two decades, Stanford enticed more than 30,000 investors to purchase more than $8 billion of these securities. Stanford used an array of agents to sell the CDs.

However, there was one major problem: Stanford was using some of the money to fund his lavish lifestyle, purchasing mansions, boats, and personal aircraft. In one year alone he spent $100 million. He continually needed more investors to pay prior investors the promised returns on their investments, to pay investors their principal amount when due, and to fund his personal lifestyle. Stanford was eventually bringing in $1 million per day from new investors.

Stanford was running a classic Ponzi scheme, in which new investors are continually needed. But Ponzi schemes all have one thing in common: they come crashing down when not enough new investors can be found. And that is what happened when a recession hit and many investors sought to redeem their CDs, while new investors became hard to come by. Stanford's Ponzi scheme collapsed.

The Securities and Exchange Commission (SEC) investigated and filed a civil complaint charging that Stanford operated a "massive Ponzi scheme" in violation of federal securities laws. Stanford's assets and those of his companies were frozen and placed in receivership. Stanford was arrested before he could flee the United States, and the federal government brought criminal charges against him. The government's star witness at the trial was the chief financial officer of Stanford's companies. Stanford was convicted on multiple counts of wire and mail fraud and obstruction of SEC proceedings.

The U.S. district court judge sentenced Stanford to 110 years in federal prison and ordered him to repay the $5.7 billion in unpaid claims. The trial judge stated that Stanford orchestrated "one of the most egregious frauds ever presented to a trial jury in federal court." The U.S. court of appeals upheld the guilty verdict and sentence. The U.S. Supreme Court refused to hear Stanford's appeal. *United States v. Stanford*, 805 F.3d 557 (United States Court of Appeals for the Fifth Circuit, 2015)

Ethics Questions

Why do Ponzi schemes initially work? Why do they eventually fail? Did Stanford act ethically in this case? What harm was done by Stanford's fraud? Should the victims share any of the blame for their losses?

Money Laundering

When criminals make money from illegal activities, they are often faced with the problem of having large sums of money and no record of how this money was earned. This could easily tip off the government to their illegal activities. To "wash" the money and make it look as though it was earned legitimately, many criminals purchase legitimate businesses and run the money through those businesses to "clean" it before they receive the money from the so-called legitimate business. The legitimate business has "cooked" books, which show faked expenditures and receipts, and is the repository for the "buried" illegal money. Restaurants, motels, and other cash businesses make excellent money laundries.

To address the problem of **money laundering**, the federal government enacted the **Money Laundering Control Act.**[7] This act makes it a crime to:

Money Laundering Control Act
A federal statute that makes it a crime to (1) engage knowingly in a *money transaction* through a financial institution involving property from an unlawful activity worth more than $10,000 and (2) engage knowingly in a *financial transaction* involving the proceeds of an unlawful activity.

- Engage knowingly in a *monetary transaction* through a financial institution involving property from an unlawful activity worth more than $10,000.

  Example Monetary transactions through a financial institution include making deposits, making withdrawals, conducting transactions between accounts, or obtaining monetary instruments, such as cashiers' checks, money orders, and travelers' checks, from a bank or another financial institution for more than $10,000.

- Engage knowingly in a *financial transaction* involving the proceeds of an unlawful activity.

  Example Financial transactions involving the proceeds of an illegal activity include buying real estate, automobiles, personal property, intangible assets, or anything else of value with money obtained from illegal activities.

Thus, money laundering itself is now a federal crime. The money that is washed could have been made from illegal gambling operations, drug dealing, fraud, or other crimes, including white-collar crimes. Persons convicted of money laundering can be fined up to $500,000 or twice the value of the property involved, whichever is greater, and sentenced to up to 20 years in federal prison. In addition, violation of the act subjects any property involved in or traceable to the offense to forfeiture to the government.

Racketeer Influenced and Corrupt Organizations Act (RICO)

Organized crime has a pervasive influence on many parts of the U.S. economy. To combat this activity, Congress enacted the Organized Crime Control Act. The **Racketeer Influenced and Corrupt Organizations Act (RICO)** is part of this act.[8] Originally, RICO was intended to apply only to organized crime. However, the broad language of the RICO statute has been used against non–organized crime defendants as well. RICO, which provides for both criminal and civil penalties, is one of the most important laws affecting business today.

Racketeer Influenced and Corrupt Organizations Act (RICO)
A federal act that provides for both criminal and civil penalties for racketeering.

Criminal RICO RICO makes it a federal crime to acquire or maintain an interest in, use income from, or conduct or participate in the affairs of an enterprise through a pattern of racketeering activity. This is called **criminal RICO**. An *enterprise* is defined as a corporation, a partnership, a sole proprietorship, another business or organization, or the government.

Racketeering activity consists of a number of specifically enumerated federal and state crimes, including activities such as gambling, arson, robbery, counterfeiting, and dealing in narcotics. Business-related crimes, such as bribery, embezzlement, mail fraud, and wire fraud, are also considered racketeering. To prove a *pattern of racketeering*, at least two of these acts must be committed by the defendant within a 10-year period. Commission of the same crime twice within this 10-year period constitutes criminal RICO as well.

Individual defendants found criminally liable for RICO violations can be fined, imprisoned for up to 20 years, or both. In addition, RICO provides for the *forfeiture* of any property or business interests (even interests in a legitimate business) that were gained because of RICO violations. This provision allows the government to recover investments made with monies derived from racketeering activities. The government may also seek civil penalties for RICO violations, which include injunctions, orders of dissolution, reorganization of business, and divestiture of the defendant's interest in an enterprise.

Civil RICO Persons injured by a RICO violation can bring a private **civil RICO** action against the violator to recover damages for injury to business or property. A successful plaintiff may recover treble damages (three times the actual loss) plus attorney's fees.

Criminal Conspiracy

A **criminal conspiracy** occurs when two or more persons enter into an *agreement* to commit a crime. To be liable for a criminal conspiracy, a person must commit an *overt act* to further the crime. The crime itself does not have to be committed, however. The government usually brings criminal conspiracy charges if (1) the defendants have been thwarted in their efforts to commit the substantive crime or (2) there is insufficient evidence to prove the substantive crime.

criminal conspiracy
A crime in which two or more persons enter into an agreement to commit a crime and an overt act is taken to further the crime.

Example Two securities brokers agree over the telephone to commit a securities fraud. They obtain a list of potential victims and prepare false financial statements necessary for the fraud. Because they entered into an agreement to commit a crime and took an overt act, the brokers are guilty of the crime of criminal conspiracy, even if they never carry out the securities fraud.

The following feature discusses the criminal liability of corporations for the acts of its officers, directors, and employees.

Business Environment

Corporate Criminal Liability

A *corporation* is a fictitious legal person that is granted legal existence by the state when certain requirements are met. A corporation cannot act on its own behalf. Instead, it must act through *agents*, such as a board of directors, officers, and employees.

Originally, under the common law, it was generally held that corporations lacked the criminal mind (*mens rea*) to be held criminally liable. Modern courts, however, impose **corporate criminal liability**. These courts have held that corporations are criminally liable for the acts of their directors, officers, and employees. Because corporations cannot be put in prison, they are usually sanctioned with fines, loss of a license or franchise, and the like.

Corporate directors, officers, and employees are individually liable for crimes that they commit on behalf of or to further the interests of the corporation. In addition, under certain circumstances, a corporate manager can be held criminally liable for the criminal activities of subordinates. To be held criminally liable, the manager must have failed to supervise the subordinates appropriately. This is an evolving area of the law.

Critical Legal Thinking Questions
Why is criminal liability imposed on a corporation? Do you think that the penalties (e.g., jail time) that are imposed on corporate executives for white-collar crimes are sufficient?

Regulatory Crimes

Federal and state governments have enacted many **regulatory statutes** that regulate various aspects of business and the environment. Some statutes make violations a criminal offense. **Regulatory crimes** include violations of securities, antitrust, environmental, consumer, employment, credit, bankruptcy, intellectual property, and other statutes. Regulatory crimes are covered in various chapters of this book.

regulatory crimes
Violations of regulatory statutes that include securities, antitrust, environmental, consumer, employment, credit, bankruptcy, intellectual property, and other statutes.

Cybercrimes

8.6 List and describe cybercrimes.

The development of computers, digital devices, email, and the internet has made it easier for criminals to perpetrate many existing crimes and has created the ability for them to commit crimes that did not exist before the digital age. These

cybercrime
A crime that is committed using computers, email, the internet, or other electronic means.

are commonly referred to as **cybercrime**. The government has had to apply existing laws to these new media and develop new laws to attack digital crimes.

One of the most pervasive monetary crimes today is internet fraud. The following feature discusses the crime of online identity theft.

Information Technology

The Internet and Identity Theft

The advent of the computer, the internet, and digital devices has made one type of crime—identity theft—easier to commit. Identity theft was around long before the computer was invented, but computers and the internet have made it much easier for criminals to obtain the information they need to commit identity theft. In **identity theft**—or ***ID theft***—one person steals information about another person to pose as that person and take the innocent person's money or property or to purchase goods and services using the victim's credit information.

To commit ID theft, thieves must first obtain certain information about the victim. This could be the victim's name, Social Security number, credit card numbers, bank account information, and other personal information. With the use of electronic devices, criminals can obtain the information they need to commit ID theft more easily. Credit card fraud is one of the crimes most commonly committed by ID thieves. An ID thief may use a victim's existing credit card or open new credit card accounts in the victim's name and purchase goods and services with these credit cards, often using the internet.

In 1998, Congress enacted the **Identity Theft and Assumption Deterrence Act**,[9] which made it a federal crime to engage in identity theft. This statute makes it a federal crime to transfer or use, without authority, the identity of another person knowingly and with the intent to commit any unlawful activity as defined by federal law and state and local felony laws. The act has been amended several times since its original passage. Violators can be sentenced to prison for up to 15 years and have any property used in the commission of ID theft forfeited to the government.

In 2008, Congress enacted the **Identity Theft Enforcement and Restitution Act**.[10] This act makes it easier to prosecute identity theft cases and permits identity theft cases to be brought in federal court even if the cybercriminal and victim live in the same state.

Most states have enacted identity theft criminal statutes.

Computer Fraud and Abuse Act

Computer Fraud and Abuse Act (CFAA)
A federal statute that makes computer fraud a distinct federal crime.

Identity Theft and Assumption Deterrence Act
A federal act that makes it a crime to transfer or use, without authority, the identity of another person knowingly and with the intent to commit any unlawful activity as defined by federal law and state and local felony laws.

The **Computer Fraud and Abuse Act (CFAA)**[11] is a federal statute that makes computer fraud a distinct federal crime. The act applies to any "protected computer" which is connected to the internet, which includes desktop and laptop computers, cellphones, smart devices, tablets, and websites. The CFAA has been amended by the **Information Infrastructure Protection Act (IIP Act)**[12] and other federal laws.

The computer-related crimes outlawed by the CFAA include:

Computer fraud. Many computer crimes occur where the protected computer is used as an accessory to committing an ordinary crime. The CFAA prohibits computer fraud, which is defined as knowingly accessing a protected device without authorization with the intent to further a fraud or obtain anything of value. The perpetrator commits two crimes: the ordinary crime and computer fraud.

Example If a person uses a computer to commit embezzlement, the perpetrator is guilty of two crimes: embezzlement and computer fraud.

Unauthorized computer access. The CFAA prohibits a person from intentionally accessing, without authorization, a protected computer and obtaining information. This commonly occurs when someone hacks into another person's computer.

Example A person surreptitiously installs spyware on the user's computer which recovers the user's personal information.

Computer damage. The CFAA prohibits intentional attacks on protected computers that disrupts or disables service, or damages or destroys the device. Here, the computer is the subject or victim of a crime.

Example The unauthorized installation of viruses, worms, trojan horses, time bombs, malware, and denial of service attacks which damage protected computers violate the CFAA.

Extortion threats. The CFAA prohibits anyone from making a threat to cause damage to a protected computer system or data with the intent to extort money or property from the victim.

Example A person secretly installs ransomware on a user's computer, which encrypts data, and then demands a ransom payment before the information is restored.

Electronic Communications Privacy Act (ECPA)
A federal statute that makes it a crime to intercept an electronic communication at the point of transmission, while in transit, after receipt by the intended recipient, or when stored by a router or server. There are some exceptions to this law.

Government Computers and Computer Espionage. The CFAA makes it a crime for a person to intentionally and without authorization gain access to a government computer. The act also makes it a crime for a person to engage in computer espionage involving classified information concerning national defense, foreign relations, or atomic energy.

Penalties. Penalties for violating the CFAA includes fines and imprisonment ranging up to a maximum of twenty years. The CFAA authorizes victims of computer-related crimes to bring civil lawsuits against violators to recover damages.

Information Technology

Electronic Communications Privacy Act

The **Electronic Communications Privacy Act (ECPA)**[13] is a federal law enacted to protect the privacy of citizens while balancing the needs of law enforcement. The ECPA, as amended, protects oral, wire, and electronic communications while the communications are being made, while they are in transit, and when they are stored on computers. The act covers traditional telephone wiretaps, smartphone interceptions, email, electronic messages, digital data, voicemail systems, recording or videotaping private face-to-face conversations, web-streaming video, and the like.

The major sections of the ECPA are the *Wiretap Act* and the *Stored Communications Act*.

Wiretap Act

The ***Wiretap Act***[14] makes it a federal crime for a third party to use an electronic, mechanical, or other device to intentionally intercept, disclose, or use the contents of any oral, wire, or electronic communication of another party at the point of transmission, while in transit, and after receipt by the intended recipient. The unauthorized recording of another's telephone conversation or reading another's email or text messages would violate the act.

Example Celeste owns a smartphone, on which she sends and receives text messages. Rasmus learns Celeste's smartphone access code. Rasmus opens Celeste's smartphone and reads her text messages. Rasmus has violated the Wiretap Act.

Federal intelligence agencies may obtain a court order to monitor telephone and internet-based conversations if they prove to a judge that they have probable cause to believe that the wiretap will help them solve a serious crime or prevent an act of terrorism. In some circumstances, wiretaps may be authorized by the attorney general.

Stored Communications Act (SCA)

The ***Stored Communications Act (SCA)***[15] makes it a federal crime for a third party to intentionally review the contents of the files of a subscriber stored by a third-party internet service provider (ISP), including records such as a subscriber's name, billing records, or IP address.

Stored electronic communications may be accessed without violating the law by (1) a party or entity that is providing the electronic communication service, such as an employer accessing stored email communications of employees placed on the employer's service; and (2) government and law enforcement entities that are investigating suspected illegal activity. In such cases, the disclosure of information of a subscriber by an ISP would be required only pursuant to a valid warrant.

The ECPA provides for criminal penalties. In addition, the ECPA provides that an injured party may sue for civil damages for violations of the ECPA.

Constitutional Protections
A suspect or defendant in a criminal case is afforded many constitutional protections, including the right to be free from unreasonable search and seizure, privilege against self-incrimination, protection against double jeopardy, right to a public jury trial, and protection against cruel and unusual punishment.

Alamy

Fourth Amendment Protection from Unreasonable Search and Seizure

8.7 Explain the Fourth Amendment protection from unreasonable search and seizure.

In many criminal cases, the government relies on information obtained from searches of individuals and businesses. The **Fourth Amendment** to the U.S. Constitution protects persons and corporations from overzealous investigative activities by the government. It protects the rights of the people from **unreasonable search and seizure** by the government. It permits people to be secure in their persons, houses, papers, and effects.

unreasonable search and seizure
Protection granted by the Fourth Amendment for people to be free from unreasonable search and seizure by the government.

Reasonable search and seizure by the government is lawful. A **search warrant** based on *probable cause* is necessary in most cases. Such a warrant specifically states the place and scope of the authorized search. General searches beyond the specified area are forbidden. A **warrantless search** is permitted only (1) incident to arrest, (2) where evidence is in "plain view," or (3) in exigent circumstances such as when it is likely that evidence will be destroyed. Warrantless searches are judged by the probable cause standard.

search warrant
A warrant issued by a court that authorizes the police to search a designated place for specified contraband, articles, items, or documents. A search warrant must be based on probable cause.

Example The police obtained a search warrant to attach a global positioning system (GPS) to a suspect's automobile, and the warrant stated that the device be installed within 10 days. The police, however, did not install the device until the 11th day. The U.S. Supreme Court held that this was an unconstitutional search and that the information obtained from the search be excluded from evidence.[16]

Exclusionary Rule

Evidence obtained from an unreasonable search and seizure is considered tainted evidence ("fruit of a tainted tree"). Under the **exclusionary rule**, such evidence can generally be prohibited from introduction at a trial or an administrative proceeding against the person searched. However, this evidence is freely admissible against other persons.

exclusionary rule
A rule that says evidence obtained from an unreasonable search and seizure can generally be prohibited from introduction at a trial or an administrative proceeding against the person searched.

The U.S. Supreme Court created a *good faith exception* to the exclusionary rule.[17] This exception allows evidence obtained illegally to be introduced as evidence against the accused if the police officers who conducted the unreasonable search reasonably believed that they were acting pursuant to a lawful search warrant.

The following is a U.S. Supreme Court case that applies the Fourth Amendment.

CASE 8.1 *U.S. SUPREME COURT CASE Search of Curtilage*

Collins v. Virginia

138 S.Ct. 1663 (2018)
Supreme Court of the United States

"When it comes to the Fourth Amendment, the home is first among equals."

—Sonia Sotomayor, Justice

Facts

Over the course of several weeks, Officers Matthew McCall and David Rhodes of the Albemarle County Police Department saw the driver of an orange and black motorcycle commit traffic violations, but on each occasion the motorcyclist evaded apprehension. After investigation, the officers determined that the motorcycle had likely been stolen and was in the possession of Ryan Collins. After using Facebook to find photographs of Collins on the motorcycle, as well as information on the address where he might be, Officer Rhodes drove to the address. Rhodes saw a vehicle with a tarp over it parked in the driveway of the house. Rhodes entered the driveway, lifted the tarp, and found an orange and black motorcycle. After taking photographs, Officer Rhodes ran the license plate and discovered that the motorcycle was stolen. Officer Rhodes did not get a search warrant. Instead, he waited, and when Collins returned home, Rhodes arrested him. At trial, Collins argued that the warrantless search on the curtilage (the land immediately surrounding the house) violated the Fourth Amendment. The trial court denied Collins's motion to suppress the evidence, and Collins was convicted of the crime of receiving stolen property. The Virginia court of appeals and the Supreme Court of Virginia upheld the conviction. Collins appealed to the U.S. Supreme Court.

Issue

Does the Fourth Amendment permit a police officer, uninvited and without a search warrant, to enter the curtilage of a home in order to search a vehicle parked in the driveway of the home?

Language of the U.S. Supreme Court

The Fourth Amendment's protection of curtilage has long been black letter law. When it comes to the Fourth Amendment, the home is first among equals. To give full practical effect to that right, the Court considers curtilage—the area immediately surrounding and associated with the home—to be part of the home itself for Fourth Amendment purposes. When a law enforcement officer physically intrudes on the curtilage to gather evidence, a search within the meaning of the Fourth Amendment has occurred. Such conduct thus is presumptively unreasonable absent a warrant.

Decision

The U.S. Supreme Court held that the warrantless search of the curtilage of the home violated the Fourth Amendment. The Court reversed the decision of the Virginia Supreme Court and remanded the case for further proceedings.

Critical Legal Thinking Questions

Should the curtilage be considered part of a home for Fourth Amendment purposes? Could Officer Rhodes have obtained a warrant under the facts of this case?

Search of Electronic Information

Most people use electronic devices to communicate with one another, including using smartphones, sending text messages, using computers, and sending emails and documents. Large amounts of data are stored on these devices. Many people use social media sites and post information and photographs to their accounts, which discuss and show many of their life activities. Searches of websites and the use of apps on smartphones show what users are interested in. Thus, people have an extreme amount of personal data and businesses have large amounts of business data stored on electronic devices.

Critical Legal Thinking Questions

Does the exclusionary rule allow some guilty parties to go free? Is this an acceptable result when balanced against the protections afforded by the Fourth Amendment?

In apprehending and prosecuting criminal defendants, the government can use electronic information taken from digital devices to prove their case. However, the government must establish probable cause that the information sought is relevant and obtain a search warrant to acquire the information.

Example Penelope is arrested on suspicion of operating an internet fraud, and is indicted. The government, in preparation for the criminal trial, can, based on probable cause, obtain a search warrant to access information on her computer and other digital devices.

One case dealing with the search of a digital device is discussed in the following feature.

Information Technology

Search of Cellphones Incident to Arrest

"Our answer to the question of what police must do before searching a cellphone seized incident to an arrest is accordingly simple—get a warrant."
—John Roberts, Chief Justice

David Riley was stopped for driving with expired registration tags. A search of the car turned up two concealed and loaded firearms. The police confiscated Riley's smartphone and went through it, finding gang-related information and a photograph of Riley in front of a car they suspected to be involved in a shooting a few weeks earlier. Based on the information retrieved from the cellphone, Riley was charged with that earlier shooting, firing at an occupied vehicle, assault with a semiautomatic weapon, and attempted murder. Riley was convicted of all charges and was sentenced to 15 years in prison. Prior to trial, Riley moved to suppress the evidence the police obtained from his cellphone, alleging that the information obtained from his phone was the fruit of an unconstitutional search in violation of the Fourth Amendment.

The U.S. Supreme Court held that the police cannot conduct a warrantless search of digital information on a person's cellphone incident to that person's arrest. The Supreme Court held that searches of a variety of personal items carried by an arrestee—billfolds, address books, wallets, and purses—is lawful. However, the Supreme Court noted that "cellphones differ in both a quantitative and qualitative sense from other objects that might be kept on an arrestee's person." The Supreme Court stated, "Our answer to the question of what police must do before searching a cellphone seized incident to an arrest is accordingly simple—get a warrant." Thus, the police must show cause and obtain a search warrant before searching an arrestee's cellphone. *Riley v. California*, 134 S.Ct. 2473, 2014 U.S. Lexis 4497 (Supreme Court of the United States, 2014)

Searches of Business Premises

Generally, the government does not have the right to search business premises without a search warrant.[18] However, certain hazardous and regulated industries are subject to warrantless searches if proper statutory procedures are met.

Example Sellers of firearms, liquor stores and bars that sell alcohol, coal mines, and the like are businesses subject to warrantless searches.

The following feature discusses a federal act that affects the disclosure of electronic communications in certain criminal investigations.

Clarifying Lawful Overseas Use of Data Act (CLOUD Act)
A federal statute the provides a streamlined process by which law enforcement agencies may obtain user information from internet, media, and tech companies.

Information Technology

CLOUD Act

In 2018, the **Clarifying Lawful Overseas Use of Data Act**, commonly called the CLOUD Act, was enacted into law.[19] This federal legislation was supported by the U.S. Department of Justice and other U.S. law enforcement agencies, as well as by tech giants such as Google, Apple, Facebook, and Microsoft.

The CLOUD Act establishes rules on how tech companies must respond to warrants issued by law enforcement agencies located both in the United States and in foreign countries. Prior to the CLOUD Act, if a law enforcement agency wanted to obtain a user's data from an internet or social media company, they had to apply for and obtain a court order, which was a long process. Also, tech companies had to try to comply with complicated and oftentimes conflicting state and national laws.

The CLOUD Act provides for a streamlined process whereby law enforcement agencies can serve warrants directly on tech companies to obtain user data. The CLOUD Act contains the following two important provisions.

1. ***Provision for U.S. law enforcement agencies to obtain access to user data stored in foreign countries.*** The CLOUD Act allows federal, state, and local law enforcement agencies located in the United States to issue warrants directly to U.S. technology companies to obtain users' electronic data that is stored in foreign countries. The warrants do not have to be issued by courts. Upon receipt of the warrant, the tech company must disclose the user's electronic data that is sought by the U.S. law enforcement agency. Thus, having electronic user data stored in foreign countries does not protect the user data from discovery by U.S. law enforcement agencies.
2. ***Provision for the United States to create executive agreements with foreign countries permitting law enforcement agencies of each country to have access to user data stored in the other country.*** The CLOUD Act permits the executive branch of the federal government to enter into *bilateral data sharing agreements* with foreign countries. Under these agreements, a foreign government may serve a warrant directly to a U.S. technology company to obtain a targeted user's electronic data. No federal official or court will review an incoming foreign warrant seeking access to the data. However, foreign governments cannot target U.S. citizens or residents. Pursuant to such agreements, U.S. government law enforcement agencies can serve warrants directly on technology companies located in participating foreign countries and obtain requested electronic data about U.S. citizens or residents. The CLOUD Act only permits warrants seeking electronic data related to serious crimes or terrorism. Information sought may include the content of emails, the identity of users (e.g., name, address, telephone number), address books, contact lists, photographs, electronic messages, files, cloud storage, and the like.

Fifth Amendment Privilege Against Self-Incrimination

8.8 Explain the Fifth Amendment privilege against self-incrimination and other privileges recognized in criminal matters.

The **Fifth Amendment** to the U.S. Constitution provides that no person "shall be compelled in any criminal case to be a witness against himself." Thus, a person cannot be compelled to give testimony against him- or herself. A person who asserts this right is described as "taking the Fifth." This protection applies to federal cases and is extended to state and local criminal cases through the Due Process Clause of the Fourteenth Amendment. The right established by the Fifth Amendment is referred to as the **privilege against self-incrimination.**

privilege against self-incrimination
The Fifth Amendment provision that a person may not be required to be a witness against him- or herself in a criminal case.

Nontestimonial evidence (e.g., fingerprints, body fluids) may be obtained without violating the Fifth Amendment.

The protection against **self-incrimination** applies only to natural persons who are accused of crimes. Therefore, artificial persons (e.g., corporations, limited liability companies, partnerships) cannot raise this protection against incriminating testimony.[20] Thus, business records of corporations, limited liability companies, and partnerships are not generally protected from disclosure, even if they incriminate individuals who work for the business. However, certain "private papers" of businesspersons (e.g., personal diaries) are protected from disclosure.

Critical Legal Thinking Questions

What is the policy behind adding the privilege against self-incrimination to the U.S. Constitution? What percentage of criminal defendants "take the Fifth" and do not take the witness stand?

Miranda Rights

Many people have not read and memorized the provisions of the U.S. Constitution. The U.S. Supreme Court recognized this fact when it decided the landmark case *Miranda v. Arizona* in 1966.[21] In that case the U.S. Supreme Court held that the Fifth Amendment privilege against self-incrimination is not useful unless a criminal suspect has knowledge of this right. Therefore, the Supreme Court required that the following warning—colloquially called the ***Miranda* rights**—be read to a criminal suspect before he or she is interrogated by the police or other government officials:

***Miranda* rights**
Rights that a suspect must be informed of before being interrogated so that the suspect will not unwittingly give up his or her Fifth Amendment right.

- You have the right to remain silent.
- Anything you say can and will be used against you.

- You have the right to consult a lawyer and to have a lawyer present with you during interrogation.
- If you cannot afford a lawyer, a lawyer will be appointed free of charge to represent you.

Any statements or confessions obtained from a suspect before he or she has been read the *Miranda* rights can be excluded from evidence at trial. In 2000, the U.S. Supreme Court upheld *Miranda* in *Dickerson v. United States*.[22] In that opinion, Chief Justice William Rehnquist stated, "We do not think there is justification for overruling *Miranda*. *Miranda* has become embedded in routine police practice to the point where the warnings have become part of our national culture."

Many police departments read an accused a more detailed version of the *Miranda* rights (see Exhibit 8.1). This is designed to cover all issues that a detainee might encounter while in police custody. Detainees may be asked to sign a statement acknowledging that the *Miranda* rights have been read to them.

Attorney–Client and Other Privileges

To obtain a proper defense an accused should tell the lawyer the truth so that the lawyer can prepare the best defense possible for the accused. However, the accused must be able to tell the attorney facts about the case without fear that the attorney will be called as a witness against the accused. This information is protected from disclosure by the **attorney–client privilege**, which is recognized by the Fifth Amendment. Either the client or the attorney can raise this privilege. For the privilege to apply, the information must be told to the attorney in his or her capacity as an attorney and not as a friend or neighbor or in other capacity.

attorney–client privilege
A rule that says a client can tell his or her lawyer anything about the case without fear that the attorney will be called as a witness against the client.

Example Cedric is accused of murder and employs Gloria, a renowned criminal attorney, to represent him. During their discussions, Cedric confesses to the murder. Gloria cannot be a witness against Cedric at his criminal trial.

At the present time in this country there is more danger that criminals will escape justice than that they will be subjected to tyranny.

Justice Oliver Wendell Holmes, Dissenting Opinion
Kepner v. United States
195 U.S. 100, 24 S.Ct. 797, 1904 U.S. Lexis 820 (1904)
Supreme Court of the United States

The Fifth Amendment has also recognized the following privileges under which an accused may keep the following individuals from being witnesses against him or her:

- **Psychiatrist/psychologist–patient privilege** so that the accused may tell the truth in order to seek help for his or her condition.
- **Priest/rabbi/minister/imam–penitent privilege** so that the accused may tell the truth in order to repent, be given help, and seek forgiveness for his or her deed.
- **Spouse–spouse privilege** so that the family will remain together.
- **Parent–child privilege** so that the family will remain together.

Exhibit 8.1 *MIRANDA* RIGHTS

POLICE DEPARTMENT
PINE SHORES, MICHIGAN

- You have the right to remain silent and refuse to answer questions. Do you understand?
- Anything you say may be used against you in a court of law. Do you understand?
- You have the right to consult an attorney before speaking to the police and to have an attorney present during questioning now or in the future. Do you understand?
- If you cannot afford an attorney, one will be appointed for you before any questioning if you wish. Do you understand?
- If you decide to answer questions now without an attorney present, you will still have the right to stop answering at any time until you talk to an attorney. Do you understand?
- Knowing and understanding your rights as I have explained them to you, are you willing to answer my questions without an attorney present?

A spouse or child who is injured by a spouse or parent (e.g., domestic abuse) may testify against the accused. In addition, if the accused discloses a plan to commit a crime in the future (e.g., murder), the accused's lawyer; psychiatrist or psychologist; or priest, rabbi, minister, or imam is required to report this to the police or other relevant authorities.

The U.S. Supreme Court has held that there is no accountant–client privilege under federal law.[23] Thus, an accountant can be called as a witness in cases that involve federal securities laws, federal mail or wire fraud, or other federal crimes. Approximately 20 states have enacted special statutes that create an **accountant–client privilege**. An accountant cannot be called as a witness against a client in a court action in a state where these statutes are in effect. However, federal courts do not recognize this privilege.

The following feature discusses immunity from prosecution.

immunity from prosecution The government's agreement not to use against a person granted immunity any evidence given by that person.

Ethics

Immunity from Prosecution

On occasion, the government may want to obtain information from a suspect who has asserted the Fifth Amendment privilege against self-incrimination. The government can often achieve this by offering the suspect **immunity from prosecution**. Immunity from prosecution means that the government agrees not to use against a person granted immunity any evidence given by that person. Once immunity is granted, the suspect loses the right to assert the Fifth Amendment privilege.

Example Grants of immunity are often given when the government wants a suspect to give information that will lead to the prosecution of other, more important, criminal suspects.

Partial grants of immunity are also available. A suspect must agree to a partial grant of immunity for it to occur.

In serious cases, the government can place a witness in a government protective program whereby, after the trial, the witness and his or her family are moved permanently to an undisclosed location, given a new identity, and provided monetary assistance. Such a witness is also usually protected prior to trial.

Ethics Questions
What is the public policy underlying the government's offering of immunity from prosecution? Is it ethical for the government to offer such immunity?

Other Constitutional Protections

8.9 Explain the protections provided by the Double Jeopardy Clause, the right to a public jury trial, the right to counsel, and protection against cruel and unusual punishment.

Besides those already discussed in this chapter, other provisions in the U.S. Constitution and Amendments guarantee and protect additional rights in the criminal process. Several of these additional rights are described in the paragraphs that follow.

Critical Legal Thinking Questions
Why was the Double Jeopardy Clause added to the U.S. Constitution? What does it prevent the government from doing?

Fifth Amendment Protection Against Double Jeopardy

The **Double Jeopardy Clause** of the Fifth Amendment protects persons from being tried twice for the same crime.

Double Jeopardy Clause A clause of the Fifth Amendment that protects persons from being tried twice for the same crime.

Example If a state tries a suspect for the crime of murder and the suspect is found not guilty, the state cannot bring another trial against the accused for the same crime. This is true even if more evidence later surfaces that would lead to conviction. The government is given the opportunity to bring its case against an accused once and cannot keep retrying the same case.

If the same act violates the laws of two or more jurisdictions, each jurisdiction may try the accused.

Example If a person kidnaps another person in one state and brings the victim across a state border into another state, the act violates the laws of two states and the federal government. Thus, three jurisdictions can prosecute the accused without violating the Double Jeopardy Clause.

If an accused is tried once and the jury reaches a *hung jury* decision—that is, the verdict is not unanimously either guilty or not guilty—the government can retry the case against the accused without violating the Double Jeopardy Clause.

Sixth Amendment Right to a Public Jury Trial

The **Sixth Amendment** guarantees that a criminal defendant has the **right to a public jury trial**. This includes the right to (1) be tried by an impartial jury of the state or district in which the alleged crime was committed, (2) confront (cross-examine) the witnesses against the accused, (3) have the assistance of a lawyer for his defense, and (4) have a speedy trial.

The **Speedy Trial Act** is a federal statute that requires that a criminal defendant in a federal case be brought to trial within 70 days after indictment.[24] Continuances may be—and often are—granted by the court to serve the "ends of justice." States also have speedy trial acts. A verdict must be unanimous to convict a defendant of a serious crime in federal or state court.[25]

Eighth Amendment Protection Against Cruel and Unusual Punishment

WEB EXERCISE
Go to **http://usdoj.gov/usao/** and go to "About" and then click on and read the Mission Statement of the U.S. Attorneys of the U.S. Department of Justice.

The **Eighth Amendment** protects criminal defendants from **cruel and unusual punishment**. For example, it prohibits the torture of criminals. However, this clause does not prohibit capital punishment.[26] The U.S. Supreme Court has held that, in capital punishment cases, death by lethal injection is not cruel and unusual punishment.[27]

Example The U.S. Supreme Court has held that the imposition of life imprisonment without the possibility of parole for a juvenile defendant convicted of murder violates the Eighth Amendment's prohibition against cruel and unusual punishment.[28]

Key Terms and Concepts

Critical Legal Thinking Cases

8.1 Criminal Fraud Timothy Durham and James Cochran owned and operated Fair Finance Company (Fair). Durham was the company's chief executive officer, and Cochran was its chief operating officer and chairman of the board. Fair was an investment company that sold interest-bearing certificates to investors with the promise of extraordinarily high interest payments and the repayment of the investor's principal in five years. Durham and Cochran conducted most of their business over the phone, luring clients to invest. Rather than investing the clients' funds, however, Durham and Cochran used the money to support their lavish lifestyles. They paid promised interest and principal to existing investors from money raised from new investors. As long as they could keep bringing in new investors, they could keep the scheme going.

Eventually the scheme began to unravel when Fair was unable to recruit enough new investors and began falling behind in making interest and principal payments to investors. Following an extensive investigation, the Federal Bureau of Investigation (FBI) seized Fair's computer and other records and arrested Durham and Cochran. Over a period of eight years they had enticed more than 5,000 investors, many of them elderly or living on modest incomes, who lost $215 million. Only $6 million of assets was recovered. The federal government sued Durham and Cochran for securities and wire fraud. Are Durham and Cochran guilty of fraud? Did Durham and Cochran act ethically in this case? *United States v. Durham*, 766 F.3d 672, 2014 U.S. App. Lexis 17267 (United States Court of Appeals for the Seventh Circuit, 2014)

8.2 Murder Gregory O. Wilson, who had been arguing earlier in the day with his girlfriend, Melissa Spear, later set her on fire in her car and walked away. Spear was transported to a hospital with third-degree burns. She remained in a coma for 45 days but was transported home before dying there, nine months after the incident.

The state of Ohio brought murder charges against Wilson. Wilson argued that he was not liable for murder because there was not sufficient causation between Wilson's act of setting Spear on fire and Spear's death nine months later to warrant a conviction for murder. Is Wilson guilty of murder? *State of Ohio v. Wilson*, 2004 Ohio App. Lexis 2503 (Court of Appeals of Ohio, 2004)

8.3 Fourth Amendment Kentucky undercover police officers set up a controlled buy of cocaine outside an apartment complex. After the deal took place, uniformed police moved in on the suspect. The suspect ran to a breezeway of an apartment building. As the officers arrived in the area, they heard a door shut. At the end of the breezeway were two apartments, one on the left and one on the right. The officers smelled marijuana smoke emanating from the apartment on the left.

The officers banged on the door as loudly as they could, while yelling "Police!" As soon as the officers started banging on the door, they heard people moving inside and things being moved inside the apartment. These noises led the officers to believe that drug-related evidence was about to be destroyed. At that point, the officers kicked in the door and entered the apartment, where they found three people, including Hollis King, his girlfriend, and a guest. The officers saw marijuana and powder cocaine in plain view. A further search turned up crack cocaine, cash, and drug paraphernalia. Police eventually entered the apartment on the right side of the breezeway and found the suspect who was the initial target of their investigation.

King was indicted for criminal violations, including trafficking in marijuana, trafficking in controlled substances, and persistent felony offender status. King filed a motion to have the evidence suppressed as the fruits of an illegal warrantless search in violation of the Fourth Amendment. The government argued that the search was a valid warrantless search that was justified by exigent circumstances. Is the warrantless search constitutional? *Kentucky v. King*, 563 U.S. 452, 131 S.Ct. 1849, 2011 U.S. Lexis 3541 (Supreme Court of the United States, 2011)

8.4 Search William Wheetley, a police officer, was on a routine patrol in his police car with Aldo, a German shepherd dog trained to detect certain narcotics (methamphetamine, marijuana, cocaine, heroin, and ecstasy). Wheetley stopped Clayton Harris's truck because it had an expired license plate. On approaching the driver's side door, Wheetley saw that Harris was visibly nervous, shaking, and breathing rapidly. Wheetley also noticed an open can of beer in the truck's cup holder. Wheetley asked Harris for consent to search the truck, but Harris refused. Wheetley then retrieved Aldo from the patrol car and walked him around Harris's truck. Aldo stopped and alerted at the driver's-side door, signaling that he had smelled drugs there. Wheetley concluded, based principally on Aldo's alert, that he had probable cause to search the truck. The search revealed 200 loose pseudoephedrine pills, 8,000 matches, a bottle of hydrochloric acid, two containers of antifreeze, and a coffee filter full of iodine crystals—all ingredients for making methamphetamine. Wheetley arrested Harris, and the state of Florida charged Harris with possession of pseudoephedrine for use in manufacturing methamphetamine. At trial, Harris moved to suppress the evidence found in his truck on the grounds that Aldo's alert had not given Wheetley probable cause for the search and therefore the evidence against Harris was inadmissible under the Fourth Amendment protection against unreasonable search and seizure. The trial court permitted the evidence to be submitted at trial. Did Aldo's alert give Wheetley probable cause to search Harris's truck? *Florida v. Harris*, 568 U.S. 237, 133 S.Ct. 1050, 2013 U.S. Lexis 1121 (Supreme Court of the United States, 2013)

8.5 Search and Seizure Government agents suspected that marijuana was being grown in the home of Danny Kyllo, who lived in a triplex building in Florence, Oregon. Indoor marijuana growth typically requires high-intensity lamps. To determine whether an amount of heat was emanating from Kyllo's home consistent with the use of such lamps, federal agents used a thermal imager to scan the triplex. Thermal imagers detect infrared radiation and produce images of the radiation. The scan of Kyllo's home, which was performed from an automobile on the street, showed that the roof over the garage and a side wall of Kyllo's home were "hot." The agents used this scanning evidence to obtain a search warrant authorizing a search of Kyllo's home. During the search, the agents found an indoor growing operation involving more than 100 marijuana plants.

Kyllo was indicted for manufacturing marijuana, a violation of federal criminal law. Kyllo moved to suppress the imaging evidence and the evidence it led to, arguing that it was an unreasonable search that violated the Fourth Amendment to the U.S. Constitution. Is the use of a thermal-imaging device aimed at a private home from a public street to detect relative amounts of heat within the home a "search" within the meaning of the Fourth Amendment? *Kyllo v. United States*, 533 U.S. 27, 121 S.Ct. 2038, 2001 U.S. Lexis 4487 (Supreme Court of the United States, 2001)

8.6 Fourth Amendment A driver of a vehicle called 911 and reported that a truck had run her off the road. She gave a description of the vehicle and its license number to the 911 dispatcher. The dispatcher relayed the information to California Highway Patrol officers, who located and stopped the truck. As the two officers approached the truck, they smelled marijuana. A search of the truck bed revealed 30 pounds of marijuana. The officers arrested the driver, Lorenzo Prado Navarette, and the passenger, José Prado Navarette (the petitioners). The petitioners moved to suppress the evidence, arguing that the traffic stop based on only another driver's report violated the Fourth Amendment. The petitioners alleged that the officers lacked reasonable suspicion of criminal activity. The California trial court denied the petitioners' motion, and the petitioners were found guilty and sentenced to 90 days in jail plus three years of probation. The California court of appeals affirmed. The petitioners appealed to the U.S. Supreme Court. Did the stop and search of the truck violate the Fourth Amendment? *Navarette v. California*, 134 S.Ct. 1683, 2014 U.S. Lexis 2930 (Supreme Court of the United States, 2014)

Ethics Cases

8.7 Ethics Case Detective William Pedraja of the Miami-Dade Police Department received a Crime Stoppers unverified tip that one of the tipper's neighbors, Joelis Jardines, was growing marijuana in his house. Detective Pedraja and Detective Bartelt and his drug detection dog, Franky, went to Jardines's home. There were no cars in the driveway, and the window blinds were closed. The two detectives and Franky went onto Jardines's porch. Franky sniffed the base of the front door and sat, alerting the detectives to the smell of drugs.

Based on this investigation, the detectives obtained a search warrant to search Jardines's home. The search revealed marijuana plants. Jardines was arrested for the crime of trafficking in marijuana. At trial, Jardines made a motion to suppress the marijuana plants as evidence on the grounds that the detectives and Franky's investigation was an unreasonable search in violation of the Fourth Amendment to the U.S. Constitution. The Florida trial court and the Florida Supreme Court held that there was an unreasonable search and suppressed the evidence. The case was appealed to the U.S. Supreme Court. Was the canine investigation an unreasonable search? Is it ethical for a defendant to assert the Fourth Amendment to suppress evidence when he knows he is guilty of the crime charged? *Florida v. Jardines*, 133 S.Ct. 1409, 2013 U.S. Lexis 2542 (Supreme Court of the United States, 2013)

8.8 Ethics Case Drunk drivers take a grisly toll on the nation's roads, killing more than 10,000 people each year—approximately one death every hour—and injuring many more victims. All states have enacted laws that prohibit motorists from driving with a blood alcohol concentration (BAC) that exceeds a specified level. Most states calculate BAC by administering a breath test to suspected drunk drivers, usually at the time and place of the traffic stop. Several states also provide a second means of calculating BAC by taking blood samples from the suspect.

Many drivers who are stopped on suspicion of drunk driving do not submit to testing when given the option. Most states have enacted implied consent laws, under which the state automatically finds a person liable for drunk driving if that person refuses to undergo a blood alcohol test. These statutes impose penalties for refusing blood alcohol testing, which usually include mandatory alcohol addiction treatment, fines, and imprisonment of repeat offenders.

Two drivers from states that require BAC testing by either a breath test or blood test were stopped for suspected drunk driving. The drivers, who faced the imposition of the penalties imposed by implied consent laws, sued, alleging that requiring the taking of BAC breath or blood tests violated their Fourth Amendment right to be free from unlawful searches. The U.S. Supreme Court heard an appeal.

Do implied consent laws that impose penalties for failing to take a BAC breath test violate the Fourth Amendment? Do implied consent laws that impose penalties for failing to take a BAC blood test violate the Fourth Amendment? Was it ethical for the drivers to protest that the evidence was not admissible against them? *Birchfield v. North Dakota*, 136 S.Ct. 2160, 2016 U.S. Lexis 4058 (Supreme Court of the United States, 2016)

Notes

1. Title 18 of the U.S. Code contains the federal criminal code.
2. Public Law 115-391.
3. Sentencing Reform Act of 1984, 18 U.S.C. Section 3551 et seq.
4. 532 U.S. 318, 121 S.Ct. 1536, 2001 U.S. Lexis 3366 (Supreme Court of the United States, 2001).
5. 18 U.S.C. Section 1341.
6. 18 U.S.C. Section 1343.
7. 18 U.S.C. Section 1957.
8. 18 U.S.C. Sections 1961–1968.
9. 18 U.S.C. Section 1028.
10. 18 U.S.C. Section 1030.
11. 18 U.S.C. Section 1030.
12. Public Law 104-294, 110 Stat. 3488.
13. 18 U.S.C. Sections 2510–2522.
14. 18 U.S.C. Section 2511.
15. 18 U.S.C. Sections 2701–2712.
16. *United States v. Jones*, 565 U.S. 400, 132 S.Ct. 945, 2012 U.S. Lexis 1063 (Supreme Court of the United States, 2012).
17. *United States v. Leon*, 468 U.S. 897, 104 S.Ct. 3405, 1984 U.S. Lexis 153 (Supreme Court of the United States, 1984).
18. *Marshall v. Barlow's, Inc.*, 436 U.S. 307, 98 S.Ct. 1816, 1978 U.S. Lexis 26 (Supreme Court of the United States, 1978).

19. H.R. 4943.
20. *Bellis v. United States*, 417 U.S. 85, 94 S.Ct. 2.179, 1974 U.S. Lexis 58 (Supreme Court of the United States, 1974).
21. 384 U.S. 436, 86 S.Ct. 1602, 1966 U.S. Lexis 2817 (Supreme Court of the United States, 1966).
22. 530 U.S. 428, 120 S.Ct. 2326, 2000 U.S. Lexis 4305 (Supreme Court of the United States, 2000).
23. 409 U.S. 322, 93 S.Ct. 611, 1973 U.S. Lexis 23 (Supreme Court of the United States, 1973).
24. 19. U.S.C. Section 316(c) (1).
25. *Ramos v. Louisiana*, No. 18-5924 (Supreme Court of the United States, 2020).
26. *Baldwin v. Alabama*, 472 U.S. 372, 105 S.Ct. 2727, 1985 U.S. Lexis 106 (Supreme Court of the United States, 1985).
27. *Baze v. Rees*, 553 U.S. 35, 128 S.Ct. 1520, 2008 U.S. Lexis 3476 (Supreme Court of the United States, 2008).
28. *Miller v. Alabama*, 567 U.S. 460, 132 S.Ct. 2455, 2012 U.S. Lexis 4873 (Supreme Court of the United States, 2012).

PART III

Contracts and E-Commerce

Henry R. Cheeseman

CHAPTER 9

Nature of Traditional and E-Contracts

NEW YORK CITY

New York City is the largest city in the United States. It is an international center of business, commerce, industry, and finance. Commerce in New York City and worldwide relies on business contracts. Contracts are the basis of many of our daily activities. They provide the means for individuals and businesses to sell and otherwise transfer property, services, and other rights. The purchase of goods is based on sales contracts; the hiring of employees is based on service contracts; the lease of an apartment, office, or commercial building is based on rental contracts; and the sale of goods and services over the internet is based on electronic contracts. The list is almost endless. Without enforceable contracts, commerce would collapse.

Henry R. Cheeseman

Learning Objectives

After studying this chapter, you should be able to:

9.1 Define *contract* and describe the elements necessary to form a valid contract.

9.2 List and describe the sources of contract law.

9.3 Explain the objective theory of contracts.

9.4 List and describe the classifications of contracts.

9.5 Define *express* and *implied-in-fact* contracts and describe the difference between them.

9.6 Define *equity* and learn how to apply the doctrine to contract disputes.

9.7 Learn how contract law applies to electronic commerce (e-commerce).

"The movement of the progressive societies has hitherto been a movement from status to contract."

— *Sir Henry Maine*
Ancient Law, Chapter 5 (1861)

Introduction to Nature of Traditional and E-Contracts

Contracts are voluntarily entered into by parties. The terms of a contract become *private law* between the parties. One court has stated that "the contract between parties is the law between them and the courts are obliged to give legal effect to such contracts according to the true interests of the parties."[1]

Most contracts are performed without the aid of the court system. This is usually because the parties feel a moral duty to perform as promised. Although some contracts, such as illegal contracts, are not enforceable, most are **legally enforceable contracts.**[2] Thus, if a party fails to perform a contract, the other party may call on the courts to enforce the contract.

This chapter introduces the study of **traditional contract law** and **electronic contract law (e-contract law)**. Topics such as the definition of *contract*, requirements for forming a contract, sources of contract law, and the various classifications of contracts are discussed.

Contracts must not be the sports of an idle hour, mere matters of pleasantry and badinage, never intended by the parties to have any serious effect whatever.

Lord Stowell
Dalrymple v. Dalrymple (1811)

legally enforceable contract
A contract in which if one party fails to perform as promised, the other party can use the court system to enforce the contract and recover damages or other remedy.

Definition of a Contract

9.1 Define *contract* and describe the elements necessary to form a valid contract.

A **contract** is an agreement that is enforceable by a court of law or equity. A simple and widely recognized definition of *contract* is provided by the *Restatement (Second) of Contracts*: "A contract is a promise or a set of promises for the breach of which the law gives a remedy or the performance of which the law in some way recognizes a duty."[3]

Parties to a Contract

Every contract involves at least two parties. The **offeror** is the party who makes an offer to enter into a contract. The **offeree** is the party to whom the offer is made (see Exhibit 9.1). In making an offer, the offeror promises to do—or to refrain from doing—something. The offeree then has the power to create a contract by accepting the offeror's offer. A contract is created if the offer is accepted. No contract is created if the offer is not accepted.

offeror
The party who makes an offer to enter into a contract.

offeree
The party to whom an offer to enter into a contract is made.

Example Raul makes an offer to Elizabeth to sell his automobile to her for $10,000. In this case, Raul is the offeror, and Elizabeth is the offeree.

Exhibit 9.1 PARTIES TO A CONTRACT

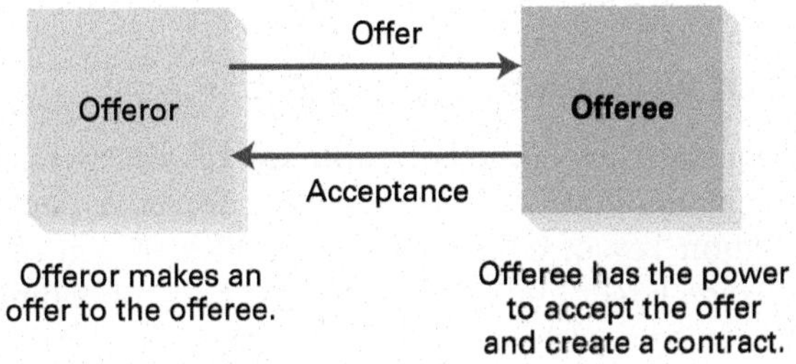
Offer
Offeror
Offeree
Acceptance
Offeror makes an offer to the offeree.
Offeree has the power to accept the offer and create a contract.

Elements of a Contract

Justice is the end of government. It is the end of civil society. It ever has been, and ever will be pursued, until it be obtained, or until liberty be lost in the pursuit.

James Madison
Fourth President of the United States
The Federalist No. 51 (1788)

For a contract to be enforceable, the following four basic requirements must be met:

1. **Agreement.** To have an enforceable contract, there must be an **agreement** between the parties. This requires an **offer** by the offeror and an **acceptance** of the offer by the offeree. There must be mutual assent by the parties.
2. **Consideration.** A promise must be supported by a bargained-for **consideration** that is legally sufficient. Money, personal property, real property, provision of services, and the like qualify as consideration.
3. **Contractual capacity.** The parties to a contract must have **contractual capacity** for the contract to be enforceable against them. Contracts cannot be enforced against parties who lacked contractual capacity when they entered into the contracts.
4. **Lawful object.** The object of a contract must be lawful. Most contracts have a **lawful object**. However, contracts that have an illegal object are void and cannot be enforced.

CONCEPT SUMMARY

ELEMENTS OF A CONTRACT

1. Agreement	3. Contractual capacity
2. Consideration	4. Lawful object

Defenses to the Enforcement of a Contract

Two *defenses* may be raised to the enforcement of contracts:

1. **Genuineness of assent.** The consent of the parties to create a contract must be genuine. This is referred to as **genuineness of assent**. If the consent is obtained by duress, undue influence, or fraud, there is no real consent.
2. **Writing and form.** The law requires that certain contracts be in writing or in a certain **form**. Failure of such a contract to be in writing or to be in proper form may be raised against the enforcement of the contract.

The requirements to form an enforceable contract and the defenses to the enforcement of contracts are discussed in this chapter and the following chapters on contract law.

Sources of Contract Law

9.2 List and describe the sources of contract law.

There are several sources of contract law in the United States, including the *common law of contracts*, the *Uniform Commercial Code*, and the *Restatement (Second) of Contracts*. The following paragraphs explain these sources in more detail.

Common Law of Contracts

common law of contracts
Contract law developed primarily by state courts.

A major source of contract law is the **common law of contracts**, which developed from early court decisions that became precedent for later decisions. There is a limited federal common law of contracts that applies to contracts made by the federal government. The larger and more prevalent body of common law has been developed from state court decisions. Thus, although the general principles remain the same throughout the country, there is some variation from state to state.

Uniform Commercial Code (UCC)

Another major source of contract law is the **Uniform Commercial Code (UCC)**. The UCC, which was first drafted by the National Conference of Commissioners on Uniform State Laws in 1952, has been amended several times. Its goal is to create a uniform system of commercial law among the 50 states. The provisions of the UCC normally take precedence over the common law of contracts. (The provisions of the UCC are discussed in Chapters 18–25 and 27 in this book.)

The UCC is divided into nine main articles. Every state has adopted at least part of the UCC. In the area of contract law, two of the major provisions of the UCC are:

- **Article 2 (Sales). Article 2 (Sales)** prescribes a set of uniform rules for the creation and enforcement of contracts for the sale of goods. These contracts are often referred to as **sales contracts**.

  Examples The sale of equipment, automobiles, computers, clothing, and such involve sales contracts subject to Article 2 of the UCC.

- **Article 2A (Leases). Article 2A (Leases)** prescribes a set of uniform rules for the creation and enforcement of contracts for the lease of goods. These contracts are referred to as **lease contracts**.

  Examples Leases of automobiles, leases of aircraft, and other leases involving goods are subject to Article 2A of the UCC.

Uniform Commercial Code (UCC)
A comprehensive statutory scheme that includes laws that cover aspects of commercial transactions.

The *Restatement of the Law of Contracts*

In 1932, the American Law Institute, a group composed of law professors, judges, and lawyers, completed the ***Restatement of the Law of Contracts***. The *Restatement* is a compilation of contract law principles as agreed on by the drafters. The *Restatement*, which is currently in its second edition, is cited in this book as the ***Restatement (Second) of Contracts***. Note that the *Restatement* is not law. However, lawyers and judges often refer to it for guidance in contract disputes because of its stature.

Restatement of the Law of Contracts
A compilation of model contract law principles drafted by legal scholars. The *Restatement* is not law.

Objective Theory of Contracts

9.3 Explain the objective theory of contracts.

The intent to enter into a contract is determined using the **objective theory of contracts**—that is, whether a reasonable person viewing the circumstances would conclude that the parties intended to be legally bound.

Example The statement "I will buy your building for $2 million" is a valid offer because it indicates the offeror's present intent to contract.

Example A statement such as "Are you interested in selling your building for $2 million?" is not an offer. It is an invitation to make an offer or an invitation to negotiate.

Offers that are made in jest, anger, or undue excitement do not include the necessary objective intent.

Example The owner of Company A has lunch with the owner of Company B. In the course of their conversation, Company A's owner exclaims in frustration, "For $200, I'd sell the whole computer division!" An offer such as that cannot result in a valid contract.

In the following case, the court discusses parties' freedom to contract.

objective theory of contracts
A theory stating that the intent to contract is judged by the reasonable person standard and not by the subjective intent of the parties.

Critical Legal Thinking Questions

Why is the objective theory of contracts applied in determining whether a contract has been created? Why is the subjective intent of the parties not considered?

CASE 9.1 *FEDERAL COURT CASE Business Contract*

Severn Peanut Co., Inc. and Travelers Property Casualty Company of America v. Industrial Fumigant Co.

807 F.3d 88 (2015)
United States Court of Appeals for the Fourth Circuit

"Its courts recognize that the right of private contract is no small part of the liberty of the citizen . . ."

—J. Harvie Wilkinson, Circuit Judge

Facts

Industrial Fumigant Co. (IFC) is a commercial company that applies pesticides for customers. Severn Peanut Co., Inc. (Severn) is a large company that produces raw, roasted, and salted peanuts. Severn and IFC entered into a Pesticide Application Agreement (PAA) whereby IFC would use the pesticide phosphine to fumigate a peanut storage dome owned by Severn that contained 20 million pounds of peanuts. Severn paid $8,604 for the fumigation service. The contract provided that the payment was not sufficient to warrant IFC to assume the risk of incidental or consequential damages to Severn's property, product, equipment, downtime, or loss of business.

The fumigation resulted in a fire and the explosion of the peanut dome, causing Severn the loss of the peanuts, loss of business, and cleanup costs. Severn's insurer, Travelers Property Casualty Company of America (Travelers), paid Severn more than $19 million to cover the cost of loss of the peanuts, lost business income, the damage to the peanut dome, and Severn's remediation and fire suppression costs. Travelers then sued IFC to recover the insurance payments, alleging that IFC breached its contract with Severn by improperly applying a dangerous pesticide while fumigating Severn's peanut dome, and was therefore responsible for Severn's losses. The U.S. district court granted summary judgment to IFC, holding that the PAA's consequential and incidental damages exclusion barred Severn's, and therefore Travelers's, claim of damages. Travelers appealed.

Issue

Is IFC liable for the losses suffered by Severn?

Language of the Court

North Carolina follows a broad policy which generally accords contracting parties freedom to bind themselves as they see fit. Its courts recognize that the right of private contract is no small part of the liberty of the citizen, and the usual and most important function of courts is therefore to enforce and maintain contracts rather than enable parties to escape their obligations. Enforcement of contractual liability limitations and damages exclusions is one aspect of this freedom of contract. Severn and IFC are sophisticated commercial entities who entered into an arm's length transaction. We are considering a rather typical agreement among two commercial entities, and we may hold them to the contract's terms.

Decision

The U.S. court of appeals affirmed the U.S. district court's grant of summary judgment in favor of IFC.

Critical Legal Thinking Questions

Should sophisticated commercial entities have freedom to contract? How did Severn protect against loss in this case? What would be the consequences if the limitation on damages in the contract had not been enforced?

Classifications of Contracts

9.4 List and describe the classifications of contracts.

There are several types of contracts. Each differs somewhat in formation, performance, and discharge. The different types of contracts are discussed in the following paragraphs.

Bilateral and Unilateral Contracts

Contracts are either *bilateral* or *unilateral*, depending on what the offeree must do to accept the offeror's offer. The language of the offeror's promise must be carefully scrutinized to determine whether it is an offer to create a bilateral or a unilateral contract. If there is any ambiguity as to which it is, it is presumed to be a bilateral contract.

Bilateral Contracts A contract is a **bilateral contract** if the offeror's promise is answered with the offeree's promise of acceptance. In other words, a bilateral contract is a "promise for a promise." This exchange of promises creates an enforceable contract. No act of performance is necessary to create a bilateral contract.

bilateral contract
A contract entered into by way of exchange of promises of the parties; "a promise for a promise."

Example Ariana, the owner of the Clothing Shop, says to Peng, a painter, "If you promise to paint my store by July 1, I will pay you $3,000." Peng says, "I promise to do so." A *bilateral contract* was created at the moment Peng promised to paint the dress shop (a promise for a promise). If Peng fails to paint the shop, Ariana can sue Peng and recover whatever damages result from his breach of contract. Similarly, Peng can sue Ariana if she refuses to pay him after he has performed as promised.

Unilateral Contracts A contract is a **unilateral contract** if the offeror's offer can be accepted only by the performance of an act by the offeree. There is no contract until the offeree performs the requested act. An offer to create a unilateral contract cannot be accepted by a promise to perform. It is a "promise for an act."

unilateral contract
A contract in which the offeror's offer can be accepted only by the performance of an act by the offeree; a "promise for an act."

Example Armand, the owner of the Computing Shop, says to Chloe, a painter, "If you paint my store by July 1, I will pay you $3,000." This offer creates a *unilateral contract*. The offer can be accepted only by the painter's performance of the requested act. If Chloe does not paint the shop by July 1, there has been no acceptance, and Armand cannot sue Chloe for damages. If Chloe paints the shop by July 1, Armand owes Chloe $3,000. If Armand refuses to pay, Chloe can sue Armand to collect payment.

Incomplete or Partial Performance Problems can arise if the offeror in a unilateral contract attempts to revoke an offer after the offeree has begun performance. Generally, an offer to create a unilateral contract can be revoked by the offeror at any time prior to the offeree's performance of the requested act. However, the offer cannot be revoked if the offeree has begun or has substantially completed performance.

A man must come into a court of equity with clean hands.

C.B. Eyre
Dering v. Earl of Winchelsea (1787)

Example Suppose Alan tells Esther that he will pay her $5,000 if she finishes the Boston Marathon. Alan cannot revoke the offer once Esther starts running the marathon.

Formal and Informal Contracts

Contracts may be classified as either *formal* or *informal*.

Formal Contracts **Formal contracts** are contracts that require a special form or method of creation. Many formal contracts require *specific words*. The *Restatement (Second) of Contracts* identifies the following types of formal contracts:[4]

formal contract
A contract that requires a special form or method of creation.

- **Negotiable instruments.** **Negotiable instruments**, which include checks, drafts, notes, and certificates of deposit, are special forms of contracts recognized by the UCC. They require a special form and language for their creation and must meet certain requirements for transfer.

- **Letters of credit.** A **letter of credit** is an agreement by the issuer of the letter to pay a sum of money on the receipt of an invoice and other documents. Letters of credit are governed by the UCC.
- **Recognizance.** In a **recognizance**, a party acknowledges in court that he or she will pay a specified sum of money if a certain event occurs.
- **Contracts under seal.** This type of contract is one to which a seal (usually a wax seal) is attached. Although no state currently requires contracts to be under seal, a few states provide that no consideration is necessary if a contract is made under seal.

informal contract (simple contract)
A contract that is not formal. Valid informal contracts are fully enforceable and may be sued upon if breached.

Informal Contracts All contracts that do not qualify as formal contracts are called **informal contracts** (or **simple contracts**). The term is a misnomer. Valid informal contracts (e.g., leases, sales contracts, service contracts) are fully enforceable and may be sued on if breached. They are called *informal contracts* only because no special form or method is required for their creation. Thus, the parties to an informal contract can use any words they choose to express their contract. Most contracts entered into by individuals and businesses are informal contracts.

In the following case, the court had to decide whether a contract was enforceable.

CASE 9.2 *STATE COURT CASE Informal Contract*

McKee v. Isle of Capri Casinos, Inc.

864 N.W.2d 518, 2015 Iowa Sup. Lexis 50 (2015)
Supreme Court of Iowa

"Gambling contracts are governed by traditional contract principles."
—Edward Mansfield, Justice

Facts

Pauline McKee was attending a family reunion at the Isle Casino Hotel Waterloo. One evening she and several members of her family gambled at the casino. McKee was playing Miss Kitty, a penny slot machine. A person wins at the Miss Kitty game by lining up different combinations of symbols from left to right on the slot machine screen. The game includes a button labeled "Touch Game Rules" in the lower left-hand corner of the screen. Tapping this button displays the rules that govern the game and a chart describing potential winning combinations of symbols. These rules do not mention any additional bonus, jackpot, or prize available to a person playing the Miss Kitty game. The rules state "MALFUNCTION VOIDS ALL PAYS AND PLAYS." A sign posted on the front of the machine reiterates "MALFUNCTION VOIDS ALL PAYS AND PLAYS." McKee did not read the rules before she played the slot machine.

While playing the game, McKee won $1.85 based on how the symbols had lined up on the slot machine screen. However, a message appeared on the screen stating "Bonus Award $41797550.16." The casino paid McKee $1.85 but refused to pay the alleged bonus, claiming it was an error and not part of the game. McKee sued the casino in district court to recover $41,797,550.16. The casino introduced evidence that the appearance of the bonus on the screen was an error in the computer system of the game. The casino made a motion for summary judgment, which was opposed by McKee. The district court held that the rules of the Miss Kitty game were an express contract between McKee and the casino. The court granted summary judgment to the casino. McKee appealed.

Issue

Was there a contract between the parties that provided for the payment of a bonus when playing the Miss Kitty slot machine?

Language of the Court

Gambling contracts are governed by traditional contract principles. We agree with the district court that the Miss Kitty rules of the game are the relevant contract here and that they form an express contract. Further, it is *undisputed that the rules of the Miss Kitty game did not provide for any kind of bonus. Hence, in our view, McKee had no contractual right to a bonus. Nor is it relevant that McKee failed to read the rules of the game before playing it. It is sufficient that those rules were readily accessible to her and she had an opportunity to read them. On the play in question, the alignment of the reels entitled McKee to a prize of $1.85, and the casino paid it to her, fulfilling its side of the contract.*

Decision

The Supreme Court of Iowa affirmed the district court's grant of summary judgment in favor of the casino.

Critical Legal Thinking Questions

Do you believe that this case was decided correctly? How many people do you think read the rules of slot machine games before playing the games? How many people do you think read software, social media, or video game contracts?

Valid, Void, Voidable, and Unenforceable Contracts

Contract law places contracts in the following categories:

1. **Valid contract.** A **valid contract** meets all the essential elements to establish a contract. In other words, it (1) consists of an agreement between the parties, (2) is supported by legally sufficient consideration, (3) is between parties with contractual capacity, and (4) accomplishes a lawful object. A valid contract is enforceable by at least one of the parties.
2. **Void contract.** A **void contract** has no legal effect. It is as if no contract had ever been created. A contract to commit a crime is void. If a contract is void, then neither party is obligated to perform the contract and neither party can enforce the contract.
3. **Voidable contract.** A **voidable contract** is a contract in which at least one party has the *option* to void his or her contractual obligations. If the contract is voided, both parties are released from their obligations under the contract. If the party with the option chooses to ratify the contract, both parties must fully perform their obligations.

   With certain exceptions, contracts may be voided by minors; insane persons; intoxicated persons; and persons acting under duress, undue influence, or fraud; and in cases involving mutual mistake.
4. **Unenforceable contract.** With an **unenforceable contract**, there is some legal defense to the enforcement of the contract. If a contract is required to be in writing under the Statute of Frauds but is not, the contract is unenforceable. The parties may voluntarily perform a contract that is unenforceable.

valid contract
A contract that meets all the essential elements to establish a contract; a contract that is enforceable by at least one of the parties.

void contract
A contract that has no legal effect; a nullity.

voidable contract
A contract in which one or both parties have the option to void their contractual obligations. If a contract is voided, both parties are released from their contractual obligations.

unenforceable contract
A contract in which the essential elements to create a valid contract are met but there is some legal defense to the enforcement of the contract.

Executory and Executed Contracts

A contract is classified as either an *executory* or an *executed* contract.

Executory Contracts A contract that has not been performed by both sides is an **executory contract**. Contracts that have been fully performed by one side but not by the other are classified as executory contracts.

Examples Suppose Darius signs a contract to purchase a new BMW automobile from Ace Motors. He has not yet paid for the car, and Ace Motors has not yet delivered the car to Darius. This is an executory contract because the contract has not yet been performed. If Darius has paid for the car but Ace Motors has not yet delivered the car to Darius, there is an executory contract because Ace Motors has not performed the contract.

executory contract
A contract that has not been fully performed by either or both sides.

executed contract
A contract that has been fully performed on both sides; a completed contract.

Executed Contracts A completed contract—that is, one that has been fully performed on both sides—is called an **executed contract**.

Example If Darius has paid for the car in the prior example and Ace Motors has delivered the car to Darius, the contract has been fully performed by both parties and is an executed contract.

Express and Implied Contracts

9.5 Define *express* and *implied-in-fact* contracts and describe the difference between them.

An **actual contract** may be either *express* or *implied-in-fact*.

Express Contract

express contract
An agreement that is expressed in written or oral words.

An **express contract** is stated in oral or written words. Most personal and business contracts are express contracts.

Examples A written agreement to buy an automobile from a dealership is an express contract because it is in written words. A license between Facebook, Inc. and a user of Facebook is an express written contract. An oral agreement to purchase a neighbor's bicycle is an express contract because it is in oral words.

In the following case, the court enforced an express contract.

Information Technology

CASE 9.3 *FEDERAL COURT CASE Express Contract*

Facebook, Inc. v. Winklevoss

640 F.3d 1034, 2011 U.S. App. Lexis 7430 (2011)
United States Court of Appeals for the Ninth Circuit

"At some point, litigation must come to an end. That point has now been reached."

—Alex Kozinski, Circuit Judge

Facts

Mark Zuckerberg, Cameron Winklevoss, Tyler Winklevoss, and Divya Narendra were schoolmates at Harvard University. The Winklevoss twins, along with Narendra, started a company called ConnectU. They alleged that Zuckerberg stole their idea and created Facebook, and they sued Facebook and Zuckerberg. The court ordered the parties to mediate their dispute. After a day of negotiations, the parties signed a handwritten, one-and-one-third-page "Term Sheet & Settlement Agreement." In the agreement, the Winklevosses agreed to give up their claims in exchange for cash and Facebook stock. The Winklevosses were to receive $20 million in cash and $45 million of Facebook stock, valued at $36 per share.

The parties stipulated that the settlement agreement was confidential and binding and "may be submitted into evidence to enforce it." The agreement granted all parties mutual releases. The agreement stated that the Winkelvosses represented and warranted that "they have no further right to assert against Facebook" and have "no further claims against Facebook and its related parties." Facebook became an extremely successful social networking site, with its value exceeding $30 billion at the time the next legal dispute arose.

Subsequently, in a lawsuit, the Winklevosses brought claims against Facebook and Zuckerberg, alleging that Facebook and Zuckerberg had engaged in fraud at the time of forming the settlement agreement. The Winklevosses alleged that Facebook and Zuckerberg had misled them into believing that Facebook shares were worth $36 per share at the time of settlement, when in fact an internal Facebook document valued the stock at $8.88 per share for tax code purposes. The Winklevosses sought to rescind the settlement agreement. The U.S. district court enforced the settlement agreement. The Winklevosses appealed.

Issue

Is the settlement agreement enforceable?

Language of the Court

The Winklevosses are sophisticated parties who were locked in a contentious struggle over ownership rights in one of the world's fastest-growing companies. They brought half-a-dozen lawyers to the mediation. When adversaries in a roughly equivalent bargaining position and with ready access to counsel sign an agreement to "establish a general peace," we enforce the clear terms of the agreement.

There are also very important policies that favor giving effect to agreements that put an end to the expensive and disruptive process of litigation. For whatever reason, the Winklevosses now want to back out. Like the district court, we see no basis for allowing them to do so. At some point, litigation must come to an end. That point has now been reached.

Decision

The U.S. court of appeals upheld the decision of the U.S. district court that enforced the settlement agreement.

Critical Legal Thinking Questions

Should the Winklevosses have had their claims of fraud decided by the court? Did anyone act unethically in this case?

Implied-in-Fact Contract

Implied-in-fact contracts are implied from the conduct of the parties. The following elements must be established to create an implied-in-fact contract:

1. The plaintiff provided property or services to the defendant.
2. The plaintiff expected to be paid by the defendant for the property or services and did not provide the property or services gratuitously.
3. The defendant was given an opportunity to reject the property or services provided by the plaintiff but failed to do so.

If these conditions are met and a defendant misappropriates and uses the plaintiff's information or property without forming an express contract and without paying for the information or property, the defendant is liable for damages for beaching an implied-in-fact contract.

implied-in-fact contract
A contract in which agreement between parties has been inferred from their conduct.

Example A screenwriter meets with a movie producer and presents a script for a movie with a novel plot and unique characters. The producer reads the script but does not enter into an express contract with the screenwriter and does not pay the screenwriter any compensation. Subsequently, the producer makes a hit movie that is very similar to the screenplay. The screenwriter can recover damages from the producer for breaching an implied-in-fact contract.

Implied-in-Law Contract (Quasi Contract)

The equitable doctrine of **implied-in-law contract**, also called **quasi contract**, allows a court to award monetary damages to a plaintiff for providing work or services to a defendant even though no actual contract existed between the parties. Recovery is generally based on the reasonable value of the services received by the defendant.

The doctrine of quasi contract is intended to prevent *unjust enrichment* and *unjust detriment*. It does not apply where there is an enforceable contract between the parties. A quasi contract is imposed where (1) one person confers a benefit on another, who retains the benefit, and (2) it would be unjust not to require that person to pay for the benefit received.

implied-in-law contract (quasi contract)
An equitable doctrine whereby a court may award monetary damages to a plaintiff for providing work or services to a defendant even though no actual contract existed. The doctrine is intended to prevent unjust enrichment and unjust detriment.

Example Georgianna is driving her automobile when she is involved in a serious accident in which she is knocked unconscious. She is rushed to Metropolitan

Critical Legal Thinking Questions

Why does the law recognize quasi contracts? Are they difficult to prove?

Hospital, where the doctors and other staff members perform the necessary medical procedures to save her life. Georgianna comes out of her coma and, after recovering, is released from the hospital. Subsequently, Metropolitan Hospital sends Georgianna a bill for its services. The charges are reasonable. Under the doctrine of quasi contract, Georgianna is responsible for any charges that are not covered by her insurance.

CONCEPT SUMMARY

CLASSIFICATIONS OF CONTRACTS

Formation	1. **Bilateral contract.** A promise for a promise. 2. **Unilateral contract.** A promise for an act. 3. **Express contract.** A contract expressed in oral or written words. 4. **Implied-in-fact contract.** A contract inferred from the conduct of the parties. 5. **Implied-in-law contract (quasi contract).** A contract implied by law to prevent unjust enrichment. 6. **Formal contract.** A contract that requires a special form or method of creation. 7. **Informal contract.** A contract that requires no special form or method of creation.
Enforceability	1. **Valid contract.** A contract that meets all the essential elements of establishing a contract. 2. **Void contract.** No contract exists. 3. **Voidable contract.** A contract in which at least one party has the option of voiding the contract. 4. **Unenforceable contract.** A contract that cannot be enforced because of a legal defense.
Performance	1. **Executed contract.** A contract that is fully performed on both sides. 2. **Executory contract.** A contract that is not fully performed by one or both parties.

Equity

9.6 Define *equity* and learn how to apply the doctrine to contract disputes.

Recall that two separate courts developed in England: the courts of law and the Chancery Court (or courts of equity). The equity courts developed a set of maxims based on fairness, equality, moral rights, and natural law that were applied in settling disputes.

equity
A doctrine that permits judges to make decisions based on fairness, equality, moral rights, and natural law.

Equity is resorted to when (1) an award of money damages "at law" would not be the proper remedy or (2) fairness requires the application of equitable principles. Today, in most states of the United States, the courts of law and equity have been merged into one court. In an action "in equity," the judge decides the equitable issue; there is no right to a jury trial in an equitable action. The doctrine of equity is sometimes applied in contract cases.

The following feature illustrates the application of the doctrine of equity.

Critical Legal Thinking

Equity

"There is only minimal delay in giving notice, the harm to the lessor is slight, and the hardship to the lessee is severe."

—Richard Abbe, Judge

A landlord leased a motel he owned to lessees for a 10-year period. The lessees had an option to extend the lease for an additional 10 years. To do so, they had to give written notice to the landlord three months before the first 10-year lease expired.

For almost 10 years, the lessees devoted most of their assets and a great deal of their energy to building up the business. During this time, they transformed a disheveled, unrated motel into a AAA three-star operation. With the landlord's knowledge, the lessees made extensive long-term improvements that greatly increased the value of both the property and the business.

Prior to three months before the end of the lease, the lessees told the landlord orally that they intended to extend the lease. The lessees instructed their accountant to give the landlord written notice of the option to extend the lease for another 10 years. Despite reminders from the lessees, the accountant failed to give the written notice within three months of the expiration of the lease. As soon as they discovered the mistake, the lessees personally delivered a written notice of renewal of the option to the landlord—13 days too late. The landlord rejected the notice as late and instituted a lawsuit to evict the lessees.

The trial and appellate courts held in favor of the lessees. The courts rejected the landlord's argument for strict adherence to the deadline for giving written notice of renewal of the lease. Instead, the courts granted equitable relief and permitted the late renewal notice. The court reasoned that "there is only minimal delay in giving notice, the harm to the lessor is slight, and the hardship to the lessee is severe." *Romasanta v. Mitton*, 189 Cal.App.3d 1026, 234 Cal.Rptr. 729, 1987 Cal. App. Lexis 1428 (Court of Appeal of California, 1987)

Critical Legal Thinking Questions

Why does the law recognize the doctrine of equity? Should the court have applied the doctrine of equity and saved the lessees from their mistake? Did the landlord act ethically in this case?

E-Commerce

9.7 Learn how contract law applies to electronic commerce (e-commerce).

During the past few decades, a new economic shift has brought the United States and the rest of the world into the information age. Computer and digital technology and the use of the internet have increased dramatically. A new form of commerce—**electronic commerce**, or **e-commerce**—is flourishing. All sorts of goods and services are now sold over the internet. You can purchase automobiles and children's toys, participate in auctions, purchase airline tickets, make hotel reservations, and purchase other goods and services. Microsoft Corporation, Google LLC, Facebook, Inc., Yahoo! Inc., and other technology companies license the use of their software over the internet.

electronic commerce (e-commerce)
The sale and lease of goods and services and other property and the licensing of software over the internet or by other electronic means.

Much of the cyberspace economy is based on **electronic contracts (e-contracts)** and **electronic licenses (e-licenses)**. Electronic licensing usually concerns computer and software information. E-commerce has created problems for forming e-contracts over the internet, enforcing e-contracts, and providing consumer protection. In many situations, traditional contract rules apply to e-contracts. Many states have adopted rules that specifically regulate e-commerce transactions. The federal government has also enacted several laws that regulate e-contracts. Contract rules that apply to e-commerce are discussed in this and the following chapters.

electronic contract (e-contract)
A contract that is formed electronically.

Key Terms and Concepts

Acceptance (188)
Actual contract (194)
Agreement (188)
Article 2 (Sales) (189)
Article 2A (Leases) (189)
Bilateral contract (191)
Common law of contracts (188)
Consideration (188)
Contract (187)
Contractual capacity (188)
Electronic commerce (e-commerce) (197)
Electronic contract (e-contract) (197)
Electronic contract law (e-contract law) (187)
Electronic license (e-license) (197)
Equity (196)
Executed contract (194)
Executory contract (193)
Express contract (194)
Form (188)
Formal contract (191)
Genuineness of assent (188)
Implied-in-fact contract (195)
Implied-in-law contract (quasi contract) (195)
Informal contract (simple contract) (192)
Lawful object (188)
Lease contract (189)
Legally enforceable contract (187)
Letter of credit (192)
Negotiable instrument (191)
Objective theory of contracts (189)
Offer (188)
Offeree (187)
Offeror (187)
Recognizance (192)
Restatement of the Law of Contracts (189)
Restatement (Second) of Contracts (189)
Sales contract (189)
Traditional contract law (187)
Unenforceable contract (193)
Uniform Commercial Code (UCC) (189)
Unilateral contract (191)
Valid contract (193)
Void contract (193)
Voidable contract (193)

Critical Legal Thinking Cases

9.1 Implied-in-Fact Contract Thomas Rinks and Joseph Shields created the Psycho Chihuahua cartoon character, which they promoted, marketed, and licensed through their company, Wrench LLC. Psycho Chihuahua is a clever, feisty cartoon dog with an attitude—a self-confident, edgy, cool dog who knows what he wants and will not back down. Rinks and Shields attended a licensing trade show in New York City, where they were approached by two Taco Bell employees, Rudy Pollak, a vice president, and Ed Alfaro, a creative services manager. Taco Bell owns and operates a nationwide chain of fast-food Mexican restaurants. Pollak and Alfaro expressed interest in the Psycho Chihuahua character for Taco Bell advertisements because they thought the character would appeal to Taco Bell's core consumers, men ages 18 to 24. Pollak and Alfaro obtained some Psycho Chihuahua materials to take back with them to Taco Bell's headquarters.

Later, Alfaro contacted Rinks and asked him to create art boards combining Psycho Chihuahua with the Taco Bell name and image. Rinks and Shields prepared art boards and sent them to Alfaro, along with Psycho Chihuahua T-shirts, hats, and stickers. Alfaro showed these materials to Taco Bell's vice president of brand management as well as to Taco Bell's outside advertising agency. Rinks suggested to Alfaro that Taco Bell should use a live Chihuahua dog manipulated by computer graphic imaging that had the personality of Psycho Chihuahua and a love for Taco Bell food. Rinks and Shields gave a formal presentation of their concept of using an animated dog to Taco Bell's marketing department. Taco Bell would not enter into an express contract with Wrench LLC, Rinks, or Shields.

Just after Rinks and Shields's presentation, Taco Bell hired a new outside advertising agency, Chiat/Day. Taco Bell gave Chiat/Day materials received from Rinks and Shields regarding Psycho Chihuahua. Three months later, Chiat/Day proposed using a Chihuahua in Taco Bell commercials. Chiat/Day claimed to have conceived this idea by itself. Taco Bell aired its Chihuahua commercials in the United States, and they became an instant success and the basis of its advertising. Taco Bell paid nothing to Wrench LLC or to Rinks and Shields. Plaintiffs Wrench LLC, Rinks, and Shields sued defendant Taco Bell to recover damages for breach of an implied-in-fact contract. Was there an implied-in-fact contract? *Wrench LLC v. Taco Bell Corporation*, 256 F.3d 446, 2001 U.S. App. Lexis 15097 (United States Court of Appeals for the Sixth Circuit, 2001)

9.2 Unilateral Contract United Airlines operated a MileagePlus frequent flyer program that allowed customers to collect rewards such as free flights and seat upgrades in exchange for patronizing United. MileagePlus rules allowed United to change the terms of the program unilaterally and without notice. United offered a Million-Mile Flyer status to Mileage Plus members after they had flown more than 1 million miles on United. Reaching this status offered additional benefits. After seeing the advertisements for the million-mile program, George Lagen changed from using other airlines to almost exclusively patronizing United. In 10 years, Lagen became a million-mile flyer and received the upgraded benefits that came with this status. However, after United merged with Continental Airlines, the airline substantially reduced the benefits of patrons who were million-mile members. Lagen sued United, alleging that United breached a unilateral contract. Lagen argued that United made an offer for a unilateral contract, and his performance of flying over 1 million miles on United created a binding unilateral contract. United argued that no unilateral contract was formed because it reserved the right to change the terms of the program whenever it wanted. Lagen appealed. Was a unilateral contract formed when Lagen flew 1 million miles on United? *Lagen v. United Continental Holdings, Inc.*, 774 F.3d 1124, 2014 U.S. App. Lexis 24216 (United States Court of Appeals for the Seventh Circuit, 2014)

9.3 Objective Theory of Contracts Attorney James Cheney Mason represented the criminal defendant Nelson Serrano, who stood accused of murdering his former business partner and the son and daughter and son-in-law of another business partner in Bartow, Florida. During Serrano's highly publicized capital murder trial, Mason participated in a television interview with *NBC News* in which he focused on the seeming implausibility of the prosecution's theory of the case. Serrano claimed he was on a business trip to Atlanta, Georgia, several hundred miles away from where the murders were committed in central Florida, and therefore he had an alibi and alleged he could not have committed the murders. Hotel security cameras confirmed that Serrano was at a La Quinta Inn in Atlanta, Georgia, before and after the murders occurred in Bartow, Florida. The prosecution argued that Serrano had committed the crimes during the 10-hour span between the times that he was seen on the security cameras. To commit the murders, Serrano would have had to slip out of the hotel and, traveling under several aliases, fly from Atlanta to Orlando, rent a car, drive to Bartow, commit the murders, return to Atlanta, drive from the airport to the La Quinta Inn, and appear on the hotel's security footage again that evening.

During the NBC interview, Mason argued that it was impossible for his client to have committed the murders in accordance with this timeline. Mason stated that it was impossible to make it off the airplane in Atlanta and back to the La Quinta Inn within the 28 minutes in the prosecution's timeline. Mason then stated, "I challenge anybody to show me, and guess what? Did they bring in any evidence to say that somebody made that route, did so? If they can do it, I'll challenge 'em. I'll pay them a million dollars if they can do it." NBC did not broadcast Mason's original interview during Serrano's trial. The jury returned a guilty verdict in Serrano's criminal case. Subsequently, NBC televised an edited version of Mason's interview on a national broadcast of its *Dateline* television program, including Mason's million-dollar challenge.

Dustin Kolodziej, a law student at the South Texas College of Law who had been following the Serrano case, saw the edited interview and decided to take up Mason's million-dollar challenge. Kolodziej recorded himself retracing Serrano's route, traveling from a flight landing at the Atlanta airport to the site of the La Quinta Inn in less than 28 minutes. Kolodziej sent Mason a copy of the recording of his journey and demanded $1 million. When Mason refused to pay, Kolodziej sued Mason in U.S. district court for breach of contract to recover $1 million. Was Mason's million-dollar challenge made on television a legitimate legal offer? *Kolodziej v. Mason*, 774 F.3d 736, 2014 U.S. App. Lexis 23816 (United States Court of Appeals for the Eleventh Circuit, 2014)

9.4 Objective Theory of Contracts Al and Rosemary Mitchell owned a small secondhand store. The Mitchells attended Alexander's Auction, where they frequently shopped to obtain merchandise for their business. While at the auction, they purchased a used safe for $50. They were told by the auctioneer that the inside compartment of the safe was locked and that no key could be found to unlock it. The safe was part of the Sumstad estate. Several days after the auction, the Mitchells took the safe to a locksmith to have the locked compartment opened. When the locksmith opened the compartment, he found $32,207 in cash. The locksmith called the City of Everett Police, who impounded the money. The City of Everett commenced an action against the Sumstad estate and the Mitchells to determine who owns the cash that was found in the safe. Who owns the money found in the safe? *City of Everett, Washington v. Mitchell*, 631 P.2d 366, 1981 Wash. Lexis 1139 (Supreme Court of Washington, 1981)

Ethics Case

9.5 Ethics Case The Lewiston Lodge of Elks sponsored a golf tournament at the Fairlawn Country Club in Poland, Maine. For promotional purposes, Marcel Motors, an automobile dealership, agreed to give any golfer who shot a hole-in-one a new Dodge automobile. Fliers advertising the tournament were posted in the Elks Club and sent to potential participants. On the day of the tournament, the new Dodge automobile was parked near the clubhouse, with one of the posters conspicuously displayed on the vehicle. Alphee Chenard Jr., who had seen the promotional literature regarding the hole-in-one offer, registered for the tournament and paid the requisite entrance fee. While playing the 13th hole of the golf course, in the presence of the other members of his foursome, Chenard shot a hole-in-one. When Marcel Motors refused to tender the automobile, Chenard sued for breach of contract. Was the contract a bilateral or a unilateral contract? Should Chenard win? Is it ethical for Marcel Motors to refuse to give the automobile to Chenard? *Chenard v. Marcel Motors*, 387 A.2d 596, 1978 Me. Lexis 911 (Supreme Judicial Court of Maine, 1978)

Notes

1. *Rebstock v. Birthright Oil & Gas Co.*, 406 So.2d 636, 1981 La. App. Lexis 5242 (Court of Appeal of Louisiana).
2. *Restatement (Second) of Contracts*, Section 1.
3. *Restatement (Second) of Contracts*, Section 1.
4. *Restatement (Second) of Contracts*, Section 6.

CHAPTER

10 Agreement

LAKEFRONT HOUSE, SAINT IGNACE, MICHIGAN
This house was purchased pursuant to a written real estate agreement.

Henry R. Cheeseman

Learning Objectives

After studying this chapter, you should be able to:

10.1 Define *agreement*.

10.2 Define *offer* and describe express and implied terms of an offer.

10.3 List and describe special types of offers, including advertisements and auctions.

10.4 Describe how offers are terminated by acts of the parties and define *counteroffer*.

10.5 Describe how offers are terminated by operation of law.

10.6 Define *acceptance* and apply the mirror image rule.

> *"When I use a word," Humpty Dumpty said, in rather a scornful tone, "it means just what I choose it to mean—neither more nor less."*
>
> *"The question is," said Alice, "whether you can make words mean so many different things."*
>
> *"The question is," said Humpty Dumpty, "which is to be master—that's all."*
>
> —*Lewis Carroll*
> *Alice's Adventures in Wonderland (1865)*

Introduction to Agreement

Contracts are voluntary agreements between parties; that is, one party makes an offer that is accepted by the other party. Assent may be expressly evidenced by the oral or written words of the parties or implied from the conduct of the parties. Without mutual assent, there is no contract.

A party to whom an offer is made may take actions other than accepting the contract. That party may reject the offer, make a counteroffer, or take other actions that do not constitute assent. Sometimes, an offer is terminated before it has been accepted, and this may be by action of the parties or operation of law.

Topics such as offer, acceptance, agreement, and termination of offers are discussed in this chapter.

Where law ends, there tyranny begins.

William Pitt the Younger
The case of John Wilkes
(speech, 1805)

Agreement

10.1 Define *agreement*.

The words *agreement* and *contract* are often used interchangeably. An **agreement** is a voluntary exchange of promises between two or more legally competent persons to do or to refrain from doing an act. An agreement requires the **mutual assent** of the parties—that is, their **"meeting of the minds"**—to perform current or future contractual duties.

The following feature describes the enforcement of a contract.

agreement
The manifestation by two or more persons of the substance of a contract.

Ethics

A Contract Is a Contract Is a Contract

"In hindsight, the agreement appears to be unfair to Marder."
—Harry Pregerson, Circuit Judge

The movie *Flashdance* tells a story of a female construction worker who is a performer at night. The movie is based on the life of Maureen Marder. Paramount Pictures and Marder signed a contract in which Paramount paid Marder $2,300 to use her life story. Marder also signed a contract that released Paramount from any further claims by Marder. The movie grossed more than $150 million in box office receipts and additional revenue from television broadcasts and rentals. Marder sued Paramount, alleging that she should be paid more money than provided in the original contract because of the success of the movie. The U.S. district court held that Marder was bound by her contract and that Paramount owed her no addition compensation. Although the court noted "In hindsight, the agreement appears to be unfair to Marder," the court concluded "the law imputes to Marder an intention corresponding to the reasonable meaning of her words and acts." This is an example of the adage "A contract is a contract is a contract." *Marder v. Lopez*, 450 F.3d 445, 2006 U.S. App. Lexis 14330 (United States Court of Appeals for the Ninth Circuit, 2006)

Ethics Questions

Did Marder act ethically when she tried to have the contract rewritten? Did Paramount take advantage of Marder by paying her so little for her life story? What would be the consequences if courts could undo contracts using hindsight?

In the following case, the court had to decide if there had been mutual assent of the parties.

CASE 10.1 *STATE COURT CASE Meeting of the Minds*

The Institute of Range and the American Mustang v. The Nature Conservancy

922 N.W.2d 1, 2018 S.D. 88 (2018)
Supreme Court of South Dakota

"Consent is mutual when the parties all agree upon the same thing in the same sense."

—Per Curiam

Facts

Dayton Hyde moved to the Black Hills of South Dakota to create a wild horse sanctuary. He formed and was president of The Institute of Range and the American Mustang (IRAM), a non-profit corporation dedicated to acquiring land and preserving a habitat for horses. The Nature Conservancy is a charitable non-profit corporation with a stated mission to conserve lands and waters upon which all life depends. The Nature Conservancy obtains conservation easements on private property by purchasing land or accepting donations from property owners.

After substantial negotiation, IRAM agreed to grant an easement on its South Dakota property to The Nature Conservancy for a payment of $230,000. The conservation easement deed was signed by Hyde on behalf of IRAM. The Nature Conservancy paid $230,000, and the deed was recorded. Eighteen years later, IRAM brought a lawsuit to have the deed declared null and void. IRAM alleged that there had been no meeting of the minds of the parties because Hyde had not read the deed and therefore did not understand the extent of the rights that he granted on behalf of IRAM. The circuit court found that there had been mutual assent of the parties and granted summary judgment to The Nature Conservancy.

Issue

Was there a meeting of the minds of the parties when the conservation easement agreement was entered into?

Language of the Court

IRAM argues that the parties did not have a meeting of the minds. We acknowledge that an enforceable contract requires mutuality of consent. Consent is mutual when the parties all agree upon the same thing in the same sense. Hyde's failure to determine the contents of the deed he was signing must be described as negligence. Hyde's negligence should not foreclose The Nature Conservancy's right to rely on Hyde's affirmative manifestation of mutual agreement and assent to be bound by the terms of the deed. To permit a party, when sued on a written contract, to admit that he signed it but deny that it expresses the agreement he made or to allow him to admit he signed it but did not read it or its stipulations would destroy the value of all contracts.

Decision

The Supreme Court of South Dakota affirmed the decision of the circuit court in favor of The Nature Conservancy.

Critical Legal Thinking Questions

Was there a meeting of the minds in this case? What would be the consequences if a party could rescind a contract because he or she did not read it?

Offer and Acceptance

A **contract** is an agreement that meets certain additional legal criteria (to be discussed in this and the following chapters) and is enforceable in a court of law. To begin with, a contract requires an *offer* and an *acceptance*.

Offer

10.2 Define *offer* and describe express and implied terms of an offer.

The process of reaching an agreement begins when one party makes an offer to another party to sell or lease property or provide services to another party. Often, prior to entering into a contract, the parties engage in preliminary negotiations about price, time of performance, and so on. At some point, one party makes an offer to the other party. The person who makes the offer is called the **offeror**, and the person to whom the offer is made is called the **offeree**. The offer sets forth the terms under which the offeror is willing to enter into the contract. The offeree has the power to create an agreement by accepting the offer.

offeror
The party who makes an offer.

offeree
The party to whom an offer has been made.

Section 24 of the *Restatement (Second) of Contracts* defines an **offer** as "the manifestation of willingness to enter into a bargain, so made as to justify another person in understanding that his assent to that bargain is invited and will conclude it." The following three elements are required for an offer to be effective:

offer
"The manifestation of willingness to enter into a bargain, so made as to justify another person in understanding that his assent to that bargain is invited and will conclude it" (Section 24 of the *Restatement [Second] of Contracts*).

1. The offeror must *objectively intend* to be bound by the offer.
2. The terms of the offer must be definite or reasonably *certain*.
3. The offer must be *communicated* to the offeree.

Generally, an offer is not effective until it is actually received by the offeree. The making of an offer is shown in Exhibit 10.1.

Express Terms

The terms of an offer must be clear enough for the offeree to be able to decide whether to accept or reject those terms. To be considered definite, an offer (and contract) generally must contain the following terms: (1) identification of the parties, (2) identification of the subject matter and quantity, (3) consideration to be paid, and (4) time of performance. Complex contracts usually state additional terms.

Most offers and contracts set forth **express terms** that identify the parties, the subject matter of the contract, the consideration to be paid by the parties, and the time of performance as well as other terms of the offer and contract.

If the terms are indefinite, the courts usually cannot enforce the contract or determine an appropriate remedy for its breach. However, the law permits some terms to be implied.

Implied Terms

The common law of contracts required an exact specification of contract terms. If one essential term was omitted, the courts held that no contract had been made. This rule was inflexible.

The modern law of contracts is more lenient. The *Restatement (Second) of Contracts* merely requires that the terms of the offer be "reasonably certain."[1] Accordingly, the court can supply a missing term if a reasonable term can be implied.[2] The definition of *reasonable* depends on the circumstances. Terms that are supplied in this way are called **implied terms**.

implied term
A term in a contract that can reasonably be supplied by the courts.

Exhibit 10.1 OFFER

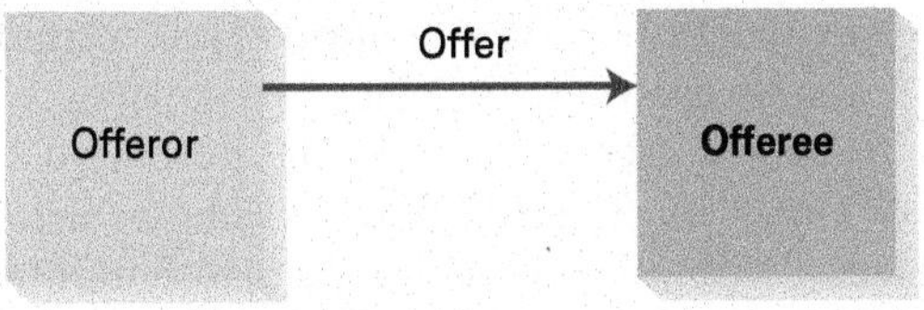

Offeror makes an offer to the offeree.

Generally, time of performance can be implied. Price can be implied if there is a market or source from which to determine the price of the item or service (e.g., the Carfax or Kelley Blue Book for a used automobile price).

The parties or subject matter of the contract usually cannot be implied if an item or a service is unique or personal, such as the construction of a house or the performance of a professional sports contract.

Communication of an Offer

A contract is a mutual promise.

William Paley
The Principles of Moral and Political Philosophy (1784)

An offer cannot be accepted if it is not communicated to the offeree by the offeror or a representative or an agent of the offeror.

Example Ms. Jones, the CEO of Ace Corporation, wants to sell a manufacturing division to Baker Corporation. She puts the offer in writing, but she does not send it. Mr. Griswald, the CFO of Baker Corporation, visits Ms. Jones's office and sees the written offer lying on her desk. Griswald tells his CEO about the offer. However, because Ms. Jones never communicated the offer to Baker Corporation, there is no offer to be accepted.

Special Offers

10.3 List and describe special types of offers, including advertisements and auctions.

There are several special types of offers. These include *advertisements, rewards*, and *auctions*.

Advertisements

advertisement
An invitation to make an offer or an actual offer.

An **advertisement** for the sale of goods, even at a specific price, is generally treated as an **invitation to make an offer**. This rule is intended to protect advertiser-sellers from the unwarranted breach of contract suits for nonperformance that would otherwise arise if the seller ran out of the advertised goods.

There is one exception to this rule: An advertisement is considered an offer if it is so definite or specific that it is apparent that the advertiser has the present intent to bind itself to the terms of the advertisement.

Example An automobile owner's advertisement to sell a "previously owned white 2019 Land Rover SUV, vehicle identification number (vin) SALMF13478A315624, $50,000" is an offer. Because the advertisement identifies the exact automobile for sale, the first person to accept the offer owns the automobile.

Rewards

reward
An award given for performance of some service or attainment. To collect a reward, the offeree must (1) have knowledge of the reward offer prior to completing the requested act and (2) perform the requested act.

An offer to pay a **reward** (e.g., for the return of lost property or the capture of a criminal) is an offer to form a unilateral contract. To be entitled to collect the reward, the offeree must (1) have knowledge of the reward offer prior to completing the requested act and (2) perform the requested act.

Example Zacharia accidentally leaves a briefcase containing $100,000 in negotiable bonds on a subway train. He places newspaper ads stating "$10,000 reward for return of briefcase left on a train in Manhattan on January 10, 2021, at approximately 10:00 a.m. Call 212-555-6789." Helena, who is unaware of the offer, finds the briefcase. She reads the luggage tag containing Zacharia's name, address, and telephone number, and she returns the briefcase to him. Helena is not entitled to the reward money because she did not know about the reward when she performed the requested act.

Auctions

In an **auction**, the seller offers goods for sale through an auctioneer. Unless otherwise expressly stated, an auction is considered an **auction with reserve**—that is, it is an invitation to make an offer. The seller retains the right to refuse the highest bid and withdraw the goods from sale. A contract is formed only when the auctioneer strikes the gavel down or indicates acceptance by some other means. The bidder may withdraw the bid prior to that time.

auction with reserve
An auction in which the seller retains the right to refuse the highest bid and withdraw the goods from sale. Unless expressly stated otherwise, an auction is an auction with reserve.

Example If an auction is an auction with reserve and an item is offered at $100,000, but the highest bid is $75,000, the auctioneer does not have to sell the item.

If an auction is expressly announced to be an **auction without reserve**, the participants reverse the roles: The seller is the offeror, and the bidders are the offerees. The seller must accept the highest bid and cannot withdraw the goods from sale. However, if the auctioneer has set a minimum bid that it will accept, the auctioneer has to sell the item only if the highest bid is equal to or greater than the minimum bid.

auction without reserve
An auction in which the seller expressly gives up the right to withdraw the goods from sale and must accept the highest bid.

CONCEPT SUMMARY

TYPES OF AUCTIONS

Type	Does the seller offer the goods for sale?
Auction with reserve	No. It is an invitation to make an offer. Because the bidder is the offeror, the seller (the offeree) may refuse to sell the goods. An auction is with reserve unless otherwise stated.
Auction without reserve	Yes. The seller is the offeror and must sell the goods to the highest bidder (the offeree). An auction is without reserve only if it is stipulated as such.

Termination of an Offer by Act of the Parties

10.4 Describe how offers are terminated by acts of the parties and define *counteroffer*.

An offer may be terminated by certain acts of the parties. The **termination of an offer by an act of the parties** consists of situations in which one party takes an action that indicates that he or she is not interested in forming a contract under the terms of the offer. Acts of the parties that terminate an offer are discussed in the following paragraphs.

Revocation of an Offer by the Offeror

Under the common law, an offeror may revoke (i.e., withdraw) an offer at any time prior to its acceptance by the offeree. Generally, an offer can be so revoked even if the offeror promised to keep the offer open for a longer time. The **revocation of an offer** may be communicated to the offeree by the offeror or by a third party and made by (1) the offeror's express statement (e.g., "I hereby withdraw my offer") or (2) an act of the offeror that is inconsistent with the offer (e.g., selling the goods to another party). Generally, a revocation of an offer is not effective until it is received by the offeree.

revocation of an offer
Withdrawal of an offer by the offeror that terminates the offer.

Offers made to the public may be revoked by communicating the revocation by the same means used to make the offer.

Example If a reward offer for a lost watch was published in two local newspapers each week for four weeks, a notice of revocation must be published in the same newspapers for the same length of time. The revocation is effective against all offerees, even those who saw the reward offer but not the notice of revocation.

Rejection of an Offer by the Offeree

rejection of an offer
Express words or conduct by the offeree to reject an offer. Rejection terminates the offer.

An offer is terminated if the offeree *rejects* it. Any subsequent attempt by the offeree to accept the offer is ineffective and is construed as a new offer that the original offeror (now the offeree) is free to accept or reject. A **rejection of an offer** may be evidenced by the offeree's express words (oral or written) or conduct. Generally, a rejection of an offer is not effective until it is actually received by the offeror.

Example Ji Eun, a sales manager for a digital company, offers to sell 10,000 software licenses to Ted, the purchasing manager of Operating Corporation, for $1 million. Ted telephones Ji Eun to say that he is not interested. This rejection terminates the offer. If Ted later decides that he wants to purchase the software licenses, a new contract must be executed by the parties.

Counteroffer by the Offeree

counteroffer
A response by an offeree that contains terms and conditions different from or in addition to those of the offer. A counteroffer terminates the previous offer.

A **counteroffer** by the offeree simultaneously terminates the offeror's offer and creates a new offer. Offerees' making of counteroffers is the norm in many transactions. A counteroffer terminates the existing offer and puts a new offer into play. The previous offeree becomes the new offeror, and the previous offeror becomes the new offeree. Generally, a counteroffer is not effective until it is actually received by the offeror.

Example Fei says to Harold, "I will sell you my house for $700,000." Harold says, "I think $700,000 is too high; I will pay you $600,000." Harold has made a counteroffer. Fei's original offer is terminated, and Harold's counteroffer is a new offer that Fei is free to accept or reject.

The following case involves the issue of a counteroffer.

CASE 10.2 *STATE COURT CASE Counteroffer*

Ehlen v. Melvin

823 N.W.2d 780, 2012 N.D. Lexis 252 (2012)
Supreme Court of North Dakota

"The parties' mutual assent is determined by their objective manifestations, not their secret intentions."

—Carol Ronning Kapsner, Justice

Facts

Paul Ehlen signed a document titled "Purchase Agreement" (Agreement) offering to purchase real estate owned by John M. and LynnDee Melvin (the Melvins) for $850,000, with closing to be within 12 days. Two days after the offer was made by Ehlen, the Melvins modified the terms of the Agreement by correcting the spelling of LynnDee Melvin's name and the description of the property, adding that the property was to be sold "as is," that the mineral rights conveyed by the Melvins were limited to the rights that they owned, and that the property was subject to a federal wetland easement and an agricultural lease. The Melvins handwrote the changes on the Agreement, initialed each change, signed the Agreement, and returned it to Ehlen. When the Melvins had not heard from Ehlen on the date of the proposed closing, they notified Ehlen that the transaction was terminated. Ehlen sued the Melvins to enforce the Purchase Agreement as modified by them, alleging that there was a binding and enforceable contract. The trial court held that the Melvins had made a counteroffer that had not been accepted by Ehlen, and therefore there was no contract. Ehlen appealed.

Issue

Was a counteroffer made by the Melvins that Ehlen accepted?

Language of the Court

The parties' mutual assent is determined by their objective manifestations, not their secret intentions. We conclude the evidence supports the court's finding that the parties did not agree to the essential terms of the agreement and the Melvins' modifications to the agreement constituted a counteroffer. Ehlen did not sign the modified agreement or initial the changes. The evidence supports the court's finding that Ehlen did not accept the Melvins' counteroffer.

Decision

The supreme court of North Dakota held that no agreement existed between Ehlen and the Melvins.

Critical Legal Thinking Questions

Did Ehlen act ethically in trying to enforce the purported contract? What would be the consequence if silence were considered acceptance?

CONCEPT SUMMARY

TERMINATION OF AN OFFER BY ACT OF THE PARTIES

Action	Description
Revocation	The offeror *revokes* (withdraws) the offer at any time prior to its acceptance by the offeree.
Rejection	The offeree rejects the offer by his or her words or conduct.
Counteroffer	A counteroffer by the offeree creates a new offer and terminates the offeror's offer.

The following feature discusses the use of an option contract to require that an offer be kept open for a specified period of time.

Business Environment

Option Contract

An offeree can prevent the offeror from revoking an offer by paying the offeror compensation to keep the offer open for an agreed period of time. This creates what is called an **option contract**. In other words, the offeror agrees not to sell the property to anyone except the offeree during the option period. An option contract is a contract in which the original offeree pays consideration (usually money) in return for the original offeror giving consideration (time of the option period). The death or incompetency of either party does not terminate an option contract unless the contract is for the performance of a personal service.

Example Ilha offers to sell a piece of real estate to Zion for $1 million. Zion wants time to investigate the property for possible environmental problems and to arrange financing if he decides to purchase the property, so he pays Ilha $25,000 to keep her offer open to him for six months. At any time during the option period, Zion may exercise his option and pay Ilha the $1 million purchase price. If Zion lets the option expire, however, Ilha may keep the $25,000 and sell the property to someone else. Often option contracts are written so that if the original offeree purchases the property, the option amount is applied to the sale price.

Termination of an Offer by Operation of Law

10.5 Describe how offers are terminated by operation of law.

An offer may be terminated by operation of law. The **termination of an offer by operation of law** includes the following situations.

option contract
A contract that is created when an offeree pays an offeror compensation to keep an offer open for an agreed-upon period of time. An option contract prevents the offeror from revoking his or her offer during the option period.

Destruction of the Subject Matter

An offer terminates if the subject matter of the offer is destroyed through no fault of either party prior to the offer's acceptance.

Example If a fire destroys an office building that has been listed for sale, the offer automatically terminates.

Death or Incompetency of the Offeror or Offeree

Prior to acceptance of an offer, the death or incompetency of either the offeror or the offeree terminates an offer. Notice of the other party's death or incompetence is not a requirement.

Example Suppose that on June 1, Shari offers to sell her house to Damian for $1 million, provided that Damian decides on or before June 15 that he will buy it. Shari dies on June 7, before Damian has made up his mind. The offer automatically terminates on June 7 when Shari dies.

Supervening Illegality

If the object of an offer is made illegal prior to the acceptance of the offer, the offer terminates. This situation, which usually occurs when a statute is enacted, or a decision of a court is announced that makes the object of the offer illegal, is called a **supervening illegality**.

supervening illegality
The enactment of a statute, regulation, or court decision that makes the object of an offer illegal. This action terminates the offer.

Example Suppose Sumitra offers to loan Edsel $1 million at a 15 percent interest rate. Prior to Edsel's acceptance of the offer, the state legislature enacts a statute that sets a usury interest rate of 10 percent. Sumitra's offer to Edsel is automatically terminated when the usury statute becomes effective.

Lapse of Time

lapse of time
A stated time period after which an offer terminates. If no time is stated, an offer terminates after a reasonable time.

An offer expires at the **lapse of time** of an offer. An offer may state that it is effective only until a certain date. Unless otherwise stated, the time period begins to run when the offer is actually received by the offeree and terminates when the stated time period expires.

Example If an offer states, "This offer is good for 10 days," the offer expires at midnight of the tenth day after the offer was made.

Example If an offer states, "This offer must be accepted by January 1, 2023," the offer expires on midnight of January 1, 2023.

CONCEPT SUMMARY

TERMINATION OF AN OFFER BY OPERATION OF LAW

Action	Description
Destruction of the subject matter	The subject matter of an offer is destroyed prior to acceptance through no fault of either party.
Death or incompetency	Prior to acceptance of an offer, either the offeror or the offeree dies or becomes incompetent.
Supervening illegality	Prior to the acceptance of an offer, the object of the offer is made illegal by statute, regulation, court decision, or other law.
Lapse of time	An offer terminates on the expiration of a stated time in the offer. If no time is stated, the offer terminates after a "reasonable time."

Acceptance

10.6 Define *acceptance* and apply the mirror image rule.

Acceptance is "a manifestation of assent by the offeree to the terms of the offer in a manner invited or required by the offer as measured by the objective theory of contracts."[3] Recall that generally (1) unilateral contracts can be accepted only by the offeree's performance of the required act and (2) a bilateral contract can be accepted by an offeree who promises to perform (or, where permitted, by performance of) the requested act.

acceptance
"A manifestation of assent by the offeree to the terms of the offer in a manner invited or required by the offer as measured by the objective theory of contracts" (Section 50 of the *Restatement [Second] of Contracts*).

Who Can Accept an Offer?

Only the offeree has the legal power to accept an offer and create a contract. Third persons usually do not have the power to accept an offer. If an offer is made individually to two or more persons, each has the power to accept the offer. Once one of the offerees accepts the offer, it terminates as to the other offeree(s). An offer that is made to two or more persons jointly must be accepted jointly.

The acceptance of an offer is illustrated in Exhibit 10.2.

Unequivocal Acceptance

An offeree's acceptance must be an **unequivocal acceptance**. That is, the acceptance must be clear and unambiguous, and it must have only one possible meaning. An unequivocal acceptance must not contain conditions or exceptions.

unequivocal acceptance
An acceptance of an offer that is clear, unambiguous, and has only one possible meaning.

Example Abraham says to Caitlin, "I will sell you my smartphone for $300." Caitlin says, "Yes, I will buy your smartphone at that price." This is an unequivocal acceptance that creates a contract.

Usually, even a "grumbling acceptance" is a legal acceptance.

Example Jordan offers to sell his smartphone to Taryn for $300. Taryn says, "Okay, I'll take the smartphone, but I sure wish you would make me a better deal." This grumbling acceptance creates an enforceable contract because it was not a rejection or a counteroffer.

An **equivocal response** by the offeree does not create a contract.

Example Halim offers to sell his smartphone to Nicole for $300. Nicole says, "I think I would like it, but I'm not sure." This is equivocation and does not amount to an acceptance.

The following feature discusses the mirror image rule.

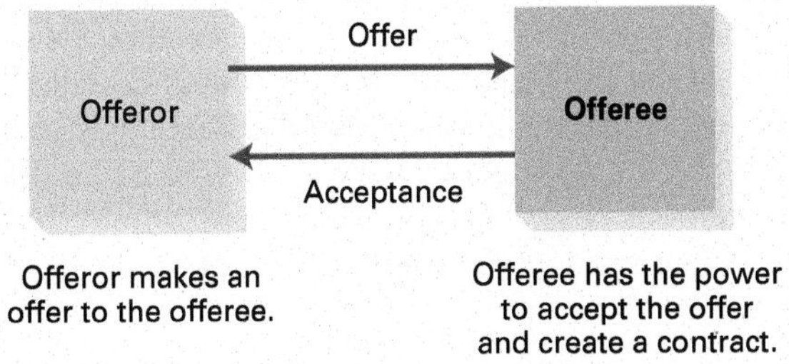
Offer
Offeror
Offeree
Acceptance
Offeror makes an offer to the offeree.
Offeree has the power to accept the offer and create a contract.

Exhibit 10.2 ACCEPTANCE OF AN OFFER

Contemporary Environment

Mirror Image Rule

For an acceptance to exist, the offeree must accept the terms as stated in the offer. This is called the **mirror image rule.** To meet this rule, the offeree must accept the terms of the offer without modification. Any attempt to accept the offer on different terms constitutes a counteroffer, which rejects the offeror's offer.

Example A seller offers to sell a specific automobile she owns for $30,000. The automobile is a certain brand, model, year, color, and condition. A buyer accepts the exact terms of the offer. Under the mirror image rule, a contract has been created.

Example If, in the previous example, the potential buyer agrees to all of the terms of the seller's offer but demands that new wheel rims be installed on the automobile to replace the existing rims, the mirror image rule has not been met, and no contract is created.

---

mirror image rule
A rule stating that, for an acceptance to exist, the offeree must accept the terms as stated in the offer.

Critical Legal Thinking Questions

What is the mirror image rule? Why is this rule applied strictly in determining whether a contract has been made?

Silence as Acceptance

Silence usually is not considered acceptance, even if the offeror states that it is. This rule is intended to protect offerees from being legally bound to offers because they failed to respond.

Example Coco sends a letter to Dwayne stating, "You have agreed to purchase my motorcycle for $4,000 unless I hear otherwise from you by Friday." Obviously, there is no contract if Dwayne ignores the letter.

Nevertheless, silence *does* constitute acceptance in the following situations:

1. The offeree has indicated that silence means assent.

   Example "If you do not hear from me by Friday, ship the order."

2. The offeree has signed an agreement indicating continuing acceptance of delivery until further notification.

   Example Book of the Month Club, a subscription-based e-commerce service that offers a selection of electronic books to its members each month, uses such an acceptance.

3. Prior dealings between the parties indicate that silence means acceptance.

   Example A fish wholesaler who delivers 30 pounds of fish to a restaurant each Friday for several years and is paid for the fish can continue the deliveries with expectation of payment until notified otherwise by the restaurant.

Time of Acceptance

acceptance-upon-dispatch rule (mailbox rule)
A rule stating that an acceptance is effective when it is dispatched, even if it is lost in transmission.

Under the common law of contracts, acceptance of a bilateral contract occurs when the offeree *dispatches* the acceptance by an authorized means of communication. This rule is called the **acceptance-upon-dispatch rule**, often referred to as the **mailbox rule** or **posting rule**. Under this rule, the acceptance is effective when it is dispatched, even if it is lost in transmission. If an offeree first dispatches a rejection and then sends an acceptance, the mailbox rule does not apply to the acceptance.[4]

An acceptance sent by a courier delivery service (e.g., FedEx, UPS) or by fax is governed by the mailbox rule. The majority of states hold that an email or text acceptance is valid when sent, while others hold that an email or text acceptance is not valid until received.

The problem of lost acceptances can be minimized by expressly altering the mailbox rule. The offeror can do this by stating in the offer that acceptance is effective only on actual receipt of the acceptance.

Example Jonathon sends a written offer to Tabetha offering to sell his home to her for $1 million. In the offer, Jonathon specifies that acceptance is only effective when he receives a written acceptance by Tabetha sent by registered mail. A contract is effective when Jonathon receives a written acceptance from Tabetha by registered mail. If Tabetha sends her acceptance by regular mail or by courier service, the acceptance is not valid even if Jonathon receives the acceptance.

CONCEPT SUMMARY

EFFECTIVE DATES OF COMMUNICATIONS

Type of Communication	Effective When
Offer	Received by offeree
Revocation of offer	Received by offeree
Rejection of offer	Received by offeror
Counteroffer	Received by offeror
Acceptance of offer for a bilateral contract	Dispatched by offeree

Mode of Acceptance

An acceptance must be **properly dispatched**. The acceptance must be properly addressed, packaged in an appropriate envelope or container, and have prepaid postage or delivery charges. Under common law, if an acceptance is not properly dispatched, it is not effective until it is received by the offeror.

proper dispatch
The proper addressing, packaging, and posting of an acceptance.

Generally, an offeree must accept an offer by an **authorized means of communication**. Most offers do not expressly specify the means of communication required for acceptance. The common law recognizes certain implied means of communication. Implied authorization may be inferred from what is customary in similar transactions, usage of trade, or prior dealings between the parties. Section 30 of the *Restatement (Second) of Contracts* permits **implied authorization** "by any medium reasonable in the circumstances." Thus, in most circumstances, a party may send an acceptance by mail, overnight delivery service, fax, email, or text.

implied authorization
A mode of acceptance that is implied from what is customary in similar transactions, usage of trade, or prior dealings between the parties.

An offer can stipulate that acceptance must be made by a specified means of communication (e.g., registered mail, telegram). Such stipulation is called **express authorization**. If the offeree uses an unauthorized means of communication to transmit the acceptance, the acceptance is not effective, even if it is received by the offeror within the allowed time period, because the means of communication was a condition of acceptance.

express authorization
A stipulation in an offer that says the acceptance must be by a specified means of communication.

CONCEPT SUMMARY

RULES OF ACCEPTANCE

Rule	Description
Unequivocal acceptance	An acceptance must be clear and unambiguous, have only one possible meaning, and not contain conditions or exceptions.
Mirror image rule	To create a contract, an offeree must accept the terms as stated in the offeror's offer, without modification. Any attempt to accept the offer on different terms constitutes a counteroffer, which rejects the offeror's offer.
Acceptance-upon-dispatch rule (mailbox rule)	Unless otherwise provided in an offer, acceptance is effective when it is dispatched by the offeree.
Proper dispatch rule	An acceptance must be properly addressed, packaged, and have prepaid postage or delivery charges to be effective when dispatched. Generally, improperly dispatched acceptances are not effective until actually received by the offeror.
Authorized means of communication	Acceptance must be by the express means of communication stipulated in the offer, or, if no means is stipulated, then by reasonable means in the circumstances.

In the following feature, a court addressed the question of whether an email acceptance of a written offer creates a contract.

Information Technology

Email Acceptance Creates an Enforceable Contract

"It is clear that a contract is formed when someone accepts a written offer by email."

—Kenneth Salinger, Justice

Carol Riselli contacted Clean Properties, Inc. and requested that it clean up a substantial release of oil that had occurred on a property owned by Riselli in Belmont, Massachusetts, on an emergency basis. Clean Properties offered to do this environmental cleanup work pursuant to the terms and conditions in a proposed written contract that it sent to Riselli, which identified the contract as Project 0941, Order 1. The proposed contract included a provision for a mechanic's lien on the property in favor of Clean Properties that made the property collateral in case Clean Properties was not paid for its services. Riselli immediately responded by email, which stated, "I agree with the terms of the contract identified as Project #0941, Order 1. Please start work right away." The email concludes with a signature block that states "Thank you, Carol J. Riselli."

Clean Properties provided services to clean up the oil but was not paid for its services. Clean Properties attempted to perfect its mechanic's lien on the property so that it could bring proceedings to have the property sold and have the sum it was owed paid from the proceeds of the sale. Riselli alleged that there was no written contract between the parties because her acceptance and signature were not in writing but were made electronically by email.

The superior court held that Riselli's email acceptance of Clean Properties' written offer created an enforceable contract. The court stated, "It is clear that a contract is formed when someone accepts a written offer by email, and that such a written contract is enforceable. Riselli's email expressed her acceptance of the written contract terms offered by Clean Properties." The court ruled that Clean Properties could perfect its remedy afforded by the mechanics lien. *Clean Properties, Inc. v. Riselli*, 2014 Mass. Super. Lexis 106 (Commonwealth of Massachusetts Superior Court, 2014)

Critical Legal Thinking Questions

Does the court's decision reflect current business practices? Was it ethical for Riselli to argue that her email response did not create a contract?

Key Terms and Concepts

Acceptance (209)
Acceptance-upon-dispatch rule (mailbox rule or posting rule) (210)
Advertisement (204)
Agreement (201)
Auction (205)
Auction with reserve (205)
Auction without reserve (205)
Authorized means of communication (211)
Contract (202)
Counteroffer (206)
Equivocal response (209)
Express authorization (211)
Express terms (203)
Implied authorization (211)
Implied term (203)
Invitation to make an offer (204)
Lapse of time (208)
Mirror image rule (210)
Mutual assent (meeting of the minds) (201)
Offer (203)
Offeree (203)
Offeror (203)
Option contract (207)
Properly dispatched (211)
Rejection of an offer (206)
Revocation of an offer (205)
Reward (204)
Supervening illegality (208)
Termination of an offer by act of the parties (205)
Termination of an offer by operation of law (207)
Unequivocal acceptance (209)

Critical Legal Thinking Cases

10.1 Mirror Image Rule Norma English made an offer to purchase a house owned by Michael and Laurie Montgomery (Montgomerys) for $272,000. In her offer, English also proposed to purchase certain personal property—paving stones and a fireplace screen worth a total of $100—from the Montgomerys. When the Montgomerys received English's offer, they made many changes to English's offer, including deleting the paving stones and fireplace screen from the personal property that English wanted. When English received the Montgomerys' counteroffer, English accepted and initialed all of the Montgomerys' changes except that English did not initial the change that deleted the paving stones and fireplace screen from the deal.

Subsequently, the Montgomerys notified English that because English had not completely accepted the terms of the Montgomerys' counteroffer, the Montgomerys were withdrawing from the deal. That same day, the Montgomerys signed a contract to sell the house to another buyer for $285,000. English sued the Montgomerys for specific performance of the contract. The Montgomerys defended, arguing that the mirror image rule was not satisfied because English had not initialed the provision that deleted the paving stones and fireplace screen. Is there an enforceable contract between English and the Montgomerys? *Montgomery v. English*, 902 So.2d 836, 2005 Fla. App. Lexis 4704 (Court of Appeal of Florida, 2005)

10.2 Agreement Wilbert Heikkila listed eight parcels of real property for sale. David McLaughlin submitted written offers to purchase three of the parcels. Three printed purchase agreements were prepared and submitted to Heikkila, with three earnest-money checks from McLaughlin. Writing on the purchase agreements, Heikkila changed the price of one parcel from $145,000 to $150,000, the price of another parcel from $32,000 to $45,000, and the price of the third parcel from $175,000 to $179,000. Heikkila also changed the closing dates on all three of the properties, added a reservation of mineral rights to all three, and signed the purchase agreements.

McLaughlin did not sign the purchase agreements to accept the changes before Heikkila withdrew his offer to sell. McLaughlin sued to compel specific performance of the purchase agreements under the terms of the agreements before Heikkila withdrew his offer. The court granted Heikkila's motion to dismiss McLaughlin's claim. McLaughlin appealed. Does a contract to convey real property exist between Heikkila and McLaughlin? *McLaughlin v. Heikkila*, 697 N.W.2d 231, 2005 Minn. App. Lexis 591 (Court of Appeals of Minnesota, 2005)

10.3 Solicitation to Make an Offer The U.S. Congress directed the Secretary of the Treasury to mint and sell a stated number of specially minted commemorative coins to raise funds to restore and renovate the Statue of Liberty. The U.S. Mint mailed advertising materials to persons, including Mary and Anthony C. Mesaros, that described the various types of coins that were to be issued. Payment could be made by check, money order, or credit card. The materials included an order form. Directly above the space provided on this form for the customer's signature was the following: "YES, Please accept my order for the U.S. Liberty Coins I have indicated."

Mary Mesaros forwarded to the Mint a credit card order of $1,675 for certain coins, including the $5 gold coin. All credit card orders were forwarded by the Mint to Mellon Bank in Pittsburgh, Pennsylvania, for verification, which took a period of time. Meanwhile, cash orders were filled immediately, and orders paid by check were filled as the checks cleared. The issuance of 500,000 gold coins was exhausted before Mesaros's credit card order could be filled. The Mint sent a letter to the Mesaroses, notifying them of this fact. The gold coin increased in value by 200 percent within the first few months of issue. Mary and Anthony C. Mesaros filed a class action lawsuit against the United States, seeking in the alternative either damages for breach of contract or a decree ordering the Mint to deliver the gold coins to the plaintiffs. Is there a contract between the Mesaroses and the United States? *Mesaros v. United States*, 845 F.2d 1576, 1988 U.S. App. Lexis 6055 (United States Court of Appeals for the Federal Circuit, 1988)

10.4 Counteroffer Glende Motor Company (Glende), an automobile dealership that sold new cars, leased premises from certain landlords. One day, fire destroyed part of the leased premises, and Glende restored the leasehold premises. The landlords received payment of insurance proceeds for the fire. Glende sued the landlords to recover the insurance proceeds. Ten days before the trial was to begin, the defendants jointly served on Glende a document titled "Offer to Compromise Before Trial," which was a settlement offer of $190,000. Glende agreed to the amount of the settlement but made it contingent on the execution of a new lease. The next day, the defendants notified Glende that they were revoking the settlement offer. Glende thereafter tried to accept the original settlement offer. Has there been a settlement of the lawsuit? *Glende Motor Company v. Superior Court*, 159 Cal.App.3d 389, 205 Cal. Rptr. 682, 1984 Cal. App. Lexis 2435 (Court of Appeal of California, 1984)

Ethics Case

10.5 Ethics Case *Mighty Morphin' Power Rangers* was a phenomenal success as a television series. The Power Rangers battled to save the universe from all sorts of diabolical plots and bad guys. They were also featured in a profitable line of toys and garments bearing the Power Rangers logo. The name and logo of the Power Rangers are known to millions of children and their parents worldwide. The claim of ownership of the logo for the Power Rangers ended up in a battle in a courtroom.

David Dees is a designer who works as d.b.a. David Dees Illustration. Saban Entertainment, Inc. (Saban), which owns the copyright and trademark to Power Rangers figures and the name "Power Ranger," hired

Dees as an independent contractor to design a logo for the Power Rangers. The contract signed by the parties was titled "Work-for-Hire/Independent Contractor Agreement." The contract was drafted by Saban with the help of its attorneys; Dees signed the agreement without the representation of legal counsel.

Dees designed the logo currently used for the Power Rangers and was paid $250 to transfer his copyright ownership in the logo. Subsequently, Dees sued Saban to recover damages for copyright and trademark infringement. Saban defended, arguing that Dees was bound by the agreement he had signed. What does the adage "A contract is a contract is a contract" mean? Does the doctrine of equity save Dees from his contract? Does Saban owe an ethical duty to pay Dees more money now that Power Rangers is a successful brand? Is Dees bound by the contract? *Dees, d/b/a David Dees Illustration v. Saban Entertainment, Inc.*, 131 F.3d 146, 1997 U.S. App. Lexis 39173 (United States Court of Appeals for the Ninth Circuit, 1997)

Notes

1. *Restatement (Second) of Contracts*, Section 204.
2. Section 87(2) of the *Restatement (Second) of Contracts* states that an offer that the offeror should reasonably expect to induce action or forbearance of a substantial character on the part of the offeree before acceptance and that does induce such action or forbearance is binding as an option contract to the extent necessary to avoid injustice.
3. *Restatement (Second) of Contracts*, Section 50(1).
4. *Restatement (Second) of Contracts*, Section 40.

CHAPTER

11

Consideration and Promissory Estoppel

BEIJING, CHINA

This is a photograph of the Forbidden City, Beijing, China. In 1999, China dramatically overhauled its contract laws by enacting the ***Unified Contract Law (UCL).*** *This new set of laws changed many outdated business and commercial contract laws. The UCL was designed to provide users with a consistent and easy-to-understand set of statutes that more closely resembled international business contracting principles. It also provides for resolution of contract disputes by the application of the rule of law. The UCL covers all the parts of contract law that should be familiar to Western businesses, including the definitions of contract, acceptance, agreement, consideration, breach of contract, and remedies.*

Henry R. Cheeseman

Learning Objectives

After studying this chapter, you should be able to:

11.1 Define *consideration* and describe the requirements of consideration.

11.2 Define *gift promise* and identify whether gift promises are enforceable.

11.3 Describe contracts that lack consideration, such as those involving illegal consideration, an illusory promise, a preexisting duty, or past consideration.

11.4 List and describe special business contracts, including output contracts, requirements contracts, and best-efforts contracts.

11.5 Define *accord and satisfaction* in settling a disputed claim.

11.6 Define and apply the equitable doctrine of *promissory estoppel*.

> *"The law has outgrown its primitive stage of formalism when the precise word was the sovereign talisman, and every slip was fatal. It takes a broader view today. A promise may be lacking, and yet the whole writing may be 'instinct with an obligation,' imperfectly expressed."*
>
> —*Benjamin N. Cardozo, Justice*
> *Wood v. Lucy, Lady Duff-Gordon*
> *222 N.Y.88, 118 N.E. 214, 1917 N.Y. Lexis 818*
> *(New York Court of Appeals, 1917)*

Introduction to Consideration and Promissory Estoppel

There is grim irony in speaking of freedom of contract of those who, because of their economic necessities, give their service for less than is needful to keep body and soul together.

Harlan Fiske Stone, Chief Justice
Morehead v. New York ex rel. Tipaldo
298 U.S. 587, 56 S.Ct. 918, 1936 U.S. Lexis 1044 (1936)
Supreme Court of the United States

To be enforceable, a contract usually must be supported by *consideration*, which is broadly defined as something of legal value. It can consist of money, property, the provision of services, the forbearance of a right, or anything else of value. Most contracts are supported by consideration.

Contracts that are not supported by consideration are usually not enforceable. This means that a party who has not given consideration cannot enforce a contract. The parties may, however, voluntarily perform a contract that is lacking in consideration. If a contract that was lacking in consideration is performed by the parties, the parties cannot subsequently assert lack of consideration to undo the performed contract. *Promissory estoppel* is an equity doctrine that permits a court to order enforcement of a contract that lacks consideration.

This chapter discusses consideration, promises that lack consideration, and equity doctrines that permit promises that lack consideration to be enforced.

Consideration

11.1 Define *consideration* and describe the requirements of consideration.

consideration
Something of legal value given in exchange for a promise.

Consideration usually must be given before a contract can exist. **Consideration** is defined as something of legal value given in exchange for a promise. Consideration can come in different forms. The most common types consist of either a tangible payment (e.g., money or property) or the performance of an act (e.g., providing legal services). Less usual forms of consideration include the forbearance of a legal right (e.g., accepting an out-of-court settlement in exchange for dropping a lawsuit) and noneconomic forms of consideration (e.g., refraining from "drinking, using tobacco, swearing, or playing cards or billiards for money"[1] for a specified time).

Written contracts are presumed to be supported by consideration. This rebuttable presumption, however, may be overcome by sufficient evidence. A few states provide that contracts made under seal cannot be challenged for lack of consideration.

Requirements of Consideration

Consideration consists of two elements: (1) Something of *legal value* must be given (i.e., either a legal benefit must be received or legal detriment must be suffered) and (2) there must be a *bargained-for exchange*. Each of these is discussed in the paragraphs that follow:

legal value
Support for a contract when either (1) the promisee suffers a legal detriment or (2) the promisor receives a legal benefit.

1. **Legal value.** Under the modern law of contracts, a contract is considered to be supported by **legal value** if (1) the promisee suffers a *legal detriment* or (2) the promisor receives a *legal benefit*.

2. **Bargained-for exchange.** To be enforceable, a contract must arise from a **bargained-for exchange**. In most business contracts, the parties engage in such exchanges. The commercial setting in which business contracts are formed leads to this conclusion.

bargained-for exchange
Exchange that parties engage in that leads to an enforceable contract.

In the following case, the court had to determine whether there was consideration.

CASE 11.1 *STATE COURT CASE Consideration*

Ferguson v. Carnes

125 So.3d 841, 2013 Fla. App. Lexis 5361 (2013)
District Court of Appeal of Florida

"A promise, no matter how slight, can constitute sufficient consideration so long as a party agrees to do something that they are not bound to do."
—Dorian Damoorgian, Justice

Facts

Thomas Ferguson and Theresa Carnes were brother and sister and the only living children of a wealthy mother. Their mother frequently threatened to disinherit both siblings. Ferguson and Carnes entered an oral agreement to afford each other assurance against disinheritance. The oral agreement provided that if one of them were disinherited, they would divide evenly between them whatever property either received from their mother's estate. The mother died with a will that named Carnes as her sole beneficiary and disinherited Ferguson. When Carnes refused to divide her inheritance with Ferguson, he sued his sister for breach of contract. Carnes alleged that the oral promise was unenforceable because it lacked consideration. The circuit court held that there was no consideration and granted Carnes summary judgment. Ferguson appealed.

Issue

Was the oral promise supported by consideration?

Language of the Court

A promise, no matter how slight, can constitute sufficient consideration so long as a party agrees to do something that they are not bound to do. The oral agreement between Ferguson and Carnes did not lack consideration. Essentially, the terms of the oral agreement delineated mutual promises. The consideration lies in the fact that each gave up the possibility of inheriting more than the other in return for ensuring that neither would be disinherited in whole or part.

Decision

The court of appeal held that the oral agreement did not lack consideration, reversed the decision of the circuit court, and remanded the case for further proceedings.

Critical Legal Thinking Questions

Do you find it interesting that one court found lack of consideration while the other court found that there was consideration? Did Carnes act ethically in backing out of her oral promise to her brother?

Gift Promise

11.2 Define *gift promise* and identify whether gift promises are enforceable.

A **gift promise**, also called a **gratuitous promise**, is unenforceable because it lacks consideration. To change a gift promise into an enforceable promise, the promisee must offer to do something in exchange—that is, in consideration—for the promise. Gift promises cause considerable trouble for persons who do not understand the importance of consideration.

gift promise (gratuitous promise)
A promise that is unenforceable because it lacks consideration.

Example On May 1, Mrs. Colby promises to give her son $10,000 on June 1. When June 1 arrives, Mrs. Colby refuses to pay the $10,000. The son cannot recover

Critical Legal Thinking Questions

Why are gift promises unenforceable if they are not supported by consideration? Do you think that many gift promises are made without the parties realizing that the promise is unenforceable?

the $10,000 because it was a gift promise that lacked consideration. If, however, Mrs. Colby promises to pay her son $10,000 if he earns an A in his business law course and the son earns the A, the contract is enforceable and the son can recover the $10,000.

A completed gift promise cannot be rescinded for lack of consideration.

Example On May 1, Mr. Goldberg promises to give his granddaughter $10,000 on June 1. If Mr. Goldberg gives the $10,000 to his granddaughter on or before June 1, it is a completed gift promise. Mr. Goldberg cannot thereafter recover the money from his granddaughter, even though the original promise lacked consideration.

The following case involves the issue of whether a gift promise was enforceable.

CASE 11.2 *STATE COURT CASE Gift Promise*

Crum v. Thornsbury

Nos. 15-1131, 15-1219 (2016)
Supreme Court of Appeals of West Virginia

"A promise to make a gift in the future or to assist in a time of need is not enforceable and does not constitute a contract."

—Menis Ketchum, Chief Justice

Facts

Walter Eugene Crum, sheriff of Mingo County, West Virginia, was killed in the line of duty. John Hubbard, Greg Smith, David Baisden, and Michael Thornsbury (respondents) visited the Crum home and assured Walter's widow, Rosana, that "they would take care of all funeral and burial costs." The expenses for Walter's casket and funeral exceeded $30,000. When the respondents did not pay for the funeral costs, Rosana sued them for breach of contract. The respondents asserted that the alleged promise lacked consideration, and therefore they were not liable to pay the funeral expenses. Finding that the gift promise lacked consideration, the circuit court dismissed each of the respondents. Rosana Crum appealed.

Issue

Did the gift promise lack consideration?

Language of the Court

A promise to make a gift in the future or to assist in a time of need is not enforceable and does not constitute a contract. The promise to make a gift in this matter is not a valid contract as it lacked consideration and mutual assent. A promise or contract where there is no valuable consideration, and where there is no benefit moving to the promisor or damage or injury to the promisee, is void. Nowhere in petitioner's complaint does she allege that there was any consideration for respondents' alleged promise to cover the cost of Sheriff Crum's funeral.

Decision

The Supreme Court of Appeals of West Virginia affirmed the judgment of the circuit court.

Critical Legal Thinking Questions

Why does the law require consideration to make a gift promise enforceable? If someone makes you a gift promise, what should you do to make it enforceable? Is it ethical for a promisor to renege on a gift promise?

Promises That Lack Consideration

11.3 Describe contracts that lack consideration, such as those involving illegal consideration, an illusory promise, a preexisting duty, or past consideration.

Some contracts seem as though they are supported by consideration even though they are not. These contracts *lack consideration* and are therefore unenforceable. Several types of contracts that fall into this category are discussed in the following paragraphs.

Illegal Consideration

A contract cannot be supported by a promise to refrain from doing an illegal act because that is **illegal consideration**. Contracts based on illegal consideration are void.

illegal consideration
A promise to refrain from doing an illegal act. Such a promise does not support a contract.

Example A person threatens a business owner by saying, "I will burn your business down unless you agree to pay me $10,000." Out of fear, the business owner promises to pay the money. This agreement is not an enforceable contract because the consideration given—not to burn down a business—is illegal consideration. Thus, the extortionist cannot enforce the contract against the business owner.

Illusory Promise

If parties enter into a contract but one or both of the parties can choose not to perform their contractual obligations, the contract lacks consideration. Such a promise, which is known as an **illusory promise** (or **illusory contract**), is unenforceable.

illusory promise (illusory contract)
A contract into which both parties enter but in which one or both of the parties can choose not to perform their contractual obligations. Thus, the contract lacks consideration.

Example A contract that provides that one of the parties has to perform only if he or she chooses to do so is an illusory contract.

Preexisting Duty

A promise lacks consideration if a person promises to perform an act or do something he is already under an obligation to do. This is called a **preexisting duty**. The promise is unenforceable because no new consideration has been given.

preexisting duty
Something a person is already under an obligation to do. A promise lacks consideration if a person promises to perform a preexisting duty.

Example Statutes prohibit police officers from demanding money for investigating and apprehending criminals and prohibit firefighters from demanding payment for fighting fires. If a person agrees to such a demand, he or she does not have to pay it because public servants are under a preexisting duty to perform their functions.

In the private sector, the preexisting duty rule often arises when one of the parties to an existing contract seeks to change the terms of the contract during the course of its performance. Such midstream changes are unenforceable: The parties have a preexisting duty to perform according to the original terms of the contract.

Sometimes a party to a contract runs into substantial *unforeseen difficulties* while performing his or her contractual duties. If the parties modify their contract to accommodate these unforeseen difficulties, the modification will be enforced even though it is not supported by new consideration.

Past Consideration

Problems of **past consideration** often arise when a party promises to pay someone some money or other compensation for work done in the past. Past consideration is not consideration for a new promise; therefore, a promise based on past consideration is not enforceable.

past consideration
A prior act or performance. Past consideration (e.g., prior acts) do not support a new contract. New consideration must be given.

Example Felipe, who has worked in management for the Analytics Corporation for 20 years, is retiring. The president of Analytics says, "Because you were such a loyal employee, Analytics will pay you a bonus of $200,000." Subsequently, the corporation refuses to pay the $200,000. Unfortunately for Felipe, he has already done the work for which he has been promised payment. The contract is unenforceable against Analytics because it is based on past consideration.

In the following case, the court had to decide whether a contract was supported by consideration.

CASE 11.3 *STATE COURT CASE Lack of Consideration*

Clemmons v. Kansas City Chiefs Football Club, Inc.

397 S.W.3d 503, 2013 Mo. App. Lexis 224 (2013)
Missouri Court of Appeals

"The agreement contains promises made only by Clemmons. . . . Nowhere did the Chiefs agree to do anything."

—Lisa White Hardwick, Judge

Facts

The Kansas City Chiefs, which is owned by the Kansas City Chiefs Football Club, Inc., is a professional football team that is a member of the National Football League (NFL). Soon after Larry Clemmons was employed by the Chiefs as an at-will employee, the Chiefs presented him with a document and told him that he had to sign it to continue his employment with the Chiefs. Clemmons signed the document, which was an arbitration agreement that required that any dispute he had with the Chiefs would be subject to arbitration by the commissioner of the NFL. The Chiefs were not bound to the arbitration agreement.

Clemmons was employed for 38 years and held the position of controller when the Chiefs terminated him when he was 60 years old. Clemmons filed a lawsuit against the Chiefs in Missouri circuit court, alleging that the Chiefs had terminated him in violation of age discrimination laws. The Chiefs filed a motion to stop the litigation and compel arbitration. Clemmons opposed the motion, arguing that the arbitration agreement was not an enforceable contract because it lacked consideration because he, and not the Chiefs, was bound by the arbitration agreement. The circuit court held that the arbitration agreement lacked consideration and was therefore unenforceable against Clemmons. He could therefore proceed with his lawsuit against the Chiefs. The Chiefs appealed.

Issue

Is the arbitration agreement enforceable?

Language of the Court

The agreement contains promises made only by Clemmons. Only Clemmons agreed that all matters in dispute should be referred to the commissioner for a binding and conclusive decision. Nowhere did the Chiefs agree to do anything. The Agreement does not contain any mutual promises by the Chiefs that constitute sufficient consideration for Clemmons's promise to forgo his right of access to the courts and arbitrate his claims against them. Because the Chiefs did not prove that the agreement was supported by consideration, they failed to establish the existence of a valid and enforceable arbitration contract.

Decision

The court of appeals affirmed the circuit court's ruling that the arbitration agreement lacked consideration and was unenforceable.

Critical Legal Thinking Questions

Did the Chiefs act ethically by making Clemmons, but not the Chiefs, subject to the arbitration agreement? Why would Clemmons want his case to be decided by a jury rather than be subject to arbitration by the commissioner of the NFL?

CONCEPT SUMMARY

CONTRACTS THAT LACK CONSIDERATION

Type of Consideration	Description of Promise
Illegal consideration	Promise to refrain from doing an illegal act.
Illusory promise	Promise in which one or both parties can choose not to perform their obligation.
Preexisting duty	Promise based on the preexisting duty of the promisor to perform.
Past consideration	Promise based on the past performance of the promisee.

Special Business Contracts

11.4 List and describe special business contracts, including output contracts, requirements contracts, and best-efforts contracts.

Generally, the courts tolerate a greater degree of uncertainty as to the issue of consideration in business contracts than in personal contracts, based on the premise that sophisticated parties know how to protect themselves when negotiating contracts. The law imposes an obligation of good faith on the performance of the parties to requirements and output contracts.

The following paragraphs describe special types of business contracts that allow a greater-than-usual degree of uncertainty concerning consideration.

Output Contract

In an **output contract**, the seller agrees to sell all of its production to a single buyer. Output contracts serve the legitimate business purposes of (1) assuring the seller of a purchaser for all its output and (2) assuring the buyer of a source of supply for the goods it needs.

output contract
A contract in which a seller agrees to sell all of its production to a single buyer.

Example Organic Foods, Inc. is a company that operates farms that produce organically grown grains and vegetables. Urban Food Markets is a grocery store chain that sells organically grown foods. Urban Food Markets contracts with Organic Foods, Inc. to purchase all the foods Organic Foods, Inc. grows organically this year. This is an example of an output contract: Organic Foods, Inc. must sell all of its output to Urban Foods Market, and Urban Foods Market must buy all of the output.

Requirements Contract

A **requirements contract** is a contract in which a buyer agrees to purchase all of its requirements for an item from one seller. Such contracts serve the legitimate business purposes of (1) assuring the buyer of a uniform source of supply and (2) providing the seller with reduced selling costs.

requirements contract
A contract in which a buyer agrees to purchase all of its requirements for an item from one seller.

Example Goodyear Tire & Rubber Company manufactures tires that are used on automobiles, SUVs, trucks, and other vehicles. Ford Motor Company manufactures trucks on which it must place tires before the trucks can be sold. Assume that Ford Motor Company enters into a contract with Goodyear Tire & Rubber Company to purchase the tires it will need for its trucks this year from Goodyear. This is an example of a requirements contract: Ford Motor Company agrees to purchase all tires that it will need from Goodyear. Goodyear may, however, sell tires to other purchasers.

Best-Efforts Contract

A **best-efforts contract** is a contract that contains a clause that requires one or both of the parties to use their *best efforts* to achieve the objective of the contract. The courts generally have held that the imposition of the best-efforts duty provides sufficient consideration to make a contract enforceable. A party can sue another company for failing to use its promised best efforts. Best-efforts contracts are most often used in business arrangements.

best-efforts contract
A contract that contains a clause that requires one or both of the parties to use their best efforts to achieve the objective of the contract.

Example Real estate listing contracts often require real estate brokers to use their best efforts to find a buyer for the listed real estate. Contracts often require underwriters to use their best efforts to sell securities on behalf of their corporate clients. Both of these contracts would be enforceable.

CONCEPT SUMMARY

SPECIAL BUSINESS CONTRACTS

Type of Contract	Description of Contract
Output contract	A contract in which the seller agrees to sell all of its production to a single buyer.
Requirements contract	A contract in which a buyer agrees to purchase all of its requirements for an item from one seller.
Best-efforts contract	A contract that contains a clause that requires one or both of the parties to use their *best efforts* to achieve the objective of the contract.

Settlement of Claims

11.5 Define *accord and satisfaction* in settling a disputed claim.

In some situations, one of the parties to a contract believes that he or she did not receive what was due. This party may attempt to reach a compromise with the other party (e.g., by paying less consideration than was provided for in the contract). If the two parties agree to a compromise, a settlement of the claim has been reached. The settlement agreement is called an **accord**. If the accord is performed, it is called a **satisfaction**. This type of settlement is called an **accord and satisfaction**, or a **compromise**.

accord
An agreement whereby the parties agree to accept something different in satisfaction of the original contract.

satisfaction
The performance of an accord.

accord and satisfaction (compromise)
The settlement of a contract dispute.

Example A retailer enters into a contract to license computer software from a technology company for $300,000. This software is to be used to keep track of inventory, accounts receivable, and other financial data. After the software is installed, the computer system works but not as well as promised. The retailer refuses to pay the full amount of the contract. To settle the dispute, the parties agree that $200,000 is to be paid as full and final payment for the software. The retailer pays the $200,000 as agreed. Here, the retailer performed the accord, so there is an accord and satisfaction.

If the accord is not satisfied, the other party can sue to enforce the accord. An accord is enforceable even though no new consideration is given because the parties reasonably disagreed as to the value of the goods or services contracted for. In the alternative, the nonbreaching party to an unperformed accord can choose to enforce the original contract rather than the accord.

Equity: Promissory Estoppel

11.6 Define and apply the equitable doctrine of *promissory estoppel*.

promissory estoppel (detrimental reliance)
An equitable doctrine that prevents the withdrawal of a promise by a promisor if it will adversely affect a promisee who has adjusted his or her position in justifiable reliance on the promise.

Promissory estoppel (or **detrimental reliance**) is an equity doctrine that permits a court to order enforcement of a contract that lacks consideration. Promissory estoppel is applied to avoid injustice. It is usually used to provide a remedy to a party who has relied on another party's promise, but that party has withdrawn its promise and is not subject to a breach of contract action because consideration is lacking.

The doctrine of promissory estoppel **estops** (prevents) promisors from revoking their promise based on lack of consideration. Therefore, the person who has *detrimentally relied* on the promise for performance may sue the promisor for performance or other remedy the court feels is fair to award in the circumstances.

For the doctrine of promissory estoppel to apply, the following elements must be shown:

1. The promisor made a promise.
2. The promisor should have reasonably expected to induce the promisee to rely on the promise.

Critical Legal Thinking Questions

What public policy supports the equity doctrine of promissory estoppel to permit the enforcement of a contract that lacks consideration? Are the elements of promissory estoppel difficult to apply?

3. The promisee actually relied on the promise and engaged in an action or forbearance of a right of a definite and substantial nature.
4. Injustice would be caused if the promise were not enforced.

In the following feature, the court was asked to apply the equity doctrine of promissory estoppel.

Now equity is no part of the law, but a moral virtue, which qualifies, moderates, and reforms the rigor, hardness, and edge of the law, and is a universal truth.

Lord Cowper
Dudley v. Dudley (1705)

Critical Legal Thinking

Doctrine of Promissory Estoppel Requires a Subcontractor to Honor Its Bid

"How could competitive bidding function at all if general contractors did not rely on subcontractors' bids?"

—William Connolly, Justice

The Evangelical Lutheran Good Samaritan Society (Samaritan), a major operator in the retirement living market, invited four large general contractors, including Weitz Company, LLC (Weitz), to bid on constructing a nursing home facility in Beatrice, Nebraska. In preparing a bid to submit to a proposed client, general contractors obtain bids from subcontractors to perform certain work on the project. Selected subcontractor bids are used by the general contractor as the basis of the bids they submit to the client.

Hands, Inc., a subcontractor doing business as H & S Plumbing and Heating (H&S), submitted a bid to Weitz for the plumbing and the heating, ventilation, and air conditioning (HVAC) parts of the Samaritan job. Other subcontractors also submitted bids to Weitz to do the work, but Weitz selected H&S's bid of $2,430,600 and included it in Weitz's own bid of $9.2 million that it submitted to Samaritan. Weitz was selected as the general contractor and signed a contract with Samaritan.

After Weitz had been awarded the contract, H&S refused to honor its bid. Weitz completed the project using other plumbing and HVAC subcontractors at greater expense than H&S's bid. Weitz sued H&S to recover damages. At trial, the owner of H&S testified that the company had "left too much money on the table" in submitting its bid to Weitz.

Because no actual contract existed between Weitz and H&S, Weitz sought to enforce H&S's bid asserting promissory estoppel. The trial court determined that Weitz reasonably and foreseeably relied on H&S's bid, and therefore H&S was estopped from reneging on its bid. The court enforced H&S's bid under promissory estoppel and awarded Weitz $292,492 in damages, which was the difference between what Weitz had to pay to the other contractors and the amount of H&S's bid.

The Supreme Court of Nebraska affirmed the decision, stating, "How could competitive bidding function at all if general contractors did not rely on subcontractors' bids? We affirm the judgment for Weitz on its promissory estoppel claim. H&S's bid was a promise, and it should have foreseen that Weitz might rely on the bid. Weitz reasonably relied on the bid by incorporating it in its own bid to the project owner. And the court could avoid injustice only by enforcing H&S's bid. We further conclude that the court correctly measured Weitz's damages." *Weitz Company, LLC v. Hands, Inc.*, 882 N.W.2d 659, 2016 Neb. Lexis 108 (Supreme Court of Nebraska, 2016)

Critical Legal Thinking Questions

What is the doctrine of promissory estoppel? Does this equity doctrine serve a useful purpose? What would have been the result in this case if promissory estoppel was not available?

Key Terms and Concepts

Accord (222)
Accord and satisfaction (compromise) (222)
Bargained-for exchange (217)
Best-efforts contract (221)
Consideration (216)
Estop (222)
Gift promise (gratuitous promise) (217)
Illegal consideration (219)
Illusory promise (illusory contract) (219)
Legal value (216)
Output contract (221)
Past consideration (219)
Preexisting duty (219)
Promissory estoppel (detrimental reliance) (222)
Requirements contract (221)
Satisfaction (222)
Unified Contract Law (UCL) (215)

Critical Legal Thinking Cases

11.1 Lack of Consideration Toll Brothers, Inc. is a real estate development company that builds and sells luxury homes across the country. Spouses Mehdi Noohi and Soheyla Bolouri (plaintiffs) deposited a total of $77,008 toward the $1,006,975 purchase price of a Toll Brothers home to be built in Maryland. The agreement for sale included an arbitration clause that required the plaintiffs—but not Toll Brothers—to submit to arbitration any disputes regarding the agreement. The agreement of sale required that the plaintiffs seek a mortgage to finance the purchase of the home. The plaintiffs applied for a mortgage from many lenders but could not get approval for a loan. Toll Brothers had not yet started to build the home and had incurred no costs at the time plaintiffs sought to rescind the agreement and obtain the return of their deposit. When Toll Brothers refused to return the deposit, the plaintiffs sued Toll Brothers in U.S. district court for breach of contract individually and on behalf of a class of other prospective buyers who allegedly lost deposits to Toll Brothers in a similar manner. Toll Brothers made a motion to have the case removed for arbitration pursuant to the arbitration clause in the agreement. The plaintiffs asserted that the arbitration clause was unenforceable because it lacked mutuality of consideration because it required only the buyer—but not the seller—to submit disputes to arbitration. Had Toll Brothers given consideration for the arbitration agreement? *Noohi v. Toll Brothers, Inc.*, 708 F.3d 599, 2013 U.S. App. Lexis 4188 (United States Court of Appeals for the Fourth Circuit, 2013)

11.2 Gift Promise Lester Cooper suffered serious injuries that caused him to be hospitalized for an extended time. While he was hospitalized, Julie Smith, whom Cooper had met the year before, and Janet Smith, Julie's mother, made numerous trips to visit him. A romantic relationship developed between Cooper and Julie Smith. While he was still in the hospital, Cooper proposed marriage to Julie, and she accepted. Cooper ultimately received a $180,000 settlement for his injuries. After being released from the hospital, Cooper moved into Janet's house and lived with Janet and Julie. Over the next couple of months, Cooper purchased a number of items for Julie, including a diamond engagement ring, a car, a computer, a tanning bed, and horses. On Julie's request, Cooper paid off Janet's car loan and paid for various improvements to Janet's house.

Several months later, the settlement money had run out, and Julie had not yet married Cooper. About six months after that, Julie and Cooper had a disagreement, and Cooper moved out of the house. Julie returned the engagement ring to Cooper. Cooper sued Julie and Janet to recover the gifts or the value of the gifts he had given them. Can Cooper recover the gifts or the value of the gifts he gave to Julie and Janet Smith? *Cooper v. Smith*, 800 N.E.2d 372, 2003 Ohio App. Lexis 5446 (Court of Appeals of Ohio, 2003)

11.3 Consideration Jack Tallas immigrated to the United States from Greece. He lived in Salt Lake City, Utah, for nearly 70 years, during which time he achieved considerable success in business, primarily as an insurance agent and landlord. Over a period of 14 years, Peter Dementas, a close personal friend of Tallas's, rendered services to Tallas, including picking up his mail, driving him to the grocery store, and assisting with the management of his rental properties. One day, Tallas met with Dementas and dictated a memorandum to him, in Greek, stating that he owed Dementas $50,000 for his help over the years. Tallas indicated in the memorandum that he would change his will to make Dementas an heir for this amount. Tallas signed the document. Tallas died seven weeks later, without having changed his will to include Dementas as an heir. He left a substantial estate. Dementas filed a claim for $50,000 with Tallas's estate. When the estate denied the claim, Dementas brought this action to enforce the contract. The estate of Tallas argued that Tallas's promise to Dementas lacked consideration and should not be enforced. Is there consideration supporting Tallas's promise to Dementas? *Dementas v. Estate of Tallas*, 764 P.2d 628, 1988 Utah App. Lexis 174 (Court of Appeals of Utah, 1988)

Ethics Case

11.4 Ethics Case Raymond P. Wirth signed a pledge agreement that stated that in consideration of his interest in education, and "intending to be legally bound," he irrevocably pledged and promised to pay Drexel University the sum of $150,000. The pledge agreement provided that an endowed scholarship would be created in Wirth's name. Wirth died months after signing the pledge but before any money had been paid to Drexel. When the estate of Wirth refused to honor the pledge, Drexel sued the estate to collect the $150,000. The administrators of the estate alleged that the pledge was unenforceable because of lack of consideration. The surrogate court denied Drexel's motion for summary judgment and dismissed Drexel's claim against the estate. Drexel appealed. Did the administrators of the estate of Wirth act ethically by refusing to honor Mr. Wirth's pledge? Was the pledge agreement supported by consideration and therefore enforceable against the estate of Wirth? *In the Matter of Wirth*, 14 A.D.3d 572, 789 N.Y.S.2d 69, 2005 N.Y. App. Div. Lexis 424 (Supreme Court of New York, Appellate Division, 2005)

Note

1. *Hamer v. Sidwa*, 124 N.Y. 538, 27 N.E. 256, 1891 N.Y. Lexis 1396 (Court of Appeals of New York, 1891).

CHAPTER

12 Capacity and Legality

Henry R. Cheeseman

PYONGYANG, NORTH KOREA

This is a presentation at the mass games of the Arirang Festival in Pyongyang, North Korea. The Democratic People's Republic of Korea (DPRK) is a dictatorship. The U.S. government makes most sales of goods and services to, and investments in, North Korea illegal. Food, medicine, and other humanitarian goods may be sold to North Korea.

Learning Objectives

After studying this chapter, you should be able to:

12.1 Define and describe the infancy doctrine.

12.2 Define *mental incompetence* and explain how it can affect contractual capacity.

12.3 Explain how intoxication may affect contractual capacity.

12.4 Describe lawful contracts and identify illegal contracts that are contrary to statutes and those that violate public policy.

12.5 Describe exculpatory agreements and identify when they are lawful.

12.6 Describe business restrictive agreements, including *confidentiality agreements*, *non-solicitation agreements*, and *noncompete agreements*.

12.7 Describe licensing statutes and identify the effects of violating these statutes.

12.8 Define *unconscionable contract* and determine when such contracts are unenforceable.

> *"An unconscionable contract is one which no man in his senses, not under delusion, would make, on the one hand, and which no fair and honest man would accept on the other."*
>
> —*Melville Fuller, Chief Justice*
> *Hume v. United States*
> *132 U.S. 406, 10 S.Ct. 134, 1889 U.S. Lexis 1888 (1889)*
> *Supreme Court of the United States*

Introduction to Capacity and Legality

Generally, the law presumes that the parties to a contract have the requisite **contractual capacity** to enter into the contract. Certain persons do not have this capacity, however, including minors, mentally incompetent persons, and persons under the influence of alcohol or drugs. The common law of contracts and many state statutes protect persons who lack contractual capacity from having contracts enforced against them. The party asserting incapacity or his or her guardian, conservator, or other legal representative bears the burden of proof.

An essential element for the formation of a contract is that the object of the contract be lawful. A contract to perform an illegal act is called an *illegal contract*. Illegal contracts are void. That is, they cannot be enforced by either party to the contract. The term *illegal contract* is a misnomer, however, because no contract exists if the object of the contract is illegal. In addition, courts hold that *unconscionable contracts* are unenforceable. An unconscionable contract is one that is so oppressive or manifestly unfair that it would be unjust to enforce it.

Many employment and business contracts contain restrictive agreements. The most common restrictive agreements are confidentiality agreements, nonsolicitation agreements, and noncompete agreements.

Capacity to contract, lawfulness of contracts, and restrictive agreements are discussed in this chapter.

Minors

12.1 Define and describe the infancy doctrine.

Minors do not always have the maturity, experience, or sophistication needed to enter into contracts with adults. Most states have enacted statutes that specify the **age of majority**. The most prevalent age of majority is 18 years of age for both men and women. Any age below the statutory age of majority is called the **period of minority**.

minor
A person who has not reached the age of majority.

Infancy Doctrine

To protect minors, the law recognizes the **infancy doctrine**, which gives minors the right to *disaffirm* (or *cancel*) most contracts they have entered into with adults. This right is based on public policy, which reasons that minors should be protected from the unscrupulous behavior of adults. In most states, the infancy doctrine is an objective standard. If a person's age is below the age of majority, the court will not inquire into the minor's knowledge, experience, or sophistication. Generally, contracts for the necessaries of life, which we discuss later in this chapter, are exempt from the scope of this doctrine.

infancy doctrine
A doctrine that allows minors to disaffirm (cancel) most contracts they have entered into with adults.

Under the infancy doctrine, a minor has the option of choosing whether to enforce a contract or not (i.e., the contract is voidable by a minor). This is called a **voidable contract**. The adult party is bound to the minor's decision. If both parties to a contract are minors, both parties have the right to disaffirm the contract.

If performance of the contract favors the minor, the minor will probably enforce the contract. Otherwise, the minor will probably disaffirm the contract. A minor may not affirm one part of a contract and disaffirm another part.

Disaffirmance

disaffirm
The act of a minor to rescind a contract under the infancy doctrine. Disaffirmance may be done orally, in writing, or by the minor's conduct.

A minor can expressly **disaffirm** a contract orally, in writing, or through his or her conduct. No special formalities are required. The contract may be disaffirmed at any time prior to the person's reaching the age of majority plus a "reasonable time." The designation of a reasonable time is determined on a case-by-case basis.

Duties of Restoration and Restitution

If a minor's contract is executory and neither party has performed, the minor can simply disaffirm the contract: There is nothing to recover because neither party has given the other party anything of value. If the parties have exchanged consideration and partially or fully performed the contract by the time the minor disaffirms the contract, however, the issue becomes one of what consideration or restitution must be made. The following rules apply:

duty of restoration
A rule that states that a minor is obligated only to return the goods or property he or she has received from the adult in the condition it is in at the time of disaffirmance.

duty of restitution
A rule that states that if a minor has transferred money, property, or other valuables to the competent party before disaffirming the contract, that party must place the minor in status quo.

- **Minor's duty of restoration.** Generally, a minor is obligated only to return the goods or property he or she has received from the adult in the condition it is in at the time of disaffirmance (subject to several exceptions, discussed later in this chapter), even if the item has been consumed, lost, or destroyed or has depreciated in value by the time of disaffirmance. This rule, called the **duty of restoration**, is based on the rationale that if a minor had to place the adult in status quo on disaffirmance of a contract, there would be no incentive for an adult not to deal with a minor.
- **Competent party's duty of restitution.** If a minor has transferred consideration—money, property, or other valuables—to a competent party before disaffirming the contract, that party must place the minor in status quo. That is, the minor must be restored to the same position he or she was in before the minor entered into the contract. This restoration is usually done by returning the consideration to the minor. If the consideration has been sold or has depreciated in value, the competent party must pay the minor the cash equivalent. This action is called the **duty of restitution**.

Example Harry, who is 17 years old (a minor), enters into a contract to purchase an automobile costing $20,000 from Gertrude, a competent adult. Gertrude, who believes that Harry is an adult and does not ask for verification of his age, delivers ownership of the automobile to Harry after she receives his payment of $20,000. Subsequently, before Harry reaches the age of 18 (the age of majority), he is involved in an automobile accident caused by his own negligence. The automobile sustains $13,000 worth of damage in the accident (the automobile is now worth only $7,000). Harry can disaffirm the contract, return the damaged automobile to Gertrude, and recover $20,000 from Gertrude. In this result, Harry recovers his entire $20,000 purchase price from Gertrude, and Gertrude is left with a damaged automobile worth only $7,000.

Most states provide that the minor owes a duty of restitution and must put the adult in status quo on disaffirmance of the contract if the minor's intentional, reckless, or grossly negligent conduct caused the loss of value to the adult's property.

On occasion, minors might misrepresent their age to adults when entering into contracts. Most state laws provide that minors who misrepresent their age must place the adult in status quo if they disaffirm the contract.

The right of a minor to disaffirm his contract is based upon sound public policy to protect the minor from his own improvidence and the overreaching of adults.

Justice Michael Sullivan
Star Chevrolet v. Green
473 So.2d 157, 1985 Miss.
Lexis 2141 (1985)
Supreme Court of Mississippi

Example If, in the prior example, Harry had recklessly caused the accident (e.g., by driving 25 miles an hour over the speed limit) or had misrepresented his age when he purchased the car, Harry can still disaffirm the contract and return the damaged automobile to Gertrude, but he can recover only $7,000 from Gertrude. In this result, Gertrude is made whole (she keeps $13,000 of Harry's money and has a damaged automobile worth $7,000). Harry has $7,000.

Ratification

If a minor does not disaffirm a contract either during the period of minority or within a reasonable time after reaching the age of majority, the contract is considered ratified (accepted). Hence, the minor (who is now an adult) is bound by the contract; the right to disaffirm the contract is lost. Note that any attempt by a minor to ratify a contract while still a minor can be disaffirmed just as the original contract can be disaffirmed.

The **ratification**, which relates back to the inception of the contract, can be expressed by oral or written words or implied from the minor's conduct (e.g., after reaching the age of majority, the minor remains silent regarding the contract).

ratification
The act of a minor after the minor has reached the age of majority by which he or she accepts a contract entered into when he or she was a minor.

Parents' Liability for Their Children's Contracts

Generally, parents owe a legal duty to provide food, clothing, shelter, and other necessaries of life for their minor children. Parents are liable for their children's contracts for necessaries of life if they have not adequately provided such items.

The parental duty of support terminates if a minor becomes *emancipated*. **Emancipation** occurs when a minor voluntarily leaves home and lives apart from his or her parents. The courts consider factors such as getting married, setting up a separate household, or joining the military in determining whether a minor is emancipated. Each situation is examined on its merits.

emancipation
The act or process of a minor voluntarily leaving home and living apart from his or her parents.

Necessaries of Life

Minors are obligated to pay for the **necessaries of life** that they contract for. Otherwise, many adults would refuse to sell these items to them. There is no standard definition of what is a necessary of life. The minor's age, lifestyle, and status in life influence what is considered necessary.

necessaries of life
Food, clothing, shelter, medical care, and other items considered necessary to the maintenance of life. Minors must pay the reasonable value of necessaries of life for which they contract.

Examples Items such as food, clothing, shelter, and medical services are generally understood to be necessaries of life. Goods and services such as automobiles, tools of trade, education, and vocational training have also been found to be necessaries of life in some situations.

The seller's recovery is based on the equitable doctrine of **quasi-contract** rather than on the contract itself. Under this theory, the minor is obligated only to pay the reasonable value of the goods or services received. Reasonable value is determined on a case-by-case basis.

The following feature discusses modern statutes that make minors liable on certain contracts.

Contemporary Environment

Special Types of Minors' Contracts

Based on public policy, many states have enacted statutes that make certain specified contracts enforceable against minors—that is, minors cannot assert the infancy doctrine against enforcement for these contracts. These usually include contracts for the following:

- Medical, surgical, and pregnancy care
- Psychological counseling
- Health insurance
- Life insurance
- The performance of duties related to stock and bond transfers, bank accounts, and the like
- Educational loan agreements
- Contracts to support children
- Artistic, sports, and entertainment contracts that have been entered into with the approval of the court

Many statutes mandate that a certain portion of the wages and fees earned by a minor (e.g., 50 percent) based on an artistic, sports, or entertainment contract be put in trust until the minor reaches the age of majority.

Mentally Incompetent Persons

12.2 Define *mental incompetence* and explain how it can affect contractual capacity.

In most contracts, the parties to the contract are mentally competent to enter into the contract. However, in certain other cases, a party to a contract may not have had the requisite mental competence to have entered into an enforceable contract. In those situations, a mentally incompetent party will not be bound to the contract.

Mental incompetence may arise because of mental illness, dementia, schizophrenia, mania, brain damage, and the like. The law protects people suffering from substantial mental incompetence from enforcement of contracts against them because such persons may not understand the consequences of their actions in entering into a contract.

To be relieved of his or her duties under a contract, a person must have been legally mentally incompetent at the time of entering into the contract. Most states use the *objective cognitive "understanding" test* to determine legal mental incompetence. Under this test, the person's mental incompetence must render that person incapable of understanding or comprehending the nature of the transaction. Mere weakness of intellect, or slight psychological or emotional problems, do not constitute mental incompetence.

In the following case, the court had to determine whether a party had the mental competence to change contracts.

CASE 12.1 *STATE COURT CASE Mental Capacity*

Ivie v. Smith

439 S.W.3d 189, 2014 Mo. Lexis 190 (2014)
Supreme Court of Missouri

"Under the common law, a contract is deemed void if a party lacks the requisite mental capacity at the time of contracting."

—Zel Fischer, Judge

Facts

Patricia Watson taught elementary school in the state of California. She retained close ties with her four half-siblings (the Ivies) who lived in Missouri. In February 2002, at age 70, Watson retired from teaching, and soon married Arnold L. Smith, age 60. At the time of their marriage, Watson had substantial income and approximately $1 million in assets, which included her home in California, several parcels of real estate in Missouri, a pension, and several bank accounts, retirement accounts, and vehicles. Smith, on the other hand, had minimal income and assets. Watson had no living children. Her property was designated to go to the Ivies upon her death.

In late 2004, Watson sold her home in California, and she and Smith moved to Missouri, where she bought a house. Watson visited several physicians in 2005, complaining about memory loss. One physician diagnosed her as suffering from moderate to severe dementia. In October 2005, Watson saw a neuropsychologist at the Mayo Clinic, who concluded that Watson suffered from dementia. In March 2006, Watson went to see a new physician who diagnosed her with Alzheimer's dementia. By May 2007, Watson could not recognize previously known family members. In June 2007, a hospital physician diagnosed Watson with dementia, probably Alzheimer's disease.

From early December 2007 to mid-January 2008, Watson retitled her bank accounts and retirement accounts to "pay on death" to Smith, and on other accounts she changed the beneficiary to Smith. On July 24, 2008, Smith obtained and filled out a change of beneficiary form for Watson's pension that would leave survivor benefits to Smith. Watson signed the form.

Watson died April 10, 2009. The Ivies filed an action, naming Smith as a defendant, to set aside the beneficiary designations and various property transfers made to Smith. The circuit court held that Watson lacked mental capacity at the time of these transactions and held that they were void. The court directed that Watson's bank accounts, retirement accounts, pension benefits, and other assets go to the Ivies. Smith appealed.

Issue

Did Watson lack contractual capacity at the time she changed beneficiary designations and retitled property to Smith?

Language of the Court

Under the common law, a contract is deemed void if a party lacks the requisite mental capacity at the time of contracting—meaning mental capacity must be present for a contract to exist at all. The record supports the conclusion that Watson lacked capacity regarding the changes to the beneficiary designations and property transfers. Therefore, substantial evidence supports the circuit court's judgment that all changes to beneficiary designations and property transfers after July 1, 2007, were void.

Decision

The Supreme Court of Missouri affirmed the circuit court's decision.

Critical Legal Thinking Questions

Was the determination of mental incapacity difficult in this case? Do you think that many cases exist where a person takes advantage of someone's mental incapacity?

The law has developed two standards concerning contracts of mentally incompetent persons: (1) adjudicated mentally incompetent and (2) mentally incompetent but not adjudicated mentally incompetent.

Adjudicated Mentally Incompetent

In certain cases, a relative, a loved one, or another interested party may institute a legal action to have someone declared legally (i.e., adjudged) mentally incompetent. If, after evidence is presented at a formal judicial or administrative hearing, the person is **adjudicated mentally incompetent**, the court will make that person a ward of the court and appoint a guardian to act on that person's behalf. Any contract entered into by a person who has been adjudged mentally incompetent is void. That is, no contract exists. This is called a **void contract**. The court-appointed guardian is the only one who has the legal authority to enter into contracts on behalf of the person who has been adjudicated mentally incompetent.

adjudicated mentally incompetent
Declared mentally incompetent by a proper court or administrative agency. A contract entered into by a person adjudged mentally incompetent is *void*.

Mentally Incompetent but Not Adjudicated Mentally Incompetent

If no formal ruling has been made about a person's mental competence but the person suffers from a mental impairment that makes him or her legally mentally incompetent—that is, the person is **mentally incompetent but not adjudicated mentally incompetent**—any contract entered into by this person is voidable.

Mentally incompetent but not adjudicated mentally incompetent
Being mentally incompetent but not having been adjudged mentally incompetent by a court or an administrative agency. A contract entered into by such person is generally *voidable*. Some states hold that such a contract is void.

Unless the other party does not have contractual capacity, he or she does not have the option to void the contract.

Some people have alternating periods of mental competency and mental incompetency. Any contracts made by such persons during a lucid interval are enforceable. Contracts made while the person was not legally competent can be disaffirmed.

A person who has dealt with a mentally incompetent person must place that person in status quo if the contract is either void or is voided by the guardian of the mentally incompetent person. Most states hold that a party who did not know he or she was dealing with a mentally incompetent person must be placed in status quo on voidance of the contract. Mentally incompetent persons are liable in *quasi-contract* to pay the reasonable value for the necessaries of life they receive.

Intoxicated Persons

12.3 Explain how intoxication may affect contractual capacity.

intoxicated person
A person who is under contractual incapacity because of ingestion of alcohol or drugs to the point of incompetence.

Most states provide that contracts entered into by certain **intoxicated persons** are voidable by those persons. The intoxication may occur because of alcohol or drugs. The contract is not voidable by the other party if that party had contractual capacity.

Generally, the contract is voidable only if the person was so intoxicated when the contract was entered into that he or she was incapable of understanding or comprehending the nature of the transaction. In most states, this rule holds even if the intoxication was self-induced. Some states allow the person to disaffirm the contract only if the person was forced to become intoxicated or did so unknowingly.

Men intoxicated are sometimes stunned into sobriety.

Lord Mansfield
R. v. Wilkes (1770)

The amount of alcohol or drugs that must be consumed for a person to be considered legally intoxicated to disaffirm contracts varies from case to case. The factors that are considered include the user's physical characteristics and his or her ability to "hold" intoxicants.

A person who disaffirms a contract based on intoxication generally must be returned to the status quo. In turn, the intoxicated person generally must return the consideration received under the contract to the other party and make restitution that returns the other party to status quo. After becoming sober, an intoxicated person can ratify the contracts entered into while intoxicated. Intoxicated persons are liable in *quasi-contract* to pay the reasonable value for necessaries they receive.

Lawful and Illegal Contracts

12.4 Describe lawful contracts and identify illegal contracts that are contrary to statutes and those that violate public policy.

lawful contract
A contract that has a lawful object.

One requirement to have an enforceable contract is that the object of the contract must be lawful. Most contracts that individuals and businesses enter into are **lawful contracts** that are enforceable. These include contracts for the sale of goods, services, real property, and intangible rights; the lease of goods; property leases; licenses; and other contracts.

illegal contract
A contract that has an illegal object. Such contracts are *void*.

Some contracts have illegal objects. A contract with an illegal object is *void* and therefore unenforceable. These contracts are called **illegal contracts**. The following paragraphs discuss various illegal contracts.

Contracts Contrary to Law

Both federal and state legislatures have enacted statutes that prohibit certain types of conduct. Administrative agencies adopt rules and regulations to enforce statutory law. And the president of the United States can issue executive orders making certain conduct illegal. Contracts to perform activities that are prohibited by law are illegal contracts. These are called **contracts contrary to law**.

contract contrary to law
A contract to perform activities that are prohibited by law.

Example An agreement between two companies to engage in price fixing in violation of federal antitrust statutes is illegal and therefore void. Thus, neither company to this illegal contract can enforce the contract against the other company.

In the following case, the court addressed the legality of contracts.

CASE 12.2 *FEDERAL COURT CASE Illegal Contract*

Ford Motor Company v. Ghreiwati Auto

2013 U.S. Dist. Lexis 159470 (2013)
United States District Court for the Eastern District of Michigan

"A contract that violates an executive order or law is unlawful and discharges performance of the contract."

—Nancy Edmunds, District Judge

Facts

Ford Motor Company manufactures automobiles, trucks, and other vehicles. In 2004, Ford entered into a dealership agreement with Ghreiwati Auto (Auto), a Syrian corporation, whereby Auto would sell and service Ford vehicles in Syria. Auto invested more than $20 million in creating its dealer network. In 2011, after civil and military hostilities developed in Syria, the president of the United States issued an executive order that imposed widespread sanctions against Syria, including prohibiting American companies from selling products and services in Syria. Violation of the executive order carries both civil and criminal penalties. Pursuant to the executive order, Ford immediately terminated its dealership agreement with Auto. Ford filed an action in U.S. district court, requesting a declaratory judgment that it did not terminate the dealership agreement improperly because the executive order made Ford's performance of the contract illegal. Auto alleged that Ford breached the dealer agreement and was liable for damages.

Issue

Did the presidential executive order make the dealership contract illegal for Ford to perform?

Language of the Court

Ford argues that the executive order renders performance of the agreement illegal, thereby permitting Ford to immediately terminate Auto's dealership agreement and discharges Ford from any duties under the agreement. The Court agrees with Ford and its arguments. A contract that violates an executive order or law is unlawful and discharges performance of the contract.

Decision

The U.S. district court held that the executive order rendered the Ford–Auto dealership agreement illegal and that Ford had therefore terminated the agreement properly.

Critical Legal Thinking Questions

Did Ford have any other course of action in this case? Did Ford have an ethical duty to reimburse Auto for its losses? Would such reimbursement have been legal?

Usury Laws

State **usury laws** set an upper limit on the annual interest rate that can be charged on certain types of loans. The limits vary from state to state. Lenders who charge a higher rate than the state limit are guilty of usury. These laws are intended to protect unsophisticated borrowers from loan sharks and others who charge exorbitant rates of interest.

usury law
A law that sets an upper limit on the interest rate that can be charged on certain types of loans.

Most states provide criminal and civil penalties for making usurious loans. Some states require lenders to remit the difference between the interest rate charged on the loan and the usury rate to the borrower. Other states prohibit lenders from collecting any interest on the loan. Still other states provide that a usurious loan is a void contract, permitting the borrower not to have to pay the interest or the principal of the loan to the lender.

Example Suppose a state has set a usurious rate of interest as any interest rate above 15 percent. Kristoff borrows $1,000 from Taylor, which requires Kristoff to pay $4,000 in one year to pay off the loan. This is a usurious loan because that amount of interest—$3,000—calculates to a 300 percent annual interest rate.

Most usury laws exempt certain types of lenders and loan transactions involving legitimate business transactions from the reach of the law. These exemptions usually include loans made by banks and other financial institutions, loans above a certain dollar amount, and loans made to corporations and other businesses.

Contracts to Commit Crimes

Contracts to commit criminal acts are void. If the object of a contract becomes illegal after the contract is entered into because the government has enacted a statute that makes it unlawful, the parties are discharged from the contract. The contract is not an illegal contract unless the parties agree to go forward and complete it.

Contract in Restraint of Trade

contract in restraint of trade
A contract that unreasonably restrains trade.

The general economic policy of this country favors competition. At common law, **contracts in restraint of trade**—that is, contracts that unreasonably restrain trade—are held to be unlawful.

Example It would be an illegal restraint of trade for Toyota, General Motors, and Ford to agree to fix the prices of the automobiles they sell. Their contract would be void and could not be enforced by any of the parties against the other parties.

Contracts Contrary to Public Policy

contract contrary to public policy
A contract that has a negative impact on society or that interferes with the public's safety and welfare.

immoral contract
A contract whose objective is the commission of an act that society considers immoral.

Certain contracts are illegal because they are contrary to public policy. **Contracts contrary to public policy** are void. Although *public policy* eludes precise definition, the courts have held contracts to be contrary to public policy if they have a negative impact on society or interfere with the public's safety and welfare.

Immoral contracts—that is, contracts whose objective is the commission of an act that society considers immoral—may be found to be against public policy. Judges are not free to define morality based on their individual views. Instead, they must look to the practices and beliefs of society when defining immoral conduct.

Example A contract that is based on sexual favors is an immoral contract and void as against public policy.

Gambling Statutes

gambling statutes
Statutes that make certain forms of gambling illegal.

All states either prohibit or regulate gambling, wagering, lotteries, and games of chance via **gambling statutes**. States provide various criminal and civil penalties for illegal gambling. There are many exceptions to wagering laws. Many states have enacted statutes that permit games of chance under a certain dollar amount, bingo games, lotteries conducted by religious and charitable organizations, and the like. Many states also permit and regulate horse racing, harness racing, dog racing, and state-operated lotteries.

In 1988, Congress enacted the **Indian Gaming Regulatory Act (IGRA),**[1] which established the framework for permitting and regulating Native American gaming casinos. There are approximately 500 such establishments in the country operated by approximately 240 of the more than 560 federally recognized tribes. Federal law permits these casinos only if the state permits such gambling.

Effects of Illegality

The **effect of illegality** is as follows: Because illegal contracts are void, the parties cannot sue for nonperformance. Further, if an illegal contract is executed, the court will generally *leave the parties where it finds them.*

Certain situations are exempt from the general rule of the effect of finding an illegal contract. If an exception applies, the innocent party may use the court system to sue for damages or to recover consideration paid under the illegal contract. Persons who can assert an exception are as follows:

effect of illegality
A doctrine that states that the courts will refuse to enforce or rescind an illegal contract and will leave the parties where it finds them.

- Innocent persons who were justifiably ignorant of the law or fact that made the contract illegal.

  Example A person who purchases insurance from an unlicensed insurance company may recover insurance benefits from the unlicensed company.

- Persons who were induced to enter into an illegal contract by fraud, duress, or undue influence.

  Example A shop owner who pays $5,000 in "protection money" to a mobster so that his store will not be burned down by the mobster can recover the $5,000.

- Persons who entered into an illegal contract who withdraw before the illegal act is performed.

  Example If the president of New Toy Corporation pays $10,000 to an employee of Old Toy Corporation to steal a trade secret from his employer but reconsiders and tells the employee not to do it before he has done it, the New Toy Corporation may recover the $10,000.

- Persons who were less at fault than the other party for entering into the illegal contract. In common law, parties to an illegal contract were considered ***in pari delicto*** (in equal fault). Some states have changed this rule and permit the less-at-fault party to recover restitution of the consideration they paid under an illegal contract from the more-at-fault party.

Critical Legal Thinking Questions
Why is an illegal contract void? Does the rule that the court "will leave the parties where it finds them" ever cause unfair results?

in pari delicto
A situation in which both parties are equally at fault in an illegal contract.

Exculpatory Agreements

12.5 Describe exculpatory agreements and identify when they are lawful.

An **exculpatory agreement** (also called a **release of liability agreement**) is a contractual provision that relieves one (or both) of the parties to a contract from tort liability for ordinary negligence. An exculpatory agreement can only relieve a party of liability for ordinary negligence. It cannot be used in a situation involving willful conduct, intentional torts, fraud, recklessness, or gross negligence. Exculpatory clauses are often found in leases, sales contracts, sporting event ticket stubs, parking lot tickets, service contracts, and the like. Such clauses do not have to be reciprocal (i.e., one party may be relieved of tort liability, whereas the other party is not).

exculpatory agreement (release of liability agreement)
A contractual provision that relieves one (or both) of the parties to a contract from tort liability for ordinary negligence.

Example Deshaun voluntarily enrolls in a parachute jump course and signs a contract containing an exculpatory clause that relieves the parachute center of liability for ordinary negligence. After receiving proper instruction, he jumps from an airplane. Unfortunately, Deshaun is injured when he is unable to steer his parachute toward the target area. He sues the parachute center for damages. Here, the court would usually enforce the exculpatory clause, reasoning that parachute jumping was a voluntary choice and did not involve an essential service.

Exculpatory clauses that either affect the public interest or result from superior bargaining power are usually found to be void as against public policy. Although the outcome varies with the circumstances of the case, the greater the degree to which the party serves the general public, the greater the chance that the exculpatory clause will be struck down as illegal. The courts will consider such factors as the type of activity involved; the relative bargaining power, knowledge, experience, and sophistication of the parties; and other relevant factors.

Example If a department store had a sign above the entrance stating, "The store is not liable for the ordinary negligence of its employees," this would be an illegal exculpatory clause and would not be enforced.

In the following case, the court had to decide whether an exculpatory agreement was enforceable.

CASE 12.3 ***STATE COURT CASE Exculpatory Agreement***

Langlois v. NOVA River Runners, Inc.

2018 Alas. Lexis 31 (2018)
Supreme Court of Alaska

"A waiver of negligence must be specifically set forth using the word 'negligence.'"

—Memorandum Decision

Facts

Stephen Morton took part in a whitewater rafting trip on Six Mile Creek near Hope, Alaska, that was operated by NOVA River Runners (NOVA). Before embarking on the rafting trip, Morton signed NOVA's liability release (Release), which states, "Although the concessionaire has taken reasonable steps to provide you with appropriate equipment and/or skilled guides so you can enjoy an activity for which you may not be skilled, we wish to remind you this activity is not without risk. Certain risks cannot be eliminated without destroying the unique character of the activity." The Release stated that some of the "inherent risks" included the loss of control of the craft, collision, capsizing, and sinking of the craft, which can result in wetness, injury, and/or drowning. The Release waived liability for the negligent acts of NOVA and its employees. Participants were asked to acknowledge that they have "read, understood, and accepted the terms and conditions stated herein" and that the agreement "shall be binding upon the participant and their estate."

Brad Cosgrove was NOVA's river manager for the trip. The trip consisted of rafting the water through three canyons. The raft capsized in the third canyon, ejecting Morton from the raft into the river. Cosgrove was able to pull Morton from the river and tried to resuscitate him. NOVA contacted emergency services and delivered Morton for further care, but he died shortly thereafter. Morton's widow, Vanessa Langlois, sued NOVA to recover wrongful death and survival damages, alleging that NOVA's negligence had caused her husband's death. NOVA moved for summary judgment, asserting that the Release barred the plaintiff's claims. Langlois alleged that the Release was not enforceable and violated public policy. The trial court granted NOVA's motion for summary judgment. Langlois appealed.

Issue

Does the Release bar the plaintiff's negligence claims?

Language of the Court

NOVA's Release clearly and repeatedly disclosed the risk of the specific injury at issue—here, death by drowning. A waiver of negligence must be specifically set forth using the word "negligence." NOVA's Release uses the word "negligence" twice. We therefore conclude that the Release brings home to the reader its intent to waive liability for negligence using simple language and emphasized text. The Release suggests an intent to exculpate NOVA from liability for acts of employee negligence.

Alaska recognizes that recreational releases from liability for negligence are not void as a matter of public policy, because to hold otherwise would impose unreasonable burdens on businesses whose patrons want to engage in high-risk physical activities. Whitewater rafting, far from being a matter of practical necessity, is an optional activity. We therefore conclude that the Release does not violate public policy.

Decision

The Supreme Court of Alaska affirmed the trial court's decision holding that the Release was enforceable and barred the plaintiff's negligence claim.

Critical Legal Thinking Questions

What purpose do release clauses serve? For what activities are they enforceable? For what activities are they not enforceable?

Restrictive Agreements in Employment and Business Contracts

12.6 Describe business restrictive agreements, including *confidentiality agreements, non-solicitation agreements,* and *noncompete agreements.*

Many employment and other contracts include **restrictive covenants**, also called **restrictive agreements**, that are designed to protect employers from employees, past employees, and others using certain secret or proprietary knowledge gained during employment or access to the company to harm the company. Many such restrictions are included as parts of comprehensive employment and business agreements, but may be included in individual contracts as well. The most common restrictive agreements are *confidentiality agreements, non-solicitation agreements*, and *noncompete agreements*. Each of these is discussed in this section.

restrictive agreements
Agreements in business and employment contracts that protect businesses and employers from employees, past employees, and others using secret or proprietary knowledge about the company to harm the company.

Confidentiality Agreements

A restrictive agreement that is often included in an employment contract and other contracts is a confidentiality agreement. A **confidentiality agreement**, or **nondisclosure agreement** or **NDA**, is an agreement whereby employees, independent consultants, and others who are privy to a company's secret or proprietary information agree not to disclose such information to any other party. Confidentiality agreements are often required to be signed by individuals or companies who are given access to confidential information about a company.

confidentiality agreement (nondisclosure agreement or NDA)
An agreement whereby employees, independent consultants, and others who are privy to a company's secret or proprietary information agree not to disclose such information to any other party.

Information that is commonly protected by confidentiality agreements includes trade secrets, intellectual property such as unpublished patent applications, business plans, secret recipes or formulas, scientific information, computer technology, proprietary software, engineering drawings and designs, prototypes and samples, sales and marketing plans, client and customer lists, and other inside information.

Example If two companies are considering merging, and each company is conducting due diligence by examining the operations of the other company, each company would sign a confidentiality agreement whereby they each agree not to disclose any confidential information that they are told or uncover while investigating the other company.

Example An inventor has invented new cutting-edge software and is trying to locate a company to partner with or to invest in the development and marketing of the software. The inventor may require signed nondisclosure agreements from any parties he discloses his invention to.

Confidentiality agreements in employment contracts include terms that prohibit an employee from disclosing secret and proprietary information about their employer that they are privy to during their employment. Such a confidentiality agreement is binding while the employee is working at the employer and also after the employee is no longer employed by the employer.Most states strictly enforce confidentiality agreements.

Non-Solicitation Agreements

non-solicitation agreement
An agreement in which employees agree that they will not solicit the clients or customers of the employer for their own benefit or for the benefit of a competitor of the employer after their employment ends.

Many employment contracts contain a non-solicitation agreement. A **non-solicitation agreement** is a contract in which employees agree that they will not solicit the clients or customers of the employer for their own benefit or for the benefit of a competitor of the employer after their employment ends. A non-solicitation agreement is often a clause in an employment agreement, but it may also be a separate agreement. A non-solicitation agreement applies whether the employee voluntarily leaves the employer or is terminated by the employer.

Customer lists are important business assets that are protected by non-solicitation agreements. For such a list to be considered protected, the employer must have spent time, money, or energy producing it. If the information is generally obtainable from other sources than the employer, the customer list is not protected.

Example An auction firm has spent millions of dollars and thousands of hours over a period of years compiling a list of wealthy investors and owners who are interested in purchasing and selling rare and expensive art pieces. The auction firm uses this list to match buyers and sellers and earns a commission on sales. This is a unique customer list that would be protected under a non-solicitation agreement. A non-solicitation agreement that prohibits an employee from later contacting these clients would be enforceable.

Example An employee works for a company that sells after-market vehicle parts to vehicle repair shops. The employer keeps a list of the vehicle repair shops. If the vehicle repair shops in the area can be readily ascertainable by using an internet search engine or other public source, this list is not protected by a non-solicitation agreement. A non-solicitation agreement that prohibits an employee from later contacting these clients would be unenforceable.

Non-solicitation agreements often prohibit employees who have left the company from soliciting other employees to leave the company. This is to prevent the raiding of a company's employees by a past employee to join him or her at a competitor or at the past employee's own competing business.

Companies can sue prior employees who violate non-solicitation agreements, obtain cease-and-desist orders preventing past employees from further violations, and obtain injunctions to prevent competitors from using the information subject to the non-solicitation agreement.

In most states, non-solicitation agreements are enforceable. This is primarily because an employee is not prevented from obtaining employment after leaving the employer, even with a competitor of the employer. Several states prohibit or severely restrict the use of non-solicitation agreements.

Covenants Not to Compete

covenant not to compete (noncompete agreement)
An agreement that provides that a seller of a business or an employee will not engage in a similar business or occupation within a specified geographical area for a specified time following the sale of the business or termination of employment.

A **covenant not to compete**, or **noncompete agreement**, is an agreement that provides that a seller of a business or an employee will not engage in a similar business or occupation within a specified geographical area for a specified time following the sale of the business or termination of employment. This agreement is often included in an employment or sale of a business contract, but it may also be a separate agreement.

Covenants not to compete are often ancillary to a legitimate sale of a business. Entrepreneurs and investors often buy and sell businesses. The sale of a business includes its "goodwill," or reputation. To protect this goodwill after the sale, the seller often enters into an agreement with the buyer whereby the seller agrees not to engage in a similar business or occupation within a specified geographic area for a specified period of time following the sale.

In the employment area, employers often do not want an employee who resigns or is terminated to work in a position that competes with the employer for a certain length of time after the employee has left the company. Employers often require an employee, before or after he or she is hired, to sign a noncompete agreement agreeing not to work for another employer or for themselves in a position that would compete with their prior employer for a certain period of time after the employee has left or been terminated by the employer.

Covenants not to compete are usually considered lawful if they are reasonable in three aspects: (1) the line of business protected, (2) the geographic area protected, and (3) the duration of the restriction. A covenant that is found to be unreasonable is not enforceable as written. The reasonableness of covenants not to compete is examined on a case-by-case basis. If a covenant not to compete is unreasonable, the courts may either refuse to enforce it or change it so that it is reasonable. Usually, the courts choose the first option.

Examples Zara is a certified public accountant (CPA) with a lucrative accounting practice in Providence, Rhode Island. Her business includes a substantial amount of goodwill with her clients. Zara sells her accounting practice to Harold. When she sells her practice to Harold, Zara agrees not to open another accounting practice in the state of Rhode Island for a 20-year period. This covenant not to compete is reasonable in the line of business protected, but it is unreasonable in geographic scope and duration. It will not be enforced by the courts as written. The covenant not to compete would be reasonable and enforceable if it only prohibited Zara from practicing as a CPA in the city of Providence for five years.

Many states enforce reasonable noncompete agreements. Some states either prohibit or severely restrict the use of covenants not to compete. Many states exempt certain professions, such as physicians, from noncompete agreements. Other states prohibit noncompete clauses in all employment contracts. The reasoning is that persons should not be prevented from obtaining employment opportunities. Most states permit covenants not to compete that are ancillary to the sale of a business.

In the following case, the court addressed the lawfulness of a covenant not to compete.

CASE 12.4 *STATE COURT CASE Covenant Not to Compete*

Friedman v. Lasco

372 P.3d 451, 383 Mont. 381 (2016)

Supreme Court of Montana

"The district court determined that the covenant not to compete was reasonable and therefore a valid covenant."

—Mike Wheat, Justice

Facts

Aaron and Constance Lasco (Lascos) owned Spirit Quest Archery, Inc., a professional archery retail sporting goods business located in Kalispell, Montana. The Lascos entered into a Purchase and Sale Agreement with Kevin and Kimber-Lee Friedman (Friedmans) whereby the Lascos sold the archery business to the Friedmans for $600,000. The sale included the business, the business assets, the goodwill of the business, and the real estate on which the business was located. The agreement contained a covenant not to compete that prohibited the Lascos from owning a business that provided archery services or archery-related sales,

(continued)

and from affiliation with any other archery sales or services provider, either as employees, independent contractors, consultants, advisors, lenders, or otherwise, within a 100-air-mile radius of the real property for a period of five years following the date of sale.

After the sale of the business was final, Aaron Lasco went to work at Sportsman & Ski Haus (Sportsman) in Kalispell, Montana, as a salesman in the hunting department. Sportsman only had a single, one-sided shopping aisle with archery equipment that did not include bows. Within a year, Lasco had played an instrumental role in establishing a new archery department at Sportsman, with multiple aisles of archery equipment, including bows, and a 20-yard shooting range. The store began to hold itself out as a professional archery shop. The Friedmans sued the Lascos for violating the noncompete agreement and petitioned the district court to issue an injunction enjoining Aaron Lasco from employment at Sportsman. The Lascos argued that the noncompete clause was unlawful. The district court held in favor of the Friedmans and granted the injunction. The Lascos appealed.

Issue

Was the injunction lawful?

Language of the Court

The district court determined that the covenant not to compete was reasonable and therefore a valid covenant. Montana law provides that contracts that restrain any person from exercising a lawful profession, trade, or business, of any kind are generally void. However, Montana law also provides some exceptions to this rule, including where a person selling the goodwill of a business may agree with the buyer to refrain from carrying on a similar business. The language of the agreement is clear and explicit regarding the goodwill of the business and supports the district court's conclusion. We conclude that the district court properly entered the injunction against the Lascos.

Decision

The Supreme Court of Montana affirmed the district court's decision.

Critical Legal Thinking Questions

Why was the covenant not to compete valid as part of the sale of the business? Under Montana law, would a covenant not to compete be valid if it were included in an employment contract?

Licensing Statutes

12.7 Describe licensing statutes and identify the effects of violating these statutes.

licensing statute
A statute that requires a person or business to obtain a license from the government prior to engaging in a specified occupation or activity.

All states have **licensing statutes** that require members of certain professions and occupations to be licensed by the state in which they practice. Lawyers, doctors, real estate agents, insurance agents, certified public accountants, teachers, contractors, hairdressers, and others are among such professionals. In most instances, a license is granted to a person who demonstrates that he or she has the proper schooling, experience, and moral character required by the relevant statute. Sometimes, a written examination is also required.

Problems arise if an unlicensed person tries to collect payment for services provided to another under a contract. Some statutes expressly provide that unlicensed persons cannot enforce contracts to provide these services. If the statute is silent on the point, enforcement depends on whether it is a *regulatory statute* or a *revenue-raising statute*:

regulatory licensing statute
A licensing statute enacted to protect the public.

- **Regulatory licensing statute.** Statutes may require persons or businesses to obtain a license from the government to qualify to practice certain professions or to engage in certain types of businesses. These statutes, which are enacted to protect the public, are called **regulatory licensing statutes**. Generally, unlicensed persons cannot recover payment for services when they do not have the required license.

Example State law provides that legal services can be provided only by lawyers who have graduated from law school and passed the appropriate bar exam.

Nevertheless, suppose Marie, a first-year law student, agrees to draft a will for Randy for a $500 fee. Because Marie is not licensed to provide legal services, she has violated a regulatory statute. She cannot enforce the contract and recover payment from Randy. Randy, even though he received services by having his will drafted, does not have to pay Marie $500.

- **Revenue-raising statute.** Licensing statutes enacted to raise money for the government are called **revenue-raising statutes**. A person who provides services pursuant to a contract without the appropriate license required by such a statute can enforce the contract and recover payment for services rendered.

revenue-raising statute
A licensing statute with the primary purpose of raising revenue for the government.

Example A state licensing statute requires licensed attorneys to pay an annual $500 renewal fee without requiring continuing education or other new qualifications. If a lawyer provides legal services but has not paid the annual licensing fee, the lawyer can still recover for her services.

Unconscionable Contracts

12.8 Define *unconscionable contract* and determine when such contracts are unenforceable.

The general rule of freedom of contract holds that if the object of a contract is lawful and the other elements for the formation of a contract are met, the courts will enforce a contract according to its terms. Although it is generally presumed that parties are capable of protecting their own interests when contracting, it is a fact of life that dominant parties sometimes take advantage of weaker parties.

In addition, many contracts that a consumer signs are **contracts of adhesion**—that is, they are preprinted forms whose terms the consumer cannot negotiate and that the consumer must sign in order to obtain a product or service. Most adhesion contracts are lawful even though there is a disparity in power of contracting.

Examples Automobile sales contracts and leases, mortgages, and apartment leases are usually contracts of adhesion.

However, when a contract is so oppressive or manifestly unfair as to be unjust, the law has developed the equity doctrine of unconscionability to prevent their enforcement. The doctrine of unconscionability is based on public policy. A contract found to be unconscionable under this doctrine is called an **unconscionable contract**.

The courts are given substantial discretion in determining whether a contract or contract clause is unconscionable. There is no single definition of *unconscionability*. This doctrine may not be used merely to save a contracting party from a bad bargain.

unconscionable contract
A contract that courts refuse to enforce in part or at all because it is so oppressive or manifestly unfair as to be unjust.

Elements of Unconscionability

The following elements must be shown to prove that a contract or a clause in a contract is unconscionable:

- The parties possessed severely unequal bargaining power.
- The dominant party unreasonably used its unequal bargaining power to obtain oppressive or manifestly unfair contract terms.
- The adhering party had no reasonable alternative.

Critical Legal Thinking Questions
What is the policy that permits a court to not enforce a contract because it is unconscionable? Is it difficult to determine when a contract is unconscionable? Are all contracts of adhesion unconscionable?

Unconscionable contracts are sometimes found where there is a consumer contract that takes advantage of uneducated, poor, or elderly people who have been persuaded to enter into an unfair contract.

If the court finds that a contract or a clause in a contract is unconscionable, it may (1) refuse to enforce the contract, (2) refuse to enforce the unconscionable clause but enforce the remainder of the contract, or (3) limit the applicability of any unconscionable clause to avoid any unconscionable result. The appropriate remedy depends on the facts and circumstances of each case. Note that because unconscionability is a matter of law, the judge may opt to decide the case without a jury trial.

Example Suppose a door-to-door salesperson sells a poor family a freezer full of meat and other foods for $3,000, with monthly payments for 60 months at 20 percent interest. If the actual cost of the freezer and the food is $1,000, this contract could be found to be unconscionable. The court could either find the entire contract unenforceable or rewrite the contract so that it has reasonable terms.

In the following feature, the court addressed the issue of whether certain contracts were unconscionable.

Critical Legal Thinking

Interest Rates of Over 1,000 Percent per Year on Consumer Loans Found Unconscionable

"We conclude that the interest rates in this case are substantively unconscionable."

—Edward Chavez, Justice

B&B Investment Group, Inc. marketed high-cost signature loans of $50 to $300 from offices located in New Mexico. B&B targeted the working poor, most of whom were less educated and financially unsophisticated individuals who were usually under or near the poverty level. Most borrowers did not have a bank account, or if they did, it was to receive government assistance deposits. The loans were for one year, on which B&B charged annual percentage interest rates ranging from 1,147 to 1,500 percent. B&B employees were instructed to describe loan costs as $1.00 or $1.50 per day, which was itself usually only half of what the loan cost daily, and to never disclose the annual percentage rate (APR).

If borrowers failed to make required loan payments, B&B would have their wages garnished so that their employers were required to make the loan payments out of the borrower's paycheck. Based on the terms of the loans, borrowers were liable for B&B's costs on collecting the debt, including attorney fees. Nonpayment of loans destroyed the credit ratings of the borrowers who missed loan payments.

The attorney general for the state of New Mexico sued B&B for unconscionable trade practices. The Supreme Court of New Mexico held that the small-principal, high-interest-rate signature loans made by B&B were unconscionable. The court stated, "We conclude that the interest rates in this case are substantively unconscionable. We hold it is grossly unreasonable and against public policy to offer installment loans at 1,147 to 1,500 percent interest."

The Supreme Court of New Mexico ordered B&B to refund all money collected on the loans that exceeded 15 percent of the loan principal and to refund any fees and penalties it collected from the borrowers. The court also issued an injunction against B&B's engaging in unfair practices in the future. *State of New Mexico v. B&B Investment Group, Inc.*, 329 P.3d 658, 2014 N.M. Lexis 230 (Supreme Court of New Mexico, 2014)

Critical Legal Thinking Questions

The general rule is "A contract is a contract is a contract" that will be enforced according to its terms. Why did the courts adopt the equity doctrine of unconscionable contract that deviates from the legal rule? In addition, the court could have voided the loan contracts entirely and let the borrowers keep the money B&B loaned to them. Do you think that the court should have imposed this penalty?

Key Terms and Concepts

Adjudicated mentally incompetent (231)
Age of majority (227)
Confidentiality agreement (nondisclosure agreement or NDA) (237)
Contract contrary to law (233)
Contract contrary to public policy (234)
Contract in restraint of trade (234)
Contract of adhesion (241)
Contractual capacity (227)
Covenant not to compete (noncompete agreement) (238)
Disaffirm (228)
Duty of restitution (228)
Duty of restoration (228)
Effect of illegality (235)
Emancipation (229)
Exculpatory agreement (release of liability agreement) (235)
Gambling statute (234)
Illegal contract (232)
Immoral contract (234)
In pari delicto (235)
Indian Gaming Regulatory Act (IGRA) (235)

Infancy doctrine (227)
Intoxicated person (232)
Lawful contract (232)
Licensing statute (240)
Mentally incompetent but not adjudicated mentally incompetent (231)
Minor (227)
Necessaries of life (229)
Non-solicitation agreement (238)
Period of minority (227)
Quasi-contract (229)
Ratification (229)
Regulatory licensing statute (240)
Restrictive covenant (restrictive agreement) (237)
Revenue-raising statute (241)
Unconscionable contract (241)
Usury law (233)
Void contract (231)
Voidable contract (227)

Critical Legal Thinking Cases

12.1 Minor Harun Fountain, a minor, was shot in the back of the head at point-blank range by a playmate. Fountain required extensive lifesaving medical services from a variety of medical service providers, including Yale Diagnostic Radiology. The expense of the services rendered by Yale to Fountain totaled $17,694. Yale billed Vernetta Turner-Tucker (Tucker), Fountain's mother, for the services. Tucker, however, declared bankruptcy and had Yale's claim against her discharged in bankruptcy. Tucker, on behalf of Fountain, sued the boy who shot Fountain and recovered damages in a settlement agreement. These funds were placed in an estate on Fountain's behalf under the supervision of the probate court.

Yale filed a motion with the probate court for payment of the $17,694 from the estate. The probate court denied the motion. Yale appealed to the trial court, which held in favor of Yale. The trial court held that minors were liable for their necessaries. Fountain's estate appealed. Is Fountain's estate liable to Yale under the doctrine of necessaries? *Yale Diagnostic Radiology v. Estate of Fountain*, 838 A.2d 179, 2004 Conn. Lexis 7 (Supreme Court of Connecticut, 2004)

12.2 Illegal Contract Andrew Parente had a criminal record. He and Mario Pirozzoli Jr. formed a partnership to open and operate the Speak Easy Café in Berlin, Connecticut, which was a bar that would serve alcohol. The owners were required to obtain a liquor license from the state of Connecticut before operating the bar. Because the state of Connecticut usually would not issue a liquor license to anyone with a criminal record, it was agreed that Pirozzoli would form a corporation called Centerfolds, Inc., to own the bar, sign the real estate lease for the bar in his name, and file for the liquor license in his name only. Pirozzoli did all of these things. Parente and Pirozzoli signed a partnership agreement acknowledging that Parente was an equal partner in the business. The state of Connecticut granted the liquor license, and the bar opened for business. Parente and Pirozzoli shared the profits of the bar. Six years later, Pirozzoli terminated the partnership and kept the business. Parente sued Pirozzoli for breach of the partnership agreement to recover the value of his alleged share of the business. Parente's share would have been $138,000. Pirozzoli defended, arguing that the partnership agreement was an illegal contract that should not be enforced against him. Is the partnership agreement an illegal contract that is void and unenforceable by the court? *Parente v. Pirozzoli*, 866 A.2d 629, 2005 Conn. App. Lexis 25 (Appellate Court of Connecticut, 2005)

12.3 Exculpatory Clause Keystone, a ski resort located in Colorado, is operated by Vail Summit Resorts, Inc. (VSRI). Teresa Brigance visited Keystone with her family for a ski vacation. Brigance participated in a ski school where she signed a liability waiver that contained the following provisions: "THIS IS A RELEASE OF LIABILITY & WAIVER OF CERTAIN LEGAL RIGHTS. I understand the dangers and risks of the Activity and ASSUME ALL INHERENT DANGERS AND RISKS of the Activity. I expressly acknowledge and assume all additional risks and dangers that may result in physical injury and/or death above and beyond the inherent dangers and risks of the Activity." In addition, the ski lift ticket stated, "Holder agrees to ASSUME ALL RISKS, inherent and otherwise. Holder agrees to hold the ski area harmless for claims to person or property." As Brigance attempted to unload from a chairlift, her left ski boot became wedged between the ground and the lift. The motion of the lift pushed Brigance forward, fracturing her left femur. Brigance filed suit against VSRI, alleging that VSRI was negligent and therefore liable for her injuries. VSRI asserted that the exculpatory waivers released it from liability. Did the exculpatory waivers release VSRI from liability to Brigance? *Brigance v. Vail Summit Resorts, Inc.*, 883 F.3d 1243 (United States Court of Appeals, 2018)

12.4 Exculpatory Clause Cynthia DeCormier participated in the Rider's Edge New Riders Course, a class for new motorcycle riders sponsored by Harley-Davidson Motor Company Group, Inc. and conducted by St. Louis Motorcycle, Inc. d/b/a/Gateway Harley-Davidson (Gateway). Before participating in the course, DeCormier signed a "Release and Waiver" that discharged Harley-Davidson and Gateway from liability, including for negligence arising out of or in connection with her participation in the program. While DeCormier was performing an exercise on the course, her motorcycle slipped and landed on her leg, causing her serious injuries. DeCormier sued Harley-Davidson and Gateway for negligence to recover damages for her injuries, alleging that the course was slippery and wet and that the instructors should not have directed her to perform motorcycle exercises at the time of her accident. Harley-Davidson and Gateway filed a motion for summary judgment, alleging that the exculpatory clause signed by DeCormier before participating in the course released them from liability. Is the exculpatory clause signed by plaintiff DeCormier enforceable? *DeCormier v. Harley-Davidson Motor Company Group, Inc.*, 446 S.W.3d 668, 2014 Mo. Lexis 215 (Supreme Court of Missouri, 2014)

Ethics Cases

12.5 Ethics Case City Segway Tours of Washington DC, LLC (CST) operated tours in which customers used Segway personal transportation vehicles to tour the city. Norman Mero and his significant other signed up for such a tour. The contract they signed prior to beginning the tour contained a release of liability clause (exculpatory clause) that stated,

> *I do hereby waive, release, acquit, and forever discharge the CST Indemnitees from any and all losses, claims, suits, causes of actions, etc. for property damages, personal injuries, or death I may suffer or sustain while riding or operating the Segway, whether arising from my own acts, actions, activities and/or omissions of those of others, except only those arising solely from the gross negligence of the CST Indemnitees.*

While riding a Segway, Mero collided with the Segway ridden by his significant other. Mero fell to the ground and fractured his right arm. Mero sued CST for negligence to recover for his injuries. CST asserted that the release of liability clause that Mero signed released it from liability. Mero argued the release of liability clause was not enforceable. Is CST liable to Mero? Did CST act ethically in placing a release of liability clause in its contract? *Mero v. City Segway Tours of Washington DC*, 962 F.Supp.2d 92, 2013 U.S. Dist. Lexis 120304 (United States District Court for the District of Columbia, 2013)

12.6 Ethics Case The United Arab Emirates (UAE), a country in the Middle East, held a competition for the architectural design of a new embassy it intended to build in Washington DC. Elena Sturdza, an architect licensed in Maryland and Texas, entered the competition and submitted a design. After reviewing all of the submitted designs, UAE notified Sturdza that she had won the competition. UAE and Sturdza entered into contract negotiations, and over the next two years, they exchanged multiple contract proposals. During that time, at UAE's request, Sturdza modified her design. She agreed to defer billing UAE for her work until the execution of their contract. At last, UAE sent Sturdza a final agreement. Sturdza informed UAE that she assented to the contract. Without explanation, however, UAE stopped communicating with Sturdza. UAE hired another architect to design the embassy. Sturdza filed suit against UAE to recover damages for breach of contract or, alternatively, under equity, to prevent unjust enrichment to UAE. UAE defended, alleging that because Sturdza did not have an architectural license issued by Washington DC, she could not recover damages. Was there an illegal contract? Was it ethical for UAE not to pay Sturdza? *Sturdza v. United Arab Emirates*, 11 A.3d 251, 2011 D.C. App. Lexis 2 (District of Columbia Court of Appeals, 2011)

Note

1. 25 U.S.C. Section 2701 et. seq.

CHAPTER

13 Genuineness of Assent and Undue Influence

CARS FOR SALE
The history of car sales has generated many cases of contracts tainted by mistake and fraud.

Pincasso/Shutterstock

Learning Objectives

After studying this chapter, you should be able to:

13.1 Define *mistake* as it applies to contracts and list the types of mistakes.

13.2 List and describe the elements necessary to prove intentional misrepresentation (fraud).

13.3 List and describe the various types of fraud.

13.4 Define *duress* and describe how it affects the enforcement of a contract.

13.5 Define and apply the equitable doctrine of *undue influence*.

> *"A contract is a contract is a contract."*
>
> —*Circuit Judge Harry Pregerson*
> *Marder v. Lopez*
> *450 F.3d 445 (2006)*
> *United States Court of Appeals*

Introduction to Genuineness of Assent and Undue Influence

Voluntary assent by the parties is necessary to create an enforceable contract. Assent is determined by the relevant facts surrounding the negotiation and formation of a contract. Assent may be manifested in any manner sufficient to show agreement, including express words or conduct of the parties.

A contract may not be enforced if the assent of one or both of the parties to the contract is not genuine or real. Genuineness of assent may be missing because a party entered into a contract based on *mistake, fraudulent misrepresentation*, or *duress*. A court may permit the rescission of a contract based on the equitable doctrine of *undue influence*.

genuineness of assent
The requirement that a party's assent to a contract be genuine.

Problems concerning **genuineness of assent** are discussed in this chapter.

Mistake

13.1 Define *mistake* as it applies to contracts and list the types of mistakes.

A **mistake** occurs when one or both of the parties to a contract have an erroneous belief about the subject matter, value, or some other aspect of the contract. Mistakes may be either *unilateral* or *mutual*. There are two primary mutual mistakes, which are a *mutual mistake of a material fact* and a *mutual mistake of value*. The law permits **rescission** of some contracts made in mistake.

rescission
An action to undo a contract.

Unilateral Mistake

unilateral mistake
A mistake in which only one party is mistaken about a material fact regarding the subject matter of a contract.

A **unilateral mistake** occurs when only one party is mistaken about a material fact regarding the subject matter of the contract. In most cases of unilateral mistake, the mistaken party is not permitted to rescind the contract. The contract is enforced on its terms.

There are three types of situations in which a contract may not be enforced due to a unilateral mistake:

1. One party makes a unilateral mistake of fact, and the other party knew (or should have known) that a mistake was made.
2. A unilateral mistake occurs because of a clerical or mathematical error that is not the result of gross negligence.
3. The mistake is so serious that enforcing the contract would be unconscionable.[1]

> *Words are chameleons, which reflect the color of their environment.*
>
> Justice Learned Hand
> *Commissioner v. National Carbide Corporation*
> 167 F.2d 304, 1948 U.S. App. Lexis 3910 (1948)
> United States Court of Appeals for the Second Circuit

Example If a buyer contracts to purchase a new automobile while thinking that there is a V-8 engine in the automobile when in fact there is a V-6 engine, this unilateral mistake does not excuse the buyer from the contract.

Mutual Mistake of a Material Fact

mutual mistake of a material fact
A mistake made by both parties concerning a material fact that is important to the subject matter of a contract.

A party may rescind a contract if there has been a **mutual mistake of a material fact.**[2] A **material fact** is a fact that is important to the subject matter of a contract. An ambiguity in a contract may constitute a mutual mistake of a material fact. An ambiguity occurs when a word or term in the contract is susceptible to more than one logical interpretation. If there has been a mutual mistake, the contract may be rescinded on the grounds that no contract has been formed because there has been no "meeting of the minds" between the parties.

Example In the celebrated case *Raffles v. Wichelhaus*,[3] which has become better known as the case of the good ship *Peerless*, the parties agreed on a sale of cotton that was to be delivered from Bombay (now Mumbai) by the ship. There were two ships named *Peerless*, however, and each party, in agreeing to the sale, was referring to a different ship. Because the sailing time of the two ships was materially different, neither party was willing to agree to shipment by the other *Peerless*. The court ruled that there was no binding contract because each party had a different ship in mind when the contract was formed.

Mutual Mistake of Value

A **mutual mistake of value** exists if both parties know the object of the contract but are mistaken as to its value. Here, the contract remains enforceable by either party because the identity of the subject matter of the contract is not at issue. If the rule were different, almost all contracts could later be rescinded by the party who got the "worst" of the deal.

mutual mistake of value
A mistake that occurs if both parties know the object of the contract but are mistaken as to its value.

Example Edith cleans her attic and finds a red and green silkscreen painting of a tomato soup can. She has no use for the painting, so she offers to sell it to Qian for $100. Qian, who thinks that the painting is "cute," accepts the offer and pays Edith $100. It is later discovered that the painting is worth $5 million because it was painted by the famous American pop artist Andy Warhol. Neither party knew this at the time they entered into the contract. It is a mistake of value. Edith cannot recover the painting.

Fraud

13.2 List and describe the elements necessary to prove intentional misrepresentation (fraud).

A misrepresentation occurs when an assertion is made that is not in accord with the facts.[4] An **intentional misrepresentation** occurs when one person consciously decides to induce another person to rely and act on a misrepresentation. Intentional misrepresentation is commonly referred to as **fraudulent misrepresentation**, or **fraud**. When fraudulent misrepresentation is used to induce another party to enter into a contract, the innocent party's assent to the contract is not genuine, and the contract is voidable by the innocent party.[5] The innocent party can either rescind the contract and obtain restitution or enforce the contract and sue for contract damages.

intentional misrepresentation (fraudulent misrepresentation or fraud)
An event that occurs when one person consciously decides to induce another person to rely and act on a misrepresentation.

Elements of Fraud

To prove fraud, the following elements must be shown:

1. The wrongdoer made a false representation of material fact.
2. The wrongdoer intended to deceive the innocent party.
3. The innocent party justifiably relied on the misrepresentation.
4. The innocent party was injured.

Each of these elements is discussed in the following list.

1. **Misrepresentation of a material fact.** A **misrepresentation of a material fact** by the wrongdoer may occur by words (oral or written) or by the conduct of a party. To be actionable as fraud, the misrepresentation must be of a past or existing *material fact*. This means that the misrepresentation must have been a significant factor in inducing the innocent party to enter into the contract. It need not have been the sole factor. Statements of opinion or predictions about the future generally do not form the basis for fraud.
2. **Intent to deceive.** To prove that a person intended to deceive an innocent party, the person making the misrepresentation must have either had

scienter ("guilty mind")
Knowledge that a representation is false or that it was made without sufficient knowledge of the truth.

knowledge that the representation was false or made it without sufficient knowledge of the truth. This is called ***scienter* (guilty mind)**. The misrepresentation must have been made with the **intent to deceive** the innocent party. Intent can be inferred from the circumstances.

3. **Reliance on the misrepresentation.** A misrepresentation is not actionable unless the innocent party to whom the misrepresentation was made relied on the misrepresentation and acted on it. An innocent party who acts in **reliance on a misrepresentation** must justify his or her reliance. Justifiable reliance is generally found unless the innocent party knew that the representation was false or the representation was so extravagant as to be obviously false.
4. **Injury to the innocent party.** To recover damages, the innocent party must prove that the fraud caused him or her **economic injury**. The measure of damages is the difference between the value of the property as represented and the actual value of the property. This measure of damages gives the innocent party the "benefit of the bargain." Instead of suing to recover damages, the buyer can rescind the contract and recover the purchase price.

A charge of fraud is such a terrible thing to bring against a man that it cannot be maintained in any court unless it is shown that he had a wicked mind.

M. R. Lord Esher
Le Lievre v. Gould (1732)

Individuals must be on guard in their commercial and personal dealings not to be defrauded. Basically, something sounding "too good to be true" is a signal that the situation might be fraudulent. Although the law permits a victim of fraud to rescind the contract and recover damages from the wrongdoer, often the wrongdoer cannot be found or the money has been spent.

Types of Fraud

13.3 List and describe the various types of fraud.

There are various types of fraud. Several of these are discussed in the following paragraphs.

Fraud in the Inception

fraud in the inception (fraud in the factum)
Fraud that occurs if a person is deceived as to the nature of his or her act and does not know what he or she is signing.

Fraud in the inception, or **fraud in the factum**, occurs if a person is deceived as to the nature of his or her act and does not know what he or she is signing. Contracts involving fraud in the inception are void rather than just voidable.

Example Heather brings her professor a grade card to sign. The professor signs the grade card on the front without reading the grade card. On the back, however, are contract terms that transfer all of the professor's property to Heather. Here, there is fraud in the inception. The contract is void.

Fraud in the Inducement

fraud in the inducement
Fraud that occurs when the party knows what he or she is signing but has been fraudulently induced to enter into the contract.

Many fraud cases concern **fraud in the inducement**. Here, the innocent party knows what he or she is signing or doing but has been fraudulently induced to enter into the contract. Such contracts are voidable by the innocent party.

Example Maximillian tells Candice that he is forming a partnership to invest in drilling for oil in an oil field and invites her to invest in this venture. There is no oil field, and Maximillian intends to use whatever money he receives from Candice for his personal expenses. Candice relies on Maximillian's statements and invests $50,000 with Maximillian. Maximillian absconds with Candice's $50,000 investment. Here, there has been fraud in the inducement. Candice has been induced to give Maximillian $50,000 based on Maximillian's misrepresentation of fact.

Candice can rescind the contract and recover the money from Maximillian, if she can find him and locate his money or property.

In the following case, the court had to decide if fraud had occurred.

CASE 13.1 ***FEDERAL COURT CASE Fraud in the Inducement***

Portugués-Santana v. Rekomdiv International, Inc.

725 F.3d 17, 2013 U.S. App. Lexis 15331 (2013)
United States Court of Appeals for the First Circuit

"In the end, Portugués got zilch for his money."
—Rogeriee Thompson, Circuit Judge

Facts

Victor Omar Portugués-Santana wanted to open a Victoria's Secret franchise in Puerto Rico. Richard Domingo, a business broker, told Santana that obtaining a Victoria's Secret franchise was a "done deal" if he hired Domingo's firm, Rekomdiv International, Inc., and hired former U.S. Senator Birch Bayh's law firm, Venable, LLP, to assist him. Portugués relied on Domingo's representations and entered into retainer agreements with Rekomdiv and Venable. Portugués paid $225,000 to Rekomdiv and $400,000 to Venable. Several months after entering into these agreements and paying the retainers, someone from Venable emailed Portugués telling him that a Victoria's Secret franchise was not available because Victoria's Secret did not use a franchise system but owned and operated its own stores. Portugués sued Domingo and Rekomdiv and Bayh and Venable for breach of contract and *dolo*—Spanish for "fraud." Venable and Bayh settled with Portugués for an undisclosed amount. Portugués's lawsuit against Domingo and Rekomdiv proceeded to trial in U.S. district court in Puerto Rico, where the jury held in favor of Portugués and awarded him $625,000 in damages. The decision was appealed.

Issue

Are Domingo and Rekomdiv liable to Portugués for *dolo*?

Language of the Court

In the end, Portugués got zilch for his money. On the verdict form the jury answered yes to the following question: "Do you find that any of the defendants incurred in dolo?" and listed each defendant's name with a space to the left of each name where the jury could mark an "X." The jury placed an "X" next to "Richard Domingo" and "Rekomdiv Int'l, Inc." When asked on the verdict form, "What damages, if any, did plaintiff sustain as the consequence of defendant's/defendants' dolo?" the jury responded the damages amounted to $625,000.

Decision

The U.S. court of appeals affirmed the U.S. district court's finding of fraud and the award of $625,000 in favor of the plaintiff.

Critical Legal Thinking Questions

What is *dolo*? Did Domingo act ethically in this case? Why do defendants settle lawsuits?

Fraud by Concealment

Fraud by concealment occurs when one party takes specific action to conceal a material fact from another party.[6]

Example Steel, Inc. contracts to buy used manufacturing equipment from United, Inc. United, Inc. does not show Steel, Inc. the invoices for repairs to the equipment even though Steel, Inc. has asked to see all of the repair invoices for the equipment. Relying on the knowledge that the equipment is in good condition and has never been repaired, Steel, Inc. purchases the equipment. If Steel, Inc. subsequently discovers that a significant repair record has been concealed by United, Inc., Steel, Inc. can sue United, Inc. for fraud by concealment.

fraud by concealment
Fraud that occurs when one party takes specific action to conceal a material fact from another party.

Whoever is detected in a shameful fraud is ever after not believed even if they speak the truth.
Phaedrus (Thrace of Macedonia) (c. 15 BCE–c. 50 CE)

CONCEPT SUMMARY

TYPES OF FRAUD

1. **Fraud in the inception (fraud in the factum).** Fraud that occurs if a person is deceived as to the nature of his or her act and does not know what he or she is signing.
2. **Fraud in the inducement.** Fraud that occurs when the party knows what he or she is signing but has been fraudulently induced to enter the contract.
3. **Fraud by concealment.** Fraud that occurs when one party takes specific action to conceal a material fact from another party.

Silence as Misrepresentation

Generally, neither party to a contract owes a duty to disclose all the facts to the other party. Ordinarily, such silence is not a misrepresentation unless (1) nondisclosure would cause bodily injury or death, (2) there is a fiduciary relationship (i.e., a relationship of trust and confidence) between the contracting parties, or (3) federal and state statutes require disclosure. The *Restatement (Second) of Contracts* specifies a broader duty of disclosure: Nondisclosure is a misrepresentation if it would constitute a failure to act in "good faith."[7]

Examples Some states require that home sellers disclose material facts about their property, such as structural problems, the existence of mold or mildew, water leaks in the foundations or walls, or unresolved disputes with adjacent landowners about the size or survey lines of the property. Some states require disclosure of suicides and other deaths that have occurred on the property within a certain time period prior to listing the property for sale. Nondisclosure of such required facts constitutes silence as misrepresentation and violates the law.

Misrepresentation of Law

Usually, a **misrepresentation of law** is not actionable as fraud. The innocent party cannot generally rescind the contract because each party to a contract is assumed to know the law that applies to the transaction, either through his or her own investigation or by hiring a lawyer. There is one major exception to this rule: The misrepresentation will be allowed as grounds for rescission of the contract if one party to the contract is a professional who should know what the law is and intentionally misrepresents the law to a less sophisticated contracting party.[8]

Innocent Misrepresentation

innocent misrepresentation
Fraud that occurs when a person makes a statement of fact that he or she honestly and reasonably believes to be true even though it is not.

An **innocent misrepresentation** occurs when a person makes a statement of fact that he or she honestly and reasonably believes to be true even though it is not. Innocent misrepresentation is not fraud. If an innocent misrepresentation has been made, the aggrieved party may rescind the contract but may not sue for damages. Often, innocent misrepresentation is treated as a mutual mistake.

In the following case, the court found fraud and awarded punitive damages.

CASE 13.2 *STATE COURT CASE Fraud*

Krysa v. Payne

176 S.W.3d 150, 2005 Mo. App. Lexis 1680 (2005)
Court of Appeals of Missouri

"Payne's conduct can only be seen as exhibiting a very high degree of reprehensibility."
—Joseph Ellis, Judge

Facts

Frank and Shelly Krysa were shopping for a truck to pull their 18-foot trailer. During the course of their search, they visited Payne's Car Company, a used car dealership owned by Emmett Payne. Kemp Crane, a used car salesman, showed the Krysas around the car lot. The Krysas saw an F-350 truck that they were interested in purchasing. Crane told the Krysas that the truck would tow their trailer and that the truck would make it to 400,000 miles, and that it was "a one-owner trade-in." The Krysas took the truck for a test-drive and decided to purchase the truck. The Krysas paid for the truck and took possession.

Later that day, the Krysas noticed that the power locks did not work on the truck. A few days later, the truck took three hours to start. The heater was not working. Mr. Krysa tried to fix some problems and noticed that the radiator was smashed up, the radiator cap did not have a seal, and the thermostat was missing. Mr. Krysa noticed broken glass on the floor underneath the front seats and that the driver's side window had been replaced. Shortly thereafter, Mr. Krysa attempted to tow his trailer, but within two miles, he had his foot to the floor trying to get the truck to pull the trailer. A large amount of smoke was pouring out of the back of the truck. Mr. Krysa also noticed that the truck was consuming a lot of oil. Mr. Krysa obtained a CARFAX report for the truck, which showed that the truck had had 13 prior owners. Evidence proved that the truck was actually two halves of different trucks that had been welded together. An automobile expert told the Krysas not to drive the truck because it was unsafe.

Mr. Krysa went back to the dealership to return the truck and get his money back. Payne would not give Krysa his money back. The Krysas sued Payne for fraudulent nondisclosure and fraudulent misrepresentation, and they sought to recover compensatory and punitive damages. The jury returned a verdict for the Krysas and awarded them $18,449 in compensatory damages and $500,000 in punitive damages. Payne appealed the award of punitive damages.

Issue

Did Payne engage in fraudulent nondisclosure, fraudulent misrepresentation, and reckless disregard for the safety of the Krysas and the public to support the award of $500,000 in punitive damages?

Language of the Court

The record clearly supports a finding that Payne acted indifferently to or in reckless disregard of the safety of the Krysas in selling them a vehicle that he knew or should have known was not safe to drive. The evidence also supported a finding that the harm sustained by the Krysas was the result of intentional malice, trickery, or deceit, and was not merely an accident. Payne's conduct can only be seen as exhibiting a very high degree of reprehensibility.

Decision

The court of appeals found that Payne's fraudulent concealment, fraudulent misrepresentation, and reckless disregard for the safety of the Krysas and the public justified the award of $500,000 of punitive damages to the Krysas.

Critical Legal Thinking Questions

Did Payne, the used car dealer, act ethically in this case? Should punitive damages have been awarded in this case?

Duress

13.4 Define *duress* and describe how it affects the enforcement of a contract.

duress
A situation in which one party threatens to do a wrongful act unless the other party enters into a contract.

Duress occurs when one party threatens to do some wrongful act unless the other party enters a contract. If a party to a contract has been forced into making the contract, the assent is not voluntary. Such a contract is not enforceable against the innocent party. Thus, if someone threatens to physically harm another person unless that person signs a contract, this is *physical duress*. If the victim of the duress signs the contract, it cannot be enforced against the victim. Duress can also occur when a threat does not involve physical harm.

Examples The threat to commit extortion unless someone enters a contract constitutes duress. A threat to bring (or not drop) a criminal lawsuit unless someone enters a contract constitutes duress even if the criminal lawsuit is well founded.[9] A threat to bring (or not drop) a civil lawsuit, however, does not constitute duress unless such a suit is frivolous or brought in bad faith.

Equitable Doctrine: Undue Influence

13.5 Define and apply the equitable doctrine of *undue influence*.

undue influence
A situation in which one person takes advantage of another person's mental, emotional, or physical weakness and unduly persuades that person to enter into a contract; the persuasion by the wrongdoer must overcome the free will of the innocent party.

The courts may permit the rescission of a contract based on the equitable doctrine of **undue influence**. Undue influence occurs when one person (the **dominant party**) takes advantage of another person's mental, emotional, or physical weakness and unduly persuades that person (the **servient party**) to enter a contract. The persuasion by the wrongdoer must overcome the free will of the innocent party. A contract entered into because of undue influence is voidable by the innocent party.[10]

The following elements must be shown to prove undue influence:

- A fiduciary or confidential relationship must have existed between the parties.
- The dominant party must have unduly used his or her influence to persuade the servient party to enter into a contract.

If there is a confidential relationship between persons—such as a lawyer and a client, a doctor and a patient, a psychiatrist and a patient—any contract made by the servient party that benefits the dominant party is presumed to be entered into under undue influence. This rebuttable presumption can be overcome through proper evidence.

Critical Legal Thinking Questions

Is it difficult to determine when undue influence has occurred? Do you think that undetected undue influence occurs very often?

Example Mr. Johnson, who is 70 years old, had a stroke and is partially paralyzed. He is required to use a wheelchair, and he needs constant nursing care. Prior to his stroke, Mr. Johnson had executed a will, leaving his property on his death equally to his four grandchildren. Edward, a licensed nurse, is hired to care for Mr. Johnson daily, and Mr. Johnson relies on Edward's care. Edward works for Mr. Johnson for two years before Mr. Johnson passes away. It is later discovered that Mr. Johnson had executed a written contract with Edward three months before he died, deeding a valuable piece of real estate to Edward. If it is shown that Edward has used his dominant and fiduciary position to unduly influence Mr. Johnson to enter into this contract, then the contract is invalid. If no undue influence is shown, the contract with Edward is valid, and Edward will receive the property deeded to him by Mr. Johnson.

Key Terms and Concepts

Dominant party (252)
Duress (252)
Economic injury (248)
Fraud by concealment (249)
Fraud in the inception (fraud in the factum) (248)
Fraud in the inducement (248)
Genuineness of assent (246)
Innocent misrepresentation (250)
Intentional misrepresentation (fraudulent misrepresentation or fraud) (247)
Intent to deceive (248)
Material fact (246)
Misrepresentation of a material fact (247)
Misrepresentation of law (250)
Mistake (246)
Mutual mistake of a material fact (246)
Mutual mistake of value (247)
Reliance on a misrepresentation (248)
Rescission (246)
Scienter (guilty mind) (248)
Servient party (252)
Undue influence (252)
Unilateral mistake (246)

Critical Legal Thinking Cases

13.1 Unilateral Mistake The County of Contra Costa, California, held a tax sale in which it offered for sale a vacant piece of property located in the city of El Cerrito. Richard J. Schultz, a carpenter, saw the notice of the pending tax sale and was interested in purchasing the lot to build a house. Prior to attending the tax sale, Schultz visited and measured the parcel, examined the neighborhood and found the houses there to be "very nice," and had a title search done that turned up no liens or judgments against the property. Schultz did not, however, check with the city zoning department regarding the zoning of the property.

Schultz attended the tax sale and, after spirited bidding, won with a bid of $9,100 and received a deed to the property. Within one week of the purchase, Schultz discovered that the city's zoning laws prevented building a residence on the lot. In essence, the lot was worthless. Schultz sued to rescind the contract. Can the contract be rescinded? *Schultz v. County of Contra Costa, California*, 157 Cal. App.3d 242, 203 Cal. Rptr. 760, 1984 Cal. App. Lexis 2198 (Court of Appeal of California, 1984)

13.2 Fraud James L. "Skip" Deupree, a developer, was building a development of townhouses called Point South in Destin, Florida. All the townhouses in the development were to have individual boat slips. Sam and Louise Butner, husband and wife, bought one of the townhouses. The sales contract between Deupree and the Butners provided that a boat slip would be built and was included in the price of the townhouse. The contract stated that permission from the Florida Department of Natural Resources (DNR) had to be obtained to build the boat slips. It is undisputed that a boat slip adds substantially to the value of the property and that the Butners relied on the fact that the townhouse would have a boat slip.

Prior to the sale of the townhouse to the Butners, the DNR had informed Deupree that it objected to the plan to build the boat slips and that permission to build them would probably not be forthcoming. Deupree did not tell the Butners this information but instead stated that there would be "no problem" getting permission from the state to build the boat slips. The Butners purchased the townhouse. When the DNR would not approve the building of the boat slips for the Butners' townhouse, they sued for damages for fraud. Who wins? *Deupree v. Butner*, 522 So.2d 242, 1988 Ala. Lexis 55 (Supreme Court of Alabama, 1988)

13.3 Undue Influence Conrad Schaneman Sr. had eight sons and five daughters. He owned an 80-acre farm in the Scottsbluff area of Nebraska. Conrad was born in Russia and could not read or write English. All of his children had frequent contact with Conrad and helped with his needs. Subsequently, however, his eldest son, Lawrence, advised the other children that he would henceforth manage his father's business affairs. After much urging by Lawrence, Conrad deeded the farm to Lawrence for $23,500. Evidence showed that at the time of the sale, the reasonable fair market value of the farm was between $145,000 and $160,000.

At the time of the conveyance, Conrad was more than 80 years old, had deteriorated in health, suffered from heart problems and diabetes, had high and uncontrollable blood sugar levels, had difficulty breathing, could not walk more than 15 feet, and had to have a jack hoist lift him in and out of the bathtub. He was for all purposes an invalid, relying on Lawrence for most of his personal needs, transportation, banking, and other business matters. After Conrad died, the conservators of the estate brought an action to cancel the deed transferring the farm to Lawrence. Can the conservators cancel the deed? *Schaneman v. Schaneman*, 206 Neb. 113, 291 N.W.2d 412, 1980 Neb. Lexis 823 (Supreme Court of Nebraska, 1980)

13.4 Duress Judith and Donald Eckstein were married and had two daughters. Years later, Judith left the marital abode in a jointly owned Volkswagen van with only the clothes on her back. She did not take the children, who were 6 and 8 years old at the time. She had no funds, and Donald promptly closed the couple's bank account. Judith was unemployed. Shortly after Judith left, Donald discovered her whereabouts and the location of the van and seized and secreted the van. Donald refused Judith's request to visit or communicate with her children and refused to allow her to retrieve her clothing. He told her that she could see the children and take her clothes only if she signed a separation agreement prepared by his lawyer. Judith contacted Legal Aid but was advised that she did not qualify for assistance.

Judith was directed to go to Donald's lawyer's office. A copy of a separation agreement was given to her to read. The separation agreement provided that Judith would (1) give custody of the children to Donald, (2) deed her interest in their jointly owned house to Donald, (3) assign her interest in a jointly owned new Chevrolet van to Donald, and (4) waive alimony, support, maintenance, court costs, attorneys' fees, and any right to inheritance in Donald's estate. By the agreement, Judith was to receive $1,100 cash, her clothes, the Volkswagen van, and any furniture she desired. Judith testified that Donald told her over an interoffice phone in the lawyer's office that if she did not sign the separation agreement, he would get her for desertion, that she would never see her children again, and that she would get nothing—neither her clothes nor the van—unless she signed the agreement. Judith signed the separation agreement. Immediately thereafter, her clothes were surrendered to her, and she was given $1,100 cash and the keys to the Volkswagen van. Donald filed for divorce. Judith filed an answer seeking to rescind the separation agreement. Can she rescind the separation agreement? *Eckstein v. Eckstein*, 38 Md. App. 506, 379 A.2d 757, 1978 Md. App. Lexis 324 (Court of Special Appeals of Maryland, 1978)

Ethics Case

13.5 Ethics Case Wells Fargo Credit Corporation (Wells Fargo) obtained a judgment of foreclosure on a house owned by Mr. and Mrs. Clevenger. The total indebtedness stated in the judgment was $207,141. The foreclosure sale was scheduled for 11:00 a.m. on a specified day at the west front door of the Hillsborough County Courthouse. Wells Fargo was represented by a paralegal who had attended more than 1,000 similar judicial sales. Wells Fargo's handwritten instruction sheet informed the paralegal to make one bid at $115,000, the tax-appraised value of the property. Because the first 1 in the number was close to the dollar sign, the paralegal misread the bid instruction as $15,000 and opened the bidding at that amount.

Harley Martin, who was attending his first judicial sale, bid $20,000. The county clerk gave ample time for another bid and then announced, "$20,000 going once, $20,000 going twice, sold to Harley. . . ." The paralegal screamed, "Stop, I'm sorry. I made a mistake!" The certificate of sale was issued to Martin. Wells Fargo filed suit to set aside the judicial sale based on its unilateral mistake. Does Wells Fargo's unilateral mistake constitute grounds for setting aside the judicial sale? Did any party act unethically in this case? *Wells Fargo Credit Corporation v. Martin*, 650 So.2d 531, 1992 Fla. App. Lexis 9927 (Court of Appeal of Florida, 1992)

Notes

1. *Restatement (Second) of Contracts*, Section 153.
2. *Restatement (Second) of Contracts*, Section 152.
3. 59 Eng. Rep. 375 (1864).
4. *Restatement (Second) of Contracts*, Section 159.
5. *Restatement (Second) of Contracts*, Sections 163 and 164.
6. *Restatement (Second) of Contracts*, Section 160.
7. *Restatement (Second) of Contracts*, Section 161.
8. *Restatement (Second) of Contracts*, Section 170.
9. *Restatement (Second) of Contracts*, Section 177.
10. *Restatement (Second) of Contracts*, Section 176.

CHAPTER 14

Statute of Frauds and Equitable Exceptions

Henry R. Cheeseman

GOLDEN PAVILION, JAPAN

In Japan, China, Korea, Vietnam, and other countries of Asia, individuals often follow the tradition of using a seal as their signature. The seal is a character or set of characters carved onto one end of a cylinder-shaped stamp—made of ivory, stone, metal, wood, plastic, or other material. A party places the end bearing the characters in ink and then applies this end to the document to be signed, leaving an ink imprint that serves as the party's signature. Government agencies and corporations often use seals on contracts. Seals are usually registered with the government. Today, however, such seals are being replaced by hand-applied signatures in many commercial transactions.

Learning Objectives

After studying this chapter, you should be able to:

14.1 List the common contracts that must be in writing under the Statute of Frauds.

14.2 Describe the UCC Statute of Frauds that applies to the sale and lease of goods.

14.3 Describe and apply the equitable doctrine of part performance.

14.4 Describe the formality of written contracts.

14.5 Describe and apply the parol evidence rule.

14.6 Define *promissory estoppel* and apply this equitable doctrine.

> *"A verbal contract isn't worth the paper it's written on."*
>
> —*Samuel Goldwyn*

Introduction to Statute of Frauds and Equitable Exceptions

Statute of Frauds: That unfortunate statute, the misguided application of which has been the cause of so many frauds.

Bacon, Viscount
Morgan v. Washington (1878)

Certain types of contracts must be in writing pursuant to the Statute of Frauds. Other issues regarding the form of a contract may arise, such as the form of signature that is required on a written contract, whether a contract can be created by the integration of several documents, whether any previous oral or written agreements between the parties can be given effect, and how contract language should be interpreted. Also, there are several equitable exceptions to the Statute of Frauds—namely, the part performance exception and the doctrine of promissory estoppel.

Issues regarding the Statute of Frauds, the formality of the writing of contracts, and equitable doctrines that allow exceptions to the Statute of Frauds are discussed in this chapter.

Statute of Frauds for Common Contracts

14.1 List the common contracts that must be in writing under the Statute of Frauds.

In 1677, the English Parliament enacted "An Act for the Prevention of Frauds and Perjuries." This statute required that certain types of contracts had to be in writing and signed by the party against whom enforcement was sought. Today, every U.S. state has enacted a **Statute of Frauds** that requires certain types of contracts to be in *writing*. This statute is intended to ensure that the terms of important contracts are not forgotten, misunderstood, or fabricated. One court stated about the Statute of Frauds, "It is the purpose of the Statute of Frauds to suppress fraud, i.e., cooked-up claims of agreement, sometimes fathered by wish, sometimes imagined in the light of subsequent events, and sometimes simply conjured up."[1]

Statute of Frauds
A state statute that requires certain types of contracts to be in writing.

The following feature identifies the types of contracts that usually must be in writing under the Statute of Frauds.

Contemporary Environment

Contracts That Must Be in Writing Under the Statute of Frauds

Although the statutes vary slightly from state to state, most states require the following types of contracts to be in writing:[2]

- Contracts involving interests in real property
- Contracts that by their own terms cannot possibly be performed within one year
- Collateral contracts in which a person promises to answer for the debt or duty of another
- Promises made in consideration of marriage
- Contracts for the sale of goods worth $500 or more
- Contracts for the lease of goods with payments of $1,000 or more
- Real estate agents' contracts
- Agents' contracts, where the underlying contract must be in writing
- Promises to write a will
- Contracts to pay debts barred by the statute of limitations or discharged in bankruptcy
- Contracts to pay compensation for services rendered in negotiating the purchase of a business
- Finder's fee contracts

Executory Contracts

Generally, an **executory agreement** (also called an **executory contract**) that is not in writing even though the Statute of Frauds requires it to be is unenforceable by either party. The Statute of Frauds is usually raised by one party as a defense to the enforcement of the contract by the other party.

Example Leana enters an oral contract to sell her house to Toshiro for $500,000, with the closing of the transaction to be in 30 days. At the time of closing, Leana refuses to sell her house to Toshiro. Toshiro cannot enforce the contract against Leana because the contract to sell the real property was oral and was not in writing.

Executed Contracts

If an oral contract that should have been in writing under the Statute of Frauds is already executed, neither party can seek to **rescind** the contract on the grounds of noncompliance with the Statute of Frauds. That is, the contract may be voluntarily performed by the parties.

Critical Legal Thinking Questions

What is the purpose of the Statute of Frauds? Why does it not apply to all contracts?

Example Alister enters an oral contract to sell his house to Indira for $500,000, with the closing of the transaction to be in 30 days. At the time of closing, Alister signs the deed to the property to Indira and Indira pays Alister the $500,000 purchase price. Under the Statute of Frauds, this contract for the sale of real estate should have been in writing to be enforceable. However, since both parties performed the oral contract, neither party can raise the Statute of Frauds to rescind the contract.

Generally, contracts listed in the Statute of Frauds must be in writing to be enforceable. There are several equity exceptions to this rule. The contracts that must be in writing pursuant to the Statute of Frauds, and the exceptions to this rule, are discussed in the following paragraphs.

Contracts Involving Interests in Real Property

Under the Statute of Frauds, any contract that transfers an ownership interest in **real property** must be in writing to be enforceable. Real property includes the land itself, buildings, trees, soil, minerals, timber, plants, crops, fixtures, and things permanently affixed to the land or buildings.

real property
The land itself, as well as buildings, trees, soil, minerals, timber, plants, crops, fixtures, and other things permanently affixed to the land or buildings.

Example Vincente enters an oral contract to sell his 100-acre farm to Greta for $500,000, with the closing of the transaction to be in 30 days. At the time of closing, Vincente refuses to sell his farm to Greta. Greta cannot enforce the contract against Vincente because the contract to sell the farm, which is real property, was oral and was not in writing.

Certain items of personal property that are permanently affixed to the real property are *fixtures* that become part of the real property.

Example Built-in cabinets in a house are fixtures that become part of the real property.

Other contracts that transfer an ownership interest in land must be in writing under the Statute of Frauds. These interests include the following:

- **Mortgages.** Borrowers often give a lender an interest in real property as security for the repayment of a loan. This action must be done through the use of a written **mortgage** or a **deed of trust**.

  Example Ida purchases a house for $500,000. She pays $100,000 toward the payment of the house and borrows $400,000 of the purchase price from Country Bank. Country Bank requires that the house be collateral for the loan and takes a mortgage on the house. Here, the mortgage between Ida and Country Bank must be in writing to be enforceable.

- **Leases.** A **lease** is the transfer of the right to use real property for a specified period of time. Most Statutes of Frauds require leases for a term of more than one year to be in writing.
- **Life estates.** On some occasions, a person is given a **life estate** in real property. In other words, the person has an interest in the real property for the

mortgage
An interest in real property given to a lender as security for the repayment of a loan.

lease
The transfer of the right to use real property for a specified period of time.

life estate
An interest in real property for a person's lifetime; upon that person's death, the interest will be transferred to another party.

person's lifetime, and the interest will be transferred to another party on that person's death. A life estate is an ownership interest that must be in writing under the Statute of Frauds.

- **Easements.** An **easement** is a given or required right to use another person's land without owning or leasing it. Easements may be either express or implied. Express easements must be in writing to be enforceable, while implied easements need not be written.

easement
A right to use someone else's land without owning or leasing it.

One-Year Rule

The Statute of Frauds states that an executory contract that cannot be performed by its own terms within one year of its formation must be in writing.[3] This **one-year rule** is intended to prevent disputes about contract terms that may otherwise occur toward the end of a long-term contract. If the performance of the contract is possible within the one-year period, the contract may be oral.

one-year rule
A rule stating that an executory contract that cannot be performed by its own terms within one year of its formation must be in writing.

The extension of an oral contract might cause the contract to violate the Statute of Frauds if the original term and the extension period exceed one year.

Example Fredericka, the owner of a store, hires Anna as the store manager for six months. This contract does not have to be in writing to be enforceable because it is for less than one year. Assume that after three months, Fredericka and Anna agree to extend the contract for an additional 11 months. At the time of the extension, the contract would be for 14 months (the three months left on the original contract plus 11 months added by the extension). The modification would have to be in writing because it exceeds the one-year rule.

In the following ethics feature, the court applied the one-year rule.

Ethics

Bonus Lost Because of the Statute of Frauds

"The end result may not seem 'fair' to Sawyer. The Statute of Frauds, by its own terms, can be considered 'harsh' in that it will bar oral agreements between parties under certain conditions. This is simply the nature of the beast."

—James Ishmael, Trial Court Judge

Barbara Lucinda Sawyer worked as a paralegal for Melbourne Mills Jr., an attorney at a law firm. Sawyer proposed that Mills and the law firm become engaged in class action lawsuits. Mills agreed to pay Sawyer an unspecified bonus when "the ship comes in." After Sawyer's assistance and persistence, the law firm became involved in pharmaceutical class action litigation. After the law firm received millions of dollars in fees from class action lawsuits, Sawyer and her husband, Steve, met with Mills to discuss Sawyer's bonus. Mills orally agreed to pay Sawyer $1,065,000 as a bonus to be paid in monthly installments over 107 months. Sawyer secretly recorded the conversation. Mills later refused to sign a written contract conveying the terms of the oral agreement.

After Mills had paid $165,000, he quit making further payments. Sawyer sued Mills to collect the remaining $900,000. Mills defended, arguing that the oral contract exceeded one year and was therefore unenforceable because it was not in writing, as required by the Statute of Frauds. The jury ruled in favor of Sawyer.

Mills made a motion to the trial court judge to refuse to enforce the oral contract against him. The trial court held that the Statute of Frauds required the bonus agreement between Sawyer and Mills to be in writing to be enforceable. Because the oral agreement exceeded one year, the court held that it did not meet the requirements of the Statute of Frauds and was therefore unenforceable. The trial court judge stated,

> *The end result may not seem "fair" to Sawyer. The Statute of Frauds, by its own terms, can be considered "harsh" in that it will bar oral agreements between parties under certain conditions. This is simply the nature of the beast.*

The court of appeals and the Supreme Court of Kentucky affirmed the trial court's decision holding that Sawyer would not receive the remainder of the promised bonus because of the Statute of Frauds. *Sawyer v. Mills*, 295 S.W.3d 79, 2009 Ky. Lexis 195 (Supreme Court of Kentucky, 2009)

Ethics Questions
Should Mills do the "moral" thing and honor his oral agreement with Sawyer? Does the Statute of Frauds sometimes assist the commission of fraud?

Guaranty Contract

A **guaranty agreement** (also called a **guaranty contract**) occurs when one person agrees to answer for the debts or duties of another person. Guaranty contracts are required to be in writing under the Statute of Frauds.[4]

In a guaranty situation, there are at least three parties and two contracts (see Exhibit 14.1). The *first contract*, which is known as the **original contract**, or **primary contract**, is between the debtor and the creditor. It does not have to be in writing (unless another provision of the Statute of Frauds requires it to be). The *second contract*, called the *guaranty contract*, is between the person who agrees to pay the debt if the primary debtor does not (i.e., the **guarantor**) and the original creditor. The guarantor's liability is secondary because it does not arise unless the party primarily liable fails to perform.

guaranty contract
A promise in which one person agrees to answer for the debts or duties of another person. It is a contract between the guarantor and the original creditor.

guarantor
A person who agrees to pay a debt if the primary debtor does not.

Example Wei, a recent college graduate, offers to purchase a new automobile on credit from a Mercedes-Benz automobile dealership. Because Wei does not have a credit history, the dealer will agree to sell the car to her only if there is a guarantor. If Wei's father signs a written guaranty contract, he becomes responsible for any payments his daughter fails to make. If Wei's father only orally guaranteed Wei's contract, he would not be bound to the guaranty because it was oral and not in writing.

The "Main Purpose" Exception If the main purpose of a transaction and an oral collateral contract is to provide pecuniary (i.e., financial) benefit to the guarantor, the collateral contract is treated like an original contract and does not have to be in writing to be enforced.[5] This exception is called the **main purpose exception**, or **leading object exception**, to the Statute of Frauds. This exception is intended to ensure that the primary benefactor of the original contract (i.e., the guarantor) is answerable for the debt or duty.

main purpose exception (leading object exception)
An exception to the Statute of Frauds that states that if the main purpose of a transaction and an oral collateral contract is to provide pecuniary benefit to the guarantor, the collateral contract does not have to be in writing to be enforced.

Example Ethel is president and sole shareholder of Computer Corporation, Inc. Assume (1) that the corporation borrows $100,000 from CityBank for working capital and (2) that Ethel orally guarantees to repay the loan if the corporation fails to pay it. CityBank can enforce the oral guaranty contract against Ethel if the corporation does not meet its obligation because the main purpose of the loan was to benefit her as the sole shareholder of the corporation.

Agents' Contracts

Many states' Statutes of Frauds require that **agents' contracts** to sell real property covered by the Statute of Frauds be in writing to be enforceable. The requirement is often referred to as the **equal dignity rule**.

equal dignity rule
A rule stating that an agent's contract to sell property covered by the Statute of Frauds must be in writing to be enforceable.

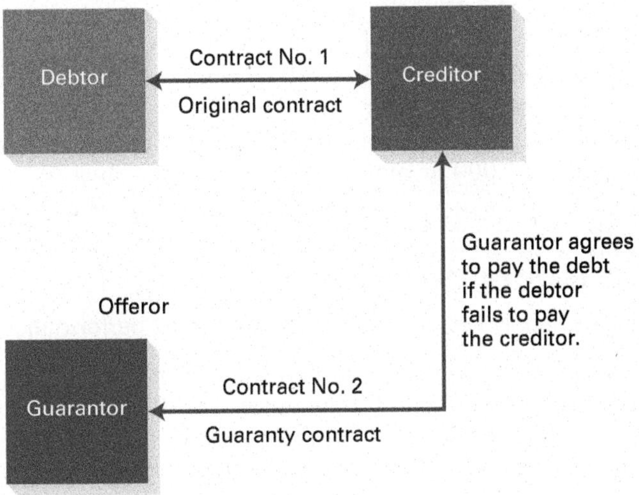

Exhibit 14.1 GUARANTY CONTRACT

Example Natalia hires Bernard, a licensed real estate broker, to sell her house. Because a contract to sell real estate must be in writing pursuant to the Statute of Frauds, the equal dignity rule requires that the real estate agent's contract be in writing as well.

Some state Statutes of Frauds expressly mandate that the real estate broker and agents' contracts must be in writing.

Promises Made in Consideration of Marriage

Under the Statute of Frauds, a unilateral promise to pay money or property in consideration for a promise to marry must be in writing.

Example A **prenuptial agreement** (also called a **premarital agreement**), which is a contract entered by parties prior to marriage that defines their ownership rights in each other's property, must be in writing.

UCC Statute of Fraud

14.2 Describe the UCC Statute of Frauds that applies to the sale and lease of goods.

The **Uniform Commercial Code (UCC)** establishes Statutes of Fraud for contracts for the sale and lease of *goods*. The UCC Statutes of Fraud are discussed in the following paragraphs.

UCC: Contract for the Sale of Goods

Section 2-201(1) of the Uniform Commercial Code
A section of the Uniform Commercial Code (UCC) stating that sales contracts for the sale of goods priced at $500 or more must be in writing.

Section 2-201(1) of the Uniform Commercial Code is the basic Statute of Frauds provision for a **sales contract**. It states that contracts for the sale of goods priced at *$500 or more* must be in writing to be enforceable. If the contract price of an original sales contract is below $500, it does not have to be in writing under the **UCC Statute of Frauds**. However, if a modification of the sales contract increases the sales price to $500 or more, the *modification* must be in writing to be enforceable.

Example Echo enters an oral contract to sell Jacob her used car for $15,000, with the delivery date to be May 1. When May 1 comes and Jacob tenders $15,000 to Echo, Echo refuses to sell her car to Jacob. The contract will not be enforced against Echo because it was an oral contract for the sale of goods costing $500 or more, and it should have been in writing.

UCC: Contract for the Lease of Goods.

Section 2A-201(1) of the Uniform Commercial Code
A section of the Uniform Commercial Code (UCC) stating that lease contracts requiring payments of $1,000 or more must be in writing.

Section 2A-201(1) of the Uniform Commercial Code is the Statute of Frauds provision that applies to the lease of goods. It states that a **lease contract** requiring a payment of *$1,000 or more* must be in writing. If a lease payment of an original lease contract is less than $1,000, it does not have to be in writing under the UCC Statute of Frauds. However, if a modification of the lease contract increases the lease payment to $1,000 or more, the *modification* must be in writing to be enforceable.

Equitable Doctrine: Part Performance

part performance
An equitable doctrine that allows the court to order an oral contract for the sale of land or transfer of another interest in real property to be specifically performed if it has been partially performed and performance is necessary to avoid injustice.

14.3 Describe and apply the equitable doctrine of part performance.

If an oral contract for the sale of land or transfer of other interests in real property has been partially performed, it may not be possible to return the parties to their *status quo*. To solve this problem, the courts have developed the equitable doctrine of **part performance**. This doctrine allows the court to order such an oral contract to be specifically performed if performance is necessary to avoid injustice. For this performance exception to apply, most courts require that the purchaser either pay part of the purchase price and take possession of the property or make valuable improvements on the property.

In the following feature, the court was asked to apply the equity doctrine of part performance.

Critical Legal Thinking

Doctrine of Part Performance Used to Enforce Oral Promise to Transfer Real Estate

"The doctrine of part performance by the purchaser is a well-recognized exception to the Statute of Frauds as applied to contracts for the sale of real property."

—Anthony Kline, Judge

Arlene and Donald Warner inherited a home at 101 Molimo Street in San Francisco. The Warners obtained a $170,000 loan on the property. Donald Warner and Kenneth Sutton were friends. Donald Warner proposed that Sutton and his wife purchase the residence. His proposal included a $15,000 down payment toward the purchase price of $185,000. The Suttons were to pay all the mortgage payments and real estate taxes on the property for five years, and at any time during the five-year period, they could purchase the house. All this was agreed to orally.

The Suttons paid the down payment and cash payments equal to the monthly mortgage to the Warners. The Suttons paid the annual property taxes on the house. The Suttons also made improvements to the property. Four and one-half years later, the Warners reneged on the oral sales/option agreement. At that time, the house had risen in value to between $250,000 and $320,000. The Suttons sued for specific performance of the sales agreement. The Warners defended, alleging that the oral promise to sell real estate had to be in writing under the Statute of Frauds and was therefore unenforceable.

The trial court applied the equitable doctrine of part performance and ordered the Warners specifically to perform the oral contract for the sale of real estate and transfer ownership of the property to the Suttons. The court of appeal agreed. *Sutton v. Warner*, 12 Cal. App.4th 415, 15 Cal. Rptr.2d 632, 1993 Cal. App. Lexis 22 (Court of Appeal of California, 1993)

Critical Legal Thinking Questions

Why was the doctrine of part performance developed? Who would have won if the Statute of Frauds were applied to this case?

Formality of the Writing

14.4 Describe the formality of written contracts.

Some written commercial contracts are long, detailed documents that have been negotiated by the parties and drafted and reviewed by their lawyers. Others are preprinted forms with blanks that can be filled in to fit the facts of a situation.

A written contract does not have to be drafted by a lawyer or formally typed to be legally binding. Generally, the law requires only a writing containing the essential terms of the parties' agreement. Thus, any writing—including letters, telegrams, invoices, sales receipts, checks, and handwritten agreements written on scraps of paper—can be an enforceable contract under this rule.

Required Signature

The Statute of Frauds and the UCC require a written contract, whatever its form, to be signed *by the party against whom enforcement is sought*. The signature of the person who is enforcing the contract is not necessary. Thus, a written contract may be enforceable against one party but not the other party.

Generally, the signature may appear anywhere on the writing. In addition, it does not have to be a person's full legal name. The person's last name, first name, nickname, initials, seal, stamp, engraving, or other symbol or mark (e.g., an *X*) that indicates the person's intent can be binding as a signature. The signature may be affixed by an authorized agent. If a signature is suspected of being forged,

WEB EXERCISE

John Hancock's bold signature on the U.S. Declaration of Independence is one of the most famous signatures in history. Go to **http://www.john-hancock-heritage.com/john-hancock-signature/** to *see this signature.*

the victim can hire handwriting experts and use modern technology to prove that it is not his or her signature.

Digital signatures on electronic documents are enforceable.

Integration of Several Writings

integration
The combination of several writings to form a single contract.

incorporation by reference
Integration made by express reference in one document that refers to and incorporates another document within it.

Both the common law of contracts and the UCC permit several writings to be integrated to form a single written contract. That is, the entire writing does not have to appear in one document to be an enforceable contract. This rule is called **integration.**

Integration may be by an *express reference* in one document that refers to and incorporates another document within it. This procedure is called **incorporation by reference**. Thus, what may often look like a simple one-page contract may actually be hundreds of pages long when the documents that are incorporated by reference are included.

Example Credit card contracts often incorporate by express reference such documents as the master agreement between the issuer and cardholders, subsequent amendments to the agreement, and such.

The meaning of words varies according to the circumstances of and concerning which they are used.

Justice Colin Blackburn
Allgood v. Blake (1873)

Several documents may be integrated to form a single written contract if they are somehow physically attached to each other to indicate a party's intent to show integration. Attaching several documents together with a staple, paper clip, or some other means may indicate integration. Placing several documents in the same container (e.g., an envelope) may also indicate integration. Such an action is called **implied integration**.

Interpreting Contract Words and Terms

When contracts are at issue in a lawsuit, courts are often called on to interpret the meaning of certain contract words or terms. The parties to a contract may define the words and terms used in their contract. Many written contracts contain a detailed definition section—usually called a **glossary**—that defines many of the words and terms used in the contract.

Counsel Randle Jackson: *In the book of nature, my lords, it is written...*
Lord Ellenborough: *Will you have the goodness to mention the page, sir, if you please?*

Lord Campbell
Lives of the Chief Justices (1857)

If the parties have not defined the words and terms of a contract, the courts apply the following **standards of interpretation**:

- *Ordinary* words are given their usual meaning according to the dictionary.
- *Technical words* are given their technical meaning, unless a different meaning is clearly intended.
- *Specific terms* are presumed to qualify *general terms*. For example, if a provision in a contract refers to the subject matter as "corn" but a later provision refers to the subject matter as "feed corn" for cattle, this specific term qualifies the general term.
- If both parties are members of the same trade or profession, words will be given their meaning as used in the trade (i.e., **usage of trade**). If the parties do not want trade usage to apply, the contract must indicate that.
- Where a preprinted form contract is used, *typed words* in a contract prevail over *preprinted words. Handwritten words* prevail over both preprinted and typed words.
- If there is an ambiguity in a contract, the ambiguity will be resolved against the party who drafted the contract.

Parol Evidence Rule

14.5 Describe and apply the parol evidence rule.

parol evidence
Any oral or written words outside the four corners of a written contract.

By the time a contract is reduced to writing, the parties usually have engaged in prior or contemporaneous discussions and negotiations or exchanged prior writings. Any oral or written words outside the *four corners* of the written contract are called **parol evidence**. *Parol* means "word."

The **parol evidence rule** was originally developed by courts as part of the common law of contracts. The UCC has adopted the parol evidence rule for sales and lease contracts.[6] The parol evidence rule states that if a written contract is a complete and final statement of the parties' agreement (i.e., a **complete integration**), any prior or contemporaneous oral or written statements that alter, contradict, or are in addition to the terms of the written contract are inadmissible in any court proceeding concerning the contract.[7] In other words, a completely integrated contract is viewed as the best evidence of the terms of the parties' agreement.

parol evidence rule
A rule stating that if a written contract is a complete and final statement of the parties' agreement, any prior or contemporaneous oral or written statements that alter, contradict, or are in addition to the terms of the written contract are inadmissible in court regarding a dispute over the contract. There are several exceptions to this rule.

Merger, or Integration, Clause

The parties to a written contract may include a clause stipulating that the contract is a complete integration and the exclusive expression of their agreement and that parol evidence may not be introduced to explain, alter, contradict, or add to the terms of the contract. This type of clause, called a **merger clause**, or an **integration clause**, expressly reiterates the parol evidence rule.

In the following case, the court had to decide if oral promises were barred by the contents of a written contract.

merger clause (integration clause)
A clause in a contract that stipulates that it is a complete integration and the exclusive expression of the parties' agreement.

CASE 14.1 *FEDERAL COURT CASE Parol Evidence Rule and Merger Clause*

In the Matter of Pilgrim's Pride Corporation

706 F.3d 636, 2013 U.S. App. Lexis 2201 (2013)
United States Court of Appeals for the Fifth Circuit

"In sum, the contracts between PPC and the growers bar PPC's oral promises because the contracts address the same subject matter as the growers' claims."
—Stephen Higginson, Circuit Judge

Facts

Pilgrim's Pride Corporation (PPC) operated a chicken processing plant in Clinton, Arkansas. PPC contracted with more than 100 chicken growers to supply the plant with poultry. The growers received chicks and feed from PPC, then raised the chicks to maturity and sold them to PPC at a price based on weight. Each grower signed the same boilerplate contract provided by PPC. The contract specified that it was "to continue on a flock to flock basis." The contract stated that either party could terminate the contract without cause between flocks, which lasted between four and nine weeks, and that PPC could end the agreement at any time for "cause or economic necessity." The contract included a merger clause representing that the contract "supersedes, voids, and nullifies" all prior agreements and oral statements, and a clause preventing oral modification of the contract.

Citing economic factors caused by an increase in the cost of chicken feed and a drop in the price of chickens, PPC idled the Clinton plant and terminated its contracts with the chicken growers. The growers sued PPC, contending that PPC officials had made oral representations that the company would maintain a long-term relationship with them and that PPC assured them that PPC "was here for the long haul." The U.S. district court held that the written contracts barred the growers' claims against PPC based on alleged oral promises. The growers appealed.

Issue

Do the contracts signed by the growers bar their claims of oral promises made by PPC?

Language of the Court

Here, the contracts between PPC and the growers bar the growers' claims because the contracts and the claims cover the same subject matter: the duration of the agreements. The essence of PPC's alleged oral representations—for example, to commit to the growers "for the long haul"—is the promise of a long-term relationship. The plain language of the contracts, however, specifies and is sure that the agreements between PPC and the growers are to "continue on a flock to flock basis"—a time period spanning between four and nine weeks. In sum, the contracts between PPC and the growers bar PPC's oral

(continued)

promises because the contracts address the same subject matter as the growers' claims.

Decision

The U.S. court of appeals affirmed the district court's ruling in favor of PPC.

Critical Legal Thinking Questions

Do you think that oral side promises are often made outside of written contracts? If the "long haul" oral promise had been made by PPC, would it have been ethical for the company to not honor it?

Exceptions to the Parol Evidence Rule

There are several major exceptions to the parol evidence rule. Parol evidence may be admitted in court if it:

- Shows that a contract is void or voidable (e.g., evidence that the contract was induced by fraud, misrepresentation, duress, undue influence, or mistake).
- Explains ambiguous language.
- Concerns *a prior course of dealing or course of performance* between the parties or a *usage of trade*.[8]
- *Fills in the gaps* in a contract (e.g., if a price term or time of performance term is omitted from a written contract, the court can hear parol evidence to imply the reasonable price or time of performance under the contract).
- Corrects an obvious clerical or typographical error. The court can *reform* the contract to reflect the correction.

In the following case, the court applied the parol evidence rule.

CASE 14.2 *STATE COURT CASE Parol Evidence Rule*

Yarde Metals, Inc. v. New England Patriots Limited Partnership

834 N.E.2d 1233, 2005 Mass. App. Lexis 904 (2005)
Appeals Court of Massachusetts

"The purchase of a ticket to a sports or entertainment event typically creates nothing more than a revocable license."

—Mel Greenberg, Judge

Facts

Yarde Metals, Inc. (Yarde) was a season ticket holder to New England Patriots professional home football games. The football team is owned by the New England Patriots Limited Partnership (Patriots). Yarde permitted a business associate to attend a Patriots game. However, the associate was ejected from the game for disorderly conduct. Subsequently, the Patriots sent Yarde a letter terminating the season ticket privileges in the future. Yarde sued the Patriots, claiming that the Patriots had breached its implied contractual right to purchase season tickets. The Patriots countered that the Patriots' written contract with season ticket holders expressly provided that the "purchase of season tickets does not entitle purchaser to renewal in a subsequent year." The Patriots asserted that because the contract with Yarde was an express written contract, Yarde's claim of an implied right to purchase season tickets in the future was parol evidence and was inadmissible to change the express terms of the contract. The trial court dismissed Yarde's case. Yarde appealed.

Issue

Does Yarde have an implied right to purchase Patriots season tickets?

Language of the Court

The purchase of a ticket to a sports or entertainment event typically creates nothing more than a revocable license. The ticket specifically stated that "purchase of season tickets does not entitle purchaser to renewal in a subsequent year." Parol evidence is not generally admissible to vary the unambiguous terms of the contract. Yarde has articulated no basis on which we can ignore the language on the ticket.

Decision

The appeals court held that there was an express written contract between Yarde and the Patriots, and that the parol evidence rule prevented Yarde's alleged implied right to purchase season tickets from becoming part of that contract. The appeals court affirmed the trial court's dismissal of Yarde's case.

Critical Legal Thinking Questions

Was it ethical for the Patriots to terminate Yarde's season ticket privileges? What would be the consequences if there were no parol evidence rule?

Equitable Doctrine: Promissory Estoppel

14.6 Define *promissory estoppel* and apply this equitable doctrine.

The doctrine of **promissory estoppel**, or **equitable estoppel**, is another equitable exception to the strict application of the Statute of Frauds. The version of promissory estoppel in the *Restatement (Second) of Contracts* provides that if parties enter into an oral contract that should be in writing under the Statute of Frauds, the oral promise is enforceable against the promisor if three conditions are met: (1) The promise induces action or forbearance of action by another, (2) the reliance on the oral promise was foreseeable, and (3) injustice can be avoided only by enforcing the oral promise.[9] Where this doctrine applies, the promisor is *estopped (prevented)* from raising the Statute of Frauds as a defense to the enforcement of the oral contract.

promissory estoppel (equitable estoppel)
An equitable doctrine that permits enforcement of oral contracts that should have been in writing. It is applied to avoid injustice.

Example Jed, who is 65 years old, owns a very large and very profitable farm and lives in a beautiful 10,000-square-foot house on the farm. Jed has no living family members except Jethro, his nephew. Jethro lives in a large city in another state where he works as a successful lawyer, and he and his family enjoy an affluent lifestyle. Jed wants Jethro to live closer to him, so Jed tells Jethro that if Jethro buys the small farm next to him, which is currently for sale, that in 10 years Jed will give his farm and house to Jethro as long as Jed can live out his remaining years with Jethro and his family in the large house on the farm. Based on this promise, Jethro agrees, gives up his lucrative law practice, buys the small farm next to Jed, and moves his family to the new farm. For 10 years Jethro works the small farm and makes a very modest living substantially below his and his family's prior lifestyle. During this time, Jed has a warm relationship with Jethro and Jethro's family. At the end of 10 years, Jethro requests that Jed honor his promise and deed the farm to him, but Jed refuses to do so. Jethro can sue Jed and acquire Jed's farm based on the doctrine of promissory estoppel. Here, Jed made an oral promise to Jethro, Jethro foreseeably relied and acted on the promise, and injustice can only be avoided by enforcing Jed's oral promise.

Key Terms and Concepts

Critical Legal Thinking Cases

14.1 Statute of Frauds Fritz Hoffman and Fritz Frey contacted the Sun Valley Company (Company) about purchasing a 1.64-acre piece of property known as the Ruud Mountain property, located in Sun Valley, Idaho, from Company. Mr. Conger, a representative of Company, was authorized to sell the property, subject to the approval of the executive committee of Company. Conger reached an agreement on the telephone with Hoffman and Frey, whereby they would purchase the property for $90,000, payable at 30 percent down, with the balance to be payable quarterly at an annual interest rate of 9.25 percent. The next day, Hoffman sent Conger a letter confirming the conversation.

The executive committee of Company approved the sale. Sun Valley Realty prepared the deed of trust, note, seller's closing statement, and other loan documents. However, before the documents were executed by either side, Sun Valley Company sold all its assets, including the Ruud Mountain property, to another purchaser. When the new owner refused to sell the Ruud Mountain lot to Hoffman and Frey, they brought this action for specific performance of the oral contract. Do Hoffman and Frey win? *Hoffman v. Sun Valley Company*, 102 Idaho 187, 628 P.2d 218, 1981 Ida. Lexis 320 (Supreme Court of Idaho, 1981)

14.2 Guaranty Contract David Brown met with Stan Steele, a loan officer with the Bank of Idaho (now First Interstate Bank), to discuss borrowing money from the bank to start a new business. After learning that he did not qualify for the loan on the basis of his own financial strength, Brown told Steele that his former employers, James and Donna West of California, might be willing to guarantee the payment of the loan. Steele talked to Mr. West, who orally stated on the telephone that he would personally guarantee the loan to Brown. Based on this guaranty, the bank loaned Brown the money. The bank sent a written guarantee to Mr. and Mrs. West for their signatures, but it was never returned to the bank. When Brown defaulted on the loan, the bank filed suit against the Wests to recover on their guaranty contract. Are the Wests liable? *First Interstate Bank of Idaho, N.A. v. West*, 107 Idaho 851, 693 P.2d 1053, 1984 Ida. Lexis 600 (Supreme Court of Idaho, 1984)

14.3 Sufficiency of a Writing Irving Levin and Harold Lipton owned the San Diego Clippers Basketball Club, a professional basketball franchise. Levin and Lipton met with Philip Knight to discuss the sale of the Clippers to Knight. After the meeting, they all initialed a three-page handwritten memorandum that Levin had drafted during the meeting. The memorandum outlined the major terms of their discussion, including subject matter, price, and the parties to the agreement. Levin and Lipton forwarded to Knight a letter and proposed sale agreement. Two days later, Knight informed Levin that he had decided not to purchase the Clippers. Levin and Lipton sued Knight for breach of contract. Knight argued in defense that the handwritten memorandum was not enforceable because it did not satisfy the Statute of Frauds. Is he correct? *Levin v. Knight*, 865 F.2d 1271, 1989 U.S. App. Lexis 458 (United States Court of Appeals for the Ninth Circuit, 1989)

Ethics Case

14.4 Ethics Case Adolfo Mozzetti, who owned a construction company, orally promised his son, Remo, that if Remo would manage the family business for their mutual benefit and would take care of him for the rest of his life, he would leave the family home to Remo. Section 2714 of the Delaware Code requires contracts for the transfer of land to be in writing, and Section 2715 of the Delaware Code requires testamentary transfers of real property to be in writing. Remo performed as requested: He managed the family business and took care of his father until the father died. When the father died, his will left the family home to his daughter, Lucia M. Shepard. Remo brought an action to enforce his father's oral promise that the home belonged to him. The daughter argued that the will should be upheld. Who wins? Did the daughter act ethically in trying to defeat the father's promise to leave the property to the son? Did the son act ethically in trying to defeat his father's will? *Shepard v. Mozzetti*, 545 A.2d 621, 1988 Del. Lexis 217 (Supreme Court of Delaware, 1988)

Notes

1. *Elias v. George Sahely & Co.*, 1983 App. Cas. (P.C.) 646, 655.
2. *Restatement (Second) of Contracts*, Section 110.
3. *Restatement (Second) of Contracts*, Section 130.
4. *Restatement (Second) of Contracts*, Section 112.
5. *Restatement (Second) of Contracts,* Section 116.
6. UCC Section 2-202 and UCC Section 2A-202.
7. *Restatement (Second) of Contracts*, Section 213.
8. UCC Sections 1-205, 2-202, and 2–208.
9. *Restatement (Second) of Contracts*, Section 139.

CHAPTER 15

Third-Party Rights and Discharge

Henry R. Cheeseman

PYRAMIDS OF GIZA, EGYPT

In many parts of the world, substantial negotiations occur before the parties devise a contract.

Learning Objectives

After studying this chapter, you should be able to:

15.1 Describe assignment of contract rights and what contract rights are assignable.

15.2 Describe delegation of duties and what duties cannot be delegated.

15.3 Define *third-party beneficiary* and distinguish between intended and incidental beneficiaries.

15.4 Define *covenant* and describe how it is an unconditional promise to perform.

15.5 Distinguish between *conditions precedent, conditions subsequent,* and *concurrent conditions.*

15.6 Explain when the performance of a contract is discharged by agreement or impossibility of performance.

15.7 Define *statute of limitations* and explain how it applies to contract disputes.

"An honest man's word is as good as his bond."

—Don Quixote de la Mancha
Part II, Book IV, Ch. 34 (1615)
Miguel de Cervantes Saavedra

Introduction to Third-Party Rights and Discharge

The parties to a contract are said to be in **privity of contract**. Contracting parties have a legal obligation to perform the duties specified in their contract. A party's duty of performance may be discharged by agreement of the parties, excuse of performance, or operation of law. If one party fails to perform as promised, the other party may enforce the contract and sue for breach.

privity of contract
The state of two specified parties being in a contract.

With two exceptions, third parties do not acquire any rights under other people's contracts. The exceptions include (1) *assignees* to whom rights are subsequently transferred and (2) *intended third-party beneficiaries* to whom the contracting parties intended to give rights under the contract at the time of contracting.

Make fair agreements and stick to them.
Confucius (551–479 BCE)

This chapter discusses the rights of third parties under a contract, conditions to performance, and ways of discharging the duty of performance.

Assignment of a Right

15.1 Describe assignment of contract rights and what contract rights are assignable.

In many cases, the parties to a contract can transfer their rights under the contract to other parties. The transfer of contractual rights is called an **assignment** or an **assignment of a right**.

assignment of rights (assignment)
The transfer of contractual rights by an obligee to another party.

Form of Assignment

A party who owes a duty of performance under a contract is called the **obligor**. A party who is owed a right under a contract is called the **obligee**. An obligee that transfers the right to receive performance is called an **assignor**. The party to whom the right has been transferred is called the **assignee**. The assignee can assign the right to yet another person (called a **subsequent assignee**, or **subassignee**). Exhibit 15.1 illustrates these relationships.

assignor
An obligee who transfers a right.

assignee
A party to whom a right has been transferred.

Generally, no formalities are required for a valid assignment of rights. Although the assignor often uses the word *assign*, other words or terms, such as *sell, transfer, convey*, and *give*, are sufficient to indicate intent to transfer a contract right.

Exhibit 15.1 ASSIGNMENT OF A RIGHT

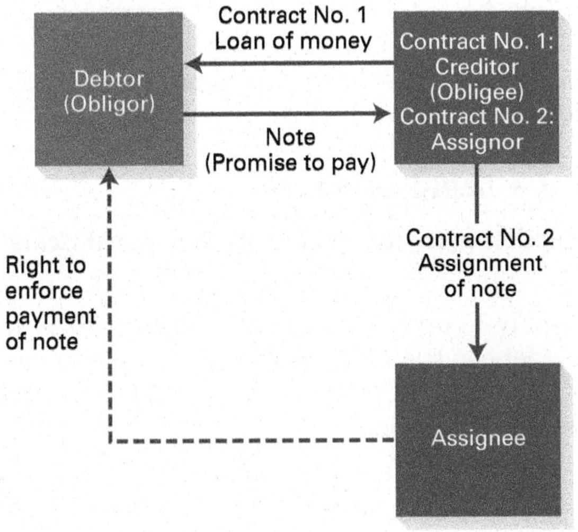

Example A retail clothing store purchases $5,000 worth of goods on credit from a manufacturer. Payment is due in 120 days. If the manufacturer needs cash before the 120-day period expires, the manufacturer (assignor) can sell its right to collect the money to another party (assignee) for some price, let's say $4,000. If the retail store is given proper notice of the assignment, it must pay $5,000 to the assignee when the 120-day period is reached.

In the United States, public policy favors a free flow of commerce. Hence, most contract rights are assignable, including sales contracts and contracts for the payment of money. The following paragraphs discuss types of contracts that present special problems for assignment.

Personal Service Contract

Contracts for the provision of personal services are generally not assignable.[1]

Example A famous actor signs a contract with a movie studio whereby she agrees to star in a romantic comedy. The movie studio cannot assign the actor's contract to another movie studio because it is a personal service contract.

The parties may agree that a **personal service contract** may be assigned.

Example Many professional sports players agree in their contracts with professional team owners that their contracts may be assigned. Therefore, the professional team that owns a player's contract can trade a player by assigning the contract to another team.

Assignment of a Future Right

If a man will improvidently bind himself up by a voluntary deed, and not reserve a liberty to himself by a power of revocation, this court will not loose the fetters he hath put upon himself, but he must lie down under his own folly.

Lord Chancellor Lord Nottingham
Villers v. Beaumont (1682)

Usually, a person cannot assign a currently nonexistent right that the person expects to have in the future (i.e., a **future right**).

Example Henrietta, an heiress worth millions of dollars, signs a will, leaving all her property to her granddaughter Anastasia. Anastasia has only an expected future right, not a current right, to the money. Anastasia cannot lawfully assign her expected future right to receive her inheritance. The assignment would be invalid.

Contract Where an Assignment Would Materially Alter the Risk

A contract cannot be assigned if the assignment would materially alter the risk or duties of the obligor.

Example Consuelo, who has a safe driving record, purchases automobile insurance from an insurance company. Consuelo cannot assign her rights to be insured to another driver because the assignment would materially alter the risk and duties of the insurance company.

Assignment of a Legal Action

The right to sue another party for a violation of personal rights cannot usually be assigned.

Example Jet is severely injured by Alesia in an automobile accident caused by Alesia's negligence. Jet can sue Alesia for the tort of negligence to recover monetary damages for his injuries. Jet's right to sue Alesia is a personal right that cannot be assigned to another person.

A legal right that arises out of a breach of contract may be assigned.

Example Andrea borrows $10,000 from Country Bank with an 8 percent interest rate. The loan is to be repaid in equal monthly installments over a five-year period. If Andrea defaults on the loan, Country Bank may sue Andrea to collect the unpaid amount of the loan. Instead, Country Bank may sell (assign) its legal right to a collection agency to recover the money Andrea still owes on the loan. In this case, Country Bank is the assignor, and the collection agency is the assignee.

Effect of an Assignment of a Right

Where there has been a valid assignment of rights, the assignee "stands in the shoes of the assignor." That is, the assignor is entitled to performance from the obligor. The unconditional assignment of a contract right extinguishes all the assignor's rights, including the right to sue the obligor directly for nonperformance.[2] An assignee takes no better rights under the contract than the assignor had.

Example If the assignor has a right to receive $10,000 from a debtor, the right to receive this $10,000 is all that the assignor can assign to the assignee.

An obligor can assert any defense he or she had against the assignor or the assignee. An obligor can raise the defenses of fraud, duress, undue influence, minority, insanity, illegality of the contract, mutual mistake, or payment by worthless check of the assignor, against enforcement of the contract by the assignee. The obligor can also raise any personal defenses (e.g., participation in the assignor's fraudulent scheme) he or she may have directly against the assignee.

Notice of Assignment

When an assignor makes an assignment of a right under a contract, the assignee is under a duty to notify the obligor that (1) the assignment has been made and (2) performance must be rendered to the assignee. If the assignee fails to provide **notice of assignment** to the obligor, the obligor may continue to render performance to the assignor, who no longer has a right to it. The assignee cannot sue the obligor to recover payment because the obligor has performed the original contract. The assignee's only course of action is to sue the assignor for damages.

That what is agreed to be done, must be considered as done.

Lord Chancellor Lord Hardwicke
Guidot v. Guidot (1745)

Example Juan borrows $10,000 from Samuel. Juan is to pay Samuel the principal amount, with 10 percent interest, over three years in 36 equal monthly payments. After six months of receiving the proper payments from Juan, Samuel assigns his right to receive future payments to Blanca. Blanca, as the assignee, owes a duty to notify Juan that he is to now make the payments to her. If Blanca fails to give Juan this notice, Juan will continue to pay Samuel. In this situation, Blanca cannot recover from Juan the money that Juan continued to pay Samuel; Blanca's only recourse is to recover the money from Samuel.

The result changes if the obligor is notified of the assignment but continues to render performance to the assignor. In such situations, the assignee can sue the obligor and recover payment. The obligor will then have to pay twice: once wrongfully to the assignor and then rightfully to the assignee. The obligor's only recourse is to sue the assignor for damages.

Anti-Assignment Clause

anti-assignment clause
A clause that prohibits the assignment of rights under the contract.

Some contracts contain an **anti-assignment clause** that prohibits the assignment of rights under the contract. Such clauses may be used if the obligor does not want to deal with or render performance to an unknown third party. Anti-assignment clauses are usually given effect.

Approval Clause

Some contracts contain an **approval clause**. Such clauses require that the obligor approve any assignment of a contract. Where there is an approval clause, many states prohibit the obligor from unreasonably withholding approval.

Successive Assignment of the Same Right

An obligee (the party who is owed performance, money, a right, or another thing of value) has the right to assign a contract right or a benefit to another party. If the obligee *fraudulently* makes successive assignments of the same right to a number of assignees, which assignee has the legal right to the assigned right? To answer this question, the following rules apply:

American rule (New York rule)
The **American rule** (or **New York rule**) provides that the first assignment in time prevails, regardless of notice.

- **American rule (New York rule).** The **American rule** (or **New York rule**) provides that the first assignment in time prevails, regardless of notice. Most states follow this rule.

  Example Whitehall (obligor) owes $10,000 to Vinnie. On April 1, Vinnie (assignor) sells (assigns) his right to collect this money to Jackson (first assignee) for the payment of $8,000. On April 15, Vinnie (assignor) sells (assigns) his right to collect this money to Maybell (second assignee) for the payment of $7,000. Maybell notifies Whitehall to make future payments to her. There has been a successive assignment of the same right. Under the American rule, Jackson, the assignee who was first in time, can recover the money from Whitehall. Maybell's only recourse is to sue Vinnie to recover her $7,000.

English rule
The **English rule** provides that the first assignee to give notice to the obligor prevails.

- **English rule.** The **English rule** provides that the first assignee to *give notice* to the obligor (the person who owes the performance, money, duty, or other thing of value) prevails.

  Example Millicent (obligor) owes $20,000 to Tony. On August 1, Tony (assignor) sells (assigns) his right to collect this money to Justin (first assignee) for the payment of $15,000. Justin does not notify Millicent of this assignment. On August 20, Tony (assignor) sells (assigns) his right to collect the money from Millicent to Marcia (second assignee) for the payment of $14,000. Marcia notifies Millicent to make future payments to her. There has been a successive assignment of the same right. Under the English rule, Marcia, the second assignee, can recover the money from Millicent because Marcia was the first to give notice of the assignment to Millicent. Justin's only recourse is to sue Tony to recover his $15,000.

Critical Legal Thinking Questions

What is a successive assignment of a right or benefit? What is the difference between the American rule and the English rule regarding successive assignments of a right?

- **Possession of tangible token rule.** The **possession of tangible token rule** provides that under either the American or English rule, if the assignor makes successive assignments of a contract right that is represented by a tangible token, such as a stock certificate or a savings account passbook, the first assignee who receives delivery of the tangible token prevails over subsequent assignees.

The same rules apply if the obligee has *mistakenly* made successive assignments of the same right to a number of assignees.

CONCEPT SUMMARY

SUCCESSIVE ASSIGNMENTS OF A RIGHT

The following rules apply if there has been a successive assignment of a contract right.

- **American Rule (New York Rule)** The *American rule* (or *New York rule*) provides that the first assignment in time prevails, regardless of notice. Most states follow this rule.
- **English Rule.** The *English rule* provides that the first assignee to *give notice* to the obligor (the person who owes the performance, money, duty, or other thing of value) prevails.
- **Possession of Tangible Token Rule.** The *possession of tangible token rule* provides that the first assignee who receives delivery of the tangible token prevails over subsequent assignees.

Delegation of a Duty

15.2 Describe delegation of duties and what duties cannot be delegated.

Unless otherwise agreed, the parties to a contract can generally transfer the performance of their duties under the contract to other parties. This transfer is called the **delegation of a duty**, or just **delegation**.

An obligor who transfers a duty is called a **delegator**. The party to whom the duty is transferred is the **delegatee**. The party to whom the duty is owed is the *obligee*. Generally, no special words or formalities are required to create a delegation of duties. Exhibit 15.2 illustrates the parties to a delegation of a duty.

delegation of duties
A transfer of contractual duties by an obligor to another party for performance.

delegator
An obligor who has transferred his or her duty.

delegatee
A party to whom a duty has been transferred.

Example A city law imposes a legal duty on homeowners to keep the sidewalk in front of their house repaired. The sidewalk in front of a homeowner's house is damaged by tree roots. The homeowner hires a contractor, who is an independent contractor, to repair the damage. Here, the homeowner is the delegator and the contractor is the delegatee.

Duties That Can and Cannot Be Delegated

If an obligee has a substantial interest in having an obligor perform the acts required by a contract, these duties cannot be transferred.[3] This restriction includes obligations under the following types of contracts:

If there's no meaning in it, said the King, that saves a world of trouble, you know, we needn't try to find any.
Lewis Carroll
Alice in Wonderland, Chapter 12 (1865)

1. Personal service contracts calling for the exercise of personal skills, discretion, or expertise

   Example If a famous singer is hired to give a concert on a college campus, another singer cannot appear in her place.

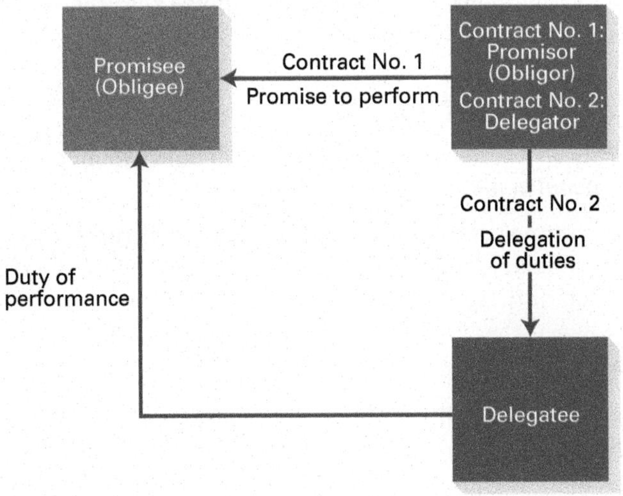

Exhibit 15.2 DELEGATION OF A DUTY

2. Contracts whose performance would materially vary if the obligor's duties were delegated

   Example If a person hires an experienced surgeon to perform a complex surgery, a recent medical school graduate cannot be substituted to perform the operation.

Often, contracts are entered into with companies or firms rather than with individuals. In such cases, a firm may designate any of its qualified employees to perform the contract.

Example If a client retains a firm of lawyers to represent him or her, the firm can **delegate** the duties under the contract to any qualified member of the firm.

Effect of Delegation of Duties

Where there has been a delegation of duties, the liability of the delegatee is determined by the following rules:

assumption of duties
A situation in which a delegation of duties contains the term *assumption, I assume the duties*, or other similar language. In such a case, the delegatee is legally liable to the obligee for nonperformance.

1. **Assumption of Duties.** Where a valid delegation of duties contains the term *assumption* or other similar language, there is an **assumption of duties** by the delegatee. Here, the obligee can sue the delegatee and recover damages from the delegatee for nonperformance or negligent performance by the delegatee.
2. **Declaration of Duties.** Where there is a valid delegation of duties but the delegatee has not assumed the duties under a contract, the delegation is called a **declaration of duties**. Here, the delegatee is not liable to the obligee for nonperformance or negligent performance, and the obligee cannot recover damages from the delegatee.

In either form of delegation, the delegator remains legally liable for the performance of the contract. If the delegatee does not perform properly, the obligee can sue the obligor-delegator for any resulting damages.

Anti-Delegation Clause

anti-delegation clause
A clause that prohibits the delegation of duties under the contract.

The parties to a contract can include an **anti-delegation clause** indicating that the duties cannot be delegated. Anti-delegation clauses are usually enforced. Some courts, however, have held that duties that are totally impersonal in nature—such as the payment of money—can be delegated despite such clauses.

Assignment and Delegation

An **assignment and delegation** occurs when there is a transfer of both rights and duties under a contract. If the transfer of a contract to a third party contains only language of assignment, the modern view holds that there is corresponding delegation of the duties of the contract.[4]

Third-Party Beneficiary

15.3 Define *third-party beneficiary* and distinguish between intended and incidental beneficiaries.

Third parties sometimes claim rights under others' contracts; this party is called a **third-party beneficiary**. Such third parties are either *intended* or *incidental beneficiaries*. Each of these designations is discussed here.

intended third-party beneficiary
A third party who is not in privity of contract but who has rights under the contract and can enforce the contract against the promisor.

Intended Beneficiary

When parties enter into a contract, they can agree that the performance of one of the parties should be rendered to or directly benefit a third party. Under such circumstances, the third party is called an **intended third-party beneficiary**.

An intended third-party beneficiary can enforce the contract against the party who promised to render performance.[5]

Examples The beneficiary may be expressly named in a contract from which he or she is to benefit ("I leave my property to my daughter Yu Yan") or may be identified by another means ("I leave my property to all my children, equally").

In the following case, the court had to decide whether a person was an intended beneficiary.

CASE 15.1 *STATE COURT CASE Third-Party Beneficiary*

Cline v. Homuth

235 Cal.App.4th 699, 185 Cal.Rptr.3d 470, 2015 Cal. App. Lexis 273 (2015)
Court of Appeal of California

"Cline reads that language to mean the release covers only the named parties. We disagree with Cline's reading."

—Elena Duarte, Judge

Facts

Colby Homuth was a teenager who had a provisional driver's license that required the supervision of an adult whenever he was driving a vehicle. On the day of the accident, Colby was driving his parents' automobile with the sole passenger being his grandmother, Berniece Homuth (Homuth). As Colby turned to go left onto another street, a motorcycle driven by Ronald Cline struck the back of Colby's vehicle. Cline was severely injured and suffered numerous broken bones. The traffic collision report concluded that Colby caused the accident. Colby's parents, Wade and Leslie Homuth, had automobile insurance with a policy limit of $100,000 for bodily injury. Cline's attorney made a demand for the policy limit and the insurance company paid the claim. Cline executed a release prepared by the insurance company that released the driver and his parents "and any other person, corporation, association, or partnership responsible in any manner or degree" from any further liability for the accident. Cline later sued Colby's grandmother, Berniece Homuth, for negligent supervision. Homuth defended, arguing that she was an intended beneficiary of the release that Cline signed. The trial court granted summary judgment to Homuth. Cline appealed.

Issue

Was Berniece Homuth an intended beneficiary of the release signed by Cline?

Language of the Court

The trial court found the language of the release unambiguously expresses a mutual intent to benefit a class of persons of which Homuth is a member; thus Homuth was entitled to enforce the release. Cline reads that language to mean the release covers only the named parties. We disagree with Cline's reading. The remaining evidence that Cline offers is that Cline would not have signed the release had he understood it to release Homuth. This evidence of undisclosed subjective intent of Cline is insufficient to establish that the parties intended that Homuth be excluded from the release.

Decision

The court of appeal found that Homuth was an intended beneficiary of the release and affirmed the trial court's grant of summary judgment in her favor.

Critical Legal Thinking Questions

What is the difference between an intended beneficiary and an incidental beneficiary? Do you think that Homuth was an intended beneficiary of the release?

Intended third-party beneficiaries are sometimes classified as either *donee* or *creditor* beneficiaries. These terms are defined in the following paragraphs. The *Restatement (Second) of Contracts* and many state statutes have dropped this distinction, however, and now refer to both collectively as *intended beneficiaries*.[6]

Donee Beneficiary

The first type of intended beneficiary is the donee beneficiary. When a person enters into a contract with the intent to confer a benefit or gift on an intended third party, the contract is called a **donee beneficiary contract**. The three persons involved in such a contract are:

donee beneficiary contract
A contract entered into with the intent to confer a benefit or gift on an intended third party.

1. The **promisee** (the contracting party who directs that the benefit be conferred on another)
2. The **promisor** (the contracting party who agrees to confer performance for the benefit of the third person)
3. The **donee beneficiary** (the third person on whom the benefit is to be conferred)

donee beneficiary
A third party on whom a benefit is to be conferred.

If the promisor fails to perform the contract, the donee beneficiary can sue the promisor directly.

Example Nina goes to Life Insurance Company and purchases a $2 million life insurance policy on her life. Nina names her husband, Joaquin, as the beneficiary of the life insurance policy—that is, he is to be paid the $2 million if Nina dies. Joaquin is an intended beneficiary of the Nina–Life Insurance Company contract. Nina makes the necessary premium payments to Life Insurance Company. She dies in an automobile accident. Life Insurance Company does not pay the $2 million life insurance benefits to Joaquin. Joaquin, as an intended beneficiary, can sue Life Insurance Company to recover the life insurance benefits. Here, Joaquin has rights as an intended third-party beneficiary to enforce the Nina–Life Insurance Company contract (see Exhibit 15.3.).

Creditor Beneficiary

The second type of intended beneficiary is the *creditor beneficiary*. A **creditor beneficiary contract** usually arises in the following situation:

creditor beneficiary contract
A contract that arises in the following situation: (1) a debtor borrows money, (2) the debtor signs an agreement to pay back the money plus interest, (3) the debtor sells the item to a third party before the loan is paid off, and (4) the third party promises the debtor that he or she will pay the remainder of the loan to the creditor.

1. A debtor (promisor) borrows money from a creditor (promisee) to purchase some item.
2. The debtor signs an agreement to pay the creditor the amount of the loan plus interest.
3. The debtor sells the item to another party before the loan is paid.
4. The new buyer (new promisor) promises the original debtor (new promisee) that he or she will pay the remainder of the loan amount to the original creditor.

Exhibit 15.3 DONEE BENEFICIARY CONTRACT

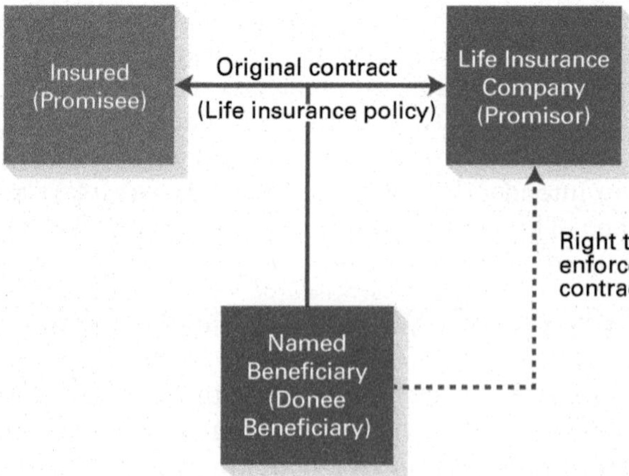

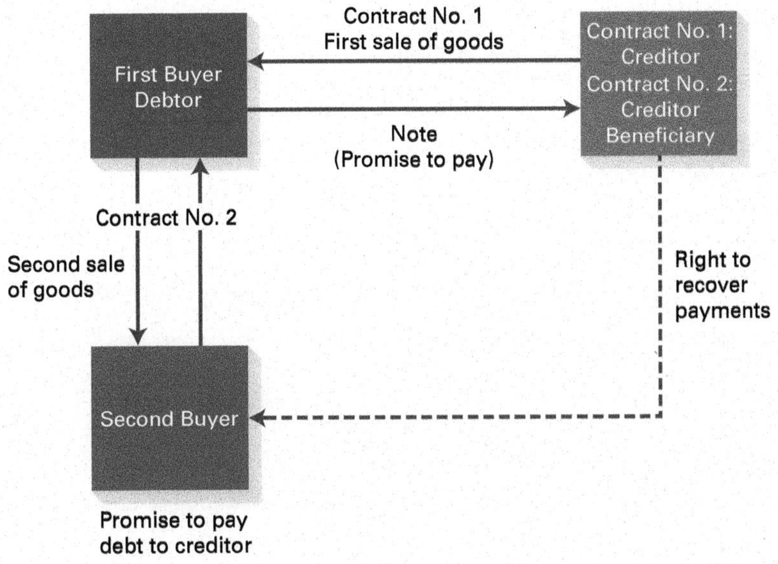

Exhibit 15.4 **CREDITOR BENEFICIARY CONTRACT**

The original creditor is now the **creditor beneficiary** of this second contract. The parties to the second contract are the original debtor (promisee of the second contract) and the new party (promisor of the second contract; see Exhibit 15.4).

creditor beneficiary
An original creditor who becomes a beneficiary under the debtor's new contract with another party.

If the new debtor (promisor) fails to perform according to the second contract, the creditor beneficiary may either (1) enforce the original contract against the original debtor-promisor or (2) enforce the new contract against the new debtor-promisor. However, the creditor can collect only once.

Example Brier Hotels obtains a loan from City Bank to build an addition to a hotel that it owns. The parties sign a promissory note requiring Brier Hotels (promisor) to pay off the loan in equal monthly installments over a period of 10 years to City Bank (promisee). With six years left before the loan will be paid, Brier Hotels sells the hotel to Palace Hotels, another chain of hotels. Palace Hotels (new promisor) agrees with Brier Hotels (new promisee) to complete the payments due to City Bank on the loan. If Palace Hotels fails to pay the loan, City Bank has two options: It can sue Brier Hotels on the original promissory note to recover the unpaid loan amount, or it can use its status as a creditor beneficiary to sue and recover the unpaid loan amount from Palace Hotels.

Incidental Beneficiary

In many instances, the parties to a contract unintentionally benefit a third party when a contract is performed. In such situations, the third party is referred to as an **incidental beneficiary**. An incidental beneficiary has no rights to enforce or sue under other people's contracts.

incidental beneficiary
A party who is unintentionally benefited by other people's contracts.

Example Kara owns a house on Residential Street. Her house, which is somewhat older, needs a new exterior coat of paint. Her neighbor Juan owns the house next door. If Kara has her house painted, Juan will benefit by having a nicer-looking house next door that may actually raise housing values on the street. Kara contracts with George, a painting contractor, to paint her house. George breaches the contract and does not paint Kara's house. Although Juan may have benefited if Kara's house had been painted, he is merely an incidental beneficiary to the Kara–George contract and has no cause of action to sue George for not painting Kara's house. Kara can sue George for breach of contract.

Generally, the public and taxpayers are only incidental beneficiaries to contracts entered into by the government on their behalf. As such, they acquire no right to enforce government contracts or to sue parties who breach these contracts.

Often, the courts are asked to decide whether a third party is an intended or an incidental beneficiary, as in the following case.

CASE 15.2 *FEDERAL COURT CASE Third-Party Beneficiary*

Does I-XI, Workers in China, Bangladesh, Indonesia, Swaziland, and Nicaragua v. Walmart Stores, Inc.

572 F.3d. 677, 2009 U.S. App. Lexis 15279 (2009)
United States Court of Appeals for the Ninth Circuit

"We agree with the district court that the language of the Standards does not create a duty on the part of Walmart to monitor the suppliers, and does not provide plaintiffs a right of action against Walmart as third-party beneficiaries."

—Ronald Gould, Circuit Judge

Facts

Walmart Stores, Inc. owns and operates a chain of large big-box discount department and warehouse stores and is the largest company in the United States. Walmart is the largest importer in the United States of foreign-produced goods. Walmart developed a code of conduct for its foreign suppliers titled "Standards for Suppliers" (Standards). These Standards require foreign suppliers to adhere to local law and local industry working conditions, such as pay, hiring forced labor, child labor, and discrimination. These Standards are incorporated into Walmart's supply contracts with foreign suppliers. The Standards provide that Walmart may make on-site inspections of production facilities and permit Walmart to cancel orders with, or terminate, any foreign supplier that fails to comply with the Standards.

Workers at foreign suppliers in China, Bangladesh, Indonesia, Swaziland, and Nicaragua who produce and sell goods to Walmart sued Walmart in U.S. district court. The foreign workers alleged that they were third-party beneficiaries to Walmart's contract with its foreign suppliers and that they were due damages from Walmart for Walmart's breach of the Standards. They alleged that their employers regularly violated the Standards and that Walmart failed to investigate working conditions at foreign suppliers, knew that the Standards were being violated, and failed to enforce the standards contained in these contracts. The U.S. district court held that the plaintiffs were not intended third-party beneficiaries to Walmart's contracts with its foreign suppliers and dismissed their lawsuit. The plaintiffs appealed.

Issue

Are the foreign workers intended third-party beneficiaries under Walmart's contracts with its foreign suppliers?

Language of the Court

We agree with the district court that the language of the Standards does not create a duty on the part of Walmart to monitor the suppliers, and does not provide plaintiffs a right of action against Walmart as third-party beneficiaries. Plaintiffs' allegations are insufficient to support the conclusion that Walmart and the suppliers intended for plaintiffs to have a right of performance against Walmart under the supply contracts.

Decision

The U.S. court of appeals held that the plaintiff foreign workers were not intended third-party beneficiaries to Walmart's contracts with its foreign suppliers. The U.S. court of appeals affirmed the dismissal of the plaintiffs' case.

Critical Legal Thinking Questions

Are Walmart's Standards illusory if the company does not consistently enforce them against foreign suppliers? Does Walmart owe a duty to require that its foreign suppliers provide the same protections to their workers as is provided to workers in the United States?

Covenants

15.4 Define *covenant* and describe how it is an unconditional promise to perform.

In contracts, parties make certain promises to each other. A **covenant** is an *unconditional* promise to perform. Nonperformance of a covenant is a breach of contract that gives the other party the right to sue. The majority of the provisions in contracts are covenants.

covenant
An unconditional promise to perform.

Example Seed Company borrows $500,000 from Rural Bank and signs a promissory note to repay the $500,000 plus 10 percent interest in one year. This promise is a covenant. That is, it is an unconditional promise to perform.

Example Mikhail enters into a written contract with Vivian to sell Vivian his house for $1 million. Closing is to be June 1. These are covenants: Mikhail owes a duty to deliver the deed to his house to Vivian, and Vivian owes a duty to pay $1 million to Mikhail. If either of the parties fails to perform, the other party can sue the breaching party for nonperformance of his or her covenant.

Conditions

15.5 Distinguish between *conditions precedent, conditions subsequent,* and *concurrent conditions.*

Some contract provisions are conditions rather than covenants. A **conditional promise** (or **qualified promise**) is not as definite as a covenant. The promisor's duty to perform or not perform arises only if the **condition** does or does not occur.[7] A conditional promise becomes a covenant if the condition is met, however.

condition
A qualification of a promise that becomes a covenant if it is met. There are three types of conditions: conditions precedent, conditions subsequent, and concurrent conditions.

Generally, contract language such as *if, on condition that, provided that, when, after*, and *as soon as* indicates a condition. A single contract may contain numerous conditions that trigger or excuse performance.

There are three primary types of conditions: *conditions precedent, conditions subsequent*, and *concurrent conditions*. Each of these is discussed in the following paragraphs.

Condition Precedent

If a contract requires the occurrence (or nonoccurrence) of an event *before* a party is obligated to perform a contractual duty, this is a **condition precedent**. The happening (or nonhappening) of the event triggers the contract or duty of performance. If the event does not occur, no duty to perform the contract arises because there is a failure of condition.

condition precedent
A condition that requires the occurrence or nonoccurrence of an event before a party is obligated to perform a duty under a contract.

Example FinTech Company offers Joan, a senior who is a finance major in college, a job. FinTech and Joan sign a three-year employment contract, but the contract contains a provision that FinTech has to hire Joan only if she graduates from college. This is a condition precedent. If Joan graduates, the condition precedent has been met and a contract is created. If FinTech refuses to hire Joan at that time, she can sue FinTech for breach of contract. If Joan does not graduate from college, however, FinTech is not obligated to hire her because there has been a failure of the condition precedent.

Condition Precedent Based on Satisfaction

Some contracts reserve the right to a party to pay for services provided by the other only if the services meet the first party's "satisfaction." The courts have developed two tests—the *personal satisfaction test* and the *reasonable person test*—to determine whether this special form of condition precedent has been met:

personal satisfaction test
A subjective test that applies to contracts involving personal taste and comfort.

1. **Personal Satisfaction Test.** The **personal satisfaction test** is a *subjective* test that applies if the performance involves personal taste and comfort

(e.g., contracts for interior decorating, contracts for tailoring clothes). The only requirement is that the person given the right to reject the contract acts in good faith.

Example Gretchen employs an artist to paint her daughter's portrait. The contract provides that Gretchen does not have to accept and pay for the portrait unless she is personally satisfied with it. This is a condition precedent based on the personal satisfaction test. Gretchen rejects the painting because she personally dislikes it. This rejection is lawful because it is based on the personal satisfaction test.

reasonable person test
An objective test that applies to commercial contracts and contracts involving mechanical fitness.

2. **Reasonable Person Test.** The **reasonable person test** is an *objective* test that is used to judge contracts involving mechanical fitness and most commercial contracts. Most contracts that require the work to meet the satisfaction of a third person (e.g., engineer, architect) are judged by this standard.

   Example E-Commerce Company hires Einstein to install an artificial intelligence system that will handle internet ordering, customer service, financial transactions, record-keeping, and all intelligence functions of the company. Einstein installs a state-of-the-art system that exceeds current industry standards. E-Commerce Company rejects the contract as not meeting its personal satisfaction. This is a breach of contract because the personal satisfaction test does not apply to this contract. Instead, the objective reasonable person test applies, and a reasonable company in the same situation would have accepted the system.

The following feature discusses a special type of condition—a "time is of the essence" condition in a contract.

Business Environment

"Time Is of the Essence" Contract

Generally, there is a breach of contract if a contract is not performed when due. Nevertheless, if the other party is not jeopardized by the delay, most courts treat the delay as a minor breach and give the nonperforming party additional time to perform.

Conversely, if a contract expressly provides **"time is of the essence"** or similar language, performance by the stated time is an express condition. There is a breach of contract if the contracting party does not perform by the stated date.

Example W Store, a large discount retail store, contracts to purchase 100,000 units of the new Violent Video Game #100 from VVG, Inc. The contract provides for delivery on October 1. If, on October 1, VVG, Inc. fails to deliver the games but can do so on October 8, which would not cause a significant loss to W Stores, delivery can be made on October 8 without there being a breach of contract.

Example Disney Company is going to release a sequel to the movie *Frozen* that is called *Unfrozen* and stars Elsa's long-lost twin sister, Eloise. Disney contracts with Toy Company to purchase 100,000,000 Eloise dolls to be manufactured by Toy Company that will be used in the promotion of the movie. The contract provides that the dolls are to be delivered to Disney on September 1 and that "time is of the essence." Toy Company does not deliver the dolls to Disney on September 1 but can complete and deliver the dolls by October 1. Here, Toy Company gets no more time. The contract was a "time is of the essence" contract that called for a delivery date of September 1, and since the dolls were not delivered on September 1, Toy Company is in breach of the contract. Disney can recover whatever damages it suffers because of the breach.

Condition Subsequent

condition subsequent
A condition whose occurrence or nonoccurrence of a specific event automatically excuses the performance of an existing contractual duty to perform.

A **condition subsequent** exists when there is a condition in a contract that provides that the occurrence or nonoccurrence of a specific event automatically excuses the performance of an existing duty to perform. That is, failure to meet the condition subsequent relieves the other party from obligation under the contract.

Example Andre, a scientist, is hired as an employee by Google.com as an artificial intelligence researcher. The three-year employment contract provides that Google.com can terminate Andre's employment anytime during the three-year employment period if he fails a random drug test. This is a condition subsequent. If Andre fails a random drug test, Google.com can terminate Andre immediately. Andre cannot sue Google.com for breach of contract.

Note that the *Restatement (Second) of Contracts* eliminates the distinction between conditions precedent and conditions subsequent. Both are referred to as "conditions."[8]

Concurrent Conditions

Concurrent conditions arise when the parties to a contract agree to render performance simultaneously—that is, when each party's absolute duty to perform is conditioned on the other party's absolute duty to perform.

concurrent condition
Condition that exists when the parties to a contract must render performance simultaneously; each party's absolute duty to perform is conditioned on the other party's absolute duty to perform.

Example Greenpeace contracts to purchase the MT Artic Sunset, a sophisticated icebreaker ship, from Marinette Marine. The contract provides that payment is due on delivery of the ship. In other words, Greenpeace's duty to pay and Marinette Marine's duty to deliver the ship are concurrent conditions. Recovery of damages is available if one party fails to respond to the other party's performance.

Implied Condition

Any of the previous types of conditions may be further classified as either express or implied conditions. An **express condition** exists if the parties expressly agree on it. An **implied-in-fact condition** is one that can be implied from the circumstances surrounding a contract and the parties' conduct.

implied-in-fact condition
A condition that can be implied from the circumstances surrounding a contract and the parties' conduct.

Example A contract in which a buyer agrees to purchase grain from a farmer implies that there is proper street access to the delivery site, that there are proper unloading facilities, and the like.

CONCEPT SUMMARY
TYPES OF CONDITIONS

Type of Condition	Description
Condition precedent	A specified event must occur or not occur before a party is obligated to perform contractual duties.
Condition subsequent	The occurrence or nonoccurrence of a specified event excuses the performance of an existing contractual duty to perform.
Concurrent condition	The parties to a contract are obligated to render performance simultaneously. Each party's duty to perform is conditioned on the other party's duty to perform.
Implied-in-fact condition	A condition implied from the circumstances surrounding a contract and the parties' conduct.

Discharge of Performance

15.6 Explain when the performance of a contract is discharged by agreement or impossibility of performance.

A party's duty to perform under a contract may be discharged by *mutual agreement* of the parties or by *impossibility of performance*. These methods of discharge are discussed in the paragraphs that follow.

Men keep agreements when it is to the advantage of neither to break them.
Solon (c. 638–558 BCE)

Discharge by Agreement

The parties to a contract may mutually agree to discharge their contractual duties under a contract. This is called **discharge by agreement**. The different methods for discharging a contract by mutual agreement are as follows:

- **Mutual Rescission.** If a contract is wholly or partially executory on both sides, the parties can agree to rescind (i.e., cancel) the contract. **Mutual rescission** requires parties to enter into a second agreement that expressly terminates the first one. **Unilateral rescission** of a contract by one of the parties without the other party's consent is not effective. Unilateral rescission of a contract constitutes a breach of that contract.
- **Substituted Contract.** The parties to a contract may enter into a new contract that revokes and discharges an existing contract. The new contract is called a **substituted contract**. If one of the parties fails to perform his or her duties under a substituted contract, the nonbreaching party can sue to enforce its terms against the breaching party. The prior contract cannot be enforced against the breaching party because it has been discharged.
- **Novation.** A **novation agreement** (commonly called **novation**) substitutes a third party for one of the original contracting parties. The new substituted party is obligated to perform a contract. All three parties must agree to the substitution. In a novation, the exiting party is relieved of liability on the contract.
- **Accord and Satisfaction.** The parties to a contract may agree to settle a contract dispute by an **accord and satisfaction**. The agreement whereby the parties agree to accept something different in satisfaction of the original contract is called an *accord*.[9] The performance of an accord is called a *satisfaction*. An accord does not discharge the original contract. It only suspends it until the accord is performed. Satisfaction of the accord discharges both the original contract and the accord. If an accord is not satisfied when it is due, the aggrieved party may enforce either the accord or the original contract.

novation agreement (novation)
An agreement that substitutes a new party for one of the original contracting parties and relieves the exiting party of liability on the contract.

accord and satisfaction
The settlement of a contract dispute.

impossibility of performance (objective impossibility)
Nonperformance that is excused if a contract becomes impossible to perform. It must be an objective, not subjective, impossibility.

The following feature discusses the discharge of a contract by impossibility of performance.

Contemporary Environment

Impossibility of Performance

Under certain circumstances, the nonperformance of contractual duties is excused—that is, discharged—because of *impossibility of performance*. **Impossibility of performance** (or **objective impossibility**) occurs if a contract becomes impossible to perform.[10] The impossibility must be an objective impossibility ("it cannot be done") rather than a subjective impossibility ("I cannot do it"). The following types of objective impossibility excuse nonperformance:

- The death or incapacity of the promisor prior to the performance of a personal service contract[11]

  Example If a professional athlete dies prior to or during a contract period, his or her contract with the team is discharged.

- The destruction of the subject matter of a contract prior to performance[12]

  Example If a building is destroyed by fire, the lessees are discharged from further performance unless otherwise provided in the lease.

- A supervening illegality that makes performance of the contract illegal[13]

  Example An art dealer contracts to purchase native art found in a foreign country. The contract is discharged if the foreign country enacts a law forbidding native art from being exported from the country before the contract is performed.

Force Majeure Clause

The parties may agree in a contract that certain events will excuse nonperformance of the contract. These clauses are called ***force majeure*** **clauses**.

force majeure **clause**
A clause in a contract in which the parties specify certain events that will excuse nonperformance.

Example A *force majeure* clause usually excuses nonperformance caused by natural disasters such as floods, tornadoes, and earthquakes. Modern clauses also often excuse performance due to labor strikes, shortages of raw materials, and the like.

Statute of Limitations

15.7 Define *statute of limitations* and explain how it applies to contract disputes.

Every state has a **statute of limitations** that applies to contract actions. Under these statutes, if an aggrieved party does not bring suit for breach of contract during a designated period after a breach of contract has occurred, that party loses the right to sue. Time periods vary from state to state. The usual period for bringing a lawsuit for breach of contract is one to five years.

statute of limitations
A statute that establishes the time period during which a lawsuit must be brought; if the lawsuit is not brought within this period, the injured party loses the right to sue.

Example Assume that a state has a statute of limitations that requires that a lawsuit alleging a breach of a written contract be brought within two years of the breach. If a contract is breached on May 1, 2022, the nonbreaching party has until May 1, 2024, to bring a lawsuit against the breaching party. If a nonbreaching party waits until May 2, 2024, or thereafter, to bring the lawsuit, the court will dismiss the lawsuit because it was not brought within the statute of limitations.

Key Terms and Concepts

Accord and satisfaction (282)
American rule (New York Rule) (272)
Anti-assignment clause (272)
Anti-delegation clause (274)
Approval clause (272)
Assignee (269)
Assignment and delegation (274)
Assignment (assignment of a right) (269)
Assignor (269)
Assumption of duties (274)
Concurrent conditions (281)
Condition (279)
Condition precedent (279)
Condition subsequent (280)
Conditional promise (qualified promise) (279)
Covenant (279)
Creditor beneficiary (277)
Creditor beneficiary contract (276)
Declaration of a duty (274)
Delegate (274)
Delegatee (273)
Delegation of a duty (delegation) (273)
Delegator (273)
Discharge by agreement (282)
Donee beneficiary (276)
Donee beneficiary contract (276)
English rule (272)
Express condition (281)
Force majeure clause (283)
Future right (270)
Implied-in-fact condition (281)
Impossibility of performance (objective impossibility) (282)
Incidental beneficiary (277)
Intended third-party beneficiary (274)
Mutual rescission (282)
Notice of assignment (271)
Novation agreement (novation) (282)
Obligee (269)
Obligor (269)
Personal satisfaction test (279)
Personal service contract (270)
Possession of tangible token rule (272)
Privity of contract (269)
Promisee (276)
Promisor (276)
Reasonable person test (280)
Statute of limitations (283)
Subsequent assignee (subassignee) (269)
Substituted contract (282)
Third-party beneficiary (274)
Time is of the essence (280)
Unilateral rescission (282)

Critical Legal Thinking Cases

15.1 Intended or Incidental Beneficiary The Phillies, L.P., the owner of the Philadelphia Phillies professional baseball team (Phillies), decided to build a new baseball stadium called Citizens Bank Park (the Project). The Phillies entered into a contract (Agreement) with Driscoll/Hunt Joint Venture (DH) whereby DH would act as the construction manager of the Project. In that capacity, DH entered into multiple contracts with subcontractors to provide material and services in constructing the Project. One such subcontractor was Ramos/Carson/DePaul, Joint Venture (RCD), which was hired to install concrete foundations for the Project. The Project was beset with numerous delays and disruptions, for which RCD claimed it was owed additional compensation from DH and the Phillies. Subcontractor RCD sued the Phillies to recover the alleged compensation, alleging it was an intended beneficiary to the Phillies–DH Agreement, thus giving it rights to recover compensation from the Phillies. The Phillies argued that RCD was merely an incidental beneficiary to the Phillies–DH Agreement and could not recover compensation from the Phillies. Was RCD an intended or an incidental beneficiary of the Phillies–DH Agreement? *Ramos/Carson/DePaul, a Joint Venture v. The Phillies, L.P.*, 2008 Phila. Ct. Com. Pl. Lexis 282 (Common Pleas Court of Philadelphia County, Pennsylvania, 2008)

15.2 Third-Party Beneficiary Eugene H. Emmick hired L. S. Hamm, an attorney, to draft his will. The will named Robert Lucas and others (Lucas) as beneficiaries. When Emmick died, it was discovered that the will was improperly drafted, violated state law, and was therefore ineffective. Emmick's estate was transferred pursuant to the state's intestate laws. Lucas did not receive the $75,000 he would have otherwise received had the will been valid. Lucas sued Hamm for breach of the Emmick–Hamm contract to recover what he would have received under the will. Who wins? *Lucas v. Hamm*, 56 Cal.2d 583, 364 P.2d 685, 15 Cal. Rptr. 821, 1961 Cal. Lexis 321 (Supreme Court of California, 1961)

15.3 Assignment William John Cunningham, a professional basketball player, entered into a contract with Southern Sports Corporation, which owned the Carolina Cougars, a professional basketball team. The contract provided that Cunningham was to play basketball for the Cougars for a three-year period. The contract contained a provision that it could not be assigned to any other professional basketball franchise without Cunningham's approval. Subsequently, Southern Sports Corporation sold its assets, including its franchise and Cunningham's contract, to the Munchak Corporation (Munchak). There was no change in the location of the Cougars after the purchase. When Cunningham refused to play for the new owners, Munchak sued to enforce Cunningham's contract. Is Cunningham's contract assignable to the new owner? *Munchak Corporation v. Cunningham*, 457 F.2d 721, 1972 U.S. App. Lexis 10272 (United States Court of Appeals for the Fourth Circuit, 1972)

15.4 Delegation of Duties C.W. Milford owned a registered quarter horse named Hired Chico. Milford sold the horse to Norman Stewart. Recognizing that Hired Chico was a good stud, Milford included the following provision in the written contract that was signed by both parties: "I, C.W. Milford, reserve two breedings each year on Hired Chico registration #403692 for the life of this stud horse regardless of whom the horse may be sold to." The agreement was filed with the County Court Clerk of Shelby County, Texas. Stewart later sold Hired Chico to Sam McKinnie. Prior to purchasing the horse, McKinnie read the Milford–Stewart contract and testified that he understood the terms of the contract. When McKinnie refused to grant Milford the stud services of Hired Chico, Milford sued McKinnie for breach of contract. Who wins? *McKinnie v. Milford*, 597 S.W.2d 953, 1980 Tex. App. Lexis 3345 (Court of Appeals of Texas, 1980)

15.5 Condition Shumann Investments, Inc. (Shumann) hired Pace Construction Corporation (Pace), a general contractor, to build Outlet World of Pasco County. In turn, Pace hired OBS Company, Inc. (OBS), a subcontractor, to perform the framing, drywall, insulation, and stucco work on the project. The contract between Pace and OBS stipulated, "Final payment shall not become due unless and until the following conditions precedent to final payment have been satisfied ... (c) receipt of final payment for subcontractor's work by contractor from owner." When Shumann refused to pay Pace, Pace refused to pay OBS. OBS sued Pace to recover payment. Who wins? *Pace Construction Corporation v. OBS Company, Inc.*, 531 So.2d 737, 1988 Fla. App. Lexis 4020 (Court of Appeal of Florida, 1988)

Ethics Case

15.6 Ethics Case Indiana Tri-City Plaza Bowl (Tri-City) leased a building from Charles H. Glueck for use as a bowling alley. The lease provided that Glueck was to provide adequate paved parking for the building. The lease gave Tri-City the right to approve the plans for the construction and paving of the parking lot. When Glueck submitted paving plans to Tri-City, it rejected the plans and withheld its approval. Tri-City argued that the plans were required to meet its personal satisfaction before it had to approve them. Evidence showed that the plans were commercially reasonable in the circumstances. A lawsuit was filed between Tri-City and Glueck. Who wins? Was it ethical for Tri-City to reject the plans? *Indiana Tri-City Plaza Bowl, Inc. v. Estate of Glueck*, 422 N.E.2d 670, 1981 Ind. App. Lexis 1506 (Court of Appeals of Indiana, 1981)

Notes

1. *Restatement (Second) of Contracts*, Sections 311 and 318.
2. *Restatement (Second) of Contracts*, Section 317.
3. *Restatement (Second) of Contracts*, Section 318(2).
4. *Restatement (Second) of Contracts*, Section 328.
5. *Restatement (Second) of Contracts*, Section 302.
6. *Restatement (Second) of Contracts*, Section 302(1)(b).
7. *Restatement (Second) of Contracts*, Section 224, defines *condition* as "an event, not certain to occur, which must occur, unless its nonperformance is excused, before performance under a contract is due."
8. *Restatement (Second) of Contracts*, Section 224.
9. *Restatement (Second) of Contracts*, Section 281.
10. *Restatement (Second) of Contracts*, Section 261.
11. *Restatement (Second) of Contracts*, Section 262.
12. *Restatement (Second) of Contracts*, Section 263.
13. *Restatement (Second) of Contracts*, Section 264.

CHAPTER

16

Breach of Contract and Remedies

RIO DE JANEIRO, BRAZIL

International contracts are entered into by businesses located in different countries.

GÃ¡bor KovÃ¡cs/123RF

Learning Objectives

After studying this chapter, you should be able to:

16.1 Describe complete, substantial, and inferior performance of contractual duties.

16.2 Describe the monetary damages that can be awarded when there is a breach of contract.

16.3 Define *compensatory damages* and describe when they can be awarded.

16.4 Define *consequential damages* and describe when they can be awarded.

16.5 Define *nominal damages* and describe when they can be awarded.

16.6 Explain mitigation of damages and describe when this is required.

16.7 Define *liquidated damages* and describe when they are awarded.

16.8 Describe rescission of a contract and the payment of restitution.

16.9 Describe the equitable remedies of specific performance, reformation, and injunction.

16.10 Identify when contract disputes are to be resolved using arbitration.

16.11 Describe torts associated with contracts, including the tort of bad faith.

"Contracts must not be sports of an idle hour, mere matters of pleasantry and badinage, never intended by the parties to have any serious effect whatsoever."

— Lord Stowell
Dalrymple v. Dalrymple
2 Hag. Con. 54 (1811)

Introduction to Breach of Contract and Remedies

There are three levels of performance of a contract: *complete, substantial*, and *inferior*. Complete (or strict) performance by a party discharges that party's duties under the contract. Substantial performance constitutes a minor breach of the contract. Inferior performance constitutes a material breach that impairs or destroys the essence of the contract. Various remedies may be obtained by a nonbreaching party if a **breach of contract** occurs—that is, if a contracting party fails to perform an absolute duty owed under a contract.[1]

Men keep their agreements when it is an advantage to both parties not to break them.

Solon
(c. 600 BCE)

breach of contract
A situation that occurs if one or both of the parties do not perform their duties as specified in the contract.

The most common remedy for a breach of contract is an award of *monetary damages*, often called the "law remedy." Monetary damages include *compensatory, consequential, liquidated*, and *nominal* damages. If a monetary award does not provide adequate relief, however, the court may order any one of several *equitable remedies*, including *specific performance, reformation*, and *injunction*. Equitable remedies are based on the concept of fairness.

This chapter discusses breach of contract and the remedies available to the nonbreaching party.

Performance and Breach

16.1 Describe complete, substantial, and inferior performance of contractual duties.

If a contractual duty has not been discharged (i.e., terminated) or excused (i.e., relieved of legal liability), the contracting party owes an absolute duty (i.e., covenant) to perform the duty. As mentioned in the chapter introduction, there are three types of performance of a contract: (1) *complete performance*, (2) *substantial performance* (or minor breach), and (3) *inferior performance* (or material breach). A breach of contract occurs if one or both parties do not perform the duties as specified in the contract. These concepts are discussed in the following paragraphs.

Complete Performance

Most contracts are discharged by the **complete performance**, or **strict performance**, of the contracting parties. Complete performance occurs when a party to a contract renders performance exactly as required by the contract. A fully performed contract is called an **executed contract**.

complete performance (strict performance)
A situation in which a party to a contract renders performance exactly as required by the contract. Complete performance discharges that party's obligations under the contract.

Tender of performance, or **tender**, also discharges a party's contractual obligations. Tender is an unconditional and absolute offer by a contracting party to perform its obligations under the contract.

tender of performance (tender)
An unconditional and absolute offer by a contracting party to perform his or her obligations under a contract.

Example Camille, who owns a women's retail store, contracts to purchase high-fashion blue jeans from a manufacturer for $100,000. At the time of performance, Camille tenders the $100,000. Camille has performed her obligation under the contract once she tenders the $100,000 to the manufacturer. The manufacturer tenders the jeans to Camille when required to do so, and Camille accepts the jeans. There is a complete performance of the contract.

Substantial Performance: Minor Breach

substantial performance
Performance by a contracting party that deviates only slightly from complete performance.

minor breach
A breach that occurs when a party renders substantial performance of his or her contractual duties.

Substantial performance occurs when there has been a **minor breach** of contract. In other words, it occurs when a party to a contract renders performance that deviates slightly from complete performance. The nonbreaching party may

Exhibit 16.1 SUBSTANTIAL PERFORMANCE: MINOR BREACH

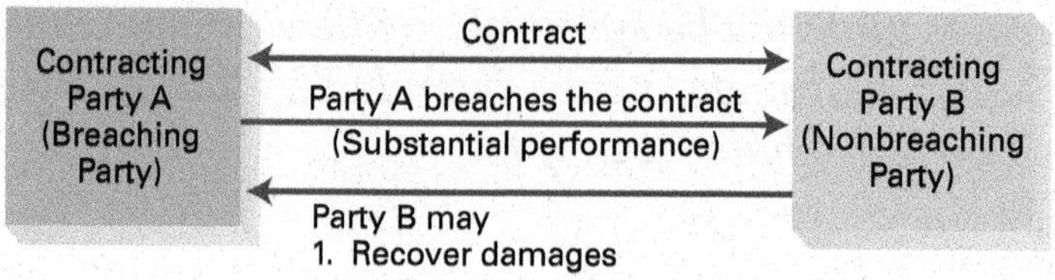

try to convince the breaching party to elevate its performance to complete performance. If the breaching party does not correct the breach, the nonbreaching party can sue to recover *damages* by (1) deducting the cost to repair the defect from the contract price and remitting the balance to the breaching party or (2) suing the breaching party to recover the cost to repair the defect if the breaching party has already been paid (see Exhibit 16.1).

Examples Rachel contracts with Beck Corporation to have Beck construct a high-rise office building for $50 million. The architectural plans call for installation of triple-pane windows in the building. Beck constructs the building exactly to plan except that it installs double-pane windows. There has been substantial performance. It would cost $4 million to install the correct windows. If Beck agrees to replace the windows and does so, its performance is elevated to complete performance, and Rachel must pay the entire contract price. However, if Rachel has to hire someone else to replace the windows, she may deduct this cost of repair of $4 million from the contract price of $50 million and remit the difference of $46 million to Beck. If Rachel had already paid the $50 million and Beck refuses to install the proper windows, Rachel can sue and recover the $4 million.

Inferior Performance: Material Breach

material breach
A breach that occurs when a party renders inferior performance of his or her contractual duties.

inferior performance
A situation in which a party fails to perform express or implied contractual obligations and impairs or destroys the essence of a contract.

A **material breach** of a contract occurs when a party renders **inferior performance** of its contractual obligations that impairs or destroys the essence of the contract. There is no clear line between a minor breach and a material breach. A determination is made on a case-by-case basis.

Where there has been a material breach of contract, the nonbreaching party may *rescind* the contract and seek restitution of any compensation paid under the contract to the breaching party. The nonbreaching party is discharged from any further performance under the contract.[2] Alternatively, the nonbreaching party may treat the contract as being in effect and sue the breaching party to recover *damages* (see Exhibit 16.2).

Example A university contracts with a general contractor to build a new 400,000-square-foot building with classroom space for 1,000 students. The contract price is $250 million. However, the completed building cannot support more than 500 students because the contractor used inferior materials. The defect cannot be repaired without rebuilding the entire structure. Because this is a material breach, the university may rescind the contract, recover any money that it has paid to the contractor, and require the contractor to remove the building. The university is discharged of any obligations under the contract and is free to employ another contractor to rebuild the building. However, assume that the

Exhibit 16.2 INFERIOR PERFORMANCE: MATERIAL BREACH

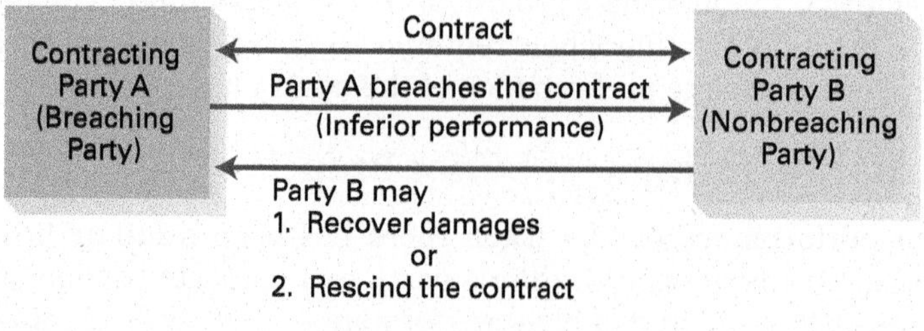

building does meet building codes so that it can be used as an administration building of the university. Thus, as an alternative remedy, the university could accept the building as an administration building, which has a value of $80 million. If the university accepts the building as an administration building, the university would owe $80 million to the contractor.

CONCEPT SUMMARY

TYPES OF PERFORMANCE

Type of Performance	Legal Consequence
Complete performance	The contract is discharged.
Substantial performance (minor breach)	The nonbreaching party may recover damages caused by the breach.
Inferior performance (material breach)	The nonbreaching party may either (1) rescind the contract and recover restitution or (2) affirm the contract and recover damages.

Anticipatory Breach

Anticipatory breach (or **anticipatory repudiation**) of a contract occurs when a contracting party informs the other party in advance that it will not perform the contractual duties when due. This type of material breach can be expressly stated or implied from the conduct of the repudiator. Where there is an anticipatory repudiation, the nonbreaching party's obligations under the contract are discharged immediately. The nonbreaching party also has the right to sue the repudiating party when the anticipatory breach occurs; there is no need to wait until performance is due.[3]

anticipatory breach (anticipatory repudiation)
A breach that occurs when one contracting party informs the other that he or she will not perform his or her contractual duties when due.

Monetary Damages

16.2 Describe the monetary damages that can be awarded when there is a breach of contract.

Where there has been a breach of a contract, the nonbreaching party may recover **monetary damages** from a breaching party. Monetary damages are available whether the breach was minor or material. Monetary damages are sometimes referred to as **dollar damages**. Several types of monetary damages may be awarded. These include *compensatory, consequential, liquidated*, and *nominal damages*. Each is discussed in the following paragraphs.

monetary damages
An award of money.

Compensatory Damages

16.3 Define *compensatory damages* and describe when they can be awarded.

Compensatory damages are intended to compensate a nonbreaching party for the loss of the bargain. In other words, they place the nonbreaching party in the same position as if the contract had been fully performed by restoring the "benefit of the bargain."

Example Leader Laboratories enters into a written contract to employ Wei as a chief operations officer of the company for three years, at a salary of $20,000 per month. After one year at work, Leader informs Wei that her employment is terminated. This is a material breach of the contract. If Wei is unable to find a comparable job, Wei can sue Leader and recover $480,000 (24 months × $20,000) as compensatory damages. However, if after six months of being unemployed Wei finds a comparable job that pays $20,000 per month, Wei can recover $120,000 from Leader (6 months × $20,000) as compensatory damages. In these examples, the damages awarded to Wei place her in the same situation as if her contract with Leader had been performed.

compensatory damages
An award of money intended to compensate a nonbreaching party for the loss of the bargain. Compensatory damages place the nonbreaching party in the same position as if the contract had been fully performed by restoring the "benefit of the bargain."

It is a vain thing to imagine a right without a remedy: for want of right and want of remedy are reciprocal.

Lord Chief Justice Holt
Ashby v. White (1703)

The amount of compensatory damages that will be awarded for breach of contract depends on the type of contract involved and which party breached the contract. The award of compensatory damages in some special types of contracts is discussed in the following paragraphs.

Sale of a Good

Compensatory damages for a breach of a sales contract involving goods are governed by the Uniform Commercial Code (UCC). The usual measure of damages for a breach of a sales contract is the difference between the contract price and the market price of the goods at the time and place the goods were to be delivered.[4]

Example Revlon, Inc. contracts to buy a piece of equipment from Greenway Supply Co. for $80,000. Greenway does not deliver the equipment to Revlon when it is required to do so. Revlon purchases the equipment from another vendor but has to pay $100,000 because the current market price for the equipment has risen. Revlon can recover $20,000 from Greenway—the difference between the market price paid ($100,000) and the contract price ($80,000)—in compensatory damages.

Construction Contract

Every unjust decision is a reproach to the law or the judge who administers it. If the law should be in danger of doing injustice, then equity should be called in to remedy it. Equity was introduced to mitigate the rigor of the law.

Lord Denning,
Master of the Rolls
Re Vandervell's Trustees Ltd (1974)
Court of Appeal

A construction contract arises when the owner of real property contracts to have a contractor build a structure or do other construction work. The compensatory damages recoverable for a breach of a construction contract vary with the stage of completion of the project when the breach occurs.

A contractor may recover the profits he or she would have made on the contract if the owner breaches the construction contract before construction begins.

Example Beta Corporation contracts to have Ace Construction Company build a building for it for $1,200,000. It will cost Ace $900,000 in materials and labor to build the building for Beta. Ace would earn $300,000 profit on the project. If Beta Corporation breaches the contract before construction begins, Ace can recover $300,000 in "lost profits" from Beta as compensatory damages.

Example Bentel Corporation contracts to have the Ace Construction Company build a building for Bentel for $1,200,000. It will cost Ace $900,000 to construct the building. Thus, Ace will make $300,000 profit on the contract. Ace begins construction and has spent $200,000 on materials and labor before Bentel breaches the contract by terminating Ace. Here, Ace can recover $500,000, which is composed of $300,000 lost profits ($1,200,000 – $900,000) plus $200,000 expended on materials and labor. The $500,000 of compensatory damages will make Ace Construction Company "whole."

If the builder breaches a construction contract either before or during construction, the owner can recover the increased cost above the contract price that he or she has to pay to have the work completed by another contractor.

Example Ethanol Corporation contracts to have the Ace Construction Company build a building for Ethanol for $1,200,000. Just before Ace is to begin work, it breaches the contract by withdrawing from the project. Ethanol seeks new bids, and the lowest bid it receives to construct the building is $1,500,000. Here, Ethanol can recover $300,000 in compensatory damages from Ace ($1,500,000 [new contract price] – $1,200,000 [Ace's original price]).

Employment Contract

An employee whose employer breaches an employment contract can recover lost wages or salary as compensatory damages. If the employee breaches the contract, the employer can recover the costs to hire a new employee plus any increase in salary paid to the replacement.

The very definition of a good award is that it gives dissatisfaction to both parties.

Sir Thomas Plumer,
Master of the Rolls
Goodman v. Sayers (1820)

Example EBM Corporation enters into a written contract to employ Mohammad as a chief financial officer of the company for three years at a salary of $30,000 per month. Before Mohammad starts work, EBM informs Mohammad that his employment is terminated. This is a material breach of the contract. If Mohammad is unable to find a comparable job, Mohammad can recover $1,080,000 (36 months × $30,000) as compensatory damages.

Consequential Damages

16.4 Define *consequential damages* and describe when they can be awarded.

A nonbreaching party can sometimes recover **consequential damages**, or **special damages**, from the breaching party. Consequential damages are *foreseeable damages* that arise from circumstances outside a contract. To be liable for consequential damages, the breaching party must know or have reason to know that the breach will cause special damages to the other party.

consequential damages (special damages)
Foreseeable damages that arise from circumstances outside a contract. To be liable for these damages, the breaching party must know or have reason to know that the breach will cause special damages to the other party.

Example Mart, a major retailer, contracts with Mattel, a major manufacturer of toys, to purchase one million of a new toy doll produced by Mattel at $20 per doll. Mart plans to sell these dolls in its stores nationwide at $50 per doll, and Mattel is aware that Mart intends to resell the dolls. The popularity of the dolls guarantees that all the dolls purchased by Mart will be sold. If Mattel breaches this contract and fails to deliver the dolls to Mart, Mart cannot purchase the dolls elsewhere because Mattel holds the copyright and trademark on the doll. Therefore, Mart can recover the lost profits on each lost sale as consequential damages from Mattel—that is, the difference between the would-be sales price of the dolls ($50) and the purchase price of each doll ($20), or $30 lost profit per doll. In total, Mart can recover $30 million in consequential damages from Mattel ($50 − $20 = $30 × 1,000,000).

Disclaimer of Consequential Damages

Consequential damages are often disclaimed in a sales or license agreement. A **disclaimer of consequential damages** means that the breaching party is not responsible to pay consequential damages. Disclaimer of consequential damages is lawful in most instances.

Example A student installs a new software program on his computer that is licensed from a software company. The license price was $100. The software was installed, but it was defective. The software causes files in the computer, including the student's class notes, Ph.D. dissertation, and other valuable information, to be deleted. These were the only copies of the files. The student suffers a loss of having his only copies of these important materials deleted because of the newly installed software. These losses are consequential damages. However, the software license contains a disclaimer stating that the licensor is not liable for consequential damages. Therefore, the student cannot recover monetary damages for his consequential damages. The student can recover $100 in compensatory damages, however, for the license price he paid for the defective software.

Nominal Damages

16.5 Define *nominal damages* and describe when they can be awarded.

A nonbreaching party can sue a breaching party to a contract for nominal damages even if no financial loss resulted from the breach. **Nominal damages** are usually awarded in a small amount, such as $1. Cases involving nominal damages are usually brought on principle. Most courts disfavor nominal damages lawsuits because they use valuable court time and resources.

nominal damages
Damages awarded when the nonbreaching party sues the breaching party even though no financial loss has resulted from the breach. Nominal damages are usually $1 or some other small amount.

Example Arianna enters into an employment contract with Micro Corporation. It is a three-year contract, and Arianna is to be paid $100,000 per year. One year later, Micro Corporation fires Arianna. The next day, Arianna finds a better position at Macro Corporation, in the same city, paying $125,000 per year on a two-year contract. Arianna has suffered no monetary damages but could bring a civil lawsuit against Micro Corporation because of its breach and recover nominal damages (such as $1).

Mitigation of Damages

16.6 Explain mitigation of damages and describe when this is required.

If a contract has been breached, the law places a duty on the innocent nonbreaching party to make reasonable efforts to *mitigate* (i.e., avoid or reduce) the resulting damages. The extent of **mitigation of damages** required depends on the type of contract involved.

mitigation of damages
A nonbreaching party's legal duty to avoid or reduce damages caused by a breach of contract.

If an employer breaches an employment contract, the employee owes a duty to mitigate damages by trying to find substitute employment. The employee is only required to accept *comparable employment*. The courts consider factors such as compensation, rank, status, job description, and geographical location in determining the comparability of jobs.

Example Darius is employed by Software, Inc., a software company located in the Silicon Valley of California, as a software manager. His contract is for three years at $200,000 per year. If Software, Inc. terminates Darius after one year, he is under a duty to mitigate the damages that would be owed to him by Software, Inc. If Darius finds a job as a software manager at another software company located in the Silicon Valley for the same salary, he is required to take the job. However, if Darius finds a job at a similar salary as a sales manager (different job) in the Silicon Valley, or if he is offered a job as a software manager at the same salary at a software company in Los Angeles, California (different location), or if he is offered a job as a software manager at a company in the Silicon Valley but at a salary of $120,000 per year (much lower salary), he is not required to accept any of these job offers because they are not comparable jobs.

If an employee who has been dismissed improperly accepts a job that is not comparable, the employee can sue the prior employer for damages.

Critical Legal Thinking Questions

What is mitigation of damages? Why does the law impose a duty on the nonbreaching party to mitigate damages?

Examples Andrew is employed as a chief financial officer of Financial Company in New York City for a salary of $200,000 per year on a three-year contract. His employer terminates Andrew with two years left on the contract. Andrew accepts employment as a financial analyst at a new employer that pays $150,000 per year. Andrew can sue his prior employer, Financial Company, and recover $100,000 ($50,000 difference in salary per year for two years).

Liquidated Damages

16.7 Define *liquidated damages* and describe when they are awarded.

Under certain circumstances, the parties to a contract may agree in advance to the amount of damages payable on a breach of contract. These damages are called **liquidated damages**. To be lawful, the actual damages must be difficult or impracticable to determine, and the liquidated amount must be reasonable in the circumstances.[5] An enforceable **liquidated damages clause** is an exclusive remedy even if actual damages are later determined to be different from the liquidated damages.

liquidated damages
Damages that parties to a contract agree in advance should be paid if the contract is breached.

The following feature demonstrates the enforcement of a liquidated damages clause.

Business Environment

Liquidated Damages Clause Limits Recovery of Damages

"The general rule of freedom of contract includes the freedom to make a bad bargain."

—David Hamilton, Circuit Judge

Environs, Inc. is an architectural firm that designs commercial and business buildings. SAMS Hotel Group, LLC signed a contract with Environs where Environs would provide architectural services for the design of a six-story hotel in Fort Wayne, Indiana, to be built by SAMS. SAMS paid Environs a fee of $70,000. The contract between the parties limited Environs's liability for breach of contract to $70,000. The hotel structure was nearly complete when serious structural defects were discovered. The county building department condemned the building and the hotel was demolished.

SAMS sued Environs, alleging that the defendant had breached its contract by providing negligent architectural services, and sought to recover its loss of more than $4.2 million. The U.S. district court found that Environs had been negligent and breached the contract, but the court enforced the liquidated damages clause and awarded SAMS $70,000. The U.S. court of appeals agreed, stating, "The undisputed facts show that the negotiating parties were two sophisticated business entities. The general rule of freedom of contract includes the freedom to make a bad bargain." *SAMS Hotel Group, LLC v. Environs, Inc.*, 716 F.3d 432, 2013 U.S. App. Lexis 11047 (United States Court of Appeals for the Seventh Circuit, 2013)

Critical Legal Thinking Questions

Was it ethical for Environs to avoid paying the full claim? How could SAMS have protected itself from the outcome of this case?

Penalty

A liquidated damages clause is considered a **penalty** if actual damages are clearly determinable in advance or if the liquidated damages are excessive or unconscionable. If a liquidated damages clause is found to be a penalty, it is unenforceable. The nonbreaching party may then recover actual damages.

Example Rent-to-Own Store is a store that rents furniture to individuals who are often not well off financially. The renter takes physical possession of the furniture. Individuals obtain title to the furniture after having paid the cost of the furniture (which is often inflated) and interest payment (often high interest rates). Mable, an elderly person who is poor, has rented and has paid enough money to have purchased a living room set, a dining room set, and a bedroom set from Rent-to-Own Store. She therefore owns these pieces of furniture. Mable then rents a smart television from Rent-to-Own Store and signs a contract that states that if Mable falls more than three months behind in her television payments, Rent-to-Own Store can recover all of the furniture she had previously purchased from the store as liquidated damages. This is an example of a liquidated damages clause that is a penalty and that would not be enforced.

In the following case, the court had to judge whether a liquidated damage clause was an unenforceable penalty.

CASE 16.1 *FEDERAL COURT CASE Liquidated Damages*

Burke v. 401 N. Wabash Venture, LLC

714 F.3d 501, 2013 U.S. App. Lexis 7199 (2013)
United States Court of Appeals for the Seventh Circuit

"Whether a provision constitutes a valid liquidated damages clause or an unenforceable penalty clause is a question of state law."

—Ann Claire Williams, Circuit Judge

Facts

401 N. Wabash Venture, LLC is the developer of a hotel and condominium building in Chicago. Michael Burke signed a contract with the developer to buy a condominium unit and two parking spaces for $2,282,130 when the building was completed. Burke paid a deposit of $456,426—20 percent of the purchase price—as required by the purchase agreement. The purchase agreement contained a liquidated damages clause that permitted the developer to retain the deposit money if Burke did not complete the purchase of the unit.

When it came time to close the purchase, Burke refused to pay the rest of the contract price and asked the developer to refund his deposit. The developer refused to refund Burke the deposit, which it kept as liquidated damages, and resold the unit at a price higher than in the purchase agreement. Burke sued the developer in U.S. district court, alleging that the liquidated damage provision was a penalty and therefore unenforceable. The developer moved to dismiss Burke's lawsuit. The U.S. district court held that the liquidated damage clause was enforceable and dismissed Burke's lawsuit. Burke appealed.

Issue

Was the liquidated damage clause an unenforceable penalty?

Language of the Court

Whether a provision constitutes a valid liquidated damages clause or an unenforceable penalty clause is a question of state law. The U.S. district court rejected the plaintiff's argument that the liquidated damage clause was a penalty because the developer sold the unit for more than the price in the plaintiff's purchase agreement, reasoning that under the terms of the agreement, it was irrelevant to the liquidated damage issue whether the unit was later resold. We also note that the 20 percent figure is not so high as to be unenforceable on public policy grounds in Illinois.

Decision

The U.S. court of appeals affirmed the district court's decision that enforced the liquidated damages agreement permitting the developer to retain the plaintiff's deposit.

Critical Legal Thinking Questions

Why do parties include liquidated damages provisions in contracts? Should it matter that the developer kept the plaintiff's deposit and sold the unit at a higher price than the plaintiff would have paid?

CONCEPT SUMMARY

TYPES OF MONETARY DAMAGES

Type of Damage	Description
Compensatory	Damages that compensate a nonbreaching party for the loss of a bargain. It places the nonbreaching party in the same position as if the contract had been fully performed.
Consequential	Damages that compensate a nonbreaching party for foreseeable special damages that arise from circumstances outside a contract. The breaching party must or should have known that these damages would result from the breach.
Nominal	Damages awarded against the breaching party even though the nonbreaching party has suffered no financial loss because of the breach. A small amount (e.g., $1) is usually awarded.
Liquidated	An agreement by the parties in advance that sets the amount of damages recoverable in case of breach. These damages are lawful if they do not cause a penalty.

Rescission and Restitution

16.8 Describe rescission of a contract and the payment of restitution.

Rescission is an action to undo a contract. It is available where there has been a material breach of contract, fraud, duress, undue influence, or mistake. Generally, to rescind a contract, the parties must make **restitution** of the consideration they received under the contract.[6] Restitution consists of returning the goods, property, money, or other consideration received from the other party. If possible, the actual goods or property must be returned. If the goods or property have been consumed or are otherwise unavailable, restitution must be made by conveying a cash equivalent. The rescinding party must give adequate notice of the rescission to the breaching party. Rescission and restitution restore the parties to the positions they occupied prior to the contract.

rescission
An action to rescind (undo) a contract. Rescission is available if there has been a material breach of contract, fraud, duress, undue influence, or mistake.

restitution
The return of goods or property received from the other party to rescind a contract. If the actual goods or property are not available, a cash equivalent must be proffered.

Example Praline's Store contracts to purchase $1,000,000 of goods from a clothing manufacturer. Praline's pays $100,000 as a down payment, and the first $200,000 worth of goods are delivered. The goods are materially defective, and the defect cannot be cured. This breach is a material breach. Praline's can rescind the contract. Praline's is entitled to receive its $100,000 down payment back from the manufacturer, and the manufacturer is entitled to receive the goods back from Praline's.

Equitable Remedies

16.9 Describe the equitable remedies of specific performance, reformation, and injunction.

Equitable remedies are available if there has been a breach of contract that cannot be adequately compensated through a legal remedy. They are also available to prevent unjust enrichment. The most common equitable remedies are *specific performance, reformation*, and *injunction*, which are discussed in the following paragraphs.

equitable remedy
A remedy that is available if there has been a breach of contract that cannot be adequately compensated through a legal remedy or to prevent unjust enrichment.

Specific Performance

An award of **specific performance** orders the breaching party to perform the acts promised in a contract. The courts have the discretion to award this remedy if the subject matter of the contract is *unique*.[7] Specific performance is available to enforce land contracts because every piece of real property is unique. Works of art, antiques, items of sentimental value, rare coins, stamps, heirlooms, and the like also fit the requirement for uniqueness. Most other personal property does not.

specific performance
A remedy that orders the breaching party to perform the acts promised in the contract. Specific performance is usually awarded in cases in which the subject matter is unique, such as in contracts involving land, heirlooms, and paintings.

Example On September 1, Ha-Yoon enters into a contract to purchase a house from Geraldine for $1 million. The closing date is set for November 1. On November 1, Ha-Yoon brings the money to the closing, but Geraldine does not appear at the closing and thereafter refuses to sell the house to Ha-Yoon. In this case, because each piece of real estate is considered unique, Ha-Yoon can bring an action of specific performance against Geraldine and obtain a court judgment ordering Geraldine to sell the house to Ha-Yoon.

Critical Legal Thinking Questions

What is the purpose of the equitable remedy of specific performance? To what types of contracts does this equitable doctrine apply? Why would a buyer seek specific performance of a contract rather than damages?

Specific performance of personal service contracts is not granted because the courts would find it difficult or impracticable to supervise or monitor performance of such a contract.

Example A concert hall contracts with a famous singer to hold a series of concerts. Later, the singer refuses to perform. Here, the concert hall cannot require the singer to perform because it is a personal service contract. The concert hall could, however, sue to recover any payments it has made to the singer and recover any damages that it may have suffered because of the breach.

The court had to decide whether to issue an order of specific performance in the following case.

CASE 16.2 *STATE COURT CASE Specific Performance*

Alba v. Kaufmann

27 A.D.3d 816, 810 N.Y.S.2d 539, 2006 N.Y. App. Div. Lexis 2321 (2006)
Supreme Court of New York, Appellate Division

"The case law reveals that the equitable remedy of specific performance is routinely awarded in contract actions involving real property, on the premise that each parcel of real property is unique."

—Bruce Crew, Judge

Facts

Jean-Claude Kaufmann owned approximately 37 acres of real property located in the town of Stephentown, Rensselaer County, New York. The property is located in a wooded area and is improved with a 19th-century farmhouse. Kaufmann and his spouse, Christine Cacace, reside in New York City and use the property as a weekend or vacation home. Kaufmann listed the property for sale for $350,000.

Richard Alba and his spouse (Albas) looked at the property and offered Kaufmann the asking price. The parties executed a contract for sale, and the Albas paid a deposit, obtained a mortgage commitment, and procured a satisfactory home inspection and title insurance. A date for closing the transaction was set. Prior to closing, Cacace sent the Albas an email, indicating that she and Kaufmann had "a change of heart" and no longer wished to go forward with the sale. The Albas sent a reply email, stating their intent to go forward with the scheduled closing. When Kaufmann refused to close, the Albas sued, seeking specific performance, and moved for summary judgment. The supreme court of New York denied the motion. The Albas appealed.

Issue

Is an order of specific performance of the real estate contract warranted in this case?

Language of the Court

The Albas plainly discharged that burden here. In short, the record demonstrates that the Albas were ready, willing, and able to close and, but for Kaufmann's admitted refusal to do so, would have consummated the transaction. As to the remedy the Albas seek, the case law reveals that the equitable remedy of specific performance is routinely awarded in contract actions involving real property, on the premise that each parcel of real property is unique. Moreover, volitional unwillingness, as distinguished from good faith inability, to meet contractual obligations furnishes neither a ground for cancellation of the contract nor a defense against its specific performance.

Decision

The appellate court, as a matter of law, granted the Albas' motion for summary judgment and ordered Kaufmann specifically to perform the real estate contract.

Critical Legal Thinking Questions

What is specific performance? Was it ethical for Kaufmann to try to back out of the contract? Was it ethical for the buyer to sue for specific performance when the seller had a "change of heart" and no longer wanted to sell?

Reformation

reformation
An equitable doctrine that permits the court to rewrite a contract to express the parties' true intentions.

Reformation is an equitable doctrine that permits the court to rewrite a contract to express the parties' true intentions. Reformation is usually available to correct clerical errors in contracts.

Example A clerical error is made during the preparation of a contract, and both parties sign the contract without discovering the error. If a dispute later arises, the court can reform the contract to correct the clerical error to read as the parties originally intended.

Injunction

An **injunction** is a court order that prohibits a person from doing a certain act. To obtain an injunction, the requesting party must show that he or she will suffer irreparable injury if the injunction is not issued.

injunction
A court order that prohibits a person from doing a certain act.

Example A professional basketball team enters into a five-year employment contract with a basketball player. The basketball player breaches the contract and enters into a contract to play for a competing professional basketball team. Here, the first team can obtain an injunction to prevent the basketball player from playing for the other team during the remaining term of the original contract.

CONCEPT SUMMARY
TYPES OF EQUITABLE REMEDIES

Type of Equitable Remedy	Description
Specific performance	A court orders the breaching party to perform the acts promised in the contract. The subject matter of the contract must be unique.
Reformation	A court rewrites a contract to express the parties' true intentions. This remedy is usually used to correct clerical errors.
Injunction	A court prohibits a party from doing a certain act. Injunctions are available in contract actions only in limited circumstances.

Arbitration of Contract Disputes

16.10 Identify when contract disputes are to be resolved using arbitration.

Many contract disputes are heard and decided by the court system. In the contract area, however, some contract disputes are heard and decided through **arbitration**. Arbitration is a nonjudicial, private resolution of a contract dispute. An arbitrator, not a judge or jury, renders a decision in the case. Most arbitration agreements stipulate **binding arbitration**, that is, the arbitrator's decision cannot be appealed to the courts. Arbitration occurs if the parties have entered into an **arbitration agreement**, either as part of their contract or as a separate agreement. Many consumer and business contracts contain arbitration clauses.

arbitration
A nonjudicial, private resolution of a contract dispute.

Examples Social media contracts, software licenses, credit card agreements, mortgages, sales contracts, automobile leases, employment contracts, electronic contracts, and many other contracts contain arbitration clauses.

The U.S. Congress has enacted the **Federal Arbitration Act (FAA)**,[8] which promotes the arbitration of contract disputes whether the dispute involves federal or state law. The U.S. Supreme Court has upheld the act's national policy favoring arbitration and the enforcement of arbitration agreements.[9]

In the following case, the court had to decide whether an arbitration clause in a contract was enforceable.

Critical Legal Thinking Questions

Why do so many form contracts contain arbitration clauses? What percent of the contracts that you enter into contain arbitration agreements?

CASE 16.3 FEDERAL COURT CASE Arbitration of a Contract Dispute

Mance v. Mercedes-Benz USA

901 F.Supp.2d 1147, 2012 U.S. Dist. Lexis 140778 (2012)
United States District Court for the Northern District of California

"The arbitration provision was highlighted, apparent, and not oppressive, and it should not have taken Mr. Mance by surprise."

—Laurel Beeler, Judge

Facts

Demetrius Mance purchased a new Mercedes-Benz E350 automobile from a Mercedes-Benz dealer in Sacramento, California. The automobile was distributed by Mercedes-Benz USA. To purchase the car, Mance signed a retail installment contract. In the contract, Mercedes-Benz warranted to preserve and maintain the utility and performance of the vehicle. The contract contained an arbitration clause that states that any claim or dispute between the parties will be decided by arbitration and not by a court proceeding. The arbitration clause was highlighted by bold, capitalized text. The arbitration clause provided for binding, nonappealable arbitration.

Mance experienced numerous problems with the automobile, but Mercedes-Benz did not repair the car satisfactorily, according to Mance. Mance filed a lawsuit in U.S. district court against Mercedes-Benz for breach of express and implied warranties, alleging that the arbitration clause was unconscionable. Mercedes-Benz made a motion for an order compelling Mance to arbitrate his claims.

Issue

Is the arbitration clause enforceable?

Language of the Court

The arbitration provision was highlighted, apparent, and not oppressive, and it should not have taken Mr. Mance by surprise. He argues that the binding arbitration would leave him with limited appeal rights, but conclusiveness is one of the primary purposes of arbitration. The arbitration clause provides Mr. Mance with a choice of two common arbitration associations and allows him to suggest an alternative. Mr. Mance's unconscionability argument fails.

Decision

The U.S. district court held that the arbitration clause was enforceable and granted Mercedes-Benz's motion to compel arbitration.

Critical Legal Thinking Questions

Is it ethical for sellers to make consumers go to arbitration rather than to court? Did Mance know that he was subject to the arbitration agreement?

Torts Associated with Contracts

16.11 Describe torts associated with contracts, including the tort of bad faith.

The recovery for breach of contract is usually limited to contract damages. A party who can prove a contract-related **tort**, however, may also recover tort damages. Tort damages include compensation for personal injury, pain and suffering, emotional distress, and possibly punitive damages. Generally, punitive damages are not recoverable for breach of contract. They are recoverable, however, for certain tortious conduct that may be associated with the nonperformance of a contract.

The major torts associated with contracts are *intentional interference with contractual relations* and *breach of the implied covenant of good faith and fair dealing*. These torts are discussed in the following paragraphs.

Intentional Interference with Contractual Relations

intentional interference with contractual relations
A tort that arises when a third party induces a contracting party to breach the contract with another party.

A party to a contract may sue any third party who intentionally interferes with the contract and causes that party injury. The third party does not have to have acted with malice or bad faith. This tort, which is known as the tort of **intentional interference with contractual relations**, usually arises when a third party induces a contracting party to breach a contract with another party. The following elements must be shown:

1. A valid, enforceable contract between the contracting parties
2. Third-party knowledge of this contract
3. Third-party inducement to breach the contract

A third party can contract with the breaching party without becoming liable for this tort if a contracting party has already breached the contract, and thus, the third party cannot be held to have induced a breach of the other parties' contract.

Example A professional football player signs a five-year contract to play football for a certain professional football team. Two years into the contract, another professional football team, with full knowledge of the player's contract with the other team, offers the player twice the amount of money that he is currently making to breach his contract and sign and play with the second football team. The player breaches his contract and signs to play for the second team. Here, the second team intentionally interfered with the player's contract with the first team. The first team can recover tort damages—including punitive damages—from the second team for the tort of intentional interference with a contract.

The following feature discusses the implied covenant of good faith and fair dealing.

Critical Legal Thinking Questions

Why is the covenant of good faith and fair dealing implied in some contracts? Is it difficult to define *bad faith*?

covenant of good faith and fair dealing

An implied covenant under which the parties to a contract not only are held to the express terms of the contract but also are required to act in "good faith" and deal fairly in all respects in obtaining the objective of the contract.

Critical Legal Thinking

Implied Covenant of Good Faith and Fair Dealing

Contracts usually are enforced based on the express terms of the contract. However, some states permit a court to imply a covenant called the **covenant of good faith and fair dealing** in certain types of contracts. Under this implied covenant the parties to a contract are not only held to the express terms of the contract but are also required to act in good faith and deal fairly in all respects in obtaining the objective of the contract.

This covenant of good faith and fair dealing is usually implied in contracts where the parties have a special relationship that involves a fiduciary duty. Contracts between insurance companies and insureds, publishing agreements between publishers and authors, and employment contracts are often included under this implied covenant.

A breach of the implied covenant of good faith and fair dealing is a *tort* for which tort damages are recoverable. A court can award punitive damages for the breach if the circumstances warrant. Breach of the implied covenant of good faith and fair dealing is often referred to as the **tort of bad faith**.

Example An automobile owner (called the insured) has an automobile insurance policy with an insurance company that provides for the payment of up to $200,000 for medical expenses, pain and suffering, and other injuries incurred by anyone who is injured if the insured causes an automobile accident.

The insured driver causes an automobile accident whereby he seriously injures another driver. The other driver incurs medical expenses of $100,000 and will suffer permanent injuries because of the accident. The injured party sues the insured and his insurance company for $1 million to recover damages for medical expenses, future medical expenses, and pain and suffering. The injured party makes an offer to the insurance company whereby he will accept the automobile insurance policy limit of $200,000 in exchange for releasing the insurance company and the insured of any future liability. This is often done to settle a case quickly and to avoid the risks of going to trial.

Although this is a reasonable settlement offer, the insurance company refuses to settle. The case goes to trial, and the jury awards the injured party $1 million. The insurance company pays the policy limit of $200,000, leaving an $800,000 judgment for the insured to pay. If the insured has any assets, they will have to be used to pay the judgment. If the insured does not have the ability to pay, he might have to file for bankruptcy.

The insured sues his insurance company, alleging that the insurance company breached the implied covenant of good faith and fair dealing by refusing to settle the lawsuit within the policy limits. Under these facts, the jury awards the insured $800,000 in compensatory damages and $2 million in punitive damages against the insurance company based on its bad faith in handling the claim.

The implied covenant of good faith and fair dealing is an evolving area of the law.

Critical Legal Thinking Questions

What is the implied covenant of good faith and fair dealing? Why is it called a tort of bad faith? Do you think that the possibility of an award of punitive damages will curtail some abusive conduct by businesses? Should this covenant be implied in all contracts?

Key Terms and Concepts

Anticipatory breach (anticipatory repudiation) (289)
Arbitration (297)
Arbitration agreement (297)
Binding arbitration (297)
Breach of contract (287)
Compensatory damages (289)
Complete performance (strict performance) (287)
Consequential damages (special damages) (291)
Covenant of good faith and fair dealing (299)
Disclaimer of consequential damages (291)
Equitable remedies (295)
Executed contract (287)
Federal Arbitration Act (FAA) (297)
Inferior performance (288)
Injunction (297)
Intentional interference with contractual relations (298)
Liquidated damages (293)
Liquidated damages clause (293)
Material breach (288)
Minor breach (287)
Mitigation of damages (292)
Monetary damages (dollar damages) (289)
Nominal damages (292)
Penalty (293)
Reformation (296)
Rescission (295)
Restitution (295)
Specific performance (295)
Substantial performance (287)
Tender of performance (tender) (287)
Tort (298)
Tort of bad faith (299)

Critical Legal Thinking Cases

16.1 Liquidated Damages A 72-story luxury condominium building was to be constructed at 845 United Nations Plaza in Manhattan, New York. Before the building was constructed, 845 UN Limited Partnership (845 UN) began selling condominiums at the building. The condominium offering plan required a nonrefundable down payment of 25 percent of the purchase price. The purchase contract provided that if a purchaser defaulted and did not complete the purchase, 845 UN could keep the 25 percent down payment as liquidated damages.

Cem Uzan and Hakan Uzan each contracted to purchase two condominium units on the top floors of the building. Both Cem and Hakan were represented by attorneys. Over the course of two years, while the building was being constructed, the brothers paid the 25 percent nonrefundable down payment of $8 million. On September 11, 2001, before the building was complete, terrorists attacked New York City by flying two planes into the World Trade Center, the city's two tallest buildings, murdering thousands of people.

Cem and Hakan sent letters to 845 UN, rescinding their purchase agreements because of the terrorist attack that occurred on September 11. Thus, 845 UN terminated the four purchase agreements and kept the 25 percent down payments on the four condominiums as liquidated damages. Cem and Hakan sued 845 UN, alleging that the money should be returned to them. However, 845 UN defended, arguing that the 25 percent nonrefundable down payment was an enforceable liquidated damages clause. Is the liquidated damage clause enforceable? *Uzan v. 845 UN Limited Partnership*, 10 A.D.3d 230, 778 N.Y.S.2d 171, 2004 N.Y. App. Div. Lexis 8362 (Supreme Court of New York, Appellate Division, 2004)

16.2 Liquidated Damages California and Hawaiian Sugar Company (C&H), a California corporation, is an agricultural cooperative owned by 14 sugar plantations in Hawaii. It transports raw sugar to its refinery in Crockett, California. Sugar is a seasonal crop, with about 70 percent of the harvest occurring between April and October. C&H requires reliable seasonal shipping of the raw sugar from Hawaii to California. Sugar stored on the ground or left unharvested suffers a loss of sucrose and goes to waste.

After C&H was notified by its normal shipper that it would be withdrawing its services at a specified date in the future, C&H commissioned the design of a large hybrid vessel—a tug of a catamaran design consisting of a barge attached to the tug. After substantial negotiation, C&H contracted with Sun Ship, Inc. (Sun Ship), a Pennsylvania corporation, to build the vessel for $25,405,000. The contract gave Sun Ship 1¾ years to build and deliver the ship to C&H. The contract also contained a liquidated damages clause calling for a payment of $17,000 per day for each day that the vessel was not delivered to C&H after the agreed-on delivery date. Sun Ship did not complete the vessel until 8½ months after the agreed-on delivery date. On delivery, the vessel was commissioned and christened the *Moku Pahu*.

During the season that the boat had not been delivered, C&H was able to find other means of shipping the crop from Hawaii to its California refinery. Evidence established that actual damages suffered by C&H because of the nonavailability of the vessel from Sun Ship were $368,000. When Sun Ship refused to pay the liquidated damages, C&H filed suit to require payment of $4,413,000 in liquidated damages under the contract. Can C&H recover the liquidated damages from Sun Ship? *California and Hawaiian Sugar Company v. Sun Ship, Inc.*, 794 F.2d 1433, 1986 U.S. App. Lexis 27376 (United States Court of Appeals for the Ninth Circuit, 1986)

16.3 **Damages** Hawaiian Telephone Company entered into a contract with Microform Data Systems, Inc. (Microform), for Microform to provide a computerized assistance system that would handle 15,000 calls per hour with a one-second response time and with a "nonstop" feature to allow automatic recovery from any component failure. The contract called for installation of the host computer no later than mid-February of the next year. Microform was not able to meet the initial installation date, and at that time, it was determined that Microform was at least nine months away from providing a system that met contract specifications. Hawaiian Telephone canceled the contract and sued Microform for damages. Did Microform materially breach the contract? Can Hawaiian Telephone recover damages? *Hawaiian Telephone Co. v. Microform Data Systems Inc.*, 829 F.2d 919, 1987 U.S. App. Lexis 13425 (United States Court of Appeals for the Ninth Circuit, 1987)

16.4 **Damages** Ptarmigan Investment Company (Ptarmigan), a partnership, entered into a contract with Gundersons, Inc. (Gundersons), a South Dakota corporation in the business of golf course construction. The contract provided that Gundersons would construct a golf course for Ptarmigan for a contract price of $1,294,129. Gundersons immediately started work and completed about one-third of the work by about three months later, when bad weather forced cessation of most work. Ptarmigan paid Gundersons for the work to that date. The following spring, Ptarmigan ran out of funds and was unable to pay for the completion of the golf course. Gundersons sued Ptarmigan and its individual partners to recover the lost profits that it would have made on the remaining two-thirds of the contract. Can Gundersons recover these lost profits as damages? *Gundersons, Inc. v. Ptarmigan Investment Company*, 678 P.2d 1061, 1983 Colo. App. Lexis 1133 (Court of Appeals of Colorado, 1983)

Ethics Cases

16.5 **Ethics Case** Liz Claiborne, Inc. (Claiborne) is a large maker of sportswear in the United States and a well-known name in fashion, with sales of more than $1 billion per year. Claiborne distributes its products through 9,000 retail outlets in the United States. Avon Products, Inc. (Avon) is a major producer of fragrances, toiletries, and cosmetics, with annual sales of more than $3 billion per year. Claiborne, which desired to promote its well-known name on perfumes and cosmetics, entered into a joint venture with Avon whereby Claiborne would make available its names, trademarks, and marketing experience and Avon would engage in the procurement and manufacture of the fragrances, toiletries, and cosmetics. The parties would equally share the financial requirements of the joint venture. During its first year of operation, the joint venture had sales of more than $16 million. In the second year, sales increased to $26 million, making it one of the fastest-growing fragrance and cosmetic lines in the country. One year later, Avon sought to "uncouple" the joint venture. Avon thereafter refused to procure and manufacture the line of fragrances and cosmetics for the joint venture. When Claiborne could not obtain the necessary fragrances and cosmetics from any other source for the fall/Christmas season, Claiborne sued Avon for breach of contract, seeking specific performance of the contract by Avon. Is specific performance an appropriate remedy in this case? Did Avon act ethically in refusing to perform the contract? *Liz Claiborne, Inc. v. Avon Products, Inc.*, 141 A.D.2d 329, 530 N.Y.S.2d 425, 1988 N.Y. App. Div. Lexis 6423 (Supreme Court of New York, 1988)

16.6 **Ethics Case** On Halloween Day, Christine Narvaez drove her automobile onto the parking lot of a busy supermarket. Narvaez had her 2-year-old grandchild with her. The youngster was riding, unconstrained, in a booster seat. Narvaez saw a friend and decided to stop for a brief chat. She parked and exited the car, leaving the keys in the ignition and the motor running. The youngster crawled behind the wheel, slipped the car into gear, and set it in motion. The car struck Marguerite O'Neill, a woman in her eighties, pinned her between the Narvaez car and another car, and slowly crushed the woman's trapped body.

O'Neill suffered a crushed hip, a broken arm, and four cracked ribs, and she lost more than 40 percent of her blood supply from internal bleeding. She spent one month in a hospital's intensive care unit and had to be placed in a nursing home and was deprived of the ability to live independently.

Narvaez carried the $20,000 minimum amount of liability insurance allowed by law. She was insured by Gallant Insurance Company. O'Neill's medical bills totaled $105,000. O'Neill sued Narvaez and her insurance company, Gallant. O'Neill's attorney demanded the policy limit of $20,000 from Gallant in settlement of O'Neill's claim and offered a complete release from liability for Narvaez. Three Gallant insurance adjusters, its claims manager, and the lawyer of the law firm representing

Gallant for the case all stated to John Moss, Gallant's executive vice president, that Gallant should accept the settlement offer. Moss rejected their advice and refused to settle the case.

One year later, on the eve of trial, Moss offered to settle for the $20,000 policy limit, but O'Neill then refused. The case went to trial, and the jury returned a verdict against Narvaez of $731,063. Gallant paid $20,000 of this amount, closed its file, and left Narvaez liable for the $711,063 excess judgment. To settle her debt to O'Neill, Narvaez assigned her claims against Gallant to O'Neill. O'Neill then sued Gallant for a bad faith tort for breaching the implied covenant of good faith and fair dealing that Gallant owed to Narvaez to settle the case. Is Gallant Insurance Company liable for a bad faith tort? Did Gallant act unethically? *O'Neill v. Gallant Insurance Company*, 769 N.E.2d 100, 2002 Ill. App. Lexis 311 (Appellate Court of Illinois, 2002)

Notes

1. *Restatement (Second) of Contracts*, Section 235(2).
2. *Restatement (Second) of Contracts*, Section 241.
3. *Restatement (Second) of Contracts*, Section 253; UCC Section 2-610.
4. UCC Sections 2-708 and 2-713.
5. *Restatement (Second) of Contracts*, Section 356(1).
6. *Restatement (Second) of Contracts*, Section 370.
7. *Restatement (Second) of Contracts*, Section 359.
8. 9 U.S.C. Section 1 *et seq.*
9. *Nitro-Lift Technologies, L.L.C. v. Howard*, 568 U.S. 17, 133 S.Ct. 500, 2012 U.S. Lexis 8897 (Supreme Court of the United States, 2012).

CHAPTER

17 Digital Law and E-Commerce

Mama_mia/Shutterstock

DIGITAL LAW AND E-COMMERCE
The development of the internet and electronic commerce has required courts to apply existing law to online commerce transactions and e-contracts, and has spurred the U.S. Congress and state legislatures to enact new laws that govern the formation and enforcement of e-contracts.

Learning Objectives

After studying this chapter, you should be able to:

17.1 Explain how email contracts and text contracts are formed.

17.2 Describe electronic commerce and web contracts.

17.3 Describe the provisions of the Electronic Signatures in Global and National Commerce Act (E-SIGN Act).

17.4 Describe electronic licensing of software and information rights.

17.5 List and describe laws that regulate unfair information technology practices.

17.6 Define *domain name* and describe how domain names are registered and protected.

> *"Through the use of chat rooms, any person with a phone line can become a town crier with a voice that resonates farther than it could from any soapbox. Through the use of web pages, mail exploders, and newsgroups, the same individual can become a pamphleteer."*
>
> — *John Paul Stevens, Justice*
> *Reno v. American Civil Liberties Union*
> *521 U.S. 844, 117 S.Ct. 2329, 1997 U.S. Lexis 4037 (Supreme Court of the United States, 1997)*

Introduction to Digital Law and E-Commerce

electronic commerce (e-commerce)
The sale, lease, or licensing of goods and services using the internet.

The internet delivers a large amount of digital content, including the streaming of movies and music. Social media sites are used by countless millions to communicate with each other. **Electronic commerce**, or **e-commerce**, using the internet, accounts for approximately 15 percent of the sale, lease, or licensing of goods and services.

Federal and state laws that existed before the advent of the information age have been applied to new digital technologies. In addition, federal and state governments have enacted new laws that apply directly to information technology. This chapter covers many of these laws and their application, including laws relating to e-commerce, e-contracts, licensing of software, the internet, social media, and other digital technology.

Email and Text Contracts

17.1 Explain how email contracts and text contracts are formed.

Electronic mail, or **email**, and **text messaging**, or **texting**, are two of the most widely used methods of communication. Using email and text messages, individuals around the world can communicate instantaneously with one another. In many instances, email and texting are replacing telephone and paper communication between individuals and businesses.

electronic mail contract (email contract)
A contract entered into by the parties by use of email.

text contract
A contract entered into by the parties by use of text messaging.

Many contracts are now completed by via email. These are referred to as **electronic mail contracts**, or **email contracts**. Contracts formed using text messaging are referred to as **text contracts**. Email and text contracts are enforceable so long as they meet the requirements necessary to form a traditional contract, including agreement, consideration, capacity, and lawful object. Traditional challenges to the enforcement of a contract, such as fraud, duress, intoxication, or insanity, may be asserted against the enforcement of email contracts.

Email and text contracts usually meet the requirements of the Statute of Frauds, which requires certain contracts to be in writing, including contracts for the sale of real estate, contracts for the sale of goods that cost $500 or more, and other contracts listed in the relevant Statute of Frauds.

The use of email and text communication is often somewhat informal. In addition, an email or text contract may not have the comprehensive formality of a paper contract that includes the final terms and conditions of the parties' agreement. The terms of the parties' agreement may have to be gleaned from several emails or texts that have been communicated between the parties. In such case, the court can integrate several emails or texts to determine the terms of the parties' agreement.

E-Commerce and Web Contracts

17.2 Describe electronic commerce and web contracts.

Electronic contracts, also called **e-contracts**, have increased as a means of conducting personal and commercial business. Internet sellers, lessors, and licensors use websites to sell and lease goods and services and to license software and other intellectual property. Websites such as **www.amazon.com**, **www.microsoft.com**, and **www.ebay.com** use the internet extensively to sell, lease, or license goods, services, and intellectual property. Assuming the elements to establish a traditional contract are present, **web contracts** are valid and enforceable.

In the following case, the court considered whether a web contract was enforceable.

web contract
A contract entered into by purchasing, leasing, or licensing goods, services, software, or other intellectual property from websites operated by sellers, lessors, and licensors.

Information Technology

CASE 17.1 *STATE COURT CASE Web Contract*

Hubbert v. Dell Corporation

835 N.E.2d 113, 2005 Ill. App. Lexis 808 (2005)
Appellate Court of Illinois

"The blue hyperlinks on the defendant's web pages, constituting the five-step process for ordering the computers, should be treated the same as a multipage written paper contract."

—Robert Hopkins, Justice

Facts

Plaintiffs Dewayne Hubbert, Elden Craft, Chris Grout, and Rhonda Byington purchased computers from Dell Corporation online through Dell's website. To make their purchase, each of the plaintiffs completed online order forms on five pages on Dell's website. On each of the five pages, Dell's terms and conditions of sale were accessible by clicking on a blue hyperlink. To understand the terms and conditions, the plaintiffs would have had to click on the blue hyperlink and read the terms and conditions of sale. On the last page of the five-page order form, the following statement appeared: "All sales are subject to Dell's Terms and Conditions of Sale."

The plaintiffs filed a lawsuit against Dell, alleging that Dell misrepresented the speed of the microprocessors included in the computers they purchased. Dell made a demand for arbitration, asserting that the plaintiffs were bound by the arbitration agreement that was contained in the terms and conditions of sale. The plaintiffs countered that the arbitration clause was not part of their web contract because the terms and conditions of sale were not conspicuously displayed as part of the web contract. The trial court sided with the plaintiffs, finding that the arbitration clause was unenforceable because the terms and conditions of sale were not adequately communicated to the plaintiffs. Dell appealed.

Issue

Were the terms and conditions of sale adequately communicated to the plaintiffs?

Language of the Court

We find that the online contract included the "Terms and Conditions of Sale." The blue hyperlink entitled "Terms and Conditions of Sale" appeared on numerous web pages the plaintiffs completed in the ordering process. The blue hyperlinks on the defendant's web pages, constituting the five-step process for ordering the computers, should be treated the same as a multipage written paper contract. The blue hyperlink simply takes a person to another page of the contract, similar to turning the page of a written paper contract. Although there is no conspicuousness requirement, the hyperlink's contrasting blue type makes it conspicuous. Because the "Terms and Conditions of Sale" were a part of the online contract, the plaintiffs were bound by the "Terms and Conditions of Sale," including the arbitration clause.

Decision

The appellate court held that Dell's terms and conditions of sale, which were accessible by clicking on a blue hyperlink and which included the arbitration clause, were part of the web contract between the plaintiffs and Dell. The appellate court reversed the decision of the trial court and held in favor of Dell.

Critical Legal Thinking Questions

Did the plaintiffs act ethically in claiming that the terms and conditions of sale were not included in their web contract? Did Dell act ethically in requiring consumers to take extra steps to read the terms and conditions? Do you read the terms and conditions of sale when you purchase goods over the internet?

Counteroffers Ineffectual Against an Electronic Agent

electronic agent
A computer program or an electronic or other automated means used independently to initiate an action or respond to electronic records or performances in whole or in part, without review or action by an individual.

In today's e-commerce, many internet sellers have websites that use electronic agents to sell goods and services. An **electronic agent** is any computer system that has been established by a seller to accept orders. Web page order systems are examples of electronic agents.

In the past, when humans dealt with each other face-to-face, by telephone, or in writing, their negotiations might have consisted of an exchange of several offers and counteroffers until agreed-on terms were reached and a contract was formed. Each new counteroffer extinguished the previous offer and became a new viable offer.

Most web pages use electronic ordering systems that do not have the ability to evaluate and accept counteroffers or to make counteroffers. Thus, counteroffers are not effective against these electronic agents.

Example Green Company has a website that uses an electronic ordering system for accepting orders for products. Freddie accesses Green Company's website and orders a product that costs $1,000. Freddie enters the product code and description, his mailing address and credit card information, and other data needed to complete the transaction. Green Company's web ordering system does not provide a method for a party to submit a counteroffer. After ordering the goods on the website, Freddie sends an email to Green Company stating, "I will accept the product I ordered if, after two weeks of use, I am satisfied with the product." However, because Freddie has placed the order with an electronic agent, Freddie has ordered the product, and his counteroffer is ineffectual.

E-Sign Act

17.3 Describe the provisions of the Electronic Signatures in Global and National Commerce Act (E-SIGN Act).

Electronic Signatures in Global and National Commerce Act (E-SIGN Act)
A federal statute that (1) recognizes electronic contracts as meeting the writing requirement of the Statute of Frauds and (2) recognizes and gives electronic signatures—e-signatures—the same force and effect as handwritten, pen-inscribed signatures on paper.

In 2000, the federal government enacted the **Electronic Signatures in Global and National Commerce Act (E-SIGN Act)**[1] to apply to digital contracting. This federal statute is designed to place the world of electronic commerce on a par with the world of paper contracts in the United States.

E-SIGN Act and Writing Requirement

One of the main features of the E-SIGN Act is that it recognizes electronic contracts as meeting the writing requirement of the Statutes of Frauds—state laws that require certain types of contracts to be in writing—for most contracts. The E-SIGN Act provides that electronically signed contracts cannot be denied effect because they are in electronic form or media, or are delivered electronically. The act also provides that record retention requirements are satisfied if the records are stored electronically.

The federal law was passed with several provisions to protect consumers. First, consumers must consent to receiving electronic records and contracts. Second, to receive electronic records, consumers must be able to demonstrate that they have access to the electronic records. Third, businesses must tell consumers that they have the right to receive hard copy documents of their transaction.

Critical Legal Thinking Questions

Does the Electronic Signatures in Global and National Commerce Act (E-SIGN Act) bring uniformity to electronic contracting? Should additional new federal laws be enacted to bring more uniformity to electronic contracting?

E-Signatures

Traditionally, a person entered into a contract by hand-writing a signature on a paper document. In the electronic age, the equivalent may be to answer a security question such as "What is your mother's maiden name?", to slide your smart card over a sensor, or to look into an iris scanner. But are electronic signatures sufficient to form an enforceable contract?

The E-SIGN Act made the answer clear by recognizing **electronic signatures**, or **e-signatures**. The act gives an e-signature the same force and effect as a handwritten, pen-inscribed signature on paper. The act is technology neutral, however, in that it does not define or decide which technologies should be used to create a legally binding signature in cyberspace. Loosely defined, a digital "signature" is some electronic method that identifies an individual. The challenge is to make sure that someone who uses a digital signature is the person he or she claims to be. The act provides that a digital signature can be verified in one of three ways:

electronic signature (e-signature)
A signature that is inscribed using an electronic means.

1. By something the signatory knows, such as a secret password or pet's name
2. By something a person has, such as a smart card, which looks like a credit card and stores personal information
3. By biometrics, which uses a device that digitally recognizes fingerprints or the retina or iris of the eye

The verification of electronic signatures has created a need for the use of scanners and other secure methods for verifying personal information.

E-Licensing of Software and Information Rights

17.4 Describe electronic licensing of software and information rights.

Much of the cyber-economy is based on electronic contracts and the licensing of computer software and information. E-commerce created problems for forming contracts over the internet, enforcing e-commerce contracts, and providing consumer protection.

License

Intellectual property and information rights are extremely important assets of many individuals and companies. Patents, trademarks, copyrights, trade secrets, data, software programs, and the like constitute valuable intellectual property and information rights.

The owners of intellectual property and information rights often wish to transfer limited rights in the property or information to parties for specified purposes and limited duration. The agreement that is used to transfer such limited rights is called a **license**, which is defined as follows:

license
A contract that transfers limited rights in intellectual property and information rights.

License means a contract that authorizes access to, or use, distribution, performance, modification, or reproduction of, information or information rights, but expressly limits the access or uses authorized or expressly grants fewer than all rights in the information, whether or not the transferee has title to a licensed copy. The term includes an access contract, a lease of a computer program, and a consignment of a copy (UCITA Section 102(a)(40)).

The parties to a license are the licensor and the licensee. The **licensor** is the party who owns the intellectual property or information rights and obligates him- or herself to transfer rights in the property or information to the licensee. The **licensee** is the party who is granted limited rights in or access to the intellectual property or information.

licensor
An owner of intellectual property or information rights who transfers rights in the property or information to the licensee.

licensee
A party who is granted limited rights in or access to intellectual property or information rights owned by a licensor.

A licensing arrangement is illustrated in Exhibit 17.1.

A license grants the contractual rights expressly described in the license and the right to use information rights within the licensor's control that are necessary to perform the expressly described rights. A license can grant the licensee the exclusive rights to use the information. An **exclusive license** means that for the specified duration of the license, the licensor will not grant to any other person rights to the same information.

Exhibit 17.1 LICENSING ARRANGEMENT

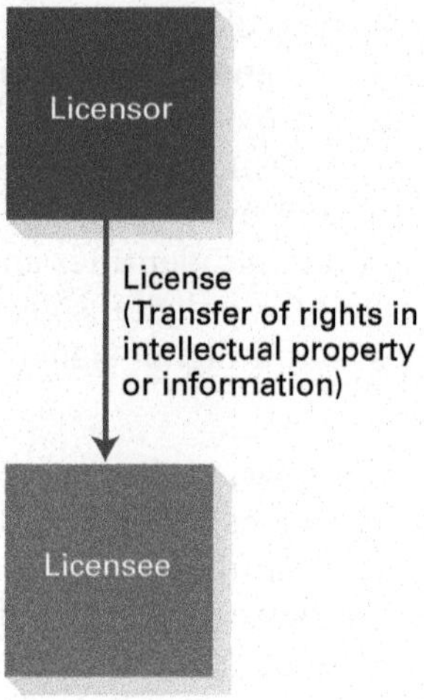

E-License

electronic license (e-license)
A contract whereby the owner of a software or a digital application grants limited rights to the owner of a computer or digital device to use the software or digital application for a limited period and under specified conditions.

Most software programs and digital applications are licensed electronically by the owner of the program or application to a user of a computer or digital device. An **electronic license**, or **e-license**, is a contract whereby the owner of software or a digital application grants limited rights to the owner of a computer or digital device to use the software or digital application for a limited period and under specified conditions. The owner of the program or application is the **electronic licensor**, or **e-licensor**, and the owner of the computer or digital device to whom the license is granted is the **electronic licensee**, or **e-licensee**.

Example Dorothea owns a computer and licenses a computer software program from SoftWare Company to use on her computer. Dorothea downloads the software onto her computer from SoftWare Company's website. There is an e-license between the two parties. SoftWare Company is the e-licensor, and Dorothea is the e-licensee.

Licensing Agreement

licensing agreement
A detailed and comprehensive written agreement between a licensor and a licensee that sets forth the express terms of their agreement.

A licensor and a licensee usually enter into a written **licensing agreement** that expressly states the terms of their agreement. Licensing agreements tend to be very detailed and comprehensive contracts. This is primarily because of the nature of the subject matter and the limited uses granted in the intellectual property or information rights.

The parties to a contract for the licensing of information owe a duty to perform the obligations stated in the contract. If a party fails to perform as required, there is a breach of the contract. Breach of contract by one party to a licensing agreement gives the nonbreaching party certain rights, including the right to recover damages or other remedies.

Unfair Business Practices in the Information Age

17.5 List and describe laws that regulate unfair information technology practices.

Consumers have always had to contend with unfair business practices. But digital technologies make it even easier for unscrupulous businesses and individuals to take advantages of consumers. State and federal governments have enacted laws that address these dangers. Several federal laws that address unfair business practices are discussed in the following paragraphs.

Telephone Consumer Protection Act (TCPA)

Telemarketers harass consumers with annoying and unwanted telephone calls and texts. Scammers often try to sell people goods or services, to convince them to invest in illegal scams, or to entice them to give up personal information that will be used to rob them of their money or property. In 1991, the **Telephone Consumer Protection Act (TCPA)**,[2] a federal statute, was enacted to curb abusive telemarketing calls, texts, and faxes. The **Federal Communications Commission (FCC)**, an administrative agency, is empowered to enforce the TCPA and to adopt rules and regulations to implement the law.

TCPA and FCC regulations prohibit unsolicited telephone calls and text messages; the use of autodialed, prerecorded, or artificial voice calls (commonly known as robocalls) to wireless telephone numbers; and the use of prerecorded or artificial voice calls to residential telephone numbers unless the caller has received the prior expressed consent of the called party. The TCPA and FCC rules also prohibit unsolicited fax advertisements. TCPA prohibits any commercial calls and texts before 8:00 a.m. and after 9:00 p.m.

In 2012, the FCC revised its TCPA rules to require telemarketers to (1) obtain prior *written* consent from consumers before robocalling them, (2) no longer use an "established business relationship" to avoid getting specific consent from consumers, and (3) provide an automated, interactive opt-out mechanism during each robocall so consumers can immediately tell the telemarketer to stop calling.

In 2020, the **Telephone Robocall Abuse Criminal Enforcement and Deterrence Act (TRACED Act)**[3] became effective. The act amends the TCPA by providing additional protections against illegal robocalls, spam calls and texts, and malicious caller ID spoofing. Spoofed calls are those in which scammers mask their identity by changing the number that is displayed on a caller ID. The TRACED Act requires telecom carriers to implement, at no extra charge, number-authentication systems to help consumers identify who is calling. Telecom carriers must alert customers of calls and texts that seem suspicious by having labels such as "scam likely" or "spam likely" appear on their phones. The authentication system also combats spoofed numbers by using digital imprints to help determine whether the number from which a call is placed is the same as the number that shows up on caller ID. Certain apps are available that provide robocall-blocking protections beyond those provided by law.

The TCPA, as amended, provides a private right of action to people who receive illegal calls, text messages, or faxes, and permits class action lawsuits. The FCC can bring enforcement actions and recover civil fines from violators. The U.S. Department of Justice can bring criminal charges against violators of the TCPA. The statute of limitations for bringing lawsuits is four years from the date of the violation. One major gap in these laws is that they do not reach spammers and robocallers located outside the United States.

Telephone Consumer Protection Act (TCPA)
A federal statute that curbs abusive telemarketing calls, texts, and faxes.

Federal Communications Commission (FCC)
A federal administrative agency that is empowered to enforce the Telephone Consumer Protection Act (TCPA) and to adopt rules and regulations to implement the law.

Telephone Robocall Abuse Criminal Enforcement and Deterrence Act (TRACED Act)
A federal statute that provides protections against illegal robocalls, spam calls and texts, and malicious caller ID spoofing.

Do-Not-Call Registry

In 2003, to facilitate the enforcement of the TCPA, Congress enacted the **Do-Not-Call Implementation Act**.[4] Pursuant to the act, the **Federal Trade Commission (FTC)**, a government agency, created and administers a **National Do-Not-Call Registry**. Consumers can place their telephone numbers on the registry and free themselves from most unsolicited telemarketing and commercial telephone calls and texts. Both wireless phones and land lines can be registered. The registry applies only to residential phones and not to business phones.

When a person registers a phone, it is recorded in the Do-Not-Call Registry the next day. Telemarketers and other businesses then have 31 days to remove the customer's phone number from their sales call list and cease calling and texting

Do-Not-Call Implementation Act
A federal statute that authorized the Federal Trade Commission (FTC) to create a registry on which consumers can place their names and personal mobile or residential telephone numbers to prevent most unsolicited commercial telephone calls and texts.

Federal Trade Commission (FTC)
A federal administrative agency that created and administers the National Do-Not-Call Registry.

National Do-Not-Call Registry
A federal registry on which consumers can place their names and personal wireless or land line telephone numbers to prevent unsolicited telemarketing and commercial telephone calls and texts.

the number. Registration of a telephone number on the Do-Not-Call Registry is permanent. The Do-Not-Call Registry also allows consumers to designate specific companies to not call or text them. The act does not limit calls by non-profit organizations, political organizations, and parties conducting surveys. However, the act does apply to telemarketers calling on behalf of these organizations. Creditors and collection agencies are exempt and may call or text parties listed on the registry unless those parties notify the creditor or agency to quit calling or texting them. The FTC can bring enforcement action against violators and recover civil fines, individuals may sue violators and recover damages, and the government can bring criminal charges against violators. More than 70 percent of Americans have registered on the Do-Not-Call Registry. To register, go online to **www.donotcall.gov**, or call 888-382-1222.

Example Dish Network LLC, a U.S. television provider, was sued by the federal government and several states for hiring third-party telemarketers that it knew were making unsolicited telephone calls to consumers listed on the Do-Not-Call Registry on behalf of Dish to drum up new customers for Dish. The court found that Dish had violated the TCPA and ordered Dish to pay $280 million in fines to the federal and state governments. The court stated, "Dish's reckless decision to use anyone with a call center without any vetting or meaningful supervision demonstrates a disregard for the consuming public." *United States v. Dish Network LLC*, 256 F.Supp.3d 810 (United States District Court for the Central District of Illinois, 2017)

Controlling the Assault of Non-Solicited Pornography and Marketing Act (CAN-SPAM Act)

Controlling the Assault of Non-Solicited Pornography and Marketing Act (CAN-SPAM Act)
A federal statute that places certain restrictions on persons and businesses that send unsolicited commercial advertising (spam) to email accounts, prohibits falsified headers, prohibits deceptive subject lines, and requires spammers to label sexually oriented email as such.

Americans are often sent **email spam**—unsolicited commercial advertising. Many email spam messages are fraudulent and deceptive, and include misleading subject lines. In 2003, Congress enacted the federal **Controlling the Assault of Non-Solicited Pornography and Marketing Act (CAN-SPAM Act).**[5]

The act (1) prohibits spammers from using falsified headers in email messages, including the originating domain name and email address; (2) prohibits deceptive subject lines that mislead a recipient about the contents or subject matter of the message; and (3) requires that recipients of spam be given the opportunity to opt out and not have the spammer send email to the recipient's address. The act requires spammers who send sexually oriented email to label it properly as such. The FTC is empowered to enforce the CAN-SPAM Act.

In effect, the CAN-SPAM Act does not necessarily end spam, but instead approves of the business use of spam so long as businesses do not lie. The act provides a civil right of action to internet service providers that suffer losses because of spam. However, the act does not provide a civil right of action to individuals who have received unsolicited spam. Individual users who receive spam can forward it to the FTC, which has authority to sue the offender and obtain damages. The CAN-SPAM Act does not regulate spam sent to Americans from other countries.

In the following case, the court was presented with an issue involving spam.

Internet Service Providers (ISPs)

Internet service providers (ISPs) are companies that provide consumers and businesses with access to the internet. ISPs provide email accounts, internet access, and storage on the internet to subscribers. ISPs offer a variety of access devices and services to connect users to the internet. There are also web-hosting services that allow users to create their own websites and provide storage space for website users.

Information Technology

CASE 17.2 FEDERAL COURT CASE Email Spam

Facebook, Inc. v. Porembski

2011 U.S. Dist. Lexis 9668 (2011)
United States District Court for the Northern District of California

"The record demonstrates that defendants willfully and knowingly violated the statutes in question by engaging in the circumvention of Facebook's security measures."

—Jeremy Fogel, District Judge

Facts

Facebook, Inc. owns and operates the social networking website located at **www.facebook.com**. Facebook users must register with the website and agree to Facebook's Statement of Rights and Responsibilities (SRR). Facebook maintains strict policies against spam or any other form of unsolicited advertising by users. Philip Porembski formed PP Web Services, LLC and registered as a Facebook user subject to Facebook's SRR. Through fraudulent misrepresentations, Porembski obtained more than 116,000 Facebook users' account information and sent more than 7.2 million spam messages to these Facebook users. Facebook filed a lawsuit in U.S. district court against Philip Porembski and PP Web Services, LLC, alleging that the defendants' spamming activities violated the federal CAN-SPAM Act. Facebook sought damages and a permanent injunction against the defendants.

Issue

Did the defendants violate the CAN-SPAM Act?

Language of the Court

The record demonstrates that defendants willfully and knowingly violated the statutes in question by engaging in the circumvention of Facebook's security measures. The court will award statutory damages of $50.00 per violation of the CAN-SPAM Act, for a total award of $360,000,000 under that Act. It is appropriate that defendants be permanently enjoined from accessing and abusing Facebook services. Facebook's request for permanent injunctive relief is granted.

Decision

The U.S. district court held that the defendants had violated the CAN-SPAM Act, awarded Facebook $360 million in damages, and issued a permanent injunction against the defendants.

Critical Legal Thinking Questions

Did Porembski act ethically in this case? Will Facebook recover its awarded damages?

A provision in the federal **Communications Decency Act** of 1996 provides, "No provider or user of an interactive computer service shall be treated as the publisher or speaker of any information provided by another information content provider."[6] Thus, ISPs are not liable for the content transmitted over their networks by email users and websites.

Communications Decency Act
A federal statute stating that internet service providers are not liable for the content transmitted over their networks by email users and websites.

Domain Names

17.6 Define *domain name* and describe how domain names are registered and protected.

Most businesses conduct e-commerce by using websites on the internet. Each website is identified by a unique Internet **domain name**. The **Internet Corporation for Assigned Names and Numbers (ICANN)** is a private nonprofit organization that oversees the registration and regulation of domain names.

domain name
A unique name that identifies an individual's or company's website.

ICANN provides for the registration of top-level domain (TLD) extensions. The stated purpose of having a great number of domain name extensions is to enhance competition and increase the choice of domain name space. There are more than 350 million domain names registered worldwide. The most widely used top-level domain extension is .com, with approximately 145 million domain names.

Examples The domain name for the publisher of this book—Pearson Education, Inc.—is **www.pearson.com**. The domain name for Microsoft Corporation is **www.microsoft.com**. The domain name for McDonald's Corporation is **www.mcdonalds.com**. The domain name for Starbucks Corporation is **www.starbucks.com**.

Registration of Domain Names

Domain names can be registered. The first step in registering a domain name is to determine whether any other party already owns the name. For this purpose, InterNIC maintains a database that contains the domain names that have been registered. The InterNIC website can be accessed at **www.internic.net**.

WEB EXERCISE
Think of an Internet domain name you would like to use for a business. Go to the Network Solutions website at **www.networksolutions.com** or another domain registration site to see if that name is available with the top-level domain extension .com.

Domain names can be registered with a variety of internet companies. An applicant must complete a registration form and pay a fee, both of which can be done online. Domain names may be registered for longer periods of time. Country-specific domain names are usually more expensive to register. Often, the companies that register domain names will do so for free if a party agrees to have that company provide hosting services for the registrant's website.

Domain Name Extensions

top-level domain (TLD)
A domain extension at the highest level in the hierarchical domain name system of the internet.

generic top-level domain (gTLD)
A top-level domain that is not restricted to any geographic or country designation.

A **top-level domain (TLD)** is a domain extension at the highest level in the hierarchical domain name system of the internet. It refers to the last part of a domain name, such as .com. The seven original TLDs were .com, .org, .net, .int, .edu, .gov, and .mil. Many additional TLDs have been added over the years. Some domain names are restricted to registrants who demonstrate eligibility to use the domain. Examples include .name, .pro, .coop, .gov, and others. **Generic top-level domains (gTLD)** are domains that are not restricted to any geographic or country designation. Several of the generic TLDs and their descriptions are listed in Exhibit 17.2.

Exhibit 17.2 COMMONLY USED TOP-LEVEL DOMAIN NAMES

WEB EXERCISE
Go to **www.networksolutions.com** or another domain registration site. See if your name is available in the .name extension.

.biz	This domain is used for small-business websites.
.club	This domain is a generic term used by people and organizations, such as tennis clubs, chess clubs, fan clubs, prominent individuals, and others.
.com	This domain represents the word *commercial* and is the most widely used extension in the world. Many businesses prefer a .com domain name because it is a highly recognized business symbol.
.coop	This domain represents the word *cooperative* and may be used by cooperative associations around the world.
.edu	This domain is for educational institutions.
.info	This domain signifies a resource website. It is an unrestricted global name that may be used by businesses, individuals, and organizations.
.int	This domain is reserved for international treaty-based organizations and United Nations agencies and organizations.
.mil	This domain is for use by the U.S. Department of Defense and its subsidiary and affiliated organizations.

.mobi	This domain is reserved for websites that are viewable on mobile devices.
.museum	This domain enables museums, museum associations, and museum professionals to register websites.
.name	This domain is for individuals, who can use it to register personalized domain names.
.net	This domain represents the word *network*, and it is most commonly used by ISPs, web-hosting companies, and other businesses that are directly involved in the infrastructure of the internet. Some businesses also choose domain names with a .net extension.
.org	This domain represents the word *organization* and is used primarily by nonprofit groups and trade associations.
.pro	This domain is available to professionals, such as doctors, lawyers, and consultants.
.work	This domain is used by people, businesses, and organizations that are associated with the employment of workers, such as employment services, recruiters, and human resource departments.
.xyz	This domain is a generic term used for any general purpose.

Specific Domain Names

Some domains identify types of business, service, profession, or activity. These include .accountants, .actor, .attorney, .auction, .bar, .blog, .boutique, .camera, .career, .church, .club, .contractor, .credit, .dating, .dentist, .email, .engineer, .expert, .finance, .food, .gift, .homes, .kitchen, .loans, .mortgage, .music, .pharmacy, .pizza, .repair, .restaurant, .services, .shop, .tech, .toys, .vacation, .website, and .yoga.

Companies can have their own company domains. These include such trademarked names such as .google, .mcdonalds, .cocacola, .microsoft, and .nike. Any business, service, or professional organization may use their name as a domain extension. In addition, companies can obtain domains for specific products, such as .iphone or .prius. Such domains will help companies with the branding of their company names and products.

Cities and other government agencies can register domains, such as .nyc (New York City), .paris (Paris, France), and .quebec (Quebec Province, Canada). Persons sharing a cultural or community identity can have their own domain, such as .lat for Latin American communities; .scot for Scottish people; .saulttribe for the Sault Ste. Marie Tribe of Chippewa Indians; .kurd for Kurds living in any country; and .ven for the Venetian community in Italy.

TLDs can be registered in languages other than English, including Arabic, Chinese, French, Russian, and Spanish.

Country Domain Names

Countries, territories, and sovereign states have top-level domains that are reserved to them. These domains are called **country code top-level domains (ccTLD)**. The country code domain for the United States is **.us**. It is open to registrations by citizens, residents, and businesses with a presence in the United States. Many countries make their domain name available for private purchase for commercial use. Examples of country code domains are listed in Exhibit 17.3.

country code top-level domain (ccTLD)
A top-level domain that is assigned to a country, territory, or sovereign state.

Exhibit 17.3 EXAMPLES OF COUNTRY DOMAIN NAMES

Afghanistan	.af	Ireland	.ie
Angola	.ao	Israel	.il
Argentina	.ar	Japan	.jp
Australia	.au	Kenya	.ke
Bangladesh	.bd	Madagascar	.mg
Bhutan	.bt	Mali	.ml
Brazil	.br	Mexico	.mx
Burkina Faso	.bf	Mongolia	.mn
Canada	.ca	New Zealand	.nz
Chile	.cl	Nigeria	.ng
China	.cn	Pakistan	.pk
Cuba	.cu	Peru	.pe
Egypt	.eg	Russia	.ru
France	.fr	Saudi Arabia	.sa
Germany	.de	South Korea	.kr
Great Britain (UK)	.gb	Turkey	.tr
Greece	.gr	United States	.us
India	.in	Venezuela	.ve
Indonesia	.id	Zambia	.zm
Iran	.ir		

WEB EXERCISE

Pick out a name of a country that is not listed in Exhibit 17.3 and find its domain name extension. Does the country allow the domain to be used by businesses and individuals?

The following feature discusses the sale of domain names.

Information Technology

Sale of Domain Names

Domain names can be very valuable. Like other property, domains names can be purchased and sold. Some domain names that have been sold, and the sales prices, include the following:

360.com	$17,000,000
Business.com	7,500,000
California.com	3,000,000
Candy.com	3,000,000
Carinsurance.com	49,700,000
Clothes.com	$4,900,000
CreditCards.com	2,750,000
Diamonds.com	7,500,000
Fb.com	8,500,000
Fund.com	12,000,000
Giftcard.com	4,000,000
Hotels.com	11,000,000
iCloud.com	6,000,000

IG.com	4,600,000
Insurance.com	35,600,000
Internet.com	18,000,000
Investing.com	$2,450,000
LasVegas.com	90,000,000
Loans.com	3,000,000
Medicare.com	4,800,000
MI.com	3,600,000
Privatejet.com	30,180,000
Shoes.com	9,000,000
Social.com	2,600,000
Tesla.com	11,000,000
Toys.com	$5,100,000
Vacationrentals.com	35,000,000
Voice.com	30,000,000
Yp.com	3,800,000
Z.com	6,800,000

Some high-profile domain names are sold privately, and their purchase price is not disclosed. These include **crypto .com**, **bitcoin.com**, and **stake.com**.

Anticybersquatting Consumer Protection Act

Sometimes a party registers a domain name of another party's trademarked name or a famous person's name, an act called **cybersquatting**. Often the domain name owner has registered the domain name with the hope of obtaining payment for the name from the trademark holder or the famous person whose name has been registered as a domain name. Trademark law is of little help in this area because trademark laws require distribution of goods or services to find infringement. Most cybersquatters do not distribute goods or services but merely sit on the internet domain names.

In 1999, the U.S. Congress enacted the **Anticybersquatting Consumer Protection Act (ACPA)**.[7] The act was specifically aimed at cybersquatters who register internet domain names of famous companies and people and hold them hostage by demanding ransom payments from the famous company or person. The act has two fundamental requirements: (1) the name must be famous, and (2) the domain name must have been registered in bad faith. Thus, the law prohibits the act of cybersquatting itself if it is done in *bad faith*.

Anticybersquatting Consumer Protection Act (ACPA)
A federal statute that permits trademark owners and famous persons to recover domain names that use their names where the domain name has been registered by another person or business in bad faith.

The first issue in applying the statute is whether the domain name is someone else's famous name. Trademarked names qualify; nontrademarked names—such as those of famous actors, singers, sports stars, and politicians—are also protected. The second issue is whether the domain name was registered in bad faith. In determining bad faith, a court may consider the extent to which the domain name resembles the trademark owner's name or the famous person's name, whether goods or services are sold under the name, the holder's offer to sell or transfer the name, whether the holder has acquired multiple internet domain names of famous companies and persons, and other factors.

The act provides for the issuance of cease-and-desist orders and injunctions against the domain name registrant. The court may order the domain name registrant to turn over the domain name to the trademark owner or famous person. The law also provides for monetary penalties. The ACPA gives owners of trademarks and persons with famous names the right to prevent the kidnapping of internet domain names by cyberpirates.

The following case involves a domain name dispute.

Information Technology

CASE 17.3 *NATIONAL ARBITRATION FORUM Domain Name*

New York Yankees Partnership d/b/a The New York Yankees Baseball Club

Claim Number FA0609000803277 (2006)
National Arbitration Forum

"Such use by Moniker is indicative of an intent to disrupt the business of the Yankees, and constitutes registration and use of the disputed domain name in bad faith."

—Harold Kalina, Judge, Retired

Facts

The New York Yankees Partnership d/b/a/ The New York Yankees Baseball Club (Yankees) is among the world's most recognized and followed sports teams, having won more than 20 World Series Championships and more than 30 American League pennants. The Yankees own the trademark for the NEW YORK YANKEES (Reg. No. 1,073,346), which was issued to the Yankees by the U.S. Patent and Trademark Office (PTO) on September 13, 1977. Moniker Online Services, Inc. (Moniker) registered the domain name <nyyankees.com>. Moniker operates a commercial website under this domain name where it offers links to third-party commercial websites that sell tickets to Yankees baseball games and sell merchandise bearing the NEW YORK YANKEES trademark without the Yankees' permission. The Yankees filed a complaint with the National Arbitration Forum alleging that Moniker had registered the domain in bad faith in violation of the ICANN Uniform Domain Dispute Resolution Policy and seeking to obtain the domain name from Moniker.

Issue

Did Moniker violate the ICANN Uniform Domain Dispute Resolution Policy (Policy)?

Language of the Arbitrator

Complainant has sufficiently demonstrated that Moniker's <nyyankees.com> domain name is confusingly similar to complainant's NEW YORK YANKEES mark. There is no evidence in the record to suggest that Moniker is commonly known by the disputed domain name. Such use by Moniker is indicative of an intent to disrupt the business of the Yankees, and constitutes registration and use of the disputed domain name in bad faith.

Decision

The arbitrator held that Moniker violated the ICANN Policy and ordered that the <nyyankees.com> domain name be transferred from Moniker to the Yankees.

Critical Legal Thinking Questions

Did Moniker act ethically in obtaining and using the <nyyankees.com> domain name and website? Do you think that the element of bad faith was shown in this case?

Key Terms and Concepts

.biz (312)
.club (312)
.com (312)
.coop (312)
.edu (291) (312)
.info (312)
.int (312)
.mil (312)
.mobi (313)
.museum (313)
.name (313)
.net (313)
.org (313)
.pro (313)
.us (313)
.xyz (313)
Anticybersquatting Consumer Protection Act (ACPA) (315)
Communications Decency Act (311)
Controlling the Assault of Non-Solicited Pornography and Marketing Act (CAN-SPAM Act) (310)
Country code top-level domain (ccTLD) (313)
Cybersquatting (315)
Domain name (311)
Do-Not-Call Implementation Act (309)
Electronic agent (306)
Electronic commerce (e-commerce) (304)
Electronic contracts (e-contracts) (304)
Electronic license (e-license) (308)
Electronic licensee (e-licensee) (308)
Electronic licensor (e-licensor) (308)
Electronic mail (email) (304)
Electronic mail contract (email contract) (304)

Critical Legal Thinking Cases

17.1 Cybersquatting Ernest & Julio Gallo Winery (Gallo) is a famous maker of wines located in California. The company registered the trademark "Ernest & Julio Gallo" with the U.S. Patent and Trademark Office in 1964. The company has spent more than $500 million promoting its brand name and has sold more than 4 billion bottles of wine. Its name has taken on a secondary meaning as a famous trademark name. Steve, Pierce, and Fred Thumann created Spider Webs Ltd., a limited partnership, to register internet domain names. Spider Webs registered more than 2,000 internet domain names, including **ernestandjuliogallo.com**. Spider Webs is in the business of selling domain names. Gallo filed suit against Spider Webs Ltd. and the Thumanns, alleging violation of the federal Anticybersquatting Consumer Protection Act (ACPA). The U.S. District Court held in favor of Gallo and ordered Spider Webs to transfer the domain name **ernestandjuliogallo.com** to Gallo. Spider Webs Ltd. appealed. Who wins? *E. & J. Gallo Winery v. Spider Webs Ltd.*, 286 F.3d 270, 2002 U.S. App. Lexis 5928 (United States Court of Appeals for the Fifth Circuit, 2002)

17.2 Internet Service Provider Someone secretly took video cameras into the locker room and showers of the Illinois State University football team. Video recordings showing undressed players were displayed on a website operated by Franco Productions. The internet site concealed the name of the person responsible. GTE Corporation, an internet service provider (ISP), provided a high-speed connection and storage space on its server so that the content of the website could be accessed. The images passed over GTE's network between Franco Productions and its customers. The football players sued Franco Productions and GTE for monetary damages. Franco Productions defaulted when it could not be located. Is GTE Corporation, the ISP, liable for damages to the plaintiff football players? *John Doe v. GTE Corporation*, 347 F.3d 655, 2003 U.S. App. Lexis 21345 (United States Court of Appeals for the Seventh Circuit, 2003)

17.3 Email Contract Little Steel Company is a small steel fabricator that makes steel parts for various metal machine shop clients. When Little Steel Company receives an order from a client, it must locate and purchase 10 tons of a certain grade of steel to complete the order. Little Steel Company sends an email message to West Coast Steel Company, a large steel company, inquiring about the availability of 10 tons of the described grade of steel. West Coast Steel Company replies by email that it has available the required 10 tons of steel and quotes $450 per ton. Little Steel Company's purchasing agent replies by email that Little Steel Company will purchase the 10 tons of described steel at the quoted price of $450 per ton. The emails are signed electronically by Little Steel Company's purchasing agent and the selling agent of West Coast Steel Company. When the steel arrives at Little Steel Company's plant, Little Steel Company rejects the shipment, claiming the defense of the Statute of Frauds. West Coast Steel Company sues Little Steel Company for damages. Who wins?

17.4 Electronic Signature David Abacus uses the internet to place an order to license software for his computer from Inet.License, Inc. (Inet) through Inet's online ordering system. Inet's web-page order form asks David to type in his name, mailing address, telephone number, email address, credit card information, computer location information, and personal identification number. Inet's electronic agent requests that David verify the information a second time before it accepts the order, which David does. The license duration is two years at a license fee of $300 per month. Only after receiving the verification of information does Inet's electronic agent place the order and send an electronic copy of the software program to David's computer, where he installs the new software program. David later refuses to pay the license fee due to Inet because he claims his electronic signature and information were not authentic. Inet sues David to recover the license fee. Is David's electronic signature enforceable against him?

Ethics Case

17.5 Ethics Case BluePeace.org is a new environmental group that has decided that the internet is the best and most efficient way to spend its time and money to advance its environmental causes. To draw attention to its websites, BluePeace.org comes up with catchy internet domain names. One is macyswearus.org, another is exxonvaldezesseals.org, and another is generalmotorscrashesdummies.org. The macyswearus.org website first shows beautiful women dressed in mink fur coats sold by Macy's Department Stores and displays graphic photos of minks being slaughtered, skinned, and made into the coats. The exxonvaldezesseals.org website first shows a beautiful, pristine bay in Alaska, with the *Exxon Valdez* oil tanker quietly sailing through the waters. Then it shows photos of the ship breaking open and spewing forth oil, followed by seals that are covered with oil, suffocating and dying on the shoreline. The website generalmotorscrashesdummies.org shows a General Motors automobile involved in normal crash tests with dummies, followed by photographs of automobile accident scenes where people and children lie bleeding and dying after an accident involving General Motors automobiles. Macy's Inc., the ExxonMobil Corporation, and the General Motors Corporation sue BluePeace.org for violating the federal Anticybersquatting Consumer Protection Act (ACPA). Who wins? Has BluePeace.org acted unethically in this case?

Notes

1. 15 U.S.C. Chapter 96.
2. 47 U.S.C. Section 227.
3. Pub. L. 116-105.
4. 15 U.S.C. Sections 6101 et seq.
5. 15 U.S.C. Sections 7701-7713.
6. 47 U.S.C. Section 230(c)(1).
7. 15 U.S.C. Section 1125(d).

PART IV

Sales and Lease Contracts and Warranties

Henry R. Cheeseman

CHAPTER

18 Formation of Sales and Lease Contracts

Henry R. Cheeseman

EQUIPMENT

The sale and lease of goods—business equipment, automobiles, consumer goods, computers, electronics, and such—make up a considerable part of the U.S. economy. A special law—the Uniform Commercial Code (UCC)—contains rules that apply to contracts for the sale and lease of goods. The UCC is a model act that many states have adopted in whole or in part as their commercial code. Article 2 of the UCC covers sales of goods, and Article 2A of the UCC covers the lease of goods.

Learning Objectives

After studying this chapter, you should be able to:

18.1 Describe the Uniform Commercial Code (UCC).

18.2 Define *sales contracts* governed by Article 2 of the UCC.

18.3 Define *lease contracts* governed by Article 2A of the UCC.

18.4 Describe the formation of sales and lease contracts and define the *firm offer rule*.

18.5 Describe acceptance and define the UCC's *additional terms rule* and *written confirmation rule*.

18.6 Describe the UCC Statute of Frauds for sales and lease contracts.

18.7 Describe how Revised Article 2 (Sales) and Article 2A (Leases) permit electronic contracting.

18.8 Describe how letters of credit facilitate international trade.

> *"Commercial law lies within a narrow compass, and is far purer and freer from defects than any other part of the system."*
>
> *—Henry Peter Brougham*
> *House of Commons of the United Kingdom, February 7, 1828*

Introduction to Formation of Sales and Lease Contracts

Most tangible items—such as books, clothing, and tools—are considered *goods*. In medieval times, merchants gathered at fairs in Europe to exchange such goods. Over time, certain customs and rules evolved for enforcing contracts and resolving disputes. These customs and rules, which were referred to as the *Law Merchant*, were enforced by "fair courts" established by the merchants. Eventually, the customs and rules of the Law Merchant were absorbed into the common law.

Laws made by common consent must not be trampled on by individuals.
George Washington
(1732–1799)

Toward the end of the 1800s, England enacted a statute (the Sale of Goods Act) that codified the common law rules of commercial transactions. In the United States, laws governing the sale of goods also developed. In 1906, the **Uniform Sales Act** was promulgated in the United States and enacted in many states. It was quickly outdated, however, as mass production and distribution of goods developed in the 20th century.

In 1949, the National Conference of Commissioners on Uniform State Laws promulgated a comprehensive statutory scheme called the *Uniform Commercial Code (UCC)*. The UCC covers most aspects of commercial transactions.

Article 2 (Sales) and *Article 2A (Leases)* of the UCC govern personal property sales and leases. These articles are intended to provide clear, easy-to-apply rules that place the risk of loss of the goods on the party most able to either bear the risk or insure against it. The common law of contracts governs whether either Article 2 or Article 2A is silent on an issue.

This chapter discusses the formation of sales and lease contracts. Subsequent chapters cover the performance, enforcement, breach, and remedies for the breach of sales and lease contracts, as well as sales and lease contract warranties.

Uniform Commercial Code

18.1 Describe the Uniform Commercial Code (UCC).

One of the major frustrations of businesspeople conducting interstate business is that they are subject to the laws of each state in which they operate. To address this problem, in 1949, the National Conference of Commissioners on Uniform State Laws promulgated the **Uniform Commercial Code (UCC)**. The following feature discusses the UCC.

Uniform Commercial Code (UCC)
A model act that includes comprehensive laws that cover most aspects of commercial transactions. All the states have enacted all or part of the UCC as statutes.

Landmark Law

Uniform Commercial Code

The UCC is a *model act* drafted by the American Law Institute and the National Conference of Commissioners on Uniform State Laws. This model act contains uniform rules that govern commercial transactions. For the UCC or any part of the UCC to become law in a state, that state needs to enact the UCC as its commercial law statute. Every state (except Louisiana, which has adopted only parts of the UCC) has enacted the UCC or the majority of the UCC as a commercial statute.

The UCC is divided into articles, with each article establishing uniform rules for a particular facet of

(continued)

commerce in this country. The articles of the UCC are the following:

Article 1	General Provisions
Article 2	Sales
Article 2A	Leases
Article 3	Negotiable Instruments
Article 4	Bank Deposits and Collections
Article 4A	Funds Transfers
Article 5	Letters of Credit
Article 6	Bulk Transfers and Bulk Sales (Repealed)
Article 7	Documents of Title
Article 8	Investment Securities
Article 9	Secured Transactions

The UCC is continually revised to reflect changes in modern commercial practices and technology.

Critical Legal Thinking Questions

What is the benefit of states having the same or similar laws regarding transactions in goods? Should uniform laws also be adopted for the provision of services, the sale of real estate, and other transactions?

Article 2 (Sales)

18.2 Define *sales contracts* governed by Article 2 of the UCC.

All states except Louisiana have adopted some version of **Article 2 (Sales)** of the UCC. Article 2 is also applied by federal courts to sales contracts governed by federal law.

Article 2 (Sales)
An article of the UCC that governs sale of goods.

What Is a Sale?

Article 2 of the UCC applies to transactions in goods [UCC 2-102]. All states have held that Article 2 applies to a **sales contract** for the sale of goods. The **sale of goods** consists of the passing of title of goods from a seller to a buyer for a price [UCC 2-106(1)].

sale of goods
The passing of title of goods from a seller to a buyer for a price.

Example The purchase of an automobile (costing $500 or more) is a sale of a good subject to Article 2, whether the automobile was paid for using cash, credit card, or another form of consideration (see Exhibit 18.1).

What Are Goods?

goods
Tangible items that are movable at the time of their identification to a contract.

Goods are defined as tangible items that are movable at the time of their identification to a contract [UCC 2-105(1)]. Specially manufactured goods and the unborn young of animals are examples of goods. Certain items are not considered goods and are not subject to Article 2. They include the following:

- Money and intangible items are not tangible goods.

  Examples Stocks, bonds, and patents are not tangible goods.

- Real estate is not a tangible good because it is not movable [UCC 2-105(1)]. However, minerals, structures, growing crops, and other items that are severable from real estate may be classified as goods subject to Article 2.

  Examples The sale and removal of a chandelier in a house is a sale of goods subject to Article 2 because its removal would not materially harm the real estate. The sale and removal of the furnace, however, would be a sale of real property because its removal would cause material harm [UCC 2-107(2)].

Exhibit 18.1 SALES TRANSACTION

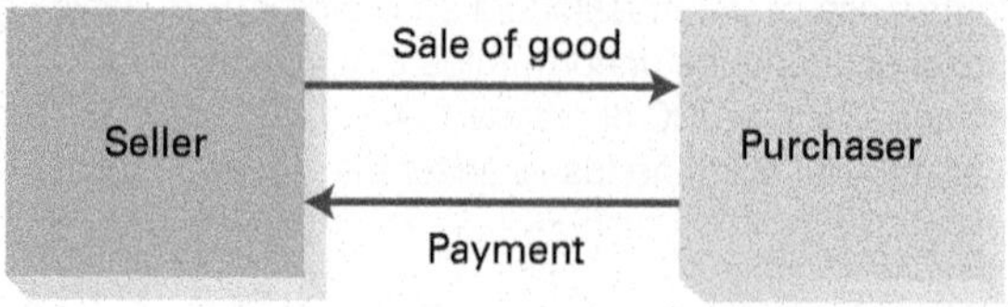

Who Are Sellers?

A manufacturer, distributor, wholesaler, dealer, or retailer who owns—i.e., has title to—the product during the chain of distribution is a seller. However, shippers, warehouses, brokers, marketers, auctioneers, bailees, and consignees, who do not take title to property during the course of a distribution but rather render services to facilitate that distribution or sale, are not sellers.

Goods versus Services

Contracts for the provision of services—including legal services, medical services, and dental services—are not covered by Article 2. Sometimes, however, a sale involves the provision of both a service and a good in the same transaction. This sale is referred to as a **mixed sale**. Article 2 applies to mixed sales only if the goods are the predominant part of the transaction. Whether the sale of goods is the predominant part of a mixed sale is decided by courts on a case-by-case basis.

mixed sale
A sale that involves the provision of a service and a good in the same transaction.

Example A medical doctor performs a surgical procedure wherein the doctor replaces a patient's diseased knee joint with an artificial knee consisting of a combination of metal and plastic. Although the artificial knee is a good, the predominant part of the transaction is the provision of medical services by the doctor. Therefore, the UCC does not apply to the transaction between the doctor and the patient.

In the following case, the court had to decide whether **Amazon.com** was a seller of a good.

CASE 18.1 *FEDERAL COURT CASE Seller*

Erie Insurance Company v. Amazon.com, Inc.

925 F.3d 135 (2019)
United States Court of Appeals for the Fourth Circuit

"When Amazon sells its own goods on its website, it has the responsibility of a seller, just as any other retailer would have."

—Paul Niemeyer, Circuit Judge

Facts

Trung Cao purchased online an LED headlamp used for cycling, camping, and hiking and gave it as a gift to his friends, Minh and Anh Nguyen. Both Cao and the Nguyens lived in Maryland. Cao purchased the headlamp on **Amazon.com**'s website, which stated that the headlamp was "sold by: Dream Light" and "fulfilled by: Amazon." Cao paid by credit card. Amazon stored Dream Light products in a warehouse in Virginia, where Dream Light retained title and risk of loss to the goods. In fulfilling Cao's order, Amazon put the headlamp in a box and shipped it by UPS. Two weeks after delivery, the headlamp malfunctioned, supposedly from a defective battery or batteries, igniting the Nguyens' house and causing $313,166 in damages. Erie Insurance Company (Erie), the Nguyens' insurer, paid the loss. Erie sued Amazon, alleging that Amazon was liable as a seller of the headlamp. Amazon argued that it was not the seller but that Dream Light was the seller. The U.S. district court held that Amazon was not the seller of the headlamp and therefore was not liable. Erie appealed.

Issue

Was Amazon the seller of the headlamp?

Language of the Court

The ordinary meaning of a seller is one that offers property for sale, with sale defined as the transfer of ownership of and title to property of one person to another for a price. Indeed, the Maryland Uniform Commercial Code adopts this definition precisely. When Dream Light shipped its headlamp to Amazon's warehouse in Virginia it was the owner of—it had title to—the headlamp. And when it transferred possession of the headlamp to Amazon, without Amazon's payment of the headlamp's price or an agreement transferring title to

(continued)

it, Amazon did not, by that simple transfer, receive title. Amazon explicitly posted on its site that Dream Light was the seller.

We conclude that Amazon was not a seller and therefore does not have the liability under Maryland law that sellers of goods have. When Amazon sells its own goods on its website, it has the responsibility of a seller, just as any other retailer would have. But when it provides a website for use by other sellers of products and facilitates those sales under its fulfilment program, it is not a seller, and it does not have the liability of a seller.

Decision

The U.S. court of appeals held that Amazon was not a UCC seller of the headlamp and was therefore not liable.

Critical Legal Thinking Questions

When you order goods on Amazon, do you know whether Amazon is the seller or a third party is the seller? Do you think that Amazon should be held liable for third-party products sold on its website?

Who Is a Merchant?

Generally, Article 2 of the UCC applies to all sales contracts, whether they involve merchants or not. However, Article 2 contains several provisions that either apply only to merchants or impose a greater duty on merchants. UCC 2-104(1) defines a **merchant** as (1) a person who deals in goods of the kind involved in the transaction or (2) a person who by occupation holds him- or herself out as having knowledge or skill peculiar to the goods involved in the transaction.

merchant
A person who (1) deals in goods of the kind involved in a transaction or (2) by occupation holds him- or herself out as having knowledge or skill peculiar to the goods involved in the transaction.

Examples A sporting goods dealer is a merchant with respect to the sporting goods he or she sells. This sporting goods dealer is not a merchant concerning the sale of a personal lawn mower to a neighbor.

Article 2A (Leases)

18.3 Define *lease contracts* governed by Article 2A of the UCC.

Personal property leases of goods are a billion-dollar industry. **Article 2A (Leases)** of the UCC directly addresses personal property leases [UCC 2A-101]. It establishes a comprehensive uniform law covering the formation, performance, and default of leases in goods [UCC 2A-102, 2A-103(h)]. Article 2A is similar to Article 2. In fact, many Article 2 provisions were simply adapted to reflect leasing terminology and practices that carried over to Article 2A.

Article 2A (Leases)
An article of the UCC that governs leases of goods.

Examples More than 30 percent of automobiles and other vehicles are leased. Commercial goods such as farm machinery, industrial equipment, aircraft, and the like are often leased.

Definition of *Lease*

A **lease** is a transfer of the right to the possession and use of named goods for a set term in return for certain consideration [UCC 2A-103(1)(i)(x)]. Leased goods can be anything from an automobile leased to an individual to a complex line of industrial equipment leased to a multinational corporation.

lease
A transfer of the right to the possession and use of named goods for a set term in return for certain consideration.

In a **lease contract**, the **lessor** is the person who transfers the right of possession and use of goods under the lease [UCC 2A-103(1)(p)]. The **lessee** is the person who acquires the right to possession and use of goods under the lease [UCC 2A-103(1)(n)].

lessor
A person who transfers the right of possession and use of goods under a lease.

lessee
A person who acquires the right to possession and use of goods under a lease.

Example Ingersoll-Rand Corporation, which manufactures robotic equipment, enters into a contract to lease robotic equipment to Dow Chemical. This is a lease contract. Ingersoll-Rand is the lessor, and Dow Chemical is the lessee (see Exhibit 18.2).

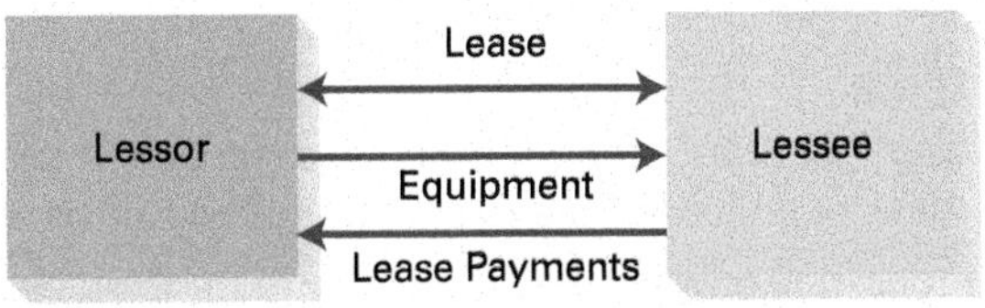

Exhibit 18.2 **LEASE**

Finance Lease

A **finance lease** is a three-party transaction consisting of a lessor, a lessee, and a **supplier** (or vendor). The lessor does not select, manufacture, or supply the goods. Instead, the lessor acquires title to the goods or the right to their possession and use in connection with the terms of the lease [UCC 2A-103(1)(g)].

finance lease
A three-party transaction consisting of a lessor, a lessee, and a supplier.

Example JetGreen Airways, a commercial air carrier, decides to lease a new airplane that is manufactured by Boeing. To finance the airplane acquisition, JetGreen goes to City Bank. City Bank purchases the airplane from Boeing, and City Bank then leases the airplane to JetGreen. Boeing is the supplier, City Bank is the lessor, and JetGreen is the lessee. City Bank does not take physical delivery of the airplane; the airplane is delivered by Boeing directly to JetGreen (see Exhibit 18.3).

Formation of Sales and Lease Contracts: Offer

18.4 Describe the formation of sales and lease contracts and define the *firm offer rule.*

As with general contracts, the formation of sales and lease contracts requires an offer and an acceptance. The UCC-established rules for each of these elements often differ considerably from common law.

A contract for the sale or lease of goods may be made in any manner sufficient to show agreement, including conduct by both parties that recognizes the existence of a contract [UCC 2-204(1), 2A-204(1)]. Under the UCC, an agreement sufficient to constitute a contract for the sale or lease of goods may be found even though the moment of its making is undetermined [UCC 2-204(2), 2A-204(2)].

Open Terms

Sometimes the parties to a sales or lease contract leave open a major term in the contract. The UCC is tolerant of open terms. According to UCC 2-204(3) and 2A-204(3), a contract does not fail because of indefiniteness if (1) the parties intended to make a contract and (2) there is a reasonably certain basis for giving an appropriate remedy. In effect, certain **open terms** are permitted to be "read into" sales or lease contracts. This rule is commonly referred to as the **gap-filling rule**. Some examples of terms that are commonly left open are listed in Exhibit 18.4.

gap-filling rule
A rule stating that an open term can be "read into" a contract.

Exhibit 18.3 **FINANCE LEASE**

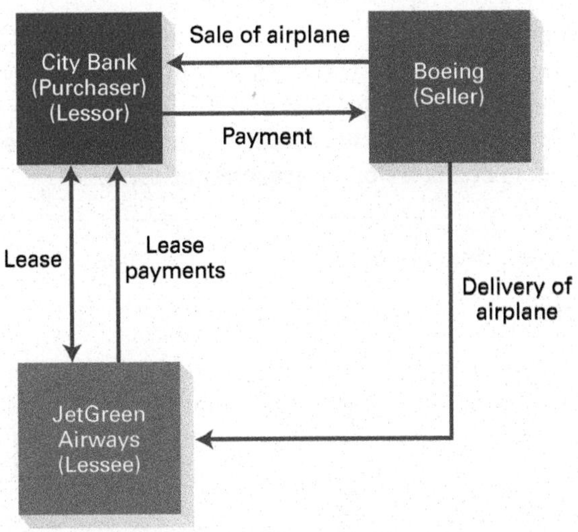

Exhibit 18.4 UCC OPEN TERMS

OPEN PRICE TERM
If a sales contract does not contain a specific price, a "reasonable price" is implied at the time of delivery. This is called an **open price term.**

Example A contract may provide that a price is to be fixed by a market rate, such as a commodities market rate.

Example A contract may provide that a price will be set or recorded by a third person or an agency, such as a government agency. For example, the federal government sets minimum prices for some agricultural products.

A contract may provide that the price will be set by another standard, either on delivery or on a set date. If the agreed-on standard is unavailable when the price is to be set, a reasonable price is implied at the time of delivery of the goods [UCC 2-305(1)]. A seller or buyer who reserves the right to fix a price must do so in good faith [UCC 2-305(2)]. When one of the parties fails to fix an open price term, the other party may opt to either (1) treat the contract as canceled or (2) fix a reasonable price for the goods [UCC 2-305(3)].

OPEN PAYMENT TERM
If the parties to a sales contract do not agree on payment terms, payment is due at the time and place at which the buyer is to receive the goods. This is called an **open payment term.**

If delivery is authorized and made by way of document of title, payment is due at the time and place at which the buyer is to receive the document of title, regardless of where the goods are to be received [UCC 2-310].

OPEN DELIVERY TERM
If the parties to a sales contract do not agree to the time, place, and manner of delivery of the goods, the place for delivery is the seller's place of business. If the seller does not have a place of business, delivery is to be made at the seller's residence. This is called an **open delivery term.**

If identified goods are located at some other place, and both parties know of this fact at the time of contracting, that place is the place of delivery [UCC 2-308].

If goods are to be shipped but the shipper is not named, the seller is obligated to make the shipping arrangements. Such arrangements must be made in good faith and within limits of commercial reasonableness [UCC 2-311(2)].

The foundation of justice is good faith.

Cicero
De Officiis, Book 1, Chapter VII (44 BCE)

OPEN TIME TERM
If the parties to a sales contract do not set a specific time of performance for any obligation under the contract, the contract must be performed within a reasonable time. If a sales contract provides for successive performance over an unspecified period of time, the contract is valid for a reasonable time [UCC 2-309]. This is called an **open time term.**

OPEN ASSORTMENT TERM
If the assortment of goods to a sales contract is left open, the buyer is given the option of choosing those goods. The buyer must make the selection in good faith and within limits set by commercial reasonableness [UCC 2-311(2)]. This is called an **open assortment term.**

The following feature discusses a unique UCC rule.

Consideration

The formation of sales and lease contracts requires consideration. However, the UCC changes the common law rule that requires the modification of a contract to be supported by new consideration. An agreement modifying a sales or lease contract needs no consideration to be binding [UCC 2-209(1), 2A-208(1)].

Business Environment

UCC Firm Offer Rule

Recall that the common law of contracts allows the offeror to revoke an offer at any time prior to its acceptance. The UCC recognizes an exception to this rule, which is called the **firm offer rule**. This rule states that a *merchant* who (1) offers to buy, sell, or lease goods and (2) gives a written and signed assurance on a separate form that the offer will be held open cannot revoke the offer for the time stated or, if no time is stated, for a reasonable time. The maximum amount of time permitted under this rule is three months [UCC 2-205, 2A-205].

Example On June 1, Sophisticated LLC, a BMW automobile dealer, offers to sell a BMW M3 coupe to Mandy for $60,000. Sophisticated LLC signs a written assurance to keep that offer open to Mandy until July 15. On July 5, Sophisticated LLC sells the car to another buyer. On July 15, Mandy tenders $60,000 for the car. Sophisticated LLC is a merchant subject to the firm offer rule. Sophisticated LLC is liable to Mandy for breach of contract. Thus, if Mandy has to pay $70,000 for the car at another dealership, she can recover $10,000 from Sophisticated LLC.

Modification of a sales or lease contract must be made in good faith [UCC 1-203]. As in the common law of contracts, modifications are not binding if they are obtained through fraud, duress, extortion, or other bad faith efforts.

firm offer rule
A UCC rule stating that a merchant who (1) makes an offer to buy, sell, or lease goods and (2) assures the other party in a separate writing that the offer will be held open cannot revoke the offer for the time stated or, if no time is stated, for a reasonable time.

Formation of Sales and Lease Contracts: Acceptance

18.5 Describe acceptance and define the UCC's *additional terms rule* and *written confirmation rule*.

Both common law and the UCC provide that a contract is created when the offeree (i.e., the buyer or lessee) sends an acceptance to the offeror (seller or lessor), not when the offeror receives the acceptance.

Examples A sales or lease contract is made when the acceptance letter is delivered to the post office. The contract remains valid even if the post office loses the letter. An e-contract is made when the offeree sends an email or another electronic document to the offeror.

Method and Manner of Acceptance

Unless otherwise unambiguously indicated by language or circumstance, an offer to make a sales or lease contract may be accepted in any manner and by any reasonable medium of acceptance [UCC 2-206(1)(a), 2A-206(1)].

Example A seller sends a telegram to a proposed buyer, offering to sell the buyer certain goods. The buyer responds by mailing a letter of acceptance to the seller. In most circumstances, mailing the letter of acceptance would be considered reasonable. If the goods were extremely perishable or if the market for the goods were very volatile, however, a faster means of acceptance (e.g., a telegram) might be warranted.

If an order or other offer to buy goods requires prompt or current shipment, the offer is accepted if the seller (1) promptly promises to ship the goods or (2) promptly ships either conforming or nonconforming goods [UCC 2-206(1)(b)]. The shipment of conforming goods signals acceptance of the buyer's offer.

Acceptance of goods occurs after the buyer or lessee has a reasonable opportunity to inspect them and signifies that (1) the goods are conforming, (2) the buyer will take or retain the goods despite their nonconformity, or (3) the buyer fails to reject the goods within a reasonable time after tender or delivery [UCC 2-513(1), 2A-515(1)].

The following feature discusses an area of the law where the UCC differs from the common law of contracts.

Business Environment

UCC Permits Additional Terms

Under common law's **mirror image rule**, an offeree's acceptance must be on the same terms as the offer. The inclusion of **additional terms** in the acceptance is considered a **counteroffer** rather than an acceptance. Thus, a counteroffer extinguishes the offeror's original offer.

UCC 2-207(1) is more liberal than the mirror image rule. It permits definite and timely expression of acceptance or written confirmation to operate as an acceptance even though the contract contains terms that are additional to or different from the offered terms, unless the acceptance is expressly conditional on assent to such terms.

If one or both parties to a sales contract are *nonmerchants*, any additional terms are considered **proposed additions** to the contract. The proposed additions do not constitute a counteroffer or extinguish the original offer. If the offeree's proposed additions are accepted by the original offeror, they become part of the contract. If they are not accepted, the sales contract is formed on the basis of the terms of the original offer [UCC 2-207(2)].

Example A salesperson at a Lexus dealership offers to sell an automobile to a buyer for $65,000. The buyer replies, "I accept your offer, but I would like to have a satellite radio in the car." The satellite radio is a proposed addition to the contract. If the salesperson agrees, the contract between the parties consists of the terms of the original offer plus the additional term regarding the satellite radio. If the salesperson rejects the proposed addition, the sales contract consists of the terms of the original offer because the buyer made a definite expression of acceptance.

---

additional terms
In certain circumstances, the UCC permits an acceptance of a sales contract to contain additional terms and to act still as an acceptance rather than a counteroffer.

accommodation
A shipment that is offered to a buyer as a replacement for the original shipment when the original shipment cannot be filled.

Accommodation Shipment

A shipment of nonconforming goods does not constitute an acceptance if the seller reasonably notifies the buyer that the shipment is offered only as an **accommodation** to the buyer [UCC 2-206(1)(b)].

Example A buyer offers to purchase 500 red umbrellas from a seller. The seller's red umbrellas are temporarily out of stock. The seller sends the buyer 500 green umbrellas and notifies the buyer that these umbrellas are being sent as an accommodation. The accommodation is a counteroffer from the seller to the buyer. The buyer is free either to accept or to reject the counteroffer.

The following feature discusses how the UCC resolves a commonplace problem that occurs between merchants.

Business Environment

UCC Battle of the Forms

When *merchants* negotiate sales contracts, they often exchange preprinted forms. These "boilerplate" forms usually contain terms that favor the drafter. Thus, an offeror who sends a standard form contract as an offer to the offeree may receive an acceptance drafted on the offeree's own form contract. This scenario—commonly called the **battle of the forms**—raises important questions: Is there a contract? If so, what are its terms? The UCC provides guidance in answering these questions.

Under UCC 2-207(2), if both parties are merchants, any additional terms contained in an acceptance become part of the sales contract unless (1) the offer expressly limits acceptance to the terms of the offer, (2) the additional terms materially alter the terms of the original contract, or (3) the offeror notifies the offeree that he or she objects to the additional terms within a reasonable time after receiving the offeree's modified acceptance.

In the battle of the forms, there is no contract if the additional terms so materially alter the terms of the original offer that the parties cannot agree on the contract. This fact-specific determination is made by the courts on a case-by-case basis.

UCC Statute of Frauds

18.6 Describe the UCC Statute of Frauds for sales and lease contracts.

The UCC includes Statute of Frauds provisions that apply to sales and lease contracts. The provisions of the **UCC Statute of Frauds** are as follows:

- All contracts for the *sale of goods* priced at *$500 or more* must be in writing [UCC 2-201(1)].
- *Lease* contracts requiring payments of *$1,000 or more* must be in writing [UCC 2A-201(1)].

Future amendments to the UCC may increase these dollar amounts.

The writing must be sufficient to indicate that a contract has been made between the parties. Except as discussed in the paragraphs that follow, the writing must be signed by the party against whom enforcement is sought or by an authorized agent or broker. If a contract falling within these parameters is not written, it is unenforceable.

Example A seller orally agrees to sell her computer to a buyer for $550. When the buyer tenders the purchase price, the seller asserts the Statute of Frauds and refuses to sell the computer to him. The seller is correct. The contract must be in writing to be enforceable because the contract price for the computer exceeds $499.99.

battle of the forms
A UCC rule stating that if both parties are merchants, then additional terms contained in the acceptance may become part of the sales contract if certain requirements are met.

UCC Statute of Frauds
A rule in the UCC that requires all contracts for the sale of goods costing $500 or more and lease contracts involving payments of $1,000 or more to be in writing.

Critical Legal Thinking Question

The UCC additional terms rule and UCC battle of the forms rule differ from the mirror image rule applicable to non-UCC contracts. Why are the UCC rules more liberal in allowing contracts to be formed?

Exceptions to the UCC Statute of Frauds

In three situations, a sales or lease contract that would otherwise be required to be in writing is enforceable even if it is not in writing [UCC 2-201(3), UCC 2A-201(4)]:

1. **Specially manufactured goods.** Buyers and lessees often order **specially manufactured goods**. If a contract to purchase or lease such goods is oral, the buyer or lessee may not assert the Statute of Frauds against the enforcement of the contract if (1) the goods are not suitable for sale or lease to others in the ordinary course of the seller's or the lessor's business and (2) the seller or lessor has made either a substantial beginning of the manufacture of the goods or commitments for their procurement.
2. **Admissions in pleadings or court.** If the party against whom enforcement of an oral sales or lease contract is sought admits in pleadings, testimony, or otherwise in court that a contract for the sale or lease of goods was made, the oral contract is enforceable against that party. However, the contract is enforceable only as to the quantity of goods admitted.
3. **Part acceptance.** An oral sales or lease contract that should otherwise be in writing is enforceable to the extent to which the goods have been received and accepted by the buyer or lessee.

   Example A lessor orally contracts to lease 20 automobiles to a lessee. The lessee accepts the first eight automobiles tendered by the lessor. This action is part acceptance. The lessee refuses to take delivery of the remaining 12 automobiles. Here, the lessee must pay for the eight automobiles it originally received and accepted. The lessee does not have to accept or pay for the remaining 12 automobiles.

The prince is not above the laws, but the laws above the prince.

Pliny the Younger
(Gaius Caecilius Secundus)
(61–113 AD)

The following feature discusses a unique UCC rule that applies to contracts between merchants.

Business Environment

UCC Written Confirmation Rule

Under the **written confirmation rule**, if both parties to an oral sales or lease contract are *merchants*, the Statute of Frauds writing requirement can be satisfied if (1) one of the parties to an oral agreement sends a written confirmation of the sale or lease within a reasonable time after contracting and (2) the other merchant does not give written notice of an objection to the contract within 10 days after receiving the confirmation. This situation is true even though the party receiving the written confirmation has not signed it. The only stipulations are that the confirmation is sufficient and that the party to whom it was sent has reason to know its contents [UCC 2-201(2)].

Example A merchant-seller in Chicago orally contracts by telephone to sell goods to a merchant-buyer in Phoenix for $100,000. Within a reasonable time after contracting, the seller sends a sufficient written confirmation to the buyer of the agreed-on transaction. The buyer, who has reason to know the contents of the written confirmation, fails to object to the contents of the confirmation in writing within 10 days after receiving it. Under the UCC, the Statute of Frauds has been met, and the buyer cannot thereafter raise it against enforcement of the contract.

---

written confirmation rule
A rule stating that if both parties to an oral sales or lease contract are merchants, the Statute of Frauds writing requirement can be satisfied if (1) one of the parties to an oral agreement sends a written confirmation of the sale or lease within a reasonable time after contracting and (2) the other merchant does not give written notice of an objection to the contract within 10 days after receiving the confirmation.

When Written Modification Is Required

Oral modification of a contract is not enforceable if the parties agree that any modification of the sales or lease contract must be signed in writing [UCC 2-209(2), 2A-208(2)]. In the absence of such an agreement, oral modifications to sales and lease contracts are binding if they do not violate the Statute of Frauds. If the oral modification brings the contract within the Statute of Frauds, it must be in writing to be enforceable.

Example A lessor and lessee enter into an oral lease contract for the lease of goods at a rent of $900. Subsequently, the contract is modified by raising the rent to $1,200. Because the modified contract rent is more than $999.99, the contract comes under the UCC Statute of Frauds, and the modification must be in writing to be enforceable.

Parol Evidence Rule

parol evidence rule
A rule stating that if a written contract is a complete and final statement of the parties' agreement, any prior or contemporaneous oral or written statements that alter, contradict, or are in addition to the terms of the written contract are inadmissible in court regarding a dispute over the contract.

The **parol evidence rule** states that when a sales or lease contract is evidenced by a writing that is intended to be a final expression of the parties' agreement or a confirmatory memorandum, the terms of the writing may not be contradicted by evidence of (1) a prior oral or written agreement or (2) a contemporaneous oral agreement (i.e., parol evidence) [UCC 2-202, 2A-202]. This rule is intended to ensure certainty in written sales and lease contracts.

Occasionally, the express terms of a written contract are not clear on their face and must be interpreted. In such cases, reference may be made to certain sources outside the contract. These sources are construed together when they are consistent with each other. If that is unreasonable, they are considered in descending order of priority [UCC 2-208(2), 2A-207(2)]:

1. **Course of performance**. Conduct of the parties concerning the contract in question.
2. **Course of dealing**. Conduct of the parties in prior transactions and contracts.
3. **Usage of trade**. Any practice or method of dealing that is regularly observed or adhered to in a place, a vocation, a trade, or an industry.

Example A cattle rancher contracts to purchase 3,000 bushels of "corn" from a farmer. The farmer delivers feed corn to the rancher. The rancher rejects this corn and demands delivery of corn that is fit for human consumption. If the parties did not have any prior course of performance or course of dealing that would indicate otherwise, usage of trade would be used to interpret the word *corn*. Thus, the delivery of feed corn would be assumed and become part of the contract.

CONCEPT SUMMARY

COMPARISON OF CONTRACT LAW AND THE LAW OF SALES

Topic	Common Law of Contract	UCC Law of Sales
Definiteness	Contract must contain all the material terms of the parties' agreement.	The UCC gap-filling rule permits terms to be implied if the parties intended to make a contract and there is reasonably certain basis for giving an appropriate remedy [UCC 2-204].
Irrevocable offers	Option contracts.	Option contracts. Firm offers by merchants to keep an offer open are binding up to three months without any consideration [UCC 2-205].
Counteroffers	Acceptance must be a mirror image of the offer. A counteroffer rejects and terminates the offeror's original offer.	Additional terms of an acceptance become part of the contract if (1) they do not materially alter the terms of the offer and (2) the offeror does not object within a reasonable time after reviewing the acceptance [UCC 2-207].
Statute of Frauds	Writing must be signed by the party against whom enforcement is sought.	Writing may be enforced against a party who has not signed a contract if (1) both parties are merchants, (2) one party sends a written confirmation of oral agreement within a reasonable time after contracting, and (3) the other party does not give written notice of objection within 10 days after receiving the confirmation [UCC 2-201].
Modification	Consideration is required.	Consideration is not required [UCC 2-209].

Electronic Sales and Lease Contracts

18.7 Describe how Revised Article 2 (Sales) and Article 2A (Leases) permit electronic contracting.

Many sales and lease contracts are now electronic. Jurisdictions recognize and enforce **electronic sales contracts (e-sales contracts)** and **electronic lease contracts (e-lease contracts)**. Following are some of the definitions for electronic commerce and their implications:

- **Electronic** means relating to technology having electrical, digital, magnetic, wireless, optical, electromagnetic, or similar capabilities. This term extends many of the provisions and rules of the UCC to cover electronic contracting of sales and lease contracts.
- **Electronic agent** means a computer program or an electronic or other automated means used independently to initiate an action or respond to electronic records or performances in whole or in part, without review or action by an individual. This definition allows for contracting for the sale and lease of goods over the internet, using websites and other electronic media to order or lease goods.
- **Electronic record (e-record)** means a record created, generated, sent, communicated, received, or stored by electronic means. This term is often used in addition to the words *writing* and *record* and thus recognizes that UCC contracts and other information may be sent or stored by electronic means rather than in tangible writings.
- **Electronic signature (e-signature** or **digital signature)** means the signature of a person that appears on an electronic record and is recognized as a lawful signature. An electronic signature may also be that of a person's electronic agent.

These definitions expand the coverage of the provisions of UCC Article 2 and Article 2A to electronic contracting of sales and lease contracts.

electronic agent
A computer program or an electronic or other automated means used independently to initiate an action or respond to electronic records or performances in whole or in part, without review or action by an individual.

electronic record (e-record)
A record created, generated, sent, communicated, received, or stored by electronic means.

EIFFEL TOWER, PARIS, FRANCE
Letters of credit are often used to facilitate the financing of international trade.

Letters of Credit

18.8 Describe how letters of credit facilitate international trade.

letter of credit (documentary credit)
A document that is issued by a bank on behalf of a buyer who purchases goods from a seller that guarantees that the bank will pay the seller.

Uniform Customs and Practice for Documentary Credits (UCP)
A set of rules promulgated by the International Chamber of Commerce (ICC) that establishes specific terms (called Incoterms) that are used to govern international letters of credit.

importer
The buyer in an international sales contract who is located in one country and who is buying goods from a seller located in another country.

exporter
The seller in an international sales contract who is located in one country and who is selling goods to a buyer located in another country.

issuing bank
The bank that issues a letter of credit on behalf of a buyer.

Letters of credit are often used to finance international trade and facilitate import-export transactions. A **letter of credit**, also known as a **documentary credit**, is a formal document issued by a bank that guarantees payment to a seller on behalf of a buyer. The International Chamber of Commerce (ICC) has promulgated the **Uniform Customs and Practice for Documentary Credits (UCP)**, which establishes specific terms (called **Incoterms**) that are almost universally accepted and used to govern international letters of credit. Most parties to international sale of goods contracts that involve letters of credit agree that the provisions of the UCP apply to their letters of credit.

In an international sales transaction, the buyer (the **importer**) and the seller (the **exporter**) are located in different countries. If the seller delivers the goods but the buyer fails to pay for the goods, difficulties may arise for the seller in obtaining payment because the buyer is located in a different country, where different legal rules and procedures may apply. Also, the unpaid seller will incur legal and other expenses in trying to recover payment. To solve this problem, the seller often requires that the buyer obtain a letter of credit from a bank whereby the seller is paid for the goods by the bank rather than by the buyer directly. Letters of credit are often used if the seller and buyer have not conducted prior business, if the reliability and creditworthiness of a buyer cannot be readily ascertained, and even between known parties to guarantee that the seller will be paid the correct amount and on time, without having to resort to legal proceedings. A letter of credit is a separate document from the sales contract.

In a letter of credit transaction, the buyer-importer goes to a bank and pays a fee to the bank to issue a letter of credit. The buyer is called the **applicant**. The bank that issues the letter of credit is called the **issuing bank**. The buyer and the bank usually have a preexisting business relationship, although this is not required. The seller is named the **beneficiary** in the letter of credit. The seller usually designates a bank to receive payment on the letter of credit once the goods are delivered to the buyer. The seller's bank is called the **nominated bank** or **accepting bank**. The seller and the nominated bank usually have a prior working relationship. The nominated bank is identified in the letter of credit. Once the goods are delivered and the buyer and seller meet the requirements set forth in the sales contract, the issuing bank will pay the nominated bank the purchase price of the goods. The nominated bank will then disperse the funds to the seller. In some instances, the issuing bank will pay the seller directly. There may be intermediary banks between the issuing bank and the nominated bank who facilitate the financial transaction. For example, a letter of credit issued by a foreign bank may be required to be additionally guaranteed by a domestic bank. The parties usually pay their own banks for services rendered, although different arrangements may be agreed to.

nominated bank (accepting bank)
The bank that accepts a letter of credit on behalf of a seller.

Example Agro-Industrial, Inc. is a Brazilian company with farming operations in Brazil. It enters into an international sales contract with Deere & Company, a U.S. company, to purchase $35 million of John Deere tractors and other farm equipment. To guarantee payment to Deere, Agro-Industrial goes to Brazil Bank and applies for, and is granted, a $35 million letter of credit that names Deere & Company the beneficiary. Deere employs Bank of America, a U.S. bank, to be its bank to receive payment on the letter of credit from Brazil Bank. In this transaction, Agro-Industrial is the buyer, importer, and applicant. Brazil Bank is the issuing bank. Deere & Company is the seller, exporter, and beneficiary. Bank of America is the nominated bank. Once the goods are delivered and all of the paperwork is in order, Brazil Bank makes the funds available to Bank of America. Deere & Company can then draw the funds from Bank of America.

Letters of credit can also be used in domestic sales and purchase transactions. Domestic letters of credit are usually governed by **Article 5 (Letters of Credit)** of the UCC, although the parties may designate that the provisions of the UCP apply to their transaction. Often, a **standby letter of credit** is used in domestic sales transactions. Rather than being the primary method for paying for goods, a standby letter of credit guarantees the seller that if the buyer does not pay for the goods, then the bank will pay the seller.

Article 5 (Letters of Credit)
An article of the Uniform Commercial Code (UCC) that governs letters of credit.

standby letter of credit
A letter of credit whereby a bank guarantees that if a buyer does not pay for the goods purchased from a seller, then the bank will pay the seller.

Letters of credit are also used to guarantee payment for the provision of services and the transfer of intellectual property. The vast majority of letters of credit are issued in electronic form, and the UCP and Article 5 have been revised to accommodate digital letters of credit and trade practices.

Key Terms and Concepts

Accommodation (328)
Additional terms (328)
Applicant (332)
Article 2 (Sales) (322)
Article 2A (Leases) (324)
Article 5 (Letters of Credit) (333)
Battle of the forms (328)
Beneficiary (332)
Counteroffer (328)
Course of dealing (330)
Course of performance (330)
Electronic (331)
Electronic agent (331)
Electronic lease contract (e-lease contract) (331)
Electronic record (e-record) (331)
Electronic sales contract (e-sales contract) (331)
Electronic signature (e-signature or digital signature) (331)
Exporter (332)
Finance lease (325)
Firm offer rule (327)
Gap-filling rule (325)
Goods (322)
Importer (332)
Incoterms (332)
Issuing bank (332)
Lease (323)
Lease contract (324)
Lessee (324)
Lessor (324)
Letter of credit (documentary credit) (332)
Merchant (324)
Mirror image rule (328)
Mixed sale (323)
Nominated bank (accepting bank) (333)
Open assortment term (326)

Critical Legal Thinking Cases

18.1 Good or Service Mr. Gulash lived in Shelton, Connecticut. He wanted an aboveground swimming pool installed in his backyard. Gulash contacted Stylarama, Inc. (Stylarama), a company specializing in the sale and construction of pools. The two parties entered into a contract that called for Stylarama to "furnish all labor and materials to construct a Wavecrest brand pool, and furnish and install a pool with vinyl liners." The total cost for materials and labor was $3,690. There was no breakdown in the contract of costs between labor and materials. After the pool was installed, its sides began bowing out, the 4-inch wooden supports for the pool rotted and misaligned, and the entire pool became tilted. Gulash brought suit, alleging that Stylarama had violated several provisions of Article 2 of the UCC. Does this transaction involve the sale of goods, making it subject to Article 2? *Gulash v. Stylarama*, 33 Conn. Supp. 108, 364 A.2d 1221, 1975 Conn. Super. Lexis 209 (Superior Court of Connecticut, 1975)

18.2 Battle of the Forms Dan Miller was a commercial photographer who had taken a series of photographs that appeared in *The New York Times*. *Newsweek* magazine wanted to use the photographs. When a *Newsweek* employee named Dwyer phoned Miller, Dwyer was told that 72 images were available. Dwyer said that he wanted to inspect the photographs, and he offered a certain sum of money for each photo *Newsweek* used. The photos were to remain Miller's property. Miller and Dwyer agreed to the price and the date for delivery. *Newsweek* sent a courier to pick up the photographs. Along with the photos, Miller gave the courier a delivery memo that set out various conditions for the use of the photographs. The memo included a clause that required *Newsweek* to pay $1,500 each if any of the photos were lost or destroyed. After *Newsweek* received the package, it decided it no longer needed Miller's work. When Miller called to have the photos returned, he was told that they had all been lost. Miller demanded that *Newsweek* pay him $1,500 for each of the 72 lost photos. Assume that the court finds Miller and *Newsweek* to be merchants. Are the clauses in the delivery memo part of the sales contract? *Miller v. Newsweek, Inc.*, 660 F.Supp. 852, 1987 U.S. Dist. Lexis 4338 (United States District Court for the District of Delaware, 1987)

18.3 Open Terms Alvin Cagle was a potato farmer in Alabama who had had several business dealings with the H. C. Schmieding Produce Co. (Schmieding). Several months before harvest, Cagle entered into an oral sales contract with Schmieding. The contract called for Schmieding to pay the market price at harvest time for all the red potatoes that Cagle grew on his 30-acre farm. Schmieding asked that the potatoes be delivered during the normal harvest months. As Cagle began harvesting his red potatoes, he contacted Schmieding to arrange delivery. Schmieding told the farmer that no contract had been formed because the terms of the agreement were too indefinite. Cagle demanded that Schmieding buy his crop. When Schmieding refused, Cagle sued to have the contract enforced. Has a valid sales contract been formed? *H. C. Schmieding Produce Co. v. Cagle*, 529 So.2d 243, 1988 Ala. Lexis 284 (Supreme Court of Alabama, 1988)

18.4 Good or Service Frances Hector entered Cedars-Sinai Medical Center (Cedars-Sinai), Los Angeles, California, for a surgical operation on her heart. During the operation, a pacemaker was installed in Hector. The pacemaker, which was manufactured by American Technology, Inc., was installed at Cedars-Sinai Medical Center by Hector's physician, Dr. Eugene Kompaniez. The pacemaker was defective, causing injury to Hector. Hector sued Cedars-Sinai Medical Center under Article 2 (Sales) of the UCC to recover damages for breach of warranty of the pacemaker. Hector alleged that the surgical operation was primarily a sale of a good and therefore covered by the UCC. Cedars-Sinai Medical Center argued that the surgical operation was primarily a service and therefore the UCC did not apply. Who wins? *Hector v. Cedars-Sinai Medical Center*, 180 Cal. App.3d 493, 225 Cal. Rptr. 595, 1986 Cal. App. Lexis 1523 (Court of Appeal of California, 1986)

Ethics Cases

18.5 Ethics Case Kurt Perschke was a grain dealer in Indiana. Perschke phoned Ken Sebasty, the owner of a large wheat farm, and offered to buy 14,000 bushels of wheat for $1.95 per bushel. Sebasty accepted the offer. Perschke said that he could send a truck for the wheat on a stated date six months later. On the day of the phone call, Perschke's office manager sent a memorandum to Sebasty, stating the price and quantity of wheat that had been contracted for. One month before the scheduled delivery, Perschke called Sebasty to arrange for the loading of the wheat. Sebasty stated that no contract had been made. When Perschke brought suit, Sebasty claimed that the contract was unenforceable because of the Statute of Frauds. Was it ethical for Sebasty to raise the Statute of Frauds as a defense? Assuming that both parties are merchants, who wins the suit? *Sebasty v. Perschke*, 404 N.E.2d 1200, 1980 Ind. App. Lexis 1489 (Court of Appeals of Indiana, 1980)

18.6 Ethics Case Gordon Construction Company (Gordon) was a general contractor in the New York City area. Gordon planned on bidding for the job of constructing two buildings for the Port Authority of New York. In anticipation of its own bid, Gordon sought bids from subcontractors. E. A. Coronis Associates (Coronis), a fabricator of structured steel, sent a signed letter to Gordon. The letter quoted a price for work on the Port Authority project and stated that the price could change based on the amount of steel used. The letter contained no information other than the price Coronis would charge for the job. One month later, Gordon was awarded the Port Authority project. Four days later, Coronis sent Gordon a telegram, withdrawing its offer. Gordon replied that it expected Coronis to honor the price that it had previously quoted to Gordon. When Coronis refused, Gordon sued. Gordon claimed that Coronis was attempting to withdraw a firm offer. Did Coronis act ethically in withdrawing its offer? Who wins? *E. A. Coronis Associates v. Gordon Construction Co.*, 90 N.J. Super. 69, 216 A.2d 246, 1966 N.J. Super. Lexis 368 (Superior Court of New Jersey, 1966)

CHAPTER 19

Title to Goods and Risk of Loss

Henry R. Cheeseman

FREIGHTER

Common carriers, such as freighters and other ships, carry goods for buyers and sellers on the Great Lakes and other waterways in the United States and on oceans and other bodies of water worldwide. Risk of loss of the goods while in transit depends on the shipping terms used in the shipping or destination contract.

Learning Objectives

After studying this chapter, you should be able to:

19.1 Describe how title to goods passes in sales contracts.

19.2 Describe what party bears the risk of loss of goods where there is no breach of the sales contract.

19.3 Describe what party bears the risk of loss of goods where there has been a breach of a sales contract.

19.4 Describe which party bears the risk of loss of goods in conditional sales contracts.

19.5 Describe what party bears the risk of loss of goods in lease contracts.

19.6 Identify who bears the risk of loss when goods are stolen and resold.

19.7 Describe the provisions of the United Nations Convention for the International Sale of Goods (CISG) and how they apply to international sales contracts.

> *"A lawyer without history or literature is a mechanic, a mere working mason: if he possesses some knowledge of these, he may venture to call himself an architect."*
>
> —*Sir Walter Scott*
> *Guy Mannering, Chapter 37 (1815)*

Introduction to Title to Goods and Risk of Loss

Under common law, the rights and obligations of the buyer, the seller, and third parties are determined based on who held technical title to the goods. Article 2 of the Uniform Commercial Code (UCC) establishes precise rules for determining the *passage of title* in sales contracts. Other provisions of Article 2 apply, irrespective of title, except as otherwise provided [UCC 2-401].

Decided cases are the anchors of the law, as laws are of the state.
Francis Bacon, First Viscount St. Alban (1561–1626)

Common law placed the **risk of loss** to goods on the party who held title to the goods. Article 2 of the UCC rejects this notion and adopts concise rules for risk of loss that are not tied to title. It also gives the parties to a sales contract the right to *insure* the goods against loss if they have an "insurable interest" in the goods.

Article 2A (Leases) of the UCC establishes rules regarding title and risk of loss for leased goods. It also gives the parties to the lease contract the right to *insure* the goods against loss if they have an "insurable interest" in the goods.

Title, risk of loss, and insurable interest for the sale and lease of goods are discussed in this chapter.

Identification of Goods and Passage of Title

19.1 Describe how title to goods passes in sales contracts.

The *identification of goods* is rather simple. It means distinguishing the goods named in a contract from the seller's or lessor's other goods. The seller or lessor retains the risk of loss of the goods until he or she identifies them in a sales or lease contract. Further, UCC 2-401(1) and 2-501 prevent title to goods from passing from the seller to the buyer unless the goods are identified in the sales contract. In a lease transaction, title to the leased goods remains with the lessor or a third party. It does not pass to the lessee.

The identification of goods and passage of title are discussed in the following paragraphs.

Identification of Goods

Identification of goods can be made at any time and in any manner explicitly agreed to by the parties of a contract. In the absence of such an agreement, the UCC mandates when identification occurs [UCC 2-501(1), 2A-217]:

identification of goods
Distinguishing of the goods named in a contract from the seller's or lessor's other goods.

- Already existing goods are identified when a contract is made and names the specific goods sold or leased.

  Examples A piece of farm machinery, a car, or a boat is identified when its serial number is listed on a sales or lease contract.

- Goods that are part of a larger mass of goods are identified when the specific merchandise is designated.

  Example If a food processor contracts to purchase 150 cases of oranges from a farmer who has 1,000 cases of oranges, the buyer's goods are identified when the seller explicitly separates or tags the 150 cases for that buyer.

future goods
Goods not yet in existence (e.g., ungrown crops, unborn stock animals).

- **Future goods** are goods not yet in existence.

Examples Unborn young animals (such as unborn cattle) are identified when the young are conceived. Crops to be harvested are identified when the crops are planted or otherwise become growing crops.

Future goods other than crops and unborn animals are identified when the goods are shipped, marked, or otherwise designated by the seller or lessor as the goods to which the contract refers.

Passage of Title to Goods

Once the goods that are the subject of a contract exist and have been identified, title to the goods may be transferred from the seller to the buyer. Article 2 of the UCC establishes precise rules for determining the **passage of title** in sales contracts. (As mentioned earlier, lessees do not acquire title to the goods they lease.)

title
Legal, tangible evidence of ownership of goods.

Under UCC 2-401(1), **title** to goods passes from the seller to the buyer in any manner and under any conditions explicitly agreed on by the parties. If the parties do not agree to a specific time, title passes to the buyer when and where the seller's performance with reference to the physical delivery is completed. This point in time is determined by applying the rules discussed in the following paragraphs [UCC 2-401(2)].

Shipment and Destination Contracts

shipment contract
A contract that requires the seller to ship the goods to the buyer via a common carrier.

destination contract
A contract that requires the seller to deliver the goods either to the buyer's place of business or to another destination specified in the sales contract.

A **shipment contract** requires the seller to ship the goods to the buyer via a common carrier. The seller is required to (1) make proper shipping arrangements and (2) deliver the goods into the carrier's hands. Title passes to the buyer at the time and place of shipment [UCC 2-401(2)(a)].

A **destination contract** requires the seller to deliver the goods either to the buyer's place of business or to another destination specified in the sales contract. Title passes to the buyer when the seller tenders delivery of the goods at the specified destination [UCC 2-401(2)(b)].

Delivery of Goods Without Moving Them

document of title
An actual piece of paper, such as a warehouse receipt or bill of lading, that is required in some transactions of pickup and delivery.

Sometimes a sales contract authorizes goods to be delivered without requiring the seller to move them. In other words, the buyer might be required to pick up goods from the seller. In such situations, the time and place of the passage of title depends on whether the seller is to deliver a **document of title** (e.g., a warehouse receipt or bill of lading) to the buyer. If a document of title is required, title passes when and where the seller delivers the document to the buyer [UCC 2-401(3)(a)].

Example If the goods named in a sales contract are located at a warehouse, title passes when the seller delivers to the buyer a warehouse receipt representing the goods.

If (1) no document of title is needed and (2) the goods are identified at the time of contracting, title passes at the time and place of contracting [UCC 2-401(3)(b)].

Example If a buyer signs a sales contract to purchase bricks from a seller, and the contract stipulates that the buyer will pick up the bricks at the seller's place of business, title passes when the contract is signed by both parties. This situation is true even if the bricks are not picked up until a later date.

The following feature discusses commonly used shipping terms.

Business Environment

Commonly Used Shipping Terms

Goods subject to a sales contract are often shipped by a common carrier such as a trucking company, a ship, or a railroad. Many sales contracts contain **shipping terms** that have different legal meanings and consequences. The following are commonly used shipping terms:

- **F.O.B. (free on board) point of shipment** requires the seller to arrange to ship the goods and put the goods in the carrier's possession. The buyer bears the shipping expense and risk of loss while the goods are in transit [UCC 2-319(1)(a)].

  Example If a shipment contract specifies "F.O.B. Anchorage, Alaska," and the goods are shipped from New Orleans, Louisiana, the buyer bears the shipping expense and risk of loss while the goods are in transit to Anchorage, Alaska.

- **F.A.S. (free alongside ship) port of shipment or F.A.S. (vessel) port of shipment** requires the seller to deliver and tender the goods alongside the named vessel or on the dock designated and provided by the buyer. The seller bears the expense and risk of loss until this is done [UCC 2-319(2)(a)]. The buyer bears shipping costs and the risk of loss during transport.

  Example If a contract specifies "F.A.S. *The Gargoyle*, New Orleans," and the goods are to be shipped to Anchorage, Alaska, the seller bears the expense and risk of loss until it delivers the goods into the hands of the vessel *The Gargoyle* in New Orleans. Once this is done, the buyer pays the shipping costs, and the risk of loss passes to the buyer during transport to Anchorage, Alaska.

- **C.I.F. (cost, insurance, and freight)** is a pricing term that means that the price includes the cost of the goods and the costs of insurance and freight. **C.&F. (cost and freight)** is a pricing term that means that the price includes the cost of the goods and the cost of freight. In both cases, the seller must, at his or her own expense and risk, put the goods into the possession of a carrier. The buyer bears the risk of loss during transportation [UCC 2-320(1), (3)].

  Example If a contract specifies "C.I.F. *The Gargoyle*, New Orleans, Louisiana" or "C.&F. *The Gargoyle*, New Orleans, Louisiana," and the goods are to be shipped to Anchorage, Alaska, the seller bears the expense and risk of loss until it delivers the goods into the hands of the vessel *The Gargoyle* in New Orleans. Once this is done, the risk of loss passes to the buyer during transport from New Orleans to Anchorage, Alaska.

- **F.O.B. (free on board) place of destination** requires the seller to bear the expense and risk of loss until the goods are tendered to the buyer at the place of destination [UCC 2-319(1)(b)].

  Example If a destination contract specifies "F.O.B. Anchorage, Alaska," and the goods are shipped from New Orleans, Louisiana, the seller bears the expense and risk of loss before and while the goods are in transit until the goods are tendered to the buyer at the port of Anchorage, Alaska.

- **Ex-ship (from the carrying vessel)** requires the seller to bear the expense and risk of loss until the goods are unloaded from the ship at its port of destination [UCC 2-322(1)(b)].

  Example If a contract specifies "Ex-ship, *The Gargoyle*, Anchorage, Alaska," and the goods are shipped from New Orleans, Louisiana, the seller bears the expense and risk of loss before the goods are loaded, during transit, and until the goods are unloaded from *The Gargoyle* at the port in Anchorage, Alaska.

- **No-arrival, no-sale contract** requires the seller to bear the expense and risk of loss of the goods during transportation. However, the seller is under no duty to deliver replacement goods to the buyer because there is no contractual stipulation that the goods will arrive at the appointed destination [UCC 2-324(a), (b)].

Risk of Loss Where There Is No Breach of the Sales Contract

19.2 Describe what party bears the risk of loss of goods where there is no breach of the sales contract.

In the case of sales contracts, common law placed the risk of loss of goods on the party who had title to the goods. Article 2 of the UCC rejects this notion and allows the parties to a sales contract to agree among them who will bear the risk of loss if the goods subject to the contract are lost or destroyed. If the parties do not have a specific agreement concerning the assessment of the risk of loss, the UCC mandates who will bear the risk.

Laws are not masters but servants, and he rules them who obeys them.

Henry Ward Beecher
Proverbs from Plymouth Pulpit (1887)

Where there has been no breach of the sales contract, the UCC provides the following rules regarding title and risk of loss.

Carrier Cases: Movement of Goods

Unless otherwise agreed, goods that are shipped via carrier (e.g., railroad, ship, truck) are considered to be sent pursuant to a *shipment contract* or a *destination contract*. Absent any indication to the contrary, sales contracts are presumed to be shipment contracts rather than destination contracts.

risk of loss in a shipment contract
The buyer bears the risk of loss during transportation.

A *shipment contract* requires the seller to deliver goods conforming to the contract to a carrier. The **risk of loss in a shipment contract** passes to the buyer when the seller delivers the conforming goods to the carrier. The buyer bears the risk of loss of the goods during transportation [UCC 2-509(1)(a)]. Shipment contracts are created in two ways. The first method requires the use of the term *shipment contract*. The second requires the use of one of the following delivery terms: F.O.B. *point of shipment*, F.A.S., C.I.F., or C.&F.

risk of loss in a destination contract
The seller bears the risk of loss during transportation.

A *destination contract* requires the seller to deliver conforming goods to a specific destination. The **risk of loss in a destination contract** is on the seller while the goods are in transport. Thus, except in the case of a no-arrival, no-sale contract, the seller is required to replace any goods lost in transit. The buyer does not have to pay for destroyed goods. The risk of loss does not pass until the goods are tendered to the buyer at the specified destination [UCC 2-509(1)(b)].

Unless otherwise agreed, destination contracts are created in two ways. The first method requires the use of the term *destination contract*. The alternative method requires the use of the following delivery terms: F.O.B. *place of destination*, ex-ship, or no-arrival, no-sale contract.

Noncarrier Cases: No Movement of Goods

Sometimes a sales contract stipulates that the buyer is to pick up the goods at either the seller's place of business or another specified location. This type of arrangement raises a question: Who bears the risk of loss if the goods are destroyed or stolen after the contract date but before the buyer picks up the goods from the seller? The UCC provides two different rules for this situation. One applies to *merchant-sellers* and the other to *nonmerchant-sellers* [UCC 2-509(3)].

- **Merchant-seller.** If the seller is a merchant, the risk of loss does not pass to the buyer until the goods are received. In other words, a merchant-seller bears the risk of loss between the time of contracting and the time the buyer picks up the goods.
- **Nonmerchant-seller.** Nonmerchant-sellers pass the risk of loss to the buyer on "tender of delivery" of the goods. Tender of delivery occurs when the seller (1) places or holds the goods available for the buyer to take delivery and (2) notifies the buyer of this fact.

Goods in the Possession of a Bailee

bailee
A holder of goods who is not a seller or a buyer (e.g., a warehouse).

Goods sold by a seller to a buyer are sometimes in the possession of a **bailee** (e.g., a warehouse). If such goods are to be delivered to the buyer without the seller moving them, the risk of loss passes to the buyer when (1) the buyer receives a negotiable document of title (e.g., warehouse receipt, bill of lading) covering the goods, (2) the bailee acknowledges the buyer's right to possession of the goods, or (3) the buyer receives a nonnegotiable document of title or other written direction to deliver *and* has a reasonable time to present the document or direction to the bailee and demand the goods. If the bailee refuses to honor the document or direction, the risk of loss remains on the seller [UCC 2-509(2)].

Risk of Loss Where There Is a Breach of the Sales Contract

19.3 Describe what party bears the risk of loss of goods where there has been a breach of a sales contract.

Special risk of loss rules apply to situations in which there has been a breach of a sales contract [UCC 2-510]. These rules are discussed in the following paragraphs.

Seller in Breach of a Sales Contract

A seller breaches a sales contract if he or she tenders or delivers nonconforming goods to the buyer. If the goods are so nonconforming that the buyer has the right to reject them, the risk of loss remains on the seller until (1) the defect or nonconformity is cured or (2) the buyer accepts the nonconforming goods.

Example A buyer orders 1,000 talking dolls from a seller. The contract is a shipment contract, which normally places the risk of loss during transportation on the buyer. However, the seller ships to the buyer totally nonconforming dolls that cannot talk. This switches the risk of loss to the seller during transit. The goods are destroyed in transit. The seller bears the risk of loss because he breached the contract by shipping nonconforming goods.

Buyer in Breach of a Sales Contract

A buyer breaches a sales contract if he or she (1) refuses to take delivery of conforming goods, (2) repudiates the contract, or (3) otherwise breaches the contract. A buyer who breaches a sales contract before the risk of loss would normally pass to him or her bears the risk of loss of any goods identified to the contract. The risk of loss rests on the buyer for only a commercially reasonable time. The buyer is liable only for any loss in excess of insurance recovered by the seller.

Risk of Loss in Conditional Sales

19.4 Describe which party bears the risk of loss of goods in conditional sales contracts.

Sellers often entrust possession of goods to buyers on a trial basis. These transactions are classified as *sales on approval, sales or returns*, and *consignment* transactions [UCC 2-326]. Title and risk of loss in these types of **conditional sales** are discussed in the following paragraphs.

conditional sale
Type of sale in which the seller entrusts possession of goods to a buyer on a trial basis.

Sale on Approval

In a **sale on approval**, there is no sale unless and until the buyer accepts the goods. A sale on approval occurs when a merchant allows a customer to take the goods for a specified period of time to see if they fit the customer's needs. The prospective buyer may use the goods to try them out during this time.

sale on approval
A type of sale in which there is no actual sale unless and until the buyer accepts the goods.

Acceptance of the goods occurs if the buyer (1) expressly indicates acceptance, (2) fails to notify the seller of rejection of the goods within the agreed-on trial period (or, if no time is agreed on, within a reasonable time), or (3) uses the goods inconsistently with the purpose of the trial (e.g., a customer resells a computer to another person).

In a sale on approval, the risk of loss and title to the goods remain with the seller. They do not pass to the buyer until acceptance [UCC 2-327(1)]. The goods are not subject to the claims of the buyer's creditors until the buyer accepts them.

Sale or Return

sale or return
A contract in which the seller delivers goods to a buyer with the understanding that the buyer may return the goods if they are not used or resold within a stated or reasonable period of time.

In a **sale or return**, the seller delivers goods to a buyer with the understanding that the buyer may return them if they are not used or resold within a stated period of time (or within a reasonable time, if no specific time is stated). The sale is considered final if the buyer fails to return the goods within the specified time or within a reasonable time, if no time is specified. The buyer has the option of returning all the goods or any commercial unit of the goods.

Example Louis Vuitton delivers 10 women's handbags to Fashion Boutique Store on a sale or return basis. The boutique pays $10,000 ($1,000 per handbag). If Fashion Boutique Store sells 6 handbags but fails to sell the other 4 handbags within a reasonable time, such as three months, it may return the unsold handbags to Louis Vuitton and can recover the compensation it paid to Louis Vuitton for the 4 returned handbags ($4,000).

In a sale or return contract, the risk of loss and title to the goods pass to the buyer when the buyer takes possession of the goods [UCC 2-327(2)]. Goods sold pursuant to a sale or return contract are subject to the claims of the buyer's creditors while the goods are in the buyer's possession.

Example In the previous example, title and risk of loss transferred to Fashion Boutique Store when it took possession of the Louis Vuitton handbags. If the Louis Vuitton handbags are destroyed while in the possession of Fashion Boutique Store, the store is responsible for their loss. It cannot recover the value of the handbags from Louis Vuitton.

Consignment

consignment
An arrangement in which a seller (the consignor) delivers goods to a buyer (the consignee) to sell on his or her behalf.

In a **consignment**, a seller (the **consignor**) delivers goods to a buyer (the **consignee**) to sell on his or her behalf. The consignee is paid a fee if it sells the goods on behalf of the consignor.

A consignment is treated as a sale or return under the UCC; that is, title and risk of loss of the goods pass to the consignee when the consignee takes possession of the goods.

Whether goods are subject to the claims of a buyer's creditors usually depends on whether the seller files a financing statement, as required by Article 9 of the UCC. If the seller files a financing statement, the goods are subject to the claims of the seller's creditors. If the seller fails to file such a statement, the goods are subject to the claims of the buyer's creditors [UCC 2-326(3)].

Risk of Loss in Lease Contracts

19.5 Describe what party bears the risk of loss of goods in lease contracts.

Critical Legal Thinking Questions

Can the parties to a sales or lease contract change the UCC risk of loss rules that would apply to their contract? If so, how?

The parties to a lease contract are the party who leases the goods (the **lessor**) and the party who receives the goods (the **lessee**). The lessor and the lessee may agree about who will bear the risk of loss of the goods if they are lost or destroyed. If the parties do not agree, the UCC provides the following risk of loss rules:

1. In the case of an **ordinary lease**, if the lessor is a merchant, the risk of loss passes to the lessee on the receipt of the goods [UCC 2A-219].
2. If the lease is a **finance lease** and the supplier is a merchant, the risk of loss passes to the lessee on the receipt of the goods [UCC 2A-219]. A finance lease is a three-party transaction consisting of a lessor, a lessee, and a supplier (or vendor).
3. If a tender of delivery of goods fails to conform to the lease contract, the risk of loss remains with the lessor or supplier until cure or acceptance [UCC 2A-220(1)(a)].

The following feature describes insuring goods against risk of loss.

Business Environment

Insuring Goods Against Risk of Loss

To protect against financial loss that would occur if goods were damaged, destroyed, lost, or stolen, the parties to sales and lease contracts should purchase insurance against such loss. If the goods are then lost or damaged, the insured party receives reimbursement from the insurance company for the loss.

To purchase insurance, a party must have an **insurable interest** in the goods. A seller has an insurable interest in goods as long as he or she retains title or has a security interest in the goods. A lessor retains an insurable interest in the goods during the term of the lease. A buyer or lessee obtains an insurable interest in the goods when they are identified in the sales or lease contract. Both the buyer and the seller or the lessee and the lessor can have an insurable interest in the goods at the same time [UCC 2-501, 2A-218].

Sale of Goods by Nonowners

19.6 Identify who bears the risk of loss when goods are stolen and resold.

Sometimes people sell goods even though they do not hold valid title to them. The UCC anticipated many of the problems this situation could cause and established rules concerning the title, if any, that could be transferred to purchasers.

Stolen Goods

In a case in which a buyer purchases goods or a lessee leases goods from a thief who has stolen them, the purchaser does not acquire title to the goods, and the lessee does not acquire any leasehold interest in the goods. The real owner can reclaim the goods from the purchaser or lessee [UCC 2-403(1)]. This is called **void title** or **void leasehold interest**.

void title
A situation in which a thief acquires no title to goods he or she steals.

Example Jack steals a truckload of consumer electronic devices that are owned by Electronics Store. The thief resells the devices to City-Mart, which does not know that the goods were stolen. If Electronics Store finds out where the electronic devices are, it can reclaim them because the thief had no title in the goods, so title was not transferred to City-Mart. There is void title. City-Mart's only recourse is against the thief, if the thief can be found.

Fraudulently Obtained Goods

A seller or lessor has **voidable title** or **voidable leasehold interest** to goods if he or she obtained the goods through fraud, if the check for the payment of the goods or lease is dishonored, or if the seller or lessor impersonated another person.

voidable title
A title that a purchaser has on goods obtained by (1) fraud, (2) a check that is later dishonored, or (3) impersonation of another person.

A person with voidable title to goods can transfer good title to a **good faith purchaser for value** or a good leasehold interest to a **good faith subsequent lessee**. A good faith purchaser or lessee for value is someone who pays sufficient consideration or rent for the goods to the person he or she honestly believes has good title to or leasehold interest in those goods [UCC 2-201(1), 1-201(44)(d)]. The real owner cannot reclaim goods from such a purchaser or lessee [UCC 2-403(1)].

good faith purchaser for value
A person to whom good title can be transferred from a person with voidable title. The real owner cannot reclaim goods from a good faith purchaser for value.

Example Max buys a Rolex watch from his neighbor Dorothy for nearly fair market value. It is later discovered that Dorothy obtained the watch from Jewelry Store with a bounced check—that is, a check for which there were insufficient funds to pay for the Rolex watch. Jewelry Store cannot reclaim the watch from Max because Max, the second purchaser, purchased the watch in good faith and for value.

buyer in the ordinary course of business
A person who, in good faith and without knowledge that the sale violates the ownership or security interests of a third party, buys goods in the ordinary course of business from a person in the business of selling goods of that kind. A buyer in the ordinary course of business takes the goods free of any third-party security interest in the goods.

entrustment rule
A rule stating that when an owner *entrusts* the possession of his or her goods to a merchant who deals in goods of that kind, the merchant has the power to transfer all rights (including title) in the goods to a buyer in the ordinary course of business.

Critical Legal Thinking Questions

Describe the buyer in the ordinary course of business rule. When does this rule apply? Is the result of this rule fair?

The following feature discusses the entrustment rule.

Ethics

Entrustment Rule

If an owner *entrusts* the possession of goods to a merchant who deals in goods of that kind, the merchant has the power to transfer all rights (including title) in the goods to a **buyer in the ordinary course of business** [UCC 2-403(2)]. The real owner cannot reclaim the goods from this buyer. This is called the **entrustment rule.**

Example Kim brings her diamond ring to Ring Store to be repaired. Ring Store both sells and repairs jewelry. Kim leaves (entrusts) her diamond ring at the store until it is repaired. Ring Store sells Kim's ring to Harold, who is going to propose marriage to Gretchen. Harold, a buyer in the ordinary course of business, acquires title to the ring. Kim cannot reclaim her ring from Harold (or Gretchen). Her only recourse is to sue Ring Store.

The entrustment rule also applies to leases. If a lessor entrusts the possession of goods to a lessee who is a merchant who deals in goods of that kind, the merchant-lessee has the power to transfer all the lessor's and lessee's rights in the goods to a buyer or sublessee in the ordinary course of business [UCC 2A-305(2)].

Ethics Questions
What is the public policy underlying the entrustment rule? What is a buyer in the ordinary course of business? Should parties who entrust others with their property be more cautious in doing so?

In the following case, the court had to decide whether a purchaser was a buyer in the ordinary course of business.

CASE 19.1 *STATE COURT CASE Entrustment Rule*

Lindholm v. Brant

925 A.2d 1048, 2007 Conn. Lexis 264 (2007)
Supreme Court of Connecticut

"Any entrusting of possession of goods to a merchant who deals in goods of that kind gives him power to transfer all rights of the entruster to a buyer in ordinary course of business."

—Chase Rogers, Justice

Facts

In 1962, Andy Warhol, a famous artist, created a silkscreen on canvas titled *Red Elvis*. Kerstin Lindholm was an art collector who, for 30 years, had been represented by Anders Malmberg, an art dealer. In 1987, with the assistance and advice of Malmberg, Lindholm purchased *Red Elvis* for $300,000.

In 2000, Malmberg told Lindholm that he could place *Red Elvis* on loan to the Louisiana Museum in Denmark if Lindholm agreed. By letter dated March 20, 2000, Lindholm agreed and gave permission to Malmberg to obtain possession of *Red Elvis*, which he did. Instead of placing *Red Elvis* on loan to the Louisiana Museum, Malmberg, claiming ownership to *Red Elvis*, immediately contracted to sell *Red Elvis* to Peter M. Brant, an art collector, for $2.9 million. Brant paid $2.9 million to Malmberg and received an invoice of sale and possession of *Red Elvis*.

Subsequently, Lindholm made arrangements to sell *Red Elvis* to a Japanese buyer for $4.6 million. Shortly thereafter, Lindholm discovered the fraud. Lindholm brought a civil lawsuit in the state of Connecticut against Brant to recover *Red Elvis*. Brant argued that he was a buyer in the ordinary course of business because he purchased *Red Elvis* from an art dealer to whom Lindholm had entrusted *Red Elvis*, and he had a claim that was superior to Lindholm's claim of ownership. The superior court of Connecticut issued a memorandum opinion that awarded *Red Elvis* to Brant.

Issue

Is Brant a buyer in the ordinary course of business who has a claim of ownership to *Red Elvis* that is superior to that of the owner Lindholm?

Language of the Court

Any entrusting of possession of goods to a merchant who deals in goods of that kind gives him power to transfer all rights of the entruster to a buyer in ordinary course of business. Once K. Lindholm entrusted Red Elvis *to Malmberg she gave him the power to transfer all of her rights as the entruster to a buyer in the ordinary course. Accordingly, because Brant has proven his special defense of being a buyer in the ordinary course, judgment will enter in favor of the defendant on all counts.*

Decision

The trial court held that Brant was a buyer in the ordinary course of business who obtained ownership to *Red Elvis* when he purchased the stolen *Red Elvis* from Malmberg. Lindholm appealed the decision of the trial court to the supreme court of Connecticut, which affirmed the decision of the trial court and awarded the *Red Elvis* to Brant. A court in Sweden convicted Malmberg of criminal fraud and sentenced him to three years in prison. A Swedish court awarded Lindholm $4.6 million in damages against Malmberg.

Critical Legal Thinking Questions

Did Malmberg act ethically in this case? Did he act criminally? Does Lindholm have some responsibility for her loss of the *Red Elvis*?

CONCEPT SUMMARY

PASSAGE OF TITLE BY NONOWNER THIRD PARTIES

Type of Transaction	Title Possessed by Seller	Innocent Purchaser	Purchaser Acquires Title to Goods
Goods acquired by theft are resold.	Void title	Good faith purchaser for value	No. Original owner may reclaim the goods.
Goods acquired by fraud or dishonored check are resold.	Voidable title	Good faith purchaser for value	Yes. Purchaser takes goods, free of claim of original owner.
Goods entrusted by owner to merchant who deals in that type of goods are resold.	No title	Buyer in the ordinary course of business	Yes. Purchaser takes goods, free of claim of original owner.

Critical Legal Thinking Questions

Describe the *good faith purchaser for value* and the *good faith subsequent lessee* rules. When do these rules apply? Is the result of these rules fair?

United Nations Convention on Contracts for the International Sale of Goods (CISG)

19.7 Describe the provisions of the United Nations Convention for the International Sale of Goods (CISG) and how they apply to international sales contracts.

International contracts of companies located around the world are often governed by the **United Nations Convention on Contracts for the International Sale of Goods (CISG)**. The CISG, a convention that codifies law for international sales contracts, was developed by the United Nations Commission on International Trade Law. More than 90 countries are signatories to the CISG. The CISG provides legal rules that govern the formation, performance, and enforcement of international sales contracts.

United Nations Convention on Contracts for the International Sale of Goods (CISG)
A model act for international sales contracts that provides legal rules that govern the formation, performance, and enforcement of international sales contracts entered into between businesses located in different countries that are signatories of the CISG, and to sales contracts not otherwise subject to the CISG if the parties select in their contract to be governed by the CISG.

SYDNEY OPERA HOUSE, SYDNEY, AUSTRALIA
The United Nations Convention for the International Sale of Goods (CISG) applies to many international contracts.

Peter Adams Photography/Alamy Stock Photo

The CISG applies to contracts for the international sale of goods when the buyer and seller have their places of business in different nations and both nations are signatories of the CISG. For example, a contract between a business entity in the United States and a business entity located in another CISG contracting nation will be governed by the CISG. However, the contracting parties may agree to exclude (i.e., opt out of) the CISG or to modify the application of the CISG to their contract. For example, the parties could stipulate that the UCC or a nation's contract law governs the international sales contract.

The CISG does not apply to contracts for the international sale of goods where one of the contracting parties is located in a CISG signatory nation and the other contracting party is located in a nation that is not a signatory to the CISG. For example, if a business entity located in the United States enters into an international sales contract with a business entity located in a non-CISG signatory country, the CISG does not apply to the contract. In this case, the UCC or a nation's contract law applies, depending on the facts of the case. The parties may designate the contract law to be applied to their contract, including the CISG.

Many of the provisions of the CISG are similar to those of the UCC. However, there are several important differences. Under the UCC, acceptance occurs when the offeree transmits its acceptance to the offeror, but under the CISG, acceptance does not occur until it is received by the offeror. Under the UCC's Statute of Frauds, all contracts for the sale of goods priced at $500 or more must be in writing. The CISG does not require that a sales contract be in writing.

Under the UCC, if both parties are merchants, additional terms contained in an acceptance become part of the sales contract unless the offeror has expressly limited acceptance to the terms of the offer, the additional terms materially alter the terms of the offer, or the offeror rejects the additional terms within a reasonable time. Under the CISG, if additional terms are added to the acceptance or the acceptance modifies the terms of the offer, then the purported acceptance is considered a rejection and counteroffer. There are other differences between the UCC and CISG as well.

The CISG is increasingly being used for international sales transactions. The CISG offers a uniform sales law for the contracting parties, and is written in plain business language that is more easily understood by contracting parties than the laws of many nations. The CISG does not apply to lease transactions in goods.

Key Terms and Concepts

Bailee (340)
Buyer in the ordinary course of business (344)
C.&F. (cost and freight) (339)
C.I.F. (cost, insurance, and freight) (339)
Conditional sale (341)
Consignee (342)
Consignment (342)
Consignor (342)
Destination contract (338)
Document of title (338)
Entrustment rule (344)
Ex-ship (from the carrying vessel) (339)
F.A.S. (free alongside ship) port of shipment or F.A.S. (vessel) port of shipment (339)
Finance lease (342)
F.O.B. (free on board) place of destination (339)
F.O.B. (free on board) point of shipment (339)
Future goods (338)
Good faith purchaser for value (343)
Good faith subsequent lessee (343)
Identification of goods (337)
Insurable interest (343)
Lessee (342)
Lessor (342)
No-arrival, no-sale contract (339)
Ordinary lease (342)
Passage of title (338)
Risk of loss (337)
Risk of loss in a destination contract (340)
Risk of loss in a shipment contract (340)
Sale on approval (341)
Sale or return (342)
Shipment contract (338)
Shipping terms (339)
Title (338)
United Nations Convention on Contracts for the International Sale of Goods (CISG) (345)
Void leasehold interest (343)
Void title (343)
Voidable leasehold interest (343)
Voidable title (343)

Critical Legal Thinking Cases

19.1 Conditional Sale Numismatic Funding Corporation (Numismatic), with its principal place of business in New York, sells rare and collector coins by mail throughout the United States. Frederick R. Prewitt, a resident of St. Louis, Missouri, responded to Numismatic's advertisement in the *Wall Street Journal*. Prewitt received several shipments of coins from Numismatic via the mail. These shipments were "on approval" for 14 days. Numismatic gave no instructions as to the method for returning unwanted coins. Prewitt kept and paid for several coins and returned the others to Numismatic, fully insured, via FedEx. Numismatic then mailed Prewitt 28 gold and silver coins worth over $60,000 on a 14-day approval. Thirteen days later, Prewitt returned all the coins via certified mail of the U.S. Postal Service and insured them for the maximum allowed, $400. Numismatic never received the coins. Numismatic sued Prewitt to recover for the value of the coins, alleging that Prewitt had an express or implied duty to ship the coins back to Numismatic by FedEx and fully insured. Prewitt argued that he was not liable for the coins because this was a sale or return contract. Who wins? *Prewitt v. Numismatic Funding Corporation*, 745 F.2d 1175, 1984 U.S. App. Lexis 17926 (United States Court of Appeals for the Eighth Circuit, 1984)

19.2 Identification of Goods Big Knob Volunteer Fire Company (Fire Co.) agreed to purchase a fire truck from Hamerly Custom Productions (Hamerly), which was in the business of assembling various component parts into fire trucks. Fire Co. paid Hamerly $10,000 toward the price two days after signing the contract. Two weeks later, it gave Hamerly $38,000 more toward the total purchase price of $53,000. Hamerly bought an engine chassis for the new fire truck on credit from Lowe and Meyer Garage (Lowe and Meyer). After installing the chassis, Hamerly painted the Big Knob Fire Department's name on the side of the cab. Hamerly never paid for the engine chassis, and the truck was repossessed by Lowe and Meyer. Fire Co. sought to recover the fire truck from Lowe and Meyer. Although Fire Co. was the buyer of a fire truck, Lowe and Meyer questioned whether any goods had ever been identified in the contract. Were they? *Big Knob Volunteer Fire Co. v. Lowe and Meyer Garage*, 487 A.2d 953, 1985 Pa. Super. Lexis 5540 (Superior Court of Pennsylvania, 1985)

19.3 Entrustment Rule Fuqua Homes, Inc. (Fuqua) is a manufacturer of prefabricated houses. MMM, a dealer of prefabricated homes, was a partnership created by two men named Kirk and Underhill. On seven occasions before the disputed transactions occurred, MMM had ordered homes from Fuqua. MMM was contacted by Kenneth Ryan, who wanted to purchase a 55-foot modular home. MMM called Fuqua and ordered a prefabricated home that met Ryan's specifications. Fuqua delivered the home to MMM and retained a security interest in it until MMM paid the purchase price. MMM installed the house on Ryan's property and collected full payment from Ryan. Kirk and Underhill then disappeared, taking Ryan's money with them. Fuqua was never paid for the prefabricated home it had manufactured. Ryan had no knowledge of the dealings between MMM and Fuqua. Fuqua claimed title to the house based on its security interest. Who has title to the home? *Fuqua Homes, Inc. v. Evanston Bldg. & Loan Co.*, 370 N.E.2d 780, 1977 Ohio App. Lexis 6968 (Court of Appeals of Ohio, 1977)

19.4 Risk of Loss All America Export-Import Corp. (All America) placed an order for several thousand pounds of yarn with A. M. Knitwear (Knitwear). On June 4, All America sent Knitwear a purchase order. The purchase order stated the terms of the sale, including language that stated that the price was F.O.B. the seller's plant. A truck hired by All America arrived at Knitwear's plant. Knitwear turned the yarn over to the carrier and notified All America that the goods were now on the truck. The truck left Knitwear's plant and proceeded to a local warehouse. Sometime during the night, the truck was hijacked, and all the yarn was stolen. All America had paid for the yarn by check but stopped payment on it when it learned that the goods had been stolen. Knitwear sued All America, claiming that it must pay for the stolen goods because it bore the risk of loss. Who wins? *A. M. Knitwear v. All America, Etc.*, 41 N.Y.2d 14, 359 N.E.2d 342, 390 N.Y.S.2d 832, 1976 N.Y. Lexis 3201 (Court of Appeals of New York, 1976)

Ethics Cases

19.5 Ethics Case John Torniero was employed by Michaels Jewelers, Inc. (Michaels). During the course of his employment, Torniero stole pieces of jewelry, including several diamond rings, a sapphire ring, a gold pendant, and several loose diamonds. Over a period of several months, Torniero sold individual pieces of the stolen jewelry to G&W Watch and Jewelry Corporation (G&W). G&W had no knowledge of how Torniero obtained the jewels. Torniero was arrested when Michaels discovered the thefts. After Torniero admitted that he had sold the stolen jewelry to G&W, Michaels attempted to recover it from G&W. G&W claimed title to the jewelry as a good faith purchaser for value. Michaels challenged G&W's claim to title in court. Who wins? Did any party act unethically in this case? *United States v. Michaels Jewelers, Inc.*, 42 UCC Rep. Serv. 141, 1985 U.S. Dist. Lexis 15142 (United States District Court for the District of Connecticut, 1985)

19.6 Ethics Case Executive Financial Services, Inc. (EFS) purchased three tractors from Tri-County Farm Company (Tri-County), a John Deere dealership owned by Gene Mohr and James Loyd. The tractors cost $48,000, $19,000, and $38,000. EFS did not take possession of the tractors but instead left the tractors on Tri-County's lot. EFS leased the tractors to Mohr-Loyd Leasing (Mohr-Loyd), a partnership between Mohr and Loyd, with the understanding and representation by Mohr-Loyd that the tractors would be leased out to farmers. Instead of leasing the tractors, Tri-County sold them to three different farmers. EFS sued and obtained judgment against Tri-County, Mohr-Loyd, and Mohr and Loyd personally for breach of contract. Because that judgment remained unsatisfied, EFS sued the three farmers who bought the tractors to recover the tractors from them. Did Mohr and Loyd act ethically in this case? Who owns the tractors, EFS or the farmers? *Executive Financial Services, Inc. v. Pagel*, 715 P.2d 381, 1986 Kan. Lexis 290 (Supreme Court of Kansas, 1986)

CHAPTER

20

Remedies for Breach of Sales and Lease Contracts

TRUCK UNLOADING GOODS

A seller or lessor is under a duty to deliver conforming goods, and the buyer or lessee is under a duty to pay for these goods. The Uniform Commercial Code (UCC) provides certain remedies to sellers and lessors and to the buyers and lessees if the other party does not perform his or her duties.

Henry R. Cheeseman

Learning Objectives

After studying this chapter, you should be able to:

20.1 Describe seller and lessor performance of sales and lease contracts.

20.2 Describe buyer and lessee performance of sales and lease contracts.

20.3 List and describe seller and lessor remedies for buyer and lessee breach of sales and lease contracts.

20.4 List and describe buyer and lessee remedies for seller and lessor breach of sales and lease contracts.

20.5 List and describe additional performance issues.

> *"Trade and commerce, if they were not made of Indian rubber, would never manage to bounce over the obstacles which legislators are continually putting in their way."*
>
> —*Henry D. Thoreau*
> *Resistance to Civil Government (1849)*

Introduction to Remedies for Breach of Sales and Lease Contracts

The buyer needs a hundred eyes, the seller not one.
George Herbert
Jacula Prudentum (1651)

Usually, the parties to a sales or lease contract owe a duty to perform the obligations specified in their agreement [UCC 2-301, 2A-301]. The seller's or lessor's general obligation is to transfer and deliver the goods to the buyer or lessee. The buyer's or lessee's general obligation is to accept and pay for the goods.

breach
Failure of a party to perform an obligation in a sales or lease contract.

tender of delivery
The obligation of a seller to transfer and deliver goods to the buyer or lessee in accordance with a sales or lease contract.

When one party **breaches** a sales or lease contract, the Uniform Commercial Code (UCC) provides the injured party with a variety of prelitigation and litigation remedies. These remedies are designed to place the injured party in as good a position as if the breaching party's contractual obligations were fully performed [UCC 1-106(1), 2A-401(1)]. The best remedy depends on the circumstances of the case.

The performance of obligations and remedies available for breach of sales and lease contracts are discussed in this chapter.

Seller and Lessor Performance

20.1 Describe seller and lessor performance of sales and lease contracts.

The seller's or lessor's basic obligation is the **tender of delivery**, or the transfer and delivery of goods to the buyer or lessee in accordance with a sales or lease contract [UCC 2-301]. Tender of delivery requires the seller or lessor to (1) put and hold conforming goods at the buyer's or lessee's disposition and (2) give the buyer or lessee any notification reasonably necessary to enable delivery of goods. The parties may agree as to the time, place, and manner of delivery. If there is no special agreement, tender must be made at a reasonable hour, and the goods must be kept available for a reasonable period of time.

Example The seller cannot telephone the buyer at 12:01 a.m. and say that the buyer has 15 minutes to accept delivery [UCC 2-503(1), 2A-508(1)].

Place of Delivery

Nobody has a more sacred obligation to obey the law than those who make the law.
Sophocles (496–406 BCE)

Many sales and lease contracts state where the goods are to be delivered. Often, the contract will say that the buyer or lessee must pick up the goods from the seller or lessor. If the contract does not expressly state the **place of delivery**, the UCC stipulates place of delivery based on the following rules:

1. **Noncarrier cases.** Unless otherwise agreed, the place of delivery is the seller's or lessor's place of business. If the seller or lessor has no place of business, the place of delivery is the seller's or lessor's residence. If the parties have knowledge at the time of contracting that identified goods are located in some other place, that place is the place of delivery.

   Example If two parties contract regarding the sale of wheat that is located in a silo, the silo is the place of delivery [UCC 2-308].

2. **Carrier cases.** Unless the parties have agreed otherwise, if delivery of goods to a buyer is to be made by carrier, the UCC establishes different rules for *shipment contracts* and *destination contracts*:

a. **Shipment contract.** A sales contract that requires the seller to send the goods to the buyer but not to a specifically named destination is a **shipment contract**. Under such contracts, the seller must put the goods in the carrier's possession and contract for the proper and safe transportation of the goods and promptly notify the buyer of the shipment [UCC 2-504]. Delivery occurs when the seller puts the goods in the carrier's possession.

shipment contract
A sales contract that requires the seller to send the goods to the buyer but not to a specifically named destination.

b. **Destination contract.** A sales contract that requires the seller to deliver goods to the buyer's place of business or another specified destination is a **destination contract**. Unless otherwise agreed, destination contracts require delivery to be tendered at the buyer's place of business or other location specified in the sales contract [UCC 2-503]. Delivery occurs when the goods reach this destination.

destination contract
A sales contract that requires the seller to deliver the goods to the buyer's place of business or another specified destination.

Perfect Tender Rule

A seller or lessor is under a duty to deliver conforming goods. If the goods or tender of delivery fail in any respect to conform to the contract, the buyer or lessee may opt (1) to reject the whole shipment, (2) to accept the whole shipment, or (3) to reject part and accept part of the shipment. This option is referred to as the **perfect tender rule** [UCC 2-601, 2A-509]. If a buyer accepts nonconforming goods, the buyer may seek remedies against the seller.

perfect tender rule
A rule that says if the goods or tender of a delivery fail in any respect to conform to the contract, the buyer may opt (1) to reject the whole shipment, (2) to accept the whole shipment, or (3) to reject part and accept part of the shipment.

Example A sales contract requires Lawn Mower Company to deliver 100 lawn mowers to Outdoor Store. When the buyer inspects the delivered goods, it is discovered that 80 lawn mowers conform to the contract and that 20 lawn mowers do not conform. Pursuant to the perfect tender rule, the buyer Outdoor Store may reject the entire shipment of lawn mowers. In the alternative, Outdoor Store can accept the 80 conforming lawn mowers and reject the 20 nonconforming lawn mowers. As another alternative, Outdoor Store may accept the whole shipment, both the conforming and the nonconforming lawn mowers, and seek remedies from Lawn Mower Company for the 20 nonconforming lawn mowers.

The UCC allows the parties to a sales or lease contract to limit the effect of the perfect tender rule. For example, they may decide that (1) only the defective or nonconforming goods may be rejected, (2) the seller or lessor may replace nonconforming goods or repair defects, or (3) the buyer or lessee will accept nonconforming goods with appropriate compensation from the seller or lessor [UCC 2-614(1)].

The following feature discusses the seller's and lessor's opportunity to cure the delivery of nonconforming goods under certain circumstances.

right to cure
An opportunity to repair or replace defective or nonconforming goods.

Contemporary Environment

Seller's and Lessor's Right to Cure

The UCC gives a seller or lessor who delivers nonconforming goods the **right to cure** the nonconformity. Although the term **cure** is not defined by the UCC, it generally means an opportunity to repair or replace defective or nonconforming goods [UCC 2-508, 2A-513].

A cure may be attempted if the time for performance has not expired and the seller or lessor notifies the buyer or lessee of his or her intention to make a conforming delivery within the contract time.

Example A lessee contracts to lease a BMW automobile from a lessor for delivery on July 1. On June 15, the lessor delivers a BMW to the lessee, and the lessee rejects it as nonconforming. The lessor has until July 1 to cure the nonconformity by delivering the BMW specified in the contract.

A cure may also be attempted if the seller or lessor had reasonable grounds to believe the nonconforming delivery would be accepted. The seller or lessor may have a further reasonable time to substitute a conforming tender.

(continued)

Example A buyer contracts to purchase 500 red dresses from a seller for delivery on July 1. On July 1, the seller delivers 500 blue dresses to the buyer. In the past, the buyer has accepted different-colored dresses than those ordered. This time, though, the buyer rejects the blue dresses as nonconforming. The seller has a reasonable time after July 1 to deliver conforming red dresses to the buyer.

Installment Contracts

An **installment contract** is a contract that requires or authorizes goods to be delivered and accepted in separate lots. Such a contract must contain a clause that states "each delivery in a separate lot" or equivalent language.

Example A contract in which the buyer orders 1,000 widgets to be delivered in four equal installments is an installment contract.

The UCC alters the perfect tender rule with regard to installment contracts. The buyer or lessee may reject the entire contract only if the nonconformity or default with respect to any installment or installments substantially impairs the value of the entire contract [UCC 2-612, 2A-510].

good faith
Every contract or duty within this Act imposes an obligation of good faith in its performance or enforcement [UCC 1-203].

reasonableness
A term used throughout the UCC to establish the duties of performance by the parties to sales and lease contracts.

commercial reasonableness
The term that establishes certain duties of merchants under the UCC.

Critical Legal Thinking Questions

Why does the UCC impose the duties of *good faith* and *reasonableness*? Are these concepts difficult to apply? Does this differ from the common law of contracts?

Destruction of Goods

The UCC provides that if goods identified in a sales or lease contract are totally destroyed without the fault of either party before the risk of loss passes to the buyer or the lessee, the contract is void. Both parties are then excused from performing the contract.

If the goods are only partially destroyed, the buyer or lessee may inspect the goods and then choose either to treat the contract as void or to accept the goods. If the buyer or lessee opts to accept the goods, the purchase price or rent will be reduced to compensate for damages [UCC 2-613, 2A-221].

Example A buyer contracts to purchase a sofa from a seller. The seller agrees to deliver the sofa to the buyer's home. The truck delivering the sofa is hit by an automobile, and the sofa is totally destroyed. Because the risk of loss has not passed to the buyer, the contract is voided, and the buyer does not have to pay for the sofa.

The following feature discusses the concepts of good faith and reasonableness that the UCC imposes on parties.

Critical Legal Thinking

UCC Imposes Duties of Good Faith and Reasonableness

Generally, the common law of contracts only obligates the parties to perform their contracts according to the **express terms** of their contract. There is no breach of contract unless the parties fail to meet these terms. However, the UCC adopts two broad principles that govern the performance of sales and lease contracts: **good faith** and **reasonableness**.

UCC 1-203 states, "Every contract or duty within this Act imposes an obligation of good faith in its performance or enforcement." Thus, both parties owe a duty of good faith to perform a sales or lease contract. Merchants are held to a higher standard of good faith than nonmerchants [UCC 2-103(1)(b)].

The words *reasonable* and *reasonably* are used throughout the UCC to establish the duties of performance by the parties to sales and lease contracts. In addition, the term **commercial reasonableness** is used to establish certain duties of merchants under the UCC.

The concepts of good faith and reasonableness extend to the "spirit" of a contract as well as the contract terms.

Critical Legal Thinking Questions

Are parties more apt to perform contracts if their conduct is judged against the UCC standards of *good faith, reasonableness*, and *commercial reasonableness*? Do these concepts promote ethical behavior?

Buyer and Lessee Performance

20.2 Describe buyer and lessee performance of sales and lease contracts.

The buyer or lessee in a sales or lease contract owes certain duties of performance under the contract. These duties are either specified in the contract itself or are created by UCC Articles 2 and 2A. Once the seller or lessor has properly tendered delivery, the buyer or lessee is obligated to accept and pay for the goods in accordance with the sales or lease contract. If there is no agreement, the provisions of the UCC apply.

Right of Inspection

Unless otherwise agreed, the buyer or lessee has the **right to inspect** goods that are tendered, delivered, or identified in a sales or lease contract prior to accepting or paying for them. If the goods are shipped, the inspection may take place after their arrival. If the inspected goods do not conform to the contract, the buyer or lessee may reject the goods and not pay for the goods [UCC 2-513(1), 2A-515(1)]. If the goods are rejected for nonconformance, the cost of inspection can be recovered from the seller [UCC 2-513(2)].

The parties may agree as to the time, place, and manner of inspection. If there is no such agreement, the inspection must occur at a reasonable time and place and in a reasonable manner. Reasonableness depends on the circumstances of the case, common usage of trade, prior course of dealing between the parties, and similar conditions. If the goods conform to the contract, the buyer pays for the inspection.

Acceptance

Acceptance occurs when the buyer or lessee takes either of the following actions after a reasonable opportunity to inspect the goods: (1) signifies to the seller or lessor in words or by conduct that the goods are conforming or that the buyer or lessee will take or retain the goods despite their nonconformity or (2) fails to effectively reject the goods within a reasonable time after their delivery or tender by the seller or lessor. Acceptance also occurs if a buyer acts inconsistently with the seller's ownership rights in the goods. Acceptance occurs if the buyer resells the goods delivered by the seller [UCC 2-606(1), 2A-515(1)].

Buyers and lessees may only accept delivery of a *commercial unit*—a unit of goods that commercial usage deems is a single whole for purpose of sale. Acceptance of a part of any commercial unit is acceptance of the entire unit [UCC 2-606(2), 2A-515(2)].

Example A commercial unit may be a single article (e.g., a machine), a set of articles (e.g., a suite of furniture or an assortment of sizes), a quantity (e.g., a bale, a gross, or a carload), or any other unit treated in use or in the relevant market as a single whole.

acceptance
An act that occurs when a buyer or lessee takes either of the following actions after a reasonable opportunity to inspect the goods that are the subject of a contract: (1) signifies to the seller or lessor in words or by conduct that the goods are conforming or that the buyer or lessee will take or retain the goods despite their nonconformity or (2) fails to effectively reject the goods within a reasonable time after their delivery or tender by the seller or lessor. Acceptance also occurs if a buyer acts inconsistently with the seller's ownership rights in the goods.

Payment

Goods that are accepted must be paid for [UCC 2-607(1)]. Unless the parties to a contract agree otherwise, **payment** is due from a buyer when and where the goods are delivered, even if the place of delivery is the same as the place of shipment. Buyers often purchase goods on credit extended by the seller. Unless the parties agree to other terms, the credit period begins to run from the time the goods are shipped [UCC 2-310]. A lessee must pay lease payments in accordance with the lease contract [UCC 2A-516(1)].

The goods can be paid for in any manner currently acceptable in the ordinary course of business (e.g., check, credit card) unless the seller demands payment in cash or unless the contract names a specific form of payment. If the seller requires

A proceeding may be perfectly legal and may yet be opposed to sound commercial principles.

Lord Justice Lindley
Verner v. General and Commercial Trust (1894)

cash payment, the buyer must be given an extension of time necessary to procure the cash. If the buyer pays by check, payment is conditional on the check being honored (paid) when it is presented to the bank for payment [UCC 2-511].

In the following case, the court had to decide whether a buyer accepted goods delivered by the seller.

CASE 20.1 *STATE COURT CASE Acceptance of Goods*

Accent Commercial Furniture, Inc. v. P. Schneider & Associates, PLLC

110 A.D.3d 1415, 974 N.Y.S.2d 175, 2013 N.Y. App. Div. Lexis 7075 (2013)
New York Supreme Court, Appellate Division

"The UCC provides that acceptance of goods takes place when the buyer fails to reject them after having reasonable opportunity to inspect them."

—William McCarthy, Judge

Facts

P. Schneider & Associates, PLLC (Schneider) contracted with Accent Commercial Furniture, Inc. (Accent) for Accent to deliver and install furniture and wall panels in Schneider's office. Schneider made a $13,250 down payment on the purchase price of $44,330. When the furniture arrived, the parties discovered that the manufacturer had used incorrect fabric on the wall panels. Three months later the correct panels were installed. Accent sent Schneider an invoice for the unpaid balance. Schneider made no further payments. After one year, Accent sued Schneider to collect the remaining balance. Schneider argued that it did not owe the money because Accent had breached the contract by originally delivering the wrong goods. Accent alleged that Schneider had accepted the goods and therefore owed the outstanding balance. The trial court granted summary judgment to Accent, ordering Schneider to pay for the goods it had accepted and not rejected. Schneider appealed.

Issue

Does Schneider owe Accent the remaining balance?

Language of the Court

The UCC provides that acceptance of goods takes place when the buyer fails to reject them after having reasonable opportunity to inspect them. Plaintiff Accent met its burden on the summary judgment motion by submitting proof that it delivered and installed the furniture and defendant Schneider accepted the furniture by retaining it without attempting to return it.

Decision

The court held that Schneider owed Accent the remaining balance of the purchase price.

Critical Legal Thinking Questions

Does the UCC add uniformity to the interpretation and enforcement of contracts involving the sale of goods? Did the purchaser act ethically in refusing to pay for the goods?

Revocation of Acceptance

A buyer or lessee who has accepted goods may subsequently revoke acceptance if (1) the goods are nonconforming, (2) the nonconformity substantially impairs the value of the goods to the buyer or lessee, and (3) one of the following factors is shown: (a) the seller's or lessor's promise to timely cure of the nonconformity is not met, (b) the goods were accepted before the nonconformity was discovered and the nonconformity was difficult to discover, or (c) the goods were accepted before the nonconformity was discovered and the seller or lessor assured the buyer or lessee that the goods were conforming.

revocation of acceptance
Reversal of acceptance.

Revocation of acceptance is not effective until the seller or lessor is so notified. In addition, the revocation must occur within a reasonable time after the buyer or lessee discovers or should have discovered the grounds for the revocation. The revocation, which must be of a lot or commercial unit, must occur before there is any substantial change in the condition of the goods (e.g., before perishable goods spoil) [UCC 2-608(1), 2A-517(1)].

Seller and Lessor Remedies

20.3 List and describe seller and lessor remedies for buyer and lessee breach of sales and lease contracts.

Often, a buyer or lessee may breach a sales or lease contract. The UCC provides various remedies to sellers and lessors if a buyer or lessee *breaches a contract*. The remedies that are available to sellers and lessors if a buyer or lessee breaches a sales or lease contract are discussed in the following paragraphs.

Right to Withhold Delivery

A seller or lessor may withhold delivery of goods in his or her possession when the buyer or lessee breaches the contract. The **right to withhold delivery** is available if the buyer or lessee wrongfully rejects or revokes acceptance of the goods, fails to make a payment when due, or repudiates the contract. If part of the goods under the contract have been delivered when the buyer or lessee materially breaches the contract, the seller or lessor may withhold delivery of the remainder of the affected goods [UCC 2-703(a), 2A-523(1)(c)].

right to withhold delivery
The right of a seller or lessor to refuse to deliver goods to a buyer or lessee on breach of a sales or lease contract by the buyer or lessee or the insolvency of the buyer or lessee.

Right to Stop Delivery of Goods in Transit

Often, sellers and lessors employ common carriers and other bailees (e.g., warehouses) to hold and deliver goods to buyers and lessees. The goods are considered to be *in transit* while they are in possession of these carriers or bailees.

A seller or lessor has the **right to stop delivery of goods in transit** if while the goods are in transit (1) the buyer or lessee repudiates the contract, (2) the buyer or lessee fails to make payment when due, or (3) the buyer or lessee otherwise gives the seller or lessor some other right to withhold or reclaim the goods. In these circumstances, the delivery can be stopped only if it constitutes a carload, a truckload, a planeload, or a larger express or freight shipment [UCC 2-705(1), 2A-526(1)]. A seller or lessor who learns of the buyer's or lessee's insolvency while the goods are in transit has a right to stop delivery of the goods in transit, regardless of the size of the shipment.

right to stop delivery of goods in transit
The right of a seller or lessor to stop delivery of goods in transit if he or she learns of the buyer's or lessee's insolvency or if the buyer or lessee repudiates the contract, fails to make payment when due, or gives the seller or lessor some other cause to withhold the goods.

Right to Reclaim Goods

In certain situations, a seller or lessor may demand the return of the goods it sold or leased that are already in the possession of the buyer or lessee. In a sale transaction, the seller or lessor has the **right to reclaim goods** in two situations. If the goods are delivered in a credit sale and the seller then discovers that the buyer was insolvent, the seller has 10 days to demand that the goods be returned [UCC 2-507(2)]. If the buyer misrepresented solvency in writing within three months before delivery [UCC 2-702(2)] or paid for goods in a cash sale with a check that bounces [UCC 2-507(2)], the seller may reclaim the goods at any time. A lessor may reclaim goods in the possession of the lessee if the lessee is in default of the contract [UCC 2A-525(2)].

right to reclaim goods
The right of a seller or lessor to demand the return of goods from the buyer or lessee under specified situations.

Right to Dispose of Goods

If a buyer or lessee breaches or repudiates a sales or lease contract before the seller or lessor has delivered the goods, the seller or lessor may resell or release the goods and recover damages from the buyer or lessee [UCC 2-703(d), 2-706(1), 2A-523(1)(e), 2A-527(1)]. The **right to dispose of goods** also arises if the seller or lessor has reacquired the goods after stopping them in transit.

right to dispose of goods
The right of a seller or lessor to dispose of goods in a good faith and commercially reasonable manner. A seller or lessor who is in possession of goods at the time the buyer or lessee breaches or repudiates a contract may in good faith resell, release, or otherwise dispose of the goods in a commercially reasonable manner and recover damages, including incidental damages, from the buyer or lessee.

The seller or lessor may recover any damages incurred on the disposition of the goods. In the case of a sales contract, damages are defined as the difference between the disposition price and the original contract price. In the case of a lease contract, damages are the difference between the disposition price and the rent the original lessee would have paid. Any profit made on the resale or release of the goods does not revert to the original buyer or lessee if the seller or lessor disposes of the goods at a higher price than the buyer or lessee contracted to pay.

The seller or lessor may also recover any **incidental damages** (reasonable expenses incurred in stopping delivery, transportation charges, storage charges, sales commission, and the like [UCC 2-710, 2A-530]) incurred on the disposition of the goods [UCC 2-706(1), 2A-527(2)].

Unfinished Goods

Sometimes a sales or lease contract is breached or repudiated before the goods are finished. In a case of **unfinished goods**, the seller or lessor may choose either (1) to cease manufacturing the goods and resell them for scrap or salvage value or (2) to complete the manufacture of the goods and resell, release, or otherwise dispose of them to another party [UCC 2-704(2), 2A-524(2)]. The seller or lessor may recover damages from the breaching buyer or lessee.

Right to Recover the Purchase Price or Rent

right to recover the purchase price or rent
The right of a seller or lessor to recover the contracted-for purchase price or rent from the buyer or lessee (1) if the buyer or lessee fails to pay for accepted goods, (2) if the buyer or lessee breaches the contract and the seller or lessor cannot dispose of the goods, or (3) if the goods are damaged or lost after the risk of loss passes to the buyer or lessee.

In certain circumstances, the UCC provides that a seller or lessor may sue the buyer or lessee to recover the purchase price or rent stipulated in a sales or lease contract. The seller or lessor has the **right to recover the purchase price or rent** in the following situations:

1. The buyer or lessee accepts the goods but fails to pay for them when the price or rent is due.
2. The buyer or lessee breaches the contract after the goods have been identified in the contract and the seller or lessor cannot resell or dispose of them.
3. The goods are damaged or lost after the risk of loss passes to the buyer or lessee [UCC 2-709(1), 2A-529(1)].

The seller or lessor may also recover incidental damages from the buyer or lessee.

Right to Recover Damages for Breach of Contract

right to recover damages for breach of contract
The right of a seller or lessor to recover damages measured as the difference between the contract price (or rent) and the market price (or rent) at the time and place the goods were to be delivered, plus incidental damages, from a buyer or lessee who repudiates the contract or wrongfully rejects tendered goods.

If a buyer or lessee repudiates a sales or lease contract or wrongfully rejects tendered goods, the seller or lessor has the **right to recover damages for breach of contract** caused by the buyer's or lessee's breach. Generally, the amount of damages is calculated as the difference between the contract price (or rent) and the market price (or rent) of the goods at the time and place the goods were to be delivered to the buyer or lessee plus incidental damages [UCC 2-708(1), 2A-528(1)].

If the preceding measure of damages will not put the seller or lessor in as good a position as performance of the contract would have, the seller or lessor has the **right to recover lost profits** that would have resulted from the full performance of the contract plus an allowance for reasonable overhead and incidental damages [UCC 2-708(2), 2A-528(2)].

Right to Cancel a Contract

A seller or lessor has the **right to cancel a contract** if the buyer or lessee breaches the contract by rejecting or revoking acceptance of the goods, failing to pay for the goods, or repudiating all or any part of the contract. The cancellation may refer only to the affected goods or to the entire contract if the breach is material [UCC 2-703(f), 2A-523(1)(a)].

The following feature discusses the UCC rule that applies to a lost volume seller.

Business Environment

Lost Volume Seller

Should a seller be permitted to recover the profits it lost on a sale to a defaulting buyer if the seller sold the goods to another buyer? It depends. If the seller had only one item or a limited number of items and could produce no more, the seller cannot recover lost profits from the defaulting buyer if the seller sold the one item to another buyer or sold the limited number of items to other buyers. This is because the seller made profits on the sale or sales.

If, however, the seller could have produced more of the item, the seller is a **lost volume seller.** In this situation, the seller can recover the profit it would have made on the sale to the defaulting buyer. This is because the seller has realized profits from the sales to the other buyers and would have also made a profit from the sale to the defaulting buyer.

Example Carpet Store purchases hundreds of oriental rugs from manufacturers that it sells to customers in its store. Mary contracts to purchase an oriental rug for $3,000 from Carpet Store. This rug cost Carpet Store $1,200. Mary defaults and does not take possession of the rug. Carpet Store sells the rug to another buyer for $3,000. Here, Carpet Store can recover lost profits from Mary because the buyer of the rug that Mary did not buy might have purchased a different rug from Carpet Store and, therefore, Carpet Store would have had two sales if Mary had not breached the sales contract. Therefore, Carpet Store can recover $1,800 of lost profits from Mary.

CONCEPT SUMMARY

SELLER'S AND LESSOR'S REMEDIES

Possession of Goods at the Time of the Buyer's or Lessee's Breach	Seller's or Lessor's Remedies
Goods in the possession of the seller or lessor	1. Withhold delivery of the goods [UCC 2-703(a), 2A-523(1)(c)]. 2. Resell or release the goods and recover the difference between the contract or lease price and the resale or release price [UCC 2-706, 2A-527]. 3. Sue for breach of contract and recover as damages the difference between the market price and the contract price [UCC 2-708(1), 2A-528(1)]. 4. A lost volume seller can sue and recover lost profits [UCC 2-708(2), 2A-528(2)]. 5. Cancel the contract [UCC 2-703(f), 2A-523(1)(a)].
Goods in the possession of a common carrier or bailee	1. Stop goods in transit [UCC 2-705(1), 2A-526(1)]. a. Carload, truckload, planeload, or larger shipment if the buyer is solvent. b. Any size shipment if the buyer is insolvent.
Goods in the possession of the buyer or lessee	1. Sue to recover the purchase price or rent [UCC 2-709(1), 2A-529(1)]. 2. Reclaim the goods [UCC 2-507(2), 2A-525(2)].

Buyer and Lessee Remedies

20.4 List and describe buyer and lessee remedies for seller and lessor breach of sales and lease contracts.

If a seller or lessor breaches a sales or lease contract, the UCC provides a variety of remedies to the buyer or lessee for the seller's or lessor's breach. These remedies are discussed in the following paragraphs.

lost volume seller
A seller who can recover lost profits from a defaulting buyer even though the seller sold the item to another buyer, where the seller has other similar items and would have made two sales had the original buyer not defaulted.

Right to Reject Nonconforming Goods or Improperly Tendered Goods

If the contracted-for goods or the seller's or lessor's tender of delivery fails to conform to a sales or lease contract in any way, the buyer or lessee has the **right to reject nonconforming goods or improperly tendered goods** and may (1) reject the whole, (2) accept the whole, or (3) accept any commercial unit and reject the rest. Nonconforming or improperly tendered goods must be rejected within a reasonable time after their delivery or tender. The seller or lessor must be notified of the rejection. The buyer or lessee must hold any rightfully rejected goods with reasonable care for a reasonable time [UCC 2-602(2), 2A-512(1)].

right to reject nonconforming goods or improperly tendered goods
The right of a buyer or lessee to reject goods that do not conform to a contract. If the goods or the seller's or lessor's tender of delivery fails to conform to the contract, the buyer or lessee may (1) reject the whole, (2) accept the whole, or (3) accept any commercial unit and reject the rest.

If the buyer or lessee chooses to reject the goods, he or she must identify defects that are ascertainable by reasonable inspection [UCC 2-601, 2A-509]. Any buyer or lessee who rightfully rejects goods is entitled to reimbursement from the seller or lessor for reasonable expenses incurred in holding, storing, reselling, shipping, and otherwise caring for the rejected goods.

Right to Recover Goods from an Insolvent Seller or Lessor

right to recover goods from an insolvent seller or lessor
The right of a buyer or lessee who has wholly or partially paid for goods before they are received to recover the goods from a seller or lessor who becomes insolvent within 10 days after receiving the first payment; the buyer or lessee must tender the remaining purchase price or rent due under the contract.

If a buyer or lessee makes partial or full payment for goods before they are received and the seller or lessor becomes insolvent within 10 days after receiving the first payment, the buyer or lessee has the **right to recover the goods from the insolvent seller or lessor**. To do so, the buyer or lessee must tender the unpaid portion of the purchase price or rent due under the sales or lease contract. Only conforming goods that are identified in the contract may be recovered [UCC 2-502, 2A-522]. This remedy is often referred to as *capture*.

Right to Obtain Specific Performance

specific performance
A decree of the court that orders a seller or lessor to perform his or her obligations under the contract; this usually occurs when the goods in question are unique, such as art or antiques.

If goods are unique or the remedy at law is inadequate, a buyer or lessee has the **right to obtain specific performance** of a sales or a lease contract. A decree of **specific performance** orders the seller or lessor to perform the contract. Specific performance is usually used to obtain possession of works of art, antiques, rare coins, and other unique items [UCC 2-716(1), 2A-521(1)].

Example A buyer enters into a sales contract to purchase a specific Rembrandt painting from a seller for $25 million. When the buyer tenders payment, the seller refuses to sell the painting to the buyer. The buyer may bring an equity action to obtain a decree of specific performance from the court, which orders the seller to sell the painting to the buyer.

Right to Replevy Goods

A buyer or lessee has the **right to replevy (recover) goods** from a seller or lessor who is wrongfully withholding the goods. The buyer or lessee must show that he or she was unable to cover or that attempts at cover will be unavailing. Thus, the goods must be scarce but not unique. **Replevin** actions are available only as to goods identified in a sales or lease contract [UCC 2-716(3), 2A-521(3)].

replevin
An action by a buyer or lessee to recover scarce goods wrongfully withheld by a seller or lessor.

The following feature discusses a buyer's and lessee's UCC right to cover.

Right to Cancel a Contract

If a seller or lessor fails to deliver conforming goods or repudiates the contract, the buyer or lessee has the **right to cancel the contract**. The buyer or lessee can also cancel a sales or lease contract if the buyer or lessee rightfully rejects the goods or justifiably revokes acceptance of the goods. The contract may be canceled with respect to the affected goods, or if there is a material breach,

Contemporary Environment

Buyer's and Lessee's Right to Cover

A buyer or lessee has the **right to cover** by purchasing or renting substitute goods if the seller or lessor fails to make delivery of the goods or repudiates the contract or if the buyer or lessee rightfully rejects the goods or justifiably revokes their acceptance. The buyer's or lessee's **cover** must be made in good faith and without unreasonable delay. If the exact commodity is not available, the buyer or lessee may purchase or lease any commercially reasonable substitute.

A buyer or lessee who rightfully covers may sue the seller or lessor to recover as damages the difference between the cost of cover and the contract price or rent. The buyer or lessee may also recover incidental and consequential damages, less expenses saved (such as delivery costs) [UCC 2-712, 2A-518].

Example University contracts to purchase 1,000 specific electronic devices from Orange Store for $300 each to be used by its faculty members. Orange Store breaches the contract and does not deliver the devices to University. University covers and contracts with Apple Store to purchase 1,000 of these electronic devices at the price of $400 per device. Here, University may recover $100,000 from Orange Store ($400 cover price − $300 contract price = $100 × 1,000 devices).

Failure of the buyer or lessee to cover does not bar the buyer from other remedies against the seller.

---

the whole contract may be canceled. A buyer or lessee who rightfully cancels a contract is discharged from any further obligations on the contract and retains his or her rights to other remedies against the seller or lessor [UCC 2-711(1), 2A-508(1)(a)].

Right to Recover Damages for Nondelivery or Repudiation

If a seller or lessor fails to deliver the goods or repudiates the sales or lease contract, the buyer or lessee has the **right to recover damages for nondelivery or repudiation**. The measure of **damages** is the difference between the contract price (or original rent) and the market price (or rent) at the time the buyer or lessee learned of the breach. Incidental and consequential damages, less expenses saved, can also be recovered [UCC 2-713, 2A-519].

Example Fresh Foods Company contracts to purchase 10,000 bushels of soybeans from Sunshine Farms for $14 per bushel. Delivery is to occur on August 1. On August 1, the market price of soybeans is $24 per bushel. Sunshine Farms does not deliver the soybeans to Fresh Foods. Fresh Foods decides not to cover and to do without the soybeans. Fresh Foods sues Sunshine for market value minus the contract price damages. It can recover $100,000 ($24 market price − $14 contract price = $10 × 10,000 bushels) plus incidental damages less expenses saved because of Sunshine's breach. Fresh Foods cannot recover consequential damages because it did not attempt to cover.

right to cover
The right of a buyer or lessee to purchase or lease substitute goods if a seller or lessor fails to make delivery of the goods or repudiates the contract or if the buyer or lessee rightfully rejects the goods or justifiably revokes their acceptance.

damages
Damages a buyer or lessee recovers from a seller or lessor who fails to deliver the goods or repudiates a contract. Damages are measured as the difference between the contract price (or original rent) and the market price (or rent) at the time the buyer or lessee learned of the breach.

Right to Recover Damages for Accepted Nonconforming Goods

A buyer or lessee may accept nonconforming goods from a seller or lessor. Even with acceptance, the buyer or lessee still has the **right to recover damages for accepted nonconforming goods** and any loss resulting from the seller's or lessor's breach. Incidental and consequential damages may also be recovered. The buyer or lessee must notify the seller or lessor of the nonconformity within a reasonable time after the breach was or should have been discovered. Failure to do so bars the buyer or lessee from any recovery. If the buyer or lessee accepts nonconforming goods, he or she may deduct all or any part of damages resulting from the breach from any part of the purchase price or rent still due under the contract [UCC 2-714(1), 2A-516(1)].

This is the kind of order which makes the administration of justice stink in the nostrils of commercial men.

A.L. Smith
L. J. Graham v. Sutton, Carden & Company (1897)

Example Retail Clothing contracts to purchase 1,000 designer dresses for $500 per dress from Manhattan Loft, a women's clothes designer and manufacturer. Retail Clothing pays for the dresses prior to delivery. After the dresses are delivered, Retail Clothing discovers that 200 of the dresses have flaws in them. Retail Clothing may accept these nonconforming dresses and sue Manhattan Loft for reasonable damages resulting from the nonconformity.

CONCEPT SUMMARY

BUYER'S AND LESSEE'S REMEDIES

Situation	Buyer's or Lessee's Remedy
Seller or lessor refuses to deliver the goods or delivers nonconforming goods that the buyer or lessee does not want.	1. Reject nonconforming goods [UCC 2-601, 2A-509]. 2. Cover and recover damages [UCC 2-712, 2A-518]. 3. Sue for breach of contract and recover damages [UCC 2-713, 2A-519]. 4. Cancel the contract [UCC 2-711(1), 2A-508(1)(a)].
Seller or lessor tenders nonconforming goods, and the buyer or lessee accepts them.	1. Sue for ordinary damages [UCC 2-714(1), 2A-516(1)]. 2. Deduct damages from the unpaid purchase or rent price [UCC 2-714(1), 2A-516(1)].
Seller or lessor refuses to deliver the goods, and the buyer or lessee wants them.	1. Sue for specific performance [UCC 2-716(1), 2A-521(1)]. 2. Replevy the goods [UCC 2-716(3), 2A-521(3)]. 3. Recover the goods from an insolvent seller or lessor [UCC 2-502, 2A-522].

Additional Performance Issues

20.5 List and describe additional performance issues.

UCC Articles 2 (Sales) and 2A (Leases) contain several other provisions that affect the parties' performance of a sales or lease contract. These provisions are discussed in the following paragraphs.

Assurance of Performance

Each party to a sales or lease contract expects that the other party will perform its contractual obligations. If one party to a contract has reasonable grounds to believe that the other party either will not or cannot perform its contractual obligations, an **adequate assurance of performance** may be demanded in writing. If it is commercially reasonable to do so, the party making the demand may suspend its performance until adequate assurance of due performance is received from the other party [UCC 2-609, 2A-401].

adequate assurance of performance
Adequate assurance of performance from the other party if there is an indication that a contract will be breached by that party.

Example A buyer contracts to purchase 1,000 bushels of wheat from a farmer. The contract requires delivery on September 1. In July, the buyer learns that floods have caused substantial crop loss in the area of the seller's farm. The farmer receives the buyer's written demand for adequate assurance on July 15. The farmer fails to give adequate assurance of performance. The buyer may suspend performance and treat the sales contract as having been repudiated.

UCC statute of limitations
A rule that provides that an action for breach of any written or oral sales or lease contract must commence within four years after the cause of action accrues. The parties may agree to reduce the limitations period to one year.

Statute of Limitations

The **UCC statute of limitations** provides that an action for breach of any written or oral sales or lease contract must commence within four years after the legal claim accrues. The parties may agree to reduce the limitations period to one year, but they cannot extend it beyond four years.

Example A buyer contracts to purchase cattle from a seller with a delivery date of July 1, 2020. The seller breaches the contract and does not deliver the cattle on July 1, 2020. Under the UCC four-year statute of limitations, the buyer has until July 1, 2024, to bring a lawsuit against the seller for breach of contract. If the buyer waits until after this date has passed, then the buyer loses the right to sue the seller. The parties could have included a provision in their contract to reduce the limitations period to one year, or July 1, 2021.

Agreements Affecting Remedies

The parties to a sales or lease contract may agree on remedies in addition to or in substitution for the remedies provided by the UCC. The parties may limit the buyer's or lessee's remedies to repair and replacement of defective goods or parts or to the return of the goods and repayment (refund) of the purchase price or rent.

Convenience is the basis of mercantile law.

Lord Mansfield
Medcalf v. Hall (1782)

The remedies agreed on by the parties are in addition to the remedies provided by the UCC unless the parties expressly provide that they are exclusive. If an exclusive remedy fails in its essential purpose (e.g., there is an exclusive remedy of repair, but there are no repair parts available), any remedy may be had, as provided in the UCC.

Liquidated Damages

The UCC permits parties to a sales or lease contract to establish in advance in their contract the damages that will be paid on a breach of the contract. Such pre-established damages, called **liquidated damages**, substitute for actual damages. In a sales or lease contract, liquidated damages are valid if they are reasonable in light of the anticipated or actual harm caused by the breach, the difficulties of proof of loss, and the inconvenience or nonfeasibility of otherwise obtaining an adequate remedy [UCC 2-718(1), 2A-504].

liquidated damages
Damages that will be paid on a breach of contract that are established in advance.

The UCC doctrine of unconscionable contract is discussed in the following ethics feature.

Ethics

UCC Doctrine of Unconscionability

UCC Article 2 (Sales) and Article 2A (Leases) have adopted the equity doctrine of **unconscionability**. Under this doctrine, a court may determine as a matter of law that a contract is an **unconscionable contract**. To prove unconscionability, there must be proof that the parties had substantially unequal bargaining power, that the dominant party misused its power in contracting, and that it would be manifestly unfair or oppressive to enforce the contract. This sometimes happens where a dominant party uses a preprinted form contract and the terms of the contract are unfair or oppressive.

If a court finds that a contract or any clause in a contract is unconscionable, the court may refuse to enforce the contract, it may enforce the remainder of the contract without the unconscionable clause, or it may so limit the application of any unconscionable clause as to avoid any unconscionable result [UCC 2-302, 2A-108]. Unconscionability is sometimes found in a consumer lease if the consumer has been induced by unconscionable conduct to enter into the lease. The doctrine of unconscionability applies to online contracts as well as traditional contracts.

Ethics Questions
Does the fact that the term *unconscionable* is somewhat vague serve any useful purpose? Does the doctrine of unconscionability encourage ethical behavior?

Key Terms and Concepts

Acceptance (353)
Adequate assurance of performance (360)
Breach (350)
Commercial reasonableness (352)
Cover (359)
Cure (351)
Damages (359)
Destination contract (351)
Express terms (352)
Good faith (352)
Incidental damages (356)
Installment contract (352)
Liquidated damages (361)
Lost volume seller (357)
Payment (353)
Perfect tender rule (351)
Place of delivery (350)
Reasonableness (352)
Replevin (358)
Revocation of acceptance (354)
Right to cancel a contract (356)
Right to cover (359)
Right to cure (351)
Right to dispose of goods (355)
Right to inspect (353)
Right to obtain specific performance (358)
Right to reclaim goods (355)
Right to recover damages for accepted nonconforming goods (359)
Right to recover damages for breach of contract (356)
Right to recover damages for nondelivery or repudiation (359)
Right to recover goods from an insolvent seller or lessor (358)
Right to recover lost profits (356)
Right to recover the purchase price or rent (356)
Right to reject nonconforming goods or improperly tendered goods (358)
Right to replevy (recover) goods (358)
Right to stop delivery of goods in transit (355)
Right to withhold delivery (355)
Shipment contract (351)
Specific performance (358)
Tender of delivery (350)
UCC statute of limitations (360)
Unconscionability (361)
Unconscionable contract (361)
Unfinished goods (356)

Critical Legal Thinking Cases

20.1 Nonconforming Goods The Jacob Hartz Seed Company, Inc. (Hartz) bought soybeans for use as seed from E. R. Coleman. Coleman certified that the seed had an 80 percent germination rate. Hartz paid for the beans and picked them up from a warehouse in Card, Arkansas. After the seed was transported to Georgia, a sample was submitted for testing to the Georgia Department of Agriculture. When the department reported a germination level of only 67 percent, Coleman requested that the seed be retested. The second set of tests reported a germination rate of 65 percent. Hartz canceled the contract after the second test, and Coleman reclaimed the seed. Hartz sought a refund of the money it had paid for the seed, claiming that the soybeans were nonconforming goods. Who wins? *Jacob Hartz Seed Co. v. Coleman*, 612 S.W.2d 91, 1981 Ark. Lexis 1153 (Supreme Court of Arkansas, 1981)

20.2 Right to Cure Connie R. Grady purchased a new Chevrolet Chevette from Al Thompson Chevrolet (Thompson). Grady gave Thompson a down payment on the car and financed the remainder of the purchase price through General Motors Acceptance Corporation (GMAC). Grady picked up the Chevette. The next day, the car broke down and had to be towed back to Thompson. Grady picked up the repaired car one day later. The car's performance was still unsatisfactory in that the engine was hard to start, the transmission slipped, and the brakes had to be pushed to the floor to function. Two weeks later, Grady again returned the Chevette for servicing. When she picked up the car that evening, the engine started, but the engine and brake warning lights came on. This pattern of malfunction and repair continued for another two months. Grady wrote a letter to Thompson, revoking the sale. Thompson repossessed the Chevette. GMAC sued Grady to recover its money. Grady sued Thompson to recover her down payment. Thompson claimed that Grady's suit was barred because the company was not given adequate opportunity to cure. Who wins? *General Motors Acceptance Corp. v. Grady*, 501 N.E.2d 68, 1985 Ohio App. Lexis 10353 (Court of Appeals of Ohio, 1985)

20.3 Specific Performance Dr. and Mrs. Sedmak (Sedmaks) were collectors of Chevrolet Corvettes. The Sedmaks saw an article in *Vette Vues* magazine concerning a new limited-edition Corvette. The limited edition was designed to commemorate the selection of the Corvette as the official pace car of the Indianapolis 500. Chevrolet was manufacturing only 6,000 of these pace cars. The Sedmaks visited Charlie's Chevrolet, Inc. (Charlie's), a local Chevrolet dealer. Charlie's was to receive only one limited-edition car, which the sales manager agreed to sell to the Sedmaks for the sticker price of $15,000. When the Sedmaks went to pick up and pay for the car, they were told that because of the great demand for the limited edition, it was going to be auctioned to the highest bidder. The Sedmaks sued the dealership for specific performance. Who wins? *Sedmak v. Charlie's Chevrolet, Inc.*, 622 S.W.2d. 694, 1981 Mo. App. Lexis 2911 (Court of Appeals of Missouri, 1981)

20.4 Right to Cover Kent Nowlin Construction, Inc. (Nowlin) was awarded a contract by the state of New Mexico to pave a number of roads. After Nowlin was awarded the contract, it entered into an agreement with Concrete Sales & Equipment Rental Company, Inc. (C&E). C&E was to supply 20,000 tons of paving material to Nowlin. Nowlin began paving the roads, anticipating C&E's delivery of materials. On the delivery date, however, C&E shipped only 2,099 tons of paving materials. Because Nowlin had a deadline to meet, the company contracted with Gallup Sand and Gravel Company (Gallup) for substitute material. Nowlin sued C&E to recover the difference between the higher price it had to pay Gallup for materials and the contract price C&E had agreed to. C&E claims that it is not responsible for Nowlin's increased costs. Who wins? *Concrete Sales & Equipment Rental Company, Inc. v. Kent Nowlin Construction, Inc.*, 746 P.2d 645, 1987 N.M. Lexis 3808 (Supreme Court of New Mexico, 1987)

Ethics Cases

20.5 Ethics Case Both Allsopp Sand and Gravel (Allsopp) and Lincoln Sand and Gravel (Lincoln) were in the business of supplying sand to construction companies. In March, Lincoln's sand dredge became inoperable. To continue in business, Lincoln negotiated a contract with Allsopp to purchase sand over the course of a year. The contract called for the sand to be loaded on Lincoln's trucks during Allsopp's regular operating season (March through November). Loading at other times was to be done by "special arrangement." By the following November, Lincoln had taken delivery of one-quarter of the sand it had contracted for. At that point, Lincoln requested that several trucks of sand be loaded in December. Allsopp informed Lincoln that it would have to pay extra for this special arrangement. Lincoln refused to pay extra, pointing out that the sand was already stockpiled at Allsopp's facilities. Allsopp also offered to supply an employee to supervise the loading. Negotiations between the parties broke down, and Lincoln informed Allsopp that it did not intend to honor the remainder of the contract. Allsopp sued Lincoln. Is it commercially reasonable for Lincoln to demand delivery of sand during December? Has Lincoln acted ethically in this case? *Allsopp Sand and Gravel v. Lincoln Sand and Gravel*, 525 N.E.2d 1185, 1988 Ill. App. Lexis 939 (Appellate Court of Illinois, 1988)

20.6 Ethics Case Saber Energy, Inc. (Saber) entered into a sales contract with Tri-State Petroleum Corporation (Tri-State). The contract called for Saber to sell Tri-State 110,000 barrels of gasoline per month for six months. Saber was to deliver the gasoline through the colonial pipeline in Pasadena, Texas. The first 110,000 barrels were delivered on time. On August 1, Saber was informed that Tri-State was canceling the contract. Saber sued Tri-State for breach of contract and sought to recover its lost profits as damages. Tri-State admitted its breach but claimed that lost profits is an inappropriate measure of damages. Who wins? Did Tri-State act ethically in canceling the contract? Did Tri-State act ethically in denying it owed damages to Saber Energy? *Tri-State Petroleum Corporation v. Saber Energy, Inc.* 845 F.2d 575, 1988 U.S. App. Lexis 6819 (United States Court of Appeals for the Fifth Circuit, 1988)

CHAPTER 21

Warranties

EXPRESS WARRANTY

The sellers of goods are liable for breach of warranties that they make. For example, when a jewelry store sells a diamond ring, it states the "four Cs" of the ring: cut, clarity, color, and carat weight. If a party purchases a ring but it does not meet the four Cs as stated by the seller, the seller has breached a warranty. The purchaser can sue the seller for breach of a warranty.

Henry R. Cheeseman

Learning Objectives

After studying this chapter, you should be able to:

21.1 Describe express warranties and distinguish them from statements of opinion.

21.2 List and describe implied warranties.

21.3 Describe the implied warranty of merchantability.

21.4 Describe the implied warranty of fitness for human consumption.

21.5 Describe the implied warranty of fitness for a particular purpose.

21.6 Identify warranty disclaimers and determine when they are lawful.

21.7 Describe the protections provided by the Magnuson-Moss Warranty Act.

21.8 List and describe warranties of title and possession.

> *"When a manufacturer engages in advertising in order to bring his goods and their quality to the attention of the public and thus to create consumer demand, the representations made constitute an express warranty running directly to a buyer who purchases in reliance thereon. The fact that the sale is consummated with an independent dealer does not obviate the warranty."*
>
> — *John Francis, Justice*
> *Henningsen v. Bloomfield Motors, Inc.*
> *161 A.2d 69, 1960 N.J. Lexis 213 (1960)*

Introduction to Warranties

The doctrine of ***caveat emptor***—"let the buyer beware"—governed the law of sales and leases for centuries. Finally, the law recognized that consumers and other purchasers and lessees of goods needed greater protection. Article 2 of the Uniform Commercial Code (UCC), adopted in whole or in part by all 50 states, establishes certain warranties that apply to the sale of goods. In addition, Article 2A of the UCC, adopted in almost all states, establishes warranties that apply to lease transactions.

A **warranty** is the buyer's or lessee's assurance that the goods meet certain standards. Warranties that are based on contract law may be either *expressly* stated or *implied* by law. If the seller or lessor fails to meet a warranty, the buyer or lessee can sue for breach of warranty.

Sales and lease warranties are discussed in this chapter.

warranty
A seller's or lessor's express or implied assurance to a buyer or lessee that the goods sold or leased meet certain quality standards.

Warranties are favored in law, being a part of a man's assurance.

Sir Edward Coke (1552–1634)
First Institute of the Laws of England, Volume 2

Express Warranty

21.1 Describe express warranties and distinguish them from statements of opinion.

An **express warranty** is created when a seller or lessor affirms that the goods he or she is selling or leasing meet certain standards of quality, description, performance, or condition [UCC 2-313(1), 2A-210(1)]. Express warranties can be written, oral, or inferred from the seller's conduct. It is not necessary to use formal words such as *warrant* or *guarantee* to create an express warranty. Express warranties can be made by mistake because the seller or lessor does not have to specifically intend to make the warranty [UCC 2-313(2), 2A-210(2)].

Sellers and lessors are not required to make express warranties. Generally, express warranties are made to entice consumers and others to buy or lease their products. That is why these warranties are often found in advertisements, brochures, catalogs, pictures, illustrations, diagrams, blueprints, and so on. Buyers and lessees can recover for breach of an express warranty if the warranty induced the buyer to purchase the product or the lessee to lease the product.

express warranty
A warranty created when a seller or lessor makes an affirmation that the goods he or she is selling or leasing meet certain standards of quality, description, performance, or condition.

Creation of an Express Warranty

An express warranty is created when a seller or lessor indicates that the goods will conform to the following:

1. All *affirmations of fact or promise* made about the goods

   Examples Promises are statements such as "This car will go 100 miles per hour" or "This house paint will last at least five years."

2. Any *description* of the goods

   Examples Descriptions of goods include terms such as *Idaho potatoes* and *Michigan cherries*.

3. Any *model* or *sample* of the goods

   Example A model of an oil-drilling rig or a sample of wheat taken from a silo creates an express warranty.

Buyers and lessees can recover for a breach of an express warranty if the warranty was a contributing factor that induced the buyer to purchase the product or the lessee to lease the product [UCC 2-313(1), 2A-210(1)]. Generally, a retailer is liable for the express warranties made by manufacturers of goods it sells. A manufacturer is not liable for express warranties made by wholesalers and retailers unless the manufacturer authorizes or ratifies a warranty.

The following feature discusses whether a statement of opinion creates an express warranty.

Contemporary Environment

Statement of Opinion (Puffing)

Many express warranties arise during the course of negotiations between a buyer and a seller or a lessor and a lessee. A seller's or lessor's **statement of opinion** (also known as **puffing**) or commendation of the goods does not create an express warranty. It is often difficult to determine whether a seller's statement is an affirmation of fact (which creates an express warranty) or a statement of opinion (which does not create a warranty). An affirmation of the value of goods does not create an express warranty [UCC 2-313(2), 2A-210(2)].

Examples A used car salesperson says, "This is the best used car available in town." This statement does not create an express warranty because it is an opinion and mere puffing. However, a statement such as "This car has been driven only 20,000 miles" is an express warranty because it is a statement of fact.

Examples Statements such as "This painting is worth a fortune" or "Others would gladly pay $20,000 for this car" do not create an express warranty because these are statements of value and not statements of fact.

---

statement of opinion (puffing)
A commendation of goods, made by a seller or lessor, that does not create an express warranty.

compensatory damages
Damages that are generally equal to the difference between the value of the goods as warranted and the actual value of the goods accepted at the time and place of acceptance.

Damages Recoverable for Breach of Warranty

Where there has been a breach of warranty, the buyer or lessee may sue the seller or lessor to recover **compensatory damages**. The amount of recoverable compensatory damages is generally equal to the difference between the value of the goods as warranted and the actual value of the goods accepted at the time and place of acceptance [UCC 2-714(2), 2A-508(4)]. A purchaser or lessee can recover for personal injuries that are caused by a breach of warranty.

Example A used car salesperson warrants that a used car has been driven only 20,000 miles. If true, that would make the car worth $20,000. The salesperson gives the buyer a "good deal" and sells the car for $16,000. Unfortunately, the car was worth only $10,000 because it had actually been driven 100,000 miles. The buyer discovers the breach of warranty and sues the salesperson for damages. The buyer can recover $10,000 ($20,000 warranted value minus $10,000 actual value). The contract price ($16,000) is irrelevant to this computation.

Implied Warranties

21.2 List and describe implied warranties.

In addition to express warranties made by a manufacturer or seller, the law sometimes *implies* warranties in the sale or lease of goods. An **implied warranty** is not expressly stated in the sales or lease contract but instead is **implied by law**.

The most common forms of implied warranties are the *implied warranty of merchantability*, the *implied warranty of fitness for human consumption*, and the *implied warranty of fitness for a particular purpose*.

These warranties are discussed in the following paragraphs.

Implied Warranty of Merchantability

21.3 Describe the implied warranty of merchantability.

If a seller or lessor of a good is a *merchant* with respect to goods of that kind, the sales contract or lease contract contains an **implied warranty of merchantability** of the goods unless this implied warranty is properly disclaimed [UCC 2-314(1), 2A-212(1)]. This implied warranty requires that the following standards be met:

1. The goods must be fit for the ordinary purposes for which they are used.

   Examples A chair must be able to safely perform the function of a chair. If a normal-sized person sits in a chair that has not been tampered with and the chair collapses, there has been a breach of the implied warranty of merchantability. If the same person is injured because he or she uses the chair as a ladder and it tips over, there is no breach of implied warranty because use as a ladder is not the ordinary purpose of a chair.

2. The goods must be adequately contained, packaged, and labeled.

   Example The implied warranty of merchantability applies to a milk bottle as well as to the milk inside the bottle.

3. The goods must be of an even kind, quality, and quantity within each unit.

   Example All the goods in a carton, package, or box must be consistent.

4. The goods must conform to any promise or affirmation of fact made on the container or label.

   Example The goods must be capable of being used safely in accordance with the instructions on the package or label.

5. The quality of the goods must pass without objection in the trade.

   Example The goods must be of such quality that other users of the goods would not object to their quality.

6. Fungible goods must meet a fair average quality for the type of good.

   Example To be classified as a certain grade, such as pearl millet grain (*Pennisetum glaucum*) or iron ore (magnetite Fe_3O_4), goods must meet the average range of quality of that grade.

In the following case, the court had to decide if the implied warranty of merchantability had been breached.

implied warranty of merchantability
Unless properly disclosed, a warranty that is implied that sold or leased goods are fit for the ordinary purpose for which they are sold or leased, as well as other assurances.

Critical Legal Thinking Questions

How do an express warranty and an implied warranty differ? What is the public policy for implying a warranty of merchantability?

Law should be like death, which spares no one.

Charles de Montesquieu (1689–1755)

CASE 21.1 *FEDERAL COURT CASE Implied Warranty of Merchantability*

Osorio v. One World Technologies, Inc.

659 F.3d 81, 2011 U.S. App. Lexis 20174 (2011)
United States Court of Appeals for the First Circuit

"Manufacturers must design products so that they are fit for the ordinary purposes for which such goods are used."

—Juan Torruella, Circuit Judge

Facts

Carlos Osorio worked at a construction site for his employer, a contractor who repairs and installs hardwood floors. The employer had purchased a

(continued)

Ryobi Model BTS 15 table saw at Home Depot for $179. The saw was manufactured by Ryobi Technologies, Inc. As Osorio was using the BTS 15 saw to make a cut along the length of a piece of wood, his left hand slipped and slid into the saw's blade, causing severe injury. Osorio sued Ryobi in U.S. district court, claiming breach of the implied warranty of merchantability. At trial, Osorio produced a witness, Dr. Stephen Gass, who invented "SawStop," a mechanism that allows a table saw to sense when the blade comes into contact with flesh, immediately stop the blade from spinning, and cause the blade to retreat into the body of the saw. Dr. Gass testified that he presented the technology to Ryobi, but the company did not incorporate this technology into its saws. The jury held that Ryobi had breached the implied warranty of merchantability by not adopting the flesh-detection technology in its saws and awarded Osorio damages of $1.5 million. Ryobi appealed.

Issue

Did Ryobi breach the implied warranty of merchantability?

Language of the Court

Manufacturers must design products so that they are fit for the ordinary purposes for which such goods are used. It is the province of the jury to determine whether a product's design is unreasonable. Considering the evidence before it, the jury simply agreed with Osorio's case and found in his favor.

Decision

The U.S. court of appeals affirmed the U.S. district court's finding that Ryobi had breached the implied warranty of merchantability.

Critical Legal Thinking Questions

Should Ryobi have adopted flesh-detection technology in its saws? What would be the impact on consumers if it did?

The implied warranty of merchantability does not apply to sales or leases by nonmerchants or to casual sales.

Examples The implied warranty of merchantability applies to the sale of a lawn mower that is sold by a merchant who is in the business of selling lawn mowers. The implied warranty of merchantability does not apply when one neighbor sells a lawn mower to another neighbor.

In the following case, the court had to decide whether there was a breach of an implied warranty of merchantability and failure to warn.

CASE 21.2 *FEDERAL COURT CASE Implied Warranty of Merchantability*

Geshke v. Crocs, Inc.

740 F.3d 74, 2014 U.S. App. Lexis 954 (2014)
United States Court of Appeals for the First Circuit

"Massachusetts law gives rise to a duty to warn only where there is some reason to suppose a warning is needed."

—Bruce Selya, Circuit Judge

Facts

Crocs, Inc. makes odd-looking shoes called CROCS, a type of soft-soled resin clog that are known for their comfort. Nancy Geshke's 9-year-old daughter, N.K., wore a pair of CROCS when she and her mother and father visited Boston. The family boarded a descending escalator operated by the Massachusetts Bay Transportation Authority (MBTA). N.K.'s CROCS-shod right foot became entrapped in the side of the moving escalator. While N.K. screamed, an MBTA worker unsuccessfully attempted to activate the escalator's emergency brake. A bystander rushed to the rescue, freeing N.K.'s foot before she reached the bottom plate. N.K. suffered injuries from the accident. Nancy Geshke, as mother and guardian of N.K., a minor, sued Crocs, Inc. for damages, alleging that it violated the implied warranty of merchantability by designing CROCS that present a heightened risk of danger to wearers using escalators, and that the manufacturer failed to warn of this risk. The U.S. district court found that the plaintiff's allegations were unsupported and entered summary judgment in favor of Crocs, Inc. Geshke appealed.

Issue

Did Crocs, Inc. breach the implied warranty of merchantability of the safety of its CROCS footwear and fail to warn of such danger?

Language of the Court

Massachusetts law gives rise to a duty to warn only where there is some reason to suppose a warning is needed. The plaintiff's case hinges on demonstrating that the defendant's product was particularly dangerous on escalators. Yet even after full discovery, the plaintiff has failed to adduce probative evidence on this point sufficient to allow a reasonable jury to find in her favor. We need to go no further. From this record, we cannot tell whether CROCS present a heightened risk of escalator entrapment.

Decision

The U.S. court of appeals affirmed the district court's grant of summary judgment in favor of Crocs, Inc.

Critical Legal Thinking Questions

Do escalators pose any general dangers of use? If so, what are these dangers?

Implied Warranty of Fitness for Human Consumption

21.4 Describe the implied warranty of fitness for human consumption.

The common law implied a special warranty—the **implied warranty of fitness for human consumption**—to food products. The UCC incorporates this warranty within the implied warranty of merchantability, and it applies to food and drink consumed on or off the seller's premises. Restaurants, grocery stores, fast-food outlets, coffee shops, bars, vending machines, and other purveyors of food and drink are all subject to this warranty. States use one of the following two tests in determining whether there has been a breach of the implied warranty of fitness for human consumption:

implied warranty of fitness for human consumption
A warranty that applies to food or drink consumed on or off the premises of restaurants, grocery stores, fast-food outlets, coffee shops, bars, vending machines, and other purveyors of food and drink.

1. **Foreign substance test.** Under the **foreign substance test**, food and drink are unmerchantable if a foreign object in that product causes injury to a person.

   Examples Under this test, the implied warranty would be breached if a person were injured by eating a nail in a cherry pie. This is because a nail is a foreign object in the cherry pie. The implied warranty would not be breached if a person were injured by eating a cherry pit in the pie. This is because the cherry pit is not a foreign object in the cherry pie.

foreign substance test
A test to determine merchantability based on foreign objects found in food.

2. **Consumer expectation test.** The majority of states have adopted the modern **consumer expectation test** to determine the merchantability of food products. Under this test, the court asks what a consumer would expect to find or not find in food or drink that is consumed.

   Examples The implied warranty would be breached if a person were injured by a chicken bone while eating a chicken salad sandwich. This is because a consumer would expect that the food producer would have removed all bones from the chicken. Under this test, the implied warranty would not be breached if a person were injured by a chicken bone while eating fried chicken. This is because a consumer would expect to find bones in fried chicken.

consumer expectation test
A test to determine merchantability based on what the average consumer would expect to find or not find in food or drink products.

In the following case, the court had to decide whether there was a breach of the implied warranty of merchantability.

CASE 21.3 *FEDERAL COURT CASE Implied Warranty of Merchantability*

Manley v. Doe

849 F.Supp.2d 594, 2012 U.S. Dist. Lexis 12514 (2012)
United States District Court for the Eastern District of North Carolina

"Manley seeks to stack inference, upon inference, upon inference to prove the malfunction of an unidentified hamburger."

—James Dever, Chief Judge

Facts

On four or five occasions over a two-month period, John Manley purchased single- or double-patty hamburgers garnished with cheese, tomatoes, pickles, onions, bacon, mayonnaise, and ketchup; a side order of french fries; and a soft drink from a Wendy's fast-food restaurant located at 350 South College Road, Wilmington, North Carolina, owned and operated by First Sun Management Corporation (First Sun), a franchisee of Wendy's. Manley paid cash and has no receipts of the purchases. Several months later, Manley experienced mild discomfort, which turned into bouts of fatigue, coughing, and choking. Manley sought medical help, but doctors were unable to diagnose his symptoms for two years. After Manley experienced gastrointestinal problems, a pulmonologist surgically removed a foreign object approximately two inches in length from Manley's lungs. It was a plastic fragment from an eating utensil that was embossed with a portion of the Wendy's logo. Manley admits that he does not recall ingesting the fragment.

Manley sued First Sun, alleging that the franchisee breached the implied warranty of merchantability associated with food by serving him a hamburger with a two-inch plastic fragment in it. Manley sought to recover damages for medical costs incurred and pain and suffering he alleged prevented him from performing his normal activities and employment obligations. First Sun defended, arguing that Manley had not identified the specific hamburger that allegedly contained the plastic fragment.

Issue

Has there been a breach of the implied warranty of merchantability?

Language of the Court

Although the fragment included the Wendy's logo, the logo's presence is not evidence that it originated in the Wendy's restaurant located at 350 South College Road. Manley seeks to stack inference, upon inference, upon inference to prove the malfunction of an unidentified hamburger. Manley's hypothesis fails to take into account the plausibility that the plastic fragment from the eating utensil entered his lung outside of a Wendy's restaurant.

Decision

The U.S. district court granted summary judgment to the defendant Wendy's franchisee First Sun Management Corporation. The U.S. court of appeals affirmed the decision.

Critical Legal Thinking Questions

Did Manley lack evidence to prove his claim? If the case went to trial, would you have voted that the defendant was liable?

Implied Warranty of Fitness for a Particular Purpose

21.5 Describe the implied warranty of fitness for a particular purpose.

implied warranty of fitness for a particular purpose
A warranty that arises when a seller or lessor warrants that the goods will meet the buyer's or lessee's expressed needs.

The UCC contains an **implied warranty of fitness for a particular purpose**. This implied warranty attaches to the sale or lease of goods if the seller or lessor has made statements that the goods will meet the buyer's or lessee's needs or purpose. This implied warranty is breached if the goods do not meet the buyer's or lessee's expressed needs. The warranty applies to both merchant and nonmerchant sellers and lessors.

The warranty of fitness for a particular purpose is implied at the time of contracting if [UCC 2-315, 2A-213]:

- The seller or lessor has reason to know the particular purpose for which the buyer is purchasing the goods or the lessee is leasing the goods.
- The seller or lessor makes a statement that the goods will serve this purpose.
- The buyer or lessee relies on the seller's or lessor's skill and judgment and purchases or leases the goods.

Example Susan wants to buy lumber to build a small deck in her backyard. She goes to Joe's Lumber Yard to purchase the lumber and describes to Joe, the owner of the lumber yard, the size of the deck she intends to build. Susan also tells Joe that she is relying on him to select the right lumber for the project. Joe selects the lumber and states that the lumber will serve Susan's purpose. Susan buys the lumber and builds the deck. The deck collapses because the lumber was not strong enough to support it. Susan can sue Joe for breach of the implied warranty of fitness for a particular purpose.

CONCEPT SUMMARY
EXPRESS AND IMPLIED WARRANTIES

Type of Warranty	How Created	Description
Express warranty	Made by the seller or lessor	Affirms that the goods meet certain standards of quality, description, performance, or condition [UCC 2-313(1), 2A-210(1)].
Implied warranty of merchantability	Implied by law if the seller or lessor is a merchant	Implies that the goods: 1. Are fit for the ordinary purposes for which they are used. 2. Are adequately contained, packaged, and labeled. 3. Are of an even kind, quality, and quantity within each unit. 4. Conform to any promise or affirmation of fact made on the container or label. 5. Pass without objection in the trade. 6. Meet a fair average quality for the type of fungible goods [UCC 2-314(1), 2A-212(1)].
Implied warranty of fitness for human consumption	Implied by law	Implies that food and drink are fit for human consumption. Each state has adopted one of the following standards: 1. Foreign substance test. A foreign object is in food or drink that causes injury. 2. Consumer expectation test. What a consumer would expect to find or not find in food or drink that is consumed.
Implied warranty of fitness for a particular purpose	Implied by law	Implies that the goods are fit for the purpose for which the buyer or lessee acquires the goods if: 1. The seller or lessor has reason to know the particular purpose for which the goods will be used. 2. The seller or lessor makes a statement that the goods will serve that purpose. 3. The buyer or lessee relies on the statement and buys or leases the goods [UCC 2-315, UCC 2A-213].

Warranty Disclaimers

21.6 Identify warranty disclaimers and determine when they are lawful.

Warranties can be disclaimed, or limited. If an *express warranty* is made, it can be limited only if the **warranty disclaimer** and the warranty can be reasonably construed with each other. All implied warranties of quality may be disclaimed. The rules for disclaiming implied warranties are discussed in the following paragraphs.

warranty disclaimer
A statement that negates express and implied warranties.

- **"As Is" Disclaimer** Expressions such as *as is*, *with all faults*, or other language that makes it clear to the buyer that there are no implied warranties disclaims all implied warranties. An **"as is" disclaimer** is often included in sales contracts for used products.

Example Sabine is a race car driver who is leaving the sport. She sells her race car to Dale "as is." After one month, the engine in the race car breaks down and has to be repaired at a cost of $35,000. Dale seeks to recover this expense from Sabine. Sabine is not liable because she sold the car to Dale "as is."

Some states follow the rule that a seller's fraudulent statements about the condition or fitness of the good being sold prevents the seller from enforcing an "as is" disclaimer. The following case applies this rule.

CASE 21.4 *STATE COURT CASE "As Is" Disclaimer*

Sorchaga v. Ride Auto, LLC

909 N.W.2d 550 (2018)
Supreme Court of Minnesota

"Sorchaga relied on Ride Auto's fraudulent statements and purchased a truck that was not fit for any purpose for which a truck is purchased."
—Lorie Gildea, Chief Justice

Facts

Esmeralda Sorchaga visited Ride Auto, LLC, a used vehicle dealer, to look for a truck to purchase. A salesperson showed Sorchaga a truck, which she took for a test drive. The test drive was short because the truck was low on fuel. Sorchaga noticed that the check engine light was on, but the salesperson explained that the truck had a faulty oxygen sensor, which Ride Auto would later correct. The salesperson told Sorchaga that the truck came with a third-party warranty from ASC Vehicle Protection Plan paid for by Ride Auto, which would cover repairs to the truck. Sorchaga purchased the truck for $12,951. The agreement stated that the sale was an "AS IS—NO WARRANTY" sale.

Immediately after Sorchaga purchased the truck, the truck would not travel faster than 40 miles an hour. Sorchaga was stopped by police while she was driving the truck because it emitted excessive smoke. When Sorchaga brought the truck back to Ride Auto, the dealer refused to repair the truck. When she called ASC she was told that the warranty did not cover a salvage truck. Ride Auto had previously purchased the truck as a salvage truck for $6,000. When Sorchaga had the truck inspected by a repair service she was told that the truck needed a full engine replacement at a cost of $20,000 and that she should not drive the truck in its unsafe condition.

Sorchaga sued Ride Auto for breach of the implied warranty of merchantability. Ride Auto countered that it was not liable because Sorchaga purchased the truck "as is." The trial court held that Ride Auto's fraudulent conduct prevented it from enforcing the "as is" disclaimer, and awarded Sorchaga $14,366 as damages and $21,949 in attorney's fees and litigation expenses. The court of appeals affirmed the decision. Ride Auto appealed.

Issue

Do a seller's fraudulent statements about the fitness and condition of a vehicle being sold prevent the seller from enforcing an "as is" disclaimer?

Language of the Court

Sorchaga relied on Ride Auto's fraudulent statements and purchased a truck that was not fit for any purpose for which a truck is purchased. To permit Ride Auto to nevertheless enforce the "as is" disclaimer in this situation would permit Ride Auto to profit from its fraud and to be effectively granted a license to mislead or conceal facts. We hold that Ride Auto's fraudulent statements about the fitness of the truck for the purpose for which a truck is purchased is a circumstance that makes the "as is" disclaimer of implied warranties in the purchase documents ineffective under Minnesota law.

Decision

The Supreme Court of Minnesota affirmed the decision that Ride Auto's fraudulent conduct prevented it from enforcing the "as is" disclaimer.

Critical Legal Thinking Questions

Should an "as is" disclaimer release a seller from liability? Is the fraudulent conduct exception helpful?

- **Disclaimer of the Implied Warranty of Merchantability** If the "as is" type of disclaimer is not used, a **disclaimer of the implied warranty of merchantability** must specifically mention the term *merchantability* for the implied warranty of merchantability to be disclaimed. These disclaimers may be oral or written.
- **Disclaimer of the Implied Warranty of Fitness for a Particular Purpose** If the "as is" type of disclaimer is not used, a **disclaimer of the implied warranty of fitness for a particular purpose** may contain general language, without specific use of the term *fitness*. The disclaimer has to be in writing.

Conspicuous Display of Disclaimer

Written disclaimers must be conspicuously displayed to be valid. A **conspicuous disclaimer** means one that is noticeable to a reasonable person [UCC 2-316, 2A-214]. A heading printed in uppercase letters or a typeface that is larger or in a different style than the rest of the body of a sales or lease contract is considered to be conspicuous. Different-color type is also considered to be conspicuous.

An inconspicuous disclaimer is not enforceable.

conspicuous disclaimer
A requirement that warranty disclaimers be noticeable to a reasonable person.

Example A disclaimer hidden in the fine print of a 10-page contract is inconspicuous and unenforceable.

The following feature discusses warranty disclaimers in software licenses.

Information Technology

Warranty Disclaimers in Social Media Software Licenses

Software and social media companies usually license their software products to users. A software license is a complex contract that contains the terms of the license. Most software licenses contain a warranty disclaimer, a limitation on liability clause, and other clauses that limit the licensor's liability. Disclaimer of warranty and limitation on liability clauses that are included in a social media software license appear below.

SOCIALMEDIA.COM, INC.
LIMITATION AND DISCLAIMERS OF WARRANTIES,
REMEDIES, AND DAMAGES

"As Is" License Our products are provided "as is," and we make no guarantees that they will always be safe, secure, or error free, or that they will function without disruptions, delays, or imperfections.

Warranty Disclaimer To the extent permitted by law, we DISCLAIM ALL WARRANTIES, WHETHER EXPRESS OR IMPLIED, INCLUDING THE IMPLIED WARRANTIES OF MERCHANTABILITY, FITNESS FOR A PARTICULAR PURPOSE, TITLE, AND NONINFRINGEMENT.

No Liability for Third-Party Conduct We do not control or direct what people and others do or say, and we are not responsible for their actions or conduct (whether online or offline) or any content they share (including offensive, inappropriate, obscene, unlawful, or other objectionable content).

Limit on Damages We cannot predict when issues might arise with our products. Accordingly, our liability shall be limited to the fullest extent permitted by applicable law, and under no circumstance will we be liable to you for any lost profits, revenues, information, or data, or for consequential, special, indirect, exemplary, punitive, or incidental damages arising out of or related to our products, even if we have been advised of the possibility of such damages.

Customer Remedies Our aggregate liability arising out of or relating to our products will not exceed the greater of $100 or the amount you have paid us in the past 12 months.

Magnuson-Moss Warranty Act

21.7 Describe the protections provided by the Magnuson-Moss Warranty Act.

Magnuson-Moss Warranty Act
A federal statute that regulates written warranties on consumer products.

The **Magnuson-Moss Warranty Act** is a federal statute that covers written warranties related to **consumer products.**[1] This act is administered by the Federal Trade Commission (FTC). *Consumer transactions* but not commercial and industrial transactions are governed by the act.

The act does not require a seller or lessor to make an *express* written warranty. However, sellers or lessors who do make express warranties are subject to the provisions of the act. If a warrantor chooses to make an express warranty, the Magnuson-Moss Warranty Act requires that the warranty be labeled as either "full" or "limited":

Critical Legal Thinking Questions

What does the Magnuson-Moss Warranty Act provide? What is the difference between a full warranty and a limited warranty?

- **Full warranty.** For a warranty to qualify as a **full warranty**, the warrantor must guarantee that a defective product will be repaired or replaced for free during the warranty period. The warrantor must indicate whether there is a time limit on the full warranty (e.g., "full 36-month warranty").
- **Limited warranty.** In a **limited warranty**, the warrantor limits the scope of the warranty in some way. A warranty that covers the costs of parts but not the labor to fix a defective product is a limited warranty.

Limited warranties are made more often by sellers and lessors than are full warranties. The act stipulates that sellers or lessors who make express written warranties related to *consumer products* are forbidden from disclaiming or modifying the implied warranties of merchantability and fitness for a particular purpose.

The act authorizes warrantors to establish an informal dispute-resolution procedure, such as arbitration. A successful plaintiff can recover damages, attorney's fees, and other costs incurred in bringing the action.

Warranties of Title and Possession

21.8 List and describe warranties of title and possession.

The UCC imposes special warranties on sellers and lessors of goods. These include a *warranty of good title*, a *warranty of no security interests*, a *warranty against infringements*, and a *warranty of no interference*. These warranties are discussed in the following paragraphs.

Warranty of Good Title

Unless they properly disclaim warranties, sellers of goods warrant that they have valid title to the goods they are selling and that the transfer of title is rightful [UCC 2-312(1)(a)]. This is called the **warranty of good title**. Persons who transfer goods without proper title breach this warranty.

warranty of good title
A warranty in which the seller warrants valid title to the goods he or she is selling and that the transfer of title is rightful.

Example Ingersoll-Rand owns a heavy-duty crane. A thief steals the crane and sells it to Turner Construction. Turner Construction does not know that the crane is stolen. If Ingersoll-Rand discovers that Turner Construction has the equipment, it can reclaim it. Turner Construction, in turn, can recover against the thief for breach of the warranty of title. This is because the thief made an implied warranty that he had good title to the equipment and that the transfer of title to Turner Construction was rightful.

warranty of no security interests
A warranty in which sellers of goods warrant that the goods they sell are delivered free from any third-party security interests, liens, or encumbrances that are unknown to the buyer.

Warranty of No Security Interests

Under the UCC, sellers of goods automatically warrant that the goods they sell are delivered free from any third-party security interests, liens, or encumbrances that are unknown to the buyer [UCC 2-312(1)(b)]. This is called the **warranty of no security interests**.

Example Albert purchases a refrigerator on credit from Appliance World, an appliance store. The store takes back a security interest in the refrigerator. Before completely paying off the refrigerator, Albert sells it to Monica for cash. Monica has no knowledge of the store's security interest in the refrigerator. After Albert misses several payments, the appliance store discovers that Monica has the refrigerator and repossesses the refrigerator. Monica can recover against Albert, based on his breach of warranty of no security interests in the goods [UCC 2-312(1)(b)].

The warranties of good title and no security interests may be excluded or modified by specific language [UCC 2-312(2)]. For example, specific language such as "seller hereby transfers only those rights, title, and interest as he or she has in the goods" is sufficient to disclaim these warranties. General language such as "as is" or "with all faults" is not specific enough to be a disclaimer to the warranties of good title and no security interests. The special nature of certain sales (e.g., sheriffs' sales) tells the buyer that the seller is not giving title warranties with the sale of the goods.

Warranty Against Infringements

Unless otherwise agreed, a seller or lessor who is a merchant regularly dealing in goods of the kind sold or leased automatically warrants that the goods are delivered free of any third-party patent, trademark, or copyright claim [UCC 2-312(3), 2A-211(2)]. This is called the **warranty against infringements**.

warranty against infringements
An automatic warranty provided by a seller or lessor who is a merchant who regularly deals in goods of the kind sold or leased that warrants that the goods are delivered free of any third-party patent, trademark, or copyright claim.

Example Adams Company, a manufacturer of machines that make shoes, sells a machine to Smith & Franklin, a shoe manufacturer. Subsequently, Nita claims that she has a patent on the machine. Nita proves her patent claim in court. Nita notifies Smith & Franklin that the machine can no longer be used without her permission and the payment of a fee to her. Smith & Franklin may rescind the sales contract with Adams Company, based on the breach of the warranty against infringement.

Warranty of No Interference

When goods are leased, the lessor warrants that no person holds a claim or an interest in the goods that arose from an act or omission of the lessor that will interfere with the lessee's enjoyment of the leasehold interest [UCC 2A-211(1)]. This is referred to as the **warranty of no interference**, or the **warranty of quiet possession**.

warranty of no interference (warranty of quiet possession)
A warranty in which the lessor warrants that no person holds a claim or an interest in the goods that arose from an act or omission of the lessor that will interfere with the lessee's enjoyment of the leasehold interest.

Example Petroleum Supplier, as lessor, leases a piece of heavy equipment to Aztec Drilling. Petroleum Supplier later gives a security interest in the equipment to City Bank as collateral for a loan. If Petroleum Supplier defaults on the loan to City Bank and City Bank repossesses the equipment from Aztec, Aztec can recover damages from Petroleum Supplier for breach of the warranty of no interference.

Key Terms and Concepts

"As is" disclaimer (372)
Caveat emptor (365)
Compensatory damages (366)
Conspicuous disclaimer (373)
Consumer expectation test (369)
Consumer products (374)
Disclaimer of the implied warranty of fitness for a particular purpose (373)
Disclaimer of the implied warranty of merchantability (373)
Express warranty (365)
Foreign substance test (369)
Full warranty (374)
Implied by law (366)
Implied warranty (366)
Implied warranty of fitness for a particular purpose (370)
Implied warranty of fitness for human consumption (369)
Implied warranty of merchantability (367)
Limited warranty (374)
Magnuson-Moss Warranty Act (374)
Statement of opinion (puffing) (366)
Warranty (365)
Warranty against infringements (375)
Warranty disclaimer (371)
Warranty of good title (374)
Warranty of no interference (warranty of quiet possession) (375)
Warranty of no security interests (374)

Critical Legal Thinking Cases

21.1 Express Warranty W. Hayes Daughtrey consulted Sidney Ashe, a jeweler, about the purchase of a diamond bracelet as a Christmas present for his wife. Ashe showed Daughtrey a diamond bracelet that he had for sale for $15,000. When Daughtrey decided to purchase the bracelet, Ashe completed and signed an appraisal form that stated that the diamonds were "H color and v.v.s. quality" (v.v.s. is one of the highest ratings in a jeweler's quality classification). After Daughtrey paid for the bracelet, Ashe put the bracelet and the appraisal form in a box. Daughtrey gave the bracelet to his wife as a Christmas present. One year later, when another jeweler looked at the bracelet, Daughtrey discovered that the diamonds were of substantially lower grade than v.v.s. Daughtrey filed a specific performance suit against Ashe to compel him to replace the bracelet with one mounted with v.v.s. diamonds or to pay appropriate damages. Has an express warranty been made by Ashe regarding the quality of the diamonds in the bracelet? Who wins? *Daughtrey v. Ashe*, 243 Va. 73, 413 S.E.2d 336, 1992 Va. Lexis 152 (Supreme Court of Virginia, 1992)

21.2 "As Is" Warranty Disclaimer Joseph Mitsch purchased a used Chevrolet Yukon SUV vehicle from Rockenbach Chevrolet. The Yukon was manufactured by General Motors Corporation (GMC) and had been driven over 36,000 miles. The purchase contract with Rockenbach Chevrolet contained the following disclaimer:

> *AS IS*
>
> *THIS USED MOTOR VEHICLE IS SOLD AS IS. THE PURCHASER WILL BEAR THE ENTIRE EXPENSE OF REPAIRING OR CORRECTING ANY DEFECTS THAT PRESENTLY EXIST OR THAT MAY OCCUR IN THE VEHICLE.*

Mitsch purchased GMC's extended service plan for the Yukon. During a period of approximately 18 months, Mitsch experienced problems with the Yukon's transmission, engine, suspension, and climate control. All the repairs were made by GMC dealerships and paid for by the GMC extended service plan. Mitsch sued Rockenbach Chevrolet for breach of the implied warranty of merchantability and sought to rescind his acceptance of the Yukon. Rockenbach Chevrolet argued that the "as is" disclaimer barred Mitsch's claim. Mitsch alleged that the "as is" disclaimer was not conspicuous, and should be voided. Is the "as is" disclaimer conspicuous and does it therefore properly disclaim the implied warranty of merchantability? *Mitsch v. Rockenbach Chevrolet*, 359 Ill. App.3d 99, 833 N.E.2d 936, 2005 Ill. App. Lexis 699 (Appellate Court of Illinois, 2005)

21.3 Implied Warranty of Fitness for a Particular Purpose Felicitas Garnica went to Mack Massey Motors, Inc. (Massey Motors) to inquire about purchasing a Jeep Cherokee that was manufactured by Jeep Eagle, for the purpose of towing a 23-foot Airstream trailer she had on order. After Garnica explained her requirements to the sales manager, he called the Airstream dealer to verify the specifications of the trailer Garnica was purchasing. The sales manager advised Garnica that the Jeep Cherokee could do the job of pulling the trailer. After she purchased the vehicle, Garnica found that it did not have sufficient power to pull the trailer. She brought the Jeep Cherokee back to Massey Motors several times for repairs for a slipping transmission. Eventually, she was told to go to another dealer. The drive shaft on the Jeep Cherokee twisted apart at 7,229 miles. Garnica sued Massey Motors and Jeep Eagle for damages, alleging breach of the implied warranty of fitness for a particular purpose. Have the defendants made and breached an implied warranty of fitness for a particular purpose? *Mack Massey Motors, Inc. v. Garnica*, 814 S.W.2d 167, 1991 Tex. Lexis 1814 (Court of Appeals of Texas, 1991)

21.4 Implied Warranty of Merchantability Nancy Denny purchased a Bronco II, a small sport-utility vehicle (SUV) that was manufactured by Ford Motor Company. Denny testified that she purchased the Bronco for use on paved city and suburban streets and not for off-road use. When Denny was driving the vehicle on a paved road, she slammed on the brakes in an effort to avoid a deer that had walked directly into her SUV's path. The Bronco II rolled over, and Denny was severely injured. Denny sued Ford Motor Company to recover damages for breach of the implied warranty of merchantability.

Denny alleged that the Bronco II presented a significantly higher risk of occurrence of rollover accidents than did ordinary passenger vehicles. Denny introduced evidence at trial that showed that the Bronco II had a low stability index because of its high center of gravity, narrow tracks, and shorter wheelbase, as well as the design of its suspension system. Ford countered that the Bronco II was intended as an off-road vehicle and was not designed to be used as a conventional passenger automobile on paved streets. Has Ford Motor Company breached the implied warranty of merchantability? *Denny v. Ford Motor Company*, 87 N.Y.2d 248, 662 N.E.2d 730, 639 N.Y.S.2d 250, 1995 N.Y. Lexis 4445 (Court of Appeals of New York, 1995)

Ethics Cases

21.5 Ethics Case Cole Energy Development Company (Cole Energy) wanted to lease a gas compressor for use in its business of pumping and selling natural gas and began negotiating with the Ingersoll-Rand Company (Ingersoll-Rand) for the lease of a gas compressor. The two parties entered into a lease agreement whereby Ingersoll-Rand leased a gas compressor to Cole Energy The lease agreement contained a section labeled "WARRANTIES." Part of the section read,

> *THERE ARE NO IMPLIED WARRANTIES OF MERCHANTABILITY OR FITNESS FOR A PARTICULAR PURPOSE CONTAINED HEREIN.*

The gas compressor that was installed failed to function properly. As a result, Cole Energy lost business. Cole Energy sued Ingersoll-Rand for the breach of an implied warranty of merchantability. Is Ingersoll-Rand liable? Has Cole-Energy acted ethically in bringing the lawsuit? Has Ingersoll-Rand acted ethically in denying liability for the failure of a product it leased? *Cole Energy Development Company v. Ingersoll-Rand Company*, 678 F.Supp. 208, 1988 U.S. Dist. Lexis 923 (United States District Court for the Central District of Illinois, 1988)

Note

1. 15 U.S.C. Sections 2301–2312.

PART

V

Negotiable Instruments, Banking, and Electronic Financial Transactions

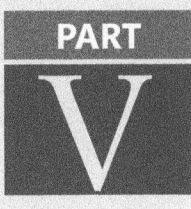

Henry R. Cheeseman

CHAPTER 22

Creation of Negotiable Instruments

Henry R. Cheeseman

COMMUNITY BANK

Individuals and businesses have checking accounts at banks. A check qualifies as a negotiable instrument. Negotiable instruments are governed by Article 3 of the Uniform Commercial Code (UCC).

Learning Objectives

After studying this chapter, you should be able to:

22.1 Define *negotiable instrument* and describe the functions of negotiable instruments.

22.2 Describe types of negotiable instruments, including drafts, checks, promissory notes, and certificates of deposit.

22.3 Identify and describe the requirements for creating a negotiable instrument.

22.4 Describe prepayment, acceleration, and extension clauses.

22.5 Distinguish between a nonnegotiable instrument and a negotiable instrument.

> *"The great object of the law is to encourage commerce."*
>
> —*Chambre, Judge*
> *Beale v. Thompson*
> *3 Bos. & Pull. 421 (1803)*

Introduction to Creation of Negotiable Instruments

Negotiable instruments (or **commercial paper**) are important for the conduct of business and individual affairs. In this country, modern commerce could not continue without them. Examples of negotiable instruments include checks (e.g., a check used by a business to purchase equipment) and promissory notes (e.g., a note executed by a borrower of money to pay for tuition). The term *instrument* means negotiable instrument [UCC 3-104(b)]. These terms are used often interchangeably.

negotiable instrument (commercial paper)
A special form of contract that satisfies the requirements established by Article 3 of the UCC.

The types of negotiable instruments and their creation are discussed in this chapter.

Negotiable Instruments

22.1 Define *negotiable instrument* and describe the functions of negotiable instruments.

To qualify as a negotiable instrument, a document must meet certain requirements established by Article 3 of the Uniform Commercial Code (UCC). If these requirements are met, a transferee who qualifies as a **holder in due course (HDC)** takes the instrument free of many defenses that can be asserted against the original payee. In addition, the document is considered an ordinary contract that is subject to contract law.

> *A trader is trusted upon his character, and visible commerce, that credit enables him to acquire wealth.*
>
> The Earl of Mansfield
> (1705–1793)
> *Lord Chief Justice of England*

The concept of **negotiation** is important to the law of negotiable instruments. The primary benefit of a negotiable instrument is that it can be used as a substitute for money. As such, it must be freely transferable to subsequent parties. Technically, a negotiable instrument is negotiated when it is originally issued. The term *negotiation*, however, is usually used to describe the transfer of negotiable instruments to subsequent transferees.

Article 3 of the UCC

Article 3 (Commercial Paper) of the Uniform Commercial Code, which was promulgated in 1952, established rules for the creation of, transfer of, enforcement of, and liability on negotiable instruments. Most states and the District of Columbia have adopted Article 3 of the UCC.

Article 3 (Commercial Paper) of the UCC
A model code that establishes rules for the creation of, transfer of, enforcement of, and liability on negotiable instruments.

In 1990, the American Law Institute and the National Conference of Commissioners on Uniform State Laws promulgated **Revised Article 3 (Negotiable Instruments) of the Uniform Commercial Code**. This article, which is called "Negotiable Instruments" instead of "Commercial Paper," is a comprehensive revision of Article 3. Revised Article 3 has been amended from time to time. Revised Article 3, as amended, is used as the basis for this and the following chapters on negotiable instruments.

Revised Article 3 (Negotiable Instruments) of the UCC
A comprehensive revision of the UCC law of negotiable instruments that reflects modern commercial practices.

Functions of Negotiable Instruments

Negotiable instruments serve the following functions:

1. **Substitutes for money.** Merchants and consumers often do not carry cash for fear of loss or theft. Further, it would be almost impossible to carry enough cash for large purchases (e.g., a car, a house). Thus, certain forms of negotiable instruments—such as checks—serve as a **substitute for money**.

2. **Credit devices.** Some forms of negotiable instruments extend credit from one party to another. A seller may sell goods to a customer based on the customer's promise to pay for the goods at a future time, or a bank may lend money to a buyer who signs a note promising to repay the money. Both of these examples represent **extensions of credit**. Without negotiable instruments, the "credit economy" of the United States and other modern industrial countries would not be possible.
3. **Record-keeping devices.** Negotiable instruments often serve as a **record-keeping device**. Banks either return checks to checking-account customers each month or allow customers to view them online. These act as a record-keeping device for the preparation of financial statements, tax returns, and the like.

Types of Negotiable Instruments

22.2 Describe types of negotiable instruments, including drafts, checks, promissory notes, and certificates of deposit.

The UCC recognizes four kinds of negotiable instruments: (1) *drafts*, (2) *checks*, (3) *promissory notes*, and (4) *certificates of deposit*. Each of these is discussed in the following paragraphs.

Draft

draft
A three-party instrument that is an unconditional written order by one party that orders a second party to pay money to a third party.

drawer of a draft
The party who writes an order for a draft.

drawee of a draft
The party who must pay the money stated in a draft. Also called the *acceptor* of a draft.

payee of a draft
The party who receives the money from a draft.

A **draft**, which is a three-party instrument, is an unconditional written order by one party (the **drawer of a draft**) that orders a second party (the **drawee of a draft**) to pay money to a third party (the **payee of a draft**) [UCC 3-104(e)]. The drawee is obligated to pay the drawer money before the drawer can order the drawee to pay this money to a third party (the payee).

For the drawee to be liable on a draft, the drawee must accept the drawer's written order to pay it. Acceptance is usually shown by the written word *accepted* on the face of the draft, along with the drawee's signature and the date. The *drawee* is called the *acceptor of a draft* because his or her obligation changes from having to pay the drawer to having to pay the payee. After the drawee accepts the draft, it is returned to the drawer or the payee. The drawer or the payee, in turn, can freely transfer it as a negotiable instrument to another party.

Example Mary owes Hector \$1,000. Hector wants Mary to pay the money to Amaya instead of to him. Hector writes out a draft that orders Mary to pay the \$1,000 to Amaya. Mary agrees to this change of obligation and writes the word "accepted" on the draft and signs the draft. Hector is the drawer, Mary is the drawee and acceptor of the draft, and Amaya is the payee. Mary is now obligated to pay Amaya \$1,000.

time draft
A draft payable at a designated future date.

sight draft (demand draft)
A draft payable on sight.

trade acceptance (bill of exchange)
A sight draft that arises when credit is extended (by a seller to a buyer) with the sale of goods. The seller is both the drawer and the payee, and the buyer is the drawee.

A draft can be either a time draft or a sight draft. A **time draft** is payable at a designated future date. Language such as "pay on January 1, 2022" or "pay 120 days after date" creates a time draft (see Exhibit 22.1). A **sight draft** is payable on sight. A sight draft is also called a **demand draft**. Language such as "on demand pay" or "at sight pay" creates a sight draft. A draft can be both a time draft and a sight draft. Such a draft would provide that it is payable at a stated time after sight. This type of draft is created by language such as "payable 90 days after sight."

Trade Acceptance. A **trade acceptance (bill of exchange)** is a sight draft that arises when credit is extended by the seller to the buyer with the sale of goods. With this type of draft, the seller is both the drawer and the payee. The buyer to whom credit is extended is the drawee. Even though only two actual parties are involved, it is considered a three-party instrument because three legal positions

Exhibit 22.1 TIME DRAFT

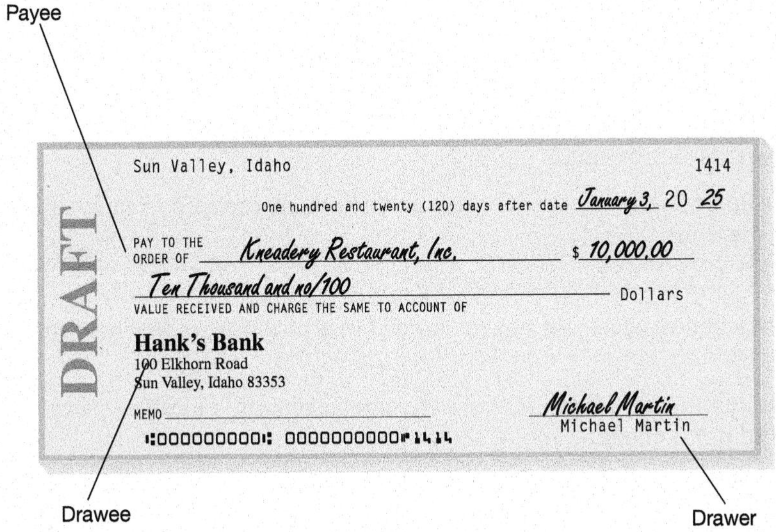

are involved. A trade acceptance is not countersigned by the drawee's bank, so it is only as good as the buyer–drawee's creditworthiness.

Check

A **check** is a distinct form of draft. It is unique in that it is drawn on a financial institution (the drawee) and is payable on demand [UCC 3-104(f)]. In other words, a check is an *order to pay* (see Exhibit 22.2). Most businesses and many individuals have checking accounts at financial institutions. Like other drafts, a check is a three-party instrument. A customer who has a checking account and writes (draws) a check is the **drawer of a check**. The financial institution on which the check is written is the **drawee of a check**. And the party to whom the check is written is the **payee of a check**.

check
A distinct form of draft drawn on a financial institution and payable on demand.

drawer of a check
The checking account holder and writer of a check.

drawee of a check
The financial institution where the drawer of a check has an account.

payee of a check
The party to whom a check is written.

Example Kosumi has a checking account at Country Bank. When Kosumi purchases a car from Popov's Motors, a car dealership, Kosumi pays for the car by writing a check on the bank made payable to Popov's Motors. Here, Kosumi is the drawer, Country Bank is the drawee, and Popov's Motors is the payee.

Exhibit 22.2 CHECK

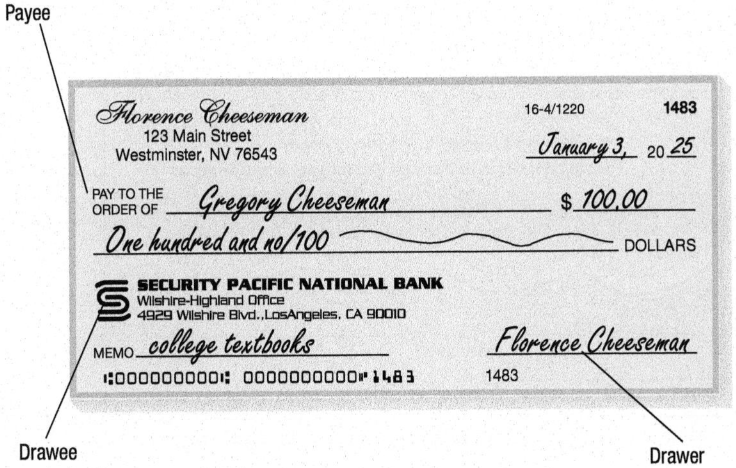

CONCEPT SUMMARY

TYPES OF ORDERS TO PAY

Order to Pay	Parties	Description
Draft	Drawer	Person who issues a draft.
	Drawee	Person who owes money to a drawer; person who is ordered to pay a draft and accepts the draft.
	Payee	Person to whom a draft is made payable.
Check	Drawer	Owner of a checking account at a financial institution; person who issues a check.
	Drawee	Financial institution where drawer's checking account is located; party who is ordered to pay a check.
	Payee	Person to whom a check is made payable.

Promissory Note

promissory note (note)
A two-party negotiable instrument that is an unconditional written promise by one party to pay money to another party.

maker of a note
The party who makes a promise to pay (borrower).

payee of a note
The party to whom a promise to pay is made (lender).

A **promissory note** (or **note**) is an unconditional written promise by one party to pay money to another party [UCC 3-104(e)]. It is a two-party instrument (see Exhibit 22.3), not an order to pay. Promissory notes usually arise when one party borrows money from another. The note is evidence of (1) the extension of credit and (2) the borrower's promise to repay the debt. A party who makes a promise to pay is the **maker of a note** (i.e., the borrower). The party to whom the promise to pay is made is the **payee of a note** (i.e., the lender). A promissory note is a negotiable instrument that the payee can freely transfer to other parties.

Example Andrew borrows $10,000 from Wei and signs a promissory note agreeing to pay Wei the principal and 10 percent annual interest over three years in equal monthly installments. Here, Andrew is the maker of the note, and Wei is the payee.

time note
A note payable at a specific time.

demand note
A note payable on demand.

The parties are free to design the terms of a note to fit their needs. Notes can be payable at a specific time (**time note**) or on demand (**demand note**). Notes can be made payable to a named payee or to "bearer." They can be payable in a single payment or in installments. The latter are called **installment notes**. Most notes require the borrower to pay interest on the principal.

Exhibit 22.3 PROMISSORY NOTE

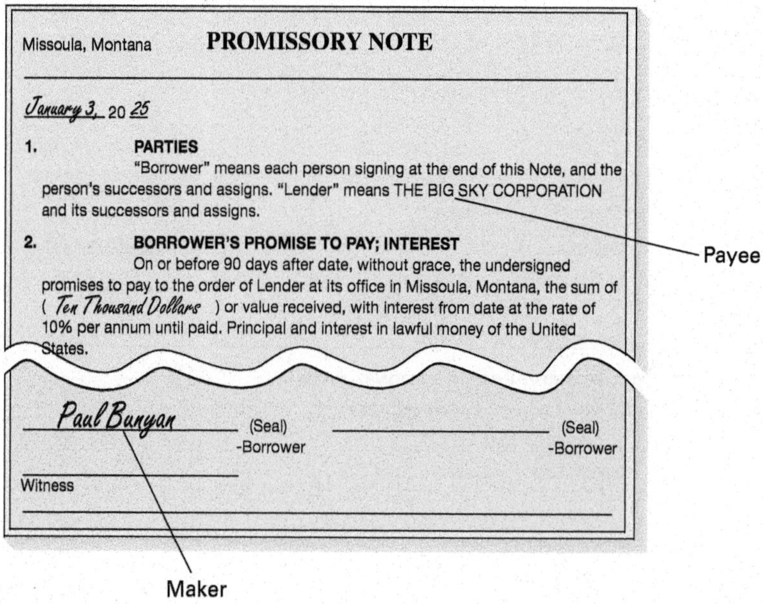
Missoula, Montana PROMISSORY NOTE

January 3, 20 25

1. PARTIES
"Borrower" means each person signing at the end of this Note, and the person's successors and assigns. "Lender" means THE BIG SKY CORPORATION and its successors and assigns.

2. BORROWER'S PROMISE TO PAY; INTEREST
On or before 90 days after date, without grace, the undersigned promises to pay to the order of Lender at its office in Missoula, Montana, the sum of (Ten Thousand Dollars) or value received, with interest from date at the rate of 10% per annum until paid. Principal and interest in lawful money of the United States.

Paul Bunyan (Seal) -Borrower   (Seal) -Borrower

Witness

Lenders sometimes require the maker of a note to post security for the repayment of the note. This security, which is called **collateral**, may be in the form of automobiles, houses, securities, or other property. If a maker fails to repay a note when it is due, the lender can foreclose and take the collateral as payment for the note. Notes are often named after the security that underlies the note. For example, notes that are secured by real estate are called **mortgage notes**, and notes that are secured by personal property are called **collateral notes**.

Certificate of Deposit

A **certificate of deposit (CD)** is a special form of note that is created when a depositor deposits money at a financial institution in exchange for the institution's promise to pay back the amount of the deposit plus an agreed-on rate of interest on the expiration of a set time period agreed on by the parties [UCC 3-104(j)].

certificate of deposit (CD)
A two-party negotiable instrument that is a special form of note created when a depositor deposits money at a financial institution in exchange for the institution's promise to pay back the amount of the deposit plus an agreed-on rate of interest on the expiration of a set time period agreed on by the parties.

The financial institution is the borrower (the **maker of a certificate of deposit**), and the depositor is the lender (the **payee of a certificate of deposit**). A CD is a two-party instrument (see Exhibit 22.4). Note that a CD is a promise to pay, not an order to pay. Unlike a regular passbook savings account, a CD is a negotiable instrument. CDs under $100,000 are commonly referred to as **small certificates of deposit (small CDs)**. CDs of $100,000 or more are usually called **jumbo certificates of deposit (jumbo CDs)**.

maker of a certificate of deposit
The financial institution that issues a CD (borrower).

Example Min has $50,000 that she would like to invest and earn income on. Min goes into City Bank and deposits her money with the bank in exchange for a certificate of deposit (CD) that bears an annual interest rate of 5 percent. Here, City Bank is the maker of the CD (borrower) and Min is the payee (lender).

payee of a certificate of deposit
The party to whom a CD is made payable; usually the depositor (lender).

CONCEPT SUMMARY
TYPES OF PROMISES TO PAY

Promise to Pay	Parties	Description
Promissory note	Maker	Party who issues a promissory note; this is usually the borrower.
	Payee	Party to whom a promissory note is made payable; this is usually the lender.
Certificate of deposit (CD)	Maker	Financial institution that issues a CD.
	Payee	Party to whom a CD is made payable; this is usually the depositor.

Exhibit 22.4 CERTIFICATE OF DEPOSIT

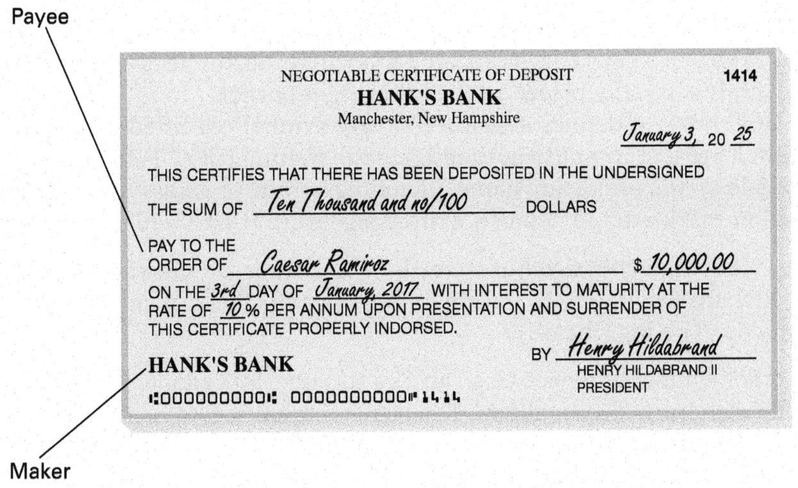

Requirements for Creating a Negotiable Instrument

22.3 Identify and describe the requirements for creating a negotiable instrument.

According to UCC 3-104(a), a negotiable instrument must:

1. Be in writing.
2. Be signed by the maker or drawer.
3. Be an unconditional promise or order to pay.
4. State a fixed amount of money.
5. Not require any undertaking in addition to the payment of money.
6. Be payable on demand or at a definite time.
7. Be payable to order or to bearer.

These requirements must appear on the *face* of the instrument. If they do not, the instrument does not qualify as negotiable. Each of these seven requirements is discussed in the paragraphs and sections that follow.

1. Be in Writing

Money speaks sense in a language all nations understand.

Aphra Behn
The Rover (1677)

A negotiable instrument must be (1) in writing and (2) permanent and portable. The **writing requirement** is met if the writing is on a preprinted form, but typewritten, handwritten, or other tangible agreements are also acceptable [UCC 1-201(46)]. The instrument can be a combination of different kinds of writing.

Example A check is often a preprinted form on which the drawer handwrites the amount of the check, the name of the payee, and the date of the check.

permanency requirement
A requirement of negotiable instruments that says they must be in a permanent state, such as written on ordinary paper.

Most writings on paper meet the **permanency requirement**. However, a writing that is on tissue paper would not meet this requirement because of its impermanence. Oral promises do not qualify as negotiable instruments because they are not clearly transferable in a manner that will prevent fraud. Tape recordings and videotapes are not negotiable instruments because they are not considered writings.

portability requirement
A requirement of negotiable instruments that says they must be able to be easily transported between areas.

The **portability requirement** is intended to ensure free transfer of an instrument.

Example A promise to pay chiseled in a tree would not qualify as a negotiable instrument because the tree is not freely transferable in commerce.

2. Be Signed by the Maker or the Drawer

signature requirement
A requirement that states that a negotiable instrument must be signed by the drawer or maker. Any symbol executed or adopted by a party with a present intent to authenticate a writing qualifies as a signature.

The UCC **signature requirement** indicates that a negotiable instrument must be *signed* by the maker if it is a note or CD and by the drawer if it is a check or draft. The maker or drawer is not liable on the instrument unless his or her signature appears on it. The signature can be placed on the instrument by the maker or drawer or by an authorized agent [UCC 3-401(a)]. Although the signature of the maker, drawer, or agent can be located anywhere on the face of the negotiable instrument, it is usually placed in the lower-right corner.

The UCC broadly defines **signature** as any symbol executed or adopted by a party with a present intent to authenticate the writing [UCC 1-201(39)]. A signature is made by the use of any name, including a trade or an assumed name, or by any word or mark used in lieu of a written signature [UCC 3-401(b)].

Examples The requisite signature can be the maker or drawer's formal name (Henry Richard Cheeseman), informal name (Hank Cheeseman), initials (HRC), or nickname (The Big Cheese).

Any other symbol or device (e.g., an *X*, a thumbprint) adopted by the signer as his or her signature also qualifies. The signer's intention to use the symbol as a signature is controlling. Typed, printed, lithographed, rubber-stamped, and other mechanical means of signing instruments are recognized as valid by the UCC.

Representative's Signature. A maker or drawer can appoint an *agent* to sign a negotiable instrument on his or her behalf. In such circumstances, the **representative's signature** binds the maker or drawer.

Example Corporations and other organizations use agents, usually corporate officers or employees, to sign the corporation's checks and other negotiable instruments. Individuals can also appoint agents to sign their negotiable instruments.

A maker or drawer is liable on a negotiable instrument signed by an authorized agent. The agent is not personally liable on the negotiable instrument if the signature properly and unambiguously discloses (1) the agent's agency status and (2) the identity of the maker or drawer [UCC 3-402(b)]. In the case of an organization, the agent's signature is proper if the organization's name is preceded or followed by the name of the authorized agent.

3. Be an Unconditional Promise or Order to Pay

To be a negotiable instrument under the requirements of UCC 3-104, a writing must contain either an unconditional order to pay (draft or check) or an unconditional promise to pay (note or CD) a fixed amount of money on demand or at a definite time. This is called the **unconditional promise or order to pay requirement**. The term *unconditional*, which is discussed in the following paragraphs, is one of the keys.

unconditional promise or order to pay requirement
A requirement that says a negotiable instrument must contain either an *unconditional promise to pay* (note or CD) or an *unconditional order to pay* (draft or check).

Order to Pay. To be negotiable, a *draft* or *check* must contain the drawer's unconditional **order to pay** a payee. The language of the order must be precise and contain the word *pay*.

Examples The words *Pay to the order of* are usually used on a check or draft. The printed word *pay* on a check is a proper order that is sufficient to make a check negotiable.

order to pay
A drawer's unconditional order to a drawee to pay a payee.

An order can be directed to one or more parties jointly, such as "to A *and* B," or in the alternative, such as "to A *or* B."

Promise to Pay. To be negotiable, a *promissory note* must contain the maker's unconditional and affirmative **promise to pay**. The mere acknowledgment of a debt is not sufficient to constitute a negotiable instrument.

promise to pay
A maker's (borrower's) unconditional and affirmative undertaking to repay a debt to a payee (lender).

Examples The statement "I owe you $100" is merely an I.O.U. It acknowledges a debt, but it does not contain an express promise to repay the money. If the I.O.U. used language such as "I promise to pay" or "the undersigned agrees to pay," however, a negotiable instrument would be created because the note would contain an affirmative obligation to pay.

Certificates of deposit (CDs) are an exception to this rule. CDs do not require an express promise to pay because the bank's acknowledgment of the payee's bank deposit and other terms of the CD clearly indicate the bank's promise to repay the certificate holder. Nevertheless, most CDs contain an express promise to pay.

Unconditional. To be negotiable, a promise or an order must be **unconditional** [UCC 3-104(a)]. A promise or an order that is **conditional** on another promise or event is not negotiable because the risk of the other promise or event not occurring would fall on the person who held the instrument. A conditional promise is not a negotiable instrument and is therefore subject to normal contract law.

unconditional
Not conditional or limited. Promises to pay and orders to pay must be unconditional in order to be negotiable.

Example Delta Air Lines, a commercial airplane company, buys a $100 million airplane from The Boeing Company, a commercial airplane manufacturer. Delta signs a promissory note that promises to pay Boeing if it is "satisfied" with the airplane. This promise is a conditional promise. The condition—that Delta is satisfied with the airplane—destroys the negotiability of the note.

Critical Legal Thinking Question

Why does the UCC require that the writing be an unconditional order to pay or an unconditional promise to pay to qualify as a negotiable instrument?

A promise or an order is conditional and, therefore, not negotiable if it states (1) an express condition to payment, (2) that the promise or order is subject to or governed by another writing, or (3) the rights or obligations with respect to the promise or order are stated in another writing. The mere reference to a different writing does not make a promise or an order conditional [UCC 3-106(a)].

Examples Dow Chemical purchases equipment from Illinois Tool Works and signs a sales contract. Dow Chemical borrows the purchase price from Citibank and executes a promissory note evidencing this debt and promising to repay the borrowed money plus interest to Citibank. The note contains the following reference: "Sales contract—purchase of equipment." This reference does not affect the negotiability of the note. The note would not be negotiable, however, if the reference stated, "This note hereby incorporates by this reference the terms of the sales contract between Dow Chemical and Illinois Tool Works of this date."

A promise or an order remains unconditional even if it refers to a different writing for a description of rights to collateral, prepayment, or acceleration.

Example An unconditional promise or order might state, "See collateral agreement dated January 15, 2025."

A promise or an order may also stipulate that payment is limited to a particular fund or source and still remain unconditional [UCC 3-106(b)].

Example An unconditional promise or order might state, "Payable out of the proceeds of the Tower Construction Contract."

4. State a Fixed Amount of Money

To be negotiable, an instrument must contain a promise or an order to pay a **fixed amount of money** [UCC 3-104(a)].

fixed amount of money
A requirement that a negotiable instrument contain a promise or an order to pay a fixed amount of money.

Fixed Amount. The fixed amount of money requirement ensures that the value of the instrument can be determined with certainty. The principal amount of the instrument must appear on the face of the instrument.

An instrument does not have to be payable with interest, but if it is, the amount of interest being charged may be expressed as either a *fixed* or *variable* rate. The amount or rate of interest may be stated or described in the instrument or may require reference to information not contained in the instrument. If an instrument provides for interest but the amount of interest cannot be determined from the description, interest is payable at the judgment rate (legal rate) in effect at the place of payment of the instrument [UCC 3-112].

Example A note that contains a promise to pay $10,000 in one year at a stated rate of 10 percent interest is a negotiable instrument because the value of the note can be determined at any time. A note that contains a promise to pay in goods or services is not a negotiable instrument because the value of the note would be difficult to determine at any given time.

Payable in Money. UCC 3-104(a) provides that the fixed amount of a negotiable instrument must be **payable in money**. The UCC defines **money** as a "medium of exchange authorized or adopted by a domestic or foreign government as part of its currency" [UCC 1-201(24)].

money
A "medium of exchange authorized or adopted by a domestic or foreign government" [UCC 1-201(24)].

Example An instrument that is "payable in $10,000 U.S. currency" is a negotiable instrument.

Instruments that are fully or partially payable in a medium of exchange other than money are not negotiable.

Examples An instrument that is "payable in $10,000 U.S. gold" is not negotiable. Although the stated amount is a fixed amount, it is not payable in a medium of exchange of the U.S. government.

Example Instruments that are payable in diamonds, commodities, goods, services, stocks, bonds, and such do not qualify as negotiable instruments.

Bad money drives out good money.

Sir Thomas Gresham (1560)

The UCC provides that an instrument may state that it is **payable in foreign currency** [UCC 3-107].

In the following case, the court had to decide the dollar amount of a specific negotiable instrument.

CASE 22.1 *STATE COURT CASE Negotiable Instrument*

Tips Family Trust v. PB Commercial LLC

459 S.W.3d 147, 2015 Tex. App. Lexis 1657 (2015)
Court of Appeals of Texas

"It is well settled that unambiguous written words prevail over arithmetic numbers in promissory notes."

—Michael Massengale, Justice

Facts

The Charles R. Tips Family Trust and the Hazel W. Tips Family Trust borrowed $1,700,000 from Patriot Bank and signed a promissory note (note) to repay the loan. The note was secured by real property owned by the trusts. Charles Watkins, a trustee of both trusts, signed a guaranty agreement with the bank agreeing to personally pay the loan if the trusts defaulted on their payments. The note, security agreement, and guaranty agreement all described the principal amount of the loan as "ONE MILLION SEVEN THOUSAND AND NO/100 ($1,700,000.00) DOLLARS." The bank loaned the trusts $1,700,000.

The trusts made payments of $595,586 before defaulting on the loan. Watkins made no payments as the guarantor. The bank sued the trusts and the guarantor to collect the balance due on the note as well as unpaid interest. PB Commercial, LLC (PBC) acquired the note while the litigation was pending, sold the property securing the note at auction for $874,125, and was substituted as the plaintiff in the case against the trusts and guarantor. PBC alleged that it was owed a balance of $815,214 of the $1,700,000 loan. The trusts and guarantor counterclaimed, arguing that the loan was for $1,007,000, the amount of the written words on the note and other agreements, and that PBC owed them approximately $189,000, which they allege was surplus money PBC received from the sale of the property. The trial court held that the note was for $1,700,000 and granted summary judgment in favor of PBC. The trusts and guarantor appealed.

Issue

Was the original principal amount of the promissory note $1,700,000 or $1,007,000?

Language of the Court

Under the Uniform Commercial Code, which governs negotiable instruments such as the note, if an instrument contains contradictory terms, typewritten terms prevail over printed terms, handwritten terms prevail over both, and words prevail over numbers. It is well settled that unambiguous written words prevail over arithmetic numbers in promissory notes. It does not matter that the discrepancy between the words and numbers is a large one. Here, the words "one million seven thousand" control over the numerals "$1,700,000" to set the amount of the promissory note and guaranty obligations.

Decision

The court of appeals held that the amount of the note was for $1,007,00, reversed the summary judgment in favor of PBC, and remanded the case for a calculation of damages that is owed to the trusts.

Critical Legal Thinking Questions

Did the UCC rule cause an injustice in this case? Did the trusts act ethically in denying that they owed $1,700,000, which was the amount of money they received from the bank?

5. Not Require Any Undertaking in Addition to the Payment of Money

To qualify as a negotiable instrument, a promise or an order to pay cannot state any other undertaking by the person promising or ordering payment to do any act in addition to the payment of money [UCC 3-104(a)(3)].

Example If a note required the maker to pay a stated amount of money *and* perform some type of service, it would not be negotiable.

A promise or an order may include authorization or power to protect collateral, dispose of collateral, and waive any law intended to protect the obligee.

6. Be Payable on Demand or at a Definite Time

For an instrument to be negotiable, it is necessary to know when the maker, drawee, or acceptor is required to pay it. UCC 3-104(a)(2) requires the instrument to be either *payable on demand* or *payable at a definite time*, as noted on the face of the instrument.

payable on demand or at a definite time
A requirement that a negotiable instrument be payable either *on demand* or *at a definite time.*

demand instrument
An instrument payable on demand.

time instrument
An instrument payable (1) at a fixed date, (2) on or before a stated date, (3) at a fixed period after sight, or (4) at a time readily ascertainable when the promise or order is issued.

Payable on Demand. Instruments that are **payable on demand** are called **demand instruments**. Demand instruments are created by language such as "payable on demand," "payable at sight," or "payable on presentment" [UCC 3-108(a)]. By definition, checks are payable on demand [UCC 3-104(f)]. Other instruments, such as notes, CDs, and drafts, can be but are not always payable on demand.

Payable at a Definite Time. Instruments that are **payable at a definite time** are called **time instruments**. UCC 3-108(b) and 3-108(c) state that an instrument is payable at a definite time if it is payable as follows:

1. At a fixed date.

   Example An instrument is payable at a definite time if it says "Payable on January 1, 2028."

2. On or before a stated date.

   Example An instrument is payable at a definite time if it says "Payable on or before January 1, 2028." In this case, the maker or drawee has the option of paying the note before—but not after—the stated maturity date.

Instruments that are payable on an uncertain act or event are not negotiable.

Example Sarah's father executes a promissory note that states, "I promise to pay to the order of my daughter, Sarah, $100,000 on the date she marries Bobby Boggs." This note is nonnegotiable because the act and date of marriage are uncertain.

7. Be Payable to Order or to Bearer

The UCC requires that negotiable instruments be either **payable to order** or **payable to bearer** [UCC 3-104(a)(1)]. Promises or orders to pay that do not meet this requirement are not negotiable.

order instrument (order paper)
An instrument that is payable (1) to the order of an identified person or (2) to an identified person or order.

Payable to Order. An instrument is an **order instrument** or **order paper** if it is payable (1) to the order of an identified person or (2) to an identified person or order [UCC 3-109(b)].

Example An instrument that states "payable to the order of IBM" or "payable to IBM or order" is a negotiable order instrument. It would not be negotiable if it stated either "payable to IBM" or "pay to IBM" because it is not payable to *order*.

An instrument can be payable to the order of the maker, the drawer, the drawee, the payee, or two or more payees together or, alternatively, to an office, an officer by his or her title, a corporation, a partnership, an unincorporated association, a trust, an estate, or another legal entity. A party to which an instrument is payable may be identified in any way, including by name, identifying number, office, or account number. An instrument is payable to the party intended by the signer of the instrument even if that party is identified in the instrument by a name or another identification that is not that of the intended party [UCC 3-110].

Examples An instrument made "payable to the order of Lovey" is negotiable. The identification of "Lovey" may be determined by evidence. On the other hand, an instrument made "payable to the order of my loved ones" is not negotiable because the payees are not ascertainable with reasonable certainty.

Payable to Bearer. A **bearer instrument** or **bearer paper** is payable to anyone in physical possession of the instrument who presents it for payment when it is due. The person in possession of the instrument is called the **bearer**. *Bearer paper* results when the drawer or maker does not make the instrument payable to a specific payee.

bearer instrument (bearer paper)
An instrument that is payable to anyone in physical possession of the instrument who presents it for payment when it is due.

Examples An instrument is payable to bearer when any of the following language is used: "payable to the order of bearer," "payable to bearer," "payable to Google or bearer," "payable to cash," or "payable to the order of cash."

In addition, any other indication that does not purport to designate a specific payee creates bearer paper [UCC 3-109(a)].

Example An instrument "payable to my dog Fido" creates a bearer instrument.

In the following case, the court held that a gambling casino marker was a negotiable instrument.

CASE 22.2 *FEDERAL COURT CASE Negotiable Instrument*

Las Vegas Sands, LLC, dba Venetian Resort Hotel Casino v. Nehme

632 F.3d 526, 2011 U.S. App. Lexis 492 (2011)
United States Court of Appeals for the Ninth Circuit

"The marker therefore was valid and enforceable as a negotiable instrument under Nevada law."

—Carlos Bea, Circuit Judge

Facts

Amine T. Nehme, a California resident, is a repeat gambler at the Venetian, a licensed casino in Las Vegas, Nevada. The Venetian is owned by Las Vegas Sands, LLC. Nehme applied for a line of credit with the Venetian by completing a standard credit application form. The bottom of the credit application provided, "Before drawing on my line of credit, if granted, I agree to sign credit instruments in the amount of the draw. Each draw against my credit line constitutes a separate loan of money. I will sign a credit instrument in the amount of the loan." By signing the credit application, Nehme agreed to repay all loans and draws against his credit line.

The Venetian approved a credit line of $500,000 to Nehme. One day, while gambling at the Venetian, Nehme signed a casino marker for $500,000 payable to the Venetian. Nehme exchanged the marker for chips and lost all $500,000 worth of chips playing blackjack. Nehme then left the Venetian with the marker outstanding. The Venetian presented the $500,000 marker to Bank of America, the bank specified on the marker, but the marker was returned for insufficient funds. The Venetian sued Nehme for failure to pay a negotiable instrument.

(*continued*)

Issue

Is the Venetian's casino marker signed by Nehme a negotiable instrument under the Nevada Uniform Commercial Code?

Language of the Court

Here, the marker is a negotiable instrument and a check because it provides a mechanism for payment of $500,000 from Bank of America to the order of the Venetian, is signed by Nehme, and is payable on demand because it states no time or date of payment. On the face of the marker, the order is unconditional and states no undertakings by Nehme other than to pay a specific sum of money. The marker therefore was valid and enforceable as a negotiable instrument under Nevada law.

Decision

The U.S. court of appeals held that the casino marker was a negotiable instrument. The court remanded the case for the determination of other issues involved in the case.

Critical Legal Thinking Questions

Did Nehme act ethically in trying not to pay his marker? Should gambling casinos advance credit to gamblers?

Prepayment, Acceleration, and Extension Clauses

22.4 Describe prepayment, acceleration, and extension clauses.

The inclusion of *prepayment, acceleration*, or *extension clauses* in an instrument does not affect its negotiability. Such clauses are commonly found in promissory notes.

A **prepayment clause** permits the maker to pay the amount due prior to the due date of the instrument.

prepayment clause
A clause in an instrument that permits the maker to pay the amount due prior to the date of the instrument.

Example A person borrows money from a bank to purchase a house. The loan is a 30-year loan, with interest and principal to be paid in equal monthly installments. If the loan agreement contains a prepayment clause, the borrower can pay off the loan at any time during the 30-year period.

An **acceleration clause** allows the payee or holder to accelerate payment of the principal amount of an instrument, plus accrued interest, on the occurrence of an event, such as missing a loan payment.

acceleration clause
A clause in an instrument that allows the payee or holder to accelerate payment of the principal amount of the instrument, plus accrued interest, on the occurrence of an event.

Example A person borrows money from a bank to purchase an automobile. The loan is a five-year loan with interest and principal to be paid in equal monthly installments. After making payments for two years, the borrower misses a payment and defaults on the loan. If the loan agreement contains an acceleration clause, the entire amount of the loan, plus accrued interest, is due and payable at the time of default.

An **extension clause** is the opposite of an acceleration clause: It allows the date of maturity of an instrument to be extended to sometime in the future. An extension clause contains the terms for extension, such as setting the interest rate during the extension period.

extension clause
A clause in an instrument that allows the date of maturity of the instrument to be extended to sometime in the future.

Example A college student borrows money from her mother for college expenses. The loan agreement provides that the student will repay the loan five years after graduation from college. The loan agreement contains an extension clause that permits the graduate to extend the loan another two years if, at the end of five years, she wants extra time to pay the loan.

Nonnegotiable Contract

22.5 Distinguish between a nonnegotiable instrument and a negotiable instrument.

If a promise or an order to pay does not meet one of the previously discussed requirements of negotiability, it is a **nonnegotiable contract** and is therefore not subject to the provisions of UCC Article 3. A promise or an order that conspicuously states that it is not negotiable or is not subject to Article 3 is not a negotiable instrument [UCC 3-104(d)] and is therefore a nonnegotiable contract.

A nonnegotiable contract is not rendered either nontransferable or unenforceable. A nonnegotiable contract can be enforced under normal contract law. If the maker or drawer of a nonnegotiable contract fails to pay it, the holder of the contract can sue the nonperforming party for breach of contract.

nonnegotiable contract
A contract that fails to meet the requirements of a negotiable instrument and, therefore, is not subject to the provisions of UCC Article 3.

Critical Legal Thinking Questions

If the writing does not meet the requirements to be a negotiable instrument, what is it? Is it still enforceable?

Key Terms and Concepts

Acceleration clause (392)
Article 3 (Commercial Paper) of the Uniform Commercial Code (381)
Bearer (391)
Bearer instrument (bearer paper) (391)
Certificate of deposit (CD) (385)
Check (383)
Collateral (385)
Collateral note (385)
Conditional (387)
Demand draft (382)
Demand instrument (390)
Demand note (384)
Draft (382)
Drawee of a check (383)
Drawee of a draft (382)
Drawer of a check (383)
Drawer of a draft (382)
Extension clause (392)
Extension of credit (382)
Fixed amount of money (388)
Holder in due course (HDC) (381)
Installment note (384)
Jumbo certificate of deposit (jumbo CD) (385)
Maker of a certificate of deposit (385)
Maker of a note (384)
Money (388)
Mortgage note (385)
Negotiable instrument (commercial paper) (381)
Negotiation (381)
Nonnegotiable contract (393)
Order instrument (order paper) (390)
Order to pay (387)
Payable at a definite time (390)
Payable in foreign currency (389)
Payable in money (388)
Payable on demand (390)
Payable to bearer (390)
Payable to order (390)
Payee of a certificate of deposit (385)
Payee of a check (383)
Payee of a draft (382)
Payee of a note (384)
Permanency requirement (386)
Portability requirement (386)
Prepayment clause (392)
Promise to pay (387)
Promissory note (note) (384)
Record-keeping device (382)
Representative's signature (387)
Revised Article 3 (Negotiable Instruments) of the Uniform Commercial Code (381)
Sight draft (demand draft) (382)
Signature (386)
Signature requirement (386)
Small certificate of deposit (small CD) (385)
Substitute for money (381)
Time draft (382)
Time instrument (390)
Time note (384)
Trade acceptance (bill of exchange) (382)
Unconditional (387)
Unconditional promise or order to pay requirement (387)
Writing requirement (386)

Critical Legal Thinking Cases

22.1 Negotiable Instrument William H. Bailey, MD, executed a note payable to California Dreamstreet, a joint venture that solicited investments for a cattle breeding operation. Bailey's promissory note read, "Dr. William H. Bailey hereby promises to pay to the order of California Dreamstreet the sum of $329,800." Four years later, Dreamstreet negotiated the note to Cooperatieve Centrale Raiffeisen-Boerenleenbank B.A. (Cooperatieve), a foreign bank. A default occurred, and Cooperatieve filed suit against Bailey to recover on the note. Is the note executed by Bailey a negotiable instrument? *Cooperatieve Centrale Raiffeisen-Boerenleenbank B.A. v. Bailey*, 710 F.Supp. 737, 1989 U.S. Dist. Lexis 4488 (United States District Court for the Central District of California, 1989)

22.2 Formal Requirements Mr. Higgins operated a used car dealership in the state of Alabama. Higgins purchased a Chevrolet Corvette. He paid for the car with a draft on his account at the First State Bank of Albertville. Soon after, Higgins resold the car to Mr. Holsonback. To pay for the car, Holsonback signed a check that was printed on a standard-sized envelope. The reason the check was printed on an envelope is that this practice made it easier to transfer title and other documents from the seller to the buyer. The envelope on which the check was written contained a certificate of title, a mileage statement, and a bill of sale. Does a check printed on an envelope meet the formal requirements to be classified as a negotiable instrument under the UCC? *Holsonback v. First State Bank of Albertville*, 394 So.2d 381, 1980 Ala. Civ. App. Lexis 1208 (Court of Civil Appeals of Alabama, 1980)

22.3 Reference to Another Agreement Holly Hill Acres, Ltd. (Holly Hill), purchased land from Rogers and Blythe. As part of its consideration, Holly Hill gave Rogers and Blythe a promissory note and mortgage. The note read, in part, "This note with interest is secured by a mortgage on real estate made by the maker in favor of said payee. The terms of said mortgage are by reference made a part hereof." Rogers and Blythe assigned this note and mortgage to Charter Bank of Gainesville (Charter Bank) as security in order to obtain a loan from the bank. Within a few months, Rogers and Blythe defaulted on their obligation to Charter Bank. Charter Bank sued to recover on Holly Hill's note and mortgage. Does the reference to the mortgage in the note cause it to be nonnegotiable? *Holly Hill Acres, Ltd. v. Charter Bank of Gainesville*, 314 So.2d 209, 1975 Fla. App. Lexis 13715 (Court of Appeal of Florida, 1975)

Ethics Case

22.4 Ethics Case Stewart P. Blanchard borrowed $50,000 from Progressive Bank & Trust Company (Progressive) to purchase a home. As part of the transaction, Blanchard signed a note secured by a mortgage. The note provided for a 10 percent annual interest rate. Under the terms of the note, payment was "due on demand, if no demand is made, then $600 monthly" beginning at a specified date. Blanchard testified that he believed Progressive could demand immediate payment only if he failed to make the monthly installments. After one year, Blanchard received notice that the rate of interest on the note would rise to 11 percent. Despite the notice, Blanchard continued to make $600 monthly payments. One year later, Progressive notified Blanchard that the interest rate on the loan would be increased to 12.75 percent. Progressive requested that Blanchard sign a form consenting to the interest rate adjustment. When Blanchard refused to sign the form, Progressive demanded immediate payment of the note balance. Progressive sued Blanchard to enforce the terms of the note. Is the note a demand instrument? Did either party act unethically in this case? *Blanchard v. Progressive Bank & Trust Company*, 413 So.2d 589, 1982 La. App. Lexis 7213 (Court of Appeal of Louisiana, 1982)

CHAPTER 23

Holder in Due Course and Transferability

BANK
Checks are cleared using the banking system.

Anton Violin/Shutterstock

Learning Objectives

After studying this chapter, you should be able to:

23.1 Describe how a nonnegotiable contract is transferred by assignment.

23.2 Describe how a negotiable instrument is transferred by negotiation.

23.3 Describe how a negotiable instrument is transferred by indorsement.

23.4 List and describe the types of indorsements.

23.5 Define *holder* and *holder in due course*.

23.6 Identify and describe the requirements for being a holder in due course.

> *A negotiable bill or note is a courier without luggage.*
>
> — *Chief Justice Gibson*
> *Overton v. Tyler*
> *3 Pa. 346, 1846 Pa. Lexis 117 (1846)*

Introduction to Holder in Due Course and Transferability

The borrower runs in his own debt.

Ralph Waldo Emerson
Essays, Vol. Compensation
(1841)

Once created, a negotiable instrument can be transferred to subsequent parties by *negotiation*. This is accomplished by placing an *indorsement* on the instrument. There are several types of indorsements, each with its own requirements and effect.

Recall that the primary purpose of commercial paper is to act as a substitute for money. For this to occur, the holder of a negotiable instrument must qualify as a *holder in due course (HDC)*. Commercial paper held by an HDC is virtually as good as money because HDCs take an instrument free of all claims and most defenses that can be asserted by other parties.

This chapter discusses the negotiation of an instrument, types of indorsements, and the requirements that must be met to qualify as an HDC.

Transfer of a Nonnegotiable Contract by Assignment

23.1 Describe how a nonnegotiable contract is transferred by assignment.

assignment
The transfer of rights under a nonnegotiable contract. The transferor is the *assignor*, and the transferee is the *assignee*.

nonnegotiable contract
A contract that lacks one or more of the requirements to be a negotiable instrument.

An **assignment** is the transfer of rights under a contract. It transfers the rights of the transferor (**assignor**) to the transferee (**assignee**). Because normal contract principles apply, the assignee acquires only the rights that the assignor possessed. Thus, any defenses to the enforcement of the contract that could have been raised against the assignor can also be raised against the assignee.

A **nonnegotiable contract** is a contract that lacks one or more of the requirements to be a negotiable instrument. An assignment occurs when a nonnegotiable contract is transferred. In the case of a negotiable instrument, assignment occurs when the instrument is transferred but the transfer fails to qualify as a negotiation under Article 3 of the Uniform Commercial Code (UCC). In this case, the transferee is an *assignee* rather than a *holder*.

Example Abraham borrows $25,000 from Joshua at 5 percent interest and signs a promissory note agreeing to repay the principal and interest in equal monthly installments over five years. This promissory note would normally be a negotiable instrument. However, the note contains a reference to another document, and by doing so it becomes a nonnegotiable instrument. If Joshua transfers the note to Maribelle, this is an assignment of rights—a transfer of a normal contract—and not a negotiation subject to Article 3 of the UCC. Joshua is the assignor, and Maribelle is the assignee. Maribelle can enforce the note against Abraham, but Abraham can raise defenses that he has against Joshua (e.g., fraud) against Maribelle.

Transfer of a Negotiable Instrument by Negotiation

23.2 Describe how a negotiable instrument is transferred by negotiation.

negotiation
The transfer of a negotiable instrument by a person other than the issuer to a person who thereby becomes a *holder*.

Negotiation is the transfer of a *negotiable instrument* by a person other than the issuer. The person to whom the instrument is transferred becomes the *holder* [UCC 3-201(a)]. The holder receives at least the rights of the transferor and may acquire even greater rights than the transferor if he or she qualifies as a holder in due course [UCC 3-302]. An HDC has greater rights because he or she is not subject to some of the defenses that could otherwise have been raised against the transferor.

The proper method of negotiation depends on whether the instrument involved is *order paper* or *bearer paper*, as discussed in the following paragraphs.

Negotiating Order Paper

An instrument that is payable to a specific payee or indorsed to a specific indorsee is an **order instrument** or **order paper**. Order paper is negotiated by delivery with the necessary indorsement [UCC 3-201(b)]. Thus, for order paper to be negotiated there must be delivery and indorsement.

order instrument (order paper)
An instrument that is payable to a specific payee or indorsed to a specific indorsee. Order paper is negotiated by (1) delivery and (2) indorsement.

Example Samuel Bennett receives a weekly payroll check from his employer, Ace Corporation, made "payable to the order of Samuel Bennett." Samuel takes the check to a local store, signs his name on the back of the check (indorsement), gives the check to the cashier (delivery), and receives cash for the check. Samuel has negotiated the check to the store. Delivery and indorsement have occurred.

Negotiating Bearer Paper

An instrument that is not payable to a specific payee or indorsee is a **bearer instrument** or **bearer paper**. Bearer paper is negotiated by *delivery*; indorsement is not necessary [UCC 3-201(b)]. Substantial risk is associated with the loss or theft of bearer paper.

bearer instrument (bearer paper)
An instrument that is not payable to a specific payee or indorsee. Bearer paper is negotiated by delivery; indorsement is not necessary.

Critical Legal Thinking Questions

What is order paper? What is bearer paper? What is the difference in the negotiation of order paper versus bearer paper?

Example Celeste draws from her checking account a $1,500 check made out to "pay to cash" and gives it to Peter. This is a bearer instrument because the check has not been made out to a named payee. There has been a negotiation because Celeste delivered a bearer instrument (the check) to Peter. Subsequently, Carmen steals the check from Peter. There has not been a negotiation because the check was not voluntarily delivered. But Carmen physically possesses the bearer instrument. The negotiation is complete if Carmen delivers the check to an innocent third party, Zhi Ruo. Zhi Ruo is a holder and may qualify as a holder in due course with all the rights in the check [UCC 3-302]. If the holder, Zhi Ruo, is an HDC, she can deposit the check in her account, and Celeste's checking account will be debited $1,500. Peter's only recourse is to recover the $1,500 from Carmen, the thief.

The following feature discusses how order and bearer paper can be converted from one to the other.

Contemporary Environment

Converting Order and Bearer Paper

An instrument can be converted from order paper to bearer paper and vice versa many times until the instrument is paid [UCC 3-109(c)]. The deciding factor is the type of indorsement placed on the instrument at the time of each subsequent transfer. Follow the indorsements in the example shown here to determine whether order or bearer paper has been created.

(continued)

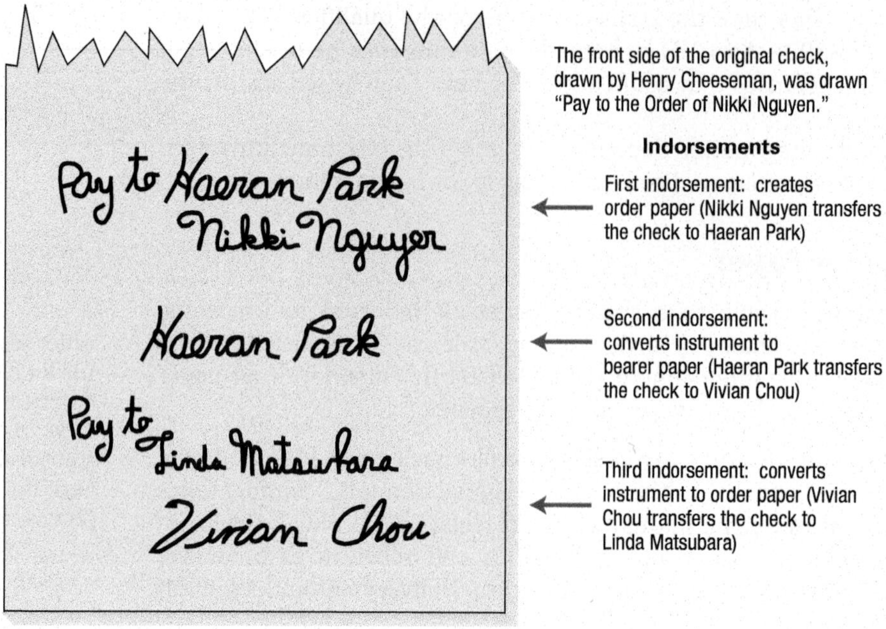

Pay to Haeran Park
Nikki Nguyen
Haeran Park
Pay to Linda Matsubara
Vivian Chou
The front side of the original check, drawn by Henry Cheeseman, was drawn "Pay to the Order of Nikki Nguyen."
Indorsements
First indorsement: creates order paper (Nikki Nguyen transfers the check to Haeran Park)
Second indorsement: converts instrument to bearer paper (Haeran Park transfers the check to Vivian Chou)
Third indorsement: converts instrument to order paper (Vivian Chou transfers the check to Linda Matsubara)

The case that follows demonstrates the risk of bearer paper.

CASE 23.1 *STATE COURT CASE Bearer Paper*

Gerber & Gerber, P.C. v. Regions Bank

596 S.E.2d 174, 2004 Ga. App. Lexis 206 (2004)
Court of Appeals of Georgia

"Accordingly, when here the payees of the cashier's checks indorsed the checks in blank, the checks then became bearer paper and could—similar to cash—be transferred by possession alone."

—Yvette Miller, Judge

Facts

Cynthia Stafford worked as a real estate closing secretary for Gerber & Gerber, P.C. (G&G), a law firm. The law firm acted as a trustee for the closing of real estate transactions. Real estate buyers would write cashier's checks for the purchase price of the real estate and make these checks payable to the seller-payee. The seller-payee in turn indorsed these checks in blank to the law firm and gave the checks to the law firm to hold during the time period for closing of their real estate transactions. This created bearer paper. Over a period of two years, Stafford stole some of these blank-indorsed cashier's checks. Stafford then personally indorsed the cashier's checks in her possession and deposited them in her personal bank account at Regions Bank. The total loss was $180,000.

Stafford confessed to the theft. She pleaded guilty to criminal charges and received a five-year jail sentence. Stafford claimed to have spent the money. G&G sued Regions Bank to recover for the checks paid to Stafford, alleging that the bank was negligent in accepting the checks from Stafford. Regions Bank moved for summary judgment, arguing that it had acted properly under the Uniform Commercial Code (UCC) in accepting the bearer blank-indorsed checks from Stafford. The trial court granted Regions Bank summary judgment as to the bearer paper. G&G appealed.

Issue

Has Regions Bank properly accepted the blank-indorsed bearer cashier's checks from Stafford?

Language of the Court

Accordingly, when here the payees of the cashier's checks indorsed the checks in blank, the checks then became bearer paper and could—similar to cash—be transferred by possession alone. Thus, Regions Bank quite properly accepted the indorsed-in-blank cashier's checks from the person in possession of them and deposited the checks into that person's account.

Decision

The court of appeals held that Regions Bank was not negligent in accepting the blank-indorsed bearer cashier's checks from Stafford and placing the money in Stafford's personal account. The court of appeals upheld the trial court's grant of summary judgment to Regions Bank.

Critical Legal Thinking Questions

Did Stafford act ethically in this case? Did G&G act ethically in suing Regions Bank to recover for Stafford's thefts?

Transfer of a Negotiable Instrument by Indorsement

23.3 Describe how a negotiable instrument is transferred by indorsement.

indorsement
The signature (and other directions) written by or on behalf of the holder somewhere on an instrument.

An **indorsement** is the signature of a signer (other than as a maker, a drawer, or an acceptor) that is placed on an instrument to negotiate it to another person. The signature may (1) appear alone, (2) name an individual to whom the instrument is to be paid, or (3) be accompanied by other words [UCC 3-204(2)]. The person who indorses an instrument is called the **indorser**. If the indorsement names a payee, this person is called the **indorsee**. Indorsements are required to negotiate order paper, but they are not required to negotiate bearer paper [UCC 3-201(b)].

An indorsement is usually placed on the reverse side of the instrument, such as on the back of a check (see Exhibit 23.1). If there is no room on the instrument, the indorsement may be written on a separate piece of paper called an **allonge**. The allonge must be affixed (e.g., stapled, taped) to the instrument [UCC 3-204(a)].

allonge
A separate piece of paper attached to an instrument on which an indorsement is written.

Exhibit 23.1 PLACEMENT OF AN INDORSEMENT

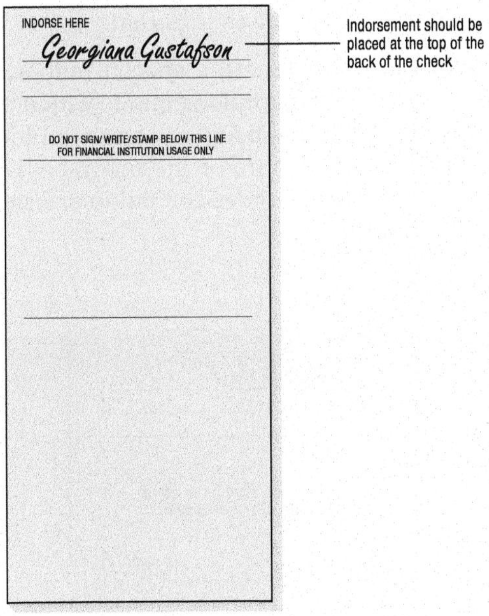
INDORSE HERE
Georgiana Gustafson
Indorsement should be placed at the top of the back of the check
DO NOT SIGN/ WRITE/ STAMP BELOW THIS LINE
FOR FINANCIAL INSTITUTION USAGE ONLY

Types of Indorsements

23.4 List and describe the types of indorsements.

There are four categories of indorsements:

1. Blank indorsement
2. Special indorsement
3. Qualified indorsement
4. Restrictive indorsement

These types of indorsements are discussed in the following paragraphs.

Blank Indorsement

blank indorsement
An indorsement that does not specify a particular indorsee. It creates *bearer paper.*

A **blank indorsement** does not specify a particular indorsee. It may consist of just a signature [UCC 3-205(b)].

Example Zandor Green draws a check "pay to the order of Victoria Rudd" and delivers the check to Victoria. Victoria indorses the check in blank by writing her signature "Victoria Rudd" on the back of the check (see Exhibit 23.2).

Order paper that is indorsed in blank becomes bearer paper. As mentioned earlier, bearer paper can be negotiated by delivery; indorsement is not required. Thus, a lost bearer paper can be presented for payment or negotiated to another holder.

Example In the prior example, assume that Victoria Rudd loses the check she has indorsed in blank and that Mari Nielsen finds the check. Mari Nielsen, who is in possession of bearer paper, can deliver it to another person without indorsing it.

Special Indorsement

special indorsement
An indorsement that contains the signature of the indorser and specifies the person (indorsee) to whom the indorser intends the instrument to be payable. It creates *order paper.*

A **special indorsement** contains the signature of the indorser and specifies the person (indorsee) to whom the indorser intends the instrument to be payable [UCC 3-205(a)]. Words of negotiation (e.g., "pay to the order of . . .") are not required for a special indorsement. Words such as "pay Emily Ingman" are sufficient to form a special indorsement. A special indorsement creates *order paper*. As mentioned earlier, order paper is negotiated by indorsement and delivery.

Example A special indorsement would be created if Betsy McKenny indorsed her check and then wrote "pay to Dan Jones" above her signature (see Exhibit 23.3). The check is negotiated when Betsy gives it to Dan.

To prevent the risk of loss from theft, a special indorsement (which creates order paper) is preferred over a blank indorsement (which creates bearer paper). A holder can convert a blank indorsement into a special indorsement by writing contract instructions over the signature of the indorser [UCC 3-205(c)]. Words such as "pay to John Jones" written above the indorser's signature are enough to convert bearer paper to order paper.

Exhibit 23.2 BLANK INDORSEMENT

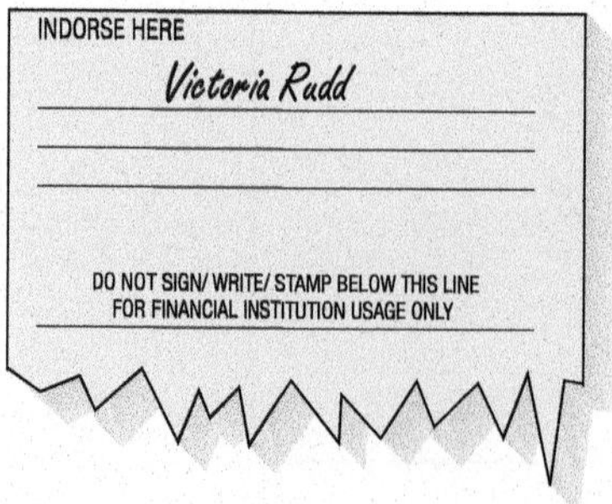

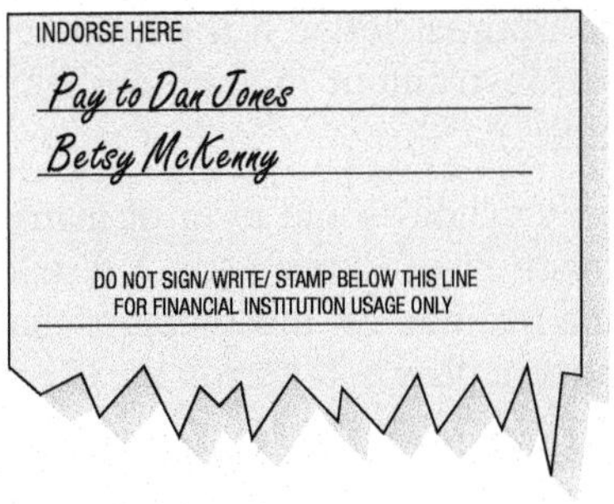
INDORSE HERE
Pay to Dan Jones
Betsy McKenny
DO NOT SIGN/ WRITE/ STAMP BELOW THIS LINE
FOR FINANCIAL INSTITUTION USAGE ONLY

Exhibit 23.3 SPECIAL INDORSEMENT

Qualified Indorsement

Generally, an indorsement is a promise by the indorser to pay the holder or any subsequent indorser the amount of the instrument if the maker, drawer, or acceptor defaults on it. This promise is called an **unqualified indorsement**. Unless otherwise agreed, the order and liability of the indorsers is presumed to be the order in which they indorse the instrument [UCC 3-415(a)].

unqualified indorsement
An indorsement whereby the indorser promises to pay the holder or any subsequent indorser the amount of the instrument if the maker, drawer, or acceptor defaults on it.

Example Cindy draws a check payable to the order of Rai. Rai (indorser) indorses the check and negotiates it to Steve (indorsee). When Steve presents the check for payment, there are insufficient funds in Cindy's account to pay the check. Rai, as an **unqualified indorser**, is liable on the check. Rai can recover from Cindy.

The UCC permits a **qualified indorsement**—that is, an indorsement that disclaims or limits liability on the instrument. A **qualified indorser** does not guarantee payment of the instrument if the maker, drawer, or acceptor defaults on it. A qualified indorsement is created by placing a notation such as "without recourse" or other similar language that disclaims liability as part of the indorsement [UCC 3-415(b)]. A qualified indorsement protects only the indorser who wrote an indorsement on the instrument. A qualified indorsement is often used by persons who sign instruments in a representative capacity.

qualified indorsement
An indorsement that includes the notation "without recourse" or similar language that disclaims liability of the indorser.

Example Suppose an insurance company that is paying a claim makes out a check payable to the order of the attorney representing the payee. The attorney can indorse the check to his client (the payee) with the notation "without recourse." This notation ensures that the attorney is not liable as an indorser if the insurance company fails to pay the check.

A qualified indorsement can be either a special qualified indorsement or a blank qualified indorsement. A *special qualified indorsement* creates order paper that can be negotiated by indorsement and delivery. A *blank qualified indorsement* creates bearer paper that can be further negotiated by delivery without indorsement (see Exhibit 23.4).

Restrictive Indorsement

Most indorsements are *nonrestrictive*. A **nonrestrictive indorsement** does not have any instructions or conditions attached to the payment of the funds.

nonrestrictive indorsement
An indorsement that has no instructions or conditions attached to the payment of the funds.

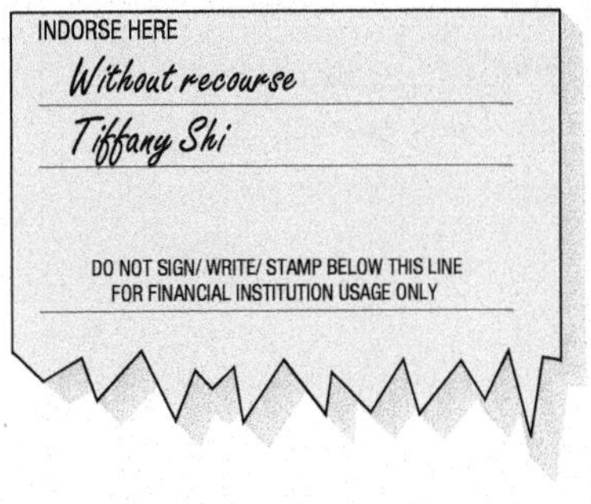
INDORSE HERE
Without recourse
Tiffany Shi
DO NOT SIGN/ WRITE/ STAMP BELOW THIS LINE
FOR FINANCIAL INSTITUTION USAGE ONLY

Exhibit 23.4 QUALIFIED INDORSEMENT

Example An indorsement is nonrestrictive if the indorsee merely signs his or her signature to the back of an instrument or includes a notation to pay a specific indorsee ("pay to Sam Smith").

restrictive indorsement
An indorsement that contains some sort of instruction from the indorser.

Occasionally, an indorser includes some form of instruction in an indorsement. This instruction is called a **restrictive indorsement**. A restrictive indorsement restricts the indorsee's rights in some manner. An indorsement that purports to prohibit further negotiation of an instrument does not destroy the negotiability of the instrument.

Example A check that is indorsed "pay to Sarah Stein only" can still be negotiated to other transferees. Because of its ineffectiveness, this type of restrictive indorsement is seldom used.

UCC 3-206 recognizes the following types of restrictive indorsements:

indorsement for deposit or collection
An indorsement that makes the indorsee the indorser's collecting agent (e.g., "For deposit only").

- **Indorsement for deposit or collection.** An indorser can indorse an instrument so as to make the indorsee his collecting agent. Such indorsement—called an **indorsement for deposit or collection**—is often done when an indorser deposits a check or another instrument for collection at a bank. Words such as *for collection*, *for deposit only*, and *pay any bank* create this type of indorsement. Banks use this type of indorsement in the collection process.

  Example Raul Martinez receives his paycheck from his employer. He indorses the back of the check "For deposit only" and signs his name under these words. Raul deposits the check at an ATM of his bank. This is an indorsement for deposit or collection. Raul's bank will send the check to the employer's bank for collection (see Exhibit 23.5).

- **Indorsement in trust.** An indorsement can state that it is for the benefit or use of the indorser or another person.

indorsement in trust (agency indorsement)
An indorsement that states that it is for the benefit or use of the indorser or another person.

  Example Checks are often indorsed to attorneys, executors of estates, real estate agents, and other fiduciaries in their representative capacity for the benefit of clients, heirs, or others. Such an indorsement is called an **indorsement in trust**, or an **agency indorsement** (see Exhibit 23.6). The indorser is not personally liable on the instrument if there is a proper trust or agency indorsement.

Exhibit 23.5 RESTRICTIVE INDORSEMENT

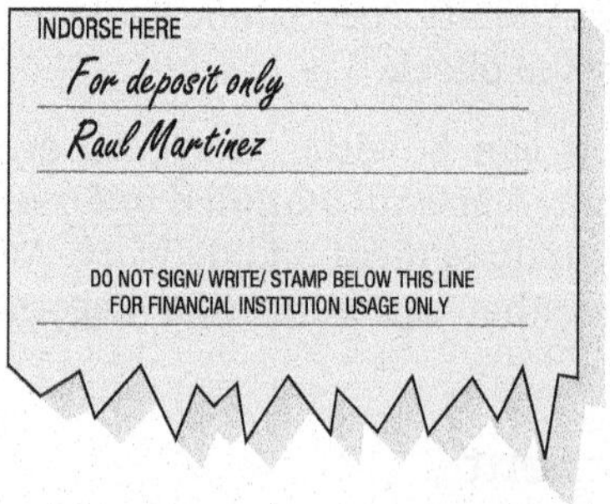
INDORSE HERE
For deposit only
Raul Martinez
DO NOT SIGN/ WRITE/ STAMP BELOW THIS LINE
FOR FINANCIAL INSTITUTION USAGE ONLY

Exhibit 23.6 TRUST INDORSEMENT

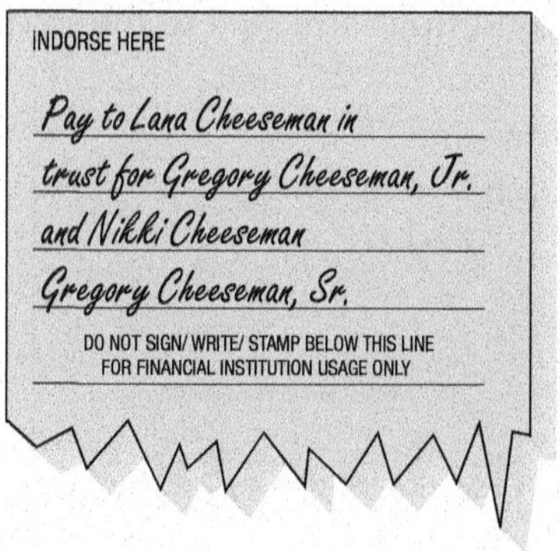
INDORSE HERE
Pay to Lana Cheeseman in
trust for Gregory Cheeseman, Jr.
and Nikki Cheeseman
Gregory Cheeseman, Sr.
DO NOT SIGN/ WRITE/ STAMP BELOW THIS LINE
FOR FINANCIAL INSTITUTION USAGE ONLY

An indorsee who does not comply with the instructions of a restrictive indorsement is liable to the indorser for all losses that occur because of such noncompliance.

Example Suppose a check is drawn "payable to Anne Spencer, attorney, in trust for Danso Assan." If Spencer indorses the check to an automobile dealer in payment for a car that she purchases personally, the automobile dealer (indorsee) has not followed the instructions of the restrictive indorsement. The automobile dealer is liable to Danso Assan for any losses that arise because of the dealer's noncompliance with the restrictive indorsement.

CONCEPT SUMMARY

TYPES OF INDORSEMENTS

Type of Indorsement	Description
Blank	Does not specify a particular indorsee (e.g., /s/Mary Jones). This indorsement creates bearer paper.
Special	Specifies the person to whom the indorser intends the instrument to be payable (e.g., "Pay to the order of John Smith" /s/Mary Jones). This indorsement creates order paper. (If it is not payable to order [e.g., "Pay to John Smith" /s/Mary Jones], it can be converted to order paper [e.g., "Pay to the order of Fred Roe" /s/John Smith].)
Unqualified	Does not disclaim or limit liability. The indorsee is liable on the instrument if it is not paid by the maker, acceptor, or drawer.
Qualified	Disclaims or limits the liability of the indorsee. There are two types: 1. Special qualified indorsement (e.g., "Pay to the order of John Smith, without recourse" /s/Mary Jones). 2. Blank qualified indorsement (e.g., "Without recourse" /s/Mary Jones).
Nonrestrictive	No instructions or conditions are attached to the payment of funds (e.g., "Pay to John Smith or order" /s/Mary Jones).
Restrictive	Conditions or instructions restrict the indorsee's rights. There are three types: 1. Indorsement prohibiting further indorsement (e.g., "Pay to John Smith only" /s/Mary Jones). 2. Indorsement for deposit or collection (e.g., "For deposit only" /s/Mary Jones). 3. Indorsement in trust (e.g., "Pay to John Smith, trustee" /s/Mary Jones).

Misspelled or Wrong Name

Where the name of the payee or indorsee is misspelled in a negotiable instrument, the payee or indorsee can indorse the instrument using the misspelled name, the correct name, or both.

Example If Susan Worth receives a check payable to "Susan Wirth," she can indorse the check by signing "Susan Wirth" or "Susan Worth" or both. A person paying or taking the instrument for value or collection may require a signature in both the misspelled and the correct versions [UCC 3-204(d)].

Multiple Payees or Indorsees

Drawers, makers, and indorsers often make checks, promissory notes, and other negotiable instruments payable to two or more payees or indorsees. The question then arises: Can the instrument be negotiated by the signature of one payee or indorsee, or are both or all of their signatures required to negotiate the instrument?

Section 3-110(d) of Revised Article 3 of the UCC and cases that have interpreted that section establish the following rules:

- If an instrument is **payable jointly** using the word *and*, both persons' indorsements are necessary to negotiate the instrument.

  Example "Pay to Shou-Yi Kang and Min-Wer Chen." Here, the indorsement signatures of *both* Shou-Yi Kang and Min-Wer Chen are required to negotiate the instrument. The indorsement signature of only one of the named persons is not sufficient to negotiate the instrument.

- If the instrument is **payable in the alternative** using the word *or*, either person's indorsement signature alone is sufficient to negotiate the instrument.

  Example "Pay to Shou-Yi Kang or Min-Wer Chen." Here, *either* Shou-Yi Kang or Min-Wer Chen can individually indorse and negotiate the instrument without the other's signature.

- If a **virgule**—a slash mark (/)—is used, courts have held that the instrument is *payable in the alternative*—that is, the instrument is treated as if the / is an "or." Thus, if a virgule is used, either person may individually negotiate the instrument.

  Example "Pay to Shou-Yi Kang/Min-Wer Chen." Here, the virgule (/) is treated as an "or," and either Shou-Yi Kang or Min-Wer Chen can individually indorse and negotiate the instrument without the other's indorsement.

Holder in Due Course

23.5 Define *holder* and *holder in due course*.

holder
A person who is in possession of a negotiable instrument that is drawn, issued, or indorsed to that person or to that person's order, or to bearer, or in blank.

Two of the most important concepts of the law of negotiable instruments are the concepts of *holder* and *holder in due course*. A **holder** is a person in possession of an instrument that is payable to a bearer or an identified person who is in possession of an instrument payable to that person [UCC 1-201(20)]. A holder is subject to all the claims and defenses that can be asserted against the transferor.

The concept of *holder in due course* is unique to the area of negotiable instruments. An HDC takes a negotiable instrument free of all claims and most defenses that can be asserted against the transferor of the instrument. Only *universal defenses*—and not *personal defenses*—may be asserted against an HDC. Thus, an HDC can acquire greater rights than a transferor.

Example Zuberi purchases an automobile from Shannen. At the time of sale, Shannen tells Zuberi that the car has had only one previous owner and has been driven only 20,000 miles. Zuberi, relying on these statements, purchases the car. He pays 10 percent down and signs a promissory note to pay the remainder of the purchase price, with interest, in 12 equal monthly installments. Shannen transfers the note to Patricia. Then Zuberi discovers that the car has actually had four previous owners and has been driven 100,000 miles. If Patricia were a holder (but not an HDC) of the note, Zuberi could assert Shannen's fraudulent representations against enforcement of the note by Patricia. Zuberi could rescind the note and refuse to pay Patricia. Patricia's only recourse would be against Shannen.

Example If in the prior example Patricia qualified as an HDC, the result would be different. Zuberi could not assert Shannen's fraudulent conduct against enforcement of the note by Patricia because this type of fraud is a *personal defense* that cannot be raised against an HDC. Therefore, Patricia could enforce the note against Zuberi. Zuberi's only recourse would be against Shannen, if she could be found.

Requirements for Holder in Due Course Status

23.6 Identify and describe the requirements for being a holder in due course.

To qualify as a **holder in due course (HDC)**, a transferee must meet the requirements established by the UCC: The person must be the *holder* of a negotiable instrument that was taken (1) for value; (2) in good faith; (3) without notice that it is overdue, dishonored, or encumbered in any way; and (4) bearing no apparent evidence of forgery, alterations, or irregularity [UCC 3-302]. These requirements are discussed in the paragraphs that follow. Exhibit 23.7 illustrates the HDC doctrine.

holder in due course (HDC)
A holder who takes a negotiable instrument for value, in good faith, and without notice that it is defective or overdue.

1. Taking for Value

Under the UCC **taking for value requirement**, the holder must have *given value* for the negotiable instrument in order to qualify as an HDC [UCC 3-302(a)(2)(i)].

taking for value requirement
A requirement that says a holder must give value for a negotiable instrument in order to qualify as an HDC.

Example Théodore draws a check "payable to the order of Adriana Silva" and delivers the check to Adriana. Adriana indorses it and gives it as a gift to her daughter. Adriana's daughter cannot qualify as an HDC because she has not given value for it. The purchaser of a limited interest in a negotiable instrument is an HDC only to the extent of the interest purchased.

Under the UCC, value has been given if the holder does the following [UCC 3-303]:

- Performs the agreed-on promise
- Acquires a security interest in or lien on the instrument
- Takes the instrument in payment of or as security for an antecedent claim
- Gives a negotiable instrument as payment
- Gives an irrevocable obligation as payment

If a person promises to perform but has not yet done so, no value has been given, and that person is not an HDC.

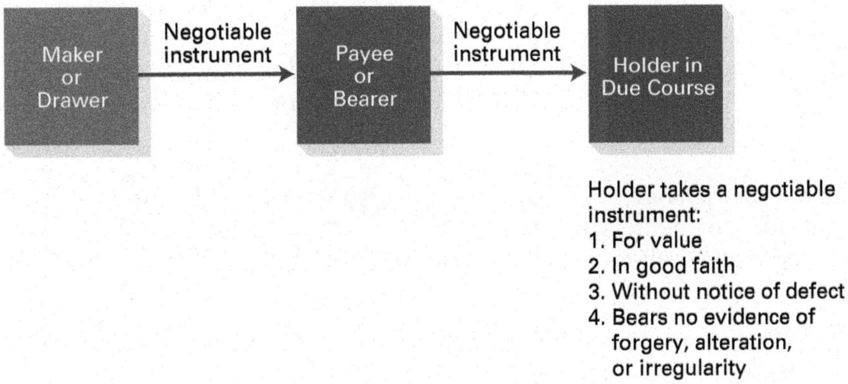

Exhibit 23.7 HOLDER IN DUE COURSE

Example Karen executes a note payable to Fred for $3,000 for goods she purchased from him. Fred transfers the note to Amy, who pays $2,500 for the note. Amy has *given value* for the negotiable instrument and therefore meets this qualification for HDC status.

2. Taking in Good Faith

taking in good faith requirement
A UCC requirement that says a holder must take the instrument in good faith in order to qualify as an HDC.

good faith
Honesty in fact in the conduct or transaction concerned. The good faith test is subjective.

Under the UCC **taking in good faith requirement**, a holder must *take* an instrument in *good faith* to qualify as an HDC [UCC 3-302(a)(2)(ii)]. **Good faith** means honesty in fact in the conduct or transaction concerned [UCC 1-201(19)]. *Honesty in fact* is a subjective test that examines the holder's actual belief. A holder's subjective belief can be inferred from the circumstances.

Example If a holder acquires an instrument from a stranger under suspicious circumstances and at a deep discount, it could be inferred that the holder did not take the instrument in good faith. A naive person who acquired the same instrument at the same discount, however, may be found to have acted in good faith and thereby qualify as an HDC. Each case must be reviewed individually.

Note that the good faith test applies only to the holder. It does not apply to the transferor of an instrument.

Example A thief steals a negotiable instrument and transfers it to Caitlyn. Caitlyn does not know that the instrument is stolen. Caitlyn meets the good faith test and qualifies as an HDC.

3. Taking Without Notice of Defect

taking without notice of defect requirement
A UCC requirement that says a person cannot qualify as an HDC if that person has notice that the instrument is defective in certain ways.

Under the UCC **taking without notice of defect requirement**, a person cannot qualify as an HDC if he or she has noticed that the instrument is defective in any of the following ways [UCC 3-302(a)(2)]:

- It is overdue.
- It has been dishonored.
- It contains an unauthorized signature or has been altered.
- There is a claim to it by another person.
- There is a defense against it.

time instrument
An instrument that specifies a definite date for payment of the instrument.

Overdue Instruments A **time instrument** is an instrument with an express due date. If a time instrument is not paid on its expressed due date, it becomes overdue the next day. This is called an **overdue time instrument**. When an instrument is not paid when due, there is some defect to its payment.

Example Suppose a promissory note is due June 15, 2025. To qualify as an HDC, a purchaser must acquire the note by 11:59 p.m. June 15, 2025. A purchaser who acquires the note on June 16, 2025, or thereafter, is only a holder and not an HDC.

dishonored instrument
An instrument that is presented for payment and payment is refused.

Dishonored Instruments An instrument is *dishonored* when it is presented for payment and payment is refused. This is called a **dishonored instrument**. A holder who takes such an instrument with notice of its dishonor cannot qualify as an HDC.

Example A person who takes a check that has been marked by the payer bank "payment refused—not sufficient funds" cannot qualify as an HDC.

4. Taking Where There Is No Evidence of Forgery, Alteration, or Irregularity

The UCC imposes a **taking where there is no evidence of forgery, alteration, or irregularity requirement**. Under this rule, a holder does not qualify as an HDC if at the time the instrument was issued or negotiated to the holder, it bore apparent evidence of forgery or alteration or was otherwise so irregular or incomplete so as to call into question its authenticity [UCC 3-302(a)(1)].

Clever and undetectable forgeries and alterations are not classified as obvious irregularities. Determining whether a forgery or an alteration is apparent and whether the instrument is so irregular or incomplete that its authenticity should be questioned are issues of fact that must be decided on a case-by-case basis.

The following feature discusses a special UCC rule.

taking where there is no evidence of forgery, alteration, or irregularity requirement
A requirement that says a holder cannot become an HDC to an instrument that is apparently forged or altered or is otherwise so irregular or incomplete as to call into question its authenticity.

shelter principle
A principle that says a holder who does not qualify as a holder in due course in his or her own right becomes a holder in due course if he or she acquires an instrument through a holder in due course.

Contemporary Environment

Shelter Principle

A holder who does not qualify as a holder in due course in his or her own right becomes a holder in due course if he or she acquires the instrument through a holder in due course. This is called the **shelter principle**.

Example Gerhard buys a used car from Debbie. He pays 10 percent down and signs a negotiable promissory note, promising to pay Debbie the remainder of the purchase price, with interest, in 36 equal monthly installments. At the time of sale, Debbie materially misrepresented the mileage of the automobile. Later, Debbie negotiates the note to Eric, who has no notice of the misrepresentation. Eric, an HDC, negotiates the note to Jaime. Assume that Jaime does not qualify as an HDC in her own right. She becomes an HDC, however, because she acquired the note through an HDC (Eric). Jaime can enforce the note against Gerhard.

Key Terms and Concepts

Allonge (399)
Assignee (396)
Assignment (396)
Assignor (396)
Bearer instrument (bearer paper) (397)
Blank indorsement (400)
Dishonored instrument (406)
Good faith (406)
Holder (404)
Holder in due course (HDC) (405)
Indorsee (399)
Indorsement (399)
Indorsement for deposit or collection (402)
Indorsement in trust (agency indorsement) (402)
Indorser (399)
Negotiation (396)
Nonnegotiable contract (396)
Nonrestrictive indorsement (401)
Order instrument (order paper) (397)
Overdue time instrument (406)
Payable in the alternative (404)
Payable jointly (404)
Qualified indorsement (401)
Qualified indorser (401)
Restrictive indorsement (402)
Shelter principle (407)
Special indorsement (400)
Taking for value requirement (405)
Taking in good faith requirement (406)
Taking where there is no evidence of forgery, alteration, or irregularity requirement (407)
Taking without notice of defect requirement (406)
Time instrument (406)
Unqualified indorsement (401)
Unqualified indorser (401)
Virgule (404)

Critical Legal Thinking Cases

23.1 Payable Jointly Murray Walter, Inc. (Walter, Inc.) was a general contractor for the construction of a waste treatment plant in New Hampshire. Walter, Inc. contracted with H. Johnson Electric, Inc. (Johnson Electric) to install the electrical system in the treatment plant. Johnson Electric purchased its supplies for the project from General Electric Supply (G.E. Supply). Walter, Inc. issued a check payable to "Johnson Electric and G.E. Supply" in the amount of $54,900, drawn on its account at Marine Midland Bank (Marine Midland). Walter, Inc. made the check payable to both the subcontractor and its material supplier, to be certain that the supplier was paid by Johnson Electric. Despite this precautionary measure, Johnson Electric negotiated the check without G.E. Supply's indorsement, and the check was paid by Marine Midland. Johnson Electric never paid G.E. Supply. G.E. Supply then demanded payment from Walter, Inc. When Walter, Inc. learned that Marine Midland had paid the check without G.E. Supply's indorsement, it demanded to be reimbursed. When Marine Midland refused, Walter, Inc. sued Marine Midland to recover for the check. Was Johnson Electric's indorsement sufficient to legally negotiate the check to Marine Midland Bank? *Murray Walter, Inc. v. Marine Midland Bank*, 103 A.D.2d 466, 480 N.Y.S.2d 631, 1984 N.Y. App. Div. Lexis 19962 (Supreme Court of New York, 1984)

23.2 Assignment FFP Operating Partners, L.P. (FFP Operating) operates a number of convenience stores and gas stations. FFP Operating executed 31 promissory notes in favor of Franchise Mortgage Acceptance Company (FMAC). In connection with the notes, FFP Marketing Company, Inc. (FFP Marketing) executed guaranties of payment in favor of FMAC for all 31 notes. Loan and security agreements were also executed in connection with all 31 transactions. The promissory notes incorporated by reference the loan, security, and guaranty agreements, which included waivers, consents, and acknowledgments. Long Lane Master Trust IV (LLMT) became a successor in interest to FMAC with respect to the promissory notes, guaranties, and associated loan documents.

FFP Operating failed to make payments on the notes to LLMT. LLMT gave notice to FFP Operating of the default, accelerated the obligations under the promissory notes, and demanded payment. The notes went unpaid. The outstanding principal of the notes was $13,212,199, with unpaid interest of $1,488,899. LLMT filed suit against FFP Operating and FFP Marketing. LLMT filed a motion for summary judgment on its claim of default under the 31 promissory notes and guaranties for the amount due. FFP Operating declared bankruptcy and was dismissed from this case. The trial court entered summary judgment in favor of LLMT against FFP Marketing. FFP Marketing appealed.

Why does LLMT want the notes to be found to be negotiable instruments? Are the 31 promissory notes negotiable instruments that can be enforced against FFP Marketing? *FFP Marketing Company, Inc. v. Long Lane Master Trust IV*, 169 S.W.3d 402, 2005 Tex. App. Lexis 5277 (Court of Appeals of Texas, 2005)

Ethics Case

23.3 Ethics Case Samuel C. Mazilly wrote a personal check that was drawn on Calcasieu-Marine National Bank of Lake Charles, Inc. (CMN Bank). The check was made payable to the order of Lee St. Mary and was delivered to him. St. Mary indorsed the check in blank and delivered it to Leland H. Coltharp Sr. in payment for some livestock. Coltharp accepted the check and took it to the City Savings Bank & Trust Company (City Savings) to deposit it. He indorsed the check as follows: "Pay to the order of City Savings Bank & Trust Company, DeRidder, Louisiana." City Savings accepted the check and forwarded it to CMN Bank for payment. The check never arrived at CMN Bank. Some unknown person stole the check while it was in transit and presented it directly to CMN Bank for payment. The teller at CMN Bank cashed the check without indorsement of the person who presented it. When CMN Bank accepted the check, was it order or bearer paper? Has the person cashing the check acted unethically and has he acted illegally? *Coltharp v. Calcasieu-Marine National Bank of Lake Charles, Inc.*, 199 So.2d 568, 1967 La. App. Lexis 5203 (Court of Appeal of Louisiana, 1967)

CHAPTER

24 Liability, Defenses, and Discharge

Henry R. Cheeseman

HONG KONG

Hong Kong is one of the world's greatest banking centers. Hong Kong is home to large domestic banks and offices of foreign banks from around the world. Banks in Hong Kong provide a wide range of financial services, including retail banking, deposit taking, trade financing, interbank wholesale transfer, and foreign exchange.

Learning Objectives

After studying this chapter, you should be able to:

24.1 Describe signature liability for negotiable instruments.

24.2 Describe primary liability for negotiable instruments.

24.3 Describe secondary liability for negotiable instruments.

24.4 Describe liability for forged indorsements and explain the imposter rule and the fictitious payee rule.

24.5 Describe warranty liability for negotiable instruments.

24.6 List and describe transfer warranties.

24.7 List and describe presentment warranties.

24.8 Describe how defenses may be raised to the payment of negotiable instruments.

24.9 List and describe the universal (real) defenses that can be raised against holder in due course status.

24.10 List and describe personal defenses that can be raised against ordinary holders of negotiable instruments.

24.11 Describe how parties are discharged from liability on negotiable instruments.

> *If one wants to know the real value of money, he needs but to borrow some from his friends.*
>
> — *Confucius*
> *Analects (ca. 500 BCE)*

Introduction to Liability, Defenses, and Discharge

If payment is not made on a negotiable instrument when it is due, the holder can use the court system to enforce the instrument. Various parties, including both signers and nonsigners, may be liable on it. Some parties are primarily liable on the instrument, while others are secondarily liable. Accommodation parties (i.e., guarantors) can also be held liable.

Once a holder qualifies as a holder in due course (HDC), the HDC takes an instrument free of most defenses that can be asserted against other parties. However, several defenses, called *universal defenses*, can be raised against the payment of the instrument to the HDC. The Uniform Commercial Code (UCC) also specifies when and how certain parties are discharged from liability on negotiable instruments.

One cannot help regretting that where money is concerned it is too much the rule to overlook moral obligations.

Vice Chancellor Malins
Ellis v. Houston (1878)

This chapter discusses the liability of parties to pay a negotiable instrument, the defenses that can be raised against the HDC, and the discharge of liability on a negotiable instrument.

Signature Liability for Negotiable Instruments

24.1 Describe signature liability for negotiable instruments.

A person cannot be held contractually liable on a negotiable instrument unless his or her signature appears on it [UCC 3-401(a)]. Therefore, this type of liability is often referred to as **signature liability**, or **contract liability**. A signature on a negotiable instrument identifies who is obligated to pay it. The signature on a negotiable instrument can be any name, word, or mark used in lieu of a written signature [UCC 3-401(b)].

signature liability (contract liability)
Liability in which a person cannot be held contractually liable on a negotiable instrument unless his or her signature appears on the instrument.

Signers of instruments sign in many different capacities, as makers of notes or certificates of deposit, drawers of drafts or checks, drawees who certify or accept checks or drafts, indorsers who indorse instruments, agents who sign on behalf of others, and accommodation parties. The location of the signature on an instrument generally determines the signer's capacity.

signer
A person signing an instrument who acts in the capacity of (1) a maker of notes or certificates of deposit, (2) a drawer of drafts or checks, (3) a drawee who certifies or accepts checks or drafts, (4) an indorser who indorses an instrument, (5) an agent who signs on behalf of others, or (6) an accommodation party.

Examples A signature in the lower-right corner of a check indicates that the signer is the drawer of the check. A signature in the lower-right corner of a promissory note indicates that the signer is the maker of the note. The signature of the drawee named in a draft on the face of the draft or another location on the draft indicates that the signer is an acceptor of the draft.

Most indorsements appear on the back or reverse side of an instrument. Unless an instrument clearly indicates that such a signature is made in some other capacity (e.g., agents who properly sign the instrument), it is presumed to be that of the indorser. Every party that signs a negotiable instrument (except qualified indorsers and agents who properly sign the instrument) is either primarily or secondarily liable on the instrument.

Signature Defined

signature
Any name, word, or mark used in lieu of a written signature; any symbol that is (1) handwritten, typed, printed, stamped, or made in almost any other manner and (2) executed or adopted by a party to authenticate a writing.

The **signature** on a negotiable instrument can be any name, word, or mark used in lieu of a written signature [UCC 3-401(b)]. In other words, a signature is any symbol that is (1) handwritten, typed, printed, stamped, or made in almost any other manner and (2) executed or adopted by a party to authenticate a writing [UCC 1-201(39)]. This rule permits trade names and other assumed names to be used as signatures on negotiable instruments.

The unauthorized signature of a person on an instrument is ineffective as that person's signature. It is effective as the signature of the unauthorized signer in favor of an HDC, however. A person who forges a signature on a check may be held liable to an HDC. An unauthorized signature may be ratified [UCC 3-403(a)].

Primary Liability for Negotiable Instruments

24.2 Describe primary liability for negotiable instruments.

Makers of promissory notes and certificates of deposit have **primary liability** for the instruments. On signing a promissory note, the maker unconditionally promises to pay the amount stipulated in the note when it is due. A maker is absolutely liable to pay the instrument, subject only to certain universal (real) defenses. The holder need not take any action to give rise to this obligation. Generally, the maker is obligated to pay a note according to its original terms. If the note was incomplete when it was issued, the maker is obligated to pay the note as completed, as long as he or she authorized the terms as they were filled in [UCC 3-412].

primary liability
Absolute liability to pay a negotiable instrument, subject to certain universal (real) defenses.

A draft or a check is an order from a drawer to pay the instrument to a payee (or other holder) according to its terms. No party is primarily liable when the draft or check is issued because such instruments are merely orders to pay. Thus, a drawee that refuses to pay a draft or a check is not liable to the payee or holder. If there has been a wrongful dishonor of the instrument, the drawee may be liable to the drawer for certain damages.

On occasion, a drawee is requested to accept a draft or check. Acceptance of a draft occurs when the drawee writes the word *accepted* across the face of the draft. The acceptor—that is, the drawee—is primarily liable on the instrument. A check, which is a special form of draft, is accepted when it is certified by a bank. The bank's certification discharges the drawer and all prior indorsers from liability on the check. Note that the bank may choose to refuse to certify the check without liability. The issuer of a cashier's check is also primarily liable on the instrument [UCC 3-411].

The great source of the flourishing state of this kingdom is its trade, and commerce, and paper currency, guarded by proper regulations and restrictions, is the life of commerce.

Justice Ashhurst
Jordaine v. Lashbrooke (1798)

Secondary Liability for Negotiable Instruments

24.3 Describe secondary liability for negotiable instruments.

Under the UCC's *indorsers' liability* rules, drawers of checks and drafts and unqualified indorsers of negotiable instruments have **secondary liability** on the instruments. This liability is similar to that of a guarantor of a simple contract. It arises when the party primarily liable on the instrument defaults and fails to pay the instrument when due.

secondary liability
Liability on a negotiable instrument that is imposed on a party only when the party primarily liable on the instrument defaults and fails to pay the instrument when due.

If an unaccepted draft or check is dishonored by the drawee or acceptor, the drawer is obliged to pay it according to its terms, either when it is issued or, if incomplete when issued, when it is properly completed [UCC 3-414(a)].

Example Tuya draws a check on her checking account at City Bank "payable to the order of Phyllis Jones." When Phyllis presents the check for payment, City Bank refuses to pay it. Phyllis can collect the amount of the check from Tuya because Tuya—the drawer—is secondarily liable on the check when it is dishonored.

Unqualified Indorser

An **unqualified indorser** has secondary liability on negotiable instruments. In other words, he or she must pay any dishonored instrument to the holder or to any subsequent indorser according to its terms, when issued or properly

unqualified indorser
Those who are secondarily liable on negotiable instruments they indorse.

completed. Unless otherwise agreed, indorsers are liable to each other in the order in which they indorsed the instrument [UCC 3-415(a)].

Example Dara borrows $10,000 from Jorge and signs a promissory note, promising to pay Jorge this amount plus 10 percent interest in one year. Jorge indorses the note and negotiates it to Frank. Frank indorses the note and negotiates it to Linda. Linda presents the note to Dara for payment when the note is due. Dara refuses to pay the note. Because Frank became secondarily liable on the note when he indorsed it to Linda, he must pay the amount of the note—$11,000—to Linda. Frank can then require Jorge to pay the note to Frank because Jorge (as payee) became secondarily liable on the note when he indorsed it to Frank. Jorge can then enforce the note against Dara. Linda could have skipped over Frank and required the payee, Jorge, to pay the note. In this instance, Frank would have been relieved of any further liability because he indorsed the instrument after the payee.

Qualified Indorser

qualified indorser
One who disclaims liability and is not secondarily liable on instruments they indorse.

A **qualified indorser** (i.e., an indorser who indorses instruments "without recourse" or similar language that disclaims liability) is not secondarily liable on an instrument because he or she has expressly disclaimed liability [UCC 3-415(b)]. The drawer can disclaim all liability on a draft (but not a check) by drawing the instrument "without recourse." In this instance, the drawer becomes a qualified drawer [UCC 3-414(e)]. Many payees, however, will not accept a draft or check that has been drawn without recourse.

Requirements for Imposing Secondary Liability

A party is secondarily liable on a negotiable instrument only if the following requirements are met:

presentment
A demand for acceptance or payment of an instrument made on the maker, acceptor, drawee, or other payer by or on behalf of the holder.

- **The instrument is properly presented for payment.** **Presentment** is a demand for acceptance or payment of an instrument made upon the maker, acceptor, drawee, or other payer by or on behalf of the holder. Presentment may be made by any commercially reasonable means, including oral, written, or electronic communication. Presentment is effective when it is received by the person to whom presentment is made [UCC 3-501].
- **The instrument is dishonored.** An instrument is a **dishonored instrument** when acceptance or payment of the instrument is refused or cannot be obtained from the party required to accept or pay the instrument within the prescribed time after presentment is duly made [UCC 3-502].
- **Notice of the dishonor is timely given to the person to be held secondarily liable on the instrument.** A secondarily liable party cannot be compelled to accept or pay an instrument unless proper **notice of dishonor** has been given. Notice may be given by any commercially reasonable means. The notice must reasonably identify the instrument and indicate that it has been dishonored. Return of an instrument given to a bank for collection is sufficient notice of dishonor. Banks must give notice of dishonor before midnight of the next banking day following the day that presentment is made. Others must give notice of dishonor within 30 days following the day on which the person receives notice of dishonor [UCC 3-503].

notice of dishonor
The formal act of letting the party with secondary liability to pay a negotiable instrument know that the instrument has been dishonored.

Liability of an Accommodation Party

accommodation party
A party who signs an instrument and lends his or her name (and credit) to another party to the instrument.

A party who signs an instrument for the purpose of lending his or her name (and credit) to another party to the instrument is the **accommodation party**. The accommodation party, who may sign an instrument as maker, drawer, acceptor, or indorser, is obliged to *pay* the instrument in the capacity in which he or she signs [UCC 3-419(a),(b)]. An accommodation party who pays an instrument can recover reimbursement from the accommodated party and enforce the instrument against him or her [UCC 3-419(e)].

There are two types of liability of an accommodation party:

1. **Guarantee of payment.** An accommodation party who signs an instrument and **guarantees payment** is *primarily liable* on the instrument. This party is called an **accommodation maker**. That is, the debtor can seek payment on the instrument directly from the accommodation maker without first seeking payment from the maker.

   Example Decha, a college student, wants to purchase an automobile on credit from ABC Motors. He does not have a sufficient income or credit history to justify the extension of credit to him alone. Decha asks his mother to cosign the note to ABC Motors, which she does. Decha's mother is an accommodation maker and is primarily liable on the note.

2. **Guarantee of collection.** An accommodation party may sign an instrument that **guarantees collection** rather than that guarantees payment of an instrument. This party is called an **accommodation indorser**. In this situation, the accommodation indorser is only *secondarily liable* on the instrument. To reserve this type of liability, the signature of the accommodation party must be accompanied by words indicating that he or she is guaranteeing collection rather than payment of the obligation. An accommodation party who guarantees collection is obliged to pay the instrument only if (1) execution of judgment against the other party has been returned unsatisfied, (2) the other party is insolvent or in an insolvency proceeding, (3) the other party cannot be served with process, or (4) it is otherwise apparent that payment cannot be obtained from the other party [UCC 3-419(d)].

guarantee of payment
A form of accommodation in which the accommodation party guarantees *payment* of a negotiable instrument; the accommodation party is *primarily liable* on the instrument.

guarantee of collection
A form of accommodation in which the accommodation party guarantees *collection* of a negotiable instrument; the accommodation party is *secondarily liable* on the instrument.

CONCEPT SUMMARY

LIABILITY OF ACCOMMODATION MAKER AND ACCOMMODATION INDORSER COMPARED

Accommodation Party	Contract Liability
Accommodation maker	Primarily liable on the instrument
Accommodation indorser	Secondarily liable on the instrument

Agent's Signature

A person may either sign a negotiable instrument personally or authorize a representative to sign the instrument on his or her behalf [UCC 3-401(a)]. The representative is the **agent**, and the represented person is the **principal**. The authority of an agent to sign an instrument is established under general agency law. No special form of appointment is necessary. If an authorized agent signs an instrument with either the principal's name or the agent's own name, the principal is bound as if the signature were made on a simple contract. It does not matter whether the principal is identified in the instrument [UCC 3-402(2)].

agent
A person who has been authorized to sign a negotiable instrument on behalf of another person.

principal
A person who authorizes an agent to sign a negotiable instrument on his or her behalf.

Example Suppose Anderson is the agent for Puttkammer. The following signatures on a negotiable instrument would bind Puttkammer on the instrument:

1. Puttkammer, by Anderson, agent
2. Puttkammer
3. Puttkammer, Anderson
4. Anderson

An authorized agent's personal liability on an instrument signed on behalf of a principal depends on the information disclosed in the signature. The agent has no liability if the signature shows unambiguously that it is made on behalf of a principal who is identified in the instrument [UCC 3-402(b)(1)].

Example Signature number 1 ("Puttkammer, by Anderson, agent") satisfies this requirement.

If an authorized agent's signature does not show unambiguously that the signature was made in a representative capacity and the agent cannot prove that the original parties did not intend the agent to be liable, the agent is liable (1) to an HDC who took the instrument without notice that the agent was not intended to be liable on the instrument and (2) to any other person other than an HDC [UCC 3-402(b)(2)].

Examples Signature number 2 ("Puttkammer") does not show unambiguously that the signature was made in a representative capacity. Signatures number 3 ("Puttkammer, Anderson") and 4 ("Anderson") place the agent at risk of personal liability to an HDC that does not have notice that the agent was not intended to be liable on the instrument. To avoid liability to a non-HDC for these signatures, the agent would have to prove that the third-party non-HDC did not intend to hold the agent liable on the instrument.

There is one exception to these rules: If an agent signs as the drawer of a check without indicating the agent's representative status and the check is payable from the account of the principal who is identified on the check, the agent is not liable on the check [UCC 3-402(c)].

Unauthorized Signature

unauthorized signature
A signature made by a purported agent without authority from the purported principal.

An **unauthorized signature** is a signature made by a purported agent without authority from the purported principal. Such a signature arises if (1) a person signs a negotiable instrument on behalf of a person for whom he or she is not an agent or (2) an authorized agent exceeds the scope of his or her authority. An unauthorized signature by a purported agent does not act as the signature of the purported principal. The purported agent is liable to any person who in good faith pays the instrument or takes it for value [UCC 3-403(a)]. The purported principal is liable if he or she ratifies the unauthorized signature [UCC 3-403(a)].

Example Max, a purported agent, signs a contract and promissory note to purchase a building for ViVi, a purported principal. Suppose that ViVi, the purported principal, likes the deal and accepts it. ViVi has ratified the transaction and is liable on the note.

Forged Indorsements

24.4 Describe liability for forged indorsements and explain the imposter rule and the fictitious payee rule.

forged indorsement
The forged signature of a payee or holder on a negotiable instrument.

Article 3 of the UCC establishes certain rules for assessing liability when a negotiable instrument has been paid over a **forged indorsement**. Generally, an unauthorized indorsement is wholly inoperative as the indorsement of the person whose name is signed [UCC 3-401(a)]. Where an indorsement on an instrument has been forged or is unauthorized, the loss falls on the party who first takes the forged instrument after the forgery.

Example Ivan draws a check payable to the order of Mallory. Leslie steals the check from Mallory, forges Mallory's indorsement, and cashes the check at a liquor store. The liquor store is liable. Ivan, the drawer, is not. The liquor store can recover from Leslie, the forger (if she can be found).

There are two exceptions to this general rule: (1) the *imposter rule* and (2) the *fictitious payee rule*. These rules are discussed in the following two ethics features.

imposter rule
A rule that states that if an imposter forges the indorsement of the named payee, the drawer or maker is liable on the instrument to any person who, in good faith, pays the instrument or takes it for value or for collection.

Ethics

Imposter Rule

An *imposter* is someone who impersonates a payee and induces the maker or drawer to issue an instrument in the payee's name and give the instrument to the imposter. If the imposter forges the indorsement of the named payee, the drawer or maker is liable on the instrument to any person who, in good faith, pays the instrument or takes it for value or for collection [UCC 3-404(a)]. This rule is called the **imposter rule**.

Example Zion purchases goods by telephone from Cynthia. Zion has never met Cynthia. Beverly goes to Zion and pretends to be Cynthia. Zion draws a check payable to the order of Cynthia and gives the check to Beverly, believing her to be Cynthia. Beverly forges Cynthia's indorsement and cashes the check at a store. Under the imposter rule, Zion is liable and the store is not because Zion was in the best position to have prevented the forged indorsement.

Ethics Questions
Does an imposter act ethically? What is the public policy underlying the imposter rule?

Ethics

Fictitious Payee Rule

A drawer or maker is liable on a forged or unauthorized indorsement under the **fictitious payee rule**. This rule applies when a person signing as or on behalf of a drawer or maker intends the named payee to have no interest in the instrument or when the person identified as the payee is a fictitious person [UCC 3-404(b)].

Example Marcia is the treasurer of Weld Corporation. As treasurer, Marcia makes out and signs the payroll checks for the company. Marcia draws a payroll check payable to the order of her neighbor Harold Green, who does not work for the company. Marcia does not intend Harold to receive this money. She indorses Harold's name on the check and names herself as the indorsee. She cashes the check at a store. Under the fictitious payee rule, Weld Corporation is liable because it was in a better position than the store to have prevented the fraud.

Ethics Questions
Does a fictitious payee act ethically? What is the public policy underlying the fictitious payee rule?

Warranty Liability for Negotiable Instruments

24.5 Describe warranty liability for negotiable instruments.

In addition to signature liability, transferors can be held liable for breaching certain **implied warranties** when negotiating instruments. **Warranty liability** is imposed whether or not the transferor signed the instrument. Note that a transferor makes an implied warranty; implied warranties are not made when a negotiable instrument is originally issued.

There are two types of implied warranties: *transfer warranties* and *presentment warranties*. Transfer and presentment warranties shift the risk of loss to the party who was in the best position to prevent the loss. This party is usually the one who dealt face-to-face with the wrongdoer.

These implied warranties are discussed in the paragraphs that follow.

fictitious payee rule
A rule that states that a drawer or maker is liable on a forged or unauthorized indorsement if the person signing as or on behalf of a drawer or maker intends the named payee to have no interest in the instrument or when the person identified as the payee is a fictitious person.

implied warranties
Certain warranties that the law implies on transferors of negotiable instruments. There are two types of implied warranties: transfer and presentment warranties.

Transfer Warranties

24.6 List and describe transfer warranties.

Any passage of an instrument other than its issuance and presentment for payment is considered a **transfer**. Any person who transfers a negotiable instrument for

transfer
Any passage of an instrument other than its issuance and presentment for payment.

transfer warranties
The following five implied warranties made by any person who transfers a negotiable instrument for consideration to a transferee who took the instrument in good faith: (1) The transferor has good title to the instrument or is authorized to obtain payment or acceptance on behalf of one who does have good title, (2) all signatures are genuine or authorized, (3) the instrument has not been materially altered, (4) no defenses of any party are good against the transferor, and (5) the transferor has no knowledge of any insolvency proceeding against the maker, the acceptor, or the drawer of an unaccepted instrument.

consideration makes the following five **transfer warranties** to the transferee. If the transfer is by indorsement, the transferor also makes these warranties to any subsequent transferee [UCC 3-416(a)]:

1. The transferor has good title to the instrument or is authorized to obtain payment or acceptance on behalf of one who does have good title.
2. All signatures are genuine or authorized.
3. The instrument has not been materially altered.
4. No defenses of any party are good against the transferor.
5. The transferor has no knowledge of any insolvency proceeding against the maker, the acceptor, or the drawer of an unaccepted instrument.

Transfer warranties cannot be disclaimed with respect to checks, but they can be disclaimed with respect to other instruments. An indorsement that states "without recourse" disclaims the transfer warranties [UCC 3-419(c)]. A transferee who took the instrument in good faith may recover damages for breach of transfer warranty from the warrantor equal to the loss suffered. The amount recovered cannot exceed the amount of the instrument plus expenses and interest [UCC 3-416(b)].

Example Bianca signs a promissory note to pay $1,000 to Adam. Adam cleverly raises the note to $10,000 and negotiates the note to Nickolas. Nickolas indorses the note and negotiates it to Matthew. When Matthew presents the note to Bianca for payment, Bianca has to pay only the original amount of the note, $1,000. Matthew can collect the remainder of the note ($9,000) from Nickolas, based on a breach of the transfer warranty. If Nickolas is lucky, he can recover the $9,000 from Adam.

Presentment Warranties

24.7 List and describe presentment warranties.

presentment warranties
Three implied warranties that a person who presents a draft or check for payment or acceptance makes to a drawee or an acceptor who pays or accepts the instrument in good faith: (1) The presenter has good title to the instrument or is authorized to obtain payment or acceptance of the person who has good title, (2) the instrument has not been materially altered, and (3) the presenter has no knowledge that the signature of the maker or drawer is unauthorized.

Any person who presents a draft or check for payment or acceptance makes the following **presentment warranties** to a drawee or an acceptor who pays or accepts the instrument in good faith [UCC 3-417(a)]:

1. The presenter has good title to the instrument or is authorized to obtain payment or acceptance of the person who has good title.
2. The instrument has not been materially altered.
3. The presenter has no knowledge that the signature of the maker or drawer is unauthorized.

A drawee who pays an instrument may recover damages for breach of presentment warranty from the warrantor. The amount that can be recovered is limited to the amount paid by the drawee less the amount the drawee received or is entitled to receive from the drawer because of the payment plus expenses and interest [UCC 3-147(b)].

Example Maureen draws a $1,000 check on City Bank "payable to the order of Paul." Paul cleverly raises the check to $10,000 and indorses and negotiates the check to Napoleon. Napoleon presents the check for payment to City Bank. As the presenter of the check, Napoleon makes the presentment warranties of UCC 3-417(a) to City Bank. City Bank pays the check as altered ($10,000) and debits Maureen's account. When Maureen discovers the alteration, she demands that the bank recredit her account, which the bank does. City Bank can recover against the presenter (Napoleon), based on breach of the presentment warranty that the instrument was not altered when it was presented. Napoleon can recover against the wrongdoer (Paul), based on breach of the transfer warranty that the instrument was not altered.

Defenses to Payment of Negotiable Instruments

24.8 Describe how defenses may be raised to the payment of negotiable instruments.

The creation of negotiable instruments may give rise to defenses against their payment. Many of these defenses arise from the underlying transactions. There are two general types of defenses: (1) *universal (real) defenses* and (2) *personal defenses*. A **holder in due course (HDC)** (or a holder through an HDC) takes an instrument free from personal defenses but not universal defenses. Personal and universal defenses can be raised against a normal **holder** of a negotiable instrument. Universal defenses and personal defenses are discussed in the following paragraphs.

Universal (Real) Defenses

24.9 List and describe the universal (real) defenses that can be raised against holder in due course status.

Universal defenses (also called **real defenses**) can be raised against both ordinary *holders* and *holders in due course* to deny the payment of negotiable instruments [UCC 3-305(b)]. If a universal defense is proven, the holder or HDC cannot recover on the negotiable instrument. The most important universal defenses are the following:

universal defense (real defense)
A defense that can be raised against both holders and HDCs.

1. **Minority** A *minor* who does not misrepresent his or her age can disaffirm negotiable instruments that the minor has issued if state law permits the minor to disaffirm simple contracts under the *infancy doctrine* [UCC 3-305(a)(1)(i)].
2. **Extreme duress** *Extreme duress* requires force or violence. If extreme duress was used to have a negotiable instrument issued (e.g., a promissory note was signed at gunpoint), then it is unenforceable [UCC 3-305(a)(1)(ii)]. (Ordinary duress is a personal defense.)
3. **Mental incapacity** A person *adjudicated mentally incompetent* by a court or other appropriate government agency cannot issue a negotiable instrument; the instrument is *void* and therefore unenforceable from its inception [UCC 3-305(a)(1)(ii)]. (Nonadjudicated mental incompetence is a personal defense.)
4. **Illegality** If an instrument arises out of an *illegal transaction*, it is unenforceable if the law declares the instrument void [UCC 3-305(a)(1)(ii)].

   Example Assume that a state's law declares gambling to be illegal and gambling contracts to be void. Gordon wins $5,000 from Jerry in an illegal poker game. Jerry, who does not have cash to immediately cover his debt, signs a promissory note promising to pay Gordon this amount plus 10 percent interest in 30 days. Gordon negotiates this note to DeLeon, an HDC. When DeLeon presents the note to Jerry for payment, Jerry raises the universal defense of illegality against the enforcement of the note by DeLeon. DeLeon's only recourse is against Gordon.

5. **Discharge in bankruptcy** Bankruptcy law is designed to relieve debtors of burdensome debts, including paying negotiable instruments. Negotiable instruments *discharged in bankruptcy* are thereafter unenforceable [UCC 3-305(a)(1)(iv).
6. **Fraud in the inception** If a person is deceived into signing a negotiable instrument, thinking that it is something else, this is *fraud in the inception* (also called *fraud in the factum* or *fraud in the execution*). An instrument obtained by fraud in the inception is unenforceable [UCC 3-305(a)(1)(iii)].

Critical Legal Thinking Questions

What is a universal (real) defense? What are the consequences to a holder in due course (HDC) if a universal defense is proven? Can HDCs protect themselves from universal defenses?

One cannot help regretting that where money is concerned it is too much the rule to overlook moral obligations.

Vice Chancellor Malins
Ellis v. Houston (1878)

7. **Forgery** *Forgery* occurs where a party places the unauthorized signature of a maker, a drawer, or an indorser on an instrument. Because the signature is wholly inoperative as that of the person whose name is signed, the instrument is unenforceable [UCC 3-403(a)]. A forged signature operates as the signature of the forger, who is liable on the instrument.
8. **Material alteration** **Material alteration** consists of adding to any part of a signed instrument, removing any part of a signed instrument, or making changes to the dollar amount of the instrument. An instrument that has been fraudulently and materially altered cannot be enforced by an ordinary holder. HDCs cannot enforce such an instrument if the alteration is apparent or obvious [UCC 3-407(b)].

Personal Defenses

24.10 List and describe personal defenses that can be raised against ordinary holders of negotiable instruments.

personal defense
A defense that can be raised against enforcement of a negotiable instrument by an ordinary holder but not against an HDC.

Personal defenses can be raised against *ordinary holders* to deny the payment of negotiable instruments [UCC 3-305(b)]. Thus, if a personal defense is proven, the holder cannot recover on the negotiable instrument. However, personal defenses cannot be raised against *HDCs* to deny the payment of negotiable instruments [UCC 3-305(b)]. Thus, even if a personal defense is proven, the HDC can still recover on the negotiable instrument. The most important personal defenses are the following:

1. **Breach of contract** If a negotiable instrument arises from a transaction where there has been a *breach of contract*, the negotiable instrument is unenforceable by a holder but is enforceable by an HDC.

   Example Minh purchases a used car from Karen and signs a promissory note promising to pay Karen the purchase price plus interest over three years. Karen, the seller, warrants that the car is in perfect working condition. A month later, the car's engine fails; the cost of repair is $5,000. Minh can raise the defense of breach of contract against Karen's attempt to enforce the negotiable instrument against him. However, if Karen negotiated the promissory note to Max, an HDC, Minh could not raise Karen's breach of warranty against Max, and Minh would have to pay the amount of the promissory note to Max. Minh's only recourse then would be to seek recovery for breach of warranty against Karen.

Critical Legal Thinking Questions

What is a personal defense? What are the consequences to a holder in due course (HDC) if a personal defense is proven? Compare this to the consequence of finding a universal defense.

2. **Fraud in the inducement** *Fraud in the inducement* occurs when a wrongdoer makes a false statement to another person to lead that person to enter into a contract with the wrongdoer and issue a negotiable instrument. Fraud in the inducement makes a negotiable instrument unenforceable by an ordinary holder but enforceable by an HDC.

   Example Heather represents to potential investors that if they pay her money that she will invest it for them and pay them interest on their investment. Heather, however, plans to use the money for her personal means. John draws a $50,000 check payable to Heather. John learns of Heather's plan, and stops payment on the check. Here, Heather is only a holder so John can raise the defense of fraud in the inception and not pay the check. However, if Heather negotiated the check to Manuel, an HDC, John could not raise Heather's fraud in the inception against Manuel, and John would have to pay the amount of the check to Manuel. John's only recourse then would be to seek recovery against Heather.

3. **Mental illness that makes a contract voidable instead of void** If mental illness is found that makes a contract *voidable* rather than void—because the drawer or maker is mentally ill but has not been adjudicated mentally ill (*nonadjudicated mentally incompetent*)—then the negotiable instrument is unenforceable by a holder but is enforceable by an HDC.

4. **Illegality of a contract that makes the contract voidable instead of void** If a contract is found to be illegal but the illegality makes the contract only *voidable* rather than void, then the negotiable instrument is unenforceable by a holder but is enforceable by an HDC.
5. **Ordinary duress or undue influence** If a person is wrongfully influenced or threatened to enter into a negotiable instrument, but the pressure is only *ordinary duress* or *undue influence* and does not amount to extreme duress, it is unenforceable by a holder but is enforceable by an HDC [UCC 3-305(a)(1)(ii)].
6. **Discharge of an instrument by payment or cancellation** If an instrument is discharged by payment or cancellation, it is unenforceable by a holder but is enforceable by an HDC.

In the following case, the court had to decide if a defense could be asserted against an HDC.

CASE 24.1 *FEDERAL COURT CASE Holder in Due Course*

Bank of Colorado v. Berwick

2011 U.S. Dist. Lexis 34373 (2011)
United States District Court for the District of Colorado

"The Court finds that Las Vegas Sands was a holder in due course."

—Christine Arguello, District Judge

Facts

Ron Bryant wanted money to obtain promotional premiums from the Venetian Resort Hotel Casino located in Las Vegas, Nevada. The Venetian is owned by Las Vegas Sands, LLC (Sands). James Berwick agreed to supply the funds to Bryant in return for a promise by Bryant to repay Berwick the next day. On October 29, 2008, Berwick purchased a cashier's check (check) in the amount of $250,000 from Bank of Colorado made payable to Ron Bryant. Thus, Bank of Colorado held $250,000 of Berwick's money until the check was presented for payment, at which time it would pay the check. Berwick transferred the check to Bryant.

The next day, October 30, Bryant presented the check to the Sands, who paid him the $250,000 value of the check. On the following day, October 31, Bryant did not repay Berwick the $250,000. On November 3, unbeknownst to the Sands, Berwick stopped payment on the check, alleging to Bank of Colorado that the check had been lost. Berwick knew that the check had not been lost. Berwick filed a police report with the Las Vegas Metro Police Department stating that Bryant had misappropriated the $250,000.

On November 8, the Sands deposited the check at its bank, but when the check was presented to the Bank of Colorado for payment it refused to pay the check because of Berwick's stop payment order. In a lawsuit in the U.S. district court, both Berwick and the Sands claimed the right to be paid the funds. The Bank of Colorado agreed to hold the funds until the court determined to whom the funds should be paid. The Sands alleged that it was a holder in due course and that Bryant's fraud on Berwick was fraud in the inducement, a personal defense that could not be raised against an HDC. Berwick claimed that he was due the funds because of his stop payment order.

Issue

Is the Sands an HDC against whom the personal defense of fraud in the inducement cannot be raised?

Language of the Court

The Court finds that Las Vegas Sands was a holder in due course. The Court finds that Las Vegas Sands is entitled to the amount of the check because it received the check in good faith and for value, without knowledge of Bryant's alleged fraudulent scheme against Berwick. Therefore, the loss must fall on Berwick; his recourse is against Bryant, who defrauded him.

Decision

The U.S. district court held that Las Vegas Sands was a holder in due course and that Bryant's fraud on Berwick was fraud in the inducement, a personal defense that could not be raised against an HDC.

Critical Legal Thinking Questions

Did Bryant act ethically? Did Berwick act ethically in trying to place his loss on the Sands?

The following feature discusses a federal consumer protection rule that affects negotiable instruments.

Contemporary Environment

FTC Rule Limits HDC Status in Consumer Transactions

In certain situations, the HDC rule can cause a hardship for consumers who sign negotiable instruments, usually promissory notes, in conjunction with the purchase of goods. If the consumer has a legitimate claim against the seller of a defective product who has negotiated the promissory note to another party, the consumer cannot raise this claim against an HDC seeking enforcement on the negotiable instrument.

To correct this harsh result, the **Federal Trade Commission (FTC)**, a federal administrative agency in charge of consumer protection, adopted the **FTC HDC rule** pursuant to its federal statutory powers. The FTC HDC rule eliminates HDC status regarding negotiable instruments arising out of certain *consumer* credit transactions.[1] This federal law takes precedence over any state's UCC.

Example Gustaf, a consumer, purchases a television on credit from Lou's Electronics. He signs a note, promising to pay the purchase price plus interest to Lou's Electronics in 12 equal monthly installments. Lou's Electronics immediately negotiates the note at a discount to City Bank for cash. City Bank is an HDC. The television is defective. Gustaf would like to stop paying for it, but under the UCC Gustaf cannot assert the personal defense of the defectiveness of a product against City Bank, an HDC, from collecting on the note. Under the UCC, Gustaf's only recourse is to sue Lou's Electronics. However, this is often an unsatisfactory result because Gustaf has no leverage against Lou's Electronics, and bringing a court action is expensive and time-consuming. However, because the FTC HDC rule eliminates HDC status for negotiable instruments arising out of consumer transactions, Gustaf can assert the otherwise personal defense of the defectiveness of the product against enforcement of the promissory note by City Bank, an HDC.

FTC HDC rule
A rule adopted by the Federal Trade Commission (FTC) that eliminates HDC status with regard to negotiable instruments that arise out of certain consumer credit transactions.

discharge
Actions or events that relieve certain parties from liability on negotiable instruments. There are three methods of discharge: (1) payment of the instrument, (2) cancellation, and (3) impairment of the right of recourse.

Critical Legal Thinking Questions
How does the FTC HDC rule affect the rights of a holder in due course (HDC)? What public policy supports this rule?

Discharge of Liability

24.11 Describe how parties are discharged from liability on negotiable instruments.

The UCC specifies when and how certain parties are **discharged** (relieved) from liability on negotiable instruments. Generally, all parties to a negotiable instrument are discharged from liability if (1) the party primarily liable on the instrument pays it in full to the holder of the instrument or (2) a drawee in good faith pays an unaccepted draft or check in full to the holder. When a party other than a primary obligor (e.g., an indorser) pays a negotiable instrument, that party and all subsequent parties to the instrument are discharged from liability [UCC 3-602].

The holder of a negotiable instrument can discharge the liability of any party to the instrument by **cancellation** [UCC 3-604]. Cancellation can be accomplished by (1) any manner apparent on the face of the instrument or the indorsement (e.g., writing *canceled* on the instrument) or (2) destruction or mutilation of a negotiable instrument with the intent of eliminating the obligation.

Intentionally striking out the signature of an indorser cancels that party's liability on the instrument and the liability of all subsequent indorsers. Prior indorsers are not discharged from liability. The instrument is not canceled if it is destroyed or mutilated by accident or by an unauthorized third party. The holder can bring suit to enforce the destroyed or mutilated instrument.

A party to a negotiable instrument sometimes posts collateral as security for the payment of the obligation. Other parties (e.g., holders, indorsers, accommodation parties) look to the credit standing of the party primarily liable on the instrument, the collateral (if any) that is posted, and the liability of secondary parties for the payment of the instrument when it is due. A holder owes a duty not to impair the rights of others when seeking recourse against the liable parties or the collateral. Thus, a holder who either (1) releases an obligor from liability or (2) surrenders the collateral without the consent of the parties who would benefit thereby discharges those parties from their obligation on the instrument [UCC 3-605(e)]. This discharge is called **impairment of the right of recourse**.

Key Terms and Concepts

Accommodation indorser (413)
Accommodation maker (413)
Accommodation party (412)
Agent (413)
Cancellation (420)
Discharge (420)
Dishonored instrument (412)
Federal Trade Commission (FTC) (420)
Fictitious payee rule (415)
Forged indorsement (414)
FTC HDC rule (420)
Guarantee of collection (413)
Guarantee of payment (413)
Holder (417)
Holder in due course (HDC) (417)
Impairment of the right of recourse (420)
Implied warranties (415)
Imposter rule (415)
Material alteration (418)
Notice of dishonor (412)
Personal defenses (418)
Presentment (412)
Presentment warranties (416)
Primary liability (411)
Principal (413)
Qualified indorser (412)
Secondary liability (411)
Signature (410)
Signature liability (contract liability) (410)
Signer (410)
Transfer (415)
Transfer warranties (416)
Unauthorized signature (414)
Universal defense (real defense) (417)
Unqualified indorser (411)
Warranty liability (415)

Critical Legal Thinking Cases

24.1 Transfer Warranty David M. Fox was a distributor of tools manufactured and sold by Matco Tools Corporation (Matco). Cox purchased tools from Matco, using a credit line that he repaid as the tools were sold. The credit line was secured by Cox's Matco tool inventory. In order to expedite payment on Cox's line of credit, Matco decided to authorize Cox to deposit any customer checks that were made payable to "Matco Tools" or "Matco" into Cox's own account. Matco's controller sent Cox's bank, Pontiac State Bank (Pontiac), a letter stating that Cox was authorized to make such deposits. Several years later, some Matco tools were stolen from Cox's inventory. The Travelers Indemnity Company (Travelers), which insured Cox against such a loss, sent Cox a settlement check in the amount of $24,960. The check was made payable to "David M. Cox and Matco Tool Co." Cox indorsed the check and deposited it in his account at Pontiac. Pontiac forwarded the check through the banking system for payment by the drawee bank. Cox never paid Matco for the stolen tools. Matco sued Pontiac for accepting the check without the proper indorsements. Is Pontiac liable? *Matco Tools Corporation v. Pontiac State Bank*. 614 F.Supp. 1059, 1985 U.S. Dist. Lexis 17234 (United States District Court for the Eastern District of Michigan, 1985)

24.2 Presentment Warranty John Waddell Construction Company (Waddell) maintained a checking account at the Longview Bank & Trust Company (Longview Bank). Waddell drafted a check from this account made payable to two payees, Engineered Metal Works (Metal Works) and E. G. Smith Construction (Smith Construction). The check was sent to Metal Works, which promptly indorsed the check and presented it to the First National Bank of Azle (Bank of Azle) for payment. The Bank of Azle accepted the check with only the indorsement of Metal Works and credited it to the account of Metal Works.

The Bank of Azle subsequently presented the check to Longview Bank through the Federal Reserve System. Longview Bank accepted and paid the check. When Waddell received the check along with its monthly checking statements from Longview Bank, a company employee noticed the missing indorsement and notified Longview Bank. Longview Bank returned the check to the Bank of Azle, and the Bank of Azle's account was debited the amount of the check at the Federal Reserve. Has the Bank of Azle breached its warranty of good title? *Longview Bank & Trust Company v. First National Bank of Azle*, 750 S.W.2d 297, 1988 Tex. App. Lexis 1377 (Court of Appeals of Texas, 1988)

Ethics Case

24.3 Ethics Case Grand Island Production Credit Association (Grand Island) is a federally chartered credit union. Carl M. and Beulah C. Humphrey, husband and wife, entered into a loan arrangement with Grand Island for a $50,000 line of credit. Mr. and Mrs. Humphrey signed a line of credit promissory note that provided, in part, "As long as the Borrower is not in default, the Association will lend to the Borrower, and the Borrower may borrow and repay and reborrow at any time from date of said 'Line of Credit' Promissory

Note in accordance with the terms thereof and prior to maturity thereof, up to an aggregate maximum amount of principal at any one time outstanding of $50,000."

Mr. Humphrey borrowed money against the line of credit to purchase cattle. Two months later, Mrs. Humphrey went to Grand Island's office and told the loan officer that she had left Mr. Humphrey and filed for divorce. She told the loan officer not to advance any more money to Mr. Humphrey for his cattle purchases. When the Humphreys failed to pay the outstanding balance on the line of credit, Grand Island sued Mr. and Mrs. Humphrey to recover the unpaid balance of $13,936.71. Is Mrs. Humphrey a co-maker of the line of credit promissory note and, therefore, primarily liable for the outstanding principal balance of the note, plus interest? Is it ethical for Mrs. Humphrey to deny liability on the promissory note in this case? *Grand Island Production Credit Association v. Humphrey*, 388 N.W.2d 807, 1986 Neb. Lexis 1185 (Supreme Court of Nebraska, 1986)

Note

1. 16 C.F.R. 433.2 (1987).

CHAPTER 25

Banking System and Electronic Financial Transactions

Henry R. Cheeseman

FEDERAL RESERVE, WASHINGTON DC
The Federal Reserve System (also known as the Federal Reserve or the Fed) was created by Congress as the central bank of the United States. The Federal Reserve has many functions, including setting monetary policy and being a check clearing system for banks.

Learning Objectives

After studying this chapter, you should be able to:

25.1 Describe the bank–customer relationship.

25.2 Describe ordinary checks and identify the parties to an ordinary check.

25.3 List and describe special forms of checks and identify the parties to these checks.

25.4 Describe when a bank must honor a check.

25.5 Identify what parties are liable for altered and forged checks.

25.6 Describe the Federal Reserve System and the collection process for checks.

25.7 Describe bank payment rules, including posting and settlement.

25.8 List and describe the various forms of electronic and online banking, cryptocurrency, and mobile payment apps.

25.9 Describe banking reform measures.

> *"Bankers have no right to establish a customary law among themselves, at the expense of other men."*
>
> — *Justice Foster*
> *Hankey v. Trotman (1746)*

Introduction to the Banking System and Electronic Financial Transactions

Money is a good servant, but a dangerous master.
Dominique Bouhours (1628–1702)

Checks are the most common form of negotiable instrument used in this country. Checks act both as substitutes for money and as record-keeping devices. There are many special forms of checks, including certified checks and cashier's checks.

The banking system is made up of international, national, regional, and community banks. Banks are highly regulated financial institutions. Banks, with the assistance of the Federal Reserve System, process checks.

Many banking transactions occur online and electronically. These include wire transfers of money, interbank transfers, and electronic consumer transactions. Financial technology, also referred to a "fintech," refers to companies that offer innovative digital financial services to customers.

This chapter discusses checks, the banking system, the regulation of financial institutions, electronic and online banking, cryptocurrency, mobile payment apps, and bank reform.

The Bank–Customer Relationship

25.1 Describe the bank–customer relationship.

creditor–debtor relationship
A relationship that is created when a customer deposits money into the bank; the customer is the creditor, and the bank is the debtor.

When a customer makes a deposit into a bank, a **creditor–debtor relationship** is formed. The customer is the *creditor* and the bank is the *debtor*. In effect, the customer is loaning money to the bank.

A **principal–agent relationship** is created if (1) the deposit is a check that the bank must collect for the customer or (2) the customer writes a check against his or her account. The customer is the *principal* and the bank is the *agent*. The bank is obligated to follow the customer's order to collect or pay the check. The rights and duties of a bank and a checking account customer are contractual. The signature card and other bank documents signed by the customer form the contract.

Uniform Commercial Code Governs Checks and Banking

Article 3 (Commercial Paper)
An article of the UCC that sets forth the requirements for negotiable instruments, including checks.

Revised Article 3 (Negotiable Instruments)
A revision of Article 3 of the UCC.

Article 4 (Bank Deposits and Collections)
An article of the UCC that establishes the rules and principles that regulate bank deposit and collection procedures.

Article 4A (Funds Transfers)
An article of the UCC that establishes rules regulating the creation and collection of and liability for wire transfers.

Various articles of the **Uniform Commercial Code (UCC)** establish rules for creating, collecting, and enforcing checks and wire transfers. These articles are the following:

- **Article 3 (Commercial Paper).** **Article 3 (Commercial Paper)** establishes the requirements for negotiable instruments. Because a check is a negotiable instrument, the provisions of Article 3 apply. **Revised Article 3 (Negotiable Instruments)** was promulgated in 1990. The provisions of Revised Article 3 serve as the basis of the discussion of Article 3 in this chapter.
- **Article 4 (Bank Deposits and Collections).** **Article 4 (Bank Deposits and Collections)** establishes the rules and principles that regulate bank deposit and collection procedures for checking accounts offered by commercial banks and check-like accounts offered by other financial institutions. Article 4 was substantially amended in 1990. The amended Article 4 serves as the basis of the discussion of Article 4 in this chapter.
- **Article 4A (Funds Transfers).** **Article 4A (Funds Transfers)** establishes rules that regulate the creation and collection of and liability for wire transfers.

Article 4A was added to the UCC in 1989. Article 4A serves as the basis of the discussion of fuds transfers in this chapter.

Ordinary Checks

25.2 Describe ordinary checks and identify the parties to an ordinary check.

Most adults and businesses have at least one checking account at a bank. A customer opens a checking account by going to a bank, completing the necessary forms (including a signature card), and making a **deposit** to the account. The bank issues checks to the customer. The customer then uses the checks to purchase goods and services.

Parties to a Check

UCC 3-104(f) defines a **check** as an order by the drawer to the drawee bank to pay a specified sum of money from the drawer's checking account to the named payee (or holder). There are three parties to an **ordinary check**:

1. **Drawer.** The **drawer of a check** is the customer who maintains the checking account and writes (draws) checks against the account.
2. **Drawee (or payer bank).** The **drawee of a check** is the bank on which a check is drawn.
3. **Payee.** The **payee of a check** is the party to whom a check is written.

ordinary check
An order by a drawer to a drawee bank to pay a specified sum of money from the drawer's checking account to the named payee (or holder).

drawer of a check
The checking account holder and writer of a check.

drawee of a check
The bank where a check drawer has an account.

payee of a check
The party to whom a check is written.

Example The Kneadery Restaurant, Inc. has a checking account at Mountain Bank. Mike Martin, the president of the Kneadery Restaurant, writes a check for $1,000 from this account, payable to Sun Valley Bakery, to pay for food supplies. The Kneadery Restaurant is the drawer, Mountain Bank is the drawee, and Sun Valley Bakery is the payee. Mountain Bank is obligated to pay the check when it is presented for payment if the Kneadery Restaurant's checking account has sufficient funds to cover the amount of the check at the time of presentment (see Exhibit 25.1).

Exhibit 25.1 ORDINARY CHECK

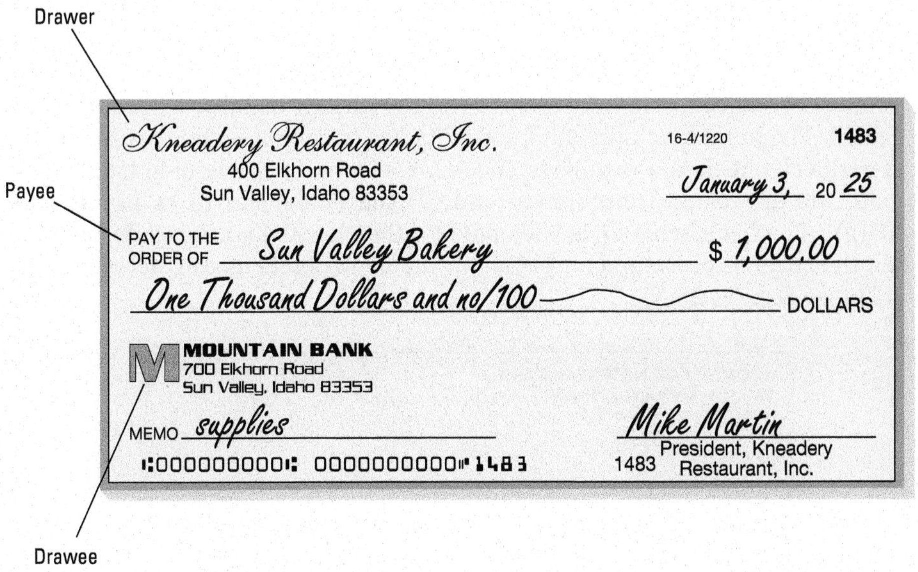

Special Types of Checks

25.3 List and describe special forms of checks and identify the parties to these checks.

If a payee fears that there may be insufficient funds in the drawer's account to pay a check when it is presented for payment or that the drawer has stopped payment of the check, the payee may be unwilling to accept an ordinary check from the drawer. However, the payee might be willing to accept a **bank check**—that is, a *certified check* or a *cashier's check*. These types of checks are usually considered "as good as cash" because the bank is solely or primarily liable for payment. These forms of checks are discussed in the following paragraphs.

bank check
A certified check or a cashier's check, the payment for which a bank is solely or primarily liable.

Certified Checks

Men such as they are, very naturally seek money or power; and power because it is as good as money.

Ralph Waldo Emerson (1803–1882)

When a bank *certifies a check*, it agrees in advance (1) to accept the check when it is presented for payment and (2) to pay the check from funds set aside from the customer's account and either placed in a special certified check account or held in the customer's account. Certified checks do not become stale. Thus, they are payable at any time from the date they are issued.

A check is a **certified check** when the bank writes or stamps the word *certified* across the face of an ordinary check. The certification should also contain the date, the amount being certified, and the name and title of the person at the bank who certifies the check. Note that a bank is not obligated to certify a check. A bank's refusal to do so is not a dishonor of a check [UCC 3-409(d)]. The drawer cannot stop payment on a certified check (see Exhibit 25.2).

certified check
A type of check for which a bank agrees in advance (*certifies*) to accept the check when it is presented for payment.

Exhibit 25.2 CERTIFIED CHECK

Cashier's Checks

A person can purchase a **cashier's check** from a bank by paying the bank the amount of the check plus a fee for issuing the check. Usually, a specific payee is named. The purchaser does not have to have a checking account at the bank.

cashier's check
A check issued by a bank for which the customer has paid the bank the amount of the check and a fee. The bank guarantees payment of the check.

A cashier's check is a two-party check for which (1) the issuing bank serves as both the drawer and the drawee and (2) the holder serves as payee [UCC 3-104(g)]. The bank, which has been paid for the check, guarantees its payment. When the check is presented for payment, the bank debits its own account [UCC 3-412] (see Exhibit 25.3).

Exhibit 25.3 CASHIER'S CHECK

Honoring Checks

25.4 Describe when a bank must honor a check.

When a customer opens a checking account at a bank, the customer impliedly agrees to keep sufficient funds in the account to pay any checks written against it. Thus, when the drawee bank receives a properly drawn and payable check, the bank is under a duty to **honor** the check and charge (debit) the drawer's account the amount of the check if there are sufficient funds in the customer's checking account at the bank [UCC 4-401(a)].

honor
To pay a drawer's properly drawn check.

Stale Checks

Occasionally, a payee or another holder in possession of a check fails to present the check immediately to the payer bank for payment. A check that has been outstanding for more than six months is considered stale, and the bank is under no obligation to pay it. A bank that pays a **stale check** in good faith may charge the drawer's account [UCC 4-404].

stale check
A check that has been outstanding for more than six months.

Incomplete Checks

Drawers sometimes write checks that omit certain information, such as the amount of the check or the payee's name, either on purpose or by mistake. Such checks are called **incomplete checks**. In such cases, the payee or any holder can complete the check, and the payer bank that in good faith makes payment on the completed check can charge the customer's account the amount of the completed check unless it has notice that the completion was improper [UCC 3-407(c), 4-401(d)(2)]. The UCC places the risk of loss of an incomplete item on the drawer.

Example Markus, who owes Harper $200, draws a check payable to Harper on his checking account at City Bank. Markus signs the check but leaves the amount blank. Harper fraudulently fills in $1,000 and presents the check to City Bank, which pays it. City Bank can charge Markus's account $1,000. Markus's only recourse is to sue Harper.

Postdated Checks

On occasion, a drawer of a check does not want a check to be cashed until sometime in the future. This is called a **postdated check**. Under UCC 4-401(c), to require a bank to abide by a postdated check, the drawer must take the following steps:

postdated check
A check that a drawer does not want cashed until sometime in the future.

1. The drawer must postdate the check to some date in the future.
2. The drawer must give *separate written notice* to the bank, describing the check with reasonable certainty and notifying the bank not to pay the check until the date on the check.

If these steps are taken and the bank pays the check before its date, the bank is liable to the drawer for any losses resulting from its act.

Stop-Payment Orders

A **stop-payment order** is an order by a drawer of a check to the payer bank not to pay or certify a check. Only the drawer can order a stop-payment order. A stop-payment order can be given orally or in writing. An *oral order* is binding on the bank for only 14 calendar days, unless confirmed in writing during this time. A *written order* is effective for six months. It can be renewed in writing for additional six-month periods [UCC 4-403]. If the payer bank fails to honor a valid stop-payment order, it must recredit the customer's account.

stop-payment order
An order by a drawer of a check to the payer bank not to pay or certify a check.

Overdrafts

If the drawer does not have enough money in an account when a properly payable check is presented for payment, the payer bank can either (1) dishonor the check or (2) honor the check and create an **overdraft** in the drawer's account [UCC 4-401(a)].

overdraft
The amount of money a drawer owes a bank after it has paid a check despite the drawer's account having insufficient funds.

If a bank dishonors a check the bank notifies the drawer of the dishonor and returns the check to the holder, marked **insufficient funds**. The holder often resubmits the check to the bank, hoping that the drawer has deposited more money into the account and the check will clear. If the check does not clear, the holder's recourse is against the drawer of the check.

A banker so very careful to avoid risk would soon have no risk to avoid.

Lord MacNaghten
Bank of England v. Vaglliano Brothers (1891)

If the bank chooses to pay the check even though there are insufficient funds in the drawer's account, it can later charge the drawer's account for the amount of the overdraft [UCC 4-401(a)]. If the drawer does not fulfill this commitment, the bank can sue to recover payment for the overdrafts and overdraft fees. Many banks offer optional expressly agreed-on overdraft protection to their customers.

Wrongful Dishonor

If a bank does not honor a check when there are sufficient funds in the drawer's account to pay a properly payable check, it is liable for **wrongful dishonor**. The payer bank is liable to the drawer for damages proximately caused by the wrongful dishonor as well as for consequential damages, damages caused by criminal prosecution, and so on. A payee or holder cannot sue the bank for damages caused by the wrongful dishonor of a drawer's check. The only recourse for the payee or holder is to sue the drawer to recover the amount of the check [UCC 4-402].

wrongful dishonor
A situation in which there are sufficient funds in a drawer's account to pay a properly payable check, but the bank does not do so.

The following ethics feature discusses federal currency reporting law.

Ethics

Federal Currency Reporting Law

The federal **Bank Secrecy Act**[1] requires financial institutions and other entities (such as retailers, car and boat dealers, antiques dealers, jewelers, and real estate brokers) to file a **Currency Transaction Report (CTR)** with the Internal Revenue Service (IRS), reporting the following:

- The receipt in a single transaction or a series of related transactions of cash in an amount greater than $10,000 (daily aggregate amount). "Cash" is not limited to currency but includes cashier's checks, bank drafts, traveler's checks, and money orders (but not ordinary checks).
- Suspected criminal activity by bank customers involving a financial transaction of $1,000 or more in funds.

The law also stipulates that it is a crime to structure or assist in structuring any transaction for the purpose of evading these reporting requirements. Financial institutions and entities may be fined for negligent violations of the currency reporting requirements. Fines may be levied for a pattern of negligent violations. Willful violations may subject the violator to civil money penalties, charges of aiding and abetting the criminal activity, and prosecution for violating money-laundering statutes.

Ethics Questions
Why were the reporting requirements adopted? Do you think that many transactions are structured to avoid the reporting statute?

Bank Secrecy Act
A federal law that requires financial institutions and other entities to report to the Internal Revenue Service (IRS) the receipt of a transaction or series of transactions in an amount greater than $10,000 in cash and suspected criminal activity involving a financial transaction of $1,000 or more in funds.

Forged Signatures and Altered Checks

25.5 Identify what parties are liable for altered and forged checks.

Major problems associated with checks and other negotiable instruments are that (1) signatures are sometimes forged and (2) the instrument itself may have been altered prior to presentment for payment. The UCC rules that apply to these situations are discussed in the following paragraphs. These rules apply to all types of negotiable instruments but are particularly important concerning checks.

Forged Signature of the Drawer

When a check is presented to the payer bank for payment, the bank is under a duty to verify the drawer's signature. This is usually done by matching the signature on the signature card on file at the bank to the signature on the check.

A check with a *forged drawer's signature* is called a **forged instrument**. A forged signature is wholly inoperative as the signature of the drawer. The check is not properly payable because it does not contain an order of the drawer. The payer bank cannot charge the customer's account if it pays a check over the forged signature. If the bank has charged the customer's account, it must recredit the account, and the forged check must be dishonored [UCC 3-401].

forged instrument
A check with a forged drawer's signature on it.

The bank can recover from the party who presented the check to it for payment only if that party had knowledge that the signature of the drawer on the check was unauthorized [UCC 3-417(a)(3)]. The forger is liable on the check because the forged signature acts as the forger's signature [UCC 3-403(a)]. Although the payer bank can sue the forger, the forger usually cannot be found or is **judgment proof**; that is, the forger does not have funds or assets to pay the judgment.

Example Zion has a checking account at Country Bank. Mildred steals one of Zion's checks, completes it by writing in $10,000 as the amount of the check, adding her name as the payee, and forges Zion's signature. Mildred indorses the check to Sam, who knows that Zion's signature has been forged. Sam indorses the check to Destiny, who is innocent and does not know of the forgery. Destiny presents the check to Country Bank, the payer bank, which pays the check. Country Bank may recover from the original forger, Mildred, and from Sam, who knew of the forgery. It cannot recover from Destiny because she did not have knowledge of the forgery.

Critical Legal Thinking Questions
What is a forged check? Explain the liability of the following parties where there has been a forged check: (1) drawer, (2) payor bank, (3) presenter of the check, and (4) forger.

Altered Checks

Sometimes a check is altered before it is presented for payment. This is an unauthorized change in the check that modifies the legal obligation of a party [UCC 3-407(a)]. The payer bank can dishonor an **altered check** if it discovers the alteration. If the payer bank pays the altered check, it can charge the drawer's account for the **original tenor** of the check but not the altered amount [UCC 3-407(c), 4-401(d)(1)].

altered check
A check that has been altered without authorization and thus modifies the legal obligation of a party.

original tenor
The original amount for which the drawer wrote a check.

If the payer bank has paid the altered amount, it can recover the difference between the altered amount and the original tenor from the party who presented the altered check for payment. This is because the presenter of the check for payment and each prior transferor *warrant* that the check has not been altered [UCC 3-417(a)(2)]. If there has been an alteration, each party in the chain of collection can recover from the preceding transferor based on a breach of this warranty. The ultimate loss usually falls on the party that first paid the altered check because that party was in the best position to identify the alteration. The forger is liable for the difference between the original tenor and the altered amount—if the forger can be found and is not judgment proof.

Example A father draws a $100 check on City Bank made payable to his daughter. The daughter alters the check to read "$1,000" and cashes the check at a liquor store. The liquor store presents the check for payment to City Bank. City Bank pays the check. The father is liable only for the original tenor of the check ($100), and City Bank can charge the father's account this amount. City Bank is liable for the $900 difference, but it can recover this amount from the liquor store for breach of the presentment warranty. This is because the liquor store was in the best position to identify the alteration. The liquor store can seek to recover the $900 from the daughter.

Critical Legal Thinking Questions
What is an altered check? Explain the liability of the following parties where there has been an altered check: (1) drawer, (2) payor bank, (3) presenter of the check, and (4) forger.

One-Year Rule

The drawer's failure to report a forged or altered check to the bank within *one year* of receiving the bank statement and canceled checks containing it relieves the bank of any liability for paying the instrument [UCC 4-406(3)]. Thus, the payer bank is not required after this time to recredit the customer's account for the amount of the forged or altered check, even if the customer later discovers the forgery or alteration. This is called the **one-year rule.**

one-year rule
A rule that states that if a drawer fails to report a forged or altered check to the bank within *one year* of receiving the bank statement and canceled checks containing it, the bank is relieved of any liability for paying the instrument.

Series of Forgeries

If the same wrongdoer engages in a **series of forgeries or alterations** on the same account, the customer must report that to the payer bank within a reasonable period of time, not exceeding 30 days from the date that the bank statement was made available to the customer [UCC 4-406(d)(2)]. The customer's failure to do so discharges the bank from liability on all similar forged or altered checks after this date and prior to notification.

The Federal Bureau of Investigation (FBI) is authorized to investigate forgeries, bank fraud, and other financial crimes.

In the following case, the court held that a checking account holder failed to review its bank statements as required by law to catch a series of forgeries by an employee.

CASE 25.1 ***STATE COURT CASE Series of Forgeries of Checks***

Spacemakers of America, Inc. v. SunTrust Bank

609 S.E.2d 683, 2005 Ga. App. Lexis 43 (2005)
Court of Appeals of Georgia

"In this case, the undisputed evidence showed that Spacemakers hired as a bookkeeper a twice-convicted embezzler who was on probation, then delegated the entire responsibility of reviewing and reconciling its bank statements to her while failing to provide any oversight on these essential tasks."
—John Ellington, Judge

Facts

Spacemakers of America, Inc. hired Jenny Triplett as its bookkeeper. Spacemakers did not inquire about any prior criminal record or conduct a criminal background check of Triplett. If it had taken those steps, it would have discovered that Triplett was on probation for 13 counts of forgery and had been convicted of theft by deception. All convictions were the result of Triplett forging checks of previous employers.

Spacemakers delegated to Triplett sole responsibility for maintaining the company's checkbook, reconciling the checkbook with monthly bank statements, and preparing financial reports. Triplett also handled the company's accounts payable and regularly presented checks to Dennis Rose, the president of Spacemakers, so he could sign them.

Just weeks after starting her job at Spacemakers, Triplett forged Rose's signature on a check for \$3,000 made payable to her husband's company, Triple M Entertainment Group, which was not a vendor for Spacemakers. By the end of her first full month of employment, Triplett had forged five more checks totaling \$22,320, all payable to Triple M. Over the next nine months, Triplett forged 59 more checks totaling approximately \$475,000. All checks were drawn against Spacemakers's bank account at SunTrust Bank. No one except Triplett reviewed the company's bank statements.

Subsequently, a SunTrust employee visually inspected a \$30,670 check. She became suspicious of the signature and called Rose. The SunTrust employee faxed a copy of the check, which was made payable to Triple M, to Rose. Rose knew that Triple M was not one of the company's vendors, and a Spacemakers employee reminded Rose that Triplett's husband owned Triple M. Rose immediately called the police, and Triplett was arrested.

Spacemakers sent a letter to SunTrust Bank, demanding that the bank credit \$523,106 to its account for the forged checks. The bank refused, contending that Spacemakers's failure to provide the bank with timely notice of the forgeries barred Spacemakers's claim. Spacemakers sued SunTrust for negligence and unauthorized payment of forged items. The trial court granted SunTrust's motion for summary judgment. Spacemakers appealed.

Issue

Did the failure of Spacemakers to uncover the forgeries and failure to provide SunTrust with timely notice of the forgeries bar its claim against SunTrust?

Language of the Court

In this case, the undisputed evidence showed that Spacemakers hired as a bookkeeper a twice-convicted embezzler who was on probation, then delegated the entire responsibility of reviewing and reconciling its bank statements to her while failing to provide any oversight on these essential tasks. There is every reason to believe that, if Spacemakers had simply reviewed its bank statements, it would have discovered the forgeries. Accordingly, we find that Spacemakers is precluded as a matter of law from asserting claims based upon the forgeries in this case.

Decision

The court of appeals held that Spacemakers was barred from recovering the value of the forged checks from SunTrust. The court of appeals affirmed the trial court's grant of summary judgment to SunTrust.

Critical Legal Thinking Questions

Did Triplett act ethically in this case? Did Spacemakers act ethically when it sued SunTrust to try to recover its losses caused by the forgeries?

The Collection Process

25.6 Describe the Federal Reserve System and the collection process for checks.

A bank is under a duty to accept deposits into a customer's account. This includes collecting checks that are drawn on other banks and made payable or indorsed to the depositor. The **collection process**, which may involve several banks, is governed by Article 4 of the UCC.

When a payee or holder receives a check, he or she can either go to the drawer's bank (the **payer bank**) and present the check for payment in cash or—as is more common—deposit the check into a bank account at his or her own bank, called the **depository bank**. (The depository bank may also serve as the payer bank if both parties have accounts at the same bank.)

The depository bank must present a check to the payer bank for collection. At this point in the process, the Federal Reserve System and other banks may be used in the collection of a check. The depository bank and these other banks are each called a **collecting bank**. Each bank in the collection process that is not the depository bank or the payer bank is called an **intermediary bank**. A bank can have more than one role during the collection process [UCC 4-105]. The check collection process is illustrated in Exhibit 25.4.

payer bank
The bank where the drawer has a checking account and on which a check is drawn.

depository bank
The bank where the payee or holder has an account.

collecting bank
The depository bank and other banks in the collection process (other than the payer bank).

intermediary bank
A bank in the collection process that is not the depository bank or the payer bank.

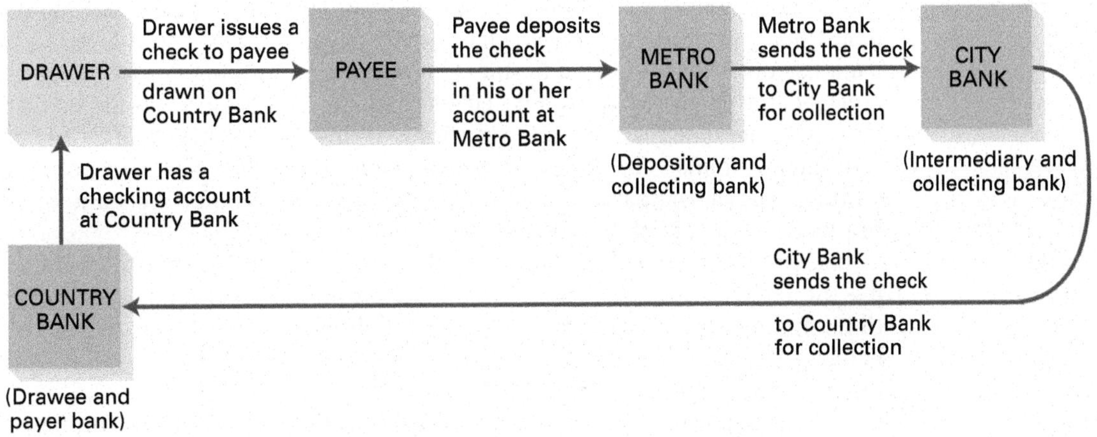

Exhibit 25.4 CHECK COLLECTION PROCESS

Federal Reserve System

Federal Reserve System
A system of 12 regional Federal Reserve banks that assist other banks in the collection of checks.

The **Federal Reserve System** (also known as the **Federal Reserve** or **the Fed**) was created by Congress as the central bank of the United States. The Federal Reserve has many functions, including being a check clearing system for banks and other depository institutions. The Federal Reserve consists of 12 regional Federal Reserve banks located in major cities in different geographical areas of the country.

Most U.S. banks have accounts at regional Federal Reserve banks. Rather than send a check directly to another bank for collection, member banks may submit paid checks to the Federal Reserve banks for collection. The Federal Reserve banks debit and credit the accounts of these banks daily to reflect the collection and payment of checks. Banks pay the Federal Reserve banks a fee for this service. In large urban areas, private clearinghouses may provide similar check collection services [UCC 4-110, 4-213(a)].

Bank Payment Rules

25.7 Describe bank payment rules, including posting and settlement.

The federal government has established rules for the payment of checks by banks and other depository institutions. The following are the major time rules that apply to depository institutions for the payment of checks.

Deferred Posting

deferred posting rule
A rule that allows banks to fix an afternoon hour of 2:00 p.m. or later as a cutoff hour for the purpose of processing items.

The **deferred posting rule** allows banks to fix an afternoon hour of 2:00 p.m. or later as a cutoff hour for the purpose of processing checks and deposits. Any check or deposit of money received after this cutoff hour is treated as being received on the next banking day [UCC 4-108]. Saturdays, Sundays, and holidays are not banking days unless the bank is open to the public for carrying on substantially all banking functions [UCC 4-104(a)(3)].

Settlement

A check is finally paid when the payer bank (1) pays the check in cash, (2) settles for the check without having a right to revoke the settlement, or (3) fails to dishonor the check within certain statutory time periods. These time periods are as follows:

A man is usually more careful of his money than he is of his principles.

Ralph Waldo Emerson (1803–1882)

"on us" item
A check that is presented for payment where the depository bank is also the payer bank. That is, the drawer and payee or holder have accounts at the same bank.

"on them" item
A check presented for payment by a payee or holder where the depository bank and the payer bank are not the same bank.

midnight deadline
The midnight of the next banking day following the banking day on which the bank received an "on them" check for collection.

1. **Deposit of cash.** A deposit of cash to an account becomes available for withdrawal at the opening of the next banking day following the deposit [UCC 4-215(a)].
2. **"On us" items.** If the drawer and the payee or holder have accounts at the *same* bank, the depository bank is also the payer bank. The check is called an **"on us" item** when it is presented for payment by the payee or holder. In this case, the bank has until the opening of business on the second banking day following the receipt of the check to dishonor it. If it fails to do so, the check is considered paid. The payee or holder can withdraw the funds at this time [UCC 4-215(e)(2)].
3. **"On them" items.** If a drawer and a payee or holder have accounts at *different* banks, the payer bank and depository bank are not the same bank. In this case, the check is called an **"on them" item.**

   Except for the collecting bank, each bank in the collection process, including the payer bank, must take proper action on an "on them" check prior to its midnight deadline. The **midnight deadline** is the midnight of the next banking day following the banking day on which the bank received an "on them" check for collection [UCC 4-104(a)(10)].

   This deadline is of particular importance to the payer bank: If the payer bank does not dishonor a check by its midnight deadline, the bank is *accountable* (liable) for the face amount of the check. It does not require that the check be properly payable [UCC 4-302(a)].

4. **Presentment across the counter.** Instead of depositing an "on them" check for collection, a depositor can physically present the check for payment at the payer bank. This is called **presentment across the counter**. In this case, the payer bank has until the end of that banking day to dishonor the check. If it fails to do so, it must pay the check [UCC 4-301(a)].

presentment across the counter
A situation in which a depositor physically presents a check for payment at the payer bank instead of depositing an "on them" check for collection.

The following feature discusses insured deposits at banks.

Contemporary Environment

FDIC Insurance of Bank Deposits

The **Federal Deposit Insurance Corporation (FDIC)** is a government agency that insures deposits at most banks and savings institutions in the United States. Each insured bank pays assessed yearly premiums based on the size of its deposits to the FDIC. If an FDIC-insured bank fails and the insured bank does not have sufficient assets to pay its depositors back their money, the FDIC will pay the depositors their lost deposits, up to certain limits.

FDIC insurance covers savings accounts, checking accounts, money market accounts, certificates of deposit, IRAs and other retirement accounts, and other types of deposits received at an insured bank. To show whether it is covered by FDIC insurance, a bank or savings institution will display the official FDIC sign.

FDIC insurance per insured bank is set at: (1) $250,000 per single account owned by one person, (2) $250,000 per co-owner for joint accounts owned by two or more persons, and (3) $250,000 per corporation, partnership, and unincorporated association accounts. IRAs and other retirement accounts are insured up to $250,000 per owner. Accounts at separate banks are each insured to these amounts. However, funds deposited in separate branches of the same bank are not separately insured.

Example Henry has $250,000 on deposit at the First National Bank and another $250,000 on deposit at Central Savings Bank. Each deposit is insured.

Example Kerry is married to Patricia. Kerry has $250,000 on deposit at the Second National Bank, Patricia has $250,000 on deposit at the bank, Kerry and Patricia have a $250,000 joint account at the bank, and Kerry's law firm (under a limited liability partnership entity) has $250,000 on deposit at the bank. Each deposit is insured.

If the FDIC is unable to cover the insured deposits, the *full faith and credit* of the U.S. government backs the FDIC. Thus, if there are major failures of many banks and the FDIC insurance fund is insufficient to cover all of the depositors' losses, then the U.S. government will pay the depositors the money owed by the FDIC.

Electronic Banking and E-Money

25.8 List and describe the various forms of electronic and online banking, cryptocurrency, and mobile payment apps.

Federal Deposit Insurance Corporation (FDIC)
A government agency that insures deposits at most banks and savings institutions ("insured banks") in the United States.

Computer and electronic technology have made it possible for banks to offer electronic deposit, withdrawal, payment, and collection services to bank customers. This technology is collectively referred to as the **electronic funds transfer system (EFTS)**. EFTS is supported by contracts among and between customers, banks, private clearinghouses, and other third parties. Some of the major forms of electronic banking services are discussed in the following paragraphs.

electronic funds transfer system (EFTS)
Computer and electronic technology that makes it possible for banks to offer electronic deposit, withdrawal, payment, and collection services to bank customers.

Automated Teller Machine

An **automated teller machine (ATM)** is an electronic machine that is located either on a bank's premises or at some other convenient location, such as a shopping center, supermarket, or stores. These devices are connected online to the bank's computers and permit the withdrawal of cash from bank accounts, provide cash advances against credit cards, accept deposits to banking accounts, allow payment of bank loans (e.g., mortgage payments) and permit other banking services. Each bank customer is issued a secret personal identification number (PIN) to access the customer's bank accounts through ATMs.

Debit Cards

debit card
A card that is issued to a holder of a bank account that permits purchases of goods and services and withdrawals of cash by deducting the amount of the purchase or withdrawal from the card holder's bank account.

Many banks issue **debit cards** to customers. Debit cards are electronically connected to a bank account of the holder of the debit card. Debit cards are often used by holders to make purchases or to make withdrawals of cash. No credit is extended. Instead, the customer's bank account is immediately debited for the amount of a purchase. Debit cards can be used at merchants that have a point-of-sale terminal or other similar electronic device. These terminals are connected online to a bank's computers. To make a purchase or withdrawal, a customer inserts a debit card into the appropriate electronic device for the amount of the purchase. If there are sufficient funds in the customer's account, the transaction will debit the customer's account and credit the merchant's account for the amount of the purchase. If there are insufficient funds in the customer's account, the purchase is rejected unless the customer has overdraft protection. At many electronic terminals, customers can also obtain cash using their debit card.

The following feature discusses federal law that governs debit cards and *consumer* electronic funds transfers.

Information Technology

Consumer Electronic Funds Transfers

Computers have made it much easier and faster for banks and their customers to conduct banking transactions. The U.S. Congress enacted the **Electronic Fund Transfer Act (EFTA)**[2] to regulate *consumer* electronic funds transfers. The Federal Reserve Board adopted **Regulation E** to further interpret the act. The EFTA and Regulation E establish the following consumer rights:

- **Unsolicited debit cards.** A bank can send unsolicited EFTS debit cards to a consumer only if the cards are not valid for use. Unsolicited cards can be validated for use by a consumer's specific request.
- **Lost or stolen debit cards.** Debit cards are sometimes lost or stolen. If a customer notifies the issuing bank within two days of learning that a debit card has been lost or stolen, the customer is liable for only $50 for unauthorized use. If a customer does not notify the bank within this two-day period, the customer's liability increases to $500. If the customer fails to notify the bank within 60 days after an unauthorized use appears on the customer's bank statement, the customer can be held liable for more than $500.
- **Evidence of transaction.** Other than for a telephone transaction, a bank must provide a customer with a written receipt of a transaction made through a computer terminal or electronic device. This receipt is *prima facie* evidence of the transaction. The receipt can be provided electronically by the bank.
- **Bank statements.** A bank must provide a monthly statement to an electronic funds transfer customer at the end of the month in which the customer conducts a transaction. The statement must include the date and amount of the transfer, the name of the retailer, the location and identification of the terminal, and the fees charged for the transaction. Bank statements must also contain the address and telephone number where inquiries or errors can be reported. The statement can be provided electronically by the bank.

A bank is liable for wrongful dishonor when it fails to pay an electronic funds transfer when there are sufficient funds in the customer's account to do so.

Online Banking

Electronic Fund Transfer Act
A federal statute that regulates *consumer* electronic funds transfers.

online banking
Electronic system that permits bank customers to check their bank statements online and pay bills from their bank accounts by using personal computers and other electronic devices.

Banks provide the service of paying recurring payments and crediting recurring deposits on behalf of customers. Direct recurring payments are commonly used to pay utility bills, insurance premiums, mortgage payments, and the like. Social Security checks, wages, and dividend and interest checks are examples of recurring direct deposits.

Banks permit customers to check their bank statements online and pay bills from their bank accounts by using personal computers and other electronic devices. This is referred to as **online banking**. To engage in online banking, a customer must enter a PIN and account name or number, the amount of the bill to be paid, and the account number of the payee to whom the funds are to be transferred.

Mobile Payment Apps

A **mobile payment app** is an app on an electronic mobile device such as a smartphone, tablet, or smartwatch that is used for the payment of goods or services. Customers can choose among many different payment apps that can be downloaded onto their electronic devices. Mobile apps are linked to a user's bank account or credit card.

mobile payment apps
A mobile payment app is an app on an electronic mobile device such as a smartphone, tablet, or smartwatch that is used for the payment of goods or services.

Most mobile apps allow for in-store purchases and online purchases. Digital apps excel in paying for small purchases. Payment at retail stores is made by passing a smart device's screen displaying the app next to a store's digital register. Payment apps enable purchasers to pay in seconds with no need to pull out a credit or debit card or cash. The most obvious benefit of a digital wallet is the elimination of a physical wallet. Many apps permit peer-to-peer (P2P) payments, thus allowing users to send money instantly to friends and family members.

Mobile payment apps are considered safer than using credit or debit cards, which can easily be lost or have their numbers stolen. Mobile apps usually provide several layers of security. If the app stores payment card information, the card numbers are almost always encrypted or tokenized for safety so that the real card number is never stored on the device. Apps are usually password-protected, and some use biometrics, such as a fingerprint, facial recognition, or iris scan, to unlock the app.

Consumers can choose from a variety of payment apps such as Apple Pay, Google Pay, Samsung Pay, Venmo, Xoom, Zelle, and others. Some apps only work with specific devices. Other apps are used for specialized type of payments.

The following feature discusses federal law that governs *commercial* electronic funds transfers.

Information Technology

Commercial Electronic Wire Transfers

Commercial wire transfers, or **wholesale wire transfers,** are electronic transfers of funds from a bank to another party. They are often used to transfer payments between businesses and financial institutions. A customer of a bank may request the bank to pay another party by wiring funds (money) to the other party's bank account. UCC Article 4A (Funds Transfers) governs *commercial wire transfers*. Article 4A applies only to **commercial electronic funds transfers;** consumer electronic funds transfers are not subject to Article 4A. The customer is liable to pay the bank for any properly paid funds transfer [UCC 4A-103(a)].

Example Boeing Aircraft Corporation wants to pay Pittsburgh Steel Company for supplies it purchased. Instead of delivering a check to Pittsburgh Steel, Boeing instructs its bank, Washington Bank, to wire the funds to Pittsburgh Steel's bank, Liberty Bank, with instructions to credit Pittsburgh Steel's account.

Trillions of dollars are transferred each day using wire transfers. A wire transfer often involves a large amount of money (multimillion-dollar transactions are common). The benefit of using wire transfers is their speed—most transfers are completed on the same day.

The following feature discusses cryptocurrency.

Information Technology

Cryptocurrency

Several forms of **cryptocurrency,** also called **digital currency** or **virtual currency,** have been developed. Virtual currency is a decentralized form of online currency that uses cryptography for security. The first major cryptocurrency was Bitcoin. Other cryptocurrencies are Ethereum, Ripple, Litecoin, Tether, and Neo. There are thousands of cryptocurrencies now available. Additional cryptocurrencies are continually being developed.

Like traditional currency, virtual currency is divided into different denominations. A digital wallet is a place to hold and store virtual money. A wallet stores digital credentials that allow a person to access and spend virtual currency. Cryptography protects access to each wallet. Virtual currency can be transferred to another party's digital wallet.

Cryptocurrency can be purchased from online exchanges, which charge a fee for making each exchange. Cryptocurrency

(continued)

can be traded by placing a buy order or a sell order with an online exchange. A sell order (ask) is an offer to sell cryptocurrency at a minimum price per virtual unit. A buy order (bid) is an offer to buy cryptocurrency at a maximum price per virtual unit. The exchange's software system matches buy and sell orders. In addition, cryptocurrency can be converted to U.S. dollars and other currencies, or to gold or silver, using a digital currency exchange.

Virtual currency can be used to purchase goods and services from merchants and companies that accept it as payment. Many companies accept bitcoin payments, including Microsoft, Overstock.com, Dell, Expedia.com, Shopify.com, Zynga, Dish Network, and Tesla.

Cryptocurrency is pseudonymous, meaning that the funds are not tied to persons or real-world entities but rather to digital addresses. Owners of virtual currency addresses are not explicitly identified. The anonymous nature of cryptocurrency is well-suited for criminal activities, such as conducting online drug sales, selling goods and services using digital black markets, illegal gambling, money laundering, and tax evasion. Use of virtual currency for illegal purposes violates existing federal and state criminal laws.

Cryptocurrencies are not regulated by any central authority or government. However, in the United States, cryptocurrency exchanges are required to register with the Financial Crimes Enforcement Network (FinCEN), a division of the Department of Treasury. Many issuances of cryptocurrencies in an initial coin offering (ICO) and securities tokens offerings (STO) must be registered with the Securities and Exchange Commission (SEC) before being sold. As virtual currency develops in importance, additional government regulation is sure to follow.

As digital technology improves, additional forms of cryptocurrencies will be developed. Several countries are working on developing their own forms of virtual currency.

cryptocurrency
A digital currency or virtual currency that is a decentralized form of online currency that uses cryptography for security.

Dodd-Frank Wall Street Reform and Consumer Protection Act
A federal statute that reforms many aspects of the banking system.

Bank Reform

25.9 Describe banking reform measures.

After the country suffered a major financial and economic depression beginning in late 2007, Congress decided that the bank system needed to be reformed. To accomplish this, Congress passed the **Dodd-Frank Wall Street Reform and Consumer Protection Act.**[3] The act was enacted in July 2010, and its most important provisions are the following:

- **Bank regulation.** The act reorganized and streamlined the federal government agencies that regulate the banking industry and increased the powers of and strengthened bank regulatory oversight by federal agencies.
- **Lending regulation.** The act requires mortgage lenders to make a reasonable and good faith determination that a borrower has the ability to repay the loan.
- **Consumer Financial Protection Bureau (CFPB).** The act created the **Consumer Financial Protection Bureau (CFPB)**, a federal regulatory agency. This agency has broad authority to regulate consumer financial products and services.

The following feature discusses using bank secrecy laws of other countries.

Global Law

Hiding Money in Offshore Banks

Each country has its own banking laws. Some countries have national banking laws that provide secrecy to account holders. That is, the country's law prohibits others—mainly government agencies of other countries—from discovering information about who has bank accounts in that country, account numbers, and amounts deposited. Banks in these countries mainly provide banking services to nonresidents. The banks are used by individuals and organizations that want to hide illegally obtained money and to avoid paying taxes. These banks are often referred to as "offshore" banks.

Bank secrecy and tax-evasion haven countries include the Cayman Islands, the Bahamas, and Bermuda in the Caribbean; Switzerland, Liechtenstein, Luxembourg, and Monaco in Europe; the Isle of Man off the coast of Great Britain; Hong Kong and Singapore in Asia; Bahrain and Dubai in the Middle East; and the micro-islands of Niue and Vanuatu in the South Pacific.

Tax evaders, money launderers, drug cartels, criminal organizations, corrupt government officials, white-collar criminals, terrorist groups, and others who want anonymity use these offshore banking countries to hide their money.

Key Terms and Concepts

Altered check (429)
Article 3 (Commercial Paper) (424)
Article 4 (Bank Deposits and Collections) (424)
Article 4A (Funds Transfers) (424)
Automated teller machine (ATM) (433)
Bank check (426)
Bank Secrecy Act (428)
Cashier's check (426)
Certified check (426)
Check (425)
Collecting bank (431)
Collection process (431)
Commercial electronic funds transfers (435)
Commercial wire transfer (wholesale wire transfer) (435)
Consumer Financial Protection Bureau (CFPB) (436)
Creditor–debtor relationship (424)
Cryptocurrency (digital currency, virtual currency) (435)
Currency Transaction Report (CTR) (428)
Debit card (434)
Deferred posting rule (432)
Deposit (425)
Depository bank (431)
Dodd-Frank Wall Street Reform and Consumer Protection Act (436)
Drawee of a check (425)
Drawer of a check (425)
Electronic Fund Transfer Act (EFTA) (434)
Electronic funds transfer system (EFTS) (433)
Federal Deposit Insurance Corporation (FDIC) (433)
Federal Reserve System (Federal Reserve or the Fed) (432)
Forged instrument (429)
Honor (427)
Incomplete check (427)
Insufficient funds (428)
Intermediary bank (431)
Judgment proof (429)
Midnight deadline (432)
Mobile payment app (435)
"On them" item (432)
"On us" item (432)
One-year rule (430)
Online banking (434)
Ordinary check (425)
Original tenor (429)
Overdraft (428)
Payee of a check (425)
Payer bank (431)
Postdated check (427)
Presentment across the counter (433)
Principal–agent relationship (424)
Regulation E (434)
Revised Article 3 (Negotiable Instruments) (424)
Series of forgeries or alterations (430)
Stale check (427)
Stop-payment order (427)
Uniform Commercial Code (UCC) (424)
Wrongful dishonor (428)

Critical Legal Thinking Cases

25.1 Cashier's Check Dr. Graham Wood purchased a cashier's check in the amount of $6,000 from Central Bank of the South (Bank). The check was made payable to Ken Walker and was delivered to him. Eleven months later, Bank's branch manager informed Wood that the cashier's check was still outstanding. Wood subsequently signed a form, requesting that payment be stopped and a replacement check issued. He also agreed to indemnify Bank for any damages resulting from the issuance of the replacement check. Bank issued a replacement check to Wood. Seven months later, Walker deposited the original cashier's check in his bank, which was paid by Bank. Bank requested that Wood repay the bank $6,000. When he refused, Bank sued Wood to recover this amount. Who wins? *Wood v. Central Bank of the South*, 435 So.2d 1287, 1982 Ala. Civ. App. Lexis 1362 (Court of Civil Appeals of Alabama, 1982)

25.2 Overdraft Louise Kalbe maintained a checking account at the Pulaski State Bank (Bank) in Wisconsin. Kalbe made out a check for $7,260, payable in cash. Thereafter, she misplaced it but did not report the missing check to the bank or stop payment on it. One month later, some unknown person presented the check to a Florida bank for payment. The Florida bank paid the check and sent it to Bank for collection. Bank paid the check even though it created a $6,542.12 overdraft in Kalbe's account. Bank requested Kalbe pay this amount. When she refused, Bank sued Kalbe to collect the overdraft. Who wins? *Pulaski State Bank v. Kalbe*, 122 Wis.2d 663, 364 N.W.2d 162, 1985 Wisc. App. Lexis 3034 (Court of Appeals of Wisconsin, 1985)

25.3 Wrongful Dishonor Larry J. Goodwin and his wife maintained a checking and a savings account at City National Bank of Fort Smith (Bank). Bank also had a customer named Larry K. Goodwin. Two loans of Larry K. Goodwin were in default. Bank mistakenly took money from Larry J. Goodwin's checking account to pay the loans. At the end of the month, the Goodwins received written notice that four of their checks, which were written to merchants, had been dishonored for insufficient funds. When the Goodwins investigated, they discovered that their checking account balance was zero and that the bank had placed their savings account on hold. After being informed of the error, Bank promised to send letters of apology to the four merchants and to correct the error. Bank, however, subsequently "bounced" several other checks of the Goodwins. Eventually, Bank notified all the parties of its error. One month later, the Goodwins closed their accounts at Bank and were paid the correct balances due. They sued the bank for consequential and punitive damages for wrongful dishonor. Who wins? *City National Bank of Fort Smith v. Goodwin*, 301 Ark. 182, 783 S.W.2d 335, 1990 Ark. Lexis 49 (Supreme Court of Arkansas, 1990)

25.4 Stale Check Charles Ragusa & Son (Ragusa), a partnership consisting of Charles and Michael Ragusa, issued a check in the amount of $5,000, payable to Southern Masonry, Inc. (Southern). The check was drawn on Community State Bank (Bank). Several days later, Southern informed Ragusa that the check had been lost. Ragusa issued a replacement check for the same amount and sent it to Southern, and that check was cashed. At the same time, Ragusa gave a verbal stop-payment order to Bank regarding the original check. Three years later, the original check was deposited by Southern into its account at the Bank of New Orleans. When the check was presented to Bank, it paid it and charged $5,000 against Ragusa's account. The partnership was not made aware of this transaction until one month later, when it received its monthly bank statement. Ragusa demanded that Bank recredit its account $5,000. When Bank refused to do so, Ragusa sued. Who wins? *Charles Ragusa & Son v. Community State Bank*, 360 So.2d 231, 1978 La. App. Lexis 3435 (Court of Appeal of Louisiana, 1978)

25.5 Postdated Check David Siegel maintained a checking account with the New England Merchants National Bank (Bank). On September 14, Siegel drew and delivered a $20,000 check payable to Peter Peters. The check was dated November 14. Peters immediately deposited the check in his own bank, which forwarded it for collection. On September 17, Bank paid the check and charged it against Siegel's account. Siegel discovered that the check had been paid when another of his checks was returned for insufficient funds. Siegel informed Bank that the check to Peters was postdated November 14 and requested that the bank return the $20,000 to his account. When Bank refused, Siegel sued for wrongful debit of his account. Must Bank recredit Siegel's account? *Siegel v. New England Merchants National Bank*, 386 Mass. 672, 437 N.E.2d 218, 1982 Mass. Lexis 1559 (Supreme Judicial Court of Massachusetts, 1982)

25.6 Stop Payment Dynamite Enterprises, Inc. (Dynamite), a corporation doing business in Florida, maintained a checking account at Eagle National Bank of Miami (Bank). Dynamite drew a check on this account, payable to one of its business associates. Before the check had been cashed or deposited, Dynamite issued a written stop-payment order to Bank. Bank informed Dynamite that it would not place a stop-payment order on the check because there were insufficient funds in the account to pay the check. Several weeks later, the check was presented to Bank for payment. By this time, sufficient funds had been deposited in the account to pay the check. Bank paid the check and charged Dynamite's account. When Dynamite learned that the check had been paid, it requested Bank to recredit its account. When Bank refused, Dynamite sued to recover the amount of the check. Who wins? *Dynamite Enterprises, Inc. v. Eagle National Bank of Miami*, 517 So.2d 112, 1987 Fla. App. Lexis 11791 (Court of Appeal of Florida, 1987)

Ethics Case

25.7 Ethics Case Mr. Gennone maintained a checking account at Peoples National Bank & Trust Company of Pennsylvania (Bank). Gennone noticed that he was not receiving his bank statements and canceled checks. When Gennone contacted Bank, he was informed that the statements had been mailed to him. Bank agreed to hold future statements so that he could pick them up in person. Gennone picked up the statements but did not reconcile the balance of the account. As a result, it was not until two years later that he discovered that beginning more than one year earlier, his wife had forged his signature on 25 checks. Gennone requested Bank to reimburse him for the amount of these checks. When Bank refused, Gennone sued Bank to recover. Did Gennone act ethically in suing the bank? Who wins? *Gennone v. Peoples National Bank & Trust Co.*, 9 U.C.C. Rep.Serv. 707, 1971 Pa. Dist. & Cnty. Dec. Lexis 551, 51 Pa. D. & C.2d 529 (Common Pleas Court of Montgomery County, Pennsylvania, 1971)

Notes

1. 31 U.S.C. 5311 et seq.
2. 15 U.S.C. 1693 et seq.
3. Public Law 111-203.

PART VI

Credit, Secured Transactions, and Bankruptcy

Henry R. Cheeseman

CHAPTER

26 Credit, Real Property Financing, and Debtors' Rights

COTTAGE, MACKINAC ISLAND, MICHIGAN
A house is often a person's most valuable asset. Homeowners often borrow money to help provide the funds to purchase a house. Usually, the lender takes back a mortgage that secures the house as collateral for the repayment of the loan. If the borrower defaults, the lender can bring a foreclosure proceeding to recover the collateral.

Henry R. Cheeseman

Learning Objectives

After studying this chapter, you should be able to:

26.1 Define *credit* and identify the parties to a credit transaction.

26.2 Define *unsecured credit* and describe the liability of the debtor.

26.3 Define *secured credit* and describe the rights of the creditor.

26.4 Describe real property financing, foreclosure procedures, and deficiency judgments.

26.5 Describe and distinguish between surety and guaranty arrangements.

26.6 List and describe collection remedies.

26.7 List and describe laws that protect debtors' rights.

"Creditors have better memories than debtors."

— *Benjamin Franklin*
Poor Richard's Almanack (1758)

Introduction To Credit, Real Property Financing, and Debtors' Rights

Words pay no debts.
William Shakespeare
Troilus and Cressida, Act III (ca. 1602)

The U.S. economy is a credit economy. Consumers borrow money to make major purchases (e.g., homes, automobiles, appliances) and use credit cards (e.g., Visa, MasterCard) to purchase goods and services at clothing stores, restaurants, and other businesses. Businesses use credit to purchase equipment, supplies, and other goods and services.

Because lenders are sometimes reluctant to lend large sums of money simply on the borrower's promise to repay, many of them take a *security interest* in the property purchased or some other property of the debtor. The property in which the security interest is taken is called *collateral*. If the debtor does not pay the debt, the creditor can foreclose on and recover the collateral.

A lender who is unsure whether a debtor will have sufficient income or assets to repay a loan may require another person to guarantee payment. If the borrower fails to repay the loan, the person who agreed to guarantee the loan is responsible for paying it.

In addition, governments have enacted consumer financial protection laws that protect consumer-debtors in credit transactions.

This chapter discusses unsecured credit, secured credit, mortgages and other security interests in real property, guaranty and surety arrangements, and consumer-debtor financial protection laws.

Credit

26.1 Define *credit* and identify the parties to a credit transaction.

In a transaction involving the extension of **credit** (either unsecured or secured), there are two parties. The party extending the credit, the **lender**, is called the **creditor**. The party borrowing the money, the **borrower**, is called the **debtor** (see Exhibit 26.1).

credit
Occurs when one party makes a loan to another party.

creditor (lender)
The lender in a credit transaction.

debtor (borrower)
The borrower in a credit transaction.

Exhibit 26.1 RELATIONSHIP BETWEEN DEBTOR AND CREDITOR

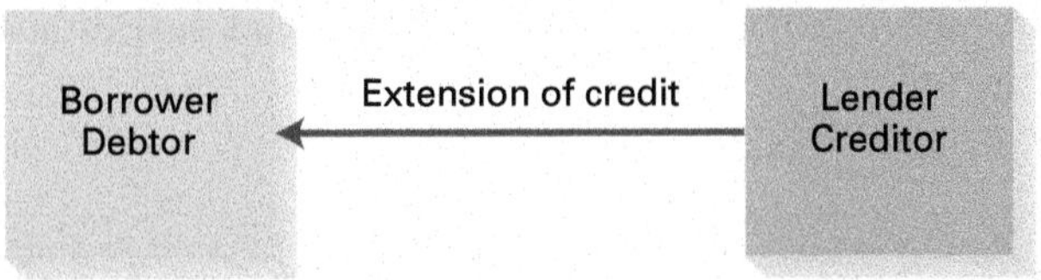

Example Prima Company goes to Urban Bank and borrows $100,000. In this case, Prima Company is the *borrower-debtor*, and Urban Bank is the *lender-creditor*.

Credit may be extended on either an *unsecured* or a *secured* basis. The following paragraphs discuss these types of credit.

Unsecured Credit

26.2 Define *unsecured credit* and describe the liability of the debtor.

Unsecured credit does not require any security (collateral) to protect the payment of the debt. Instead, the creditor relies on the debtor's promise to repay the principal (plus any interest) when it is due. The creditor is called an **unsecured creditor**. In deciding whether to make the loan, the unsecured creditor considers the debtor's credit history, income, and other assets. If the debtor fails to make

unsecured credit
Credit that does not require any security (collateral) to protect the payment of the debt.

the payments, the creditor may bring legal action and obtain a judgment against the debtor. If the debtor is **judgment proof** (i.e., has little or no property or no income that can be garnished), the creditor may never collect.

Example Arnold borrows $15,000 from Hae-Won. Hae-Won lends the money to Arnold without taking an interest in collateral for the loan. This is an unsecured loan. Hae-Won is relying on Arnold's credit standing when she makes the loan. If Arnold defaults on the loan, Hae-Won has no collateral to foreclose on. Hae-Won's recourse is to sue Arnold to recover the unpaid loan amount.

Secured Credit

26.3 Define *secured credit* and describe the rights of the creditor.

To minimize the risk associated with extending unsecured credit, a creditor may require a security interest in the debtor's property (**collateral**). The collateral secures payment of the loan. This type of credit is called **secured credit**. The creditor who has a security interest in collateral is called a **secured creditor**, or **secured party**. Security interests may be taken in real, personal, intangible, and other property. If the debtor fails to make the payments when due, the collateral may be repossessed to recover the outstanding amount. Generally, if the sale of the collateral is insufficient to repay the loan plus interest, the creditor may bring a lawsuit against the debtor to recover a deficiency judgment for the difference.

secured credit
Credit that requires security (collateral) that secures payment of the loan.

Rather go to bed supperless than rise in debt.

Benjamin Franklin
(1706–1790)

Example Sarah purchases an automobile from a car dealership. She borrows part of the purchase price from a lender. The lender requires Sarah to give it a security interest in the automobile to secure the loan. This is a secured credit transaction with the automobile being collateral for the loan. If Sarah defaults and fails to make the required payments, the lender can repossess the automobile.

Real Property Financing

26.4 Describe real property financing, foreclosure procedures, and deficiency judgments.

Owners of real estate can create **security interests in real property**. This occurs if an owner borrows money from a lender and pledges real estate as security for repayment of the loan.

Mortgage

mortgage
An arrangement where an owner of real property borrows money from a lender and pledges the real property as collateral to secure the repayment of the loan.

mortgagor (owner-debtor)
The owner-debtor in a mortgage transaction.

mortgagee (creditor)
The creditor in a mortgage transaction.

A person who owns a piece of real property has an ownership interest in that property. A property owner who borrows money from a creditor may use the real estate as collateral for repayment of the loan. This type of collateral arrangement, known as a **mortgage**, is a *two-party instrument*. The **mortgagor** is the **owner-debtor**, and the **mortgagee** is the **lender-creditor**. The parties to a mortgage are illustrated in Exhibit 26.2.

Example General Electric purchases a manufacturing plant for $10 million, pays $2 million cash as a down payment, and borrows the remaining $8 million from City Bank. General Electric is the debtor, and City Bank is the creditor. To secure

Exhibit 26.2 PARTIES TO A MORTGAGE

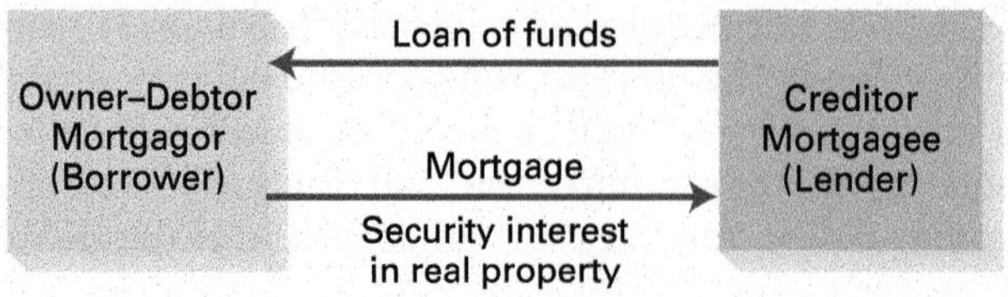

the loan, General Electric gives a mortgage on the plant to City Bank. This is a secured loan, with the plant being collateral for the loan. General Electric is the mortgagor, and City Bank is the mortgagee. If General Electric defaults on the loan, the bank may take action under state law to foreclose and take the property.

When a mortgage is repaid in full, the lender files a written document called a **reconveyance**, sometimes referred to as **satisfaction of a mortgage**, with the county recorder's office, which is proof that the mortgage has been paid.

Note and Deed of Trust

Some states' laws provide for the use of a *deed of trust and note* in place of a mortgage. The **note** is the instrument that is evidence of the borrower's debt to the lender; the **deed of trust** is the instrument that gives the creditor a security interest in the debtor's property that is pledged as collateral.

A deed of trust is a *three-party instrument*. Under it, legal title to the real property is placed with a **trustee** (usually a trust corporation) until the amount borrowed has been paid. The owner-debtor is called the **trustor**. Although legal title is vested in the trustee, the trustor has full legal rights to possession of the real property. The lender-creditor is called the **beneficiary**. Exhibit 26.3 illustrates the relationship between the parties.

note
An instrument that is evidence of a borrower's debt to the lender.

deed of trust
An instrument that gives a creditor a security interest in the debtor's real property that is pledged as collateral for a loan.

Exhibit 26.3 PARTIES TO A NOTE AND DEED OF TRUST

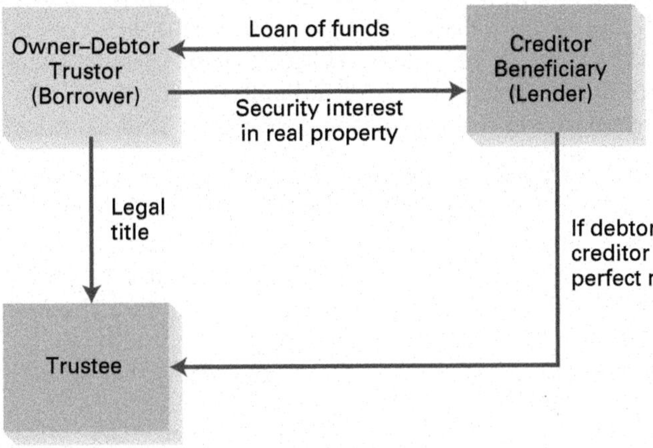

When the loan is repaid, the trustee files a written *reconveyance* with the county recorder's office, which transfers title to the real property to the borrower-debtor.

Debt is the prolific mother of folly and of crime.

Benjamin Disraeli
Henrietta Temple (1837)

Recording Statute

Most states have enacted **recording statutes** that require a mortgage or deed of trust to be recorded in the **county recorder's office** in the county in which the real property is located. These filings are public record and alert the world that a mortgage or deed of trust has been recorded against the real property. This record gives potential lenders or purchasers of real property the ability to determine whether there are any existing liens (mortgages) on the property.

recording statute
A statute that requires a mortgage or deed of trust to be recorded in the county recorder's office of the county in which the real property is located.

The **nonrecordation of a mortgage** or deed of trust does not affect either the legality of the instrument between the mortgagor and the mortgagee or the rights and obligations of the parties. In other words, the mortgagor is obligated to pay the amount of the mortgage according to the terms of the mortgage, even if the document is not recorded. However, an improperly recorded document is not effective against either (1) subsequent purchasers of the real property or (2) other mortgagees or lienholders who have no notice of the prior mortgages.

Example Eileen purchases a house for $500,000. She borrows $400,000 from Boulevard Bank and gives the bank a mortgage on the house for this amount. Boulevard Bank fails to record the mortgage. Eileen then applies to borrow $400,000

By no means run in debt.

George Herbert
The Temple (1633)

from Advance Bank. Advance Bank reviews the real estate recordings and finds no mortgage recorded against the property, so it lends Eileen $400,000. Advance Bank records its mortgage. Later, Eileen defaults on both loans. In this case, Advance Bank can foreclose on the house because it recorded its mortgage. Boulevard Bank, even though it made the first loan to Eileen, does not get the house and can only sue Eileen to recover the unpaid loan.

Foreclosure Sale

foreclosure sale
A legal procedure by which a secured creditor causes the judicial sale of the secured real estate to pay a defaulted loan.

A debtor that does not make the required payments on a secured real estate transaction is in **default**. All states permit **foreclosure sales**. Under this method, the debtor's default may trigger a legal court action for foreclosure. Any party having an interest in the property—including owners of the property and other mortgagees or lienholders—must be named as defendants. If the mortgagee's case is successful, the court will issue a judgment that orders the real property to be sold at a judicial sale. The procedures for a foreclosure action and sale are mandated by state statute. Any surplus must be paid to the mortgagor.

Example Isabella borrows $500,000 from Country Bank to buy a house. Isabella (mortgagor) gives a mortgage to Country Bank (mortgagee), making the house collateral to secure the loan. Later, Isabella defaults on the loan. Country Bank can foreclose on the property and follow applicable state law to sell the house at a judicial sale. If the house sells for $575,000, the bank keeps $500,000 and must remit $75,000 to Isabella. Most state statutes permit the mortgagee-lender to recover the costs of the foreclosure and judicial sale from the sale proceeds before remitting the surplus to the mortgagor-borrower.

power of sale
A power stated in a mortgage or deed that permits foreclosure without court proceedings and sale of the property through an auction.

Most states permit foreclosure by **power of sale**, although this must be expressly conferred in the mortgage or deed of trust. Under a power of sale, the procedure for that sale is provided in the mortgage or deed of trust itself. No court action is necessary. Some states have enacted statutes that establish the procedure for conducting the sale. Such a sale must be by auction for the highest price obtainable. Any surplus must be paid to the mortgagor.

In the following case, the courts had to decide the priority of mortgages and a lien on a piece of real property.

CASE 26.1 ***STATE COURT CASE Mortgages and Liens***

Old Republic National Title Insurance Company v. Fifth Third Bank

2008 Ohio App. Lexis 4423 (2008)
Court of Appeals of Ohio

"The recording statute sets forth the general rule that the first mortgage recorded shall have preference over subsequently recorded mortgages."

—Patrick Dinkelacker, Judge

Facts

James and Heather McCarthy (McCarthy) owned a house in Cincinnati, Ohio. The house was purchased with a mortgage loan from Countrywide Home Loans, which recorded its mortgage in the appropriate county recorder's office. Subsequently, the following events occurred:

- March 10—McCarthy borrowed money from Fifth Third Bank and gave the bank a mortgage on their house. Fifth Third Bank did not record the mortgage.
- March 10—McCarthy went to Centex Home Equity Company to refinance the original mortgage loan from Countrywide.
- March 19—Centex's title search revealed Countrywide's loan but did not reveal Fifth Third's unrecorded mortgage.
- March 24—The law firm of Santen and Hughes recorded a lien judgment on McCarthy's house for failure to pay for legal services.

- April 1—McCarthy closed on the Centex loan. Centex was not informed that McCarthy had previously obtained a loan from Fifth Third. Centex did not conduct a new title search, so it was not aware of the law firm's recorded lien. The proceeds from Centex's loan were used to pay off Countrywide's mortgage. Centex notified its agent, Buckeye Title Company (Buckeye), to record Centex's mortgage within 24 hours. Buckeye failed to record Centex's mortgage.
- April 15—Fifth Third recorded its mortgage.
- May 2—Centex recorded its mortgage.

When Santen and Hughes commenced a foreclosure action against McCarthy's house, Fifth Third and Centex were brought into the suit. The trial court held that the Santen and Hughes lien had first priority. As to the mortgages, the court applied the doctrine of equity and ruled that Centex's first-in-time but later recorded mortgage had priority over Fifth Third's later-made but previously recorded mortgage. Fifth Third appealed.

Issue

What is the priority of the lien and two mortgages on McCarthy's house?

Language of the Court

Under Ohio law, lien priority is determined by the time of filing. The recording statute sets forth the general rule that the first mortgage recorded shall have preference over subsequently recorded mortgages. Lien priority in this case is hereby established as follows: the Santen and Hughes lien has first priority, the Fifth Third mortgage has second priority, and the Centex mortgage has third priority.

Decision

The court of appeals reversed the decision of the trial court and ruled that the priority of the security interests on McCarthy's house were by the recording date: first, Santen and Hughes; second, Fifth Third; and third, Centex.

Critical Legal Thinking Questions

Was it ethical for Centex to argue that its unrecorded mortgage should take priority over Fifth Third's prior recorded mortgage?

Deficiency Judgment

Some states permit a mortgagee to bring a separate legal action to recover a deficiency from the mortgagor. If the mortgagee is successful, the court will award a **deficiency judgment** that entitles the mortgagee to recover the amount of the judgment from the mortgagor's other property.

Example Rolf buys a house for $800,000. He puts $200,000 down and borrows $600,000 from a bank, which takes a mortgage on the property to secure the loan. Rolf defaults, and when the bank forecloses on the property, it is worth only $500,000. There is a deficiency of $100,000 ($600,000 loan – $500,000 foreclosure sale price). The bank can recover the $100,000 deficiency from Rolf's other property. The bank has to bring a legal action against Rolf to do so.

The following feature describes anti-deficiency statutes.

deficiency judgment
A judgment of a court that permits a secured lender to recover other property or income from a defaulting debtor if the collateral is insufficient to repay the unpaid loan.

anti-deficiency statute
A statute that prohibits deficiency judgments regarding certain types of mortgages, such as those on residential property.

Contemporary Environment

Anti-Deficiency Statutes

Several states have enacted **anti-deficiency statutes** that prohibit deficiency judgments regarding certain types of mortgages, such as loans for the original purchase of residential property. Anti-deficiency statutes usually apply only to **first purchase money mortgages** (i.e., mortgages that are taken out to purchase houses). Second mortgages and other subsequent mortgages, even mortgages that refinance the first mortgage, usually are not protected by anti-deficiency statutes.

Example Assume that a house is located in a state that has an anti-deficiency statute. Qian buys the house for $800,000. She puts $200,000 down and borrows $600,000 of the purchase price from First Bank, which takes a mortgage on the property to secure the loan. This is a first purchase money mortgage. Subsequently, Qian borrows $100,000 from Second Bank and gives a second mortgage to Second Bank to secure the loan. Qian defaults

(continued)

on both loans, and when she defaults, the house is worth only $500,000. Both banks bring foreclosure proceedings to recover the house. First Bank can recover the house worth $500,000 at foreclosure. However, First Bank has a deficiency of $100,000 ($600,000 loan – $500,000 foreclosure sale price). Because of the state's anti-deficiency statute, First Bank cannot recover this deficiency from Qian; First Bank can recover only the house in foreclosure and must write off the $100,000 loss. Second Bank's loan, a second loan, is not covered by the anti-deficiency statute. Therefore, Second Bank can sue Qian to recover its $100,000 deficiency from Qian's other property.

Right of Redemption

right of redemption
A right that allows the mortgagor to redeem real property after default and before foreclosure. It requires the mortgagor to pay the full amount of the debt incurred by the mortgagee because of the mortgagor's default.

The common law and many state statutes give the mortgagor the right to redeem real property after default and before foreclosure. This right, called the **right of redemption**, requires the mortgagor to pay the full amount of the debt—that is, principal, interest, and other costs—incurred by the mortgagee because of the mortgagor's default. Redemption of a partial interest is not permitted. On redemption, the mortgagor receives title to the property, free and clear of the mortgage debt. Several states allow the mortgagor to redeem real property for a specified period (usually six months or one year) after foreclosure. This is called the **statutory period of redemption**.

The following feature describes liens that contractors and laborers can obtain on real property.

Business Environment

Construction Liens on Real Property

Owners of real property often hire contractors, architects, and laborers (e.g., painters, plumbers, roofers, bricklayers, furnace installers) to make improvements to the real property. The contractors and laborers expend the time to provide their services as well as money to provide the materials for the improvements. Their investments are protected by state statutes that permit them to file a **construction lien** (also known as a **mechanic's lien**) against the improved real property. Construction liens are often called by more specific names, such as a *supplier's lien* (also called *material person's lien*) for those parties supplying materials, *laborer's lien* for persons providing labor, and *design professional's lien* for those parties providing architectural and design services.

The lienholder must file a **notice of lien** with the county recorder's office in the county in which the real property subject to the lien is located. When a lien is properly filed, the real property to which the improvements have been made becomes security for the payment of these services and materials. In essence, the lienholder has the equivalent of a mortgage on the property. If the owner defaults, the lienholder may foreclose on the lien, sell the property, and satisfy the debt plus interest and costs out of the proceeds of the sale. Any surplus must be paid to the owner-debtor. Mechanic's liens are usually subject to the debtor's right of redemption.

Most state statutes permit an owner of real property to have subcontractors, laborers, and material persons who will provide services or materials to a real property project to sign a written **release of lien** contract (also called a **lien release**) releasing any lien they might otherwise assert against the property. A lien release can be used by the property owner to defeat a statutory lienholder's attempt to obtain payment.

Example Landowner, which owns an undeveloped piece of property, hires General Contractor, a general contractor, to build a house on the property. General Contractor hires Roofing Company, a roofer, as a subcontractor to put the roof on the house. When the house is complete, Landowner pays General Contractor the full contract price for the house but has failed to obtain a lien release from Roofing Company. General Contractor fails to pay Roofing Company for the roofing work. Roofing Company files a mechanic's lien against the house and demands payment from Landowner. Here, Landowner must pay Roofing Company for the roofing work; if Landowner does not, Roofing Company can foreclose on the house, have it sold, and satisfy the debt out of the proceeds of the sale. To prevent foreclosure, Landowner must pay Roofing Company for its work. Landowner ends up paying twice for the roofing work—once to General Contractor, the general contractor, and a second time to Roofing Company, the subcontractor. Landowner's only recourse is to sue General Contractor to recover its payment.

Example Suppose in the preceding example that Landowner obtained a lien release from Roofing Company, the subcontractor, before or at the time Landowner paid General Contractor, the general contractor. If General Contractor fails to pay Roofing Company, the subcontractor, then Roofing Company could not file a lien against Landowner's house because it had signed a lien release. In this situation, Roofing Company's only recourse would be to sue General Contractor to recover payment for its services.

Henry R. Cheeseman

PINE SHORES, MICHIGAN
*Most states permit the transfer and sale of real property pursuant to a **land sale contract** or **land contract**. In this contract, the owner of real property agrees to sell the property to a purchaser, who agrees to pay the purchase price to the owner-seller over an agreed-on period of time. Often, making such a loan is referred to as "carrying the paper." Land sales contracts are often used to sell undeveloped property, farms, and the like. If the purchaser defaults, the seller may declare forfeiture and retake possession of the property.*

land sale contract (land contract)
An arrangement in which the owner of real property sells property to a purchaser and extends credit to the purchaser.

construction lien (mechanic's lien)
A contractor's, laborer's, supplier's, or design professional's statutory lien that makes the real property to which services or materials have been provided security for the payment of the services and materials.

lien release
A written document signed by a contractor, subcontractor, laborer, or material person, waiving his or her statutory lien against real property.

Surety and Guaranty Arrangements

26.5 Describe and distinguish between surety and guaranty arrangements.

Sometimes a creditor refuses to extend credit to a debtor unless a third person agrees to become liable on the debt. The third person's credit becomes the security for the credit extended to the debtor. This relationship may be either a *surety arrangement* or a *guaranty arrangement*. These arrangements are discussed in the following paragraphs.

Surety Arrangement

In a strict **surety arrangement**, a third person—known as the **surety** or **co-debtor**—promises to be liable for the payment of another person's debt. A person who acts as a surety is commonly called an **accommodation party** or **co-signer**. Along with the principal debtor, the surety is **primarily liable** for paying the principal debtor's debt when it is due. If the principal debtor defaults on paying the debt, the creditor can bring a legal action against the surety to recover the unpaid debt. The creditor does not have to sue the principal debtor first.

surety arrangement
An arrangement in which a third party promises to be *primarily liable* with the borrower for the payment of the borrower's debt.

Example Ivy, a college student, wants to purchase a new BMW automobile. She goes to Auto Dealer and finds exactly the car she wants, and she wants to finance the car. Auto Dealer will not sell the car to Ivy on credit based on her own credit standing. Auto Dealer requires Ivy to find a co-signer on the purchase and credit contract. Ivy asks her mother to co-sign on the agreement. When Ivy's mother signs as a co-signer, she is now a surety. Ivy's mother is equally bound by the contract with Ivy. Ivy's mother is *primarily liable* with Ivy on the loan. If Ivy does not pay, Auto Dealer may immediately bring legal action against Ivy's mother for payment. Auto Dealer does not have to sue Ivy first.

Guaranty Arrangement

In a **guaranty arrangement**, a third person, the **guarantor**, agrees to pay the debt of the principal debtor if the debtor defaults and does not pay the debt when it is due. In this type of arrangement, the guarantor is **secondarily liable** on the debt.

guaranty arrangement
An arrangement in which a third party promises to be *secondarily liable* for the payment of another's debt.

In other words, the guarantor is obligated to pay the debt if the principal debtor defaults on the debt and the creditor has not been able to collect the debt from the debtor.

Example Ivan, a college student, wants to purchase a new computer, printer, and other electronic equipment on credit from Electronics Retail, Inc. Electronics will not sell the computer and other equipment to Ivan unless he can get someone to guarantee the payment. Ivan asks his roommate, Edward, to guarantee the payment. Edward agrees, and he is placed on the credit agreement as a guarantor. Edward is *secondarily liable*: If Ivan fails to make the necessary payment, Electronics must first attempt unsuccessfully to recover the payments from Ivan before taking legal action against Edward to recover payment.

In the following case, the court had to determine if a personal guaranty was enforceable.

CASE 26.2 *FEDERAL COURT CASE Personal Guaranty*

Avnet, Inc. v. Catalyst Resource Group, LLC

791 F.3d 899, 2015 U.S. App. Lexis 11423 (2015)
United States Court of Appeals for the Eighth Circuit

"The personal guaranty did not expressly state it was not assignable."

—Kermit Bye, Circuit Judge

Facts

David Wild is the sole owner and member of a limited liability company called Braveheart Equity Holdings, LLC (Braveheart). Braveheart, in turn, was an owner and member of another limited liability company, Catalyst Resources Group, LLC (Catalyst). Catalyst borrowed $500,000 from Laurus Technologies, Inc. (Laurus). Wild signed a personal guaranty to pay the loan if Catalyst failed to do so. Several years later, Laurus assigned the Catalyst promissory note to Avnet, Inc. When Catalyst did not repay the loan when due, Avnet contacted Catalyst to demand payment of the loan. When Catalyst did not pay the loan, Avnet contacted Wild to honor his personal guaranty. Wild refused to do so. Avnet sued Wild in U.S. district court to recover the unpaid loan. Wild argued that he was not bound to pay Avnet because his personal guaranty had been to Laurus and not to Avnet, and that he had not intended that his guaranty be assigned to any other party. The district court concluded that Avnet could enforce Wild's personal guaranty and granted summary judgment in Avnet's favor. Wild appealed.

Issue

Is Wild bound by his personal guaranty even though the guaranty had been assigned to another party?

Language of the Court

The assignment from Laurus to Avnet did not materially change Wild's duties under the guaranty, or materially increase the burden or risk imposed upon him. Before the assignment, Wild was bound by the guaranty to repay the loan should Catalyst fail to do so. After the assignment, Wild had the same obligation to repay the loan should Catalyst fail to do so. The personal guaranty did not expressly state it was not assignable. In addition, Wild's undisclosed intentions are immaterial because the guaranty itself contains no language clearly identifying to a potential assignee that the note and guaranty were not assignable.

Decision

The U.S. court of appeals affirmed the district court's grant of summary judgment to Avnet that enforced Wild's personal guaranty.

Critical Legal Thinking Questions

Why do you think Laurus required Wild to personally guaranty the loan to Catalyst? Was Wild's assertion that he did not intend that his personal guaranty be assigned persuasive?

Defenses of a Surety or Guarantor

Generally, the defenses the principal debtor has against the creditor may also be asserted by a surety or guarantor.

Example If credit has been extended for the purchase of a piece of machinery that proves to be defective, both the debtor and the surety can assert the defect as a defense to liability. The defenses of fraudulent inducement to enter into the surety or guaranty agreement and duress may also be cited as personal defenses to liability.

CONCEPT SUMMARY

SURETY AND GUARANTY CONTRACTS

Type of Arrangement	Party	Liability
Surety contract	Surety	Primarily liable. The surety is a co-debtor who is liable to pay the debt when it is due.
Guaranty contract	Guarantor	Secondarily liable. The guarantor is liable to pay the debt if the debtor defaults and the creditor has been unsuccessful in collecting the debt from the debtor.

Collection Remedies

26.6 List and describe collection remedies.

Once a creditor has obtained a judgment against a debtor, the creditor can petition the court for a *postjudgment order* to obtain property in possession of the debtor or a third party to satisfy the judgment. In some cases, a court can issue a *prejudgment order* to tie up property of the debtor during the court proceedings. The most common **collection remedies** are discussed in the following paragraphs:

Writ of Attachment

Attachment is a **prejudgment court order** that permits the seizure of a debtor's property that is in the debtor's possession while a lawsuit against the debtor is pending. To obtain a **writ of attachment**, a creditor must follow the procedures of state law, give the debtor notice, and post a bond with the court.

writ of attachment
A prejudgment court order that permits the seizure of a debtor's property while a lawsuit is pending.

Example Taryn sues Justin for fraud. Taryn lost a large sum of money to Justin when she invested in what she alleges was a fraudulent investment scheme. Because it may take more than one year before the case is heard, Taryn is afraid that Justin will transfer any money or property he has to avoid having to pay a judgment if he loses at trial. Taryn can immediately make a motion to the court to have the court issue a writ of attachment ordering the seizure of Justin's property, pending the outcome of the lawsuit. The court will do so if it determines that there is some merit to Taryn's claim against Justin and there is justification to believe that Justin might dispose of his property prior to the trial.

Writ of Execution

Execution is a **postjudgment court order** that permits the seizure of the debtor's property that is in the possession of the debtor. Certain property is exempt from levy (e.g., tools of trade, clothing, homestead exemption). A **writ of execution** is a court order directing the sheriff or other government officials to seize the debtor's property in the debtor's possession and authorizing a judicial sale of that

writ of execution
A postjudgment court order that permits the seizure of the debtor's property that is in the possession of the debtor.

property. The proceeds are used to pay the creditor the amount of the final judgment. Any surplus must be paid to the debtor.

Example Aamir wins a $25,000 judgment against Nicole. Nicole refuses to pay the amount of the judgment to Aamir. Aamir can obtain a postjudgment writ of execution from the court whereby the court directs the sheriff to seize Nicole's automobile and other property and have them sold at public auction to satisfy the judgment she owes Aamir.

Writ of Garnishment

writ of garnishment
A postjudgment court order that permits the seizure of a debtor's property that is in the possession of third parties.

Garnishment is a *postjudgment court order* that permits the seizure of a debtor's property that is in the possession of third parties. The creditor (also known as the **garnishor**) must go to court to seek a **writ of garnishment**. A third party in this situation is called a **garnishee**. Common garnishees are employers who possess wages due a debtor, banks in possession of funds belonging to the debtor, and other third parties in the possession of property of the debtor.

Example Yuming wins a $30,000 judgment against Lisa. Lisa refuses to pay the amount of the judgment to Yuming. Lisa works for E-Communications Company. Yuming obtains a postjudgment writ of garnishment from the court whereby the court orders E-Communications Company to pay 25 percent of Lisa's weekly disposable earnings (after taxes) directly to Yuming. Thus, after receiving this writ of garnishment, E-Communications Company must deduct the amount of the garnishment from Lisa's wages before she is paid and remit this amount to Yuming until the judgment is paid.

Title III of the Consumer Credit Protection Act
A federal law that permits debtors who are subject to a writ of garnishment to retain a specified percentage or amount of their earnings.

To protect debtors from abusive and excessive garnishment actions by creditors, Congress enacted **Title III of the Consumer Credit Protection Act.**[1] This federal law allows debtors who are subject to a writ of garnishment to retain the greater of (1) 75 percent of their weekly disposable earnings (after taxes) or (2) an amount equal to 30 hours of work paid at federal minimum wage. State law limitations on garnishment control are often more stringent than federal law.

CONCEPT SUMMARY

COLLECTION REMEDIES

Type of Collection Remedy	Period When Collection Remedy Occurs	Debtor's Property in the Possession of This Party
Attachment	Prejudgment	Debtor
Execution	Postjudgment	Debtor
Garnishment	Postjudgment	Third party

Consumer Financial Protection

26.7 List and describe laws that protect debtors' rights.

Consumer Financial Protection Bureau (CFPB)
A federal administrative agency that is responsible for enforcing federal consumer financial protection statutes.

In many consumer credit transactions, the lender is an institution or party that has greater leverage than the borrower. In the past, this sometimes led to lenders taking advantage of debtors. To rectify this problem, the federal government has enacted many consumer financial protection statutes that protect debtors from abusive, deceptive, and unfair credit practices. Many of these **consumer financial protection** laws are discussed in the following paragraphs.

Contemporary Environment

Consumer Financial Protection Bureau

In 2010, Congress created a new federal government agency called the **Consumer Financial Protection Bureau (CFPB)**. The bureau has authority to supervise all participants in the consumer finance and mortgage area, including depository institutions, such as commercial and savings banks, and non-depository parties, such as insurance companies, mortgage brokers, credit-counseling firms, debt collectors, and debt buyers. The bureau provides uniform model forms that covered parties can use to make required disclosures.

The bureau has authority to prohibit unfair, deceptive, or abusive acts or practices regarding consumer financial products and services. The bureau is a watchdog over credit cards, debit cards, mortgages, payday loans, and other consumer financial products and services. The automobile industry is exempt from bureau supervision and is subject to oversight by the Federal Trade Commission (FTC).

The bureau has authority to enforce federal consumer financial protection laws and is authorized to adopt rules to interpret and enforce the provisions of the acts it administers. The bureau has investigative and subpoena powers and may refer matters to the U.S. attorney general for criminal prosecution.

Truth-in-Lending Act

The **Truth-in-Lending Act (TILA)**[2] is one of the first federal consumer protection statutes enacted by Congress. The TILA, as amended, requires creditors to make certain disclosures to debtors in consumer transactions (e.g., retail installment sales, automobile loans) and real estate loans on the debtor's principal dwelling. The TILA covers only creditors that regularly (1) extend credit for goods or services to consumers or (2) arrange such credit in the ordinary course of their business. **Consumer credit** is defined as credit extended to natural persons for personal, family, or household purposes.

Truth-in-Lending Act (TILA)
A federal statute that requires creditors to make certain disclosures to debtors in consumer transactions and real estate loans on the debtor's principal dwelling.

Regulation Z **Regulation Z**, an administrative agency regulation, sets forth detailed rules for compliance with the TILA.[3] The TILA and Regulation Z require the creditor to disclose the following information to the consumer-debtor:

Regulation Z
A regulation that sets forth detailed rules for compliance with the TILA.

- Cash price of the product or service
- Down payment and trade-in allowance
- Unpaid cash price
- Finance charge, including interest, points, and other fees paid for the extension of credit
- **Annual percentage rate (APR)** of the finance charges
- Charges not included in the finance charge (such as appraisal fees)
- Total dollar amount financed
- Date the finance charge begins to accrue
- Number, amounts, and due dates of payments
- Description of any security interest
- Penalties to be assessed for delinquent payments and late charges
- Prepayment penalties
- Comparative costs of credit (optional)

The uniform disclosures required by the TILA and Regulation Z are intended to help consumers shop for the best credit terms.

Consumer Leasing Act

Consumers often opt to lease consumer products, such as automobiles, rather than purchase them. The **Consumer Leasing Act (CLA)**[4] is a federal statute that extends the TILA's coverage to lease terms in consumer leases. The CLA applies to lessors who engage in leasing or arranging leases for consumer goods in the

Consumer Leasing Act (CLA)
A federal statute that extends the TILA's coverage to lease terms in consumer leases.

ordinary course of their business. Casual leases (such as leases between consumers) are not subject to the CLA. Creditors that violate the CLA are subject to the civil and criminal penalties provided in the TILA.

Fair Credit Billing Act (FCBA)
A federal statute requiring that creditors promptly acknowledge in writing consumer billing complaints and investigate billing errors and that affords consumer-debtors other protection during billing disputes.

Fair Credit Billing Act

The **Fair Credit Billing Act (FCBA)**[5] is a federal statute that regulates billing errors involving consumer credit. The act requires that creditors promptly acknowledge in writing consumer billing complaints and investigate billing errors. The act prohibits creditors from taking actions that adversely affect the consumer's credit standing until the investigation is completed. The act affords other protection during disputes. The amendment requires creditors to post payments promptly to the consumer's account and either refund overpayments or credit them to the consumer's account.

The following ethics feature discusses the Credit CARD Act of 2009.

Credit Card Accountability Responsibility and Disclosure Act (Credit CARD Act)
A federal statute that requires disclosures to consumers concerning credit card terms, adds transparency to the creditor-debtor relationship, and eliminates many of the abusive practices of credit card issuers.

Ethics

Credit CARD Act

Credit card companies, including banks and other issuers of credit cards, have long engaged in unfair, abusive, deceptive, and unethical practices that took advantage of consumer-debtors; however, most of the practices did not violate the law. This changed when, in 2009, Congress enacted the **Credit Card Accountability Responsibility and Disclosure Act**, more commonly referred to as the **Credit CARD Act.**[6]

Here are some of the main provisions of the Credit CARD Act:

- The terms of the credit card agreement must be written in plain English and in no less than 12-point font (thus avoiding "legalese" and fine-print agreements).
- Credit cards cannot be issued to individuals under the age of 21 (the previous minimum age was 18) unless they have a co-signer (e.g., parent) or they can prove they have the means to pay credit card expenses.
- Payments above the minimum payment must be applied to pay higher-interest balances first (previously, issuers applied payments to lower-interest balances first). The minimum payment can be applied to pay off lowest-interest-rate balances first.
- Card companies cannot retroactively increase interest rates on existing balances.
- If cardholders cancel a card, they have the right to pay off existing balances at the existing interest rate and existing payment schedule (e.g., current minimum monthly payment).
- Cardholders who have been subject to an interest rate increase because of default, but then pay on time for six months, must have the interest rate returned to the interest rate that applied prior to the default and rate increase.
- The universal default rule cannot be applied retroactively to existing balances that the cardholders have on their credit cards. The **universal default rule** (which was used extensively by credit card companies prior to the act) allowed *all* credit card companies with whom a cardholder had a credit card to raise the interest rate on the card, including on the existing balances, if the cardholder was late in making a payment to *any* credit card company. The act does not eliminate the universal default rule; it allows credit card companies to apply the rule only to future balances.
- Credit card companies must place a notice on each billing statement that notifies the cardholder how long it would take to pay off the existing balance plus interest if the cardholder were to make minimum payments on the card.
- Credit card companies must place a notice on each billing statement that notifies the cardholder what monthly payment would be necessary for the cardholder to pay off the balance plus interest in 36 months.

The Credit CARD Act does not limit how high an interest rate can be charged on a credit card. The act does not apply to commercial or business credit cards. Violations of the act are subject to criminal prosecution and civil lawsuits.

Ethics Questions

Have credit card companies acted unethically in the past? Is the universal default rule justified or was it just greed on the part of the credit card companies?

Fair Credit Reporting Act

The **Fair Credit Reporting Act (FCRA)**[7] is a federal statute that regulates credit reporting companies that gather credit information about consumers. These include credit bureaus that compile and sell credit reports for a fee, medical information companies, and tenant screening services. This act protects consumers who are the subject of a **credit report** by setting rules for consumer reporting agencies.

Fair Credit Reporting Act (FCRA)
A federal statute that protects a consumer who is the subject of a credit report by setting rules for credit bureaus to follow and permitting consumers to obtain information from credit reporting businesses.

credit report
Information about a person's credit history that can be secured from a credit reporting agency.

Information in a consumer credit report can only be provided to parties who have a purpose for obtaining the information, such as a bank, credit card company, or merchant who may be extending credit to a consumer, or an insurance company, prospective employer, or prospective landlord. Users of the information for credit, insurance, employment, and other purposes must notify the consumer when an adverse action is taken on the basis of such reports. A credit report cannot be supplied to anyone who does not have a legitimate purpose for using the report as provided in the act.

Consumers may request the following information at any time: (1) the nature and substance of all the information in their credit file, (2) the sources of this information, and (3) the names of recipients of their credit report. If a consumer challenges the accuracy of pertinent information contained in a credit file, the agency may be compelled to reinvestigate. If the reporting company cannot find an error, despite the consumer's complaint, consumers may file a 100-word written statement of their version of the disputed information. If a consumer reporting agency or user violates the FCRA, an injured consumer may bring a civil action against the violator and recover actual damages. The FCRA also provides for criminal penalties.

The **Fair and Accurate Credit Transactions Act (FACTA)**[8] gives consumers the right to obtain one free credit report every 12 months from the three nationwide credit reporting agencies (Equifax, Experian, and TransUnion). Consumers may purchase, for a reasonable fee, their credit score and receive information on how the credit score is calculated. The act permits consumers to place fraud alerts on their credit files.

Fair Debt Collection Practices Act

The **Fair Debt Collection Practices Act (FDCPA)**[9] is a federal statute that protects consumer-debtors from abusive, deceptive, and unfair practices used by **debt collectors**. The FDCPA expressly prohibits debt collectors from using certain practices: (1) harassing, abusive, or intimidating tactics (e.g., threats of violence, obscene or abusive language); (2) false or misleading representations (e.g., posing as a police officer or an attorney); and (3) unfair or unconscionable practices (e.g., threatening the debtor with imprisonment).

Fair Debt Collection Practices Act (FDCPA)
A federal act that protects consumer-debtors from abusive, deceptive, and unfair practices used by debt collectors.

A debt collector is not allowed to contact a debtor in some circumstances, including the following:

1. At any inconvenient time. The FDCPA provides that convenient hours are between 8:00 a.m. and 9:00 p.m., unless this time is otherwise inconvenient for the debtor (e.g., the debtor works a night shift and sleeps during the day).
2. At inconvenient places, such as at places of worship or social events.
3. At the debtor's place of employment, if the employer objects to such contact.
4. If the debtor is represented by an attorney.
5. If the debtor gives a written notice to the debt collector that he or she refuses to pay the debt or does not want the debt collector to contact him or her again.

The FDCPA limits the contact that a debt collector may have with third persons other than the debtor's spouse or parents. Such contact is strictly limited. Unless the court has given its approval, third parties can be consulted only for the purpose of locating a debtor, and a third party can be contacted only once. A debt collector may not inform a third person that a consumer owes a debt that is in the process of collection. A debtor may bring a civil action against a debt collector for intentionally violating the FDCPA.

Equal Credit Opportunity Act

Equal Credit Opportunity Act (ECOA)
A federal statute that prohibits discrimination in the extension of credit based on sex, marital status, race, color, national origin, religion, age, or receipt of income from public assistance programs.

The **Equal Credit Opportunity Act (ECOA)**[10] is a federal statute that prohibits discrimination in the extension of credit based on sex, marital status, race, color, national origin, religion, age, or receipt of income from public assistance programs. The ECOA applies to all creditors that extend or arrange credit in the ordinary course of their business, including banks, savings and loan associations, automobile dealers, real estate brokers, credit card issuers, and so on.

The creditor must notify the applicant within 30 days regarding the action taken on a credit application. If the creditor takes an *adverse action* (i.e., denies, revokes, or changes the credit terms), the creditor must provide the applicant with a statement containing the specific reasons for the action. If a creditor violates the ECOA, the consumer may bring a civil action against the creditor and recover actual damages (including for emotional distress and embarrassment).

Fair Credit and Charge Card Disclosure Act

Fair Credit and Charge Card Disclosure Act
An amendment to the TILA that requires disclosure of certain credit terms on credit card and charge card solicitations and applications.

The **Fair Credit and Charge Card Disclosure Act**[11] is a federal statute that requires disclosure of credit terms on credit card and charge card solicitations and applications. The regulations adopted under the act require that any direct written solicitation to a consumer display, in tabular form, the following information: (1) the APR, (2) any annual membership fee, (3) any minimum or fixed finance charge, (4) any transaction charge for use of the card for purchases, and (5) a statement that charges are due when the periodic statement is received by the debtor.

Violations of consumer financial protection statutes are subject to fines, criminal prosecution, and civil lawsuits.

Key Terms and Concepts

Annual percentage rate (APR) (451)
Anti-deficiency statute (445)
Attachment (449)
Beneficiary (creditor) (443)
Collateral (442)
Collection remedies (449)
Construction lien (mechanic's lien) (446)
Consumer credit (451)
Consumer financial protection (450)
Consumer Financial Protection Bureau (CFPB) (451)
Consumer Leasing Act (CLA) (451)
County recorder's office (443)
Credit (441)
Credit Card Accountability Responsibility and Disclosure Act (Credit CARD Act) (452)
Credit report (453)
Creditor (lender) (441)
Debt collector (453)
Debtor (borrower) (441)
Deed of trust (443)
Default (444)
Deficiency judgment (445)
Equal Credit Opportunity Act (ECOA) (454)
Execution (449)
Fair and Accurate Credit Transactions Act (FACTA) (453)
Fair Credit and Charge Card Disclosure Act (454)
Fair Credit Billing Act (FCBA) (452)
Fair Credit Reporting Act (FCRA) (453)
Fair Debt Collection Practices Act (FDCPA) (453)
First purchase money mortgage (445)
Foreclosure sale (444)
Garnishee (450)
Garnishment (450)
Garnishor (450)
Guarantor (447)
Guaranty arrangement (447)
Judgment proof (442)
Land sale contract (land contract) (447)
Lien release (release of lien) (446)
Mortgage (442)

Mortgagee (lender-creditor) (442)
Mortgagor (owner-debtor) (442)
Nonrecordation of a mortgage (443)
Note (443)
Notice of lien (446)
Postjudgment court order (449)
Power of sale (444)
Prejudgment court order (449)
Primarily liable (447)
Reconveyance (satisfaction of a mortgage) (443)
Recording statute (443)
Regulation Z (451)
Right of redemption (446)
Secondarily liable (447)
Secured credit (442)
Secured creditor (secured party) (442)
Security interest in real property (442)
Statutory period of redemption (446)
Surety (co-debtor, accommodation party, or co-signer) (447)
Surety arrangement (447)
Title III of the Consumer Credit Protection Act (450)
Trustee (443)
Trustor (443)
Truth-in-Lending Act (TILA) (451)
Universal default rule (452)
Unsecured credit (441)
Unsecured creditor (441)
Writ of attachment (449)
Writ of execution (449)
Writ of garnishment (450)

Critical Legal Thinking Cases

26.1 Lien Ironwood Exploration, Inc. (Ironwood) owned a lease on oil and gas property located in Duchesne County, Utah. Ironwood contracted to have Lantz Drilling and Exploration Company, Inc. (Lantz) drill an oil well on the property. Thereafter, Lantz rented equipment from Graco Fishing and Rental Tools, Inc. (Graco) for use in drilling the well. Graco billed Lantz for these rentals, but Lantz did not pay. Graco filed a notice of a lien on the well in the amount of $19,766. Ironwood, which had paid Lantz, refused to pay Graco. Graco sued to foreclose on its lien. Who wins? *Graco Fishing and Rental Tools, Inc. v. Ironwood Exploration, Inc.*, 766 P.2d 1074, 1988 Utah Lexis 125 (Supreme Court of Utah, 1988)

26.2 Foreclosure Atlantic Ocean Kampgrounds, Inc. (Atlantic) borrowed $60,000 from Camden National Bank (Camden National) and executed a note and mortgage on property located in Camden, Maine, securing that amount. Maine permits strict foreclosure. Atlantic defaulted on the loan, and Camden commenced strict foreclosure proceedings pursuant to state law. After the one-year period of redemption, Camden National sold the property to a third party in an amount in excess of the mortgage and costs of the foreclosure proceeding. Atlantic sued to recover the surplus from Camden National. Who wins? *Atlantic Ocean Kampgrounds, Inc. v. Camden National Bank*, 473 A.2d 884, 1984 Me. Lexis 666 (Supreme Judicial Court of Maine, 1984)

26.3 Redemption Elmer and Arletta Hans, husband and wife, owned a parcel of real property in Illinois. They borrowed $100,000 from First Illinois National Bank (First Illinois) and executed a note and mortgage to First Illinois, making the real estate security for the loan. The security agreement authorized First Illinois to take possession of the property on the occurrence of a default and required the Hanses to execute a quitclaim deed in favor of First Illinois. The state of Illinois recognizes the doctrine of redemption. When the Hanses defaulted on the loan, First Illinois filed a lawsuit, seeking an order requiring the Hanses to immediately execute a quitclaim deed to the property. Must the Hanses execute the quitclaim deed before the foreclosure sale? *First Illinois National Bank v. Hans*, 493 N.E.2d 1171, 1986 Ill. App. Lexis 2287 (Appellate Court of Illinois, 1986)

26.4 Deficiency Judgment Sally Fitch obtained a loan from Buffalo Federal Savings and Loan Association (Buffalo Federal). She signed a promissory note for $130,000 with interest at 17 percent. The loan was secured with a real estate mortgage on property owned by Fitch located in Johnson County, Wyoming. Wyoming did not have an anti-deficiency statute. Four years later, Fitch was in default on the note. When she was unable to pay the loan to current status, Buffalo Federal sent her a notice of foreclosure. After publication of proper public notice, the sheriff conducted the sale as advertised on the steps of the Johnson County Courthouse. The property sold for a high bid of $66,000. Buffalo Federal applied the $66,000 to the $150,209 balance on the note and sued Fitch to recover a judgment for the deficiency of $84,209. Who wins? *Fitch v. Buffalo Federal Savings and Loan Association*, 751 P.2d 1309, 1988 Wyo. Lexis 27 (Supreme Court of Wyoming, 1988)

Ethics Cases

26.5 Ethics Case Jessie Lynch became seriously ill and needed medical attention. Her sister, Ethel Sales, took her to Forsyth County Memorial Hospital in North Carolina for treatment. Lynch was admitted for hospitalization. Sales signed Lynch's admission form, which included the following section:

> *The undersigned, in consideration of hospital services being rendered or to be rendered by Forsyth County Memorial Hospital Authority, Inc., in Winston-Salem, N.C., to the above patient, does hereby guarantee payment to Forsyth County Hospital Authority, Inc., on demand all charges for said services and incidentals incurred on behalf of such patient.*

Lynch received care and services rendered by the hospital until her discharge more than 30 days later. The total bill during her hospitalization amounted to $7,977. When Lynch refused to pay the bill, the hospital instituted an action against Lynch and Sales to recover the unpaid amount. Is Sales liable? Did Sales act ethically in denying liability? Did she have a choice when she signed the contract? *Forsyth County Memorial Hospital Authority, Inc. v. Sales*, 346 S.E.2d 212, 1986 N.C. App. Lexis 2432 (Court of Appeals of North Carolina, 1986)

26.6 Ethics Case Elizabeth Valentine purchased a home in Philadelphia, Pennsylvania. She applied for and received a home loan from Salmon Building and Loan Association (Salmon) for the purpose of paneling the cellar walls and redecorating the house. Salmon took a security interest in the house as collateral for the loan. Although Salmon gave Valentine a disclosure document, nowhere on the document were finance charges disclosed. The document did notify Valentine that Salmon had a security interest in the house. More than two years later, Valentine sued Salmon (which had since merged with Influential Savings and Loan Association) to rescind the loan. Who wins? Did Salmon act ethically in this case? *Valentine v. Influential Savings and Loan Association*, 572 F.Supp. 36, 1983 U.S. Dist. Lexis 15884 (United States District Court for the Eastern District of Pennsylvania, 1983)

Notes

1. 15 U.S.C. Sections 1671 et seq.
2. 15 U.S.C. Sections 1601–1667.
3. 12 C.F.R. 226.
4. 15 U.S.C. Sections 1667–1667f.
5. 15 U.S.C. Sections 1666–1666j.
6. Public Law 24, 123 Stat. 1734–1766.
7. 15 U.S.C. Sections 1681–1681u.
8. 15 U.S.C. Sections 1681–1681x.
9. 15 U.S.C. Sections 1692–1692o.
10. 15 U.S.C. Sections 1691–1691f.
11. 15 U.S.C. Sections 1637c–g.

CHAPTER 27

Secured Transactions

FARM EQUIPMENT

People often purchase cars, trucks, motorcycles, equipment, boats, and other personal property using credit that is extended by banks, sellers, or other lenders. Often, the lender takes back a security interest in the property, which becomes collateral for the loan. This is called a secured transaction. If this combine is purchased using a loan from a bank, the bank, as the lender, would take a security interest in the combine as collateral. Secured transactions are governed by Article 9 of the Uniform Commercial Code (UCC).

Stephen Mcsweeny/123RF

Learning Objectives

After studying this chapter, you should be able to:

27.1 Define *secured transaction* and describe Article 9 of the Uniform Commercial Code (UCC).

27.2 Describe how a security interest in personal property is created.

27.3 Describe the perfection of a security interest by filing a financing statement and other means.

27.4 Explain the UCC rule for determining priority among conflicting claims.

27.5 Define *default* and describe the remedies available to the secured party if there is a default.

"Debtors are liars."

—*George Herbert,*
Jacula Prudentum (1651)

Introduction to Secured Transactions

Never spend your money before you have it.
Thomas Jefferson (1743–1826)
Third president of the United States

Many items of *personal property* are purchased with credit rather than with cash. Because lenders are reluctant to lend large sums of money simply on the borrower's promise to repay, many of them take a *security interest* in either the item purchased or some other personal property of the debtor. The property in which a security interest is taken is called *collateral*. When a creditor extends credit to a debtor and takes a security interest in some property of the debtor, it is called a *secured transaction*. If the debtor does not pay the debt, the creditor can foreclose on and recover the collateral.

This chapter discusses secured transactions in personal property.

Secured Transactions in Personal Property

27.1 Define *secured transaction* and describe Article 9 of the Uniform Commercial Code (UCC).

personal property
Tangible property, such as equipment, vehicles, furniture, and jewelry, as well as intangible property, such as securities, patents, trademarks, and copyrights.

Revised Article 9 (Secured Transactions)
An article of the Uniform Commercial Code that governs secured transactions in personal property.

2010 Amendments to Revised Article 9
Amendments to Revised Article 9 that address modern commercial issues and expand the use of electronic methods in secured transactions.

Individuals and businesses purchase or lease various forms of tangible and intangible **personal property**. *Tangible personal property* includes equipment, vehicles, furniture, computers, clothing, jewelry, and other physical possessions. *Intangible personal property* includes securities, patents, trademarks, and copyrights.

Personal property is often sold on credit. This means the purchaser-debtor borrows money from a lender-creditor to purchase the personal property. Sometimes a lender extends **unsecured credit** to a debtor to purchase personal property. In this case, the creditor takes no interest in any collateral to secure the loan but bases the decision to extend credit on the credit standing of the debtor. If the debtor defaults on the loan, the creditor must sue the debtor to try to recover the unpaid loan amount.

In some credit transactions, particularly those involving large or expensive items, a creditor may agree to extend credit only if the purchaser pledges some personal property as collateral for the loan. This is called **secured credit**. If the debtor defaults on the loan, the creditor may seek to recover the collateral under a lawful foreclosure action.

The following feature describes Article 9 of the Uniform Commercial Code.

Landmark Law

Article 9—Secured Transactions

Article 9 (Secured Transactions) of the Uniform Commercial Code (UCC) governs secured transactions in which personal property is used as collateral for a loan or the extension of credit. In 2001, after years of study and debate, the National Conference of Commissioners on Uniform State Laws and the American Law Institute issued **Revised Article 9 (Secured Transactions)** of the UCC. Most states have enacted Revised Article 9 as the secured transactions statute within their states. Revised Article 9 includes modern and efficient rules that govern secured transactions in personal property, and it contains many new provisions that recognize the importance of e-commerce, including rules for the creation, filing, and enforcement of electronic secured transactions.

In 2010, Revised Article 9 was amended. The **2010 Amendments to Revised Article 9** address commercial issues that arose since the adoption of Revised Article 9, clarify information to be included on financing statements, add new provisions recognizing the importance of the use of electronic media for secured transactions, and other issues. The material in this chapter that covers secured transactions is based on the provisions of Revised Article 9, including the 2010 amendments. The act and amendments will be referred to as Article 9 in this chapter.

Article 9 does not apply to transactions involving real estate mortgages, landlord's liens, artisan's or mechanic's liens, liens on wages, judicial liens, and the like. These types of liens are covered by other laws.

Secured Transaction

When a creditor extends credit to a debtor and takes a security interest in some personal property of the debtor, it is called a **secured transaction**. The **secured party** is the seller, lender, or other party in whose favor there is a security interest. If the debtor defaults and does not repay the loan, generally the secured party can foreclose and recover the collateral. Article 9 recognizes the importance of electronic transactions and authorizes the use of electronic records.

secured transaction
A transaction that is created when a creditor makes a loan to a debtor in exchange for the debtor's pledge of personal property as security.

Some of the words commonly used in secured transactions are listed and defined in Exhibit 27.1.

Exhibit 27.1 DEFINITIONS USED IN SECURED TRANSACTIONS

1. **Authenticate.** Means to sign a document, or to adopt or accept an electronic record by electronic signature (electronic symbol, sound, or process) [UCC 9-102(a)(7)].
2. **Debtor.** A **debtor** is a person who has an ownership or other interest (other than a secured interest) in the collateral, whether or not the person is the obligor, or is a seller of promissory notes, accounts, chattel paper, or payment intangibles [UCC 9-102(a)(28)].

   Example Oil Corporation, a major oil producing company, purchases a large piece of oil field equipment from Equipment Corporation, a large oil equipment manufacturer, on credit, and gives Equipment Corporation a secured interest in the collateral. Oil Corporation is the debtor.
3. **Secured party.** A person in whose favor a security interest is created or provided for under a security agreement, agricultural lien, or a person to which promissory notes, accounts, chattel paper, or payment intangibles have been sold [UCC 9-102(a)(73)].

   Example In the prior example, Equipment Corporation is the secured party.
4. **Security interest.** An interest in the collateral, such as personal property or fixtures, that secures payment or performance of an obligation [UCC 1-201(b)(35)].

   Example In the previous example, Oil Corporation, the debtor, gave Equipment Corporation, the creditor, a security interest in equipment.
5. **Security agreement.** An agreement that creates or provides for a security interest [UCC 9-102(a)(74)].

   Example In the prior example, Equipment Corporation, the creditor, would, as a condition of the credit sale, have required Oil Corporation, the debtor, to sign a security agreement giving Equipment Corporation a security interest in the equipment, making the equipment collateral for the loan.
6. **Collateral.** The property that is subject to a security agreement [UCC 9-102(a)(12)].

   Example In the prior example, the oil field equipment is the collateral for the security agreement.
7. **Financing statement.** The record or records composed of an initial financing statement and any filed record relating to the initial filing statement [UCC 9-102(a)(39)]. This is *Form UCC-1 (UCC Financing Statement)*. The financing statement is usually filed with the appropriate state office (filing office) to give public notice of the secured party's security interest in the collateral and to establish priority of claims in case there are competing interests in the secured property. Most states permit the filing of electronic financing statements

(continued)

Example In the prior example, if Equipment Corporation (the secured creditor) files a financing statement, it has given public notice of its secured interest in the collateral, the oil field equipment. The financing statement must name Oil Corporation as the debtor.

8. **Record. Record** means information that is inscribed on a tangible medium or that is stored in an electronic or other medium and is retrievable in perceivable form [UCC 9-102(a)(70)]. The term *record* is now used in most of the provisions of Article 9 in place of the term *writing*, further recognizing the importance of e-commerce.
9. **Public organic record.** A **public organic record** is a record that is available to the public for inspection that is the correct source of the debtor's name that appears on a financing statement [UCC 9-102(a)(68)].

   Examples The articles of incorporation of a corporation, public formation records of other business entities, public records that create a business trust, and such.

10. **Registered organization.** A **registered organization** is an organization that is formed under the laws of a state or the United States [UCC 9-102(a)(71)].

    Examples Corporations, limited liability companies, limited partnerships, general partnerships, sole proprietorships, business trusts, and such.

Two-Party Secured Transaction

two-party secured transaction
Occurs when a seller sells goods to a buyer on credit and retains a security interest in the goods.

Exhibit 27.2 illustrates a **two-party secured transaction**. Such transactions occur, for example, when a seller sells goods to a buyer on credit and retains a security interest in the goods.

Example A retail dealer sells supplies and equipment to a contractor on credit. The dealer retains a security interest in the supplies and equipment, which are collateral for the loan. This is a two-party secured transaction. The contractor is the purchaser and debtor, and the retail dealer is the seller and secured creditor.

Three-Party Secured Transaction

three-party secured transaction
Occurs when a seller sells goods to a buyer who has obtained financing from a third-party lender who takes a security interest in the goods sold.

A three-party secured transaction arises when a seller sells goods to a buyer who has obtained financing from a third-party lender (e.g., a bank) and the **third-party lender** takes a security interest in the goods. Exhibit 27.3 illustrates a **three-party secured transaction**.

Example A business purchases an airplane from an airplane manufacturer. The business obtains a loan to purchase the airplane from a bank, which obtains a security interest in the airplane. The airplane manufacturer is paid for the airplane out of the proceeds of the loan. This is a three-party secured transaction. The airplane manufacturer is the seller, the purchasing business is the buyer and debtor, and the bank is the lender and secured creditor.

Exhibit 27.2 TWO-PARTY SECURED TRANSACTION

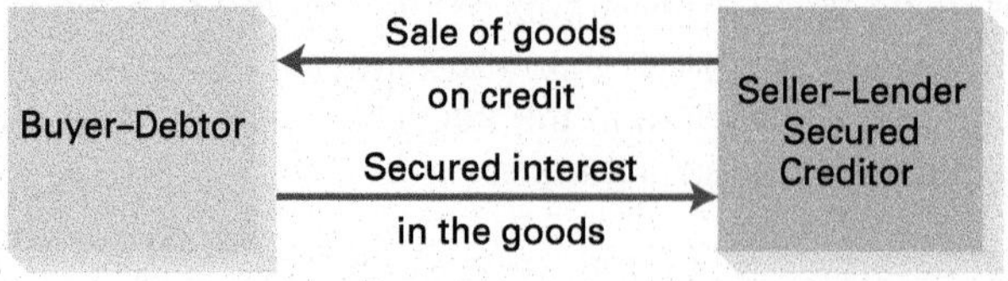

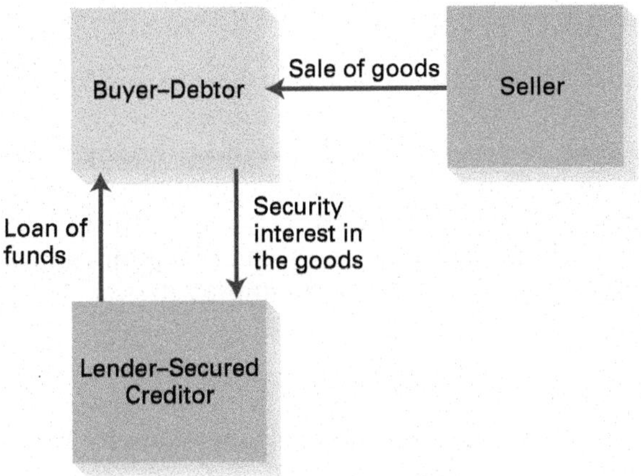

Exhibit 27.3 THREE-PARTY SECURED TRANSACTION

Personal Property Subject to a Security Agreement

A security interest may be given in various types of personal property that becomes **collateral** for the loan. This includes *tangible personal property* and *intangible personal property* [UCC 9-102(a)(12)].

collateral
Personal property that is subject to a security agreement.

Tangible Collateral

Tangible personal property is personal property that can be touched and can be moved from one place to another. It is distinguishable from real property that is attached to one location and is not movable. It is also distinguishable from intangible property, which cannot be touched, such as checking accounts, stocks and bonds, and patents.

The UCC uses the term *goods* to define tangible personal property that can be used as collateral for secured transactions. **Goods** means all things that are movable when a security interest attaches to the goods, including such things as standing timber, unborn young of animals, grown and growing crops, manufactured homes, and removable fixtures [UCC 9-102(a)(44)]. Categories of goods that can be used as **tangible collateral** for secured transactions are listed and described in Exhibit 27.4.

goods
All things that are movable when a security interest attaches to the goods.

tangible collateral
Goods that can be used as collateral for secured transactions.

Exhibit 27.4 TANGIBLE COLLATERAL

1. **Accessions.** Goods that are physically united with other goods in such a manner that the identity of the original goods is not lost [UCC 9-102(a)(1)].

   Example A DVD player that is installed in an automobile.

2. **Consumer good.** A good bought or used primarily for personal, family, or household purposes [UCC 9-102(a)(23)].

   Examples Household televisions, computers, electronic devices, furniture, and furnishings.

3. **Equipment.** Goods other than inventory, farm products, or consumer goods [UCC 9-102(a)(33)]. These goods are often used for business purposes.

   Examples Moving cranes and assembly line equipment.

4. **Farm products.** Goods with respect to which the debtor is engaged in farming operations, including crops growing or grown, aquatic goods, livestock (born and unborn), and supplies used or produced in farming operations [UCC 9-102(a)(34)].

   Examples Wheat, fish, cattle, milk, apples, and unborn calves.

5. **Inventory.** Goods (other than farm products) that are held for sale or lease or to be furnished under a contract of service, raw materials, work in progress, or materials used or consumed in a business [UCC 9-102(a)(48)].

   Example Iron ore that is used to make steel.

Intangible Collateral

Intangible personal property is an item that has no physical substance and cannot be touched or held. This includes such things as security investments, intellectual property such as copyrights, and the like. Intangible personal property is distinguishable from real property and physical tangible property. Intangible personal property can be used as collateral for secured transactions. Categories of intangible property that can be used as **intangible collateral** for secured transactions are listed and described in Exhibit 27.5.

intangible collateral
Items that have no physical substance that can be used as collateral for secured transactions.

Creating a Security Interest

27.2 Describe how a security interest in personal property is created.

Article 9 sets forth the requirements that must be met to create a security interest in personal property. These requirements are discussed in the following paragraphs.

Security Agreement and Attachment

If a creditor extends credit to a debtor to purchase personal property, the creditor remains an unsecured creditor unless the creditor obtains a security interest in the property (or some other personal property) of the debtor to secure the loan. This is accomplished by attaching a **security interest** to the personal property. The personal property to which a security interest attaches is called collateral. **Attachment** means that the creditor has an enforceable security interest against the debtor and can satisfy the debt out of the designated collateral [UCC 9-203(a)].

attachment
A situation in which a creditor has an enforceable security interest against a debtor and can satisfy the debt out of the designated collateral.

A security interest is enforceable against the debtor if (1) value has been given for the security interest, (2) the debtor has rights in the collateral (or power to transfer rights in the collateral to a third party), and (3) the debtor has authenticated a **security agreement** that provides a description of the collateral [9-203(b)]. Giving value is similar to giving consideration for a contract. In order for a security interest to be enforceable, the debtor must have a current or future legal right in or the right to possession of the collateral.

security agreement
A written document signed by a debtor that creates a security interest in personal property.

Authenticate means that the debtor signs a physical security agreement or provides an electronic signature to an electronic record of the security agreement by attaching or associating an electronic sound, symbol, or process to the record [UCC 9-102(a)(7)]. Thus, electronic security agreements are recognized and enforceable. A security agreement is a contract between the creditor and the debtor, and it is an enforceable contract as long as the requirements for creating the security agreement have been met.

authenticate
The act of signing a document or adopting or accepting an electronic record by electronic signature (electronic symbol, sound, or process).

A security agreement is an agreement that creates or provides for a security interest [UCC 9-102(a)(74)]. A security agreement must (1) describe the collateral clearly so that it can be readily identified; (2) contain the debtor's promise to repay the creditor, including terms of repayment (e.g., interest rate, time of payment); and (3) set forth the creditor's rights on the debtor's default. A security interest attaches to collateral when it becomes enforceable against the debtor with respect to the collateral [UCC 9-203(a)].

A security agreement is not necessary to give a creditor a secured interest in the debtor's property if the creditor is in possession of the collateral. Possession alone gives the creditor a security interest in the personal property [UCC 9-313(a)].

Floating Lien

floating lien
A security interest in property that was not in the possession of the debtor when the security agreement was executed.

A security agreement may include a provision that provides that the security interest attaches to property that was not originally in the possession of the debtor when the agreement was executed. This interest is called a **floating lien**.

Exhibit 27.5 INTANGIBLE COLLATERAL

1. **Accounts.** An **account** is a right to receive payment of a monetary obligation for property that has been or is to be sold, leased, licensed, assigned, or otherwise disposed of; for services rendered or to be rendered, including contract rights; for policies of insurance; for a secondary obligation incurred or to be incurred; for winnings from a government-sponsored or authorized lottery; for use of a credit card; and for health care insurance receivables [UCC 9-102(a)(2)].

   Example A doctor provides medical services to patients, and the patients owe the doctor money for the services. The doctor can pledge the payments due from the patients as collateral to obtain a loan.

2. **Chattel paper. Chattel paper** is a record or records that evidences both a monetary obligation and a security interest in specific goods and software used in the goods [UCC 9-102(a)(11)]. Chattel paper indicates that a holder is owed money and has a security interest in valuable goods associated with the debt. It is personal property in its own right, distinct from the property it relates to. **Tangible chattel paper** means chattel paper evidenced by a record or records consisting of information that is inscribed on a tangible medium (written) [UCC 9-102(a)(79)]. **Electronic chattel paper** means chattel paper evidenced in a record or records consisting of information stored in an electronic medium [UCC 9-102(a)(31)].

   Example An equipment lessor leases equipment to businesses and takes a security interest in the equipment as security for the payment of the rental payments. This is chattel paper. The equipment lessor can sell its interest in the lease payments and security agreements to another party.

3. **Deposit account.** A **deposit account** means a demand, time, savings, passbook, or similar account maintained with a bank or other financial institution. The term does not include investment property or accounts evidenced by an instrument [UCC 9-102(a)(29)].

   Examples A checking or savings account at a bank.

4. **Instrument.** An **instrument** means a negotiable instrument or any other writing that evidences a right to the payment of money that in the ordinary course of business is transferred by delivery with any necessary indorsement or assignment. The term does not include investment property [UCC 9-102(a)(47)].

   Examples Negotiable instruments such as promissory notes, checks, and drafts.

5. **Investment property. Investment property** means a security, whether certificated or uncertificated, securities account, security entitlement, or commodity contract or account [UCC 9-102(a)(49)].

   Examples Stocks, bonds, commodities future contracts, and other investment securities.

6. **General intangible.** A **general intangible** means any personal property other than accounts, chattel paper, deposit accounts, documents, goods, instruments, investment property, letters of credit, money, and oil, gas, or other minerals prior to extraction [UCC 9-102(a)(42)]. This definition is a catch-all or residual category of collateral that includes types of intangible personal property not covered by the other more recognized categories.

   Examples Patents, copyrights, and trademarks and other intellectual property, literary rights and royalties, rights to collect money pursuant to annuity contracts, licenses such as liquor licenses and commercial fishing licenses, proceeds to an impending lawsuit, and general and limited partnership interests.

No further action must be taken by the secured party when future events specified in the original filing statements occur. A floating lien can attach to *after-acquired property, sale proceeds*, and *future advances*. These are discussed in the following paragraphs.

after-acquired property
Property that a debtor acquires after a security agreement is executed.

- **After-acquired property.** Many security agreements contain a clause that gives the secured party a security interest in **after-acquired property** of the debtor. After-acquired property is property that the debtor acquires after the security agreement is executed [UCC 9-204(a)].

  Example A manufacturing company borrows $100,000 from a bank and gives the bank a security interest in both its current and after-acquired inventory. If the manufacturing company defaults on its loan to the bank, the bank can recover available original inventory and after-acquired inventory as necessary to satisfy its secured claim.

sale proceeds
The resulting assets from the sale, exchange, or disposal of collateral subject to a security agreement.

- **Sale proceeds.** Unless otherwise stated in a security agreement, if a debtor sells, exchanges, or disposes of collateral subject to such an agreement, the secured party automatically has the right to receive the **sale proceeds** of the sale, exchange, or disposition [UCC 9-102(a)(64), 9-203(f), 9-315(a)].

  Example An equipment manufacturer sells equipment to a retail business on credit and takes a security interest in the sold equipment. If the debtor sells the equipment, the secured creditor has the right to receive the sale proceeds.

future advances
Funds advanced to a debtor in the future as prearranged in a security agreement.

- **Future advances.** A security agreement may provide that the collateral secures **future advances** or other value. Future advances are funds advanced to a debtor in the future under terms prearranged in a security agreement. A security agreement may provide that accounts, chattel paper, payment intangibles, or promissory notes are sold in connection with future advances or other value [UCC 9-204(c)].

  Example A company establishes a $1 million continuous, revolving five-year line of credit at a bank that allows it to borrow up to $1 million and to repay and re-borrow money from the line of credit during the five-year period as long as the total outstanding loan amount at any one time does not exceed $1 million. At the time of executing the line of credit, the company signs a security agreement that makes its patents collateral for the line of credit. At the time that the loan agreement and security agreement are signed, the company borrows $500,000 against the line of credit. Two years later, the technology company pays back the $500,000. One year after that, the company borrows $1 million against the outstanding line of credit. This loan is secured by the patents.

Perfecting a Security Interest

27.3 Describe the perfection of a security interest by filing a financing statement and other means.

perfection of a security interest
A process that establishes the right of a secured creditor against other creditors who claim an interest in the collateral.

The concept of **perfection of a security interest** establishes the right of a secured creditor against other creditors who claim an interest in the collateral. The process of perfection is not required by law. Thus, a creditor retains its security interest in the collateral whether or not the creditor perfects its interest. However, perfection of a security interest allows a creditor to claim priority status over other creditors who may later obtain a security interest in the collateral.

Perfection of a security interest is a legal process. The three main methods of perfecting a security interest under the UCC are (1) perfection by filing a *financing statement*, (2) perfection by possession of collateral, and (3) perfection by a purchase money security interest in consumer goods. These three main methods of perfecting a security interest are discussed in the following paragraphs.

Perfection by Filing a Financing Statement

Often, a creditor's physical possession of collateral is impractical because it would deprive the debtor of use of the collateral (e.g., farm equipment, industrial machinery, consumer goods). At other times, it is simply impossible (e.g., accounts receivable).

The filing of a **financing statement** by a secured party with the secretary of state or other designated state government office (filing office) is the most common method for perfecting the secured party's security interest in collateral [UCC 9-501]. This is called **perfection by filing a financing statement**. Financing statements are effective for five years from the date of filing.

financing statement
A document filed by a secured creditor with the appropriate government office that constructively notifies the world of the creditor's security interest in personal property. Financing statements are effective for five years from the date of filing.

A uniform financing statement form, **UCC Financing Statement (Form UCC-1)**, is used in all states [UCC 9-521(a)]. A financing statement can be filed electronically using a state's e-filing system [UCC 9-102(a)(18)]. A financing statement is usually assigned a file number, and the date and time of the filing are recorded. To be enforceable, a financing statement must contain the name of the debtor, list the name and address of the secured party or a representative of the secured party, and indicate the collateral covered by the financing statement [UCC 9-502(a)]. Article 9 requires the debtor's name to appear on a financing statement as follows:

UCC Financing Statement (Form UCC-1)
A uniform financing statement form that is used in all states.

- **Individual debtor's name.** If the debtor is an individual, a financing statement is sufficient only if it contains the debtor's name as shown on an unexpired driver's license issued by the debtor's resident state. This is an "only if" rule; that is, if a debtor has an unexpired driver's license, the name on the driver's license must be used as the name of the debtor on a financing statement. If an individual debtor does not have an unexpired driver's license, the financing statement must provide either the individual name of the debtor (the legal name) or the debtor's surname and first personal name [UCC 9-503(a)(4)(5) Alternative A]. Most states follow this rule.
- **Registered organization name.** If a debtor is a registered organization, then the organization's name used on the public organic record of the state of organization or jurisdiction of organization must be used to identify the debtor in a financing statement. This name can be found on a corporation's articles of incorporation, a limited liability company's articles of organization, and so on [UCC 503(a)(1)]. If the debtor is an organization that has a name but is not a registered organization, the financing statement shall provide the organization's name [UCC 9-503(a)(6)(A)].
- **No organization name.** If the debtor is an entity without a legal organization name, then a financing statement must contain the individual names of partners, members, associates, or other persons comprising the debtor. For example, this would be the individual names of partners in a general partnership [UCC 9-503(a)(6)(B)].
- **Trust.** If the debtor is a trust and it is a registered organization, the debtor's name on the financing statement must be the registered name. If a trust is not a registered organization, then the name of the settlor or testator shall be used as the name of the debtor on the financing statement [UCC 9-503(a)(3)(A)].

Critical Legal Thinking Questions
What is a financing statement? What does the proper filing of a financing statement accomplish? What are the consequences if a financing statement is filed improperly?

A financing statement is not rendered ineffective if it does not include the trade name of the debtor [UCC 9-503(b)(1)]. A financing statement that provides only the debtor's trade name does not provide the name of the debtor sufficiently [UCC 9-503(c)]. Minor errors and omissions on a financing statement do not change its effectiveness unless the error or omission makes the financing statement seriously misleading [UCC 9-506(a)].

A debtor must notify the creditor if he or she or an entity changes their name. If the name on a financing statement becomes insufficient as the name of the debtor and renders the statement seriously misleading, the financing statement is effective for a grace period of four months [UCC 9-507(c)]. A creditor may file an amendment to the financing statement. Therefore, a creditor must be vigilant in checking to determine if a debtor's name has changed.

State law specifies where a financing statement must be filed. A state may choose either the secretary of state or the county recorder's office in the county of the debtor's residence or, if the debtor is not a resident of the state, in the county where the goods are kept or in another county office, or both. If the collateral is minerals, timber, or a fixture filing, the filing office is where mortgages are filed in the state where the collateral is located [UCC 9-501(a)(1)].

A filing office may refuse a filing statement if the statement does not contain the name of the debtor or the secured party, if it is not submitted by the approved method of communication, or if the filer has not paid the requisite filing fee [UCC 9-516(b)].

Financing statements are available for review by the public. They serve as *constructive notice* to the world that a creditor claims an interest in a property. A **continuation statement** may be filed up to six months prior to the expiration of a financing statement's five-year term. Such statements are effective for a new five-year term. Succeeding continuation statements may be filed [Revised UCC 9-515(d), (e)]. A financing statement filed in connection with a manufactured-home transaction is effective for a period of 30 years from the date of filing [UCC 9-515(b)].

continuation statement
A document filed by a secured creditor with the appropriate government office to extend the five-year term of a financing statement for an additional five-year term. Successive continuation statements may be filed.

Service companies such as CSC and others provide professional services for filing and searching UCC-1 financing statements.

In the following case, the court had to determine whether the filing of a financing statement was effective.

CASE 27.1 *STATE COURT CASE Filing a Financing Statement*

Pankratz Implement Company v. Citizens National Bank

130 P.3d 57, 2006 Kan. Lexis 141 (2006)
Supreme Court of Kansas

"Thus, Pankratz's financing statement using the misspelled name of the debtor, while prior in time, was seriously misleading ..."

—Robert Davis, Justice

Facts

Rodger House purchased a tractor on credit from Pankratz Implement Company. House signed a note and security agreement that made the tractor collateral for the repayment of the debt. The creditor filed a financing statement with the Kansas secretary of state using the misspelled name of the debtor, "Roger House," rather than the correct name of the debtor, "Rodger House." One year later, House obtained a loan from Citizens National Bank (CNB). House gave a security interest to CNB by pledging all equipment that he owned and that he may own in the future as collateral for the loan. CNB filed a financing statement with the Kansas secretary of state using the correct name of the debtor, "Rodger House."

Several years later, while still owing money to Pankratz and CNB, House filed for bankruptcy. Pankratz filed a lawsuit in Kansas trial court to recover the tractor. CNB challenged the claim, alleging that it should be permitted to recover the tractor. The trial court found that Pankratz's misspelling of the debtor's first name on its financing statement was a minor error and granted summary judgment to Pankratz. The court of appeals held that Pankratz's misspelling of House's first name was seriously misleading and held in favor of CNB. Pankratz appealed.

Issue

Is Pankratz's filing of the financing statement under the wrong first name of the debtor seriously misleading?

Language of the Court

Because the primary purpose of a financing statement is to provide notice to third parties that the creditor has an interest in the debtor's property and the financing statements are indexed under the debtor's name, it is particularly important to require exactness in the name used, the debtor's legal name. We conclude that Pankratz's filed financing statement was "seriously misleading."

Decision

The supreme court of Kansas held that the misspelling of the debtor's name misled creditors and was therefore ineffectual in giving CNB notice of Pankratz's security interest in the tractor. The state supreme court affirmed the court of appeals judgment in CNB's favor.

Critical Legal Thinking Questions

Did either party act unethically in this case? Or was this a legitimate legal dispute?

Perfection by Possession of Collateral

A secured party may perfect a security interest in goods, tangible chattel, tangible negotiable documents, tangible chattel paper, instruments, and money by taking possession of the collateral [UCC 9-313(a)]. Thus, no financing statement has to be filed if the secured party has physical possession of the collateral [UCC 9-310(a)(6)]. This is known as **perfection by possession of collateral**. The rationale behind this rule is that if someone other than the debtor is in possession of the property, a potential creditor is on notice that another party may claim an interest in the debtor's property. A secured party who holds the debtor's property as collateral must use reasonable care in the custody and preservation of the collateral [UCC 9-207(a].

perfection by possession of collateral
A rule stating that if a secured creditor has physical possession of the collateral, no financing statement has to be filed; the creditor's possession is sufficient to put other potential creditors on notice of the creditor's secured interest in the property.

Example Karen borrows $3,000 from Ignacio and gives her motorcycle to him as security for the loan. Ignacio does not file a financing statement. Another creditor obtains a judgment against Karen. This creditor cannot recover the motorcycle from Ignacio. Even though Ignacio has not filed a financing statement, his security interest in the motorcycle is perfected because he has possession of the motorcycle.

A security interest in deposit accounts (e.g., bank accounts), investment property (e.g., stocks), letter of credit rights, electronic chattel paper, and electronic documents may be perfected by possession or control of the collateral [UCC 9-314].

Perfection by a Purchase Money Security Interest in Consumer Goods

Sellers and lenders often extend credit to consumers to purchase consumer goods. **Consumer goods** include furniture, televisions, home appliances, electronic devices, and other goods used primarily for personal, family, or household purposes.

A creditor who extends credit to a consumer to purchase a consumer good under a written security agreement obtains a **purchase money security interest** in the consumer good. The agreement automatically perfects the creditor's security interest at the time of the sale. This is called **perfection by a purchase money security interest in consumer goods**. The creditor does not have to file a financing statement or take possession of the goods to perfect the security interest. This is called **perfection by attachment**, or the **automatic perfection rule** [UCC 9-309(1)].

purchase money security interest
An interest a creditor automatically obtains when the creditor extends credit to a consumer to purchase consumer goods.

Example A consumer buys a $1,500 smart television for her home on credit extended by the seller, a retail store. The seller requires the consumer to sign a security agreement making the television collateral for the credit. The store has a purchase money security interest in the television that is automatically perfected at the time of the sale.

In a consumer credit transaction, the secured party may file a financing statement indicating its security interest in the property.

CONCEPT SUMMARY

METHODS OF PERFECTING A SECURITY INTEREST

Perfection Method	How Created
Financing statement	Creditor files a financing statement with the appropriate government office.
Possession of collateral	Creditor obtains physical possession of the collateral.
Purchase money security interest	Creditor extends credit to a debtor to purchase consumer goods and obtains a security interest in the goods.

termination statement
A document filed by a secured party that ends a secured interest because the debt has been paid.

certificate of title statutes
State statutes that provide for filing of certificates of title for motor vehicles, trailers, mobile homes, boats, farm tractors, or the like that may specify security interests held in the property.

Termination Statement

Because most original financing statements expire after five years, and continuation statements also usually expire after five years, a secured party has no duty to file a termination statement regarding nonconsumer transactions unless demanded to do so by the debtor. If a financing statement covers consumer goods, the secured party must file a **termination statement** with the appropriate state filing office within one month after the debt is paid or 20 days after receipt of the debtor's written demand, whichever occurs first [UCC 9-513(a), (b)]. If the affected secured party fails to file or send the termination statement as required, the secured party is liable for any other losses caused to the debtor.

The following feature describes certificate of title laws.

Contemporary Environment

Certificate of Title Statutes

The filing of a financing statement is not necessary or effective to perfect a security interest in property subject to a state statute covering motor vehicles, trailers, mobile homes, boats, farm tractors, or the like, which provides for a security interest to be indicated on the certificate of title as a condition or result of perfection [UCC 9-311(a)(2)]. The state statute is usually referred to as a **certificate of title statute.** A secured party's interest in the property must be indicated on the personal property's **certificate of title** [UCC 9-102(a)(10)]. In some states, the lienholder possesses the certificate of title until the loan has been paid, at which time the certificate of title will be transferred to the owner. Duration and renewal of a security interest in property subject to a certificate of title statute is determined by that statute.

Example A person purchases a car from an automobile dealer and obtains a loan from Ally Financial, Inc., a car finance company, to complete the purchase. The name Ally Financial, Inc. is placed on the car's certificate of title as the lienholder. This perfects the lender's security interest in the car. If the purchaser later defaults on the loan, the lender can repossess the vehicle and take whatever other legal action is necessary to recover payment of the loan.

If a lender fails to place its name on a certificate of title, the loan is still valid pursuant to the loan documents signed by the parties, but the lender's security interest is not perfected for purposes of priority. If the lender files a UCC Article 9 financing statement concerning its security interest in personal property subject to a certificate of title law, but does not place its name on the certificate of title, the lender's security interest is not perfected for purposes of priority. Most state certificate of title laws require lenders to release the title within 10 days after a loan is paid off.

Priority of Claims

27.4 Explain the UCC rule for determining priority among conflicting claims.

Two or more creditors often claim an interest in the same collateral or property. The priority of the claims is determined according to (1) whether the claim is unsecured or secured and (2) the time at which secured claims were attached or perfected. The UCC rules for establishing creditors' **priority of claims** are as follows:

priority of claims
The order in which conflicting claims of creditors in the same collateral are solved.

1. **Secured versus unsecured claims.** A creditor who has the only secured interest in the debtor's collateral has priority over creditors with unsecured interests.
2. **Competing unperfected security interests.** If two or more secured parties claim an interest in the same collateral but neither has a perfected claim, the first to attach has priority [UCC 9-322(a)(3)].
3. **Perfected versus unperfected claims.** If two or more secured parties claim an interest in the same collateral but only one has perfected a security interest, the perfected security interest has priority [UCC 9-322(a)(2)].
4. **Competing perfected security interests.** If two or more secured parties have perfected security interests in the same collateral, the first to perfect (e.g., by filing a financing statement or by taking possession of the collateral) has priority [UCC 9-322(a)(1)].
5. **Perfected secured claims in fungible, commingled goods.** If a security interest in goods is perfected but the goods are later commingled with other goods in which there are also perfected security interests and the goods become part of a product or mass and lose their identity, the security interests rank equal and according to the ratio that the original cost of goods of each security interest bears to the cost of the total product or mass [UCC 9-336].

Critical Legal Thinking Question

What could be the consequences if a secured creditor does not file a financing statement or otherwise perfect its security interest in personal property? Explain.

The following feature describes the concept of a buyer in the ordinary course of business.

buyer in the ordinary course of business
A person who, in good faith and without knowledge of another's ownership or security interest in goods, buys the goods in the ordinary course of business from a person in the business of selling goods of that kind.

Contemporary Environment

Buyer in the Ordinary Course of Business

A **buyer in the ordinary course of business** who purchases goods from a merchant takes the goods free of any perfected or unperfected security interest in the merchant's inventory, even if the buyer knows of the existence of the security interest. This rule is necessary because buyers would be reluctant to purchase goods if a merchant's creditors could recover those goods if the merchant defaulted on loans owed to secured creditors. This rule does not apply to persons who buy farm products from a person engaged in farming operations [UCC 9-320(a)].

A buyer in the ordinary course of business is a person who buys goods in good faith, without knowledge that the sale violates the rights of another person in the goods, and in the ordinary course, from a party (other than a pawnbroker) in the business of selling goods of that kind [UCC 1-201(9)]. The buyer in the ordinary course of business rule is often applied to inventory collateral.

Example A car dealership finances all its inventory of new automobiles at a bank. That, is, the dealership borrows money from the bank to purchase vehicles from an automobile manufacturer, which are then displayed at the dealership. The bank takes a security interest the dealership's inventory of cars and perfects this security interest. Basil, a buyer in the ordinary course of business, purchases a car from the dealership. The bank cannot recover the car from Basil even if dealership defaults on its payments to the bank.

Default and Remedies

27.5 Define *default* and describe the remedies available to the secured party if there is a default.

Article 9 of the UCC defines the rights, duties, and remedies of the secured party and the debtor in the event of **default**. The term *default* is not defined. Instead, the parties are free to define it in their security agreement. Events such as failing to make scheduled payments when due, bankruptcy of the debtor, breach of the warranty of ownership as to the collateral, and other such events are commonly defined in security agreements as default.

default
Failure to make scheduled payments when due, bankruptcy of the debtor, breach of the warranty of ownership as to the collateral, and other events defined by the parties in a security agreement.

On default by a debtor, the secured party may reduce a claim to judgment, foreclose and recover the collateral, or otherwise enforce a security interest by any available judicial procedure [UCC 9-601(a)]. The UCC provides the secured party with the remedies discussed in the following paragraphs.

Taking Possession of the Collateral

repossession
A right granted to a secured creditor to take possession of the collateral on default by the debtor.

Many secured parties seek to cure a default by **taking possession of the collateral**. This is usually done by **repossession** of the goods from the defaulting debtor. A secured party may repossess the collateral pursuant to judicial process or without judicial process if the self-help repossession of the collateral does not breach the peace [UCC 9-609(b)].

Example A consumer purchases a new automobile from an automobile dealer on credit and gives the dealer a secured interest in the automobile. The dealer properly files a financing statement. If the debtor defaults on the loan, the creditor can repossess the vehicle from any publicly accessible place, such as if the car is parked on the street, in the parking lot of a store, and even from an unsecured driveway. The creditor cannot enter a private building or a secured area. Such action would be considered a breach of the peace. Thus, the vehicle cannot be repossessed from the debtor's enclosed garage.

Many debtors peacefully allow a secured creditor to repossess goods. If necessary, however, a secured creditor may obtain a court judgment or warrant to repossess personal property. In reality, many secured creditors of business equipment, farm implements, and other non-consumer goods do not use repossession, usually because the equipment may be large and expensive to move, or its value is not what is used to be. The same is true of less expensive consumer items whose value has decreased substantially.

After legally repossessing the goods, the secured party can either (1) retain the collateral or (2) sell, lease, license, or otherwise dispose of it and satisfy the debt from the proceeds of the sale or disposition. There is one caveat: The secured party must act in good faith, with commercial reasonableness, and with reasonable care to preserve the collateral in the party's possession [UCC 9-603, 9-610(a), 9-620].

Credit card debt is unsecured. If a credit card holder fails to make required payments, the credit card company cannot repossess goods purchased with the credit card. Purchases made with a debit card do not involve an extension of credit.

Retention of the Collateral

retention of the collateral
A secured creditor's repossession and retention of the collateral upon a debtor's default.

In the event of a debtor's default, a secured creditor who repossesses collateral may propose the **retention of the collateral** in satisfaction of the debtor's obligation. Notice of the proposal must be sent to the debtor unless the debtor has signed a written statement renouncing this right. In the case of consumer goods, no other notice need be given [UCC 9-620(a)].

Disposing of the Collateral

disposition of collateral
A secured creditor's repossession of collateral on a debtor's default and selling, leasing, or otherwise disposing of it in a commercially reasonable manner.

In the event of a debtor's default, a secured party who chooses not to retain the collateral may sell, lease, or otherwise dispose of the collateral in its current condition or following any commercially reasonable preparation or processing. **Disposition of collateral** may be by public or private proceeding. The method, manner, time, place, and terms of the disposition must be commercially reasonable [UCC 9-610].

The secured party must notify the debtor in writing about the time and place of any public or private sale or any other intended disposition of the collateral unless the debtor has signed a statement renouncing or modifying the right to receive such notice. In the case of consumer goods, no other notification need be sent.

The proceeds from a sale, a lease, or another disposition are applied in the following order: (1) to pay reasonable expenses of collection and enforcement incurred by the secured party; (2) to pay the indebtedness owed to the secured party; (3) to pay subordinate (junior) security interests. The debtor is entitled to receive any surplus that remains [UCC 9-608(a)].

Deficiency Judgment

Unless otherwise agreed, after a debtor's default, if the proceeds from the disposition of collateral are not sufficient to pay the expenses incurred by the secured party for the collection and enforcement of the debt and to satisfy the debt to the secured party, the debtor is personally liable to the secured party for the payment of the deficiency. The secured party may bring an action to recover a **deficiency judgment** against the debtor [UCC 9-608(a)(4)].

deficiency judgment
A judgment of a court that permits a secured lender to recover other property or income from a defaulting debtor if the collateral is insufficient to repay the unpaid loan.

Example Genevieve borrows $30,000 from a bank to purchase a new automobile. She signs a security agreement giving the bank a purchase money security interest in the automobile. Genevieve defaults when she still owes $24,250 of the debt. The bank repossesses the automobile and sells it at a public auction for $17,000. The selling expenses and sales commission are $1,250. This amount is deducted from the sale proceeds, and the remaining $15,750 of cash is applied to the unpaid $24,250. Genevieve remains personally liable to the bank for the $8,500 deficiency.

The parties may agree in their security agreement that the debtor will not be liable for any deficiency. If the underlying transaction is the sale of accounts, chattel paper, payment intangibles, or promissory notes, the debtor is not entitled to any surplus and is not liable for any deficiency [UCC 9-608(b)].

In the following case, the court addressed the issue of a deficiency judgment regarding the sale of goods.

CASE 27.2 *STATE COURT CASE Deficiency Judgment*

John Deere Construction & Forestry Co. v. Parham

755 S.E.2d 825, 2014 Ga. App. Lexis 104 (2014)
Court of Appeals of Georgia

"Deere subsequently filed this deficiency action, seeking the remaining balance due under the terms of the Loan."

—Carla McMillan, Judge

Facts

John Deere Construction & Forestry Co. (Deere) manufactures and sells farm and other equipment. Carl S. Parham purchased a Deere 700 Crawler Dozer though a Deere dealership for commercial and agricultural use. Parham executed a Loan Contract and Security Agreement (Loan) in favor of Deere to finance the purchase for a total of $84,568. Parham agreed to pay 60 equal monthly payments and granted Deere a purchase money security interest in the Dozer. Parham defaulted on the loan by failing to make required payments at a time when $74,423 was still due on the loan.

Deere repossessed the Dozer, and after notifying Parham of his redemption rights, which he did not exercise, sold the Dozer for $40,000. Deere filed a deficiency action, seeking to recover from Parham the remaining balance due. Deere filed a motion for summary judgment. Parham also filed a motion for summary judgment, arguing that he had not been

(continued)

given proper notice of the sale as required by the state Retail Installment Act that applied to sales of goods for personal, family, or household use. The trial court held in favor of Parham. Deere appealed.

Issue

Was the sale for commercial and agricultural use?

Language of the Court

Deere subsequently filed this deficiency action, seeking the remaining balance due under the terms of the Loan. Because the Dozer was purchased for commercial and agricultural purposes, and not for personal, family, or household use, we find that the Loan does not fall within the definition of a "good" pursuant to the Retail Installment Act.

Decision

The court of appeals reversed the grant of summary judgment to Parham. Thus, Deere can proceed to recover the deficiency judgment from Parham.

Critical Legal Thinking Questions

What is a deficiency judgment? Should purchasers of goods be more alert as to the consequences if they do not completely pay for goods subject to a security agreement?

Redemption Rights

In the event of a debtor's default, the debtor or another secured party may redeem the collateral before the priority lienholder has disposed of it, entered into a contract to dispose of it, or discharged the debtor's obligation by having exercised a right to retain the collateral. The **right of redemption** may be accomplished by payment of all obligations secured by the collateral, all expenses reasonably incurred by the secured party in retaking and holding the collateral, and any attorneys' fees and other legal expenses provided for in the security agreement and not prohibited by law [UCC 9-623].

Relinquishing the Security Interest and Proceeding to Judgment on the Underlying Debt

judgment
A right granted to a secured creditor to relinquish its security interest in the collateral and sue a defaulting debtor to recover the amount of the underlying debt.

When a debtor defaults, instead of repossessing the collateral, a secured creditor may relinquish the security interest in the collateral and proceed to **judgment** against the debtor to recover the underlying debt. This course of action is rarely chosen unless the value of the collateral has been reduced below the amount of the secured interest and the debtor has other assets from which to satisfy the debt [UCC 9-601(a)].

Example Suppose Jacob borrows $100,000 from First Bank to purchase a piece of equipment, and First Bank perfects its security interest in the equipment for this amount. Jacob defaults when he owes $80,000 on the loan. If the equipment has gone down in value to $60,000 at the time of default but Jacob has other personal assets to satisfy the debt, it may be in the bank's best interest to relinquish its security interest, sue Jacob, and proceed to judgment on the underlying debt.

artisan's lien
A statutory lien given to workers on personal property to which the workers furnish services or materials in the ordinary course of business.

If the secured creditor obtains a judgment against the debtor but the debtor has no money to pay the judgment, the secured creditor can proceed to take possession of the collateral.

The following feature discusses artisan's liens on personal property.

Business Environment

Artisan's Liens on Personal Property

If a worker in the ordinary course of business furnishes services or materials to someone with respect to goods, and obtains a lien on the goods as authorized by law, this **artisan's lien** prevails over all other security interests in the goods, including security interests obtained under Article 9. Thus, an artisan's lien is often called a **super-priority lien**. An artisan's lien is possessory; that is, the artisan must be in possession of the property to affect an artisan's lien [UCC 9-333].

Example Whitaker borrows money from First Bank to purchase an automobile. First Bank has a purchase money security interest in the car and files a financing statement. The automobile is involved in an automobile accident, and Whitaker takes the car to Eleanor's Repair Shop (Eleanor's) to be repaired. Eleanor's retains an artisan's lien on the car for the amount of the repair work. When the repair work is completed, Whitaker refuses to pay, so Eleanor's retains Whitaker's car. He also defaults on his payments to First Bank. If the car is sold to satisfy the liens, Eleanor's artisan's lien is paid in full before First Bank is paid anything.

Key Terms and Concepts

2010 Amendments to Revised Article 9 (458)
Accession (461)
Account (463)
After-acquired property (464)
Article 9 (Secured Transactions) (458)
Artisan's lien (super-priority lien) (473)
Attachment (462)
Authenticate (462)
Buyer in the ordinary course of business (469)
Certificate of title (468)
Certificate of title statute (468)
Chattel paper (463)
Collateral (461)
Consumer goods (467)
Continuation statement (466)
Debtor (459)
Default (469)
Deficiency judgment (471)
Deposit account (463)
Disposition of collateral (470)
Electronic chattel paper (463)
Equipment (461)
Farm products (461)
Financing statement (465)
Floating lien (462)
Future advances (464)
General intangible (463)
Goods (461)
Instrument (463)
Intangible collateral (462)
Intangible personal property (462)
Inventory (461)
Investment property (463)
Judgment (472)
Perfection by a purchase money security interest in consumer goods (467)
Perfection by attachment (automatic perfection rule) (467)
Perfection by filing a financing statement (465)
Perfection by possession of collateral (467)
Perfection of a security interest (464)
Personal property (458)
Priority of claims (469)
Public organic record (460)
Purchase money security interest (467)
Record (460)
Registered organization (460)
Repossession (470)
Retention of the collateral (470)
Revised Article 9 (Secured Transactions) (458)
Right of redemption (472)
Sale proceeds (464)
Secured credit (458)
Secured party (459)
Secured transaction (459)
Security agreement (462)
Security interest (462)
Taking possession of the collateral (470)
Tangible chattel paper (463)
Tangible collateral (461)
Tangible personal property (461)
Termination statement (468)
Third-party lender (460)
Three-party secured transaction (460)
Two-party secured transaction (460)
UCC Financing Statement (Form UCC-1) (465)
Unsecured credit (458)

Critical Legal Thinking Cases

27.1 Financing Statement PSC Metals, Inc. (PSC) entered into an agreement whereby it extended credit to Keystone Consolidated Industries, Inc., and took back a security interest in personal property owned by Keystone. PSC filed a financing statement with the state, listing the debtor's trade name, "Keystone Steel & Wire Co.," rather than its corporate name, "Keystone Consolidated Industries, Inc." When Keystone went into bankruptcy, PSC filed a motion with the bankruptcy court to obtain the personal property securing its loan. Keystone's other creditors and the bankruptcy trustee objected, arguing that because PSC's financing statement was defectively filed, PSC did not have a perfected security interest in the personal property. If this were true, then PSC would become an unsecured creditor in Keystone's bankruptcy proceeding. Is the financing statement filed in the debtor's trade name, rather than in its corporate name, effective? *In re FV Steel and Wire Company*, 310 B.R. 390, 2004 Bankr. Lexis 748 (United States Bankruptcy Court for the Eastern District of Wisconsin, 2004)

27.2 Financing Statement C&H Trucking, Inc. (C&H) borrowed $19,747.56 from S&D Petroleum Company, Inc. (S&D). S&D hired Clifton M. Tamsett to prepare a security agreement naming C&H as the debtor and giving S&D a security interest in a new Mack truck. The security agreement prepared by Tamsett declared that the collateral also secured "any other indebtedness or liability of the debtor to the secured party direct or indirect, absolute or contingent, due or to become due, now existing or hereafter arising, including all future advances or loans which may be made at the option of the secured party."

Tamsett failed to file a financing statement or the executed agreement with the appropriate government office. C&H subsequently paid off the original debt, and S&D continued to extend new credit to C&H. Two years later, when C&H owed S&D more than $17,000, S&D learned that (1) C&H was insolvent, (2) the Mack truck had been sold, and (3) Tamsett had failed to file the security agreement. Does S&D have a security interest in the Mack truck? Is Tamsett liable to S&D? *S&D Petroleum Company, Inc. v. Tamsett*, 144 A.D.2d 849, 534 N.Y.S.2d 800, 1988 N.Y. App. Div. Lexis 11258 (Supreme Court of New York, 1988)

27.3 Floating Lien Joseph H. Jones and others (debtors) borrowed money from Columbus Junction State Bank (Bank) and executed a security agreement in favor of Bank. Bank perfected its security interest by filing financing statements covering "equipment, farm products, crops, livestock, supplies, contract rights, and all accounts and proceeds thereof" with the Iowa secretary of state. Four years and 10 months later, Bank filed a continuation statement with the Iowa secretary of state. Four years and 10 months after that, Bank filed a second continuation statement with the Iowa secretary of state. Two years later, the debtors filed for Chapter 7 liquidation bankruptcy. The bankruptcy trustee collected $10,073 from the sale of the debtors' crops and an undetermined amount of soybeans harvested on farmland owned by the debtors. The bankruptcy trustee claimed the funds and soybeans on behalf of the bankruptcy estate. Bank claimed the funds and soybeans as a perfected secured creditor. Who wins? *In re Jones*, 79 B.R. 839, 1987 Bankr. Lexis 1825 (United States Bankruptcy Court for the Northern District of Iowa, 1987)

27.4 Purchase Money Security Interest Prior Brothers, Inc. (PBI) began financing its farming operations through Bank of California, N.A. (Bank). Bank's loans were secured by PBI's equipment and after-acquired property. Bank immediately filed a financing statement, perfecting its security interest. Two years later, PBI contacted the International Harvester dealership in Sunnyside, Washington, about the purchase of a new tractor. A retail installment contract for a model 1066 International Harvester tractor was executed. PBI took delivery of the tractor "on approval," agreeing that if it decided to purchase the tractor, it would inform the dealership of its intention and would send a $6,000 down payment. The dealership received a $6,000 check and immediately filed a financing statement concerning the tractor. Subsequently, when PBI went into receivership, the dealership filed a complaint, asking the court to declare that its purchase money security interest in the tractor had priority over Bank's security interest. Does the dealership's purchase money security interest in the tractor have priority over Bank's security interest? *In the Matter of Prior Brothers, Inc.*, 632 P.2d 522, 1981 Wash. App. Lexis 2507 (Court of Appeals of Washington, 1981)

27.5 Buyer in the Ordinary Course of Business Heritage Ford Lincoln Mercury, Inc. (Heritage) was in the business of selling new cars. Heritage entered into an agreement with Ford Motor Credit Company (Ford) whereby Ford extended a continuing line of credit to Heritage to purchase vehicles. Heritage granted Ford a purchase money security interest in all motor vehicles it owned and thereafter acquired and in all proceeds from the sale of such motor vehicles. Ford immediately filed its financing statement with the secretary of state. When the dealership experienced financial trouble, two Heritage officers decided to double-finance certain new cars by issuing dealer papers to themselves and obtaining financing for two new cars from First National Bank

& Trust Company of El Dorado (Bank). The loan proceeds were deposited in the dealership's account to help with its financial difficulties. The cars were available for sale. When the dealership closed its doors and turned over the car inventory to Ford, Bank alleged that it had priority over Ford because the Heritage officers were buyers in the ordinary course of business. Who wins? *First National Bank and Trust Company of El Dorado v. Ford Motor Credit Company*, 646 P.2d 1057, 1982 Kan. Lexis 280 (Supreme Court of Kansas, 1982)

Ethics Cases

27.6 Ethics Case Mike Thurmond operated Top Quality Auto Sales, a used car dealership. Top Quality financed its inventory of vehicles by obtaining credit under a financing arrangement with Indianapolis Car Exchange (ICE). ICE filed a financing statement that listed Top Quality's inventory of vehicles as collateral for the financing.

Top Quality sold a Ford truck to Bonnie Chrisman, a used car dealer, who paid Top Quality for the truck. Chrisman in turn sold the truck to Randall and Christina Alderson, who paid Chrisman for the truck. When Chrisman filed to retrieve the title to the truck for the Aldersons, it was discovered that Top Quality had not paid ICE for the truck. ICE requested that the Indiana Bureau of Motor Vehicles place a lien in its favor on the title of the truck. When ICE refused to release the lien on the truck, the Aldersons sued ICE to obtain title to the truck. The Aldersons asserted that Chrisman, and then they, were buyers in the ordinary course of business and therefore acquired the truck free of ICE's financing statement. ICE filed a counterclaim to recover the truck from the Aldersons. Are Chrisman and the Aldersons buyers in the ordinary course of business who took the truck free from ICE's security interest in the truck? Did ICE have a legitimate claim in this case? *Indianapolis Car Exchange v. Alderson*, 910 N.E.2d 802, 2009 Ind. App. Lexis (Court of Appeals of Indiana, 2009)

27.7 Ethics Case Harder & Sons, Inc., an International Harvester dealership in Ionia, Michigan, sold a used International Harvester 1066 diesel tractor to Terry Blaser on an installment contract. Although the contract listed Blaser's address as Ionia County, Blaser informed Harder at the time of purchase that he was going to work and live in Barry County. Blaser took delivery of the tractor at his Ionia County address three days later. On that same day Harder filed a financing statement that was executed by Blaser with the installment contract, in Barry County. The State of Michigan UCC requires an Article 9 financing statement to be filed in the debtor's county of residence. The contract and security agreement were immediately assigned to International Harvester Credit Corporation (International Harvester).

Blaser subsequently moved to Barry County for about three months, then to Ionia County for a few months, then to Kent County for three weeks, and then to Muskegon County, where he sold the tractor to Jay and Dale Vos. At the time of sale, Blaser informed the Vos brothers that he owned the tractor. He did not tell them that it was subject to a lien. The Vos brothers went to First Michigan Bank & Trust Company (Bank) to obtain a loan to help purchase the tractor. When the Bank checked the records of Ionia County and found that no financing statement was filed against the tractor, it made a $7,000 loan to the Vos brothers to purchase the tractor. About six months later, International Harvester filed suit to recover the tractor from the Vos brothers on the grounds that it had a prior perfected security interest. Did Blaser act ethically in this case? Who wins? *International Harvester Credit Corporation v. Vos*, 290 N.W.2d 401, 1980 Mich. App. Lexis 2430 (Michigan Court of Appeals, 1980)

CHAPTER 28 Bankruptcy and Reorganization

OUT OF BUSINESS
Businesses that run into hard economic times often go out of business.

Carolyn Franks/Shutterstock

Learning Objectives

After studying this chapter, you should be able to:

28.1 Describe bankruptcy law and list the types of bankruptcy.

28.2 Describe bankruptcy procedures, including filing petitions for bankruptcy proceedings.

28.3 Describe how the bankruptcy estate is determined.

28.4 List and describe the exempt property that a debtor is permitted to keep.

28.5 Describe the provisions of a Chapter 7 liquidation bankruptcy.

28.6 Describe a Chapter 13 adjustment of debts of an individual with regular income bankruptcy.

28.7 Describe how businesses are reorganized in Chapter 11 bankruptcy.

"A trifling debt makes a man your debtor, a large one makes him your enemy."

— *Lucius Annaeus Seneca*
Epistulae Morales ad Lucilium (ca. 65)

Introduction to Bankruptcy and Reorganization

The extension of credit from creditors to debtors in commercial and personal transactions is important to the viability of the U.S. and world economies. On occasion, however, borrowers become overextended and are unable to meet their debt obligations. The founders of our country thought that the plight of debtors was so important that they included a provision in the U.S. Constitution giving Congress the authority to establish uniform federal bankruptcy laws. Congress has enacted bankruptcy laws pursuant to this power. The goal of bankruptcy laws is to balance the rights of debtors and creditors and provide methods for debtors to be relieved of some debt to obtain a **fresh start**.

I will pay you some, and, as most debtors do, promise you indefinitely.
William Shakespeare
Henry IV, part 2 (ca. 1596–1599)

Prior to 2005, the most recent overhaul of federal bankruptcy law occurred in 1978. The 1978 law was structured to make it easier for debtors to be relieved of much of their debt by declaring bankruptcy; it was deemed "debtor friendly" because it allowed many debtors to escape their unsecured debts.

fresh start
The goal of federal bankruptcy law to grant a debtor relief from some burdensome debts while protecting creditors by requiring the debtor to pay more of the debts than would otherwise have been required prior to the 2005 act.

After a decade of lobbying by credit card companies and banks, Congress enacted the Bankruptcy Abuse Prevention and Consumer Protection Act of 2005. The 2005 act makes it much more difficult for debtors to escape their debts under federal bankruptcy law. The 2005 act has been criticized by consumer groups for being too "creditor friendly."

This chapter discusses federal bankruptcy law, bankruptcy procedure, the different types of bankruptcy, and business reorganization under bankruptcy law.

Bankruptcy Law

28.1 Describe bankruptcy law and list the types of bankruptcy.

Article I, Section 8, Clause 4 of the U.S. Constitution states, "The Congress shall have the power … to establish … uniform laws on the subject of bankruptcies throughout the United States." Bankruptcy law is exclusively federal law; there are no state bankruptcy laws. Congress enacted the original federal Bankruptcy Act in 1878.

Types of Bankruptcy

The Bankruptcy Code is divided into chapters. Chapters 1, 3, and 5 set forth definitions and general provisions that govern case administration. The provisions of these chapters generally apply to all forms of bankruptcy.

Four special chapters of the Bankruptcy Code provide different types of bankruptcy under which individual and business debtors may be granted remedy. They are as follows:

Chapter	Type of Bankruptcy
Chapter 7	Liquidation
Chapter 11	Reorganization
Chapter 12	Adjustment of Debts of a Family Farmer or Fisherman with Regular Income
Chapter 13	Adjustment of Debts of an Individual with Regular Income

Most bankruptcies are filed by consumers. Approximately 750,000 consumer-debtors file personal bankruptcy each year, Approximately 20,000 businesses file for business bankruptcy each year. Bankruptcy petitions may be filed by the debtor without the assistance of an attorney or filing service. If the debtor uses an attorney or filing service, their fees must be paid. The following feature discusses federal bankruptcy law.

Landmark Law

Bankruptcy Code

Over the years, Congress has adopted various bankruptcy laws. Federal **bankruptcy law** was completely revised by the **Bankruptcy Reform Act of 1978.**[1] The 1978 act made it easier for debtors to rid themselves of unsecured debt, primarily by filing for Chapter 7 liquidation bankruptcy.

Subsequently, credit card companies, commercial banks, and other businesses lobbied Congress to pass a new bankruptcy act that would reduce the ability of some debtors to relieve themselves of unwanted debt through bankruptcy. In response, Congress enacted the **Bankruptcy Abuse Prevention and Consumer Protection Act of 2005.**[2] The 2005 act substantially amended federal bankruptcy law, making it much more difficult for debtors to escape unwanted debt through bankruptcy.

Federal bankruptcy law, as amended, is called the **Bankruptcy Code**, which is contained in Title 11 of the U.S. Code. The Bankruptcy Code establishes procedures for filing for bankruptcy, resolving creditors' claims, and protecting debtors' rights.

Bankruptcy Reform Act of 1978
A federal act that substantially changed federal bankruptcy law. The act made it easier for debtors to file for bankruptcy and have their unpaid debts discharged. This act was considered debtor friendly.

Bankruptcy Abuse Prevention and Consumer Protection Act of 2005
A federal act that substantially amended federal bankruptcy law. This act makes it more difficult for debtors to file for bankruptcy and have their unpaid debts discharged.

Bankruptcy Code
The name given to federal bankruptcy law, as amended.

U.S. bankruptcy courts
Special federal courts that hear and decide bankruptcy cases.

U.S. Trustee
A federal government official who is responsible for handling and supervising many of the administrative tasks of a bankruptcy case.

Bankruptcy Courts

Congress created a system of federal bankruptcy courts. These special **U.S. bankruptcy courts** are necessary because the number of bankruptcies would otherwise overwhelm the federal district courts. The bankruptcy courts are part of the federal court system, and one bankruptcy court is attached to each of the 94 U.S. district courts in the country. Bankruptcy judges, specialists who hear bankruptcy proceedings, are appointed for 14-year terms. The relevant district court has jurisdiction to hear appeals from bankruptcy courts.

Federal law establishes the office of the **U.S. Trustee**. A U.S. Trustee is a federal government official who has responsibility for handling and supervising many of the administrative tasks associated with a bankruptcy case.[3] A U.S. Trustee is empowered to perform many of the tasks that the bankruptcy judge previously performed.

Bankruptcy Procedure

28.2 Describe bankruptcy procedures, including filing petitions for bankruptcy proceedings.

The Bankruptcy Code requires that certain procedures be followed for the commencement and prosecution of a bankruptcy case. These procedures are discussed in the following paragraphs.

Prepetition and Postpetition Counseling

Individuals filing for bankruptcy must receive **prepetition counseling** within 180 days prior to filing a petition for bankruptcy. This includes counseling on types of credit, the use of credit, and budget analysis. The counseling is to be provided by not-for-profit credit counseling agencies approved by the U.S. Trustee.

Before an individual debtor receives a discharge in a Chapter 7 or Chapter 13 bankruptcy, the debtor must receive **postpetition counseling** by attending a personal financial management course approved by the U.S. Trustee. This course is designed to provide the debtor with information on responsible use of credit and personal financial planning.

Filing a Bankruptcy Petition

A bankruptcy case is commenced when a **petition for bankruptcy** is filed with a bankruptcy court. Two types of petitions can be filed:

petition for bankruptcy
A document filed with a bankruptcy court that starts a bankruptcy proceeding.

1. **Voluntary petition.** A **voluntary petition** is a petition filed by the debtor. A voluntary petition can be filed by the debtor in Chapter 7 (liquidation), Chapter 11 (reorganization), Chapter 12 (family farmer or fisherman), and Chapter 13 (adjustment of debts) bankruptcy cases. The petition has to state that the debtor has debts.
2. **Involuntary petition.** An **involuntary petition** is a petition that is filed by a creditor or creditors and places the debtor into bankruptcy. An involuntary petition can be filed in Chapter 7 (liquidation) and Chapter 11 (reorganization) cases; an involuntary petition cannot be filed in Chapter 12 (family farmer or fisherman) or Chapter 13 (adjustment of debts) cases.

voluntary petition
A petition filed by a debtor that states that the debtor has debts.

involuntary petition
A petition filed by creditors of a debtor that alleges that the debtor is not paying his or her debts as they become due.

An individual debtor must submit the following **schedules** on filing a voluntary petition: a list of secured and unsecured creditors, with addresses; a list of all property owned; a statement of the financial affairs of the debtor; a statement of the debtor's monthly income; current income and expenses; evidence of payments received from employers within 60 days prior to the filing of the petition; and a copy of the debtor's federal income tax return for the most recent year ending prior to the filing of the petition. In addition, an individual debtor must file a certificate stating that he or she has received the required prepetition credit counseling. All forms must be sworn under oath and signed by the debtor.

Bankruptcy petitions, along with supporting documents, may be filed electronically with bankruptcy courts.

WEB EXERCISE
Go to **www.ftc.gov/bcp/edu/pubs/consumer/credit/cre41.shtm** and read information from the Federal Trade Commission (FTC) about credit counseling before filing for bankruptcy.

Attorney Certification

Bankruptcy law requires an **attorney certification** whereby an attorney who represents a client in bankruptcy must certify the accuracy of the information contained in the bankruptcy petition and the schedules, under penalty of perjury. If any factual discrepancies are found, the attorney is subject to monetary fines and sanctions.

If an attorney represents a debtor in bankruptcy, the attorney must conduct a thorough investigation of the debtor's financial position and schedules to determine the accuracy of the information contained in the petition and schedules.

Order for Relief

The filing of either a voluntary petition or an unchallenged involuntary petition constitutes an **order for relief**. If the debtor challenges an involuntary petition, a trial is held to determine whether an order for relief should be granted. If an order is granted, the case is accepted for further bankruptcy proceedings. In the case of an involuntary petition, the debtor must file the same schedules filed by voluntary petition debtors.

order for relief
An order that occurs on the filing of either a voluntary petition or an unchallenged involuntary petition or an order that is granted after a trial of a challenged involuntary petition.

Meeting of the Creditors

Within a reasonable time after the court grants an order for relief (not less than 10 days or more than 30 days) the court must call a **meeting of the creditors** (also called the **first meeting of the creditors**). The bankruptcy judge cannot attend the meeting. The debtor must appear and submit to questioning, under oath, by creditors. Creditors may ask questions regarding the debtor's financial affairs,

meeting of the creditors (first meeting of the creditors)
A meeting of the creditors in a bankruptcy case must occur within a reasonable time after an order for relief. The debtor must appear at this meeting.

disposition of property prior to bankruptcy, possible concealment of assets, and similar matters. The debtor may have an attorney present at this meeting.

Proof of Claim and Proof of Interest

proof of claim
A document required to be filed by a creditor that states the amount of the claim against the debtor.

A creditor must file a **proof of claim** stating the amount of the claim against the debtor. The document for filing a proof of claim is provided by the court. The proof of claim must be timely filed, which generally means within six months of the first meeting of the creditors. A secured creditor whose claim exceeds the value of the collateral may submit a proof of claim and become an unsecured claimant as to the difference. An equity security holder (e.g., a shareholder of a corporation) must file a **proof of interest**.

proof of interest
A document required to be filed by an equity security holder that states the amount of interest against the debtor.

Bankruptcy Trustee

bankruptcy trustee
A legal representative of the debtor's estate.

A **bankruptcy trustee** must be appointed in Chapter 7 (liquidation), Chapter 12 (family farmer or family fisherman), and Chapter 13 (adjustment of debts) bankruptcy cases. A trustee may be appointed in a Chapter 11 (reorganization) case on a showing of fraud, dishonesty, incompetence, or gross mismanagement of the affairs of the debtor by current management. Trustees, who are often lawyers, accountants, or business professionals, are entitled to receive reasonable compensation for their services and reimbursement for expenses. Once appointed, a trustee becomes the legal representative of the debtor's estate and has the power to sell and buy property, invest money, and the like.

The following feature discusses the automatic stay of bankruptcy law.

automatic stay
The suspension of certain legal actions by creditors against a debtor or the debtor's property.

Contemporary Environment

Automatic Stay

The filing of a voluntary or an involuntary petition automatically *stays*—that is, suspends—certain legal actions by creditors against the debtor or the debtor's property. This is called an **automatic stay**. The stay, which applies to collection efforts of secured and unsecured creditors, is designed to prevent a scramble for the debtor's assets in a variety of court proceedings. The following creditor actions are stayed:

- Instituting or maintaining legal actions to collect prepetition debts
- Enforcing judgments obtained against the debtor
- Obtaining, perfecting, or enforcing liens against the property of the debtor
- Nonjudicial collection efforts, such as self-help activities (e.g., repossession of an automobile)

Actions to recover domestic support obligations (e.g., alimony, child support), the dissolution of a marriage, and child custody cases are not stayed in bankruptcy. Criminal actions against the debtor are also not stayed.

Discharge of Debts

discharge in bankruptcy
A court order that relieves a debtor of the legal liability to pay debts that were not paid in the bankruptcy proceeding.

In Chapter 7 (liquidation), Chapter 11 (reorganization), Chapter 12 (family farmer and family fisherman), and Chapter 13 (adjustment of debts) bankruptcies, if the requirements are met, the court grants the debtor a discharge of all or some of the debts. When a **discharge in bankruptcy** is granted, the debtor is relieved of responsibility to pay the discharged debts. In other words, the debtor is no longer legally liable to pay the discharged debts. Discharge is one of the primary reasons a debtor files for bankruptcy. The specifics of discharge under each type of bankruptcy are discussed in this chapter.

Certain debts are not dischargeable in bankruptcy. Creditors who have nondischargeable claims against the debtor may participate in the distribution of the bankruptcy estate. The creditor may pursue the nondischarged balance against the debtor after bankruptcy. Debts that are not discharged in bankruptcy are listed and described in Exhibit 28.1.

Critical Legal Thinking Questions

What is the public policy that allows debtors to discharge debts in bankruptcy? When a discharge is granted, does any party suffer a detriment?

Exhibit 28.1 DEBTS THAT CANNOT BE DISCHARGED IN BANKRUPTCY

The following debts are not dischargeable in bankruptcy:

- Claims for income or gross receipts taxes owed to federal, state, or local governments accrued within three years prior to the filing of the petition for bankruptcy
- Certain fines and penalties payable to federal, state, and local governmental units
- Claims based on the debtor's liability for causing willful or malicious injury to a person or property
- Claims arising from fraud, larceny, or embezzlement by the debtor while acting in a fiduciary capacity
- Domestic support obligations and alimony, maintenance, and child support payments resulting from a divorce decree or separation agreement
- Unscheduled claims
- Claims based on a consumer-debtor's purchase of luxury goods or services of more than $725 from a single creditor on or within 90 days of the order for relief
- Cash advances of more than $1,000 obtained by a consumer-debtor by use of a revolving line of credit or credit cards on or within 70 days of the order for relief
- Judgments and consent decrees against the debtor for liability incurred because of the debtor's operation of a motor vehicle, a vessel, or an aircraft while legally intoxicated
- A debt that would result in a benefit to the debtor that outweighs the detrimental consequences to a spouse, former spouse, or child of the debtor
- An amount owed to a pension, profit-sharing, or stock bonus plan and loans owed to employee retirement plans

In the following case, the court had to decide if a bankruptcy discharge should be denied.

CASE 28.1 *FEDERAL COURT CASE Bankruptcy Discharge*

In re Resler

583 B.R. 238 (2018)
United States Bankruptcy Court for Idaho

"A total bar to discharge is an extreme penalty."
—Terry Myers, Chief Bankruptcy Judge

Facts

Timothy and Kimberly Resler had been married more than 20 years when Timothy purchased a diamond and platinum ring for Kimberly. The ring was appraised for $46,295, and the Reslers added a rider to their homeowner's insurance policy insuring the ring for that amount. Subsequently, the Reslers (Debtors) filed for bankruptcy. The Debtors' bankruptcy schedules listed several items of jewelry with a total value of $9,250. After the U.S. Trustee (UST) requested copies of insurance policies, the Debtors amended their schedules to reflect a "Ladies' platinum and diamond band" worth $2,000. Debtors provided the insurance policy that insured the ring, but Timothy had handwritten on the insurance policy that the ring was Kimberly's mother's ring and that her mother had paid them to insure the ring while she lived with them.

The UST brought an adversary proceeding objecting to the Debtors' discharge. During discovery, the Debtors acknowledged that the ring was Kimberly's ring, but that Kimberly had thrown it in a lake after she and Timothy had a marital dispute. On the eve of trial, Timothy hired a diver who "discovered" the real ring in the lake, and the Debtors delivered the ring to the UST at trial. The UST insisted that the Debtors' discharge be denied because they concealed property and knowingly made false statements.

(continued)

Issue

Should the Debtors' discharge be denied?

Language of the Court

A total bar to discharge is an extreme penalty. After careful consideration of the entirety of the evidentiary record and—importantly—the evaluation of the credibility of Timothy and Kimberly, the Court finds Debtors concealed the ring. The Court further finds that both Timothy and Kimberly concealed the ring with intent to hinder, delay, and defraud Trustee. The UST met its burden of showing that Debtors' discharge should be denied.

Decision

The U.S. bankruptcy court denied bankruptcy discharge to the Debtors.

Critical Legal Thinking Questions

Did the Debtors act ethically in this case? What are the consequences to the Debtors by being denied discharge?

Reaffirmation Agreement

reaffirmation agreement
An agreement entered into by a debtor with a creditor prior to discharge whereby the debtor agrees to pay the creditor a debt that would otherwise be discharged in bankruptcy. Certain requirements must be met for a reaffirmation agreement to be enforced.

A debtor and a creditor can enter into a **reaffirmation agreement**, whereby the debtor agrees to pay the creditor for a debt that is dischargeable in bankruptcy. This might occur if the debtor wishes to repay a debt to a family member, to a bank, or to another party. A reaffirmation agreement must be entered into before discharge is granted and must be filed with the court. Approval by the court is required if the debtor is not represented by an attorney. If the debtor is represented by an attorney, the attorney must certify that the debtor voluntarily entered into the reaffirmation agreement and understands the consequences of the agreement. Even if the debtor is represented by an attorney, court approval is required if the agreement will cause undue hardship on the debtor or his or her family.

Bankruptcy Estate

28.3 Describe how the bankruptcy estate is determined.

bankruptcy estate
The debtor's property and earnings that comprise the estate of a bankruptcy proceeding.

The **bankruptcy estate** is created on the commencement of a bankruptcy case. It includes all the debtor's legal and equitable interests in real, personal, tangible, and intangible property, wherever located, that exist when the petition is filed, and all interests of the debtor and the debtor's spouse in community property. Certain *exempt property* (as discussed later in this section) is not part of the bankruptcy estate.

Gifts, inheritances, life insurance proceeds, and property from divorce settlements that the debtor is entitled to receive within 180 days after the petition is filed are part of the bankruptcy estate. Earnings from property of the estate—such as rents, dividends, and interest payments—are property of the estate.

Earnings from services performed by an individual debtor are not part of the bankruptcy estate in a Chapter 7 liquidation bankruptcy. However, the 2005 act provides that a certain amount of postpetition earnings from services performed by the debtor that are earned for up to five years after the order for relief may be required to be paid as part of the completion of Chapter 12 (family farmer or family fisherman), Chapter 11 (reorganization), and Chapter 13 (adjustment of debts) cases.

Fraudulent Transfer of Property Prior to Bankruptcy

fraudulent transfer
A transfer of a debtor's property or an obligation incurred by a debtor within two years of the filing of a petition, where (1) the debtor had actual intent to hinder, delay, or defraud a creditor or (2) the debtor received less than a reasonable equivalent in value.

The bankruptcy court may void certain **fraudulent transfers** of a debtor's property made by the debtor within two years prior to filing a petition for bankruptcy. To void a transfer or an obligation, the court must find that (1) the transfer was made or the obligation was incurred by the debtor with the actual intent to hinder, delay, or defraud a creditor or (2) the debtor received less than a reasonable equivalent in value.

Example Ida owes her unsecured creditors $100,000. On February 9, Ida knows that she is insolvent. Ida owns a Mercedes-Benz automobile that is worth $55,000. On February 9, Ida sells her Mercedes-Benz automobile to her friend, Wei, for $30,000. Wei is a bona fide purchaser who does not know of Ida's financial situation. On July 1, Ida files for Chapter 7 liquidation bankruptcy while still owing the $100,000 to her unsecured creditors. The court can void Ida's sale of her automobile to Wei as a fraudulent transfer because it occurred within two years of the petition and Ida received less than a reasonable equivalent in value. Because Wei was a bona fide purchaser, the court must repay Wei the purchase price of $30,000 to recover the automobile from her.

The following ethics feature discusses debtors' fraudulent transfers of property prior to declaring bankruptcy.

Ethics

Fraudulent Transfer of Property Prior to Bankruptcy

"Here, the trustee seeks turnover of the diamonds."

—Thomas Catliota, Bankruptcy Judge

Minh Vu Hoang (Hoang) owned businesses and purchased and sold real estate. When she filed for bankruptcy, she listed ownership interests in 10 business entities and five parcels of real estate. A bankruptcy trustee was appointed who, in turn, hired a forensic accountant to determine if Hoang had interests in any other properties. It was discovered that Hoang owned interests in dozens of businesses and real estate properties that were not disclosed in her bankruptcy schedules. These properties were owned under fictitious names, alter-ego entities, slush funds, and agents' names. In more than 60 adversarial proceedings, many of these properties were acquired for the bankruptcy estate. The forensic accountant identified that Hoang had used cash proceeds from the sale of a piece of real property that should have been an asset of the bankruptcy estate to purchase 48 carats of diamonds worth $171,000. These diamonds had not been disclosed or turned over to the bankruptcy trustee. The bankruptcy trustee made a motion to the bankruptcy court to recover the diamonds as assets of the bankruptcy estate. Hoang asserted her Fifth Amendment right and did not testify at the bankruptcy hearing.

The U.S. bankruptcy court held that the diamonds are property of the bankruptcy estate. The court stated, "The cash used by Hoang to purchase the diamonds was proceeds of property of the estate and thus the diamonds are proceeds from property of the estate and therefore property of the estate." The bankruptcy court entered an order that required Hoang to turn over the diamonds to the bankruptcy trustee. The U.S. district court affirmed the bankruptcy court's decision. *In Re Hoang*, 2012 Bankr. Lexis 4355 (United States Bankruptcy Court for the District of Maryland, 2012)

Ethics Questions

Do you think there are many fraudulent transfers by debtors prior to their filing of bankruptcy petitions? What items or assets are likely to be involved in fraudulent transfers prior to bankruptcy?

Exempt Property

28.4 List and describe the exempt property that a debtor is permitted to keep.

Because the Bankruptcy Code is not designed to make the debtor a pauper, certain property is exempt from the bankruptcy estate. **Exempt property** is property of the debtor that he or she can keep and that does not become part of the bankruptcy estate. The creditors cannot claim the property.

The Bankruptcy Code establishes a list of property and assets that a debtor can claim as exempt property. The federal exemptions, with the dollar limits, are listed in Exhibit 28.2.[4] Federal exemptions are adjusted every three years to reflect changes in the consumer price index.

exempt property
Property that may be retained by the debtor pursuant to federal or state law that does not become part of the bankruptcy estate.

WEB EXERCISE
Use an internet search engine and find the bankruptcy exemptions of your state.

Exhibit 28.2 FEDERAL EXEMPTIONS FROM THE BANKRUPTCY ESTATE

The following property is exempt from the bankruptcy estate:

1. Interest up to $25,150 in equity in property used as a residence, mobile homes, and burial plots (called the "homestead exemption")
2. Interest up to $4,000 in value in one motor vehicle
3. Interest up to $625 per item in household goods and furnishings, wearing apparel, appliances, books, animals, crops, or musical instruments, up to an aggregate value of $13,400 for all items
4. Interest in jewelry up to $1,700
5. Interest in any property the debtor chooses (including cash) up to $1,325, plus up to $12,575 of any unused portion of the homestead exemption
6. Interest up to $2,525 in value in implements, tools, or professional books used in the debtor's trade
7. Any unmatured life insurance policy owned by the debtor
8. Professionally prescribed health aids
9. Many government benefits, regardless of value, including Social Security benefits, welfare benefits, unemployment compensation, veterans benefits, disability benefits, and public assistance benefits
10. Certain rights to receive income, including domestic support payments (e.g., alimony, child support), certain pension benefits, profit sharing, and annuity payments
11. Interests in wrongful death benefits and life insurance proceeds to the extent necessary to support the debtor or his or her dependents
12. Personal injury awards up to $25,150, except for pain and suffering
13. Retirement funds that are in a fund or an account that is exempt from taxation under the Internal Revenue Code and defined benefit plans up to any amount; the exemption for individual retirement accounts (IRAs) and ROTH IRAs shall not exceed $1,362,800 for an individual unless the interests of justice require this amount to be increased

State Exemptions

The Bankruptcy Code permits states to enact their own exemptions. States that do so may (1) give debtors the option of choosing between federal and state exemptions or (2) require debtors to follow state law. The exemptions available under state law are often more liberal than those provided by federal law.

Homestead Exemption

homestead exemption
Equity in a debtor's home that the debtor is permitted to retain.

The federal Bankruptcy Code permits homeowners to claim a **homestead exemption** in their principal residence of $25,150, or $50,300 if married and filing jointly. If the debtor's equity in the property (i.e., the value above the amount of the mortgages and liens) exceeds the exemption limits, the trustee may sell the property to realize the excess value for the bankruptcy estate.

Example Assume that a debtor owns a principal residence worth $500,000 that is subject to a $400,000 mortgage and the debtor therefore owns $100,000 of equity in the property. The debtor files a petition for Chapter 7 liquidation bankruptcy. The trustee may sell the home, pay off the mortgage, pay the debtor $25,150 (applying the federal exemption), and use the remaining proceeds of $74,850 for distribution to the debtor's creditors.

WEB EXERCISE
Use an internet search engine and find the homestead exemption of your state.

Homestead exemptions under many state laws are usually higher than the federal exemption. Most states exempt between $30,000 and $100,000 of equity in a debtor's principal residence from the bankruptcy estate. However, some states have no dollar amount limit on their homestead exemptions, while others have very high dollar homestead exemptions. The 2005 act limits **abusive homestead**

exemptions. It provides that a debtor may not exempt an amount greater than $170,350 under a state law homestead exemption if the property was acquired by the debtor within 40 months before the filing of the petition for bankruptcy.

Chapter 7—Liquidation

28.5 Describe the provisions of a Chapter 7 liquidation bankruptcy.

Chapter 7—Liquidation (also called **straight bankruptcy**) is a familiar form of bankruptcy.[5] In this type of bankruptcy proceeding, the debtor is permitted to keep a substantial portion of his or her assets (exempt assets). The debtor's non-exempt property is sold for cash, and the cash is distributed to the creditors; any of the debtor's unpaid debts are discharged. The debtor's future income, even if the debtor becomes rich, cannot be reached to pay the discharged debt. Thus, a debtor would be left to start life anew, without the burden of the prepetition debts. Approximately 475,000 Chapter 7 bankruptcies are filed each year.

Chapter 7—Liquidation (straight bankruptcy)
A form of bankruptcy in which the debtor's nonexempt property is sold for cash, the cash is distributed to the creditors, and any unpaid debts are discharged.

The U.S. Supreme Court described a Chapter 7 bankruptcy as follows.

> *Chapter 7 allows a debtor to make a clean break from his financial past, but at a steep price: prompt liquidation of the debtor's assets. When a debtor files a Chapter 7 petition, his assets, with specified exemptions, are immediately transferred to a bankruptcy estate. Crucially, however, a Chapter 7 estate does not include the wages a debtor earns or the assets he acquires after the bankruptcy filing. Thus, while a Chapter 7 debtor must forfeit virtually all his prepetition property, he is able to make a "fresh start" by shielding from creditors his postpetition earnings and acquisitions.*[6]

Example Annabelle finds herself overburdened with debt, particularly credit card debt. Assume that Annabelle qualifies for Chapter 7 bankruptcy. When she files for Chapter 7 bankruptcy, her unsecured credit is $100,000. Annabelle has few assets, and most of those are exempt property (e.g., her clothes, some furniture). Her nonexempt property is $10,000, which will be sold to raise cash. The $10,000 in cash will be distributed to her debtors on a pro rata basis—that is, each creditor will receive 10 cents for every dollar of debt owed. The other $90,000 is *discharged*—that is, the creditors must absorb this loss. Annabelle is free from this debt forever. She is given a fresh start, and her future earnings are hers.

A man may be a bankrupt, and yet be honest, for he may become so by accident, and not of purpose to deceive his creditors.
Roll, Chief Justice
Rooke v. Smith (1651)

Qualifications for Chapter 7 Bankruptcy

One of the purposes of the 2005 act's changes to Chapter 7 was to force many debtors out of Chapter 7 liquidation bankruptcy and into Chapter 13 debt adjustment bankruptcy, which requires debtors to pay some of their future income to pay off prepetition debts. Thus, the 2005 act reduces the number of debtors who qualify for Chapter 7 liquidation bankruptcy. To accomplish this, the 2005 act added two tests, the *median income test* and the *means test,* to determine whether a debtor qualifies to obtain a discharge of debts under Chapter 7:

- **Test 1: Median Income Test.** The first step in determining whether a debtor qualifies for Chapter 7 relief is to apply the **median income test**. A **state's median income** is defined as that income where half of the state's families of a specified size have incomes above that figure and half of the state's families of that size have incomes below that figure. The median income for a family of two will differ from the median income for a family of three and so on.

  If a family has median family income *equal to or below* the state's median family income for the size of the debtor's family, the debtor qualifies for Chapter 7 bankruptcy. The debtor may proceed with the Chapter 7 case and be granted discharge of unsecured debts. Thus, for debtors at or below the state median income, the 2005 act makes no changes in the ability to obtain Chapter 7 relief.

median income test
A bankruptcy rule that states that if a debtor's median family income is at or below the state's median family income for a family the same size as the debtor's family, the debtor can receive Chapter 7 relief.

WEB EXERCISE
Use an internet search engine and find the median income for a family of four in your state.

Example Assume that a state's median income for a family of four is $75,000. If the median income of the debtor's family of four is $60,000, the debtor qualifies for Chapter 7 bankruptcy relief.

If a family has median family income that is *higher* than the state's median family income for the size of the debtor's family, the debtor does not automatically qualify for a Chapter 7 bankruptcy. A second test, the *means test*, is applied to see if the debtor qualifies for Chapter 7 bankruptcy.

means test
A bankruptcy rule that applies to a debtor who has a median family income that exceeds the state's median family income for families the same size as the debtor's family. A debtor in this category qualifies for Chapter 7 bankruptcy if the debtor has disposable income below an amount determined by bankruptcy law but does not qualify for Chapter 7 bankruptcy if he or she has disposable income above an amount determined by bankruptcy law.

- **Test 2: Means Test.** The **means test** is a calculation that establishes a bright-line test to determine whether the debtor has sufficient *disposable income* to pay prepetition debts out of postpetition income. **Disposable income** is determined by taking the debtor's actual income and subtracting expenses for a typical family the same size as the debtor's family. Income is the actual income of the debtor. However, expenses are determined by using preestablished government tables and not the actual expenses of the family. A complicated formula is used to calculate the debtor's disposable income and thus determine whether the debtor qualifies for Chapter 7 bankruptcy.

  If, because of the application of the means test, a debtor is determined to have a sufficient disposable income as determined by bankruptcy law, the debtor does not qualify for Chapter 7 bankruptcy. The petition for Chapter 7 bankruptcy will be denied by the bankruptcy court. Usually these debtors will file for Chapter 13 bankruptcy (discussed later in this chapter).

  If, however, using the means test calculation, a debtor is determined to have an insufficient amount of disposable income as determined by bankruptcy law, the debtor qualifies for Chapter 7 bankruptcy. These debtors may be granted Chapter 7 discharge of debts.

  Thus, some of the debtors that have income above the state's median income for the debtor's size of family will qualify for Chapter 7, and some will not.

Statutory Distribution of Property

If a debtor qualifies for a Chapter 7 liquidation bankruptcy, the **nonexempt property** of the bankruptcy estate must be distributed to the debtor's secured and unsecured creditors pursuant to statutory priority established by the Bankruptcy Code. The claims of secured creditors to the debtor's nonexempt property have priority over the claims of unsecured creditors.

It is the policy of the law that the debtor be just before he be generous.

Justice Edward Finch
Hearn 45 St. Corp. v. Jano 283 N.Y. 139, 27 N.E.2d 814, 1940 N.Y. Lexis 926 (1940)

As to secured creditors, the following two situations can result:

1. **Oversecured secured creditor.** If the value of the collateral securing the secured loan exceeds the secured interest, the secured creditor is an **oversecured creditor**. In this case, the property is usually sold, and the secured creditor is paid the amount of its secured interest (i.e., the principal and accrued interest) and reasonable fees and costs resulting from the debtor's default. The excess becomes available to satisfy the claims of the debtor's unsecured creditors.
2. **Undersecured secured creditor.** If the value of the collateral securing the secured loan is less than the secured interest, the secured creditor is an **undersecured creditor**. In this case, the property is usually awarded to the secured creditor. The secured creditor then becomes an unsecured creditor as to the amount still owed to it, which consists of unpaid principal and interest and reasonable fees and costs of the debtor's default.

Small debts are like small shot; they are rattling on every side, and can scarcely be escaped without a wound; great debts are like cannon; of loud noise, but little danger.

Samuel Johnson
Letters to Joseph Simpson (1759)

If personal property of an individual debtor secures a claim or is subject to an unexpired lease (e.g., an automobile lease) and is not exempt property, the debtor must (1) surrender the personal property, (2) redeem the property by paying the secured lien in full, or (3) assume the unexpired lease.

Unsecured claims are to be satisfied out of the bankruptcy estate in the order of their statutory priority, as established by the Bankruptcy Code. The **statutory priority of unsecured claims** is set forth in Exhibit 28.3.

Exhibit 28.3 PRIORITY OF UNSECURED CREDITOR CLAIMS

1. Unsecured claims for domestic support obligations owed to a spouse, former spouse, or child of the debtor
2. Fees and expenses of administering the estate, including court costs, trustee fees, attorney's fees, appraisal fees, and other costs of administration
3. In an involuntary bankruptcy, secured claims of "gap" creditors who sold goods or services on credit to the debtor in the ordinary course of the debtor's business between the date of the filing of the petition and the date of the appointment of the trustee or issuance of the order for relief (whichever occurred first)
4. Unsecured claims for wages, salary, commissions, severance pay, and sick leave pay earned by the debtor's employees within 180 days immediately preceding the filing of the petition, up to $13,650 per employee
5. Unsecured claims for contributions to employee benefit plans based on services performed within 180 days immediately preceding the filing of the petition, up to $13,650 per employee, but only to the extent that payments under item 4 above have not reached $13,650; thus, the payments under items 4 and 5 can total only $13,650

   Example If an employee is owed $7,000 of unpaid priority benefits but has been paid $13,650 or more for priority unpaid wages, the employee receives no priority payment for unpaid benefits. He or she is still owed $7,000 for unpaid benefits, but the $7,000 becomes a nonpriority unsecured claim.

   Example If an employee has been paid $5,000 for priority unpaid wages, the employee can recover up to $8,650 of priority benefits owed.

6. Farm producers and fishermen against debtors who operate grain storage facilities or fish storage or processing facilities, respectively, up to $6,725 per claim
7. Unsecured claims for cash deposited by a consumer with the debtor prior to the filing of the petition in connection with the purchase, lease, or rental of property or the purchases of services that were not delivered or provided by the debtor, up to $3,025 per claim
8. Unsecured claims for unpaid income and gross receipts taxes owed to governments incurred during the three years preceding the bankruptcy petition and unpaid property taxes owed to governments incurred within one year preceding the bankruptcy petition
9. Commitment by the debtor to maintain the capital of an insured depository institution such as a commercial bank or savings bank
10. Claims against the debtor for personal injuries or death caused by the debtor while he or she was intoxicated from using alcohol or drugs

A debtor can be granted Chapter 7 relief only after eight years following Chapter 7 or Chapter 11 relief and only after six years following Chapter 12 or Chapter 13 relief.

Chapter 7 Discharge

In a Chapter 7 bankruptcy, the property of the estate is sold, and the proceeds are distributed to satisfy allowed claims. The remaining unpaid debts that the debtor incurred prior to the date of the order for relief are discharged. *Discharge* means that the debtor is no longer legally responsible for paying those claims. The major benefit of a **Chapter 7 discharge** is that it is granted quite soon after the petition is filed. The individual debtor is not responsible for paying prepetition debts out of postpetition income, as would be required in other forms of bankruptcy.

Chapter 7 discharge
The termination of the legal duty of an individual debtor to pay unsecured debts that remain unpaid on the completion of a Chapter 7 proceeding.

Example Suppose that at the time that Aldo is granted Chapter 7 relief, he still owes $50,000 of unsecured debt that there is no money in the bankruptcy estate to pay. This debt is composed of credit card debt, an unsecured loan from a friend, and unsecured credit from a department store. This $50,000 of unsecured credit is discharged. This means that Aldo is relieved of this debt and is not legally liable for its repayment. The unsecured creditors must write off this debt.

Acts That Bar Discharge

Any party of interest may file an objection to the discharge of a debt. The court then holds a hearing. Discharge of unsatisfied debts is denied if the debtor:

- Made false representations about his or her financial position when obtaining an extension of credit
- Transferred, concealed, removed, or destroyed property of the estate with the intent to hinder, delay, or defraud creditors within one year before the date of the filing of the petition
- Falsified, destroyed, or concealed records of his or her financial condition
- Failed to account for any assets
- Failed to submit to questioning at the meeting of the creditors (unless excused)
- Failed to complete an instructional course concerning personal financial management (unless excused)

If a discharge is obtained through fraud of the debtor, any party of interest may bring a motion to have the bankruptcy revoked. The bankruptcy court may revoke a discharge within one year after it is granted.

Beggars can never be bankrupt.
Thomas Fuller
Gnomologia (1732)

In the following case, the U.S. Supreme Court addressed the issue of whether a debt was dischargeable in bankruptcy.

CASE 28.2 *U.S. SUPREME COURT CASE Bankruptcy Fraud*

Husky International Electronics, Inc. v. Ritz

136 S.Ct. 1581, 2016 U.S. Lexis 3048 (2016)
Supreme Court of the United States

"The Bankruptcy Code prohibits debtors from discharging debts obtained by false pretenses, a false representation, or actual fraud."
—Sonia Sotomayor, Justice

Facts

Husky International Electronics, Inc. (Husky) sold electronic components to Chrysalis Manufacturing Corp. (Chrysalis), on credit, which incurred a debt to Husky of $163,999. Daniel Lee Ritz Jr. owned 30 percent of Chrysalis's common stock and served as a director of the company. During a one-year period, Ritz drained Chrysalis of assets it could have used to pay creditors of Chrysalis like Husky by transferring large sums of Chrysalis's funds to other entities Ritz controlled. Ritz transferred $52,600 to CapNet Risk Management, Inc., a company he owned in full; $121,831 to CapNet Securities Corp., a company in which he owned an 85 percent interest; $99,386 to Dynalyst Manufacturing Corp., a company in which he owned a 25 percent interest; and made additional transfers to other companies he controlled.

When Chrysalis did not pay the $163,999 debt it owed Husky, Husky filed a lawsuit against Ritz seeking to hold him personally responsible for the debt. Husky argued that Ritz's intercompany-transfer scheme was actual fraud under Texas law that allows creditors to hold shareholders responsible for corporate debt. Ritz filed for Chapter 7 bankruptcy. In that proceeding, Husky argued that Ritz could not discharge the debt in bankruptcy because the intercompany-transfer scheme constituted actual fraud that was not dischargeable in bankruptcy.

The U.S. district court held that Ritz was personally liable to Husky for the debt, but that the debt could be discharged in bankruptcy. U.S. court of appeals affirmed the decision that the debt could be discharged in bankruptcy. Husky appealed to the U.S. Supreme Court.

Issue

Is Ritz's debt to Husky dischargeable in bankruptcy?

Language of the U.S. Supreme Court

The Bankruptcy Code prohibits debtors from discharging debts obtained by false pretenses, a false representation, or actual fraud. The historical meaning of actual fraud provides even stronger evidence that the phrase has long encompassed the kind of conduct alleged to have occurred here: a transfer scheme designed to hinder the collection of debt. From the beginning of English bankruptcy practice, courts and legislatures have used the term fraud to describe a debtor's transfer of assets that, like Ritz's scheme, impairs a creditor's ability to collect the debt.

Decision

The U.S. Supreme Court held that the Bankruptcy Code exempted from discharge false representation schemes. The Supreme Court reversed the decision of the court of appeals and remanded the case for final disposition.

Critical Legal Thinking Questions

What was Ritz's intercompany-transfer scheme designed to accomplish? Did Ritz act ethically in this case?

As the following feature shows, special rules apply for the discharge of student loans in bankruptcy.

Critical Legal Thinking

Discharge of Student Loans in Bankruptcy

Until their graduation from college and professional schools, many students have borrowed money to pay tuition and living expenses. At this point, when a student might have large student loans and very few assets, he or she might be inclined to file for bankruptcy in an attempt to have the student loans discharged.

To prevent such abuse of bankruptcy law, Congress amended the Bankruptcy Code to make it more difficult for people to have their **student loans** discharged in bankruptcy. Student loans are defined to include loans made by or guaranteed by governmental units; loans made by nongovernmental commercial institutions such as banks; and funds for scholarships, benefits, or stipends granted by educational institutions.

The Bankruptcy Code now states that student loans cannot be discharged in any form of bankruptcy unless their nondischarge would cause an undue hardship to the debtor and his or her dependents. **Undue hardship in bankruptcy** is construed strictly and is difficult for a debtor to prove unless the debtor can show severe physical or mental disability or inability to pay for basic necessities, such as food or shelter, for his or her family.

Co-signers (e.g., parents who guarantee their child's student loan) must also meet the heightened undue hardship test to discharge their obligation.

Critical Legal Thinking Questions

Why did the U.S. Congress make the discharge of student loans more difficult than the discharge of other loans? What is undue hardship?

Chapter 13—Adjustment of Debts of an Individual With Regular Income

28.6 Describe a Chapter 13 adjustment of debts of an individual with regular income bankruptcy.

Chapter 13—Adjustment of Debts of an Individual with Regular Income is a rehabilitation form of bankruptcy for individuals.[7] Chapter 13 permits a qualified

Chapter 13—Adjustment of Debts of an Individual with Regular Income
A rehabilitation form of bankruptcy that permits bankruptcy courts to supervise the debtor's plan for the payment of unpaid debts in installments over the plan period.

debtor to propose a plan to pay all or a portion of the debts owed in installments over a specified period of time, pursuant to the requirements of Chapter 13. The bankruptcy court supervises the debtor's plan for the payment.

The debtor has several advantages under Chapter 13. These include avoiding the stigma of Chapter 7 liquidation, retaining more property than is exempt under Chapter 7, and incurring fewer expenses than in a Chapter 7 proceeding. The creditors have advantages, too: They may recover a greater percentage of the debts owed them than they would recover under a Chapter 7 bankruptcy.

Chapter 13 petitions are usually filed by individual debtors who do not qualify for Chapter 7 liquidation bankruptcy and by homeowners who want to protect nonexempt equity in their residence. Chapter 13 enables debtors to catch up on secured credit loans, such as home mortgages, and avoid repossession and foreclosure. Approximately 300,000 Chapter 13 bankruptcies are filed each year.

Filing a Chapter 13 Petition

individual with regular income
An individual whose income is sufficiently stable and regular to enable the individual to make payments under a Chapter 13 plan.

A Chapter 13 proceeding can be initiated only through the voluntary filing of a petition by an individual debtor with regular income. A creditor cannot file an involuntary petition to institute a Chapter 13 case. An **individual with regular income** means an individual whose income is sufficiently stable and regular to enable him or her to make payments under a Chapter 13 plan. Regular income may be from any source, including wages, salary, or commissions, and from investments, Social Security income, pension income, or public assistance. The debts of the individual debtor must be primarily consumer debt. **Consumer debt** means debts incurred by an individual for personal, family, or household purposes. The petition must be filed in good faith.

The petition must state that the debtor desires to obtain an extension or a composition of debts, or both.

extension
Provides a longer period of time for the debtor to pay his or her debts.

An **extension** provides for a longer period of time for the debtor to pay the debts.

Example A debtor who is obligated to pay a debt within one year petitions the bankruptcy court to extend the time in which to pay the debt to three years.

composition
Provides for the reduction of a debtor's debts.

A **composition** provides for the reduction of a debtor's debts.

Example A debtor who owes an unsecured creditor $10,000 petitions the court to reduce the unsecured debt owed the creditor to $7,000.

Limitations on Who Can File for Chapter 13 Bankruptcy

Bankruptcy law establishes dollar limits on the secured and unsecured debt that a debtor may have in order to qualify to file for Chapter 13 bankruptcy. Only an individual with regular income alone or with a spouse who owes individually or with a spouse (1) noncontingent, liquidated, unsecured debts of not more than $419,275 and (2) secured debts of not more than $1,257,850 may file a petition for Chapter 13 bankruptcy. Individual debtors who exceed these dollar limits do not qualify for Chapter 13 bankruptcy. Sole proprietorships, because they are owned by individuals, may file for Chapter 13 bankruptcy.

Property of a Chapter 13 Estate

The property of a Chapter 13 estate consists of all nonexempt property of the debtor at the commencement of the case and nonexempt property acquired after the commencement of the case but before the case is closed. In addition, the property of the estate includes earnings and future income earned by the debtor after the commencement of the case but before the case is closed. This ensures that prepetition creditors receive payments from the debtor's postpetition earnings and income.

The debtor remains in possession of all of the property of the estate during the completion of the plan except as otherwise provided by the plan. If the debtor is self-employed, the debtor may continue to operate the business. Alternatively, the court may order that a trustee operate the business, if necessary.

Chapter 13 Plan of Payment

The debtor's **Chapter 13 plan of payment** must be filed not later than 90 days after the order for relief. The debtor must file information about his or her finances, including a budget of estimated income and expenses during the period of the plan. The Chapter 13 plan may be either up to three years or up to five years, depending on a complicated calculation specified in the Bankruptcy Code.

Chapter 13 plan of payment
A plan that lays out a debtor's plan for paying his or her disposable income to prepetition creditors during a Chapter 13 plan period.

The plan must be submitted to secured and unsecured creditors for acceptance. The plan is confirmed as to a secured creditor or an unsecured creditor if that creditor accepts the plan. If a secured creditor does not accept the plan, the court may still confirm the plan if the secured creditor will be paid in full, including arrearages, during the plan. If an unsecured creditor objects to the plan, the court may still confirm the plan if the debtor agrees to commit all disposable income during the plan period to pay the unsecured creditors. However, during the plan period, unsecured creditors might not receive full payment of the debt owed to them.

Disposable income is defined as current monthly income less amounts reasonably necessary to be spent for the maintenance or support of the debtor and the debtor's dependents. Expenses include amounts necessary to pay domestic support obligations and charitable donations that do not exceed 15 percent of the debtor's gross income for the year the charitable donations are made. If a debtor earns more than the median income of the state, expenses are determined by the objective Internal Revenue Service (IRS) standards.

Debt rolls a man over and over, binding him hand and foot, and letting him hang upon the fatal mesh until the long-legged interest devours him.

Henry Ward Beecher
Proverbs from Plymouth Pulpit (1887)

The U.S. Supreme Court described a Chapter 13 bankruptcy as follows.

> *A wholly voluntary alternative to Chapter 7, Chapter 13 allows a debtor to retain his property if he proposes, and gains court confirmation of, a plan to repay his debts over a three- to five-year period. Payments under a Chapter 13 plan are usually made from a debtor's "future earnings or other future income." Accordingly, the Chapter 13 estate from which creditors may be paid includes both the debtor's property at the time of his bankruptcy petition, and any wages and property acquired after filing. A Chapter 13 trustee is often charged with collecting a portion of a debtor's wages through payroll deduction, and with distributing the withheld wages to creditors. Proceedings under Chapter 13 can benefit debtors and creditors alike. Debtors are allowed to retain their assets, commonly their home or car. And creditors, entitled to a Chapter 13 debtor's "disposable" post-petition income, usually collect more under a Chapter 13 plan than they would have received under a Chapter 7 liquidation.*[8]

Confirmation of a Chapter 13 Plan of Payment

The court can confirm a Chapter 13 plan of payment if the prior requirements are met and if (1) the plan was proposed in good faith, (2) the plan passes the feasibility test (i.e., the debtor must be able to make the proposed payments), (3) the plan is in the best interests of the creditors (i.e., the present value of the payments must equal or exceed the amount that the creditors would receive in a Chapter 7 liquidation proceeding), (4) the debtor has paid all domestic support obligations owed, and (5) the debtor has filed all applicable federal, state, and local tax returns.

The debtor must begin making the planned installment payments to the trustee in equal monthly installments. The trustee is responsible for remitting these payments to the creditors. The trustee is paid for administering the plan.

A Chapter 13 plan may be modified if the debtor's circumstances materially change. For example, if the debtor's income subsequently decreases, the court may decrease the debtor's payments under the plan.

Chapter 13 Discharge

The court grants an order discharging the debtor from all unpaid unsecured debts covered by the plan after all the payments required under the plan are completed (which could take up to three years or up to five years). This is called a Chapter 13 discharge. The debtor must certify that all domestic support payments have been paid before discharge is granted. Most unpaid taxes are not discharged.

Chapter 13 discharge
A discharge in a Chapter 13 case that is granted to the debtor after the debtor's plan of payment is completed (which could be up to three or up to five years).

A debtor cannot be granted **Chapter 13 discharge** if the debtor has received discharge under Chapter 7, 11, or 12 within the prior four-year period or Chapter 13 relief within the prior two-year period of the order for relief in the current Chapter 13 case.

Chapter 11—Reorganization

28.7 Describe how businesses are reorganized in Chapter 11 bankruptcy.

Chapter 11—Reorganization
A bankruptcy method that allows the reorganization of the debtor's financial affairs under the supervision of the bankruptcy court.

Chapter 11—Reorganization of the Bankruptcy Code provides a method for reorganizing a debtor's financial affairs under the supervision of the bankruptcy court.[9] The goal of Chapter 11 is to reorganize the debtor with a new capital structure so that the debtor emerges from bankruptcy as a viable concern. This option, which is referred to as **reorganization bankruptcy**, is often in the best interests of debtors and creditors.

Chapter 11 is available to partnerships, corporations, limited liability companies, and other business entities. Most Chapter 11 proceedings are filed by corporations and other businesses that want to reorganize their capital structure by receiving discharge of a portion of their debts and obtaining relief from burdensome contracts and to emerge from bankruptcy as *going concerns*. Chapter 11 is also filed by wealthy individual debtors who do not qualify for Chapter 7 or Chapter 13 bankruptcy. Approximately 7,000 Chapter 11 bankruptcies are filed each year.

Debtor-in-Possession

debtor-in-possession
A debtor who is left in place to operate the business during the reorganization proceeding.

In most Chapter 11 cases, the debtor is left in place to operate the business during the reorganization proceeding. In such cases, the debtor is called a **debtor-in-possession**. The court may appoint a trustee to operate the debtor's business only on a showing of cause, such as fraud, dishonesty, or gross mismanagement of the affairs of the debtor by current management.

The debtor-in-possession is empowered to operate the debtor's business during the bankruptcy proceeding. This power includes authority to enter into contracts, purchase supplies, incur debts, and so on. Credit extended by postpetition unsecured creditors in the ordinary course of business is given automatic priority as an administrative expense in bankruptcy.

Creditors' Committees

creditors' committee
A committee of unsecured creditors that is appointed by the court to represent the class of unsecured claims. The court can also appoint committees for secured creditors and for equity holders.

After an order for relief is granted, the court appoints a **creditors' committee** composed of representatives of the class of unsecured claims. The court may also appoint a committee of secured creditors and a committee of equity holders. Generally, the parties holding the seven largest creditor claims or equity interests are appointed to their requisite committees. Committees may appear at bankruptcy court hearings, participate in the negotiation of a plan of reorganization, assert objections to proposed plans of reorganization, and the like.

Automatic Stay in Chapter 11

The filing of a Chapter 11 petition stays (suspends) actions by creditors to recover the debtor's property. This automatic stay suspends certain legal actions against the debtor or the debtor's property, including the ability of creditors to foreclose on assets given as collateral for their loans to the debtor. This automatic stay is extremely important to a business trying to reorganize under Chapter 11 because the debtor needs to keep its assets to stay in business.

Poor bankrupt.
William Shakespeare
Romeo and Juliet (ca. 1594)

Example Big Oil Company owns a manufacturing plant and has borrowed $50 million from a bank, using the plant as collateral for the loan. If Big Oil Company files for Chapter 11 bankruptcy, the automatic stay prevents the bank from foreclosing and taking the property. Once out of bankruptcy, Big Oil Company must pay the bank any unpaid arrearages and begin making the required loan payments again.

executory contract or unexpired lease
A contract or lease that has not been fully performed. With the bankruptcy court's approval, a debtor may reject executory contracts and unexpired leases in bankruptcy.

The following feature discusses how executory contracts and unexpired leases are treated in a Chapter 11 bankruptcy.

Business Environment

Executory Contracts and Unexpired Leases

A major benefit of Chapter 11 bankruptcy is that the debtor is given the opportunity to accept or reject certain executory contracts and unexpired leases. **Executory contracts** or **unexpired leases** are contracts or leases that have not been fully performed.

A contract to purchase goods or supply goods at a later date is an executory contract. A 20-year office lease that has eight years left until it is completed is an unexpired lease. Other executory contracts and unexpired leases may include consulting contracts, contracts to purchase or provide services, equipment leases, warehouse leases, automobile and equipment leases, leases for office and commercial space, and the like.

Under the Bankruptcy Code, a debtor-in-possession (or trustee) in a Chapter 11 proceeding is given authority to assume or reject executory contracts. In general, the debtor rejects unfavorable executory contracts and assumes favorable executory contracts. The debtor is not liable for damages caused by the rejection of executory contracts and unexpired leases in bankruptcy.

Examples Big Oil Company enters into a contract to sell oil to another company, and the contract has two years remaining when Big Oil files for Chapter 11 bankruptcy. This is an *executory contract*. Big Oil Company has leased an office building for 20 years from a landlord to use as its headquarters, and it has 15 years left on the lease when it declares bankruptcy. This is an *unexpired lease*. In the Chapter 11 reorganization proceeding, Big Oil Company can reject (get out of) the executory contract or the unexpired lease or both without any liability; it can keep one or the other or both if doing so is in its best interests.

Labor Union and Retiree Benefits Contracts

Debtors that file for Chapter 11 reorganization sometimes have collective bargaining agreements with labor unions that require the payment of agreed-on wages and other benefits to union member-employees for some agreed-on period in the future. Debtors also often have contracts to pay union and nonunion retired employees and their dependents' medical, surgical, hospitalization, dental, and death benefits (retiree benefits). In a Chapter 11 case, union members and union retirees are represented by the responsible labor union. The court appoints a committee to represent nonunion retirees.

Critical Legal Thinking Questions
What is the public policy that allows businesses to file for Chapter 11 bankruptcy? Who benefits from Chapter 11 bankruptcy?

The debtor and the representatives of the union members and retirees can voluntarily agree to modification of the union collective bargaining agreement and retiree benefits. If such an agreement is not reached, the debtor must confer in good faith with the union and retirees' representative, but if a settlement cannot be reached, the debtor can petition the bankruptcy court to reject the union agreement or to modify retiree benefits. The court can reject a union contract or modify retirees' benefits if the court finds that the "balance of equities" favors rejection or modification and the rejection or modification is necessary to the debtor's reorganization.

Discharge of Debts

In its bankruptcy reorganization, the debtor usually proposes to reduce its *unsecured debt* so that it can come out of bankruptcy with fewer debts to pay than when it filed for bankruptcy. The bankruptcy court permits the debtor to *discharge* the amount of unsecured credit that would make its plan of reorganization feasible. Unsecured credit is discharged on a pro rata basis.

Example Big Oil Company has $100 million in secured debts (e.g., real estate mortgages, personal property secured transactions) and $100 million in unsecured credit when it files for Chapter 11 bankruptcy. In its plan of reorganization, Big Oil Company proposes to eliminate 60 percent—$60 million—of its unsecured credit. If the court approves, then Big Oil will emerge from bankruptcy owing only $40 million of prepetition unsecured debt. The other $60 million is discharged, and the creditors can never recover these debts in the future.

Chapter 11 Plan of Reorganization

Chapter 11 plan of reorganization
A plan that sets forth a proposed new capital structure for a debtor to assume when it emerges from Chapter 11 reorganization bankruptcy.

The debtor has the exclusive right to file a **Chapter 11 plan of reorganization** with the bankruptcy court within the first 120 days after the date of the order for relief. This period may be extended up to 18 months. The debtor has the right to obtain creditor approval of the plan, but if the debtor fails to do so, any party of interest (e.g., a trustee, a creditor, or an equity holder) may propose a plan.

The plan of reorganization sets forth the proposed new financial structure of the debtor. This includes the portion of the unsecured debts proposed to be paid by the debtor and the unsecured debt the debtor proposes to have discharged. The plan must specify the executory contracts and unexpired leases that the debtor proposes to reject that have not previously been rejected in the bankruptcy proceeding. The plan also designates how equity holders are to be treated, describes any new equity investments that are to be made in the debtor, and includes other relevant information.

The debtor must supply the creditors and equity holders with a *disclosure statement* that contains adequate information about the proposed plan of reorganization so that they can make an informed judgment about the plan.

Chapter 11 Confirmation of a Plan of Reorganization

confirmation of a Chapter 11 plan of reorganization
The bankruptcy court's approval of a plan of reorganization.

acceptance method
A method whereby the court confirms a plan of reorganization if the creditors accept the plan and if other requirements are met.

cram-down provision
A provision whereby the court confirms a plan of reorganization over an objecting class of creditors if certain requirements are met.

There must be **confirmation of a Chapter 11 plan of reorganization** by the bankruptcy court for the debtor to be reorganized under Chapter 11. The bankruptcy court confirms a plan of reorganization under the **acceptance method** if (1) the plan is in the best interests of the creditors because the creditors would receive at least what they would receive in a Chapter 7 liquidation bankruptcy, (2) the plan is feasible (i.e., the new reorganized company is likely to succeed), and (3) each class of creditors accepts the plan (i.e., at least one-half the number of creditors who represent at least two-thirds of the dollar amount of the debt vote to accept the plan).

If a class of creditors does not accept the plan, the plan can be confirmed by the court by using the Bankruptcy Code's **cram-down provision**. In order for the court to confirm a plan over the objection of a class of creditors, at least one class of creditors must have voted to accept the plan.

Example BigDotCom Corporation has financial difficulties and has filed for Chapter 11 reorganization. At the time of filing for Chapter 11, the corporation has $100 million of secured credit, $100 million of unsecured credit, and common stockholders whose equity securities are now worthless. The corporation files a plan of reorganization whereby the corporation (1) keeps the secured assets for the business, pays the secured creditors any arrearages owed, and has the secured creditors retain their secured interests in the secured assets; (2) reduces unsecured debt by $45 million and discharges $55 million of unsecured debt; (3) eliminates the interests of the equity holders; (4) rejects specified executory contracts and unexpired leases; (5) eliminates several unprofitable product lines; (6) provides for the payment of required unpaid taxes; and (7) accepts the investment of $30 million in capital from an investment bank that wants to invest in the corporation. If this plan is approved by the court, $55 million of the corporation's unsecured debt is discharged. The corporation emerges from Chapter 11 as a reorganized going concern.

Small Business Bankruptcy

The Bankruptcy Code permits a "small business," defined as one with total debts of less than $2,725,625, to use a simplified, fast-track form of Chapter 11 reorganization bankruptcy. **Small business bankruptcy** provides an efficient and cost-saving method for small businesses to reorganize under Chapter 11.

Henry R. Cheeseman

BLAINE COUNTY, IDAHO

Chapter 12 Bankruptcy

Chapter 12—Adjustment of Debts of a Family Farmer or Fisherman with Regular Income[10] of the federal Bankruptcy Code contains special provisions for the reorganization bankruptcy of family farmers and family fishermen. Under Chapter 12, only the debtor may file a voluntary petition for bankruptcy. To qualify, a family farmer cannot have debt that exceeds $4,441,400, and a family fisherman cannot have debt that exceeds $2,044,225. The debtor files a plan of reorganization.

The plan may modify secured and unsecured credit and assume or reject executory contracts and unexpired leases. The plan period is usually three years, although a court may increase the period to up to five years, based on showing of cause. To confirm a plan of reorganization, the bankruptcy court must find the plan to be feasible. During the plan period, the debtor makes the debt payments required by the plan. When the family farmer or family fisherman has completed making the payments required by the plan, the bankruptcy court grants the debtor discharge of all the debts provided for by the plan. Approximately 500 Chapter 12 bankruptcies are filed each year.

Key Terms and Concepts

Abusive homestead exemption (484)
Acceptance method (494)
Article I, Section 8, Clause 4 of the U.S. Constitution (477)
Attorney certification (479)
Automatic stay (480)
Bankruptcy Abuse Prevention and Consumer Protection Act of 2005 (478)
Bankruptcy Code (478)
Bankruptcy estate (482)
Bankruptcy law (478)
Bankruptcy Reform Act of 1978 (478)
Bankruptcy trustee (480)
Chapter 7 discharge (488)
Chapter 7—Liquidation (straight bankruptcy) (485)
Chapter 11 plan of reorganization (494)
Chapter 11— Reorganization (492)
Chapter 12—Adjustment of Debts of a Family Farmer or Fisherman with Regular Income (495)
Chapter 13—Adjustment of Debts of an Individual with Regular Income (489)
Chapter 13 discharge (492)
Chapter 13 plan of payment (491)
Composition (490)
Confirmation of a Chapter 11 plan of reorganization (494)
Consumer debt (490)
Cram-down provision (494)
Creditors' committee (492)
Debtor-in-possession (492)
Discharge in bankruptcy (480)
Disposable income (486)
Executory contract (493)
Exempt property (483)
Extension (490)
Fraudulent transfer (482)
Fresh start (477)
Homestead exemption (484)
Individual with regular income (490)
Involuntary petition (479)
Means test (486)
Median income test (485)
Meeting of the creditors (first meeting of the creditors) (479)
Nonexempt property (486)
Order for relief (479)
Oversecured creditor (486)
Petition for bankruptcy (479)
Postpetition counseling (478)
Prepetition counseling (478)
Proof of claim (480)
Proof of interest (480)
Reaffirmation agreement (482)
Reorganization bankruptcy (492)
Schedules (479)
Small business bankruptcy (495)
State's median income (485)
Statutory priority of unsecured claims (487)
Student loan (489)
U.S. bankruptcy courts (478)
U.S. Trustee (478)
Undersecured creditor (486)
Undue hardship in bankruptcy (489)
Unexpired lease (493)
Voluntary petition (479)

Critical Legal Thinking Cases

28.1 Bankruptcy Estate Dr. Morris Lebovitz and Kerrye Hill Lebovitz, husband and wife, were residents of the state of Tennessee. Dr. Lebovitz filed for bankruptcy protection as a result of illness. Mrs. Lebovitz (Debtor) filed for bankruptcy because she had cosigned on a large loan with Dr. Lebovitz. The Debtor is the owner of the following pieces of jewelry: a Tiffany 5-carat diamond engagement ring (purchase price $40,000 to $50,000), a pair of diamond stud earrings of approximately 1 carat each, a diamond drop necklace of approximately 1 carat, and a Cartier watch. All of these items were gifts from Dr. Lebovitz.

Tennessee opted out of the federal bankruptcy exemption provisions and adopted its own bankruptcy exemption provisions. Tennessee does not provide for an exemption for jewelry. The state does provide for an exemption for "necessary and proper wearing apparel." Debtor claimed that her jewelry was necessary and proper wearing apparel and was therefore exempt property from the bankruptcy estate. The bankruptcy trustee filed an objection to the claim of exemption, arguing that the Debtor's jewelry does not qualify for an exemption and should be part of the bankruptcy estate. Does Debtor's jewelry qualify as necessary and proper wearing apparel, and should it thus be exempt property from the bankruptcy estate? *In re Lebovitz*, 344 B.R. 556, 2006 Bankr. Lexis 1044 (United States Bankruptcy Court for the Western District of Tennessee, 2006)

28.2 Automatic Stay James F. Kost filed a voluntary petition for relief under Chapter 11 of the Bankruptcy Code. First Interstate Bank of Greybull (First Interstate) held a first mortgage on the debtor's residence near Basin, Wyoming. Appraisals and other evidence showed that the house was worth $116,000. The debt owed to First Interstate was almost $103,000 and was increasing at a rate of $32.46 per day. The debtor had only an 11.5 percent equity cushion in the property. Further evidence showed that (1) the Greybull/Basin area was suffering from tough economic times, (2) there were more than 90 homes available for sale in the area, (3) the real estate market in the area was declining, (4) the condition of the house was seriously deteriorating and the debtor was not financially able to make the necessary improvements, and (5) the insurance on the property had lapsed. First Interstate moved for a relief from stay so that it could foreclose on the property and sell it. Should the motion be granted? *In re Kost*, 102 B.R. 829, 1989 U.S. Dist. Lexis 8316 (United States District Court for the District of Wyoming, 1989)

28.3 Student Loan Donald Wayne Doyle (Debtor) obtained a guaranteed student loan to enroll in a school for training truck drivers. Due to his impending divorce, Debtor never attended the program. The first monthly installment of approximately $50 to pay the student loan became due. Two weeks later, Debtor filed a voluntary petition for Chapter 7 bankruptcy. Debtor, age 29, earned approximately $1,000 per month at an hourly wage of $7.70 as a truck driver, a job that he had held for 10 years. Debtor resided on a farm where he performed work in lieu of paying rent for his quarters. Debtor was paying monthly payments of $89 on a bank loan for his former wife's vehicle, $200 for his truck, $40 for health insurance, $28 for car insurance, $120 for gasoline and vehicular maintenance, $400 for groceries and meals, and $25 for telephone charges. In addition, a state court had ordered Debtor to pay $300 per month to support his children, ages four and five. Debtor's parents were assisting him by buying him $130 of groceries per month. Should Debtor's student loan be discharged in bankruptcy? *In re Doyle*, 106 B.R. 272, 1989 Bankr. Lexis 1772 (United States Bankruptcy Court for the Northern District of Alabama, 1989)

28.4 Discharge Margaret Kawaauhau sought treatment from Dr. Paul Geiger for a foot injury. Dr. Geiger examined Kawaauhau and admitted her to the hospital to attend to the risks of infection. Although Dr. Geiger knew that intravenous penicillin would have been a more effective treatment, he prescribed oral penicillin, explaining that he thought that his patient wished to minimize the cost of her treatment. Dr. Geiger then departed on a business trip, leaving Kawaauhau in the care of other physicians. When Dr. Geiger returned, he discontinued all antibiotics because he believed that the infection had subsided. Kawaauhau's condition deteriorated over the next few days, requiring the amputation of her right leg below the knee. Kawaauhau and her husband sued Dr. Geiger for medical malpractice. The jury found Dr. Geiger liable and awarded the Kawaauhaus $355,000 in damages. Dr. Geiger, who carried no malpractice insurance, filed for bankruptcy in an attempt to discharge the judgment. Is a debt arising from a medical malpractice judgment that is attributable to negligent or reckless conduct dischargeable in bankruptcy? *Kawaauhau v. Geiger*, 523 U.S. 57, 118 S.Ct. 974, 1998 U.S. Lexis 1595 (Supreme Court of the United States, 1998)

Ethics Cases

28.5 Ethics Case Peter and Geraldine Tabala (Debtors), husband and wife, purchased a house in Clarkstown, New York. They purchased a Carvel ice cream business for $70,000 with a loan obtained from People's National Bank. In addition, the Carvel Corporation extended trade credit to Debtors. Two years after getting the bank loan, Debtors conveyed their residence to their three daughters, ages 9, 19, and 20, for no consideration. Debtors continued to reside in the house and to pay maintenance expenses and real estate taxes due on the property. On the date of transfer, Debtors owed obligations in excess of $100,000. Five months after conveying their residence to their daughters, Debtors filed a petition for Chapter 7 bankruptcy. The bankruptcy trustee moved to set aside Debtors' conveyance of their home to their daughters as a fraudulent transfer. Did the Debtors act ethically in this case? Who wins? *In re Tabala*, 11 B.R. 405, 1981 Bankr. Lexis 3663 (United States Bankruptcy Court for the Southern District of New York, 1981)

28.6 Ethics Case John Reaves is the sole owner and president of a small business called Speedsportz, LLC, which refurbishes exotic automobiles. Reaves had been in this business for about 30 years when he met Angela Lieben. Shortly after meeting, they started dating, and Lieben moved in with Reaves, who hired her as his company's office manager and bookkeeper. Lieben's duties included paying bills, reconciling bank statements, and entering information in the company's accounting software. Several years later, Reaves ended their relationship and terminated Lieben's employment. Reaves then discovered irregularities in the company's bank statements, checks that were written with unauthorized and forged signatures, cash that was missing, and unauthorized ATM withdrawals. The total amount stolen was $49,232. Evidence showed that Lieben had previously been convicted of forgery. Lieben subsequently filed for personal bankruptcy. Speedsportz and Reaves filed documents with the bankruptcy court, alleging that Lieben's debt from her defalcations was not dischargeable in bankruptcy because they had been committed by fraud or embezzlement. Did debtor Lieben's defalcations result from fraud or embezzlement and were therefore not dischargeable in bankruptcy? Did Lieben act ethically in filing for bankruptcy in this case? *Speedsportz v. Lieben*, 2013 Bankr. Lexis 3783 (United States Bankruptcy Court for the Northern District of Georgia, 2013)

Notes

1. 11 U.S.C. Sections 101–1330.
2. Public Law 109-8, 119 Stat. 23 (2005).
3. 28 U.S.C. Sections 586–589b
4. 11 U.S.C. Section 522d.
5. 11 U.S.C. Sections 701–784.
6. *Harris v. Viegelahn*, 135 S.Ct. 1829, 2015 U.S. Lexis 3203 (Supreme Court of the United States, 2015)
7. 11 U.S.C. Sections 1301–1330.
8. *Harris v. Viegelahn*, 135 S.Ct. 1829, 2015 U.S. Lexis 3203 (Supreme Court of the United States, 2015)
9. 11 U.S.C. Sections 1101–1174.
10. 11 U.S.C. Sections 1201–1231.

PART

VII Agency, Employment, and Labor Law

Henry R. Cheeseman

CHAPTER 29

Agency Formation and Termination

REAL ESTATE AGENT

One of the most recognizable types of agent is a real estate agent. Often, homeowners hire a real estate agent to sell their house. The real estate agent is an independent contractor who may be given agency powers by the seller. Real estate agents are usually paid on a commission basis.

Henry R. Cheeseman

Learning Objectives

After studying this chapter, you should be able to:

29.1 Define *agency* and identify the parties to a principal–agent relationship.

29.2 Describe a principal–independent contractor relationship.

29.3 Describe how express and implied agencies are created.

29.4 Define *apparent agency*.

29.5 List and describe the duties of a principal.

29.6 List and describe the duties of an agent.

29.7 Describe how an agency is terminated.

"Let every eye negotiate for itself, and trust no agent."

—*William Shakespeare*
Much Ado About Nothing (1598)

Introduction to Agency Formation and Termination

If businesspeople had to conduct all their business personally, the scope of their activities would be severely curtailed. Partnerships would not be able to operate, corporations could not act through managers and employees, and sole proprietorships would not be able to hire employees. The use of agents (or agency), which allows one person to act on behalf of another, solves this problem.

The crowning fortune of a man is to be born to some pursuit which finds him employment and happiness, whether it be to make baskets, or broad swords, or canals, or statues, or songs.
Ralph Waldo Emerson
(1803–1882)

Examples Agency relationships include a salesperson who sells goods for a store, an executive who works for a corporation, and a partner who acts on behalf of a partnership.

Some agents are *independent contractors*. That is, they are outside contractors who are employed by a principal to conduct limited activities for the principal.

Examples An attorney who is hired to represent a client and a real estate broker who is employed by an owner to sell the owner's house are independent contractors.

Agency is governed by a large body of common law known as **agency law**. The formation of agencies, the formation of an independent contractor relationship, the duties of principals and agents, and termination of agencies are discussed in this chapter.

agency law
The large body of common law that governs agency; a mixture of contract law and tort law.

Employment and Agency

29.1 Define *agency* and identify the parties to a principal–agent relationship.

Agency relationships are formed by the mutual consent of a principal and an agent. Section 1(1) of the ***Restatement (Second) of Agency*** defines **agency** as a fiduciary relationship "which results from the manifestation of consent by one person to another that the other shall act in his behalf and subject to his control, and consent by the other so to act." The *Restatement (Second) of Agency* is the reference source for the rules of agency law in this chapter.

A party who employs another person to act on his or her behalf is called a **principal**. A party who agrees to act on behalf of another is called an **agent**. The principal–agent relationship is commonly referred to as an agency. This relationship is depicted in Exhibit 29.1.

agency
The principal-agent relationship.

principal
A party who employs another person to act on his or her behalf.

agent
A party who agrees to act on behalf of another.

Exhibit 29.1 PRINCIPAL–AGENT RELATIONSHIP

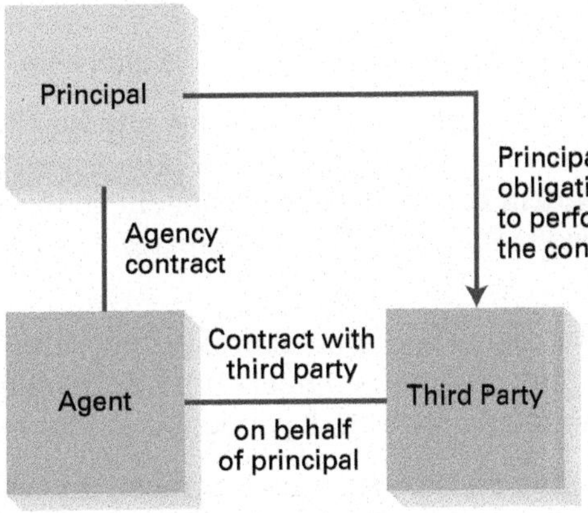

Persons Who Can Initiate an Agency Relationship

Any person who has the capacity to contract can appoint an agent to act on his or her behalf. Generally, persons who lack **contractual capacity**, such as insane persons and minors, cannot appoint agents. However, the court can appoint legal guardians or other representatives to handle the affairs of insane persons, minors, and others who lack capacity to contract. With court approval, these representatives can enter into enforceable contracts on behalf of the persons they represent.

An agency can be created only to accomplish a lawful purpose. Agency contracts that are created for illegal purposes or are against public policy are void and unenforceable.

Example A principal cannot hire an agent to kill another person.

Some agency relationships are prohibited by law.

Example Unlicensed agents cannot be hired to perform the duties of certain licensed professionals (e.g., doctors, lawyers).

Principal–Agent Relationship

principal–agent relationship
A relationship formed when an employer hires an employee and gives that employee authority to act and enter into contracts on the employer's behalf.

A **principal–agent relationship** is formed when an employer hires an employee and gives that employee authority to act and enter contracts on the employer's behalf. The extent of this authority is governed by any express agreement between the parties and implied from the circumstances of the agency.

Examples The president of a corporation usually has the authority to enter into major contracts on the corporation's behalf, and a supervisor on the corporation's assembly line may have the authority only to purchase the supplies necessary to keep the line running.

Employer–Employee Relationship

employer–employee relationship
A relationship that results when an employer hires an employee to perform some task or service but the employee has not been authorized to enter into contracts on behalf of the employer.

An **employer–employee relationship** exists when an employer hires an employee to perform some form of physical service but does not give that person agency authority to enter contracts.

Example A welder on General Motors Corporation's automobile assembly line is employed to perform a physical task but is not given authority to enter contracts.

Although the employee in an employer–employee relationship may not have contracting authority, the principal is still liable for tortious conduct of its employees committed while acting within the *scope of their employment*.

Independent Contractor

29.2 Describe a principal–independent contractor relationship.

principal–independent contractor relationship
The relationship between a principal and an independent contractor who is not an employee of the principal but who has been employed by the principal to perform a certain task on behalf of the principal.

Principals often employ *outsiders*—that is, persons and businesses that are not employees—to perform certain tasks on their behalf. These persons and businesses are called independent contractors. Independent contractors operate their own business or profession. This arrangement creates a **principal–independent contractor relationship**.

Examples Doctors, dentists, consultants, stockbrokers, architects, certified public accountants, real estate brokers, and plumbers are examples of those in professions and trades who commonly act as independent contractors.

A principal can authorize an independent contractor to enter into contracts. Principals are bound by the authorized contracts of their independent contractors.

Critical Legal Thinking Question
What is the difference between (1) a principal–agent relationship, (2) an employer–employee relationship, and (3) a principal–independent contractor relationship?

Example If a client authorizes an attorney to settle a case within a certain dollar amount and the attorney does so, the settlement agreement is binding.

Formation of an Agency

29.3 Describe how express and implied agencies are created.

An agency and the resulting authority of an agent can arise in any of the following four ways: *express agency, implied agency, agency by ratification*, and *apparent agency*. These types of agencies are discussed in the paragraphs that follow.

Express Agency

Express agency is the most common form of agency. In an express agency, the agent has the authority to contract or otherwise act on the principal's behalf, as expressly stated in the agency agreement. Express agency occurs when a principal and an agent expressly agree to enter into an agency agreement with each other. Express agency contracts can be either oral or written unless the Statute of Frauds stipulates that they must be written.

Example In most states, a real estate broker's contract to sell real estate must be in writing.

If a principal and an agent enter into an **exclusive agency contract** the principal cannot employ any agent other than the exclusive agent. If the principal does so, the exclusive agent can recover damages from the principal. If an agency is not an exclusive agency, the principal can employ more than one agent to try to accomplish a stated purpose.

The following feature describes the creation of a special form of express agency.

express agency
An agency that occurs when a principal and an agent expressly agree to enter into an agency agreement with each other.

power of attorney
An express agency agreement that is often used to give an agent the power to sign legal documents on behalf of the principal.

general power of attorney
A power of attorney in which a principal confers broad powers on the agent to act in any matters on the principal's behalf.

special power of attorney
A power of attorney in which a principal confers powers on an agent to act in specified matters on the principal's behalf.

Contemporary Environment

Power of Attorney

A **power of attorney** is one of the most formal types of express agency agreements. It is often used by a principal to give an agent the power to sign legal documents on behalf of the principal. The agent is called an **attorney-in-fact** even though he or she does not have to be a lawyer. Powers of attorney must be written. Usually, they must also be notarized. There are two kinds of powers of attorney:

1. General power of attorney. A **general power of attorney** confers broad powers on the agent to act in any matters on the principal's behalf.

   Example A person who is going on a long trip gives a general power of attorney to his brother to make all decisions on his behalf while he is gone. This general power of attorney includes the power to purchase or sell stocks or real estate, pursue or defend lawsuits, and to make all other relevant decisions.

2. Special power of attorney. A **special power of attorney** confers limited powers on an agent to act on behalf of a principal. The agent is restricted to perform those powers enumerated by the agreement. This is often referred to as a **limited power of attorney**.

   Example A person who has her house listed for sale but who is going on a trip gives her sister a special power of attorney to make decisions regarding the selling of her house while she is gone, including accepting offers to sell the house and signing documents and deeds necessary to sell the house.

A principal can make a power of attorney a **durable power of attorney**, which remains effective even though the principal is incapacitated.

Implied Agency

In many situations, a principal and an agent do not expressly create an agency. Instead, the agency is implied from the conduct of the parties. This type of agency is referred to as an **implied agency**. The extent of the agent's authority is determined from the facts and circumstances of the situation.

implied agency
An agency that occurs when a principal and an agent do not expressly create an agency, but it is inferred from the conduct of the parties.

Example A homeowner employs a real estate broker to sell his house. A water pipe breaks and begins to leak water into the house. If the homeowner cannot be contacted, the real estate broker has implied authority to hire a plumber to repair the pipe to stop the water leak. The homeowner is responsible for paying for the repairs.

Agency by Ratification

agency by ratification
An agency that occurs when (1) a person misrepresents him- or herself as another's agent when in fact he or she is not and (2) the purported principal ratifies the unauthorized act.

Agency by ratification occurs when (1) a person misrepresents him- or herself as another's agent when in fact he or she is not and (2) the purported principal ratifies (accepts) the unauthorized act. In such cases, the principal is bound to perform, and the agent is relieved of any liability for misrepresentation.

Example Bill Livingston sees a house for sale and thinks his friend Sherry Maxwell would want to buy it. Bill enters into a contract to purchase the house from the seller and signs the contract "Bill Livingston, agent for Sherry Maxwell." Because Bill is not Sherry Maxwell's agent, she is not bound to the contract. If Sherry agrees to purchase the house, however, there is an agency by ratification. On ratification of the contract, Sherry Maxwell is obligated to purchase the house.

In the following case, the court had to decide whether an agency relationship existed.

CASE 29.1 *STATE COURT CASE Scope of Employment*

Matthews v. Food Lion, LLC

695 S.E.2d 828, 2010 N.C. App. Lexis 1151 (2010)
North Carolina Court of Appeals

"In the event that an employee is engaged in some private matter of his own or outside the legitimate scope of his employment the employer is no longer responsible for the negligence of the employee."

—Beasley, Judge

Facts

Brigitte Hall was a part-time cashier at a grocery store owned and operated by Food Lion, LLC. When Hall's shift was over, she punched the time clock to end her work shift and headed toward the bathroom before leaving the premises. Hall entered the bathroom at a brisk pace and, on opening the door, struck Diamond Matthews, knocking Matthews to the floor. Employees at Food Lion called 911. Rescue assistants accompanied Matthews to the hospital. Matthews sued Hall and Food Lion to recover damages for negligence under the doctrine of *respondeat superior*, which holds a principal liable for the acts of its agents. Food Lion filed a motion for summary judgment, alleging that Hall was not acting within the scope of her employment at the time of the incident. The trial court granted summary judgment in favor of Food Lion. Matthews appealed.

Issue

Was Hall acting within the scope of her employment at the time of the accident?

Language of the Court

The evidence establishes that Food Lion has no control over the actions of its employees once they have "clocked out" of work. Hall was not acting within the scope of her employment at the time of the incident and Hall had completely departed from the course of business of her employer. Therefore, Hall was acting outside the scope of her employment at the time she entered the bathroom and Food Lion is not liable under the theory of respondeat superior.

Decision

The court of appeals held that Hall was not acting within the scope of her employment at the time of the accident. The court of appeals affirmed the trial court's grant of summary judgment for Food Lion.

Critical Legal Thinking Questions

Should Food Lion have denied liability in this case? Was this a close case to decide? Did any party act unethically in this case?

In the following case, the court had to decide whether an agency relationship was created.

CASE 29.2 *STATE COURT CASE Agency Relationship*

Bosse v. Brinker Restaurant Corporation, d.b.a. Chili's Grill and Bar

2005 Mass. Super. Lexis 372 (2005)
Superior Court of Massachusetts

"No information indicates that Chili's had any effective control over the patron."

—Mitchell Sikora, Judge

Facts

Brendan Bosse and Michael Griffin were a part of a group of four teenagers eating a meal at a Chili's restaurant in Dedham, Massachusetts. Chili's is owned by Brinker Restaurant Corporation (collectively, "Chili's"). After they finished eating, the teenagers decided not to pay. They exited the building, got in their car, and drove away, heading north up Route 1.

A patron of the restaurant saw the teenagers leave without payment. He followed them in his white sport-utility vehicle. The teenagers saw him following them. A high-speed chase ensued through Dedham side streets. The patron used his cell phone to call the Chili's manager. The manager called 911 and reported the incident and the location of the car chase. The teenagers' car collided with a cement wall, and Bosse and Griffin were seriously injured. The Chili's patron drove past the crash scene and was never identified.

Bosse and Griffin sued Chili's for compensatory damages for their injuries. The plaintiffs argued that the patron was an agent of Chili's and therefore that Chili's was liable to the plaintiffs based on the doctrine of *respondeat superior*. Chili's filed a motion for summary judgment, arguing that the patron was not its agent.

Issue

Is the restaurant patron who engaged in the high-speed car chase an agent of Chili's?

Language of the Court

The evidence is insufficient to create a genuine issue whether Chili's appointed or authorized the patron to act as a posse to conduct the chase. No information indicates any preliminary communication between the patron and restaurant manager. No member of Chili's house staff joined in the pursuit. The plaintiffs argue that Chili's effectively assented to an agency relationship by acceptance of the patron's reconnaissance reports during the course of the chase; and by failure to instruct him to break off the chase. That circumstance is not enough. No information indicates that Chili's had any effective control over the patron.

Decision

The superior court held that the restaurant patron who engaged in the high-speed chase in which the plaintiffs were injured was not the agent of Chili's restaurant. The superior court granted summary judgment to Chili's. The appeals court of Massachusetts affirmed the decision.

Critical Legal Thinking Questions

Why do you think the plaintiffs sued Chili's? Do you think they had a very good chance of winning the lawsuit against Chili's? Is the restaurant patron who instituted the chase liable?

Apparent Agency

29.4 Define *apparent agency*.

Apparent agency (or **agency by estoppel**) arises when a principal creates the appearance of an agency that in actuality does not exist. Where an apparent agency is established, the principal is **estopped** (stopped) from denying the agency relationship and is bound to contracts entered into by the apparent agent while acting within the scope of the apparent agency. Note that the principal's actions—not the agent's—create an apparent agency.

apparent agency (agency by estoppel)
Agency that arises when a principal creates the appearance of an agency that does not exist.

Example Georgia Pacific, Inc. interviews Albert Iorio for a sales representative position. Iorio, accompanied by Jane Franklin, the national sales manager, visits retail stores located in the open sales territory. While visiting one store, Franklin tells the store manager, "I wish I had more sales reps like Albert." Nevertheless, Iorio is not hired. If Iorio later enters into contracts with the store on behalf of Georgia Pacific and Franklin has not controverted the impression of Iorio that she left with the store manager, the company will be bound to the contract.

In the following case, the court had to decide whether an apparent agency existed.

CASE 29.3 *FEDERAL COURT CASE Apparent Agency*

Webster v. CDI Indiana, LLC

917 F.3d 574 (2019)
United States Court of Appeals for the Seventh Circuit

"A medical provider is liable if a patient reasonably relied on its apparent authority over the wrongdoer."

—Amy St. Eve, Circuit Judge

Facts

Courtney Webster had outpatient surgery for rectal cancer. One year later her medical examinations showed no further signs of cancer. A few years later, Webster had a gastroenterologist conduct a colonoscopy, which revealed a large mass. The gastroenterologist referred Webster to CDI Indiana, LLC (CDI), a diagnostic imaging facility, to have a CT scan. CDI hired an independent contractor, Medical Scanning Consultants (MSC), to conduct the CT scan. In turn, MSC hired Dr. Brian Walker, a radiologist and independent contractor, to conduct the CT scan. Dr. Walker missed Webster's cancer despite the image showing a tumor in the space where Webster's rectal cancer had originally occurred.

Two years later, after Webster complained of pain, it was discovered that the tumor had increased in size and that the cancer had metastasized in her lungs and liver. The delay in diagnosing Webster's cancer resulted in a dramatic reduction of her prospects for survival. Webster sued CDI to recover damages for medical malpractice. CDI defended, arguing that it was not liable because it did not directly employ Dr. Walker. The jury found that Dr. Walker was an apparent agent of CDI and awarded Webster $15 million against CDI. CDI appealed.

Issue

Was Dr. Walker an apparent agent of CDI?

Language of the Court

A medical provider is liable if a patient reasonably relied on its apparent authority over the wrongdoer. Webster believed that CDI had provided the health care services in relation to her CT scan. CDI's argument that Dr. Walker was an independent contractor hired by MSC, therefore, is of no moment unless Webster was aware of any such contractual relationship. She was not; Webster testified at trial that she had no idea about the contractual relationship among MSC, CDI, and Dr. Walker and she was never provided information that the physician who would be interpreting her CT scan was not subject to CDI's control or supervision.

Decision

The U.S. court of appeals affirmed the judgment and the award of damages.

Critical Legal Thinking Questions

Would the result of this case have been different if Webster had been informed that MSC and Dr. Walker were independent contractors and not employees of CDI?

CONCEPT SUMMARY
FORMATION OF AGENCY RELATIONSHIPS

Type of Agency	Formation	Enforcement of the Contract
Express	Authority is expressly given to the agent by the principal.	Principal and third party are bound to the contract.
Implied	Authority is implied from the conduct of the parties, custom and usage of trade, or act incidental to carrying out the agent's duties.	Principal and third party are bound to the contract.
By ratification	Acts of the agent are committed outside the scope of his or her authority.	Principal and third party are not bound to the contract unless the principal ratifies the contract.
Apparent	Authority is created when the principal leads a third party to believe that the agent has authority.	Principal and third party are bound to the contract.

Principal's Duties

29.5 List and describe the duties of a principal.

The principal owes certain duties to agents and independent contractors. These duties are discussed in the following paragraphs.

Principal's Duty to Compensate

A principal owes a **duty to compensate** an agent for services provided. Usually, the agency contract (whether written or oral) specifies the compensation to be paid. The principal must pay this amount either on the completion of the agency or at some other mutually agreeable time.

duty to compensate
A duty that a principal owes to pay an agreed-on amount to the agent either upon the completion of the agency or at some other mutually agreeable time.

If there is no agreement about the amount of compensation, the law implies a promise that a principal will pay the agent the customary fee paid in the industry. If the compensation cannot be established by custom, the principal owes a duty to pay the reasonable value of the agent's services.

Contingency Fee Certain types of agents traditionally perform their services on a **contingency fee** basis. Under this type of arrangement, the principal owes a duty to pay the agent an agreed-on contingency fee only if the agency is completed. Real estate brokers, finders, lawyers, and salespersons often work on a contingency fee basis.

Example Freida, who is driving her automobile, is injured when another driver negligently causes an automobile accident. Freida hires a lawyer to represent her on a 35 percent contingency fee basis. If the lawyer wins the case for Freida in court, or settles the case with Freida's approval, the lawyer will earn 35 percent of whatever is collected from the defendant. If the lawyer does not win or settle the lawsuit, the lawyer gets paid nothing.

Principal's Duty to Reimburse

duty to reimburse
Unless otherwise agreed, the principal owes a duty to reimburse the agent for expenses incurred by the agent on behalf of the principal.

In carrying out an agency, an agent may spend his or her own money on the principal's behalf. Unless otherwise agreed, the principal owes a **duty to reimburse** the agent for all such expenses if they were (1) authorized by the principal, (2) within the scope of the agency, and (3) necessary to discharge the agent's duties in carrying out the agency.

Example A principal must reimburse an agent for authorized business trips taken on the principal's behalf.

Principal's Duty to Indemnify

duty to indemnify
A principal owes a duty to indemnify the agent for any losses the agent suffers because of the principal's conduct.

A principal also owes a **duty to indemnify** the agent for any losses the agent suffers because of the principal's conduct. This duty usually arises when an agent is held liable for the principal's misconduct.

Example An agent enters an authorized contract with a third party on the principal's behalf, the principal fails to perform on the contract, and the third party recovers a judgment against the agent. The agent can recover indemnification of this amount from the principal.

Principal's Duty to Cooperate

duty to cooperate
Unless otherwise agreed, the principal owes a duty to cooperate with and assist the agent in the performance of the agent's duties and the accomplishment of the agency.

Unless otherwise agreed, the principal owes a **duty to cooperate** with and assist the agent in the performance of the agent's duties and the accomplishment of the agency.

Example Unless otherwise agreed, a principal who employs a real estate agent to sell a house owes a duty to allow the agent to show the house to prospective purchasers during reasonable hours.

Agent's Duties

29.6 List and describe the duties of an agent.

The agent owes certain duties to a principal. These duties are discussed in the following paragraphs.

Agent's Duty to Perform

duty to perform
An agent's duty to a principal that includes (1) performing the lawful duties expressed in the contract and (2) meeting the standards of reasonable care, skill, and diligence implicit in all contracts.

An agent who enters a contract with a principal has two distinct obligations: (1) to perform the lawful duties expressed in the contract and (2) to meet the standards of reasonable care, skill, and diligence implicit in all contracts. Collectively, these duties are referred to as the agent's **duty to perform**. Normally, an agent is required to render the same standard of care, skill, and diligence that a fictitious reasonable agent in the same occupation would render in the same locality and under the same circumstances.

Examples A general medical practitioner in a rural area would be held to the standard of a reasonable general practitioner in rural areas. A brain surgeon would be held to the standard of a reasonable brain surgeon.

An agent who does not perform his or her express duties or who fails to use the standard degree of care, skill, or diligence is liable to the principal for damages.

Agent's Duty to Notify

duty to notify
An agent owes a duty to notify the principal of important information concerning the agency.

In an agency, the agent usually learns information that is important to the principal. This information may come from third parties or other sources. An agent owes a duty to notify the principal of important information learned concerning the agency. The agent's duty to notify the principal of such information is called the **duty to notify**. The agent is liable to the principal for any injuries resulting from a breach of this duty.

Information learned by an agent in the course of an agency is *imputed* to the principal. The legal rule of **imputed knowledge** means that the principal is assumed to know what the agent knows. This is so even if the agent does not tell the principal certain relevant information.

imputed knowledge
Information that is learned by an agent that is attributed to the principal.

Example Sonia, who owns a piece of vacant real estate, hires Matthew, a licensed real estate broker, to list the property for sale. Ian, an adjacent property owner to Sonia's property, tells Matthew that a chemical plant has polluted his property and probably Sonia's property. Sonia does not know this fact, and Matthew does not tell Sonia this information. Sonia sells the property to Macy. It is later discovered that the property Macy bought from Sonia is polluted. In this example, the information that Matthew was told about the possible pollution of the property is imputed to Sonia. Sonia will be held liable to Macy.

Agent's Duty to Account

Unless otherwise agreed, an agent owes a duty to maintain an accurate accounting of all transactions undertaken on the principal's behalf. This **duty to account** (sometimes called the **duty of accountability**) includes keeping records of all property and money received and expended during the course of the agency. A principal has a right to demand an accounting from the agent at any time, and the agent owes a legal duty to make the accounting. This duty also requires the agent to (1) maintain a separate account for the principal and (2) use the principal's property in an authorized manner.

duty to account (duty of accountability)
A duty that an agent owes to maintain an accurate accounting of all transactions undertaken on the principal's behalf.

Any property, money, or other benefit received by the agent in the course of an agency belongs to the principal. If an agent breaches the agency contract, the principal can sue the agent to recover damages caused by the breach.

Termination of an Agency

29.7 Describe how an agency is terminated.

An agency contract can be terminated by an *act of the parties*, by an *unusual change of circumstances*, by *impossibility of performance*, and by *operation of law*.

Termination of an Agency by an Act of the Parties

An agency contract is similar to other contracts in that it can be terminated by an act of the parties (**termination of an agency by act of the parties**). An agency can be terminated by the following acts.

termination of an agency by an act of the parties
A situation in which the parties to an agency contract terminate their contract by mutual agreement or when a previously agreed on event occurs.

1. The mutual assent of the parties.

   Example A principal hires a lawyer to represent her in a lawsuit until the lawsuit is resolved. If the principal and the lawyer voluntarily agree to terminate the relationship prior to the resolution of the case by trial or settlement, the agency is terminated.

2. If a stated time has lapsed.

   Example If an agency agreement states, "This agency agreement will terminate on August 1, 2028," the agency terminates when that date arrives.

3. If a specified purpose is achieved.

   Example If a homeowner hires a real estate broker to sell the owner's house within six months and the house sells after three months, the agency terminates on the sale of the house.

4. The occurrence of a stated event.

Example If a principal employs an agent to take care of her dog until she returns from a trip, the agency terminates when the principal returns from the trip.

Shortly his fortune shall be lifted higher;
True industry doth kindle honour's fire.
William Shakespeare
The Life and Death of Lord Cromwell (1602)

Notice of Termination The termination of an agency extinguishes an agent's actual authority to act on the principal's behalf. If the principal fails to give the proper **notice of termination of an agency** to a third party, however, the agent still has apparent authority to bind the principal to contracts with these third parties. To avoid this liability, the principal needs to provide the following notices:

- **Direct notice** of termination to all persons with whom the agent dealt. The notice may be oral or written unless required to be in writing.
- **Constructive notice** of termination to any third party who has knowledge of the agency but with whom the agent has not dealt.

Example Notice of the termination of an agency that is printed in a newspaper that serves the vicinity of the parties is constructive notice.

Generally, a principal is not obliged to give notice of termination to strangers who have no knowledge of the agency. Constructive notice is valid against strangers who assert claims of apparent agency.

Termination of an Agency by an Unusual Change of Circumstances

termination of an agency by an unusual change of circumstances
A situation in which an agency terminates because an unusual change in circumstances has occurred that would lead the agent to believe that the principal's original instructions should no longer be valid.

An agency terminates when there is an unusual change in circumstances (**termination of an agency by an unusual change of circumstances**) that would lead the agent to believe that the principal's original instructions should no longer be valid.

Example An owner of a farm employs a real estate agent to sell the farm for $1 million. The agent thereafter learns that oil has been discovered on the property—a discovery that makes the land worth $5 million. The agency terminates because of this change in circumstances.

Termination of an Agency by Impossibility of Performance

termination of an agency by impossibility of performance
A situation in which an agency terminates because a situation arises that makes the fulfillment of the agency impossible.

An agency relationship terminates if a situation arises that makes its fulfillment impossible. The following circumstances can lead to **termination of an agency by impossibility of performance**:

- The loss or destruction of the subject matter of the agency.

  Example A principal employs an agent to sell his horse, but the horse dies before it is sold. The agency relationship terminates at the moment the horse dies.

- The loss of a required qualification.

  Example A principal employs a licensed real estate agent to sell her house but the real estate agent's license is revoked before he can sell the principal's house. The agency relationship terminates when the real estate agent's license is revoked.

- A change in the law.

  Example A company employs an agent to purchase oil from another country and to import the oil into the United States. If the president of the United States issues an executive order that makes importing oil from that country into the United States illegal, the agency contract terminates when the law becomes effective.

Termination of an Agency by Operation of Law

Agency contracts can be terminated by operation of law (**termination of an agency by operation of law**). An agency contract is terminated by operation of law in the following circumstances:

termination of an agency by operation of law
A situation in which an agency terminates because of the occurrence of legally specified events.

1. The death of either the principal or the agent
2. The insanity of either the principal or the agent
3. The bankruptcy of the principal
4. The outbreak of a war between the principal's country and the agent's country

If an agency terminates by operation of law, there is no duty to notify third parties about the termination.

Wrongful Termination

The termination of an agency extinguishes the power of the agent to act on behalf of the principal. If the principal's or agent's termination of an agency contract breaches the contract, the other party can sue to recover damages for **wrongful termination** of an agency.

wrongful termination
The termination of an agency contract in violation of the terms of the agency contract. The nonbreaching party may recover damages from the breaching party.

Example A principal employs a licensed real estate agent to sell his house. The agency contract gives the agent an exclusive listing for four months. After one month, the principal unilaterally terminates the agency. The agent can no longer act on behalf of the principal. Because the principal did not have the right to terminate the contract, however, the agent can sue him and recover damages (i.e., lost commission) for wrongful termination.

Key Terms and Concepts

Agency (501)
Agency by ratification (504)
Agency law (501)
Agent (501)
Apparent agency (agency by estoppel) (505)
Attorney-in-fact (503)
Constructive notice (510)
Contingency fee (507)
Contractual capacity (502)
Direct notice (510)
Durable power of attorney (503)
Duty to account (duty of accountability) (509)
Duty to compensate (507)
Duty to cooperate (508)
Duty to indemnify (508)
Duty to notify (508)
Duty to perform (508)
Duty to reimburse (507)
Employer–employee relationship (502)
Estopped (505)
Exclusive agency contract (503)
Express agency (503)
General power of attorney (503)
Implied agency (503)
Imputed knowledge (509)
Notice of termination of an agency (510)
Power of attorney (503)
Principal (501)
Principal–agent relationship (502)
Principal–independent contractor relationship (502)
Restatement (Second) of Agency (501)
Special power of attorney (limited power of attorney) (503)
Termination of an agency by act of the parties (509)
Termination of an agency by an unusual change of circumstances (510)
Termination of an agency by impossibility of performance (510)
Termination of an agency by operation of law (511)
Wrongful termination (511)

Critical Legal Thinking Cases

29.1 Scope of Employment Lapp Roofing and Sheet Metal Company, Inc. is a corporation headquartered in Dayton, Ohio. The company provides construction services in several states. Lapp Roofing sent James Goldick and other Lapp Roofing employees to work on a roofing project in Wilmington, Delaware. Lapp Roofing entrusted Goldick, as job supervisor, with a white Ford van to transport the workers to the job site and to provide transportation to meals and other necessities. Lapp Roofing's company policy prohibited employees from driving company vehicles for personal purposes.

While in Wilmington, Goldick and another Lapp Roofing employee, James McNees, went to Gators Bar and Restaurant. Goldick, after eating and drinking for several hours, was ejected from the bar. Shortly thereafter, Goldick drove the company van onto the curb in front of the bar, striking and injuring seven individuals. Subsequently, the police stopped the van and apprehended Goldick. Goldick was arrested and pleaded guilty to criminal assault charges. Christopher M. Keating and the other injured individuals filed a personal injury lawsuit against Goldick and Lapp Roofing. Lapp Roofing defended, alleging that it was not liable because Goldick's negligent conduct was committed outside the scope of his employment. Is Goldick's negligent conduct committed within the scope of his employment for Lapp Roofing, thus making Lapp Roofing liable? *Keating v. Goldick and Lapp Roofing and Sheet Metal Company, Inc.*, 2004 Del. Super. Lexis 102 (Superior Court of Delaware, 2004)

29.2 Independent Contractor Mercedes Connolly and her husband purchased airline tickets and a tour package for a tour to South Africa from Judy Samuelson, a travel agent conducting business as International Tours of Manhattan. Samuelson sold tickets for a variety of airline companies and tour operators, including African Adventurers, which was the tour operator for the Connollys' tour. Mercedes fell while trying to cross a six-inch-deep stream while the tour group was on a walking tour to see hippopotami in a river at a game reserve. In the process, she injured her left ankle and foot. She sued Samuelson for damages. Is Samuelson liable? *Connolly v. Samuelson*, 671 F.Supp. 1312, 1987 U.S. Dist. Lexis 8308 (United States District Court for the District of Kansas, 1987)

29.3 Agent Nicholas Brown was a student at Georgia Tech University and a member of the Ramblin' Reck spirit club. The board of regents of the University System of Georgia (University) owns a 1930 Ford Model A automobile called the Ramblin' Reck, which is the mascot of Georgia Tech University. Members of the club are responsible for driving the car at sporting events, parades, campus-sponsored events, and throughout campus to raise school spirit. During its use, several club members drive and sit in the car, while two other members stand on the running boards of the vehicle. When the vehicle needed some repairs, Eco-Clean, Inc. installed new handles on the vehicle's doors using wood screws one-half to three-quarters of an inch long.

One day when the club members drove the Model A from a fraternity house, Brown stood on the passenger side running board, grasping an interior handle with one hand and the exterior handle with the other. After the car had gone one block, the driver turned left onto another street. When the driver took the turn the handle Brown was holding onto snapped off, and he fell from the running board. Brown struck his head on the road and lost consciousness. Eyewitnesses testified that the car accelerated through a red light and that the car was turning at an unusually high rate of speed at the time of the accident. Brown fractured his right temporal bone and was hospitalized for four days. Brown permanently lost his sense of taste and smell, as well as the hearing in one ear.

Brown sued Georgia Tech University and Eco-Clean to recover damages for negligence. Brown asserted that the University negligently promoted the unsafe use of the car by students on public roads and that the University is vicariously liable for the negligence of its agents, including the driver who was driving the Ramblin' Reck on the University's behalf at the time of the accident. Was the driver of the car an agent of the University? *Eco-Clean, Inc. v. Brown*, 749 S.E.2d 4, 2013 Ga. App. Lexis 913 (Court of Appeals of Georgia, 2013)

29.4 Scope of Employment Kenya Massey and Raymond Rodriquez entered a Starbucks coffee shop in Manhattan, New York. The couple ordered two beverages from a Starbucks employee and paid for the drinks. When Massey and Rodriquez moved toward the seating area while waiting for their drinks to be prepared, Karen Morales, the shift supervisor at the store, told Massey and Rodriquez that they could not sit down because the store was closing. Massey informed Morales that when she received her drinks, she and Rodriquez intended to sit and enjoy them at Starbucks.

Morales instructed a Starbucks employee to cancel Massey's beverage order and refund Massey's money. Massey asked to speak with a manager. Morales identified herself as the manager and told Massey to "get a life." At that point, Starbucks employee Melissa Polanco told Massey, "I get off at 10:00, and we can go outside." Massey and Rodriquez exited and walked away from the store while Massey and the employees yelled profanities at each other. Massey continued to walk away, and Polanco ran after and caught her, then punched Massey in the face. Morales then jumped on Massey's back, and a scuffle ensued. A pedestrian passerby finally separated the parties. Massey's face was bleeding when she got up.

The Starbucks employees who were involved in the altercation were terminated by Starbucks. Massey sued Starbucks for damages for the injuries she suffered. Starbucks moved for summary judgment, alleging that the employees were not acting within the scope of their employment when they assaulted Massey. Were the employees who injured Massey acting within their scope of employment? *Massey v. Starbucks Corporation*, 2004 U.S. Dist. Lexis 12993 (United States District Court for the Southern District of New York, 2004)

29.5 Imputed Knowledge Iota Management Corporation entered into a contract to purchase the Bel Air West Motor Hotel in St. Louis, Missouri, from Boulevard Investment Company. The agreement contained the following warranty: "Seller has no actual notice of any substantial defect in the structure of the Hotel or in any of its plumbing, heating, air-conditioning, electrical, or utility systems." When the buyer inspected the premises, no leaks in the pipes were visible. Iota purchased the hotel for $2 million. When Iota removed some of the walls and ceilings during remodeling, it found evidence of prior repairs to leaking pipes and ducts, as well as devices for catching water (e.g., milk cartons, cookie sheets, buckets). The estimate to repair these leaks was $500,000. Evidence at trial showed that Cecil Lillibridge, who was Boulevard's maintenance supervisor for the four years prior to the motor hotel's sale, had actual knowledge of these problems and had repaired some of the pipes. Iota sued Boulevard to rescind the contract. Is Boulevard liable? *Iota Management Corporation v. Boulevard Investment Company*, 731 S.W.2d 399, 1987 Mo. App. Lexis 4027 (Court of Appeals of Missouri, 1987)

Ethics Case

29.6 Ethics Case The Hagues, husband and wife, owned a 160-acre tract that they decided to sell. They entered into a listing agreement with Harvey C. Hilgendorf, a licensed real estate broker, that gave Hilgendorf the exclusive right to sell the property for a period of 12 months. The Hagues agreed to pay Hilgendorf a commission of 6 percent of the accepted sale price if a bona fide buyer was found during the listing period.

By letter five months later, the Hagues terminated the listing agreement with Hilgendorf. Hilgendorf did not acquiesce to the termination, however. One month later, Hilgendorf presented an offer to the Hagues from a buyer willing to purchase the property at the full listing price. The Hagues ignored the offer and sold the property to another buyer. Hilgendorf sued the Hagues for breach of the agency agreement. Did the Hagues act ethically in this case? Who wins the lawsuit? *Hilgendorf v. Hague*, 293 N.W.2d 272, 1980 Iowa Sup. Lexis 882 (Supreme Court of Iowa, 1980)

CHAPTER 30

Liability of Principals, Agents, and Independent Contractors

MODERN BUILDING
The construction of most new buildings requires the work of employees of the general contractor and the use of independent subcontractors.

Pavel L Photo and Video/Shutterstock

Learning Objectives

After studying this chapter, you should be able to:

30.1 Describe the duty of loyalty owed by an agent to a principal.

30.2 Describe the tort liability of principals and agents to third parties.

30.3 Describe the liability of agents and principals for intentional torts.

30.4 Describe the principal's and agent's liability on third-party contracts.

30.5 Define *independent contractor* and describe the liability of independent contractors.

> *"People might not get all they work for in this world, but they most certainly work for all they get."*
>
> —*Frederick Douglass (1818–1895)*

Introduction to Liability of Principals, Agents, and Independent Contractors

Principals and agents owe certain duties to each other and are liable to each other for breaching these duties. When acting for the principal, an agent often enters into contracts and otherwise deals with third parties. Agency law has established certain rules that make principals, agents, and independent contractors liable to third persons for certain contracts. In addition, agents and independent contractors sometimes engage in negligent or other tortious conduct when acting on behalf of principals. Agency law establishes the liability of principals, agents, and independent contractors for such conduct.

This chapter discusses contract and tort liability of principals, agents, and independent contractors to each other and to third parties.

The law, wherein, as in a magic mirror, we see reflected not only our lives, but the lives of all men that have been! When I think on this majestic theme, my eyes dazzle.

Oliver Wendell Holmes, Jr.
To the Suffolk Bar Association (1885)

Agent's Duty of Loyalty

30.1 Describe the duty of loyalty owed by an agent to a principal.

Because the agency relationship is based on trust and confidence, an agent owes the principal a duty of loyalty in all agency-related matters. Thus, an agent owes a duty not to act adversely to the interests of the principal. If this duty is breached by an agent, the agent is liable to the principal. The most common breaches of the **duty of loyalty of agents** are discussed in the following paragraphs.

duty of loyalty of agents
A fiduciary duty owed by an agent not to act adversely to the interests of the principal.

Self-Dealing

Agents are generally prohibited from undisclosed **self-dealing** with the principal. An agent who engages in undisclosed self-dealing with the principal has violated the duty of loyalty to the principal. If there has been undisclosed self-dealing by an agent, the principal can rescind the purchase and recover the money paid to the agent. As an alternative, the principal can ratify the purchase.

Example A real estate agent who is employed to purchase real estate for a principal cannot secretly sell his or her own property to the principal. However, the deal is lawful if the principal agrees to buy the property after the agent discloses ownership of the property.

Usurping an Opportunity

Sometimes an agent is offered a business opportunity or another opportunity that is meant for the principal or that the principal is entitled to be informed about and have the opportunity to accept or reject. An agent cannot personally engage in **usurping an opportunity** that belongs to the principal. A third-party offer to an agent must be conveyed to the principal. The agent cannot appropriate the opportunity for him- or herself unless the principal rejects it after due consideration. If the agent does so, the principal can recover the opportunity from the agent.

Example An agent works for a principal that is in the business of real estate development. The principal is looking for vacant land to purchase to develop. A third party who owns and wants to sell his vacant land tells an agent of the principal of the availability of the land. The agent, without informing the principal, purchases the land for personal use. This is a violation of the agent's duty of loyalty.

Competing with the Principal

Agents are prohibited from **competing with the principal** during the course of an agency unless the principal agrees. The reason for this rule is that an agent cannot meet the duty of loyalty when personal interests conflict with the principal's interests. The principal may recover the profits made by the agent as well as damages caused by the agent's conduct, such as lost sales. An agent is free to compete with the principal when the agency has ended unless the parties have entered into an enforceable covenant-not-to-compete.

Example An agent works as a salesperson for a principal who owns an automotive parts business. The agent's job is to sell the principal's automotive parts to auto repair shops and other purchasers. While doing so, the agent also works as a salesperson for a competing seller of automotive parts. This example demonstrates a conflict of interest, and the agent has violated the duty of loyalty.

Misuse of Confidential Information

The way to wealth is as plain as the way to market. It depends chiefly on two words, industry and frugality: that is, waste neither time nor money, but make the best use of both. Without industry and frugality nothing will do, and with them everything.

Benjamin Franklin
(1706–1790)

During an agency, the agent often acquires *confidential information* about the principal's affairs (e.g., business plans, technological innovations, customer lists, trade secrets). The agent is under a legal duty not to disclose or **misuse confidential information** either during or after the course of the agency.

If the agent violates this duty, the principal can recover damages, lost profits, and any remuneration the agent received from another party to obtain the confidential information. The principal can also obtain an injunction ordering a third party to return the confidential information and to not use such information. There is no prohibition against using general information, knowledge, or experience acquired during an agency in later employment.

Example An agent works for a principal who owns and operates a bank that specializes in serving wealthy clients. Over many years, the bank has carefully developed a unique and selective list of wealthy individuals that it serves or is courting to serve. The agent quits his job at the bank and is hired by another bank. The agent takes the list of wealthy clients developed by his previous employer and discloses the list to his new employer. This is a violation of the agent's duty of loyalty.

Most are engaged in business the greater part of their lives, because the soul abhors a vacuum and they have not discovered any continuous employment for man's nobler faculties.

Henry David Thoreau
(1817–1862)

Dual Agency

An agent cannot meet a duty of loyalty to two parties with conflicting interests. **Dual agency** occurs when an agent acts for two or more different principals in the same transaction. This practice is generally prohibited unless all the parties involved in the transaction agree to it. If an agent acts as an undisclosed dual agent, he or she must forfeit all compensation received in the transaction. Some agents, such as middlemen and finders, are not considered dual agents. This is because they only bring interested parties together; they do not take part in any negotiations.

Example A real estate broker is hired by a homeowner to sell the owner's house. The broker is approached by a person interested in purchasing the house. The real estate broker agrees to accept compensation from the proposed purchaser if the agent can get the seller to agree to a lower price than the asking price. The real estate owner accomplishes this and recovers a fee from both the seller and buyer of the house. The agent has violated her duty of loyalty by acting as a dual agent.

Tort Liability of Principals and Agents to Third Parties

30.2 Describe the tort liability of principals and agents to third parties.

A principal and an agent are each personally liable for their own **tortious conduct**. Principals are liable for tortious conduct committed by agents while they are acting within the scope of authority given to them by the principal. The agent, however, is liable for the tortious conduct of the principal only if he or she directly or indirectly participates in or aids and abets the principal's conduct.

The courts have applied a broad and flexible standard in interpreting scope of authority in the context of employment. Although other factors may also be considered, the courts rely on the following factors to determine whether an agent's conduct occurred within the scope of employment:

- Was the act specifically requested or authorized by the principal?
- Was it the kind of act that the agent was employed to perform?
- Did the act occur substantially within the time period of employment authorized by the principal?
- Did the act occur substantially within the location of employment authorized by the employer?
- Was the agent advancing the principal's purpose when the act occurred?

Where liability is found, tort remedies are available to the injured party. These remedies include recovery for medical expenses, lost wages, pain and suffering, emotional distress, and, in some cases, punitive damages. As discussed in the following paragraphs, the three main sources of **tort liability** for principals and agents are *negligence, intentional torts*, and *misrepresentation*.

Negligence

Principals are liable for the negligent conduct of agents acting within their **scope of employment**. This liability is based on the common law doctrine of **respondeat superior** ("let the master answer"), which in turn is based on the legal theory of **vicarious liability** (liability without fault). In other words, the principal is liable because of the employment contract with the negligent agent, not because the principal was personally at fault.

The doctrine of **negligence** rests on the principle that if someone (i.e., the principal) expects to derive certain benefits from acting through others (i.e., an agent), that person should also bear the liability for injuries caused to third persons by the negligent conduct of an agent who is acting within the scope of employment.

Example Algorithm Corporation employs Harriet as its marketing manager. Harriet is driving her automobile to attend a meeting with a client on behalf of her employer. On her way to the meeting, Harriet is involved in an automobile accident that is caused by her negligence, and several people are seriously injured. In this example, Harriet is personally liable to the injured parties. In addition, Algorithm Corporation is liable as the principal because Harriet was acting within the scope of her employment when she caused the accident.

Frolic and Detour

Agents sometimes act during the course of their employment to further their own interests rather than the principal's interests. An agent might take a detour to run a personal errand while on assignment for the principal. This is commonly referred to as **frolic and detour**. Negligence actions stemming from frolic and

respondeat superior
A rule stating that an employer is liable for the tortious conduct of its employees or agents while they are acting within the scope of the employer's authority.

vicarious liability
Liability without fault. Vicarious liability occurs where a principal is liable for an agent's tortious conduct because of the employment contract between the principal and agent, not because the principal was personally at fault.

Critical Legal Thinking Questions

What is the doctrine of *respondeat superior*? What is the doctrine of *vicarious liability*? Why does the law recognize these doctrines?

frolic and detour
A situation in which an agent does something during the course of employment to further his or her own interests rather than the principal's.

detour are examined on a case-by-case basis. Agents are always personally liable for their tortious conduct in such situations. Principals are generally relieved of liability if the agent's frolic and detour is substantial. If the deviation is minor, however, the principal is liable for the injuries caused by the agent's tortious conduct.

Example A salesperson stops at home for lunch while on an assignment for his principal. After lunch and while leaving his home in his car, the agent hits and injures a pedestrian. The principal would be liable if the agent's home were not too far out of the way from the agent's assignment. The principal would not be liable, however, if an agent who is on an assignment for his employer in Cleveland, Ohio, deviates from his assignment and drives to a nearby city to meet a friend and is involved in an accident. The facts and circumstances of each case determine its outcome.

Coming and Going Rule

coming and going rule (going and coming rule)
A rule stating that a principal is generally not liable for injuries caused by its agents and employees while they are on their way to or from work.

Under the common law, a principal is generally not liable for injuries caused by its agents and employees while they are on their way to or from work. This so-called **coming and going rule**, which is sometimes referred to as the **going and coming rule**, applies even if the principal supplies the agent's automobile or other transportation or pays for gasoline, repairs, and other automobile operating expenses. This rule is quite logical: Because principals do not control where their agents and employees live, they should not be held liable for tortious conduct of agents on their way to and from work. This rule applies even if the employer pays for the vehicle or vehicle expenses for the employee.

Example Miremba works as a professor at a university. Her home is 20 miles from the campus. One morning Miremba is driving to work when her negligence causes an automobile accident in which several pedestrians are injured. In this example, Miremba is personally liable for her negligence, but the university is not liable because of the coming and going rule.

Dual-Purpose Mission

dual-purpose mission
A situation that occurs when a principal requests an employee or agent to run an errand or do another act for the principal while the agent is undertaking his or her own personal business.

Sometimes principals request that agents run errands or conduct other acts on their behalf while the agent or employee is on personal business. In this case, the agent is on a **dual-purpose mission**. That is, the agent is acting partly for him- or herself and partly for the principal. Most jurisdictions hold both the principal and the agent liable if the agent injures someone while on such a mission.

Example Suppose a principal asks an employee to drop off a package at a client's office on the employee's way home. If the employee negligently injures a pedestrian while on this dual-purpose mission, the principal is liable to the pedestrian.

Liability for Intentional Torts

30.3 Describe the liability of agents and principals for intentional torts.

Intentional torts include acts such as assault, battery, false imprisonment, and other intentional conduct that causes injury to another person. A principal is not liable for the intentional torts of agents and employees that are committed outside the principal's scope of business.

Example If an employee attends a sporting event after working hours and gets into a fight with another spectator at the event, the employer is not liable. This is because the fight was a personal affair and outside the employee's business responsibilities.

However, a principal is liable under the doctrine of vicarious liability for intentional torts of agents and employees committed within the agent's scope of employment. The courts generally apply one of the two following tests in determining whether an agent's intentional torts were committed within the agent's scope of employment:

1. **Motivation test.** Under the **motivation test**, if the agent's motivation for committing an intentional tort is to promote the principal's business, the principal is liable for any injury caused by the tort. If an agent's motivation for committing the intentional tort is personal, however, the principal is not liable, even if the tort takes place during business hours or on business premises.

   Example Under the motivation test, an employer—the principal—is not liable if an employee, who is motivated by jealousy, injures someone on the job who dated her boyfriend. In this example, the motivation of the employee was personal and not work related.

2. **Work-related test.** Some jurisdictions have rejected the motivation test as being too narrow. These jurisdictions apply the **work-related test** instead. Under this test, if an agent commits an intentional tort within a work-related time or space—for example, during working hours or on the principal's premises—the principal is liable for any injuries caused by the agent's intentional torts. Under this test, the agent's motivation is immaterial.

   Example Under the work-related test, an employer—the principal—is liable if an employee, who was motivated by jealousy, injures someone on the work premises and during work hours who dated her boyfriend. In this example, the motivation of the employee is not relevant. What is relevant is that the intentional tort was committed on work premises and during the employee's work hours.

motivation test
A test that determines whether an agent's motivation in committing an intentional tort is to promote the principal's business; if so, the principal is liable for any injury caused by the tort.

work-related test
A test that determines whether an agent committed an intentional tort within a work-related time or space; if so, the principal is liable for any injury caused by the agent's intentional tort.

In the following case, the court faced the issue of whether an employer was liable for an employee's intentional tort.

CASE 30.1 *STATE COURT CASE Employee's Intentional Tort*

Burlarley v. Wal-Mart Stores, Inc.

904 N.Y.S.2d 826, 2010 N.Y. App. Div. Lexis 6278 (2010)
Appellate Division of the Supreme Court of New York

"In our view, the court properly concluded that throwing a full bag of heavy items at an unsuspecting customer's face as a 'joke' is not commonly done by a cashier and, indeed, substantially departs from a cashier's normal methods of performance."

—Thomas Mercure, Judge

Facts

After an hour of shopping at a Walmart store, Michael Burlarley and his wife proceeded to the checkout. The cashier, joking with the couple in an effort to make her work shift "go a little faster," pretended to ring up items for vastly more than their price and threw various items at Michael. Michael, not amused, told her to stop, and the cashier initially complied. When Michael turned away, however, the cashier threw a bag containing a pair of shoes and shampoo at him, striking Michael in the face. Michael sued Walmart to recover damages. Walmart filed a motion for summary judgment, alleging that the cashier's actions were personally motivated and that Walmart was not liable under the state's motivation test. The trial court granted summary judgment to Walmart. Michael appealed.

(continued)

Issue

Is Walmart vicariously liable for the personally motivated acts of its cashier?

Language of the Court

In our view, the court properly concluded that throwing a full bag of heavy items at an unsuspecting customer's face as a "joke" is not commonly done by a cashier and, indeed, substantially departs from a cashier's normal methods of performance. Moreover, the cashier's actions arose not from any work-related motivation, but rather her desire to pass the time and relieve mounting frustration with her job.

Decision

Applying the motivation test, the appellate court held that Walmart was not vicariously liable for the intentional tort of its cashier. The appellate court affirmed the trial court's grant of summary judgment in favor of Walmart.

Critical Legal Thinking Questions

Was it ethical for Walmart to deny liability for its employee's actions in this case? If the court applied the work-related test, would the outcome of the case be different?

Misrepresentation

intentional misrepresentation (fraud or deceit)
A deceit in which an agent makes an untrue statement that he or she knows is not true.

Intentional misrepresentation is also known as **fraudulent misrepresentation** or **fraud** or **deceit**. An intentional misrepresentation occurs when an agent makes a statement that the agent knows is not true.

An **innocent misrepresentation** occurs when an agent negligently makes a misrepresentation to a third party.

A principal is liable for the intentional and innocent misrepresentations made by an agent acting within the scope of employment. The third party can either (1) rescind the contract with the principal and recover any consideration paid or (2) affirm the contract and recover damages.

Example Assume that a car salesperson is employed to sell the principal's car, and the principal tells the agent that the car was repaired after it was involved in a major accident. If the agent intentionally tells the buyer that the car was never involved in an accident, the agent has made an intentional misrepresentation. Both the principal and the agent are liable for this misrepresentation.

CONCEPT SUMMARY

TORT LIABILITY OF PRINCIPALS AND AGENTS TO THIRD PARTIES

Agent's Conduct	Agent Liable?	Principal Liable?
Negligence	Yes	The principal is liable under the doctrine of respondeat superior if the agent's negligent act was committed within his or her scope of employment.
Intentional tort	Yes	*Motivation test:* The principal is liable if the agent's motivation in committing the intentional tort was to promote the principal's business.
	Yes	*Work-related test:* The principal is liable if the agent committed the intentional tort within work-related time and space.
Misrepresentation	Yes	The principal is liable for the intentional and innocent misrepresentations made by an agent acting within the scope of his or her authority.

Contract Liability of Principals and Agents to Third Parties

30.4 Describe the principal's and agent's liability on third-party contracts.

Bad laws are the worst sort of tyranny.
Edmund Burke (1729–1797)

Agency law imposes **contract liability** on principals and agents, depending on the circumstances. A principal who authorizes an agent to enter into a contract with a third party is liable on the contract. Thus, the third party can enforce the contract against the principal and recover damages from the principal if the principal fails to perform it.

The agent can also be held liable on the contract in certain circumstances. Imposition of such liability depends on whether the agency is classified as *fully disclosed, partially disclosed*, or *undisclosed*.

Fully Disclosed Agency

A **fully disclosed agency** results if a third party entering into a contract knows (1) that the agent is acting as an agent for a principal and (2) the actual identity of the principal. The third party has the requisite knowledge if the principal's identity is disclosed to the third party by either the agent or some other source.

fully disclosed agency
An agency in which a contracting third party knows (1) that the agent is acting for a principal and (2) the identity of the principal.

In a fully disclosed agency, the contract is between the principal and the third party. Thus, the principal, who is called a **fully disclosed principal**, is liable on the contract. The agent is not liable on the contract, however, because the third party relied on the principal's credit and reputation when the contract was made.

Example Aiko decides to sell her house and hires John, a real estate broker, to list and sell the house for a price of $1 million. They agree that John will disclose the existence of the agency and the identity of the principal to interested third parties. John shows the house to Leena, a prospective buyer, and discloses to Leena that he is acting as an agent for Aiko. Leena agrees to buy the house, and John signs the contract on behalf of Aiko. Aiko, the principal, is liable on the contract, but John, the agent, is not.

The **agent's signature** on a contract entered into on the principal's behalf is important. It can establish the agent's status and therefore his or her liability. For instance, in a fully disclosed agency, the agent's signature must clearly indicate that the agent is acting as an agent for a specifically identified principal.

Examples Proper agent's signatures include "Catherine Adams, agent for Juan Perez" and "Juan Perez, by Catherine Adams, agent."

Partially Disclosed Agency

A **partially disclosed agency** occurs if an agent discloses his or her agency status but does not reveal the principal's identity, and the third party does not know the principal's identity from another source. The nondisclosure may be because the principal instructs the agent not to disclose his or her identity to the third party or the agent forgets to tell the third party the principal's identity. In this kind of agency, the principal is called a **partially disclosed principal**.

partially disclosed agency
An agency in which a contracting third party knows that the agent is acting for a principal but does not know the identity of the principal.

In a partially disclosed agency, both the principal and the agent are liable on third-party contracts. This is because the third party must rely on the agent's reputation, integrity, and credit because the principal is unidentified. If the agent is made to pay the contract, the agent can sue the principal for indemnification. The third party and the agent can agree to relieve the agent's liability.

Example A principal, Nigel Jones, and an agent, Marcia McKee, agree that the agent will represent the principal to purchase a business and that the agent will disclose the existence of the agency and identity of the principal to third parties. The agent finds a suitable business and contracts to purchase the business on behalf of the principal, but the agent mistakenly signs the contract "Marcia McKee, agent," omitting the principal's name. This is a partially disclosed agency. The principal is liable on the contract with the third party, and the agent is also liable.

Undisclosed Agency

undisclosed agency
An agency in which a contracting third party does not know of either the existence of the agency or the principal's identity.

An **undisclosed agency** occurs when a third party is unaware of the existence of an agency. The principal is called an **undisclosed principal**. Undisclosed agencies are lawful. They are often used when the principal feels that the terms of the contract would be changed if the principal's identity were known. For example, a wealthy party may use an undisclosed agency to purchase property if she thinks that the seller would raise the price of the property if her identity were revealed.

In an undisclosed agency, both the principal and the agent are liable on the contract with the third party because the agent, by not divulging agency status, becomes a principal to the contract. Because the third party does not know the existence of a principal, the third party relies on the reputation and credit of the agent in entering into the contract.

Critical Legal Thinking Questions
What is an undisclosed agency? When would an undisclosed agency be used?

If the principal fails to perform the contract, the third party can recover against the principal or the agent. If the agent is made to pay the contract, he or she can recover indemnification from the principal. An undisclosed agency can be created either expressly or by mistake.

Example Walt Disney Company wants to open a new theme park in Chicago but first needs to acquire land for the park. Disney employs Saul Arnold as an agent to work on its behalf to acquire the needed property, with an express agreement that the agent will not disclose the existence of the agency to a third-party seller. If a seller agrees to sell the needed land and the agent signs his name "Saul Arnold," it is an undisclosed agency. Disney is liable on the contract with the third-party seller, and so is the agent.

Agent Exceeding the Scope of Authority

implied warranty of authority
A warranty of an agent who enters into a contract on behalf of another party that he or she has the authority to do so.

ratification of a contract
A situation in which a principal accepts an agent's unauthorized contract.

An agent who enters into a contract on behalf of another party impliedly warrants that he or she has the authority to do so. This is called the agent's **implied warranty of authority**. If the agent exceeds the scope of his or her authority, the principal is not liable on the contract. The agent, however, is liable to the third party for breaching the implied warranty of authority. To recover, the third party must show (1) reliance on the agent's representation and (2) ignorance of the agent's lack of status. A principal is bound on the contract only if the principal *ratifies* the contract—that is, accepts it as his or her own. This is called **ratification of a contract**.

Example Henry hires April, a real estate broker, to find him a house in a specified area for $1 million or less. Henry specifies that the house must be at least 4,000 square feet and must be a two-story house, with four bedrooms and four bathrooms. Henry, the principal, gives April, the agent, authority to sign a contract on his behalf to purchase such a home. April finds a house she thinks Henry would want to own that is 6,000 square feet and costs $1.5 million. April signs a contract with the seller as the disclosed agent of Henry. Here, April has exceeded her authority, and Henry is not bound to purchase the house. April, on the other hand, is bound to the contract to purchase the house. If, however, Henry likes the $1.5 million house, he can ratify the contract with the seller. If Henry does so, he is bound to the contract with the seller.

CONCEPT SUMMARY

CONTRACT LIABILITY OF PRINCIPALS AND AGENTS TO THIRD PARTIES

Type of Agency	Principal Liable?	Agent Liable?
Fully disclosed	Yes	No, unless the agent (1) acts as a principal or (2) guarantees the performance of the contract
Partially disclosed	Yes	Yes, unless the third party relieves the agent's liability
Undisclosed	Yes	Yes
Nonexistent	No, unless the principal ratifies the contract	Yes, the agent is liable for breaching the implied warranty of authority

Independent Contractor

30.5 Define *independent contractor* and describe the liability of independent contractors.

Principals often employ outsiders—that is, persons and businesses that are not employees—to perform certain tasks on their behalf. These persons and businesses are called **independent contractors**. For example, lawyers, doctors, dentists, consultants, stockbrokers, architects, certified public accountants, real estate brokers, and plumbers are examples of people who commonly act as independent contractors. The party that employs an independent contractor is called a *principal*.

independent contractor
"A person who contracts with another to do something for him who is not controlled by the other nor subject to the other's right to control with respect to his physical conduct in the performance of the undertaking" [*Restatement (Second) of Agency*].

Example Jessica is a lawyer who has her own law firm and specializes in real estate law. Ignacio, a real estate developer, hires Jessica to represent him in the purchase of land. Ignacio is the principal, and Jessica is the independent contractor.

A principal–independent contractor relationship is depicted in Exhibit 30.1.

Factors for Determining Independent Contractor Status

Section 2 of the *Restatement (Second) of Agency* defines *independent contractor* as "a person who contracts with another to do something for him who is not controlled by the other nor subject to the other's right to control with respect to his

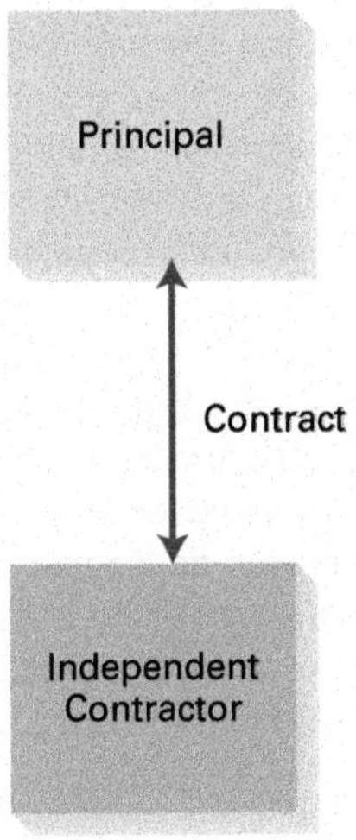

Exhibit 30.1 PRINCIPAL–INDEPENDENT CONTRACTOR RELATIONSHIP

physical conduct in the performance of the undertaking." Independent contractors usually work for a number of clients, have their own offices, hire employees, and control the performance of their work.

The crucial factor in determining whether someone is an independent contractor or an employee is the **degree of control** that the principal has over that party. Critical factors in determining independent contractor status include the following:

- Whether the worker is engaged in a distinct occupation or an independently established business
- The length of time the agent has been employed by the principal
- The amount of time that the agent works for the principal
- Whether the principal supplies the tools and equipment used in the work
- The method of payment, whether by time or by the job
- The degree of skill necessary to complete the task
- Whether the worker hires employees to assist him or her
- Whether the employer has the *right to control* the manner and means of accomplishing the desired result

If an examination of these factors shows that the principal asserts little control, the person is an independent contractor. Substantial control indicates an employer–employee relationship. Labeling someone an independent contractor is only one factor in determining whether independent contractor status exists.

The following feature examines whether FedEx drivers are employees or independent contractors.

Critical Legal Thinking Questions

Is it difficult to apply the factors for determining whether a person is an independent contractor or an employee? A plaintiff injured by that person usually wants which status to be found?

Critical Legal Thinking

Are FedEx Drivers Independent Contractors?

"FedEx has established an employment relationship with its delivery drivers but dressed that relationship in independent contractor clothing."

—William Fletcher, Circuit Judge

FedEx Ground Package System, Inc. (FedEx) is a company that delivers packages to businesses and residences. FedEx contracts with drivers to drive trucks and deliver packages to customers. FedEx classified the drivers as independent contractors and not as employees. By classifying the drivers as independent contractors, FedEx saved millions of dollars of wages, overtime pay, health care costs, workers' compensation, pensions, Social Security contributions, and unemployment insurance.

FedEx drivers in many states sued FedEx, arguing that they were employees and not independent contractors and had therefore been deprived of unpaid wages, overtime pay, and other employee benefits. Should the FedEx drivers be classified as independent contractors or as employees? To determine the answer, the courts examined the following facts:

- FedEx structures drivers' workloads to ensure that the drivers work between 9.5 and 11 hours every working day. Drivers must arrive at a designated FedEx terminal every morning to pick up the packages they are designated to deliver each day.
- FedEx drivers must deliver every package that is assigned to them by FedEx each day, and within specified time periods negotiated between FedEx and its customers. After each delivery, drivers must use an electronic scanner to send data about the delivery to FedEx.
- FedEx requires its drivers to provide their own vehicles, which must be approved by FedEx. FedEx requires that the vehicle have specific dimensions, and that all vehicles contain shelves with specific dimensions. FedEx dictates the colors, logos, numbers, and insignia of the vehicle. In their contract with FedEx, the drivers authorize FedEx to pay for vehicle licensing, taxes, and fees, and to deduct these costs from the drivers' pay.
- FedEx offers a package by which it sells drivers vehicles, uniforms, scanners, and other necessary equipment. The required uniform includes a uniform shirt with the FedEx logo, uniform pants or shorts, dark shoes and socks, and, if the driver wears a jacket or cap, a uniform jacket and cap with the FedEx logo. FedEx deducts the cost of the clothes and equipment from the drivers' pay.
- FedEx provides a boilerplate contract that each driver must sign to become a FedEx driver. FedEx's contract identifies drivers as independent contractors. FedEx can terminate the contract at any time for cause, which includes violations of any of FedEx's rules and procedures. A driver can terminate the contract with 30 days' written notice.

- Drivers are paid as independent contractors, and FedEx does not deduct federal or state income taxes, or Social Security or Medicare taxes, from the drivers' pay. Drivers are responsible for paying these taxes themselves.

Most courts that have addressed this issue of whether FedEx drivers are independent contractors or employees have found that FedEx drivers are employees rather than independent contractors. For example, the U.S. Court of Appeals for the Ninth Circuit found that more than 2,300 FedEx drivers in California were employees and not independent contractors. FedEx settled the lawsuit by agreeing to classify the drivers as employees and paying $226 million in damages. *Alexander v. FedEx Ground Package System, Inc.*, 765 F.3d 981 (United States Court of Appeals for the Ninth Circuit, 2014)

In a separate case, FedEx settled class action lawsuits brought by drivers in 19 states for mislabeling them as independent contractors. FedEx agreed to classify the drivers as employees and to pay $227 million to settle the claims of more than 12,000 drivers. Payments to individual drivers ranged from $250 to $116,000. *In re FedEx Ground Package System Inc. Employment Practices Litigation* (United States District Court for the Northern District of Indiana, 2017) The settlements, however, do not include an admission of guilt by FedEx. Additional lawsuits have been brought by FedEx drivers in other states.

Critical Legal Thinking Questions

Prior to reading this case, did you think FedEx drivers were employees or independent contractors? Why did FedEx classify the drivers are independent contractors rather than as employees? Did FedEx act ethically in doing so?

Liability for an Independent Contractor's Torts

Generally, a principal is not liable for the torts of its independent contractors. Independent contractors are personally liable for their own torts. The rationale behind this rule is that principals do not control the means of how the results are accomplished.

If we are industrious, we shall never starve; for, at the workingman's house hunger looks in, but dares not enter. Nor will the bailiff or the constable enter, for industry pays debts, while despair increaseth them.
Benjamin Franklin (1706–1790)

Example Qixia hires Zachary, a lawyer and an independent contractor, to represent her in a court case. While driving to the courthouse to represent Qixia at trial, Zachary negligently causes an automobile accident in which Mildred is severely injured. Zachary is liable to Mildred because he caused the accident. Qixia is not liable to Mildred because Zachary was an independent contractor when he caused the accident.

Principals cannot avoid liability for an **inherently dangerous activity** that they assign to independent contractors. For example, the use of explosives, clearing of land by fire, crop dusting, and other inherently dangerous activities involve special risks. In these cases, a principal is liable for the negligence of the independent contractor the principal hired to perform the dangerous task.

Liability for an Independent Contractor's Contracts

A principal can authorize an independent contractor to enter into contracts. Principals are bound by the authorized contracts of their independent contractors.

Nature seems to have taken a particular care to disseminate her blessings among the different regions of the world, with an eye to their mutual intercourse and traffic among mankind, that the nations of the several parts of the globe might have a kind of dependence upon one another and be united together by their common interest.
Joseph Addison (1672–1719)

Example Suppose a client hires a lawyer as an independent contractor to represent her in a civil lawsuit against a defendant to recover monetary damages. If the client authorizes the lawyer to settle a case within a certain dollar amount and the lawyer does so, the settlement agreement is binding.

If an independent contractor enters into a contract with a third party on behalf of the principal without express or implied authority from the principal to do so, the principal is not liable on the contract.

In the following case, the court had to decide whether an automobile dealership was an independent contractor or an agent of an automobile manufacturer.

CASE 30.2 *STATE COURT CASE Independent Contractor*

Thornton v. Ford Motor Company

297 P.3d 413 (2012)
Court of Civil Appeals of Oklahoma

"Ford did not have the right to control day-to-day operations and activities of the dealership."

—William Hetherington, Judge

Facts

Ford Motor Company (Ford), a manufacturer of automobiles and other vehicles, grants licenses to independently owned and operated dealerships to sell Ford vehicles. Ford granted a dealership to Ibex, LLC to operate a dealership in Nowata, Oklahoma. Ibex operated the dealership under the name Nowata Ford. Ford's dealership agreement provides that dealerships are not agents but are independent contractors. Seven months after opening, Ibex closed the business. Prior to closing its doors, Ibex executed a bogus check, failed to deliver vehicles and title certificates on purchased vehicles, and did not pay money owed to customers who traded in vehicles at the dealership. Customers injured by this conduct sued Ibex and Ford to recover damages for breach of contract and fraud. The plaintiffs alleged that Ibex was both an actual agent and an apparent agent of Ford, and therefore Ford should be held liable for Ibex's actions. Ford moved for summary judgment, arguing that Ibex was an independent contractor and not an actual or apparent agent of Ford. The trial court denied Ford's motion. The trial court held Ibex liable, and also held Ford liable for actual damages, attorney fees, and costs. Ford appealed.

Issue

Is Ibex an actual or apparent agent of Ford, or is Ibex an independent contractor?

Language of the Court

Ford argues that the dealership is an independent dealer, instead of an actual agent. If the facts show actual control by the principal, an agency is established regardless of the contract language. Ford did not have the right to control day-to-day operations and activities of the dealership. Concerning hiring, directing, and controlling, the court made findings which clearly support that the dealership was not Ford's actual agent.

Apparent authority exists only to the extent that it is reasonable for the third person dealing with the agent to believe that the agent is authorized. The customers' position focuses on arguing Ford clothed Nowata Ford with apparent authority by placing the Ford trademark oval sign on the dealerships' premises. Other than Ford's trademark sign, the customers have failed to present any evidence of Ford's manifestation or conduct which would reasonably lead them to believe that the dealership was authorized to sell motor vehicles on behalf of Ford.

Decision

The court of appeals held that Ibex was an independent contractor and not the actual or apparent agent of Ford.

Critical Legal Thinking Questions

What were the key elements for the court finding in favor of Ford? Prior to reading this case, did you think that automobile dealerships were owned by automobile manufacturers?

The following feature discusses whether an agency relationship exists between U.S. companies and third-party suppliers located in another country.

Ethics

Are U.S. Retailers Liable for Unsafe Working Conditions of Suppliers Located in Foreign Countries?

"Defendants' only contact with the garment factories in Bangladesh was through a system of indirect sourcing."

—Mary Johnston, Judge

One day, cracks were noticed in Rana Plaza, an eight-story commercial building in Savar, Bangladesh, where thousands of garment factory employees worked. The building was evacuated, and an engineer declared Rana Plaza unsafe and requested a more thorough inspection by public authorities. Despite knowing that the building was unsafe, managers demanded that workers return to work the next day, and most workers did. On that day, Rana Plaza collapsed, killing more than 1,000 people and injuring more than 2,000 others.

J.C. Penney Corporation, Inc. (Penney) and Walmart Stores, Inc. (Walmart), retailers with stores located in the United States and other countries, had clothing manufactured for them by third-party contractors located in the collapsed building. Many of the factory workers killed and injured worked for these contractors. Penney and Walmart are each incorporated in Delaware.

Persons living in Bangladesh who are relatives of workers killed or injured in the building collapse brought a lawsuit against Penney and Walmart in Delaware state court alleging that the defendants knew or should have known of the structural issues plaguing Rana Plaza, and that the defendants acted negligently in failing to ensure safe and healthy working conditions for the garment factory employees at Rana Plaza. The plaintiffs filed a class action lawsuit on behalf of other similarly situated workers and their representatives.

Penney and Walmart filed motions to dismiss the lawsuit, asserting that the law imposed no duty of care on them for negligent actions of independent third-party factory owners in Bangladesh. The Superior Court of Delaware agreed with Penney and Walmart and dismissed the plaintiffs' case. The court held that the clothing manufacturers operating in Rana Plaza were independent contractors of Penney and Walmart, and therefore the defendants were not liable for the clothing manufacturers' negligence.

The court stated, "The employer of an independent contractor is not liable for physical harm caused to another by the act of omission of the contractor or his servants. Defendants' only contact with the garment factories in Bangladesh was through a system of indirect sourcing. Defendants were not plaintiffs' direct employer." The court dismissed the plaintiffs' action against Penney and Walmart. *Rahaman v. J.C. Penney Corporation, Inc. and Walmart Stores, Inc.*, C.A. No. N15C-07-174 MMJ (Superior Court of Delaware, 2016)

Ethics Questions

Do you think that retailers like Penney and Walmart who have clothing and other goods manufactured in foreign countries are aware of the conditions under which foreign workers manufacture those goods? Did Penney and Walmart act ethically in not ensuring safe working conditions for the factory workers in Bangladesh?

Key Terms and Concepts

Agent's signature (521)
Coming and going rule (going and coming rule) (518)
Competing with the principal (516)
Contract liability (521)
Degree of control (524)
Dual agency (516)
Dual-purpose mission (518)
Duty of loyalty of agents (515)
Frolic and detour (517)
Fully disclosed agency (521)
Fully disclosed principal (521)
Implied warranty of authority (522)
Independent contractor (523)
Inherently dangerous activity (525)
Innocent misrepresentation (520)
Intentional misrepresentation (fraudulent misrepresentation or fraud or deceit) (520)
Intentional tort (518)
Misuse of confidential information (516)
Motivation test (519)
Negligence (517)
Partially disclosed agency (521)
Partially disclosed principal (521)
Ratification of a contract (522)
Respondeat superior (517)
Scope of employment (517)
Self-dealing (515)
Tort liability (517)
Tortious conduct (517)
Undisclosed agency (522)
Undisclosed principal (522)
Usurping an opportunity (515)
Vicarious liability (517)
Work-related test (519)

Critical Legal Thinking Cases

30.1 Frolic and Detour Jesse Spires was employed as a welder by Johnson Welded Products, Inc. Johnson Welded Products provides a lunchroom equipped with a microwave, refrigerator, and vending machine for sandwiches, snacks, and drinks. Spires worked a shift that ran from 3:15 p.m. until 12:15 a.m. One day at work, Spires was on his way to a friend's house for lunch during his lunch break, driving his own pickup truck, when he collided with Donald Siegenthaler, who was riding a motorcycle. The collision, which was the result of Spires's negligence, caused injury to Siegenthaler. Siegenthaler sued Johnson Welded Products, alleging that Spires was an agent of Johnson Welded Products at the time of the accident and that Johnson Welded Products was vicariously liable under the doctrine of respondeat superior. Johnson Welded Products argued that Spires was on personal business and a frolic and detour when he caused the accident. Is Spires an agent of Johnson Welded Products, acting within the scope of his employment, at the time of the accident that injured Siegenthaler? *Siegenthaler v. Johnson Welded Products, Inc.*, 2006 Ohio App. Lexis 5616 (Court of Appeals of Ohio, 2006)

30.2 Agent Marc Brandon worked for Warner Bros. Entertainment, Inc. (Warner) as vice president of antipiracy internet operations. Brandon drove his car from his home in southern California to the Burbank Airport, where he parked his car in an airport parking lot. Brandon then flew to a three-day conference in Sunnyvale, California, that was sponsored by one of Warner's antipiracy vendors. Warner approved Brandon's trip and paid for his airfare, hotel, and airport parking.

When Brandon left the conference, he flew back to the Burbank Airport, where he retrieved his car from the parking lot. On his way home from the airport, his route took him past his Warner office location. He continued toward his house, not stopping at the Warner office, using his normal route from the office to his home. Approximately two or three miles past the office, he was involved in an automobile collision with Jared Southard. One or both cars struck and injured pedestrians Chuenchomporn Jeewarat, Tipphawan Tantisriyanurak, and Kanhathai Vutthicharoen. Vutthicharoen died of her injuries. Jeewarat, Tantisriyanurak, and Vutthicharoen's heirs sued Brandon, Southard, and Warner to recover damages for negligence and respondeat superior. Warner filed a motion for summary judgment, alleging that because Brandon was taking his normal route home, Warner was protected from liability by the coming and going rule. Does the coming and going rule protect Warner from liability? *Jeewarat v. Warner Bros. Entertainment, Inc.*, 177 Cal. App.4th 427, 98 Cal. Rptr.3d 837, 2009 Cal. App. Lexis 1478 (Court of Appeal of California, 2009)

30.3 Independent Contractor Delta Tau Delta, Inc. is a national fraternity that grants charters to local fraternities at colleges and universities. Delta Tau Delta granted a charter to the Beta Psi local fraternity at Wabash College in Crawfordsville, Indiana. The national fraternity offers its brand to the local fraternity, along with informational resources and organizational guidance. The national fraternity does not control the operation of the local fraternity or its members. The national fraternity disapproves of hazing and irresponsible and underage drinking and requires new local chapter members to take an online educational program concerning these topics. The national fraternity can suspend local fraternity charters where hazing and underage drinking occur.

During a hazing incident of pledges of the Beta Psi fraternity at Wabash College, alcohol was served, including to minors. During the hazing, Johnny Dupree Smith, a first-year-student at Wabash College and a minor, died from acute alcohol ingestion. Stacy and Robert Smith, Johnny's parents, brought a wrongful death action against the local fraternity Beta Psi, the national fraternity Delta Tau Delta, and Wabash College to recover damages for the death of their son. The plaintiffs reached a settlement with Wabash College. The plaintiffs alleged that the local fraternity chapter was negligent, that it and its members were the agents of the national fraternity, and that the national fraternity was vicariously liable for their negligence. The national fraternity made a motion for summary judgment, arguing that the local fraternity and its members were not the national fraternity's agents. Is there an agency relationship between the local fraternity and its members and the national fraternity? *Smith v. Delta Tau Delta, Inc.*, 9 N.E.3d 154, 2014 Ind. Lexis 450 (Supreme Court of Indiana, 2014)

30.4 Tort Liability Ray Johnson and his 8-year-old son David were waiting for a "Walk" sign before crossing a street in downtown Salt Lake City. A truck owned by Newspaper Agency Corporation (NAC) and operated by its employee, Donald Rogers, crossed the intersection and jumped the curb, killing David and injuring Ray. Before reporting for work on the evening of the accident, Rogers had consumed approximately seven mixed drinks containing vodka and had chugalugged a 27-ounce drink containing two mini-bottles of tequila. His blood alcohol content after the accident was 0.18 percent.

Evidence showed that the use of alcohol and marijuana was widespread at NAC and that the company made no effort to curtail such use. Evidence further showed that NAC vehicles were returned with beer cans in them and that, on one occasion, an NAC supervisor who had observed drivers smoking marijuana had told them to "do it on the road." Ray Johnson sued Rogers and NAC for the wrongful death of his child, David, and for physical injury to Ray. Is NAC liable? *Johnson v. Rogers*, 763 P.2d 771, 1988 Utah Lexis 81 (Supreme Court of Utah, 1988)

30.5 Independent Contractor Frankie and Trena Gibbs and Joel and Madeira Glenn were members of the Gatlin Creek Baptist Church in Thomasville, Georgia, which both couples attended. The church held a fundraiser during which members would help other members with projects, and the member for whom the work was done would make a donation to the church's youth ministry. As part of the fundraiser, Frankie Gibbs, who had no experience using a chainsaw, asked Joel Glenn, who was experienced with using a chainsaw, to trim branches on a tree on Gibbs's property.

When Glenn arrived at Gibbs's property with his own chainsaw and ladder, Gibbs showed Glenn which limbs on the tree he wanted trimmed. Glenn climbed to the very top of an A-type ladder, straddled the ladder—one foot on each side—and began trimming the tree. However, after he made a cut on a limb, the limb snapped off and hit the top of the ladder, knocking the ladder backward. Glenn fell forward, head first, and landed on his back. Glenn died from the fall. Madeira Glenn sued the Gibbs to recover damages, alleging that her deceased husband was an agent of the Gibbs and that, as principals, the Gibbses had breached the ordinary duty of care they owed to Glenn as an invitee on their property. Gibbs defended, asserting that Glenn was an independent contractor with a duty of his own to make certain his work area was safe, to take all precautions, and to exercise ordinary care for his own safety. Was Joel Glenn an independent contractor or was he an agent of the Gibbses? *Glenn v. Gibbs*, 746 S.E.2d 658, 2013 Ga. App. Lexis 639 (Court of Appeals of Georgia, 2013)

Ethics Case

30.6 Ethics Case Hercules, Inc. is a large chemical corporation. Its operation in Brunswick, Georgia, extracts resins from tree stumps, processes the resins into chemical compounds, and sells them to manufacturers. Hercules purchases tree stumps from various parties, including D. Hays Trucking, Inc. (Hays). Hays owns its own equipment and delivery vehicles, hires its own truckers and other employees, pays for its employees' workers' compensation coverage, and withholds federal and state taxes from employees' paychecks. Hays directed the work of its employees who pulled the stumps from the ground and the truckers who delivered the stumps to Hercules.

One night, Mr. Hays was driving a tractor-trailer owned by D. Hays Trucking, Inc. loaded with 80,000 pounds of pine stumps from Alabama to the Hercules plant in Georgia. Just prior to midnight, when he was 10 miles from the Hercules plant, Mr. Hays crashed the tractor-trailer into a car driven by Phyllis Lewis, killing her. Mr. Hays was driving the truck approximately 10 to 15 miles per hour over the 65-mile-per-hour speed limit, and there were no skid marks from the truck prior to the collision.

Preston Lewis, the executor of the estate of Phyllis Lewis, brought suit in U.S. district court against Mr. Hays, D. Hays Trucking, Inc., and Hercules, Inc., to recover damages for negligence. Hercules made a motion for summary judgment, alleging that D. Hays Trucking, Inc. was an independent contractor and therefore Hercules could not be held liable for its negligence. Is D. Hays Trucking, Inc. an independent contractor or an employee of Hercules? Did Lewis act ethically in suing Hercules, Inc.? *Lewis v. D. Hays Trucking, Inc.*, 701 F.Supp.2d 1300, 2010 U.S. Dist. Lexis 28035 (United States District Court for the Northern District of Georgia, 2010)

CHAPTER

31 Employment, Worker Protection, and Immigration Law

STATUE OF LIBERTY, NEW YORK HARBOR
In 1886, the people of France gave the Statue of Liberty to the people of the United States in recognition of the friendship between the two countries that was established during the American Revolution. "The New Colossus," a sonnet by Emma Lazarus (1849–1887), is engraved on a tablet attached to the base of the Statue of Liberty. It reads, in part: "Give me your tired, your poor, /your huddled masses yearning to breathe free, /the wretched refuse of your teeming shore. /Send these, the homeless, tempest-tossed to me, /I lift my lamp beside the golden door!"

Henry R. Cheeseman

Learning Objectives

After studying this chapter, you should be able to:

31.1 Define *term employee* and *at-will employee*.

31.2 Describe workers' compensation programs and the benefits available.

31.3 Describe employers' duty to provide safe working conditions under the Occupational Safety and Health Act.

31.4 Describe the minimum wage, overtime pay, and other rules of the Fair Labor Standards Act.

31.5 Describe the protections afforded by the Family and Medical Leave Act.

31.6 Describe the protections afforded by the Consolidated Omnibus Budget Reconciliation Act.

31.7 Describe the protections afforded by the Employee Retirement Income Security Act.

31.8 Describe unemployment compensation and how persons qualify for benefits.

31.9 Describe Social Security and how persons qualify for benefits.

31.10 Describe immigration laws and foreign guest worker visas.

> *"It is difficult to imagine any grounds, other than our own personal economic predilections, for saying that the contract of employment is any the less an appropriate subject of legislation than are scores of others, in dealing with which this Court has held that legislatures may curtail individual freedom in the public interest."*
>
> —*Harlan Stone, Justice*
> *Dissenting opinion, Morehead v. New York (1936) 298 US 587 (1936)*

Introduction to Employment, Worker Protection, and Immigration Law

Generally, the employer–employee relationship is subject to the common law of contracts and agency law. This relationship is also highly regulated by federal and state governments that have enacted myriad laws that protect workers from unsafe working conditions, require employers to provide workers' compensation to employees injured on the job, prohibit child labor, require minimum wages and overtime pay to be paid to workers, require employers to provide time off to employees with certain family and medical emergencies, and require employers to provide other employee protections and rights.

Poorly paid labor is inefficient labor, the world over.

Henry George (1839–1887)
Progress and Poverty (1879)

Today, many high-technology and other businesses rely on employees who are foreign nationals. U.S. immigration laws provide that visas may be issued by the federal government to a specified number of foreign nationals to work in the United States. In addition, immigration law regulates the employment relationship.

This chapter discusses employment law, term and at-will employees, workers' compensation, occupational safety, pay and hour laws, family and medical leave rules, unemployment benefits, Social Security, and immigration law.

Term Employment and Employment at Will

31.1 Define *term employee* and *at-will employee*.

Sole proprietorships, partnerships, companies, and corporations often hire employees to work for the business. Employees are then obligated to perform the tasks for which they have been employed. The term of their employment depends on whether they have been hired as a *term employee* or an *at-will employee*. These two types of employment are discussed in the following paragraphs.

Term Employment

Term employment occurs when an employer and an employee enter a contract for a specified time. An employee who is employed under a term contract is a **term employee**. An employer who terminates a term employee without cause during the stated period is liable for **wrongful discharge** and owes damages to the employee. Where there is an employment contract for a stated term, an employer may terminate an employee for cause without being liable for damages.

term employee
An employee who has an employment contract with an employer for a stated time.

Examples A company employs a chief executive officer (CEO) for a period of five years with a stated annual salary of $1 million. If the employer terminates the CEO after three years without cause, the employer owes $2 million to the terminated employee. If, however, during the time of the contract, the CEO is found stealing corporate funds, the CEO can be terminated for cause without payment of damages.

At-Will Employment

at-will employee
An employee who does not have a term employment contract.

Most employees, including most managers, are **at-will employees**. This is because they do not have term contracts with their employer. An at-will employee can be terminated without cause at any time by the employer. The employee has no redress to recover damages from the employer. At-will employees may also be terminated for cause, but a showing of cause is not necessary for the employer to terminate the employee.

Example A software designer has been hired by an internet company as an at-will employee. After six months, the employer terminates the employee without cause. The employee has no claim for damages from the employer.

Exceptions

There are certain exceptions where employees, including at-will employees, cannot be legally terminated. Following are the most common exceptions:

labor union exception
A rule that restricts an employer's ability to discharge an at-will employee who is a member of a labor union. Certain procedures must be followed to seek the discharge of a union-represented employee.

public policy exception
A law that states that employees, including at-will employees, cannot be discharged by an employer if such discharge violates public policy.

statutory exception
A law that prohibits employers from refusing to hire, not promoting, or discharging at-will or term employees in violation of federal and state statutes.

- **Labor union exception.** Under the **labor union exception**, federal and state statutes restrict employers' ability to discharge employees who are union members protected by labor laws and collective bargaining agreements between the employer and the union. Certain procedures must be followed to seek the discharge of union-represented employees.
- **Public policy exception.** Under the **public policy exception**, employees, including at-will employees, cannot be discharged by an employer if such discharge violates public policy. Discharging an employee for serving as a juror, for refusing to do an act in violation of the law (e.g., refusing to dispose of toxic waste in violation of environmental laws), for refusing to engage in illegal research (e.g., research that violates animal protection laws), for refusing to distribute defective products, and the like have been held to violate public policy.
- **Statutory exception.** Certain **statutory exceptions** prohibit employers from refusing to hire, not promoting, or discharging employees in violation of federal and state statutes. Employees cannot be discharged because of their race, national origin, color, gender, religion, age, disabilities, or their status as members of other protected classes as specified in federal and state antidiscrimination laws. Thus, even at-will employees can recover damages and other remedies from employers for detrimental employment decisions in violation of these statutes.

In the following case, the court addressed the issue of at-will employment.

CASE 31.1 *STATE COURT CASE At-Will Employment*

Dore v. Arnold Worldwide, Inc.

46 Cal.Rptr.3d 668, 39 Cal.4th 384, 139 P.3d 56 (2006)
Supreme Court of California

"At-will employment may be ended by either party at any time without cause, for any or no reason."

—Kathryn Werdegar, Justice

Facts

Brook Dore applied for an available management supervisor position at the Los Angeles office of Arnold Worldwide, Inc. (AWI). She was interviewed by several AWI officers. AWI offered Dore the job during a telephone conversation, and Dore accepted the offer. AWI sent Dore a three-page letter that confirmed the offer and stated the terms of employment, including compensation and benefits. A separate paragraph in the letter stated, "Brook, please know that as with all our company employees, your employment with Arnold Communications, Inc. is at will. This simply means that Arnold Communications has the right to terminate your employment at any time just as you have the right to terminate your employment with Arnold Communications, Inc. at any time." Dore read, signed, and returned the letter.

After two years of employment, AWI terminated Dore as an employee. Dore sued AWI, alleging breach of contract, breach of the implied covenant of good faith and fair dealing, intentional infliction of emotional distress, and fraud. Dore alleged that because the agreement did not state whether termination would be with or without cause, it was therefore ambiguous, and the at-will clause could not be enforced. Dore also alleged that AWI, through various oral representations and conduct, led him to understand that there existed between himself and AWI an implied-in-fact contract that provided that he would not be discharged from his employment except for cause. AWI asserted that Dore was an at-will employee who could be terminated at any time without cause. The trial court held that Dore was an at-will employee who had been properly terminated by AWI. The trial court granted summary judgment to AWI. The court of appeals reversed and remanded the case for trial. Dore appealed to the Supreme Court of California.

Issue

Was Dore an at-will employee who could be terminated without cause?

Language of the Court

The language of the parties' written agreement is unambiguous. AWI's letter plainly states that Dore's employment with AWI was at-will. That AWI's letter went on to define at-will employment as employment that may be terminated at any time did not introduce ambiguity rendering the letter susceptible of being interpreted as allowing for an implied agreement that Dore could be terminated only for cause. At-will employment may be ended by either party at any time without cause, for any or no reason. We conclude that AWI's letter contained no ambiguity, patent or latent, in its termination provisions.

Decision

The Supreme Court of California agreed with the trial court that Dore was an at-will employee who had been properly terminated by AWI. The supreme court reversed the decision of the court of appeals.

Critical Legal Thinking Questions

What is the difference between term employment and at-will employment? Are more jobs term employment or at-will employment?

Workers' Compensation

31.2 Describe workers' compensation programs and the benefits available.

Many types of employment are dangerous, and many workers are injured on the job each year. Under common law, employees who were injured on the job could sue their employers for negligence. This time-consuming process placed the employee at odds with the employer. In addition, there was no guarantee that the employee would win the case. Ultimately, many injured workers—or the heirs of deceased workers—were left uncompensated.

Workers' compensation acts were enacted by states in response to the unfairness of that result. These acts create an administrative procedure for workers to receive **workers' compensation** for injuries that occur on the job.

workers' compensation
Compensation paid to workers and their families when workers are injured in connection with their jobs.

Under workers' compensation, an injured worker files a claim with the appropriate state government agency, often called the **workers' compensation board** or **workers' compensation commission**. Next, that entity determines the legitimacy of the claim. If the worker disagrees with the agency's findings, the decision may be appealed through the state court system. Workers' compensation benefits are usually paid according to preset limits established by statute or regulation. The amounts that are recoverable vary from state to state.

Workers' Compensation Insurance

workers' compensation insurance
Insurance that employers obtain and purchase from private insurance companies or from government-sponsored programs. Some states permit employers to self-insure.

States usually require employers to purchase **workers' compensation insurance** from private insurance companies or to contribute to state funds to cover workers' compensation claims. Some states permit employers to self-insure if they demonstrate that they have the ability to pay workers' compensation claims. Many large companies self-insure.

Employment-Related Injury

employment-related injury
An injury to an employee that arises out of and occurs in the course of employment.

For an injury to be compensable under workers' compensation, the claimant must prove that he or she was harmed by an **employment-related injury**. Thus, injuries that arise out of and in the course of employment are compensable.

Examples If an employee is injured in an automobile accident while driving to a business lunch, the injury is covered by workers' compensation. However, if an employee is injured in an automobile accident while driving to an off-premises restaurant during a personal lunch hour, the injury is not covered by workers' compensation.

In addition to covering physical injuries, workers' compensation insurance covers stress and mental illness that are employment related.

Exclusive Remedy

exclusive remedy
The sole remedy for employees who are covered by workers' compensation and have been injured on the job. Workers who are covered by workers' compensation give up their right to sue their employer for damages.

Workers' compensation is an **exclusive remedy**. Thus, workers cannot both receive workers' compensation and sue their employers in court for damages. Workers' compensation laws make a trade-off: An injured worker qualifies for workers' compensation benefits and does not have to spend time and money to sue the employer, which comes with a possible risk of not winning. The employer has to pay for workers' compensation insurance but does not have to incur the expense and risk of a lawsuit.

Example A professor is covered by the university's workers' compensation insurance. While teaching a class, the professor is injured after tripping over a power cord that was lying on the floor in the classroom. In this case, the professor's sole remedy is to recover workers' compensation. The professor cannot sue the university to recover damages.

Workers' compensation acts do not bar injured workers from suing responsible third parties to recover damages.

WEB EXERCISE
Go to **http://www.dir.ca.gov/dwc/WCFaqIW.html#1** to learn more about workers' compensation. Read the first four questions and answers.

Example A worker who is covered by workers' compensation insurance is operating a machine while at work. The worker is injured when the machine breaks. The worker can recover workers' compensation benefits but cannot sue the employer. If it is proven that a defect in the machine has caused the injury, the worker can sue the manufacturer to recover damages caused by the defective machine.

Workers can sue an employer in court to recover damages for employment-related injuries if the employer does not carry workers' compensation insurance or does not self-insure if permitted to do so. If an employer intentionally injures a worker, the worker can collect workers' compensation benefits and can also sue the employer.

The following case involves a workers' compensation claim.

CASE 31.2 *STATE COURT CASE Workers' Compensation*

Wal-Mart Stores v. Henle

843 N.W.2d 476, 2014 Iowa App. Lexis 73 (2014)
Court of Appeals of Iowa

"Industrial disability does not require a state of absolute helplessness."

—Mary Tabor, Justice

Facts

Julie Henle worked in the inventory department of the Marshalltown, Iowa, Wal-Mart Store. She was a manual laborer, whose work included unloading delivery trucks, climbing ladders to stock shelves, and driving forklifts. Henle was injured when a 60-pound stack of plastic totes fell 15 feet, striking her on the head and left shoulder, knocking her to the floor. She received treatment in a hospital emergency room for contusions, abrasions, and lacerations over her eye and left temple. The injury caused Henle to suffer chronic headaches and dizziness. After the injury, she had trouble concentrating and was diagnosed with mood disorders. Henle saw five different doctors, including a neurologist. One year after the injury, a doctor performing an independent medical evaluation determined that Henle suffered 40 percent impairment of the whole person. At that time, Henle was 55 years old. The doctor prescribed future medical treatments and continued treatment by a chronic pain specialist.

In an arbitration proceeding, the Worker's Compensation Commissioner concluded that Henle was permanently and totally disabled from competitive employment and ordered Wal-Mart to make total disability payments to Henle in the future and to pay Henle a lump sum payment for unpaid past disability payments. Wal-Mart appealed, and Henle filed for judicial entry of judgment of the workers' compensation award. The district court found the commissioner's award of permanent total disability was supported by the evidence and granted Henle's request to reduce the award to judgment. Wal-Mart appealed.

Issue

Was the award of permanent total disability warranted in this case?

Language of the Court

Wal-Mart appears to argue an employee must suffer from 100 percent impairment to qualify for total disability. This is incorrect. Industrial disability does not require a state of absolute helplessness. The pertinent question is whether jobs exist in the community for which the injured employee can realistically compete. The commissioner found the types of accommodations needed for Henle to work are not available in the general labor market.

Decision

The court of appeals upheld the finding of permanent total disability and the award of workers' compensation benefits.

Critical Legal Thinking Questions

What is the public policy that underlies workers' compensation laws? Why did Wal-Mart challenge the commissioner's findings?

Occupational Safety

31.3 Describe employers' duty to provide safe working conditions under the Occupational Safety and Health Act.

In 1970, Congress enacted the **Occupational Safety and Health Act**[1] to promote safety in the workplace. Almost all private employers are within the scope of the act, but federal, state, and local governments are exempt. Industries regulated by other federal safety legislation are also exempt.[2] The act also established the **Occupational Safety and Health Administration (OSHA)**, a federal administrative agency within the Department of Labor that is empowered to enforce the act. The act imposes

Occupational Safety and Health Act
A federal act enacted in 1970 that promotes safety in the workplace.

Occupational Safety and Health Administration (OSHA)
A federal administrative agency that is empowered to enforce the Occupational Safety and Health Act.

record-keeping and reporting requirements on employers and requires them to post notices in the workplace to inform employees of their rights under the act.

OSHA is empowered to adopt rules and regulations to interpret and enforce the Occupational Safety and Health Act. OSHA has adopted thousands of regulations to enforce the safety standards established by the act.

OSHA is empowered to inspect places of employment for health hazards and safety violations. If a violation is found, OSHA can issue a written citation that requires the employer to abate or correct the situation. Contested citations are reviewed by the Occupational Safety and Health Review Commission. Its decision is appealable to the Court of Appeals for the Federal Circuit. Employers who violate the act, OSHA rules and regulations, or OSHA citations are subject to both civil and criminal penalties.

Federal law permits states to develop and operate their own safety and health programs with OSHA's approval and monitoring. State plans must set work safety and health standards that are at least as effective as OSHA standards. Many state plans provide for increased safety standards and the assessment of greater fines and penalties than those of OSHA. State claims are filed with an appropriate state agency. Approximately half of the states have adopted such plans.

Specific Duty Standards

specific duty standards
OSHA standards that set safety rules for specific equipment, procedures, types of work, unique work conditions, and so on.

Many of the OSHA standards are **specific duty standards**. That is, these rules are developed for and apply to specific equipment, procedures, types of work, individual industries, unique work conditions, and so on.

Examples OSHA standards establish safety requirements for safety guards on saws, set maximum exposure levels for hazardous chemicals, and regulate the location of machinery in the workplace.

General Duty Standard

general duty standard
An OSHA standard that requires an employer to provide a work environment free from recognized hazards that have caused or are likely to cause death or serious physical harm to employees.

The Occupational Safety and Health Act contains a **general duty standard** that imposes on an employer a duty to provide employees with a work environment that is free from recognized hazards that have caused or are likely to cause death or serious physical harm to its employees. This general duty standard is a catchall provision that applies even if no specific workplace safety regulation addresses the situation.

Example A factory worker who is walking toward an assigned work station trips over some boxes stored on the floor. This would be a violation of the OSHA general duty requirement to provide safe working conditions.

In the following case, the court had to determine if an employer had violated the general duty standard.

CASE 31.3 *FEDERAL COURT CASE General Duty Standard*

SeaWorld of Florida, LLC v. Perez, Secretary, United States Department of Labor

748 F.3d 1202, 2014 U.S. App. Lexis 6660 (2014)
United States Court of Appeals for the District of Columbia

"The remedy imposed for SeaWorld's violations does not change the essential nature of its business."

—Judith Rogers, Circuit Judge

Facts

SeaWorld of Florida, LLC, operates a theme park in Orlando, Florida, that is designed to entertain and educate paying customers by displaying and studying marine animals. Dawn Brancheau, a 15-year veteran trainer at SeaWorld, was interacting with Tilikum, an orca (commonly known as a killer whale), during a performance before an audience in a pool at SeaWorld, when the killer whale grabbed her and refused to release her. She suffered traumatic injuries and drowned. A customer had taken a video of the performance. Although Brancheau was the only SeaWorld employee killed by an animal, Brancheau's death was the third fatality associated with Tilikum during a 30-year period.

There are no specific duty standards regulating how trainers work with killer whales. Secretary of Labor Tom Perez issued citations to SeaWorld for violating the general duty clause of the Occupational Safety and Health Act by exposing animal trainers to the recognized hazard of injury or drowning when working with killer whales during performances and training. The secretary determined that SeaWorld had violated the general duty standard, held that trainers should not be allowed any contact with killer whales unless they are protected by physical barriers or decking systems, and imposed a $12,000 fine. SeaWorld petitioned for review.

Issue

Did SeaWorld violate the general duty clause?

Language of the Court

The remedy imposed for SeaWorld's violations does not change the essential nature of its business. There will still be human interactions and performances with killer whales; the remedy will simply require that they continue with increased safety measures. With distance and physical barriers between Tilikum and trainers, Tilikum can still perform almost the same behaviors performed when no barriers were present.

Decision

The U.S. court of appeals denied SeaWorld's petition for review.

Critical Legal Thinking Questions

What does the general duty clause require? Was the fine sufficient in this case? Does this case raise issues concerning animal rights?

Fair Labor Standards Act

31.4 Describe the minimum wage, overtime pay, and other rules of the Fair Labor Standards Act.

In 1938, Congress enacted the **Fair Labor Standards Act (FLSA)** to protect workers.[3] The FLSA applies to private employers and employees engaged in the production of goods for interstate commerce. The **U.S. Department of Labor** is empowered to enforce the FLSA. Private civil actions are also permitted under the FLSA.

Fair Labor Standards Act (FLSA)
A federal act enacted in 1938 to protect workers. It prohibits child labor and spells out minimum wage and overtime pay requirements.

Child Labor

The FLSA regulates **child labor** by restricting the types of occupations and jobs that children under the age of 18 may engage in. The Department of Labor has adopted the following regulations regarding lawful child labor:

1. Children under the age of 14 cannot work in nonhazardous or hazardous occupations, with limited exceptions approved by the Department of Labor (e.g., child actors).
2. Children ages 14 and 15 may work in a limited set of occupations approved by the Department of Labor (e.g., restaurant waiters) with restrictions on work hours, and in nonhazardous agricultural jobs outside of school hours.
3. Children ages 16 and 17 may work unlimited hours in nonhazardous occupations and in nonhazardous and hazardous agriculture jobs.
4. Children of any age may work in nonhazardous agricultural jobs, outside of school hours, with parental consent, when certain conditions are met concerning farm size, nature and duration of work, and other requirements.

The Department of Labor determines which occupations are hazardous (e.g., mining, roofing, working with explosives). The FLSA forbids the use of oppressive child labor and makes it unlawful to ship goods produced by businesses that use oppressive child labor. The Department of Labor may conduct workplace inspections and investigations to determine whether oppressive child labor is employed.

Persons age 18 and older may work at any occupation, whether it is hazardous or not.

Minimum Wage

Critical Legal Thinking Questions

Should the minimum wage be increased? What are the economic consequences of raising the minimum wage?

The FLSA requires employers to pay all employees a minimum hourly wage. The **federal minimum wage** is set by Congress and can be changed. As of 2019, the federal minimum wage was set at $7.25 per hour. The Department of Labor permits employers to pay less than the minimum wage to students and apprentices. An employer may reduce the minimum wage by an amount equal to the reasonable cost of food and lodging provided to employees.

There is a special minimum wage rule for tipped employees. An employee who earns tips can be paid $2.13 an hour by an employer if that amount plus the tips received equals at least the minimum wage. If an employee's tips and direct employer payment do not together equal the minimum wage, the employer must make up the difference.

WEB EXERCISE

Using **www.google.com** or other internet search engine, find the minimum wage for your state.

The federal government periodically reviews whether the minimum wage should be increased.

The following feature discusses state and local government minimum wage laws.

Business Environment

State and Local Government Minimum Wage and Living Wage Laws

Federal law permits state and local governments to set higher minimum wage laws than those provided by FLSA. The majority of states have enacted **state minimum wage** laws that set minimum wages at a rate higher than the federal rate.

Examples Washington ($13.50), California ($13), Massachusetts ($12.75), Arizona ($12), Colorado ($12), and Maine ($12).

Some cities and counties have enacted minimum wage requirements that establish minimum wage rates that are higher than the federal or state levels. These laws are often referred to as **living wage laws**.

Examples Hourly living wages of the following cities are: Seattle, Washington ($16.39); Mountain View, California ($16.05); San Francisco, California ($15); New York, New York ($15); Los Angeles, California ($15); and Portland, Oregon ($13.25). Living wages are usually adjusted on an annual basis.

Labor unions and employers often agree to pay scales for union workers that exceed minimum wages required by law. Many companies set minimum wages for their employees that are higher than federal and state rates. These include Bank of America, Facebook, Costco, Amazon, Ben & Jerry's, JP Morgan Chase, and others.

Overtime Pay

The FLSA requires employers to pay certain employees who work more than 40 hours per week **overtime pay** for each hour worked beyond 40 hours at a rate not less than one and a half times their regular per hour pay. Each week is treated separately. Averaging hours over two or more weeks is not permitted. Thus, if an employee works 50 hours one week and 30 hours the next, the employer owes the employee 10 hours of overtime pay for the first week. FLSA does not require overtime pay for work on Saturdays, Sundays, holidays, or regular days of rest, unless overtime is worked on those days.

Some employees qualify for overtime pay, and some employees do not. Employees who qualify for overtime pay are called **nonexempt employees.** Employees who do not qualify for the overtime pay are called **exempt employees.**

Blue-Collar Workers

Manual laborers and other blue-collar workers who perform work involving repetitive operations with their hands, physical skill, and energy are nonexempt employees who are entitled to be paid overtime pay under federal law. Examples of blue-collar workers include production line workers and laborers, carpenters, electricians, mechanics, plumbers, ironworkers, craft workers, longshoremen, maintenance workers, and construction workers. Blue-collar workers are required to be paid overtime no matter how highly paid they might be. Blue-collar workers often learn their occupation through apprenticeships, through on-the-job training, and by attending trade schools.

Example Ophelia is a licensed plumber employed by Green Construction Company at an hourly wage of $30, which is $1,200 per week. At this wage, for every overtime hour Ophelia works, her employer owes her $45 ($30 + $15 overtime pay). If one week she works 40 hours, the employer owes her wages of $1,200 (40 hours × $30). If the next week she works 30 hours, her employer owes her $900 (30 hours × $30). If the next week she works 60 hours, her employer owes her $2,100 (40 regular hours × $30 plus 20 overtime hours × $45).

First Responders

Police officers, firefighters, paramedics, emergency medical technicians, ambulance personnel, and other first responders are required to be paid overtime pay regardless of rank or pay level.

White-Collar Workers

There is often a general belief that salaried employees do not have to be paid overtime pay. This is not the case. The FLSA requires that white-collar workers be paid overtime pay unless they are explicitly made exempt from the requirement.

Under the FLSA, certain executive, administrative, professional, and other white-collar employees are exempt from being paid overtime if minimum wage and/or duty tests are met. These exemptions are often referred to as **EAP exemptions** or **white-collar exemptions**. Categories of white-collar workers who do not have to be paid overtime include:

EAP exemptions (white-collar exemptions) Exemptions from federal overtime pay rules for white-collar workers who are paid a salary above a certain dollar amount and/or perform certain job duties.

- **Executive employees.** The **executive employee exemption** applies to employees (1) who earn a salary of at least $684 per week and (2) whose primary duty is managing the enterprise or a department or subdivision of the enterprise. These executives customarily and regularly direct the work of two or more full-time employees, and have the authority to hire and fire employees. CEOs, midlevel managers, project managers, and shift managers customarily fit in this category.
- **Administrative employees.** The **administrative employee exemption** applies to employees (1) who earn a salary of at least $684 per week and (2) whose primary duty is office or nonmanual work that is related to the management or general business operations of the employer or the employer's customers. The employee's duty must also include the exercise of discretion and independent judgment with respect to matters of significance. Payroll and finance employees, public relations representatives, and quality control employees customarily fit in this category.

- **Learned professionals.** The **learned professional employee exemption** applies to employees (1) who earn a salary of at least $684 per week and (2) who perform work requiring advanced knowledge that is predominantly intellectual in character. The advanced knowledge must be in a field of science or learning, and the advanced knowledge must have been acquired through a prolonged course of specialized intellectual instruction. Lawyers, dentists, accountants, architects, engineers, and pharmacists fit in this category.
- **Creative professionals.** The **creative employee exemption** applies to employees (1) who earn a salary of at least $684 per week and (2) whose primary duty must be in the performance of work that requires invention, imagination, originality, or talent in a recognized field of artistic or creative endeavor. Writers, novelists, screenplay writers, musicians, artists, painters, graphic designers, actors, cartoonists, composers, and conductors fit in this category.
- **Highly compensated employees.** The **highly compensated employee exemption** applies to employees who (1) are paid a total annual compensation of at least $107,432 (which must include a salary of at least $684 per week) and (2) perform office or nonmanual work, and customarily and regularly perform at least one of the duties of an exempt executive, administrative, or learned professional, employee. Employees who earn commissions, nondiscretionary bonuses, or other nondiscretionary incentive compensation fit into this category.
- **Computer employees.** The **computer employee exemption** applies to employees (1) who earn a salary of at least $684 per week or are paid at a rate of at least $27.63 an hour and (2) whose primary duty consists of higher-level systems-analyst techniques and procedures or the design or development of computer systems or programs. This exemption is meant for positions such as network analyst, developer, and software engineer; it is not meant for lower-level computer support roles.
- **Outside sales representatives.** The **outside sales representative exemption** applies to employees whose primary duty is making sales or obtaining orders or contracts or services or for the use of facilities for which consideration will be paid by a client or customers, and the employee must be customarily and regularly engaged away from the employer's place of business. The minimum salary threshold does not apply to outside sales employees.
- **Teachers.** The **teacher exemption** applies to employees whose primary duty is teaching, tutoring, instructing, or lecturing, and who are performing that duty as an employee of an educational establishment. Educational establishments include elementary school systems, secondary educational systems, institutions of higher education, and other educational institutions. The exemption extends to online and remote teaching. The minimum salary threshold does not apply to teachers.

White-collar employees who do not fall into one of the above exemptions must be paid overtime pay. This may be because they are not paid a salary high enough to qualify for an exemption or they do not perform work that meets the job duty requirements of an exemption.

Example An administrative assistant works for an employer but does not do work that meets the duty requirement for an administrative employee exemption. The administrative assistant must be paid overtime.

Example A person who is employed as a singer by a recording company is paid $650 per week. The singer is being paid less than the threshold minimum salary of $684 per month required for a creative employee exemption. The singer must be paid overtime.

The federal overtime dollar thresholds for determining exemptions are updated every three years.

Job Titles and Employee Duties

Job titles do not establish exempt status. Employees who are designated by their employers to be in an exempt class must actually be performing the duties required for that exemption. Sometimes employers falsely assign employees job titles that would place them in an exempt status and thus not qualify them for overtime pay. Doing so violates the FLSA.

Example A big-box store labels a worker who stocks shelves with goods as a "manager" in an attempt to avoid paying the employee overtime. The employee can file an action to be properly classified and recover unpaid overtime wages.

The following feature discusses a Supreme Court case in which workers alleged that they were due overtime pay.

Critical Legal Thinking

Payment of Overtime Pay to Workers

"The Department of Labor describes the workday as roughly the period from 'whistle to whistle.'"

—John Paul Stevens, Justice

IBP, Inc., produces fresh beef, pork, and related meat products. At its plant in Pasco, Washington, it employed approximately 178 workers in its slaughter division and 800 other workers. All workers must wear gear such as outer garments, hardhats, earplugs, gloves, aprons, leggings, and boots. IBP requires employees to store their equipment and tools in company locker rooms, where the workers don and doff their equipment and protective gear.

The pay of production workers is based on time spent cutting and bagging meat. Pay begins with the first piece of meat and ends with the last piece of meat. IBP employees filed a class action lawsuit against IBP to recover compensation for the time spent walking between the locker room and the production floor before and after their assigned shifts. The employees alleged that IBP was in violation of the Fair Labor Standards Act (FLSA).

The U.S. Supreme Court held that the time spent by employees walking between the locker room and the production areas of the plant was compensable under the Fair Labor Standards Act. The Supreme Court stated, "The Department of Labor describes the workday as roughly the period from 'whistle to whistle.' Any walking time that occurs after the beginning of the employee's first principal activity and before the end of the employee's last principal activity is covered by the FLSA." *IBP, Inc. v. Alvarez*, 546 U.S. 21, 126 S.Ct. 514, 2005 U.S. Lexis 8373 (Supreme Court of the United States, 2005)

Critical Legal Thinking Questions

Why were the workers of IBP awarded overtime pay for the time spent walking between the locker room and the production floor? Was it ethical for IBP not to pay its employees for this time?

Family and Medical Leave Act

31.5 Describe the protections afforded by the Family and Medical Leave Act.

In 1993, Congress enacted the **Family and Medical Leave Act (FMLA)**.[4] This act guarantees workers unpaid time off from work for family and medical emergencies and other specified situations. The act, which applies to companies with 50 or more workers as well as to federal, state, and local governments, covers about half of the nation's workforce. To be covered by the act, an employee must have worked for the employer for at least one year and must have performed more than 1,250 hours of service during the previous 12-month period.

Family and Medical Leave Act (FMLA)
A federal act that guarantees workers up to 12 weeks of unpaid leave in a 12-month period to attend to family and medical emergencies and other specified situations.

Covered employers are required to provide up to 12 weeks of unpaid leave during any 12-month period due to the following:

1. The birth of and care for a child
2. The placement of a child with an employee for adoption or foster care
3. A serious health condition that makes the employee unable to perform his or her duties
4. Care for a spouse, child, or parent with a serious health problem

Critical Legal Thinking Questions

What are the provisions of the Family and Medical Leave Act? What are the public policies that are promoted by the act?

A leave because of the birth of a child or the placement of a child for adoption or foster care must be taken in one continuous period unless the employer allows the leave to be taken in intervals. Other leaves do not have to be taken at one time and may be taken in intervals. The employer may require medical proof of claimed serious health conditions.

An eligible employee who takes leave must, on returning to work, be restored to either the same or an equivalent position with equivalent employment benefits and pay. The restored employee is not entitled to the accrual of seniority during the leave period, however. A covered employer may deny restoration to a salaried employee who is among the highest-paid 10 percent of that employer's employees if the denial is necessary to prevent "substantial and grievous economic injury" to the employer's operations.

Consolidated Omnibus Budget Reconciliation Act

31.6 Describe the protections afforded by the Consolidated Omnibus Budget Reconciliation Act.

Consolidated Omnibus Budget Reconciliation Act (COBRA)
A federal law that permits employees and their beneficiaries to continue their group health insurance after an employee's employment has ended.

The **Consolidated Omnibus Budget Reconciliation Act (COBRA)** of 1985[5] provides that an employee of a private employer or the employee's beneficiaries must be offered the opportunity to continue group health insurance after the voluntary or involuntary termination of a worker's employment or the loss of coverage due to certain qualifying events defined in the law. The employer must notify covered employees and their beneficiaries of their rights under COBRA. To continue coverage, a person must pay the required group rate premium. Under most circumstances, COBRA coverage is available for 18 months after employment has ended. Government employees are subject to parallel provisions found in the Public Health Service Act.

Employee Retirement Income Security Act

31.7 Describe the protections afforded by the Employee Retirement Income Security Act.

Employee Retirement Income Security Act (ERISA)
A federal act designed to prevent fraud and other abuses associated with private pension funds.

Employers are not required to establish pension plans for their employees. If they do, however, they are subject to the record-keeping, disclosure, fiduciary duty, and other requirements of the **Employee Retirement Income Security Act (ERISA)**.[6] ERISA is a complex act designed to prevent fraud and other abuses associated with private pension funds. Federal, state, and local government pension funds are exempt from its coverage. ERISA is administered by the Department of Labor.

Among other things, ERISA requires pension plans to be in writing and to name a pension fund manager. The pension fund manager owes a fiduciary duty to act as a "prudent person" in managing the fund and investing its assets. No more than 10 percent of a pension fund's assets can be invested in the securities of the sponsoring employer.

Vesting occurs when an employee has a nonforfeitable right to receive pension benefits. First, ERISA provides for immediate vesting of each employee's own contributions to the plan. Second, it requires employers' contributions to be either (1) totally vested after five years (*cliff vesting*) or (2) gradually vested over a seven-year period and completely vested after that time.

Unemployment Compensation

31.8 Describe unemployment compensation and how persons qualify for benefits.

unemployment compensation
Compensation that is paid to workers who are temporarily unemployed.

In 1935, Congress established an **unemployment compensation** program to assist workers who are temporarily unemployed. Under the **Federal Unemployment Tax Act (FUTA)**[7] and state laws enacted to implement the program, employers are required to pay unemployment contributions (taxes). The tax rate and unemployment wage level are subject to change. Employees do not pay unemployment taxes.

State governments administer unemployment compensation programs under general guidelines set by the federal government. Each state establishes its own eligibility requirements and the amount and duration of the benefits. To collect benefits, applicants must be able to work and be available for work and seeking employment. Workers who have been let go because of bad conduct (e.g., illegal activity, drug use on the job) or who voluntarily quit work without just cause are not eligible to receive unemployment benefits.

Social Security

31.9 Describe Social Security and how persons qualify for benefits.

In 1935, Congress established the federal **Social Security** system to provide limited retirement and death benefits to certain employees and their dependents. The Social Security system is administered by the **Social Security Administration**. Today, Social Security benefits include (1) retirement benefits, (2) survivors' benefits to family members of deceased workers, (3) disability benefits, and (4) medical and hospitalization benefits (Medicare).

Social Security
A federal system that provides limited retirement and death benefits to covered employees and their dependents.

Under the **Federal Insurance Contributions Act (FICA)**,[8] employees must make contributions (i.e., pay taxes) into the Social Security fund. An employee's employer must pay a matching amount. Social Security does not operate like a savings account. Instead, current contributions are used to fund current claims. The employer is responsible for deducting employees' portions from their wages and remitting the entire payment to the federal government.

Under the **Self-Employment Contributions Act**,[9] self-employed individuals must pay Social Security contributions, too. The amount of tax self-employed individuals must pay is equal to the combined employer–employee amount.

Failure to submit Social Security taxes subjects the violator to interest payments, penalties, and possible criminal liability. Social Security taxes may be changed by an act of Congress.

Immigration Law and Employment

31.10 Describe immigration laws and foreign guest worker visas.

The United States is a country of immigrants. Immigration has been a major source of population growth throughout the country's history and has led to cultural diversity across the nation. Prior to 1921, there were few restrictions on immigration to the United States. In 1921, the United States enacted an immigration quota law that established limits on the number of immigrants who could be admitted to the United States from each foreign country each year. This country-of-origin immigration quota system is no longer in effect today.

All persons born or naturalized in the United States, and subject to the jurisdiction thereof, are citizens of the United States and of the States wherein they reside.

Fourteenth Amendment to the United States Constitution (July 9, 1868)

Mexico, China, India, and the Philippines are the leading countries of origin of immigrants to the United States. Other countries with significant immigration to the United States include the Dominican Republic, Vietnam, South Korea, Cuba, Colombia, and Haiti.

Immigration is primarily governed by federal law. The **Immigration Act of 1990**,[10] the **Immigration Reform and Control Act of 1986**,[11] other federal statutes, presidential executive orders, and government regulations regulate immigration, the employment of immigrants in the United States, and naturalization and citizenship. Currently, the immigration laws of this country are administered by the **U.S. Citizenship and Immigration Services (USCIS)**, which is part of the U.S. Department of Homeland Security. The USCIS processes immigrant and nonimmigrant visa and naturalization petitions.

U.S. Citizenship and Immigration Services (USCIS)
A federal agency empowered to enforce U.S. immigration laws.

Form I-9, Employment Eligibility Verification
A form completed by prospective employees that demonstrates that they are authorized to work in the United States. The information must be verified by the employer.

Foreign nationals who qualify and have met the requirements to do so may become citizens of the United States. During their swearing-in ceremony, they must swear the **Oath of Citizenship**. More than 1 million persons are naturalized as U.S. citizens each year.

The following feature discusses the employment eligibility verification requirements of employers.

Business Environment

Employment Eligibility Verification

The law requires employers to employ only individuals who may legally work in the United States—either U.S. citizens or foreign citizens who have the necessary authorization. The Immigration Reform and Control Act of 1986 requires employers to attest to their employees' immigration status and makes it illegal for employers to knowingly recruit undocumented workers.

Employers are required to have prospective employees complete a portion of **Form I-9, Employment Eligibility Verification**, and employers must obtain a completed Form I-9 for every employee, regardless of citizenship status or national origin. An employer cannot require a person to complete a Form I-9 before the employee accepts a job offer. A Form I-9 can be completed using a computer.

Employers must examine evidence that establishes a prospective employees' (1) identity and (2) employment eligibility.

The following documents establish both *identity* and *employment eligibility*: (1) U.S. Passport or U.S. Passport Card; (2) Permanent Resident Card or Alien Registration Receipt Card; or (3) foreign passport that contains an immigrant visa.

Applicants may also submit one document that establishes *identity* and a second document that establishes *employment eligibility*. Documents that establish *identity* include: (1) driver's license or ID card issued by a state; (2) ID card issued by federal, state, or local government agencies or entities; (3) school ID card with a photograph; (4) voter registration card; (5) U.S. military card or draft record; (6) Native American tribal document; or (7) driver's license issued by a Canadian government authority.

Documents that establish *employment eligibility* include: (1) Social Security card; (2) certification of report of birth issued by the U.S. Department of State; (3) original or certified copy of birth certificate issued by a state, county, municipal authority, or territory of the United States; (4) U.S. Citizen ID Card; or (5) employment authorization document issued by the U.S. Department of Homeland Security.

If the employer, after reviewing the evidence provided, determines that the applicant is eligible for employment, the employer completes the remaining portion of Form I-9. Employers can use the federal government's USCIS **E-Verify** internet-based system to verify the employment eligibility of their employees after hire. E-Verify compares information from an applicant's Form I-9 to U.S. Department of Homeland Security and Social Security Administration records to confirm employment eligibility within seconds. If E-Verify does not verify a person's right to work, then the employer may terminate the employee.

Employers do not have to file Form I-9 forms with the USCIS. They must maintain Form I-9s and copies of supporting documents on file during the course of employment, and for a certain time after the employee stops working for the employer as determined by a government-specified formula. These records may be stored electronically. Form I-9s must be available for inspection by authorized officials of the U.S. Department of Homeland Security, U.S. Department of Labor, and U.S. Department of Justice.

Federal immigration law imposes civil and criminal penalties on employers who knowingly hire undocumented workers. The employer must post notices in the workplace outlining the contents of the law.

Temporary Visitors

B-1 visa
A visa issued to persons seeking temporary entry to the United States for business purposes.

B-2 visa
A visa issued to persons seeking temporary entry to the United States for tourism and non-business purposes.

Foreign persons may be permitted to enter the United States for temporary visits. A **B-1 visa** can be issued to persons seeking temporary entry to the United States for business purposes. A **B-2 visa** can be granted to persons seeking temporary entry to the United States for tourism or non-business reasons, such as visiting family members in the United States. B-1 and B-2 are nonimmigrant visas. The maximum period of stay for a B-1 or B-2 visa is six months, although the United States may restrict an applicant's stay to less than six months.

A **Visa Waiver Program (VWP)** allows citizens or nationals of designated countries to come to the United States for business or travel without a B visa for stays of not more than 90 days. Approximately 40 countries are participants in this program, including most European countries, Australia, Chile, Japan, New Zealand, Singapore, South Korea, and Taiwan.

Student Visa

Students from foreign countries who wish to study at colleges and universities or English language programs in the United States must obtain an **F-1 visa**. A student visa is a nonimmigrant visa. The foreign national must obtain an acceptance letter from the sponsoring U.S. academic institution. Spouses and unmarried children under the age of 21 of an F-1 student qualify for an **F-2 visa** and may stay in the United States as long as the F-1 holder retains a legal status.

F-1 visa
A visa issued to foreign nationals to study at colleges and universities and English language programs in the United States.

An F-1 visa holder may remain in the United States for up to 60 days beyond the completion of his or her studies. However, F-1 visa holders who have graduated or attended an academic program for at least nine months are eligible to apply for **optional practical training (OPT)**. This program allows approved F-1 visa holders to work in the United States to get practical training in a field related to the student's major area of study without obtaining an additional work visa. Approved applicants in nontechnology fields are permitted up to 12 months of practical training. OPT may be granted for up to three years for students who have earned a degree in science, technology, engineering, and mathematics (STEM) fields. During the OPT period, the holder may work full time, part time, or as an entrepreneur, and the job may be a paid job or a nonpaid job such as an internship.

Optional practical training (OPT)
A program that allows F-1 visa holders to temporarily work in the United States to get practical training after graduation or completion of at least nine months of an academic program.

H-1B Foreign Guest Worker Visa

An **H-1B Foreign Guest Worker visa**, or **H-1B visa**, is a nonimmigrant visa that allows U.S. employers to employ in the United States foreign nationals who are skilled in specialty occupations. A **foreign guest worker** under an H-1B visa must have a bachelor's degree or higher and a "specialty occupation" such as engineering, mathematics, computer science, physical sciences, or medicine. A foreign guest worker must be sponsored by a U.S. employer. Employers, not individual applicants, apply for H-1B visas for proposed foreign guest workers. The USCIS determines H-1B eligibility.

H1-B Foreign Guest Worker visa (H-1B visa)
A visa that allows U.S. employers to employ foreign nationals in the United States who are skilled in specialty occupations. These workers are called *foreign guest workers*.

The number of H-1B visas is limited. H-1B visa holders are permitted to bring their immediate family members (i.e., spouse and unmarried children under age 21) to the United States under the **H-4 visa** category as dependents.

The duration of the stay for a worker on an H-1B visa is three years, which can be extended another three years. During this time, an employer may sponsor an H-1B holder for lawful permanent resident status, which, if issued, permits the foreign national to eventually obtain U.S. citizenship if he or she so desires.

EB-1 Extraordinary Ability Visa

An **EB-1 Extraordinary Ability visa**, or **EB-1 visa**, is a nonimmigrant visa that allows U.S. employers to employ in the United States foreign nationals who possess extraordinary ability for certain types of employment. The three categories of foreign guest workers who can qualify for an EB-1 visa are (1) persons who can demonstrate extraordinary ability in the sciences, arts, education, business, or athletics through sustained national or international acclaim; (2) professors and researchers who can demonstrate international recognition for outstanding achievements in a particular academic field; and (3) multinational managers or executives employed by a firm outside the United States and who seek to continue working for that firm in the United States. Employers must file for the visa for workers in categories (2) and (3), whereas applicants in category (1) can file for the visa themselves. The USCIS determines EB-1 eligibility. EB-1 visa holders are permitted to bring their immediate family members

EB-1 Extraordinary Ability visa (EB-1 visa)
A visa that allows U.S. employers to employ foreign nationals in the United States who possess exceptional qualifications for certain types of employment.

(i.e., spouse and unmarried children under age 21) to the United States as dependents. Persons who are granted EB-1 status may become U.S. citizens, usually in five years.

EB-5 Investor Visa

EB-5 Investor visa (EB-5 visa)
A visa that permits persons who invest a required amount of money in a commercial enterprise located in the United States, and who meet other established requirements, to immigrate to the United States.

The **EB-5 Investor visa**, or **EB-5 visa**, permits entrepreneurs who invest a required amount of money in a commercial enterprise in the United States and who meet other requirements to immigrate to the United States. To qualify, an investor must invest a minimum of $1.8 million in a U.S. business. The required investment is decreased to $900,000 for designated rural or high-unemployment areas. These amounts are adjusted for inflation every five years.

The entrepreneur's investment can be used to create a new business, purchase an existing business that will be reorganized into a new business, or expand an existing business by creating a 40 percent increase in its net worth or a 40 percent increase in the number of employees employed by the business. The investment must create or preserve the equivalent of 10 new full-time positions (excluding the investor and his or her immediate family) where each worker is employed for at least 35 hours per week.

An applicant for an investment visa must submit a business plan for the business, evidence of the funds that are to be invested in the business, and relevant financial and other documents to the USCIS. If an investor meets the qualifications for an EB-5 visa and is approved by the USCIS, the investor and dependents will be granted conditional residency in the United States. Within 90 days of the expiration of the two-year conditional period, the investor must file evidence with the USCIS to show that the necessary conditions have been met and therefore can be removed. If the conditions have been met, the investor and dependents will be granted lawful permanent residency in the United States.

H-2A Temporary Agricultural Worker Visa

WEB EXERCISE
The COVID-19 pandemic disrupted virtually every aspect of the U.S. immigration system. Go to **www.uscis.gov** and find out the current status for processing visa applications and the provision of other immigration services.

The **H-2A Temporary Agricultural Worker visa**, or **H-2A visa**, is a nonimmigrant visa that allows U.S. employers to employ foreign nationals to perform agricultural work. A foreign guest worker must be sponsored by a U.S. employer or an association of agricultural producers. The employer must demonstrate that there are not enough U.S. workers who are able, willing, qualified, and available to do the temporary or seasonal agricultural work. Initial employment can be for one year, which may be extended twice, each time for a one-year period. Dependents may accompany the foreign worker but cannot be employed in the United States. There is no annual cap on visas for H-2A workers.

H-2B Temporary Nonagricultural Worker Visa

The **H-2B Temporary Nonagricultural Worker visa**, or **H-2B visa**, is a nonimmigrant visa that allows U.S. employers to employ foreign nationals to perform nonagricultural work on a one-time, seasonal, peak-load, or intermittent basis. A foreign guest worker must be sponsored by a U.S. employer. Employers such as motels and restaurants and other businesses in seasonal markets (e.g., summer destinations, ski resorts) often use H-2B workers. The employer must establish that there are insufficient U.S. workers available to perform the temporary services or labor. Initial employment can be for one year, and may be extended twice, each time for a one-year period. Dependents may accompany the foreign worker but cannot be employed in the United States. There is an annual cap on H-2A visas.

Key Terms and Concepts

Administrative employee exemption (539)
At-will employee (532)
B-1 visa (544)
B-2 visa (544)
Child labor (537)
Computer employee exemption (540)
Consolidated Omnibus Budget Reconciliation Act (COBRA) (542)
Creative employee exemption (540)
EAP exemptions (white-collar exemptions) (539)
EB-1 Extraordinary Ability visa (EB-1 visa) (545)
EB-5 Investor visa (EB-5 visa) (546)
E-Verify (544)
Employee Retirement Income Security Act (ERISA) (542)
Employment-related injury (534)
Exclusive remedy (534)
Executive employee exemption (539)
Exempt employee (539)
F-1 visa (545)
F-2 visa (545)
Fair Labor Standards Act (FLSA) (537)
Family and Medical Leave Act (FMLA) (541)
Federal Insurance Contributions Act (FICA) (543)
Federal minimum wage (538)
Federal Unemployment Tax Act (FUTA) (542)
Foreign guest worker (545)
Form I-9, Employment Eligibility Verification (544)
General duty standard (536)
H-1B Foreign Guest Worker visa (H-1B visa) (545)
H-2A Temporary Agricultural Worker visa (H-2A visa) (546)
H-2B Temporary Nonagricultural Worker visa (H-2B visa) (546)
H-4 visa (545)
Highly compensated employee exemption (540)
Immigration Act of 1990 (543)
Immigration Reform and Control Act of 1986 (543)
Labor union exception (532)
Learned professional employee exemption (540)
Living wage laws (538)
Nonexempt employee (539)
Oath of Citizenship (544)
Occupational Safety and Health Act (535)
Occupational Safety and Health Administration (OSHA) (535)
Optional Practical Training (OPT) (545)
Outside sales representative exemption (540)
Overtime pay (538)
Public policy exception (532)
Self-Employment Contributions Act (543)
Social Security (543)
Social Security Administration (543)
Specific duty standards (536)
State minimum wage (538)
Statutory exception (532)
Teacher exemption (540)
Term employee (531)
U.S. Citizenship and Immigration Services (USCIS) (543)
U.S. Department of Labor (537)
Unemployment compensation (542)
Vesting (542)
Visa Waiver Program (VWP) (544)
Workers' compensation (533)
Workers' compensation acts (533)
Workers' compensation board (workers' compensation commission) (533)
Workers' compensation insurance (534)
Wrongful discharge (531)

Critical Legal Thinking Cases

31.1 At-Will Employment Jeremy Hoven was employed as a pharmacist by Walgreen Company (Walgreens). Hoven experienced an armed robbery at a Walgreens store during his first year of work. Hoven asked Walgreens to increase security systems, including adding a panic-button device, but Walgreens did not comply with his requests. Hoven subsequently obtained a permit to carry a concealed weapon, then purchased a handgun, which he brought to work, concealed in his pocket. During his fifth year of employment, two masked individuals with guns entered the store. One of the robbers pointed a gun at Hoven. Hoven backed away and fired his gun multiple times. No one was injured during the incident. Walgreens fired Hoven, asserting that he was an at-will employee that the company could fire at any time without cause. Hoven sued Walgreens, alleging that Walgreens violated public policy because it violated the "right to bear arms" language of the Second Amendment to the U.S. Constitution. Did Walgreens violate public policy when it terminated Hoven as an employee? *Hoven v. Walgreen Company*, 751 F.3d 778, 2014 U.S. App. Lexis 10146 (United States Court of Appeals for the Sixth Circuit, 2014)

31.2 Fair Labor Standards Act Integrity Staffing Solutions, Inc. (Integrity) provides warehouse staffing to **Amazon.com** throughout the United States. Integrity warehouse employees retrieve products from shelves and package those products for delivery to Amazon customers. Integrity requires its employees to undergo an after-work antitheft security screening before leaving the warehouse at the end of each day. During this screening, employees remove items such as wallets, keys, and belts from their persons and pass through metal detectors. This process takes about 25 minutes. Jesse Busk and Laurie Castro, who worked as hourly employees of Integrity in Nevada warehouses, brought a class action lawsuit alleging that Integrity violated the Fair Labor Standards Act (FLSA) by not paying workers for this time and therefore owed them pay for the time spent during the security screenings. Is the time spent waiting for and undergoing the security screenings compensable under the FLSA? *Integrity Staffing Solutions, Inc. v. Busk*, 135 S.Ct. 513, 2014 U.S. Lexis 8293 (Supreme Court of the United States, 2014)

31.3 **Overtime Pay** Congress enacted an exemption to the Fair Labor Standards Act (FLSA) overtime pay requirements that specifically applies to businesses engaged in selling vehicles or implements to consumers. The exemption provides that the FLSA overtime pay rules do not apply to "any salesman, partsman, or mechanic primarily engaged in selling or servicing automobiles, trucks, or farm implements, if he is employed by a nonmanufacturing establishment primarily engaged in the business of selling such vehicles or implements to ultimate purchasers."

Hector Navarro worked as a service advisor for Encino Motorcars, LLC (Encino) in a Mercedes-Benz dealership in California. Service advisors interact with customers and sell them services for their vehicles; suggest repair and maintenance services; follow up with customers as the services are performed; and explain the repair and maintenance work when customers return for their vehicles. Navarro and other service advisors sued Encino for back pay, alleging that Encino had violated the FLSA by failing to pay them overtime. Encino defended, asserting that service advisors are exempt from overtime pay. Are service advisors exempt employees for the purpose of overtime pay? *Encino Motorcars LLC v. Navarro*, 138 S.Ct. 1134 (Supreme Court of the United States, 2018)

31.4 **Workers' Compensation** Abigail Caudle was a 26-year-old apprentice electrician who worked for Raven Electric, Inc. (Raven). Raven was hired to complete the electrical work in remodeling a building in Anchorage, Alaska, where the electricians were to tear out old light fixtures. Raven did have temporary lights set up at the job site, so the light switches Caudle was working on were turned off, but no one had turned off the power at the electrical panel or otherwise disconnected power to the lights. Caudle began to remove the wire nuts from a light fixture and was electrocuted. Caudle was pronounced dead at the hospital less than an hour later.

Raven carried workers' compensation insurance. Because Caudle was unmarried and had no dependents at the time of her death, the Alaska Workers' Compensation Act limited Raven's liability to $10,000 in funeral expenses and the payment of $10,000. Marianne Burke, Caudle's nondependent mother, filed a workers' compensation claim seeking death benefits as a dependent, claiming that in the future she could have been dependent on her daughter. Is Burke entitled to workers' compensation death benefits for her daughter's death? *Burke v. Raven Electric, Inc.*, 420 P.3d 1196 (Supreme Court of Alaska, 2018)

Ethics Cases

31.5 **Ethics Case** Chad Kelley, an account manager with Coca-Cola Enterprises, Inc., attended a mandatory corporate kickoff event celebrating the release of a new Coca-Cola product. As part of a team-building event, all employees in attendance, including Kelley, were encouraged to canoe down a three-mile stretch of a river. Kelley and a coworker paddled on the river without incident. Thereafter, Kelley walked up an embankment to the parking lot and waited for a bus to arrive to take him back to his vehicle. While Kelley waited for the bus, a number of employees, including John Whitaker, who was in charge of the entire event, were seen splashing in the river, tipping canoes, and getting everyone wet. A short time later, Whitaker, who was soaking wet, and Marcus Hall, a Coca-Cola distribution manager, grabbed Kelley and tried to pull him down the embankment and into the river. When their efforts failed, Hall grabbed Kelley and slammed him to the ground, causing Kelley to injure his neck. As a result of the incident, Kelley was treated for a herniated disc and a cervical dorsal strain.

Kelley filed a claim for workers' compensation. Coca-Cola opposed the claim, asserting that because Kelley was involved in employee horseplay, he was not entitled to workers' compensation benefits. Is Kelley entitled to workers' compensation benefits? Did Coca-Cola act ethically in trying to avoid paying workers' compensation benefits?

Kelley v. Coca-Cola Enterprises, Inc., 2010 Ohio App. Lexis 1269 (Court of Appeals of Ohio, 2010)

31.6 **Ethics Case** R. Williams Construction Company (Williams) was constructing a sewer project at a building site. Williams had constructed a trench that was 10 to 12 feet deep, 13 feet wide at the top, and 45 feet long. An earthen slope at one end of the trench provided the only access to and egress from the bottom of the trench.

Groundwater seeped into the soil continuously. Williams used submersible pumps to remove the groundwater that seeped into the trench. Two of Williams's employees, Jose Aguiniga and Adam Palomar, were responsible for cleaning the pumps and did so throughout each working day, as needed.

On the day before the accident, a shoring system that supported the walls of the trench had been removed. On the day of the accident, Aguiniga and Palomar entered the unshored trench to clean the pumps and remained there for about 15 minutes. As the two men were exiting the trench, the north end wall collapsed, burying Aguiniga completely and Palomar almost completely. Aguiniga died, and Palomar was severely injured. The U.S. Occupational Safety and Health Administration (OSHA) conducted an investigation and cited Williams for violating OSHA trench safety standards by failing to ensure that no worker would have to travel more than 25 feet to reach a safe point of egress and for failing to ensure that the walls of the excavation were either sloped or supported. Did Williams violate the OSHA trench safety standards? Did Williams act ethically in denying liability? *R. Williams Construction Company v. Occupational Safety and Health Review Commission*, 464 F.3d 1060, 2006 U.S. App. Lexis 24646 (United States Court of Appeals for the Ninth Circuit, 2006)

Notes

1. 29 U.S.C. Sections 651–678.
2. For example, the Railway Safety Act and the Coal Mine Safety Act regulate workplace safety of railway workers and coal miners, respectively.
3. 29 U.S.C. Sections 201–206.
4. 29 U.S.C. Sections 2601, 2611–2619, 2651–2654.
5. 29 U.S.C. Sections 1161–1169.
6. 29 U.S.C. Sections 1001 et seq.
7. 26 U.S.C. Sections 3301–3310.
8. 26 U.S.C. Sections 3101–3125.
9. 26 U.S.C. Sections 1401–1403.
10. Public Law 101-649, 104 Stat. 4978.
11. 29 U.S.C. Section 1802.

CHAPTER

32 Labor Law

Henry R. Cheeseman

U.S. DEPARTMENT OF LABOR, WASHINGTON DC
The U.S. Department of Labor is a cabinet-level department of the federal government that is responsible for administering and enforcing a "bill of rights" for labor union members.

Learning Objectives

After studying this chapter, you should be able to:

32.1 List and describe federal labor law statutes.

32.2 Describe how a union is organized.

32.3 Describe the process of collective bargaining.

32.4 Describe union security agreements.

32.5 Define state right-to-work laws and describe how they work.

32.6 Describe employees' right to strike and when strikes are illegal.

32.7 Describe employees' right to picket and when picketing is illegal.

32.8 Explain how labor's bill of rights affects internal union affairs.

"Labor is superior to capital, and deserves much the higher consideration."

—Abraham Lincoln (1809–1865)
Sixteenth president of the United States

Introduction to Labor Law

Prior to the industrial revolution, employees and employers had somewhat equal bargaining power. Once the country became industrialized in the late 1800s, large corporate employers had much more bargaining power than their employees did. In response, beginning in the 1930s, federal legislation was enacted that gave employees the right to form and join labor unions.

Through collective bargaining with employers, labor unions obtained better working conditions, higher wages, and greater benefits for their members. Labor unions have the right to strike and to engage in picketing in support of their positions. However, there are some limits on these activities.

This chapter discusses labor law, organization of unions, collective bargaining, strikes and picketing, state right-to-work laws, and labor's bill of rights.

A truly American sentiment recognizes the dignity of labor and the fact that honor lies in honest toil.

Grover Cleveland
Twenty-second and twenty-fourth president of the United States
Letter accepting his nomination for president (1884)

Labor Law

32.1 List and describe federal labor law statutes.

The **American Federation of Labor (AFL)** was formed in 1886. Only skilled craft workers such as silversmiths and artisans were permitted to belong. In 1935, the **Congress of Industrial Organizations (CIO)** was formed. The CIO permitted semiskilled and unskilled workers to become members. In 1955, the AFL and CIO combined to form the **AFL-CIO**. Individual unions (e.g., United Auto Workers, United Steel Workers) may choose to belong to the AFL-CIO, but not all unions opt to join.

During the 1930s, federal statutes were enacted that gave workers certain rights and protections. Since then, these statutes have been amended and other statutes have been added that protect workers' rights to form and join labor unions and to bargain with employers for employment benefits and protections.

Today, approximately 11 percent of wage and salary workers in the United States belong to labor unions. Less than 6 percent of private-sector employees belong to unions.

Originally, labor unions were primarily formed by industrial workers, and these unions remain important today. For example, the International Brotherhood of Teamsters has more than 1.4 million members, the United Auto Workers has approximately 1 million members, the United Steel Workers of America and the International Brotherhood of Electrical Workers each have more than 700,000 members, and the Longshore and Warehouse Union has more than 400,000 members.

The fastest-growing private-sector union membership is in service occupations such as health care workers, hotel workers, hospitality workers, and so on. For example, the Services Employees International Union has more than 1.5 million members, and the American Nurses Association has more than 150,000 members. Professional baseball, basketball, football, and hockey players belong to labor unions.

Government workers form and join unions. More than 35 percent of public-sector employees belong to unions, including heavily unionized occupations such as teachers, police officers, and firefighters. The largest labor union in the United States is the National Education Association of the United States, with more than 2.7 million members. The American Federation of State, County, and Municipal Employees has more than 1.5 million members.

WEB EXERCISE
Visit the website of the International Brotherhood of Teamsters at **www.teamster.org**. What types of workers belong to this union? Read one of the news articles.

WEB EXERCISE
Visit the website of the Women's National Basketball Players Association (WNBPA) at **www.wnbpa.com** and read about the WNBPA's labor union.

National Labor Relations Act (NLRA) (Wagner Act)
A federal statute enacted in 1935 that establishes the right of employees to form and join labor organizations.

Labor unions were instrumental in forming political parties in many countries. The Labour Party of the United Kingdom and the Labour Party of Canada are examples. Although labor unions in the United States have not formed their own political party, they are influential in the politics of the country.

The following feature lists and describes major federal labor laws of the United States.

Landmark Law

Federal Labor Law Statutes

The major federal statutes that regulate the labor–management relationship are as follows:

- **Norris-LaGuardia Act.** Enacted in 1932, the **Norris-LaGuardia Act** stipulates that it is legal for employees to organize.[1]
- **National Labor Relations Act (NLRA).** The **National Labor Relations Act (NLRA)**, also known as the **Wagner Act**, was enacted in 1935.[2] The NLRA establishes the right of employees to form and join labor organizations, to bargain collectively with employers, and to engage in concerted activity to promote these rights.
- **Labor Management Relations Act.** In 1947, Congress enacted the **Labor Management Relations Act**, also known as the **Taft-Hartley Act.**[3] This act (1) expands the activities that labor unions can engage in, (2) gives employers the right to engage in free-speech efforts against unions prior to a union election, and (3) gives the president of the United States the right to seek an injunction (for up to 80 days) against a strike that would create a national emergency.
- **Labor Management Reporting and Disclosure Act.** In 1959, Congress enacted the **Labor Management Reporting and Disclosure Act**, also known as the **Landrum-Griffin Act.**[4] This act regulates internal union affairs and establishes the rights of union members.
- **Railway Labor Act.** The **Railway Labor Act** of 1926, as amended in 1934, covers employees of railroad and airline carriers.[5]

These federal statutes, rules and regulations adopted pursuant to these statutes, and court decisions interpreting and applying the statutes and their associated rules and regulations are collectively referred to as **labor law**.

National Labor Relations Board

National Labor Relations Board (NLRB)
A federal administrative agency that oversees union elections, prevents employers and unions from engaging in illegal and unfair labor practices, and enforces and interprets certain federal labor laws.

The National Labor Relations Act created the **National Labor Relations Board (NLRB)**. The NLRB is an administrative body composed of five members appointed by the president and approved by the Senate. The NLRB oversees union elections, prevents employers and unions from engaging in illegal and unfair labor practices, and enforces and interprets certain federal labor laws. The decisions of the NLRB are enforceable in court.

Organizing a Union

32.2 Describe how a union is organized.

Section 7 of the NLRA
A federal law that gives employees the right to form, join, and assist labor unions; to bargain collectively with employers; and to engage in concerted activity to promote these rights.

appropriate bargaining unit (bargaining unit)
A group of employees that a union is seeking to represent.

Section 7 of the NLRA gives employees the right to join or form a union. Section 7 provides that employees shall have the right to self-organize; to form, join, or assist labor organizations; to bargain collectively through representatives of their own choosing; and to engage in other concerted activities for collective bargaining or other mutual aid protection.

The group that a union is seeking to represent—which is called the **appropriate bargaining unit**, or **bargaining unit**—must be defined before the union can petition for an election. This group can be the employees of a single company or plant, a group within a single company (e.g., maintenance workers at all of a company's plants), or an entire industry (e.g., nurses at all hospitals in the country). Managers and professional employees may not belong to unions formed by employees whom they manage.

Types of Union Elections

To have a vote on whether to establish a union, union organizers attempt to obtain signatures of employees from the identified bargaining unit on *consent cards* indicating their interest in having an election on whether to establish a union. If the organizers get fewer than 30 percent of the employees to sign consent cards, a union election will not be held.

If at least 30 percent of the employees in a bargaining unit sign consent cards indicating that they are interested in joining or forming a union, the NLRB can be petitioned to investigate and to set an election date. In many of these situations, elections are contested by the employer. The NLRB is required to supervise all **contested elections**. A simple majority vote of employees (more than 50 percent) wins the election, and if this occurs, the union is certified. If 50 percent or fewer employees vote for the union, the union is not certified.

contested election
An election for a union that an employer's management contests. The NLRB must supervise this type of election.

Example If 51 of 100 employees vote for the union, the union is certified as the bargaining agent for all 100 employees.

If a majority of employees (more than 50 percent) sign the consent cards indicating their desire to form and join a union, the employer may agree not to contest the result and can recognize the union without a vote. In this case, the union is certified. If management still wants an election to be held, a **consent election** may be held without NLRB supervision. To certify the union, more than 50 percent of the employees must vote for establishing a union.

If employees no longer want to be represented by a union, a **decertification election** is held. Decertification elections must be supervised by the NLRB.

Union Solicitation on Company Property

If union solicitation is being conducted by employees, an employer may restrict solicitation activities to the employees' free time (e.g., coffee breaks, lunch breaks, before and after work). The activities may also be limited to nonworking areas, such as the cafeteria, restroom, or parking lot. Off-duty employees may be barred from union solicitation on company premises, and nonemployees (e.g., union management) may be prohibited from soliciting on behalf of the union anywhere on company property. Employers may dismiss employees who violate these rules.

WEB EXERCISE
Go to the website of the National Labor Relations Board (NLRB) at **www.nlrb.gov**. What is the stated purpose of the NLRB?

An exception to this rule applies if the location of the business and the living quarters of the employees place the employees beyond the reach of reasonable union efforts to communicate with them. This exception, called the **inaccessibility exception**, applies to logging camps, mining towns, company towns, and the like.

Illegal Interference with an Election

Section 8(a) of the NLRA makes it an **unfair labor practice** for an employer to interfere with, coerce, or restrain employees from exercising their statutory right to form and join unions. Examples of unfair labor practices by an employer include:

Section 8(a) of the NLRA
A law that makes it an unfair labor practice for an employer to interfere with, coerce, or restrain employees from exercising their statutory right to form and join unions.

- Threatening employees with loss of jobs or benefits if they join or vote for a union
- Threatening to close a plant if the employees select a union to represent them
- Threatening employees with loss of benefits if they support a union
- Questioning employees about their union sympathies or activities
- Promising benefits to employees to discourage their union support
- Assigning employees more difficult tasks or punishing them for engaging in union or protected concerted activity
- Transferring, laying off, or terminating employees for pro-union activities

An employer may not form a company union.

Section 8(b) of the NLRA A law that makes it an unfair labor practice for a labor union to interfere with, coerce, or threaten employees in exercising their statutory right to form and join unions.

Section 8(b) of the NLRA prohibits unions from engaging in unfair labor practices that interfere with lawful company business or a union election. Examples of unfair labor practices by a labor union include:

- Threatening employees that they will lose their jobs unless they support the union
- Seeking the suspension, discharge, or other punishment of an employee for not being a union member
- Refusing to process employee grievances because an employee has criticized union officials
- Fining employees who have validly resigned from a union
- Fining or punishing employees for crossing an unlawful picket line
- Engaging in picket line misconduct, such as threatening or assaulting non-strikers, or barring them from the employer's premises
- Striking over issues unrelated to employment terms and conditions
- Coercing neutral parties into a labor dispute

When an unfair labor practice of an employer or labor union has been discovered, the NLRB or the courts may issue a cease-and-desist order or an injunction to restrain unfair labor practices and may set aside the election and order a new election.

Collective Bargaining

32.3 Describe the process of collective bargaining.

collective bargaining The act of negotiating contract terms between an employer and the members of a union.

collective bargaining agreement A contract entered into by an employer and a union during a collective bargaining procedure.

compulsory subjects of collective bargaining Wages, hours, and other terms and conditions of employment.

Once a union has been elected, the employer and the union discuss the terms of employment of union members and try to negotiate a contract that embodies these terms. The act of negotiating is called **collective bargaining**, and the resulting contract is called a **collective bargaining agreement**. The employer and the union must negotiate with each other in good faith. Among other things, this prohibits making take-it-or-leave-it proposals.

The subjects of collective bargaining are classified as follows:

- **Compulsory subjects.** Wages, hours, and other terms and conditions of employment are **compulsory subjects** of collective bargaining.

  Examples Fringe benefits, health benefits, retirement plans, work assignments, safety rules, and the like.

- **Permissive subjects.** Subjects that are not compulsory or illegal are **permissive subjects** of collective bargaining. These subjects may be bargained for if the company and union agree to do so.

  Examples The size and composition of the supervisory force, location of plants, corporate reorganizations, and the like.

- **Illegal subjects.** Certain topics are **illegal subjects** of collective bargaining and therefore cannot be subjects of negotiation or agreement.

  Examples Permitting discrimination or recognizing closed shops.

Union Security Agreements

32.4 Describe union security agreements.

To obtain the greatest power possible, elected unions sometimes try to install a **union security agreement**. There are several types of security agreements often used in the private sector (in states without right-to-work laws):

union shop A workplace in which an employee must join the union within a certain number of days after being hired.

- **Union shop.** Under a **union shop** agreement, an employer may hire anyone, whether he or she belongs to a union or not. However, new employees must join the union within a certain time period (e.g., 30 days) after being hired.

Felix Lipov/Shutterstock

School
Approximately 35 percent of public-sector employees belong to unions, including heavily unionized occupations such as teachers, police officers, and firefighters.

Thus, employees of the bargaining unit have to become union members after being hired and must pay union dues as a condition of retaining employment. If an employee quits the union or does not pay the required dues, the employer must terminate the employee. Union shops are not permitted in states that have enacted right-to-work laws.

- **Agency shop.** Under an **agency shop** agreement, an employer may hire anyone, whether he or she belongs to a union or not. After employees are hired, they do not have to join the union. If the employee joins the union, then he or she pays union dues. If the employee does not join the union, he or she must pay an agency fee to the union. This fee includes an amount to help pay for the costs of collective bargaining. A nonunion employee cannot be assessed fees for non–collective bargaining union activities, such as political campaigning and the like. The agency fee prevents the free rider problem that would occur if an employee did not have to pay union dues or their equivalent but was the recipient of union collective bargaining activities. Agency shops are not permitted in states that have enacted right-to-work laws.

agency shop
A workplace in which an employee does not have to join the union but must pay an agency fee to the union.

On proper notification by the union, union and agency shop employers are required to deduct union dues and agency fees from employees' wages and forward these dues to the union. This is called **dues checkoff**.

Closed shop agreements are illegal in the United States. Under a **closed shop** agreement, an employer could only hire employees who were already members of the union. The employer could not hire employees who were not members of the union. Federal law makes closed shops illegal.

State Right-to-Work Laws

32.5 Define state right-to-work laws and describe how they work.

States can enact **right-to-work laws** either by constitutional amendment or by statute. If a state enacts a right-to-work law, individual employees cannot be forced to join a union or pay union dues and fees, even though a labor union has been elected by other employees. Thus, state right-to-work laws outlaw union and agency shops. A place of employment where a worker is not required to join or financially support a union is called an **open shop**.

right-to-work law
A law enacted by a state that stipulates that individual employees cannot be forced to join a union or pay union dues and fees even though a labor union has been elected to represent fellow employees.

open shop
A place of employment where a worker is not required to join or financially support a union.

Critical Legal Thinking Questions

What are the consequences for workers if a state adopts a right-to-work law? What are the consequences for employers?

Right-to-work laws have been points of contention. Many state governments and businesses support right-to-work laws to attract new businesses to a non-union environment. Unions usually vehemently oppose the enactment of right-to-work laws because they erode union power.

The following feature discusses right-to-work laws.

Business Environment

State Right-to-Work Laws

The following states have enacted right-to-work laws.

Arizona	Nevada
Arkansas	North Carolina
Florida	North Dakota
Georgia	Oklahoma
Idaho	South Carolina
Indiana	South Dakota
Iowa	Tennessee
Kansas	Texas
Kentucky	Utah
Louisiana	Virginia
Michigan	West Virginia
Mississippi	Wisconsin
Nebraska	Wyoming

State right-to-work laws do not prohibit the establishment of labor unions, but they do make it so employees do not have to join unions or pay union dues unless they have voluntarily joined the union. In right-to-work states, employees may terminate their union membership and become nonmembers.

Example The miners of a mining company vote to form a union. If the state has a right-to-work law, individual miners do not have to join the union nor pay agency fees. Only miners who voluntarily join the union must pay union dues. A miner who has voluntarily joined the union may terminate her union membership at any time.

In states with right-to-work laws, elected unions represent all employees of the bargaining unit—members and nonmembers—during collective bargaining, wage negotiations, and other matters. Nonmembers cannot personally negotiate pay or other employment issues. Unions also represent all employees of the bargaining unit, including nonmembers, in grievance procedures. Nonmembers may be required to pay a fee for this service.

The remedies for violation of right-to-work laws vary from state to state but usually include damages to persons injured by the violation, injunctive relief, and criminal penalties.

In states that do not have right-to-work laws, union and agency shops are permitted.

In the following case, the U.S. Supreme Court addressed whether an agency fee arrangement is lawful in the nonfederal government public sector.

CASE 32.1 *U.S. SUPREME COURT CASE Public-Sector Unions*

Janus v. American Federation of State, County, and Municipal Employees, Council 31

138 S.Ct. 2448 (2018)
Supreme Court of the United States

"The idea of public-sector unionization and agency fees would astound those who framed and ratified the Bill of Rights."

—Samuel Alito, Justice

Facts

Government employees of state and political subdivisions of Illinois are permitted to form unions. Most individuals of the bargaining unit join the union and pay union fees. However, individual employees of the bargaining unit are not obligated to join the union, but if they do not do so, they are assessed an agency fee that must be paid to the union. Nonmembers cannot be assessed a fee that will fund the union's political and ideological projects, but they do have to pay for lobbying, advertising, and other unspecified services. Here, the total chargeable amount for nonmember agency fees was 78 percent of full union dues.

Mark Janus is employed by the Illinois Department of Healthcare and Family Services as a child support specialist. He has not joined the public-sector union that represents his bargaining unit, but he is required to pay $535 in agency fees per year. Janus opposes many positions taken by the union that he does not think reflect the best interests of Illinois citizens. Janus sued the union, alleging that the compulsory payment of agency fees violates his right to free speech and association guaranteed by the First Amendment to the U.S. Constitution. The U.S. district court dismissed Janus's complaint, and the U.S. court of appeals affirmed. Janus appealed to the U.S. Supreme Court.

Issue

Do compulsory public-sector union agency fee arrangements violate the First Amendment to the Constitution?

Language of the U.S. Supreme Court

The First Amendment, made applicable to the States by the Fourteenth Amendment, forbids abridgement of the freedom of speech. We have held time and again that freedom of speech includes both the right to speak freely and the right to refrain from speaking at all. The right to eschew association for expressive purposes is likewise protected. Freedom of association presupposes a freedom not to associate. Forced associations that burden protected speech are impermissible.

The idea of public-sector unionization and agency fees would astound those who framed and ratified the Bill of Rights. It is hard to estimate how many billions of dollars have been taken from nonmembers and transferred to public-sector unions in violation of the First Amendment. Those unconstitutional exactions cannot be allowed to continue indefinitely. States and public-sector unions may no longer exact agency fees from nonconsenting employees.

Decision

The U.S. Supreme Court held that public-sector agency shop arrangements violate the First Amendment and are unconstitutional. Public-sector employees cannot be required to pay agency fees to a union. The Supreme Court reversed the decision of the U.S. court of appeals.

Note: The *Janus* case creates a right-to-work situation for state, county, and municipal government employees. Employees of a bargaining unit that has elected a union may voluntarily join the union and pay union dues, or become nonmembers and not have to pay union dues or agency fees.

Critical Legal Thinking Questions

Why was the First Amendment applied to this labor law case? Is the decision in this case applicable to private-sector unions? Why or why not? Does this decision create a free rider problem?

Federal Employees

Federal government employees have the right to organize and join labor unions. Federal workers and their union representatives are regulated by the **Civil Service Reform Act**[6] enacted in 1978. Under this act, federal government employees may voluntarily choose to join a union or choose not to join a union. Workers who join federal unions voluntarily pay membership dues, and nonmembers of the bargaining unit do not have to pay agency fees. This puts federal workers on par with workers in right-to-work states.

Federal employee unions may negotiate with respect to personnel matters, but they cannot bargain over wages, hours, and benefits. Federal workers cannot participate in a strike or picketing that would interfere with the operation of a federal agency. Only informational picketing is allowed while a worker is not on duty.

All that harms labor is treason to America.
Abraham Lincoln (1809–1865)
Sixteenth president of the United States

Example Air traffic controllers who went on strike lost their jobs and were replaced with other workers.

Strikes

32.6 Describe employees' right to strike and when strikes are illegal.

strike
A cessation of work by union members in order to obtain economic benefits or correct an unfair labor practice.

The NLRA gives union management the right to recommend that a union call a **strike** if a collective bargaining agreement cannot be reached. In a strike, union members refuse to work. Strikes are permitted by federal labor law. Before there can be a strike, a majority of the union's members must vote in favor of the action.

Cooling-Off Period

cooling-off period
A mandatory 60 days' notice before a strike can commence.

Before a strike, a union must give 60-day notice to the employer that the union intends to strike. It is illegal for a strike to begin during the mandatory 60-day **cooling-off period**. The 60-day period is designed to give the employer and the union enough time to negotiate a settlement of the union grievances and avoid a strike. Any strike without a proper 60-day notice is illegal, and the employer may dismiss the striking workers.

No-Strike Clause

no-strike clause
A clause in a collective bargaining agreement whereby a union agrees it will not strike during an agreed-on period of time.

An employer and a union can agree in a collective bargaining agreement that the union will not strike during a particular period of time. The employer gives economic benefits to the union and, in exchange, the union agrees that no strike will be called for the set time. It is illegal for a strike to take place in violation of a negotiated **no-strike clause**, and an employer may dismiss union members who strike in violation of a no-strike clause.

Illegal Strikes

Most strikes are lawful strikes. However, several types of strikes have been held to be illegal and are not protected by federal labor law. The following are **illegal strikes**:

- **Violent strikes.** In **violent strikes**, striking employees cause substantial damage to the property of the employer or a third party. Courts usually tolerate a certain amount of isolated violence before finding that an entire strike is illegal.
- **Sit-down strikes.** In **sit-down strikes**, striking employees continue to occupy the employer's premises. Such strikes are illegal because they deny the employer's statutory right to continue its operations during the strike.
- **Partial or intermittent strikes.** In **partial strikes**, or **intermittent strikes**, employees strike part of the day or workweek and work the other part. This type of strike is illegal because it interferes with the employer's right to operate its facilities at full capacity.
- **Wildcat strikes.** In **wildcat strikes**, individual union members go on strike without proper authorization from the union. The courts have recognized that a wildcat strike becomes lawful if it is quickly ratified by the union.

An employer can discharge workers who participated in illegal strikes, who then have no rights to reinstatement.

Crossover and Replacement Workers

Individual members of a union do not have to honor a strike. They may (1) choose not to strike or (2) return to work after joining the strikers for a time. Employees who choose either of these options are known as **crossover workers**.

Once a strike begins, the employer may continue operations by using management personnel and hiring **replacement workers** to take the place of the striking employees. Replacement workers can be hired on either a temporary or a permanent basis. If replacement workers are given permanent status, they do not have to be dismissed when the strike is over.

Employer Lockout

If an employer reasonably anticipates a strike by some of its employees, it may prevent those employees from entering the plant or premises. This is called an **employer lockout**.

employer lockout
An act of an employer to prevent employees from entering the work premises when the employer reasonably anticipates a strike.

Example The National Basketball Association (NBA) is a professional basketball league with teams located in Canada and the United States. The National Basketball Players Association, a labor union, represents the players. One year, after a collective bargaining agreement had expired and the owners and players could not reach an agreement, the NBA owners locked the players out. The team owners and the union eventually reached an agreement, but not before part of the season was canceled.

Picketing

32.7 Describe employees' right to picket and when picketing is illegal.

Striking union members often engage in **picketing** in support of their strike. Picketing usually takes the form of the striking employees and union representatives walking in front of the employer's premises, carrying signs that announce their strike, identify the issues, and criticize the employer. Picketing is used to put pressure on an employer to settle a strike. The right to picket is implied from the NLRA.

picketing
The action of strikers walking in front of an employer's premises, carrying signs announcing their strike.

Example Union members of a large grocery chain engage in a union-sanctioned strike over issues of pay and benefits. The union members can picket the employer. This may consist of the employees carrying signs bearing messages announcing the strike, identifying the issues, and criticizing the employer.

Picketing is lawful unless it (1) is accompanied by violence, (2) obstructs customers from entering the employer's place of business, (3) prevents nonstriking employees from entering the employer's premises, or (4) prevents pickups and deliveries at the employer's place of business. An employer may seek an injunction against unlawful picketing.

Example Union members picketing a large grocery store and blocking customers from entering the store are engaging in illegal picketing.

In the following case, the court examined the lawfulness of union picketing.

CASE 32.2 *FEDERAL COURT CASE Union Picketing*

Ahern, National Labor Relations Board v. International Longshore and Warehouse Union

721 F.3d 1122, 2013 U.S. App. Lexis 13652 (2013)
United States Court of Appeals for the Ninth Circuit

"The district court's awards sought to coerce the union and its members to comply with the court's injunctions and to compensate injured parties for actual losses caused by the union's and its members' contumacious conduct."

—Raner Collins, District Judge

Facts

Export Grain Terminal, LLC (EGT) was going to begin operating a grain terminal at Port Washington. The International Longshore and Warehouse Union represents dock workers on the West Coast of the United States. When EGT announced that it was going to hire non-union employees to operate the grain terminal, members of the union began picketing at EGT's terminal site.

The union's picketing and trespassing resulted in the destruction of EGT's property and the harassment of its employees and contractors, including but not limited to: breaking and stealing signs; tearing down gates; pushing railroad cars out of their rail sheds; verbally and physically assaulting EGT employees and contractors; impeding ingress and egress to and from the EGT facility; harassing and threatening bodily harm and/or death to EGT employees and other individuals who crossed the picket line; blocking the rail lines so that railroad cars were unable to make scheduled deliveries to EGT; damaging vehicles, including throwing eggs at, pushing, spitting on, and keying vehicles driven by EGT employees; following EGT employees and contractors as they left the facility; dropping black plastic bags filled with manure from an aircraft onto EGT property; and dropping nails on the roads leading to the entrances to the facility.

One night, several hundred people associated with the union picketed on the railroad tracks outside of the port and refused to allow a train to make a delivery to EGT's facility; the next day, more than 100 cars converged on EGT's facility, and picketers armed with garden shears, baseball bats, and metal pipes approached EGT's facility; picketers broke windows, threatened the on-duty security guards, and threw rocks at the guards; one security guard's car was driven into a drainage ditch; the picketers dumped a load of corn from a train onto the railroad tracks, cut the air hoses and broke the metal couplings that connected the train cars, knocked down a portion of the fence surrounding the EGT facility, and damaged the lights on the EGT conveyor system.

EGT filed charges with the National Labor Relations Board (NLRB). The NLRB petitioned the U.S. district court, which issued a temporary restraining order and then an injunction prohibiting the union from engaging in picket line violence, threats and property damage, mass picketing and blocking of ingress and egress at the EGT facility, and restraining or coercing employees of EGT or any other person doing business in relation to the EGT facility. The district court found the union in contempt and ordered the union to pay damages to EGT and the NLRB. The union appealed.

Issue

Did the union engage in unfair labor practices?

Language of the Court

Civil contempt proceedings serve two purposes: (1) coercing compliance with a court order; and (2) compensating the prevailing party. EGT therefore is entitled to compensation for its actual damages. The district court's awards sought to coerce the union and its members to comply with the court's injunctions and to compensate injured parties for actual losses caused by the union's and its members' contumacious conduct.

Decision

The U.S. court of appeals upheld the district court's injunctions and award of damages.

Critical Legal Thinking Questions

Why did the union and its members act with such hostility in this case? What consequences would a strike by the longshoreman's union have on the U.S. economy?

Secondary Boycott Picketing

secondary boycott picketing
A type of picketing in which a union tries to bring pressure against an employer by picketing the employer's suppliers or customers.

Unions sometimes try to bring pressure against an employer by picketing the employer's suppliers or customers. Such **secondary boycott picketing** is lawful only if it is product picketing (i.e., if the picketing is against the primary employer's product). The picketing is illegal if it is directed against the neutral employer instead of the struck employer's product.

Example Union members go on strike against their employer, a toy manufacturer. The union members picket retail stores that sell the manufacturer's toy products. They carry signs announcing their strike and request that consumers not buy toy products manufactured by their employer. This is lawful secondary boycott picketing.

Example Union members go on strike against their employer, a toy manufacturer. The union members picket retail stores that sell the manufacturer's toy products.

They carry signs requesting that consumers not shop at the retail stores. This is unlawful secondary boycott picketing.

Internal Union Affairs

32.8 Explain how labor's bill of rights affects internal union affairs.

A union may adopt **internal union rules** to regulate the operation of the union, acquire and maintain union membership, and the like. The undemocratic manner in which many unions were formulating these rules prompted Congress in 1959 to enact **Title I of the Landrum-Griffin Act**. Title I—often referred to as **labor's "bill of rights"**—gives each union member equal rights and privileges to nominate candidates for union office, to vote in elections, and to participate in membership meetings. It further guarantees union members the rights of free speech and assembly, provides for due process (notice and hearing), and permits union members to initiate judicial or administrative action.

A union may discipline members for participating in certain activities, including (1) walking off the job in a nonsanctioned strike, (2) working for wages below union scale, (3) spying for an employer, and (4) any other unauthorized activity that has an adverse economic impact on the union. A union may not punish a union member for participating in a civic duty, such as testifying in court against the union.

The following feature discusses a federal act that regulates the closing of plants by employers.

Title I of the Landrum-Griffin Act (labor's "bill of rights")
Labor's "bill of rights," which gives each union member equal rights and privileges to nominate candidates for union office, vote in elections, and participate in membership meetings.

Worker Adjustment and Retraining Notification Act (WARN Act) (Plant Closing Act)
A federal act that requires employers with 100 or more employees to give their employees 60 days' notice before engaging in certain plant closings or layoffs.

Business Environment

Worker Adjustment and Retraining Notification Act

In 1988, Congress enacted the **Worker Adjustment and Retraining Notification Act**, also called the **WARN Act or Plant Closing Act**.[7] The act requires employers with 100 or more employees to give their employees 60 days' notice before engaging in certain plant closings or layoffs. If employees are represented by a union, the notice must be given to the union; if they are not, the notice must be given to the employees individually. The act covers the following actions:

- **Plant closings.** A **plant closing** is a permanent or temporary shutdown of a single site that results in a loss of employment for 50 or more employees during any 30-day period.
- **Mass layoffs.** A **mass layoff** is a reduction of 33 percent of the employees or at least 50 employees during any 30-day period.

An employer is exempted from having to give such notice if:

- The closing or layoff is caused by business circumstances that were not reasonably foreseeable at the time that the notice would have been required.
- The business was actively seeking capital or business that, if obtained, would have avoided or postponed the shutdown and the employer believed in good faith that giving notice would have precluded it from obtaining the needed capital or business.

Key Terms and Concepts

AFL-CIO (551)
Agency shop (555)
American Federation of Labor (AFL) (551)
Appropriate bargaining unit (bargaining unit) (552)
Civil Service Reform Act (557)
Closed shop (555)
Collective bargaining (554)
Collective bargaining agreement (554)
Compulsory subjects (554)
Congress of Industrial Organizations (CIO) (551)
Consent election (553)
Contested election (553)
Cooling-off period (558)
Crossover worker (558)
Decertification election (553)
Dues checkoff (555)
Employer lockout (559)
Illegal strike (558)

Illegal subjects (554)
Inaccessibility exception (553)
Internal union rules (561)
Labor law (552)
Labor Management Relations Act (Taft-Hartley Act) (552)
Labor Management Reporting and Disclosure Act (Landrum-Griffin Act) (552)
Mass layoff (561)
National Labor Relations Act (NLRA) (Wagner Act) (552)
National Labor Relations Board (NLRB) (552)
No-strike clause (558)
Norris-LaGuardia Act (552)
Open shop (555)
Partial strike (intermittent strike) (558)
Permissive subjects (554)
Picketing (559)
Plant closing (561)
Railway Labor Act (552)
Replacement worker (558)
Right-to-work laws (555)
Secondary boycott picketing (560)
Section 7 of the NLRA (552)
Section 8(a) of the NLRA (553)
Section 8(b) of the NLRA (554)
Sit-down strike (558)
Strike (558)
Title I of the Landrum-Griffin Act (labor's "bill of rights") (561)
Unfair labor practice (553)
Union security agreement (554)
Union shop (554)
Violent strike (558)
Wildcat strike (558)
Worker Adjustment and Retraining Notification Act (WARN Act) (Plant Closing Act) (561)

Critical Legal Thinking Cases

32.1 Unfair Labor Practice Teamsters Union (Teamsters) began a campaign to organize the employees at a Sinclair Company (Sinclair) plant. When the president of Sinclair learned of the Teamsters' drive, he talked with all of his employees and emphasized the results of a long strike 13 years earlier that he claimed "almost put our company out of business," and he expressed worry that the employees were forgetting the "lessons of the past." He emphasized that Sinclair was on "thin ice" financially, that the Teamsters' "only weapon is to strike," and that a strike "could lead to the closing of the plant" because Sinclair had manufacturing facilities elsewhere. He also noted that because of the employees' ages and the limited usefulness of their skills, they might not be able to find reemployment if they lost their jobs. Finally, he sent literature to the employees stating that "the Teamsters Union is a strike happy outfit" and that they were under "hoodlum control," and included a cartoon showing the preparation of a grave for Sinclair and other headstones containing the names of other plants allegedly victimized by unions. The Teamsters lost the election 7 to 6 and then filed an unfair labor practice charge with the NLRB. Has Sinclair violated labor law? Who wins? *N.L.R.B. v. Gissel Packing Co.*, 395 U.S. 575, 89 S.Ct. 1918, 1969 U.S. Lexis 3172 (Supreme Court of the United States, 1969)

32.2 Right-to-Work Law Mobil Oil Corporation (Mobil) had its headquarters in Beaumont, Texas. It operated a fleet of eight oceangoing tankers that transported its petroleum products from Texas to ports on the East Coast. A typical trip on a tanker from Beaumont to New York took about five days. No more than 10 to 20 percent of the seamen's work time was spent in Texas. The 300 or so seamen who were employed to work on the tankers belonged to the Oil, Chemical & Atomic Workers International Union, AFL-CIO (Union), which had an agency shop agreement with Mobil. The state of Texas enacted a right-to-work law. Mobil sued Union, claiming that the agency shop agreement was unenforceable because it violated the Texas right-to-work law. Who wins? *Oil, Chemical & Atomic Workers International Union, AFL-CIO v. Mobil Oil Corp.*, 426 U.S. 407, 96 S.Ct. 2140, 1976 U.S. Lexis 106 (Supreme Court of the United States, 1976)

32.3 Unfair Labor Practice Frouge Corporation (Frouge) was the general contractor on a housing project in Philadelphia. The carpenter employees of Frouge were represented by the Carpenters' International Union (Union). Traditional jobs of carpenters included taking blank wooden doors and mortising them for doorknobs, routing them for hinges, and beveling them to fit between the doorjambs. Union had entered into a collective bargaining agreement with Frouge that provided that no member of Union would handle any doors that had been fitted prior to being furnished to the job site. The housing project called for 3,600 doors. Frouge contracted for the purchase of premachined doors that were already mortised, routed, and beveled. When Union ordered its members not to hang the prefabricated doors, the National Woodwork Manufacturers Association filed an unfair labor practice charge against Union with the NLRB. Is Union's refusal to hang prefabricated doors lawful? *National Woodwork Manufacturers Association v. N.L.R.B.*, 386 U.S. 612, 87 S.Ct. 1250, 1967 U.S. Lexis 2858 (Supreme Court of the United States, 1967)

32.4 Illegal Strike The employees of the Shop Rite Foods, Inc. (Shop Rite) warehouse in Lubbock, Texas, elected the United Packinghouse, Food and Allied Workers (Union) as its bargaining agent. Negotiations for a collective bargaining agreement began. Three months later, when an agreement had not yet been reached, Shop Rite found excessive amounts of damage to merchandise in its warehouse and concluded that it was being intentionally caused by dissident employees as a pressure tactic to secure concessions from Shop Rite. Shop Rite notified the Union representative that employees caught doing such acts would be terminated; the Union representative in turn notified the employees.

A Shop Rite manager observed an employee in the flour section—where he had no business being—making quick motions with his hands. The manager found several bags of flour that had been cut. The employee was immediately fired. Another employee (a fellow Union member) led about 30 other employees in an immediate walkout. The company discharged these employees and refused to rehire them. The employees filed a grievance with the NLRB. Can they get their jobs back? *N.L.R.B. v. Shop Rite Foods, Inc.*, 430 F.2d 786, 1970 U.S. App. Lexis 7613 (United States Court of Appeals for the Fifth Circuit, 1970)

32.5 Replacement Workers The union (Union) member-employees of the Erie Resistor Company (Company) struck Company over the terms of a new collective bargaining agreement that was being negotiated between Company and Union. Company continued production operations during the strike by hiring new workers and crossover union members who were persuaded to abandon the strike and come back to work. Company promised all replacement workers super seniority. This would take the form of adding 20 years to the length of a worker's actual service for the purpose of future layoffs and recalls. Many union members accepted the offer. Union filed an unfair labor practice charge with the NLRB. Is Company's offer of the super seniority lawful? *N.L.R.B. v. Erie Resistor Co.*, 373 U.S. 221, 83 S.Ct. 1139, 1963 U.S. Lexis 2492 (Supreme Court of the United States, 1963)

32.6 Union Shop Agreement Screen Actors Guild (SAG) is a labor union that represents performers in the entertainment industry. Lakeside Productions (Lakeside), an entertainment production company, signed a collective bargaining agreement with SAG, making SAG the exclusive union for performers that Lakeside hired for its productions. The collective bargaining agreement contained a union shop security clause, which provided that any performer who worked for Lakeside must be a member of SAG. Under the union shop agreement, an employee must become a member of the union after being employed, and the employer must terminate an employee if she does not become a union member during this period. The state did not have a right-to-work law.

Naomi Marquez, a part-time actor, auditioned for a one-line role in a TV episode to be filmed by Lakeside, and she won the part. When Marquez did not pay the $500 membership fee to SAG, Lakeside hired another actor for the part. Marquez sued SAG and Lakeside, alleging that the union shop security clause was unlawful. Does the union shop security clause negotiated between Lakeside Productions and SAG violate federal labor law? *Marquez v. Screen Actors Guild, Inc.*, 525 U.S. 33, 119 S.Ct. 292, 1998 U.S. Lexis 7110 (Supreme Court of the United States, 1998)

Ethics Case

32.7 Ethics Case American Ship Building Company (American) operated a shipyard in Chicago, Illinois, where it repaired Great Lakes ships during the winter months, when freezing on the Great Lakes rendered shipping impossible. The workers at the shipyard were represented by several labor unions. The unions notified American of their intention to seek modification of the current collective bargaining agreement when it expired three months later. On five previous occasions, agreements had been preceded by strikes (including illegal strikes) that were called just after the ships had arrived in the shipyard for repairs so that the unions increased their leverage in negotiations with the company.

Based on this history, American displayed anxiety as to the unions' strike plans and possible work stoppage. On the day that the collective bargaining agreement expired, after extensive negotiations, American and the unions reached an impasse in their collective bargaining. American decided to lay off most of the workers at the shipyard. It sent them the following notice: "Because of the labor dispute which has been unresolved, you are laid off until further notice." The unions filed unfair labor practice charges with the NLRB. Did American act ethically in locking out the employees? Are American's actions legal? *American Ship Building Company v. N.L.R.B.*, 380 U.S. 300, 85 S.Ct. 955, 1965 U.S. Lexis 2310 (Supreme Court of the United States, 1965)

Notes

1. 29 U.S.C. Sections 101–110, 113–115.
2. 29 U.S.C. Sections 151–169.
3. 29 U.S.C. Section 141 et seq.
4. 29 U.S.C. Section 401 et seq.
5. 45 U.S.C. Sections 151–162, 181–188.
6. Public Law 95-454.
7. 29 U.S.C. Section 2102.

CHAPTER 33

Equal Opportunity in Employment

U.S. CAPITOL, WASHINGTON DC
The U.S. Congress has enacted important laws that protect individuals from discrimination in the workplace and in other areas of society.

Tonobalaguer/123RF

Learning Objectives

After studying this chapter, you should be able to:

33.1 Describe the functions of the Equal Employment Opportunity Commission.

33.2 Describe the scope of coverage of Title VII of the Civil Rights Act of 1964.

33.3 Identify race and color discrimination that violates Title VII.

33.4 Identify national origin discrimination that violates Title VII.

33.5 Define *gender discrimination* and describe the scope of protection against gender discrimination.

33.6 Describe how members of the LGBTQ+ community are protected from job discrimination.

33.7 Describe racial, sexual, and other forms of harassment.

33.8 Describe an employer's duty to make reasonable accommodation for employees' religions.

33.9 List and describe defenses that may be raised by an employer against a charge of violating Title VII.

33.10 Describe the scope of coverage of the Equal Pay Act.

33.11 Describe the scope of coverage of the Age Discrimination in Employment Act.

33.12 Describe the protections afforded by the Americans with Disabilities Act.

33.13 Define *genetic information discrimination.*

33.14 Explain the protections afforded employees from employer retaliation.

33.15 Describe employment protections for veterans and military personnel.

33.16 Define *affirmative action* in employment.

> *"What people have always sought is equality of rights before the law. For rights that were not open to all equally would not be rights."*
>
> — *Cicero (106 BCE–43 BCE)*
> *De Officilis, Book II, Chapter XII*

Introduction to Equal Opportunity in Employment

Under common law, employers could terminate an employee at any time and for any reason. In this same vein, employers were free to hire and promote anyone they chose, without violating the law. This situation often created unreasonable hardship on employees and erected employment barriers to certain minority classes.

Starting in the 1960s, Congress began enacting a comprehensive set of federal laws that eliminated major forms of **employment discrimination**. These laws, which were passed to guarantee **equal opportunity in employment** to all employees and job applicants, have been broadly interpreted by the federal courts, particularly the U.S. Supreme Court. States have also enacted antidiscrimination laws. Many state and local governments have adopted laws that prevent discrimination in employment.

This chapter discusses equal opportunity in employment laws.

equal opportunity in employment
The rights of all employees and job applicants (1) to be treated without discrimination and (2) to be able to sue employers if they are discriminated against.

Equal Employment Opportunity Commission

33.1 Describe the functions of the Equal Employment Opportunity Commission.

The **Equal Employment Opportunity Commission (EEOC)** is the federal agency responsible for enforcing most federal antidiscrimination laws. The members of the EEOC are appointed by the U.S. president. The EEOC is empowered to conduct investigations, interpret the statutes, encourage conciliation between employees and employers, and bring suits to enforce the law. The EEOC can also seek injunctive relief.

The EEOC has jurisdiction to investigate charges of **discrimination** based on race, color, national origin, gender, religion, age, disability, and genetic information.

Equal Employment Opportunity Commission (EEOC)
The federal administrative agency that is responsible for enforcing most federal antidiscrimination laws.

Complaint Process

If a person believes that he or she has been discriminated against in the workplace, he or she cannot immediately file a lawsuit against the employer. The complainant must first file a complaint with the EEOC. The EEOC often requests that the parties try to resolve their dispute through mediation. If mediation does not work, the EEOC will investigate the charge. If the EEOC finds a violation, it will decide whether to sue the employer. If the EEOC sues the employer, the complainant cannot sue the employer. In this case, the EEOC represents the complainant. If the EEOC finds a violation and chooses not to bring suit or does not find a violation, the EEOC will issue a **right to sue letter** to the complainant. This gives the complainant the right to sue the employer.

WEB EXERCISE
Go to **www.eeoc.gov/field/index.cfm**. Find the location and address of the EEOC field office that serves your area.

right to sue letter
A letter issued by the EEOC if it chooses not to bring an action against an employer that authorizes a complainant to sue the employer for employment discrimination.

If a state has a **Fair Employment Practices Agency (FEPA)**, the complainant may file a claim with the FEPA instead of the EEOC. Often a complainant will file a complaint with a FEPA if state law provides protection from discrimination not covered by federal laws or if the FEPA's procedure permits a filing date that is longer than that of the EEOC. The FEPA complaint process is similar to that of the EEOC.

Lilly Ledbetter Fair Pay Act of 2009

The Civil Rights Act provides that a rejected applicant for a job or an employee who suffers pay discrimination must file a discrimination lawsuit within 180 days of the employer's act that causes the discrimination.

Lilly Ledbetter Fair Pay Act
A federal statute that permits a complainant to file an employment discrimination claim against an employer within 180 days of the most recent paycheck violation and to recover back pay for up to two years preceding the filing of the claim if similar violations occurred during the two-year period.

The **Lilly Ledbetter Fair Pay Act**[1], a federal statute enacted in 2009, provides that each discriminatory pay decision restarts the statutory 180-day clock. Thus, a plaintiff can file a claim against an employer within 180 days of the most recent paycheck violation. The act provides that a court can award back pay for up to two years preceding the filing of the claim if similar violations occurred during the prior two-year period. The act applies to female and male plaintiffs.

Example A female is hired by an employer as an employee. During a 36-month period, the employer engages in pay act violations and underpays the female employee each pay period. In this example, the female employee has 180 days from the date of the last paycheck violation to file her claim. If she files the claim and the employer is found to have violated the law during the three-year period, the female employee can recover back pay for the two years preceding the date of the last paycheck violation.

Title VII of the Civil Rights Act of 1964

33.2 Describe the scope of coverage of Title VII of the Civil Rights Act of 1964.

Prior to the passage of major federal antidiscrimination laws in the 1960s, much discrimination existed in this country. In the 1960s, Congress enacted several major federal statutes that outlawed discrimination against various members of society.

Congress enacted the **Civil Rights Act of 1964**[2], a historical and sweeping civil rights law that prohibits discrimination based on race, color, national origin, sex, and religion in public accommodations (e.g., motels, hotels, restaurants, theaters) by state and municipal government public facilities, by government agencies that receive federal funds, and by employers.

Title VII of the Civil Rights Act of 1964
A title of a federal statute enacted to eliminate job discrimination based on five protected classes: *race, color, religion, sex*, and *national origin*.

One of the major provisions of the Civil Rights Act of 1964 is *Title VII*, which governs the employment relationship. Title VII of the Civil Rights Act of 1964 is discussed in the following feature.

Landmark Law

Title VII of the Civil Rights Act of 1964

Title VII of the Civil Rights Act of 1964 makes illegal job discrimination based on the following five protected classes: race, color, religion, sex, and national origin.[3] Section 703(a)(2) of Title VII, as amended, provides, in pertinent part, the following:

It shall be an unlawful employment practice for an employer

(1) to fail or refuse to hire or to discharge any individual, or otherwise to discriminate against any individual with respect to his compensation, terms, conditions, or privileges of employment, because of such individual's race, color, religion, sex, or national origin; or

(2) to limit, segregate, or classify his employees or applicants for employment in any way which would deprive or tend to deprive any individual of employment opportunities or otherwise adversely affect his status as an employee, because of such individual's race, color, religion, sex, or national origin.

Scope of Coverage of Title VII

Title VII of the Civil Rights Act of 1964 applies to (1) employers with 15 or more employees, (2) all employment agencies, (3) labor unions with 15 or more members, (4) state and local governments and their agencies, and (5) most federal government employers. Native American tribes and tax-exempt private clubs are expressly excluded from coverage. Other portions of the Civil Rights Act of 1964 prohibit discrimination in housing, education, and other facets of life.

Title VII prohibits discrimination in hiring; decisions regarding promotion or demotion; payment of compensation and fringe benefits; availability of job training and apprenticeship opportunities; referral systems for employment; decisions regarding dismissal; work rules; and any other "term, condition, or privilege" of employment. Any employee of a covered employer, including undocumented immigrants, may bring actions for employment discrimination under Title VII.

U.S. citizens employed by U.S.-controlled companies in foreign countries are covered by Title VII. Foreign nationals employed in foreign countries by U.S.-controlled companies are not covered by Title VII.

Title VII prohibits two major forms of employment discrimination: *disparate-treatment discrimination* and *disparate-impact discrimination*. These are discussed in the following paragraphs.

Disparate-Treatment Discrimination

Disparate-treatment discrimination occurs when an employer treats a specific *individual* less favorably than others because of that person's race, color, national origin, sex, or religion. In these situations, complainants must prove that (1) they are a member of a Title VII protected class, (2) they applied for and were qualified for the employment position, (3) they were rejected despite this, and (4) the employer kept the position open and sought applications from persons with the complainant's qualifications.

disparate-treatment discrimination
A form of discrimination that occurs when an employer discriminates against a specific individual because of his or her race, color, national origin, sex, or religion.

Example A member of a minority race applies for a promotion to a position advertised as available at his company. The minority applicant, who is qualified for the position, is rejected by the company, which hires a nonminority applicant for the position. The minority applicant sues under Title VII. He has a *prima facie* case of illegal discrimination. The burden of proof shifts to the employer to prove a nondiscriminatory reason for its decision. If the employer offers a reason, such as saying that the minority applicant lacked sufficient experience, the burden shifts back to the minority applicant to prove that this was just a *pretext* (i.e., not the real reason) for the employer's decision.

Disparate-Impact Discrimination

Disparate-impact discrimination occurs when an employer discriminates against an entire protected *class*. Many disparate-impact cases are brought as class action lawsuits. This type of discrimination is often proven through statistical data about an employer's employment practices. The plaintiff must demonstrate a *causal link* between the challenged practice and the statistical imbalance. Showing a statistical disparity between the percentages of protected class employees and the percentage of the population that the protected class makes within the surrounding community is not enough, by itself, to prove discrimination. Disparate-impact discrimination can occur when an employer adopts a work rule that is neutral on its face but is shown to cause an adverse impact on a protected class.

disparate-impact discrimination
A form of discrimination that occurs when an employer discriminates against an entire protected class. An example is discrimination in which a racially neutral employment practice or rule causes an adverse impact on a protected class.

Example If an employer has a rule that all applicants for an executive position must be at least 5 feet 8 inches tall, this looks like a neutral rule because it applies to both men and women. However, because this rule is unrelated to the performance of an executive position and eliminates many more women than men from being hired or promoted to an executive position, it is disparate-impact sex discrimination, in violation of Title VII.

Remedies for Violations of Title VII

A successful plaintiff in a Title VII action can recover back pay and reasonable attorney's fees. The courts also have broad authority to grant equitable remedies. For instance, the courts can order reinstatement, grant fictional seniority, and issue injunctions to compel the hiring or promotion of protected minorities.

A court can award compensatory and **punitive damages** against an employer in a case involving an employer's malice or reckless indifference to federally protected rights. The sum of compensatory and punitive damages is capped at different amounts of money, depending on the size of the employer.

Title VII imposes liability on employers. Courts have routinely refused to hold individual employees liable under Title VII or other federal antidiscrimination laws.

Race and Color Discrimination

33.3 Identify race and color discrimination that violates Title VII.

A smile or a tear has not nationality; joy and sorrow speak alike to all nations, and they, above all the confusion of tongues, proclaim the brotherhood of man.
Frederick Douglass (1818–1895)

Title VII of the Civil Rights Act of 1964 was enacted primarily to prohibit employment discrimination based on a person's *race* and *color*. Title VII provides equal opportunity in employment for minority job applicants and minority employees seeking promotion.

Race Discrimination

The EEOC recognizes the following racial classifications.

Racial Group	Description
African American	A person having origins in any of the Black racial groups of Africa.
Asian	A person having origins in any of the original peoples of the Far East, Southeast Asia, or the Indian subcontinent.
Caucasian	A person having origins in any of the original peoples of Europe, the Middle East, and North Africa.
Native American	A person having origins in any of the original peoples of North, South, or Central America.
Pacific Islander	A person having origins in any of the original peoples of Hawaii and the Pacific Islands.

race discrimination
Employment discrimination against a person because of his or her race.

Race discrimination in employment violates Title VII.

Example National Corporation has a job opening for its chief executive officer position. The employer receives applications for this position from many persons, including Darin Thomas, who is an African American. Thomas is the best-qualified applicant for the job. If National Corporation does not hire Thomas because of his race, the company has engaged in race discrimination, in violation of Title VII. This would be disparate-treatment discrimination.

Example If an employer refuses to hire or promote all persons of a racial class, then the company has engaged in employment discrimination in violation of Title VII. This would be disparate-impact discrimination.

Color Discrimination

Color refers to the color or complexion of a person's skin. Discrimination by an employer based on color violates Title VII. **Color discrimination** cases are not brought as often as cases involving other forms of discrimination.

color discrimination
Employment discrimination against a person because of his or her color; for example, a light-skinned person of a race discriminates against a dark-skinned person of the same race.

Example If a light-skinned member of a race refuses to hire a dark-skinned member of the same race, this constitutes color discrimination, in violation of Title VII.

Unlawful discrimination occurs if an employer treats a person unfavorably because he or she is married to or associates with a person of a certain race or color, or because of a person's connection with a race-based organization or group.

Example An employer violates Title VII if it discriminates against job applicants or employees who belong to the National Association for the Advancement of Colored People (NAACP).

The following feature discusses the Civil Rights Act of 1866.

Landmark Law

Civil Rights Act of 1866

The **Civil Rights Act of 1866** was enacted after the Civil War. **Section 1981** of this act states that all persons "have the same right . . . to make and enforce contracts . . . as is enjoyed by white persons."[4] This law was enacted to give African Americans, just freed from slavery, the same right to contract as whites. Section 1981 expressly prohibits racial discrimination; it has also been held to forbid discrimination based on national origin.

Employment decisions are covered by Section 1981 because the employment relationship is contractual. Although most racial and national origin employment discrimination cases are brought under Title VII, a complainant might bring an action under Section 1981 for two reasons: (1) A private plaintiff can bring an action without going through the procedural requirements of Title VII, and (2) there is no cap on the recovery of compensatory or punitive damages under Section 1981.

National Origin Discrimination

33.4 Identify national origin discrimination that violates Title VII.

Civil Rights Act of 1866
A federal statute enacted after the Civil War that states that all persons "have the same right . . . to make and enforce contracts . . . as is enjoyed by white persons." This act prohibits race and national origin discrimination.

Title VII of the Civil Rights Act of 1964 prohibits employment discrimination based on *national origin*. **National origin** refers to the place of origin of a person's ancestors; physical, linguistic, or cultural characteristics; or heritage. **National origin discrimination** includes discrimination against employees or job applicants of a nationality (e.g., persons of Irish descent), against persons who come from a country (e.g., Iran), against persons of a certain culture (e.g., Hispanics), or against persons because of their accent. Discrimination by an employer based on a person's national origin or heritage violates Title VII.

national origin discrimination
Employment discrimination against a person because of his or her heritage, cultural characteristics, or the country of the person's ancestors.

Example National Corporation has a position for chief operations officer open. Several persons from within the company apply for a promotion to this position. Naseem al-Gharsi, one of the applicants, whose national origin is Yemen, has a Ph.D. in information sciences and 10 years' work experience and has been with the company for five years in the capacity of operations manager. Although al-Gharsi is the best-qualified person for the position, al-Gharsi is not promoted because of his Arabic heritage, and a less-qualified person is promoted. The company has engaged in national origin discrimination, in violation of Title VII.

There is a great difference between nationality and race. Nationality is the miracle of political independence. Race is the principle of physical analogy.

Benjamin Disraeli (1804–1881)

National origin discrimination occurs if an employer treats a person unfavorably because they are married to or associate with a person of a certain national origin.

An employer may not base an employment decision on an employee's foreign accent unless the accent seriously interferes with the employee's job performance.

Gender Discrimination

33.5 Define *gender discrimination* and describe the scope of protection against gender discrimination.

Title VII of the Civil Rights Act of 1964 prohibits job discrimination based on gender. The act, as amended, plus the EEOC's rules and court decisions, prohibits employment discrimination based on *gender, pregnancy*, and *sexual orientation*. In addition, *sexual harassment* is also prohibited.

Gender Discrimination

sex discrimination (gender discrimination)
Discrimination against a person because of his or her gender.

Title VII prohibits employment discrimination based on gender. **Sex discrimination**, also known as **gender discrimination**, occurs when an employer treats a job applicant or employee unfavorably because of that person's sex. Although the prohibition against sex discrimination applies equally to men and women, the majority of Title VII sex discrimination cases are brought by women. Approximately 80 percent of sexual discrimination claims are filed by women and 20 percent are filed by men.

Sex discrimination in violation of Title VII occurs when an employer engages in **direct sex discrimination**.

Example An employer refuses to hire a qualified job applicant or to promote a qualified employee because of his or her gender.

Title VII also prohibits any form of gender discrimination in which sexual favors are requested to obtain a job or be promoted. This is called **quid pro quo sex discrimination**.

Example A manager refuses to promote a woman unless she engages in sexual activities with him.

Sex-plus discrimination occurs when an employer does not discriminate against a class as a whole but treats a subset of the class differently. Courts have held that sex-plus discrimination violates Title VII of the Civil Rights Act of 1964.

Example An employer does not discriminate against women in general but does discriminate against married women or women with children.

Sex discrimination can also involve treating someone less favorably because of his or her connection with an organization or group that is generally associated with people of a certain sex.

Example An employer violates Title VII if it discriminates against female job applicants or employees who belong to the National Organization for Women (NOW).

Pregnancy Discrimination Act

Pregnancy Discrimination Act
A federal act that forbids employment discrimination because of pregnancy, childbirth, or related medical conditions.

In 1978, the **Pregnancy Discrimination Act** was enacted as an amendment to Title VII.[5] The act forbids employment discrimination against a female job applicant or employee because of her pregnancy, childbirth, or a medical condition related to pregnancy or childbirth.

Example Susan, a 30-year-old college graduate, goes on a job interview for an open position at a company. The interviewer asks Susan if she plans on having children, if that would affect her ability to come to work every day or to perform her duties, and if it would affect her ability to travel on company business. The company

Andrea Izzotti/123RF

U.S. SUPREME COURT, WASHINGTON DC

The U.S. Supreme Court has decided many major cases concerning rights and safeguards provided by federal equal opportunity in employment statutes.

refuses to hire Susan because she is a woman who might have children. This is a violation of the Pregnancy Discrimination Act.

It is unlawful to harass a woman because of her pregnancy, childbirth, or a medical condition related to pregnancy or childbirth when the harassment is so severe that it creates a hostile work environment.

Sexual Orientation and Gender Identity Discrimination

33.6 Describe how members of the LGBTQ+ community are protected from job discrimination.

Sexual orientation refers to an individual's romantic or sexual attraction to persons of the opposite sex or gender, the same sex or gender, or both sexes or more than one gender, or the person's lack of sexual attraction to others. A heterosexual is a person who is sexually attracted to persons of the opposite sex. The term *lesbian* often refers to a woman who is romantically, sexually, or emotionally attracted to women. The term *gay* often refers to a man who is romantically, physically, or emotionally attracted to men. The term *bisexual* often refers to a person who is romantically, physically, or emotionally attracted to both men and women.

Gender identity generally refers to an individual's internal sense of being a man, a woman, neither, or both. It focuses on one's behavior, expression, self-image, appearance, dress, speech patterns, and preferences. The term *transgender* identifies individuals whose gender identity or gender expression differs from what is typically associated with the sex they were assigned at birth.

The commonly used initialism **LGBTQ** stands for **lesbian, gay, bisexual, transgender, and queer or questioning**. The letter *Q* in LGBTQ often refers to the term *queer*, which is used by some individuals who consider other

sexual orientation (sexual identity)
Refers to an individual's romantic or sexual attraction to persons of the opposite sex or gender, the same sex or gender, or both sexes or more than one gender, or the person's lack of sexual attraction to others.

gender identity
Refers to an individual's internal sense of being a man, a woman, neither, or both.

LGBTQ
Commonly used initialism that stands for lesbian, gay, bisexual, transgender, and queer or questioning. The term *LGBTQ* generally refers to an individual's sexual orientation or gender identity.

LGBTQ+
An initialism often used to ensure inclusion of the entire spectrum of sexual orientation and gender identity.

sexual orientation discrimination
Employment discrimination based on a person's sexual orientation.

gender identity discrimination
Employment discrimination based on a person's gender identity.

terms too restrictive, and by other individuals who are questioning their sexuality and gender identity. The initialism **LGBTQ+** is often used to ensure inclusion of the entire spectrum of sexual orientation and gender identity. There are many other terms that identify persons who do not align with dominant concepts of gender.

Employment discrimination based on a person's sexual orientation is called **sexual orientation discrimination**. Employment discrimination based on a person's gender identity is called **gender identity discrimination**.

The following U.S. Supreme Court decision addresses whether Title VII prohibits employment discrimination against gay and transgender person.

CASE 33.1 *U.S. SUPREME COURT CASE Gay and Transgender Discrimination*

Bostock v. Clayton County, Georgia

140 S.Ct. 1731, 2020 U.S. Lexis 3252 (2020)
Supreme Court of the United States

"An individual's homosexuality or transgender status is not relevant to employment decisions."
—Neil Gorsuch, Justice

Facts

The U.S. Supreme Court consolidated three cases that started in the same way: an employer fired a long-time employee shortly after the employee revealed that he or she is gay or transgender—and allegedly for no reason other than the employee's sexuality or transgender status. Each employee brought suit under Title VII alleging unlawful discrimination on the basis of sex. The three cases are:

- Gerald Bostock was fired by Clayton County, Georgia after a decade of employment when his employer was notified that he participated in a gay recreational softball league. The Eleventh Circuit held that Title VII does not prohibit employers from firing employees for being gay.
- Donald Zada was fired by Altitude Express after working several seasons as a skydiving instructor because he mentioned that he was gay. The Second Circuit concluded that sexual orientation discrimination violates Title VII.
- Aimee Stephens, after first presenting herself as a male and working for R. G. & G. R. Harris Funeral Homes for six years, was fired when she notified her employer that she was transgender and planned to live and work as a woman. The Sixth Circuit held that Title VII bars employers from firing employees because of their transgender status.

The U.S. Supreme Court granted certiorari to resolve the disagreement among courts of appeals over the scope of Title VII's protections for gay and transgender persons.

Issue

Does Title VII prohibit employment discrimination against gay and transgender individuals?

Language of the U.S. Supreme Court

Today, we must decide whether an employer can fire someone simply for being homosexual or transgender. The answer is clear. An employer who fires an individual for being homosexual or transgender fires that person for traits or actions it would not have questioned in members of a different sex. Sex plays a necessary and undisguisable role in the decision, exactly what Title VII forbids.

Title VII's message is simple but momentous: An individual employee's sex is not relevant to the selection, evaluation, or compensation of employees. The statute's message for our cases is equally simple and momentous: An individual's homosexuality or transgender status is not relevant to employment decisions. That's because it is impossible to discriminate against a person for being homosexual or transgender without discriminating against the individual based on sex.

By discriminating against homosexuals, the employer intentionally penalizes men for being attracted to men and women for being attracted to women. By discriminating against transgender persons, the employer unavoidably discriminates against persons with one sex identified at birth and another today. Title VII prohibits all forms of discrimination because of sex, however they may manifest themselves or whatever other labels might attach to them.

Decision

The U.S. Supreme Court, in a 6-3 decision, held that Title VII prohibits employment discrimination against gay and transgender individuals.

Critical Legal Thinking Questions

Was the word "sex" limited as used in Title VII? Do you think that legislators who enacted VII in 1964 anticipated the Supreme Court's decision?

LGBTQ+ Employment Rules

The EEOC interprets the prohibition in Title VII against sex discrimination to include members of the LGBTQ+ community. The EEOC rules prohibit employment discrimination against LGBTQ+ job applicants and employees. The EEOC lists the following as examples of unlawful LGBTQ+-related sex discrimination:

- Failing to hire an applicant, failing to promote an employee, or firing an employee because he is gay or she is lesbian
- Failing to hire an applicant, failing to promote an employee, or firing an employee because the person is transgender
- Discriminating in terms, conditions, or privileges of employment, such as paying a lower salary to an employee because of his or her sexual orientation or gender identity
- Failing to hire an applicant, failing to promote an employee, or firing an employee because the person is transgender or is planning a gender reassignment medical procedure
- Harassing an employee because of his or her sexual orientation or gender identity by using derogatory terms, making sexually oriented comments, or making disparaging remarks
- Intentionally and persistently failing to use the name and gender pronoun that corresponds to the gender identity with which the employee identifies

Many state laws and hundreds of city codes and county ordinances prohibit employers from discriminating against employees and job applicants based on their sexual orientation. Some state and local laws prohibit employment discrimination based on gender identity.

Harassment

33.7 Describe racial, sexual, and other forms of harassment.

Sometimes supervisors and coworkers engage in conduct that is offensive because it is sexually, racially, ethnically, or religiously charged. Such conduct is referred to as **harassment**. The target of the harassment can be a job applicant or an employee.

Examples Lewd remarks, offensive or sexually or racially oriented jokes, name calling, slurs, intimidation, ridicule, mockery, and insults or put-downs are harassment.

The U.S. Supreme Court has held that harassment that is so severe or frequent that it creates a **hostile work environment** violates Title VII. To determine what conduct creates a hostile work environment, the U.S. Supreme Court has stated,

> *We can say that whether an environment is "hostile" or "abusive" can be determined only by looking at all the circumstances. These may include the frequency of the discriminatory conduct; its severity; whether it is physically threatening or humiliating, or a mere offensive utterance; and whether it unreasonably interferes with an employee's work performance.*[6]

hostile work environment
A work environment where harassment of an employee because of his or her race, national origin, or gender is frequent, severe, humiliating, or physically threatening, or interferes with an employee's work performance.

An isolated incident or offhand remark that is not very serious and that does not create a hostile work environment or adverse employment decision does not violate Title VII.

Affirmative Defense

In some situations, an employer is not liable for harassment if it can prove an **affirmative defense**. An employer can prove an affirmative defense if the following is established:

1. The employer exercised reasonable care to prevent, and promptly correct, any sexual harassing behavior, and
2. The plaintiff-employee unreasonably failed to take advantage of any preventive or corrective opportunities provided by the employer or to otherwise avoid harm.

The defendant-employer has the burden of proving the affirmative defense. In determining whether the defense has been proven, a court considers (1) whether the employer has an anti-harassment policy, (2) whether the employer had a complaint mechanism in place, (3) whether employees were informed of the anti-harassment policy and complaint procedure, and (4) other factors that the court deems relevant.

Classification of Harasser

Determining the liability of an employer for harassing conduct of an employee involves different liability rules depending on whether the harassing employee is a *coworker* or *supervisor*. The following liability rules apply.

- **Coworker** If an employee who harasses another employee is a **coworker**, the employer is liable if it was *negligent* in controlling the working situation. In this situation, an employer may not invoke an affirmative defense.

  Example An employer knew or reasonably should have known about harassment but failed to take remedial action. Here, the employer is liable because it failed to control the working situation where the harassment occurred.

WEB EXERCISE
Go to **www.eeoc.gov/eeoc/newsroom**. Under the term "Press Releases" replace "Search all releases" with "sexual harassment" and click on the "Search" button. Read an EEOC press release of a case involving sexual harassment.

If an employer was not negligent in controlling the workplace where coworker harassment occurred, the employer may invoke an affirmative defense.

- **Supervisor** If the employee who harasses another employee is a supervisor, the rules of employer liability are different. For Title VII purposes, a **supervisor** is narrowly defined as a person who is empowered by the employer to take tangible employment actions against the victim, such as making decisions regarding hiring and firing, promotion and demotion, reassignment, or a significant change in benefits. A person who does not have such authority is considered a coworker for Title VII purposes even if that person has some supervisory responsibilities.

If a supervisor harasses an employee by causing a *tangible employment action*, such as the victim being terminated, demoted, or denied employment benefits, then the employer is *strictly liable* for the harassing supervisor's conduct. That is, the employer cannot raise a defense to avoid liability.

Example A supervisor harasses an employee because she is African American and then demotes her without cause. The employer is strictly liable for this conduct and cannot raise a defense against the imposition of strict liability.

If a supervisor harasses an employee but *no tangible employment action* is taken, that is, the victim is not terminated, demoted, or denied employment benefits, then the employer is *vicariously liable* unless it can prove an affirmative defense.

Most employers require employees to take training courses, either in person or online, that inform employees of what constitutes harassment, the business's anti-harassment policy, the complaint procedure, and other relevant information.

CONCEPT SUMMARY

LIABILITY OF AN EMPLOYER FOR AN EMPLOYEE'S HARASSMENT

Harassing Party	Liability of Employer
Coworker	Employer is liable if it was *negligent* in controlling the workplace.
Supervisor	Employer is *strictly liable* for a harassing supervisor's conduct if a tangible employment action is taken against the victim (e.g., the victim is fired, demoted, or denied employment benefits).
	Employer is *vicariously liable* for a harassing supervisor's conduct where no tangible employment action is taken and the employer cannot prove an affirmative defense.

Racial and National Origin Harassment

It is unlawful to harass a person because of his or her race, color, or national origin if the harassment is so severe that it creates a hostile work environment. Harassment based on race or color is referred to as **racial harassment**. Harassment based on national origin is referred to as **national origin harassment**.

racial harassment
Racial slurs, offensive or derogatory remarks about a person's race, offensive name calling, or the display of racially offensive symbols.

Examples Racial slurs, offensive or derogatory remarks about a person's race or color or national origin, offensive name calling, or the display of offensive symbols about a person's race or national origin are racial or national origin harassment.

national origin harassment
Offensive or derogatory remarks about a person's national origin, offensive name calling, or the display of offensive symbols impinging a person's national origin.

Example A supervisor harasses an employee by repeatedly making offensive remarks about the victim's race or national origin or ethnicity or accent. The supervisor does not, however, fire, demote, or take other adverse employment decisions against the victim. The victim notifies the employer's human resources department, but the employer takes no action to remedy the harassing conduct. In this example, the employer is vicariously liable because of the supervisor's harassment and because it cannot prove an affirmative defense.

Sexual Harassment

Sometimes supervisors and coworkers engage in conduct that is offensive because it is sexually charged. Such conduct is referred to as **sexual harassment** or **gender harassment**. Sexual harassment is an insidious and pervasive type of harassment in the workplace. The victim and the harasser can be either a man or a woman, but women make up the majority of sexual harassment victims. It was not until 1986 that the U.S. Supreme Court first recognized sexual harassment as a violation of Title VII.[7]

sexual harassment (gender harassment)
Lewd remarks, touching, intimidation, posting of indecent materials, and other verbal or physical conduct of a sexual nature that occurs on the job.

The U.S. EEOC defines sexual harassment as follows:

1. It is unlawful to harass a person (an applicant or employee) because of that person's sex. Harassment can include sexual harassment or unwelcome sexual advances, requests for sexual favors, and other verbal or physical harassment of a sexual nature.
2. Harassment does not have to be of a sexual nature, however, and can include offensive remarks about a person's sex. For example, it is illegal to harass a woman by making offensive comments about women in general.
3. Both the victim and the harasser can be either a woman or a man, and the victim and harasser can be the same sex.

4. Although the law doesn't prohibit simple teasing, offhand comments, or isolated incidents that are not very serious, harassment is illegal when it is so frequent or severe that it creates a hostile or offensive work environment or when it results in an adverse employment decision (such as the victim being fired or demoted).
5. The harasser can be the victim's supervisor, a supervisor in another area, a coworker, or someone who is not an employee of the employer, such as a client or customer.

The EEOC receives more than 12,000 complaints of sexual harassment each year. This does not include the complaints of sexual harassment filed with state and local equal employment opportunity agencies. In addition, many sexual harassment cases are settled without notice being given to any government agency, while a substantial number of sexual harassment incidents are not reported at all.

In determining whether a woman has been sexually harassed, the EEOC and courts apply a **reasonable woman standard**, which allows cases to be analyzed from the perspective of the complainant and not that of the defendant. This rule exists because a woman and a man may have differing opinions as to what is lawful or unlawful conduct.

reasonable woman standard A standard that is applied in determining whether sexual discrimination or sexual harassment has occurred that allows a case to be analyzed from the perspective of the female complainant and not of the defendant.

Example If a female employee alleges that she has been sexually harassed by a man, a court will determine the lawfulness of the conduct based on what a reasonable woman would have believed was unlawful conduct and not on what the defendant man believed was lawful conduct.

Following is a list of examples of sexual harassment.

- Making lewd or sexually oriented jokes or remarks
- Displaying offensive or sexually explicit objects, pictures, cartoons, posters, calendars, pornography, and screen savers in the workplace
- Sharing sexually inappropriate images or videos, such as pornography, with coworkers
- Making offensive remarks about a person's sex
- Making unwelcome sexual advances
- Repeatedly asking a person out on dates or to have sex
- Requesting sexual favors
- Sexual ridiculing, insulting, or name calling
- Sending suggestive letters, notes, emails, or texts
- Making unwanted telephone calls
- Making sexually suggestive sounds or gestures
- Making sexual comments about a person's appearance, clothing, or body parts
- Staring in a sexually suggestive or offensive manner
- Sharing sexual anecdotes
- Inappropriate touching, including patting, rubbing, stroking, pinching, or purposely brushing up against another person
- Asking sexually intrusive questions, such as questions about someone's sexual history
- Making offensive comments about women or men in general
- Making physical threats
- Stalking a person
- Sexual assault

The victim and harasser can be of the same sex. Thus, **same-sex harassment**, also called **same-gender harassment**, violates Title VII.[8]

Other Types of Harassment

Harassment based on age (40 and older), pregnancy, disability, sexual preference, and genetic information also violates Title VII.

The following feature discusses harassment caused by sending offensive emails, text messages, and other electronic communications.

Information Technology

Offensive Electronic Communications Constitute Sexual and Racial Harassment

The use of email, texting, and other electronic forms of communication in business has increased efficiency and information sharing among employees. Managers and workers can communicate with each other, send documents, and keep each other informed about business developments. Electronic communication has also increased the exposure of employees to sexual and racial harassment and therefore employers to lawsuits. The standard of whether an electronic communication creates an illegal hostile work environment is the same as that for measuring harassment in any other context: The offensive conduct must be severe and cannot consist of isolated or trivial remarks and incidents.

Email, texting, and other forms of electronic harassment differ from other incidents of harassment because they are subtle and insidious. Unlike verbal and some other forms of harassment, however, electronic harassment creates evidence that is often recoverable and therefore provides harassed employees the ability to prove the harassment. Employers must adopt policies pertaining to the use of email, texting, and other electronic communications and make their employees aware that certain electronic communications constitute harassment and violate the law. Employers should make periodic inspections and audits of stored electronic communications to ensure that employees are complying with company anti-harassment policies.

Religious Discrimination

33.8 Describe an employer's duty to make reasonable accommodation for employees' religions.

Title VII prohibits employment discrimination based on a person's religion. *Religions* include traditional religions, such as Buddhism, Christianity, Hinduism, Islam, and Judaism; other religions that recognize a supreme being; and religions based on ethical or spiritual tenets.

The right of an employee to practice his or her religion is not absolute. Under Title VII, an employer is under a duty to make a *reasonable accommodation* for an employee's religious observances, practices, or beliefs if doing so does not cause an *undue hardship* on the employer. An employer is liable for **religious discrimination** if it does not make a reasonable accommodation for an employee's religious observances, practices, or beliefs that could be done without causing an undue hardship on the employer.

religious discrimination
Occurs when an employer does not make a reasonable accommodation for an employee's religious observances, practices, or beliefs that could be done without causing an undue hardship on the employer.

Undue hardship may occur if the requested accommodation would be costly, compromise workplace safety, decrease workplace efficiency, infringe on the rights of other employees, or require other employees to do more than their share of potentially hazardous or burdensome work.

Employees often request an accommodation to observe their religious holidays. Common accommodations to accomplish this include flexible scheduling, voluntary shift substitutions or swaps, and job reassignments. The extent of the accommodation depends on factors such as the size of the employer, the importance of the employee's position, and the availability of alternative workers.

Example An employer with 500 employees could most likely make a reasonable accommodation for a Jewish employee who chooses not to work on the holy day of Yom Kippur. With so many employees, it would likely not cause an undue hardship on the employer to get another worker to cover for one day.

Employers must also accommodate dress and grooming practices if it would not cause an undue hardship to do so.

Examples Accommodations could include permitting the wearing of particular head coverings, such as a Jewish yarmulke or a Muslim headscarf, and wearing certain hairstyles and facial hair, such as Rastafarian dreadlocks or the uncut hair and beard of a Sikh.

Title VII prohibits workplace or job segregation based on religion, such as assigning an employee to a noncontact position because of actual or feared customer preference. Religious discrimination occurs if an employer treats an employee or job applicant differently because he or she is married to or associated with an individual of a particular religion.

It is illegal to harass a person because of his or her religion. Such harassment violates Title VII if it is so severe that it creates a hostile work environment.

Example A supervisor or coworker frequently makes offensive remarks about a person's religious beliefs or practices.

Title VII expressly permits religious organizations to give preference in employment to individuals of their religion. For example, if a person applies for a job with a religious organization but does not subscribe to its religious tenets, the organization may refuse to hire that person.

Defenses to a Title VII Action

33.9 List and describe defenses that may be raised by an employer against a charge of violating Title VII.

Title VII and case law recognize several defenses to a charge of discrimination under Title VII. Employers can select or promote employees based on *merit*. Merit decisions are often based on work, educational experience, and professionally developed ability tests. To be lawful under Title VII, such a requirement must be job-related.

Many employers maintain *seniority* systems that reward long-term employees. Higher wages, fringe benefits, and other preferential treatment (e.g., choice of working hours, choice of vacation schedule) are examples of such rewards. Seniority systems provide an incentive for employees to stay with the company. Such systems are lawful if they are not the result of intentional discrimination.

Bona Fide Occupational Qualification

bona fide occupational qualification (BFOQ)
A true job qualification. Employment discrimination based on a protected class other than race or color is lawful if it is *job-related* and a *business necessity*. This exception is narrowly interpreted by the courts.

Discrimination based on protected classes other than race or color is permitted if it is shown to be a **bona fide occupational qualification (BFOQ)**. Thus, an employer can justify discrimination based on gender in some circumstances. To be legal, a BFOQ must be both *job related* and a *business necessity*.

Examples Allowing only women to be locker room attendants in a women's gym is a valid BFOQ. Prohibiting men from being managers or instructors at the same gym would not be a BFOQ.

CONCEPT SUMMARY

TITLE VII OF THE CIVIL RIGHTS ACT

Covered employers and employment decisions	1. **Employers.** Employers with 15 or more employees for 20 weeks in the current or preceding year, all employment agencies, labor unions with 15 or more members, state and local governments and their agencies, and most federal government employers. 2. **Employment decisions.** Decisions regarding hiring; promotion; demotion; payment of salaries, wages, and fringe benefits; dismissal; job training and apprenticeships; work rules; or any other term, condition, or privilege of employment. Decisions to admit partners to a partnership are also covered.

Protected classes	1. **Race.** A broad class of individuals with common characteristics (e.g., African American, Caucasian, Asian, Native American). 2. **Color.** The color of a person's skin (e.g., light-skinned person, dark-skinned person). 3. **National origin.** A person's country of origin or national heritage (e.g., Italian, Hispanic). 4. **Sex.** A person's sex, whether male or female. Includes sexual harassment and discrimination against women who are pregnant. 5. **Religion.** A person's religious beliefs. An employer has a duty to reasonably accommodate an employee's religious beliefs if doing so does not cause an undue hardship on the employer.
Types of discrimination	1. **Disparate-treatment discrimination.** Discrimination against a specific individual because that person belongs to a protected class. 2. **Disparate-impact discrimination.** Discrimination in which an employer discriminates against a protected class. A neutral-looking employment rule that causes discrimination against a protected class is disparate-impact discrimination.
Defenses	1. **Merit.** Job-related experience, education, or unbiased ability test. 2. **Seniority.** Length of time an employee has been employed by the employer. Intentional discrimination based on seniority is unlawful. 3. **Bona fide occupational qualification (BFOQ).** Discrimination based on sex, religion, or national origin is permitted if it is a valid BFOQ for the position. Qualification based on race or color is not a permissible BFOQ.
Remedies	1. **Equitable remedy.** The court may order the payment of back pay, issue an injunction awarding reinstatement, grant fictional seniority, or order some other equitable remedy. 2. **Damages.** The court can award compensatory damages in cases of intentional discrimination. The court can award punitive damages in cases involving an employer's malice or reckless indifference to federally protected rights.

Equal Pay Act

33.10 Describe the scope of coverage of the Equal Pay Act.

Discrimination often takes the form of different pay scales for men and women performing the same job. The **Equal Pay Act**, a federal statute passed in 1963, protects both sexes from pay discrimination based on sex.[9] The act covers all levels of private-sector employees and state and local government employees. Federal workers are not covered, however.

Equal Pay Act
A federal statute that protects both sexes from pay discrimination based on sex. It extends to jobs that require equal skill, equal effort, equal responsibility, and similar working conditions.

The act prohibits disparity in pay for jobs that require *equal skill* (i.e., equal experience), *equal effort* (i.e., mental and physical exertion), *equal responsibility* (i.e., equal supervision and accountability), or *similar working conditions* (e.g., dangers of injury, exposure to the elements). To make this determination, the courts examine the actual requirements of jobs to determine whether they are equal and similar. If two jobs are determined to be equal and similar, an employer cannot pay disparate wages to members of different sexes.

Job content, not job titles, determines whether positions are substantially equal. All forms of pay are covered by the Equal Pay Act, including salary, overtime pay, bonuses, profit sharing plans, insurance, vacation and holiday pay, reimbursement of expenses, and benefits.

Employees can bring a private cause of action against an employer for violating the Equal Pay Act. Back pay and liquidated damages are recoverable. The employer must increase the wages of the discriminated-against employee to eliminate the unlawful disparity of wages. The wages of other employees may not be lowered.

Example Both Adrianna, a woman, and François, a man, meet the educational requirements for a particular entry-level job, and are both hired as staff accountants by a company to perform exactly the same duties. The company pays

François a salary that is 20 percent higher than Adrianna's salary; its action is a violation of the Equal Pay Act.

Criteria That Justify a Differential in Wages

The Equal Pay Act expressly provides four criteria that justify a differential in payment systems:

- Seniority
- Merit (so long as there is some identifiable measurement standard)
- Quantity or quality of product (i.e., commission, piecework, or quality-control–based payment systems are permitted)
- "Any factor other than sex" (i.e., shift differentials, such as night versus day shifts)

The employer bears the burden of proving these defenses.

Example Omar, a college graduate, has been working for a company for five years as a staff accountant. Camila, a new college graduate with no experience, is hired by the company as a staff accountant, with the same job duties and responsibilities as Omar. Omar is paid a 20 percent higher salary than Camila. This differential is justified based on seniority and therefore does not violate the Equal Pay Act.

Age Discrimination

33.11 Describe the scope of coverage of the Age Discrimination in Employment Act.

Some employers have discriminated against employees and prospective employees based on their age. Primarily, employers have often refused to hire older workers. The **Age Discrimination in Employment Act (ADEA)**, a federal statute that was passed in 1967, prohibits certain **age discrimination** practices.[10]

Age Discrimination in Employment Act (ADEA)
A federal statute that prohibits age discrimination practices against employees who are 40 years and older.

The ADEA protects employees who are 40 and older from job discrimination based on their age. The ADEA prohibits age discrimination in all employment decisions, including hiring, promotions, payment of compensation, and other terms and conditions of employment. Employers cannot use employment advertisements that discriminate against applicants covered by the ADEA. The **Older Workers Benefit Protection Act (OWBPA)** amended the ADEA to prohibit age discrimination with regard to employee benefits.[11]

Older Workers Benefit Protection Act (OWBPA)
A federal statute that prohibits age discrimination regarding employee benefits.

Example Wayne, who is 50 years old, applies for an open position as manager at Big Box Retail Stores, Inc. Wayne meets the job requirements of having a college degree and prior experience as a store manager and is otherwise qualified for the job. The employer refuses to hire Wayne because of his age and instead hires someone who is 30. This is age discrimination in violation of ADEA.

Because persons under 40 are not protected by the ADEA, an employer can maintain an employment policy of hiring only workers who are 40 years of age or older without violating the ADEA. Under ADEA, an employer can maintain an employment practice whereby it gives preferential treatment to older workers over younger workers when they are both within the 40-years-and-older category.

Example An employer can legally prefer to hire persons 50 years of age and older over persons age 40 to 49.

He who would pass the declining years with honor and comfort, should when young, consider that he one day might become old, and remember when he is old, that he had once been young.
Joseph Addison (1672–1719)

Discrimination can occur when the victim and the person who inflicted the discrimination are both over 40. It is unlawful to harass a person because of his or her age if it is so severe that it creates a hostile work environment.

Example A supervisor or coworker frequently makes offensive remarks about a person's age.

The ADEA permits age discrimination where a bona fide occupational qualification (BFOQ) is shown. A BFOQ may be asserted as a necessary qualification of the job or for public safety.

Example Hiring a young person to play a young character in a movie or play is a lawful BFOQ. Setting an age limit for pilots would be a lawful BFOQ for public safety reasons.

The ADEA is administered by the EEOC. Private plaintiffs can also sue under the ADEA. A successful plaintiff in an ADEA action can recover back wages, attorney's fees, and equitable relief, including hiring, reinstatement, and promotion. Where a violation of the ADEA is found, the employer must raise the wages of the discriminated-against employee. It cannot lower the wages of other employees.

Many state laws protect persons under the age of 40 from being discriminated against.

Americans with Disabilities Act (ADA)
A federal statute that imposes obligations on employers and providers of public transportation, telecommunications, and public accommodations to accommodate individuals with disabilities.

Discrimination Against Individuals with Disabilities

33.12 Describe the protections afforded by the Americans with Disabilities Act.

Title I of the ADA
A title of a federal statute that prohibits employment discrimination against qualified individuals with disabilities in regard to job application procedures, hiring, compensation, training, promotion, and termination.

The **Americans with Disabilities Act (ADA)**[12] is a federal statute that was signed into law in 1990. The ADA, as amended, protects individuals with disabilities from discrimination in many facets of life. Title I of the ADA requires that employers make reasonable accommodations for individuals with disabilities that do not cause undue hardship to the employer. Title II requires that public agencies and public transportation be accessible to persons with disabilities. Title III requires public accommodations and commercial facilities—such as motels and hotels, recreation facilities, public transportation, schools, restaurants, and stores—to reasonably accommodate individuals with disabilities. And Title VI requires telecommunications companies to provide functionally equivalent services to persons who are deaf or hard of hearing and to persons with speech impairments.

The following feature discusses Title I of the ADA, which prohibits employment discrimination against persons with covered disabilities.

Americans with Disabilities Act Amendments Act (ADAAA)
A federal act that amends the Americans with Disabilities Act by expanding the definition of disability, requiring that the definition of disability be broadly construed, and requiring commonsense assessments in applying certain provisions of the ADA.

Landmark Law

Title I of the Americans with Disabilities Act

Title I of the Americans with Disabilities Act[13] prohibits employment discrimination against qualified individuals with disabilities in regard to job application procedures, hiring, compensation, training, promotion, and termination. Title I covers employers with 15 or more employees. The U.S. government and corporations wholly owned by the United States are exempt from Title I coverage.

Title I of the ADA is administered by the EEOC. An aggrieved individual must first file a charge with the EEOC, which may take action against the employer or permit the individual to pursue a private cause of action. If a disability discrimination lawsuit is successful, the court can issue an injunction against the employer, order the hiring or reinstatement (with back pay) of the discriminated-against individual, award attorney's fees, and order the employer to pay compensatory and punitive damages to the discriminated-against individual; the dollar amounts are subject to the same caps as Title VII damages.

Congress passed the **Americans with Disabilities Act Amendments Act (ADAAA)** of 2008,[14] which amended the ADA. The primary purposes of the ADAAA were to expand the definition of disability, require that the definition of disability be broadly construed, and require commonsense assessments in applying the provisions of the ADA and ADAAA.

The ADA, as amended by the ADAAA, provides expansive protections for individuals with disabilities in the workplace. The following discussion is based on the cumulative provisions of the ADA and the ADAAA.

Qualified Individual with a Disability

qualified individual with a disability
A person who has a physical or mental impairment that substantially limits a major life activity who, with or without reasonable accommodation, can perform the essential functions of the job that person desires or holds.

A **qualified individual with a disability** is a person who can show that he or she has a disability in one of three ways:

1. A physical (physiological) or mental (psychological) impairment that substantially limits one or more major life activities, such as walking, talking, seeing, hearing, or learning.
2. A history of such impairment, such as cancer.
3. Regarded as having such impairment even if he or she does not have the impairment.

The ADAAA's mandate is to construe the term *disability* broadly. The person with a disability must, with or without reasonable accommodation, be able to perform the essential functions of the job that person desires or holds.

A **physiological impairment** includes any physical disorder or condition, cosmetic disfigurement, or anatomical loss affecting one or more of the following body systems: neurological, musculoskeletal, special sense organs, respiratory, cardiovascular, reproductive, digestive, genitourinary, hemic and lymphatic, skin, and endocrine.

Examples Deafness, blindness, speech impediments, partial or complete missing limbs, mobility impairments requiring the use of a wheelchair, autism, cancer, cerebral palsy, diabetes, epilepsy, HIV/AIDS, multiple sclerosis, and muscular dystrophy.

Impairment also includes **mental or psychological disorders**, such as intellectual disability, organic brain syndrome, emotional or mental illness, and specific learning disabilities.

Examples Major depression, bipolar disorder, posttraumatic stress disorder, obsessive-compulsive disorder, and schizophrenia.

Limits on Employer Questions

Title I of the ADA limits an employer's ability to inquire into or test for an applicant's disabilities. Title I prohibits an employer from asking a job applicant about the existence, nature, and severity of a disability. An employer may inquire, however, about the applicant's ability to perform job-related functions. Preemployment medical examinations before a job offer are forbidden. Once a job offer has been made, an employer may require a medical examination and may condition the offer on the examination results, as long as all entering employees are subject to such an examination. The information obtained must be kept confidential.

Reasonable Accommodation

reasonable accommodation
Under Title I of the ADA, an employer's duty to *reasonably accommodate* an individual's disability if doing so does not cause an *undue hardship* to the employer.

Under Title I, an employer is under the obligation to make a **reasonable accommodation** for a disability of an employee as long as such accommodation does not cause an undue hardship on the employer.

If an employer makes a reasonable accommodation to accommodate an individual's disability, there is no violation of the ADA. However, if an employer does not make a reasonable accommodation that could be made without causing an undue hardship, the employer has violated the ADA.

Examples Reasonable accommodations may include making facilities readily accessible to individuals with disabilities, providing part-time or modified work schedules, acquiring equipment or devices, modifying examination and training materials, and providing qualified readers or interpreters.

Undue Hardship

Employers are not obligated to provide accommodations that would impose an **undue hardship**—that is, actions that would require significant difficulty or expense. In determining what constitutes undue hardship of Title I of the Americans with Disabilities Act, the EEOC and the courts consider factors such as the nature and cost of accommodation, the overall financial resources of the employer, and the employer's type of operation. What may be significantly difficult or expensive for a small employer may not cause an undue hardship for a large employer. If the needed accommodation would cause an undue hardship for the employer, there is no violation of the ADA if the employer does not make the accommodation.

Uncovered Conditions

The ADA does not consider some impairments or illnesses or certain conditions to be disabilities. In fact, the act expressly states that certain impairments are not covered by the ADA. Temporary or nonchronic impairments of short duration with few or no residual effects usually are not considered disabilities.

Examples Common colds, seasonal or common influenzas, sprained joints, minor or nonchronic gastrointestinal disorders, broken bones that are expected to heal completely, and seasonal allergies that do not substantially limit a person's major life activities are not considered disabilities.

Pregnancy is not considered a disability under the ADA. However, impairments resulting from pregnancy, such as preeclampsia, are disabilities under the ADA.

A current user of illegal drugs or an alcoholic who uses alcohol or is under the influence of alcohol at the workplace is not covered by the ADA. However, former users of illegal drugs and recovering alcoholics could meet the definition of disability if they have successfully completed a supervised rehabilitation program or are participating in a supervised rehabilitation program (e.g., Narcotics Anonymous, Alcoholics Anonymous).

It is unlawful to harass a job applicant or an employee because he or she has a disability, had a disability in the past, or is believed to have a physical or mental impairment. Harassment could include, for example, offensive remarks about a person's disability. The ADA also protects people from employment discrimination based on their relationship with a person with a disability.

Genetic Information Discrimination

33.13 Define *genetic information discrimination*.

There have been and will continue to be tremendous advances in developing genetic tests that identify a person's DNA and other genetic information. With *genetic information*, it is possible to determine a person's propensity to be stricken by many diseases, such as diabetes, heart disease, Huntington's disease, Lou Gehrig's disease, Alzheimer's disease, multiple sclerosis, certain types of cancers, and other diseases. With genetic information, preventive steps can be instituted, including medical, pharmaceutical, dietary, and exercise interventions.

However, genetic information can be misused, possibly by employers if they have access to or knowledge of an applicant's or an employee's genetic information or his or her family's genetic information. Such misuse is called **genetic information discrimination**.

genetic information discrimination
Discrimination based on information from which it is possible to determine a person's propensity to be stricken by diseases.

Example An employer might discriminate against an applicant or employee if it had information that the person's family members have been stricken by a debilitating or a fatal disease and, because of genetics, the applicant or employee is at increased risk of suffering from the same disease.

Genetic Information Nondiscrimination Act

Genetic Information Nondiscrimination Act (GINA)
A federal statute that makes it illegal for an employer to discriminate against job applicants and employees based on genetic information.

To address this concern, Congress enacted the **Genetic Information Nondiscrimination Act (GINA)** in 2008.[15] **Title II of the Genetic Information Nondiscrimination Act** makes it illegal for an employer to discriminate against job applicants and employees based on genetic information. Thus, an employer may not use genetic information in making employment decisions, including decisions to hire, promote, provide benefits to, and terminate employees. GINA is administered by the EEOC and other federal government agencies. Remedies for violations include corrective action and monetary fines. Individuals have a right to pursue private lawsuits to seek hiring, reinstatement, back pay, and compensatory and punitive damages.

Inadvertent discovery of genetic information (the "water cooler" exemption) and voluntary submission of genetic information to an employer (e.g., as part of a wellness program) do not violate the act. The misuse of such information does violate the act. Under GINA, it is illegal to harass an applicant or employee because of his or her genetic information.

Protection from Retaliation

33.14 Explain the protections afforded employees from employer retaliation.

Federal antidiscrimination laws prohibit employers from engaging in **retaliation** against an employee for filing a charge of discrimination or participating in a discrimination proceeding concerning race, color, national origin, gender, religion, age, disability, genetic information, and other forms of discrimination. Acts of retaliation include dismissing, demoting, or harassing the employee, or using other methods of reprisal.

Example Greta files a gender discrimination claim with the EEOC that states her employer has engaged in sex discrimination in violation of Title VII. The employer does not promote Greta when she qualifies for a promotion because she filed this claim. This is illegal retaliation.

Veterans and Military Personnel

33.15 Describe employment protections for veterans and military personnel.

Uniformed Services Employment and Reemployment Rights Act of 1994 and Veterans' Benefits Act of 2010
Federal statutes that provide protections and grant employment benefits to persons who serve or have served in the U.S. military services.

The federal government has enacted laws that provide employment protections for veterans of military service and for military personnel. **The Uniformed Services Employment and Reemployment Rights Act of 1994 (USERRA)**,[16] as amended by the **Veterans' Benefits Act of 2010**,[17] is a federal statute that applies to all civilian and government employers in the United States and U.S. employers operating in foreign countries.

The law protects and grants employment benefits to persons who serve or have served in the U.S. military services (Air Force, Army, Coast Guard, Marines, and Navy) or who is or has been a member of the Reserves or National Guard. The law covers all military service, whether voluntary or involuntary.

The USERRA does the following:

- Prohibits employers from engaging in employment and wage discrimination against persons because of their past military service or their current or future military obligations.

- Requires employers to rehire returning service members who had previously been its employees at a job—with comparable status, pay, benefits, and seniority—that the person would have retained had he or she not been absent for military service. If the service member cannot qualify for reemployment for that position, the law allows for alternative reemployment positions. A person must serve less than five years in military service to qualify for reemployment.
- Requires employers to rehire persons with service-connected disabilities if the disability can be reasonably accommodated.

Employees are required to give advance written or verbal notice to their employer of their military duty unless giving notice is impossible, unreasonable, or precluded by necessity. A person must file an application for reemployment with his or her previous employer on release from military service.

Affirmative Action

33.16 Define *affirmative action* in employment.

Title VII of the Civil Rights Act of 1964 outlawed discrimination in employment based on race, color, national origin, sex, and religion. The law clearly prohibited any further discrimination based on these protected classes. However, did the federal statute intend to grant a favorable status to the classes of persons who had been previously discriminated against? In a series of cases, the U.S. Supreme Court upheld the use of **affirmative action** to make up for egregious past discrimination, particularly discrimination based on race.

affirmative action
A policy that provides that certain job preferences will be given to minority or other protected-class applicants when an employer makes an employment decision.

Affirmative Action Plan

Employers often adopt an **affirmative action plan** that provides that certain job preferences will be given to members of minority racial and ethnic groups, women, and other protected-class applicants when making employment decisions. Such plans can be adopted voluntarily by employers, undertaken to settle a discrimination action, or ordered by the courts.

To be lawful, an affirmative action plan must be *narrowly tailored* to achieve some *compelling interest*. Employment quotas based on a specified number or percentage of minority applicants or employees are unlawful. If a person's minority status is only one factor of many factors considered in an employment decision, that decision will usually be considered lawful.

Reverse Discrimination

Title VII also protects members of majority classes from discrimination. Lawful affirmative action plans have an effect on members of majority classes. The courts have held that if an affirmative action plan is based on pre-established numbers or percentage quotas for hiring or promoting minority applicants, then it causes illegal **reverse discrimination**. In such cases, the members of the majority class may sue under Title VII and recover damages and other remedies for reverse discrimination.

reverse discrimination
Discrimination against a group that is usually thought of as a majority.

Thomas Barrat/Shutterstock

University of Chicago

Title IX of the Education Amendments of 1972, also named the ***Patsy Mink Equal Opportunity in Education Act,***[18] *is a federal law that prohibits gender discrimination at colleges, universities, secondary schools, and elementary schools that receive federal government financial assistance. Although Title IX is commonly known for its application to student-athletes who participate in college and university sports programs, it requires equal treatment based on sex regarding every aspect of education, including financial assistance, housing, student health services, counseling, employment, and the like. Title IX applies to both men and women. The U.S. Department of Education enforces Title IX and has the authority to adopt regulations in doing so.*

Key Terms and Concepts

Affirmative action (585)
Affirmative action plan (585)
Affirmative defense (574)
Age discrimination (580)
Age Discrimination in Employment Act (ADEA) (580)
Americans with Disabilities Act (ADA) (581)
Americans with Disabilities Act Amendments Act (ADAAA) (581)
Bona fide occupational qualification (BFOQ) (578)
Civil Rights Act of 1866 (569)
Civil Rights Act of 1964 (566)
Color discrimination (569)
Coworker (574)
Direct sex discrimination (570)
Discrimination (565)
Disparate-impact discrimination (567)
Disparate-treatment discrimination (567)
Employment discrimination (565)
Equal Employment Opportunity Commission (EEOC) (565)
Equal opportunity in employment (565)
Equal Pay Act (579)
Fair Employment Practices Agency (FEPA) (566)
Gender identity (571)
Gender identity discrimination (572)
Genetic information discrimination (583)
Genetic Information Nondiscrimination Act (GINA) (584)
Harassment (573)
Hostile work environment (573)
LGBTQ (lesbian, gay, bisexual, transgender, and queer or questioning) (571)
LGBTQ+ (entire spectrum of sexual orientation and gender identity) (572)
Lilly Ledbetter Fair Pay Act of 2009 (566)
Mental or psychological disorders (582)
National origin (569)
National origin discrimination (569)
National origin harassment (575)
Older Workers Benefit Protection Act (OWBPA) (580)
Physiological impairments (582)
Pregnancy Discrimination Act (570)
Punitive damages (568)
Qualified individual with a disability (582)

Quid pro quo sex discrimination (570)
Race discrimination (568)
Racial harassment (575)
Reasonable accommodation (582)
Reasonable woman standard (576)
Religious discrimination (577)
Retaliation (584)
Reverse discrimination (585)
Right to sue letter (565)
Same-sex harassment (same-gender harassment) (576)
Section 1981 of the Civil Rights Act of 1866 (569)
Sex discrimination (gender discrimination) (570)
Sex-plus discrimination (570)
Sexual harassment (gender harassment) (575)
Sexual orientation (571)
Sexual orientation discrimination (572)
Supervisor (574)
Title I of the Americans with Disabilities Act (581)
Title II of the Genetic Information Nondiscrimination Act (584)
Title VII of the Civil Rights Act of 1964 (566)
Title IX of the Education Amendments of 1972 (Patsy Mink Equal Opportunity in Education Act) (586)
Undue hardship (583)
Uniformed Services Employment and Reemployment Rights Act (USERRA) (584)
Veterans' Benefits Act of 2010 (584)

Critical Legal Thinking Cases

33.1 Sexual Harassment The Pennsylvania State Police (PSP) hired Nancy Drew Suders as a police communications operator for the McConnellsburg barracks. Suders's supervisors were Sergeant Eric D. Easton, station commander at the McConnellsburg barracks; Patrol Corporal William D. Baker; and Corporal Eric B. Prendergast. These three supervisors subjected Suders to a continuous barrage of sexual harassment that ceased only when she resigned from the force. Easton would bring up the subject of people having sex with animals each time Suders entered his office. He told Prendergast, in front of Suders, that young girls should be given instruction in how to gratify men with oral sex. Easton would also sit down near Suders, wearing Spandex shorts, and spread his legs apart. Baker repeatedly made obscene gestures in Suders's presence and shouted out vulgar comments inviting sex. Baker made these gestures as many as five to 10 times per night throughout Suders's employment at the barracks. Further, Baker would rub his rear end in front of her and remark "I have a nice ass, don't I?"

Five months after she was hired, Suders contacted Virginia Smith-Elliot, PSP's equal opportunity officer, and stated that she was being harassed at work and was afraid. Smith-Elliot's response appeared to Suders to be insensitive and unhelpful. Two days later, Suders resigned from the force. Suders sued PSP, alleging that she had been subjected to sexual harassment and constructively discharged and forced to resign. The employer argued that Suders should not be allowed to bring her case because she had resigned. Can Suders prevail on her sexual harassment claim? *Pennsylvania State Police v. Suders*, 542 U.S. 129, 124 S.Ct. 2342, 2004 U.S. Lexis 4176 (Supreme Court of the United States, 2004)

33.2 Sexual Harassment Teresa Harris worked as a manager at Forklift Systems Incorporated (Forklift), an equipment rental company, for 2½ years. Charles Hardy was Forklift's president. Throughout Harris's time at Forklift, Hardy often insulted her because of her sex and made her the target of unwanted sexual innuendos. Hardy told Harris on several occasions, in the presence of other employees, "You're a woman, what do you know?" and "We need a man as the rental manager." Again, in front of others, he suggested that the two of them "go to the Holiday Inn to negotiate Harris's raise." He made sexual innuendos about Harris's and other women's clothing.

Six weeks before Harris quit her job, Harris complained to Hardy about his conduct. Hardy said he was surprised that Harris was offended, claimed he was only joking, and apologized. He also promised he would stop, and based on this assurance, Harris stayed on the job. But two weeks later, Hardy began anew. While Harris was arranging a deal with one of Forklift's customers, he asked her, again in front of other employees, "What did you do, promise the guy some sex Saturday night?" One month later, Harris collected her paycheck and quit. Harris then sued Forklift, claiming that Hardy's conduct was sexual harassment that created a hostile work environment for her because of her gender. Who wins? *Harris v. Forklift Systems Incorporated*, 510 U.S. 17, 114 S.Ct. 367, 1993 U.S. Lexis 7155 (Supreme Court of the United States, 1993)

33.3 National Origin Discrimination Irma Rivera is a Hispanic woman who was born in Puerto Rico. She began working for Baccarat, Inc. (Baccarat), a distributor of fine crystal, as a sales representative in its retail store in Manhattan. Eight years later, Rivera was the top sales representative at the Baccarat store. Jean Luc Negre became the new president of Baccarat, with ultimate authority for personnel decisions. Subsequently, Negre angrily told Rivera that he did not like her attitude and that he did not want her to speak Spanish on the job. Ms. Rivera testified that during her one face-to-face meeting with Mr. Negre, he specifically stated that he did not like her accent. Six months later, Dennis Russell, the chief financial officer of Baccarat, notified Rivera that Negre had made a decision to terminate her. Rivera pressed Russell to tell her why she was being fired. According to Rivera, he replied, "Irma, he doesn't want Hispanics." Negre also terminated Ivette Brigantty, another Hispanic sales representative. Evidence showed that Rivera and Brigantty were terminated because of their accent when speaking English. The store retained its non-Hispanic salesperson. Rivera sued Baccarat for national origin discrimination, in violation of Title VII of the Civil Rights Act. Has Baccarat engaged in unlawful national origin discrimination? *Rivera v. Baccarat, Inc.*, 10 F.Supp.2d 318, 1998 U.S. Dist. Lexis 9099 (United States District Court for the Southern District of New York, 1998)

33.4 **Bona Fide Occupational Qualification (BFOQ)** Johnson Controls, Inc. (Johnson Controls) manufactures batteries. Lead is the primary ingredient in the manufacturing process. Exposure to lead entails health risks, including risk of harm to a fetus carried by a female employee. To protect unborn children from such risk, Johnson Controls adopted an employment rule that prevented pregnant women and women of childbearing age from working at jobs involving lead exposure. Only women who were sterilized or could prove they could not have children were not affected by the rule. Consequently, most female employees were relegated to lower-paying clerical jobs at the company.

Several female employees filed a class action suit, challenging the fetal-protection policy as sex discrimination, in violation of Title VII of the Civil Rights Act. Johnson Controls defended, asserting that its fetal-protection policy was justified as a bona fide occupational qualification (BFOQ). Is the company's fetal-protection policy a BFOQ, or does it constitute sex discrimination, in violation of Title VII? *International Union, United Automobile, Aerospace and Agricultural Implement Workers of America, UAW v. Johnson Controls, Inc.*, 499 U.S. 187, 111 S.Ct. 1196, 1991 U.S. Lexis 1715 (Supreme Court of the United States, 1991)

33.5 **Retaliation** Miriam Regalado and Eric Thompson, who were engaged to be married, both worked at North American Stainless, LP (NAS). Regalado filed a charge with the Equal Employment Opportunity Commission (EEOC), alleging sex discrimination by NAS, in violation of Title VII. Three weeks later, NAS fired Thompson. Thompson filed a charge with the EEOC, claiming that NAS fired him to retaliate against Regalado for filing her charge against NAS. Thompson sued NAS, alleging third-party retaliation in violation of Title VII. The U.S. district court granted summary judgment to NAS, and the U.S. court of appeals upheld this decision. The court of appeals reasoned that Thompson, as a third party, was not included in the class of persons who could bring a retaliation case under Title VII. Thompson appealed to the U.S. Supreme Court. Does Title VII permit a third-party retaliation claim against an employer? *Thompson v. North American Stainless, LP*, 562 U.S. 170, 131 S.Ct. 863, 2011 U.S. Lexis 913 (Supreme Court of the United States, 2011)

Ethics Cases

33.6 **Ethics Case** Dianne Rawlinson, age 22, was a college graduate whose major course of study was correctional psychology. After graduation, she applied for a position as a correctional counselor (prison guard) with the Alabama Board of Corrections. Her application was rejected because she failed to meet the minimum 120-pound weight requirement of an Alabama statute that also established a height minimum of 5 feet 2 inches. Rawlinson brought a class action lawsuit against Dothard, who was the director of the Department of Public Safety of Alabama. Does the height–weight requirement constitute a bona fide occupational qualification (BFOQ) that justified the sex discrimination in this case? *Dothard, Director, Department of Public Safety of Alabama v. Rawlinson*, 433 U.S. 321, 97 S.Ct. 2720, 1977 U.S. Lexis 143 (Supreme Court of the United States, 1977)

33.7 **Ethics Case** PGA Tour, Inc., is a nonprofit entity that sponsors professional golf tournaments. The PGA has adopted a set of rules that apply to its golf tour. One rule requires golfers to walk the golf course during PGA-sponsored tournaments. Casey Martin is a talented amateur golfer who won many high school and university golf championships. Martin has been afflicted with Klippel-Trenaunay-Weber syndrome, a degenerative circulatory disorder that obstructs the flow of blood from his right leg to his heart. The disease is progressive and has atrophied his right leg. Walking causes Martin pain, fatigue, and anxiety, with significant risk of hemorrhaging.

When Martin turned professional, he qualified for the PGA Tour. He made a request to use a golf cart while playing in PGA tournaments. When the PGA denied his request, Martin sued the PGA for violation of the Americans with Disabilities Act (ADA) for not making reasonable accommodations for his disability. Did the PGA owe a duty of social responsibility to accommodate Martin's disability? Does the ADA require the PGA Tour, Inc., to accommodate Casey Martin, a professional golfer with a disability, by permitting him to use a golf cart while playing in PGA-sponsored golf tournaments? *PGA Tour v. Martin*, 532 U.S. 661, 212 S.Ct. 1879, 2001 U.S. Lexis 4115 (Supreme Court of the United States, 2001)

Notes

1. Public Law No 111-2, 123 Stat. 5 (2009).
2. Public Law 88-352.
3. 42 U.S.C. Section 2000e-2.
4. 42 U.S.C. Section 1981.
5. Public Law 95-555.
6. *Harris v. Forklift Systems, Inc.*, 510 U.S. 17, 114 S.Ct. 367, 1993 U.S. Lexis 7155 (Supreme Court of the United States).
7. *Meritor Savings Bank v. Vinson*, 477 U.S. 57, 106 S.Ct. 2399, 1986 U.S. Lexis 108 (Supreme Court of the United States).
8. *Omcale v. Sundowner Offshore Services, Incorporated*, 523 U.S. 75, 118 S.Ct. 998, 1998 U.S. Lexis 1599 (Supreme Court of the United States).
9. 29 U.S.C. Section 206(d).
10. 29 U.S.C. Sections 621–634.
11. Public Law 101-433.
12. 42 U.S.C. Sections 12101 et seq.
13. 42 U.S.C. Sections 12111–12117.
14. Public Law 110-325 (2008).
15. Public Law 110-233, 122 Stat. 881.
16. 38 U.S.C. Sections 4301–4335.
17. Public Law 111-175.
18. 20 U.S.C. Sections 1681–1688.

PART

VIII

Business Organizations, Partnerships, Corporations, Limited Liability Companies, Investor Protection, and Business Ethics

Henry R. Cheeseman

CHAPTER

34 Entrepreneurship, Sole Proprietorships, and General Partnerships

Henry R. Cheeseman

SAINT IGNACE, MICHIGAN
Many small businesses operate as sole proprietors, partnerships, and companies.

Learning Objectives

After studying this chapter, you should be able to:

34.1 Define *entrepreneurship* and describe the types of organizations that an entrepreneur can use to operate a business.

34.2 Define *sole proprietorship* and describe the liability of a sole proprietor.

34.3 Define *general partnership* and describe how general partnerships are formed and operated.

34.4 List and describe the rights of general partners.

34.5 List and describe the duties of general partners.

34.6 Describe the liability of general partners and general partnerships.

34.7 Describe the dissociation of a partner and the dissolution and winding up of a general partnership.

"One of the most fruitful sources of ruin to a man of the world is the recklessness or want of principle of partners, and it is one of the perils to which every man exposes himself who enters into a partnership."

—*Vice Chancellor Richard Malins*
Mackay v. Douglas, 14 Eq. 106 AT 118 (1872)

Introduction to Entrepreneurship, Sole Proprietorships, and General Partnerships

A person who wants to start a business must decide whether the business should operate as one of the major forms of business organization—*sole proprietorship, general partnership, limited partnership, limited liability partnership, limited liability company*, or *corporation*—or under other available legal business forms. The selection depends on many factors, including the ease and cost of formation, the capital requirements of the business, the flexibility of management decisions, government restrictions, personal liability, and tax considerations.

It has been uniformly laid down in this Court, as far back as we can remember, that good faith is the basis of all mercantile transactions.
Justice Buller
Salomons v. Nissen (1788)

This chapter discusses entrepreneurship, sole proprietorships, and general partnerships.

Entrepreneurship

34.1 Define *entrepreneurship* and describe the types of organizations that an entrepreneur can use to operate a business.

An **entrepreneur** is a person who forms and operates a business. An entrepreneur may start a business alone or may cofound a business with others. Most businesses started by entrepreneurs are small or midsize businesses.

entrepreneur
A person who forms and operates a new business either alone or with others.

Examples Entrepreneurs operate business and service firms such as retail stores, restaurants, and wholesale distributors; technology businesses; e-commerce and online businesses, media and software development, and other electronic-related companies; practices operated by professionals such as lawyers, doctors, dentists, and insurance and real estate agents; service-based organizations such as those operated by plumbers, electricians, contractors, and building tradespeople; and other businesses and professions.

Some entrepreneurial businesses grow into substantial organizations.

Examples Mark Zuckerberg and others founded Facebook, Inc., an extremely successful social networking service; Oprah Winfrey started her own publication, media, and entertainment companies, and other successful businesses; David Filo and Jerry Yang founded Yahoo!, a leader in providing internet services; Jack Ma and others founded Alibaba Group, an online services and business-to-business platform; Jack Dorsey, Evan Williams, and others started Twitter, Inc., an online social networking platform; and Travis Kalanick and Garrett Camp founded Uber Technologies, Inc., a gig-economy ridesharing company.

Every day, entrepreneurs around the world create new businesses that hire employees, provide new products and services, and contribute to the growth of economies.

Entrepreneurial Forms of Conducting Business

Entrepreneurs contemplating starting a business have many options when choosing the legal form in which to conduct the business. Each of these forms of business has advantages and disadvantages for the entrepreneurs. The major forms for conducting businesses and professions are:

It is when merchants dispute about their own rules that they invoke the law.
Judge Brett
Robinson v. Mollett (1875)

- Sole proprietorship
- General partnership
- Limited partnership

- Limited liability limited partnership
- Limited liability partnership
- Limited liability company
- Corporation

Certain requirements must be met to establish and operate each of these forms of business. These requirements are discussed in this chapter and the chapters that follow.

Sole Proprietorship

34.2 Define *sole proprietorship* and describe the liability of a sole proprietor.

sole proprietorship
A form of business in which the owner is actually the business; the business is not a separate legal entity.

sole proprietor
The owner of a sole proprietorship.

A **sole proprietorship** is the simplest form of business organization. There is only one owner of the business, who is called the **sole proprietor**. There is no separate legal entity. Sole proprietorship is the most common form of business in the United States. Many small businesses—and a few large ones—operate as sole proprietorships. There are more than 20 million sole proprietorships in the United States, comprising more than 70 percent of the businesses in the country.

There are several major advantages to operating a business as a sole proprietorship:

- Forming a sole proprietorship is easy and inexpensive.
- The owner has the right to make all management decisions concerning the business, including those involving hiring and firing employees.
- The sole proprietor owns the business and has the right to receive all of the business's profits.
- A sole proprietorship can be easily transferred or sold if and when the owner desires to do so; no other approval (e.g., from partners or shareholders) is necessary.

d.b.a
A designation for a business that is operating under a trade name; it means "doing business as."

This business form has important disadvantages, too. For example, a sole proprietor's access to capital is limited to personal funds plus any loans the proprietor can obtain. A sole proprietor is legally responsible for the business's contracts, and for the torts the proprietor or any employees commit in the course of employment.

fictitious business name statement
A document filed with the state that designates a trade name of a business, the name and address of the applicant, and the address of the business.

Creation of a Sole Proprietorship

Creating a sole proprietorship is easy. There are no formalities, and no federal or state government approval is required. Some local governments require all businesses, including sole proprietorships, to obtain licenses to do business within the city.

The following feature discusses the requirement for a business to file for a trade name under certain circumstances.

Business Environment

Using a Trade Name

A sole proprietorship can operate under the name of the sole proprietor or a **trade name**. For example, the author of this book can operate a sole proprietorship under the name "Henry R. Cheeseman" or under a trade name such as "The Big Cheese." Operating under a trade name is commonly designated as **d.b.a. (doing business as)** (e.g., Henry R. Cheeseman, d.b.a. "The Big Cheese").

Most states require all businesses—including sole proprietorships, general partnerships, limited partnerships, limited liability limited partnerships, limited liability companies, limited liability partnerships, and corporations—that operate under a trade name to file a **fictitious business name statement** (or **certificate of trade name**) with the appropriate government agency. The statement must contain the name and address of the applicant, the trade name, and the address of the business. Most states also require notice of the trade name to be published in a newspaper of general circulation serving the area in which the applicant does business.

These requirements are intended to disclose the real owner's name to the public. Noncompliance can result in a fine. Some states prohibit violators from maintaining lawsuits in the state's courts. If a sole proprietor does not choose a trade name, then the name of the business is the sole proprietor's full name.

Personal Liability of a Sole Proprietor

A sole proprietor bears the risk of loss of the business; that is, the owner will lose their entire capital contribution if the business fails. In addition, the sole proprietor has **unlimited personal liability** for the debts and obligations of the sole proprietorship (see Exhibit 34.1). Therefore, creditors may recover claims against the business from the sole proprietor's personal assets (e.g., home, automobile, bank accounts).

unlimited personal liability of a sole proprietor
The personal liability of a sole proprietor for all the debts and obligations of a sole proprietorship.

Exhibit 34.1 SOLE PROPRIETORSHIP

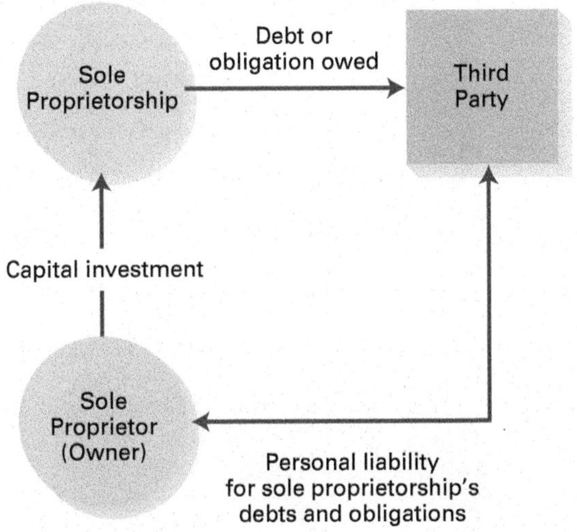

Example Esther forms a new business to develop a custom mobile app and operates the business as a sole proprietorship. Esther files the proper fictitious business name statement and publishes the necessary notice of the use of the trade name. She contributes $50,000 of her personal funds to the business and borrows $200,000 from a bank in the name of the business. After one year, Esther closes the business because it is unsuccessful. At the time it is closed, the business has no assets, owes the bank $200,000, and owes other debts of $45,000. Here, Esther, the sole proprietor, is personally liable to pay the bank and all the debts of the sole proprietorship from her personal assets.

Taxation of a Sole Proprietorship

A sole proprietorship is not a separate legal entity, so it does not pay taxes at the business level. Instead, the earnings and losses from a sole proprietorship are reported on each sole proprietor's personal income tax filing. A sole proprietorship business earns income and pays expenses while operating the business. A sole proprietor has to file tax returns and pay taxes to state and federal governments. For federal income tax purposes, a sole proprietor must prepare a personal income tax, **Form 1040**, and report the income or loss from the sole proprietorship on his or her personal income tax form. The income or loss from the sole proprietorship is reported on **Schedule C (Profit or Loss from Business)**, which must be attached to the taxpayer's Form 1040.

Critical Legal Thinking Questions

What are the benefits of being the owner of a sole proprietorship? What are the detriments?

General Partnership

34.3 Define *general partnership* and describe how general partnerships are formed and operated.

General partnerships have been recognized since ancient times. State partnership laws provide for the formation, operation, and dissolution of general partnerships. There are more than 2 million general partnerships in the United States.

A general partnership is a voluntary association of two or more persons for carrying on a for-profit business as co-owners. The formation of a general partnership creates certain rights and duties among partners and between the partners and third parties. These rights and duties are established in the partnership agreement and by law. General partners are personally liable for the debts and obligations of the partnership (see Exhibit 34.2).

The following feature discusses the Uniform Partnership Act (UPA) and Revised Uniform Partnership Act (RUPA).

Exhibit 34.2 GENERAL PARTNERSHIP

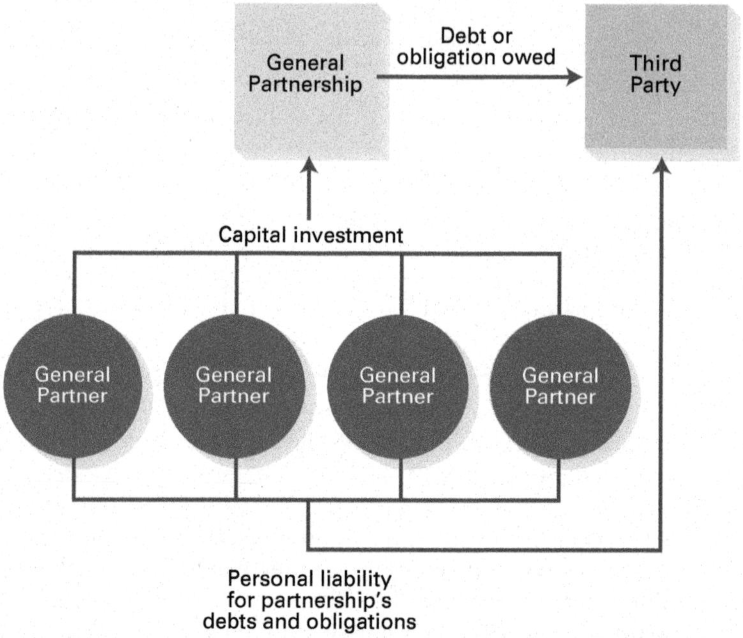

Uniform Partnership Act (UPA)
A model act that codified partnership law.

Revised Uniform Partnership Act (RUPA)
A model act that revised partnership law. The RUPA has been adopted by the majority of states.

Landmark Laws

Uniform Partnership Act and Revised Uniform Partnership Act

In 1914, the National Conference of Commissioners on Uniform State Laws, a group of lawyers, judges, and legal scholars, promulgated the **Uniform Partnership Act (UPA)**. The UPA is a model act that codifies general partnership law. Its goal was to establish consistent partnership law that was uniform throughout the United States. A model act does not become a state's law until a state adopts it as a state statute. The UPA was adopted in whole or in part by most states.

In 1997, the **Revised Uniform Partnership Act (RUPA)**, a revised uniform partnership law, was issued by the National Conference of Commissioners on Uniform State Laws. The RUPA has been adopted by the majority of states and replaces the UPA in those states. Louisiana has not adopted the UPA or the RUPA and has its own partnership law, which is somewhat similar to these uniform laws. The RUPA was amended in 2011 and 2013.

The RUPA and the UPA cover most problems that arise in the formation, operation, and dissolution of general partnerships. Other rules of law or equity govern if there is no applicable provision in the uniform partnership law. The partnership law and other laws of the jurisdiction in which a partnership has its chief executive office govern relations among the partners and between the partners and the partnership.

The RUPA and the UPA form the basis of the study of general partnerships in this chapter. Many states that have adopted the RUPA refer to their partnership acts as a "Uniform Partnership Act."

general partnership (ordinary partnership or partnership)
A voluntary association of two or more persons to carry on as co-owners of a business for profit.

Formation of a General Partnership

A business must meet four criteria to qualify as a **general partnership**. It must be (1) a voluntary association of two or more persons (2) carrying on a business (3) as co-owners (4) for profit [RUPA 202(a); UPA 6(1)]. A general partnership is sometimes referred to as an **ordinary partnership** or **partnership**. The partners of a general partnership are called **general partners**, but are also referred to as **ordinary partners** or **partners**.

general partners (ordinary partners or partners)
Partners of a general partnership.

A general partnership is a **voluntary association** of two or more persons. All partners must agree to the participation of each co-partner. A person cannot be forced to be a partner or to accept another person as a partner. The definition of a general partner includes natural persons, corporations, limited liability companies, limited partnerships, limited liability partnerships, joint ventures, estates, trusts, associations, and governments and governmental agencies. Other legal or commercial entities may also be general partners in a general partnership [RUPA 101(10)].

To qualify as a general partnership, a business—a trade, an occupation, or a profession—must be carried on. The business must have a **profit motive**, but failing to make a profit does not disqualify the business as a partnership.

Co-ownership of a business is essential to create a partnership. The interest that a partner owns of a partnership is called an **ownership interest**. The most important factors in determining co-ownership are whether the parties share the business's profits and management responsibility. Receipt of a share of business profits is *prima facie* evidence of a general partnership. No inference of the existence of a general partnership is drawn if profits are received in payment of (1) a debt owed to a creditor in installments or otherwise; (2) wages or compensation owed to an employee or payment owed to an independent contractor; (3) rent owed to a landlord or others; (4) an annuity or retirement or health benefit owed to a widow, widower, or representative of a deceased partner; (5) interest or other charges owed on a loan; or (6) consideration for the sale of goodwill of a business or other property [RUPA 202(c)(3); UPA 7]. An agreement to share losses of a business is strong evidence of a general partnership.

The right to participate in the management of a business is important evidence for determining the existence of a general partnership, but it is not conclusive evidence because the right to participate in management is sometimes given to employees, creditors, and others. It is compelling evidence of the existence of a general partnership if a person is given the right to share in profits, losses, and management of a business. Courts will examine all relevant factors in determining whether there is a partnership.

It is the privilege of a trader in a free country, in all matters not contrary to law, to regulate his own mode of carrying it on according to his own discretion and choice.

Baron Alderson
Hilton v. Eckersly (1855)

A relationship that is called a "joint venture" is a general partnership only if it meets the requirements for being a partnership.

CONCEPT SUMMARY
GENERAL PARTNERSHIP REQUIREMENTS

1. Voluntary association of two or more persons
2. Carrying on a business
3. As co-owners
4. For profit

A general partnership may be formed with little or no formality, and may even be created inadvertently. Thus, a partnership may be formed by a written agreement, an oral agreement, or an electronic record, or it may be implied from the circumstances.

Example Janelle, Ezra, and Collette meet after a business law class. They orally agree to pool an equal amount of money and join together to start an e-commerce business to make a profit. Their agreement is sealed with a handshake. Their actions create a partnership.

Although it is not usually required to do so, a general partnership may file a written statement with the state recording that it is a partnership. This statement is often referred to as a **certificate of partnership** or a **statement of partnership** [RUPA 105].

Name of the General Partnership

A general partnership can operate under the names of any one or more of the general partners or under a fictitious business name. A general partnership must file a fictitious business name statement—d.b.a. (doing business as)—with the appropriate government agency to operate under a trade name. The general partnership usually must publish a notice of the use of the trade name in a newspaper of general circulation where the partnership does business. The name selected by the partnership cannot indicate that it is a corporation (e.g., it cannot contain the term *Inc.*) and cannot be similar to the name used by any existing business entity. If a general partnership does not operate using a selected legal partnership name, then the name of the partnership is the last names of the partners.

Duration of a General Partnership

partnership at will (at-will partnership)
A partnership created with no fixed duration.

There are two types of general partnerships: *partnerships at will* and *partnerships for a term*. A **partnership at will**, sometimes referred to as an **at-will partnership**, is a partnership in which the partners have agreed to form a partnership but have not agreed to a fixed duration of the partnership.

Example Three partners form a partnership to develop a new form of social media software, but they have not agreed as to how long the partnership will last or when it will end. They have created an at-will partnership.

partnership for a term (term partnership)
A partnership created for a fixed duration.

A partnership with a fixed duration is a **partnership for a term**, which is sometimes referred to as a **term partnership**. In this type of partnership, the partners have agreed that their partnership will terminate at some date in the future, upon the completion of an undertaking, or upon the happening of a specified event.

general partnership agreement (articles of general partnership or articles of partnership)
A contract between the general partners that sets forth the terms and conditions of their relationship as partners.

Examples Three partners create a partnership and agree that the partnership will terminate at the end of five years. Three partners create a partnership to construct a building and agree that the partnership will terminate when the real estate project is completed. In both situations the partners have created a partnership for a term.

Most states require the articles of general partnership to state the duration of the partnership, whether perpetual or limited. Some states require that the articles state the duration of the partnership only if the partnership has a limited term.

The following feature describes a general partnership agreement.

Business Environment

General Partnership Agreement

A partnership agreement is a contract between the general partners that sets forth the terms and conditions of their relationship as partners. The agreement may be written, oral, an electronic record, or implied from the conduct of the parties [RUPA 101(7)]. Most partnership agreements are written documents. General partnerships that exist for more than one year or are authorized to deal in real estate must be in writing under the Statute of Frauds. A partnership agreement is called a **general partnership agreement**, or **articles of general partnership**, or **articles of partnership**.

The general partners may tailor the structure of the partnership to meet their business needs. The parties can agree to almost any terms in their partnership agreement, except terms that are illegal. A partnership agreement may contain provisions regarding the division of profits and losses, who will manage the partnership, whether the partnership will be continued if a partner withdraws from the partnership, and how other important partnership decisions will be made.

The provisions of a partnership agreement take priority over the language of a state's limited partnership statute unless prohibited by law. If partners do not have a partnership agreement, then the rules of the state's partnership law become the *default rules* that govern the partnership and the relationship of the partners to the partnership and to each other. If there is a partnership agreement but it fails to provide for an essential term or contingency, the provisions of the relevant partnership law apply and serve as a gap-filling device to the partners' agreement.

The partnership agreement can be short and simple or long and complex. Most large partnerships and partnerships among sophisticated parties usually have detailed partnership agreements that govern the partnership's operations. However, many small and informal partnerships may not have a partnership agreement, and therefore the provisions of a state's partnership law become their partnership agreement.

The consent of all of the partners is required to amend a partnership agreement. It is good practice and highly recommended that partners put their partnership agreement in writing. A written document is important evidence of the terms of the agreement, particularly if a dispute arises among the partners. A partner is liable to the partnership and to the other partners for breaching the partnership agreement.

Partnership Property

All property acquired by the partnership, by transfer or otherwise, becomes partnership property and belongs to the partnership and not to the partners. Under the entity theory of the RUPA, the property belongs outright to the partnership [RUPA 203]. Under the UPA's aggregate theory, the partners are co-owners of the partnership's property as tenants in partnership [UPA 8(1) and 25(1)].

Taxation of General Partnerships

General partnerships do not pay federal income taxes. Instead, the income and losses of partnership flow onto and have to be reported on the partners' income tax returns. This is called **flow-through taxation**. A general partnership has to file an **information return** with the government, telling the government how much income was earned or the amount of losses incurred by the partnership. This way, the government tax authorities can trace whether partners are correctly reporting their income or losses.

flow-through taxation
A tax rule that provides that the income and losses of a general partnership are reported on the owner's personal income tax return.

Rights of General Partners

34.4 List and describe the rights of general partners.

The partners of a general partnership have certain rights. These are discussed in the following paragraphs.

Right to Participate in Management

In the absence of an agreement to the contrary, each general partner has an equal **right to participate in management** and conduct of partnership business [RUPA 401(f); UPA 18(e)]. In other words, each partner has one vote, regardless of the proportional size of their capital contribution or share in the partnership's profits. A simple majority decides most ordinary partnership matters. If the vote is tied, the action being voted on is defeated.

right to participate in management
The right of general partners to participate in the management of a general partnership. General partners have an equal vote in management unless otherwise agreed.

Example Selene, George, Maria, and Dimitri form a general partnership. They contribute $200,000 in capital to the partnership in the following amounts: Selene contributes $60,000 (30 percent), George contributes $10,000 (5 percent), Maria contributes $100,000 (50 percent), and Dimitri contributes $30,000 (15 percent). The partners have not agreed on how voting rights are allocated. Here, although the capital contributions of the partners differ significantly, each of the four partners has an equal say in the business.

If the partners do not want the partnership controlled by equal voting rights, and they want to allocate voting rights on a different basis, they can provide for that in their partnership agreement.

Example Partners may allocate voting rights based on partners' capital contributions to the partnership.

The partners can, in their partnership agreement, delegate management responsibility to a managing partner or a committee of partners. A partnership

statement of partnership authority
A statement filed by a general partnership with the secretary of state that states the authority, or limitations on the authority, of some or all of the partners to enter into certain transactions on behalf of the partnership.

may file a **statement of partnership authority** with the secretary of state that states the authority, or limitations on the authority, of some or all of the partners to enter into certain transactions on behalf of the partnership [RUPA 303(a)].

Right to Share in Profits

right to share in profits
The right of partners to share in the profits of a general partnership. Partners have an equal right to share the profits unless otherwise agreed.

Unless otherwise agreed, general partners have the right to an equal share in the partnership's profits and losses no matter what the amount of their capital contribution to the partnership [RUPA 401(b); UPA 18(a)]. The **right to share in profits** of the partnership is considered to be the right to share in the earnings from the investment of capital. Unless otherwise agreed, each partner is chargeable with a share of the partnership losses in proportion to the partner's share of the profits.

Example Selene, George, Maria, and Dimitri form a general partnership. They contribute $200,000 in capital to the partnership in the following amounts: Selene contributes $60,000 (30 percent), George contributes $10,000 (5 percent), Maria contributes $100,000 (50 percent), and Dimitri contributes $30,000 (15 percent). The partners have not agreed as to how profits will be divided. Assume that the partnership makes $100,000 profit for the year. Although the capital contributions of the partners differ significantly, each of the four partners will share equally in the profits of the business—each will receive $25,000.

If the partners want to override the preceding rules and share in profits or losses based on any different formula, they need to provide for this in their partnership agreement.

Examples Partnership agreements often provide that profits be allocated based on partners' capital contributions.

Right to Compensation

No nation was ever ruined by trade.
Benjamin Franklin
(1706–1790)

Unless otherwise agreed, a partner is not entitled to payment or renumeration for services performed for the partnership (except for reasonable compensation for services rendered in winding up the business of the partnership) [RUPA 401(h); UPA 18(f)]. Under this rule, partners are not entitled to receive a salary for providing services to the partnership unless agreed to by the partners. It is implied that general partners will devote full time and service to the partnership. Thus, unless otherwise agreed, income earned by partners from providing services elsewhere belongs to the partnership.

A partnership agreement may provide that a partner or partners be paid for providing services to the partnership. The partnership agreement can specify the salary or compensation to be paid or it can designate how to or who will make such a determination. The agreement may also provide that income earned from other sources does not belong to the partnership.

Right to Indemnification

Partners sometimes incur personal travel, business, and other expenses on behalf of the partnership. A general partner is entitled to **indemnification** (i.e., reimbursement) for such expenditures if they are reasonably incurred in the ordinary and proper conduct of the business [RUPA 401(c); UPA 18(b)].

Right to Return of Capital

On termination of a general partnership, the partners are entitled to have their capital contributions returned to them. However, this right is subordinated to the rights of creditors, who must be paid their claims first.

Right to Information

Each general partner has the right to demand true and full information from any other partner of all things affecting the partnership. This is known as the **right to information**. The corollary to this rule is that each partner has a duty to provide such information on the receipt of a reasonable demand. The partnership books (e.g., financial records, tax records) must be kept at the partnership's principal place of business, and the partnership must provide partners and their agents and attorneys access to the books and records. The partners have an absolute right to inspect and copy these records [RUPA 403; UPA 19 and 20].

right to information
The right of partners to demand true and full information from other partners about all things affecting the partnership.

Action for an Accounting and Right to Sue

Under the UPA, general partners are not permitted to sue the partnership or other partners at law. Instead, they have the right to bring an **action for an accounting** against other partners. An action for an accounting is a formal judicial proceeding in which the court is authorized to review the partnership and the partners' transactions and to award each partner his or her share of the partnership assets [UPA 24]. An accounting allows the court to balance the equities, adjust the accounts of the parties, and render a money judgment for or against partners, according to the balance struck.

action for an accounting
A formal judicial proceeding in which the court is authorized to review the partnership and the partners' transactions and award each partner his or her share of the partnership assets.

Example If a partner suspects that another partner is committing fraud by stealing partnership assets, the partner can bring an action for an accounting.

The RUPA permits the partnership or partners the **right to sue** at law, and a court may grant relief without requiring an accounting [RUPA 405]. Thus, a partnership may directly sue a partner to recover damages for breach of the partnership agreement or for the violation of a duty owed to the partnership. A partner may directly sue the partnership or another partner for legal or equitable relief. An action at law may, but need not, include an action for an accounting.

right to sue
The right of a partner to sue the partnership or other partners at law.

Example Four partners form a general partnership. Three partners believe that the fourth partner has breached the partnership agreement, causing a loss to the partnership. The partnership can bring a lawsuit against the suspected partner and recover any losses incurred by the partnership that are caused by a proven breach of the partnership agreement.

Duties of General Partners

34.5 List and describe the duties of general partners.

General partners owe certain duties to each other and to the partnership. The duties of partners are discussed in the following paragraphs.

Duty of Loyalty

General partners are in a fiduciary relationship with one another. As such, they owe each other a **duty of loyalty**. This duty is imposed by law and cannot be waived. If there is a conflict between partnership interests and personal interests, the partner must choose the interest of the partnership. The RUPA lists the specific acts that violate a partner's duty of loyalty, while the UPA lists some prohibited acts and allows for the implication of other violating acts [RUPA 404(b); UPA 21]. Some of the more common forms of breach of the duty of loyalty include:

duty of loyalty
A fiduciary duty that a general partner owes not to act adversely to the interests of the general partnership.

- **Self-dealing.** Undisclosed **self-dealing** occurs when a partner deals personally with the general partnership, such as buying or selling goods or property to the partnership. Such actions are permitted only if full disclosure is made and the consent of the other partners is obtained.

Example Giovanni is a partner in a general partnership that is looking for a piece of real property on which to build a new store. Giovanni owns a desirable piece of property. To sell the property to the partnership, Giovanni must first disclose his ownership interest and receive his co-partners' consent.

- **Usurping a partnership opportunity.** If a third party offers a business opportunity to a general partner in his or her partnership status, the partner cannot usurp the partnership opportunity for him- or herself before offering it to the partnership. This is called **usurping an opportunity**. If, when offered the opportunity, the partnership rejects the opportunity, the partner is free to pursue the opportunity.

Example Ada, Mandla, and Ingrid are general partners who own a general partnership that develops and builds commercial real estate projects such as office buildings, warehouses, and the like. One day, a person who owns a piece of vacant real estate approaches Ada and offers to sell the real estate to the general partnership. Ada sees that the price is excellent, so she purchases the real estate for herself and does not bring the opportunity to the partnership. Ada has usurped a partnership opportunity.

Fraud is infinite in variety; sometimes it is audacious and unblushing; sometimes it pays a sort of homage to virtue, and then it is modest and retiring; it would be honesty itself, if it could only afford it.
Lord MacNaghten *Reddaway v. Banham* (1896)

- **Competing with the partnership.** A general partner may not compete with the partnership without the permission of the other partners. This breach of loyalty is referred to as **competing with the partnership**.

Example A partner of a general partnership that operates an automobile dealership cannot open a competing automobile dealership without the co-partners' permission.

- **Making secret profits.** General partners may not make a **secret profit** from partnership business. The partnership can recover the secret profit.

Example A partner who accepts a bribe (i.e., a kickback) from a supplier has made a secret profit. The secret profit belongs to the partnership.

- **Committing a breach of confidentiality.** General partners owe a duty to keep partnership information confidential. Failure to do so is a **breach of confidentiality**.

Example Trade secrets, customer lists, and other secret information are confidential. A partner who misuses this information—either personally or by transferring the information to someone else—has breached confidentiality.

- **Misusing partnership property.** General partners owe a duty not to use partnership property for personal use. If a general partner does so, it constitutes a **misuse of property**.
- **Representing any party who has interests adverse to those of the partnership.**

Example A partnership engages in providing engineering services. If a partner acts as an agent for a competing engineering services business in negotiating a contract, the partner has breached her duty of loyalty.

A general partner who breaches the duty of loyalty holds any ill-gotten gains in trust for the partnership, and must disgorge the profits made from the breach to the partnership. In addition, a partner is liable to the partnership and to the other partners for damages caused by his or her breach of loyalty.

Under the UPA, the duty of loyalty cannot be waived [UPA 103]. Under the RUPA, the duty of loyalty cannot be eliminated, but a partnership agreement may identify specific types or categories of activities that do not violate the duty of loyalty, if not manifestly unreasonable [RUPA 103(b)(3)].

Example A partnership is engaged in real estate development. Under the RUPA, a partnership agreement may permit individual partners to trade in real estate on their own accounts without offering the opportunity to the partnership and without getting prior permission from the other partners.

A partner owes a **duty to account** to the partnership for any property, profit, or benefit derived by the partner in the conduct of partnership business or derived from the use of partnership property, including the appropriation of partnership property. This is also called the **duty of accountability**.

Duty of Limited Care

The RUPA imposes a statutory **duty of limited care** that general partners owe to the partnership and to the other partners. A general partner owes a duty not to engage in the following conduct that injures the partnership or other partners [RUPA 404(c)]:

1. Known violation of law
2. Intentional misconduct
3. Reckless conduct
4. Grossly negligent conduct

A partner is liable for any damages the partnership or other partners incur because of such conduct. The statutory duty is a limited duty in that it does not include liability for ordinary negligence. Thus, if a partner commits an ordinarily negligent act that is not grossly negligent, he or she is not liable to the partnership or to other partners

duty of limited care
A fiduciary duty that a general partner owes not to engage in: (1) known violation of the law, (2) intentional misconduct, (3) reckless conduct, or (4) grossly negligent conduct that injures the partnership or other partners. This duty does not include liability for ordinary negligence.

Example Basil is a partner in a general partnership. While engaging in partnership business, Basil accidentally causes an automobile accident that severely injures the other driver. The injured driver sues the partnership and recovers $400,000 in damages from the partnership. If Basil was texting a friend while driving, and the court finds this conduct to be grossly negligent, Basil is liable to the partnership for the $400,000 it paid to the injured party. If the court determines that Basil was ordinarily negligent when he caused the accident—for example, he did not see a stop sign—he will not be liable for any losses caused to the partnership.

There is no statutory duty of care under the UPA, although a common law duty of care, including that for negligence, is recognized by some courts.

Duty to Inform

General partners owe a **duty to inform** their co-partners of any information concerning partnership business and affairs that they possess that is reasonably required for the proper exercise of the other partners' rights and duties [RUPA 403(c); UPA 20]. A partner is liable for damages caused by failing to inform other partners of relevant information.

A partner's knowledge, notice, or receipt of a notice concerning any matters relating to the partnership affairs is immediately imputed to the partnership and other partners. Thus, the partnership and other partners are charged with the knowledge of the information even without being informed by the partner possessing the information [RUPA 102(f); UPA 12]. This is called **imputed knowledge**.

duty to inform
The duty a partner owes to inform partners of information that the partner possesses that is relevant to the business and affairs of the partnership.

Example Cecile and Ambrosia are partners. Cecile knows that a piece of real property owned by their general partnership contains dangerous toxic wastes but fails to inform Ambrosia of this fact. Even though Ambrosia does not have actual knowledge of this fact, it is imputed to the partnership and thus to Ambrosia.

Duty of Obedience

The **duty of obedience** requires general partners to adhere to the provisions of the partnership agreement and the decisions of the partnership. A partner who breaches this duty is liable to the partnership for any damages caused by the breach.

duty of obedience
A duty that requires partners to adhere to the provisions of the partnership agreement and the decisions of the partnership.

Example Jodie, Bart, and Denise form a general partnership to develop real property. Their partnership agreement specifies that acts of the partners are limited to those necessary to accomplish the partnership's purpose. Suppose Bart, acting alone, loses $100,000 of partnership funds in commodities trading. Bart is personally liable to the partnership for the lost funds because he breached the partnership agreement.

Liability of General Partners and General Partnerships

34.6 Describe the liability of general partners and general partnerships.

A general partnership is liable for certain acts of general partners. A general partnership is liable for authorized contracts and debts entered into by partners on behalf of the partnership, and for tortious conduct committed by partners while acting within the scope of partnership business. This liability is referred to as the **liability of a general partnership**.

liability of a general partnership
Liability that is imposed on a general partnership for contracts and debts of the partnership and for tortious conduct committed by partners while acting within the scope of partnership business.

Partners of a general partnership have **unlimited personal liability** for the contracts and torts of the partnership. This could lead to the seizure and sale of a partner's personal assets to pay partnership obligations. Thus, there is substantial personal financial risk of being a partner in a general partnership. Tort and contract liability of general partners and general partnerships are discussed in the following paragraphs.

unlimited personal liability of a general partner
A general partner is personally liable for the contracts and debts of the general partnership, and for the torts (e.g., negligence, fraud) and breaches of trust committed by partners while acting on the partnership business.

Tort Liability of General Partnerships

A general partnership is liable for loss or injury caused to a person, or for a penalty incurred, as a result of a wrongful act or omission, or other actionable conduct, of a partner acting in the ordinary course of business of the partnership or with authority of the partnership [RUPA 305(a); UPA 13]. Thus, a general partnership is liable for tortious conduct committed while partners are acting within the scope of partnership business. The tort could be caused by a partner's negligent act, a breach of trust (e.g., embezzlement from a customer's account), breach of fiduciary duty, fraud, intentional tort, or another form of tort.

Example A partner, while driving his automobile on partnership business, negligently causes an automobile accident that injures another driver. The partnership is liable for the damages caused to the injured person.

Contract Liability of General Partnerships

A general partnership must act through its agents—that is, its partners. Each general partner is an **agent** of the partnership for the purpose of its business. An act of a partner, including the execution of a contract in the partnership name for apparently carrying on in the ordinary course the partnership business or business of the kind carried on by the partnership, binds the partnership [RUPA 301(1); UPA 9(1)]. Partnership contracts include contracts with suppliers, customers, lenders, landlords, employees, and others. A general partnership is liable if it does not perform these contracts.

agent
Each general partner is an agent of the partnership for the purpose of its business, and an act of a partner in the ordinary course of the partnership business binds the partnership.

Example A partner, while acting within her partnership authority, signs a contract to purchase equipment on credit to be used by the partnership. The partnership is bound to perform this contract and to pay for the equipment when the loan is due. If the partnership fails to pay the loan when it is due, the lender can sue the partnership to recover the amount of the funds due.

Tort Liability of General Partners

While acting on partnership business, a general partner might commit a tort that causes injury to a third person. The partnership is liable for damages caused by such tortious conduct. Under both the RUPA and the UPA, general partners have **joint and several liability** for the tort liability of the partnership [RUPA 306(a); UPA 15(a)]. This means that a plaintiff may sue all of the partners in a lawsuit (jointly) or some or one of the partners in a lawsuit (individually) to recover unpaid tort liability of a partnership.

joint and several liability
The personal liability of general partners where a plaintiff can sue all or some or any one of the partners jointly or individually to recover unpaid tort liability of the general partnership [RUPA Section 306(a); UPA Section 15(a)]. The RUPA imposes joint and several liability on general partners for unpaid contract liability of a general partnership [RUPA Section 306(a)].

A plaintiff must obtain a judgment against the partnership and exhaust the partnership's assets before recovering against the separate assets of a partner [RUPA 307(d)]. Further, a judgment against the partnership is not by itself a judgment against a partner. A judgment creditor must obtain a judgment against a partner before that partner is personally liable [RUPA 307(c)]. A plaintiff may sue the partnership and all, some, or one partner in the same action. Or a plaintiff may sue the partnership first and if a judgment is obtained, but not paid by the partnership, the plaintiff can then sue all, some, or one partner in a subsequent action to recover the unpaid judgment. If a plaintiff sues one or some partners but the judgment is not satisfied, the plaintiff can bring subsequent actions against other partners until the judgment amount is fully paid.

Under joint and several liability, one partner among co-partners could end up paying the entire judgment. A general partner who is made to pay more than his or her proportionate share of the judgment may seek indemnification in a subsequent lawsuit from those partners who were not named in a plaintiff's lawsuit or who were named but were not made to pay the judgment.

Example Onyx, DeShawn, and Sage form a general partnership. While acting on partnership business, Onyx negligently causes an automobile accident that severely injures a pedestrian. The pedestrian sues the partnership and DeShawn, who is wealthy, but does not sue Onyx or Sage, and is awarded a judgment of $1 million. After recovering $100,000 from the partnership, the extent of the partnership's assets, the injured pedestrian recovers the unpaid $900,000 from DeShawn. DeShawn is left to recover indemnification from Onyx and Sage. If Onyx and Sage have no assets, DeShawn ends up paying the entire $900,000.

Contract Liability of General Partners

The RUPA imposes *joint and several liability* on general partners for unpaid contract liability of a general partnership [RUPA 306(a)].

The UPA does not impose joint and several liability on general partners for unpaid contract liability of a general partnership. Instead, under the UPA, general partners have **joint liability** for the contract liability of the partnership [UPA 15(b)]. This means that a plaintiff who sues to recover on a partnership contract must name the partnership and all of the partners as defendants in the same lawsuit. The omission of one partner in the action means the lawsuit will be dismissed.

joint liability
The personal liability of general partners where a plaintiff who sues to recover on a partnership contract must name the partnership and all of the partners as defendants in a joint action.

Example Zachary, Vivienne, and Pari form a general partnership. The partnership enters into a contract and borrows $1 million from a bank. When the partnership begins to fail, it stops payment on the debt it owes to the bank. The partnership has $100,000 of assets and still owes the bank $1 million. Assume the doctrine of joint liability is applicable. The bank sues the partnership and Vivienne, who is wealthy, but does not sue Zachery or Pari. The lawsuit will be dismissed.

However, if all of the partners have been joined in the lawsuit, the plaintiff wins a judgment, and the partnership's assets have been exhausted but the judgment is not satisfied, the plaintiff can recover the balance from any one of the partners.

Critical Legal Thinking Question

How do *joint and several liability* and *joint liability* differ?

If the judgment is not then fully paid, the plaintiff may recover against another partner, and so on. Thus, one partner, or several partners, may be required to pay the entire unpaid judgment. The result under joint liability is the same as under joint and several liability as long as a plaintiff meets the pleading burden of naming all of the partners in the initial lawsuit against the partnership.

The following feature describes the liability of incoming partners.

Business Environment

Liability of Incoming Partners

A new **incoming partner** who is admitted to a general partnership is not personally liable for any partnership obligations incurred before the person's admission as a partner (**antecedent debts**). However, the incoming partner is liable for the existing debts and obligations of the partnership up to the extent of the incoming partner's capital contribution. The incoming partner is personally liable for debts and obligations incurred by the general partnership after he or she became a partner [RUPA 306(b); UPA 17].

Example On February 1, Ella is admitted as a new general partner to an existing general partnership and invests $100,000 as her capital contribution. As of that date, the partnership owes $500,000 of preexisting debt. On June 1, the general partnership borrows $1 million of new debt. On November 1, the partnership goes bankrupt, has no assets, but still owes both debts. Ella has lost her capital contribution of $100,000, which the partnership has spent. She is not personally liable for the $500,000 of existing debt owed by the partnership when she joined the partnership, but she is personally liable for the $1 million of debt that the partnership borrowed after she became a partner.

incoming partner
A new partner who is admitted to a general partnership.

Dissociation of a Partner and the Dissolution and Winding Up of a General Partnership

34.7 Describe the dissociation of a partner and the dissolution and winding up of a general partnership.

The RUPA introduces a new concept called *dissociation* that changes the law governing partnership breakups. Both the RUPA and the UPA provide rules for the dissolution of a general partnership. The concepts of dissociation and dissolution are discussed in the following paragraphs.

Dissociation of a Partner

dissociation
A change in the relation of partners caused by any partner ceasing to be associated in the carrying on of partnership business that does not cause the dissolution of the partnership [RUPA Section 601].

Under the RUPA, **dissociation** is a change in the relation of partners caused by any partner ceasing to be associated in the carrying on of a term partnership's business that does not cause the dissolution of the partnership.

The events that cause the dissociation of a partner but not the dissolution of the partnership include: (1) death of a partner; (2) bankruptcy of a partner; (3) a partner's transfer of all interest in the partnership; (4) expulsion of a partner as provided for in the partnership agreement; (5) expulsion of a partner because it is unlawful to carry on business with that partner; (6) corporate partner's charter is revoked; (7) a partnership that is a partner is dissolved; (8) wrongful dissociation by a partner; (9) a judicial determination that a partner breached the partnership agreement; or (10) a judicial determination that a partner engaged in conduct that makes it impracticable to carry on business with the partner. These events only cause dissolution if within 90 days of their occurrence at least half the partners vote to dissolve the partnership [RUPA 601].

buyout
The purchase of a dissociating partner's interest in the partnership where there is a dissociation of a partner that does not cause the dissolution of the partnership.

If a partner is dissociated from a partnership without resulting in the dissolution of the partnership, the partnership shall cause the dissociated partner's interest to be purchased. The **buyout** may be by the partnership or by the remaining partners. The buyout price is the greater of (1) the liquidation value or (2) the value based on the sale of the entire business as a going concern [RUPA 701(a) and (b)]. If the dissociating partner does not believe the price to be fair, the partner may bring a legal action to have a court determine the buyout price [RUPA 701(i)].

The UPA does not recognize the concept of dissociation.

Dissolution of a Partnership

Both the RUPA and the UPA provide for the dissolution of a general partnership upon the occurrence of certain events. **Dissolution** is a change in the relation of partners caused by any partner ceasing to be associated in the carrying on of partnership business that causes the partnership to end, be wound up, and be terminated.

dissolution
A change in the relation of partners caused by any partner ceasing to be associated in the carrying on of partnership business that causes the partnership to end, be wound up and terminated.

The RUPA and the UPA provide that a general partnership is dissolved and must be wound up and terminated in the following situations:

1. The general partners of an at-will partnership or a term partnership may specify in their partnership agreement events that will dissolve their partnership. The partnership is dissolved upon the occurrence of a such an event, and will be wound up and terminated [RUPA 801(3); UPA 31(1)(c)].
2. An at-will partnership is dissolved by receipt of a notice from a general partner of his or her express will to withdraw from the partnership [RUPA 801(1); UPA 31(1)(b)].
3. A term partnership is dissolved upon the expiration of the stated term of the partnership or the completion of the specified undertaking of the partnership [RUPA 801(2)(iii); UPA 31(1)(a)].
4. A partnership for a term can be dissolved before the expiration of its term or the completion of its specified goal upon the express will of all of the general partners; that is, all of the general partners vote to dissolve and wind up the term partnership [RUPA 801(2)(i); UPA 31(1)(c)].

The UPA does not provide for dissociation of a partner, but only provides for the dissolution of a general partnership. Thus, events listed in the RUPA that cause the dissociation of a partner but not the dissolution of the partnership, would, under the UPA, automatically cause the dissolution of the partnership [UPA 31 and 32].

The merchant has no country.
Thomas Jefferson (1743–1826)
Third president of the United States

Example Under the RUPA, the death of a partner is considered a dissociation of the partner, which does not cause the dissolution of the partnership; the partnership continues. Under the UPA, the death of the partner automatically causes the dissolution of the partnership; the partnership must be wound up and terminated.

The following feature describes the liability of outgoing partners.

Business Environment

Liability of Outgoing Partners

The withdrawal or other dissociation of a partner from a general partnership where the partnership is continued does not discharge the liability of the **outgoing partner** for existing partnership debts and obligations. Thus, the outgoing partner remains personally liable for the debts and obligations of the partnership at the time he or she withdraws or otherwise disassociates from the partnership. The outgoing partner is not liable for any new debts and obligations incurred by the general partnership after the dissociation or dissolution [RUPA 703(a)].

Example On March 1, Max, a partner of an at-will partnership, withdraws from the partnership. The partnership is continued by the other partners. As of that date, the partnership owes $500,000 of preexisting debt. On June 1, the partnership borrows $1 million of new debt. On November 1, the partnership goes bankrupt, has no assets, but still owes both debts. Max is personally liable for the $500,000 of existing debt owed by the partnership when he withdrew from the partnership, but he is not personally liable for the $1 million of debt that the partnership borrowed after he left the partnership.

Wrongful Withdrawal

A partner has the *power* to withdraw from a general partnership at any time, whether it is a partnership at will or a partnership for a term. A partner who withdraws from an at-will partnership has the *right* to do so and is therefore not liable to the partnership for his or her withdrawal. A partner who withdraws from a partnership for a definite term prior to the expiration of the term or the completion of the undertaking does not have the right to do so. Under the RUPA, a partner's wrongful withdrawal is called a **wrongful dissociation**. Under the UPA, a partner's wrongful withdrawal is called a **wrongful dissolution**. The partner is liable for damages caused by his or her wrongful withdrawal [RUPA 602(c); UPA 38(2)].

wrongful dissociation
A situation in which a partner wrongfully dissociates from a partnership.

wrongful dissolution
A situation in which a partner wrongfully causes the dissolution of a partnership.

If a partner wrongfully withdraws from a term partnership prior to the expiration of the specified term or the accomplishment of the specified object of the partnership, and the partnership continues in business, the withdrawing member is paid the liquidation value of his or her interest on the date of expiration of the term, unless the partner can establish that an earlier payment will not cause undue hardship to the business of the partnership [RUPA 701(h)].

Notice of Dissociation and Notice of Dissolution

The dissociation of a partner terminates that partner's **actual authority** to enter into contracts or act on behalf of the partnership. The dissolution of a partnership terminates all partners' actual authority to enter into contracts or otherwise act on behalf of the partnership except as necessary for the winding up of the partnership. However, unless curtailed, a dissociating partner or the partners of a dissolving partnership have **apparent authority** to enter into unauthorized contracts on behalf of the partnership.

Therefore, to limit liability for unauthorized contracts, a partnership should give immediate **actual notice** of the dissociation of the partner to its creditors, parties with whom the partnership has dealt, and parties that the partnership knows have knowledge of the dissociating partner's membership in the partnership. Actual notice of the dissolution of a partnership should be given to these same parties. Actual notice may be in writing, a phone call, email, text, or other type of communication. Actual notice terminates a third party's ability to enforce contracts against a partnership entered into purportedly on behalf of the partnership with a dissociating partner or a partner of a dissolved partnership.

Under the RUPA, a continuing partnership or the dissociating partner may file a **statement of dissociation** with the secretary of state stating the name of the partnership and the name of the partner who has dissociated from the partnership [RUPA 704]. The RUPA authorizes a partnership or partner of a dissolving partnership to file a **statement of dissolution** with the secretary of state stating the name of the partnership and that the partnership has dissolved and is winding up its business [RUPA 805]. Third parties are deemed to have notice of dissociation or dissolution 90 days after the statement is filed. The filing of these statements constitutes **constructive notice** of the dissociation or dissolution.

statement of dissociation
A statement that is filed with the appropriate state agency that states the name of the partnership from which a partner is dissociating and the name of the partner who has dissociated from the partnership.

statement of dissolution
A statement that is filed with the appropriate state agency that states the name of a dissolved partnership and that the partnership has dissolved and is winding up its business.

Constructive notice under the UPA consists of publishing a notice of dissolution in a newspaper of general circulation serving the area where the business of the partnership was regularly conducted [UPA 35(1)]. Because the UPA does not recognize the concept of dissociation, there are no rules for notice concerning dissociation.

Winding Up of a General Partnership

Unless a partnership is continued, the partnership continues after dissolution only for the purpose of **winding up** its business. The process of winding up consists of the liquidation (sale) of partnership assets and the distribution of the cash proceeds to satisfy claims against the partnership. The surviving partners have

winding up
The process of liquidating a partnership's assets and distributing the proceeds to satisfy claims against the partnership.

the right to wind up the partnership. If a surviving partner performs the winding up, that partner is entitled to reasonable compensation for his or her services [RUPA 401(h); UPA 18(f)].

Distribution of Assets on Dissolution

After partnership assets have been liquidated and reduced to cash, the proceeds are distributed to satisfy claims against the partnership. The RUPA and the UPA differ as to the priority of distributions.

Under the RUPA claims are paid in the following order [RUPA 807(a)]:

1. Creditors (including partners who are creditors)
2. Settlement of partners' accounts

Under the UPA claims are paid in the following order [UPA 40(b)]:

1. Creditors (except partners who are creditors)
2. Creditor-partners
3. Capital contributions
4. Profits

The RUPA considers all creditors, including partners who are creditors, equally. The UPA gives priority to the payment of non-partner creditors, which must be paid in full before partner creditors are paid. If there are insufficient funds to pay creditors of a class in full, the creditors will be paid proportionately for their claims. If the partnership cannot satisfy its creditors' claims, the partners are personally liable for the partnership's debts and obligations.

After creditors' claims have been paid, partners are first paid cash in an amount equal to their capital contributions that have not been previously returned, and are then paid their share of the profits of the partnership. A partnership agreement may provide for a different distribution among partners.

Termination of a General Partnership

After the winding up of its business is completed, the partnership automatically terminates, which ends the legal existence of the partnership [RUPA 802(a); UPA 30].

The following feature discusses use of a continuation agreement for a general partnership.

continuation agreement
An agreement among the partners of a general partnership that specifies if and under what conditions a partnership will continue upon the occurrence of certain events.

Business Environment

Continuation Agreement

It is good practice for the partners of a general partnership to enter into a **continuation agreement** that expressly sets forth the events that allow for continuation of the partnership. The agreement can be part of a partnership agreement, or it can be a separate agreement entered into at any time by the partners. A continuation agreement can address most issues, and its provisions take precedent over the rules of the RUPA and the UPA unless they otherwise are contrary to law. A continuation agreement cannot prohibit a general partner from withdrawing from a partnership.

The partners may specify in their partnership agreement how the withdrawal, death, or other dissociation of a partner from the partnership will be handled. This includes specifying under what circumstances a partnership will continue, the amount to be paid to outgoing partners or a formula for determining this amount, when the money will be paid, and other details. It is best practice to have a written continuation agreement. The partnership can operate under the existing name of the partnership even if it contains the name of a dissociated, withdrawn, or deceased partner.

When a partnership is continued, the partnership is composed of the remaining partners and any new partners admitted to the partnership. Existing creditors have equal status with new creditors of the partnership.

Key Terms and Concepts

Action for an accounting (601)
Actual authority (608)
Actual notice (608)
Agent (604)
Antecedent debt (606)
Apparent authority (608)
Breach of confidentiality (602)
Buyout (606)
Certificate of partnership (statement of partnership) (597)
Competing with the partnership (602)
Constructive notice (608)
Continuation agreement (609)
Co-ownership (597)
d.b.a. (doing business as) (594)
Dissociation (606)
Dissolution (607)
Duty of limited care (603)
Duty of loyalty (601)
Duty of obedience (603)
Duty to account (duty of accountability) (603)
Duty to inform (603)
Entrepreneur (593)
Fictitious business name statement (certificate of trade name) (594)
Flow-through taxation (599)
Form 1040 (595)
General partner (ordinary partner or partner) (597)
General partnership (ordinary partnership or partnership) (596)
General partnership agreement (articles of general partnership or articles of partnership) (598)
Imputed knowledge (603)
Incoming partner (606)
Indemnification (600)
Information return (599)
Joint and several liability (605)
Joint liability (605)
Liability of a general partnership (604)
Misuse of property (602)
Outgoing partner (607)
Ownership interest (597)
Partnership at will (at-will partnership) (598)
Partnership for a term (term partnership) (598)
Profit motive (597)
Revised Uniform Partnership Act (RUPA) (596)
Right to information (601)
Right to participate in management (599)
Right to share in profits (600)
Right to sue (601)
Schedule C (Profit or Loss from Business) (595)
Secret profit (602)
Self-dealing (601)
Sole proprietor (594)
Sole proprietorship (594)
Statement of dissociation (608)
Statement of dissolution (608)
Statement of partnership authority (600)
Trade name (594)
Uniform Partnership Act (UPA) (596)
Unlimited personal liability of a general partner (604)
Unlimited personal liability of a sole proprietor (595)
Usurping an opportunity (602)
Voluntary association (597)
Winding up (608)
Wrongful dissociation (608)
Wrongful dissolution (608)

Critical Legal Thinking Cases

34.1 Sole Proprietorship James Schuster was a sole proprietor doing business as (d.b.a.) Diversity Heating and Plumbing (Diversity Heating). Diversity Heating was in the business of selling, installing, and servicing heating and plumbing systems. George Vernon and others (Vernon) owned a building that needed a new boiler, and they hired Diversity Heating to install it. Diversity Heating installed the boiler and gave a warranty that the boiler would not crack for 10 years. Four years later, James Schuster died. On that date, James's son, Jerry Schuster, inherited his father's business and thereafter ran the business as a sole proprietorship d.b.a. Diversity Heating and Plumbing. One year later, the boiler installed in Vernon's building broke and could not be repaired. Vernon demanded that Jerry Schuster honor the warranty and replace the boiler. When Jerry Schuster refused to do so, Vernon had the boiler replaced at a cost of $8,203 and sued Jerry Schuster to recover this amount for breach of warranty. Jerry Schuster argued that he was a sole proprietor and as such he was not liable for the business obligations his father had incurred while operating his own sole proprietorship. Is Jerry Schuster liable for the warranty made by his father? *Vernon v. Schuster, d/b/a/ Diversity Heating and Plumbing*, 688 N.E.2d 1172, 1997 Ill. Lexis 482 (Supreme Court of Illinois, 1997)

34.2 Liability of General Partners Jose Pena and Joseph Antenucci were medical doctors who were partners in a medical practice. Both doctors treated Elaine Zuckerman during her pregnancy. Her son, Daniel Zuckerman, was born with severe physical problems. Elaine, as Daniel's mother and natural guardian, brought a medical malpractice suit against both doctors. The jury found that Pena was guilty of medical malpractice but that Antenucci was not. The amount of the verdict totaled $4 million. The trial court entered judgment against Pena but not against Antenucci. Plaintiff Zuckerman made a posttrial motion for judgment against both defendants. Is Antenucci jointly and severally liable for the medical malpractice of his partner, Pena? *Zuckerman v. Antenucci*, 478 N.Y.S.2d 578, 1984 N.Y.Misc. Lexis 3283 (Supreme Court of New York, 1984)

34.3 Tort Liability Thomas McGrath was a partner in the law firm Tarbenson, Thatcher, McGrath, Treadwell & Schoonmaker. One day, at approximately 4:30 p.m., McGrath went to a restaurant–cocktail establishment in Kirkland, Washington. From that time until about 11:00 p.m., he imbibed considerable alcohol while socializing and discussing personal and firm-related business. After 11:00 p.m., McGrath did not discuss firm business but continued to socialize and drink until approximately 1:45 a.m., when he and Fredrick Hayes, another bar patron, exchanged words. Shortly thereafter, the two encountered each other outside, and after another exchange, McGrath shot Hayes. Hayes sued McGrath and the law firm for damages. Who is liable? *Hayes v. Tarbenson, Thatcher, McGrath, Treadwell & Schoonmaker*, 749 P.2d 178, 1988 Wash. App. Lexis 27 (Court of Appeals of Washington, 1988)

Ethics Case

34.4 Ethics Case John Gilroy, an established commercial photographer in Kalamazoo, Michigan, had a small contractual clientele of schools for which he provided student portrait photographs. Robert Conway joined Gilroy's established business, and they formed a partnership called Skylight Studios. Both partners solicited schools with success, and gross sales, which were $40,000, increased every year and amounted to over $200,000 six years later.

Conway notified Gilroy that the partnership was dissolved. Gilroy discovered that Conway had closed up the partnership's place of business and opened up his own business, had purchased equipment and supplies in preparation for opening his own business and charged them to the partnership, had taken with him the partnership's employees and most of its equipment, had personally taken over the business of some customers by telling them the partnership was being dissolved, and had withdrawn partnership funds for personal use. Gilroy sued Conway for an accounting, alleging that Conway had converted partnership assets. Did Conway act ethically in this case? Who wins? *Gilroy v. Conway*, 391 N.W.2d 419, 1986 Mich. App. Lexis 2633 (Court of Appeals of Michigan, 1986)

CHAPTER

35 Limited Partnerships and Special Partnerships

Pglam/E+/123RF

OIL FIELD

Businesses such as real estate ventures, energy and natural resource developments, and investment funds operate as limited partnerships.

Learning Objectives

After studying this chapter, you should be able to:

35.1 Define and describe a *limited partnership*.

35.2 Describe the formation of a limited partnership.

35.3 Identify and describe the liability of limited partnerships, general partners, and limited partners of limited partnerships.

35.4 Describe how a limited partnership is managed.

35.5 Describe the rights and duties of general partners and limited partners.

35.6 Describe partner dissociation, identify when a limited partnership may be continued, and describe the process of dissolution and winding up of a limited partnership.

35.7 Define and describe a *limited liability limited partnership*.

“There are a great many of us who will adhere to that ancient principle that we prefer to be governed by the power of laws, and not by the power of men.”

— *Woodrow Wilson*
Speech, September 25, 1912

Introduction to Limited Partnerships, Limited Liability Limited Partnerships, and Special Partnerships

All states have enacted statutes that provide for the creation of *limited* partnerships. Limited partnerships are most often used for short-term projects, but they may be also used for long-term ventures. Because of tax benefits, families sometimes form limited partnerships to operate family businesses. These are called *family limited partnerships*. Limited partnerships that are listed and publicly traded on stock exchanges are called *master limited partnerships*. Some states permit the formation of a special form of partnership, called a *limited liability limited partnership*.

Man is an animal that makes bargains; no other animal does this—no dog exchanges bones with another.
Adam Smith (1723–1790)

This chapter discusses the formation, operation, and dissolution of limited partnerships, family limited partnerships, master limited partnerships, and limited liability limited partnerships.

Limited Partnership

35.1 Define and describe a *limited partnership*.

Today, all states have enacted statutes that provide for the creation of a **limited partnership**, also called an **LP**.

limited partnership
A partnership that has two types of partners:(1) general partners and (2) limited partners.

Definition of a Limited Partnership

A limited partnership is a partnership with two types of partners: (1) general partners and (2) limited partners. An LP must have one or more general partners and one or more limited partners [ULPA (2001) 104; RULPA 101(7)]. There are no upper limits on the number of general or limited partners allowed in a limited partnership. A limited partnership is an entity distinct from its partners [ULPA (2001) 104(a); RULPA 104(a)].

General partners and limited partners of a limited partnership have different responsibilities and different degrees of liability. A **general partner** invests capital, manages the partnership, and is personally liable for partnership obligations. A **limited partner** invests capital, often does not participate in management, and is not personally liable for partnership obligations beyond his or her capital contribution (see **Exhibit 35.1**).

general partner
A partner in a limited partnership who invests capital, manages the partnership, and is personally liable for partnership obligations.

limited partner
A partner in a limited partnership who invests capital, often does not participate in management, and is not personally liable for partnership obligations beyond his or her capital contribution.

A person becomes a general partner or a limited partner as provided in the limited partnership agreement or with the consent of all the partners [ULPA (2001) 301 and 401; RULPA 301 and 401]. A person can be both a general partner and a limited partner. Any person—including individuals, general partnerships, corporations, limited liability corporations, limited partnerships, limited liability partnerships, joint ventures, estates, trusts, associations, governments, governmental agencies, and other legal or commercial entities—may be a general or limited partner of a limited partnership.

General partners are the principals of the business. They usually have the idea for the business, develop a business plan, and make decisions and manage the business to attain its goals. Limited partners' investments make up most of the

Exhibit 35.1 LIMITED PARTNERSHIP

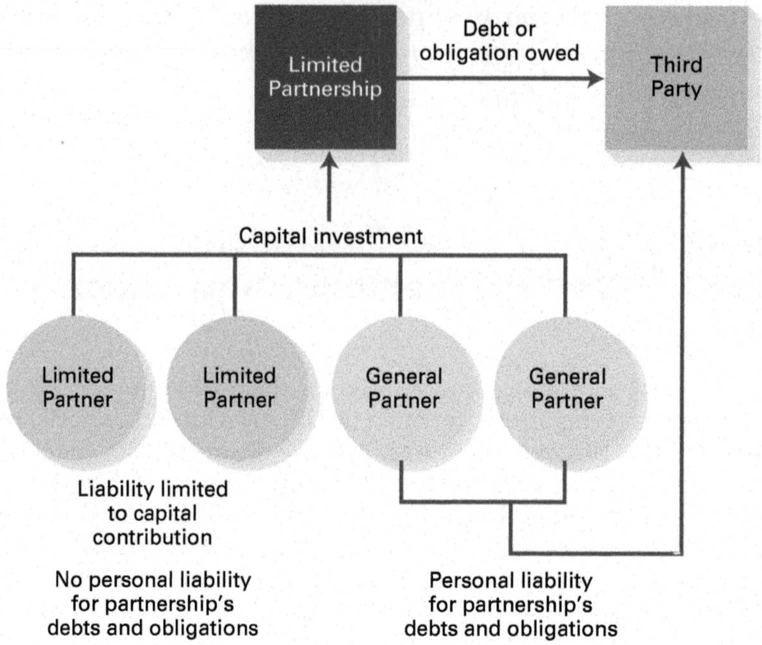

funding of a limited partnership. Usually, general partners put in approximately 10 to 20 percent of the funds, and the limited partners provide the rest of the funds for the venture.

If the business fails, general partners lose their investment and are also personally liable for unpaid partnership obligations. Limited partners are considered passive investors. They could lose their investment but are not personally liable for the obligations of the limited partnership. Limited partners function similarly to shareholders in a corporation; that is, they provide capital to the enterprise and expect to make a profit from their investment.

Businesses That Operate as Limited Partnerships

Some limited partnerships are large, such as those used to construct and operate major real estate developments.

Example One famous limited partnership is the Boston Red Sox Baseball Club Limited Partnership, which owns and operates the Boston Red Sox professional baseball team.

Some limited partnerships are small, particularly those in which one person or a few people want to engage in a business but need funds from investors to do so.

Four things belong to a judge: to hear courteously, to answer wisely, to consider soberly, and to decide impartially.
Socrates (470–399 BCE)

Example Asher and Cloe want to open a new restaurant called 1000 South. They form a limited partnership with themselves as the general partners, and they seek limited partner investments from family and friends.

A limited partnership may be conducted for any lawful purpose [ULPA (2001) 104(b); RULPA 104(b)]. A limited partnership has a perpetual duration unless otherwise agreed by the partners [ULPA (2001) 104(c); RULPA 104(c)]. Many limited partnerships are formed for a duration of a predetermined length of time or to complete a specific undertaking.

Example A film company decides to produce a full-length feature film. The film company decides on the movie to produce, the story line, and other details of the movie. The film company seeks to raise capital to fund the movie and forms a limited partnership to do so. The film company becomes the general partner, and the limited partnership sells ownership interests to limited partners who provide the majority of the funds. This is a short-term project that is particularly suited for the use of a limited partnership.

One of the major drawbacks for investors who are limited partners in a limited partnership is that their investment usually is not liquid because there is no readily available market for buying and selling most limited partnership interests. During the operation of the partnership, limited partners may be paid a quarterly distribution, if feasible. Upon the liquidation of the limited partnership, if the limited partnership has been successful, general partners frequently are paid 50 percent or more of the gain, and the limited partners are paid the rest of the gain.

The following feature discusses the Revised Uniform Limited Partnership Act and the Uniform Limited Partnership Act (2001).

Revised Uniform Limited Partnership Act and Uniform Limited Partnership Act (2001)
Uniform model acts that provide modern and comprehensive rules for the formation, operation, and dissolution of limited partnerships.

Landmark Laws

Revised Uniform Limited Partnership Act and Uniform Limited Partnership Act (2001)

In 1916, the National Conference of Commissioners on Uniform State Laws (NCCUSL), a group of lawyers, judges, and legal scholars, promulgated the **Uniform Limited Partnership Act (ULPA)**. The ULPA is a model act that contains a uniform set of provisions for the formation, operation, and dissolution of limited partnerships. A uniform model act does not become the law of a state until the state adopts the act. Most states enacted the ULPA as their limited partnership law.

In 1976, the NCCUSL promulgated the **Revised Uniform Limited Partnership Act (RULPA)**, a model limited partnership act that provides more modern and comprehensive rules for the formation, operation, and dissolution of limited partnerships. This act was revised in 1985. The majority of states adopted the 1985 version of RULPA. This RULPA superseded the ULPA in the states that have adopted it.

In 2001, the NCCUSL promulgated a new uniform model limited partnership act called the **Uniform Limited Partnership Act (2001)** or **ULPA (2001)**, which is sometimes referred to as **Re-RULPA**. The ULPA (2001) is a stand-alone act that provides updated, more flexible, and comprehensive rules for the formation, operation, and dissolution of limited partnerships. The ULPA (2001) recognizes modern-day uses of limited partnerships by sophisticated parties seeking strong centralized management with passive limited partners having little control over management. The ULPA (2001) has been adopted by the majority of states. This act was amended in 2011 and 2013.

Many states, whether they have adopted the 1985 model act or the 2001 model act, call their limited partnership law the "Uniform Limited Partnership Act." The ULPA (2001) and RULPA 1985 version provide the foundations for the discussion of limited partnership law in this chapter.

Formation of a Limited Partnership

35.2 Describe the formation of a limited partnership.

The creation of a limited partnership is formal and requires public disclosure. The entity must comply with the statutory requirements of the limited partnership law of the state. The law of the state in which the limited partnership is organized governs the partnership, its internal affairs, and the liability of its partners [ULPA (2001) 106; RULPA 901].

Certificate of Limited Partnership

In order for a limited partnership to be formed, two or more partners must sign a **certificate of limited partnership** and file it with the secretary of state of the state in which the limited partnership is formed [ULPA (2001) 201(a); RULPA 201(a)]. The certificate must state:

certificate of limited partnership
A document that two or more persons must sign and file with the secretary of state of the state of organization that forms a limited partnership.

- Name of the limited partnership
- Street and mailing address of its designated office
- Name and street and mailing address of its initial agent for service of process
- Name and street and mailing address of each general partner

Some states require the disclosure of additional information, such as the general character of the business, the capital provided by each partner, and such. The partners may include other matters in the certificate that do not violate the law. The limited partnership is formed when the certificate of limited partnership is filed with the secretary of state, which is in writing and is often filed in electronic format. A certificate of limited partnership must be amended to reflect the admission or withdrawal of a general partner, and may be amended to reflect other matters [ULPA (2001) 202; RULPA 202(a)].

Capital contributions of general and limited partners may consist of tangible and personal property, including money, property, services performed, promissory notes, and agreements to contribute cash or property or to perform future services [ULPA (2001) 501; RULPA 501].

limited partnership agreement (articles of limited partnership)
An agreement that sets forth the rights and duties of general and limited partners; the terms and conditions regarding the operation, termination, and dissolution of a partnership; and other details of the limited partnership.

Name of a Limited Partnership

The name of a limited partnership must contain the phrase "limited partnership" or the abbreviation "L.P." or "LP" [ULPA (2001) 108(b); RULPA 108(b)]. The name of a limited partnership may contain the name of any partner [ULPA (2001) 108(a); RULPA 108(b)]. A limited partnership that operates under a fictitious business name must file a fictitious business name statement—d.b.a. (doing business as)—with the appropriate government agency to operate under a trade name.

The following feature describes a limited partnership agreement.

Business Environment

Limited Partnership Agreement

A limited partnership agreement among the partners is not necessary as long as the parties have met the tests for forming a partnership. If there is a limited partnership agreement, it may be written, oral, implied, an electronic record, or any combination of these [ULPA (2001) 102(13); RULPA 101(9)]. Because of the complexity of a limited partnership, and the fact that the partnership can only be formed by filing a certificate of limited partnership with the secretary of state, most limited partnerships have written limited partnership agreements. A written document is important evidence of the terms of the agreement, particularly if a dispute arises among the partners.

A **limited partnership agreement** (also called the **agreement of limited partnership**) sets forth the rights and duties of the general and limited partners; the terms and conditions regarding the operations, termination, and dissolution of the partnership; and so on. Thus, partners may tailor the structure of the partnership to meet their business needs. The provisions of a partnership agreement expressly control over the language of the state's limited partnership law unless otherwise provided by law.

Examples A limited partnership agreement may allocate profits or losses of the partnership based on any formula chosen by the partners; delegate management responsibility to any party, including one or a committee of the partners; establish voting rights of the partners; and provide for other matters.

It is important to note that if partners do not have a partnership agreement, then the default rules of the state's limited partnership law become the rules that govern the partnership and the relationship of the partners to the partnership and to each other. Most large limited partnerships and limited partnerships among sophisticated parties have long and detailed agreements that govern most aspects of the partnership's operation and are therefore not regulated by most of the default rules of a state's limited partnership law.

Admission of a New Partner

New general and limited partners may be admitted to an existing limited partnership by the specific written consent of each general and limited partner or as provided in a partnership agreement [ULPA (2001) 401 and 301; RULPA 401 and 301]. Upon the admission of a new general partner, the limited partnership must amend its certificate of limited partnership to reflect this change [ULPA

(2001) 202(b)(1); RULPA 202(b)(1)]. Most limited partnership agreements provide specific methods for the admission of new general and limited partners to the partnership.

Foreign Limited Partnership

A limited partnership is a **domestic limited partnership** in the state in which it is organized. It is a **foreign limited partnership** in all other states. Before transacting business in a foreign state, a limited partnership must file an application to transact business with that state's secretary of state. If the application conforms to that state's law, a **certificate of authority** permitting the foreign limited partnership to transact business in that state will be issued [ULPA (2001) 902 and 904; RULPA 902 and 904]. Once registered, a foreign limited partnership may use the courts of the foreign state to enforce its contracts and other rights [ULPA (2001) 907; RULPA 907]. A foreign limited partnership must conform to the law of the host state. However, a foreign partnership's internal affairs are governed by its state of organization [ULPA (2001) 901(a); RULPA 901(a)].

domestic limited partnership
A limited partnership in the state in which it is organized.

foreign limited partnership
A limited partnership in all other states besides the state in which it is organized.

Taxation of a Limited Partnership

Limited partnerships do not pay federal income taxes. Instead, there is **flow-through taxation** whereby the income and losses of the partnership flow onto and have to be reported on the general and limited partners' personal income tax returns. A limited partnership has to file an **information return** with the government, telling the government how much income was earned or the amount of losses incurred by the partnership. This way, government tax authorities can trace whether general and limited partners are correctly reporting their income or losses.

flow-through taxation
A tax rule that provides that the income and losses of a limited partnership are reported on the owner's personal income tax return.

Liability of Limited Partnerships, General Partners, and Limited Partners

35.3 Identify and describe the liability of limited partnerships, general partners, and limited partners of limited partnerships.

A limited partnership is liable for certain acts of its partners. General partners and limited partners have different degrees of liability, depending on the circumstances. The liability of limited partnerships, general partners, and limited partners is discussed in the following paragraphs.

Liability of a Limited Partnership

Each general partner is an **agent** of the limited partnership for the purpose of its activities [ULPA (2001) 402; RULPA 402]. As such, general partners may enter into contracts with third parties and take other actions on behalf of the limited partnership. A limited partnership is liable for loss or injury caused to a person, or for a penalty incurred, as a result of a wrongful act or omission, or other actionable conduct, of a general partner acting in the ordinary course of business of the partnership or with authority of the limited partnership [ULPA (2001) 403(a); RULPA 403(a)]. This is referred to as the **liability of a limited partnership**. Thus, a limited partnership is liable for authorized contracts and debts of the partnership and for tortious conduct committed while partners are acting within the scope of partnership business.

agent
Each general partner is an agent of the partnership for the purpose of its business, and an act of a partner in the ordinary course of the partnership business binds the partnership.

liability of a limited partnership
Liability that is imposed on a limited partnership for contracts and debts of the partnership and for tortious conduct committed while general partners are acting within the scope of partnership business.

Example There are three general partners of a limited partnership. One of the general partners, while driving an automobile and acting on partnership business, negligently causes an automobile accident that severely injures a pedestrian. Here, the limited partnership is liable for the damages caused by the negligence of the general partner.

A limited partner does not have the right or the power to act for or bind the limited partnership [ULPA (2001) 302; RULPA 302]. A limited partner only has the power to act for or bind the partnership if authorized to do so in a capacity different from that of being a limited partner. A limited partnership may employ a limited partner as an agent or employee with authority to bind the partnership to contracts.

Liability of General Partners

unlimited personal liability
A general partner is personally liable for the contracts and debts of the limited partnership, and for the torts (e.g., negligence, fraud) and breaches of trust committed by partners while acting on partnership business.

joint and several liability
The personal liability of general partners where a plaintiff can sue all or some or any one of the general partners individually to recover unpaid contract and tort liability of the limited partnership.

The general partners of a limited partnership have **unlimited personal liability** for the debts and obligations of the limited partnership, whether arising from contracts, torts, or breaches of trust. Thus, plaintiffs may recover unpaid claims against the partnership from a general partner's personal assets. General partners have **joint and several liability** for unpaid limited partnership obligations, which means that a general partner may be held individually responsible for unpaid contract and tort liability of the limited partnership [ULPA (2001) 404(a); RULPA 404(a)].

Before a plaintiff can recover against the personal assets of general partners, the plaintiff must obtain a judgment against the limited partnership and a writ of execution to obtain payment of the judgment against the partnership that has not been satisfied in whole or in part [ULPA (2001) 405(c); RULPA 405(c)]. General partners may be named in the lawsuit against the partnership, or they may be sued in separate actions following the nonpayment of a judgment by the partnership. Judgment can only be collected against the partners who are sued [ULPA (2001) 405(a); RULPA 405(a)]. A general partner who is made to pay more than his or her proportionate share of liability may seek indemnification from partners who have not paid their share of the loss.

Example There are three general partners of a limited partnership. When the limited partnership defaults on a debt, the creditor sues the partnership and one partner, who is the wealthiest of the partners. The partnership fails to pay the judgment. The creditor recovers the entire judgment from the named partner. That partner can recover indemnification from the other two general partners if they have the money to pay their share.

A person admitted as a general partner into an existing limited partnership is not personally liable for any limited partnership obligation incurred before the person's admission as a general partner [ULPA (2001) 404(a); RULPA 404(a)].

Liability of Limited Partners

limited liability of limited partners
Limited partners are liable only for the debts and obligations of a limited partnership up to their capital contribution; they are not personally liable for the debts and obligations of a limited partnership.

Limited partners have limited liability for the debts and obligations of the limited partnership. An obligation of a limited partnership, whether arising in contract, tort, or otherwise, is not the obligation of any limited partner. A limited partner is not personally liable, directly or indirectly, by way of contribution or otherwise, for an obligation of a limited partnership solely by reason of being a limited partner. Limited partners are liable only for the debts and obligations of the limited partnership up to their capital contributions invested in the limited partnership, which may be lost if the limited partnership fails or does not have sufficient money to pay its obligations. This is called **limited liability of limited partners**. Thus, the liability shield for limited partners is analogous to liability shield of corporate shareholders [ULPA (2001) 303; RULPA 303].

Example Three general partners and 100 limited partners are individual partners in Conversion LP, a limited partnership formed to convert a large apartment building into condominiums. The 103 partners each contribute $100,000 to the venture. Partway through the project, the real estate market collapses and the venture fails. The limited partnership has no funds except for a partially completed project, which is sold. After the sales proceeds of the incomplete project are paid to creditors and other claimants, the limited partnership still owes unpaid banks, creditors, and other claimants \$5 million. The limited partners lose their investment in the limited partnership, but are not personally liable for the unpaid debts and obligations of the limited partnership. The general partners are personally liable for the unpaid debts and obligations.

A previous version of limited partnership law held that a limited partner who participated in the management and control of a limited partnership lost his or her liability shield and was personally liable as a general partner. However, limited partnership laws currently in effect in most states hold that even if a limited partner participates in the management and control of the limited partnership, the limited partner is not liable as a general partner but maintains his or her limited liability status.

The following feature discusses master limited partnerships.

master limited partnership (MLP)
A limited partnership that is listed on a stock exchange and has units that are publicly traded. Also called *publicly traded partnership (PTP).*

unit (limited partnership unit)
An ownership interest in a master limited partnership that is traded on an organized securities exchange.

Business Environment

Master Limited Partnership

Certain limited partnerships qualify to be a **master limited partnership (MLP)**, often called a **publicly traded partnership (PTP)**. An MLP is a limited partnership whose limited partnership interests are traded on organized securities exchanges such as the New York Stock Exchange and the NASDAQ. A **unit**, also called a **limited partnership unit**, is an ownership interest in a master limited partnership that is traded on an organized securities exchange. A limited partner who owns units of master limited partnerships is called a **unit holder**. MLPs are first sold as an initial public offering; thereafter the units are traded on the exchanges.

MLPs have two classes of partners:

1. General partners are owners who are responsible for managing the day-to-day operations of the MLP. General partners on average have a small ownership interest in the venture, usually 2 percent or less of the MLP. They usually receive compensation based on the partnership's business performance. Most general partners of MLPs are corporations.
2. Limited partners are investors who purchase units in the MLP and provide the majority of the capital funds required for the business's operations. Limited partners often own 98 percent or more of the MLP. Limited partners are usually public investors.

An investment in an MLP is liquid because it can be sold on an exchange. MLPs combine the tax benefits of normal partnership, the unique tax benefits of an MLP, and the liquidity of a publicly traded company. Because of the complexity of the business, the sophistication of the MLP general partners, and the fact that MLP units are listed on exchanges, MLPs have detailed written partnership agreements that govern the management, operation, and dissolution of the partnership.

To qualify as an MLP, federal tax law requires that the business must generate 90 percent or more of its revenue from depletable natural resources, minerals, or real estate activities. Qualifying businesses include petroleum and natural gas extraction, mining, propane, oilfield services, refineries, energy processing plants, energy storage facilities, pipelines, rail terminals, and marine transportation vessels. MLPs can also invest in real estate ventures. MLPs cannot be used to operate nonqualifying businesses.

Management of a Limited Partnership

35.4 Describe how a limited partnership is managed.

General partners have the right to manage and control the affairs of a limited partnership. Limited partners can be given authority to act on behalf of the limited partnership.

Management Authority of General Partners

General partners have a right to participate in the management of a limited partnership. Any matter relating to the activities of the limited partnership may exclusively be decided by the general partner or general partners [ULPA (2001) 406(a); RULPA 406(a)]. Unless otherwise provided in a partnership agreement,

right to participate in management
The right of general partners to participate in the management of a limited partnership. General partners have an equal vote in management unless otherwise agreed.

each general partner has an equal **right to participate in management** and conduct of limited partnership business. In other words, each general partner has one vote, regardless of the proportional size of their capital contribution or their share in the partnership's profits. A simple majority decides most ordinary partnership matters. If the vote is tied, the action being voted on is defeated.

If the partners do not want the partnership controlled by equal voting rights, and they want to allocate voting rights on a different basis than a state's partnership law provides, they can do so in their partnership agreement.

Examples Partners may want to allocate greater voting rights to a partner who has spent a greater amount of time organizing the partnership or who has contributed a greater amount of capital to the partnership.

The general partners can, in their limited partnership agreement, delegate management responsibility to a managing partner or a committee of partners. The agreement may also restrict the management powers of certain general partners.

Management Authority and Permissive Activities of Limited Partners

Limited partners do not have the right to engage in management and control activities of the limited partnership unless the partnership agreement or the general partners grant them this authority. Under most state limited partnership laws, limited partners who are permitted to and do engage in the management and control activities of a limited partnership do not lose their limited liability status [ULPA (2001) 303; RULPA 303].

Under limited partnership law, limited partners have the legal right to vote on the following issues: amend the limited partnership agreement; sell, transfer, exchange, lease, or mortgage substantially all of the assets of the limited partnership; expulse a general or limited partner; change the nature of the business of the limited partnership; approve a plan of merger; or dissolve the limited partnership. Limited partners do not lose their limited liability status for exercising these rights.

It is the privilege of a trader in a free country, in all matters not contrary to law, to regulate his own mode of carrying it on according to his own discretion and choice.

Baron Alderson
Hilton v. Eckersly (1855)

Rights and Duties of General and Limited Partners

35.5 Describe the rights and duties of general partners and limited partners.

General and limited partners have certain rights and owe certain duties to the limited partnership and other partners. Some of the duties and rights of partners are discussed in the following paragraphs.

Right to Information

General and limited partners have the right to inspect and copy information related to partnership documents and the financial affairs of the partnership [ULPA (2001) 304 and 407(a); RULPA 304 and 407(a)]. The limited partnership and each general partner owe a duty to furnish general partners with information concerning the partnership's activities reasonably required for the proper exercise of the general partner's rights and duties [ULPA (2001) 407(b); RULPA 407(b)].

General Partners' Duty of Loyalty

duty of loyalty
A fiduciary duty that a general partner owes to the limited partnership and to other partners not to act adversely to the interests of the limited partnership.

A general partner of owes a fiduciary **duty of loyalty** to the limited partnership and to other partners not to act adversely to the interests of the limited partnership. Some of the ways that a general partner breaches his or her duty of loyalty include: (1) misusing partnership property; (2) competing with the partnership; (3) adversely dealing with the partnership; (3) usurping a partnership opportunity; (4) making secret profits; and (5) representing any party who has interests adverse to those of the partnership.

A general partner owes a **duty to account** to the limited partnership for any property, profit, or benefit derived by the partner in the conduct of partnership business or derived from the use of partnership property [ULPA (2001) 408(b); RULPA 408(b)].

duty to account
A duty owed by a general partner of a limited partnership to account for any property, profit, or benefit derived by the partner in the conduct of partnership business or derived from the use of partnership property.

Example A general partner who accepts bribes while conducting partnership business has breached her duty of loyalty and owes the amount of the money accepted to the partnership.

General Partners' Duty of Limited Care

General partners owe a **duty of limited care** to the limited partnership and to the other partners. A partner owes a duty of care not to engage in the following conduct that injures the partnership or other partners: (1) known violation of law; (2) intentional misconduct; (3) reckless conduct; and (4) grossly negligent conduct. A partner is liable for any damages the partnership or other partners incur because of such conduct. This duty is a limited duty because it does not include liability for ordinary negligence. Thus, if a partner commits an ordinarily negligent act that is not grossly negligent, he or she is not liable to the partnership or other partners [ULPA (2001) 408(c); RULPA 408(c)].

duty of limited care
A fiduciary duty that a general partner of a limited partnership owes not to engage in: (1) known violation of the law, (2) intentional misconduct, (3) reckless conduct, or (4) grossly negligent conduct that injures the partnership or other partners. This duty does not include liability for ordinary negligence.

Example A general partner's reckless driving causes an automobile accident that injures another driver. The partner is liable for damages assessed against the partnership. If the general partner's negligent driving caused the accident, the partner is not liable for the damages assessed against the partnership.

Limited Partners Do Not Owe a Duty of Loyalty or a Duty of Care

A limited partner does not owe a duty of loyalty or a duty of care to the limited partnership or to other partners by reason of being a limited partner [ULPA (2001) 304; RULPA 304].

Example A limited partner may engage in a business that competes with the limited partnership.

The following feature discusses family limited partnerships.

family limited partnership (FLP)
A limited partnership that is formed to own family businesses and investments.

Contemporary Environment

Family Limited Partnership

Because of tax benefits, limited partnerships are often used in estate planning. A **family limited partnership (FLP)** is a limited partnership used to establish and operate family businesses and investments and to distribute ownership interests from parents to children and from grandparents to grandchildren. A limited partnership is particularly suited to create an entity that has a strong, centralized management and passive limited partners with little capacity to exit the partnership. FLPs provide substantial estate and gift tax benefits.

As a limited partnership, an FLP must have a least one general partner and one limited partner. Generally, senior family members, such as parents or grandparents, who have substantial assets, are the general partners who contribute assets to the FLP and manage its business and assets. The general partners give all or a portion of their assets to the FLP in exchange for a small general partnership interest and a large limited partnership interest. The children or grandchildren are, or sometime later become, the limited partners. Over time, the senior family members give their limited partnership interests to their children or grandchildren.

The general partners usually make the management decisions of the FLP, and limited partners often do not participate in the management unless given management powers by the general partners. General partners are personally liable for the debts and liabilities of the partnership, and limited partners have limited liability and are not personally liable for the debts and obligations of the FLP.

The following case involves a dispute concerning a family limited partnership.

CASE 35.1 ***STATE COURT CASE Family Limited Partnership***

Gibson v. Gibson Family Limited Partnership

877 N.W.2d 597, 2016 S.D. 26 (2016)
Supreme Court of South Dakota

"As the sole general partner, Delores is responsible for the management of the partnership."

—Steven Zinter, Justice

Facts

Delores Gibson created the Gibson Family Limited Partnership (GFLP) for estate planning reasons. She deeded 2,060 acres of farm and ranch land that she owned to the partnership. Delores, as the general partner, kept 8.4 percent interest. Her sons, Michael and Greg Gibson, the limited partners, each received a 45.8 percent interest in the partnership. Neither Michael nor Greg paid for their interests in the partnership, and they had no significant duties. Pursuant to the partnership agreement, Delores, the general partner, was responsible for the management of the partnership and had sole authority to decide with whom the partnership conducts business and whether to distribute income. The partnership agreement provided that the limited partners could not withdraw from the partnership.

Michael and Greg jointly farmed and ranched on the 2,060 acres. After four years, the brothers split, and each started his own cattle and farming operation. GFLP loaned Greg $350,000, and then leased the 2,060 acres to Champaygn Ranch, a business owned by Greg and his wife, for a 20-year term. Michael sued Delores and GFLP, alleging that Delores breached her fiduciary duty. The jury held in favor of GFLP and Delores. Subsequently, GFLP entered into a contract to sell 830 acres of the leased property to Greg for $1,100,000. The money became property of GFLP. The lease on the remaining 1,230 acres was continued. GFLP made no distributions to partners.

Michael filed suit against GFLP and Delores, alleging that Delores breached her fiduciary duty as GFLP's general partner because of GFLP's transactions with Greg, and for failure to make partnership distributions. Michael also sought equitable relief, demanding his dissociation from GFLP and payment for his ownership interest. At trial, evidence was presented that the sale price for the 830 acres was fair market value. The jury found that Delores had not breached her fiduciary duty, and the court denied Michael's equity claim to quit the partnership and be paid for his interest in the partnership. Michael appealed the court's denial of his claim to quit the partnership and be paid value.

Issue

Can Michael dissociate from GFLP and be paid for his ownership interest?

Language of the Court

As the sole general partner, Delores is responsible for the management of the partnership. The is no dispute that GFLP is a limited partnership. Michael was not entitled to withdraw under the limited partnership agreement. Under the partnership agreement, Delores was not required to make distributions, and she had complete discretion to decide with whom and how to conduct partnership business.

Decision

The Supreme Court of South Dakota held that Michael, as a limited partner, could not withdraw from GFLP and be paid for his ownership interest.

Ethics Questions

What family dynamics played out in this case? If Michael had the right to withdraw from the partnership and be paid for his ownership interest, would Delores have created the family limited partnership?

Dissociation, Dissolution, and Winding Up of a Limited Partnership

35.6 Describe partner dissociation, identify when a limited partnership may be continued, and describe the process of dissolution and winding up of a limited partnership.

Limited partnership law recognizes two related, but distinct, concepts: *dissociation* and *dissolution*. **Dissociation** means a change in a partner's relationship with a limited partnership caused by his or her ceasing to be associated with the partnership's business. **Dissolution** means the end of a limited partnership's active business, leading to the winding up of its affairs and the eventual termination of the partnership.

dissociation
A change in a partner's relationship with a limited partnership caused by his or her ceasing to be associated with the partnership's business.

dissolution
The end of a limited partnership's active business, leading to winding up of its affairs and the eventual termination of the partnership.

Dissociation of Limited Partners

A limited partner does not have the *right* to withdraw from a limited partnership before the limited partnerships terminates [ULPA (2001) 601(a); RULPA 601(a)]. Termination of a term partnership occurs if the duration date of the partnership is reached, if the undertaking of the partnership is completed, or if the partnership is terminated by the general partners prior to end of its specified duration. An at-will partnership is terminated when the partners vote to terminate the partnership, upon the occurrence of an event specified in partnership agreement, or as provided in the state's partnership law.

Most limited partnership agreements expressly reiterate that limited partners may not withdraw from the partnership. However, a limited partnership agreement may provide that limited partners can withdraw from the partnership and that their partnership interest will be purchased at a predetermined amount or by a specified valuation formula.

When a limited partner wrongfully withdraws from a limited partnership, he or she loses rights as a partner and becomes a transferee entitled to distributions from the partnership [ULPA (2001) 602(a)(1); RULPA 602(1)]. If a limited partner dies, his heirs or beneficiaries are entitled to partnership distributions but do not become partners. If a partner becomes insolvent or bankrupt, and creditors obtain the limited partner's ownership interest, the creditors are mere transferees who have no partnership rights except to receive partnership distributions.

The dissociation of a limited partner does not cause the dissolution of the partnership. The limited partnership continues.

Dissociation of General Partners

A general partner is dissociated from a limited partnership by withdrawing from the partnership or by the occurrence of an event specified in the partnership agreement or limited partnership law that causes such dissociation.

A general partner is dissociated from a limited partnership: (1) when a general partner gives notice to the limited partnership of his or her express will to withdraw as a general partner; (2) upon the occurrence of an event provided in a partnership agreement as causing the partner's dissociation; (3) through the partner's expulsion as provided in the partnership agreement; (4) through the expulsion by unanimous consent of partners because it is unlawful to carry on business with the partner, the partner has transferred his or her interest in the partnership, or a corporate or other entity partner has lost their charter; (5) when there is a judicial determination that a person is incapable of performing his or her duties as a general partner because the partner materially breached the partnership agreement or engaged in wrongful conduct that makes it impractical to carry on partnership business; (6) when the partner becomes a debtor in bankruptcy; (7) when the individual partner dies, or a guardian or conservator is appointed for the partner; or (8) upon the termination of the corporate or entity partner's charter or articles [ULPA (2001) 603; RULPA 603].

The dissociation of a general partner terminates that partner's right to participate in management or to be actively involved in partnership operations. A dissociated general partner remains liable for the obligations incurred by the partnership prior to his or her withdrawal or dissociation, but is not liable for obligations of the partnership incurred after his or her withdrawal [ULPA (2001) 607(a); RULPA 607(a)].

Dissolution of a Limited Partnership

The dissociation of a partner does not automatically cause the dissolution of the limited partnership. Limited partnership law provides that a limited partnership dissolves only in the following situations:

1. Upon the happening of an event specified in the partnership agreement as causing dissolution [ULPA (2001) 801(1); RULPA 801(1)].
2. Upon the consent of all general partners and limited partners who own a majority of the rights to receive distributions as limited partners (e.g., limited partners who own more than 50 percent of the dollar value of the limited partners' ownership interests). For purposes of this calculation, distribution rights owned by non-partner transferees are irrelevant [ULPA (2001) 801(2); RULPA 801(2)].
3. If, upon application of a partner, a court issues a judicial decree that finds that it is not reasonably practical to carry on the activities of the partnership [ULPA (2001) 802; RULPA 802].
4. Within 90 days after the dissociation of a general partner, all general partners and limited partners owning the majority of the rights to receive distributions consent to dissolution. For purposes of this calculation, distribution rights owned by non-partner transferees are irrelevant. If this vote is reached, the partnership is dissolved. If this vote is not reached, the limited partnership continues [ULPA (2001) 801(3); RULPA 801(3)].

Example A limited partnership has four general partners who each own 2.5 percent of the partnership, seven limited partners who each own 10 percent of the partnership, and two non-partner transferees of limited partners' ownership interests (one creditor, one heir) who each own 10 percent of the partnership. One of the general partners dies. This is a dissociation. Within 90 days of the dissociation, a partner vote is held in which one general partner and three limited partners vote to dissolve the partnership. The limited partnership is not dissolved for two different reasons: (1) not all general partners voted for dissolution; and (2) only three of seven qualified equal-ownership limited partners voted for dissolution. The limited partnership has not been dissolved and continues operations.

Continuation Agreement

Many limited partnership agreements expressly provide for the continuation of the limited partnership upon the withdrawal or dissociation of a general partner. This is called a **continuation agreement**. The agreement usually specifies the process for carrying on the business, a purchase price or a formula for determining the purchase price that will be paid to a withdrawing or dissociating general partner for his or her ownership interest, whether buyout price will be paid at the time of withdrawal or at the time of liquidation of the partnership, and procedures for the continuation of the business.

Wrongful Dissociation

Sometimes a partner's dissociation from a limited partnership is considered a **wrongful dissociation**. A general partner's dissociation from a limited partnership is wrongful if: (1) the partner withdraws in breach of an express provision in the partnership agreement; (2) the partner withdraws from a term partnership prior to the expiration of the term or the accomplishment of the undertaking of the partnership; (3) the partner is expelled by judicial determination of wrongful conduct or material breach of the limited partnership agreement; or (4) a general partner is dissociated by becoming a debtor in bankruptcy. A general partner who wrongfully dissociates from a limited partnership is liable to the partnership and to the other partners for damages caused by his or her wrongful dissociation [ULPA (2001) 604; RULPA 604].

Example A general partner withdraws from a five-year term partnership, two years prior to the end of the term. Here, there is a wrongful dissociation. The partner is liable if her departure causes damage to the reputation of the partnership, or causes third parties such as banks or suppliers not to deal with the partnership.

Winding Up and Termination

Unless a partnership is continued, a limited partnership continues after dissolution only for the purpose of **winding up** its business [ULPA (2001) 803(a); RULPA 803(a)]. After partnership assets have been liquidated and reduced to cash, the proceeds are distributed to satisfy claims against the partnership. Claims are paid in the following order [ULPA (2001) 812; RULPA 812]:

winding up
The process of liquidating a limited partnership's assets and distributing the proceeds to satisfy claims against the partnership.

1. Creditors (including partners who are creditors)
2. Settlement of partners' accounts

A limited partnership is terminated when the winding up of its business is completed. Termination ends the legal existence of the limited partnership.

Limited Liability Limited Partnership

35.7 Define and describe a *limited liability limited partnership*.

The majority of states permit a relatively new form of entity called a **limited liability limited partnership (LLLP)**. An LLLP is a special form of a limited partnership in which all partners—limited partners and general partners—have limited liability for the debts and obligations of the partnership, whether arising in contract, tort, or otherwise [ULPA (2001) 404(c); RULPA 404(c)]. Thus, none of the partners, not even the general partners, are personally liable for the debts and obligations of the LLLP. The debts of an LLLP are solely the responsibility of the LLLP (see **Exhibit 35.2**). This form of partnership eliminates the need for an individual to obtain a limited liability shield by creating a corporation to be a general partner of a limited partnership, instead allowing individuals to be direct partners with no personal liability exposure.

limited liability limited partnership (LLLP)
A special type of limited partnership where both the general and limited partners have limited liability for the debts and obligations of the limited partnership, and are not personally liable for the debts and obligations of the LLLP.

In order for a limited liability limited partnership to be formed, two or more partners must sign a **certificate of limited liability limited partnership** and file it with the secretary of state of the state in which the limited partnership is formed. An existing limited partnership may convert to an LLLP. An LLLP must identify itself by using the phrase "limited liability limited partnership" or the abbreviation "L.L.L.P." or "LLLP" after the partnership name.

certificate of limited liability limited partnership
A document that two or more persons must sign and file with the secretary of state of the state of organization that forms a limited liability limited partnership.

The general partners have management responsibility of the LLLP. Limited partners may participate in the management of a LLLP if authorized to do so by the general partners without losing their limited liability shield. The LLLP partnership agreement may specify that certain or all general partners or limited partners have a say in how the partnership's business will be run.

Exhibit 35.2 LIMITED LIABILITY LIMITED PARTNERSHIP (LLLP)

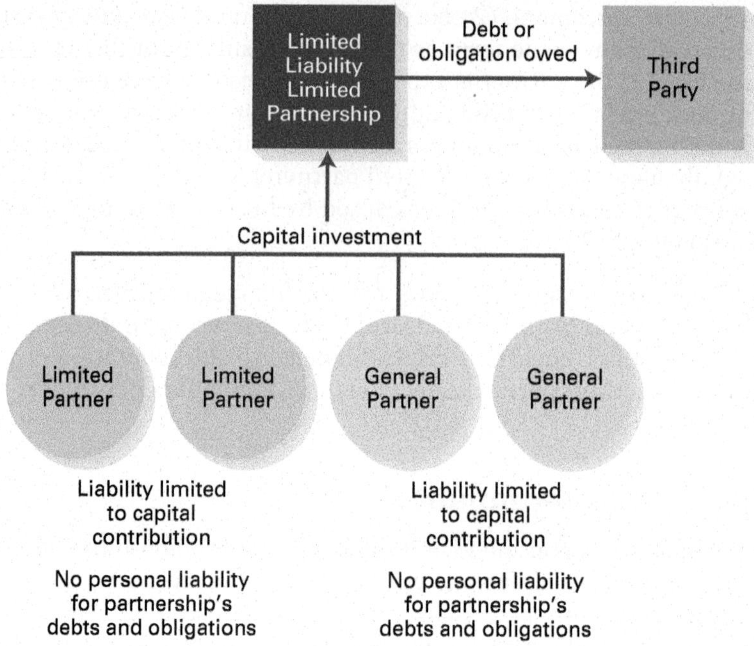

Key Terms and Concepts

Agent (617)
Certificate of authority (617)
Certificate of limited liability limited partnership (625)
Certificate of limited partnership (615)
Continuation agreement (624)
Dissociation (623)
Dissolution (623)
Domestic limited partnership (617)
Duty of limited care (621)
Duty of loyalty (620)
Duty to account (621)
Family limited partnership (FLP) (621)
Flow-through taxation (617)
Foreign limited partnership (617)
General partner (613)
Information return (617)
Joint and several liability (618)
Liability of a limited partnership (617)
Limited liability of limited partners (618)
Limited liability limited partnership (LLLP) (625)
Limited partner (613)
Limited partnership (LP) (613)
Limited partnership agreement (articles of limited partnership) (616)
Master limited partnership (MLP) (publicly traded partnership [PTP]) (619)
Revised Uniform Limited Partnership Act (RULPA) (615)
Right to participate in management (620)
Uniform Limited Partnership Act (ULPA) (615)
Uniform Limited Partnership Act (2001) (ULPA [2001] or Re-RULPA) (615)
Unit (limited partnership unit) (619)
Unit holder (619)
Unlimited personal liability (618)
Winding up (625)
Wrongful dissociation (624)

Critical Legal Thinking Cases

35.1 Liability of Limited Partners Virginia Partners, Ltd. (Virginia Partners), a limited partnership organized under the laws of Florida, conducted business in Kentucky but failed to register as a foreign limited partnership, as required by Kentucky law. Robert Day was injured in Garrard County, Kentucky, by a negligent act of Virginia Partners. At the time of the accident, Day was a bystander observing acid being injected into an abandoned oil well by Virginia Partners. The injury occurred when a polyvinyl chloride (PVC) valve failed, causing a hose to rupture from its fitting and spray nitric acid on Day, severely injuring him. Day sued Virginia Partners and its limited partners to recover damages. Are the limited partners liable? *Virginia Partners, Ltd. v. Day*, 738 S.W.2d 837, 1987 Ky. App. Lexis 564 (Court of Appeals of Kentucky, 1987)

35.2 Liability of Partners Raugust-Mathwig, Inc., a corporation, was the sole general partner of a limited partnership. Calvin Raugust was the major shareholder of this corporation. The three limited partners were Cal-Lee Trust; W.J. Mathwig, Inc.; and W.J. Mathwig, Inc., and Associates. All three of the limited partners were valid corporate entities. Although the limited partnership agreement was never executed and a certificate of limited partnership was not filed with the state, the parties opened a bank account and began conducting business.

John Molander, an architect, entered into an agreement with the limited partnership to design a condominium complex and professional office building to be located in Spokane, Washington. The contract was signed on behalf of the limited partnership by its corporate general partner. Molander provided substantial architectural services to the partnership, but neither project was completed because of a lack of financing. Molander sued the limited partnership, its corporate general partner, the corporate limited partners, and Calvin Raugust individually to recover payments allegedly due him. Against whom can Molander recover? *Molander v. Raugust-Mathwig, Inc.*, 722 P.2d 103, 1986 Wash. App. Lexis 2992 (Court of Appeals of Washington, 1986)

Ethics Case

35.3 Ethics Case Robert K. Powers and Lee M. Solomon were among other limited partners of the Cosmopolitan Chinook Hotel (Cosmopolitan), a limited partnership. Cosmopolitan entered into a contract to lease and purchase neon signs from Dwinell's Central Neon (Dwinell's). The contract identified Cosmopolitan as a "partnership" and was signed on behalf of the partnership, "R. Powers, President." At the time the contract was entered into, Cosmopolitan had taken no steps to file its certificate of limited partnership with the state, as required by limited partnership law. The certificate was not filed with the state until several months after the contract was signed. When Cosmopolitan defaulted on payments due under the contract, Dwinell's sued Cosmopolitan and its general and limited partners. Have the limited partners acted ethically in denying liability on the contract? Are the limited partners liable? *Dwinell's Central Neon v. Cosmopolitan Chinook Hotel*, 587 P.2d 191, 1978 Wash. App. Lexis 2735 (Court of Appeals of Washington, 1978)

CHAPTER

36

Limited Liability Companies and Limited Liability Partnerships

Henry R. Cheeseman

CHICAGO, ILLINOIS

Many businesses operate as limited liability companies (LLCs), and many professionals operate their businesses as limited liability partnerships (LLPs). These forms of business provide limited liability to their owners.

Learning Objectives

After studying this chapter, you should be able to:

36.1 Define *limited liability partnership (LLP)* and describe the formation of an LLP.

36.2 Describe the liability of an LLP and the limited liability of the partners of an LLP.

36.3 Define *limited liability company (LLC)*.

36.4 Describe the process of organizing an LLC.

36.5 Describe the liability of an LLC and the limited liability of members of an LLC.

36.6 Compare the management of a member-managed LLC and a manager-managed LLC.

36.7 Determine when members and managers owe fiduciary duties of loyalty and care to an LLC.

36.8 Describe the dissociation of members, and the dissolution and winding up of an LLC.

> "*Justice is the end of government. It is the end of civil society. It ever has been, and ever will be pursued, until it be obtained, or until liberty be lost in the pursuit.*"
>
> —*James Madison*
> *The Federalist, No. 51 (1788)*

Introduction to Limited Liability Companies and Limited Liability Partnerships

Most states have enacted laws that permit certain types of professionals, such as accountants, lawyers, and doctors, to operate as *limited liability partnerships (LLPs)*. The owners of an LLP have limited liability for debts and obligations of the partnership, the partners manage the partnership, and the LLP is taxed as a partnership. Most LLP laws are quite similar, although some differences do exist between these state statutes.

Business will be either better or worse.
Calvin Coolidge (1872–1933)
Thirtieth president of the United States

Owners may choose to operate a business as a *limited liability company (LLC)*. An LLC is an unincorporated business entity that combines the most favorable attributes of general partnerships, limited partnerships, and corporations. The owners of an LLC have limited liability for debts and obligations of the business, they can manage the business, and the LLC may elect to be taxed as a partnership. All states permit the formation of LLCs. Most LLC laws are quite similar, although some differences do exist between these state statutes.

This chapter discusses the formation and operation of LLPs and LLCs, the liability of the partners of LLPs and the owners of LLCs, and other issues involving LLPs and LLCs.

Limited Liability Partnership (LLP)

36.1 Define *limited liability partnership (LLP)* and describe the formation of an LLP.

All 50 states and the District of Columbia have enacted legislation to permit the creation of a special type of partnership called a **limited liability partnership (LLP)**. In most states, the law restricts the use of LLPs to certain types of professionals, such as accountants, lawyers, doctors, and architects. Several states permit nonprofessionals to form LLPs. An LLP is a partnership that has two or more partners.

limited liability partnership (LLP)
A special form of partnership in which all partners are limited partners, and there are no general partners.

Unlike a general partnership or limited partnership, in which general partners are personally liable for the debts and obligations of the partnership, in an LLP none of the partners are personally liable for the debts and obligations of the LLP. Thus, all partners are treated as limited partners regarding liability. As in a general partnership, all the partners in an LLP may manage the affairs of the LLP. For most purposes other than the partners' limited liability shield, the operation of an LLP is treated as a general partnership.

Uniform Limited Liability Partnership Amendments (ULLPA)
Amendments to the Revised Uniform Partnership Act (RUPA) that provides for the formation and operation of limited liability partnerships.

The following feature discusses LLP law.

Landmark Law

Uniform Limited Liability Partnership Amendments (ULLPA)

In 1996, the National Conference of Commissioners on Uniform State Laws adopted the **Uniform Limited Liability Partnership Amendments (ULLPA)** to the Uniform Partnership Act. These LLP amendments now appear as part of the **Revised Uniform Partnership Act (RUPA)** [RUPA Article 10 Limited Liability Partnership]. The RUPA was amended in 2011 and 2013.

(continued)

The ULLPA amends the RUPA to provide modern rules for the formation, operation, and termination of LLPs. The ULLPA, along with relevant provisions of the RUPA, covers most problems that arise in the formation, operation, liability of LLPs and members, and the dissolution of LLPs. Many states have adopted the RUPA, as amended by the ULLPA, as their LLP law. Some states permit LLPs to be formed pursuant to separate LLP statutes. State statutes that govern LLPs are commonly referred to as **limited liability partnership codes** or **limited liability partnership acts.**

The ULLPA and the RUPA form the basis of the study of LLPs in this chapter.

Formation of a Limited Liability Partnership

articles of limited liability partnership (statement of qualification)
The formal documents that must be filed at the secretary of state's office of the state of organization of a limited liability partnership to form the LLP.

LLPs are creatures of state law. An LLP can only be created pursuant to the laws of the state in which the LLP is being organized. An LLP is a general partnership that has filed **articles of limited liability partnership** or a **statement of qualification** pursuant to RUPA Section 1001 [RUPA 101(5)]. In some states, an LLP is a general partnership that has elected to become an LLP. In other states, LLP law permits the direct formation of an LLP without first being organized as a general partnership. An LLP may amend its statement of qualification by filing **articles of amendment**, sometimes called a **statement of amendment,** with the secretary of state [RUPA 1001(h)].

The LLP is a **domestic limited liability partnership** in the state in which it is organized. LLP law of that state governs the formation, operation, and termination of the LLP. An LLP may do business in other states, however. To do so, the LLP must register as a **foreign limited liability partnership** in any state in which it intends to conduct business [RUPA 1102].

Name of a Limited Liability Partnership

The name of a limited liability partnership must contain the phrase "Registered Limited Liability Partnership" or "Limited Liability Partnership" or the abbreviation "R.L.L.P." or "L.L.P." or "RLLP" or "LLP" [RUPA 1002]. This notifies businesses and consumers that they are dealing with an entity in which no partner is personally liable for the debts and obligations of the partnership. An LLP must file a fictitious business name statement—d.b.a. (doing business as)—with the appropriate government agency to operate under a trade name.

The following feature describes an LLP's limited liability partnership agreement.

Business Environment

Limited Liability Partnership Agreement

Although one is not required in many states, most LLPs have a written **limited liability partnership agreement.** A written document is important evidence of the terms of the LLP agreement, particularly if a dispute arises among the partners. The partners may tailor the structure of the partnership to meet their business needs. The partners can agree to almost any terms in their partnership agreement, except terms that are illegal.

The provisions of the partnership agreement take priority over the language of a state's LLP law unless the provision violates LLP law or other law. If partners do not have a partnership agreement, then the rules of the state's LLP law become the *default rules* that govern the LLP and the relationship of the partners to the LLP and to each other.

Taxation of a Limited Liability Partnership

LLPs enjoy the *flow-through* tax benefit of other types of partnerships—that is, there is no tax paid at the partnership level, and all profits and losses are reported on the individual partners' income tax returns. Thus, there is no double taxation of the entity and the owners.

Right to Participate in Management

One of the benefits of an LLP is that all partners are allowed to be involved in the management of the LLP. Each partner of an LLP has an equal **right to participate in management** and conduct of partnership business [RUPA 401(f)]. Unless otherwise agreed, each partner has one vote, regardless of the proportional size of his or her capital contribution or share in the partnership's profits. A simple majority decides most ordinary partnership matters [RUPA 401(j)]. A limited liability partnership agreement may provide for voting rights based on capital contributions or some other basis.

Right to Share in Profits

Unless otherwise agreed in the LLP partnership agreement, each partner of an LLP has an equal **right to share in profits** of the partnership. Each partner is chargeable with a share of the partnership losses in proportion to the partner's share of the LLP's profits [RUPA 401(b)]. The partners also have an equal right to share in the earnings from the investment of capital. An equal sharing of profits may not be what partners intend if capital contributions are not the same. Therefore, an LLP agreement can provide that profits and losses be allocated in proportion to the partners' capital contributions or in any other manner.

Liability of an LLP and Limited Liability of Partners

36.2 Describe the liability of an LLP and the limited liability of the partners of an LLP.

The LLP must deal with third parties in conducting partnership business. This includes partners entering into contracts with third parties on behalf of the LLP. Partners, as well as employees and agents of the LLP, sometimes injure third parties while conducting partnership business. The liability of LLPs and their partners is discussed in the following paragraphs.

Liability of a Limited Liability Partnership

An LLP is liable for loss or injury caused to a person, or for a penalty incurred, as a result of a wrongful act or omission, or other actionable conduct, of a partner acting in the ordinary course of business of the partnership or with authority of the partnership [RUPA 305(a)]. A partner who enters into a contract in the LLP's name, for carrying on the ordinary course of the partnership's business, binds the partnership [RUPA 301(1)]. An LLP is liable for contracts entered into on behalf of the partnership.

Sometimes, partners, employees, or agents of LLPs commit tortious conduct that causes injury to a third person. This tort could be caused by a negligent act, a breach of trust, or an intentional tort. The LLP is liable if the act is committed while the person is acting within the ordinary course of partnership business. The contract and tort **liability of a limited liability partnership** is demonstrated in the following examples.

liability of a limited liability partnership
A limited liability partnership is liable for loss or injury caused to a person, or for a penalty incurred, as a result of a wrongful act or omission, or other actionable conduct, of a partner acting in the ordinary course of business of the partnership or with authority of the partnership.

Example A partner of an LLP, while acting within partnership authority, signs a contract to purchase equipment on credit to be used by the partnership. The LLP must perform this contract and pay for the equipment when the loan is due.

Example A partner of an LLP, while acting on partnership business, negligently causes an automobile accident that injures another person. The LLP is liable for the damages caused to the injured person.

Limited Liability of Partners of an LLP

In an LLP, there does not have to be a general partner who is personally liable for the debts and obligations of the partnership. Instead, *all* partners have limited liability [RUPA 306(c)]. Unless they are personally at fault, none of the partners is personally liable for the debts and obligations of the partnership beyond his or her capital contribution. Thus, partners of an LLP have a full liability shield from personal liability for claims against the LLP. (see **Exhibit 36.1**). The **limited liability of partners of limited liability partnerships** is shown in the following example.

limited liability of partners of LLPs
The liability of LLP partners for the LLP's debts, obligations, and liabilities is limited only to the extent of their capital contributions. Partners of an LLPs are not personally liable for the LLP's debts, obligations, and liabilities.

Example An LLP that has four partners enters into a contract to lease office space from a landlord for a five-year period. Two years later, the LLP fails and is unable to pay for the remaining two years' rent. The landlord sues both the LLP and the partners for breach of contract. The LLP is liable but has no money to pay. The partners are not personally liable for the LLP's obligation to the landlord.

The LLP shield protects partners against *vicarious liability*; that is, liability for the acts or omissions of other partners. This protection is significant for professionals who do not want to be held liable for another partner's professional malpractice. The LLP shield does not protect a partner from liability for his or her own conduct.

Critical Legal Thinking Questions
How does an LLP differ from a general partnership? How does an LLP differ from a limited partnership?

Example Four medical doctors form an LLP to provide surgical services. While performing an operation, one of the doctors is negligent, causing severe injuries to a patient. The patient incurs personal and emotional injuries and is awarded $2 million at trial. Here, the LLP is liable, and the doctor who was negligent is personally liable for medical malpractice, but the other three doctors are not personally liable.

A significant number of accounting firms now operate as LLPs. Each of the "Big Four" accounting firms—Deloitte LLP; PricewaterhouseCoopers LLP; Ernst & Young LLP; and KPMG LLP—operate as LLPs. In addition, many law firms, medical practices, and other professional groups operate as LLPs. The U.S. affiliate of the world's largest law firm, DLA Piper LLP, operates as an LLP.

If an LLP partnership agreement does not provide otherwise, an LLP can convert to a general partnership upon approval of all of the partners. The conversion takes place when the cancelation of the statement of qualification as an LLP is filed with the secretary of state [RUPA Section 1001(h)].

Exhibit 36.1 LIMITED LIABILITY PARTNERSHIP (LLP)

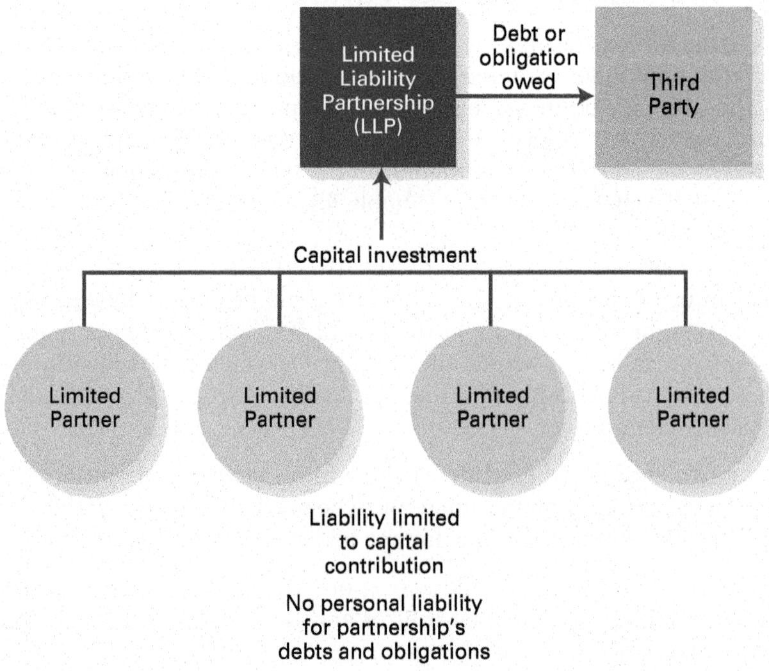

Continuation Agreement

It is good practice for the partners of an LLP to enter into a continuation agreement that expressly sets forth the events that allow for continuation of the limited liability partnership upon dissociation and dissolution. The partners may specify in their partnership agreement how the withdrawal, death, or other dissociation of a partner from the partnership will be handled. This includes specifying under what circumstances a partnership will continue, the amount to be paid to outgoing partners or a formula for determining this amount, when the money will be paid, and other details. It is best practice to have a written continuation agreement. When a partnership is continued, the partnership is composed of the remaining partners and any new partners admitted to the partnership. Existing creditors have equal status with new creditors of the partnership.

limited liability company (LLC)
An unincorporated business entity that combines the most favorable attributes of general partnerships, limited partnerships, and corporations.

Limited Liability Company (LLC)

36.3 Define *limited liability company (LLC)*.

member
An owner of an LLC.

Many entrepreneurs who begin new businesses choose a **limited liability company (LLC)** as their legal form for conducting business. More than 2 million new LLCs are formed each year in the United States. All 50 states and the District of Columbia have enacted legislation to permit the creation and use of LLCs.

Uniform Limited Liability Company Act (ULLCA)
A model act that provides comprehensive and uniform laws for the formation, operation, and dissolution of LLCs.

An LLC is created pursuant to the laws of the state in which the LLC is being organized. These statutes, commonly referred to as **limited liability company codes** or **limited liability company acts**, regulate the formation, operation, and dissolution of LLCs. An owner of an LLC is usually called a **member** (some states refer to owners of LLCs as *shareholders*).

Revised Uniform Limited Liability Company Act (RULLCA)
A revision of the ULLCA.

The following feature discusses the Uniform Limited Liability Company Act and the Revised Uniform Limited Liability Company Act.

Landmark Laws

Uniform Limited Liability Company Act and Revised Uniform Limited Liability Company Act

In 1996, the National Conference of Commissioners on Uniform State Laws (a group of lawyers, judges, and legal scholars) issued the **Uniform Limited Liability Company Act (ULLCA)**. The ULLCA codifies LLC law. Its goal is to establish comprehensive LLC law that is uniform throughout the United States. The ULLCA covers most problems that arise in the formation, operation, and termination of LLCs. The ULLCA is not law unless a state adopts it as its LLC statute. The ULLCA was revised in 2006. This revision is called the **Revised Uniform Limited Liability Company Act (RULLCA)**, which is also referred to as **Re-ULLCA** and **Uniform Limited Liability Company Act (2006)**. The RULLCA was amended in 2011 and 2013.

Previously, many states adopted all or part of the ULLCA as their LLC law. Currently, many states are adopting or have adopted all or part of the RULLCA as their LLC law. Some states have adopted separate LLC statutes. A state legislature may amend its LLC statutes at any time. The courts interpret LLC statutes to decide LLC and member disputes. The ULLCA and the RULLCA form the basis of the study of LLCs in this chapter.

Separate Legal Entity and Powers

An LLC is a separate legal entity (or legal person) distinct from its members [ULLCA 201; RULLCA 108(a)]. LLCs are treated as artificial persons that have the same powers as an individual to do all things necessary or convenient to carry on its business or affairs, including owning and transferring personal property; holding title to and selling, leasing, and mortgaging real property; making contracts and guarantees; borrowing and lending money; suing and being sued; and taking other actions to conduct the affairs and business of the LLC.

Taxation of LLCs

flow-through taxation
A situation where no tax is imposed at the entity level, and income and losses of the business are reported on owners' individual tax returns.

Under the Internal Revenue Code and regulations adopted by the Internal Revenue Service (IRS) for federal income tax purposes, an LLC is taxed as a partnership unless it elects to be taxed as a corporation. Thus, an LLC is not taxed at the entity level, but its income or losses are reported on the members' individual income tax returns. This is called **flow-through taxation**. This avoids double taxation at the individual and business level. Most LLCs accept the default status of being taxed as a partnership instead of electing to be taxed as a corporation.

Formation of an LLC

36.4 Describe the process of organizing an LLC.

The ULLCA and the RULLCA authorize that an LLC may be organized by one or more persons [ULLCA 202(a); RULLCA 201(a)]. Any person—including individuals, general partnerships, corporations, limited liability companies, limited partnerships, limited liability partnerships, joint ventures, estates, trusts, associations, governments, governmental agencies, and other legal or commercial entities—may be members of a limited liability company [ULLCA 101(14); RULLCA 102(15)]. All 50 states and the District of Columbia permit single-owner LLCs. Thus, a sole proprietor can obtain the benefit of the limited liability shield of an LLC. An existing business, such as a sole proprietorship, partnership, or corporation, may convert to an LLC.

The ULLCA permits an LLC to be formed to conduct business. Some states prohibit professionals (e.g., doctors, accountants) from operating as LLCs. Under the RULLCA, an LLC may have any lawful purpose, whether it is for profit or not [RULLCA 108(b)]. The RULLCA permits nonprofit corporations and unincorporated nonprofit associations to be members of an LLC [RULLCA 102(15)].

In business, sir, one has no friends, only correspondents.
Alexandre Dumas (1802–1870)

Example Parents want to establish a girls' soccer league for grade-school-age girls. To do so would expose the parents to potential personal liability should a participant get hurt while playing the game. Operating the soccer league as an LLC shields the parents from personal liability for such accidents.

State of Organization

An LLC can be organized in only one state, even though it can conduct business in all other states. For the sake of convenience, many LLCs, particularly small ones, choose as the state of organization the state in which the LLC will be doing most of its business. Delaware is often chosen as the state of organization for larger LLCs because of the pro-business environment of its LLC code. Nevada is also often selected as a state to form an LLC because of its favorable LLC law.

The LLC is a **domestic limited liability company** in the state in which it is organized. An LLC may do business in other states, however. To do so, the LLP must register as a **foreign limited liability company** in any state in which it wants to conduct business [ULLCA 1002; RULLCA 802]. LLC law of the state of organization governs the internal operation of the LLC.

Example Data Analytics LLC is formed under the laws of Delaware and files for and receives permission to conduct business operations in Florida. It is a domestic LLC in Delaware and a foreign LLC in Florida.

Name of a Limited Liability Company

When starting a new LLC, the organizers must choose a name for the entity. The name must contain the words "Limited Liability Company" or "Limited Company" or the abbreviation "L.L.C.," "LLC," "L.C.," or "LC." "Limited" may be abbreviated as "Ltd.," and "company" may be abbreviated as "Co." [ULLCA 105(a); RULLCA 112(a)]. An LLC must file a fictitious business name statement—d.b.a. (doing business as)—with the appropriate government agency to operate under a trade name.

Articles of Organization

An LLC is formed by delivering **articles of organization**, which some states call a **certificate of organization**, to the office of the secretary of state of the state of organization for filing. The filing of this document by the secretary of state is conclusive proof that the organizers have satisfied all the conditions necessary to create the LLC. The document must set forth the name of the LLC, the address of its initial office, the name and address of the initial agent for service of process, and other information required by the state or deemed relevant by the organizers [ULLCA 203; RULLCA 201(b)].

articles of organization (certificate of organization)
The formal documents that must be filed at the secretary of state's office of the state of organization of an LLC to form the LLC.

A sample articles of organization is set forth in **Exhibit 36.2**. An LLC can amend its articles of organization or certificate of organization at any time by filing articles of amendment, sometimes called a statement of amendment, with the secretary of state [ULLCA 204; RULLCA 202].

WEB EXERCISE
Use **www.google.com** to find and read the forms necessary to form a limited liability company in your state.

Exhibit 36.2 ARTICLES OF ORGANIZATION

ARTICLES OF ORGANIZATION
FOR FLORIDA LIMITED LIABILITY COMPANY

ARTICLE I - NAME

The name of the Limited Liability Company is
iCitrusSystems.com

ARTICLE II - ADDRESS

The mailing address and street address of the principal office of the Limited Liability Company is
3000 Dade Boulevard
Suite 200
Miami Beach, Florida 33139

ARTICLE III - DURATION

The period of duration for the Limited Liability Company shall be
50 years

ARTICLE IV - MANAGEMENT

The Limited Liability Company is to be managed by a manager and the name and address of such manager is
Susan Escobar
1000 Collins Avenue
Miami Beach, Florida 33141

____
Thomas Blandford

____
Pam Rosales

The following feature describes an LLC's operating agreement.

Business Environment

Limited Liability Company Operating Agreement

Members of an LLC may enter into a **limited liability company operating agreement** that regulates the affairs of the company and the conduct of its business and governs relations among the members, managers, and the company [ULLCA 103(a); RULLCA 105(a)]. In most cases the provisions agreed to in the operating agreement take precedence over the rules of the ULLCA and the RULLCA. The operating agreement may be oral, written, a record, or implied. Most agreements are written or a record. The use of the word "record" permits electronic agreements. An operating agreement may be amended. If members of an LLC do not have an operating agreement, then the rules of the state's LLC law become the *default rules* that govern the LLC and the relationship of the members to the LLC and to each other.

limited liability company operating agreement
An agreement entered into among members that governs the affairs and business of the LLC and the relations among members, managers, and the LLC.

at-will limited liability company
An LLC that has no specified term of duration.

term limited liability company
An LLC that has a specified term of duration.

Duration of an LLC

An LLC is an **at-will limited liability company** (i.e., with no specified term) unless it is designated as a **term limited liability company** and the duration of the term is specified in the articles of organization [ULLCA 203(a)(5); RULLCA 104(c)]. The duration of a term LLC may be specified in any manner that sets forth a specific and final date for the dissolution of the LLC.

Examples Periods specified as "50 years from the date of filing of the articles of organization" and "the period ending January 1, 2050" are valid to create a term LLC.

Capital Contribution and Distributable Interest

A member's capital contribution to an LLC may be in the form of money, personal property, real property, other tangible property, intangible property (e.g., a patent), services performed, contracts for services to be performed, promissory notes, or other agreements to contribute money or property [ULLCA 401; RULLCA 402].

A member's interest in an LLC is evidenced by their capital contribution. Most interests are measured in units. The LLC keeps a written ledger or an electronic record of all members' interests. An LLC's operating agreement may provide that a member's ownership interest may be evidenced by a **certificate of interest** issued by the LLC [ULLCA 501(c); RULLCA 208(a)]. The certificate of interest acts the same as a stock certificate that is issued by a corporation. Certificates of interest are often evidenced by electronic records.

certificate of interest
A document or electronic record that evidences a member's ownership interest in a limited liability company.

distributional interest
A member's ownership interest in an LLC that entitles the member to receive distributions of money and property from the LLC.

A member's ownership interest in an LLC is called a **distributional interest**. A member's distributional interest in an LLC is personal property and may be transferred in whole or in part unless restricted by the LLC [RULLCA 502(a)]. A member who transfers his or her distributional interest is not released from liability for the existing debts, obligations, and liabilities of the LLC. A transfer of an interest in an LLC does not entitle the transferee to become a member of the LLC or to exercise any right of a member. A transfer entitles the transferee to receive only the share of the profits or other distributions from the LLC to which the transferor would have been entitled [ULLCA 502; RULLCA 502(b)].

Whatever the human law may be, neither an individual nor a nation can commit the least act of injustice against the obscurest individual without having to pay the penalty for it.

Henry David Thoreau (1817–1862)

Share in Profits and Distributions

The members of an LLC may agree how profits, losses, and distributions will be shared by members. If there is not such agreement, the ULLCA provides that profits and losses are allocated according to the value of each member's capital contribution to the LLC.

Example Vladimir and Irene form an LLC. Vladimir contributes $75,000 capital, and Irene contributes $25,000 capital. If the LLC makes $100,000 in profits, Vladimir receives $75,000 of the profits and Irene receives $25,000 of the profits.

The RULLCA provides that if there is no prior agreement, then profits and losses will be shared *per capita*; that is, equally among members even if their capital contributions to the LLC were not equal [RULLCA 404(a)].

Example Vladimir and Irene form an LLC. Vladimir contributes $75,000 capital, and Irene contributes $25,000 capital. If the LLC makes $100,000 in profits, Vladimir and Irene share the profits equally—they each receive $50,000.

Liability of an LLC and Limited Liability of Members of an LLC

36.5 Describe the liability of an LLC and the limited liability of members of an LLC.

In the course of conducting business, the agents and employees of an LLC may enter into contracts on behalf of the LLC. Sometimes, however, the LLC may not perform these contracts. In addition, the agents or employees of an LLC may be involved in accidents or otherwise cause harm to third parties when acting on LLC business. These third parties—whether in contract disputes or tort disputes—will look to be compensated for their loss or injuries.

The following paragraphs discuss the liability of the LLC, its members, and its managers.

Liability of a Limited Liability Company

An LLC is liable for loss or injury caused to a person, or for a penalty incurred, as a result of a wrongful act or omission by a member, a manager, an agent, or an employee of the LLC who commits the wrongful act while acting within the ordinary course of business of the LLC or with authority of the LLC [ULLCA 302]. An LLC is liable for members' or managers' tortious conduct and for contracts entered on behalf of the company while they are acting within LLC authority. The **liability of a limited liability company** is demonstrated in the following examples.

liability of a limited liability company
A limited liability company is liable for loss or injury caused to a person, or for a penalty incurred, as a result of a wrongful act or omission, or other actionable conduct, of a member acting in the ordinary course of business of the company or with authority of the company.

Example A manager of an LLC, acting within company authority, signs a contract with a landlord to lease office premises for the company for a five-year period. The LLC is bound to perform this contract and to pay the rental costs when due.

Example A member, while acting on authorized company business, negligently causes an automobile accident in which another person is injured. The LLC is liable for the damages caused to the injured person.

Limited Liability of Members of an LLC

The general rule is that members of a limited liability company are not personally liable to third parties for the debts, obligations, and liabilities of an LLC beyond their capital contribution. Members have limited liability (see **Exhibit 36.3**). The debts, obligations, and liabilities of an LLC, whether arising from contracts, torts, or otherwise, are solely those of the LLC [ULLCA 303(a); RULLCA 304(a)]. This is called **limited liability of members of limited liability companies**.

limited liability of members of limited liability companies
The liability of LLC members for the LLC's debts, obligations, and liabilities is limited to the extent of their capital contributions. Members of an LLCs are not personally liable for the LLC's debts, obligations, and liabilities.

Example Five members form an LLC. Each member invests $30,000 capital in the LLC. The LLC purchases $300,000 of supplies and materials on credit from a supplier. After some time, the LLC experiences financial difficulty and goes out of business with no assets, but it still owes the supplier-creditor $250,000. In this case, the five members have each lost their $30,000 capital investment but are not personally liable for the $250,000 debt still owed by the LLC to the creditor.

Exhibit 36.3 LIMITED LIABILITY COMPANY (LLC)

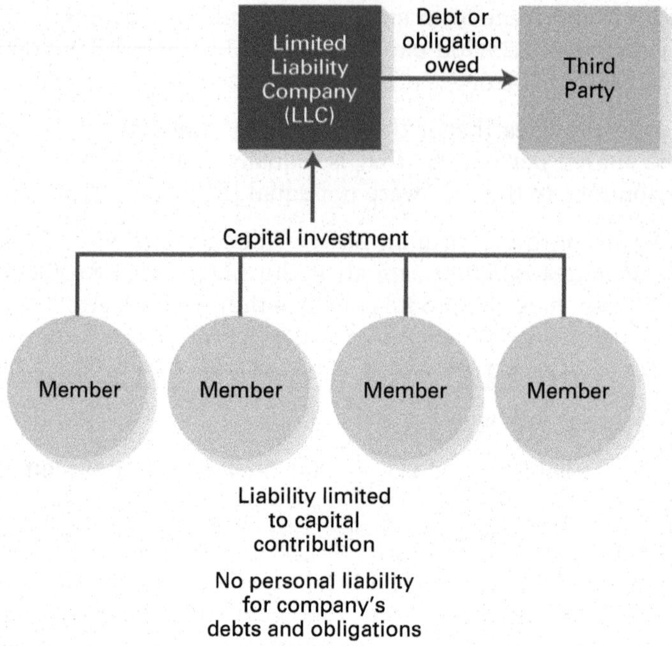

The failure of an LLC to observe the usual company formalities is not grounds for imposing personal liability on the members of the LLC. For example, if the LLC does not keep minutes of the company's meetings, the members do not become personally liable for the LLC's debts. Managers of LLCs are not personally liable for the debts, obligations, and liabilities of the LLC they manage.

If a member, manager, or employee of an LLC, while acting on behalf of the LLC, intentionally or negligently injures or kills a person, that member, manager, or employee is personally liable for injuries and damages caused by their conduct.

Example Bai, Matias, and Bjork form an LLC to own and operate a business. Each member contributes $40,000 capital. While driving his automobile on LLC business, Bjork accidentally causes an automobile accident that significantly injures another driver. The injured driver can recover damages from the LLC because Bjork was acting within the scope of the ordinary business of the LLC when the accident occurred. The injured person can also recover damages from the personal property of Bjork because he committed the negligent act. Bai and Matias have limited liability of the capital contributions they made to the LLC, but they are not personally liable to the injured person.

In the following case, the court addressed the issue of the limited liability of a member of an LLC.

CASE 36.1 *STATE COURT CASE Limited Liability Company*

Siva v. 1138 LLC

2007 Ohio 4667, 2007 Ohio App. Lexis 4202 (2007)
Court of Appeals of Ohio

"Finally, the evidence did not show that Siva was misguided as to the fact he was dealing with a limited liability company."

—Susan Brown, Judge

Facts

Five members—Richard Hess, Robert Haines, Lisa Hess, Nathan Hess, and Zack Shahin—formed a limited liability company called 1138 LLC. Ruthiran Siva owned a commercial building located at 1138 Bethel Road, Franklin County, Ohio. Siva entered into a written lease agreement with 1138 LLC whereby 1138 LLC leased premises in Siva's commercial building for a term of five years at a monthly rental of $4,000. 1138 LLC began operating a bar on the premises. Six months later, 1138 LLC was in default and in breach of the lease agreement. Siva sued 1138 LLC and Richard Hess to recover damages. Siva received a default judgment against 1138 LLC, but there was no money in 1138 LLC to pay the judgment. Hess, who had been sued personally, defended, arguing that as a member-owner of the LLC, he was not personally liable for the debts of the LLC. The trial court found in favor of Hess and dismissed Siva's complaint against Hess. Siva appealed.

Issue

Is Richard Hess, a member-owner of 1138 LLC, personally liable for the debt owed by the LLC to Siva?

Language of the Court

Based upon the evidence presented, a reasonable trier of fact could have concluded that 1138 LLC became insolvent due to unprofitable operations. Moreover, even if the record suggests poor business judgment by Hess, it does not demonstrate that he formed 1138 LLC to defraud creditors. Finally, the evidence did not show that Siva was misguided as to the fact he was dealing with a limited liability company. Siva's counsel drafted the lease agreement and Siva acknowledged at trial he did not ask any of the owners of 1138 LLC to sign the lease in an individual capacity.

Decision

The court of appeals held that Hess, as a member-owner of 1138 LLC, was not personally liable for the debt that the LLC owed to Siva. The court of appeals affirmed the decision of the trial court that dismissed Siva's complaint against Hess.

Critical Legal Thinking Questions

Did Hess owe an ethical duty to pay the debt owed by 1138 LLC to Siva? Did Siva act ethically by suing Hess personally to recover the debt owed by the 1138 LLC?

Management of an LLC

36.6 Compare the management of a member-managed LLC and a manager-managed LLC.

An LLC can be either a *member-managed LLC* or a *manager-managed LLC*. An LLC is a member-managed LLC unless it is designated as a manager-managed LLC in its articles of organization or in its operating agreement [ULLCA 203(a)(6); RULLCA 407(a)]. The distinctions between these two are as follows:

- **Member-managed LLC.** In this type of LLC, the members of the LLC have the right to manage the LLC.
- **Manager-managed LLC.** In this type of LLC, the members designate a manager or managers to manage the LLC and, by doing so, they delegate their management rights to the manager or managers. The designated manager or managers have the authority to manage the LLC, and the members no longer have the right to manage the LLC.

If the members do not designate the LLC to be either a member-managed or manager-managed LLC, the LLC is considered a member-managed LLC.

Member-Managed LLC

In a **member-managed limited liability company**, each member has equal rights in the management and conduct of the affairs of the LLC, regardless of the size of their capital contribution. Any matter relating to the ordinary business of the LLC may be decided by the member, or, if there is more than one member, then by the majority of members [ULLCA 404(a); RULLCA 407(b)].

member-managed limited liability company
An LLC that has not designated that it is a manager-managed LLC in its articles of organization and is managed by its members.

Example Allison, Jason, Stacy, Lan-Wei, and Ivy establish an LLC. Allison contributes $100,000 capital, and the other four members each contribute $25,000 capital. When deciding whether to add a new line of products to the business, Stacy, Lan-Wei, and Ivy vote to add the line, while Allison and Jason vote against it. The line of new products is added to the LLC's business because three members voted yes, while two members voted no. It does not matter that the three members who voted yes contributed $75,000 in capital collectively versus $125,000 in capital contributed by the two members who voted no.

However, members of an LLC may establish voting rights in their operating agreement that are based on capital contributions or other agreement.

Manager-Managed LLC

manager-managed limited liability company
An LLC that has designated in its articles of organization that it is a manager-managed LLC and whose nonmanager members give their management rights over to designated managers.

In a **manager-managed limited liability company**, the members designate a manager or managers to manage the affairs of the LLC. A manager may be a member or nonmember of the LLC. Each manager has equal rights to manage the LLC. Any matter relating to the ordinary business of the LLC may be decided by the manager, or, if there is more than one manager, then by the majority of the managers [ULLCA 404(b); RULLCA 407(c)]. In a manager-managed LLC, the nonmanager members no longer have the right to manage the ordinary affairs of the LLC. A manager must be appointed by a vote of a majority of the members; managers may also be removed by a vote of the majority of the members [ULLCA 404(b)(3); RULLCA 407(c)(4)].

Certain actions cannot be delegated to managers but must be voted on by all members of the LLC. Under the ULLCA, these include (1) amending the articles of organization, (2) amending the operating agreement, (3) admitting new members, (4) consenting to dissolve the LLC, (5) consenting to merge the LLC with another entity, and (6) selling, leasing, or disposing of all or substantially all of the LLC's property [ULLCA 404(c)]. The RULLCA simplifies this by requiring the vote or consent of all members to (1) amend the operating agreement or (2) undertake an act outside the ordinary course of the company's activities and affairs [RULLCA 407(c)(3)].

CONCEPT SUMMARY

MANAGEMENT OF AN LLC

Type of LLC	Description
Member-managed LLC	The members do not designate managers to manage the LLC. The LLC is managed by its members.
Manager-managed LLC	The members designate certain members or nonmembers to manage the LLC. The LLC is managed by the designated managers; nonmanager members have no right to manage the LLC.

Agency Authority to Bind an LLC to Contracts

Laws too gentle are seldom obeyed; too severe, seldom executed.
Benjamin Franklin
Poor Richard's Almanack (1756)

The designation of an LLC as member-managed or manager-managed is important in determining who has authority to bind the LLC to contracts. The following rules apply:

- **Member-Managed LLC.** Under the ULLCA, all members of a member-managed LLC have agency authority to bind the LLC to contracts [ULLCA Section 301(a)(1)].

  Example Yolanda, Darius, and Farhod form a member-managed LLC. Each one of them can bind the LLC to a contract with a third party such as a supplier, purchaser, or landlord.

  The RULLCA provides that a member is not automatically an agent of an LLC solely by reason of being a member but must be given agency authority to bind the LLC to a contract [RULLCA 301(a)].

  Example Five members form an LLC and do not appoint a manager to manage the business. However, they vote to give two of the members the authority to enter into contracts on behalf of the LLC. The other three members do not have authority to enter into contracts on behalf of the LLC.

- **Manager-managed LLC.** In a manager-managed LLC, a manager has authority to bind the LLC to contracts. Nonmanager members cannot bind the LLC to contracts.

  Example Alexis, Derek, Ashley, and Sadia form an LLC. They designate the LLC as a manager-managed LLC and name Alexis as the manager. Alexis, the manager, enters into a contract to purchase goods from a supplier for the LLC. Derek, a nonmanager member, enters into a contract to lease equipment on behalf of the LLC. The LLC is bound to the contract entered into by Alexis, the manager, but is not bound to the contract entered into by Derek, a nonmanager member.

An LLC is bound to contracts that members or managers have properly entered into on its behalf in the ordinary course of business [ULLCA 301; RULLCA 304].

CONCEPT SUMMARY

AGENCY AUTHORITY TO BIND AN LLC TO CONTRACTS

Type of LLC	Agency Authority
Member-managed LLC	Under the ULLCA all members have agency authority to bind the LLC to contracts; under the RULLCA a member must be given agency authority to bind an LLC to a contract.
Manager-managed LLC	Under the ULLCA and RULLCA a manager has authority to bind the LLC to contracts; the nonmanager members cannot bind the LLC to contracts.

Fiduciary Duties of Members of an LLC

36.7 Determine when members and managers owe fiduciary duties of loyalty and care to an LLC.

Certain members and managers of an LLC owe fiduciary duties to the LLC they own or manage. These duties include the *duty of loyalty* and the *duty of care*. The special liability rules for LLCs, their members, and their managers are discussed in the following paragraphs.

Duty of Loyalty

A member of a member-managed LLC and a manager of a manager-managed LLC owe a *fiduciary* **duty of loyalty** to the LLC and to members to act honestly and faithfully in their dealings with and on behalf of an LLC. The duty of loyalty includes the duty not to make secret profits or benefits; usurp the LLC's opportunities; deal with the LLC while having an adverse interest with the LLC; compete with the LLC; or represent any party who has interests adverse to those of the LLC [ULLCA 409(a) and (b); RULLCA 409(a) and (b)]. A member of a member-managed LLC or a manager of a manager-managed LLC who violates their duty of loyalty is liable for damages caused to the LLC and its members.

duty of loyalty
A duty owed by a member of a member-managed LLC and a manager of a manager-managed LLC to be honest in their dealings with the LLC and to not act adversely to the interests of the LLC.

Example Ester, Yi, Maria, and Enrique form a member-managed LLC that conducts online auctions. Ester secretly starts a competing business to conduct online auctions. Ester is liable for breaching her duty of loyalty to the LLC and to Yi, Maria, and Enrique. Ester is liable for any secret profits she made, and her business will be shut down.

Example Ester, Yi, Maria, and Enrique form a manager-managed LLC and hire Zola, a nonmember, as the manager. Zola embezzles money from the LLC. Zola has violated her duty of loyalty and owes the amount she has embezzled to the LLC.

Limited Duty of Care

A member of a member-managed LLC and a manager of a manager-managed LLC owe a *fiduciary* duty of care to the LLC and members not to engage in (1) a known violation of law, (2) intentional misconduct, (3) reckless conduct, or (4) grossly negligent conduct that injures the LLC and members. A member of a member-managed LLC or a manager of a manager-managed LLC is liable to the LLC for any damages the LLC incurs because of such conduct [ULLCA 409(a) and (c); RULLCA 409(g)(1)]. This duty is a **limited duty of care** because it does not include ordinary negligence. Thus, if a covered member or manager commits an ordinarily negligent act that is not grossly negligent, he or she is not liable to the LLC. A member of a member-managed LLC or a manager of a manager-managed LLC who violates their limited duty of care is liable to the LLC and its members.

limited duty of care
A duty owed by a member of a member-managed LLC and a manager of a manager-managed LLC not to engage in (1) a known violation of law, (2) intentional misconduct, (3) reckless conduct, or (4) grossly negligent conduct that injures the LLC.

Example Charlene is a member of a member-managed LLC. While engaging in LLC business, Charlene accidentally hits Zubin, a pedestrian, with her automobile and severely injures him. Zubin sues the LLC and recovers $1 million in damages. If the court determines that Charlene was ordinarily negligent when she caused the accident—for example, she was driving the speed limit and did not see Zubin because the sun was in her eyes—she will not be liable to the LLC for any losses caused to the LLC by her ordinary negligence. If instead the court determines that Charlene grossly negligent—for example, she was driving 65 mph in a 35 mph zone—she is liable to the LLC for the $1 million it was ordered to pay Zubin.

No Fiduciary Duty Owed

A member of a manager-managed LLC who is not a manager owes no fiduciary duty of loyalty or care to the LLC or its members [ULLCA 409(h)(1); RULLCA 409(g)(1)]. Basically, a nonmanager member of a manager-managed LLC is treated equally to a shareholder in a corporation.

Example Felicia is a member of a 30-person manager-managed LLC that is engaged in buying, developing, and selling real estate. Felicia is not a manager of the LLC but is just a member-owner. A third party approaches Felicia with the opportunity to purchase a large and valuable piece of real estate that is ripe for development for a price that is below fair market value. Felicia knows that the LLC is looking to purchase such a parcel of real estate. However, as a nonmanager member of a manager-managed LLC, Felicia owes no duty to offer the opportunity to the LLC. She may purchase the piece of real estate for herself without violating any duty to the LLC.

Critical Legal Thinking Questions
Describe the advantages of operating as an LLC versus operating as a (1) sole proprietorship, (2) general partnership, (3) limited partnership, and (4) corporation.

The following feature compares an LLC to other forms of business and highlights the advantages of an LLC over other forms of business.

Business Environment

Advantages of Operating a Business as an LLC

The LLC has become popular as a form of conducting business because it combines the best attributes of different forms of business into one entity. These include: (1) providing limited liability to all owners, similar to the limited liability of shareholders of a corporations and limited partners of limited partnerships; (2) giving owners the ability to manage the business, similar to the ability of general partners of general and limited partnerships but without personal liability; (3) allowing a single owner to own a business but without the personal liability of a sole proprietorship; (4) providing owners the authority to designate professional managers to manage the business, equivalent to managers of corporations; and (5) permitting flow-through taxation similar to that of partnerships, and similar to that of an S corporation but without the limitations on the number and type of owners, filing requirements, and other limitations of that entity.

Dissociation, Dissolution, and Winding up of an LLC

36.8 Describe the dissociation of members, and the dissolution and winding up of an LLC.

At times, a member of an LLC may wish to leave the LLC. This event, or other events, may cause the dissolution of the LLC. If an LLC is dissolved, the affairs of the LLC must be wound up. The dissociation of members, and the dissolution and winding up of an LLC, are discussed in the following paragraphs.

Dissociation of a Member

Unless provided otherwise in the operating agreement, a member may withdraw from an LLC, rightfully or wrongfully, at any time [ULLCA 602(a); RULLCA 601(a)]. Upon a member withdrawing from an LLC, that member's right to participate in the management and conduct of the affairs of the LLC terminates [ULLCA 603(b)(1); RULLCA 603(a)(1)]. The members may specify in their operating agreement, if there is one, how the withdrawal of a member will be handled. If there is no such agreement, then the following default rules apply.

Under ULLCA, upon the withdrawal of a member from an LLC there is a **dissociation** of a member from the LLC. If a member withdraws from an at-will LLC and the other members want the LLC to continue in business, the LLC is required to purchase the withdrawing member's interest in the LLC for fair value as determined at the time of dissociation [ULLCA 603(a)(1) and 701(a)(1)]. If the dissociating member does not believe the price to be fair, the member may bring a legal action to have a court determine the buyout price [ULLCA 701(e)]. The problem with the ULLCA's approach is that the required payment to the withdrawing member may be financially difficult for the LLC to make and may end up causing the LLC to be dissolved and terminated.

RULLCA treats a member's withdrawal from an LLC differently than does the ULLCA. Under the RULLCA, if a member withdraws from an at-will LLC, the LLC is not required to purchase the withdrawing member's interest at the time of withdrawal. Thus, under RULLCA, the LLC will suffer no financial loss at the time of a member's withdrawal and may continue in business as if nothing happened. The withdrawing member retains the right to be paid their share of the profits and other distributions of the LLC [RULLCA 603(a)(3)]. The withdrawing member's investment remains with the LLC, and the withdrawing member is paid the liquidation value along with the other members when the LLC is dissolved and wound up at some future date.

Under both the ULLCA and RULLCA, if a member withdraws from a term LLC prior to the expiration of the specified term or the accomplishment of the specified object of the LLC, and the LLC continues in business, the withdrawing member is paid the liquidation value of his interest on the date of expiration of the term [ULLCA 603(a)(2)(ii); RULLCA 603(a)(3)].

A member who wrongfully withdraws from a term LLC prior to the expiration of the term or the accomplishment of a specified object of the LLC is liable for damages caused to the LLC or other members of the LLC by such **wrongful dissociation** [ULLCA 602(c); RULLCA 601(c)].

wrongful dissociation
A member withdrawing from (1) a term LLC prior to the expiration of the term or (2) an at-will LLC when the operating agreement eliminates a member's power to withdraw.

Dissolution of an LLC

The **dissolution** of an LLC occurs (1) upon the expiration of the term of the LLC; (2) with the consent of all members of the LLC; (3) with the consent of the number or percentage of members specified in the operating agreement; (4) upon the occurrence of an event or circumstance that the operating agreement states causes dissolution; (5) when, on application by a member, a court issues an order finding that the conduct of substantially all of the LLC's activities is unlawful or that it is not reasonably practical to carry on the LLC's activities; or (6) when, on application by a member, a court issues an order finding that the managers or members in control of the LLC have acted in a manner that is illegal or fraudulent or in a manner that is oppressive and is harmful to the applicant [ULLCA 801; RULLCA 701]. A state may administratively dissolve an LLC if it does not pay state taxes or fees when due or fails files its annual report with the state [RULLCA 705].

The dissolution of an LLC does not end its existence but does change the purpose of its existence to that of taking the steps necessary to wind up its affairs. This includes notifying creditors and members, filing the necessary papers with the state, paying necessary income and business taxes, closing bank accounts, and the like.

Winding Up an LLC's Business

winding up
The liquidation of a limited liability company's assets and the distribution of the proceeds to satisfy claims against the company.

If an LLC is not continued, the LLC is wound up. The process of **winding up** an LLC consists of the liquidation (sale) of the LLC's assets and the distribution of the proceeds to satisfy claims against the LLC. After LLC assets have been liquidated and reduced to cash, the proceeds are distributed to satisfy claims against the LLC in the following order:

1. Creditors (including members who are creditors)
2. Settlement of members' accounts

If there are insufficient funds to pay all creditors, creditors with secured or priority claims will be paid first, and unsecured creditors will be paid proportionately for their claims. If the creditors are paid in full, the excess amount is distributed to members in an amount equal to their contributions that have not been previously returned. If the amount to be distributed to members is less than their unpaid contributions, the money will be distributed in proportion to the value of their claims. If the amount to be distributed to members exceeds their unpaid contributions, the excess will be distributed equally. An operating agreement may provide for a different distribution to members [ULLCA 806; RULLCA 708].

articles of termination (certificate of termination)
A document that is filed with the secretary of state to terminate an LLC.

After dissolution and winding up, an LLC may terminate its existence by filing **articles of termination** or a **certificate of termination** with the secretary of state of the state of organization of the LLC [ULLCA 805].

Continuation Agreement

continuation agreement
An agreement that provides that an LLC will be continued following the dissociation of a member or other specified event.

The members of a limited liability company can enter into a **continuation agreement** that expressly sets forth the events that allow for continuation of the business. The provisions of a continuation agreement take precedent over the rules of the ULLCA and RULLCA unless they otherwise are contrary to law. The members may specify in their agreement how the withdrawal, death, or other dissociation of a member from the LLC will be handled. This includes specifying under what circumstances the LLC will continue, the amount to be paid to outgoing members or a formula for determining this amount, when the money will be paid, and other details. It is best practice to have a written continuation agreement. Existing creditors have equal status with new creditors of the LLC.

The following feature discusses the professional limited liability company (PLLC).

professional limited liability company (PLLC)
A type of limited liability company that can be formed and operated by accountants, lawyers, doctors, and other designated professionals that has the benefits and attributes of an LLC.

Business Environment

Professional Limited Liability Company (PLLC)

More than half of the states permit professionals to form and do business as a **professional limited liability company (PLLC)**. This means that accountants, lawyers, doctors, and other designated professionals can form a PLLC and have the benefits and attributes of an LLC.

In most states, all owners of a PLLC must be licensed. To form a PLLC, the state licensing board of the professional wishing to form a PLLC must approve the articles of organization. Upon obtaining the licensing board's approval, the professional must comply with the LLC law of the state regarding the filing of the articles of organization with the secretary of state. Unlike LLPs, which require two or more partners, many states permit PLLCs to have multiple owners or a single owner. The professionals who form a PLLC should enter into an operating agreement that addresses the issues faced by the PLLC.

If granted PLLC status, the name of the PLLC must contain the phrase "Professional Limited Liability Company" or the abbreviation "P.L.L.C." or "PLLC." A state's LLC law usually applies to the operation, dissolution, winding up, or continuation of a PLLC. A PLLC and an LLC offer the same liability protection to its members.

In states that recognize PLLCs, many of the rules that apply to LLCs apply to PLLCs. PLLCs have the same management structure and tax benefits. Members of a PLLC are not liable for the malpractice of other professionals of the PLLC. Like an LLC, a PLLC does not shield professionals from liability for their own malpractice.

Key Terms and Concepts

Articles of amendment (statement of amendment) (630)
Articles of limited liability partnership (statement of qualification) (630)
Articles of organization (certificate of organization) (635)
Articles of termination (certificate of termination) (644)
At-will limited liability company (636)
Certificate of interest (636)
Continuation agreement (644)
Dissociation (643)
Dissolution (643)
Distributional interest (636)
Domestic limited liability company (634)
Domestic limited liability partnership (630)
Duty of loyalty (641)
Flow-through taxation (634)
Foreign limited liability company (634)
Foreign limited liability partnership (630)
Liability of a limited liability company (637)
Liability of a limited liability partnership (631)
Limited duty of care (642)
Limited liability company (LLC) (633)
Limited liability company codes (limited liability company acts) (633)
Limited liability company operating agreement (636)
Limited liability of members of limited liability companies (637)
Limited liability of partners of limited liability partnerships (632)
Limited liability partnership (LLP) (629)
Limited liability partnership agreement (630)
Limited liability partnership codes (limited liability partnership acts) (630)
Manager-managed limited liability company (639)
Member (633)
Member-managed limited liability company (639)
Professional limited liability company (PLLC) (644)
Revised Uniform Limited Liability Company Act (RULLCA or Re-ULLCA or Uniform Limited Liability Company Act [2006]) (633)
Revised Uniform Partnership Act (RUPA) (629)
Right to participate in management (631)
Right to share in profits (631)
Term limited liability company (636)
Uniform Limited Liability Company Act (ULLCA) (633)
Uniform Limited Liability Partnership Amendments (ULLPA) (629)
Winding up (644)
Wrongful dissociation (643)

Critical Legal Thinking Cases

36.1 Limited Liability Dale C. Bone was a member of Roscoe, LLC, an LLC organized under the laws of North Carolina. Roscoe, LLC purchased two acres of land near the town of Apex, North Carolina. Apex approved Roscoe, LLC's plan to construct and operate a propane gas bulk storage and distribution facility on the land. This use was permitted under Apex's zoning ordinance. Daylene Page and other homeowners in the area sued Roscoe, LLC and Dale C. Bone, alleging that the gas storage facility, if constructed, would constitute a nuisance.

After the trial court denied the plaintiffs' motion to obtain a preliminary injunction against construction of the facility, the plaintiffs dismissed the lawsuit. Subsequently, Bone sued the plaintiffs to recover the attorneys' fees he had spent in defending against the plaintiffs' lawsuit. Bone alleged that he should have not been named a defendant in the lawsuit because he was a member of Roscoe, LLC and would have had no personal liability in the lawsuit. Should the plaintiffs who sued Bone be required to pay his legal fees in fighting the lawsuit? Why or why not? *Page v. Roscoe, LLC*, 497 S.E.2d 422, 1998 N.C. App. Lexis 169 (Court of Appeals of North Carolina, 1998)

36.2 Liability of Members Harold, Jasmine, Caesar, and Yuan form **Microhard.com**, LLC, a limited liability company, to sell computer hardware and software on the Internet. **Microhard.com**, LLC hires Heather, a recent graduate of the University of Chicago and a brilliant software designer, as an employee. Heather's job is to design and develop software that will execute a computer command when the computer user thinks of the next command he or she wants to execute. Using Heather's research, **Microhard.com**, LLC develops the Third Eye software program that does this. **Microhard.com**, LLC sends Heather to the annual Comdex computer show in Las Vegas, Nevada, to unveil this revolutionary software.

While Heather is in Las Vegas, she rents an automobile to get from the hotel to the computer show and to meet interested buyers at different locations in Las Vegas. Driving from her hotel to the site of the Comdex computer show, Heather negligently causes an accident in which she runs over Harold Singer, a pedestrian. Singer, who suffers severe physical injuries, sues **Microhard.com**, LLC, Heather, Harold, Jasmine, Caesar, and Yuan to recover monetary damages for his injuries. Who is liable?

36.3 Manager-Managed LLC Juan, Min-Yi, and Chelsea form Unlimited, LLC, a limited liability company that operates a chain of women's retail clothing stores that sell eclectic women's clothing. The company is a manager-managed LLC, and Min-Yi has been designated in the articles of organization filed with the secretary of state as the manager of Unlimited, LLC. Min-Yi sees a store location on Rodeo Drive in Beverly Hills, California, that she thinks would be an excellent location for an Unlimited Store. Min-Yi enters into a five-year lease on behalf of Unlimited, LLC with Landlord, Inc., the owner of the store building, to lease the store at $100,000 rent per year. While visiting Chicago, Chelsea sees a store location on North Michigan Avenue that she thinks is a perfect location for an Unlimited store. Chelsea enters into a five-year lease on behalf of Unlimited, LLC with Real Estate, Inc., the owner of the store building, to lease the store location at $100,000 rent per year. Is Unlimited, LLC bound to either of these leases?

36.4 Duty of Loyalty Ally is a member and a manager of a manager-managed limited liability company called Movers & You, LLC. The main business of Movers & You, LLC is moving large corporations from old office space to new office space in other buildings. After Ally has been a member-manager of Movers & You, LLC for several years, she decides to join her friend Lana and form another LLC, called Lana & Me, LLC. This new LLC provides moving services that move large corporations from old office space to new office space. Ally becomes a member-manager of Lana & Me, LLC while retaining her member-manager position at Movers & You, LLC. Ally does not disclose her new position at Lana & Me, LLC to the other members or managers of Movers & You, LLC. Several years later, the other members of Movers & You, LLC discover Ally's other ownership and management position at Lana & Me, LLC. Movers & You, LLC sues Ally to recover damages for her working for Lana & Me, LLC. Is Ally liable?

Ethics Cases

36.5 Ethics Case Angela, Yoko, Cherise, and Serena want to start a new business that designs and manufactures toys for children. At a meeting in which the owners want to decide what type of legal form to use to operate the business, Cherise states:

We should use a limited liability company to operate our business because this form of business provides us, the owners, with a limited liability shield, which means that if the business gets sued and loses, we the owners are not personally liable to the injured party except up to our capital contribution in the business.

The others agree and form a limited liability company called Fuzzy Toys, LLC to conduct the member-managed business. Each of the four owners contributes $50,000 as her capital contribution to the LLC. Fuzzy Toys, LLC, purchases $800,000 of liability insurance from Allied Insurance Company, and starts doing business. Fuzzy Toys, LLC designs and produces "Heidi," a new toy doll and female action figure. Heidi is an instant success, and Fuzzy Toys, LLC produces and sells millions of these female action figures. After a few months, however, the LLC starts getting complaints that one of the parts of the female action figure is breaking off quite regularly, and some children are swallowing the part. The concerned member-managers of Fuzzy Toys, LLC issue an immediate recall of the female action figure, but before all of the dolls are returned for a refund, Catherine, a 7-year-old child, swallows the toy's part and is severely injured. Catherine, through her mother, sues Fuzzy Toys, LLC, Allied Insurance Company, Angela, Yoko, Cherise, and Serena to recover damages for product liability. At the time of suit, Fuzzy Toys, LLC, has $200,000 of assets. The jury awards Catherine $10 million for her injuries. Who is liable to Catherine and for how much? How much does Catherine recover? Did Angela, Yoko, Cherise, and Serena act ethically in setting up their toy business as an LLC? Explain.

36.6 Ethics Case Christopher, Melony, Xie, and Ruth form **iNet.com**, LLC, a limited liability company. The four members are all Ph.D. scientists who have been working together in a backyard garage to develop a handheld wireless device that lets you receive and send email, surf the internet, use a word processing program that can print to any printer in the world, view cable television stations, and keep track of anyone you want anywhere in the world as well as zoom in on the person being tracked without that person knowing you are doing so. This new device, called Eros, costs only $29 but makes the owners $25 profit per unit sold.

The owners agree that they will buy a manufacturing plant and start producing the unit in six months. Melony, who owns a one-quarter interest in **iNet.com**, LLC, decides she wants "more of the action" and soon, so she secretly sells the plans and drawings for the new Eros unit to a competitor for $100 million. The competitor comes out with exactly the same device, called Zeus, in one month and beats **iNet.com**, LLC to market. The LLC, which later finds out about Melony's action, suffers damages of $100 million because of it. Is Melony liable to **iNet.com**, LLC? Explain. Did Melony act ethically in this case?

CHAPTER 37

Corporate Formation and Financing

Henry R. Cheeseman

STOCK CERTIFICATE

Corporations have existed since medieval Europe, when individual charters were granted by the ruler, usually a monarch (king or queen). In the United States today, corporations are created by meeting the requirements established by state corporation codes. A corporation is owned by its shareholders, who elect members of the board of directors to make policy decisions, and who, in turn, employ corporate officers to run the day-to-day operations of the corporation. In the past, ownership interests in corporations were recognized by the issuance of stock certificates to shareholders. Today, ownership interests are more likely to be recorded electronically on the books and records of the corporation or a transfer agent designated by the corporation.

Learning Objectives

After studying this chapter, you should be able to:

37.1 Define *corporation* and list the major characteristics of a corporation.

37.2 Describe the limited liability of shareholders of a corporation.

37.3 List and describe the classifications of corporations.

37.4 Describe the process of incorporating and forming a corporation.

37.5 Describe the powers that a corporation possesses.

37.6 Describe how a corporation is financed by equity securities and define *common stock* and *preferred stock*.

37.7 Describe how a corporation is financed by debt securities.

37.8 Describe how a corporation is dissolved and terminated.

> "*A corporation is an artificial being, invisible, intangible, and existing only in the contemplation of law. Being the mere creature of the law, it possesses only those properties which the charter of its creation confers upon it, either expressly or as incidental to its very existence. These are such as supposed best calculated to effect the object for which it was created. Among the most important are immortality, and, if the expression may be allowed, individuality; properties by which a perpetual succession of many persons are considered as the same, and may act as a single individual.*"
>
> —*Chief Justice John Marshall*
> *Dartmouth College v. Woodward*
> *4 Wheaton 518, 636 (1819)*

Introduction to Corporate Formation and Financing

Corporations are the most dominant form of business organization in the United States, generating more than 85 percent of the country's gross business receipts. Corporations range in size from one owner to thousands of owners. **Shareholders** are owners of a corporation who elect the board of directors and vote on fundamental changes in the corporation.

States have enacted **general corporation statutes** that permit corporations to be formed without the separate approval of the legislature. Today, most corporations are formed pursuant to general corporation laws of the states.

The formation and financing of corporations are discussed in this chapter.

corporation
A fictitious legal entity that is created according to statutory requirements.

shareholders
Owners of a corporation who elect the board of directors and vote on fundamental changes in the corporation.

Nature of the Corporation

37.1 Define *corporation* and list the major characteristics of a corporation.

Corporations can be created only pursuant to the laws of the state of incorporation. These laws—commonly referred to as **corporation codes**—regulate the formation, operation, and dissolution of corporations. The state legislature may amend its corporate codes at any time. Such changes may require a corporation's articles of incorporation to be amended.

The following feature discusses the Revised Model Business Corporation Act and Model Business Corporation Act (2016).

corporation code (general corporation statute)
A state statute that regulates the formation, operation, and dissolution of corporations.

Landmark Law

Model Business Corporation Act (MBCA)

The Committee on Corporate Laws of the American Bar Association first drafted the **Model Business Corporation Act (MBCA)** in 1950. The model act was intended to provide a uniform law regulating the formation, operation, and termination of corporations.

In 1984, the committee completely revised the MBCA and issued the **Revised Model Business Corporation Act (RMBCA)**. This model act modernized the uniform law regulating the formation, operation, and termination of corporations. Some provisions of the RMBCA have been amended since 1984, and some new provisions have been added. Most states have adopted the RMBCA, as well as the amendments to the RMBCA.

In 2016, the committee promulgated the **Model Business Corporation Act (2016)**, also referred to as the **MBCA.** The 2016 model act is based on the structure of the RMBCA, contains most of the provisions of the RMBCA, includes amendments that have been made to the RMBCA, adds new provisions, and includes changes that bring corporate law in line with advances in electronic technology. The 2016 model

(continued)

act is a free-standing, comprehensive, modern business corporation statute. Many states have adopted the model act in full, while some states have substantially adopted the act while making changes unique to their state. The 2016 model act serves as the basis for the discussion of corporation law in this text, and is referred to as the "MBCA."

The courts interpret state corporation statutes to decide individual corporate and shareholder disputes. A body of common law, as developed by the courts, has evolved concerning corporate and shareholder rights and obligations. There is no general federal corporation law governing the formation and operation of private corporations.

The Corporation as a Legal "Person"

Model Business Corporation Act (2016) (MBCA)
A model act that is a free-standing business corporation statute that provides the most comprehensive and modern corporation law for the formation, operation, and dissolution of corporations.

A corporation is a separate **legal entity** (or **legal person**) for most purposes. Corporations are treated, in effect, as artificial persons created by the state that can sue or be sued in their own names, enter into and enforce contracts, hold title to and transfer property, and be found civilly and criminally liable for violations of law. Because corporations cannot be put in prison, the normal criminal penalty is the assessment of a fine, loss of a license, or another sanction.

Characteristics of a Corporation

Corporations have unique characteristics. Some of the major **characteristics of a corporation** are:

- **Free transferability of shares.** Corporate shares are **freely transferable** by a shareholder via sale, assignment, pledge, or gift unless they are issued pursuant to certain exemptions from securities registration. Shareholders may agree among themselves as to restrictions on the transfer of shares. National securities markets, such as the New York Stock Exchange and NASDAQ, have been developed for the organized sale of securities of larger publicly traded corporations.
- **Perpetual existence.** Corporations exist in **perpetuity** unless a specific duration is stated in a corporation's articles of incorporation [MBCA 3.02]. The existence of a corporation may be voluntarily terminated by the shareholders. The death, insanity, or bankruptcy of a shareholder, a director, or an officer of a corporation does not affect a corporation's existence.
- **Centralized management.** A corporation usually has **centralized management** composed of the board of directors and officers of the corporation. The **board of directors** makes policy decisions concerning the operation of a corporation. The members of the board of directors are elected by the shareholders. The directors, in turn, appoint **corporate officers** to run the corporation's day-to-day operations. Together, the directors and officers form the **corporate management**.

board of directors
A panel of persons who are elected by the shareholders that makes policy decisions concerning the operation of a corporation.

corporate officers
Employees of a corporation who are appointed by the board of directors to manage the day-to-day operations of the corporation.

Limited Liability of Shareholders

37.2 Describe the limited liability of shareholders of a corporation.

One of the most important features of a corporation is that its owners—its shareholders—are not responsible for the corporation's debts and obligations. Generally, the shareholders have only *limited liability*. The **limited liability of shareholders** means that shareholders are liable only to the extent of their capital contributions to the corporation; that is, they can lose their investment in the corporation. However, shareholders do not have personal liability for the corporation's debts, obligations, or liabilities [MBCA 6.22(b)]. As separate legal entities, corporations are liable for their own debts and obligations (see **Exhibit 37.1**).

limited liability of shareholders
A general rule of corporate law that provides that generally, shareholders are liable only to the extent of their capital contributions for the debts and obligations of their corporation and are not personally liable for the debts and obligations of the corporation.

Example Axel, Vivi, and Katsu form AI Corporation, a corporation organized under the corporate law of the state of New York, and each contributes $200,000 capital. The corporation borrows $1 million from Global Bank. One year later, AI

Exhibit 37.1 **CORPORATION**

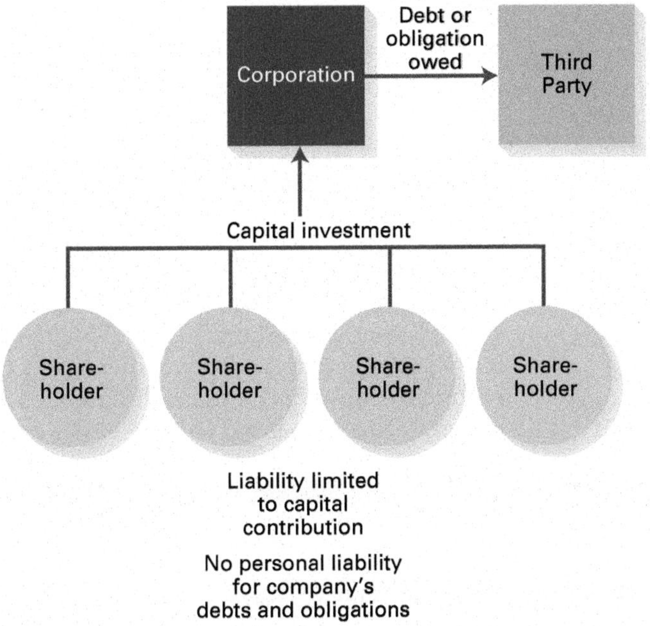

Corporation goes bankrupt and defaults on the $1 million loan owed to Global Bank. At that time, AI Corporation's only asset is $100,000 cash, which Global Bank recovers. Axel, Vivi, and Katsu, as shareholders, each lose their $200,000 capital contribution, which AI Corporation has spent. However, Axel, Vivi, and Katsu are not personally liable for the $900,000 still owed to Global Bank.

In the following case, the court was asked to decide the liability of a shareholder for a corporation's debts.

CASE 37.1 *STATE COURT CASE Shareholder's Limited Liability*

Menendez v. O'Niell

986 So.2d 255 (2008)
Court of Appeal of Louisiana

"As a general rule, a corporation is a distinct legal entity, separate from the individuals who comprise them, and individual shareholders are not liable for the debts of the corporation."

—Duke Welch, Judge

Facts

A vehicle driven by Michael O'Niell crashed while traveling on Louisiana Highway 30. Vanessa Savoy, a 19-year-old passenger in the vehicle, sustained severe injuries as a result of the collision. O'Niell, who was under the legal drinking age, had been drinking at Fred's Bar and Grill prior to the accident. Fred's Bar is owned by Triumvirate of Baton Rouge, Inc., a corporation. Marc Fraioli is the sole shareholder and president of Triumvirate. Fraioli was not at Fred's Bar the night that O'Niell was served alcohol at the bar. Savoy, through a legal representative, brought a lawsuit against O'Niell, O'Niell's automobile insurance company, Triumvirate corporation, and Fraioli seeking damages for her injuries. Savoy alleged that O'Niell was intoxicated at the time of the accident and that his drinking caused the collision. Savoy alleged that Triumvirate was liable for serving O'Niell alcohol when he was underage and that Fraioli was liable as the owner of Triumvirate.

Fraioli filed a motion for summary judgment asserting that, as the shareholder of Triumvirate, he was not liable for the corporation's debts. The trial court granted summary judgment to Fraioli and dismissed him as a defendant in the case. Savoy appealed.

Issue

Is Fraioli personally liable for the debts of Triumvirate, a corporation of which he is the sole shareholder?

(continued)

Language of the Court

As a general rule, a corporation is a distinct legal entity, separate from the individuals who comprise them, and individual shareholders are not liable for the debts of the corporation. Mr. Fraioli met his burden of proving Triumvirate's corporate existence. Plaintiff failed to offer any evidence identified by law as indicia that Mr. Fraioli and Triumvirate are not actually separate entities. The involvement of a sole or majority shareholder in a corporation is not sufficient alone, as a matter of law, to establish a basis for disregarding the corporate entity.

Decision

The court of appeal held that Fraioli was not personally liable for the debts of the Triumvirate corporation, of which he was the sole shareholder. The court of appeal affirmed the trial court's grant of summary judgment, dismissing Fraioli from the case.

Critical Legal Thinking Questions

What reasons could there be for Fraioli to operate his business as a corporation rather than as a sole proprietorship? Was it ethical for Fraioli to assert the corporate shield to avoid liability in this case?

Classifications of Corporations

37.3 List and describe the classifications of corporations.

Critical Legal Thinking Questions

What does *limited liability* of shareholders mean? What would be the economic consequences if shareholders were held personally liable for corporate debts and obligations?

There are several different types of corporations. The classifications of corporations are discussed in the following paragraphs.

For-Profit Corporations

for-profit corporation (profit corporation)
A corporation created to conduct a business for profit that can distribute profits to shareholders in the form of dividends.

publicly held corporation
A corporation that has many shareholders and whose securities are often traded on national stock exchanges.

closely held corporation (privately held corporation)
A corporation owned by one or a few shareholders.

professional corporation (P.C.)
A corporation formed by lawyers, doctors, or other professionals.

not-for-profit corporation (nonprofit corporation)
A corporation formed to operate charitable institutions, colleges, universities, and other not-for-profit entities. These corporations have no shareholders.

A **for-profit corporation**, or **profit corporation**, is a private corporation that is created to conduct a business for profit and that can distribute profits to shareholders in the form of dividends. They are owned by private parties, not by the government. They range from small one-owner corporations to large multinational corporations such as **Amazon.com**, Inc.

A **publicly held corporation** is a for-profit corporation that has many shareholders. Often, they are large corporations with thousands of shareholders, and their shares are usually traded on organized securities markets.

Examples Walmart, Inc.; Facebook, Inc.; Starbucks Corporation; Apple Inc.; Microsoft Corporation; Exxon Mobile Corporation; Apple, Inc.; UnitedHealth Group, Inc.; and Alphabet, Inc. are examples of publicly held corporations.

A **closely held corporation**, or **privately held corporation**, in contrast, is a for-profit corporation whose shares are usually owned by a few shareholders who are often family members, relatives, or friends. Privately held corporations can also be large corporations that are owned by individuals and entities, whose shares are not traded on public exchanges.

Example S. C. Johnson & Son, Inc. (commonly referred to as "S. C. Johnson, A Family Company"), is a privately owned global company with more than 10,000 employees.

A **professional corporation** is a private corporation formed by professionals such as lawyers, accountants, physicians, and dentists. The abbreviations P.C. (professional corporation), P.A. (professional association), and S.C. (service corporation) often identify professional corporations.

Not-for-Profit Corporations

A **not-for-profit corporation**, or a **nonprofit corporation**, is a private corporation that is formed for charitable, educational, religious, or scientific purposes. Although not-for-profit corporations may make a profit, they are prohibited by law from distributing this profit to their members, directors, or officers. States have statutes that govern the formation, operation, and dissolution of nonprofit corporations. The American Bar Association (ABA) has promulgated the **Model Nonprofit Corporation Act (MNCA)**, which provides comprehensive and modern law for the formation, operation, and dissolution of nonprofit corporations.

Government-Owned Corporations

A **government-owned corporation** (or **public corporation**) is formed by a government entity to meet a specific governmental or political purpose. Many public corporations are formed pursuant to state law. Most cities and towns are formed as corporations, as are most water, school, sewage, and park districts. A local government corporation is often called a **municipal corporation**.

government-owned corporation (public corporation)
A corporation formed to meet a specific governmental or political purpose.

Examples The federal government charters and owns a number of corporations, including the Corporation for Public Broadcasting (CPB), the Federal Deposit Insurance Corporation (FDIC), and the Tennessee Valley Authority (TVA).

Domestic, Foreign, and Alien Corporations

A corporation is a **domestic corporation** in the state in which it is incorporated. It is a **foreign corporation** in all other states and jurisdictions.

domestic corporation
A corporation in the state in which it was formed.

foreign corporation
A corporation in any state or jurisdiction other than the one in which it was formed.

Example Starbucks Corporation, a major coffee company and coffee house chain, is incorporated in the state of Washington. It is a domestic corporation in Washington. Starbucks conducts business in the other 49 states. Starbucks is a foreign corporation in these other 49 states.

An **alien corporation** is a corporation that is incorporated in another country. In most instances, alien corporations are treated as foreign corporations.

alien corporation
A corporation that is incorporated in another country.

CONCEPT SUMMARY
TYPES OF CORPORATIONS

Type of Corporation	Description
Domestic	A corporation is a domestic corporation in the state in which it is incorporated.
Foreign	A corporation is a foreign corporation in states other than the one in which it is incorporated.
Alien	A corporation is an alien corporation in the United States if it is incorporated in another country.

Holding Company

A **holding company** is a corporation that owns and operates a variety of other corporations and entities as subsidiaries. A holding company is often referred to as a **conglomerate**. A holding company usually owns 50 percent or more of a subsidiary company's stock so that it can elect the majority of the board members and influence the operations of its subsidiaries. Many subsidiary corporations and entities are wholly owned by the holding company.

holding company (conglomerate)
A corporation that owns and operates a variety of other corporations and entities as subsidiaries.

Examples Amazon.com, Inc. is a major publicly traded holding company that owns Whole Foods Markets, Audible, CreateSpace, Goodreads, IMDb, and other subsidiaries. JPMorgan Chase & Co. is a multinational publicly traded holding company that owns more than 40 subsidiaries, including JPMorgan Chase Bank, Chase Bank USA, and JPMorgan Securities LLC, among others.

Alphabet, Inc., a publicly traded corporation, is a parent company that owns Google LLC and various other wholly owned subsidiaries, including Calico, Chronicle, and Google Fiber.

Incorporation Procedure

37.4 Describe the process of incorporating and forming a corporation.

They [corporations] cannot commit treason, nor be outlawed, nor excommunicated, for they have no souls.
Lord Edward Coke
Case of Sutton's Hospital (1612)

Corporations are creatures of statute. Thus, the organizers of a corporation must comply with the state's corporation code to form a corporation. The procedure for **incorporating a corporation** varies somewhat from state to state, but the general procedure is discussed in the following paragraphs.

Selecting a State for Incorporating a Corporation

A corporation can be incorporated in only one state, even though it can do business in all other states in which it qualifies to do business. In choosing a state for incorporation, the incorporators, directors, and/or shareholders must consider the corporation law of the states under consideration.

For the sake of convenience, most corporations (particularly small ones) choose the state in which the corporation will be doing most of its business as the state for incorporation. Large corporations generally opt to incorporate in the state with the laws that are most favorable to the corporation's internal operations (e.g., Delaware).

Selecting a Corporate Name

The corporation is, and must be, the creature of the state. Into its nostrils the state must breathe the breath of a fictitious life for otherwise it would be no animated body but individualistic dust.
Frederic William Maitland
Introduction to Gierke, Political Theories of the Middle Ages (1915)

When starting a new corporation, the organizers must choose a name for the entity. To ensure that the name selected is not already being used by another business, the organizers should do the following:

- Choose a name for the corporation. The name must contain the word "corporation," "incorporated," "company," or "limited" or the abbreviation "Corp.," "Inc.," "Co.," or "Ltd." [MBCA 401(a)].
- Make sure the name chosen does not contain any word or phrase that indicates or implies that the corporation is organized for any purpose other than those stated in the articles of incorporation. For example, a corporate name cannot contain the word "bank" if it is not authorized to conduct the business of banking.
- Make sure that the name is distinguishable from other corporate and business names recorded at the secretary of state's office.
- Determine whether the name selected is trademarked by another company and is therefore unavailable for use.
- Determine whether the chosen name is similar to other nontrademarked names and is therefore unavailable for use.
- Determine whether the name selected is available as a domain name on the internet. If the domain name is already owned by another person or business, the new corporation cannot use this domain name to conduct e-commerce. Therefore, it may be advisable to select another corporate name.

The following feature discusses an important issue that should be considered when adopting a corporate name.

Information Technology

Choosing a Domain Name for a Corporation

Prior to or on forming a corporation and selecting a corporate name, the incorporators should check to see if the domain name for their corporate name is available. If it is available, the corporation should register the **domain name**. The domain name will identify the corporation's website to describe its business, post notices, and provide corporate information. This domain name often provides a platform from which to conduct e-commerce. Corporations can also register trade names as domain names. Corporations usually select the .com suffix for their corporate domain name. Large corporations often have many trade names.

Examples Amazon.com, Inc. operates a website using the domain name **www.amazon.com**. Nike, Inc. operates a website using the domain name **www.nike.com**. Wal-Mart Stores, Inc. operates websites using the domain names www.walmart.com and www.samsclub.com. Williams and Sonoma, Inc. operates websites using the domain names www.williams-sonoma.com and www.potterybarn.com.

Companies are permitted to use their corporate names, trade names, or brand names as domain name suffixes.

Examples Coca-Cola Company could use the domain names www.softdrinks.cocacola, www.cola.coke, www.sprite.cocacola, www.orange.fanta, www.minutemaid.cocacola, or other combinations.

Promoters

A **promoter** is a person who organizes and starts a corporation and finds the initial investors to finance the corporation. Promoters sometimes enter into contracts on behalf of a corporation prior to its actual incorporation. **Promoters' contracts** include leases, sales contracts, contracts to purchase real or personal property, employment contracts, and the like. **Promoters' liability** and the corporation's liability on promoters' contracts follow these rules:

promoter
A person who organizes and starts a corporation, negotiates and enters into contracts in advance of its formation, and finds the initial investors to finance the corporation.

promoters' contracts
A collective term for such items such as leases, sales contracts, contracts to purchase property, and employment contracts entered into by promoters on behalf of the proposed corporation prior to its actual incorporation.

- All persons purporting to act as or on behalf of a corporation, knowing there was no incorporation, are jointly and severally liable for all liabilities created while so acting [MBCA 2.04].

  Example A promoter attempts to start a corporation. Before filing the articles of incorporation, the promoter signs a five-year lease for office space for the planned corporation. When the promoter cannot raise sufficient investment funds, the corporation is never formed. The promoter is personally liable for the lease payments.

- If the corporation is formed, it becomes liable on a promoter's contract only if it agrees to become bound to the contract. A resolution of the board of directors binds the corporation to a promoter's contract.
- Even if the corporation agrees to be bound to the contract, the promoter remains liable on the contract unless the parties enter into a **novation agreement** or **novation**, a three-party agreement in which the corporation agrees to assume the contract liability of the promoter with the consent of the third party. After a novation, the corporation is solely liable on the promoter's contract.

Promoters often become shareholders, directors, or officers of the corporation.

Articles of Incorporation

articles of incorporation (corporate charter)
The basic governing document of a corporation. It must be filed with the secretary of state of the state of incorporation.

The **articles of incorporation** (or **corporate charter**) is the basic governing document of a corporation. It must be drafted and filed with the secretary of state of the state of incorporation. A party who signs the articles of

WEB EXERCISE
To view the articles of incorporation of Microsoft Corporation, go to **https://www.microsoft.com/en-us/Investor/corporate-governance/policies.aspx** and click on "Articles of Incorporation."

incorporation is called an **incorporator** [MBCA 2.01]. The articles of incorporation must include the following [MBCA 2.02(a)]:

- The name of the corporation.
- The number of shares the corporation is authorized to issue. If more than one class of shares is authorized, both the number of authorized shares of each class and the description of the rights of each class must be included.
- The address of the corporation's initial registered office and the name of the initial registered agent.
- The name and address of each incorporator.

The articles of incorporation may also include provisions concerning (1) the period of duration (which may be perpetual), (2) the purpose or purposes for which the corporation is organized, (3) limitation or regulation of the powers of the corporation, (4) regulation of the affairs of the corporation, or (5) any provision that would otherwise be contained in the corporation's bylaws.

Exhibit 37.2 illustrates simple sample articles of incorporation.

ARTICLES OF INCORPORATION
OF
THE BIG CHEESE CORPORATION

ONE: The name of this corporation is:

THE BIG CHEESE CORPORATION

TWO: The purpose of this corporation is to engage in any lawful act or activity for which a corporation may be organized under the General Corporation Law of California other than the banking business, the trust company business, or the practice of a profession permitted to be incorporated by the California Corporations Code.

THREE: The name and address in this state of the corporation's initial agent for service of process is:

Nikki Nguyen, Esq.
1000 Main Street
Suite 800
Los Angeles, California 90010

FOUR: This corporation is authorized to issue only one class of shares which shall be designated common stock. The total number of shares it is authorized to issue is 1,000,000 shares.

FIVE: The names and addresses of the persons who are appointed to act as the initial directors of this corporation are:

Shou-Yi Kang	100 Maple Street Los Angeles, California 90005
Frederick Richards	200 Spruce Road Los Angeles, California 90006
Jessie Quian	300 Palm Drive Los Angeles, California 90007
Richard Eastin	400 Willow Lane Los Angeles, California 90008

SIX: The liability of the directors of the corporation from monetary damages shall be eliminated to the fullest extent possible under California law.

SEVEN: The corporation is authorized to provide indemnification of agents (as defined in Section 317 of the Corporations Code) for breach of duty to the corporation and its stockholders through bylaw provisions or through agreements with the agents, or both, in excess of the indemnification otherwise permitted by Section 317 of the Corporations Code, subject to the limits on such excess indemnification set forth in Section 204 of the Corporations Code.

IN WITNESS WHEREOF, the undersigned, being all the persons named above as the initial directors, have executed these Articles of Incorporation.

Dated: January 1, 2022

Exhibit 37.2 ARTICLES OF INCORPORATION

A corporation's articles of incorporation can be amended to contain any provision that could have been lawfully included in the original document [MBCA 10.01(a)]. An amendment must show that (1) the board of directors adopted a *resolution* recommending the amendment and (2) the shareholders voted to approve the amendment [MBCA 10.03]. After the amendment has been approved, the corporation must file **articles of amendment** with the secretary of state of the state of incorporation [MBCA 10.06].

A corporation may change its state of incorporation by meeting the requirements of state laws to do so [MBCA 9.20]. A corporation may also convert to a noncorporate entity—for example, to a limited liability company—by meeting the requirements of state laws to do so [MBCA 9.30].

E-Filing of Articles of Incorporation and Corporate Documents

Most states permit or require articles of incorporation to be filed electronically using a document upload service. States provide the format for using electronic signatures to sign the articles. Payment of the requisite filing fee is normally accepted using a credit card. Electronic copies are usually available in a secure PDF/A format. Most other corporate documents, such as amendments to the articles of incorporation, corporate annual reports, and articles of dissolution of the corporation, may or must be e-filed.

Corporate Status

Corporate existence begins when the articles of incorporation are filed. The secretary of state's filing of the articles of incorporation is *conclusive proof* that the corporation has satisfied all conditions of incorporation. After that, only the state can bring a proceeding to cancel or revoke the incorporation or involuntarily dissolve the corporation. Third parties cannot thereafter challenge the existence of the corporation or assert its lack of existence as a corporation as a defense against the corporation. The corollary to this rule is that failure to file articles of incorporation is conclusive proof of the nonexistence of a corporation [MBCA 2.03].

general-purpose clause
A clause that can be included in the articles of incorporation that permits the corporation to engage in any lawful activity.

limited-purpose clause
A clause that can be included in the articles of incorporation that stipulates the activities that the corporation can engage in. The corporation can engage in no other purposes or activities.

Benefit corporation (B corporation or B corp)
A corporation that requires directors and officers to make decisions to accomplish general public benefits and stipulated specific public benefit purposes stated in the articles of incorporation and to consider stakeholders other than shareholders, such as employees, customers, suppliers, and the community, when making corporate decisions.

Purpose of a Corporation

A corporation can be formed for any lawful purpose. Most corporations include a **general-purpose clause** in their articles of incorporation, which expressly provides that the corporation can engage in any lawful activity. A corporation may also choose to limit its purpose or purposes by including a **limited-purpose clause** in the articles of incorporation [MBCA 3.01(a)]. Such a clause stipulates that the corporation can only engage in expressly stated purposes and activities, or it can expressly restrict the purposes and activities that the corporation may engage in. A corporation with a limited-purpose clause can engage in no other purposes or activities.

Example A limited-purpose clause could state that a corporation may only engage in the business of real estate development.

The following feature discusses benefit corporations.

Ethics

Benefit Corporations

Under the traditional corporate form, directors must keep shareholder benefits foremost and act with a goal of maximizing profits. In general, corporations have the power to make donations for the public welfare or for charitable, scientific, and educational purposes [MBCA 3.02(m)]. However, the traditional corporate purpose of advancing the financial interests of shareholders limits the extent to which the corporation can support social and charitable programs.

Many states have enacted legislation that permits a new form of corporation called a **benefit corporation**, often

(continued)

referred to as a **B corporation or B corp**. Unlike traditional corporations, where the shareholder is the main stakeholder, B corps allow directors and officers to consider benefits to society and to other stakeholders—including employees, customers, suppliers, and the community—when making corporate decisions. **Model Benefit Corporation Legislation** (MBCL) has been promulgated that provides a model act for the creation and operation of a benefit corporation.

A benefit corporation is a regular for-profit corporation that has designated a mission or missions additional to those of the pure profit motive. A benefit corporation's stated purpose may be to create **general public benefits**, such as considering social issues in its decision making. B corps can also identify **specific public benefits**, such as reducing the company's carbon footprint, engaging in sustainability efforts, promoting economic opportunities for low-income individuals or communities, improving human health, promoting the arts or sciences, or giving a percentage of its profits to charity. Shareholders can sue the benefit corporation's directors it they fail to carry out the corporation's general and special missions.

To become a benefit corporation, a corporation must elect to be so in its articles of incorporation. A new corporation can make this election when filing its initial articles of incorporation. An existing corporation can make this election by filing an amendment to its existing articles of incorporation. A vote of two-thirds of the shares of each class of stock of a corporation is necessary to elect B corporation status. Other than for a B corporation's social mission, benefit corporations are subject to the general corporate law of the state of incorporation. There are no tax benefits to being a B corp. In most states, each B corp must prepare an annual **benefit report** that assesses its social and environmental performance. The report must be delivered to shareholders and posted on the company's public website.

B Lab, a nonprofit corporation, can be hired by a corporation to certify that it is meeting its stated social missions. B corps are not required to seek such certification, but many do. A corporation that meets B Lab standards is called a **certified benefit corporation** and can display B Lab's Certified B Corporation logo.

Examples Patagonia, Inc. is a registered benefit corporation. Ben and Jerry's Homemade Holdings, Inc. is a certified benefit corporation.

Ethics Questions

What is the purpose of a benefit corporation? Why would investors purchase shares in a benefit corporation? What type of companies are more apt to be benefit corporations?

Registered Agent

registered agent
A person or corporation that is empowered to accept service of process on behalf of a corporation.

The articles of incorporation must identify a **registered office** with a designated **registered agent** (either an individual or a corporation) in the state of incorporation [MBCA 5.01]. The registered office may be any place of corporate business, and the registered agent may be an officer of the corporation. However, the registered office does not have to be the same as a corporation's place of business, and the registered agent does not have to be an employee of the corporation. In fact, many corporations designate their regular legal counsel as their registered agent and the lawyer's place of business as the registered office. A statement of change of the registered agent or location of the registered office must be filed with the secretary of state if either the registered agent or the registered office is changed. Foreign corporations must designate a registered agent and registered office in states in which they conduct business. The registered agent is the corporation's agent for service of process, notice, or demand to be served on the corporation.

Example If someone is suing a corporation, the complaint and summons are served on the registered agent.

If no registered agent is named or the registered agent cannot be found at the registered office with reasonable diligence, service may be made by mail or alternative means. If service of process is still ineffectual, the secretary of state becomes the agent of the corporation, to which process, notice, or demand may be served [MBCA 5.04].

The following feature discusses an election that can be made when forming a corporation.

Business Environment

Close Corporation Election

Several states permit corporations to elect **close corporation** status under state corporation law if certain requirements are met. Where available, close corporations are often used for small corporations owned by family members, when it is not anticipated that the corporation will ever be taken public, and when the principals do not want to make public disclosure of corporate activities or earnings.

Generally, only corporations with 50 or fewer shareholders (in some states, 30 or fewer shareholders) may elect statutory close corporation (SCC) status. To choose this status, two-thirds of the shares of each class of shares of the corporation must approve the election. The articles of incorporation must contain a statement that the corporation is a statutory close corporation. In essence, a close corporation is not a new form of entity, but is a corporation that has met the requisite requirements and has elected in its articles of incorporation to be a close corporation.

A close corporation may dispense with some of the formalities of operating a corporation. For example, if all the shareholders approve, a close corporation may operate without a board of directors, without bylaws, and without keeping minutes of meetings. A statutory close corporation need not hold annual shareholders' meetings unless one or more shareholders demand in writing that such meetings be held. In effect, the affairs of the corporation are managed by the shareholders, who can treat the corporation as a partnership for governance purposes. Selecting statutory close corporation status does not affect the limited liability of shareholders.

Corporate Bylaws

In addition to the articles of incorporation, corporations are governed by their **bylaws**. Either the incorporators or the initial directors can adopt the bylaws of the corporation. The bylaws are much more detailed than are the articles of incorporation. Bylaws may contain any provisions for managing the business and affairs of the corporation that are not inconsistent with law or the articles of incorporation [MBCA 2.06]. They do not have to be filed with any government official. Today, most corporations provide their bylaws online. The bylaws are binding on the directors, officers, and shareholders of the corporation. The bylaws govern the internal management structure of a corporation.

close corporation
A small corporation that has met specified requirements and has elected in its articles of incorporation to be a statutory close corporation. As such, the corporation may dispense with many corporate formalities.

bylaws
A detailed set of rules adopted by the board of directors after a corporation is incorporated that contains provisions for managing the business and the affairs of the corporation.

Examples Bylaws typically specify the time and place of the annual shareholders' meeting, how special meetings of shareholders are called, the time and place of annual and monthly meetings of the board of directors, how special meetings of the board of directors are called, the notice required for meetings, the quorum necessary to hold a shareholders' or board meeting, the required vote necessary to enact a corporate matter, the corporate officers and their duties, the committees of the board of directors and their duties, where the records of the corporation are kept, directors' and shareholders' rights to inspect corporate records, the procedure for transferring shares of the corporation, and other provisions.

Sample provisions of corporate bylaws are set forth in **Exhibit 37.3**.

The shareholders of the corporation have the absolute right to amend or repeal the bylaws of a corporation. The board of directors has the authority to amend or repeal the bylaws unless the articles of incorporation reserves that power exclusively to the shareholders [MBCA 10.20].

WEB EXERCISE
To view the bylaws of Microsoft Corporation, go to **https://www.microsoft.com/en-us/investor/corporate-governance/policies.aspx** and click on "Bylaws."

BYLAWS
OF
THE BIG CHEESE CORPORATION

ARTICLE I Offices

Section 1. Principal Executive Office. The corporation's principal executive office shall be fixed and located at such place as the Board of Directors (herein called the "Board") shall determine. The Board is granted full power and authority to change said principal executive office from one location to another.

Section 2. Other Offices. Branch or subordinate offices may be established at any time by the Board at any place or places.

ARTICLE II Shareholders

Section 1. Annual Meetings. The annual meetings of shareholders shall be held on such date and at such time as may be fixed by the Board. At such meetings, directors shall be elected and any other proper business may be transacted.

Section 2. Special Meetings. Special meetings of the shareholders may be called at any time by the Board, the Chairman of the Board, the President, or by the holders of shares entitled to cast not less than ten percent of the votes at such meeting. Upon request in writing to the Chairman of the Board, the President, any Vice President or the Secretary by any person (other than the Board) entitled to call a special meeting of shareholders, the officer forthwith shall cause notice to be given to the shareholders entitled to vote that a meeting will be held at a time requested by the person or persons calling the meeting, not less than thirty-five nor more than sixty days after the receipt of the request. If the notice is not given within twenty days after receipt of the request, the persons entitled to call the meeting may give the notice.

Section 3. Quorum. A majority of the shares entitled to vote, represented in person or by proxy, shall constitute a quorum at any meeting of shareholders. If a quorum is present, the affirmative vote of a majority of the shares represented and voting at the meeting (which shares voting affirmatively also constitute at least a majority of the required quorum) shall be the act of the shareholders, unless the vote of a greater number or voting by classes is required by law or by the Articles, except as provided in the following sentence. The shareholders present at a duly called or held meeting at which a quorum is present may continue to do business until adjournment, notwithstanding the withdrawal of enough shareholders to leave less than a quorum, if any action taken (other than adjournment) is approved by at least a majority of the shares required to constitute a quorum.

ARTICLE III Directors

Section 1. Election and term of office. The directors shall be elected at each annual meeting of the shareholders, but if any such annual meeting is not held or the directors are not elected thereat, the directors may be elected at any special meeting of shareholders held for that purpose. Each director shall hold office until the next annual meeting and until a successor has been elected and qualified.

Section 2. Quorum. A majority of the authorized number of directors constitutes a quorum of the Board for the transaction of business. Every act or decision done or made by a majority of the directors present at a meeting duly held at which a quorum is present shall be regarded as the act of the Board, unless a greater number be required by law or by the Articles. A meeting at which a quorum is initially present may continue to transact business notwithstanding the withdrawal of directors, if any action taken is approved by at least a majority of the required quorum for such meeting.

Section 3. Participation in Meetings by Conference Telephone. Members of the Board may participate in a meeting through use of conference telephone or similar communications equipment, so long as all members participating in such meeting can hear one another.

Section 4. Action Without Meeting. Any action required or permitted to be taken by the Board may be taken without a meeting if all members of the board shall individually or collectively consent in writing to such action. Such consent or consents shall have the same effect as a unanimous vote of the Board and shall be filed with the minutes of the proceedings of the Board.

Exhibit 37.3 BYLAWS

Organizational Meeting of the Board of Directors

organizational meeting
A meeting that must be held by the initial directors of a corporation after the articles of incorporation are filed.

An **organizational meeting** of the initial directors of a corporation must be held after the articles of incorporation are filed. At this meeting, the directors must adopt the bylaws, appoint corporate officers, and transact such other business as may come before the meeting [MBCA 2.05].

Examples Actions taken at the meeting may include accepting share subscriptions, approving the form of the stock certificate, authorizing the issuance of the shares, ratifying or adopting promoters' contracts, authorizing the reimbursement of promoters' expenses, selecting a bank, choosing an auditor, forming committees of the board of directors, fixing the salaries of officers, hiring employees, authorizing the filing of applications for government licenses to transact the business of the corporation, and empowering corporate officers to enter into contracts on behalf of the corporation. **Exhibit 37.4** contains sample corporate resolutions from an organizational meeting of a corporation.

Corporate Seal

Most corporations adopt a **corporate seal** [MBCA 3.02(b)]. Generally, the seal is a design that contains the name of the corporation and the date of incorporation. It is imprinted by the corporate secretary on certain legal documents (e.g., real

MINUTES OF FIRST MEETING
OF
BOARD OF DIRECTORS
OF
THE BIG CHEESE CORPORATION
January 2, 2022
10:00 A.M.

The Directors of said corporation held their first meeting on the above date and at the above time pursuant to required notice.

The following Directors, constituting a quorum of the Board of Directors, were present at such meeting:

Shou-Yi Kang
Frederick Richards
Jessie Quian
Richard Eastin

Upon motion duly made and seconded, Shou-Yi was unanimously elected Chairman of the meeting and Frederick Richards was unanimously elected Secretary of the meeting.

1. Articles of Incorporation and Agent for Service of Process

The Chairman stated that the Articles of Incorporation of the Corporation were filed in the office of the California Secretary of State. The Chairman presented to the meeting a certified copy of the Articles of Incorporation. The Secretary was directed to insert the copy in the Minute Book. Upon motion duly made and seconded, the following resolution was unanimously adopted:

RESOLVED, that the agent named as the initial agent for service of process in the Articles of Incorporation of this corporation is here by confirmed as this corporation's agent for the purpose of service of process.

2. Bylaws

The matter of adopting Bylaws for the regulation of the affairs of the corporation was next considered. The Secretary presented to the meeting a form of Bylaws, which was considered and discussed. Upon motion duly made and seconded, the following recitals and resolutions were unanimously adopted:

WHEREAS, there has been presented to the directors a form of Bylaws for the regulation of the affairs of this corporation; and

WHEREAS, it is deemed to be in the best interests of this corporation that said Bylaws be adopted by this Board of Directors as the Bylaws of this corporation;

NOW, THEREFORE, BE IT RESOLVED, that Bylaws in the form presented to this meeting are adopted and approved as the Bylaws of this corporation until amended or repealed in accordance with applicable law.

RESOLVED FURTHER, that the Secretary of this corporation is authorized and directed to execute a certificate of the adoption of said Bylaws and to enter said Bylaws as so certified in the Minute Book of this corporation, and to see that a copy of said Bylaws is kept at the principal executive or business office of this corporation in California.

3. Corporate Seal

The secretary presented for approval a proposed seal of the corporation. Upon motion duly made and seconded, the following resolution was unanimously adopted:

RESOLVED, that a corporate seal is adopted as the seal of this corporation in the form of two concentric circles, with the name of this corporation between the two circles and the state and date of incorporation within the inner circle.

4. Stock Certificate

The Secretary presented a proposed form of stock certificate for use by the corporation. Upon motion duly made and seconded, the following resolution was unanimously adopted:

RESOLVED, that the form of stock certificate presented to this meeting is approved and adopted as the stock certificate of this corporation.

The secretary was instructed to insert a sample copy of the stock certificate in the Minute Book immediately following these minutes.

5. Election of officers

The Chairman announced that it would be in order to elect officers of the corporation. After discussion and upon motion duly made and seconded, the following resolution was unanimously adopted:

RESOLVED, that the following persons are unanimously elected to the offices indicated opposite their names

Title	Name
Chief Executive Officer	Shou-Yi Kang
President	Frederick Richards
Secretary and Vice President	Jessie Quian
Treasurer	Richard Eastin

There being no further business to come before the meeting, on motion duly made, seconded and unanimously carried, the meeting was adjourned.

Exhibit 37.4 **MINUTES OF AN ORGANIZATIONAL MEETING OF THE BOARD OF DIRECTORS**

estate deeds) that are signed by corporate officers or directors. The seal is usually affixed using a metal stamp.

The following feature discusses an election that can be made regarding federal tax obligations.

Business Environment

S Corporation Election for Federal Tax Purposes

A **C corporation** is a corporation that does not qualify to or does not elect to be federally taxed as an S corporation. Any corporation with more than 100 shareholders is automatically a C corporation for federal income tax purposes. A C corporation must pay federal income tax at the corporate level. In addition, if a C corporation distributes its profits to shareholders in the form of dividends, the shareholders must pay personal income tax on the dividends. With a C corporation, there is **double taxation**; that is, one tax paid at the corporate level and another paid at the shareholder level.

Congress enacted the **Subchapter S Revision Act** to allow the shareholders of some corporations to avoid double taxation by electing Subchapter S corporation status.[1] If a corporation elects to be taxed as an **S corporation**, it pays no federal income tax at the corporate level. As in a partnership, the corporation's income or loss flows to the shareholders' individual income tax returns. Shareholders pay the tax on the corporation's profits even if the income is not distributed. Subchapter S election only affects the *taxation* of a corporation; it does not affect attributes of corporate form, including limited liability.

Corporations that meet the following criteria can elect to be taxed as S corporations:

- The corporation must be a domestic corporation.
- The corporation cannot be a member of an affiliated group of corporations.
- The corporation can have no more than 100 shareholders.
- Shareholders must be individuals, estates, or certain trusts. Corporations, partnerships, or other entities cannot be shareholders.
- Shareholders must be citizens or residents of the United States. Nonresident aliens cannot be shareholders.
- The corporation cannot have more than one class of stock. Shareholders do not have to have equal voting rights.

An S corporation election is made by filing **Form 2553** with the Internal Revenue Service (IRS). The election can be rescinded by shareholders who collectively own at least a majority of the shares of the corporation. If the election is rescinded, however, another S corporation election cannot be made for five years.

C corporation
A corporation that does not qualify for or has not elected to be taxed as an S corporation. Where there is a C corporation, there is double taxation; that is, a C corporation pays taxes at the corporate level and shareholders pay taxes on dividends paid by the corporation.

S corporation
A corporation that has met certain requirements and has elected to be taxed as an S corporation for federal income tax purposes. An S corporation pays no federal income tax at the corporate level. The S corporation's income or loss flows to the shareholders and must be reported on the shareholders' individual income tax returns.

foreign registration statement
A statement that must be filed by a foreign corporation with the secretary of state of a state other than the state of its own jurisdiction before conducting business in the other state.

Foreign Corporations

A corporation that is organized in one state is considered a foreign corporation in the other states.

A foreign corporation may register to do business in another state by delivering a **foreign registration statement** to the secretary of state of the state in which it wishes to conduct business [MBCA 15.02(a)]. The statement must contain the name of the corporation, the jurisdiction of its formation, the address of the foreign corporation's principal office, the name and address of the foreign corporation's registered agent and other information in the host state, the names and addresses of its directors and principal officers, and a description of the nature of the business it will conduct in the host state [MBCA 15.03]. Some states require that a foreign corporation *qualify* to conduct business in the state. The foreign corporation must file an application containing information similar to that outlined above, provide other required information, and obtain a **certificate of authority** to conduct business in the host state. A corporation of another country is considered a foreign corporation and must comply with a host state's business laws. The law of the state of jurisdiction of a foreign corporation governs the internal affairs of the foreign corporation [MBCA 15.03].

Corporate Powers

37.5 Describe the powers that a corporation possesses.

A corporation's **express powers** are found in (1) the U.S. Constitution, (2) state constitutions, (3) federal and state statutes, (4) federal and state administrative agency rules, (5) state corporation codes, (6) articles of incorporation, (7) bylaws, and (8) resolutions of the board of directors.

A corporation has the same powers as an individual to do all things necessary or convenient to carry out its business and affairs. A corporation has the power to sue and be sued; to purchase, own, and lease real and personal property; to sell, mortgage, or lease corporate property; to make contracts; to borrow or lend money; to appoint officers, employees, and agents; to invest and reinvest funds; to issue notes and bonds and other obligations; and to take other actions necessary to conduct the business and affairs of the corporation [MBCA 3.02].

Ultra Vires Act

An act by a corporation or its officers or directors that is beyond their express or implied powers is called an ***ultra vires* act** (literally "beyond the powers"). *Ultra vires* acts are not limited to illegal acts but also encompass acts beyond the powers of the corporation or its officers and directors. If an *ultra vires* act is anticipated but has not yet occurred, plaintiff shareholders or corporations can sue for an injunction to prevent the act; if the act has occurred, they can sue to set aside the act and to recover damages.

ultra vires act
An act by a corporation that is beyond its express or implied powers.

The assertion of the *ultra vires* doctrine has been sharply reduced by modern corporate law. The RMBCA limits the *ultra vires* doctrine to three situations: (1) by the corporation or shareholders against officers or directors for exceeding their authority; (2) by shareholders against a corporation to enjoin the commission of an *ultra vires* act; and (3) by the attorney general of the state of incorporation to dissolve a corporation or to enjoin it from transacting unauthorized business [MBCA 3.04].

Example A shareholder could bring an *ultra vires* action to enjoin directors from selling real estate owned by the corporation if the sale would violate corporate restrictions.

Financing the Corporation—Equity Securities

37.6 Describe how a corporation is financed by equity securities and define *common stock* and *preferred stock*.

A corporation needs to finance the operation of its business. The most common way to do this is by selling *equity securities* and *debt securities*. **Equity securities** (or **stocks**) represent ownership rights in the corporation. Equity securities can be *common stock* and *preferred stock*. These are discussed in the following paragraphs.

equity securities (stocks)
Representation of ownership rights to a corporation.

Common Stock

Common stock is an equity security that represents the residual value of a corporation. Common stock has no preferences. That is, creditors and preferred shareholders must receive their required interest and dividend payments before common shareholders receive anything. Common stock does not have a fixed maturity date. If a corporation is liquidated, the creditors and preferred shareholders are paid the value of their interests first, and the common shareholders are paid the value of their interests (if any) last.

common stock
A type of equity security that represents the *residual* value of a corporation.

Common stock can be issued in classes or series. A corporation's articles of incorporation must authorize one or more classes of shares that together have full voting rights [MBCA 6.01(b)(1)]. A corporation's articles of incorporation may authorize one or more classes of common stock that may have special, conditional, or limited voting rights [MBCA 6.01(c)(1)]. A person who owns common stock is called a **common stockholder**.

common stockholder
A person who owns common stock.

Common stockholders have the right to elect directors and to vote on mergers and other important matters. In return for his or her investment, a common stockholder usually receives a **dividend** declared by the board of directors, which is often paid quarterly. Common stockholders have limited liability and may lose their investment, but they are not personally liable for the obligations of the corporation.

Par Value and No Par Value Shares Common shares are sometimes categorized as either par or no par. **Par value shares** are common stock on which the corporation has set the lowest price at which the shares may be issued by the corporation. This price does not affect the market value of the shares. Most shares that are issued by corporations are **no par value shares**. No par value shares are not assigned par value. Although a corporation may set a par value of shares in its articles of incorporation, most corporations no longer do so [MBCA 2.02(b)(1)(iv)].

Preferred Stock

preferred stock
A type of equity security that is given certain preferences and rights over common stock.

preferred stockholder
A person who owns preferred stock.

dividend preference
The right of a preferred stockholder to receive a fixed dividend at stipulated periods during the year (e.g., quarterly).

Preferred stock is an equity security that is given certain *preferences and rights over common stock* [MBCA 6.01(c)]. The owner of a preferred stock is called a **preferred stockholder**. Like common stockholders, preferred stockholders have limited liability and may lose their investment, but they are not personally liable for the obligations of the corporation.

Preferred stock can be issued in classes or series. One class of preferred stock can be given preference over another class of preferred stock. Preferred stockholders generally are not given the right to vote for the election of directors, or similar rights. However, they are often given the right to vote if there is a merger or if the corporation has not made the required dividend payments for a certain period of time (e.g., three years). Preferences of preferred stock must be set forth in the articles of incorporation.

The following feature discusses preferred stock preferences.

Business Environment

Preferred Stock Preferences

Preferred stock may have any of the following preferences:

- **Dividend preference.** A **dividend preference** is the right to receive a **fixed dividend** at set periods during the year (e.g., quarterly) [MBCA 6.01(c)(4)]. The dividend rate is usually a set percentage of the initial offering price.

  Example A stockholder purchases $10,000 of a preferred stock that pays a 6 percent dividend annually. The stockholder has the right to receive $600 each year as a dividend on the preferred stock.

- **Liquidation preference.** The right to be paid before common stockholders if the corporation is dissolved and liquidated is called a **liquidation preference** [MBCA 6.01(c)(4)]. A liquidation preference is normally a stated dollar amount.

  Example A corporation issues a preferred stock that has a liquidation preference of $200. This means that if the corporation is dissolved and liquidated, the holder of each preferred share will receive at least $200 before the common shareholders receive anything. Note that because the corporation must pay its creditors first, there may be insufficient funds to pay this preference.

- **Cumulative dividend right.** Corporations must pay a preferred dividend if they have the earnings to do so. Sometimes, however, corporations are not able to pay preferred stock dividends when they are due. **Cumulative preferred stock** provides that any missed dividend payment must be paid in the future to the preferred shareholders before the common shareholders can be paid any dividends [MBCA 6.01(c)(3)]. The amount of unpaid cumulative dividends is called dividend **arrearages**. Usually, arrearages can be accumulated for only a limited period of time (e.g., three years).

  With **noncumulative preferred stock**, there is no right of accumulation. In other words, the corporation does not have to pay any missed dividends.

  Example A corporation issues cumulative preferred stock that requires the payment of a quarterly dividend of $1.00 per share. The corporation falls behind on six quarterly payments—$6.00 per share of preferred stock. The next quarter, the corporation makes a profit of $7.00 per share. The corporation must pay the $6.00 per share of arrearages to the preferred shareholders plus this quarter's payment of $1.00 per share. Thus, the common shareholders receive nothing.

- **Right to participate in profits. Participating preferred stock** allows a preferred stockholder to participate in the profits of the corporation along with the common stockholders [MBCA 6.01(c)(4)]. Participation is in addition to the fixed dividend paid on preferred stock. The terms of participation vary widely. Usually, the common stockholders must be paid a stipulated dollar amount of dividends before participation is allowed. **Nonparticipating preferred stock** does not give the holder a right to participate in the profits of the corporation beyond the fixed dividend rate. Most preferred stock falls into this category.

- **Conversion right.** **Convertible preferred stock** permits the preferred stockholders to convert their shares into common stock [MBCA 6.01(c)(2)]. The terms and exchange rate of the conversion are established when the shares are issued. The holders of convertible preferred stock usually exercise this option if the corporation's common stock significantly increases in value. Preferred stock that does not have a conversion feature is called **nonconvertible preferred stock**. Nonconvertible stock is more common than convertible stock.

Redeemable Preferred Stock

Redeemable preferred stock (or **callable preferred stock**) permits a corporation to redeem (i.e., buy back) the preferred stock at some future date [MBCA 6.01(c)(2)]. The terms of the redemption are established when the shares are issued. The price paid for redeemed shares may be fixed in the articles of incorporation or determined in accordance with an agreed upon formula. Corporations usually redeem the shares when the current interest rate falls below the dividend rate of the preferred shares. Preferred stock that is not redeemable is called **nonredeemable preferred stock**. Nonredeemable stock is more common than redeemable stock.

redeemable preferred stock (callable preferred stock)
Stock that permits a corporation to buy back the preferred stock at some future date.

CONCEPT SUMMARY
PREFERRED STOCK PREFERENCES

Type of Share	Description
Dividend preference	The right to receive a fixed dividend at stipulated periods during the year (e.g., quarterly).
Liquidation preference	The right to be paid a stated dollar amount if the corporation is dissolved and liquidated.
Cumulative preferred stock	The right to be paid any past missing dividend payments (arrearages) in the future before the common shareholders can be paid any dividends.
Participating preferred stock	The right to participate in the profits of the corporation along with the common shareholders.
Convertible preferred stock	The right of preferred stockholders to convert their shares into common stock.

Electronic Registration of Stock Ownership

A common or preferred shareholder's ownership interest in a corporation is registered electronically on the records of the corporation or its transfer agent. Prior to electronic registration of stock ownership, corporations issued a **common stock certificate** to owners of common stock and a **preferred stock certificate** to owners of preferred stock printed on paper to show evidence of their ownership interest in the corporation. Many certificates had beautiful designs. However, electronic registration has almost completely supplanted paper stock certificates. Corporations are no longer required by law to issue paper certificates, and most do not [MBCA 6.26]. Many paper certificates of the past have become collector's items.

WEB EXERCISE
Use the website **www.google.com** and find a copy of a stock certificate of The Walt Disney Company.

Authorized Shares

Shares of stock that a corporation can issue are authorized in the articles of incorporation. A corporation can have one or more than one class of stock. The number of shares provided for in the articles of incorporation is called **authorized shares**.

authorized shares
The number of shares provided for in the articles of incorporation.

The articles of incorporation must set forth any classes of shares and series within a class, and the number of shares of each class and series, that the corporation is authorized to issue. If more than one class or series of shares is authorized, the articles of incorporation must prescribe a distinguishing designation for each class or series and must describe the terms, including preferences, rights, and limitations, of that class or series [MBCA 6.01(a)].

Example Facebook, Inc. has a dual-class share structure. Class A common stock has one vote per share and is traded on NASDAQ (symbol FB). Class B common stock, which is owned by Mark Zuckerberg and former or present key figures at Facebook, has 10 votes per share and is not traded publicly. Class B stock, which makes up about 18 percent of the company's stock, controls 70 percent of the shareholder votes at Facebook. Zuckerberg himself controls 60 percent of the voting power at Facebook.

A vote of the shareholders is required to amend the articles of incorporation to authorize additional shares of an existing class of stock or to create a new class of stock and specify the number of shares of the new class of stock.

Issued and Outstanding Shares

issued shares
Authorized shares that have been sold by a corporation.

unissued shares
Authorized shares that a corporation has available to issue, including shares that the corporation has not issued and shares that were originally issued by the corporation but that have been repurchased by the corporation and have not yet been reissued.

outstanding shares
Shares that are in shareholder hands, whether they are originally issued shares or shares that have been repurchased by the corporation and reissued. Only outstanding shares have the right to vote.

The board of directors of a corporation may authorize the issue (sale) of the shares authorized by the articles of incorporation [MBCA 6.03(a)]. Authorized shares that have been sold by the corporation are called **issued shares**. Not all authorized shares have to be issued at the same time or issued at all. **Unissued shares** are shares that a corporation has available to issue, including shares that the corporation has not issued and shares that were originally issued by the corporation but that have been repurchased by the corporation and have not yet been reissued. The board of directors can vote to issue unissued shares at any time without shareholder approval. However, the power to issue shares may be reserved to the shareholders in the articles of incorporation [MBCA 6.21(a)].

A corporation is permitted to repurchase its own shares. Repurchased shares were once commonly called **treasury shares**. The MBCA eliminates the concept of treasury shares, and treats repurchased shares as authorized but unissued shares [MBCA 6.31].

A corporation may issue the number of shares of each class of stock authorized by the articles of incorporation. Shares that are in shareholder hands, whether they are originally issued shares or shares that have been repurchased by the corporation and reissued, are called **outstanding shares** [MBCA 6.03]. Only outstanding shares have the right to vote.

Shares may be issued in exchange for consideration consisting of tangible or intangible property or benefit to the corporation, including cash, promissory notes, services performed, contracts for services performed, or other securities of the corporation [MBCA 6.21(b)]. In the absence of fraud, the judgment of the board of directors or shareholders as to the value of consideration received for shares is conclusive. Shareholder approval is required for the corporation to issue shares, other than for cash, that will result in an increase of more than 20 percent of the voting power of outstanding shares.

CONCEPT SUMMARY

TYPES OF SHARES

Type of Share	Description
Authorized	Shares authorized by the corporation's articles of incorporation.
Issued	Shares sold by the corporation.
Outstanding	Shares that are in the hands of shareholders. These shares have the right to vote.

Financing the Corporation—Debt Securities

37.7 Describe how a corporation is financed by debt securities.

A corporation often raises funds by issuing debt securities [MBCA 3.02(g)]. **Debt securities** (also called **fixed income securities**) establish a debtor–creditor relationship in which the corporation borrows money from the investor to whom the debt security is issued. The corporation promises to pay interest on the amount borrowed and to repay the principal at some stated maturity date in the future. The corporation is the *debtor*, and the holder is the *creditor*.

debt securities (fixed income securities)
Securities that establish a debtor-creditor relationship in which the corporation borrows money from the investor to whom a debt security is issued.

Types of Debt Instruments

Debt instruments are usually classified based on the term (time to maturity) of the instrument and whether the instrument is secured or not. There are three classifications of debt securities:

- **Debenture.** A **debenture** is a *long-term* (often 30 years or more), *unsecured* debt instrument that is based on a corporation's general credit standing. If the corporation encounters financial difficulty, unsecured debenture holders are treated as general creditors of the corporation (i.e., they are paid only after the secured creditors' claims are paid).
- **Bond.** A **bond** is a *long-term* debt security that is *secured* by some form of *collateral* (e.g., real estate, personal property). Thus, bonds are the same as debentures except that they are secured. Secured bondholders can foreclose on the collateral in the event of nonpayment of interest or principal, or other specified events.
- **Note.** A **note** is a *short-term* debt security with a maturity of five years or less. Notes can be either *unsecured* or *secured*. They usually do not contain a conversion feature. They are sometimes made redeemable.

debenture
A long-term unsecured debt instrument that is based on a corporation's general credit standing.

bond
A long-term debt security that is secured by some form of collateral.

note
A debt security with a maturity of five years or less.

CONCEPT SUMMARY

TYPES OF DEBT INSTRUMENTS

Debt Instrument	Description
Debenture	A *long-term, unsecured* debt instrument that is based on a corporation's general credit rating.
Bond	A *long-term* debt security that is *secured* by some form of property. The property securing the bond is called *collateral*. In the event of nonpayment of interest or principal or other specified events, bondholders can foreclose on and obtain the collateral.
Note	A *short-term* debt instrument with a maturity of five years or less. Notes can be unsecured or secured.

Indenture Agreement

The terms of a debt security are commonly contained in a contract between the corporation and the holder; this contract is known as an **indenture agreement** (or simply an **indenture**). The indenture generally contains the maturity date of the debt security, the required interest payment, the collateral (if any), rights to conversion into common or preferred stock, call provisions, any restrictions on the corporation's right to incur other indebtedness, the rights of holders on default, and so on. It also establishes the rights and duties of the indenture trustee. Generally, a trustee is appointed to represent the interest of the debt security holders. Bank trust departments often serve in this capacity.

indenture agreement (indenture)
A contract between a corporation and a holder that contains the terms of a debt security.

The following feature discusses why the state of Delaware attracts corporate formations.

Business Environment

Delaware Corporation Law

The state of Delaware is the corporate haven of the United States. More than 50 percent of the publicly traded corporations in the United States, including 65 percent of the Fortune 500 companies, are incorporated in Delaware. In total, more than 500,000 business corporations are incorporated in Delaware. But why?

Remember that the state in which a corporation is incorporated determines the law that applies to the corporation. The corporation code of the state of incorporation applies to details such as election of directors, requirements for a merger to occur, and laws for fending off corporate raiders. Even if a corporation does no business in Delaware, it can obtain the benefits of Delaware corporation law by incorporating in Delaware.

On the legislative side, Delaware has enacted the **Delaware General Corporation Law**. This law is the most advanced corporation law in the country, and the statute is written to be of particular benefit to large corporations. For example, the legislature has enacted a state antitakeover statute that makes it difficult to take over a Delaware corporation unless the corporation's directors waive the state's antitakeover law and agree to be taken over.

On the judicial side, Delaware has a special court—the **court of chancery**—that hears and decides business cases. This court usually interprets Delaware corporation law favorably for large corporations in matters such as electing corporate boards of directors, eliminating negligence liability of outside directors, and upholding the antitakeover provisions of the Delaware corporation code. The decisions of the chancery court are made by judges who are experts at deciding corporate law disputes, thus there are no emotional juries to worry about. Appeals from the court of chancery are brought directly to the supreme court of Delaware.

The state of Delaware makes a substantial sum of money each year on fees charged to corporations incorporated within the state. Delaware is the "business state," providing advanced corporate laws and an expert judiciary for deciding corporate disputes.

Critical Legal Thinking Questions

Why does Delaware provide corporation-friendly state laws? Should corporations be permitted to "shop" for the best state corporation laws?

Dissolution of a Corporation

37.8 Describe how a corporation is dissolved and terminated.

The life of a corporation may be dissolved voluntarily by the owners or involuntarily by the state. This is called the **dissolution** of the corporation.

voluntary dissolution
Dissolution upon recommendation of the board directors and a majority vote of the shares entitled to vote of a corporation that has begun business or issued shares.

administrative dissolution
Involuntary dissolution of a corporation that is ordered by the secretary of state if a corporation has failed to comply with certain procedures required by law.

judicial dissolution
Dissolution of a corporation through a court proceeding instituted by the state.

Dissolution

The methods for dissolving corporations are:

- **Voluntary dissolution.** A corporation can be voluntarily dissolved. If the corporation has not commenced business or issued any shares, it may be dissolved by a vote of the majority of the incorporators or initial directors [MBCA 14.01]. After that, the corporation can be voluntarily dissolved if the board of directors recommends dissolution and a majority of shares entitled to vote (or a greater number, if required by the articles of incorporation or bylaws) votes for dissolution as well [MBCA 14.02]. For a **voluntary dissolution** to be effective, **articles of dissolution** must be filed with the secretary of state of the state of incorporation. A corporation is dissolved on the effective date of the articles of dissolution [MBCA 14.03].
- **Administrative dissolution.** The secretary of state can obtain **administrative dissolution** of a corporation if (1) it failed to file an annual report, (2) it failed for 60 days to maintain a registered agent in the state, (3) it failed for 60 days after a change of its registered agent to file a statement of such change with the secretary of state, (4) it did not pay its franchise fee, or (5) the period of duration stated in the corporation's articles of incorporation has expired [MBCA 14.20]. If the corporation does not cure the default within 60 days of being notified of it, the secretary of state issues a **certificate of dissolution** that dissolves the corporation [MBCA 14.21].
- **Judicial dissolution.** A corporation can be involuntarily dissolved by a judicial proceeding. **Judicial dissolution** can be instituted by the attorney general of

the state of incorporation if the corporation (1) procured its articles of incorporation through fraud or (2) exceeded or abused the authority conferred on it by law [MBCA 14.30]. If a court dissolves a corporation, the court enters a **decree of dissolution** that specifies the date of dissolution [MBCA 14.33].

Winding Up, Liquidation, and Termination

A dissolved corporation continues its corporate existence but may not carry on any business except as required for the **winding up** and liquidation of its business and affairs [MBCA 14.05]. In a voluntary dissolution, the liquidation is usually carried out by the board of directors. If the dissolution is involuntary or the dissolution is voluntary but the directors refuse to carry out the liquidation, a court-appointed receiver carries out the winding up and liquidation of the corporation [MBCA 14.32].

winding up
The process by which a dissolved corporation's assets are collected, liquidated, and distributed to creditors, preferred shareholders, and common shareholders.

Termination of a corporation occurs only after the winding up of the corporation's affairs, the liquidation of its assets, and the distribution of the proceeds to the claimants. The liquidated assets are paid to claimants according to the following priority: (1) expenses of liquidation and creditors according to their respective liens and contract rights, (2) preferred shareholders according to their liquidation preferences and contract rights, and (3) common stockholders.

termination of a corporation
The end of a corporation that occurs after winding up the corporation's affairs, liquidating its assets, and distributing the proceeds and property to the claimants.

The dissolution of a corporation does not impair any rights or remedies available against the corporation or its directors, officers, or shareholders for any right or claim existing or incurred prior to dissolution.

Key Terms and Concepts

Administrative dissolution (668)
Alien corporation (653)
Arrearages (664)
Articles of amendment (657)
Articles of dissolution (668)
Articles of incorporation (corporate charter) (655)
Authorized shares (665)
B Lab (658)
Benefit corporation (B corporation or B corp) (657)
Benefit report (658)
Board of directors (650)
Bond (667)
Bylaws (659)
C corporation (662)
Centralized management (650)
Certificate of authority (662)
Certificate of dissolution (668)
Certified benefit corporation (658)
Characteristics of a corporation (650)
Close corporation (659)
Closely held corporation (privately held corporation) (652)
Common stock (663)
Common stock certificate (665)
Common stockholder (663)
Convertible preferred stock (665)
Corporate management (650)
Corporate officers (650)
Corporate seal (660)
Corporation (649)
Corporation code (649)
Court of chancery (668)
Cumulative preferred stock (664)
Debenture (667)
Debt securities (fixed income securities) (667)
Decree of dissolution (669)
Delaware General Corporation Law (668)
Dissolution (668)
Dividend (663)
Dividend preference (664)
Domain name (655)
Domestic corporation (653)
Double taxation (662)
Equity securities (stocks) (663)
Express powers (662)
Fixed dividend (664)
For-profit corporation (profit corporation) (652)
Foreign corporation (653)
Foreign registration statement (662)
Form 2553 (662)
Freely transferrable (650)
General corporation statutes (649)
General public benefits (658)
General-purpose clause (657)
Government-owned corporation (public corporation) (653)
Holding company (653)
Incorporating a corporation (654)
Incorporator (656)
Indenture agreement (indenture) (667)
Issued shares (666)
Judicial dissolution (668)
Legal entity (legal person) (650)
Limited liability of shareholders (650)
Limited-purpose clause (657)
Liquidation preference (664)

Model Benefit Corporation Legislation (MBCL) (658)
Model Business Corporation Act (MBCA) (649)
Model Business Corporation Act (2016) (MBCA) (649)
Model Nonprofit Corporation Act (MNCA) (653)
Municipal corporation (653)
No par value share (664)
Nonconvertible preferred stock (665)
Noncumulative preferred stock (664)
Nonparticipating preferred stock (665)
Nonredeemable preferred stock (665)
Not-for-profit corporation (nonprofit corporation) (652)
Note (667)
Novation agreement (novation) (655)
Organizational meeting (660)
Outstanding shares (666)
Par value share (664)
Participating preferred stock (664)
Perpetuity (650)
Preferred stock (664)
Preferred stock certificate (665)
Preferred stockholder (664)
Professional corporation (652)
Promoter (655)
Promoters' contracts (655)
Promoters' liability (655)
Publicly held corporation (652)
Redeemable preferred stock (callable preferred stock) (665)
Registered agent (658)
Registered office (658)
Revised Model Business Corporation Act (RMBCA) (649)
S corporation (662)
Shareholder (649)
Specific public benefits (658)
Subchapter S Revision Act (662)
Termination of a corporation (669)
Treasury shares (666)
Ultra vires act (663)
Unissued shares (666)
Voluntary dissolution (668)
Winding up (669)

Critical Legal Thinking Cases

37.1 Legal Entity Jeffrey Sammak was the owner of a contracting business known as Senaco. Sammak decided to enter the coal reprocessing business. Sammak attended the Coal Show in Chicago, Illinois, at which he met representatives of the Deister Co., Inc. (Deister). Deister was incorporated under the laws of Pennsylvania. Sammak began negotiating with Deister to purchase equipment to be used in his coal reprocessing business. Deister sent Sammak literature, guaranteeing a certain level of performance for the equipment. Sammak purchased the equipment and after it was installed, he became dissatisfied with its performance. Sammak believed that Deister breached an express warranty and wanted to sue. Can a suit be brought against a corporation such as Deister? *Blackwood Coal v. Deister Co., Inc.*, 626 F.Supp. 727, 1985 U.S. Dist. Lexis 12767 (United States District Court for the Eastern District of Pennsylvania, 1985)

37.2 Corporation Hutchinson Baseball Enterprises, Inc. (Hutchinson, Inc.) was incorporated under the laws of Kansas. Some of the purposes of the corporation, according to its bylaws, were to "promote, advance, and sponsor baseball, which shall include Little League and Amateur baseball, in the Hutchinson, Kansas, area." The corporation was involved in a number of activities, including leasing a field for American Legion teams, furnishing instructors as coaches for Little League teams, conducting a Little League camp, and leasing a baseball field to a local junior college for a nominal fee. Hutchinson, Inc. raised money through ticket sales to amateur baseball games, concessions, and contributions. Any profits were used to improve the playing fields. Profits were never distributed to the corporation's directors or members. What type of corporation is Hutchinson, Inc.? *Hutchinson Baseball Enterprises, Inc. v. Commissioner of Internal Revenue*, 696 F.2d 757, 1982 U.S. App. Lexis 23179 (United States Court of Appeals for the Tenth Circuit, 1982)

37.3 Corporation Leo V. Mysels was the president of Florida Fashions of Interior Design, Inc. (Florida Fashions). Florida Fashions, which was a Pennsylvania corporation, had never registered to do business in the state of Florida. While acting in the capacity of a salesperson for the corporation, Mysels took an order for goods from Francis E. Barry. The transaction took place in Florida. Barry paid Florida Fashions for the goods ordered. When Florida Fashions failed to perform its obligations under the sales agreement, Barry brought suit in Florida. What type of corporation is Florida Fashions in regard to the state of Pennsylvania and to the state of Florida? Can Florida Fashions defend itself in a lawsuit? *Mysels v. Barry*, 332 So.2d 38, 1976 Fla. App. Lexis 14344 (Court of Appeal of Florida, 1976)

37.4 Promoters' Contracts Martin Stern Jr. was an architect who worked in Nevada. Nathan Jacobson asked Stern to draw plans for Jacobson's new hotel/casino, the Kings Castle at Lake Tahoe. Stern agreed to take on the project and immediately began preliminary work. At this time, Stern dealt directly with Jacobson, who referred to the project as "my hotel." One month later, Stern wrote to Jacobson, detailing, among other things, the architect's services and fee. The two men subsequently discussed Stern's plans and set Stern's fee at $250,000. Three months later, Jacobson formed Lake Enterprises, Inc. (Lake Enterprises), a Nevada corporation of which Jacobson was the sole shareholder and president. Lake Enterprises was formed for the purpose of owning the new casino. During this period, Stern was paid monthly by checks drawn on an account belonging to another corporation controlled by Jacobson. Stern never agreed to contract with any of these corporations and always dealt exclusively with Jacobson. When Stern was not paid the full amount of his architectural fee, he sued Jacobson to recover. Jacobson claimed that he was not personally liable for any of Stern's fee because a novation had taken place. Who wins? *Jacobson v. Stern*, 605 P.2d 198, 1980 Nev. Lexis 522 (Supreme Court of Nevada, 1980)

37.5 **Preferred Stock** Commonwealth Edison Co. (Commonwealth Edison), through its underwriters, sold 1 million shares of preferred stock at an offering price of $100 per share. Commonwealth Edison wanted to issue the stock with a dividend rate of 9.26 percent, but its major underwriter, First Boston Corporation (First Boston), advised that a rate of 9.44 percent should be paid. According to First Boston, a shortage of investment funds existed, and a higher dividend rate was necessary for a successful stock issue. Commonwealth Edison's management was never happy with the high dividend rate being paid on this preferred stock. Nine months later, Commonwealth Edison's vice chairman was quoted in the report of the annual meeting of the corporation as saying "we were disappointed at the 9.44 percent dividend rate on the preferred stock we sold last August, but we expect to refinance it when market conditions make it feasible." Commonwealth Edison, pursuant to the terms under which the stock was sold, bought back the 1 million shares of preferred stock at a price of $110 per share. What type of preferred stock is this? *The Franklin Life Insurance Company v. Commonwealth Edison Company*, 451 F.Supp. 602, 1978 U.S. Dist. Lexis 17604 (United States District Court for the Southern District of Illinois, 1978)

Ethics Case

37.6 **Ethics Case** John A. Goodman was a real estate salesperson in the state of Washington. Goodman sold to Darden, Doman & Stafford Associates (DDS), a general partnership, an apartment building that needed extensive renovation. Goodman represented that he personally had experience in renovation work. During the course of negotiations on a renovation contract, Goodman informed the managing partner of DDS that he would be forming a corporation to do the work. A contract was executed in August between DDS and "Building Design and Development (In Formation), John A. Goodman, President." The contract required the renovation work to be completed by October 15. Goodman immediately subcontracted the work, but the renovation was not completed on time. DDS also found that the work that was completed was of poor quality. Goodman did not file the articles of incorporation for his new corporation until November 1. The partners of DDS sued Goodman to hold him liable for the renovation contracts. Goodman denied personal liability. Was it ethical for Goodman to deny liability? Is Goodman personally liable? *Goodman v. Darden, Doman & Stafford Associates*, 670 P.2d 648, 1983 Wash. Lexis 1776 (Supreme Court of Washington, 1983)

Note

1. 26 U.S.C. Section 6242 et seq.

CHAPTER 38

Corporate Governance and The Sarbanes-Oxley Act

Uladzik Kryhin/Shutterstock

GOOGLE LLC

Many major technology corporations are located in the Silicon Valley area of California.

Learning Objectives

After studying this chapter, you should be able to:

38.1 Define *shareholder* and describe the rights of shareholders of corporations.

38.2 Define *board of directors* and describe the duties of members of boards of directors of corporations.

38.3 Define *corporate officer* and describe the duties and scope of authority of corporate officers.

38.4 Describe the duty of obedience of corporate directors and officers.

38.5 Describe directors' and officers' duty of care and define the *business judgment rule*.

38.6 Describe directors' and officers' duty of loyalty and how this duty is breached.

38.7 Describe how the Sarbanes-Oxley Act affects corporate governance.

> *"Corporation: An ingenious device for obtaining individual profit without individual responsibility."*
>
> —*Ambrose Bierce*
> *The Devil's Dictionary (1911)*

Introduction to Corporate Governance and the Sarbanes-Oxley Act

Shareholders, directors, and officers have different rights in managing a corporation. The shareholders elect the directors and vote on other important issues affecting the corporation. The directors are responsible for making policy decisions and employing officers. The officers are responsible for the corporation's day-to-day operations.

As a legal entity, a corporation can be held liable for the acts of its directors and officers and for authorized contracts entered into on its behalf. The directors and officers of a corporation have certain rights and owe certain duties to the corporation and its shareholders. A director or an officer who breaches any of these duties can be held personally liable to the corporation, to its shareholders, or to third parties. Except in a few circumstances, shareholders do not owe a fiduciary duty to other shareholders or to the corporation and are not personally liable for the debts and obligations of the corporation.

In response to financial frauds and scandals uncovered at major corporations, Congress enacted the Sarbanes-Oxley Act of 2002 (SOX). This federal statute establishes rules to improve corporate governance, prevent fraud, and add transparency to corporate operations.

This chapter discusses the rights, duties, and liability of corporate shareholders, directors, and officers. It also discusses the provisions of the Sarbanes-Oxley Act.

The director is really a watchdog, and the watchdog has no right, without the knowledge of his master, to take a sop from a possible wolf.

Lord Justice Bowen
Re The North Australian Territory Co. Ltd. (1891)

Corporations, which should be the carefully restrained creatures of the law and the servants of the people, are fast becoming the people's masters.

Glover Cleveland (1837–1908)
Twenty-second/twenty-fourth president of the United States

Shareholders

38.1 Define *shareholder* and describe the rights of shareholders of corporations.

A corporation's **shareholders** own the corporation (see **Exhibit 38.1**). Nevertheless, they are not agents of the corporation (i.e., they cannot bind the corporation to contracts), and the only management duty they have is the right to vote on matters such as the election of directors and the approval of fundamental changes in the corporation.

shareholders
Owners of a corporation who elect the board of directors and vote on fundamental changes in the corporation.

Exhibit 38.1
SHAREHOLDERS

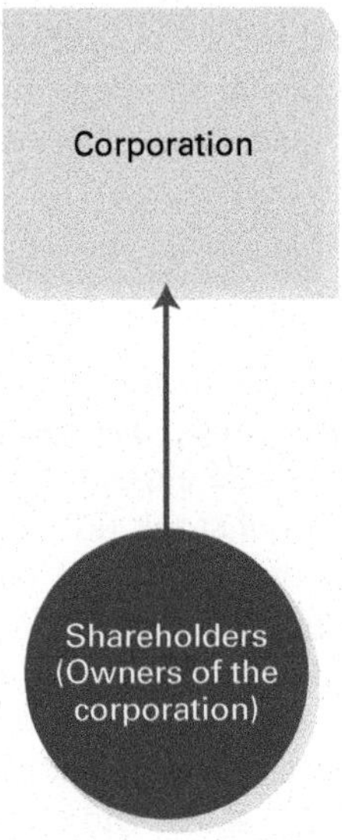

Shareholders' Meetings

annual shareholders' meeting
A meeting of the shareholders of a corporation that must be held by the corporation to elect directors and to vote on other matters.

Annual shareholders' meetings are held to elect directors, choose an independent auditor, and take other actions. These meetings must be held at the times fixed in the bylaws [MBCA 7.01]. If a meeting is not held within either 15 months of the last annual meeting or six months after the end of the corporation's fiscal year, whichever is earlier, a shareholder may petition the court to order the meeting held [MBCA 7.03].

special shareholders' meetings
Meetings of shareholders that may be called to consider and vote on important or emergency issues, such as a proposed merger or amending the articles of incorporation.

Special shareholders' meetings may be called by the board of directors, the holders of at least 10 percent of the voting shares of the corporation, or any other person authorized to do so (e.g., the president) by the articles of incorporation or bylaws [MBCA 7.02]. Special meetings may be held to consider important or emergency issues, such as a merger or consolidation of the corporation with one or more other corporations, the removal of directors, amendment of the articles of incorporation, or dissolution of the corporation.

Any act that can be taken at a **shareholders' meeting** can be taken without a meeting if all the corporate shareholders sign a written consent approving the action [MBCA 7.04(a)]. A corporation may include in its articles of incorporation a provision that permits shareholder action by less than unanimous consent [MBCA 7.04(b)].

Notice of a Shareholders' Meeting A corporation is required to give the shareholders notice of the place, day, and time of annual and special meetings. Usually the notice is given in writing, although many states permit electronic notification. Unless required by the articles, the purposes of the annual meeting need not be stated. For a special meeting, the purposes of the meeting must be stated, and only those matters can be considered at the meeting. The notice must be given not less than 10 days or more than 50 days before the date of the meeting [MBCA 7.05]. Shareholders may participate in any meeting by means of remote communication if authorized to do so by the board of directors [MBCA 7.09]. If the required notice is not given or is defective, any action taken at the meeting is void.

Proxies

proxy
A shareholder's authorizing of another person to vote the shareholder's shares at the shareholders' meetings in the event of the shareholder's absence.

Shareholders do not have to attend a shareholders' meeting to vote. Shareholders may vote by *proxy*; that is, they can appoint another person (the proxy) as their agent to vote at a shareholders' meeting by signing an appointment form or by an electronic transmission. The proxy may be directed exactly how to vote the shares or may be authorized to vote the shares at his or her discretion. The written document or electronic transmission is often called the **proxy**. Unless otherwise stated, a proxy is valid for 11 months [MBCA 7.22]. Most states allow corporations to send shareholders a one-page notice that proxy materials are available electronically on a publicly accessible website and allow shareholders to vote electronically.

Voting Shares

At least one class of shares of stock of a corporation must have voting rights. Commonly, each share is granted one vote. However, corporations may grant more than one vote per share to some classes of stock and less than one vote or no votes per share to other classes of stock [MBCA 6.01(c)(1)].

record date
A date specified in corporate bylaws that determines whether a shareholder may vote at a shareholders' meeting.

Only shareholders who own stock as of a set date may vote at a shareholders' meeting. This date, which is called the **record date**, is set forth in the corporate bylaws. If the bylaws do not designate a record date, then the board of directors can set the date. The record date may not be more than 70 days before the shareholders' meeting [MBCA 7.07]. The corporation must prepare a **shareholders list** that contains the names and addresses of the shareholders as of the record date and the class and number of shares owned by each shareholder. This list must be available for inspection at the corporation's main office. The corporation is not required to include email addresses or electronic contact information of shareholders [MBCA 7.20].

Quorum and Vote: Majority Rule Unless otherwise provided in the articles of incorporation, if a majority of shares entitled to vote are represented at a meeting in person or by proxy, there is a **quorum to hold the meeting of the shareholders.** Once a quorum is present, the withdrawal of shares does not affect the quorum of the meeting.

quorum to hold a meeting of the shareholders
The required number of shares that must be represented in person or by proxy to hold a shareholders' meeting. The RMBCA establishes a majority of outstanding shares as a quorum.

Unless otherwise provided in the articles of incorporation, the affirmative *vote* of the majority of the *voting* shares represented at a shareholders' meeting constitutes an act of the shareholders for actions other than for the election of directors [MBCA 7.25].

Example A corporation has 20,000 shares outstanding. A shareholders' meeting is duly called to amend the articles of incorporation, and 10,001 shares are represented at the meeting. A quorum is present because a majority of the shares entitled to vote are represented. Suppose that 5,001 shares are voted in favor of the amendment. The amendment passes. In this example, just over 25 percent of the shares of the corporation bind the other shareholders to the action taken at the shareholders' meeting.

Modifying Voting or Quorum Requirements

The articles of incorporation of a corporation may provide for a greater quorum or voting requirement than a majority quorum or vote.

Example The articles could provide for a 60 percent quorum before shareholders could vote to consider the purchase of another corporation. Without attaining this quorum, the shareholders' meeting cannot be held.

Example The articles of incorporation could require an 80 percent vote of the shares voting at a meeting to approve a merger. Without attaining this vote, the corporation cannot merge with another corporation. This is often referred to as a **supramajority voting requirement** or **supermajority voting requirement.**

supramajority voting requirement (supermajority voting requirement)
A requirement that a greater than majority of shares constitutes a quorum of the vote of the shareholders.

An amendment to the articles of incorporation that adds, changes, or deletes a quorum or voting requirement must meet the same quorum requirement or be adopted by the same vote required to take action under the quorum or voting requirements then in effect or proposed to be adopted, whichever is greater [MBCA 7.27].

Examples A voting requirement that requires 80 percent of the votes attending a meeting to approve a merger can only be removed by an 80 percent vote of the votes attending the shareholder meeting to consider removing this requirement. If a proposal is to increase a majority voting requirement to an 80 percent voting requirement, the change must be approved by 80 percent of the shares that vote at the meeting to consider enacting the proposed requirement.

Straight (Noncumulative) Voting for Directors

Unless otherwise required by a corporation's articles of incorporation, voting for the election of directors is by the **straight voting (noncumulative voting)** method [MBCA 7.28(a)]. This voting method is quite simple: Each shareholder votes the number of shares he or she owns for candidates for each of the positions open for election. Thus, a majority shareholder can elect the entire board of directors.

straight voting (noncumulative voting)
A system in which each shareholder votes the number of shares he or she owns for candidates for each of the open positions.

Example A corporation has 10,000 outstanding shares. Bianca owns 6,500 shares (65 percent), and Levi owns 3,500 shares (35 percent). Suppose that six directors

cumulative voting
A system in which a shareholder can accumulate all of his or her votes and vote them all for one candidate or split them among several candidates.

of the corporation are to be elected from a potential pool of 18 candidates. Bianca casts 6,500 votes for each of her six chosen candidates. Levi casts 3,500 votes for each of his six chosen candidates, who are different from those favored by Bianca. Each of the six candidates Bianca votes for wins, with 6,500 votes each. None of the candidates Levi votes for wins.

The following feature discusses cumulative voting.

Business Environment

Cumulative Voting for Directors

A corporation's articles of incorporation may provide for **cumulative voting** for the election of directors. This means that each shareholder is entitled to multiply the number of shares he or she owns by the number of directors to be elected and cast the accumulative number for a single candidate or distribute the accumulative number among two or more candidates [MBCA 7.28(b) and (c)]. Cumulative voting gives a minority shareholder a better opportunity to elect someone to the board of directors.

Example A corporation has cumulative voting. The corporation has 10,000 outstanding shares. Alexander owns 6,500 shares (65 percent), and Camilla owns 3,500 shares (35 percent). Suppose that 6 directors of the corporation are to be elected from a potential pool of 18 candidates. Alexander and Camilla make calculated assumptions as to which candidates the other will vote for. Alexander cumulates his votes (6,500 × 6 = 39,000 votes), and casts 9,750 votes for each of his 4 favored candidates, whom he assumes Camilla will not vote for. Camilla cumulates her votes (3,500 × 6 = 21,000 votes) and casts 10,500 votes for each of her 2 favored candidates, who are different from those favored by Alexander. Alexander elects 4 of the 6 directors, and Camilla elects 2 of the 6 directors.

Shareholder Agreements and Voting Arrangements

Sometimes shareholders may agree in advance as to how a corporation will be operated or how their shares will be voted. These agreements are usually only used in small, closely held corporations. Three of these agreements are:

- **Shareholder agreement.** Shareholders are permitted to enter into various **shareholder agreements** regarding the operation of a corporation. Such agreements must be by the unanimous consent of all shareholders and may be contained in the articles of incorporation or bylaws of the corporation or in a separate agreement. A shareholder agreement can (1) eliminate the board of directors or restrict the discretion or powers of the board; (2) establish who shall be the directors and officers of the corporation; (3) divide voting powers among the shareholders and enact weighted voting rights; (4) appoint one of the shareholders or another person to manage the corporation; (5) require dissolution of the corporation at the request of one or more shareholders; and (6) include other powers and restrictions allowed by the MBCA [MBCA 7.32].

voting trust
An arrangement in which the shareholders transfer their stock certificates to a trustee who is empowered to vote the shares.

- **Voting trust.** A **voting trust** is an arrangement whereby shareholders transfer their stock certificates to a trustee. Legal title to these shares is held in the name of the trustee. In exchange, **voting trust certificates** are issued to the shareholders. The trustee of the voting trust is empowered to vote the shares held by the trust. The trust may either specify how the trustee is to vote the shares or authorize the trustee to vote the shares at his discretion. The members of the trust retain all other incidents of ownership of the stock. A voting trust agreement must be in writing, and it must be filed with the corporation and be open to inspection by shareholders of the corporation. The MBCA does not limit the duration of a living trust [MBCA 7.30]. Some states limit the duration of a living trust to 10 years but provide that the trust may be extended for 10-year periods.
- **Shareholder voting agreement.** Two or more shareholders may enter into an agreement that stipulates how they will vote their shares for the election of

directors or other matters that require a shareholder vote. **Shareholder voting agreements** are not limited in duration and do not have to be filed with the corporation. They are specifically enforceable [MBCA 7.31]. Shareholder voting agreements can be either revocable or irrevocable [MBCA 7.22(d)].

shareholder voting agreement
An agreement between two or more shareholders that stipulates how they will vote their shares.

Restrictions on the Sale of Shares

Generally, shareholders have the right to transfer their shares. However, sometimes shareholders may want to restrict the ability of other shareholders to transfer their shares to parties who are not currently shareholders. Thus, shareholders may enter into agreements with one another to prevent unwanted persons from becoming owners of the corporation [MBCA 6.27]. Two of these restrictive methods are:

- **Right of first refusal.** A **right of first refusal** is an agreement that shareholders enter whereby they grant each other the right of first refusal to purchase shares they are going to sell. A selling shareholder must offer to sell his or her shares to the other parties to the agreement before selling them to anyone else. If the shareholders do not exercise their right of first refusal, the selling shareholder is free to sell his or her shares to another party. A right of first refusal may be granted to the corporation as well.
- **Buy-and-sell agreement.** Shareholders sometimes enter into a **buy-and-sell agreement** that requires selling shareholders to sell their shares to the other shareholders or to the corporation at the price specified in the agreement. The price of the shares is normally determined by a formula that considers, among other factors, the profitability of the corporation. The purchase of shares of a deceased shareholder pursuant to a buy-and-sell agreement is often funded by proceeds from life insurance.

right of first refusal
An agreement that requires a selling shareholder to offer his or her shares for sale to the other parties to the agreement before selling them to anyone else.

buy-and-sell agreement
An agreement that requires selling shareholders to sell their shares to the other shareholders or to the corporation at the price specified in the agreement.

Preemptive Rights

Preemptive rights give existing shareholders the right to purchase new shares being issued by the corporation in proportion to their current ownership interests [MBCA 6.30]. This right can prevent a shareholder's interest in the corporation from being *diluted* when the corporation issues new shares. Shareholders do not automatically have preemptive rights; they only have preemptive rights if it is expressly provided in a corporation's articles of incorporation. Shareholders are given a reasonable time (e.g., 30 days) to exercise their preemptive rights. If a shareholder does not exercise the preemptive rights during this time, the shares can then be sold to anyone.

preemptive rights
Rights that give existing shareholders the option of subscribing to new shares being issued in proportion to their current ownership interests.

Example Canonical Corporation has 10,000 outstanding shares, of which Phoebe owns 1,000 shares (10 percent). Assume that the corporation plans to raise more capital by issuing another 10,000 shares of stock. With preemptive rights, Phoebe must be offered the option to purchase 1,000 of the 10,000 new shares before they are offered to the public. If she does not purchase them, and all of the shares are sold, her ownership in the corporation will be diluted from 10 percent to 5 percent.

Dividends

Profit corporations operate to make a profit. The objective of the shareholders is to share in those profits through capital appreciation, the receipt of dividends, or both. The board of directors may authorize the corporation to make distributions, including the payment of a **dividend**, to its shareholders. Dividends are paid at the discretion of the board of directors.

The directors are responsible for determining when, where, how, and how much will be paid in dividends. Dividends are usually paid quarterly and in cash

dividend
A distribution of profits of the corporation to shareholders.

(via check or electronic transfer). The directors may opt to retain the profits in the corporation to be used for corporate purposes instead of paying dividends. This authority cannot be delegated to a committee of the board of directors or to officers of the corporation. A distribution to shareholders cannot be made if it would cause the corporation not to be able to pay its debts in the usual course of business or would leave the corporation insolvent [MBCA 6.40].

When a corporation declares a dividend, it sets a date, usually a few weeks prior to the actual payment, that is called the *record date*. Persons who are shareholders on that date are entitled to receive the dividend, even if they sell their shares before the payment date. Once declared, a cash or property dividend cannot be revoked. Shareholders can sue to recover declared but unpaid dividends.

stock dividend
Additional shares of stock distributed as a dividend.

Corporations may issue additional shares of stock as a dividend. A **stock dividend** is not a distribution of corporate assets. Stock dividends are distributed in proportion to the existing ownership interests of shareholders, so they do not increase a shareholder's proportionate ownership interest. A stock dividend allows investors to increase their holdings without receiving a taxable payment.

derivative lawsuit (derivative action)
A lawsuit a shareholder brings against an offending party on behalf of a corporation when the corporation fails to bring the lawsuit.

Example Quinn owns 1,000 shares (10 percent) of the 10,000 outstanding shares of Metal Corporation. If Metal Corporation declares a stock dividend of 20 percent, Quinn will receive a stock dividend of 200 shares. He now owns 1,200 shares—or 10 percent—of a total of 12,000 outstanding shares.

The following feature discusses derivative lawsuits brought by shareholders.

Business Environment

Derivative Lawsuits

If a corporation is harmed by someone, the directors of the corporation have the authority to bring a legal action on behalf of the corporation against the offending party to recover damages or other relief. If the corporation fails to bring the lawsuit, shareholders have the right to bring the lawsuit on behalf of the corporation. This is called a **derivative lawsuit** or **derivative action** [MBCA Section 7.40].

A shareholder can bring a derivative action if he or she (1) was a shareholder of the corporation at the time of the act complained of, (2) fairly and adequately represents the interests of the corporation, and (3) made a written demand on the corporation to take suitable action and either the corporation rejected the demand or 90 days have passed since the date of the demand. Demand must be made whether the complaint is against a third party or against an insider such as a director or corporate officer [MBCA 7.41 and 7.42]. This is referred to as the **universal demand rule**. Some states, however, excuse a shareholder from making a demand on the directors before bringing the derivative lawsuit if it would be futile to make such demand. This is called the **futility exception**.

Example The parties accused of the wrongdoing are the corporation's own directors. It would most likely be futile to demand that the directors sue themselves. Under the futility exception, demand would be excused. If the universal demand rule applied, demand would not be excused.

If the corporation believes that the demanded action is warranted, the corporation can bring a legal action against the alleged wrongdoer. However, there is no obligation on the part of the corporation to respond to the demand. If the corporation does not take action, then the shareholder may commence a derivative lawsuit, on behalf of the corporation, against the third party alleged to have committed the injurious act. If the corporation commences an inquiry into the allegations made in the demand or complaint, the court may stay any derivative proceedings for such period as the court deems appropriate [MBCA 7.43].

A court will dismiss a derivative proceeding upon motion of (1) a majority of qualified directors present at a meeting, (2) a majority vote of a committee of directors appointed by the directors, or (3) an independent panel of one or more persons appointed by the court upon a motion of the corporation, if the movant, in good faith after conducting a reasonable inquiry, has determined that the maintenance of the derivative action is not in the best interests of the corporation [MBCA 7.44]

If a derivative action is not dismissed by the court, the shareholders may pursue the claim on behalf of the corporation against the named defendant. If a shareholder's derivative action is successful, any award goes into the corporate treasury. The plaintiff-shareholder is entitled to recover payment for reasonable expenses, including attorneys' fees, incurred in bringing and maintaining the derivative action. Any settlement of a derivative action requires court approval. If a derivative action is unsuccessful, a plaintiff-shareholder is liable for the defendant's expenses if the court finds that the proceedings were commenced or maintained without reasonable cause or for an improper purpose [MBCA 7.46].

Piercing the Corporate Veil

Shareholders of a corporation generally have **limited liability** (i.e., they are liable for the debts and obligations of the corporation only to the extent of their capital contribution), and they are not personally liable for the debts and obligations of the corporation. However, if a shareholder or shareholders dominate a corporation and misuse it for improper purposes, a court of equity can *disregard the corporate entity* and hold the shareholders of the corporation personally liable for the corporation's debts and obligations. This equity doctrine is commonly referred to as **piercing the corporate veil**. The piercing the corporate veil doctrine is also called the **alter ego doctrine** because the corporation has become the *alter ego* of the shareholder or shareholders.

piercing the corporate veil (alter ego doctrine)
A doctrine that says if a shareholder dominates a corporation and uses it for improper purposes, a court of equity can disregard the corporate entity and hold the shareholder personally liable for the corporation's debts and obligations.

The judge, and not the jury, decides whether to pierce the corporate veil and impose personal liability on a shareholder. Courts will pierce the corporate veil if (1) the corporation has been formed with insufficient capital (i.e., *thin capitalization*) or (2) separateness has not been maintained between the corporation and its shareholders. Courts often allow piercing of the corporate veil if a shareholder has commingled personal and corporate assets, paid personal expenses from corporate accounts, failed to hold required shareholders' meetings, or failed to maintain corporate records.

The piercing the corporate veil doctrine was asserted in the following case.

CASE 38.1 *STATE COURT CASE Piercing the Corporate Veil*

Lunneborg v. My Fun Life Corporation

21 P.3d 187 (2018)
Supreme Court of Idaho

"The lines between the Edwards' personal assets and the assets of MFL were heavily blurred."

—Richard Bevan, Justice

Facts

Dan Edwards was the sole shareholder of My Fun Life Corporation (MFL), a company that sold memberships for access to discount travel accommodations. Dan's wife, Carrie, was Executive Vice President of the company. MFL hired Thomas Lunneborg as its Chief Operating Officer (COO). The employment contract provided that Lunneborg would be paid $60,000 severance pay if he was terminated without cause. Two months after beginning employment, MFL terminated Lunneborg, alleging that it had cause to do so. Lunneborg sued MFL for breach of contract to recover $60,000 severance pay. Lunneborg also sued Edwards, asserting that MFL's corporate veil can be pierced to reach Edwards' personal assets to satisfy any potential judgment against MFL.

Evidence showed that MFL did not observe any corporate formalities, issue any stock certificates, conduct regular corporate meetings, keep corporate minutes, or appoint corporate officers through any formal process. MFL did not pay any dividends, but made distributions to Edwards and his family members, and regularly made payments for family personal expenses. Corporate credit cards were routinely used to purchase personal items. Corporate and personal funds were commingled. Edwards transferred funds among MFL and four other businesses that he owned without loan documents, contracts, or notes evidencing these transfers.

The district court determined that Lunneborg was terminated without cause and the MFL owed him $60,000 severance pay, which was trebled to $180,000 pursuant to the Idaho Wage Claims Act. The court also awarded Lunneborg $160,000 in attorney's fees. The court pierced MFL's corporate veil and held that Edwards was personally liable for the judgment. Edwards appealed.

Issue

Should MFL's corporate shield be pierced?

Language of the Court

The trial court did not err in finding facts that demonstrated a unity of interest and ownership between Edwards and MFL to a degree that the separate personalities of MFL and the Edwards no longer existed. The lines between the Edwards' personal assets and the assets of MFL were heavily blurred. Instead of paying *the severance to Lunneborg as provided in his employment contract, the Edwards drained MFL of all income and assets by diverting those assets and income to themselves. The Edwards were very successful in this diversion to the extent that they left MFL with $5.11 of assets. The district court held to allow the Edwards to escape personal liability would be to sanction an injustice and create an inequitable result.*

Decision

The Supreme Court of Idaho affirmed the district court's decision.

Critical Legal Thinking Questions

Why is piercing the corporate veil considered an equitable remedy? Did Edwards act ethically in this case?

Board of Directors

38.2 Define *board of directors* and describe the duties of members of boards of directors of corporations.

board of directors
A panel of decision makers who are elected by the shareholders.

Every corporation must have a board of directors (except smaller corporations whose shareholders unanimously agree not to have a board of directors) [MBCA 8.01(a)]. The members of the **board of directors** of a corporation are elected by the shareholders of the corporation. The board of directors is responsible for formulating *policy decisions* that affect the management, supervision, control, and operation of the corporation (see **Exhibit 38.2**) [MBCA 8.01(b)]. Such policy decisions include determining business plans and strategy, selecting and removing the top officers of the corporation, appointing members to board committees, assessing risks, determining the capital structure of the corporation, and determining whether the corporation has effective information and reporting systems.

Selecting Directors

A director need not be a resident of the state of incorporation of the corporation or a shareholder of the corporation unless the articles or bylaws so prescribe. The articles of incorporation or bylaws may prescribe reasonable qualifications of directors or nominees for directors, and the qualification will be considered lawful [MBCA 8.02]. Qualifications could include having certain business experience, expertise, education, professional licenses or certifications, length of service, shareholding, residence, or other qualifications that may benefit the corporation.

A board of directors can consist of one or more individuals as specified in or fixed in accordance with the articles of incorporation or bylaws. The number of directors can be changed by amendment to, or in the manner provided in, the articles of incorporation or the bylaws [MBCA 8.03(a) and (b)]. Unless otherwise provided in the articles of incorporation, the directors are permitted to fix their own compensation [MBCA 8.11]. The articles of incorporation or bylaws can establish a variable range

Exhibit 38.2 BOARD OF DIRECTORS

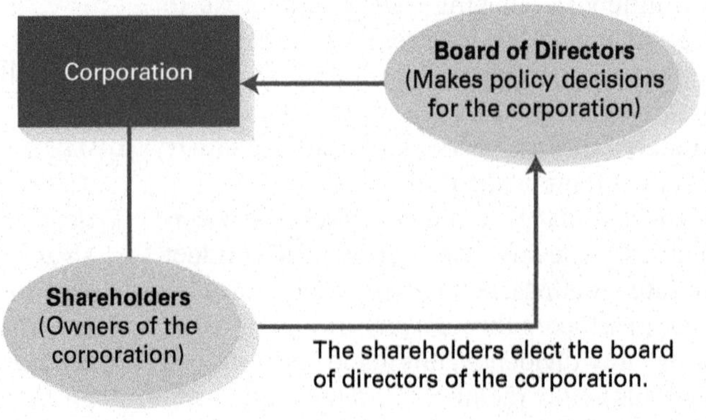

for the size of the board of directors. The exact number of directors within the range may be changed from time to time by the board of directors or the shareholders.

Boards of directors are typically composed of inside and outside directors. An **inside director** is a person who is also an officer of the corporation. For example, the president of the corporation often sits as a director of the corporation. An **outside director** is a person who sits on the board of directors of a corporation but is not an officer of that corporation. Outside directors are often officers and directors of other corporations, bankers, lawyers, professors, and so on. An outside director is often referred to as an **independent director**.

inside director
A member of the board of directors who is also an officer of the corporation.

outside director (independent director)
A member of a board of directors who is not an officer of the corporation.

CONCEPT SUMMARY

CLASSIFICATION OF DIRECTORS

Classification	Description
Inside director	A person who is also an officer of the corporation
Outside director (independent director)	A person who is not an officer of the corporation

Term of Office

The terms of the initial directors of a corporation expire at the first shareholders' meeting at which directors are elected. Directors are elected at the first annual shareholders' meeting and at each annual shareholders' meeting thereafter, unless their terms are staggered [MBCA 8.05]. The articles of incorporation may provide for staggering the terms of directors into two or three groups, with each group containing one-half or one-third of the total, as near as may be [MBCA 8.06]. These are called **staggered terms**.

The law does not permit the stockholders to create a sterilized board of directors.
Justice Collins
Manson v. Curtis
223 N.Y. 313, 119 N.E. 559, 1918 N.Y. Lexis 1186 (1918)
Court of Appeals of New York

Example A board of directors consists of 9 directors. The board can be divided into three classes of 3 directors each, with each class to be elected to serve a three-year term. Only 3 directors of the 9-member board would come up for election each year. This 9-member board could also be divided into two classes—one with 5 and the other with 4 directors—with each class to be elected to a two-year term.

Vacancies on a board of directors can occur because of death, illness, the resignation of a director before the expiration of his or her term, or an increase in the number of positions on the board. The shareholders may remove a director with or without cause unless the articles of incorporation provide that directors may be removed only for cause [MBCA 8.08(a)]. Vacancies can be filled by the shareholders or the remaining directors [MBCA Section 8.10].

Meetings of the Board of Directors

The directors of a corporation can act only as a board. They cannot act individually on the corporation's behalf unless there is only one board member. Every director has the right to participate in any meeting of the board of directors. Each director has one vote.

The board of directors may hold regular and special meetings [MBCA 8.20(a)]. **Regular meetings of a board of directors** are held at the times and places established in the bylaws. Unless otherwise provided in the articles of incorporation, regular meetings can be held without notice of the date, time, place, or purpose of the meeting [MBCA 8.22(a)]. The board can call **special meetings of the board of directors** [MBCA 8.20(a)]. Special meetings are usually convened for such reasons as issuing new shares, considering proposals to merge with other corporations, or adopting maneuvers to defend against hostile takeover attempts. Special meetings require a two-day notice unless otherwise provided in the articles or bylaws [MBCA 8.22(b)].

A corporation is an artificial being, invisible, intangible, and existing only in contemplation of law.
John C. Marshall
Dartmouth College v. Woodward 17 U.S. 518, 1819 U.S. Lexis 330 (1819)
Supreme Court of the United States of America

The board of directors may act without a meeting if all the directors sign written consents that set forth the actions taken [MBCA 8.21]. Meetings of the board are permitted by use of any means of communication in which the directors participating may simultaneously hear each other during the meeting [MBCA 8.20(b)]. This permits conference calls, video meetings, and other forms of electronic meetings.

quorum to hold a meeting of the board of directors
The number of directors necessary to hold a board meeting or transact business of the board.

Quorum and Voting Requirements A simple majority of the fixed number of directors established in the articles of incorporation or bylaws constitutes a **quorum to hold a meeting of the board of directors** to transact business. If the corporation has a variable-size board, then quorum is the majority of the number of directors in office. If a quorum is attained, the approval or disapproval of a majority of the board members present binds the entire board to the action taken.

Example A corporation has 20 directors. Eleven directors attend a properly held board of directors meeting. There is quorum because a majority of the board members are present (11 of 20 directors are in attendance). If a vote is taken on a matter, and 6 members vote in favor of the action, then a majority vote has been cast (6 of 11 directors voted for the action). The act voted upon is that of the board of directors.

The articles of incorporation may authorize a quorum to consist of no fewer than one-third of the fixed or prescribed number of directors. The articles of incorporation or the bylaws can require a greater than majority of directors to constitute a quorum or a greater than majority vote to constitute an act of the board [MBCA 8.24].

Resolutions of the Board of Directors

resolution
A vote taken by the board of directors of a corporation that authorizes certain actions to be taken on behalf of the corporation.

The board of directors authorizes actions to be taken on behalf of the corporation by adopting **resolutions** at board of directors' meetings. A resolution is put forward by a member of the board, usually seconded by another board member, and then put to the vote of the members of board of directors present at the meeting. The majority of resolutions pass, but some resolutions do not. Corporate resolutions are recorded in the written **minutes** of the board of directors' meetings and specify the action taken by the board of directors. Resolutions can be adopted for many subjects that affect the corporation.

Examples Resolutions taken by the board of directors can include authorizing the corporation to enter contracts and leases, employ an accountant or other professionals, appoint a new officer, declare a dividend, authorize entering into a banking relationship, and issue shares of stock.

The board may initiate certain actions that require shareholders' approval. These actions are initiated when the board of directors adopts a resolution that approves a transaction and recommends that it be submitted to the shareholders for a vote.

Committees of the Board of Directors

The board of directors may create **committees of the board of directors** and appoint board members to serve on the committees. Committees may exercise the powers of the board of directors to the extent authorized by the board of directors or specified in the articles of incorporation or bylaws [MBCA 8.20]. Small corporations usually do not appoint committees. Publicly held companies that are regulated by the Securities and Exchange Commission (SEC) and traded on stock exchanges are required to have the following three committees:

audit committee
A committee of the board of directors that oversees the integrity of financial statements, the independence of corporate auditors, and compliance with legal and regulatory requirements.

- **Audit committee.** The **audit committee** oversees the integrity of financial statements, public audits of the company by certified public accountants, internal audits of the company, and compliance with legal and regulatory requirements. The audit committee must be composed of independent members of the board of directors.

- **Compensation committee.** The **compensation committee** is responsible for human resources policies and procedures, employee benefit plans, and executive and employee compensation.
- **Corporate governance and nominating committee.** The **corporate governance and nominating committee** examines the eligibility of nominees for the board of directors, reviews corporate governance principles and practices, and recommends board members' compensation.

Many large corporations have an **executive committee**, usually consisting of the chairman of the board, chief executive officer, and other key directors and officers, that has the power to act as the full board in case of emergencies. Some corporations have a **social responsibility committee** that oversees corporate efforts to address social and environmental concerns. Corporations can create ad hoc committees to address specific issues as they arise, such as to examine a proposed merger or an important development project.

The following feature discusses how modern corporation codes authorize electronic communications.

corporate electronic communications
Digital and electronic communications by corporations with shareholders, among directors, with regulatory agencies, and with others.

Information Technology

Corporate E-Communications

Most state corporation codes permit the use of **corporate electronic communications (corporate e-communications)** to communicate to shareholders, among directors, with regulatory agencies, and with others. For example, the Delaware General Corporation Law recognizes the following uses of electronic technology:

- Delivery of notices to shareholders may be made electronically if the shareholder consents to the delivery of notices in this form.
- Proxy solicitation for shareholder votes may be made by electronic transmission.
- The list of shareholders of a corporation that must be made available during the 10 days prior to a shareholders' meeting may be made available either at the principal place of business of the corporation or by posting the list on an electronic network.
- Shareholders who are not physically present at a meeting may be deemed present, participate in, and vote at the meeting by electronic communication; a meeting may be held solely by electronic communication, without a physical location.
- The election of directors of the corporation may be held by electronic transmission.
- Directors' actions by unanimous consent may be taken by electronic transmission.

The use of electronic transmissions, electronic networks, and communications by email, text, and other electronic means makes the operation and administration of corporate affairs more efficient.

Corporate Officers

38.3 Define *corporate officer* and describe the duties and scope of authority of corporate officers.

Corporate officers are responsible for the day-to-day functioning and operation of a corporation. Major corporate officers are elected by the board of directors at such time and by such manner as prescribed in the corporation's bylaws. The bylaws or the board of directors can authorize duly appointed officers to appoint assistant officers. The same individual may simultaneously hold more than one office in the corporation [MBCA 8.40]. The directors can delegate certain management authority to the officers of the corporation (see **Exhibit 38.3**).

corporate officers
Employees of a corporation who are appointed by the board of directors to manage the day-to-day operations of the corporation.

At a minimum, most corporations have the following officers: a *president*, one or more *vice presidents*, a *secretary*, and a *treasurer*. Each corporate officer has the authority to perform the functions described in the bylaws, prescribed by the directors, or prescribed by officers rightfully appointed by the directors [MBCA 8.41].

An officer of a corporation may be removed at any time, with or without cause, by the board of directors, by an appointing officer, or by other officers who are authorized to do so. The board only has to determine that the best interests of the corporation

Exhibit 38.3 CORPORATE OFFICERS

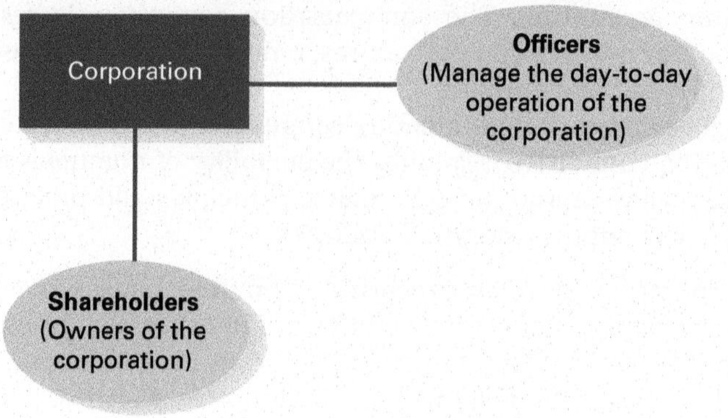

will be served by such removal [MBCA 8.43(b)]. Officers who are removed in breach of an employment contract or against the law (e.g., if the removal violates equal opportunity in employment laws) can sue the corporation for damages.

Agency Authority of Officers

WEB EXERCISE
To view the standards of business conduct of Microsoft Corporation, go to **https://www.microsoft.com/en-us/Investor/corporate-governance/policies.aspx** and click on "Microsoft Standards of Business Conduct."

Officers and agents of a corporation have such authority as may be provided in the bylaws of the corporation, as determined by the board of directors, or as authorized by officers [MBCA 8.41]. Because they are agents, officers have the express authority granted to them, as well as implied authority and apparent authority, to bind a corporation to contracts.

A corporation can *ratify* an unauthorized act of a corporate officer or agent. For example, suppose an officer acts outside the scope of his or her employment and enters into a contract with a third person. If the corporation accepts the benefits of the contract, it has ratified the contract and is bound by it. Officers are liable on an unauthorized contract if the corporation does not ratify it.

CONCEPT SUMMARY

MANAGEMENT OF A CORPORATION

Group	Function
Shareholders	Owners of the corporation. They vote on the directors and other major actions to be taken by the corporation.
Board of directors	Elected by the shareholders. Directors are responsible for making policy decisions and employing the major officers for the corporation. The board may initiate certain actions that require shareholders' approval.
Officers	Officers are responsible for the day-to-day operation of the corporation, including acting as agents for the corporation and hiring other officers and employees.

Duty of Obedience

38.4 Describe the duty of obedience of corporate directors and officers.

The directors and officers of a corporation must act within the authority conferred on them by the state's corporation code, the articles of incorporation, the corporate bylaws, and the resolutions adopted by the board of directors. This duty is called the **duty of obedience**. Directors and officers who intentionally or negligently engage in conduct beyond their authority are personally liable for any resultant damages caused to the corporation or its shareholders.

duty of obedience
A duty that directors and officers of a corporation have to act within the authority conferred on them by state corporation codes, the articles of incorporation, the corporate bylaws, and the resolutions adopted by the board of directors.

Example The articles of incorporation of a corporation authorize the corporation to invest in real estate only. If a corporate officer invests corporate funds in cattle futures contracts, the officer is liable to the corporation for any losses suffered.

Duty of Care

38.5 Describe directors' and officers' duty of care and define the *business judgment rule.*

The directors and officers of a corporation owe certain fiduciary duties when making decisions and taking action on behalf of the corporation. One such duty is the **duty of care**. The duty of care requires corporate directors and officers to use *care and diligence* when acting on behalf of the corporation. The MBCA establishes standards of conduct for both directors and officers.

duty of care
A duty of corporate directors and officers to use care and diligence when acting on behalf of the corporation.

To meet their duty of care, the directors and officers must discharge their duties (1) in good faith, (2) with the care that a person in a like position would reasonably exercise under similar circumstances, and (3) in a manner they reasonably believe to be in the best interests of the corporation [MBCA 8.30(a) and (b); MBCA 8.42(a)]. A director or officer of a small closely held corporation would be held to a different standard than a director or officer of a large publicly traded corporation. Also, facts and circumstances surrounding the decision must be considered. A decision that requires a fast response (e.g., an emergency) is treated differently than a decision that is arrived at over a long period of time (e.g., entering a new industry).

A director or an officer who breaches the duty of care is personally liable to the corporation and its shareholders for any damages caused by the breach. Such breaches, which are normally caused by **negligence**, often involve a director's or an officer's failure to (1) make a reasonable investigation of a corporate matter, (2) attend board meetings on a regular basis, (3) properly supervise a subordinate who causes a loss to the corporation through embezzlement or other action, or (4) keep adequately informed about corporate affairs. Courts examine alleged breaches of the duty of care on a case-by-case basis.

negligence
Failure of a corporate director or officer to exercise the duty of care while conducting the corporation's business.

In discharging his or her duties, a director must disclose to other board members information he or she possesses necessary for co-directors to discharge their duties [MBCA 8.30(c)]. A director is entitled to rely on information, reports, statements, and financial statements prepared and presented by officers and employees, legal counsel, public accountants, and board committees who the director believes to be reliable and competent [MBCA 8.30(d)–(f)].

business judgment rule
A rule that says directors and officers are not liable to the corporation or its shareholders for honest mistakes of judgment.

The following feature discusses the business judgment rule.

Business Environment

Business Judgment Rule

The determination of whether a corporate director or officer has met his or her duty of care is measured as of the time the decision is made; the benefit of hindsight is not a factor. Directors and officers are accorded a presumption that their decisions are based on sound business judgment, and a court cannot substitute its own notion of what is or is not sound business judgment if the board made its decision based on a proper investigation, in good faith, and with a reasonable belief that their actions were in the corporation's best interest. Thus, directors and officers are not liable to the corporation or its shareholders for honest mistakes of judgment. This is called the **business judgment rule**. If not for the protection afforded by the business judgment rule, many high-risk but socially desirable endeavors might not be undertaken.

Example Smart technology is included in automobiles and vehicles. After conducting considerable research and investigation, the directors of Super-Smart Corporation, a major automobile company, make a decision to produce a line of "super-smart" automobiles and vehicles based on the company's newly patented and the most highly developed information technology in the industry. The company spends one year designing and producing the vehicles and successfully launches a sales campaign in which thousands of the company's new super-smart vehicles are immediately sold. However, soon after the introduction of the super-smart vehicles, another automobile company, Genius Corporation, patents a newly invented and previously unknown technology, and produces even smarter "genius" vehicles. The Super-Smart Corporation's sales of super-smart vehicles and stock price plummet as the sales of the Genius Company's genius vehicles dramatically increase. The shareholders of the Super-Smart Corporation sue the board of directors of the company to recover their losses, alleging negligence on the part of company management. Because the judgment of the corporate management was based on reliable research and information at the time that they made their decision to produce the super-smart vehicles, their judgment is shielded by the business judgment rule.

Critical Legal Thinking Question

Explain the business judgment rule. What would be the consequences if this rule were not recognized by the law?

Limitation or Elimination of Liability for Negligent Conduct

The articles of incorporation may contain a provision that limits or eliminates the liability of a director to the corporation or its shareholders for monetary damages for his or her negligent conduct [MBCA 8.31(a)(1)(i)]. Most large corporations have this provision in their articles of incorporation. If directors can be held liable for negligence, corporations may find it difficult to attract persons to be members of boards of directors.

Example A director sits on the board of directors of a corporation that has included the release of liability provision in its articles of incorporation. At a board meeting the director votes for the corporation to develop and sell a new product. The product subsequently is found to be defectively designed, and plaintiffs who are injured sue the corporation and its directors for negligence. The director is not liable, even if it is shown that he or she did not conduct a proper investigation prior to approving the product.

The articles cannot contain a provision that eliminates liability for a director's intentional misconduct, the receipt of a benefit to which the director is not entitled, or a violation of criminal law [MBCA 2.02(b)(4)].

Duty of Loyalty

38.6 Describe directors' and officers' duty of loyalty and how this duty is breached.

duty of loyalty
A duty that directors and officers have not to act adversely to the interests of the corporation and to subordinate their personal interests to those of the corporation and its shareholders.

Directors and officers of a corporation owe a fiduciary duty to act honestly. This duty, called the **duty of loyalty**, requires directors and officers to subordinate their personal interests to those of the corporation and its shareholders. Most breaches of loyalty occur when a director or officer has an interest that conflicts with that of the corporation, fails to disclose this conflict, and profits financially from an undisclosed transaction. Generally, if a director or an officer breaches the duty of loyalty and makes a profit or gain on a transaction, the corporation can sue the director or officer to recover the profit or gain. Some of the most common breaches of the duty of loyalty are discussed in the following paragraphs.

Usurping a Corporate Opportunity

The general rule is that directors and officers may not personally usurp (steal) a corporate opportunity for themselves. If **usurping an opportunity** is proven, the corporation can (1) acquire the opportunity from the director or officer and (2) recover any profits made by the director or officer. However, a director or officer is personally free to take advantage of a corporate opportunity if it is fully disclosed and presented to the directors of the corporation or those acting on behalf of the corporation, and the corporation rejects it [MBCA 8.70(a)(1)]. Further, a provision may be included in the articles of incorporation that limits or eliminates the duty of a director or officer to offer the corporation a business opportunity [MBCA 2.02(b)(6)].

Example A corporation is in the business of developing and constructing retail and office building projects. An officer of the corporation is offered an opportunity to purchase a parcel of real estate that the corporation might be interested in developing. If the officer does not disclose the opportunity to the corporation or if the corporation does not have a provision in its articles of incorporation that excuses the officer from disclosing the opportunity, the officer breaches the duty of loyalty if the officer purchases the real estate parcel for private use.

Self-Dealing

Did you ever expect a corporation to have a conscience, when it has no soul to be damned, and no body to be kicked?

Lord Edward Thurlow, first Baron Thurlow (1731–1806)

Generally, a contract or transaction entered into by a corporate director or officer with his or her corporation without full disclosure by the director or officer of his or her interest in the transaction is voidable by the corporation. Such contracts are called conflicting interest transactions, which is often referred to as **self-dealing**. Relatives of, and entities controlled by, a director or officer are included in this prohibition if the director or officer knows that the relative or entity is entering into a transaction with the corporation. Contracts of a corporation to purchase property from, sell property to, or make loans to corporate directors or officers where the directors or officers have not disclosed their interest in the transaction can be voided by the corporation. In the alternative, the corporation can affirm the contract and recover any profits from the self-dealing director or officer.

Example A director works for a corporation that is involved in developing real estate projects and knows that the corporation is looking for property to purchase in a certain geographical area. The director informs her twin brother, who purchases the most desirable parcel of property in the area. The director's brother offers to sell the property to the corporation, the director does not inform the corporation of her interest in the property, and the corporation votes to purchase the property at a price higher than what the director's brother paid. The twins share the profit from the transaction. Here, the director has violated her duty of loyalty. The corporation can void the transaction and recover its purchase price, or it can affirm the purchase and recover any profits made by the director and her brother.

If an officer is selling real estate to his corporation, the director must not only disclose his or her interest in the land, but also if there are any hidden defects (e.g., pollution).

Contracts and transactions with corporate directors or officers are enforceable and do not violate their duty of loyalty if (1) their interest in the transaction is disclosed to the corporation and a majority of disinterested directors approve the transaction, (2) their interest in the transaction is disclosed to the corporation and a majority of disinterested shareholders approve the transaction, or (3) the officer or director does not disclose his or her interest in the transaction but the transaction is fair to the corporation (e.g., the corporation did not pay more than fair market value). These safe harbor rules are expressly provided for directors in the MBCA [MBCA 8.61(b)], and are usually provided to officers by common law.

Competing with the Corporation

Directors and officers cannot engage in activities where they will be **competing with the corporation** unless they make full disclosure and a majority of the disinterested directors or shareholders approve the activity. If directors or officers compete with the corporation without full disclosure and permission, they have engaged in unfair competition and breached their duty of loyalty. The corporation can recover any profits made by the director or officer from the nonapproved competition and any other damages caused to the corporation.

Example Jamie works as a corporate officer for an insurance brokerage company. The corporation represents insurance companies that sell insurance to consumers and businesses. Jamie, without getting the corporation's permission, opens a competing insurance brokerage business. This would be an example of competing with the corporation. Jamie's employer could recover profits and damages from Jamie.

Making a Secret Profit

It appears to me that the atmosphere of the temple of Justice is polluted by the presence of such things as companies.

Lord Justice James
Wilson v. Church (1879)

If a director or an officer breaches the duty of loyalty and makes a **secret profit** on a transaction, the corporation can sue the director or officer to recover the secret profit. In making the secret profit, the director or officer has violated his or her duty of loyalty.

Example Leonid is the purchasing agent for a corporation. His duties require him to negotiate and execute contracts to purchase supplies and equipment for the corporation. Dalia, a sales representative for an equipment supplier, pays Leonid a 10 percent kickback of the price of the supplies and equipment Leonid purchases for the corporation from Dalia. Leonid's corporate employer can sue and recover the secret profits—the kickbacks—Leonid received from Dalia.

Misuse of Corporate Property

A director or officer of a corporation breaches his or her duty of loyalty by misusing corporate property or information. Such **misuse of property** includes using corporate property for personal purposes. It also includes misappropriating the corporation's trade secrets, stealing electronic data or information and using it personally or selling it to a third party, stealing a password to confidential corporate information and accessing the information for personal use or for the benefit of third parties, and the like. These are all breaches of a director's or officer's duty of loyalty, and the corporation can recover damages from the wrongdoer and obtain injunctions against further use of its confidential information.

WEB EXERCISE
To view the finance code of professional conduct of Microsoft Corporation, go to **https://www.microsoft.com/en-us/investor/corporate-governance/policies.aspx** and click on "Microsoft Finance Code of Professional Conduct."

Sarbanes-Oxley Act

38.7 Describe how the Sarbanes-Oxley Act affects corporate governance.

Sarbanes-Oxley Act of 2002 (SOX)
A federal statute that establishes rules to improve corporate governance, prevent fraud, and add transparency to corporate operations.

In 2002, Congress enacted the federal **Sarbanes-Oxley Act (SOX)**.[1] The act establishes far-reaching rules regarding corporate governance. The goals of the Sarbanes-Oxley Act are to improve corporate governance rules, eliminate conflicts of interest, and instill confidence in investors and the public that management will run public companies in the best interests of all constituents.

The following ethics feature discusses some of the major provisions of the Sarbanes-Oxley Act that regulate corporate governance.

Ethics

The Sarbanes-Oxley Act Improves Corporate Governance

The Sarbanes-Oxley Act is a federal statute that has changed the rules of corporate governance in important respects. Several major provisions of the act regarding corporate governance are discussed in the following list.

- **CEO and CFO certification.** The chief executive officer (CEO) and chief financial officer (CFO) of a public company must file a statement accompanying each annual and quarterly report called the **CEO and CFO certification**. This statement certifies that the signing officer has reviewed the report; that, based on the officer's knowledge, the report does not contain any untrue statement of a material fact or omit any material fact that would make the statement misleading; and that the financial statement and disclosures fairly present, in all material aspects, the operation and financial condition of the company. A knowing and willful violation is punishable by up to 20 years in prison and a monetary fine.
- **Reimbursement of bonuses and incentive pay.** If a public company is required to restate its financial statements because of material noncompliance with financial reporting requirements, the CEO and CFO must reimburse the company for any bonuses, incentive pay, or securities trading profits made because of the noncompliance.
- **Prohibition on personal loans.** The act prohibits public companies from making personal loans to their directors or executive officers.
- **Penalties for tampering with evidence.** The act makes it a crime for any person to knowingly alter, destroy, mutilate, conceal, or create any document to impair, impede, influence, or obstruct any federal investigation. A violation is punishable by up to 20 years in prison and a monetary fine.

- **Prohibition of persons who have committed fraud from acting as an officer or a director.** The Securities and Exchange Commission (SEC), a federal government agency, may issue an order prohibiting any person who has committed securities fraud from acting as an officer or a director of a public company.

Although the Sarbanes-Oxley Act applies only to publicly held companies, privately held companies and nonprofit organizations are also influenced by the act's accounting and corporate governance rules.

Ethics Questions
Does the CEO and CFO certification requirement reduce corporate fraudulent conduct? Does the Sarbanes-Oxley Act promote more ethical behavior from corporate officers and directors?

Key Terms and Concepts

Annual shareholders' meeting (674)
Audit committee (682)
Board of directors (680)
Business judgment rule (685)
Buy-and-sell agreement (677)
CEO and CFO certification (688)
Committees of the board of directors (682)
Compensation committee (683)
Competing with the corporation (687)
Corporate electronic communications (corporate e-communications) (683)
Corporate governance and nominating committee (683)
Corporate officers (683)
Cumulative voting (676)
Derivative lawsuit (derivative action) (678)
Dividend (677)
Duty of care (685)
Duty of loyalty (686)
Duty of obedience (684)
Executive committee (683)
Futility exception (678)
Inside director (681)
Limited liability (679)
Minutes (682)
Misuse of property (688)
Negligence (685)
Outside director (independent director) (681)
Piercing the corporate veil (alter ego doctrine) (679)
Preemptive rights (677)
Proxy (674)
Quorum to hold a meeting of the board of directors (682)
Quorum to hold a meeting of the shareholders (675)
Record date (674)
Regular meeting of a board of directors (681)
Resolution (682)
Right of first refusal (677)
Sarbanes-Oxley Act (SOX) (688)
Secret profit (688)
Self-dealing (687)
Shareholder agreement (676)
Shareholder voting agreement (677)
Shareholders (673)
Shareholders' list (674)
Shareholders' meeting (674)
Social responsibility committee (683)
Special meeting of a board of directors (681)
Special shareholders' meeting (674)
Staggered terms (681)
Stock dividend (678)
Straight voting (noncumulative voting) (675)
Supramajority voting requirement (supermajority voting requirement) (675)
Universal demand rule (678)
Usurping an opportunity (686)
Voting trust (676)
Voting trust certificate (676)

Critical Legal Thinking Cases

38.1 Proxy George Gibbons, William Smith, and Gerald Zollar were all shareholders in GRG Operating, Inc. (GRG). Zollar contributed $1,000 of his own funds so that the corporation could begin to do business. In exchange for this contribution, Gibbons and Smith both granted Zollar the right to vote their shares of GRG stock. They gave Zollar a signed form that stated that "Gibbons and Smith, for a period of 10 years from the date hereof, appoint Zollar as their proxy. This proxy is solely intended to be an irrevocable proxy." A year after the agreement was signed, Gibbons and Smith wanted to revoke their proxies. Can they? *Zollar v. Smith*, 710 S.W.2d 155, 1986 Tex. App. Lexis 12900 (Court of Appeals of Texas, 1986)

38.2 Dividends Gay's Super Markets, Inc. (Super Markets) was a corporation formed under the laws of the state of Maine. Hannaford Bros. Company held 51 percent of the corporation's common stock. Lawrence F. Gay and his brother Carrol were both minority shareholders in Super Markets. Lawrence Gay was also the manager of the corporation's store at Machias, Maine. One day, he was dismissed from his job. At the meeting of Super Markets's board of directors, a decision was made not to declare a stock dividend for the prior year. The directors cited expected losses from increased competition and the expense of opening a new store as reasons for not paying a dividend. Lawrence Gay claims that the reason for not paying a dividend was to force him to sell his shares in Super Markets. Lawrence sued to force the corporation to declare a dividend. Who wins? *Gay v. Gay's Super Markets, Inc.*, 343 A.2d 577, 1975 Me. Lexis 391 (Supreme Judicial Court of Maine, 1975)

38.3 Duty of Loyalty Edward Hellenbrand ran a comedy club known as the Comedy Cottage in Rosemont, Illinois. The business was incorporated, with Hellenbrand and his wife as the corporation's sole shareholders. The corporation leased the premises in which the club was located. Hellenbrand hired Jay Berk as general manager of the club. Two years later, Berk was made vice president of the corporation and given 10 percent of its stock. Hellenbrand experienced health problems and moved to Nevada, leaving Berk to manage the daily affairs of the business. Four years later, the ownership of the building where the Comedy Cottage was located changed hands. Shortly thereafter, the club's lease on the premises expired. Hellenbrand instructed Berk to negotiate a new lease. Berk arranged a month-to-month lease but had the lease agreement drawn up in his name instead of that of the corporation. When Hellenbrand learned of Berk's move, he fired him. Berk continued to lease the building in his own name and opened his own club, the Comedy Company, Inc., there. Hellenbrand sued Berk for an injunction to prevent Berk from leasing the building. Who wins? *Comedy Cottage, Inc. v. Berk*, 495 N.E.2d 1006, 1986 Ill. App. Lexis 2486 (Appellate Court of Illinois, 1986)

38.4 Piercing the Corporate Veil M.R. Watters was the majority shareholder of several closely held corporations, including Wildhorn Ranch, Inc. (Wildhorn). All these businesses were run out of Watters's home in Rocky Ford, Colorado. Wildhorn operated a resort called the Wildhorn Ranch Resort in Teller County, Colorado. Although Watters claimed that the ranch was owned by the corporation, the deed for the property listed Watters as the owner. Watters paid little attention to corporate formalities, holding corporate meetings at his house, never taking minutes of those meetings, and paying the debts of one corporation with the assets of another. In August 1986, two guests of Wildhorn Ranch Resort drowned while operating a paddleboat at the ranch. The family of the deceased guests sued for damages. Is Watters personally liable? *Geringer v. Wildhorn Ranch, Inc.*, 706 F.Supp. 1442, 1988 U.S. Dist. Lexis 15701 (United States District Court for the District of Columbia, 1988)

Ethics Cases

38.5 Ethics Case Lawrence Gaffney was the president and general manager of Ideal Tape Company (Ideal). Ideal, which was a subsidiary of Chelsea Industries, Inc. (Chelsea), was engaged in the business of manufacturing pressure-sensitive tape. Gaffney recruited three other Ideal executives to join him in starting a tape manufacturing business. The four men remained at Ideal for the two years it took them to plan the new enterprise. During this time, they used their positions at Ideal to travel around the country to gather business ideas, recruit potential customers, and purchase equipment for their business. At no time did they reveal to Chelsea their intention to open a competing business. The new business was incorporated as Action Manufacturing Company (Action). When executives at Chelsea discovered the existence of the new venture, Gaffney and the others resigned from Chelsea. Chelsea sued them for damages. Did Gaffney act unethically? Who wins? *Chelsea Industries, Inc. v. Gaffney*, 449 N.E.2d 320, 1983 Mass. Lexis 1413 (Supreme Judicial Court of Massachusetts, 1983)

38.6 Ethics Case Jon-T Chemicals, Inc. (Chemicals) was an Oklahoma corporation engaged in the fertilizer and chemicals business. John H. Thomas was its majority shareholder and its president and board chairman. Chemicals incorporated Jon-T Farms, Inc. (Farms), as a wholly owned subsidiary, to engage in the farming and land-leasing business. Chemicals invested $10,000 to establish Farms. All the directors and officers of Farms were directors and officers of Chemicals, and Thomas was its president and board chairman. In addition, Farms used officers, computers, and accountants of Chemicals without paying a fee, and Chemicals paid the salary of Farms's only employee. Chemicals made regular informal advances to pay Farms's expenses. These payments reached $7.5 million.

Thomas and Farms engaged in a scheme whereby they submitted fraudulent applications for agricultural subsidies from the federal government under the Uplands Cotton Program. Because of these applications, the Commodity Credit Corporation, a government agency, paid more than $2.5 million in subsidies to Thomas and Farms. After discovering the fraud, the federal government obtained criminal convictions against Thomas and Farms. In a separate civil action, the federal government obtained a $4.7 million judgment against Thomas and Farms, finding them jointly and severally liable for the tort of fraud. Farms declared bankruptcy, and Thomas was unable to pay the judgment. Because Thomas and Farms were insolvent, the federal government sued Chemicals to recover the judgment. Was Farms the alter ego of Chemicals, permitting the United States to pierce the corporate veil and recover the judgment from Chemicals? Did Thomas act ethically in this case? *United States of America v. Jon-T Chemicals, Inc.*, 768 F.2d 686, 1985 U.S. App. Lexis 21255 (United States Court of Appeals for the Fifth Circuit, 1985)

Note

1. Public Law 107-204.

CHAPTER

39 Corporate Acquisitions and Multinational Corporations

Henry R. Cheeseman

TAJ MAHAL, INDIA

India is home to many large multinational corporations. The Tata Group, the largest private company in India, is a conglomerate that comprises more than 100 companies, exports goods and services to over 80 countries, has approximately 300,000 employees, and has more than $100 billion in sales, with over half of that beyond India. It owns interests in communications, information technology, power, steel, automobiles, hotels, electricity, and other industries. Tata Motors purchased the British vehicle brands Jaguar and Land Rover from Ford Motor Company.

Learning Objectives

After studying this chapter, you should be able to:

39.1 Describe the process of soliciting proxies from shareholders and engaging in a proxy contest.

39.2 Define *shareholder resolution* and identify when a shareholder can include a resolution in proxy materials.

39.3 Describe the process for approving a merger, acquisition, and share exchange.

39.4 Define *tender offer* and describe defensive maneuvers to prevent hostile takeovers.

39.5 Describe state antitakeover statutes.

36.6 Examine the use of multinational corporations in conducting international business.

> *"Corporations and other associations, like individuals, contribute to the discussion, debate, and the dissemination of information and ideas that the First Amendment seeks to foster. Political speech is indispensable to decision making in a democracy, and this is no less true because the speech comes from a corporation rather than an individual."*
>
> —*Justice Anthony Kennedy*
> *Citizens United v. Federal Election Commission*
> *558 U.S. 310, 130 S.Ct. 876, 2010 U.S. Lexis 766 (2010)*

Introduction to Corporate Acquisitions and Multinational Corporations

During its existence, a corporation may go through certain **fundamental changes**, many of which it must seek shareholder approval to enact. This requires the solicitation of votes or proxies from shareholders. Persons who want to take over the management of a corporation often conduct proxy contests to try to win over shareholder votes.

Corporations often engage in acquisitions of other corporations or businesses. This may occur by friendly merger or by hostile tender offer. In defense, a corporation may erect certain barriers or impediments to a hostile takeover.

What passes in the world for talent or dexterity or enterprise is often only a want of moral principle.
William Hazlitt (1778–1830)

Multinational corporations conduct international business around the world. This is usually done through a variety of business arrangements, including branch offices, subsidiary corporations, and the like.

This chapter discusses fundamental changes to a corporation, including the solicitation of proxies, mergers, sale or lease of assets, hostile tender offers, and defensive strategies to prevent hostile takeovers. It also examines the use of multinational corporations in conducting international business.

Proxy Solicitation and Proxy Contests

39.1 Describe the process of soliciting proxies from shareholders and engaging in a proxy contest.

Corporate shareholders have the right to vote on the election of directors, mergers, charter amendments, and the like. Unless otherwise provided in the articles of incorporation, each outstanding share is entitled to one vote. The articles of incorporation can allocate different voting rights to different classes of shares [MBCA 7.21(a)]. Shares owned by the corporation, directly or indirectly, are not entitled to vote [MBCA 7.21(b)].

Example One class of stock could be allocated one vote per share, while a different class of stock could be allocated 10 votes per share.

Shareholders can exercise their power to vote either in person or by proxy [MBCA 7.22]. The **proxy** authorizes another person—the proxy holder—to vote the shares at the shareholders' meeting as directed by the shareholder. The proxy holder is often a director or an officer of the corporation. The appointment of a proxy is effective when a signed appointment form or electronic transmission of the appointment is received by the officer or agent of the corporation authorized to court votes [MBCA 7.22(c)]. Voting by proxy is commonly used in large corporations that have thousands of shareholders located across the country and around the world.

proxy
A person who is granted authority to vote the shares of a shareholder.

The Model Business Corporation Act of 2016 (MBCA) uses the word "proxy" to mean the person who is granted authority to vote. The word "proxy" is also often used to refer to the document—the proxy card—that grants another party the right to vote shares.

Federal Proxy Rules

Section 14(a)
A provision of the Securities Exchange Act of 1934 that gives the SEC the authority to regulate the solicitation of proxies.

proxy statement
A document that fully describes (1) the matter for which a proxy is being solicited, (2) who is soliciting the proxy, and (3) any other pertinent information.

e-proxy rule
A rule of the Securities and Exchange Commission (SEC) that permits corporations subject to SEC jurisdiction to post proxy materials electronically on a designated website.

Section 14(a) of the Securities Exchange Act of 1934 gives the Securities and Exchange Commission (SEC) the authority to regulate the solicitation of proxies.[1] The federal proxy rules promote full disclosure. In other words, management or any other party soliciting proxies from shareholders must prepare a **proxy statement** that fully describes (1) the matter for which the proxy is being solicited, (2) who is soliciting the proxy, and (3) any other pertinent information.

A copy of the proxy, the proxy statement, and all other solicitation material must be filed with the SEC at least 10 days before the materials are made available to the shareholders. If the SEC requires additional disclosures, the solicitation can be held up until these disclosures are made. All filing can be made electronically.

The SEC, a federal government agency, adopted an **e-proxy rule** that allows corporations to send shareholders a one-page notice that proxy materials are available electronically on a publicly accessible website, rather than sending a full package of written proxy materials to shareholders. The SEC rule applies to publicly traded corporations and other corporations subject to SEC jurisdiction. The SEC rule does not apply to small corporations that are not subject to SEC jurisdiction.

Antifraud Provision

Sometimes different groups of shareholders will oppose the action proposed to be taken by the corporation or the persons presented by the corporation for the election to the board of directors. In such cases, different groups of shareholders may distribute their own proxy materials that inform shareholders of their competing position and seek to obtain the proxy votes of shareholders. This would lead to proxy materials being received by shareholders from two or more competing groups, which are called *proxy contests*.

antifraud provision
Section 14(a) of the Securities Exchange Act of 1934, which prohibits misrepresentations or omissions of a material fact in proxy materials.

proxy contest
A contest in which opposing factions of shareholders and managers solicit proxies from other shareholders; the side that receives the greatest number of votes wins the proxy contest.

Section 14(a) of the Securities Exchange Act of 1934 is an **antifraud provision** that prohibits material misrepresentations or omissions of a material fact in the proxy materials. Known false statements of facts, reasons, opinions, or beliefs in proxy solicitation materials are actionable. Violations of this rule can result in civil and criminal actions by the SEC and the U.S. Department of Justice, respectively. Thus, shareholders who are injured by a material misrepresentation or omission in proxy materials can sue the wrongdoer and recover damages. The court can also order a new election if a violation is found.

The following feature discusses a proxy contest for the election of the board of directors of a corporation.

Business Environment

Proxy Contest

Directors of a corporation are elected at the annual shareholders' meeting. A special meeting can also be called to elect directors of a corporation. **Incumbent directors** are the current directors of a corporation. One or more shareholders may oppose the actions taken by the incumbent directors and want to have some or all of these directors removed and replaced. The insurgent shareholders offer their own slate of proposed directors, called the **insurgent directors**, to replace the current directors. The insurgent shareholders can challenge the incumbent directors in a **proxy contest**, in which both sides solicit proxies from the other shareholders.

The vote is taken at the annual meeting of the shareholders or at a special meeting of the shareholders if one has been called. The side that receives the greatest number of votes wins the proxy contest, and its slate of directors becomes the directors of the corporation. In a proxy contest, management must either (1) provide a list of shareholders to the dissenting group or (2) mail or make available electronically to shareholders the proxy solicitation materials of the challenging group.

Example Data Mining Corporation currently has a six-member board of directors. The annual meeting of the shareholders is approaching. Management proposes that the incumbent board members be elected. Camila, who owns 15 percent of the stock of the corporation, is dissatisfied with the decisions made by the incumbent board of directors. She proposes a slate of directors, consisting of herself and five other persons, to become members of the board of directors of the corporation and replace the incumbent directors. The corporation has noncumulative voting. Camila institutes a proxy contest whereby both management and Camila seek the votes (proxies) of other shareholders. Camila convinces other shareholders controlling 36 percent of the shares of the corporation to vote for her slate of directors. With her 15 percent of the shares, and another 36 percent of the shares, Camila's slate of directors wins and will replace the incumbent directors.

Example Campbell Soup Company, a 150-year-old food company, was challenged in a proxy contest for the election of board members by an activist hedge fund investor and others who were not satisfied with how the company was being run. A number of the heirs to the Campbell fortune, who own 40 percent of the stock of the company, reached an agreement with the challengers, whereby Campbell added two directors selected by challengers to sit on Campbell's board of directors. In return, the challengers dropped their proxy contest.

WEB EXERCISE
Go to **https://www.sec.gov/Archives/edgar/data/16732/000119312518321046/d650399ddfan14a.htm** to view a copy of a proxy statement in a proxy contest involving Campbell Soup Company.

Shareholder Resolution

39.2 Define *shareholder resolution* and identify when a shareholder can include a resolution in proxy materials.

At times, shareholders may wish to submit issues for a vote to other shareholders. The Securities Exchange Act of 1934 and SEC rules permit a shareholder to submit a resolution to be considered by other shareholders if, prior to submitting the proposal, the shareholder owned $2,000 of the company's stock for three years, $15,000 of stock for two years, or $25,000 of stock for one year. The resolution cannot exceed 500 words. A **shareholder resolution**, also called a **shareholder proposal**, is usually made when the corporation is soliciting proxies from its shareholders.

shareholder resolution
A resolution that a shareholder who meets certain ownership requirements may submit to other shareholders for a vote. Many shareholder resolutions concern social issues.

If management does not oppose a resolution, it may be included in the proxy materials issued by the corporation. Even if management is not in favor of a resolution, a shareholder has a right to have the shareholder resolution included in the corporation's proxy materials if it (1) relates to the corporation's business, (2) concerns a *policy issue* (and not the day-to-day operations of the corporation), and (3) does not concern the payment of dividends. The SEC rules on whether a resolution can be included in a company's proxy materials when submitted to shareholders. About half of proposed shareholder resolutions are denied inclusion in proxy materials, usually on the grounds that they would interfere with a company's ordinary business.

Examples Shareholder resolutions have been presented concerning protecting the environment; reducing plastic pollution in the waterways and oceans; reducing global warming; setting greenhouse gas (GHG) targets; achieving sustainability; disclosing human rights violations; prohibiting U.S. corporations from purchasing goods manufactured or grown in other countries using forced and child labor; paying living wages above legal minimum wages; protecting human rights; disclosing lobbying and election expenditures; disclosing supply chain effects on deforestation; prohibiting animal cruelty; improving board and executive officer diversity; protecting the political viewpoints of employees; and promoting socially responsible and ethical conduct.

Critical Legal Thinking Questions
Do many shareholder resolutions have a chance of being adopted? If a shareholder knows that its resolution probably will not be adopted, why bother sponsoring a resolution?

Most shareholder resolutions have a slim chance of being enacted because large-scale investors usually support management; however, they can cause a corporation to change the way it does business. For example, to avoid the adverse publicity such issues can create, some corporations voluntarily adopt changes proposed in shareholder resolutions. Others negotiate settlements with the sponsors of resolutions to get the measures off the agenda before the annual shareholders' meetings.

The following feature is a shareholder resolution submitted to the Coca-Cola Company.

Ethics

Coca-Cola Shareholder Resolution on Sugar and Public Health

The Coca-Cola Company is the world's largest producer of sugary beverages. Coca-Cola, the company's number one soda brand, is sold in almost every country in the world. Sodas and sugary drinks produced by Coca-Cola and other beverage companies have been identified as one of the main contributing factors in the rise of obesity of children in the United States and other countries. The following shareholder proposal was submitted and included in the 2019 Proxy Statement of The Coca-Cola Company.

Coca-Cola Company
SHAREHOLDER PROPOSAL ON SUGAR AND PUBLIC HEALTH
Filer: John C. Harrington

Whereas, *the most serious issues continue to be related to the public health and safety impacts of our Company's beverages, including syrups and sugary drinks, and the growing national health epidemic relating to increasing uses of sugar in our diet;*

Whereas, *our Company continues to be the target of multiple campaigns related to our Company's products that contribute to general level of decline in public health of consumers, including reports that 1 in 3 U.S. children born in the year 2000 will develop diabetes, resulting from poor diet, as the increase in obesity in turn increases the risk of diabetes, hypertension, heart disease, cancers, asthma, arthritis, reproductive complications, and premature death;*

Whereas, *our Company continues to directly market sugary drinks with advertising directly influencing children's food preferences, diets, and health;*

Whereas, *the American Academy of Pediatrics released a policy statement calling for a total ban on child targeted and interactive junk food advertising as a response to concerns regarding childhood obesity;*

Whereas, *shareholders believe our Company should be part of the solution to solving the problem of the obesity epidemic in working with healthcare professionals and experts in diet and nutrition, not promoting advertising campaigns to shift the blame from poor diet causing obesity to lack of exercise.*

Be It, Therefore, Resolved, *that shareholders request the board of directors issue a report on Sugar and Public Health, with support from a group of independent and nationally recognized scientists and scholars providing critical feedback on our Company's sugar products marketed to consumers, especially those Coke products targeted to children and young consumers. Such report to shareholders should be produced at reasonable expense, exclude proprietary or legally privileged information, and be published, no later than November 1, 2019, and include an assessment of risks to the Company's finances and reputation associated with changing scientific understanding of the role of sugar in disease causation.*

The Coca-Cola Company recommended that shareholders vote against the proposal. The proposal was defeated. To read the full shareholder proposal and the company's response, go to pages 95–96 of The Coca-Cola Company 2019 Proxy Statement located at the following website: https://www.sec.gov/Archives/edgar/data/21344/000120677419000735/ko_courtesy-pdf.pdf

Ethics Questions

The American Heart Association (AHA) recommends that persons under 18 years of age should consume fewer than 25 grams of added sugar per day, an average adult man fewer than 37.5 grams, and an average adult woman fewer than 25 grams. A 12-ounce can of Coke contains 39 grams of added sugar, or about 9.5 teaspoons of sugar. Should Coca-Cola reduce the amount of added sugar in a can of Coke? Why or why not?

Mergers and Acquisitions

39.3 Describe the process for approving a merger, acquisition, and share exchange.

Corporations often agree to combine in friendly acquisitions or combinations of one another. This may occur through merger, share exchange, or sale of assets. These types of combinations are discussed in the following paragraphs.

Merger

A **merger** is a combination of two corporations where one corporation is absorbed into another corporation; one corporation survives, and the other corporation ceases to exist. The corporation that continues to exist is called the **surviving corporation**. The other corporation, which ceases to exist, is called the **merged corporation** [MBCA 11.02].

The surviving corporation gains all the rights, privileges, powers, duties, obligations, and liabilities of the merged corporation. Title to property owned by the merged corporation transfers to the surviving corporation, without formality or deeds [MBCA 11.07]. The shareholders of the merged corporation receive stock or securities of the surviving corporation or other consideration, as provided in the plan of merger. A corporation can also merge with an unincorporated entity such as a limited liability company.

merger
A transaction in which one corporation is absorbed into another corporation and ceases to exist.

surviving corporation
The corporation that continues to exist after a merger.

merged corporation
The corporation that is absorbed in the merger and ceases to exist after the merger.

Example Corporation A and Corporation B merge, and it is agreed that Corporation A will absorb Corporation B. Corporation A is the surviving corporation. Corporation B is the merged corporation. The representation of this merger is A + B = A (see **Exhibit 39.1**).

Example Amazon.com, Inc. paid $13.7 billion cash to acquire Whole Foods Market, Inc. This was accomplished through a merger agreement between Walnut Merger Sub, Inc., a wholly owned subsidiary of Amazon, with Whole Foods Market, Inc. Since the merger, Whole Foods has continued as the surviving corporation, and Walnut Merger Sub ceased to exist. Amazon operates Whole Foods as a wholly owned subsidiary.

Consolidation

A **consolidation** occurs when two or more corporations combine to form an entirely new corporation. A consolidation mimics all of the factors associated with a merger except that neither of the original companies survive the consolidation. Instead, a new company is created. The two consolidated corporations are called *merged corporations* and cease to exist. The new corporation is called the **consolidated corporation**. The articles of incorporation of the new corporation replace the articles of incorporation of the merged corporations.

consolidation
The combination of two corporations in which a new corporation is created and the two merging corporations cease to exist.

consolidated corporation
A new corporation that is formed by the consolidation of two corporations.

Example Corporation A and Corporation B consolidate to form a new corporation called Corporation C. Both Corporation A and B cease to exist. A symbolic representation of this combination is A + B = C.

Exhibit 39.1 MERGER

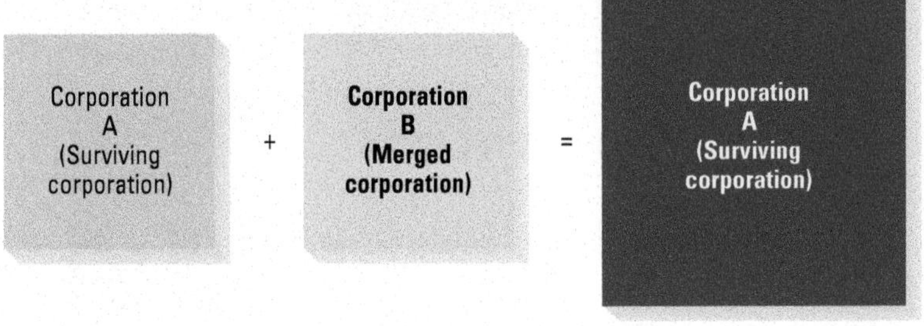

The new corporation accedes to all the rights, privileges, powers, duties, obligations, and liabilities of the merged corporations. Title to property owned by the merged corporations transfers to the new corporation, without any formality. The shareholders receive stock or other securities in the consolidated corporation or other agreed-upon consideration. The results of a consolidation are similar to a merger, except that neither of the combining corporations survive. Combining corporations might choose a consolidation over a merger if a stronger new image is desired. Consolidation is not often used because it is generally advantageous for one of the corporations to survive.

Share Exchange

share exchange
A situation in which one corporation acquires all the shares of another corporation, and both corporations retain their separate legal existence.

parent corporation
The corporation that owns the shares of the subsidiary corporation in a share exchange.

subsidiary corporation
The corporation that is owned by the parent corporation in a share exchange.

One corporation can acquire all of the shares of another corporation through a **share exchange**. In a share exchange, one corporation buys the shares of another corporation by paying for the acquired corporation's shares with its own shares [MBCA 11.03(a)]. The acquiring corporation and the acquired corporation must agree on the exchange ratio for the shares. After the exchange, both corporations still exist and have not been merged. One corporation owns all the shares of the other corporation. Following a share exchange, the acquiring corporation (the **parent corporation**) owns all the shares of the acquired corporation (the **subsidiary corporation**). A share exchange is sometimes referred to as a **stock-for-stock merger**.

Example Corporation A wants to acquire Corporation B. Corporation A offers to exchange its own shares for the shares of Corporation B, and Corporation B's shareholders approve the transaction. After the share exchange, Corporation A owns all the stock of Corporation B. Corporation B shareholders, who have received a payment with the shares of Corporation A, are now shareholders of Corporation A. Corporation A is the parent corporation, and Corporation B is the wholly owned subsidiary of Corporation A (see **Exhibit 39.2**).

Required Approvals for a Merger or Share Exchange

An ordinary merger or share exchange requires that the plan of merger or the plan of share exchange (1) be adopted by the board of directors of both corporations, and (2) be approved by the majority vote of the shares of the non-surviving corporation in a merger, or the majority vote of the shareholders of the acquired corporation in a share exchange [MBCA 11.04(a) and (b)]. The vote of the shareholders of the surviving corporation of a merger, or the shareholders of a acquiring corporation in a share exchange, is not required [MBCA 11.04.(h) and (l)]. However, the articles of incorporation can require these votes.

Exhibit 39.2 SHARE EXCHANGE

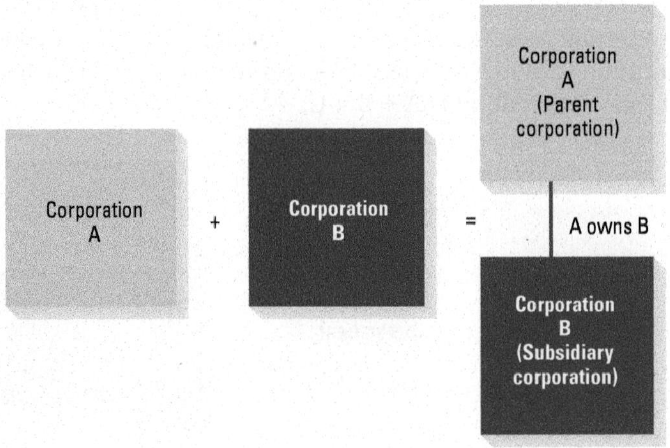

Upon completion of a merger, **articles of merger** must be filed with the secretary of state by the surviving corporation. Upon the completion of a share exchange, **articles of share exchange** must be filed with the secretary of state by the acquiring corporation. If a new corporation has been created, its articles of incorporation must be filed with the secretary of state [MBCA 11.06].

Short-Form Merger

If a parent corporation owns 90 percent or more of the outstanding shares of the subsidiary corporation, the parent may merge the subsidiary into itself without the approval of the directors or shareholders of the subsidiary corporation [MBCA 11.05]. The approval of the shareholders of the parent corporation is also not required. All that is required is the approval of the board of directors of the parent corporation [MBCA Section 11.05]. This is called a **short-form merger**.

short-form merger
A merger between a parent corporation and a subsidiary corporation that does not require the approval of the shareholders of either corporation or the approval of the board of directors of the subsidiary corporation.

Sale or Lease of Assets

A corporation may sell, lease, exchange, transfer, mortgage, and dispose of assets in the regular course of business without shareholder approval [MBCA 12.01]. However, the disposition of all or substantially all of a corporation's property that would leave the corporation without significant continuing business activity requires (1) the recommendation of the board of directors and (2) an affirmative vote of the majority of the shares of the corporation. This rule prevents the board of directors from selling or transferring all or most of the assets of the corporation without shareholder approval. However, the MBCA contains a safe harbor provision that provides that shareholder approval is not required if, after the sale or transfer, the corporation retains business activity that represents at least (1) 25 percent of total assets, or (2) either 25 percent of income from continuing operations or 25 percent of revenues of continuing operations [MBCA 12.02].

The following feature discusses dissenting shareholder appraisal rights.

dissenting shareholder appraisal rights (appraisal rights)
The rights of shareholders who object to a proposed merger, share exchange, or sale or lease of all or substantially all of the property of a corporation to have their shares valued by the court and receive cash payment of this value from the corporation.

Business Environment

Dissenting Shareholder Appraisal Rights

Some shareholders may object to an ordinary or short-form merger, share exchange, or disposition of assets of a corporation, even though the transaction received the required approvals. This is usually because the shareholder does not believe that he or she is being paid fair value for his or her shares. Objecting shareholders are provided a statutory right to dissent and bring a procedure to try to obtain a greater payment for their shares [MBCA 13.02]. This is referred to as a **dissenting shareholder appraisal right, or an appraisal right**. Shareholders have no other recourse unless the transaction is unlawful or fraudulent.

A corporation must notify shareholders of the existence of their appraisal rights before a transaction can be voted on [MBCA 13.20]. To obtain appraisal rights, a dissenting shareholder must (1) deliver written notice of the intent to demand payment of his or her shares to the corporation before the vote is taken and (2) not vote these shares in favor of the proposed action. The shareholder must deposit the share certificates with the corporation [MBCA 13.21]. Shareholders who fail to comply with these statutory procedures lose their appraisal rights.

As soon as the proposed merger, share exchange, or disposition of assets is taken, the corporation must pay each dissenting shareholder the amount the corporation estimates to be the fair value of the shares, plus accrued interest [MBCA 13.24]. If the dissenter is dissatisfied, the corporation must petition the court to determine the fair value of the shares [MBCA 13.30].

Appraisers may be appointed to help the court determine the fair value of the shares. After a hearing, the court will issue an order declaring the fair value of the shares. If the court determines a fair value higher than that accepted by the other shareholders, the dissenting shareholder is paid this amount; the shareholders who previously sold their shares will not be paid this higher amount. However, if the court determines that the share value is less than that paid in the transaction, the dissenting shareholder is paid this lower amount. Court costs and appraisal fees are usually paid by the corporation. However, the court can assess these costs against the dissenters if it finds that they have acted arbitrarily, vexatiously, or in bad faith [MBCA 13.31].

The following case involves dissenting shareholder appraisal rights.

CASE 39.1 STATE COURT CASE Dissenting Shareholder Appraisal Rights

Global GT LP v. Golden Telecom, Inc.

993 A.2d 497, 2010 Del. Ch. Lexis 76 (2010)
Court of Chancery of Delaware

"As is typical, the outcome of this appraisal proceeding largely depends on my acceptance, rejection, or modification of the views of the parties' valuation experts."

—Leo Strine, Vice Chancellor

Facts

Golden Telecom, Inc. was a Russian-based telecommunications company that was listed on the NASDAQ. Shares of Golden Telecom were purchased for $105 per share by Vimpel-Communications (VimpelCom), a major Russian provider of mobile telephone services whose largest stockholders were also the largest stockholders of Golden Telecom. Golden Telecom's management recommended that stockholders accept the offer. A total of 94.4 percent of Golden Telecom stockholders tendered their shares at the $105 offer price. The remaining stockholders exercised their appraisal rights. At trial, Golden Telecom's valuation expert witness came up with the value of $88 per share, pointing out that Golden Telecom stockholders received a generous $105 for their shares. The dissenters' valuation expert came up with a value of $139 per share, claiming that the $105 offer price was too low.

Issue

What is the appraisal value of Golden Telecom stock?

Language of the Court

As is typical, the outcome of this appraisal proceeding largely depends on my acceptance, rejection, or modification of the views of the parties' valuation experts. After making my determinations, I generated a per share value of $125.49 per share, which I supplement with an award of interest at the applicable statutory rate.

Decision

The court entered judgment that Golden Telecom shares were worth $125.49 per share at the time of the merger. The dissenting shareholders were awarded the $20.49 per share above the $105 offer price that the other shareholders were paid.

Critical Legal Thinking Questions

Did Golden Telecom's management act ethically in recommending $105 per share? Was there any conflict of interest in this case?

target corporation
The corporation that is proposed to be acquired in a tender offer situation.

tender offer
An offer that an acquirer makes directly to a target corporation's shareholders in an effort to acquire the target corporation.

tender offeror
The party that makes a tender offer.

hostile tender offer
A tender offer that is made without the permission of the target company's board of directors or without any prior attempt by a tender offeror to acquire the target company through a voluntary merger or purchase.

Tender Offer

39.4 Define *tender offer* and describe defensive maneuvers to prevent hostile takeovers.

Recall that a merger or a share exchange requires the approval of the board of directors and shareholders of the corporation whose shares are to be acquired. If the board of directors of the target corporation does not agree to a merger or an acquisition, the corporation that is trying to effectuate the merger or share exchange can make an offer directly to the shareholders of the **target corporation** to purchase their shares. This is called a **tender offer**, and the corporation making the offer is called the **tender offeror**. The shareholders of the target corporation can each make an individual decision about whether to sell their shares to the tender offeror (see **Exhibit 39.3**).

Tender offers that are made without the permission of the target company's board of directors are referred to as **hostile tender offers**. Hostile tender offers can also be made without any prior attempt by a tender offeror to acquire the target company through a voluntary merger or purchase.

Exhibit 39.3 **TENDER OFFER**

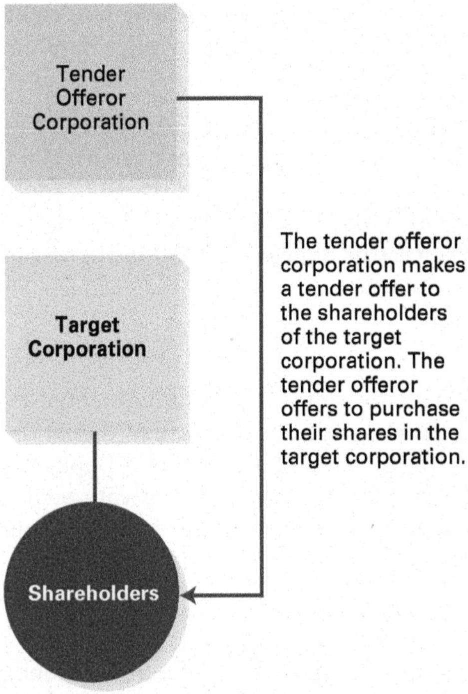
Tender Offeror Corporation
Target Corporation
Shareholders
The tender offeror corporation makes a tender offer to the shareholders of the target corporation. The tender offeror offers to purchase their shares in the target corporation.

Example Tech, Inc. wants to merge with Digital, Inc., but the board of directors of Digital, Inc. refuses to approve the transaction. Tech, Inc. makes a tender offer to the shareholders of Digital, Inc. to acquire the shares they own of Digital, Inc. This is a hostile tender offer in which Tech, Inc. is the tender offeror and Digital, Inc. is the target corporation.

To make a tender offer, the tender offeror's board of directors must approve the offer, although the tender offeror's shareholders do not have to approve the tender offer. The offer can be made for all or a portion of the shares of the target corporation. In a tender offer, the tendering corporation and the target corporation retain their separate legal status. However, a successful tender offer is sometimes followed by a merger of the two corporations.

Tender Offer Rules

The **Williams Act** is an amendment to the Securities Exchange Act of 1934.[2] This act regulates all tender offers, whether they are made with securities, cash, or other consideration, and it establishes certain disclosure requirements and antifraud provisions. The Williams Act does not require a tender offeror to notify either the management of the target company or the Securities and Exchange Commission until the offer is made. Detailed information regarding the terms, conditions, and other information concerning the tender offer must be disclosed at that time. Tender offers are governed by the following SEC rules:

Williams Act
An amendment to the Securities Exchange Act of 1934 that specifically regulates tender offers.

- The offer cannot be closed before 20 business days after the commencement of the tender offer.
- The offer must be extended for 10 business days if the tender offeror increases the number of shares it will take or the price it will pay for the shares.
- The **fair price rule**, also called the **best price rule**, requires that all shareholders be paid the same price in a tender offer. Thus, any increase in price paid for shares tendered must be offered to all shareholders, even those who have previously tendered their shares.
- The **pro rata rule** holds that the shares must be purchased on a pro rata basis if too many shares are tendered.

fair price rule (best price rule)
A rule that says any increase in price paid for shares tendered must be offered to all shareholders, even those who have previously tendered their shares.

pro rata rule
A rule that says shares must be purchased on a pro rata basis if too many shares are tendered.

Section 13(d) of the Securities Exchange Act of 1934
A law that requires that any party that acquires 5 percent or more of any equity security of a company registered with the Securities and Exchange Commission (SEC) must report the acquisition to the SEC and disclose its intentions regarding the acquisition.

- A shareholder who tenders shares has the absolute right to withdraw them at any time prior to the closing of the tender offer. The dissenting shareholder's appraisal rights are not available.

Section 13(d) of the Securities Exchange Act of 1934 requires that any party that acquires 5 percent or more of any equity security of a company registered with the SEC must report the acquisition to the SEC and disclose its intentions regarding the acquisition. This is public information. Thus, at such time, the corporation will be on notice that that party has an interest in the corporation and may be a future tender offeror.

Antifraud Provision

Section 14(e) of the Williams Act
A provision of the Williams Act that prohibits fraudulent, deceptive, and manipulative practices in connection with a tender offer.

Section 14(e) of the Williams Act prohibits fraudulent, deceptive, and manipulative practices in connection with a tender offer.[3] Violations of this section may result in the SEC bringing civil charges or the U.S. Department of Justice bringing criminal charges. The courts have implied a private civil cause of action under Section 14(e). Therefore, a shareholder who has been injured by a violation of Section 14(e) can sue the wrongdoer for damages.

Fighting a Tender Offer

The incumbent management of the target of a hostile tender offer may not want the corporation to be taken over by the tender offeror. Therefore, it may engage in various activities to impede and defeat the tender offer. Incumbent management may use some of the following strategies and tactics in defending against hostile tender offers:

crown jewel
A valuable asset of a target corporation that the tender offeror particularly wants to acquire through a tender offer.

white knight merger
The merger of a target corporation of a tender offer with a friendly corporation that promises to leave the target corporation and/or its management intact.

- **Persuasion of shareholders.** Media campaigns are often organized to convince shareholders that the tender offer is not in their best interests.
- **Delaying lawsuits.** Lawsuits may be filed, alleging that the tender offer violates securities laws, antitrust laws, or other laws. The time gained by this tactic gives management the opportunity to erect or implement other defensive maneuvers.
- **Selling a crown jewel.** Assets such as profitable divisions or real estate that is particularly attractive to outside interests—a **crown jewel**—may be sold. This tactic makes the target corporation less attractive to the tender offeror.
- **Adopting a poison pill.** A **poison pill** is a defensive strategy that is built into the target corporation's articles of incorporation, corporate bylaws, or contracts and leases. For example, contracts and leases may provide that they will expire if the ownership of the corporation changes hands. These tactics make the target corporation more expensive to the tender offeror.
- **White knight merger.** A **white knight merger** is a merger of the target corporation with a friendly corporation—that is, a corporation that promises to leave the target corporation and/or its management intact.
- **Reverse tender offer.** In a **reverse tender offer**, the target corporation makes an offer to the shareholders of the tender offeror to purchase the shares that they own of the tender offeror. Thus, the target corporation tries to purchase the tender offeror.
- **Issuing additional stock.** Placing additional stock on the market increases the number of outstanding shares that the tender offeror must purchase in order to gain control of the target corporation.
- **Creating an employee stock ownership plan.** A company may create an **employee stock ownership plan (ESOP)** and place a certain percentage of the corporation's securities (e.g., 15 percent) in it. The ESOP is then expected to vote the shares it owns against the potential acquirer in a proxy contest or

tender offer because the beneficiaries (i.e., the employees) have a vested interest in keeping the company intact.
- **Flip-over and flip-in rights plans.** These plans provide that existing shareholders of the target corporation may convert their shares for a greater number (e.g., twice the value) of shares of the acquiring corporation (**flip-over rights plan**) or debt securities of the target corporation (**flip-in rights plan**). Rights plans are triggered if the acquiring firm acquires a certain percentage (e.g., 20 percent) of the shares of the target corporation. They make it more expensive for the acquiring firm to take over the target corporation.
- **Greenmail and standstill agreements.** Most tender offerors purchase a block of stock in the target corporation before making an offer. Occasionally, the tender offeror will agree to give up its tender offer and agree not to purchase any further shares if the target corporation agrees to buy back the stock at a premium over fair market value. This payment is referred to as **greenmail**. The agreement of the tender offeror to abandon its tender offer and not purchase any additional stock is called a **standstill agreement**.

greenmail
The purchase by a target corporation of its stock from an actual or perceived tender offeror at a premium over fair market value.

There are many other strategies and tactics that target companies initiate and implement in defending against a tender offer.

Business Judgment Rule

The members of the board of directors of a corporation owe a fiduciary duty to the corporation and its shareholders. This duty, which requires the board to act carefully and honestly, is truly tested when a tender offer is made for the stock of the company. That is because shareholders and others then ask whether the board's initiation and implementation of defensive measures were taken in the best interests of the shareholders or to protect the board's own interests and jobs.

The legality of defensive strategies is examined using the **business judgment rule**. This rule protects the decisions of a board of directors that acts on an informed basis, in good faith, and in the honest belief that an action taken was in the best interests of the corporation and its shareholders.[4] In the context of a tender offer, the defensive measures chosen by the board must be reasonable in relation to the threat posed.[5]

State Antitakeover Statutes

39.5 Describe state antitakeover statutes.

Many states have enacted antitakeover statutes that are aimed at protecting corporations with ties to the state. An **antitakeover statute** is enacted by the state legislature. Antitakeover statutes are usually enacted to protect local state businesses from being taken over by other businesses, particularly out-of-state businesses, which might close certain plants located in the state, move certain business operations out of the state, lay off employees who are residents of the state, and cause a decrease in state tax revenues.

antitakeover statute
A statute enacted by a state legislature that protects corporations incorporated in or doing business in the state from the hostile takeovers.

State antitakeover statutes apply to corporations that are incorporated in the state. Many antitakeover statutes also cover corporations that have their principal office in the state or have a certain percentage of their shareholders who are residents of the state (e.g., 10 percent) or have residents of the state who own a certain percentage of the corporation's stock (e.g., 10 percent).

Because Delaware provides the most powerful antitakeover laws, many large corporations incorporate in Delaware.

The following feature discusses an important U. S. law that relates to acquisitions.

Global Law

Foreign Acquisitions of U.S. Companies

The **Exon-Florio Foreign Investment Provision** is a federal law that mandates that the president of the United States suspend, prohibit, or dismantle the merger, acquisition, or takeover of a U.S.-based company by a foreign company, person, or enterprise owned by a foreign government or agency if there is credible evidence that the acquisition threatens to impair the national security of the United States.[6] The law has been used to prohibit the acquisition of U.S. companies by foreign companies, particularly in sensitive areas such as defense systems, airlines, telecommunications, information technology, and advanced computing.

In 2018, the scope of prohibited foreign transactions was expanded by the enactment of the **Foreign Investment Risk Review Modernization Act (FIRRMA)**.[7] This federal statute (1) prevents the purchase, acquisition, or lease of real estate by or to a foreign person that is located in close proximity to U.S. military installations, ports, airports, or government facilities; (2) prohibits non-controlling investments in U.S. businesses that give a foreign person access to material, nonpublic information that involves critical technologies, critical infrastructure, or sensitive personal data of U.S. citizens; (3) prohibits joint ventures between foreign persons and U.S. businesses where U.S.-origin technology is transferred; and (4) prohibits any transaction, transfer, agreement, or arrangement designed to circumvent foreign acquisitions laws. A foreign person is an individual, a business, or an entity owned by a foreign government or agency.

The **Committee on Foreign Investment in the United States (CFIUS)** is an interagency committee of 16 U.S. departments and agencies that assists the president in overseeing the national security risks of foreign investment in the U.S. economy. CFIUS is delegated executive power to review and reject foreign acquisitions and investments deemed to violate the law. Although decisions by CFIUS are appealable, this is of limited practical value because final determinations by the president are not subject to judicial review.

Multinational Corporations

39.6 Examine the use of multinational corporations in conducting international business.

Exon-Florio Foreign Investment Provision
A federal law that mandates that the president of the United States suspend, prohibit, or dismantle the merger, acquisition, or takeover of a U.S.-based company by a foreign company, person, or enterprise owned by a foreign government or agency if there is credible evidence that the acquisition threatens to impair the national security of the United States.

Many of the largest corporations in the world are **multinational corporations**—that is, corporations that operate in many countries. These corporations are also called **transnational corporations**. Some multinational corporations operate across borders by using branch offices, while others use subsidiary corporations. Multinational corporations also include corporations that do business in other countries through a variety of means, such as agents, business alliances, strategic partnerships, franchising, and other arrangements.

multinational corporation (transnational corporation)
A corporation that operates in many countries.

Examples The Coca-Cola Company, a U.S. company, sells its products in almost every country; McDonald's Corporation, a U.S. company, has approximately 40,000 restaurants in more than 120 countries; Sony Corporation, a Japanese company, sells its electronic products in almost every country; Nestlé S.A., a Swiss multinational company, distributes its food products worldwide; Starbucks, a U.S. company, operates more than 30,000 coffee houses in over 80 countries; Royal Dutch Shell is a Netherlands oil and energy company that operates on every continent; and Petróleo Brasileiro S.A. (Petrobras) is a Brazilian multinational petroleum company. Thousands of other multinational companies could be added to this list.

International Branch Office

international branch office
An office of a multinational corporation that is located in a foreign country.

A multinational corporation can conduct business in another country by using an **international branch office**. A branch office is not a separate legal entity but merely an office of the corporation. As such, the corporation is liable for the contracts of the branch office and is also liable for the torts committed by personnel of the branch office. There is no liability shield between the corporation and the branch office (see **Exhibit 39.4**).

Example A U.S. corporation that is incorporated under the laws of Delaware opens a branch office in India. If an employee at the branch office in India negligently

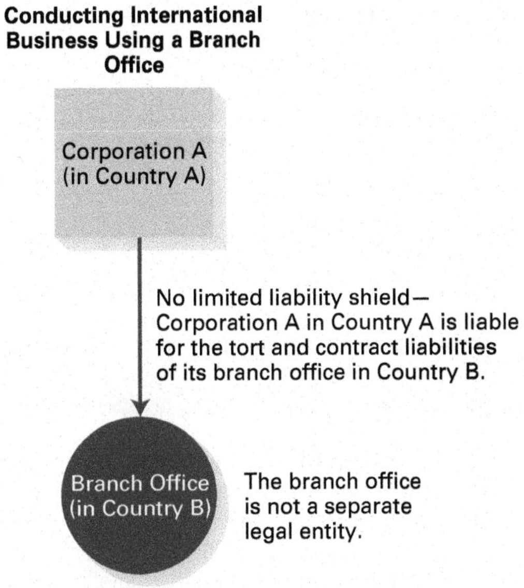
Conducting International Business Using a Branch Office
Corporation A (in Country A)
No limited liability shield—Corporation A in Country A is liable for the tort and contract liabilities of its branch office in Country B.
Branch Office (in Country B)
The branch office is not a separate legal entity.

Exhibit 39.4 INTERNATIONAL BRANCH OFFICE

injures a person in India, the corporation based in the United States is wholly liable for the injured person's damages.

International Subsidiary Corporation

A multinational corporation can conduct business in another country by using an **international subsidiary corporation**. The subsidiary corporation is organized under the laws of the foreign country. The subsidiary corporation is a separate corporation from the parent corporation. The parent corporation usually owns all or the majority of the subsidiary corporation (see **Exhibit 39.5**).

Because the subsidiary corporation is a separate legal entity, the parent corporation is not liable for the contracts of or torts committed by the subsidiary corporation. There is a liability shield between the parent corporation and the subsidiary corporation.

Example A U.S. corporation that is incorporated under the laws of Delaware creates a subsidiary corporation in Brazil that is formed under the laws of Brazil. The

international subsidiary corporation
A corporation that is organized under the laws of the foreign country and is owned by a multinational corporation.

Foreign Corrupt Practices Act (FCPA)
A federal statute that makes it illegal for a U.S. citizen or resident and U.S. companies or their officers, directors, agents, shareholders, employees, partners, or intermediaries to bribe a foreign official, a foreign political party official, a candidate for foreign political office, or an official of a public international organization, where the bribe is intended to influence the official's act or decision such that the bribing party obtains or retains business or secures an improper advantage.

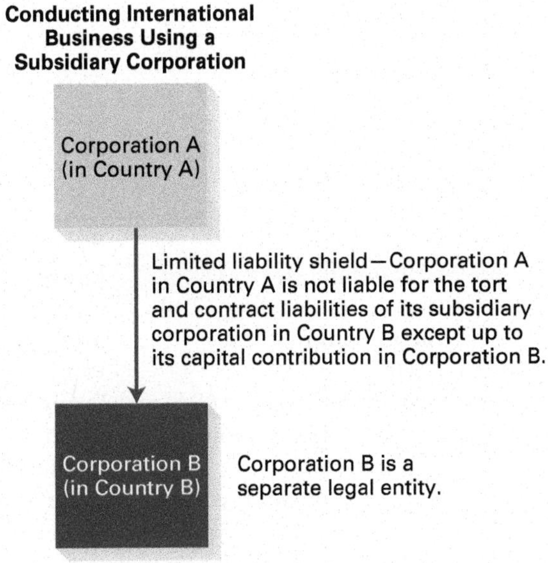
Conducting International Business Using a Subsidiary Corporation
Corporation A (in Country A)
Limited liability shield—Corporation A in Country A is not liable for the tort and contract liabilities of its subsidiary corporation in Country B except up to its capital contribution in Corporation B.
Corporation B (in Country B)
Corporation B is a separate legal entity.

Exhibit 39.5 INTERNATIONAL SUBSIDIARY CORPORATION

U.S. company is the parent corporation, and the Brazilian company is the subsidiary corporation. If an employee of the Brazilian company negligently injures a person in Brazil, only the Brazilian subsidiary corporation is liable; the parent corporation in the United States is not liable aside from the fact that it may lose its capital contribution in the Brazilian corporation.

The following feature discusses the Foreign Corrupt Practices Act.

Global Law

Foreign Corrupt Practices Act

Payment of bribes occurs in the course of operating some businesses. U.S. laws make the payment of bribes illegal in the United States. However, payment of bribes also occurs in the course of conducting international business. To prevent U.S. companies from engaging in this type of conduct, the U.S. Congress enacted the **Foreign Corrupt Practices Act (FCPA)**.[8] The FCPA was enacted primarily to prevent corporate bribery of foreign officials.

The FCPA, as amended, makes it illegal for a U.S. citizen or resident and U.S. companies or their officers, directors, agents, shareholders, employees, partners, or intermediaries to bribe a foreign official, a foreign political party official, a candidate for foreign political office, or an official of a public international organization, where the bribe is intended to influence the official's act or decision such that the bribing party obtains or retains business or secures an improper advantage. Foreign officials include individuals who work for companies that are owned or managed by foreign governments, such as state-owned enterprises.

The act prohibits the offer, promise, or payment of money, assets, or anything of value. The FCPA has worldwide application and covers unlawful payments made in the United States or outside the country. Payments to foreign officials are legal if the payment is permitted by the written laws of the foreign country. Illegal payments made to expedite the performance of a foreign official's routine duties (e.g., issuing a customs duty permit) usually do not violate the act. The FCPA prohibits payments made with a corrupt motive. Innocent mistakes are not illegal under the FCPA.

The FCPA is enforced by the U.S. Department of Justice, which can bring criminal charges, and the SEC, which can assess civil penalties for violations of the act.

The **United Nations Convention Against Corruption (UNCAC)** is an international anti-corruption treaty that requires signatory countries to adopt anti-corruption laws, to cooperate in criminal matters and assist each other in investigating suspected violators, and to return proceeds gained from corruption. The United States was a leader in developing and promoting the treaty. The United States and more than 180 other countries are member states. There is now increased enforcement of anti-corruption laws in many countries of the world.

Key Terms and Concepts

Antifraud provision (694)
Antitakeover statute (703)
Articles of merger (699)
Articles of share exchange (699)
Business judgment rule (703)
Committee on Foreign Investment in the United States (CFIUS) (704)
Consolidated corporation (697)
Consolidation (697)
Crown jewel (702)
Dissenting shareholder appraisal right (appraisal right) (699)
E-proxy rule (694)
Employee stock ownership plan (ESOP) (702)
Exon-Florio Foreign Investment Provision (704)
Fair price rule (best price rule) (701)
Flip-in rights plan (703)
Flip-over rights plan (703)
Foreign Corrupt Practices Act (FCPA) (706)
Foreign Investment Risk Review Modernization Act (FIRRMA) (704)
Fundamental changes (693)
Greenmail (703)
Hostile tender offer (700)
Incumbent director (694)
Insurgent director (694)
International branch office (704)
International subsidiary corporation (705)
Merged corporation (697)
Merger (697)
Multinational corporation (transnational corporation) (704)
Parent corporation (698)
Poison pill (702)
Pro rata rule (701)
Proxy (693)
Proxy contest (694)
Proxy statement (694)
Reverse tender offer (702)
Section 13(d) of the Securities Exchange Act of 1934 (702)

Section 14(a) of the Securities Exchange Act of 1934 (694)
Section 14(e) of the Williams Act (702)
Share exchange (stock-for-stock merger) (698)
Shareholder resolution (shareholder proposal) (695)
Short-form merger (699)
Standstill agreement (703)
Subsidiary corporation (698)
Surviving corporation (697)
Target corporation (700)
Tender offer (700)
Tender offeror (700)
United Nations Convention Against Corruption (UNCAC) (706)
White knight merger (702)
Williams Act (701)

Critical Legal Thinking Cases

39.1 Shareholder Resolution The Medical Committee for Human Rights (Committee), a nonprofit corporation organized to advance concerns for human life, received a gift of shares of Dow Chemical (Dow) stock. Dow manufactured napalm, a chemical defoliant that was used during the Vietnam conflict. Committee objected to the sale of napalm by Dow primarily because of its concerns for human life. Committee owned sufficient shares for a long enough time to propose a shareholders' resolution, as long as it met the other requirements to propose such a resolution. Committee proposed that the following resolution be included in the proxy materials circulated by management for the annual shareholders' meeting:

> *RESOLVED, that the shareholders of the Dow Chemical company request that the Board of Directors, in accordance with the law, consider the advisability of adopting a resolution setting forth an amendment to the composite certificate of incorporation of the Dow Chemical Company that the company shall not make napalm.*

Dow's management refused to include the requested resolution in its proxy materials. Committee sued, alleging that its resolution met the requirements to be included in the proxy materials. Who wins? *Medical Committee for Human Rights v. Securities and Exchange Commission*, 432 F.2d 659, 1970 U.S. App. Lexis 8284 (United States Court of Appeals for the District of Columbia Circuit, 1970)

39.2 Dissenting Shareholder Appraisal Rights Over a period of several years, the Curtiss-Wright Corporation (Curtiss-Wright) purchased 65 percent of the stock of Dorr-Oliver Incorporated (Dorr-Oliver). Curtiss-Wright's board of directors decided that a merger with Dorr-Oliver would be beneficial to Curtiss-Wright. The board voted to approve a merger of the two companies and to pay $23 per share to the stockholders of Dorr-Oliver. The Dorr-Oliver board and 80 percent of Dorr-Oliver's shareholders approved the merger. The merger became effective. John Bershad, a minority shareholder of Dorr-Oliver, voted against the merger but thereafter tendered his 100 shares and received payment of $2,300. Bershad subsequently sued, alleging that the $23 per share paid to Dorr-Oliver shareholders was grossly inadequate. Can Bershad obtain minority shareholder appraisal rights? *Bershad v. Curtiss-Wright Corporation*, 535 A.2d 840, 1987 Del. Lexis 1313 (Supreme Court of Delaware, 1987)

39.3 Tender Offer Mobil Corporation (Mobil) made a tender offer to purchase up to 40 million outstanding common shares of stock in Marathon Oil Company (Marathon) for $85 per share in cash. It further stated its intentions to follow the purchase with a merger of the two companies. Mobil was primarily interested in acquiring Marathon's oil and mineral interests in certain properties, including the Yates Field. Marathon directors immediately held a board meeting and determined to find a white knight. Negotiations developed between Marathon and United States Steel Corporation (U.S. Steel). Two weeks later, Marathon and U.S. Steel entered into an agreement whereby U.S. Steel would make a tender offer for 30 million common shares of Marathon stock at $125 per share, to be followed by a merger of the two companies.

The Marathon–U.S. Steel agreement was subject to the following two conditions: (1) U.S. Steel was given an irrevocable option to purchase 10 million authorized but unissued shares of Marathon common stock for $90 per share (or 17 percent of Marathon's outstanding shares), and (2) U.S. Steel was given an option to purchase Marathon's interest in oil and mineral rights in Yates Field for $2.8 billion (Yates Field option). The Yates Field option could be exercised only if U.S. Steel's offer did not succeed and if a third party gained control of Marathon. Evidence showed that Marathon's interest in Yates Field was worth up to $3.6 billion. Marathon did not give Mobil either of these two options. Mobil sued, alleging that these two options violated Section 14(e) of the Williams Act. Who wins? *Mobil Corporation v. Marathon Oil Company*, 669

F.2d 366, 1981 U.S. App. Lexis 14958 (United States Court of Appeals for the Sixth Circuit, 1981)

39.4 State Antitakeover Statute The state of Wisconsin enacted an antitakeover statute that protects corporations that are incorporated in Wisconsin and have their headquarters, substantial operations, or 10 percent of their shares or shareholders in the state. The statute prevents any party that acquires a 10 percent interest in a covered corporation from engaging in a business combination (e.g., merger) with the covered corporation for three years unless approval of management is obtained in advance of the combination. Wisconsin firms cannot opt out of the law. This statute effectively eliminates hostile leveraged buyouts because buyers must rely on the assets and income of the target company to help pay off the debt incurred in effectuating the takeover.

Universal Foods (Universal) was a Wisconsin corporation covered by the statute. Amanda Acquisition Corporation (Amanda) commenced a cash tender offer for up to 75 percent of the stock of Universal. Universal asserted the Wisconsin law. Is Wisconsin's antitakeover statute lawful? *Amanda Acquisition Corporation v. Universal Foods*, 877 F.2d 496, 1989 U.S. App. Lexis 9024 (United States Court of Appeals for the Seventh Circuit, 1989)

Ethics Case

39.5 Ethics Case Fruehauf Corporation (Fruehauf) is engaged in the manufacture of large trucks and industrial vehicles. The Edelman Group (Edelman) made a cash tender offer for the shares of Fruehauf for $48.50 per share. The stock had sold in the low $20-per-share range a few months earlier. Fruehauf's management decided to make a competing management-led leveraged buyout (MBO) tender offer for the company in conjunction with Merrill Lynch. The MBO would be funded using $375 million borrowed from Merrill Lynch, $375 million borrowed from Manufacturers Hanover Bank, and $100 million contributed by Fruehauf. The total equity contribution to the new company under the MBO would be only $25 million: $10 million to $15 million from management and the rest from Merrill Lynch. In return for their equity contributions, management would receive between 40 and 60 percent of the new company.

Fruehauf's management agreed to pay $30 million to Merrill Lynch for brokerage fees that Merrill Lynch could keep even if the deal did not go through. Management also agreed to a no-shop clause whereby they agreed not to seek a better deal with another bidder. Incumbent management received better information about the goings-on. They also gave themselves golden parachutes that would raise the money for management's equity position in the new company.

Edelman informed Fruehauf's management that it could top their bid, but Fruehauf's management did not give them the opportunity to present their offer. Management's offer was accepted. Edelman sued, seeking an injunction against management taking over the corporation. Did Fruehauf's management act unethically in this case? Did Fruehauf's management act legally in this case? *Edelman v. Fruehauf Corporation*, 798 F.2d 882, 1986 U.S. App. Lexis 27911 (United States Court of Appeals for the Sixth Circuit, 1986)

Notes

1. 15 U.S.C. Section 78n(a).
2. 15 U.S.C. Sections 78n(d), 78n(e).
3. 15 U.S.C. Section 78n(e).
4. *Smith v. Van Gorkom*, 488 A.2d 858, 1985 Del. Lexis 421 (Supreme Court of Delaware, 1985).
5. *Unocal Corporation v. Mesa Petroleum Company*, 493 A.2d 946, 1985 Del. Lexis 482 (Supreme Court of Delaware, 1985).
6. 50 U.S.C. app. Section 2170.
7. H.R. 5841 115th Cong. 2d. (2018).
8. 15 U.S.C. Sections 78dd-1 et seq.

CHAPTER

40 Franchises and Special Forms of Business

Henry R. Cheeseman

SOUTH KOREA

In 1999, Starbucks Corporation, in partnership with a Korean corporation, opened its first coffee shop in Seoul, South Korea. There are now more than 1,300 outlets located throughout the country. Seoul now boasts more Starbucks locations than New York City. In deference to local customs, Starbucks signs at its outlets are in Hangeul, the Korean alphabet.

Learning Objectives

After studying this chapter, you should be able to:

40.1 Define *franchise* and describe the various forms of franchises.

40.2 Describe federal and state franchise disclosure laws.

40.3 Describe a franchise agreement and the terms of a franchise agreement.

40.4 Identify the tort and contract liability of franchisors and franchisees.

40.5 Define *apparent agency* and explain how it applies in certain situations.

40.6 Describe how franchising agreements can be terminated.

40.7 Define *licensing* and describe how trademarks and intellectual property are licensed.

40.8 Define *joint venture* and describe how joint ventures are used in business.

40.9 Define *strategic alliance* and describe how strategic alliances are used in business.

"It has been uniformly laid down in this Court, as far back as we can remember, that good faith is the basis of all mercantile transactions."

—Buller, Judge
Salomons v. Nisson (1788)

Introduction to Franchises and Special Forms of Business

Whatever the human law may be, neither an individual nor a nation can commit the least act of injustice against the obscurest individual without having to pay the penalty for it.

Henry David Thoreau
(1817–1862)

Franchising is an important method for distributing goods and services to the public. Originally pioneered by the automobile and soft drink industries, franchising today is used in many other forms of business. More than 700,000 franchise outlets in the United States account for more than 25 percent of retail sales and about 15 percent of the country's gross domestic product (GDP).

Special forms of business are used in domestic and international commerce. *Licensing* permits one business to use another business's trademarks, service marks, trade names, and other intellectual property in selling goods or services. *Joint ventures* allow two or more businesses to combine their resources to pursue a single project or transaction. *Strategic alliances* are often used to enter foreign markets.

This chapter discusses franchises, licensing, joint ventures, and strategic alliances that are used in domestic and international commerce.

Franchise

40.1 Define *franchise* and describe the various forms of franchises.

franchise
An arrangement whereby one party (the *franchisor*) licenses another party (the *franchisee*) to use the franchisor's intellectual property and business model in the distribution of goods and services.

franchisor (licensor)
The party who grants the franchise and license to a franchisee in a franchise arrangement.

franchisee (licensee)
The party who is granted the franchise and license by a franchisor in a franchise arrangement.

A **franchise** is established when one party, the **franchisor (licensor)**, licenses another party, the **franchisee (licensee)**, to use the franchisor's trade name, trademarks, commercial symbols, patents, copyrights, and business model in the distribution and selling of goods and services. Generally, the franchisor and the franchisee are established as separate corporations. The term *franchise* refers to both the agreement between the parties and the franchise outlet.

Franchising has several advantages. For example, the franchisor can reach lucrative new markets, the franchisee has access to the franchisor's knowledge and resources while running an independent business, and consumers are assured of uniform product quality.

A typical franchise arrangement is illustrated in **Exhibit 40.1**.

Exhibit 40.1 FRANCHISE ARRANGEMENT

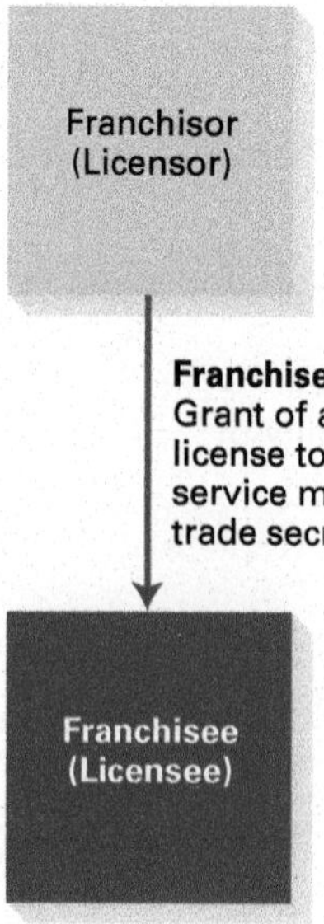

Types of Franchises

There are four basic forms of franchises: (1) *distributorship franchise*, (2) *processing plant franchise*, (3) *chain-style franchise*, and (4) *area franchise*. They are discussed in the following list.

- **Distributorship franchise.** In a **distributorship franchise**, the franchisor manufactures a product and licenses a retail dealer to distribute the product to the public.

  Example Ford Motor Company manufactures automobiles and franchises independently owned automobile dealers (franchisees) to sell them to the public.

distributorship franchise An arrangement by which a franchisor manufactures a product and licenses a franchisee to distribute the product to the public.

- **Processing plant franchise.** In a **processing plant franchise**, the franchisor provides a secret formula, or another exclusive product, to the franchisee. The franchisee then manufactures the product at its own location and distributes it to retail dealers.

  Example Coca-Cola Company, which owns the secret formulas for making Coca-Cola and other soft drinks, sells syrup concentrate to regional bottling companies, which add water and sweeteners and produce and distribute soft drinks under the Coca-Cola name and other brand names.

processing plant franchise An arrangement by which a franchisor provides a secret formula or process to the franchisee and the franchisee manufactures the product and distributes it to retail dealers.

- **Chain-style franchise.** In a **chain-style franchise**, the franchisor licenses the franchisee to make and sell its products or services to the public from a retail outlet serving an exclusive geographical territory. The product is made or the service is provided by the franchise. Most fast-food franchises use this form.

  Example Domino's Pizza, Inc. franchises independently owned restaurant franchises that make and sell pizzas and other food products to the public under the Domino's name.

chain-style franchise An arrangement where a franchisor licenses a franchisee to make and sell its products or distribute its services to the public from a retail outlet serving an exclusive territory.

- **Area franchise.** In an **area fravnchise**, also called an **area development franchise** or **master franchise**, the franchisor authorizes the franchisee to negotiate and sell franchises on behalf of the franchisor. The area franchisee is called a **subfranchisor** (see **Exhibit 40.2**). An area franchise is granted for a certain

area franchise An arrangement by which a franchisor authorizes a franchisee to negotiate and sell franchises on its behalf in designated areas. The area franchisee is called a *subfranchisor*.

Exhibit 40.2 AREA FRANCHISE

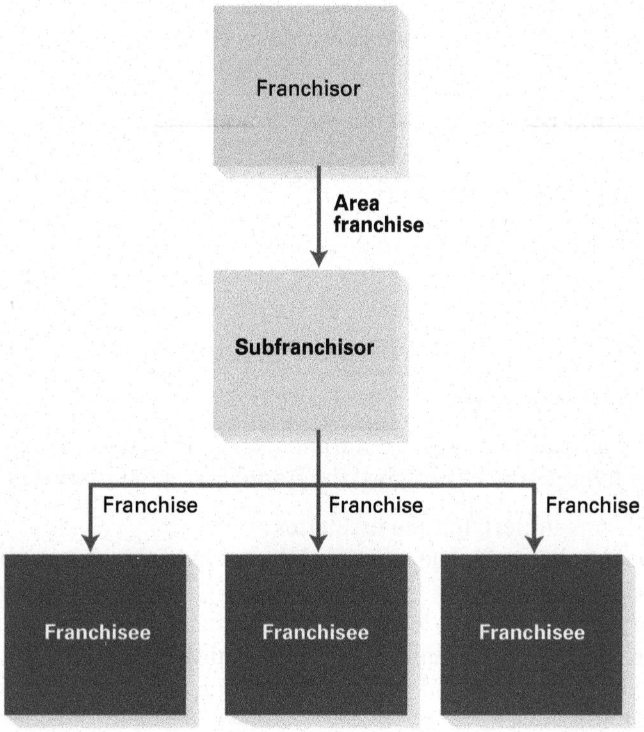

designated geographical area, such as a state, a region, or another agreed-on area. Area franchises are often used when a franchisor wants to enter a market in another country.

Example McDonald's Corporation granted a master franchise to Arcos Dorados Holdings, Inc. to operate McDonald's franchises in 20 countries of Latin America and the Caribbean.

Franchise Disclosure Laws

40.2 Describe federal and state franchise disclosure laws.

In the past, some franchisors have given false information to prospective franchisees about how successful they will be if they become a franchisee. Often, these disclosures or nondisclosures constituted fraud. To address this problem, the federal government and several state governments have adopted mandatory disclosure requirements that franchisors must make to prospective franchisees. These disclosure requirements are discussed in the following paragraphs.

FTC Franchise Rule

Federal Trade Commission (FTC)
A federal government agency that is empowered to enforce federal franchising rules.

FTC franchise rule
A rule issued by the Federal Trade Commission that requires franchisors to make full presale disclosures to prospective franchisees.

The **Federal Trade Commission (FTC)**, a federal administrative agency empowered to regulate franchising, has adopted the **FTC franchise rule**. The FTC rule requires franchisors to make full *presale* disclosures nationwide to prospective franchisees.[1] The FTC does not require the registration of the disclosure document with the FTC prior to its use, but the FTC rule requires the disclosures discussed in the following paragraphs.

Disclosure of Sales or Earnings Projections Based on Actual Data

The FTC franchise rule states that if a franchisor makes sales or earnings projections for a potential franchise location that are based on the actual sales, income, or profit figures of an existing franchise, the franchisor must disclose the following:

- The number and percentage of its actual franchises that have obtained such results.
- A cautionary statement in at least 12-point boldface type that reads, "Caution: Some outlets have sold (or earned) this amount. There is no assurance you'll do as well. If you rely upon our figures, you must accept the risk of not doing so well."

Disclosure of Sales or Earnings Projections Based on Hypothetical Data

The FTC franchise rule states that if a franchisor makes sales or earnings projections based on hypothetical examples, the franchisor must disclose the following:

- The assumptions underlying the estimates.
- The number and percentage of actual franchises that have obtained such results.
- A cautionary statement in at least 12-point boldface print that reads, "Caution: These figures are only estimates of what we think you may earn. There is no assurance you'll do as well. If you rely upon our figures, you must accept the risk of not doing so well."

FTC Franchise Notice

The FTC requires that the following statement, called the **FTC franchise notice**, appear in at least 12-point boldface type on the cover of a franchisor's required disclosure statement to prospective franchisees:

> ***To protect you, we've required your franchisor to give you this information. We haven't checked it, and don't know if it's correct. It should help you make up your mind. Study it carefully. While it includes some information about your contract, don't rely on it alone to understand your contract. Read all of your contract carefully. Buying a franchise is a complicated investment. Take your time to decide. If possible, show your contract and this information to an advisor, like a lawyer or an accountant. If you find anything you think may be wrong or anything important that's been left out, you should let us know about it. It may be against the law. There may also be laws on franchising in your state. Ask your state agencies about them.***

FTC franchise notice
A statement required by the Federal Trade Commission to appear in at least 12-point boldface type on the cover of a franchisor's required disclosure statement to prospective franchisees.

If a franchisor violates FTC disclosure rules, the wrongdoer is subject to an injunction against further franchise sales, civil fines, and an FTC civil action on behalf of injured franchisees to recover damages from the franchisor that were caused by the violation.

State Disclosure Laws

Most states have enacted franchise laws that require franchisors to register and deliver disclosure documents to prospective franchisees. State franchise administrators developed a uniform disclosure document called the **Uniform Franchise Offering Circular (UFOC)**.

Uniform Franchise Offering Circular (UFOC)
A uniform disclosure document that requires a franchisor to make specific presale disclosures to prospective franchisees.

The UFOC and state laws require a franchisor to make specific presale disclosures to prospective franchisees. Information that must be disclosed includes a description of the franchisor's business, balance sheets and income statements of the franchisor for the preceding three years, material terms of the franchise agreement, any restrictions on the franchisee's territory, reasons permitted for the termination of the franchise, and other relevant information.

The UFOC satisfies both state regulations and the FTC.

Franchise Agreement

40.3 Describe a franchise agreement and the terms of a franchise agreement.

A prospective franchisee must apply to the franchisor for a franchise. The **franchise application** often includes detailed information about the applicant's previous employment, financial and educational history, and credit status. If an applicant is approved, the parties enter into a **franchise agreement** that sets forth the terms and conditions of the franchise. Franchise agreements do not usually have much room for negotiation. Generally, the agreement is a standard-form contract prepared by the franchisor. Most states require franchise agreements to be in writing.

franchise agreement
An agreement that a franchisor and franchisee enter into that sets forth the terms and conditions of a franchise.

A franchisor's ability to maintain the public's perception of the quality of the goods and services associated with its trade name, **trademarks**, and **service marks** is the essence of its success. Most franchisors license the use of their trade names, trademarks, and service marks to their franchisees.

trademark and service mark
A distinctive mark, symbol, name, word, motto, or device that identifies the goods or services of a particular franchisor.

Franchisors are often owners of **trade secrets**, including product formulas, business plans and models, and other ideas. Franchisors license and disclose many of their trade secrets to franchisees.

trade secrets
Ideas that make a franchise successful but that do not qualify for trademark, patent, or copyright protection.

Examples The formula for the Coca-Cola soft drink, the recipe for McDonald's Big Mac special sauce, and the ingredients for KFC's original recipe are all trade secrets.

The following feature describes many terms of a McDonald's franchise.

Business Environment

McDonald's Franchise

McDonald's Corporation is the world's largest chain of hamburger fast-food restaurants. McDonald's serves approximately 70 million customers each day at more than 35,000 restaurants that operate in more than 120 countries. More than two-thirds of the company's revenues come from outside the United States. McDonald's Corporation grants franchises to qualified applicants. These franchisees own approximately 70 percent of McDonald's outlets; the company owns and operates the rest. Because of its size, experience, and reputation, McDonald's has one of the highest cost structures for franchisees, as can be seen from the following McDonald's franchise agreement, used here as an example. Franchise agreements usually cover the following topics:

- **Licensing of intellectual property.** A franchise agreement usually contains a *license* that grants the franchisee the right to use certain intellectual property—such as trademarks, service marks, trade secrets, trade names, logos, patents, and copyrights—that are owned by the franchisor. Often, the importance of this intellectual property is what prompts a party to become a franchisee of the franchisor.

  Example McDonald's licenses to franchisees the rights to use its trademarks and service marks, such as "McDonald's," "Big Mac," "Chicken McNuggets," "Quarter Pounder," "McChicken," "McMuffin," "I'm Lovin' It," "Happy Meal," Ronald McDonald, and its design, the Golden Arches, and other intellectual property.

- **Initial license fee.** An **initial license fee** is a lump-sum payment for the privilege of being granted a franchise.

  Example The initial franchise fee for a McDonald's franchise is approximately $45,000.

- **Royalty fees.** A **royalty fee** is a fee for the continued use of the franchisor's trade name, property, and assistance that is often computed as a percentage of the franchisee's gross sales. Royalty fees are usually paid monthly.

  Example McDonald's charges its franchisees a royalty fee for the use of McDonald's name that is approximately 12.5 percent of monthly gross sales.

- **Assessment fee.** An **assessment fee** is a fee for such things as advertising and promotional campaigns and administrative costs, billed either as a flat monthly fee or an annual fee or as a percentage of gross sales.

  Example McDonald's charges its franchisees approximately 4 percent of new sales and puts this money in a special fund to pay for advertising and promotion. McDonald's partners with movie studios promoting the release of movies such as *Minions, Angry Birds,* and other child-friendly movies.

- **Lease fees.** A **lease fee** is a payment for any land or equipment leased from the franchisor, billed either as a flat monthly fee or an annual fee or as a percentage of gross sales or other agreed-on amount.

  Example McDonald's owns the real estate on which a franchisee operates its franchise. McDonald's charges a franchisee rent, which is calculated as a percentage of monthly net sales. This runs between about 5 and 20 percent of monthly net sales.

- **Cost of supplies.** **Cost of supplies** involves payment for supplies purchased from the franchisor.

  Example If a franchisee purchases the cups, wrappers, plastic tableware, and other items from McDonald's, the franchisee is responsible for paying McDonald's for these supplies. McDonald's has licensed other suppliers to sell supplies to McDonald's franchisees, but such suppliers must be preapproved by McDonald's and meet the quality-control standards set by McDonald's.

- **Consulting fees and other expenses.** Many franchisors charge the franchisee a monthly or annual **consulting fee** for expert help in conducting business.
- **Territory.** One of the most important issues regarding a franchise is what geographical **territory** the franchisee will be assigned. This designation will appear in the franchise agreement. Some franchise agreements grant an **exclusive territory** to a franchisee. However, some franchise agreements do not designate exclusive territories and permit a franchisor to locate additional franchisees within specified areas.

  Example McDonald's does not grant exclusive geographical territories to its franchisees.

- **Quality-control standards.** The franchisor's most important assets are its name and reputation. The **quality-control standards** set out in a franchise agreement—such as the franchisor's right to make periodic inspections of the franchisee's premises and operations—are intended to protect these assets. Failure to meet the proper standards can result in loss of the franchise.
- **Training requirements.** Franchisees and their personnel are usually required to attend training programs either onsite or at the franchisor's training facilities.

  Example McDonald's requires that a new franchisee go through a rigorous 9- to 12-month training program before opening a franchise.

- **Covenant not to compete.** A **covenant not to compete** prohibits franchisees from competing with the franchisor during a specific time and in a specified area after the termination of the franchise. Unreasonable (overextensive) covenants not to compete are void.

- **Arbitration clause.** Most franchise agreements contain an **arbitration clause**, which provides that any claim or controversy arising from the franchise agreement or an alleged breach thereof is subject to arbitration.
- **Duration.** A franchise agreement will set forth the duration of the franchise.

  Example McDonald's grants franchises for a 20-year initial term that can be renewed for 20 years if the franchisee meets certain conditions.

- **Other terms and conditions.** Capital requirements are included in a franchise agreement. Other terms and conditions may include restrictions on the use of the franchisor's trade name, trademarks, and logo; standards of operation; record-keeping requirements; sign requirements; hours of operation; prohibition as to the sale or assignment of the franchise; conditions for the termination of the franchise; and other specific terms pertinent to the operation of the franchise and the protection of the parties' rights.
- **Total investment.** The franchise agreement often specifies the total investment that a franchisee must provide in order to be granted the franchise.

  Example The total investment by a franchisee to open a McDonald's franchise ranges from about $1 million to $2 million.

Liability of Franchisor and Franchisee

40.4 Identify the tort and contract liability of franchisors and franchisees.

If a franchise is properly organized and operated, the franchisor and franchisee are separate legal entities. Therefore, the franchisor deals with the franchisee as an **independent contractor**. Franchisees are liable on their own contracts and are liable for their own torts (e.g., negligence), as are franchisors for their own contracts and torts. Generally, neither party is liable for the contracts or torts of the other.

Critical Legal Thinking Questions

What is the public policy that supports the general rule that franchisors are not liable for the torts of a franchisee? Is this rule fair?

Example Suppose that McDonald's Corporation, a fast-food restaurant franchisor, grants a franchise to Gion Corporation, the franchisee. Gion Corporation enters into a loan agreement with City Bank whereby it borrows $1 million. Gion Corporation, the franchisee and debtor, is liable on the loan. McDonald's Corporation, the franchisor, is not liable on the loan.

In the following case, the court had to decide whether a franchisor was liable for a franchisee's actions.

CASE 40.1 *FEDERAL COURT CASE Franchise Liability*

Salazar v. McDonald's Corporation

944 F.3d 1024 (2019)
United States Court of Appeals for the Ninth Circuit

"McDonald's does not retain a general right of control over day-to-day aspects of work at the franchises."

—Susan Graber, Circuit Judge

Facts

The Haynes Family Limited Partnership (Haynes) operated eight McDonald's franchises in California. The franchise agreements required Haynes to pay fees to McDonald's and to maintain quality-control standards set by McDonald's. Plaintiffs Guadalupe Salazar, Genoveva Lopez, and Judith Zarate worked at a Haynes-operated McDonald's franchise. They sued Haynes and McDonald's on behalf of a class of approximately 1,400 employees of Haynes-operated McDonald's franchises. They allege that Haynes and McDonald's denied them overtime pay, meal and rest breaks, and other benefits in violation of wage and hour statutes. The plaintiffs alleged that Haynes and McDonald's were joint employers. Haynes reached a settlement with the plaintiffs. The U.S. district court entered summary judgment in favor of McDonald's, finding that McDonald's was not a joint employer with Haynes. The plaintiffs appealed.

Issue

Is McDonald's, the franchisor, a joint employer with Haynes, its franchisee, and therefore liable for wage and hour violations of its franchisee?

(continued)

Language of the Court

Haynes selects, interviews, and hires employees for its franchises. It trains new employees and sets their wages, which are paid from Haynes' bank account. Haynes sets employees' schedules and monitors their time entries. Haynes also supervises, disciplines, and fires employees. There is no evidence that McDonald's performs any of those functions. The district court properly ruled that McDonald's is not an employer under the control definition, which requires control over the wages, hours, or working conditions. McDonald's does not retain a general right of control over day-to-day aspects of work at the franchises.

Decision

The U.S. court of appeals held that McDonald's was not a joint employer with its franchisee and was therefore not liable for the franchisee's violations of wage and hour statutes.

Ethics Questions

What would be the consequences if franchisors were held liable for the conduct of their franchisees? Did Haynes breach its ethical duty in this case?

In the following case, the court had to decide whether a franchisor was a proper defendant in a lawsuit against a franchisee.

CASE 40.2 *STATE COURT CASE Franchise Liability*

Espinosa v. Accor North America, Inc.

174 So.3d 123, 2015 La. App. Lexis 1366 (2015)
Court of Appeal of Louisiana

"The actual authority of a franchisor is similar to that of an independent contractor."

—Terri Love, Judge

Facts

Accor North America LLC is a franchisor that grants franchises to operate Motel 6 motels. Bayou Hospitality LLC obtained a franchise to operate a Motel 6 in New Orleans, Louisiana. Jorge Espinosa was staying at the Bayou Motel 6 when he was shot by an armed robber in the motel parking lot. The shooting rendered Espinosa paraplegic. Espinosa sued Bayou, alleging that it was negligent because a portion of the motel's fence around the parking lot was missing, thus enabling the armed robber to enter the premises and shoot him. Espinosa also sued Accor, alleging that Accor, as the franchisor, was vicariously liable for the alleged negligence of the Bayou franchisee. Accor filed a motion for summary judgment, contending that it owed no duty to Espinosa because it did not control the day-to-day operations of the Bayou Motel 6 franchise. The court granted Accor's motion for summary judgment and removed Accor as a defendant in the case. Espinosa appealed.

Issue

Is the franchisor liable for the franchisee's negligence?

Language of the Court

Vicarious liability does not apply when an independent contractor relationship exists. The most important test in determining whether or not an independent contractor relationship exists involves the control over the work. The actual authority of a franchisor is similar to that of an independent contractor. The franchise agreement provides that the safety and security of the motel patrons was Bayou's sole responsibility. Bayou was solely responsible for all employee decisions. Accor did not manage the motel. Conclusively, the evidence demonstrates that Accor did not have the authority to exercise control over the day-to-day operations of the motel.

Decision

The court of appeals affirmed the trial court's decision that Accor, the franchisor, was not liable for the shooting of Espinosa by a third party at the Bayou Motel 6 franchise.

Critical Legal Thinking Questions

Do you think patrons stay at chain motels because they rely on the safety of these motels? Should franchisors be liable for franchisees' negligent conduct?

Apparent Agency

40.5 Define *apparent agency* and explain how it applies in certain situations.

If a franchisee is the *actual* or *apparent agent* of the franchisor, the franchisor is responsible for the torts committed and contracts entered while the franchisee was acting within the scope of the agency. Actual agency is created when a franchisor expressly or implicitly makes a franchisee its agent and is, therefore, liable for the contracts and torts committed by the franchisee while the franchisee is acting within the scope of the agency. Franchisors very seldom appoint franchisees as their agents.

Apparent agency is created when a franchisor leads a third person to believe that the franchisee is its agent. For example, a franchisor and franchisee who use the same trade name and trademarks and make no effort to inform the public of their separate legal status may find themselves in such a situation. However, mere use of the same name does not automatically make a franchisor liable for the franchisee's actions. The court's decision of whether an apparent agency has been created depends on the facts and circumstances of the case.

In the following case, the court had to decide whether an apparent agency existed.

apparent agency
Agency that arises when a franchisor creates the appearance that a franchisee is its agent when in fact an actual agency does not exist.

Critical Legal Thinking Questions

What is the public policy that makes a franchisor liable for the negligence of a franchisee under the doctrine of apparent agency? How can a franchisor protect against such liability?

CASE 40.3 *STATE COURT CASE Apparent Agency*

Kids R Kids International, Inc. v. Cope

769 S.E.2d 616 (2015)
Court of Appeals of Georgia

"To establish the required elements of apparent agency, it is not enough that the plaintiff believe that an agency relationship exists."

—Sara Doyle, Presiding Judge

Facts

Kids R Kids International, Inc (KRK), a franchisor of daycare centers, granted a franchise to Gonzales Foods, Inc. to operate a day care center. Veronica Higgs Cope enrolled her 3-year-old son at the center. At the time of enrollment, Cope signed a single-page enrollment agreement that stated "KRK—No. 31—475 South Deshon Road—while a KRK franchise, is independently owned and operated and that neither KRK nor any KRK center other than the one whose name appears at the heading of this form is responsible for the action or obligations of this center." A framed document stating that Gonzales Foods, Inc. was a franchisee of KRK was hanging on the wall next to the front desk. Cope's 3-year-old son sustained injuries to his face when he collided with a metal gate in the play area at school. Cope filed a negligence action against Gonzales and KRK. Cope alleged that Gonzales was an apparent agent of KRK. KRK filed a summary judgment motion, which was denied by the trial court. KRK appealed.

Issue

Was Gonzales, the franchisee, the apparent agent of KRK, the franchisor?

Language of the Court

To establish the required elements of apparent agency, it is not enough that the plaintiff believe that an agency relationship exists. It must be established that the principal held out the agent as its agent. Cope cannot demonstrate justifiable reliance given her express acknowledgment in the enrollment agreement that the day care center was a franchise and that KRK was not responsible for the actions or inactions of the facility.

Decision

The Court of Appeals of Georgia ordered that summary judgment be granted to KRK.

Critical Legal Thinking Questions

Did Cope have sufficient knowledge that Gonzales Foods was not the agent of KRK? Did KRK properly notify Cope that it was not liable for the negligence of its franchisee?

Termination of a Franchise

40.6 Describe how franchising agreements can be terminated.

Most franchise agreements permit a franchisor to terminate the franchise *for cause*. For example, the continued failure of a franchisee to pay franchise fees or meet legitimate quality-control standards would be deemed just cause. However, unreasonably strict application of a just cause termination clause constitutes wrongful termination. A single failure to meet a quality-control standard, for example, is not cause for termination.

A **termination-at-will clause** in a franchise agreement is generally held to be void on the grounds that it is unconscionable. The rationale for this position is that the franchisee has spent time, money, and effort developing the franchise. If a franchise is terminated without just cause, the franchisee can sue the franchisor for wrongful termination. The franchisee can recover damages caused by the unlawful termination and recover the franchise.

Breach of the Franchise Agreement

A lawful franchise agreement is an enforceable contract. Each party owes a duty to adhere to and perform under the terms of the franchise agreement. If the agreement is breached, the aggrieved party can sue the breaching party for rescission of the agreement, restitution, and damages.

If a franchisor terminates a franchise agreement without just cause, the franchisee can sue the franchisor for **wrongful termination**. The franchisee can recover damages caused by the wrongful termination and recover the franchise.

wrongful termination
Termination of a franchise without just cause.

licensing
A business arrangement that occurs when the owner of intellectual property (the *licensor*) contracts to permit another party (the *licensee*) to use the intellectual property.

licensor
The party who grants a license.

licensee
The party to whom a license is granted.

Licensing

40.7 Define *licensing* and describe how trademarks and intellectual property are licensed.

Licensing is an important business arrangement in both domestic and international markets. **Licensing** occurs when one business or party that owns trademarks, service marks, trade names, and other intellectual property, the **licensor**, contracts to permit another business or party, the **licensee**, to use its trademarks, service marks, trade names, and other intellectual property in the distribution of goods, services, software, and digital information. This is called a **license**. A license arrangement is illustrated in **Exhibit 40.3**.

Exhibit 40.3 LICENSE ARRANGEMENT

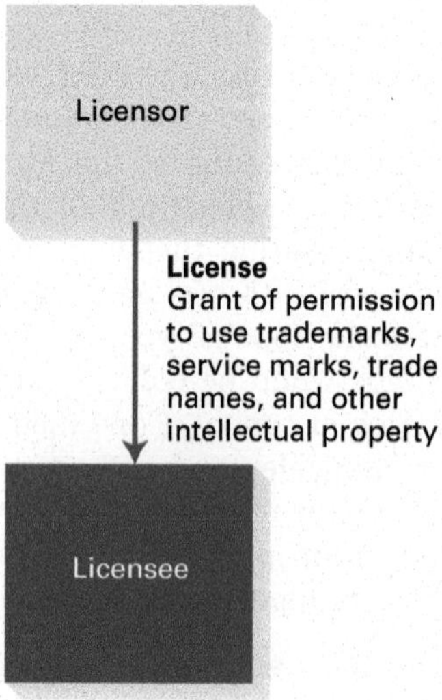

Example The Walt Disney Company, which owns copyrights and trademarks associated with the animated movie *Frozen* and its fictional characters, including Princess Elsa, Princess Anna, Kristoff, the reindeer Sven, and the snowman Olaf, can grant a license to a toy manufacturer to make and sell toy figures of these fictional characters. The Walt Disney Company is the licensor, and the toy manufacturer is the licensee.

Joint Venture

40.8 Define *joint venture* and describe how joint ventures are used in business.

A **joint venture** is an arrangement in which two or more business entities combine their resources to pursue a single project or transaction. Each party to a joint venture is called a **joint venturer**. Joint ventures resemble partnerships, except that partnerships are usually formed to pursue ongoing business operations rather than to focus on a single project or transaction. Unless otherwise agreed, joint venturers have equal rights to manage a joint venture. Joint venturers owe each other the fiduciary duties of loyalty and care. If a joint venturer violates these duties, it is liable for the damages the breach causes.

joint venture
An arrangement in which two or more business entities combine their resources to pursue a single project or transaction.

Joint Venture Partnership

If a joint venture is operated as a partnership, then each joint venturer is considered a partner of the joint venture. This is called a **joint venture partnership** (see **Exhibit 40.4**). In a joint venture partnership, each party is liable for the debts and obligations of the partnership.

joint venture partnership
A partnership owned by two or more joint venturers that is formed to operate a joint venture.

Example A new oil field is discovered in northern Canada. Two large oil companies, ChevronTexaco Corporation and ConocoPhillips Company, would each like to drill for oil there, but neither one has sufficient resources to do so alone. They join together to form a joint venture partnership, and each contributes $100 million capital to the joint venture. If the joint venture fails and the joint venture owes $1 billion to its creditors, which it cannot pay, ChevronTexaco and ConocoPhillips are each responsible for the joint venture's unpaid debts and obligations. This is because they are partners in the joint venture.

Joint Venture Corporation

In pursuing a joint venture, joint venturers often form a corporation, called a **joint venture corporation** (see **Exhibit 40.5**), to operate the joint venture. The joint venturers are shareholders of the corporation. The corporation is liable for

joint venture corporation
A corporation owned by two or more joint venturers that is created to operate a joint venture.

Exhibit 40.4 JOINT VENTURE PARTNERSHIP

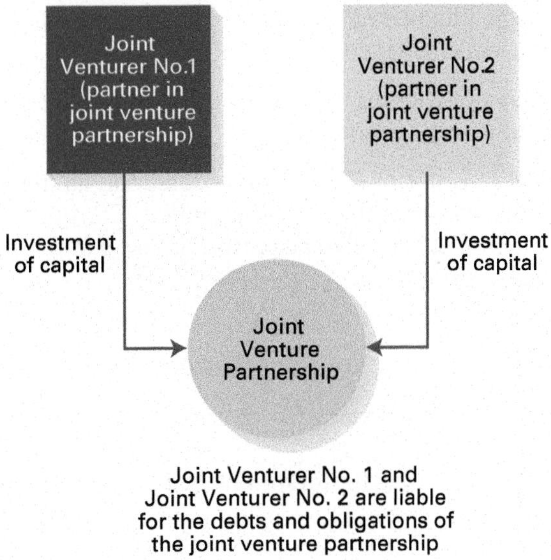

Exhibit 40.5 JOINT VENTURE CORPORATION

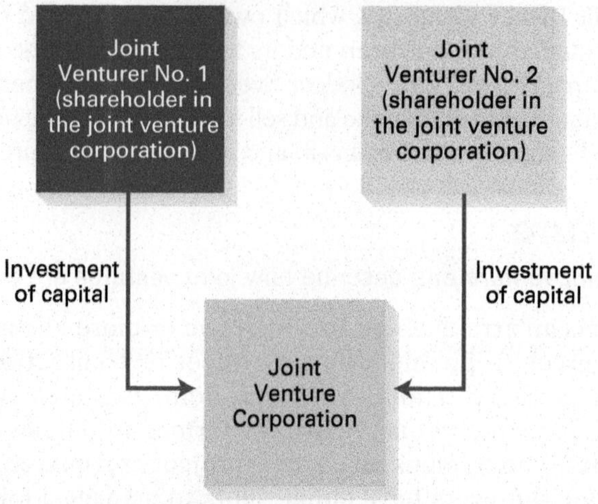

Joint Venturer No. 1 and Joint Venturer No. 2 are liable for the debts and obligations of the joint venture corporation only up to their capital contributions in the joint venture corporation

its debts and obligations, but the joint venturers are liable for the debts and obligations of the corporation only up to their capital contributions.

Example Suppose that in the preceding example, ChevronTexaco Corporation and ConocoPhillips Company form a third corporation, called Canadian Energy Corporation, to operate a joint venture. ChevronTexaco and ConocoPhillips each contribute $100 million capital to Canadian Energy Corporation, and each becomes a shareholder of Canadian Energy Corporation. If the joint venture fails and Canadian Energy Corporation owes $1 billion to its creditors, which it cannot pay, ChevronTexaco and ConocoPhillips each lose their $100 million capital contributions but are not liable for any further unpaid debts or obligations of Canadian Energy Corporation.

Strategic Alliance

40.9 Define *strategic alliance* and describe how strategic alliances are used in business.

strategic alliance
An arrangement between two or more companies whereby they agree to ally themselves and work together to accomplish a designated objective.

A **strategic alliance** is an arrangement between two or more companies whereby they agree to ally themselves and work together to accomplish a designated objective. A strategic alliance allows the companies to reduce risks, share costs, combine technologies, and extend their markets.

Example Companies often enter strategic alliances when they decide to expand internationally into foreign countries.

Strategic alliances do not have the same protection as mergers, joint ventures, or franchising, and sometimes they are dismantled. Consideration must always be given to the fact that a strategic alliance partner is also a future potential competitor.

Key Terms and Concepts

Apparent agency (717)
Arbitration clause (715)
Area franchise (area development franchise or master franchise) (711)
Assessment fee (714)
Chain-style franchise (711)
Consulting fee (714)
Cost of supplies (714)
Covenant not to compete (714)
Distributorship franchise (711)
Exclusive territory (714)
Federal Trade Commission (FTC) (712)
Franchise (710)
Franchise agreement (713)

Franchise application (713)
Franchisee (licensee) (710)
Franchisor (licensor) (710)
FTC franchise notice (713)
FTC franchise rule (712)
Independent contractor (715)
Initial license fee (714)
Joint venture (719)
Joint venture corporation (719)
Joint venture partnership (719)
Joint venturer (719)
Lease fee (714)
License (718)
Licensee (718)
Licensing (718)
Licensor (718)
Processing plant franchise (711)
Quality-control standards (714)
Royalty fee (714)
Service mark (713)
Strategic alliance (720)
Subfranchisor (711)
Termination-at-will clause (718)
Territory (714)
Trade secret (713)
Trademark (713)
Uniform Franchise Offering Circular (UFOC) (713)
Wrongful termination (718)

Critical Legal Thinking Cases

40.1 Agency Re/Max International, Inc. (Re/Max) is the owner and licensor of Re/Max trademarks and sells Re/Max franchises. Re/Max, through a subfranchisor, granted a franchise to Re/Max Midtown to operate a Re/Max franchise in Illinois (the franchisee). The Re/Max franchise agreement provided that the franchisee was an independent contractor and was not an agent of Re/Max. Nascimento, a licensed real estate sales agent, was hired by the franchisee as an independent contractor. The franchisee had no daily control over Nascimento's activities. He could find and list houses for sale and show houses to prospective buyers, but he was not required to attend any office meetings or to spend time in the office or to work a specific number of hours per week. The franchisee did not provide him with any employment benefits. Nascimento was paid commissions on houses he sold and owed the franchisee a fee for each house sold. Nascimento was to use his own car in showing properties and was to personally purchase insurance on the car.

One of Nascimento's prospective clients was Ana Maria de Oliveira Fernandes. Nascimento gave Fernandes a business card that stated that the franchisee he worked for was an independent contractor. One day while Nascimento was driving Fernandes to look at real estate properties, his car collided with another vehicle and Fernandes was seriously injured. At the time of the accident Nascimento had failed to pay his insurance premium and his insurance coverage had lapsed. Fernandes sued Re/Max, alleging that Nascimento was the actual or apparent agent of Re/Max and therefore that Re/Max was liable to her for her injuries. Re/Max defended, asserting that Nascimento was not its actual or apparent agent. Is Re/Max liable for the automobile accident caused by Nascimento? *Oliveira-Brooks v. Re/Max International*, 865 N.E.2d 252, 2007 Ill. App. Lexis 250 (Appellate Court of Illinois, 2007)

40.2 Tort Liability Southland Corporation (Southland) owns the 7-Eleven trademark and licenses franchisees to operate convenience stores using this trademark. Each franchise is independently owned and operated. The franchise agreement stipulates that the franchisee is an independent contractor who is authorized to make all inventory, employment, and operational decisions for the franchise.

Timothy Cislaw, 17 years old, died of respiratory failure. His parents filed a wrongful death action against the franchisee, a Costa Mesa, California, 7-Eleven franchise store, and Southland, alleging that Timothy's death resulted from his consumption of Djarum Specials (clove cigarettes) sold at the Costa Mesa, California, 7-Eleven franchise store. The Costa Mesa 7-Eleven was franchised to Charles Trujillo and Patricia Colwell-Trujillo. Southland defended, arguing that it was not liable for the alleged tortious conduct of its franchisee because the franchisee was an independent contractor. The plaintiffs alleged that the franchisee was Southland's agent and therefore that Southland was liable for its agent's alleged negligence of selling the clove cigarettes to their son. Was the Costa Mesa franchisee an agent of Southland, thus making Southland liable for the alleged tortious conduct of its franchisee? Does the doctrine of apparent agency apply? Who wins? *Cislaw v. Southland Corporation*, 4 Cal. App.4th 1284, 6 Cal. Rptr.2d 386, 1992 Cal. App. Lexis 375 (Court of Appeal of California, 1992)

40.3 Trademark Ramada Inns, Inc. (Ramada Inns) is a franchisor that licenses franchisees to operate motor hotels using the Ramada Inns trademarks and service marks. The Gadsden Motel Company (Gadsden), a partnership, purchased a motel in Attalla, Alabama, and entered into a franchise agreement with Ramada Inns to operate it as a Ramada Inns motor hotel. Five years later, the motel began receiving poor ratings from Ramada Inns inspectors, and Gadsden fell behind on its monthly franchise fee payments. Despite prodding from Ramada Inns, the motel never met the Ramada Inns operational standards again.

One year later, Ramada Inns properly terminated the franchise agreement, citing quality deficiencies and Gadsden's failure to pay past-due franchise fees. The termination notice directed Gadsden to remove any materials or signs identifying the motel as a Ramada. Gadsden continued using Ramada Inns signage, trademarks, and service marks inside and outside the motel. Ramada Inns sued Gadsden for trademark infringement. Who wins? *Ramada Inns, Inc. v. Gadsden Motel Company*, 804 F.2d 1562, 1986 U.S. App. Lexis 34279 (United States Court of Appeals for the Eleventh Circuit, 1986)

40.4 Termination of a Franchise Kawasaki Motors Corporation (Kawasaki), a Japanese corporation, manufactures motorcycles that it distributes in the United States through its subsidiary, Kawasaki Motors Corporation, U.S.A. (Kawasaki USA). Kawasaki USA is a franchisor that grants franchises to dealerships to sell Kawasaki motorcycles. Kawasaki USA granted the Kawasaki Shop of Aurora, Inc. (Dealer), a franchise to sell Kawasaki motorcycles in Aurora, Illinois. The franchise changed locations twice. Both moves were within the 5-mile exclusive territory granted Dealer in the franchise agreement.

Dealer did not obtain Kawasaki USA's written approval for either move, as required by the franchise agreement. Kawasaki USA acquiesced to the first move but not the second. At the second new location, Dealer also operated Honda and Suzuki motorcycle franchises and was negotiating to operate a Yamaha franchise. The Kawasaki franchise agreement expressly permitted multiline dealerships. Kawasaki USA objected to the second move, asserting that Dealer had not received written approval for the move, as required by the franchise agreement. Evidence showed, however, that the real reason Kawasaki objected to the move was because it did not want its motorcycles to be sold at the same location as other manufacturers' motorcycles. Kawasaki terminated Dealer's franchise. Dealer sued Kawasaki USA for wrongful termination. Who wins? *Kawasaki Shop of Aurora, Inc. v. Kawasaki Motors Corporation, U.S.A.*, 544 N.E.2d 457, 1989 Ill. App. Lexis 1442 (Appellate Court of Illinois, 1989)

40.5 Liability of a Franchisor Domino's Pizza, LLC is a franchisor that grants franchises to independent contractors who own and operate pizza restaurants under the Domino's name. Domino's, as the franchisor, granted a franchise to TDBO, Inc., the franchisee, to operate a franchise restaurant in Gorham, Maine. Domino's and TDBO entered into a franchise agreement that established quality-control, marketing, and operational standards. TDBO owned its own equipment, purchased its supplies, maintained its own records and bank accounts, and hired and determined the wages of its employees. The franchisee paid royalty payments to Domino's. The franchise agreement expressly stated that TDBO was an independent contractor and that Domino's was not liable for TDBO's debts and obligations.

Edward Langen, an employee of TDBO, was driving a vehicle while delivering a Domino's pizza when he negligently caused an accident that injured Paul Rainey, who was riding a motorcycle. Rainey sued Langen, TDBO, and Domino's, alleging negligence and vicarious liability. Domino's made a motion for summary judgment, asserting that it was not vicariously liable for its franchisee's negligence. Can Domino's be held vicariously liable for the alleged negligence of its franchisee? *Rainey v. Domino's Pizza LLC*, 998 A.2d 342 (Supreme Judicial Court of Maine, 2010)

Ethics Case

40.6 Ethics Case Southland Corporation (Southland) owns the 7-Eleven trademark and licenses franchisees throughout the country to operate 7-Eleven stores. The franchise agreement provides for fees to be paid to Southland by each franchisee based on a percentage of gross profits. In return, franchisees receive a lease of premises, a license to use the 7-Eleven trademark and trade secrets, advertising merchandise, and bookkeeping assistance. Vallerie Campbell purchased an existing 7-Eleven store in Fontana, California, and became a Southland franchisee. The franchise was designated number #13974 by Southland. As part of the purchase, Campbell applied to the state of California for transfer of the beer and wine license from the prior owner. Southland also executed the application. California approved the transfer and issued the license to "Campbell Vallerie Southland number #13974."

An employee of Campbell's store sold beer to Jesse Lewis Cope, a minor who was allegedly intoxicated at the time. After drinking the beer, Cope drove his vehicle and struck another vehicle. Two occupants of the other vehicle, Denise Wickham and Tyrone Crosby, were severely injured, and a third occupant, Cedrick Johnson, was killed. Johnson (through his parents), Wickham, and Crosby sued Southland—but not Campbell—to recover damages. Is Southland legally liable for the tortious acts of its franchisee? Is it morally responsible? *Wickham v. The Southland Corporation*, 168 Cal. App.3d 49, 213 Cal. Rptr. 825, 1985 Cal. App. Lexis 2070 (Court of Appeal of California, 1985)

Note

1. 116 CFR Section 436.

CHAPTER 41

Securities Law and Investor Protection

Henry R. Cheeseman

NEW YORK STOCK EXCHANGE
This is the home of the New York Stock Exchange (NYSE) in New York City. The NYSE, nicknamed the Big Board, is the premier stock exchange in the world. It lists the stocks and securities of approximately 3,000 of the world's largest companies for trading. The NYSE dates to 1792, when several stockbrokers met under a buttonwood tree on Wall Street. The NYSE is located at 11 Wall Street, and the site has been designated a National Historic Landmark. The NYSE is now operated by NYSE Euronext, which was formed when the NYSE merged with the fully electronic stock exchange Euronext.

Learning Objectives

After studying this chapter, you should be able to:

41.1 List and describe major federal securities laws.

41.2 Define a *security*.

41.3 Define an *initial public offering* and describe how securities are registered with the Securities and Exchange Commission.

41.4 Define an *emerging growth company (EGC)* and describe the requirements for issuing securities as such.

41.5 Describe the requirements for issuing securities pursuant to SEC Regulation A.

41.6 Define a *well-known seasoned investor* and describe how securities can be issued pursuant to a shelf registration.

41.7 List and describe offerings that are exempt from registration, such as the nonissuer, intrastate, private placement, and small offering exemptions.

41.8 Define *crowdfunding* and describe how capital is raised using crowdfunding.

41.9 Define *initial coin offering (ICO)* and *security token offering (STO)* and describe how they are regulated by federal securities laws.

41.10 Describe civil and criminal penalties for violating the Securities Act of 1933.

41.11 Describe how trading in securities is regulated by federal securities laws.

41.12 Define *insider trading* and describe the liability for engaging in insider trading.

41.13 Describe short-swing profit transactions that violate securities laws.

41.14 Describe how state laws regulate securities transactions.

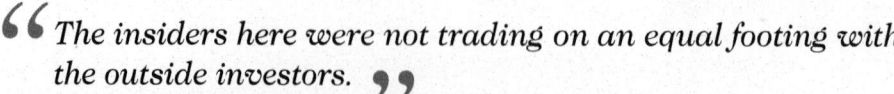

> *"The insiders here were not trading on an equal footing with the outside investors."*
>
> —*Sterry Waterman, Circuit Judge*
> *Securities and Exchange Commission v. Texas Gulf Sulphur Company*
> *401 F.2d 833, 1968 U.S. App. Lexis 5797 (1968)*

Introduction to Securities Law and Investor Protection

He will lie, sir, with such volubility that you would think truth were a tool.

William Shakespeare
All's Well That Ends Well (1604)

Prior to the 1920s and 1930s, the securities markets in this country were not regulated by the federal government. Securities were issued and sold to investors with little, if any, disclosure. Fraud in these transactions was common. To respond to this lack of regulation, in the early 1930s Congress enacted federal securities statutes, including the *Securities Act of 1933* and the *Securities Exchange Act of 1934,* to regulate the securities markets. The federal securities statutes were designed to require disclosure of information to investors, provide for the regulation of securities issues and trading, and prevent fraud. In 2012, Congress enacted the *Jumpstart Our Business Startups Act* (*JOBS Act*) to make it easier for smaller businesses to raise capital.

Today, many securities are issued over the internet and through crowdfunding sites. These e-securities transactions are subject to federal regulation.

This chapter discusses federal securities laws, public and private securities offerings, e-securities transactions, securities fraud and insider trading, and investor protection.

Securities Law

41.1 List and describe major federal securities laws.

The federal and state governments have enacted statutes that regulate the issuance and trading of securities. These are referred to collectively as **securities law**. The primary purpose of these laws is to promote full disclosure to investors and to prevent fraud in the issuance and trading of securities. These federal and state statutes are enforced by federal and state regulatory authorities, respectively.

The following feature discusses major federal securities statutes.

Landmark Laws

Federal Securities Laws

Following the stock market crash of 1929, Congress enacted a series of statutes designed to regulate securities markets. These **federal securities statutes** are designed to require disclosure to investors and to prevent securities fraud. Three of the primary securities statutes that have been enacted by the federal government to regulate securities are:

- **Securities Act of 1933.** The Securities Act of 1933 is a federal statute that primarily regulates the *issuance of securities* by companies and other businesses.[1] This act applies to the original issue of securities, including initial public offerings (IPOs) by new public companies and the sale of new securities by existing companies. The primary purpose of this act is to require full and honest disclosure of information to investors at the time of the issuance of the securities. The act also prohibits fraud during the sale of issued securities. Securities that are issued online are regulated by the 1933 act.

- **Securities Exchange Act of 1934** The Securities Exchange Act of 1934 is a federal statute designed primarily to prevent fraud in the *subsequent trading* of securities.[2] This act has been applied to prohibit insider trading and other frauds in the purchase and sale of securities in the after markets, such as trading on securities exchanges and other purchases and sales of securities. The act also requires continuous reporting—annual reports, quarterly reports, and other reports—to investors and to the Securities and Exchange Commission (SEC). Securities that are sold online and on electronic stock exchanges are regulated by the 1934 act.
- **Jumpstart Our Business Startups Act (JOBS Act).** In 2012, Congress enacted the Jumpstart Our Business Startups Act (JOBS Act).[3] The purpose of this federal statute is to make it easier for start-up companies to raise capital through IPOs. The law also mandates that the SEC adopt rules to allow small businesses to use crowdfunding to raise capital using online equity marketplaces, amends several of the exemptions from registration, and permits the use of public and internet advertising in many circumstances.

Securities and Exchange Commission

The Securities Exchange Act of 1934 created the **Securities and Exchange Commission (SEC)**, a federal administrative agency that is empowered to administer federal securities law. The SEC is an agency composed of five members who are appointed by the president. The major responsibilities of the SEC are:

- Adopting **rules and regulations** that further the purpose of the federal securities statutes. These rules have the force of law.
- Investigating alleged securities violations and bringing enforcement actions against suspected violators. These enforcement actions may include recommendations of criminal prosecution. Criminal prosecutions of violations of federal securities laws are brought by the U.S. Department of Justice.
- Bringing a civil action to recover monetary damages from violators of securities laws. A **whistle-blower bounty program** allows a person who provides information that leads to a successful SEC action in which more than $1 million is recovered to receive 10 to 30 percent of the money collected.
- Regulating the activities of securities brokers and advisors. This includes registering brokers and advisors and taking enforcement action against those who violate securities laws.

Most public company documents are now available online. The SEC requires both foreign and domestic companies to file documents using **EDGAR**, the SEC's electronic data and records system. Anyone can access and download this information.

Securities and Exchange Commission (SEC)
The federal administrative agency that is empowered to administer federal securities laws. The SEC can adopt rules and regulations to interpret and implement federal securities laws.

WEB EXERCISE
Go to the website of the Securities and Exchange Commission, at **www.sec.gov**. Click on "About" and then click on "What We Do" and read the introduction.

EDGAR
The electronic data and record system of the Securities and Exchange Commission (SEC).

Reporting Companies

The Securities Exchange Act of 1934 requires certain companies, called **reporting companies**, to file periodic reports with the SEC and to their shareholders. These include **annual reports (Form 10-K)** and **quarterly reports (Form 10-Q)**. **Monthly reports**, also called **current reports (Form 8-K)**, must be filed within 10 days of the end of the month in which a material event (such as a merger) occurs.

A reporting company includes companies whose securities (equity or debt) are listed on a national securities exchange, and issuers who have made a registered offering of securities (equity or debt) under the Securities Act of 1933. Reporting companies also include companies whose total assets exceed $10 million and whose equity securities of record are held by either 2,000 persons or 500 persons who are not accredited investors. Shares held by persons who received them pursuant to employment compensation plans are excluded from this calculation.

WEB EXERCISE
Visit the website of EDGAR at **www.sec.gov/edgar.shtml**. Click on "About EDGAR." Read the first two paragraphs of "Important Information About EDGAR."

reporting company
A company that must file periodic reports with the Securities and Exchange Commission.

Securities Exchanges

The **New York Stock Exchange (NYSE)** is operated by **NYSE Euronext**, which was formed when the NYSE merged with the fully electronic stock exchange Euronext. The NYSE lists the stocks and securities of approximately 3,000 of

New York Stock Exchange (NYSE)
A stock exchange that is operated by NYSE Euronext, which was formed when the New York Stock Exchange (NYSE) merged with the fully electronic stock exchange Euronext.

the world's largest companies for trading. These companies include Walmart Inc.; Ford Motor Company; IBM Corporation; Twitter, Inc.; Citigroup Inc.; Oracle Corporation; General Electric Company; Pfizer Inc.; Chevron Corporation; The Coca-Cola Company; United States Steel Corporation; AT&T Inc.; Alibaba Group Holdings Ltd.; China Mobile Ltd.; Toyota Motor Corp.; and others.

The **National Association of Securities Dealers Automated Quotation System (NASDAQ)** is an *electronic stock market*. NASDAQ has the largest trading volume of any securities exchange in the world, trading the stocks and securities of more than 3,000 U.S. and foreign companies. These companies include Microsoft Corporation; Apple Inc.; Starbucks Corporation; Amazon.com, Inc.; PepsiCo, Inc.; Alphabet Inc.; Facebook, Inc.; Intel Corporation; Baidu, Inc.; Amgen Inc.; Cisco Systems, Inc.; and others. NASDAQ, located in New York City, owns interests in electronic stock exchanges around the world.

National Association of Securities Dealers Automated Quotation System (NASDAQ)
An electronic stock market.

There are many other important stock exchanges throughout the world, including the Japan Exchange Group, Shanghai Stock Exchange, Euronext, London Stock Exchange, Hong Kong Stock Exchange, Deutsche Börse, Toronto Stock Exchange, National Stock Exchange of India, Shenzhen Stock Exchange, Bombay Stock Exchange, and Korea Exchange.

E-Securities Transactions

The internet has become an important vehicle for the disclosure of information about companies, online trading, and the public issuance of securities. Securities—stocks and bonds—are purchased and sold online worldwide by millions of persons and businesses each day. Individuals and businesses can open accounts at online stockbrokers, such as Charles Schwab, Ameritrade, and others, and freely trade securities and manage their accounts online. **Electronic securities transactions**, or **e-securities transactions**, are common in issuing stocks and other securities to the public, trading in securities, filing information with the SEC, and disseminating information to investors. Securities laws generally permit the use of the internet, websites, social media, and other types of electronic media in the issuance and trading of securities and the dissemination of information.

Definition of *Security*

41.2 Define a *security*.

Congress has enacted the Securities Act of 1933, the Securities Exchange Act of 1934, and several other securities statutes to regulate the issuance and sale of securities. For these federal statutes to apply, however, a **security** must first be found. Federal securities laws define securities as follows:

security
(1) An interest or instrument that is common stock, preferred stock, a bond, a debenture, or a warrant; (2) an interest or instrument that is expressly mentioned in securities acts; or (3) an investment contract.

investment contract
A flexible standard for defining a security.

***Howey* test**
A test stating that an arrangement is an investment contract if there is an investment of money by an investor in a common enterprise and the investor expects to make profits based on the sole or substantial efforts of the promoter or others.

- **Common securities.** Interests or instruments that are commonly known as securities are **common securities**.

  Examples Common stock, preferred stock, bonds, debentures, and warrants are common securities.

- **Statutorily defined securities.** Interests or instruments that are expressly mentioned in securities acts are **statutorily defined securities**.

  Examples The securities acts specifically define preorganization subscription agreements; interests in oil, gas, and mineral rights; and deposit receipts for foreign securities as securities.

- **Investment contracts.** ***Investment contract*** is a statutory term that permits courts to define these contracts as securities. The courts apply the ***Howey* test**[4] to determine whether an arrangement is an investment contract and therefore a security. Under this test, an arrangement is considered an investment contract if there is an investment of money by an investor in a common enterprise and the investor expects to make profits based on the sole or substantial efforts of the promoter or others.

Examples A limited partnership interest is an investment contract because the limited partner expects to make money based on the effort of the general partners. Pyramid schemes in which persons give money to a promoter who promises them a high rate of return on their investment are investment contracts because the investors expect to make money from the efforts of the promoter.

CONCEPT SUMMARY

DEFINITION OF *SECURITY*

Type of Security	Definition
Common securities	Interests or instruments that are commonly known as securities, such as common stock, preferred stock, debentures, and warrants.
Statutorily defined securities	Interests and instruments that are expressly mentioned in securities acts as being securities, such as interests in oil, gas, and mineral rights.
Investment contracts	A flexible standard for defining a security. Under the *Howey* test, a security exists if an investor invests money in a common enterprise and expects to make a profit from the significant efforts of others.

Mutual funds sell shares to the public, make investments in stocks and bonds for the long term, and are restricted from investing in risky investments. Because mutual funds are sold to the public, they must be registered with the SEC.

Initial Public Offering (IPO)

41.3 Define an *initial public offering* and describe how securities are registered with the Securities and Exchange Commission.

The Securities Act of 1933 primarily regulates the issuance of securities by corporations, limited partnerships, and companies. **Section 5 of the Securities Act of 1933** requires securities offered to the *public* by use of the mail, internet, or any facility of interstate commerce to be **registered** with the SEC by means of a registration statement and an accompanying prospectus.

A business or party selling securities to the public is called an **issuer**. An issuer may be a new company (e.g., Facebook) that is selling securities to the public for the first time. This is referred to as **going public**. Or the issuer may be an established company (e.g., General Motors Corporation) that sells a new security to the public. The issuance of new securities by an issuer is called an **initial public offering (IPO)**.

Many issuers of securities employ **investment bankers**, which are independent securities companies, to sell their securities to the public. Issuers pay a fee to investment bankers for this service.

A company that is contemplating making a public offering of securities may hold discussions with institutional investors to **test the waters** to help the company gauge investor interest in a planned IPO before deciding whether to go forward with it.

Securities Act of 1933
A federal statute that primarily regulates the issuance of securities by corporations, limited partnerships, and associations.

Section 5 of the Securities Act of 1933
A section that requires an issuer to register its securities with the SEC prior to selling them to the public.

initial public offering (IPO)
The sale of securities by an issuer to the public.

Registration Statement

A company that is issuing securities to the public must file a written **registration statement** with the SEC. The general form for registering with the SEC is **Form S-1**. The issuer's lawyer normally prepares the S-1 filing registration statement with the help of the issuer's managers, accountants, underwriters, and other professionals. The registration statement is filed electronically with the SEC.

registration statement
A document that an issuer of securities files with the SEC and that contains required information about the issuer, the securities to be issued, and other relevant information.

A registration statement must contain descriptions of (1) the securities being offered for sale; (2) the registrant's business; (3) the management of the registrant, including compensation, stock options and benefits, and material transactions with the registrant; (4) pending litigation; (5) how the proceeds from the offering will be used; (6) government regulation; (7) the degree of competition in the industry; and (8) any special risk factors. In addition, a registration statement must be accompanied by financial statements certified by certified public accountants.

Registrants do not have to file as an exhibit any document that is incorporated by reference in the filing, but instead are required to provide hyperlinks to the documents incorporated by reference.

Registration statements usually become effective 20 business days after they are filed unless the SEC requires additional information to be disclosed. A new 20-day period begins each time a registration statement is amended. At the registrant's request, the SEC may accelerate the effective date (i.e., not require the registrant to wait 20 days after the last amendment is filed). The date that the registration becomes effective is called the **effective date**.

The SEC does not pass judgment on the merits of the securities offered. It decides only whether the issuer has met the disclosure requirements.

Prospectus

preliminary prospectus
A written disclosure document that must be submitted to the SEC along with the registration statement and given to prospective purchasers of the securities.

A **preliminary prospectus** is a written disclosure document that must be submitted to the SEC along with the registration statement. A preliminary prospectus contains much of the information included in the registration statement. This prospectus is used as a selling tool by the issuer. It is provided to prospective investors to enable them to evaluate the financial risk of an investment. The issuer must make a **final prospectus** (which includes the final price of the securities and any amendments required by the SEC) available to purchasers before or at the time of purchase. The required prospectus must be made available on the SEC website.

A prospectus must contain the following language in capital letters and bold (usually red) type:

> *THESE SECURITIES HAVE NOT BEEN APPROVED OR DISAPPROVED BY THE SECURITIES AND EXCHANGE COMMISSION OR ANY STATE SECURITIES COMMISSION, NOR HAS THE SECURITIES AND EXCHANGE COMMISSION OR ANY STATE SECURITIES COMMISSION PASSED UPON THE ACCURACY OR ADEQUACY OF THIS PROSPECTUS. ANY REPRESENTATION TO THE CONTRARY IS A CRIMINAL OFFENSE.*

Initial Public Offerings

WEB EXERCISE
Select several of the listed companies and check to see what their current share price is versus the price at which they went public.

The following are examples of companies that have gone public. The public exchange and the ticker symbol of each company is listed in parentheses. Facebook, Inc., a social media and technology company (NASDAQ FB); General Motors Company, a large automobile manufacturer (NYSE GM); Tesla Inc., an American electric vehicle and lean energy company (NASDAQ TSLA); Dropbox, Inc., a file hosting and cloud storage service (NASDAQ DBX); and Levi Strauss & Co., a venerable American clothing company famous for making denim jeans (NYSE LEVI).

E-Public Offerings

Companies are now issuing shares of stock over the internet. This includes companies that are making **electronic initial public offerings**, or **e-initial public offerings (e-IPOs)**, by selling stock to the public for the first time. E-securities offerings provide an efficient way to distribute securities to the public.

Example When Google Inc., the web-based search engine, went public, it conducted its IPO online.

Direct Public Offering (DPO)

A **direct public offering (DPO)** occurs when a company sells its securities directly to the public without using an underwriter, investment banker, broker-dealer, or another intermediary. The company thus avoids many of the costs of an initial public offering. DPOs are attractive to companies with a loyal and established customer base. Many DPOs do not have to be registered with the SEC because they qualify for an exemption from registration. The company may choose to list the shares on a stock exchange at a later date. A company may also conduct a DPO by initially listing its shares on a stock exchange and authorizing the exchange to determine the opening price and accept the buy orders.

direct public offering (DPO)
A security offering in which a company sells its securities directly to the public without using an underwriter, investment banks, broker-dealers, or other intermediaries.

Example Spotify Technology S.A., a Swedish music streaming and media service, conducted a DPO by listing its shares on the New York Stock Exchange (NYSE SPOT). Slack Technologies, Inc., a corporate messaging app developer, also conducted a DPO by listing its shares on the NYSE (NYSE WORK).

Cross-Border IPO

Foreign companies go public on stock exchanges in their own countries. Often, they subsequently list their shares on other stock exchanges as well. Companies based in foreign jurisdictions can raise capital on U.S. stock exchanges in a **cross-border IPO**. Thus, the company is listed both in its domestic country as well as on a U.S. stock exchange. Many cross-border IPOs are made on NASDAQ. Companies based in China, the United Kingdom, Canada, and Israel make the most cross-border IPOs.

cross-border IPO
An initial public offering made in the United States by a company based in a foreign country.

Sale of Unregistered Securities

The sale of securities that should have been registered with the SEC but were not violates the Securities Act of 1933. Investors who have purchased such **unregistered securities** can rescind their purchase and recover damages. The U.S. government can impose criminal penalties on any person who willfully violates the Securities Act of 1933.

Example Suppose Space Corporation sold shares of its stock to the public at $8 per share. Within months, the price of the stock dropped to $2. Space Corporation did not register its stock offering with the SEC. Because there has been a sale of unregistered securities, the purchasers can rescind their purchase of the stock and get their money back (in the unlikely case that the seller can be recovered from). If the management of Space Corporation willfully did not register the securities, the U.S. government can file a criminal lawsuit to seek criminal penalties.

Emerging Growth Company

41.4 Define an *emerging growth company (EGC)* and describe the requirements for issuing securities as such.

The **Jumpstart Our Business Startups Act (JOBS Act)** is a federal statute that is designed to make it easier for start-up companies to raise capital through securities offerings. The JOBS Act creates a new category of issuer under federal securities laws called the **emerging growth company (EGC)**. Private companies that meet certain requirements can go public using the less restrictive EGC method rather than using a traditional IPO. EGC status is often referred to as the **IPO on-ramp**. Most companies that are planning an initial public offering of securities qualify to do so under the new EGC rules.

The Jumpstart Our Business Startups Act (JOBS Act)
A federal statute that makes it easier for start-up companies to raise capital through securities offerings.

emerging growth company (EGC)
A class of public company created by the JOBS Act that may issue securities pursuant to less restrictive rules than a traditional initial public offering. Commonly referred to as the *IPO on-ramp*.

For an existing company to qualify as an EGC to conduct an IPO, the company must (1) have less than $1.07 billion in annual gross revenue in its most recently completed fiscal year (the dollar amount to be indexed for inflation every five years), (2) have issued no more than $1 billion in debt, and (3) have less than $700 million in stock outstanding after an IPO.

By qualifying as an EGC, the company is exempt from a broad range of requirements typically imposed on companies pursuing a traditional IPO. The main benefits for qualifying as an EGC are the following:

confidential draft registration statement
A registration statement that may be filed by an emerging growth company (EGC) with the Securities and Exchange Commission that remains confidential unless the company chooses to go forward with a public offering.

- An EGC may submit a **confidential draft registration statement** for a confidential, non-public staff review by the SEC. This confidential filing allows companies to withdraw a proposed IPO without having to disclose confidential business information.
- An EGC may communicate with institutional investors ahead of a proposed offering to test the waters to help the company gauge investor interest before deciding whether to go forward with the offering.
- An EGC needs to provide only two years of audited financial statements when filing an IPO registration to issue securities, not the three years of audited financial statements that would be required in a traditional IPO.
- Qualification allows EGCs to file for registration of securities using a streamlined process and with less disclosure of financial information than is required for non-EGC IPOs.

The JOBS Act helps EGCs to decide whether to go public and significantly reduces the costs if they choose to do so. A company can retain EGC status for only five years after its IPO. At that time, the company becomes subject to the full reporting requirements of the SEC. EGCs now dominate the IPO market, with more than 80 percent of private companies that now go public doing so as EGCs.

Examples Companies that have gone public as emerging growth companies include Twitter, Inc., an online social networking and microblogging service (NYSE TWTR); Uber Technologies, Inc., a major ride-sharing app (NYSE UBER); and Pinterest, Inc., a social media web and mobile application company (NYSE PINS).

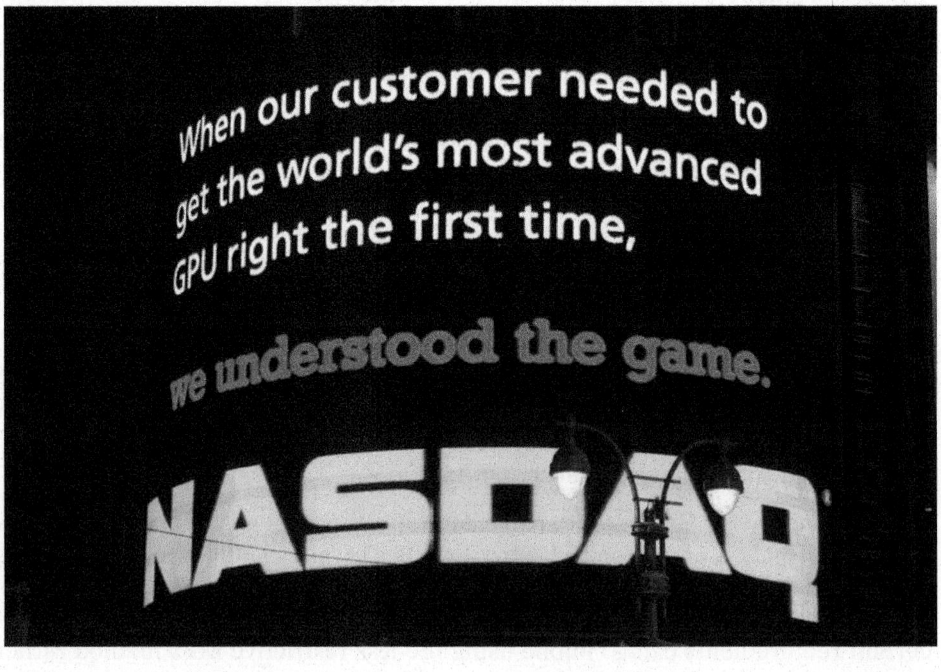

Henry R. Cheeseman

NASDAQ
NASDAQ is the world's largest electronic securities exchange. It lists more than 3,000 U.S. and global companies and corporations.

Regulation A Securities Offering

41.5 Describe the requirements for issuing securities pursuant to SEC Regulation A.

Recognizing that not all companies want to conduct a full registration IPO but would like to raise a limited amount of money from selling securities to the public, the SEC adopted Regulation A to accommodate smaller securities offerings. **SEC Regulation A** is an exemption from full registration or emerging growth company registration that allows entrepreneurs, mature start-ups, midsize companies, and even large companies to raise a limited amount of equity or debt capital from the public and to publicly and electronically advertise their offerings. A Regulation A offering is often referred to as a **limited public offering**.

Regulation A can be used by both nonreporting and reporting companies. Regulation A offerings are particularly attractive to reporting companies that are not listed on national exchanges. Insiders can sell their shares in a Regulation A offering. Regulation A cannot be used by foreign issuers, except those from Canada.

Because it is a public offering, a Regulation A offering is often referred to as a **mini-IPO**. Regulation A is divided into two tiers. An issuer can choose to offer securities using either one of the following:

- **Tier 1** permits the issuer to raise up to $20 million in a 12-month period. There is no limit on the amount of securities that any person can purchase of the issue.
- **Tier 2** permits an issuer to raise up to $75 million in a 12-month period. There is no limit on the amount of securities that an accredited investor can purchase, but a nonaccredited investor—sometimes referred to as a *main street investor*—can only purchase securities up to 10 percent of their annual income or net worth per year, whichever is greater.

Issuers that conduct offerings pursuant to Regulation A are required to electronically file an **offering statement** with the SEC. This statement requires less disclosure than a registration statement and is less costly to prepare. The issuer must provide potential investors with an **offering circular** prior to the purchase of securities, and with a final prospectus after being qualified by the SEC. Purchasers of Regulation A securities may sell their shares without limitation. Regulation A offerings are subject to the antifraud provisions of the federal securities laws.

Prior to making a Regulation A offering or submitting Regulation A offering materials to the SEC, the proposed issuer can test the waters to see whether there is sufficient investor interest to proceed with a Regulation A offering. This can be done by soliciting indications of interest from potential investors. If sufficient interest exists, the company will probably proceed with the offering, but if sufficient interest does not exist, the company will probably not make the offering.

There are three primary reasons that companies might use Regulation A offerings: (1) purchasers of Regulation A securities may immediately resell them and do not have to hold them for a period of time before reselling; (2) companies can offer shares to both accredited and nonaccredited investors; and (3) companies may engage in public advertising campaigns to market and promote the offering. Some Regulation A offerings are done through online equity crowdfunding platforms, which handle the logistics of the offering and accept investments online.

The following feature discusses a small company offering registration.

SEC Regulation A
A regulation that permits an issuer to sell securities to the public pursuant to a simplified registration process. Tier 1 permits an issuer to sell up to $20 million of securities within a 12-month period. Tier 2 permits an issuer to sell up to $50 million of securities within a 12-month period. Often referred to as a *limited public offering or mini-IPO*.

offering statement
A statement that an issuer that is issuing securities pursuant to Regulation A must file with the SEC.

Small Company Offering Registration (SCOR)
A method for small companies to sell up to $1 million of securities during a 12-month period to the public by using a question-and-answer disclosure form called Form U-7.

WEB EXERCISE
Go to **http://com.ohio.gov/documents/U-7.pdf**. Review this Form U-7 to determine what information an issuer must provide when completing the form.

Business Environment

Small Company Offering Registration

Small businesses often need to raise capital and must find public investors to buy company stock. The SEC has adopted the **Small Company Offering Registration (SCOR)** for corporations and limited liability companies proposing to raise $1 million or less in any 12-month period from a public offering of securities. The SEC requires that a **SCOR form (Form U-7)** be completed by the company and be made available to potential investors. Form U-7 is a question-and-answer disclosure form that small businesses can complete and file without the services of an expensive securities lawyer. Form U-7 doubles as a prospectus.

SCOR form questions require the issuer to develop a business plan that states specific company goals and how it intends to reach them. The SCOR form is available only to domestic businesses. The offering price of the common stock of a SCOR offering may not be less than $5 per share. Although companies using SCOR offerings are exempt from federal registration with the SEC, SCOR requires the offering to be registered with the state. Most states have adopted this form of registration. Most SCOR offerings are sold directly to the public by the issuer.

Well-Known Seasoned Investor

41.6 Define a *well-known seasoned investor* and describe how securities can be issued pursuant to a shelf registration.

well-known seasoned investor (WKSI)
A large company that, if it meets certain requirements, may file a registration statement with the Securities and Exchange Commission that, when it becomes effective, is a shelf registration that permits the company to issue securities to the public during a three-year period without filing a new registration statement for each offering.

exempt securities
Securities that are exempt from registration with the SEC.

The SEC has created a category of issuer called a **well-known seasoned investor (WKSI)**. To qualify as a WKSI, an issuer must have either (1) issued $1 billion of securities in the previous three years or (2) have at least $700 million of outstanding equity securities owned by nonaffiliate investors. For these companies, the SEC permits a **shelf registration** (or shelf offering or shelf prospectus). A shelf offering allows an issuer to register a new issue of security without selling the entire issue at once. A WKSI files the documents for a shelf registration with the SEC and is then permitted in the future to take securities "off the shelf" and sell the securities to the public using multiple offerings over a three-year period without filing a separate prospectus for each offering. A shelf registration allows an issuer to quickly issue securities when they are needed or when market conditions are optimal without waiting for the SEC to review a newly filed registration statement. The underlying reason for allowing shelf registration is that the public has access to substantial historical and current information and financial data about large public companies that qualify to use a shelf registration. A WKSI must keep the information of the shelf prospectus current.

The following feature lists securities that are exempt from registration.

Business Environment

Exempt Securities

Certain securities are exempt from registration with the SEC before being issued. These securities are usually offered by certain institutions, or the securities have certain characteristics that federal laws and the SEC believe do not require SEC oversight when they are issued. Once a security is exempt, it is exempt forever. It does not matter how many times the security is transferred. **Exempt securities** include the following:

- Securities issued by any government in the United States (e.g., municipal bonds issued by city governments)
- Short-term notes and drafts that have a maturity date that does not exceed nine months (e.g., **commercial paper** issued by corporations)
- Securities issued by nonprofit issuers, such as religious institutions, charitable institutions, and colleges and universities
- Securities of financial institutions (e.g., banks, savings associations) that are regulated by the appropriate banking authorities
- Insurance and annuity contracts issued by insurance companies
- Stock dividends and stock splits
- Securities issued in a corporate reorganization in which one security is exchanged for another security

Exempt Transactions

41.7 List and describe offerings that are exempt from registration, such as the nonissuer, intrastate, private placement, and small offering exemptions.

The Securities Act of 1933 primarily regulates the issuance of securities by corporations, limited partnerships, other businesses, and individuals. Pursuant to the Securities Act of 1933 and rules adopted by the SEC, some securities that would otherwise have to be registered with the SEC before being issued (e.g., common stock) are *exempt from registration* with the SEC because the offering meets requirements established by the act and SEC rules. These are called **exempt transactions**. The securities sold pursuant to an exempt transaction do not have to be registered with the SEC.

exempt transaction
An offering of securities that does not have to be registered with the SEC because the offering meets specified requirements established by securities laws and the SEC.

Example An issuer sells common stock to investors. Normally, such an offering would have to be registered with the SEC. If this common stock is sold in an issuance that qualifies as an exempt transaction, however, the sale of the stock does not have to be registered with the SEC before being issued.

Critical Legal Thinking Questions

What is an *exempt transaction*? Why does the government permit securities to be issued without having to register them with the SEC?

Exempt transactions that do not have to be registered with the SEC are subject to the antifraud provisions of the federal securities laws. Therefore, the issuer must provide investors with adequate information, such as annual reports, quarterly reports, proxy statements, and financial statements, even though a registration statement is not required.

The most widely used transaction exemptions include the *nonissuer exemption, intrastate offering exemptions, private placement exemptions*, and *small offering exemption*. These exempt transactions are discussed in the paragraphs that follow.

Nonissuer Exemption

Nonissuers, such as average investors, do not have to file a registration statement prior to reselling securities they have purchased. This **nonissuer exemption** exists because the Securities Act of 1933 exempts from registration those securities transactions not made by an issuer, an underwriter, or a dealer.

nonissuer exemption
An exemption from registration stating that securities transactions not made by an issuer, an underwriter, or a dealer do not have to be registered with the SEC (e.g., normal purchases of securities by investors).

Example An investor who owns shares of Apple Inc. can resell those shares to another investor at any time without having to register with the SEC.

Intrastate Offering Exemptions

Section 3(a)(11) of the Securities Act of 1933 provides that an issue of securities by a local business to local investors in one state is exempt from the registration requirements. There are two different intrastate offering exemptions, one provided by *SEC Rule 147* and another by *SEC Rule 147A*. These are called the **intrastate offering exemptions**. There is no dollar limit on the amount of securities that can be raised and no limit on the number of investors that can purchase securities under either Rule 147 or Rule 147A.

intrastate offering exemptions
Exemptions from registration that permit local businesses to raise capital from local investors without the need to register with the Securities and Exchange Commission. There are two intrastate offering exemptions, one provided under SEC Rule 147 and another under SEC Rule 147A.

SEC Rule 147 **SEC Rule 147** allows an issuer to raise capital from purchasers who are residents of one state without registering the offering with the SEC. Under Rule 147, an issuer can only make offers to in-state residents or to persons who the issuer reasonably believes are in-state residents. This prevents issuers from using general advertising or online advertising that would readily be viewed by out-of-state parties. In order to qualify for a Rule 147 exemption, the following requirements must be met:

SEC Rule 147
Permits an offeror to sell securities to purchasers who are residents of the state of which the issuer is a resident and in which the issuer has its principal place of business and is doing business. Offers and sales may not be made to out-of-state residents.

1. The issuer must be incorporated or organized in the state where it offers and sells securities.
2. The issuer has its principal place of business in the state, which is defined as the location in which the officers, partners, or managers of the entity primarily direct, control, and coordinate its activities.

3. The issuer is "doing business" in the state in which the securities are *offered* and *sold*. The doing business test is satisfied if the issuer meets one of the following four criteria: (a) derives at least 80 percent of its gross revenue within the state, (b) has at least 80 percent of its assets within the state, (c) uses at least 80 percent of the offering's net proceeds within the state, or (d) has the majority of its employees based within the state.
4. The company obtains a written representation from each purchaser providing the residency of that purchaser.

Example If a corporation has its principal place of business in Arizona, is doing business in Arizona, but is incorporated in Nevada, it cannot offer and sell securities under the Rule 147 exemption to residents of Arizona or Nevada.

SEC Rule 147A
Permits an offeror to sell securities to purchasers who are residents of the state in which the issuer has its principal place of business and is doing business. The offeror does not have to be a resident of the state and may use general solicitation and advertising, including by electronic communications. Sales may not be made to out-of-state residents.

SEC Rule 147A **SEC Rule 147A** is a separate intrastate offering exemption than Rule 147. Rule 147A is identical to Rule 147 in that it requires that the issuer's place of business to be in the state in which the securities are to be sold, the issuer must be doing business in that state, and the securities can only be sold to residents of that state. Rule 147A differs from Rule 147 in two important ways. First, Rule 147A allows issuers to use general advertising and online communications to advertise their securities offerings, even if such marketing would be visible to out-of-state residents. Second, the issuer does not have to be a resident of the state in which the securities are sold. This recognizes the reality that corporations and other issuers that have their principal office and primarily do business in one state often choose to incorporate in a different state that has preferred corporation laws (e.g., Delaware, Nevada).

Example A corporation that has its principal place of business in Michigan and is doing business in Michigan, but is incorporated in Delaware, can sell securities to residents of Michigan pursuant to a Rule 147A exemption.

private placement exemptions
Exemptions from registration with the Securities and Exchange Commission of an issue of securities that does not involve a public offering. There are two private placement exemptions, one provided under SEC Rule 506(b) and another under SEC Rule 506(c).

When Rule 147A was adopted, Rule 147 was retained because several states' securities laws were coordinated with the provisions of this rule and not with Rule 147A. Under both 147 and 147A, for six months after issuance, the securities can only be resold to residents of that state. Once the six-month period has passed, the securities may be sold to investors located outside the state of issuance.

Private Placement Exemptions

Section 4(a)(2) of the Securities Act of 1933 provides that an issue of securities that does not involve a public offering is exempt from the registration requirements. The SEC adopted Regulation D, which provides two different **private placement exemptions**, *SEC Rule 506(b)* and *SEC Rule 506(c)*. There is no dollar limit on the amount of securities that can be sold pursuant to these exemptions and no limit on how much each investor can invest. There is no limit on the frequency with which an issuer may use this exemption. Rule 506(b) and Rule 506(c) are discussed in the following paragraphs.

SEC Rule 506(b)
An exemption from registration that permits issuers to raise any amount of capital from an unlimited number of accredited investors and no more than 35 nonaccredited investors without having to register the offering with the SEC. General solicitation of or advertising of the offering to the public is not permitted.

accredited investor
A person, a corporation, a company, an institution, or an organization that meets the net worth, income, asset, position, and other requirements established by the SEC to qualify as an accredited investor.

SEC Rule 506(b) **SEC Rule 506(b)** allows issuers to raise an unlimited amount of money from an unlimited number of *accredited investors* and no more than 35 *unaccredited investors* without having to register the offering with the SEC. An **accredited investor** is defined as follows:

1. Any natural person who has individual net worth or joint net worth with a spouse that exceeds $1 million, to be calculated by excluding the value of the person's primary residence.
2. A natural person with income exceeding $200,000 in each of the two most recent years or joint income with a spouse exceeding $300,000 for those years and a reasonable expectation of the same income level in the current year.

3. A charitable organization, a corporation, a partnership, a trust, or an employee benefit plan with assets exceeding $5 million.
4. A bank, an insurance company, a registered investment company, a business development company, or a small business investment company.
5. Insiders of the issuers, such as directors, executive officers, or general partners of the entity selling the securities.
6. A business in which all the equity owners are accredited investors.

The rationale underlying the private placement exemption is that accredited investors have the sophistication to understand the risk involved with the investment and can also afford to lose their money if the investment fails. Under Rule 506(b), accredited investors self-certify their status by signing a statement that they qualify as an accredited investor.

The law permits no more than 35 **nonaccredited investors** to purchase securities pursuant to a Rule 506(b) private placement exemption. These nonaccredited investors are usually friends and family members of the insiders. Nonaccredited investors must be sophisticated investors, however, either through their own experience and education or through representatives (e.g., accountants, lawyers, business managers). General selling efforts, such as general solicitation of or advertising to the public, are not permitted if there are to be any nonaccredited investors. Thus, an issuer must have had a preexisting relationship with every investor before making an offer to them to invest.

nonaccredited investor
An investor who does not meet the qualifications to be an accredited investor.

SEC Rule 506(c) **SEC Rule 506(c)** is a private placement exemption that allows an issuer to raise an unlimited amount of money from only *accredited investors*; no nonaccredited investors can be sold securities. Rule 506(c) is sometimes referred to as the "accredited investor rule." Issuers must exercise reasonable due diligence and take reasonable steps to verify the accredited investor status of investors claiming to be accredited investors. Self-certification is not permitted. In a Rule 506(c) offering, because there are no nonaccredited investors, an issuer may use public solicitation and advertising, including the internet, websites, social media, and other media, regarding the offering.

SEC Rule 506(c)
An exemption from registration that permits issuers to raise any amount of capital from an unlimited number of accredited investors without having to register the offering with the SEC. General solicitation and advertising of the offering to the public, including using the internet, is permitted.

Many emerging businesses use the private placement exemptions to raise capital. In addition, many large, established companies use this exemption to sell securities, such as bonds, to a single investor or to a very small group of investors, such as pension funds and investment companies.

Small Offering Exemption

SEC Rule 504 of Regulation D provides a **small offering exemption** that exempts from SEC registration the sale of securities not exceeding $10 million during a 12-month period. The securities may be sold to an unlimited number of accredited and unaccredited investors, but general solicitation or advertising to the public is not permitted. A company conducting a security offering under Rule 504 must file a notice with the SEC on **Form D** within 15 days after the first sale of securities. Companies that are already SEC reporting companies cannot use this exemption. Generally, sale of the securities issued pursuant to a Rule 504 offering are restricted securities that cannot be resold for one year.

SEC Rule 504 (small offering exemption)
An exemption from registration that permits the sale of securities not exceeding $5 million during a 12-month period.

Crowdfunding

41.8 Define *crowdfunding* and describe how capital is raised using crowdfunding.

The JOBS Act created a new funding mechanism called **crowdfunding** for entrepreneurs and small businesses to raise small amounts of capital by selling securities to public investors using online portals. Crowdfunding is used by companies that do not want to meet the requirements and expense of issuing

crowdfunding
A process that allows small companies to raise capital up to $1,070,000 during a 12-month period from many small-dollar investors through a public offering using public solicitation, including social media and the internet.

SEC Regulation Crowdfunding (Regulation CF)
A regulation issued by the Securities and Exchange Commission that sets forth the rules for a crowdfunding offering.

securities pursuant to a registered offering and do not qualify for or do not wish to comply with the restrictions of other exemptions from registration.

The following feature discusses crowdfunding, which is an offering that is exempt from registration with the SEC.

Information Technology

Regulation Crowdfunding

Crowdfunding is an evolving method of raising money via the internet to fund businesses and a variety of projects. The SEC adopted **SEC Regulation Crowdfunding**, also called **Regulation CF**, which sets forth the rules for a crowdfunding offering. Crowdfunding offerings are exempt from registration with the SEC. Crowdfunding requires securities of an issuer to be sold online to the public exclusively using an intermediary internet-based **funding portal** or **web platform**. Funding portals must be approved by and register with the SEC. Many crowdfunding portals have launched to fill this role, including Kickstarter, Indiegogo, Patreon, CircleUp, RocketHub, Fundable, Crowdfunder, and Funding Circle. The web platform usually charges about 5 percent of the money raised.

Crowdfunding allows small companies to raise a maximum aggregate amount of $5 million during a 12-month period from many small-dollar investors. The issuer can use one or more crowdfunding offerings to reach the aggregate amount. Individual investors are limited in the amounts they can invest in all Regulation Crowdfunding offerings over the course of a 12-month period. Securities purchased in a crowdfunding transaction cannot be resold for a period of one year except to the issuer of the securities or an accredited investor.

Example UNYQ, a designer and producer of personalized prosthetics, raised $1.5 million through a crowdfunding offering.

An issuer conducting a Regulation Crowdfunding offering must electronically file an offering statement on **Form C** with the SEC before fundraising can begin. The issuer must disclose the name, address, legal status of the business, and its website; the type of security, price of the security, and number of securities offered; the name of the funding portal through which the securities will be sold; the use of proceeds; the risk associated with the investment; and two years of financial information. An issuer can advertise the offering, including using email and social media. The advertised information must be factual and contain the name and link to the funding portal. Non-U.S. companies and registered companies cannot use the crowdfunding exemption.

Donation-based crowdfunding can also be used to raise money for charities and social causes. Many charitable crowdfunding efforts are done to help individuals in need of assistance. Several crowdfunding portals that focus on donation and charitable causes include Causes, Fundly, CrowdRise, GoFundMe, Give, Charitable, and Mighty Cause.

Example Habitat for Humanity Global Village raised $20 million in a crowdfunding campaign.

Initial Coin Offering (ICO) and Security Token Offering (STO)

41.9 Define *initial coin offering (ICO)* and *security token offering (STO)* and describe how they are regulated by federal security laws.

cryptocurrency
A digital currency that works as a medium of exchange and serves as virtual cash.

A **cryptocurrency** is a digital currency that works as a medium of exchange and serves as virtual cash. Bitcoin and Ethereum are examples of cryptocurrencies. Cryptocurrencies can be used to purchase goods, services, investments, or digital assets from sellers willing to accept such currency. Bitcoin and Ethereum are not in themselves considered securities, but rather are electronic mediums of exchange.

Initial Coin Offering (ICO)

initial coin offering (ICO)
The issuance of crypto coins or tokens by an issuer to investors.

utility tokens (utility coins)
Tokens or coins that are issued pursuant to an initial coin offering (ICO), which are then used to purchase goods or services or are held for investment.

Some businesses raise capital through an **initial coin offering (ICO)**. ICO issuers are primarily small start-up companies and persons seeking to raise money to develop new products or services or to expand their business.

In an ICO, the issuer accepts payment from investors in Bitcoin or another cryptocurrency, or in money, and then issues its own crypto coins or tokens to the investors. Investors receive **utility tokens**, also called **utility coins**, which can then be used to purchase goods or services or held for investment. Purchasers of the utility coins are not issued stock in the company and have no equity interest or voting rights. Investors are relying on the increase in the value of the digital coins they have been issued. ICOs are made on the internet and are touted using websites, social media, and other electronic media. ICO issuers, by calling their coins "utility tokens," have argued that their tokens are not securities and are thus exempt from federal securities laws.

In 2020, the SEC issued guidelines wherein it stated that ICOs would be examined to determine whether they were "investment contracts" as defined by the *Howey* test, and therefore securities that were subject to federal securities laws and SEC regulation. In applying this definition, the SEC has found that most ICOs were securities and were therefore subject to securities laws and SEC regulation. The SEC held that merely calling coins "utility tokens" does not remove them from being securities. The SEC has brought a significant number of cyber enforcement actions against ICO issuers for selling unregistered securities.

Security Token Offering (STO)

As an alternative to the ICO, issuers of cryptocurrency offerings began conducting **security token offerings (STOs)**, which are public offerings in which tokenized digital securities, known as **security tokens**, are sold and traded on cryptocurrency exchanges. Unlike ICOs, which have no collateral, STOs provide token holders with some form of ownership or equity over a tangible asset that belongs to the company, either in full or fractionalized. Holders of security tokens are also often given voting rights, rights to the payment of dividends, and other such rights. Simply put, the security tokens provided by STOs are an investment contract in electronic form, powered by blockchain and the smart contract system. STOs are basically tokenized IPOs.

security token offering (STO)
The issuance of tokenized digital securities by an issuer to investors.

security tokens
Tokens that are issued pursuant to a security token offering (STO), which is an investment that can be sold or traded on cryptocurrency markets.

STOs are therefore subject to federal securities laws and SEC regulation. STO issues must either be registered with the SEC or qualify for an exemption from registration. Most STOs qualify for an exemption from registration. Exchanges are being developed on which security token offerings can be traded. Although ICOs will continue to be offered, the STO market is expected to increase substantially. Digital asset securities, sometimes called smart securities, issued pursuant to STOs, provide safer investment environments.

Liability for Violations of the Securities Act of 1933

41.10 Describe civil and criminal penalties for violating the Securities Act of 1933.

Various provisions of the Securities Act of 1933 impose civil and criminal penalties on parties who violate the act or rules and regulations adopted thereunder. The provisions that impose civil and criminal liability are discussed in the following paragraphs.

Civil Liability: Section 11 of the Securities Act of 1933

Private parties who have been injured by certain registration statement violations by an issuer or others may bring a **civil action** against the violator under **Section 11 of the Securities Act of 1933**. Plaintiffs may recover monetary damages when a registration statement on its effective date misstates or omits a material fact. Civil liability under Section 11 is imposed on those who (1) defraud investors intentionally or (2) are negligent in not discovering the fraud. Thus, the issuer, certain corporate officers (e.g., chief executive officer, chief financial officer, chief accounting officer), directors, signers of the registration statement, underwriters, and experts (e.g., accountants who certify financial statements and lawyers who issue legal opinions that are included in a registration statement) may be liable.

Section 11 of the Securities Act of 1933
A provision of the Securities Act of 1933 that imposes civil liability on persons who intentionally defraud investors by making misrepresentations or omissions of material facts in the registration statement or who are negligent for not discovering the fraud.

due diligence defense
A defense to a Section 11 action that, if proven, makes the defendant not liable.

All defendants except the issuer may assert a **due diligence defense** against the imposition of Section 11 liability. If this defense is proven, the defendant is not liable. To establish a due diligence defense, the defendant must prove that after reasonable investigation, he or she had reasonable grounds to believe and did believe that, at the time the registration statement became effective, the statements contained therein were true and there was no omission of material facts.

Civil Liability: Section 12 of the Securities Act of 1933

Section 12 of the Securities Act of 1933
A provision of the Securities Act of 1933 that imposes civil liability on any person who violates the provisions of Section 5 of the act.

Private parties who have been injured by certain securities violations may bring a civil action against the violator under **Section 12 of the Securities Act of 1933**. Violations include selling securities pursuant to an unwarranted exemption and making misrepresentations concerning the offer or sale of securities. The purchaser's remedy for a violation of Section 12 is either to rescind the purchase or to sue for damages.

Example Technology Inc., a corporation, issues securities to investors without qualifying for any of the exempt transactions permitted under the Securities Exchange Act. The securities decrease in value. In this example, the issuer has issued unregistered securities to the public. The investors can sue the issuer to rescind the purchase agreement and get their money back, or they can sue and recover monetary damages.

Government Actions for Violations of the Securities Act of 1933

The U.S. government may bring actions against those who violate the provisions of the Securities Act of 1933. These actions including the following:

- **SEC Actions.** The SEC may take the following actions against parties who violate the Securities Act of 1933. The SEC may (1) issue a **consent decree** whereby a defendant agrees not to violate securities laws in the future but does not admit to having violated securities laws in the past; (2) bring an action in U.S. district court to obtain an **injunction** to stop challenged conduct; and (3) request that the court grant ancillary relief, such as *disgorgement of profits* by the defendant.
- **Criminal Liability.** **Section 24 of the Securities Act of 1933** imposes *criminal liability* on any person who *willfully* violates either the act or the rules and regulations adopted thereunder.[5] A violator may be fined, imprisoned, or both. Criminal actions are brought by the Department of Justice. There is a six-year statute of limitations for criminal prosecution of violations of the Securities Act of 1933.

Section 24 of the Securities Act of 1933
A provision of the Securities Act of 1933 that imposes criminal liability on any person who willfully violates the act, or the rules or regulations adopted thereunder.

Trading in Securities

41.11 Describe how trading in securities is regulated by federal securities laws.

Securities Exchange Act of 1934
A federal statute that primarily regulates trading in securities.

Unlike the Securities Act of 1933, which regulates the original issuance of securities, the **Securities Exchange Act of 1934** primarily regulates *subsequent trading*. The act contains provisions that assess civil and criminal liability on violators of the 1934 act and rules and regulations adopted thereunder.

Section 10(b) and Rule 10b-5

Section 10(b) of the Securities Exchange Act of 1934
A provision of the Securities Exchange Act of 1934 that prohibits the use of manipulative and deceptive devices in the purchase or sale of securities in contravention of the rules and regulations prescribed by the SEC.

Section 10(b) of the Securities Exchange Act of 1934 is one of the most important sections in the 1934 act.[6] Section 10(b) prohibits the use of manipulative and deceptive devices in contravention of the rules and regulations prescribed by the SEC. Pursuant to its rule-making authority, the SEC has adopted **SEC Rule 10b-5**,[7] which provides the following:

> *It shall be unlawful for any person, directly or indirectly, by use of any means or instrumentality of interstate commerce or of the mails, or of any facility of any national securities exchange,*
> a. *to employ any device, scheme, or artifice to defraud,*
> b. *to make any untrue statement of a material fact or to omit to state a material fact necessary in order to make the statements made, in light of the circumstances under which they were made, not misleading, or*
> c. *to engage in any act, practice, or course of business that operates or would operate as a fraud or deceit upon any person, in connection with the purchase or sale of any security.*

SEC Rule 10b-5
A rule adopted by the SEC to clarify the reach of Section 10(b) against deceptive and fraudulent activities in the purchase and sale of securities.

All transfers of securities, whether they are made on a stock exchange, in the over-the-counter market, in a private sale, or in connection with a merger, are subject to this rule. Only conduct involving ***scienter*** (intentional conduct) violates Section 10(b) and Rule 10b-5. Negligent conduct is not a violation.

scienter
Intentional conduct. *Scienter* is required for a violation of Section 10(b) and Rule 10b-5 to occur.

Civil Liability: Section 10(b) of the Securities Exchange Act of 1934

Although Section 10(b) and Rule 10b-5 do not expressly provide for a private right of action, courts have *implied* such a right. Generally, a private plaintiff may bring a *civil action* and seek rescission of the securities contract or to recover damages (e.g., disgorgements of the illegal profits by the defendants) where there has been intentional conduct that violates Section 10(b) and rules adopted by the SEC. Private securities fraud claims must be brought within two years after discovery or five years after the violation occurs, whichever is shorter.

Government Actions for Violations of the Securities Exchange Act of 1934

The U.S. government may bring actions against those who violate the provisions of the Securities Exchange Act of 1934. These actions including the following:

- **SEC Civil Actions.** The SEC may investigate suspected violations of the Securities Exchange Act of 1934 and of the rules and regulations adopted thereunder. The SEC may enter into *consent decrees* with defendants, seek *injunctions* in U.S. district court, and seek court orders requiring defendants to *disgorge* illegally gained profits. The **Insider Trading Sanctions Act**[8] permits the SEC to obtain a **civil penalty** of up to three times the illegal profits gained, or up to three times the losses avoided on insider trading. The fine is payable to the U.S. Treasury.
- **Criminal Liability. Section 32 of the Securities Exchange Act of 1934** makes it a criminal offense to willfully violate the provisions of the act or the rules and regulations adopted thereunder,[9] or to willfully and knowingly make or cause to be made any false or misleading statement in any application, report, or other document required to be filed with the SEC pursuant to the act or any rule or regulation adopted thereunder. A person who willfully violates the Securities Exchange Act of 1934 can be fined, imprisoned, or both. A corporation or another entity may be fined. There is a six-year statute of limitations for criminal prosecution of violations of the Securities Exchange Act of 1934.

Insider Trading Sanctions Act
A federal statute that permits the SEC to obtain a civil penalty of up to three times the illegal benefits received from insider trading.

Section 32 of the Securities Exchange Act of 1934
A provision of the Securities Exchange Act of 1934 that imposes criminal liability on any person who willfully violates the 1934 act, or the rules or regulations adopted thereunder.

Insider Trading

41.12 Define *insider trading* and describe the liability for engaging in insider trading.

One of the most important purposes of Section 10(b) and Rule 10b-5 is to prevent insider trading and tipper-tippee trading in securities based on the use of material nonpublic information available to insiders that is sometimes made available to tippees. Insider trading and tipper-tippee trading are discussed in the following paragraphs.

Insider Trading

insider trading
Trading that occurs when an insider makes a profit by personally purchasing shares of a corporation prior to public release of favorable information or by selling shares of a corporation prior to the public disclosure of unfavorable information.

Insider trading occurs when a company employee or company advisor uses material nonpublic information to make a profit by trading in the securities of the company. This practice is considered illegal because it allows insiders to take advantage of the investing public.

In the ***Matter of Cady, Roberts & Company***,[10] the SEC announced that the duty of an insider who possesses material nonpublic information is either to (1) abstain from trading in the securities of the company or (2) disclose the information to the person on the other side of the transaction before the insider purchases or sells the securities.

Section 10(b) insiders
(1) Officers, directors, and employees at all levels of a company; (2) lawyers, accountants, consultants, and agents and representatives who are hired by the company on a temporary and nonemployee basis to provide services or work to the company; and (3) others who owe a fiduciary duty to the company.

For purposes of Section 10(b) and Rule 10b-5, **Section 10(b) insiders** are defined as (1) officers, directors, and employees at all levels of a company; (2) lawyers, accountants, consultants, and agents and representatives who are hired by the company on a temporary and nonemployee basis to provide services or work to the company; and (3) others who owe a fiduciary duty to the company.

Example A corporation has its annual audit conducted by an independent certified public accounting (CPA) firm. The accounting firm provides the results of its audit to Bianca, the chief financial officer (CFO) of the corporation. The results show that company profits are up substantially. This is material nonpublic information until the results are made public. If Bianca, an insider, purchases stock in the corporation before the financial results are made public, she is liable for insider trading.

Example If in the prior example, an auditor of the CPA firm purchases stock in the audited corporation before the financial information is made public, he is an insider in possession of nonpublic information and is liable for insider trading.

Tipper-Tippee Liability

tipper
A person who discloses material nonpublic information to another person.

tippee
A person who receives material nonpublic information from a tipper.

A person who discloses material nonpublic information to another person is called a **tipper**. A person who receives such information is known as a **tippee**. A tippee is liable for acting on material information that he or she knew or should have known was not public. The tipper is liable for the profits made by the tippee. This is called **tipper–tippee liability**. If the tippee tips other persons, both the tippee (who is now a tipper) and the original tipper are liable for the profits made by these remote tippees. The remote tippees are liable for their own trades if they knew or should have known that they possessed material inside information.

Example Nicole is the CFO of Max Steel Corporation. In her position, she learns of a confidential offer to buy the company for twice its current stock price, and that the company has accepted the offer. This is material nonpublic information. Nicole calls her brother Caleb and tells him the news. Caleb knows Nicole's position at Max Steel. Caleb purchases stock in Max Steel based on this confidential information and makes a significant profit by selling the shares after the merger is made public. Here there is illegal tipping. Nicole, the tipper, and Caleb, the tippee, could be held civilly liable and criminally guilty of violating Section 10(b) and Rule 10b-5.

SEC Rule 10b5-1
An SEC rule that prohibits the trading in the security of any issuer on the basis of material nonpublic information obtained in a breach of duty of trust or confidence owed to the person who is the source of the information.

Misappropriation Theory

Sometimes a person who possesses inside information about a company is not an employee or a temporary insider of that company. Instead, the party may be an *outsider* to the company. The SEC adopted **SEC Rule 10b5-1**, which prohibits outsiders from trading in the security of any issuer on the basis of material nonpublic information that is obtained by a breach of duty of trust or confidence owed to the person who is the source of the information. Thus, an outsider's misappropriation of information in violation of his or her fiduciary duty—and trading on that information—violates Section 10(b) and Rule 10b5-1. This rule is called the **misappropriation theory**.

misappropriation theory
A rule that imposes liability under Section 10(b) and Rule 10b5-1 on an *outsider* who misappropriates information about a company, in violation of his or her fiduciary duty, and then trades in the securities of that company.

In the following case, the court applied the misappropriation theory to decide whether a defendant committed securities fraud.

CASE 41.1 *FEDERAL COURT CASE Misappropriation Theory*

United States v. Kanodia

943 F.3d 499 (2019)
United States Court of Appeals for the First Circuit

"Consequently, the jury could conclude that Kanodia knew that information about Apollo was not his to share."

—Jeffrey Howard, Chief Judge

Facts

Amit Kanodia, an experienced real estate investor, met Shahana Basu, a U.S. licensed lawyer, through an online dating service, and the two were later married. Basu accepted the chief legal officer position at Apollo Tyres (Apollo) in New Delhi, India. Basu helped secretly negotiate Apollo's purchase of Cooper Tires (Cooper), an American company. She was sent to New York City to conduct Apollo's due diligence on Cooper and lived with Kanodia at the Waldorf Hotel.

Basu told Kanodia details of the secret transaction. Kanodia disclosed to his two closest friends, Ifthikar Ahmed, a venture capitalist, and Steven Watson, a semi-retired businessman with a Harvard MBA, information about Apollo's proposed acquisition of Cooper. Kanodia continually updated his friends on the transaction, usually in person, to avoid detection. Kanodia informed his friends that neither he nor Basu could trade in Cooper's stock because they could have easily been detected. Instead, they made a deal with Ahmed and Watson to pay them a kickback on any profits made from trading on the inside information.

Kanodia told Ahmed and Watson that Apollo planned to purchase Cooper for $35 per share. This was material nonpublic information. Ahmed and Watson purchased Cooper shares at $24 and $25 per share. Shortly thereafter, a public announcement was made disclosing Apollo's acquisition of Cooper for $35 per share. Ahmed and Watson sold their shares, with Ahmed making $1.1 million in profits, and Watson making $167,000 in profits. Kanodia opened a new bank account, and Ahmed wired $220,000 into it, and Watson wrote a $22,500 check that was deposited into the account.

The Federal Bureau of Investigation (FBI) investigated, and interviewed Watson about his trades. Watson made a plea deal in exchange for his cooperation. Basu went to India, and Ahmed fled the country. The United States sued Kanodia, alleging that Kanodia's tips to Ahmed and Watson constituted insider trading under the misappropriation theory of securities fraud. Watson was the primary witness against Kanodia. Based on Watson's testimony and other evidence, the jury convicted Kanodia, an outsider to the Apollo-Cooper acquisition, of violating Section 10(b) and Rule 10b-5 for tipping inside information given to him by his wife to Ahmed and Watson. Kanodia was sentenced to 20 months in prison. Kanodia appealed his conviction.

Issue

Is Kanodia guilty of securities fraud under the misappropriation theory?

(continued)

Language of the Court

Outsiders who owe insiders a duty not to trade on inside information violate Section 10(b) and Rule 10b-5 when an outsider (the tipper) tips another outsider (the tippee) in exchange for personal benefit. The jury could infer that Kanodia, an entrepreneur with an MBA, was sophisticated enough to know that Basu's disclosures violated her duty of confidentiality to Apollo. Consequently, the jury could conclude that Kanodia knew that information about Apollo was not his to share. The government introduced more than enough evidence to sustain Kanodia's conviction.

Decision

The court of appeals affirmed the criminal conviction of Kanodia.

Ethics Questions

Should the insider trading rules be extended to include outsiders like Kanodia? Was it fair that only Kanodia was convicted? Would you make a plea deal if you were in a situation like Watson?

Aiders and Abettors

aiders and abettors
Parties who knowingly assist principal actors in the commission of securities fraud.

Many principal actors in a securities fraud obtain the knowing assistance of other parties to complete the fraud successfully. These other parties are known as **aiders and abettors**. The U.S. Supreme Court has held that aiders and abettors are not civilly liable under Section 10(b)-5 and Rule 10b-5.[11] Aiders and abettors can, however, be held criminally liable.

Short-Swing Profits

41.13 Describe short-swing profit transactions that violate securities laws.

Section 16 statutory insider
A person who is an executive officer, a director, or a 10 percent shareholder of an equity security of a reporting company.

Section 16(a) of the Securities Exchange Act of 1934 defines any person who is an executive officer, a director, or a 10 percent shareholder of an equity security of a reporting company as a **Section 16 statutory insider** who is subject to the rules of Section 16. Statutory insiders must file reports with the SEC that disclose their ownership and trading in the company's equity securities. A person who becomes an insider must file a form with the SEC within 10 days of becoming an insider that discloses his or her equity ownership interest in the company. If an insider acquires or disposes of any equity securities of the company at any time, the transaction must be reported to the SEC within two business days of the transaction. Section 16 reports must be submitted electronically to the SEC and be made available on the company's website. Insiders do not have to furnish Section 16 reports to the company on paper.

Section 16(b)

Section 16(b) of the Securities Exchange Act of 1934
A section of the Securities Exchange Act of 1934 requiring that any profits made by a statutory insider on transactions involving *short-swing profits* belong to the corporation.

short-swing profits
Profits that are made by statutory insiders on trades involving equity securities of their corporation that occur within six months of each other.

Section 16(b) of the Securities Exchange Act of 1934 requires that any profits made by a statutory insider on transactions involving **short-swing profits**—that is, trades involving equity securities occurring within six months of each other—belong to the corporation.[12] Section 16(b) covers purchase and sale transactions as well as sale and purchase transactions. The corporation may bring a legal action to recover these profits. Involuntary transactions, such as forced redemption of securities by the corporation or an exchange of securities in a bankruptcy proceeding, are exempt. Section 16(b) is a strict liability provision. Generally, no defenses are recognized. Neither intent nor the possession of inside information need be shown.

Example Nadia is the president of a corporation and a statutory insider who does not possess any inside information. On February 1, she purchases 1,000 shares of her employer's stock at $10 per share. On June 1, she sells the stock for $14 per share. The corporation can recover the $4,000 profit because the trades occurred within six months of each other.

Section 16 Rules

The SEC has adopted the following rules under Section 16:

- It defines *officer* to include only executive officers who perform *policy-making* functions. Officers who run day-to-day operations but are not responsible for policy decisions are not included.

  Examples Policy-making executives include the CEO, the president, vice presidents in charge of business units or divisions, the CFO, the principal accounting officer, and so on.

- It relieves insiders of liability for transactions that occur within six months before becoming an insider.

  Example If a noninsider buys shares of a company on January 15, is hired by the company and becomes an insider on March 15, and sells the shares on May 15, there is no liability.

- It states that insiders are liable for transactions that occur within six months of the last transaction engaged in while an insider.

  Example If an insider buys shares in her company on April 30 and leaves the company on May 15, the shares cannot be sold before October 30. If they are, the former insider violates Section 16(b).

CONCEPT SUMMARY
SECTION 10(B) AND SECTION 16(B) COMPARED

Element	Section 10(b) and Rule 10b-5	Section 16(b)
Covered securities	All securities.	Securities required to be registered with the SEC under the 1934 act.
Inside information	Defendant made a misrepresentation or traded on inside (or perhaps misappropriated) information.	Short-swing profits recoverable whether or not they are attributable to misappropriation or inside information.
Recovery	Belongs to the injured purchaser or seller.	Belongs to the corporation.

State "Blue-Sky" Laws

41.14 Describe how state laws regulate securities transactions.

Most states have enacted securities laws. **State securities laws** generally require the registration of certain securities, provide exemptions from registration, and contain broad antifraud provisions. State securities laws are usually applied when smaller companies are issuing securities within that state. The **Uniform Securities Act** has been adopted by many states, which coordinate state securities laws with federal securities laws.

State securities laws are often referred to as *"blue-sky" laws* because they help prevent investors from purchasing a piece of the blue sky. The state that has most actively enforced its securities laws is New York. The office of the New York state attorney has brought many high-profile criminal fraud cases in recent years.

state securities laws ("blue-sky" laws)
State laws that regulate the issuance and trading of securities.

WEB EXERCISE
Visit the website of the Office of the New York State Attorney at **www.ag.ny.gov**. Click on "Divisions" and then click on "Investor Protection Bureau" and read the description of what the New York Investor Protection Bureau does.

Key Terms and Concepts

Accredited investor (734)
Aiders and abettors (742)
Annual report (Form 10-K) (725)
Civil action (737)
Civil penalty (739)
Commercial paper (732)
Common securities (726)
Confidential draft registration statement (730)
Consent decree (738)
Cross-border IPO (729)
Crowdfunding (735)
Cryptocurrency (736)
Direct public offering (DPO) (729)
Due diligence defense (738)
EDGAR (725)
Effective date (728)
Electronic initial public offering (e-initial public offering or e-IPO) (728)
Electronic securities transactions (e-securities transactions) (726)
Emerging growth company (EGC) (729)
Exempt securities (732)
Exempt transaction (733)
Federal securities statutes (724)
Final prospectus (728)
Form C (736)
Form D (735)
Form S-1 (727)
Funding portal (web platform) (736)
Going public (727)
Howey test (726)
Initial coin offering (ICO) (736)
Initial public offering (IPO) (727)
Injunction (738)
Insider trading (740)
Insider Trading Sanctions Act (739)
Intrastate offering exemption (733)
Investment banker (727)
Investment contract (726)
IPO on-ramp (729)
Issuer (727)
Jumpstart Our Business Startups Act (JOBS Act) (729)
Limited public offering (mini-IPO) (731)
Matter of Cady, Roberts & Company (740)
Misappropriation theory (741)
Monthly report (current report, Form 8-K) (725)
Mutual fund (727)
National Association of Securities Dealers Automated Quotation System (NASDAQ) (726)
New York Stock Exchange (NYSE) (725)
Nonaccredited investor (735)
Nonissuer exemption (733)
NYSE Euronext (725)
Offering circular (731)
Offering statement (731)
Preliminary prospectus (728)
Private placement exemptions (734)
Quarterly report (Form 10-Q) (725)
Registered (727)
Registration statement (727)
Reporting company (725)
Rules and regulations (725)
Scienter (739)
SCOR form (Form U-7) (732)
SEC Regulation A (731)
SEC Regulation Crowdfunding (Regulation CF) (736)
SEC Rule 10b-5 (739)
SEC Rule 10b5-1 (741)
SEC Rule 147 (733)
SEC Rule 147A (734)
SEC Rule 504 (735)
SEC Rule 506(b) (734)
SEC Rule 506(c) (735)
Section 5 of the Securities Act of 1933 (727)
Section 10(b) of the Securities Exchange Act of 1934 (738)
Section 10(b) insider (740)
Section 11 of the Securities Act of 1933 (737)
Section 12 of the Securities Act of 1933 (738)
Section 16 statutory insider (742)
Section 16(a) of the Securities Exchange Act of 1934 (742)
Section 16(b) of the Securities Exchange Act of 1934 (742)
Section 24 of the Securities Act of 1933 (738)
Section 32 of the Securities Exchange Act of 1934 (739)
Securities Act of 1933 (727)
Securities and Exchange Commission (SEC) (725)
Securities Exchange Act of 1934 (738)
Securities law (724)
Security (726)
Security token (737)
Security token offering (STO) (737)
Shelf registration (732)
Short-swing profits (742)
Small Company Offering Registration (SCOR) (732)
Small offering exemption (735)
State securities laws (743)
Statutorily defined securities (726)
Test the waters (727)
Tier 1 (731)
Tier 2 (731)
Tippee (740)
Tipper (740)
Tipper–tippee liability (740)
Uniform Securities Act (743)
Unregistered securities (729)
Utility token (utility coin) (736)
Well-known seasoned investor (WKSI) (732)
Whistle-blower bounty program (725)

Critical Legal Thinking Cases

41.1 Definition of *Security* Farmer's Cooperative of Arkansas and Oklahoma (Co-Op) was an agricultural cooperative that had approximately 23,000 members. To raise money to support its general business operations, Co-Op sold promissory notes to investors that were payable on demand. Co-Op offered the notes to both members and nonmembers, advertised the notes as an "investment program," and offered an interest rate higher than that available on savings accounts at financial institutions. More than 1,600 people purchased the notes, worth a total of $10 million. Subsequently, Co-Op filed for bankruptcy. A class of holders of the notes filed suit against Ernst & Young, a national firm of certified public accountants that had audited Co-Op's financial statements, alleging that Ernst & Young had violated Section 10(b) of the Securities Exchange Act of 1934. Are the notes issued by Co-Op securities? *Reeves v. Ernst & Young*, 494 U.S. 56, 110 S.Ct. 945, 1990 U.S. Lexis 1051 (Supreme Court of the United States, 1990)

41.2 Insider Trading Atul Bhagat worked for NVIDIA Corporation (Nvidia). Nvidia competed for and won a multimillion-dollar contract to develop a video game console for Microsoft Corporation. On receiving the news, Nvidia's chief executive officer (CEO) sent company-wide emails announcing the contract award, advising Nvidia employees that the information should be kept confidential, and imposing a trading blackout on the purchase of Nvidia stock by employees for several days. Within roughly 20 minutes after the final email was sent, Bhagat purchased a large quantity of Nvidia stock. Bhagat testified that he read the emails roughly 40 minutes after he purchased the stock.

The United States brought criminal charges against Bhagat in U.S. district court, charging him with insider trading in violation of Section 10(b) of the Securities Exchange Act of 1934 and SEC Rule 10b-5 adopted thereunder. Bhagat stuck with his story regarding his purchase of Nvidia stock. Based on circumstantial evidence, the jury convicted Bhagat of insider trading. Bhagat appealed. Is Bhagat criminally guilty of insider trading? *United States v. Bhagat*, 436 F.3d 1140, 2006 U.S. App. Lexis 3008 (United States Court of Appeals for the Ninth Circuit, 2006)

41.3 Tipper-Tippee Matthew Kluger, a lawyer, worked at several of the largest law firms in America and primarily engaged in mergers and acquisitions legal work. He became the lynchpin of a three-person scheme whereby he would pass material nonpublic inside information as to what companies were planning to merge on to his friend Kenneth Robinson, the go-between, who in turn relayed the information to Garrett Bauer, a professional stock trader. Bauer would then execute trades based on the information. Over the course of 17 years, the co-conspirators reaped more than $47 million in profits, which were split between them. Eventually, their activities were uncovered by the Federal Bureau of Investigation (FBI). The case was referred to the U.S. Department of Justice for criminal prosecution. After evidence of the scheme was uncovered, Robinson agreed to cooperate with the government and, unbeknownst to Kluger and Bauer, began taping their conversations. This led to the criminal arrests of Kluger, Bauer, and Robinson. The United States brought criminal charges against the three conspirators in U.S. district court for violating Section 10(b) of the Securities Exchange Act of 1934 and SEC Rule 10b-5 adopted thereunder. Did the defendants violate the securities laws as charged? *United States v. Kluger*, 722 F.3d 549, 2013 U.S. App. Lexis 13880 (United States Court of Appeals for the Third Circuit, 2013)

41.4 Misappropriation Theory Patrick O'Neill was an executive at Eastern Bank (Eastern), and Robert Bray was a contractor and real estate developer. They were both members of the Oakley Country Club (Oakley) and were friends for 15 years. One day when the men were privately together in the Oakley pub room, Bray told O'Neill that he needed to make a "big score" to fund a real estate project. At the time, O'Neill, as part of his work at Eastern, was evaluating whether Eastern should acquire Wainwright Bank & Trust Co. (Wainwright), a local, publicly traded bank. This was confidential information. O'Neill took a napkin, penned the word "Wainwright" on it, and slid it across the bar to Bray. Bray wordlessly took the napkin and slipped it into his pocket. The next day Bray called his stock broker and purchased $550,000 in Wainwright stock. Two weeks later, when Eastern publicly announced its acquisition of Wainwright, the stock of Wainwright increased in value, and Bray sold his stock and made a $300,000 profit. O'Neill did not purchase shares of Wainwright. The United States sued Bray for criminal securities fraud for violating Section 10(b) of the Securities Exchange Act of 1934 and Rule 10b-5 under the misappropriation theory. Is Bray guilty of securities fraud? *United States v. Bray*, 853 F.3d 18 (United States Court of Appeals for the First Circuit, 2017)

41.5 Securities Fraud Francis Lorenzo was the director of investment banking at Charles Vista, LLC, a registered broker-dealer. In a public filing, Waste2Energy stated that its total assets were worth about $14 million. This figure included intangible assets, namely, intellectual property, valued at more than $10 million. Waste2Energy hired Lorenzo's firm, Charles Vista, to sell to investors $15 million worth of debentures, which is unsecured debt. Subsequently, Lorenzo discovered that Waste2Energy's intellectual property was worthless and that its total assets amounted to less than $400,000. However, Lorenzo sent two emails to prospective investors describing the investment in Waste2Energy as having "layers of protection," including $10 million in "confirmed assets." Lorenzo signed the emails with his own name and identified himself as "Vice President—Investment Banking." Many of the persons who Lorenzo sent the emails to purchased Waste2Energy's debentures and lost their money. The SEC brought a civil proceeding against Lorenzo for committing securities fraud by sending false and misleading statements to investors with intent to defraud them in violation of Section 10(b) of the Securities Exchange Act of 1934 and Rule 10b-5. Is Lorenzo liable for violating securities laws? *Lorenzo v. Securities and Exchange Commission*, 139 S.Ct. 1094 (Supreme Court of the United States, 2019)

Ethics Cases

41.6 Ethics Case James O'Hagan was a partner in the law firm Dorsey & Whitney in Minneapolis, Minnesota. Grand Metropolitan PLC (Grand Met), a company based in London, England, hired Dorsey & Whitney to represent it in a secret tender offer for the stock of the Pillsbury Company, headquartered in Minneapolis. While this transaction was still secret, O'Hagan began purchasing call options for Pillsbury stock. Each call option gave O'Hagan the right to purchase 100 shares of Pillsbury stock at a specified price.

O'Hagan continued to purchase call options for two months, and he became the largest holder of call options for Pillsbury stock. O'Hagan also purchased 5,000 shares of Pillsbury common stock at $39 per share. These purchases were all made while Grand Met's proposed tender offer for Pillsbury remained secret to the public. When Grand Met publicly announced its tender offer one month later, Pillsbury stock increased to nearly $60 per share. O'Hagan sold his Pillsbury call options and common stock, making a profit of more than $4.3 million.

The U.S. Department of Justice charged O'Hagan with criminally violating Section 10(b) and Rule 10b-5. This was not a case of classic insider trading because O'Hagan did not trade in the stock of his law firm's client, Grand Met, but the government alleged that O'Hagan was liable under the misappropriation theory for trading in Pillsbury stock by engaging in deceptive conduct by misappropriating the secret information about Grand Met's tender offer from his employer, Dorsey & Whitney, and from its client, Grand Met. Did O'Hagan act ethically in this case? Did O'Hagan act illegally in this case? *United States v. O'Hagan*, 521 U.S. 642, 117 S.Ct. 2199, 1997 U.S. Lexis 4033 (Supreme Court of the United States, 1997)

41.7 Ethics Case Matthew Martoma worked as a portfolio manager at S.A.C. Capital Advisors (SAC), a hedge fund. Martoma managed an investment portfolio that was focused on pharmaceutical and health care companies and became interested in Elan Corporation (Elan), which was developing an experimental drug, bapineuzumab, to treat Alzheimer's disease.

To obtain information about bapineuzumab, Martoma contacted Dr. Sidney Gilman, a doctor involved in the nonpublic clinical trials being conducted on the drug. Dr. Gilman had an obligation to maintain the confidentiality of the information about the bapineuzumab clinical trials. Martoma arranged for 43 consultations with Dr. Gilman, paying $1,000 per hour to obtain nonpublic information about the ongoing clinical trials. Based on Dr. Gilman's reports of initial success, on Martoma's advice SAC purchased shares of Elan.

Subsequently, Dr. Gilman discovered that the results of the drug trials questioned the efficiency of bapineuzumab. Dr. Gilman shared this nonpublic information with Martoma. On Martoma's advice, SAC sold shares it owned of Elan stock at a profit and then entered into short-sale transactions that would be profitable if Elan's stock decreased in value. Eight days later, Dr. Gilman publicly reported the questionable results of the clinical trial, and the price of Elan's stock dropped by 42 percent. SAC profited by its short sales.

The trades that Martoma advised SAC to make resulted in $80 million of gains and $194 million of adverted losses for SAC. Martoma was paid a bonus of $9 million by SAC based on the inside information about Elan. After a government investigation, the United States brought criminal charges against Martoma as a tippee for violating Section 10(b) of the Securities Act of 1934 and Rule 10b-5. Is Martoma guilty of securities fraud? Did Martoma act ethically in this case? Did Dr. Gilman act ethically in this case? *United States v. Martoma*, 869 F.3d 58 (United States Court of Appeals for the Second Circuit, 2017)

Notes

1. 15 U.S.C. Section 77a et seq., 48 Stat. 74.
2. 15 U.S.C. Section 78a et seq., 48 Stat. 881.
3. H.R. 3606—112th Congress.
4. *Securities and Exchange Commission v. W. J. Howey Co.*, 328 U.S. 293, 66 S.Ct. 1100, 1946 U.S. Lexis 3159 (Supreme Court of the United States).
5. 15 U.S.C. Section 77x.
6. 15 U.S.C. Section 78j(b).
7. 17 C.F.R.240.10b-5.
8. 15 U.S.C. Section 78ff (1984).
9. Pub. L. 98–376.
10. 40 SEC 907 (1961).
11. *Stoneridge Investment Partners, LLC. v. Scientific-Atlanta, Inc.*, 552 U.S. 148, 128 S.Ct. 761, 2008 U.S. Lexis 1091 (Supreme Court of the United States).
12. 15 U.S.C. Section 78p(b).

CHAPTER 42 Ethics and Social Responsibility of Business

BUSINESS ETHICS
Businesses are compelled to obey the law. In some circumstances, they may be able to obey the law but engage in conduct that would be deemed by many to be unethical. Do businesses owe a duty to act ethically in the conduct of their business even though the law would permit unethical conduct?

Henry R. Cheeseman

Learning Objectives

After studying this chapter, you should be able to:

42.1 Describe how law and ethics intertwine.

42.2 Describe and apply the moral theories of business ethics.

42.3 Describe and apply the theories of the social responsibility of business.

42.4 Define *public benefit corporation* and describe the social purposes served by these corporations.

> *"Ethical considerations can no more be excluded from the administration of justice, which is the end and purpose of all civil laws, than one can exclude the vital air from his room and live."*
>
> —*John F. Dillon*
> *Laws and Jurisprudence of England and America Lecture I (1894)*

Introduction to Ethics and Social Responsibility of Business

He who seeks equality must do equity.

Joseph Story (1779–1845)
Former justice of the U.S. Supreme Court
Equity Jurisprudence (1836)

Businesses organized in the United States are subject to its laws. They are also subject to the laws of other countries in which they operate. In addition, businesspersons owe a duty to act ethically in the conduct of their affairs, and businesses owe a social responsibility not to harm society.

Although most laws are based on ethical standards, not all ethical standards have been enacted as law. While the law establishes a minimum degree of conduct expected by persons and businesses in society, ethics demands more. This chapter discusses business ethics and the social responsibility of business.

Ethics and the Law

42.1 Describe how law and ethics intertwine.

Ethics and the law are intertwined. Sometimes the rule of **law** and the rule of **ethics** demand the same response by a person confronted with a problem.

ethics
A set of moral principles or values that governs the conduct of an individual or a group.

Example Federal and state laws make bribery unlawful. A person violates the law if he or she bribes a judge for a favorable decision in a case. Ethics would also prohibit this conduct.

Sometimes, however, the law demands certain conduct but a person's ethical standards are contrary.

Example Federal law prohibits employers from hiring certain undocumented workers. Suppose an employer advertises the availability of a job and receives no response except from a person who cannot prove citizenship of this country or does not possess a required visa. The worker and the worker's family are destitute. Should the employer violate the law and hire this person? The law says no, but ethics may say yes.

And in some situations, the law may permit an act that is ethically wrong.

Example Occupational safety laws set minimum standards for emissions of dust from toxic chemicals in the workplace. Suppose a company can reduce the emission below the legal standard by spending additional money. The only benefit from the expenditure would be better employee health. Ethics would require the extra expenditure; the law would not (see **Exhibit 42.1**).

Exhibit 42.1 LAW AND ETHICS

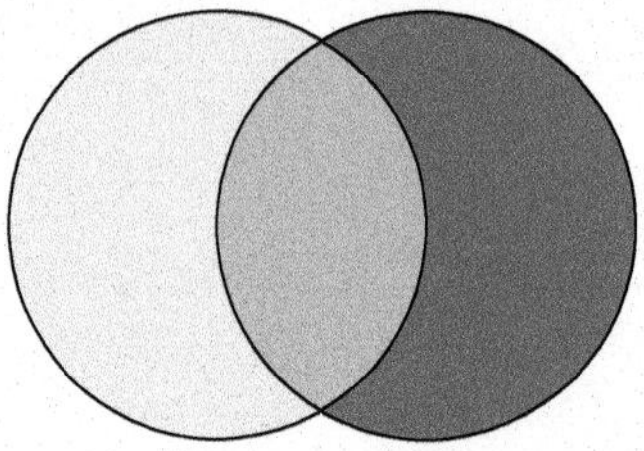

In the following U.S. Supreme Court case, the court examined the lawfulness of Wal-Mart knocking off another company's product design.

CASE 42.1 *U.S. SUPREME COURT CASE Business Ethics*

Wal-Mart Stores, Inc. v. Samara Brothers, Inc.

529 U.S. 205, 120 S.Ct. 1339, 2000 U.S. Lexis 2197 (2000)
Supreme Court of the United States

"Their suspicions aroused, however, Samara officials launched an investigation, which disclosed that Wal-Mart was selling the knockoffs of Samara's outfits."

—Antonin Scalia, Justice

Facts

Samara Brothers, Inc. (Samara) is a designer and manufacturer of children's clothing. Samara sold its clothing to retailers, which in turn sold the clothes to consumers. Wal-Mart Stores, Inc. operates a large chain of budget warehouse stores that sell thousands of items at very low prices. Wal-Mart contacted one of its suppliers, Judy-Philippine, Inc. (JPI), about the possibility of making a line of children's clothes just like Samara's successful line. Wal-Mart sent photographs of Samara's children's clothes to JPI (with the name "Samara" readily discernible on the labels of the garments) and directed JPI to produce children's clothes exactly like those in the photographs. JPI produced a line of children's clothes for Wal-Mart that copied the designs, colors, and patterns of Samara's clothing. Wal-Mart then sold this line of children's clothing in its stores.

Samara discovered that Wal-Mart was selling the knockoff clothes at a price that was lower than Samara's retailers were paying Samara for its clothes. After sending unsuccessful cease-and-desist letters to Wal-Mart, Samara sued, alleging that Wal-Mart stole Samara's trade dress in violation of Section 43(a) of the Lanham Act. The U.S. district court held in favor of Samara and awarded damages. The U.S. court of appeals affirmed the award to Samara. Wal-Mart appealed to the U.S. Supreme Court.

Issue

Must a product's design have acquired a secondary meaning before it is protected as trade dress?

Language of the U.S. Supreme Court

Their suspicions aroused, however, Samara officials launched an investigation, which disclosed that Wal-Mart was selling the knockoffs of Samara's outfits. The Lanham Act, in Section 43(a), requires that a producer show that the allegedly infringing feature is likely to cause confusion with the product for which protection is sought. In an action for infringement of unregistered trade dress a product's design is protectable only upon a showing of secondary meaning.

Decision

The Supreme Court reversed the decision of the U.S. court of appeals and remanded the case for further proceedings consistent with its opinion.

Critical Legal Thinking Questions

Even though Wal-Mart was found not to have violated the law, was its conduct ethical? Did Wal-Mart's conduct cause economic harm to Samara?

Business Ethics

42.2 Describe and apply the moral theories of business ethics.

How can ethics be measured? The answer is very personal: What one person considers ethical another may consider unethical. However, there do seem to be some universal rules about what conduct is ethical and what conduct is not. The following material discusses five major theories of ethics: (1) *ethical fundamentalism*, (2) *utilitarianism*, (3) *Kantian ethics*, (4) *Rawls's social justice theory*, and (5) *ethical relativism*.

Ethical Fundamentalism

Under **ethical fundamentalism**, a person looks to an *outside source* for ethical rules or commands. This may be a book (e.g., the Bible, the Koran) or a person (e.g., Karl Marx). Critics argue that ethical fundamentalism does not permit people to determine right and wrong for themselves. Taken to an extreme, the result could be considered unethical under most other moral theories. For example, a literal interpretation of the maxim "an eye for an eye" would permit retaliation.

ethical fundamentalism
A theory of ethics in which a person looks to an outside source for ethical rules or commands.

The following case demonstrates unethical conduct.

CASE 42.2 *FEDERAL COURT CASE Ethics*

Securities and Exchange Commission v. Zada

787 F.3d 375 (2015)
United States Court of Appeals for the Sixth Circuit

"Any reasonable jury would find that Zada lied to investors"

—Raymond Kethledge, Circuit Judge

Facts

Joseph Paul Zada presented himself to friends and acquaintances as an extremely wealthy man. Zada told potential investors that he had connections with the royal family in Saudi Arabia, and that if they invested money with him that he would use it to purchase oil on their account and pay them a 40 percent return in two months. Zada raised $56 million from 60 investors and gave them promissory notes issued by him or his company, Zada Enterprises.

Zada's connections with the royal family only existed in his imagination. And Zada never bought any oil, but instead used the investor's money to pay for his lavish lifestyle. The scheme was eventually uncovered and the Securities and Exchange Commission (SEC) brought a civil fraud action against Zada. The U.S. district court held that Zada had sold unregistered securities in violation of antifraud provisions of federal securities law. The court ordered Zada to pay the investors the $56 million he had stolen and an additional $56 million as a civil penalty. Zada appealed, alleging that the investors only loaned him the money and he did not sell them an investment, so federal securities fraud laws did not apply.

Issue

Did Zada commit fraud?

Language of the Court

If the notes are sold to a wide range of unsophisticated people the notes are more likely to be securities. Here, Zada sold the notes to a variety of laypersons. Zada's victims thought they were making lucrative investments in oil. The notes are therefore securities, which means that Zada was required to comply with the Securities Acts. Any reasonable jury would find that Zada lied to the investors.

Decision

The U.S. court of appeals affirmed the district court's judgment.

Critical Legal Thinking Questions

Did Zada violate ethical principles? Do you think that he knew he was committing fraud? Was his promise to pay the investors a 40 percent return within two months "too good to be true"? Do the investors share responsibility for their plight?
Do you think that the investors will receive their money back?

Utilitarianism

utilitarianism
A theory of ethics stating that people must choose the action or follow the rule that provides the greatest good to society.

WEB EXERCISE
Visit the website about making changes at Wal-Mart at **www.changewalmart.org.** What is one of the issues currently being discussed on this site?

Utilitarianism is a moral theory with origins in the works of Jeremy Bentham (1748–1832) and John Stuart Mill (1806–1873). This moral theory dictates that people must choose the action or follow the rule that provides the *greatest good to society*. This does not mean the greatest good for the greatest number of people.

Example If an action would increase the good of 25 people by 1 unit each and an alternative action would increase the good of 1 person by 26 units, then, according to utilitarianism, the latter action should be taken.

Utilitarianism has been criticized because it is difficult to estimate the "good" that will result from different actions, it is difficult to apply in an imperfect world, and it treats morality as if it were an impersonal mathematical calculation.

Example A company is trying to determine whether it should close an unprofitable plant located in a small community. Utilitarianism would require that the benefits to shareholders from closing the plant be compared with the benefits to employees, their families, and others in the community from keeping it open.

Henry R. Cheeseman

POTALA PALACE, TIBET
A person's culture helps shape his or her ethical values.

Kantian Ethics

Immanuel Kant (1724–1804) is the best-known proponent of **Kantian ethics**, also called **duty ethics** or **deontological ethics**. Kant believed that people owe moral duties that are based on *universal rules*. Kant's philosophy is based on the premise that people can use reasoning to reach ethical decisions. His ethical theory would have people behave according to the *categorical imperative* "Do unto others as you would have them do unto you."

Kantian ethics (duty ethics or deontological ethics)
A theory of ethics stating that people owe moral duties that are based on universal rules, such as the categorical imperative "Do unto others as you would have them do unto you."

Example According to Kantian ethics, keeping a promise to abide by a contract is a moral duty even if that contract turns out to be detrimental to the obligated party.

The universal rules of Kantian ethics are based on two important principles: (1) consistency—that is, all cases are treated alike, with no exceptions—and (2) reversibility—that is, the actor must abide by the rule he or she uses to judge the morality of someone else's conduct. Thus, if you are going to make an exception for yourself, that exception becomes a universal rule that applies to all others.

Example If you rationalize that it is acceptable for you to engage in deceptive practices, it is acceptable for competitors to do so also.

A criticism of Kantian ethics is that it is difficult to reach consensus on what the universal rules should be.

The following case involves the issue of ethics.

CASE 42.3 *FEDERAL COURT CASE Business Ethics*

Wysong Corporation v. APN, Inc.

889 F.3d 267 (2018)
United States Court of Appeals for the Sixth Circuit

"Reasonable consumers know that marketing involves some level of exaggeration—what the law calls 'puffery.'"

—Amul Thapar, Circuit Judge

Facts

Wysong Corporation is a producer and seller of high-grade pet foods. Six of Wysong's competitors manufacture and sell pet food using advertisements and placing labels on their packages that

(continued)

contain photographs of delectable lamb chops, T-bone steaks, chicken breasts, and other premium cuts of meat when in fact the pet food inside the packages is made from trimmings left over after the premium cuts of meat have been sliced away for human use. Wysong sued these competitors under **Section 43 of the Lanham Act,**[1] a federal statute that allows a competitor to sue another competitor for engaging in unfair competition, including false advertising and misleading labeling. The U.S. district court dismissed Wysong's lawsuit for failure to state a valid claim. Wysong appealed.

Issue

Have the defendant pet food manufacturers engaged in false advertising and misleading labeling?

Language of the Court

Surely a reasonable consumer could understand the defendants' packaging as indicating the type of animal from which the food was made (e.g., chicken) but not the precise cut used (e.g., chicken breast). Reasonable consumers know that marketing involves some level of exaggeration—what the law calls "puffery." Mere puffery is not actionable under the Lanham Act.

Think, for instance, of a reasonable consumer at a fast-food drive-through. Does he expect that the hamburger he receives at the window will look just like the one pictured on the menu? Of course not. He knows that puffery is a fact of life. The same is true here. It is not plausible that reasonable consumers believe most of the (cheap) dog food they encounter in the pet-food aisle is in fact made of the same sumptuous (and more costly) ingredients they find a few aisles over in the people-food sections. The puffery defense is such an obvious impediment to Wysong's success.

Decision

The U.S. court of appeals upheld the decision of the U.S. district court.

Critical Legal Thinking Questions

What is an outrageous example of puffery that you know of? Is it ethical for businesses to engage in puffery? Should producers and sellers be more honest in advertising and labeling their products?

Rawls's Social Justice Theory

John Locke (1632–1704) and Jean-Jacques Rousseau (1712–1778) proposed a *social contract* theory of morality. Under this theory, each person is presumed to have entered into a social contract with all others in society to obey moral rules that are necessary for people to live in peace and harmony. This implied contract states, "I will follow the rules if everyone else does." These moral rules are then used to solve conflicting interests in society.

The leading proponent of the modern justice theory was John Rawls (1921–2002), a philosopher at Harvard University. Under **Rawls's social justice theory**, also called the **social contract theory**, fairness is considered the essence of justice. The principles of justice should be chosen by persons who do not yet know their station in society—thus, their "veil of ignorance" would permit the fairest possible principles to be selected.

Rawls's social justice theory (social contract theory)
A theory of ethics asserting that fairness is the essence of justice. The theory says that each person is presumed to have entered into a social contract with all others in society to obey moral rules that are necessary for people to live in peace and harmony.

Example Pursuant to Rawls's social justice theory, the principle of equal opportunity in employment would be promulgated by people who would not yet know if they were in a favored class.

As a caveat, Rawls also proposed that the least advantaged in society must receive special assistance to realize their potential. Rawls's theory of social justice is criticized for two reasons. First, establishing the blind "original position" for choosing moral principles is impossible in the real world. Second, many persons in society would choose not to maximize the benefit to the least advantaged persons in society.

The ethical conduct of Apple is questioned in the following case.

Ethics

France Fines Apple for Secretly Slowing Down Older iPhones

France's consumer watchdog agency was alerted to a practice followed by Apple, Inc. Consumers reported that their older iPhones were slowing down, and they did not think that the phones should be doing so. France investigated and discovered that Apple indeed was deliberately slowing down older iPhones. It did so by using software updates to the older phones that were specifically designed to limit the older phones' performance. Apple was doing this secretly, without notifying the users of the phones that the updates were purposely limiting their use. When users of these phones downloaded Apple updates, they were, unbeknownst to them, installing software that actually "down dated" the phone's performance. Apple finally admitted that it had in fact been engaging in this practice without telling its customers. Apple was required to pay a fine of $41 million for its actions.

Ethics Questions

Why would Apple secretly slow down these older iPhones? Should Apple have been transparent and disclosed to users of these iPhones that their phones were being intentionally slowed down?

Ethical Relativism

Ethical relativism holds that individuals must decide what is ethical based on *their own feelings* about what is right and wrong. Under this moral theory, if people meet their own moral standard in reaching a decision, no one can criticize them for it. Thus, there are no universal ethical rules to guide a person's conduct. This theory has been criticized because action that is usually thought to be unethical (e.g., committing fraud) would not be unethical if the perpetrator thought it was in fact ethical. Many philosophers believe that ethical relativism is deeply flawed and is not an acceptable moral theory.

ethical relativism
A theory of ethics stating that individuals must decide what is ethical based on their own feelings about what is right and wrong.

Example Some U.S. companies do not pay bribes in the U.S. because doing so is considered wrong and is illegal, while simultaneously operating in other countries and paying bribes there because the practice is widespread and seldom prosecuted.

The following case concerns the nondisclosure of evidence in a lawsuit.

CASE 42.4 *U.S. SUPREME COURT CASE Nondisclosure of Evidence*

Goodyear Tire & Rubber Company v. Haeger

137 S.Ct. 1178, 2017 U.S. Lexis 2613 (2017)
Supreme Court of the United States

"That uncertainty points toward demanding a do-over."

—Elena Kagan, Justice

Facts

Leroy, Donna, Barry, and Suzanne Haeger sued the Goodyear Tire & Rubber Company to recover monetary damages for injuries they suffered after the family's motorhome swerved off the road and flipped over. The plaintiffs alleged that a Goodyear G159 tire on the vehicle caused the accident because the tire was not designed to withstand the level of heat generated when the tire was used on a motorhome at highway speeds. Discovery in the case lasted several years. The plaintiffs repeatedly demanded that Goodyear turn over internal test results for the G159, but the company's responses were both slow and unrevealing in content. The parties finally settled the case for an undisclosed sum of money.

Later, the plaintiffs' lawyer learned that Goodyear had disclosed a set of test results in another case that had not been disclosed to the plaintiffs that showed that the G159 tire got unusually hot at speeds between 55 and 65 miles per hour. The plaintiffs sued Goodyear to recover their entire attorneys' fees of $2.7 million for the case. The U.S. district court awarded the plaintiffs this amount of damages, and the U.S. court of appeals affirmed the judgment. Goodyear appealed to the U.S. Supreme Court,

(continued)

alleging that the award of attorneys' fees should not be the entire amount expended by the plaintiffs, but should be limited to an amount determined to be related to Goodyear's misconduct.

Issue

Should the plaintiffs recover their entire attorneys' fees of $2.7 million?

Language of the U.S. Supreme Court

Goodyear, the U.S. district court found, had engaged in a years-long course of bad-faith behavior. Here, the conduct arose to a truly egregious level. Federal courts possess the ability to fashion an appropriate sanction for conduct which abuses the judicial process. A sanctioning court must determine which fees were incurred because of, and solely because of, the misconduct at issue. No such finding lies behind the $2.7 million award. That uncertainty points toward demanding a do-over.

Decision

The U.S. Supreme Court held that the plaintiffs cannot automatically recover the entire attorneys' fees spent on the case but can recover the amount of attorneys' fees caused by Goodyear's withholding of evidence. The Supreme Court remanded the case for a determination of this amount.

Critical Legal Thinking Questions

Did Goodyear act ethically in this case? Should the plaintiffs be awarded the entire amount they spent on attorneys' fees? Do you think the amount of damages that will be awarded will prevent similar conduct in the future?

CONCEPT SUMMARY

THEORIES OF ETHICS

Theory	Description
Ethical fundamentalism	Persons look to an outside source (e.g., the Bible, the Koran) or a central figure for ethical guidelines.
Utilitarianism	Persons choose the alternative that would provide the greatest good to society.
Kantian ethics	A set of universal rules that establish ethical duties.
	The rules are based on reasoning and require (1) consistency in application and (2) reversibility.
Rawls's social justice theory	Moral duties are based on an implied social contract. Fairness is justice. The rules are established from an original position of a "veil of ignorance."
Ethical relativism	Individuals decide what is ethical, based on their own feelings as to what is right or wrong.

Social Responsibility of Business

42.3 Describe and apply the theories of the social responsibility of business.

Businesses do not operate in a vacuum. Decisions made by businesses have far-reaching effects on society. In the past, many business decisions were based solely on a cost–benefit analysis and how they affected the bottom line. Such decisions, however, may cause negative externalities for others.

Example The dumping of hazardous wastes from a manufacturing plant into a river affects the homeowners, farmers, and others who use the river's waters.

Social responsibility requires corporations and businesses to act with awareness of the consequences and impact that their decisions will have on others. Thus, corporations and businesses are considered to have some degree of responsibility for their actions.

Four theories of the **social responsibility of business** are discussed in the following paragraphs: (1) *maximize profits*, (2) *moral minimum*, (3) *stakeholder interest*, and (4) *corporate citizenship*.

social responsibility of business
A theory stating that corporations and businesses should act with awareness of the consequences and impact that their decisions will have on others.

Maximize Profits

The traditional view of the social responsibility of business is that business should **maximize profits** for shareholders. This view, which dominated business and the law during the 19th century, holds that the interests of other constituencies (e.g., employees, suppliers, residents of the communities in which businesses are located) are not important in and of themselves.

maximize profits
A theory of social responsibility stating that a corporation owes a duty to take actions that maximize profits for shareholders.

Milton Friedman, who won the Nobel Prize in economics when he taught at the University of Chicago, advocated the theory of maximizing profits for shareholders. Friedman asserted that in a free society, "there is one and only one social responsibility of business—to use its resources and engage in activities designed to increase its profits so long as it stays within the rules of the game, which is to say, engages in open and free competition without deception and fraud."[2]

The following feature discusses an extensive fraud committed by a large corporation.

Critical Legal Thinking

Volkswagen Emissions Scandal

"Americans expect corporations to operate honestly and provide accurate information."

—U.S. government

The Volkswagen Group is a German company that manufactures and sells automobiles worldwide. Some of its brand-name automobiles include Audi, Porsche, Jetta, Passat, Beetle, and Golf. Volkswagen produced a new diesel engine, but it was unable to develop one that met U.S. environmental standards, which limit the amount of nitrogen oxide (NOx) pollution that an automobile can emit. Therefore, Volkswagen would not be able to sell its new diesel cars in the United States.

The executives and engineers at Volkswagen built software into their diesel cars that could detect when their diesel automobiles were being tested by equipment of the U.S. Environmental Protection Agency (EPA). At that time, the software activated a short program whereby the emissions of the vehicle would fall below EPA emission standards. The software could detect when an automobile was not being tested and was being driven on roads, at which time the software would disable the temporary pollution controls. Volkswagen's diesel vehicles spewed NOx emissions 40 times greater than the level permitted by law.

Volkswagen sold more than 500,000 diesel vehicles containing the trick software in the United States. Several scientists discovered the deception, and the Volkswagen emission scandal was made public. When confronted with the truth, Volkswagen executives lied and destroyed relevant evidence.

The U.S. government brought civil fraud and criminal charges against Volkswagen. Consumers who purchased these vehicles—which could not be driven because they violated emission standards—brought civil class action lawsuits against Volkswagen. Eventually, Volkswagen agreed to pay $16 billion to settle the class action civil claims. Pursuant to the settlement, car owners sold their vehicles back to Volkswagen. In a settlement reached with the U.S. government, Volkswagen pleaded guilty to three criminal counts and agreed to pay $4.3 billion in fines.

Critical Legal Thinking Questions

How pervasive was the emission fraud? How did Volkswagen get away with its fraudulent scheme for so long a period? How many executives and engineers at Volkswagen would have had to participate in the deception for it to work? Should the Volkswagen executives serve jail time?

Moral Minimum

Some proponents of corporate social responsibility argue that a corporation's duty is to *make a profit while avoiding causing harm to others*. This theory of social responsibility is called the **moral minimum**. Under this theory, so long as business avoids or corrects the social injury it causes, it has met its duty of social responsibility.

moral minimum
A theory of social responsibility stating that a corporation's duty is to make a profit while avoiding causing harm to others.

The ultimate justification of the law is to be found, and can only be found, in moral considerations.

Lord MacMillan
Law and Other Things (1937)

Example A corporation that pollutes a body of water and then compensates those whom the pollution has injured has met its moral minimum duty of social responsibility.

The legislative and judicial branches of government have established laws that enforce the moral minimum of social responsibility for corporations.

Section 406 of the Sarbanes-Oxley Act
A section of the act that requires a public company to disclose whether it has adopted a code of ethics for senior financial officers.

Examples Occupational safety laws establish minimum safety standards for protecting employees from injuries in the workplace. Consumer protection laws establish safety requirements for products and make manufacturers and sellers liable for injuries caused by defective products.

The following feature discusses how the landmark Sarbanes-Oxley Act promotes ethics in business.

Ethics

Sarbanes-Oxley Act Requires Public Companies to Adopt Codes of Ethics

In the late 1990s and early 2000s, many large corporations in the United States were found to have engaged in massive financial frauds. Many of these frauds were perpetrated by the chief executive officers and other senior officers of the companies. Financial officers, such as chief financial officers and controllers, were also found to have been instrumental in committing these frauds. In response, Congress enacted the **Sarbanes-Oxley Act of 2002**, which makes certain conduct illegal and establishes criminal penalties for violations.[3] In addition, the Sarbanes-Oxley Act prompts companies to encourage senior officers of public companies to act ethically in their dealings with shareholders, employees, and other constituents.

Section 406 of the Sarbanes-Oxley Act requires a public company to disclose whether it has adopted a **code of ethics** for senior financial officers, including its principal financial officer and principal accounting officer. In response, public companies have adopted codes of ethics for their senior financial officers. Many public companies have voluntarily included all officers and employees in the coverage of their codes of ethics.

Ethics Questions
How effective will a code of ethics be in preventing unethical conduct? Can you recall any situation that you may have read about in which officers of a public company acted unethically?

Stakeholder Interest

stakeholder interest
A theory of social responsibility stating that a corporation must consider the effects that its actions have on persons other than its shareholders.

Businesses have relationships with all sorts of people besides their shareholders, including employees, suppliers, customers, creditors, and the local community. Under the **stakeholder interest** theory of social responsibility, a corporation must consider the effects its actions have on these *other stakeholders*. For example, a corporation would violate the stakeholder interest theory if it viewed employees solely as a means of maximizing shareholder wealth.

The stakeholder interest theory is criticized because it is difficult to harmonize the conflicting interests of stakeholders.

Example In deciding to close an unprofitable manufacturing plant, certain stakeholders would benefit (e.g., shareholders and creditors), whereas other stakeholders would not (e.g., current employees and the local community).

Corporate Citizenship

corporate citizenship
A theory of social responsibility stating that a business has a responsibility to do good.

The **corporate citizenship** theory of social responsibility argues that business has a responsibility to do good. That is, each business is responsible for helping to solve social problems that it did little, if anything, to cause.

Example Under the corporate citizenship theory of social responsibility, corporations owe a duty to subsidize schools and help educate children.

This theory contends that corporations owe a duty to promote the same social goals as individual members of society. Proponents of this "do good" theory argue that corporations owe a debt to society to make it a better place and that this duty arises because of the social power bestowed on them. That is, this social power is a gift from society and should be used to good ends.

A major criticism of this theory is that the duty of a corporation to do good cannot be expanded beyond certain limits. There is always some social problem that needs to be addressed, and corporate funds are limited. Further, if this theory were taken to its maximum limit, potential shareholders might be reluctant to invest in corporations.

WEB EXERCISE

Visit the website of Starbucks Corporation at **www.starbucks.com**. Either play a video or read information from the "Social Impact" section about the company's ethical sourcing of coffee.

CONCEPT SUMMARY

THEORIES OF SOCIAL RESPONSIBILITY

Theory	Social Responsibility
Maximize profits	To maximize profits for stockholders
Moral minimum	To avoid causing harm and to compensate for harm caused
Stakeholder interest	To consider the interests of all stakeholders, including stockholders, employees, customers, suppliers, creditors, and the local community
Corporate citizenship	To do good and solve social problems

The outsourcing of jobs by U.S. companies to workers in foreign countries is discussed in the following feature.

Global Law

Outsourcing of U.S. Jobs

Companies in the United States often outsource or offshore work that could otherwise be performed by U.S. workers. **Outsourcing** means that the U.S. company has hired an independent third-party company in another country to produce the good or service. **Offshoring** means that the U.S. company has relocated a business function to another country, retains ownership of the division or unit, but hires foreign workers to do the work. The term *outsourcing* is often used to encompass both outsourcing and offshoring.

The production of many of the goods that are eventually sold in the United States (e.g., clothing, athletic shoes, toys, furniture, electronic products, pharmaceuticals, vehicles, solar panels) is outsourced. The largest manufacturing outsourcing country is China. Other countries, including Mexico, Vietnam, Malaysia, Ukraine, Bangladesh, and Indonesia, also produce manufactured goods for U.S. companies. Companies in the United States often outsource knowledge-based work and services (e.g., customer service, claims processing, payroll processing, information technology-enabled services, product design, research and development, back-office services such as accounting and record-keeping, marketing, and other services) to foreign countries. The largest white-collar outsourcing country is India. The Philippines, Brazil, Argentina, Poland, Romania, and other countries also provide such services.

Examples Nike outsources the bulk of the manufacturing of its shoes and clothing; Apple outsources the production of iPhones, iPads, and other electronic products; the majority of Walmart's products are outsourced; and many U.S. prescription drugs are entirely produced in foreign countries.

The reason U.S. companies outsource the production of goods and the provisions of services is that they can be produced or provided at a lower cost in foreign countries. This is because workers in most foreign countries where the goods and services have been outsourced to are paid less than workers in the United States. This leads to U.S. companies making higher profits when they sell the foreign-made goods in the United States.

Additionally, by having their goods made in foreign countries, companies often avoid the expenses of complying with U.S. worker protection laws that would apply if the products were made in the United States. These include occupational safety laws that require workplace safety measures; workers' compensation laws that pay workers if they are injured on the job; fair labor standards laws that prevent child labor and

(continued)

require the payment of minimum wages and overtime wages; laws that allow workers to form and join unions; laws that require employers to provide health insurance to employees; laws that require employers to pay Social Security taxes to the U.S. government for employees; laws that prohibit discrimination based on race, sex, disability, age, and other protected classes; and laws that require companies to pay business taxes in the United States. To avoid compliance with and therefore the costs of these laws, U.S. companies outsource the production of their goods to workers in other countries.

Although some foreign workers are provided benefits available to U.S. workers, many are not. Many workers in foreign companies that produce goods for U.S.-based companies are provided none of the safety and other protections afforded to U.S. workers. In fact, some U.S. companies have been accused of ignoring human rights violations in their supply chains, such as using child labor in Africa's cobalt mines and coca plantations, as well permitting unsafe and oppressive working conditions in third-party–operated foreign manufacturing plants.

Some foreign countries have a very well-educated and professional workforce. For example, India has a large English-speaking and increasingly skilled population that provides professional services to U.S. companies.

Ethics Questions

Is it ethical for U.S. companies to export the production of goods to foreign workers in countries that provide a lower level of worker protections and benefits than those required by law in the United States? Who benefits by having goods made in foreign countries? Can U.S. manufacturers police worker safety and human rights violations in their offshore manufacturing supply chains? Is there a danger in allowing most prescription drugs and medical devices used in the United States to be made in foreign countries?

Public Benefit Corporations

42.4 Define *public benefit corporation* and describe the social purposes served by these corporations.

Most states have passed legislation creating a new form of corporation, called the **public benefit corporation**, often referred to as a **benefit corporation** or **B corporation** or **B corp**. A benefit corporation is a for-profit corporation, but with missions additional to the pure profit-motive. One purpose of a B corporation is to generate benefits for society. Unlike traditional corporations, in which the shareholder is the main stakeholder, B corps by law allow directors and officers to consider other stakeholders in making corporate decisions. These stakeholders include employees, customers, suppliers, and the community.

Public benefit corporation (benefit corporation or B corporation or B corp)
A corporation that requires directors and officers to make decisions to accomplish general public benefits and stipulated specific public benefit purposes stated in the articles of incorporation and to consider stakeholders other than shareholders, such as employees, customers, suppliers, and the community, when making corporate decisions.

A benefit corporation's stated purpose is to create *general public benefits*. This includes considering social issues and protecting the environment. In addition, B corps can name *specific public benefit purposes*, such as reducing the company's carbon footprint, engaging in sustainability efforts, giving 25 percent of their profits to charity, and the like. B corps are sometimes referred to as *mission-driven businesses* and *social purpose corporations*. Most states have enacted legislation that permits B corps.

Examples Patagonia, Inc. is a registered benefit corporation. Ben and Jerry's Homemade Holdings, Inc. is a certified benefit corporation.

Key Terms and Concepts

Code of ethics (756)
Corporate citizenship (756)
Ethical fundamentalism (749)
Ethical relativism (753)
Ethics (748)
Ethics and the law (748)
Kantian ethics (duty ethics or deontological ethics) (751)
Law (748)
Maximize profits (755)
Moral minimum (755)
Offshoring (757)
Outsourcing (757)
Public benefit corporation (benefit corporation or B corporation or B corp) (758)
Rawls's social justice theory (social contract theory) (752)
Sarbanes-Oxley Act of 2002 (756)
Section 43 of the Lanham Act (752)
Section 406 of the Sarbanes-Oxley Act (756)
Social responsibility of business (755)
Stakeholder interest (756)
Utilitarianism (750)

Ethics Cases

42.1 Ethics Case Starbucks Corporation and Starbucks U.S. Brands LLC (Starbucks) is a famous purveyor of specialty coffees and products sold in more than 10,000 locations worldwide. Starbucks owns more than 60 valid trademarks and service marks (marks) under which it operates retail stores and an official website where it sells coffee and other products. "Starbucks" is one of the most recognizable trademarked brand names in the United States and around the world.

Wolfe's Borough Coffee, Inc., doing business as Black Bear Micro Roastery (Black Bear), manufactures and sells roasted coffee beans and related products via internet order and from retail outlets. Black Bear uses the trademarked names "Mister Charbucks," "Mr. Charbucks," and "Charbucks Blend." Starbucks sued Black Bear, alleging that the defendant caused trademark dilution in violation of the Federal Trademark Dilution Act by blurring of the name Charbucks with Starbucks and causing a likelihood of confusion. Starbucks requested that the court issue an injunction prohibiting Black Bear from using Charbucks marks. Was Black Bear's use of the Charbucks name legal? Was Black Bear's use of the Charbucks name ethical? Do you think that the defendant was consciously using the name recognition of the famous Starbucks marks when it used the "Charbucks" name? *Starbucks Corporation v. Wolfe's Borough Coffee, Inc.*, 736 F.3d 198 (United States Court of Appeals for the Second Circuit, 2013)

42.2 Ethics Case POM Wonderful, LLC (POM) is a grower of pomegranates and a maker and distributor of pomegranate juices and juice blends. POM produces and sells a pomegranate-blueberry juice blend that consists of 85 percent pomegranate juice and 15 percent blueberry juice.

The Coca-Cola Company's Minute Maid Division makes a juice blend that contains 0.3 percent pomegranate juice, 0.2 percent blueberry juice, and 0.1 percent raspberry juice. The Coca-Cola pomegranate-blueberry juice is actually made with 99.4 percent apple and grape juices. Despite the minuscule amount of pomegranate and blueberry juices in the blend, the front label of the Coca-Cola product displays the words "POMEGRANATE" and "BLUEBERRY" in all capital letters on two separate lines. Below those words, Coca-Cola placed the phrase "flavored blend of 5 juices" in much smaller type. Coca-Cola's front label also displays a vignette of blueberries, grapes, and raspberries in front of a halved pomegranate and a halved apple.

POM sued Coca-Cola under Section 43 of the Lanham Act, which allows one competitor to sue another to recover damages for unfair competition arising from false and misleading product descriptions. Coca-Cola defended, arguing that POM could not sue it for violating Section 43. Can POM bring an unfair competition lawsuit under Section 43 of the Lanham Act against Coca-Cola that challenges the truthfulness of a food label? Did Coca-Cola act ethically in prominently labelling their fruit drink "POMEGRANATE" and "BLUEBERRY" when in fact it only contained 0.3 percent pomegranate juice and 0.2 percent blueberry juice? *POM Wonderful, LLC v. Coca-Cola Company*, 134 S.Ct. 2228, 2014 U.S. Lexis 4165 (Supreme Court of the United States, 2014)

42.3 Ethics Case Bayer Corporation (Bayer) is a large pharmaceutical company that produces prescription drugs, including its patented antibiotic Cipro. Bayer sold Cipro to private health providers and hospitals, including Kaiser Permanente Medical Care Program, one of the largest health maintenance organizations in the United States. Bayer also sold Cipro to the federal government's Medicaid program, which provides medical insurance to the poor. Federal law contains a "best price" rule that prohibits a company that sells a drug to Medicaid from charging Medicaid a price higher than the lowest price for which it sells the drug to private purchasers.

Bayer's executives came up with a plan whereby Bayer would put a private label on its Cipro and not call it Cipro and sell the antibiotic to Kaiser and other private purchasers at a 40 percent discount. Bayer continued to charge Medicaid the full price. One day, George Couto, a Bayer executive, attended a staff meeting at which it was disclosed that Bayer kept $97 million from Medicaid by using the discounted private labeling program for Kaiser and other health care companies. Couto notified the federal government of Bayer's scheme. The U.S. Department of Justice filed criminal and civil charges against Bayer. Is Bayer guilty of violating the law? Did Bayer act ethically? *United States ex. rel. Estate of George Couto v. Bayer Corporation* (United States District Court for the District of Massachusetts, 2003)

Notes

1. 15 U.S.C. Section 1125.
2. Milton Friedman, "The Social Responsibility of Business Is to Increase Its Profits," *New York Times Magazine*, September 13, 1970.
3. Public Law 107-204 (2002).

PART IX

Government Regulation

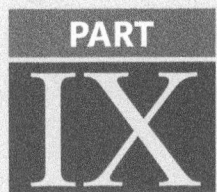

Henry R. Cheeseman

CHAPTER

43 Administrative Law and Regulatory Agencies

Henry R. Cheeseman

FEDERAL TRADE COMMISSION, WASHINGTON DC

The federal and state and local governments have enacted statutes and ordinances that regulate businesses and protect consumers and others. The Federal Trade Commission (FTC) is an administrative agency that is responsible for enforcing consumer protection laws, antitrust statutes, and other federal laws.

Learning Objectives

After studying this chapter, you should be able to:

43.1 Define *administrative law*.

43.2 Describe cabinet-level departments of the federal government.

43.3 Describe federal administrative agencies and explain their functions.

43.4 Describe state and local administrative agencies and explain their functions.

43.5 Describe administrative procedure and provisions of the Administrative Procedure Act.

43.6 List and describe the powers of administrative agencies.

43.7 Explain the procedure for judicial review of administrative agency decisions.

43.8 List and describe the statutes that require disclosure of administrative agency actions and protections of individual rights.

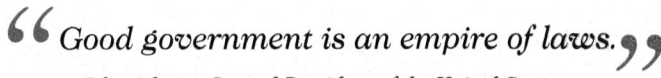

"Good government is an empire of laws."

—*John Adams, Second President of the United States*
Thoughts on Government (1776)

Introduction to Administrative Law and Regulatory Agencies

Businesses are generally free to produce goods or services, enter into contracts, and otherwise conduct business as they see fit. However, businesses are subject to substantial federal, state, and local government regulation. Government regulation is designed to protect employees and the public from unsafe and abusive practices by businesses. Many times, when a regulatory statute is enacted, an administrative agency is created to enforce the law. Regulatory agencies—and the industries, businesses, and professionals they regulate—are governed by a body of *administrative law*. Because of their importance, administrative agencies are informally referred to as the "fourth branch of government."

This chapter examines administrative law and regulatory agencies.

The independent agencies collectively constitute, in effect, a headless fourth branch of the U.S. government.

PHH Corporation v. Consumer Financial Protection Bureau
839 F.3d 1 (2016)
United States Court of Appeals for the District of Columbia Circuit

Administrative Law

43.1 Define *administrative law*.

Administrative law is law enacted by governments that regulates industries and businesses and professionals. Administrative laws are often referred to as **regulatory statutes**.

Administrative agencies are created by federal, state, and local governments to enforce regulatory statutes. Government agencies range from large, complex federal agencies, such as the Department of Homeland Security, to local zoning boards. There are more than 100 federal administrative agencies. Thousands of other administrative agencies have been created by state and local governments.

Governments often create administrative agencies to administer and enforce new statutes or laws (see **Exhibit 43.1**). Sometimes when the legislative branch enacts a new statute, it authorizes an existing administrative agency to administer and enforce the law.

administrative law
Law that governments enact to regulate industries, businesses, and professionals.

administrative agencies
Agencies that governments create to enforce regulatory statutes.

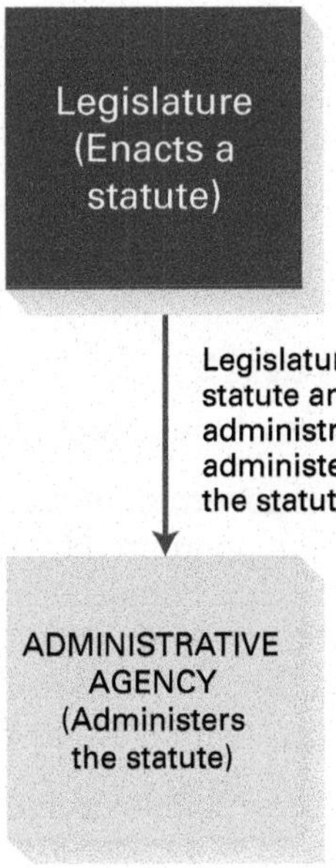

Exhibit 43.1
ADMINISTRATIVE AGENCY

Example When Congress enacted the Securities Act of 1933 and the Securities Exchange Act of 1934, it created the Securities and Exchange Commission (SEC), a federal administrative agency, to administer and enforce those statutes.

General Government Regulation

general government regulation
Laws that regulate businesses and industries collectively.

General government regulation consists of laws that regulate businesses and industries collectively. That is, most of the industries and businesses in the United States are subject to these laws. These laws do not regulate a specific industry but apply to all industries and businesses except those that are specifically exempt from certain regulations.

No nation was ever ruined by trade.

Benjamin Franklin
(1706–1790)

Examples The National Labor Relations Board (NLRB), a federal administrative agency, is empowered to regulate the formation and operation of labor unions in most industries and businesses in the United States. The federal Occupational Health and Safety Administration (OSHA) is authorized to regulate workplace safety for most industries and businesses in the country. The U.S. Equal Employment Opportunity Commission (EEOC) enforces equal opportunity in employment laws that cover most workers in the United States.

Specific Government Regulation

specific government regulation
Laws that regulate a specific industry or type of business.

Specific government regulation consists of laws that regulate specific industries; that is, an industry is subject to administrative laws that are adopted to regulate that industry. Industry-specific administrative agencies are created to administer those laws.

Examples The Federal Communications Commission (FCC) issues licenses and regulates the operation of television and radio stations. The Federal Aviation Administration (FAA) regulates the operation of commercial airlines. The federal Office of the Comptroller of the Currency regulates the licensing and operation of national banks.

CONCEPT SUMMARY
GOVERNMENT REGULATION OF BUSINESS

Type of Regulation	Description
General government regulation	Government regulation that applies to many industries (e.g., antidiscrimination laws).
Specific government regulation	Government regulation that applies to a specific industry (e.g., banking laws).

Cabinet-Level Departments

43.2 Describe cabinet-level departments of the federal government.

cabinet-level departments
Federal departments that advise the president and are responsible for enforcing specific administrative statutes enacted by Congress.

Cabinet-level departments of the federal government answer directly to the president. Each department is led by a person appointed by the president, subject to confirmation by a majority vote of the U.S. Senate. Cabinet-level departments advise the president and are responsible for enforcing specific laws enacted by Congress.

There are 15 cabinet-level departments, which are as follows:

1. **Department of Agriculture**—Oversees policies relating to food, agriculture, farming, and rural development.

2. **Department of Commerce**—Promotes the nation's economy, supports business and industry, and oversees telecommunications and technical policies.
3. **Department of Defense**—Provides the military for the country and advises on international security.
4. **Department of Education**—Promotes national education and works to keep the U.S. competitive.
5. **Department of Energy**—Advances U.S. energy policy security and addresses environmental issues.
6. **Department of Health and Human Services**—Overseas all health-related issues, including health and safety laws.
7. **Department of Homeland Security**—Focuses on national security, terrorism, and immigration policy.
8. **Department of Housing and Urban Development**—Oversees issues related to national housing and cities.
9. **Department of Interior**—Protects and manages natural resources, wildlife, and land.
10. **Department of Justice**—Enforces the law and protects public safety.
11. **Department of Labor**—Protects the welfare of U.S. workers and promotes a strong workforce.
12. **Department of State**—Develops foreign policy, negotiates treaties, and represents the United States at the United Nations.
13. **Department of Transportation**—Promotes safe and efficient transportation throughout the United States.
14. **Department of Treasury**—Develops financial and economic policies, regulates money, and collects taxes.
15. **Department of Veterans Affairs**—Administers programs that provide assistance to military veterans.

The Department of Homeland Security is discussed in the following feature.

U.S. Department of Homeland Security (DHS)
A cabinet-level federal administrative agency whose mission is to enforce laws to prevent terrorist attacks and related criminal activities.

Landmark Law

U.S. Department of Homeland Security

On September 11, 2001, the World Trade Center buildings in New York City were destroyed, and the Pentagon in Washington DC was damaged by terrorist attacks. In 2002, Congress enacted the **Homeland Security Act (HSA)**,[1] which created the federal cabinet-level **U.S. Department of Homeland Security (DHS)**. The creation of DHS was the largest government reorganization in more than 50 years.

The act placed 22 federal agencies with approximately 200,000 employees under the umbrella of DHS, which is the second-largest government agency after the Department of Defense. DHS contains the Bureau of Customs and Border Protection, the Bureau of Citizenship and Immigration Services, the U.S. Secret Service, the Federal Emergency Management Agency, the Federal Computer Incident Response Center, the National Domestic Preparedness Office, the U.S. Coast Guard, and portions of the Federal Bureau of Investigation, Treasury Department, Commerce Department, Justice Department, and other federal government agencies.

The mission of DHS is to enforce laws to prevent domestic terrorist attacks and related criminal activities, reduce vulnerability to terrorist attacks, minimize the harm caused by such attacks, and assist in recovery in the event of a terrorist attack. DHS provides services in the following critical areas: (1) border and transportation security, including protecting airports, seaports, and borders and providing immigration and visa processing; (2) chemical, biological, radiological, and nuclear countermeasures, including metering the air for biological agents and developing vaccines and treatments for biological agents; (3) information analysis and infrastructure protection, including protecting communications systems, power grids, transportation networks, telecommunications, and cyber systems; and (4) emergency preparedness and response to terrorist incidents, including training first responders and coordinating government disaster relief.

Federal Administrative Agencies

43.3 Describe federal administrative agencies and explain their functions.

federal administrative agencies
Government agencies created by the U.S. Congress that have broad regulatory powers over key areas of the national economy.

Administrative agencies that are created by the U.S. Congress are called **federal administrative agencies**. Congress has created many federal administrative agencies that have broad regulatory powers over key areas of the national economy.

Examples The Securities and Exchange Commission (SEC), which regulates the issuance and trading of securities; the Federal Trade Commission (FTC), which enforces federal antitrust and consumer protection laws; and the Federal Communications Commission (FCC), which regulates radio and television broadcasting and telecommunications, are examples of federal independent agencies.

State and Local Administrative Agencies

43.4 Describe state and local administrative agencies and explain their functions.

state administrative agencies
Agencies created by legislative branches of states to administer state regulatory laws.

All states create administrative agencies to enforce and interpret state regulatory law. **State administrative agencies** have a profound effect on business. They are empowered to enforce state statutes and adopt rules and regulations to interpret the statutes they are empowered to administer.

Examples Most states have corporation departments to enforce state corporation law and regulate the issuance of securities, banking departments to license and regulate the operation of banks, fish and game departments to regulate fishing and hunting within the state's boundaries, workers' compensation boards to decide workers' compensation claims for injuries that occur on the job, and environmental protection departments to regulate the land, waterways, and other environmental issues.

local administrative agencies
Agencies created by cities, municipalities, counties, and other local government bodies to administer local regulatory law.

Local governments such as cities, municipalities, and counties create **local administrative agencies** to administer local regulatory law.

Examples Cities adopt and enforce zoning laws, building codes, and so on.

Administrative Procedure

43.5 Describe administrative procedure and provisions of the Administrative Procedure Act.

My reading of history convinces me that most bad government has grown out of too much government.

Thomas Jefferson
(1743–1826)
Third President of the United States

Administrative law is a combination of *substantive* and *procedural law*. **Substantive administrative law** is law that an administrative agency enforces—federal statutes enacted by Congress or state statutes enacted by state legislatures. **Procedural administrative law** establishes the procedures that must be followed by an administrative agency while enforcing substantive laws.

Examples Congress created the federal Environmental Protection Agency (EPA) to enforce federal environmental laws that protect the environment. This is an example of substantive law—laws enacted to protect the environment. In enforcing these laws, the EPA must follow certain established procedural rules (e.g., notices, hearings). These are examples of procedural law.

The following feature discusses the Administrative Procedure Act.

Landmark Law

Administrative Procedure Act

In 1946, Congress enacted the **Administrative Procedure Act (APA)**.[2] This act is very important because it establishes procedures that federal administrative agencies must follow in conducting their affairs. The APA establishes notice requirements of actions the federal agency plans on taking. It requires hearings to be held in most cases, and it requires certain procedural safeguards and protocols to be followed at these proceedings.

The APA also establishes how **rules and regulations** can be adopted by federal administrative agencies. This includes providing notice of proposed rulemaking, granting a time period for receiving comments from the public regarding the proposed rulemaking, and holding hearings to take evidence. The APA provides a procedure for receiving evidence and hearing requests for the granting of federal licenses (e.g., to operate a national bank). The APA also establishes notice and hearing requirements and rules for conducting agency adjudicative actions, such as actions to take away certain parties' licenses (e.g., a securities broker's licenses).

Most states have enacted administrative procedural acts that govern state administrative procedures.

Administrative Law Judge

An **administrative law judge (ALJ)** presides over an administrative proceeding. ALJs decide questions of law and fact concerning a case. Each ALJ is an employee of an administrative agency. Both the administrative agency and the respondent may be represented by counsel. Witnesses may be examined and cross-examined, evidence may be introduced, objections may be made, and so on. There is no jury.

An ALJ's decision is issued in the form of an **administrative order**. The order must state the reasons for the ALJ's decision. The order becomes final if it is not appealed. An appeal consists of a review by the administrative agency. Further appeal can be made to the appropriate federal court (in federal agency actions) or state court (in state agency actions).

Administrative Procedure Act (APA)
A federal statute that establishes procedures to be followed by federal administrative agencies while conducting their affairs.

administrative law judge (ALJ)
An employee of an administrative agency who presides over an administrative proceeding and decides questions of law and fact concerning cases.

administrative order
A decision issued by an administrative law judge.

Powers of Administrative Agencies

43.6 List and describe the powers of administrative agencies.

When an administrative agency is created, certain powers are delegated to it. The agency has only the legislative, judicial, and executive powers that are so delegated to it, which collectively are called the **delegation doctrine**. Thus, an agency can adopt a rule or regulation (a legislative function), prosecute a violation of the statute or rule (an executive function), and adjudicate the dispute (a judicial function). The courts have upheld this combined power of administrative agencies as being constitutional. If an administrative agency acts outside the scope of its delegated powers, it commits an unconstitutional act.

Administrative agencies have been delegated legislative powers that consist of substantive rulemaking, interpretive rulemaking, issuing statements of policy, and granting licenses. Administrative agencies have also been delegated certain executive powers and judicial powers. Legislative, executive, and judicial powers are discussed in the following paragraphs.

The following feature discusses administrative agency rulemaking.

delegation doctrine
A doctrine that says that when an administrative agency is created, it is delegated certain powers; the agency can use only the legislative, judicial, and executive powers that are delegated to it.

substantive rule
A rule issued by an administrative agency that has the force of law and to which covered persons and businesses must adhere.

Critical Legal Thinking

Administrative Agency Rulemaking

Most federal statutes expressly authorize an administrative agency to engage in **rulemaking** and to issue **substantive rules**. A substantive rule is much like a statute: It has the force of law, and covered persons and businesses must adhere to it. Violators may be held civilly or criminally liable, depending on the rule. All substantive rules are subject to judicial review.

(continued)

A federal administrative agency that proposes to adopt a substantive rule must follow procedures set forth in the APA.[3] This means the agency must do the following:

1. Publish a general notice of the proposed rule in the ***Federal Register***. The notice must include:
   a. The time, place, and nature of the rulemaking proceeding
   b. The legal authority pursuant to which the rule is proposed
   c. The terms or substance of the proposed rule or a description of the subject and issues involved
2. Give interested persons an opportunity to participate in the rulemaking process. This may involve oral hearings.
3. Review all written and oral comments. Then the agency announces its *final rule* in the matter. This procedure is often referred to as *notice-and-comment rulemaking*, or **informal rulemaking**.
4. Require, in some instances, **formal rulemaking**. Here, the agency must conduct a trial-like hearing at which the parties may present evidence, engage in cross-examination, and present rebuttal evidence.

Administrative agencies can issue an **interpretive rule** that interprets existing statutory language. Such rules do not establish new laws. Neither public notice nor public participation is required. Administrative agencies may also issue a **statement of policy**. Such a statement announces a proposed course of action that an agency intends to follow in the future. Statements of policy do not have the force of law. Again, public notice and participation are not required.

Critical Legal Thinking Questions

Why are administrative agencies granted rulemaking powers? Do administrative rules have much impact on businesses? Do administrative rules have much impact on consumers? Some people assert that administrative agencies have gotten too big and impact the ability of companies to conduct business. Do you agree?

---

interpretive rule
A rule issued by an administrative agency that interprets existing statutory language.

government license
Permission that an administrative agency grants to persons or businesses to conduct certain types of commerce or professions.

Granting Licenses

Statutes often require the issuance of a **government license** before a person can enter certain types of industries (e.g., banks, television and radio stations, commercial airlines) or professions (e.g., doctors, lawyers, dentists, certified public accountants, contractors). The administrative agency that regulates the specific area involved is granted licensing power to determine whether to grant a license to an applicant.

Applicants must usually submit detailed applications to the appropriate administrative agency. In addition, the agency usually accepts written comments from interested parties and holds hearings on the matter. Courts generally defer to the expertise of administrative agencies in licensing matters.

Judicial Authority

judicial authority
Authority of an administrative agency to adjudicate cases in an administrative proceeding.

Many administrative agencies have **judicial authority** to adjudicate cases through an administrative proceeding. Such a proceeding is initiated when an agency serves a complaint on a party the agency believes has violated a statute or an administrative rule or order.

procedural due process
Due process that requires the respondent to be given proper and timely notice of the allegations or charges against him or her and an opportunity to present evidence on the matter.

In adjudicating cases, an administrative agency must comply with the Due Process Clause of the U.S. Constitution (and with the state constitution, where applicable). **Procedural due process** requires the respondent to be given proper and timely notice of the allegations or charges against him or her and an opportunity to present evidence on the matter.

Executive Power

executive power
Power that administrative agencies are granted, such as to investigate and prosecute possible violations of statutes, administrative rules, and administrative orders.

Administrative agencies are usually granted **executive powers**, such as the power to investigate and prosecute possible violations of statutes, administrative rules, and administrative orders.

To perform these functions successfully, an agency must often obtain information from the persons and businesses under investigation as well as from other sources. If the required information is not supplied voluntarily, the agency may issue an administrative subpoena to search the business premises; this is called an **administrative search**.

An **administrative subpoena** is issued to a business or person subject to the agency's jurisdiction. The subpoena directs the party to disclose the requested information to the administrative agency. The administrative agency can seek judicial enforcement of the subpoena if the party does not comply with the subpoena.

administrative subpoena
An order that directs the subject of the subpoena to disclose the requested information.

CONCEPT SUMMARY
POWERS OF ADMINISTRATIVE AGENCIES

Power	Description of Power
1. Legislative Power	
A. Substantive rulemaking	To adopt rules that advance the purpose of the statutes that the agency is empowered to enforce. These rules have the force of law. Public notice and participation are required.
B. Interpretive rulemaking	To adopt rules that interpret statutes. These rules do not establish new laws. Neither public notice nor participation is required.
C. Statements of policy	To announce a proposed course of action the agency plans to take in the future. These statements do not have the force of law. Public participation and notice are not required.
D. Licensing	To grant licenses to applicants (e.g., television station licenses, bank charters) and to suspend or revoke licenses.
2. Judicial Power	The power to adjudicate cases through an administrative proceeding. This includes the power to issue a complaint, hold a hearing by an administrative law judge (ALJ), and issue an order deciding the case and assessing remedies.
3. Executive Power	The power to prosecute violations of statutes and administrative rules and orders. This includes the power to investigate suspected violations, issue administrative subpoenas, and conduct administrative searches.

Fourth Amendment to the U.S. Constitution

Sometimes a physical inspection of business premises is crucial to an investigation. Most inspections by administrative agencies are considered "searches" that are subject to the **Fourth Amendment** to the U.S. Constitution. The Fourth Amendment protects persons (including businesses) from **unreasonable search and seizure**. Searches by administrative agencies are generally considered to be reasonable within the meaning of the Fourth Amendment if:

unreasonable search and seizure
Any search and seizure by the government that violates the Fourth Amendment to the U.S. Constitution.

- The party voluntarily agrees to the search.
- The search is conducted pursuant to a validly issued *search warrant*.
- A warrantless search is conducted in an emergency situation.
- The business is part of a special industry where warrantless searches are automatically considered valid (e.g., liquor sales, firearm sales).
- The business is part of a hazardous industry (e.g., coal mines), and a statute expressly provides for nonarbitrary warrantless searches.

Evidence from an unreasonable search and seizure ("tainted evidence") is inadmissible in court.

Judicial Review of Administrative Agency Actions

43.7 Explain the procedure for judicial review of administrative agency decisions.

Critical Legal Thinking Questions

Why are administrative agencies referred to as the "fourth branch of the government"? What purposes do administrative agencies serve? What are some criticisms of administrative agencies?

Many federal statutes expressly provide for **judicial review of administrative agency actions**. Where an enabling statute does not provide for review, the APA authorizes judicial review of federal administrative agency actions.[4] A party who appeals the decision of an administrative agency is called the **petitioner**.

Decisions of federal administrative agencies can be appealed to the appropriate federal court (see **Exhibit 43.2**). Decisions of state administrative agencies can be appealed to the proper state court.

In the following case, the U.S. Supreme Court decided the legality of an administrative agency's rule.

CASE 43.1 *U.S. SUPREME COURT CASE Administrative Agency Rule*

Environmental Protection Agency v. EME Homer City Generation, L.P.

134 S.Ct. 1584, 2014 U.S. Lexis 3108 (2014)
Supreme Court of the United States

"Air pollution is transient, heedless of state boundaries."

—Ruth Bader Ginsburg, Justice

Facts

Air pollution emitted in one state often causes harm in other states. To tackle this problem, Congress enacted the Good Neighbor Provision of the Clean Air Act, which instructs states to prohibit in-state sources from emitting air pollutants in amounts that will contribute significantly to downwind states' ability to meet national air quality standards set by the Environmental Protection Agency (EPA). Pursuant to the Good Neighbor Provision, the EPA adopted the Cross-State Air Pollution Rule (called the Transport Rule), which permits the EPA to consider costs when assessing reductions in air pollution that upwind states must make to improve air quality in downwind states. A group of state and local governments challenged the Transport Rule, alleging that the EPA exceeded its authority when it included cost as a factor in determining the amount of pollution upwind states must eliminate. They contend that the EPA should use a proportional standard when requiring upwind states to reduce air pollution, irrespective of the cost of their doing so. The U.S. court of appeals vacated the Transport Rule. The EPA appealed to the U.S. Supreme Court.

Issue

Is the EPA's Transport Rule, which permits the consideration of cost when assessing the amount of air pollution that upwind states must eliminate to reduce air pollution in downwind states, a valid rule?

Language of the U.S. Supreme Court

Air pollution is transient, heedless of state boundaries. Pollutants generated by upwind sources are often transported by air currents, sometimes over hundreds of miles, to downwind states. We hold that the text of the statute supports EPA's position. We routinely accord dispositive effect to an agency's reasonable interpretation of ambiguous statutory language.

Decision

The U.S. Supreme Court upheld the EPA's adoption of the Transport Rule.

Critical Legal Thinking Questions

Should upwind states be held responsible for air pollution they cause to downwind states? Was the EPA's adoption of the Transport Rule a valid interpretation of a statute?

Exhibit 43.2 **APPEAL OF A FEDERAL ADMINISTRATIVE AGENCY DECISION**

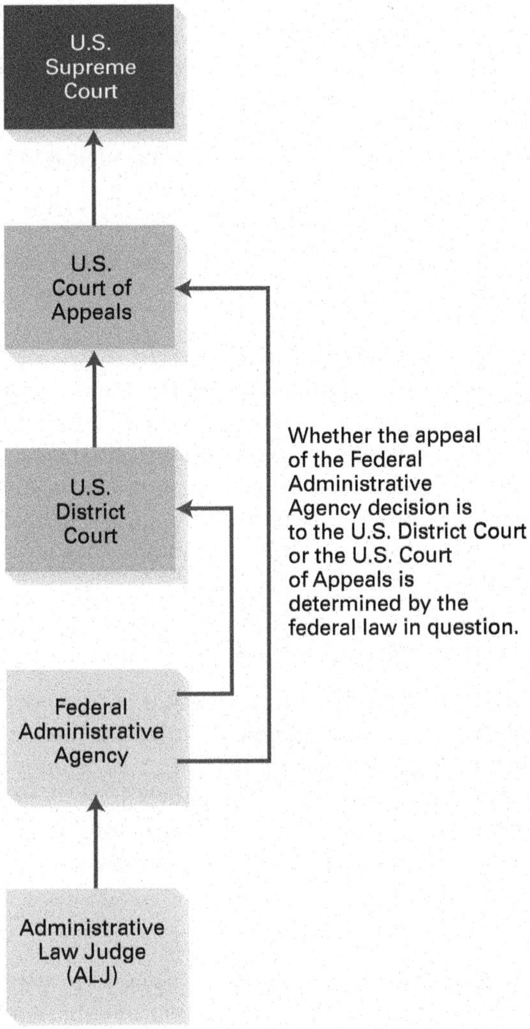
U.S.
Supreme
Court
U.S.
Court of
Appeals
U.S.
District
Court
Federal
Administrative
Agency
Administrative
Law Judge
(ALJ)
Whether the appeal of the Federal Administrative Agency decision is to the U.S. District Court or the U.S. Court of Appeals is determined by the federal law in question.

Individual Rights and Disclosures of Agency Actions

43.8 List and describe the statutes that require disclosure of administrative agency actions and protections of individual rights.

Public concern over possible secrecy of administrative agency actions led Congress to enact several statutes that promote public disclosure of federal administrative agency actions and protect parties from overly intrusive agency actions. Several of these statutes are discussed in the following paragraphs.

The following feature discusses the Freedom of Information Act.

Freedom of Information Act
A federal act that gives the public access to documents in the possession of federal administrative agencies.

Contemporary Environment

Freedom of Information Act

The **Freedom of Information Act**[5] was enacted to give the public access to most documents in the possession of federal administrative agencies. The act requires federal administrative agencies to publish agency procedures, rules, regulations, interpretations, and other such information in the *Federal Register*. The act also requires agencies to publish quarterly indexes of certain documents. In addition, the act specifies time limits for agencies to respond to requests

(continued)

for information, sets limits on copying charges, and provides for disciplinary action against agency employees who refuse to honor proper requests for information.

For purposes of privacy, the following documents are exempt from disclosure: (1) documents classified by the president in the interest of national security; (2) documents that are statutorily prohibited from disclosure; (3) records whose disclosure would interfere with law enforcement proceedings; (4) medical, personnel, and similar files; and (5) documents containing trade secrets or other confidential or privileged information. Decisions by federal administrative agencies not to publicly disclose documents requested under the act are subject to judicial review in the proper U.S. district court.

Government in the Sunshine Act

Government in the Sunshine Act
A federal act that opens most federal administrative agency meetings to the public.

The **Government in the Sunshine Act**[6] was enacted to open most federal administrative agency meetings to the public. There are some exceptions to this rule. These include meetings (1) where a person is accused of a crime, (2) concerning an agency's issuance of a subpoena, (3) where attendance of the public would significantly frustrate the implementation of a proposed agency action, and (4) concerning day-to-day operations. Decisions by federal administrative agencies to close meetings to the public are subject to judicial review in the proper U.S. district court.

Equal Access to Justice Act

Equal Access to Justice Act
A federal act that protects persons from harassment by federal administrative agencies.

Congress enacted the **Equal Access to Justice Act**[7] to protect persons from harassment by federal administrative agencies. Under this act, a private party who is the subject of an unjustified federal administrative agency action can sue to recover attorneys' fees and other costs. The courts have generally held that the agency's conduct must be extremely outrageous before an award will be made under the act. A number of states have similar statutes.

Privacy Act

Privacy Act
A federal act that states that federal administrative agencies can maintain only information about an individual that is relevant and necessary to accomplish a legitimate agency purpose.

The federal **Privacy Act**[8] concerns individual privacy. It stipulates that federal administrative agencies can maintain only information about an individual that is relevant and necessary to accomplish a legitimate agency purpose. The act affords individuals the right to have access to agency records concerning themselves and to correct these records. Many states have enacted similar privacy acts.

CONCEPT SUMMARY

INDIVIDUAL RIGHTS AND DISCLOSURE OF AGENCY ACTIONS

Act	Provisions of the Act
Freedom of Information Act	Requires that documents of federal administrative agencies be open to the public; there are certain exemptions from this requirement. The act requires agencies to publish their procedures, rules, regulations, and other information in the *Federal Register*.
Government in the Sunshine Act	Requires that meetings of federal administrative agencies be open to the public; there are certain exemptions from this requirement.
Equal Access to Justice Act	Gives a private party who was subject to an unjustified federal administrative agency action the right to sue and recover attorneys' fees and costs.
Privacy Act	Requires that federal administrative agencies maintain only information about an individual that is relevant and necessary to accomplish a legitimate agency purpose. Also gives individuals access to these records and a right to correct the records.

Key Terms and Concepts

Administrative agencies (763)
Administrative law (763)
Administrative law judge (ALJ) (767)
Administrative order (767)
Administrative Procedure Act (APA) (767)
Administrative search (768)
Administrative subpoena (769)
Cabinet-level departments (764)
Delegation doctrine (767)
Equal Access to Justice Act (772)
Executive power (768)
Federal administrative agencies (766)
Federal Register (768)
Formal rulemaking (768)
Fourth Amendment (769)
Freedom of Information Act (771)
General government regulation (764)
Government in the Sunshine Act (772)
Government license (768)
Homeland Security Act (HSA) (765)
Informal rulemaking (768)
Interpretive rule (768)
Judicial authority (768)
Judicial review of administrative agency actions (770)
Local administrative agencies (766)
Petitioner (770)
Privacy Act (772)
Procedural administrative law (766)
Procedural due process (768)
Regulatory statutes (763)
Rulemaking (767)
Rules and regulations (767)
Specific government regulation (764)
State administrative agencies (766)
Statement of policy (768)
Substantive administrative law (766)
Substantive rule (767)
Unreasonable search and seizure (769)
U.S. Department of Homeland Security (DHS) (765)

Critical Legal Thinking Cases

43.1 Government Regulation George Carlin, a satiric humorist, recorded a 12-minute monologue called "Filthy Words." He began by referring to his thoughts about "the words you couldn't say on the public airwaves" and then proceeded to list those words, repeating them over and over again in a variety of colloquialisms. At about 2:00 in the afternoon, a New York radio station, owned by Pacifica Foundation (Pacifica), broadcast Carlin's "Filthy Words" monologue. A father who heard the broadcast while driving with his young son filed a complaint with the Federal Communications Commission (FCC), a federal administrative agency charged with regulating broadcasting. The Federal Communications Act forbids the use of "any obscene, indecent, or profane language by means of radio communications." The FCC issued an order granting the complaint, and it informed Pacifica that the order would be considered in future licensing decisions involving Pacifica. Is the FCC regulation legal? *Federal Communications Commission v. Pacifica Foundation*, 438 U.S. 726, 98 S.Ct. 3026, 1978 U.S. Lexis 135 (Supreme Court of the United States, 1978)

43.2 Administrative Search The Federal Mine Safety and Health Act requires the secretary of labor to develop detailed mandatory health and safety standards to govern the operation of the nation's mines. The act provides that federal mine inspectors are to inspect underground mines at least four times a year and surface mines at least twice a year to ensure compliance with these standards and to make inspections to determine whether previously discovered violations have been corrected. The act also grants mine inspectors "a right of entry to, upon or through any coal or other mine" and states that "no advance notice of an inspection shall be provided to any person."

A federal mine inspector attempted to inspect quarries owned by Waukesha Lime and Stone Company (Waukesha) to determine whether all 25 safety and health violations uncovered during a prior inspection had been corrected. Douglas Dewey, Waukesha's president, refused to allow the inspector to inspect the premises without first obtaining a search warrant. Are the warrantless searches of stone quarries authorized by the Mine Safety and Health Act constitutional? *Donovan, Secretary of Labor v. Dewey*, 452 U.S. 594, 101 S.Ct. 2534, 1980 U.S. Lexis 58 (Supreme Court of the United States, 1980)

Ethics Case

43.3 Ethics Case A statute of the state of Wisconsin forbids the practice of medicine without a license granted by the Examining Board (Board), a state administrative agency composed of practicing physicians. The statute specifically prohibits certain acts of professional misconduct. Board may investigate alleged violations, issue charges against a licensee, hold hearings, and rule on the matter. Board also has the authority to warn and reprimand violators, suspend or revoke their licenses, and institute criminal actions.

Dr. Larkin was a physician licensed to practice medicine in the state of Wisconsin. Board sent a notice to Larkin that it would hold a hearing to determine whether Larkin had engaged in prohibited acts. Larkin was represented by counsel at the hearing. At the hearing evidence was introduced and witnesses gave testimony. Board found Larkin guilty and temporarily suspended his license to practice medicine. Larkin then filed suit, alleging that it was an unconstitutional violation of due process to permit an administrative agency to adjudicate a charge that it had investigated and brought. Is there a violation of due process? Did Larkin act ethically in challenging the authority of the administrative agency? *Withrow v. Larkin*, 421 U.S. 35, 95 S.Ct. 1456, 1975 U.S. Lexis 56 (Supreme Court of the United States, 1975)

Notes

1. Public Law 107-295 (2002).
2. 5 U.S.C. Sections 551–706.
3. 5 U.S.C. Section 553.
4. U.S.C. Section 702.
5. U.S.C. Section 702.
6. U.S.C. Section 552(b).
7. 5 U.S.C. Section 504.
8. 5 U.S.C. Section 552(a).

CHAPTER

44 Consumer Protection and Product Safety

Henry R. Cheeseman

INTERSTATE 75, MICHIGAN

I-75 is part of the interstate highway system that traverses the United States. The National Highway Traffic Safety Administration (NHTSA) is the federal administrative agency that writes and enforces motor vehicle safety standards.

Learning Objectives

After studying this chapter, you should be able to:

44.1 Describe government regulation of meat, poultry, and egg products by the U.S. Department of Agriculture.

44.2 Describe government regulation of food, drugs, cosmetics, and medical devices by the Food and Drug Administration (FDA).

44.3 Describe government requirements and restrictions on the disclosure of nutrition facts and other safety information.

44.4 Describe federal laws that regulate product safety.

44.5 Describe federal laws that regulate automobile, vehicle, bus, and motorcycle safety.

44.6 Identify and describe unfair and deceptive business practices.

44.7 Describe state and local consumer protection laws.

> *"I should regret to find that the law was powerless to enforce the most elementary principles of commercial morality."*
>
> — *Lord Herschell*
> *Reddaway v. Banham (1896)*

Introduction to Consumer Protection and Product Safety

Waste no more time arguing about what a good man should be. Be one.

Marcus Aurelius
(121–180) Meditations

Originally, sales transactions in this country were guided by the principle of ***caveat emptor*** ("let the buyer beware"). This led to abusive practices by businesses that sold adulterated food products and other unsafe products and that engaged in deceptive practices. In response, federal and state governments have enacted a variety of statutes that regulate the safety of food, drugs, cosmetics, toys, consumer products, and vehicles. In addition, governments have enacted laws that prohibit false and deceptive business practices. These laws are collectively referred to as **consumer protection laws**.

consumer protection laws
Federal and state statutes and regulations that promote product safety and prohibit abusive, unfair, and deceptive business practices.

This chapter covers consumer protection; food, drug, and cosmetic safety laws; vehicle and product safety laws; unfair and deceptive practices; and consumer financial protection laws.

Food Safety—U.S. Department of Agriculture (USDA)

44.1 Describe government regulation of meat, poultry, and egg products by the U.S. Department of Agriculture.

The safety of food is an important concern in the United States and worldwide. In the United States, federal statutes have given the **U.S. Department of Agriculture (USDA)**, a federal administrative agency, primary responsibility for regulating meat, poultry, eggs, and other food products.[1] The USDA has adopted labeling requirements for meat, poultry, and egg products. Nutrition labeling for raw fruits and vegetables and raw seafood is voluntary. Many sellers of these products provide point-of-purchase nutrition information.

U.S. Department of Agriculture (USDA)
A federal administrative agency that is responsible for regulating the safety of meat, poultry, and egg products.

Adulterated Food and False and Misleading Statements

The USDA conducts inspections of food processing and storage facilities and can initiate legal proceedings against food manufacturers and processors where meat, poultry, or egg products have been prepared, packed, or stored under unsanitary conditions. The USDA may bring actions against parties who distribute or sell adulterated food—defined as food that is in whole or in part filthy, putrid, or otherwise unfit for food—or for making **false and misleading statements** or using misleading and deceptive labeling in the sale of meat and poultry products.

The following case involves a USDA action against a food storage company.

CASE 44.1 *FEDERAL COURT CASE Adulterated Food*

United States v. LaGrou Distribution Systems, Incorporated

466 F.3d 585, 2006 U.S. App. Lexis 25986 (2006) United States Court of Appeals for the Seventh Circuit

"The conditions at LaGrou's cold storage warehouse at 2101 Pershing Road in Chicago were enough to turn even the most enthusiastic meat-loving carnivore into a vegetarian."

—William Bauer, Judge

Facts

LaGrou Distribution Systems, Incorporated, operated a cold storage warehouse and distribution center in Chicago, Illinois. The warehouse stored raw, fresh, and frozen meat, poultry, and other food products that were owned by customers who paid LaGrou to provide storage. More than 2 million pounds of food went into and out of the warehouse each day.

The warehouse had a rat problem for a considerable time. LaGrou workers consistently found rodent droppings and rodent-gnawed products, and they caught rats in traps throughout the warehouse daily. The manager of the warehouse and the president of LaGrou were aware of this problem and discussed it weekly. The problem became so bad that workers were assigned to "rat patrols" to search for rats and to put out traps to catch rats. At one point, the rat patrols were trapping as many as 50 rats per day. LaGrou did not inform its customers of the rodent infestation. LaGrou would throw out products that had been gnawed by rats.

One day, a food inspector for the U.S. Department of Agriculture (USDA) went to the LaGrou warehouse and discovered the rat problem. The following morning, 14 USDA inspectors and representatives of the federal Food and Drug Administration (FDA) arrived at the warehouse to begin an extensive investigation. The inspectors found the widespread rat infestation and the contaminated meat. The contaminated meat could transmit bacterial, viral, parasitic, and fungal pathogens, including *E. coli* and *Salmonella*, which could cause severe illness in human beings.

The USDA ordered the warehouse shut down. Of the 22 million pounds of meat, poultry, and other food products stored at the warehouse, 8 million pounds were found to be adulterated and were destroyed. The remaining product had to be treated with strict decontamination procedures. The U.S. government brought charges against LaGrou for violating federal food safety laws. The U.S. district court ordered LaGrou to pay restitution of $8.2 million to customers who lost product and to pay a $2 million fine. In addition, it sentenced LaGrou to a five-year term of probation. LaGrou appealed.

Issue

Had LaGrou knowingly engaged in the improper storage of meat, poultry, and other food products, in violation of federal food safety laws?

Language of the Court

The conditions at LaGrou's cold storage warehouse at 2101 Pershing Road in Chicago were enough to turn even the most enthusiastic meat-loving carnivore into a vegetarian. According to Dr. Bonnie Rose, the USDA microbiologist who testified, LaGrou's warehouse was the "worst case" she had seen in her 28 years with the USDA. The instructions in this case explained that in order to convict LaGrou, the jury had to find that an authorized agent or employee of LaGrou knowingly stored products under unsanitary conditions. LaGrou's president, managers, and several employees were aware of the unsanitary conditions in the Pershing Road warehouse.

Decision

The U.S. court of appeals upheld the U.S. district court's finding that LaGrou had knowingly engaged in the improper storage of meat, poultry, and other food products, in violation of federal food safety laws. The court of appeals affirmed the judgment of the district court, except that it reduced the fine from $2 million to $1.5 million.

Critical Legal Thinking Questions

Did LaGrou management knowingly engage in improper storage of food products? Do you think that the penalties imposed on LaGrou were sufficient?

Organic Foods Production Act

Organic Foods Production Act
A federal statute that establishes a program for producers and handlers of agricultural foods produced using organic methods to be certified as organic.

The **Organic Foods Production Act (OFPA)**, a federal statute, was enacted in 1990.[2] Pursuant to the act, the USDA established a certification program for producers and handlers of agricultural products that have been produced using organic methods. To be sold or labeled as "organic," a food product must contain at least 95 percent organic ingredients with no synthetic growth hormones, antibiotics, pesticides, biotechnology, synthetic ingredients, or irradiation used in production or processing.

For crops to be certified as organic, they must be grown on land that has been free of prohibited pesticides and substances for at least three years before harvest, crops must have been grown in carefully managed soil, and the land must have buffer zones to protect the crops from the flow of unwanted substances from nearby farms. For livestock to be certified as organic, the livestock must be fed organic foods, no growth hormones may be used in the food, the animals cannot be overcrowded, and the animals must be given allotted time outdoors in direct sunlight.

genetically modified organisms (G.M.O.s or GMOs)
Plants and animals modified by laboratory techniques such as genetic engineering and biotechnology. Also referred to as *living modified organisms (L.M.O.s or LMOs)*.

Once certified, the approved producers, processors, and handlers may affix a label on their products that states "Meets USDA Organic Requirements." Organic labels can be found on produce, dairy, meat, processed food, condiments, and beverages. A person who knowingly sells or labels a product as organic in violation of the act is subject to civil monetary penalties, and anyone who makes a false statement to the USDA may be criminally prosecuted.

The following feature discusses federal disclosure law for bioengineered foods.

Contemporary Environment

Bioengineered Food Disclosure Law

Many foods are genetically modified. The term **genetically modified organism (G.M.O. or GMO)** refers to plants and animals modified by laboratory techniques such as genetic engineering and biotechnology. GMOs are also referred to as **living modified organisms (L.M.O.s or LMOs)**. Genetic modification creates combinations of plants, animals, bacteria, and virus genes that cannot be created through conventional breeding or crossbreeding and that do not occur in nature. Foods can be genetically modified to be more resistant to disease, to be more tolerant of herbicides, to be more nutritious, and to taste better.

Examples Corn can be altered to prevent insects from attacking it. Soybean crops can be altered to make them immune to weed killers. Apples can be modified to turn less brown when they are cut or bruised.

Many persons have safety and health concerns about using GMO foods and want to know whether the products they are buying and eating contain GMOs. In 2016, Congress enacted the **National Bioengineered Food Disclosure Law**.[3] As required by the law, USDA adopted **National Bioengineered Food Disclosure Standards (NBFDS or Standards)** that require foods that have been genetically modified to contain a label disclosing this information.[4] The Standards apply to manufacturers, retailers, and importers of food products. The term **bioengineered (or BE)** is used in federal laws when referring to genetically modified organisms. Many producers that grow non-GMO products market them by placing the term "Non-GMO" on their products.

Food, Drugs, and Cosmetics Safety—Food and Drug Administration (FDA)

44.2 Describe government regulation of food, drugs, cosmetics, and medical devices by the Food and Drug Administration (FDA).

Food, Drug, and Cosmetic Act
A federal statute that provides the basis for the regulation of much of the testing, manufacture, distribution, and sale of food, drugs, cosmetics, and medical products.

The **Food, Drug, and Cosmetic Act (FDCA or FDC Act)**[5] is a federal statute that regulates the safety of food, drugs, cosmetics, and medical devices. The FDCA has been amended many times since its original passage. The specific areas regulated by the FDCA are discussed in the following paragraphs.

The following feature discusses the FDCA.

Landmark Law

Food, Drug, and Cosmetic Act

The Food, Drug, and Cosmetic Act (FDCA or FDC Act) was enacted in 1938. This federal statute, as amended, regulates the testing, manufacture, distribution, and sale of food, drugs, cosmetics, and medical devices in the United States. The **Food and Drug Administration (FDA)** is the federal administrative agency empowered to enforce the FDCA.

Before certain food additives, drugs, cosmetics, and medical devices can be sold to the public, they must receive FDA approval. An applicant must submit to the FDA an application that contains relevant information about the safety and uses of the product. The FDA, after considering the evidence, will either approve or deny the application.

The FDA can seek search warrants and conduct inspections; obtain orders for the seizure, recall, and condemnation of products; seek injunctions; and turn over suspected criminal violations to the U.S. Department of Justice for prosecution.

Regulation of Food

The FDCA gives the FDA authority to regulate the safety of food products and the labeling of food products. The FDA is authorized to determine whether adulterated food has been distributed or sold or if false and misleading statements have been made or improper labeling has been used in the sale or distribution of food.

Food and Drug Administration (FDA)
The federal administrative agency that administers and enforces the federal Food, Drug, and Cosmetic Act and other federal consumer protection laws.

Adulterated Food

The FDCA prohibits the shipment, distribution, or sale of **adulterated food.** Food is deemed adulterated if (1) it consists in whole or in part of any "filthy, putrid, or decomposed substance" or if it is otherwise "unfit for food;" (2) it has been prepared, packed, or held under unsanitary conditions; (3) it contains an unsafe food additive, color additive, animal drug, or pesticide chemical residue; (4) it contains any poisonous or deleterious substance that may render the food injurious to health; or (5) its container is composed of any poisonous or deleterious substance that may render the food injurious to health.

adulterated food
Food that consists in whole or in part of any filthy, putrid, or decomposed substance; is unfit for food; has been prepared, packed, or held under unsanitary conditions; or fails to meet other specified conditions.

It is unlawful to alter food by adding a substance to increase the food's bulk or weight, to reduce its quality or strength, or make it appear more valuable than it is. This is called **economic adulteration.** Note that food does not have to be entirely pure to be distributed or sold; it only must be *unadulterated*.

False and Misleading Labeling or Packaging

The FDCA prohibits **false and misleading labeling or packaging** of food products, dietary supplements, and vitamins and minerals. A manufacturer may be held liable for deceptive or misleading labeling or packaging.

false and misleading labeling or packaging
Labels on food products, dietary supplements, vitamins, and minerals, and the packaging of such items, that is misleading or deceptive.

A food item is deemed false or misbranded if (1) the labeling is false or misleading; (2) the advertising is false and misleading; (3) the label contains an inaccurate statement of the quantity of the contents in terms of weight, measure, or numerical count; (4) the food contains artificial flavoring, coloring, or chemical preservatives, and it does not bear a label that discloses this fact; (5) the container is made, formed, or filled to be misleading; (6) it is a food for which a standard of quality has been prescribed, and its quality falls below this standard; (7) any word, statement, or information required to be disclosed by law (e.g., nutrition information) is not disclosed; (8) it is a dietary supplement, and the label fails to list the name and quantity of each ingredient; or (9) it is a vitamin or mineral and its label is false or misleading.

Regulation of Drugs

Drug Efficacy Amendment
A federal law that gives the FDA broad powers to license new drugs in the United States.

The FDCA gives the FDA the authority to regulate the testing, manufacture, distribution, and sale of drugs. The **Drug Efficacy Amendment** to the FDCA was enacted in 1962, and has since been amended. This law gives the FDA broad powers to license new drugs in the United States. After a new drug application is filed, the FDA holds a hearing and investigates the merits of the application. This process can take many years. The FDA may withdraw approval of any previously licensed drug.

This law requires all users of prescription and nonprescription drugs to receive proper directions for use (including the method and duration of use) and adequate warnings about any related side effects. The manufacture, distribution, or sale of adulterated or misbranded drugs is prohibited.

Regulation of Cosmetics

WEB EXERCISE
Visit the website of the Food and Drug Administration at **www.fda.gov**. Click on "Cosmetics" and read a recent article posted on the site.

The FDA's definition of *cosmetics* includes substances and preparations for cleansing, altering the appearance of, and promoting the attractiveness of a person. Eye shadow and other facial makeup products are examples of cosmetics subject to FDA regulation. Ordinary household soap is expressly exempted from this definition.

The FDA has issued regulations that require cosmetics to be labeled, to disclose ingredients, and to contain warnings if they are carcinogenic (i.e., cancer causing) or otherwise dangerous to a person's health. The manufacture, distribution, or sale of adulterated or misbranded cosmetics is prohibited. The FDA may remove from commerce any cosmetics that contain unsubstantiated claims of preserving youth, increasing virility, growing hair, and so on.

Regulation of Medical Devices

Medical Device Amendments
Federal law that gives the FDA broad powers to regulate medical devices in the United States.

In 1976, Congress enacted the **Medical Device Amendments** to the FDCA. These amendments, which have since been amended, give the FDA authority to regulate medical devices such as heart pacemakers, kidney dialysis machines, defibrillators, surgical equipment, and other diagnostic, therapeutic, and health devices. The mislabeling of such devices is prohibited. The FDA is empowered to remove "quack" devices from the market.

Food and Product Labeling

44.3 Describe government requirements and restrictions on the disclosure of nutrition facts and other safety information.

Many food companies either made unfounded health claims for their food products or did not disclose necessary information for consumers to make educated choices when deciding what foods to purchase and consume. To address these concerns, the federal government has enacted several important statutes that require the disclosure of relevant information about food products that is presented in understandable terms and in proper disclosure formats.

Nutrition Labeling

Nutrition Labeling and Education Act
A federal statute that requires food manufacturers to disclose on food labels nutritional information about the food.

In 1990, Congress passed a sweeping truth-in-labeling law called the **Nutrition Labeling and Education Act (NLEA).**[6] This act requires food manufacturers and processors to provide a statement of ingredients and nutrition information on many foods and prohibits them from making scientifically unsubstantiated health claims. The NLEA applies to packaged foods and other foods regulated by the FDA. Pursuant to authority provided in the act, the FDA adopted and implemented rules for the disclosure of the required information. As a result, nutrition fact labels now appear on most packaged foods and beverages.

The following feature discusses a new nutrition facts label developed by the FDA.

Contemporary Environment

Nutrition Facts Label

To address confusing and false food product labeling, in 2016 the FDA announced a new **nutrition facts label**[7] for food products, which became effective in 2021. The label requires the disclosure of relevant nutritional information and is designed to make this information visible to consumers. Required information on the nutrition facts label includes:

- **Serving size.** Serving sizes must be based on amounts of the foods and beverages that people actually consume in one sitting. Serving size must be written in a common household measure (e.g., cup, tablespoon, piece, slice, fraction [e.g., ¼ pizza], fluid ounce) or other common household equipment used to package food (e.g., jar, tray). The FDA has set standard serving sizes for most foods. Food producers and sellers cannot deviate from FDA-established serving sizes.

Examples The serving size of soda is 12 ounces; the serving size of nuts is 1 ounce (about ¼ cup); the serving size for ready-to-eat cereal is ¾ cup; the serving size for cooked whole-grain cereal such as oatmeal is 1 cup.

For products that could be consumed in one sitting or multiple sittings, a dual-column label is required that shows all required nutrition information in both a per serving and per package/per unit basis. Consumers will be easily able to understand how many calories and nutrients they are getting if they eat or drink the entire package/unit at one time.

- **Nutrients.** The amount of calcium, iron, vitamin D, and potassium is required to be disclosed. The amount of vitamins A and C can be voluntarily disclosed.
- **Fats.** The label requires "Total Fat," "Saturated Fat," and "Trans Fat" to be disclosed.
- **Sugars.** The label requires the disclosure of total sugars. "Added sugars" must be disclosed on the label, stated in grams and as the percent of the daily value of calories (e.g., 20 percent).
- **Cholesterol and other information.** The label requires the disclosure of the amounts of cholesterol, sodium, total carbohydrates, dietary fiber, and protein that the food or beverage contains.
- **Grams and daily value.** All items must be listed in grams and in percent of Daily Value based on a person's consumption of 2,000 calories a day. The % Daily Value (%DV) helps consumers understand the nutrition information in the context of a total daily diet.

The nutrition facts label provides a simple presentation of information, with easy-to-read typeface and bolded number of calories and serving size declarations.

Food Label Claims

The FDA has established legal definitions for some of the most commonly used **food label claims**, including: Fat Free, Low Fat, and Reduced Fat; Sugar Free, No Added Sugar, and Reduced Sugar; Calorie Free, Low Calorie, and Reduced Calorie; Cholesterol Free, Low Cholesterol, and Reduced Cholesterol; Lean and Extra Lean; Light; Gluten Free; and High Fiber.[8]

Examples Sugar Free means the food has less than 0.5 grams of sugar per serving, and the food contains no ingredient that is a sugar. Calorie Free means the food has less than 5 calories per serving. Fat Free means that there is less than 0.5 grams of fat per serving.

The FDA has not established legal definitions for the terms "Natural" or "Healthy." For example, potato chips are often labeled "Natural" because nothing except what would be expected to be in potato chips is added. Thus, the words "natural" or "healthy" on food labels mean absolutely nothing.

nutrition facts label
A label required by federal law that must appear on certain food and beverage items that discloses calorie and nutrition information in a visible and understandable format.

food label claims
Claims made on food labels regarding calories, cholesterol, fat, sugar, and other information. The FDA has established legal definitions for most commonly used food label claims.

Menu Labeling Rule

Did you know that a Big Mac meal (Big Mac burger, medium fries, and medium soft drink) contains 1,100 calories, 44 grams of fat, and 68 grams of sugar; a Baskin Robbins large Oreo and chocolate shake contains 1,730 calories and 184 grams of sugar; a tub of original flavor Pringles contains 980 calories and 64 grams of fat; and a large-size bucket of buttered popcorn at the movie theater contains 1,200 calories and 60 grams of saturated fat? Well, you do now.

WEB EXERCISE
Use www.google.com and find the calorie count and grams of fat of a food item that you have eaten at a fast food or other restaurant.

Compare these figures with the fact that a person needs approximately 2000 calories, less than 13 grams of saturated fat, and fewer than 38 grams or 9 teaspoons of added sugar per day.

Menu Labeling Rule
A regulation that requires restaurants and retail food establishments with 20 or more locations and vending machine operators who own or operate 20 or more vending machines to disclose calorie counts of their food items.

Family Smoking Prevention and Tobacco Control Act (Tobacco Control Act)
A federal statute that authorizes the FDA to place restrictions on distributing, advertising, and marketing tobacco products to children.

The FDA adopted a **Menu Labeling Rule**[9] that requires restaurants and retail food establishments with 20 or more locations to disclose calorie counts of their food items and to supply information on how many calories a healthy person should eat in a day. The law went into effect in 2018.

The law applies to establishments selling restaurant-type food, including sit-down and fast-food restaurants, cafeterias and coffee shops, grocery stores and convenience stores, foods purchased at drive-through windows, take-out facilities and delivery food services, entertainment facilities, foods that you serve yourself from a salad or hot food bar, and alcoholic drinks when they are listed on menus. The calorie disclosures are required to be made on menus and menu boards, including drive-through menu boards. Calorie labeling also applies to vending machine operators who own or operate 20 or more vending machines.

The following feature discusses regulations on the marketing and advertising of tobacco products and electronic cigarettes.

Ethics

Regulation of Tobacco Products and Electronic Nicotine Delivery Systems

More than 35 million adults in the United States smoke cigarettes. Almost 90 percent of adult smokers started smoking before the age of 18. By 2019, one-third of high school students had used e-cigarettes or pods in the prior month. Use of e-cigarettes and pods is a good predictor of later cigarette use. Cigarettes, e-cigarettes, and other tobacco products contain nicotine, a highly addictive and dangerous chemical.

In 2009, the U.S. Congress enacted the **Family Smoking Prevention and Tobacco Control Act**, often called the **Tobacco Control Act**.[10] The act gives the FDA the authority to regulate tobacco products. The FDA has adopted rules that regulate cigarettes, cigars, and other traditional tobacco products, as well as e-cigarettes and other electronic nicotine delivery systems (ENDS). Federal law restricts the sale and distribution of cigarettes, e-cigarettes, and other tobacco products in the following ways:

- Bans the sales of tobacco products to minors. A person must be 21 years or older to purchase tobacco-related products, including e-cigarettes and vaping products. It is illegal for a retailer to sell any tobacco product to anyone under 21.
- Bans free giveaways of samples of tobacco products as promotional items.
- Prohibits tobacco-brand sponsorships of sports and entertainment events or other social or cultural events.
- Prohibits vending machine sales (except in adult-only facilities).

To make cigarettes more appealing to youngsters, the tobacco industry began adding flavors to their traditional tobacco products. This marketing strategy had its desired effect as tobacco use by young persons increased substantially. The FDA now bans the sale of candy, fruit, and other flavored cigarettes and traditional tobacco products except for menthol.

When statistics showed a high use of flavored electronic tobacco products by young persons—95 percent of minors who used e-cigarettes and pods used flavor varieties—the FDA banned the sale of flavored (e.g., mint, chocolate, cinnamon, etc.) self-contained cartridge e-cigarettes and pods, except those that are tobacco or menthol flavored. The removal of these flavored products from the marketplace is aimed at decreasing minors' desire to use e-cigarettes and pods. Open-tank refillable vaping devices, disposables, and refillable vape pods are not covered by the flavor ban.

Federal law requires health warnings to appear on cigarette and other tobacco products' packages and advertising. Packages and advertisements of ENDS must contain the following statement: "WARNING: This product contains nicotine. Nicotine is an addictive chemical."

Ethics Questions

Why do you think tobacco and ENDS manufacturers added flavoring to their products? Do you think that the target market was tweens and teenagers or adults? Have the executives at these companies acted unethically?

Product Safety—Consumer Product Safety Commission (CPSC)

44.4 Describe federal laws that regulate product safety.

Defective and faulty products cause injuries to consumers. In order to address this problem, Congress enacted the **Consumer Product Safety Act (CPSA)**[11] and created the **Consumer Product Safety Commission (CPSC)** to enforce the provisions of the act. The CPSC is an independent federal administrative agency empowered to adopt rules and regulations to interpret and enforce the CPSA, to require recall notices to be issued to consumers where violations of the act have been found, and to seek other remedies for violations of the act.

Consumer Product Safety Act
A federal statute that regulates potentially dangerous consumer products and that created the Consumer Product Safety Commission.

Consumer Product Safety Commission (CPSC)
A federal administrative agency empowered to adopt rules and regulations to interpret and enforce the Consumer Product Safety Act.

General Use Products

The CPSC regulates thousands of consumer products and issues **product safety standards** to ensure the safety of these products. Consumer products regulated by the CPSC include clothing, household products, refrigerators and dishwashers, cookware, computers and electronic devices, furniture, lights, power tools, lawnmowers, golf carts, snowmobiles, ATVs, other consumer products. A manufacturer or importer of a general use (non-children's) consumer product must certify that its product complies with all applicable product safety rules and regulations.

Toys and Children's Products

The **Consumer Product Safety Improvement Act (CPSIA)** was enacted in 2008.[12] The act sets new requirements for the testing and documentation of safety of products, and also decreases the levels of acceptable possible harmful substances.

One of the primary goals of the act is to provide protection to children by requiring toys and products that are used by children to be safe. Pursuant to the act, the CPSC has adopted safety standards for products such as tricycles, bicycles, skateboards, toys, dolls, action figures, school supplies, educational material, and bedding. The act also imposes safety standards for electronics and video games. The CPSC has adopted special infant and toddler safety standards for products such as cradles, cribs, strollers, high chairs, gates, and changing tables. The CPSC has established additional safety standards for children's products containing lead, lead in paint, and phthalates.

For children's toy and products, a manufacturer or importer must certify in writing to the CPSC that its children's product or toy complies with all applicable product safety rules and regulations. Only children's products and toys that are certified as meeting CPSC safety standards may be sold or distributed. If a consumer product is found to be imminently hazardous—that is, if its use causes an unreasonable risk of death or serious injury or illness—the manufacturer can be required to recall, repair, or replace the product or take other corrective action.

Consumer Product Safety Improvement Act
A federal statute that mandates that toys and products that are to be sold for use by children 12 and under must be tested and certified as meeting Consumer Product Safety Commission children's safety standards.

WEB EXERCISE
Go to **https://www.cpsc.gov/recalls**. Read about three recent recalls of unsafe products by the Consumer Product Safety Commission.

Automobile and Vehicle Safety—National Highway Traffic Safety Administration (NHTSA)

44.5 Describe federal laws that regulate automobile, vehicle, bus, and motorcycle safety.

The **National Traffic and Motor Vehicle Safety Act**[13] is a federal statute that regulates the safety of automobiles, SUVs, vans, trucks, electric-powered vehicles, self-driving vehicles, school buses, and motorcycles. The act created the **National Highway Traffic Safety Administration (NHTSA)**, a federal administrative agency that is part of the U.S. Department of Transportation, to administer the act. The

National Traffic and Motor Vehicle Safety Act
A federal statute that regulates the safety of automobiles, SUVs, vans, trucks, electric-powered vehicles, self-driving vehicles, school buses, and motorcycles.

National Highway Traffic Safety Administration (NHTSA)
A federal administrative agency that administers and issues regulations to enforce the National Traffic and Motor Vehicle Safety Act.

NHTSA issues regulations pursuant to its authority granted in the act. The agency may require recall notices to be issued to consumers where violations of the safety standards have been found.

The following feature describes federal motor vehicle safety standards for automobiles and other vehicles.

Contemporary Environment

Federal Motor Vehicle Safety Standards (FMVSS)

To reduce the number of fatalities and injuries caused by automobiles, buses, and other vehicles, the NHTSA has adopted safety regulations called the **Federal Motor Vehicle Safety Standards (FMVSS)**.[14] The standards are divided into three categories: (1) crash avoidance, (2) crashworthiness, and (3) post-crash survivability. These standards include safety standards for occupant crash protection, side impact protection, roof crush resistance, rear impact protection, occupant protection in interior impact, exterior protection, and windshield safety. Other FMVSS regulations set safety standards for brake systems, seat belts, tires and rims, warning devices, steering controls, head restraints, child restraint systems, and the like.

The NHTSA sets additional safety standards that apply to electric-powered vehicles, such as regulating electrolyte spillage and electrical shock protection. The NHTSA has issued safety standards that apply specifically to automated driving system vehicles, commonly referred to as self-driving vehicles. Because more than 90 percent of serious crashes are caused by human error, the government is promoting the development of driver assistance technologies.

Federal Motor Vehicle Safety Standards (FMVSS)
Safety regulations that have been issued by the National Highway Traffic Safety Administration (NHTSA) to reduce the number of fatalities and injuries caused by automobiles and other vehicles.

If a vehicle regulated by the NHTSA is found to be imminently hazardous—that is, if its use causes an unreasonable risk of death or serious injury or illness—the manufacturer can be required to recall, repair, or replace the product or take other corrective action. The NHTSA can seek injunctions, bring actions to seize hazardous vehicles, seek civil penalties for intentional violations of the act or of NHTSA rules, and seek criminal penalties for knowing and willful violations of the act or of NHTSA rules.

Unfair and Deceptive Practices—Federal Trade Commission (FTC)

44.6 Identify and describe unfair and deceptive business practices.

Federal Trade Commission (FTC)
A federal administrative agency empowered to enforce the Federal Trade Commission Act and other federal consumer protection statutes.

Section 5 of the FTC Act
A provision in the FTC Act that prohibits unfair methods of competition and unfair or deceptive acts or practices.

The **Federal Trade Commission Act (FTC Act)** was enacted in 1914.[15] The **Federal Trade Commission (FTC)** was created the following year to enforce the FTC Act as well as other federal consumer protection statutes.

Section 5 of the FTC Act, as amended, prohibits **unfair methods of competition and unfair or deceptive acts or practices.**[16] It has been used extensively to regulate business conduct. This section gives the FTC the authority to bring an administrative proceeding to attack a deceptive or unfair practice. If the FTC finds a violation of Section 5, it may issue a cease-and-desist order, an affirmative disclosure to consumers, corrective advertising, or the like. The FTC may sue in court to obtain compensation on behalf of consumers. A decision of the FTC may be appealed to federal court.

False and Deceptive Advertising

Advertising is **false and deceptive advertising** under Section 5 of the FTC Act if it (1) contains misinformation or omits important information that is likely to mislead a "reasonable consumer" or (2) makes an unsubstantiated claim (e.g., "This product is 33 percent better than our competitor's"). Proof of actual deception is not required. Statements of opinion and sales talk (e.g., "This is a great car") do not constitute false and deceptive advertising. Section 5 of the FTC Act can be used to prohibit unfair and deceptive business practices.

Example Kentucky Fried Chicken entered into an agreement with the FTC whereby KFC withdrew television commercials in which it claimed that its "fried chicken can, in fact, be part of a healthy diet."

The following ethics feature discusses a case involving false advertising by a seller on Amazon.com.

Ethics

False Product Claims and Fake Reviews on Amazon

"The making of the representations constitute a deceptive act or practice and the making of false advertisements in violation of Section 5(a) of the FTC Act."

—Alden Abbott, General Counsel, Federal Trade Commission

Cure Encapsulations, Inc. was a company that sold a weight loss supplement containing garcinia cambogia, a plant from Indonesia, using Amazon's online shopping site. The company advertised that the plant contributed to significant weight loss. The company paid a third-party website to write five-star Amazon reviews that would keep the supplement's Amazon rating above 4.3 out of 5 stars. The fake reviews claimed, among other false statements, that the supplement worked as a "powerful appetite suppressant" and "literally blocks fat from forming."

In truth, the plant used in Cure Encapsulations' supplement does not contribute to weight loss. After an investigation, the FTC brought charges against Cure Encapsulations and the company's owner for engaging in false and misleading advertising and having fake reviews posted on Amazon. The complaint stated, "The making of the representations constitute a deceptive act or practice and the making of false advertisements in violation of Section 5(a) of the FTC Act."

The FTC found that the company's claims, and those of the third-party review provider, were false and unsubstantiated in violation of Section 5(a) of the FTC Act. The FTC and Cure Encapsulations and the company's owner reached a settlement whereby the company was required to pay a $12.8 million fine, agreed to never again make unsubstantiated weight loss claims, agreed not to use third parties to write false product reviews, and was required to notify all customers who purchased the weight loss supplement. *Federal Trade Commission v. Cure Encapsulations, Inc.*, Case No. 1:19-cv-00982 (United States District Court for the Eastern District of New York, 2019)

Ethics Questions

When you shop for products on Amazon.com, do you rely on consumer reviews? Do you think that there are very many fake reviews on Amazon's online shopping site? Did the owner of Cure Encapsulations act ethically?

State and Local Consumer Protection Laws

44.7 Describe state and local consumer protection laws.

Many states have enacted various **state consumer protection laws** that prohibit fraudulent and deceptive and unfair trade practices that harm consumers. States usually create an administrative agency to enforce state consumer protection laws, which include the ability to conduct inspections, hold administrative hearings, and impose penalties for violations of the laws.

Some local governments, such as cities and towns, have also enacted **local consumer protection laws** that regulate the safety of restaurant food, prohibit deceptive and false advertising, and the like. Local governments usually have agencies that are empowered to enforce these laws.

WEB EXERCISE
Use **www.google.com** and find a state or local consumer protection law.

Examples California, Hawaii, New York, Oregon, and many other states ban single-use plastic bags. Seattle and other cities ban plastic straws, stir sticks, and utensils.

Key Terms and Concepts

Adulterated food (779)
Bioengineered (BE) (778)
Caveat emptor (776)
Consumer Product Safety Act (CPSA) (783)
Consumer Product Safety Commission (CPSC) (783)
Consumer Product Safety Improvement Act (CPSIA) (783)
Consumer protection laws (776)
Drug Efficacy Amendment (779)
Economic adulteration (779)
False and deceptive advertising (784)
False and misleading statements (776)
False and misleading labeling or packaging (779)
Family Smoking Prevention and Tobacco Control Act (Tobacco Control Act) (782)
Federal Motor Vehicle Safety Standards (FMVSS) (784)
Federal Trade Commission (FTC) (784)
Federal Trade Commission Act (FTC Act) (784)
Food and Drug Administration (FDA) (779)
Food, Drug, and Cosmetic Act (FDCA or FDC Act) (778)
Food label claims (781)
Genetically modified organism (G.M.O. or GMO) (778)
Living modified organism (L.M.O. or LMO) (778)
Local consumer protection laws (785)
Medical Device Amendment (780)
Menu Labeling Rule (782)
National Bioengineered Food Disclosure Law (778)
National Bioengineered Food Disclosure Standards (NBFDS or Standards) (778)
National Highway Traffic Safety Administration (NHTSA) (783)
National Traffic and Motor Vehicle Safety Act (783)
Nutrition facts label (781)
Nutrition Labeling and Education Act (NLEA) (780)
Organic Foods Production Act (OFPA) (778)
Product safety standards (783)
Section 5 of the Federal Trade Commission Act (784)
State consumer protection laws (785)
Unfair methods of competition and unfair or deceptive acts or practices (784)
U.S. Department of Agriculture (USDA) (776)

Critical Legal Thinking Cases

44.1 False Advertising Bronson Partners, LLC; Martin Howard; H & H Marketing; and Sandra Howard (collectively, Bronson) advertised and sold two purportedly miraculous weight loss products. Bronson advertised that its Chinese Diet Tea "SHEDS POUND AFTER POUND OF FAT—FAST!" Bronson's advertisements claimed the tea "eliminates an amazing 91 percent of absorbed sugars," "prevents 83 percent of fat absorption," and "doubles your metabolic rate to burn calories fast." Bronson claimed that its Bio-Slim Patch would achieve "LASTING weight loss." The advertisements promised that by "carrying on with your normal lifestyle" and wearing the patch, "repulsive, excess, ugly fatty tissue will disappear at a spectacular rate." The claims were bogus. The FTC sued Bronson for engaging in deceptive advertising in violation of Section 5 of the FTC Act. Did Bronson engage in false advertising in violation of the FTC Act? *Federal Trade Commission v. Bronson Partners, LLC*, 654 F.3d 359, 2011 U.S. App. Lexis 17203 (United States Court of Appeals for the Second Circuit, 2011)

44.2 Deceptive Practices Innovative Marketing, Inc. (IMI) and several of its high-level executives and founders, including Kristy Ross, a vice president of IMI, operated a massive internet-based scheme that tricked consumers into purchasing computer security software, referred to as "scareware." The internet advertisements would advise consumers that a scan of their computers had been performed and had detected a variety of dangerous files, like viruses, spyware, and illegal pornography, when no scans were ever conducted. Computers users would then pay IMI to install its scareware on their computers. The advertisements could also cause consumers to automatically download unwanted IMI products. The scheme raked in millions of dollars from unsuspecting consumers. FTC sued IMI, Ross, and other executives and founders for violating Section 5 of the FTC Act. Ross hired counsel and defended against the lawsuit. Did IMI and Ross engage in false advertising and deceptive practices in violation of Section 5 of the FTC Act? *Federal Trade Commission v. Ross*, 743 F.3d 886, 2014 U.S. App. Lexis 3476 (United States Court of Appeals for the Fourth Circuit, 2014)

Ethics Case

44.3 Ethics Case POM Wonderful, LLC produces, markets, and sells pomegranate-based products, including drinks and pills. POM products are contained in distinctively designed bottles. In a series of advertisements, POM touted that daily consumption of its products could treat, prevent, or reduce the risk of various ailments, including heart disease, prostate cancer, and erectile dysfunction. However, the claims were not supported by any controlled human clinical trial studies or other evidence. Therefore, there was no scientific evidence of a relationship between consumption of POM products and the treatment or prevention of heart disease, prostate cancer, erectile dysfunction, or other diseases. The FTC filed an administrative complaint against POM alleging that the company made false, misleading, and unsubstantiated representations in violation of Section 5 of the FTC Act. The FTC's complaint alleged that POM's advertisements mischaracterized the evidence concerning the health benefits of POM's products. Did POM make false, misleading, and deceptive advertising claims in violation of Section 5 of the FTC Act? Did the company act ethically in making the advertising and marketing claims? *POM Wonderful, Inc. v. Federal Trade Commission*, 777 F.3d 478, 2015 U.S. App. Lexis 1489 (United States Court of Appeals for the District of Columbia, 2015)

Notes

1. 21 U.S.C. Section 601 et seq.; 21 U.S.C. Section 451 et seq.; and 21 U.S.C. Section 1031 et seq.
2. 7 U.S.C. Sections 6501–6524.
3. Public Law 114–216.
4. 7 C.F.R. 66.
5. 21 U.S.C. Section 301 et seq.
6. Public Law 101–535, 104 Stat. 2353.
7. 21 C.F.R. 101.
8. 21 C.F.R. 101.54; 21 C.F.R. 101.56; 21 C.F.R. 101.60; 21 C.F.R. 101.62; and 21 C.F.R. 101.91.
9. 21 CFR 101.11.
10. Public Law 111–31, 123 Stat. 1776–1858.
11. 15 U.S.C. Section 2051 et seq.
12. Public Law 110–314.
13. 49 U.S.C. Chapter 301.
14. 49 C.F.R. 571.
15. 15 U.S.C. Sections 41–58.
16. 15 U.S.C. Section 45.

CHAPTER 45

Environmental Protection

SUN VALLEY, IDAHO
Federal and state governments have enacted many statutes to protect water, air, and the environment from pollution.

Henry R. Cheeseman

Learning Objectives

After studying this chapter, you should be able to:

45.1 Describe environmental protection and identify when an environmental impact statement must be completed.

45.2 Describe the Clean Air Act and national ambient air quality standards.

45.3 Describe the Clean Water Act and effluent water standards.

45.4 Explain how environmental laws regulate the use of toxic substances and the disposal of hazardous wastes.

45.5 Describe how the Endangered Species Act protects endangered and threatened species and their habitats.

45.6 Describe state environmental protection laws.

> *"Nature is painting for us, day after day, pictures of infinite beauty."*
>
> *—John Ruskin (1819–1900)*

Introduction to Environmental Protection

Businesses and consumers generate air pollution, water pollution, and hazardous and toxic wastes that cause harm to the environment and human health. Pollution has reached alarming rates in the United States and the rest of the world. Pollution causes injury and death to various forms of wildlife, pollutes drinking water, pollutes the air we breathe, and harms human health and the environment.

Federal and state governments have enacted environmental protection laws to contain the levels of pollution and clean up hazardous waste sites in the United States. Many laws provide both civil and criminal penalties. These laws are collectively referred to as *environmental protection laws*. The United States has some of the strongest national environmental protection laws in the world.

This chapter covers environmental protection laws.

The nation behaves well if it treats the natural resources as assets which it must turn over to the next generation increased, and not impaired, in value.

Theodore Roosevelt (1858–1919)
Twenty-Sixth President of the United States

Environmental Protection

45.1 Describe environmental protection and identify when an environmental impact statement must be completed.

In the 1970s, the federal government began enacting statutes to protect our nation's air and water from pollution, to regulate hazardous wastes, and to protect wildlife. In many instances, states have enacted their own environmental laws that now coexist with federal law. These laws provide both civil and criminal penalties. **Environmental protection** is one of the most important, and costly, issues facing business and society today.

Environmental Protection Agency

In 1970, Congress created the **Environmental Protection Agency (EPA)** to coordinate the enforcement of the federal **environmental protection laws**. The EPA has broad rulemaking powers to adopt regulations to advance the laws that it is empowered to administer. The agency also has adjudicative powers to hold hearings, make decisions, and order remedies for violations of federal environmental laws. In addition, the EPA can initiate judicial proceedings in court against suspected violators of federal environmental laws.

Environmental Protection Agency (EPA)
A federal administrative agency created by Congress to coordinate the implementation and enforcement of the federal environmental protection laws.

Environmental Impact Statement

The **National Environmental Policy Act (NEPA)** became effective January 1, 1970.[1] The NEPA, as amended, mandates that the federal government consider the "adverse impact" of proposed legislation, rulemaking, or other federal government action on the environment before the action is implemented. The EPA administers the NEPA and has the authority to adopt regulations for the enforcement of the act.

National Environmental Policy Act
A federal statute mandating that the federal government consider the adverse impact a federal government action would have on the environment before the action is implemented.

The NEPA and EPA regulations require that an **environmental impact statement (EIS)** be prepared by the federal government for any proposed legislation or major federal action that significantly affects the quality of the natural and human environment.

Examples The federal government must prepare an EIS for proposed construction projects involving highways, bridges, waterways, nuclear power plants, and so on.

environmental impact statement (EIS)
A document that must be prepared for any proposed legislation or major federal action that significantly affects the quality of the natural and human environment.

The purpose of an EIS is to provide enough information about the environment to enable the federal government to determine the feasibility of the project.

An EIS must (1) describe the affected environment, (2) describe the impact of the proposed federal action on the environment, (3) identify and discuss alternatives to the proposed action, (4) list the resources that will be committed to the action, and (5) contain a cost–benefit analysis of the proposed action and alternative actions. Expert professionals, such as engineers, geologists, and accountants, may be consulted during the preparation of an EIS.

Once an EIS is prepared and published, interested parties can submit comments to the EPA. After comments have been received and reviewed, the EPA issues an order that states whether the proposed federal action may proceed. An EIS can be challenged in court by environmentalists and other interested parties. Many projects have been blocked or altered because of such challenges.

I know that our bodies were made to thrive only in pure air, and the scenes in which pure air is found.

John Muir (1838–1914)

Most states and many local governments have enacted laws that require an EIS to be prepared regarding proposed state and local government action as well as private development. State and local laws often require private parties who want to build resorts, housing projects, or other major developments to file an EIS or equivalent document. These projects can be challenged in state court.

Example A real estate developer proposes to build a 100-house project on private land. Environmentalists challenge the development, arguing that it will destroy a wildlife habitat. The developer and environmentalists may settle the case. For example, the developer might agree to build fewer houses or to give part of the property to the government for a wildlife preserve.

Air Pollution

45.2 Describe the Clean Air Act and national ambient air quality standards.

air pollution
Pollution caused by factories, homes, vehicles, and other sources, that affects the air.

Clean Air Act
A federal statute that provides comprehensive regulation of air quality in the United States.

One of the major problems facing the United States is **air pollution**. The **Clean Air Act (CAA)**[2] was enacted in 1963 to assist states in dealing with air pollution. The act has been amended several times, most recently by the **Clean Air Act Amendments** of 1990.[3] The Clean Air Act, as amended, provides comprehensive regulation of air quality in the United States.

Sources of Air Pollution

Substantial amounts of air pollution are emitted by **stationary sources of air pollution** (e.g., industrial plants, oil refineries, petrochemical plants, public utilities). The CAA requires states to identify major stationary sources and develop plans to reduce air pollution from these sources.

Automobile and other vehicle emissions are major sources of air pollution in the United States. In an effort to control emissions from these **mobile sources of air pollution**, the CAA requires air pollution controls to be installed on motor vehicles. Emission standards have been set for automobiles, trucks, buses, motorcycles, and airplanes. In addition, the CAA authorizes the EPA to regulate air pollution caused by fuel and fuel additives.

National Ambient Air Quality Standards

national ambient air quality standards (NAAQS)
Standards for certain pollutants set by the EPA that protect (1) human beings (primary level) and (2) vegetation, matter, climate, visibility, and economic values (secondary level).

The CAA directs the EPA to establish **national ambient air quality standards (NAAQS)** for certain pollutants. These standards are set at two different levels: primary (to protect human beings) and secondary (to protect vegetation, climate, visibility, and economic values). Specific standards have been established for carbon monoxide, nitrogen oxide, sulfur oxide, ozone, lead, and particulate matter.

Although the EPA establishes air quality standards, the states are responsible for their enforcement. The federal government has the right to enforce these air pollution standards if the states fail to do so. Each state is required to prepare a

state implementation plan (SIP) that sets out how the state plans to meet the federal standards. The EPA has divided the country into **air quality control regions (AQCRs)**. Each region is monitored to ensure compliance.

In the following case, the U.S. Supreme Court addressed an issue concerning the regulation of air emissions.

CASE 45.1 *U.S. SUPREME COURT CASE Air Pollution*

Michigan v. Environmental Protection Agency

135 S.Ct. 2699, 2015 U.S. Lexis 4256 (2015)
Supreme Court of the United States

"No regulation is appropriate if it does significantly more harm than good."

—Antonin Scalia, Justice

Facts

The Clean Air Act directs the Environmental Protection Agency to regulate emissions of hazardous air pollutants from power plants if the EPA finds such regulation "appropriate and necessary." Pursuant to this authority, the EPA issued a regulation that would require power plants to spend $9.6 billion per year to prevent certain forms of air pollution. The benefits from this expenditure were $4 million to $6 million per year. Thus, the costs to power plants were between 1,600 and 2,400 times as great as the benefits from reduced emissions of hazardous air pollutants. The EPA did not take into account costs of compliance when issuing its regulation. Business organizations and 23 states challenged the EPA's refusal to consider cost when deciding to regulate power plants. The U.S. court of appeals upheld the EPA's decision. The U.S. Supreme Court agreed to hear the appeals of the petitioner business organizations and states.

Issue

Was it reasonable for the EPA to refuse to consider cost when deciding to regulate emissions of power plants?

Language of the U.S. Supreme Court

Read naturally in the present context, the phrase "appropriate and necessary" requires at least some attention to cost. One would not say that it is even rational, never mind appropriate, to impose billions of dollars in economic costs in return for a few dollars in health or environmental benefits. No regulation is appropriate if it does significantly more harm than good. The EPA must consider cost—including, most importantly, cost of compliance—before deciding whether regulation is appropriate and necessary.

Decision

The U.S. Supreme Court held that the EPA acted unreasonably when it did not consider cost when it regulated emissions from power plants. The Supreme Court reversed the decision of the U.S. court of appeals and remanded the case for further proceedings.

Critical Legal Thinking Questions

Should cost of compliance be considered when imposing air pollution regulations? Or is the environment so fragile that cost should not be considered when imposing air pollution regulations?

Nonattainment Areas

A region that does not meet air quality standards is designated a **nonattainment area**. A nonattainment area is classified into one of five categories—*marginal, moderate, serious, severe*, or *extreme*—based on the degree to which it exceeds the ozone standard. Deadlines are established for areas to meet the attainment level. States that fail to meet air quality standards are subject to sanctions such as loss of federal funds for state projects and limitations on the development of new sources of pollution (e.g., industrial plants).

nonattainment area
A geographical area that does not meet established air quality standards.

The following feature discusses a modern source of air pollution.

Contemporary Environment

Indoor Air Pollution

The Environmental Protection Agency states that air inside some buildings may be 100 times more polluted than outside air. Doctors increasingly attribute a wide range of symptoms to **indoor air pollution**, or **sick building syndrome**. Indoor air pollution has two primary causes. To reduce dependence on foreign oil, many recently constructed office buildings have been highly insulated and built with sealed windows and no outside air ducts. As a result, no fresh air enters many workplaces. This lack of fresh air can cause headaches, fatigue, and dizziness among workers.

The other chief cause of sick building syndrome, which is believed to affect up to one-third of U.S. office buildings, is hazardous chemicals and construction materials. In the office, these include everything from asbestos to noxious fumes emitted from copy machines, carbonless paper, and cleaning fluids. In the home, radon, an odorless gas that is emitted from the natural breakdown of uranium in soil, poses a particularly widespread danger. Radon gas damages and may destroy lung tissue. The costs of eliminating these conditions can be colossal.

The EPA does not regulate indoor air. Many state laws and some municipal building codes regulate the amount of lead, mold, radiation, mercury, and other dangerous chemicals that are permitted in buildings and building materials. Sick building syndrome is likely to spawn a flood of litigation, with a wide range of parties being sued. Insurance companies will undoubtedly be drawn into costly lawsuits stemming from indoor air pollution.

BOSTON, MASSACHUSETTS
Pollution of waterways by industry and humans has caused severe ecological and environmental problems, including making water sources unsafe for human consumption, and for fish, birds, and animals to live.

Henry R. Cheeseman

Water Pollution

45.3 Describe the Clean Water Act and effluent water standards.

water pollution
Pollution of lakes, rivers, oceans, and other bodies of water.

Clean Water Act
A federal statute that establishes water quality standards and regulates water pollution.

Water pollution affects human health, recreation, agriculture, and business. The federal government has enacted a comprehensive scheme of statutes and regulations to prevent and control water pollution. In 1948, Congress enacted the **Federal Water Pollution Control Act (FWPCA)**[4] to regulate water pollution. This act has been amended several times. As amended, it is simply referred to as the **Clean Water Act (CWA)**.[5] This act is administered by the EPA.

Pursuant to the CWA, the EPA has established water quality standards that define which bodies of water can be used for public drinking water, recreation (e.g., swimming), propagation of fish and wildlife, and agricultural and industrial uses. States are primarily responsible for enforcing the provisions of the CWA and EPA regulations adopted thereunder. If a state fails to do so, the federal government may enforce the act.

Point Sources of Water Pollution

The CWA authorizes the EPA to establish water pollution control standards for **point sources of water pollution**. Point sources are sources of pollution that are stationary. Point source dischargers of pollutants are required to maintain monitoring equipment, keep samples of discharges, and keep records.

Critical Legal Thinking Questions

If environmental laws had not been enacted, would businesses have protected the environment? What are the economic consequences of having environmental protection laws?

Examples Mines, manufacturing plants, electric utility plants, paper mills, and municipal sewage plants are examples of point sources of water pollution.

In the following case, the court found criminal violations of federal environmental protection statutes.

CASE 45.2 *FEDERAL COURT CASE Environmental Pollution*

United States v. Maury

695 F.3d 227, 2012 U.S. App. Lexis 19474 (2012)
United States Court of Appeals for the Third Circuit

"Defendants were found to have illegally pumped contaminated water into storm drains and, as a result, into the Delaware River."

—Julio Fuentes, Circuit Judge

Facts

The Atlantic States Cast Iron Pipe Company operates a pipe foundry in Phillipsburg, New Jersey. The plant, which produces iron pipes for municipal water pipes, sits on a 33-acre facility located one mile from the Delaware River. The facility has several large drains that lead to municipal storm sewers, which in turn have an outfall pipe that feeds into the Delaware River. During the production process, scrap iron and steel are melted in a furnace at extremely high heat. The molten metal is cast into pipes, which are sent to the finishing department, where they are cooled with water, ground, lined with cement, and painted. John Prisque was the plant manager. Jeffrey Maury was the maintenance superintendent, and Craig Davidson was the finishing superintendent; both reported to Prisque.

The plant's process produces contaminated wastewater. The plant was supposed to pump the wastewater into large holding tanks located outside the building, where the wastewater stayed until it could be legally disposed of. During production, however, the workers were instructed to pump wastewater into the tanks even though the tanks were too full to handle more wastewater. The result was that the tanks overflowed and the contaminated wastewater flowed down the roadway alongside the plant and into the nearby storm drains. Night-shift employees were instructed to pump the wastewater directly onto the roadway outside the plant, and the wastewater then flowed into the storm drains. All of the contaminated wastewater flowed into the Delaware River. Prisque, Maury, and Davidson had knowledge of these facts and ordered that the wastewater be handled in this fashion. On many occasions, New Jersey residents reported seeing oil slicks on the Delaware River. These discharges were eventually traced to the company's facility by government officials.

In addition, the painting of the pipes on the inside generated large volumes of hazardous paint waste. Employees were told to use shovels to scoop the waste into 55-gallon drums and to seal the drums with duct tape. Instead of disposing of these waste materials legally, managers, including Prisque, ordered workers to burn these drums of waste paint in the plant's furnace at night, causing chemical air pollution.

Based on the evidence, the company, Prisque, Maury, and Davidson were charged with criminal violations of the Clean Water Act; the company and Prisque were charged with criminal violations of the Clean Air Act; and individual defendants were charged with lying to investigators. Following an eight-month criminal trial in which more than 100 witnesses testified, many of them employees at the plant, the jury of the U.S. district court convicted the defendants. The court sentenced Prisque to 70 months' imprisonment, Maury to 30 months' imprisonment, and Davidson to six months' imprisonment. The court fined the company $8 million. The defendants appealed their convictions.

(continued)

Issue

Are the defendants guilty of violating environmental protection statutes?

Language of the Court

Defendants were found to have illegally pumped contaminated water into storm drains and, as a result, into the Delaware River, and to have unlawfully burned 50-gallon drums of paint waste in a furnace and emitted the fumes from those activities into the air. The jury found that the defendants engaged in a conspiracy to commit these acts and to impede the resulting federal investigation. In light of the district court's fine handling of these extraordinarily complicated proceedings, we will affirm the final judgments of convictions and sentences in this case.

Decision

The U.S. court of appeals affirmed the judgment of the U.S. district court.

Critical Legal Thinking Questions

Did the individual defendants act ethically in this case? Did the employees who carried out the managers' orders act ethically? Did the individual defendants receive sufficient punishment?

Thermal Pollution

thermal pollution
Heated water or material discharged into waterways that upsets the ecological balance and decreases the oxygen content.

The Clean Water Act expressly forbids **thermal pollution** because the discharge of heated water or materials into the nation's waterways can upset the ecological balance, decrease the oxygen content of water, and harm fish, birds, and other animals that use the waterways.[6] Sources of thermal pollution (e.g., electric utility companies, manufacturing plants) are subject to the provisions of the CWA and regulations adopted by the EPA.

Examples Electric utility plants and manufacturing plants often cause thermal pollution by discharging heated water or materials into the water. This heated water or material could harm fish in the water as well as birds and other animals that use the water.

Wetlands

wetlands
Areas that are inundated or saturated by surface water or groundwater and that support vegetation typically adapted for life in such conditions.

Wetlands are defined as areas that are inundated or saturated by surface water or groundwater and that support vegetation typically adapted for life in saturated soil conditions. Wetlands include swamps, marshes, bogs, and similar areas that support birds, animals, and vegetation. The Clean Water Act regulates the discharge of dredged or fill material into navigable waters and wetlands that have a significant nexus to navigable waters. The **U.S. Army Corps of Engineers (USACE)** is authorized to enforce this statute and to issue permits for discharge of dredged or fill material into navigable waters and qualified wetlands in the United States. The CWA forbids the filling or dredging of navigable waters and qualified wetlands unless a permit has been obtained from the Army Corps of Engineers.

Example Denzel owns 40 acres of beachfront property in a rural area that fronts an inland lake. On Denzel's property, there is high ground on which houses can be built and ponds and wetland areas that cannot support buildings. The ponds and wetlands are created because water from the lake flows into the ponds and wetlands on the property. The ponds are therefore considered navigable waters under the Clean Water Act. Swans and other birds and animals use the wetlands as their habitat. Denzel secretly fills in the ponds and wetlands to create more hard ground on which additional houses can be built. The Army Corps of Engineers is empowered to bring proceedings against Denzel to correct his illegal act and to report Denzel for criminal proceedings.

Safe Drinking Water Act

The **Safe Drinking Water Act (SDWA)**,[7] enacted in 1974 and subsequently amended, authorizes the EPA to establish national primary drinking water standards (setting the minimum quality of water for human consumption). The act prohibits the dumping of wastes into wells used for drinking water. The states are primarily responsible for enforcing the act. If a state fails to do so, the federal government can enforce the act.

Safe Drinking Water Act
A federal statute that authorizes the EPA to establish national primary drinking water standards.

Ocean Pollution

The **Marine Protection, Research, and Sanctuaries Act (MPRSA)**,[8] also called the **Ocean Dumping Act**, which was enacted in 1972, extends environmental protection to the oceans. It (1) requires a permit for dumping wastes and other foreign materials into ocean waters and (2) establishes marine sanctuaries in ocean waters as far seaward as the edge of the continental shelf. The CWA authorizes the U.S. government to clean up oil spills and spills of other hazardous substances in ocean waters within 12 miles of the shore and on the continental shelf and to recover the cleanup costs from responsible parties.

Marine Protection, Research, and Sanctuaries Act
A federal statute that extends limited environmental protection to the oceans.

There have been several major oil spills from oil tankers and oil drilling facilities in ocean waters off the coast of the United States. These oil spills have caused significant damage to plant, animal, and human life as well as to their habitats. In response, in 1990, Congress enacted the federal **Oil Pollution Act (OPA)**,[9] which is administered by the U.S. Coast Guard. This act, as amended, requires the oil industry to adopt procedures and contingency plans to respond to and clean up oil spills. A tanker owner-operator must prove that it is fully insured to cover any liability that may occur from an oil spill. The act also requires oil tankers to have double hulls.

Oil Pollution Act
A federal statute that requires the oil industry to take measures to prevent oil spills and to respond to and clean up oil spills.

The following ethics feature discusses the BP oil spill in the Gulf of Mexico.

Ethics

BP Oil Spill in the Gulf of Mexico

In 2010, the *Deepwater Horizon* oil spill—commonly referred to as the **BP oil spill**—occurred in the Gulf of Mexico. This oil spill was caused by a leak in a mobile offshore oil drilling rig called *Deepwater Horizon*. This rig was drilling on a platform owned by BP p.l.c. (formerly British Petroleum), a global oil and gas company headquartered in London. An exploratory well was being drilled at a depth of approximately 5,000 feet when an explosion occurred, killing 11 workers and injuring many others. This explosion caused a seafloor oil gusher that began spilling oil into the ocean waters and continued for more than three months. The spill spread more than 200 million gallons of oil over a 5,000-square-mile area of the Gulf of Mexico before the leak was finally capped.

The oil spill caused extensive damage to more than 1,300 miles of coastline, particularly in the Gulf states. Thousands of marine animals were killed, and tens of thousands of birds perished as well. Hundreds of species of marine animals and birds specific to the area continue to be at risk of possible extinction. BP spent $14 billion in initial response costs.

The BP oil spill was the largest in U.S. history; in fact, it was more than 20 times larger than the previous largest oil spill, the *Exxon-Valdez* oil spill in the waters off the coast of Alaska.

Thousands of civil lawsuits against BP and the other parties were filed by individuals and businesses seeking to recover damages caused by the oil spill. BP established a $20 billion trust fund to cover individual compensation claims. Many individual claims have been settled while others are still being litigated.

In 2013, BP plead guilty to 11 counts of felony manslaughter and paid $4.5 billion to settle criminal charges. In 2015, the federal government and five affected states—Texas, Louisiana, Mississippi, Alabama, and Florida—announced a $20 billion settlement of claims arising from the incident. The settlement requires BP to engage in a massive cleanup in the Gulf Coast area to restore wildlife, habitat, and water quality. The U.S. district court approved the settlement in 2016. *In re: Oil Spill by the Oil Rig "Deepwater Horizon" in the Gulf of Mexico*, 2016 U.S. Dist. Lexis 165001 (United States District Court for the Eastern District of Louisiana, 2016)

Ethics Questions
How many individuals' lives were severely affected by the BP oil spill? Do you think that all of them will be fully compensated? Are the damages difficult to assess? Do you think that the environment will fully recover from the oil spill?

Toxic Substances and Hazardous Wastes

45.4 Explain how environmental laws regulate the use of toxic substances and the disposal of hazardous wastes.

toxic substances
Chemicals used by agriculture, industry, business, mining, and households that cause injury to humans, birds, animals, fish, and vegetation.

hazardous waste
Waste that may cause or significantly contribute to an increase in mortality or serious illness or pose a hazard to human health or the environment if improperly managed.

Many chemicals used by agriculture, industry, business, mining, and households contain **toxic substances** that cause cancer, birth defects, and other health-related problems in human beings as well as injury or death to birds, fish, other animals, and vegetation. Many chemical compounds that are used in the manufacture of products are toxic (e.g., PCBs, asbestos). In addition, agriculture, mining, industry, other businesses, and households generate wastes that often contain hazardous substances that can harm the environment or pose danger to human health. The mishandling and improper disposal of **hazardous wastes** can cause air, water, and land pollution.

Examples Hazardous wastes consist of garbage, sewage, industrial discharges, old equipment, and so on, that are discharged or placed in the environment.

Toxic Substances Control

Toxic Substances Control Act
A federal statute that authorizes the EPA to regulate toxic substances.

In 1976, Congress enacted the **Toxic Substances Control Act (TSCA)**[10] and gave the EPA authority to administer the act. The act requires the EPA to identify **toxic air pollutants** that present a substantial risk of injury to human health or the environment. So far, more than 200 chemicals have been listed as toxic, including asbestos, mercury, vinyl chloride, benzene, beryllium, and radionuclides.

The act requires the EPA to establish standards for toxic chemicals and requires stationary sources to install equipment and technology to control emissions of toxic substances. The act requires manufacturers and processors to test new chemicals to determine their effects on human health and the environment and to report the results to the EPA before the chemicals are marketed. The EPA also requires special labeling of toxic substances.

Frank R. Lautenberg Chemical Safety for the 21st Century Act
A federal statute that requires the EPA to evaluate the safety of existing chemicals used in commerce and to make an affirmative determination on proposed new chemicals before they can be manufactured and distributed in commerce.

In 2016, the **Frank R. Lautenberg Chemical Safety for the 21st Century Act (Lautenberg Chemical Safety Act)** was signed into law.[11] This act amends the TSCA by mandating that the EPA evaluate the safety of existing chemicals used in commerce, make an affirmative determination on proposed new chemicals before they can be manufactured and distributed in commerce, take immediate regulatory action to address risks from toxic chemicals, and provide the public with important information about the risks of chemicals.

The EPA may limit or prohibit the manufacture and sale of toxic substances, and it can remove them from commerce if it finds that they pose an imminent hazard or an unreasonable risk of injury to human health or the environment.

Insecticides, Fungicides, and Rodenticides

Federal Insecticide, Fungicide, and Rodenticide Act
A federal statute that requires pesticides, herbicides, fungicides, and rodenticides to be registered with the EPA; the EPA may deny, suspend, or cancel registration.

Farmers and ranchers use chemical pesticides, herbicides, fungicides, and rodenticides to kill insects, weeds, and pests. Evidence shows that the use of some of these chemicals on food and their residual accumulation in soil pose health hazards. In 1947, Congress enacted the **Federal Insecticide, Fungicide, and Rodenticide Act (FIFRA)**, which gave the federal government authority to regulate pesticides and related chemicals. This act, which was substantially amended in 1972,[12] is administered by the EPA. Under the act, pesticides must be registered with the EPA before they can be sold. The EPA may suspend the registration of a pesticide that it finds poses an imminent danger or emergency.

Hazardous Waste

land pollution
Pollution of the land that is generally caused by hazardous waste being disposed of improperly.

Resource Conservation and Recovery Act
A federal statute that authorizes the EPA to regulate facilities that generate, treat, store, transport, and dispose of hazardous wastes.

The disposal of hazardous wastes sometimes causes **land pollution**. In 1976, Congress enacted the **Resource Conservation and Recovery Act (RCRA)**,[13] which regulates the disposal of new hazardous wastes. This act, which has been amended several times, authorizes the EPA to regulate facilities that generate, treat, store, transport, and dispose of hazardous wastes. States have primary responsibility for implementing the standards established by the act and EPA regulations.

The act defines *hazardous waste* as a solid waste that may cause or significantly contribute to an increase in mortality or serious illness or pose a hazard to human health or the environment if managed improperly. The EPA has designated substances that are toxic, radioactive, corrosive, or ignitable as hazardous and can add to the list of hazardous wastes as needed.

The EPA also establishes standards and procedures for the safe treatment, storage, disposal, and transportation of hazardous wastes. Under the act, the EPA is authorized to regulate underground storage facilities, such as underground gasoline tanks.

The following feature discusses an important environmental law.

WEB EXERCISE

Go to **www.epa.gov/superfund/** and find the EPA Superfund site closest to your hometown. How far away is the polluted site from your hometown? Why is it listed as a Superfund site?

Comprehensive Environmental Response, Compensation, and Liability Act (Superfund)
A federal statute that authorizes the federal government to deal with hazardous wastes. The act creates a monetary fund to finance the cleanup of hazardous waste sites.

Landmark Law

Superfund

In 1980, Congress enacted the **Comprehensive Environmental Response, Compensation, and Liability Act (CERCLA)**, which is commonly called the **Superfund.**[14] The act is administered by the EPA and gives the federal government a mandate to deal with hazardous wastes that have been spilled, stored, or abandoned. The act provides for the creation of a government fund to finance the cleanup of hazardous waste sites (hence the name *Superfund*). The fund is financed through taxes on chemicals, feedstock, motor fuels, and other products that contain hazardous substances.

The Superfund requires the EPA to (1) identify sites in the United States where hazardous wastes have been disposed of, stored, abandoned, or spilled and (2) rank these sites regarding the severity of the risk. The hazardous waste sites with the highest ranking receive first consideration for cleanup.

The EPA can order a responsible party to clean up a hazardous waste site. If that party fails to do so, the EPA can spend Superfund money to clean up the site and recover the cost of the cleanup from responsible parties. The Superfund imposes **strict liability**—that is, liability without fault. The EPA can recover the cost of the cleanup from (1) the generator who deposited the wastes, (2) the transporter of the wastes to the site, (3) the owner of the site at the time of the disposal, and (4) the current owner and operator of the site. The EPA has the authority to clean up hazardous sites quickly to prevent fire, explosion, contamination of drinking water, and other imminent dangers.

Nuclear Waste

Nuclear-powered fuel plants create **nuclear wastes** that maintain a high level of *radioactivity*. Radioactivity can cause injury and death to humans and other life and can also cause severe damage to the environment. Accidents, human error, and faulty construction are among the major causes of **radiation pollution**.

The **Nuclear Regulatory Commission (NRC)**, which was created by Congress in 1977, licenses the construction and opening of commercial nuclear power plants. It continually monitors the operation of nuclear power plants and may close a plant if safety violations are found. The EPA is empowered to set standards for radioactivity in the environment and to regulate the disposal of radioactive waste. The EPA also regulates thermal pollution from nuclear power plants and emissions from uranium mines and mills. The **Nuclear Waste Policy Act (NWPA)** of 1982[15] mandates that the federal government select a permanent site for the disposal of nuclear wastes.

radiation pollution
Emissions from radioactive wastes that can cause injury and death to humans and other life and can cause severe damage to the environment.

Nuclear Regulatory Commission (NRC)
A federal agency that licenses the construction and opening of commercial nuclear power plants.

Emergency Planning and Community Right-to-Know Act

The **Emergency Planning and Community Right-to-Know Act (EPCRA)**, which was enacted in 1986, is a federal statute that is designed to help communities prepare for chemical emergencies.[16] The act requires parties to report on the storage, use, and releases of hazardous substances to federal and state governmental authorities. The EPCRA requires state and local governments to use this information to prepare for and protect their communities from potential risks.

Emergency Planning and Community Right-to-Know Act
A federal statute that is designed to help communities prepare for chemical emergencies.

Endangered Species

45.5 Describe how the Endangered Species Act protects endangered and threatened species and their habitats.

Endangered Species Act
A federal statute that protects endangered and threatened species of wildlife.

Many species of birds, fish, reptiles, and animals are endangered or threatened with extinction. The reduction of certain species of wildlife may be caused by environmental pollution, real estate development, or hunting. The **Endangered Species Act (ESA)** was enacted in 1973.[17] The act, as amended, protects *endangered* and *threatened* species of wildlife. The U.S. secretary of the interior is empowered to declare a form of wildlife as endangered or threatened.

The act requires the EPA and the Department of Commerce to designate *critical habitats* for each endangered and threatened species. Real estate and other development in these areas is prohibited or severely limited. The secretary of commerce is empowered to enforce the provisions of the act as to marine species. In addition, the Endangered Species Act, which applies to both government and private persons, prohibits the taking of any endangered species. *Taking* is defined as an act intended to "harass, harm, pursue, hunt, shoot, wound, kill, trap, capture, or collect" an endangered animal.

Numerous other federal laws protect wildlife. Many states have enacted statutes that protect and preserve wildlife.

The following critical legal thinking case discusses a classic U.S. Supreme Court decision concerning the Endangered Species Act.

Critical Legal Thinking

Endangered Species

"It may seem curious to some that the survival of a relatively small number of three-inch fish among all the countless millions of species extant would require the permanent halting of a virtually completed dam for which Congress has expended more than $100 million."

—Warren Burger, Chief Justice

The Tennessee Valley Authority (TVA) is a wholly owned public corporation of the United States. It operates a series of dams, reservoirs, and water projects that provide electric power, irrigation, and flood control to areas in several southern states. With appropriations from Congress, the TVA began construction of the Tellico Dam on the Little Tennessee River.

Seven years after construction began, a previously unknown species of perch called the *Percina tanasi*—or "snail darter"—was found in the Little Tennessee River. After further investigation, it was determined that approximately 10,000 to 15,000 of these three-inch fish existed in the river's waters that would be flooded by the operation of the Tellico Dam. The snail darter is not found anywhere else in the world. The impounding of the water behind the Tellico Dam would destroy the snail darter's food and oxygen supplies, thus causing its extinction.

The dam was completed, but a Tennessee conservation group filed an action seeking to enjoin the TVA from closing the gates of the dam and impounding the water in the reservoir on the grounds that those actions would violate the Endangered Species Act by causing the extinction of the snail darter. The U.S. district court held in favor of the TVA. The U.S. court of appeals reversed and issued a permanent injunction, halting the operation of the Tellico Dam. The TVA appealed to the U.S. Supreme Court.

The U.S. Supreme Court held that the Endangered Species Act prohibited the impoundment of the Little Tennessee River by the Tellico Dam. The Court affirmed the injunction ordered by the U.S. court of appeals against the operation of the dam. The Supreme Court stated:

> *It may seem curious to some that the survival of a relatively small number of three-inch fish among all the countless millions of species extant would require the permanent halting of a virtually completed dam for which Congress has expended more than $100 million. We conclude, however, that the explicit provisions of the Endangered Species Act required precisely this result.*

Eventually, after substantial research and investigation, it was determined that the snail darter could live in another habitat that was found for it. After the snail darter was removed to this new location, the TVA was permitted to close the gates of the Tellico Dam and begin its operation. *Tennessee Valley Authority v. Hill, Secretary of the Interior*, 437 U.S. 153, 98 S.Ct. 2279, 1978 U.S. Lexis 33 (Supreme Court of the United States, 1978)

Critical Legal Thinking Questions
What purpose does the Endangered Species Act serve? Was the strict application of the Endangered Species Act warranted in this case?

State Environmental Protection Laws

45.6 Describe state environmental protection laws.

Many state and local governments have enacted statutes and ordinances to protect the environment. Most states require that an environmental impact statement (EIS) or a report be prepared for any proposed state action. In addition, under their police power to protect the "health, safety, and welfare" of their residents, many states require private industry to prepare EISs for proposed developments. Some states have enacted special environmental statutes to protect unique areas within their boundaries.

Examples Florida has enacted laws to protect the Everglades subtropical landscape, California has enacted laws to protect its Pacific Ocean coastline, Washington has enacted laws to protect the water ecosystem of Puget Sound, and Alaska has enacted laws to protect its wilderness areas.

The following feature discusses global environmental protection.

Global Law

International Environmental Protection

Henry R. Cheeseman

MONGOLIA

Even places like the rural country of Mongolia feel the effects of pollution caused by the industrialized countries of the world. Scientists and others have been concerned that greenhouse gases that are released into the air—particularly from carbon dioxide created by burning coal, oil, and gas, as well as deforestation—are causing an increase in atmospheric temperature that could lead to extreme weather events, changes in agricultural yields, increases in diseases, and the extinction of species. The United States has some of the strongest national environmental protection laws in the world. However, the United States is not a party to several international environmental treaties, including the ***Kyoto Protocol****, an international treaty that sets binding obligations on industrialized countries to reduce the emission of greenhouse gases; the* ***Stockholm Convention on Persistent Organic Pollutants (POPS)****, an international treaty that would eliminate or reduce high-risk toxic chemicals; and the Paris Agreement, a United Nations–sponsored treaty dealing with greenhouse gas emissions mitigation.*

Key Terms and Concepts

Air pollution (790)
Air quality control regions (AQCRs) (791)
BP oil spill (795)
Clean Air Act (CAA) (790)
Clean Air Act Amendments (790)
Clean Water Act (CWA) (792)
Comprehensive Environmental Response, Compensation, and Liability Act (CERCLA or Superfund) (797)
Emergency Planning and Community Right-to-Know Act (EPCRA) (797)
Endangered Species Act (ESA) (798)
Environmental impact statement (EIS) (789)
Environmental protection (789)
Environmental Protection Agency (EPA) (789)
Environmental protection laws (789)
Federal Insecticide, Fungicide, and Rodenticide Act (FIFRA) (796)
Federal Water Pollution Control Act (FWPCA) (792)
Frank R. Lautenberg Chemical Safety for the 21st Century Act (Lautenberg Chemical Safety Act) (796)
Hazardous waste (796)
Indoor air pollution (sick building syndrome) (792)
Land pollution (796)
Marine Protection, Research, and Sanctuaries Act (MPRSA or Ocean Dumping Act) (795)
Mobile sources of air pollution (790)
National ambient air quality standards (NAAQS) (790)
National Environmental Policy Act (NEPA) (789)
Nonattainment area (791)
Nuclear Regulatory Commission (NRC) (797)
Nuclear Waste Policy Act (NWPA) (797)
Nuclear wastes (797)
Oil Pollution Act (OPA) (795)
Point sources of water pollution (793)
Radiation pollution (797)
Resource Conservation and Recovery Act (RCRA) (796)
Safe Drinking Water Act (SDWA) (795)
State implementation plan (SIP) (791)
Stationary sources of air pollution (790)
Strict liability (797)
Thermal pollution (794)
Toxic air pollutants (796)
Toxic substances (796)
Toxic Substances Control Act (TSCA) (796)
U.S. Army Corps of Engineers (USACE) (794)
Water pollution (792)
Wetlands (794)

Critical Legal Thinking Cases

45.1 Wetlands Leslie Salt Company owned a 153-acre tract of undeveloped land south of San Francisco. The property abutted the San Francisco National Wildlife Refuge and was approximately one-quarter mile from Newark Slough, a tidal arm of San Francisco Bay. Originally, the property was pastureland. The first change occurred in the early 1900s, when Leslie's predecessors constructed facilities to manufacture salt on the property. They excavated pits and created large, shallow, watertight basins. Salt production was stopped in 1959. The construction of a sewer line and public roads on and around the property created ditches and culverts. Newark Slough is connected to the property by these culverts, and tidewaters reach the property. Water accumulates in the ponds, ditches, and culverts, providing wetland vegetation to wildlife and migratory birds and fish that live in the ponds.

More than 25 years later, Leslie started to dig a ditch to drain the property and began construction to block the culvert that connected to the Newark Slough. The Army Corps of Engineers issued a cease-and-desist order against Leslie. Leslie challenged the order. Who wins? *Leslie Salt Co. v. United States*, 896 F.2d 354, 1990 U.S. App. Lexis 1524 (United States Court of Appeals for the Ninth Circuit, 1990)

45.2 Clean Water Act The Reserve Mining Company (Reserve) owned and operated a mine in Minnesota that was located on the shores of Lake Superior and produced hazardous waste. Reserve obtained a permit from the state of Minnesota to dump its wastes into Lake Superior. The permits prohibited discharges that would "result in any clouding or discoloration of the water outside the specific discharge zone" or "result in any material adverse effects on public water supplies." Reserve discharged its wastes into Lake Superior for years. Evidence showed that the discharges caused discoloration of surface waters outside the zone of discharge and contained carcinogens that adversely affected public water supplies. The United States sued Reserve for engaging in unlawful water pollution. Who wins? *United States v. Reserve Mining Company*, 543 F.2d 1210, 1976 U.S. App. Lexis 6503 (United States Court of Appeals for the Eighth Circuit, 1976)

45.3 Hazardous Waste Douglas Hoflin was the director of the Public Works Department for Ocean Shores, Washington. Over a period of seven years, the department purchased 3,500 gallons of paint for road maintenance. As painting jobs were finished, the 55-gallon drums that had contained the paint were returned to the department's yard. The paint contained hazardous substances such as lead.

When 14 of the drums were discovered to contain unused paint, Hoflin instructed employees to haul the paint drums to the city's sewage treatment plant and bury them. The employees dug a hole on the grounds of the treatment plant and dumped in the drums. Some of the drums were rusted and leaking. The hole was not deep enough, so the employees crushed the drums with a front-end loader to make them fit. The refuse was then covered with sand. Almost two years later, one of the city's employees reported the incident to state authorities, who referred the matter to the EPA. Investigation showed that the paint had contaminated the soil. The United States brought criminal charges against Hoflin for aiding and abetting the illegal dumping of hazardous waste. Who wins? *United States v. Hoflin*, 880 F.2d 1033, 1989 U.S. App. Lexis 10169 (United States Court of Appeals for the Ninth Circuit, 1989)

Ethics Case

45.4 Ethics Case Metropolitan Edison Company owned and operated two nuclear-fueled power plants at Three Mile Island near Harrisburg, Pennsylvania. Both power plants were licensed by the NRC after extensive proceedings and investigations, including the preparation of the required environmental impact statements. When one of the power plants was shut down for refueling, the other plant suffered a serious accident that damaged the reactor. The governor of Pennsylvania recommended an evacuation of all pregnant women and small children, and many area residents left their homes for several days. As it turned out, no dangerous radiation was released.

People Against Nuclear Energy (PANE), an association of area residents who opposed further operation of the nuclear power plants at Three Mile Island, sued to enjoin the plants from reopening. They argued that the reopening of the plants would cause severe psychological health damage to persons living in the vicinity and serious damage to the stability and cohesiveness of the community. Are these reasons sufficient to prevent the reopening of the nuclear power plants? Is it socially responsible for the federal government to permit the operation of nuclear power plants? *Metropolitan Edison Company v. People Against Nuclear Energy*, 460 U.S. 766, 103 S.Ct. 1556, 1983 U.S. Lexis 21 (Supreme Court of the United States, 1983)

Notes

1. 42 U.S.C. Sections 4321–4370d.
2. Public Law 88–206.
3. 42 U.S.C. Sections 7401–7671q.
4. 33 U.S.C. Sections 1251–1376, 62 Stat. 1155.
5. 33 U.S.C. Sections 1251–1367.
6. 33 U.S.C. Section 1254(t).
7. 21 U.S.C. Section 349 and 300f–300j-25.
8. 16 U.S.C. Sections 1431 et seq., 33 U.S.C. Sections 1401–1445.
9. 33 U.S.C. Sections 2701–2761.
10. 15 U.S.C. Sections 2601–2692.
11. Public Law 114–182, 130 Stat. 448.
12. 7 U.S.C. Sections 135 et seq.
13. 42 U.S.C. Sections 6901–6986.
14. 42 U.S.C. Sections 9601–9675.
15. 42 U.S.C. Sections 10101–10270.
16. 42 U.S.C. 11001–11050, 100 Stat. 1728.
17. 16 U.S.C. Sections 1531–1544.

CHAPTER 46

Antitrust Law and Unfair Trade Practices

Cate_89/Shutterstock

FENWAY PARK, BOSTON, MASSACHUSETTS
In 1922, the U.S. Supreme Court held that professional baseball leagues were exempt from antitrust laws because they were not engaged in interstate commerce.[1] *The merits of this exemption have been debated ever since.*

Learning Objectives

After studying this chapter, you should be able to:

46.1 List and describe the major federal antitrust statutes and the enforcement of federal antitrust laws.

46.2 Describe the restraints of trade that violate Section 1 of the Sherman Act.

46.3 Identify acts of monopolization that violate Section 2 of the Sherman Act.

46.4 Explain how the lawfulness of mergers is examined under Section 7 of the Clayton Act.

46.5 Describe tying arrangements that violate Section 3 of the Clayton Act.

46.6 List and describe the types of price discrimination that violate Section 2 of the Clayton Act.

46.7 Describe antitrust acts and unfair methods of competition that violate Section 5 of the Federal Trade Commission Act.

46.8 List and describe express and implied exemptions from antitrust laws.

46.9 Describe the scope of state antitrust laws.

"While competition cannot be created by statutory enactment, it can in large measure be revived by changing the laws and forbidding the practices that killed it, and by enacting laws that will give it heart and occasion again. We can arrest and prevent monopoly."

—*Woodrow Wilson*
Twenty-Eighth President of the United States
Speech, August 7, 1912

Introduction to Antitrust Law and Unfair Trade Practices

The U.S. economic system was built on the theory of freedom of competition. After the Civil War, however, the U.S. economy changed from a rural and agricultural economy to an industrialized and urban one. Many large industrial trusts were formed during this period. These arrangements resulted in a series of monopolies in basic industries such as oil and gas, sugar, cotton, and whiskey.

Because the common law could not deal effectively with these monopolies, Congress enacted a comprehensive system of **antitrust laws** to limit anticompetitive behavior. Almost all industries, businesses, and professions operating in the United States were affected. Although many states have also enacted antitrust laws, most actions in this area are brought under federal law.

This chapter discusses antitrust laws.

People of the same trade seldom meet together, even for merriment and diversion, but that the conversation ends in a conspiracy against the public, or in some contrivance to raise prices.

Adam Smith
The Wealth of Nations (1776)

antitrust laws
A series of laws enacted to limit anticompetitive behavior in almost all industries, businesses, and professions operating in the United States.

Federal Antitrust Law

46.1 List and describe the major federal antitrust statutes and the enforcement of federal antitrust laws.

Federal antitrust law comprises several major statutes that prohibit certain anticompetitive and monopolistic practices. The **federal antitrust statutes** are broadly drafted to reflect the government's enforcement policy and to allow it to respond to economic, business, and technological changes. Federal antitrust laws provide for both government and private lawsuits.

The following feature describes the major federal antitrust statutes.

WEB EXERCISE
Go to **www.usdoj.gov/atr** and read the U.S. Justice Department's overview of the Antitrust Division.

Landmark Laws

Federal Antitrust Statutes

After the Civil War, the United States became a leader of the Industrial Revolution. Behemoth companies and trusts were established. The most powerful of these were John D. Rockefeller's Standard Oil Company, Andrew Carnegie's Carnegie Steel, Cornelius Vanderbilt's New York Central Railroad System, and J.P. Morgan's banking house. These corporations dominated their respective industries, with many obtaining monopoly power. For example, the Rockefeller oil trust controlled 90 percent of the country's oil-refining capacity. Mergers and monopolization of industries were rampant.

During the late 1800s and early 1900s, Congress enacted a series of antitrust laws aimed at curbing abusive and monopoly practices by businesses. During this time, Congress enacted the following federal statutes:

- The **Sherman Antitrust Act**[2] (or **Sherman Act**) is a federal statute, enacted in 1890, that makes certain restraints of trade and monopolistic acts illegal.
- The **Clayton Antitrust Act**[3] (or **Clayton Act**) is a federal statute, enacted in 1914, that regulates mergers and prohibits certain exclusive dealing arrangements.
- The **Federal Trade Commission Act (FTC Act)**[4] is a federal statute, enacted in 1914, that prohibits unfair methods of competition.
- The **Robinson-Patman Act**[5] is a federal statute, enacted in 1930, that prohibits price discrimination.

Each of these important statutes is discussed in this chapter.

Government Actions

The federal government is authorized to bring a **government action** to enforce federal antitrust laws. Government enforcement of federal antitrust laws is divided between the **Antitrust Division of the Department of Justice** and the **Bureau of Competition of the Federal Trade Commission**. The Sherman Act is the only major antitrust act that includes criminal sanctions. Intent is the prerequisite for criminal liability under this act. Penalties for individuals include fines and prison terms; corporations may be fined.

The government may seek **civil damages**, including *treble damages*, for violations of antitrust laws.[6] Broad remedial powers allow the courts to order a number of civil remedies, including orders for divestiture of assets, cancellation of contracts, liquidation of businesses, and licensing of patents. Private parties cannot intervene in public antitrust actions brought by the government.

Private Actions

Section 4 of the Clayton Act
A section stating that anyone injured in his or her business or property by the defendant's violation of any federal antitrust law (except the Federal Trade Commission Act) may bring a private civil action and recover from the defendant treble damages plus reasonable costs and attorney's fees.

treble damages
Damages that may be awarded in a successful civil antitrust lawsuit, in an amount that is triple the amount of actual damages.

Section 4 of the Clayton Act permits any person who suffers antitrust injury in his or her "business or property" to bring a **private civil action** against the offenders.[7] Consumers who have to pay higher prices because of an antitrust violation have recourse under this provision. To recover damages, plaintiffs must prove that they suffered **antitrust injury** caused by the prohibited act.

Successful plaintiffs may recover **treble damages** (i.e., triple the amount of the actual damages), plus reasonable costs and attorney's fees. Damages may be calculated as lost profits, an increase in the cost of doing business, or a decrease in the value of tangible or intangible property caused by the antitrust violation. This rule applies to all violations of the Sherman Act, the Clayton Act, and the Robinson-Patman Act. Only actual damages—not treble damages—may be recovered for violations of the FTC Act. A private plaintiff has four years from the date on which an antitrust injury occurred to bring a private civil treble-damages action. Only damages incurred during this four-year period are recoverable. This statute is *tolled* (i.e., does not run) during a suit by the government.

Effect of a Government Judgment

government judgment
A judgment obtained by the government against a defendant for an antitrust violation that may be used as *prima facie* evidence of liability in a private civil treble-damages action.

A **government judgment** obtained against a defendant for an antitrust violation may be used as *prima facie* evidence of liability in a private civil treble-damages action. Antitrust defendants often opt to settle government-brought antitrust actions by entering a plea of ***nolo contendere*** in a criminal action or a **consent decree** in a government civil action. These pleas usually subject the defendant to penalty without an admission of guilt or liability.

Section 16 of the Clayton Act permits the government or a private plaintiff to obtain an injunction against anticompetitive behavior that violates antitrust laws.[8] Only the FTC can obtain an injunction under the FTC Act.

Restraints of Trade: Section 1 of the Sherman Act

46.2 Describe the restraints of trade that violate Section 1 of the Sherman Act.

In 1890, Congress enacted the *Sherman Act* in order to outlaw anticompetitive behavior. The Sherman Act has been called the "Magna Carta of free enterprise."[9]

Section 1 of the Sherman Act is intended to prohibit certain concerted anticompetitive activities. It provides the following:

> *Every contract, combination in the form of trust or otherwise, or conspiracy, in restraint of trade or commerce among the several states, or with foreign nations, is hereby declared to be illegal. Every person who shall make any contract or engage in any combination or conspiracy hereby declared to be illegal shall be deemed guilty of a felony.*[10]

In other words, Section 1 makes illegal *contracts, combinations*, and *conspiracies* in restraint of trade. Thus, it applies to unlawful conduct by two or more parties. The agreement may be written, oral, or inferred from the conduct of the parties.

The following feature discusses the rule of reason and the *per se* rule used to judge the lawfulness of restraints of trade.

Section 1 of the Sherman Act
A section that prohibits contracts, combinations, and conspiracies in restraint of trade.

rule of reason
A rule stating that only unreasonable restraints of trade violate Section 1 of the Sherman Act. The court must examine the pro- and anticompetitive effects of a challenged restraint.

***per se* rule**
A rule that is applicable to restraints of trade considered inherently anticompetitive. Once this determination is made about a restraint of trade, the court will not permit any defenses or justifications to save it.

Business Environment

Rule of Reason and *Per Se* Rule

The U.S. Supreme Court has developed two different tests for determining the lawfulness of a restraint. These two tests—the *rule of reason* and the *per se rule*—are discussed in the following paragraphs.

Rule of Reason

If Section 1 of the Sherman Act were read literally, it would prohibit almost all contracts. In the landmark case ***Standard Oil Company of New Jersey v. United States***,[11] the Supreme Court adopted the **rule of reason** standard for analyzing Section 1 cases. This rule holds that only an **unreasonable restraint of trade** violates Section 1 of the Sherman Act. Reasonable restraints are lawful. The courts examine the following factors in applying the rule of reason to a case:

- The pro- and anticompetitive effects of the challenged restraint
- The competitive structure of the industry
- The firm's market share and power
- The history and duration of the restraint
- Other relevant factors

***Per Se* Rule**

The Supreme Court adopted the ***per se* rule**, which is applicable to restraints of trade that are considered inherently anticompetitive. No balancing of pro- and anticompetitive effects is necessary in such cases: Such a restraint is automatically in violation of Section 1 of the Sherman Act. When a restraint is characterized as a *per se* violation, no defenses or justifications for the restraint will save it, and no further evidence need be considered. Restraints that are not characterized as *per se* violations are examined using the rule of reason.

CONCEPT SUMMARY

RESTRAINTS OF TRADE: SECTION 1 OF THE SHERMAN ACT

Rule	Description
Rule of reason	Requires a balancing of pro- and anticompetitive effects of the challenged restraint. Restraints that are found to be unreasonable are unlawful and violate Section 1 of the Sherman Act. Restraints that are found to be reasonable are lawful and do not violate Section 1 of the Sherman Act.
Per se rule	Applies to restraints that are inherently anticompetitive. No justification for the restraint is permitted. Such restraints automatically violate Section 1 of the Sherman Act.

Horizontal Restraints of Trade

horizontal restraint of trade
A restraint of trade that occurs when two or more competitors at the same *level of distribution* enter into a contract, combination, or conspiracy to restrain trade.

A **horizontal restraint of trade** occurs when two or more competitors at the *same level of distribution* enter into a contract, combination, or conspiracy to restrain trade (see **Exhibit 46.1**). Many horizontal restraints fall under the *per se* rule; others are examined under the rule of reason. The most common forms of horizontal restraint are discussed in the following paragraphs.

Exhibit 46.1 HORIZONTAL RESTRAINT OF TRADE

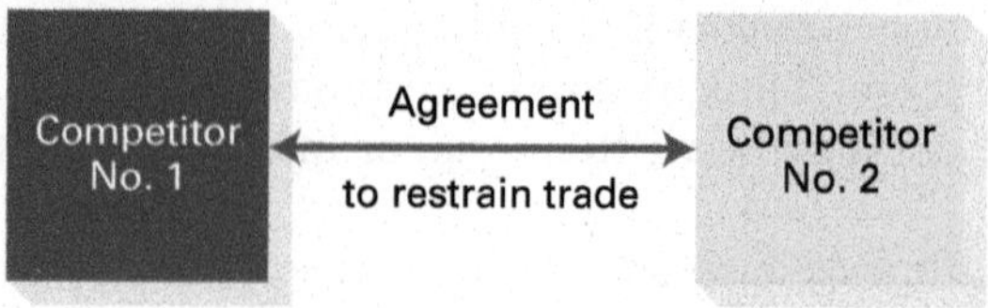

Price Fixing

price fixing
A restraint of trade that occurs when competitors in the same line of business agree to set the price of the goods or services they sell, raising, depressing, fixing, pegging, or stabilizing the price of a commodity or service.

Horizontal **price fixing** occurs when competitors in the same line of business agree to set the price of goods or services they sell. Price fixing is defined as raising, depressing, fixing, pegging, or stabilizing the price of a commodity or service. Illegal price fixing includes setting minimum or maximum prices or fixing the quantity of a product or service to be produced or provided. Although most price fixing agreements occur between sellers, an agreement among buyers to agree to the price they will pay for goods or services is also price fixing. The plaintiff bears the burden of proving a price fixing agreement.

Price fixing is a *per se* violation of Section 1 of the Sherman Act. No defenses or justifications of any kind—such as "the price fixing helps consumers or protects competitors from ruinous competition"—can prevent the *per se* rule from applying.

Example If the three largest automobile manufacturers agreed among themselves what prices to charge automobile dealers for this year's models, they would be engaging in sellers' illegal *per se* price fixing.

Example If the three largest automobile manufacturers agreed among themselves what price they would pay to purchase tires from tire manufactures, they would be engaging in buyers' illegal *per se* price fixing.

The following feature discusses a *per se* horizontal restraint of trade.

Ethics

Tech Companies Settle Lawsuit for Agreeing Not to Solicit Each Other's Employees

Adobe Inc.; Apple Inc.; Google Inc.; Intel Corporation; Intuit Inc.; Lucasfilm Ltd.; and Pixar (defendants) are high-tech companies with principal places of business in the San Francisco/Silicon Valley area of California. In a free labor market, these companies would compete for high-tech talent to hire as employees. One way of doing so is by cold calling, which includes communicating directly with and soliciting current employees of other companies, either orally, in writing, telephonically, or electronically.

After receiving complaints from certain high-tech employees, the U.S. Department of Justice (DOJ) investigated alleged anticompetitive behavior by the defendant companies. The charges were that the defendants had entered into nonsolicitation agreements amongst themselves to not cold call employees of the other companies in order to prevent a bidding war for the best talent in the area, thus depressing salaries of the affected employees. The defendants were accused of memorializing agreements in CEO-to-CEO emails and other documents, including "Do Not Call" lists, putting each firm's high-tech employees off limits to other defendants.

After receiving documents produced by the defendants and interviewing witnesses, the DOJ concluded that the defendants had entered into anticompetitive agreements that eliminated a significant form of competition that deprived employees from receiving competitively important information and access to better job opportunities. The DOJ concluded that the nonsolicitation agreements limited salaries for high-tech employees and held that the defendants had entered into agreements that were naked horizontal restraints of trade that were *per se* violations of Section 1 of the Sherman Act.

The DOJ filed complaints in federal court against the defendants for conspiracy to violate antitrust laws. Eventually, the DOJ and the defendants settled the case by agreeing to stipulated judgments whereby the defendants were enjoined from attempting to enter into, maintaining, or enforcing any agreement with any other person or company, or in any way refraining from soliciting, cold calling, recruiting, or otherwise competing for employees of any other person or company. In reaching this agreement, the defendants were not required to admit to any wrongdoing or violation of the law. *United States v. Adobe Systems Inc.* and *United States v. Lucasfilm, Inc.*, 2011 WL 2636850 (United States District Court for the District of Columbia, 2011)

Ethics Questions

Why did the DOJ and the defendants enter into a settlement rather than going to trial? Should the defendants have been required to pay damages to the high-tech employees who had been injured by the defendants? Was it right for the government to agree to allow the defendants to not admit to any wrongdoing?

Division of Markets

Competitors who agree that each will serve only a designated portion of the market are engaging in a **division of markets** (or **market sharing**), which is a *per se* violation of Section 1 of the Sherman Act. Each market segment is considered a small monopoly served only by its designated "owner." Horizontal market sharing arrangements include division by geographical territories, customers, and products.

division of markets (market sharing)
A restraint of trade in which competitors agree that each will serve only a designated portion of the market.

Example Three national breweries agree among themselves that each one will be assigned one-third of the country as its geographical "territory," and each agrees not to sell beer in the other two companies' territories. This arrangement is a *per se* illegal geographical division of markets.

Example The three largest sellers of media software agree that each can sell media software to only one designated media software purchaser and not to any other media software purchasers. This arrangement is a *per se* illegal product division of markets.

Group Boycott

A **group boycott** (or **refusal to deal**) occurs when two or more competitors at one level of distribution agree not to deal with others at a different level of distribution. A group boycott could be a *group boycott by sellers* or a *group boycott by purchasers*.

group boycott (refusal to deal)
A restraint of trade in which two or more competitors at one level of distribution agree not to deal with others at another level of distribution.

If a group of sellers agrees not to sell their products to a certain buyer, they would be engaging in a **group boycott by sellers**.

Example A group of high-fashion clothes designers and sellers agree not to sell their clothes to a certain discount retailer, such as Walmart. This is a group boycott by sellers (see **Exhibit 46.2**).

Exhibit 46.2 GROUP BOYCOTT BY SELLERS

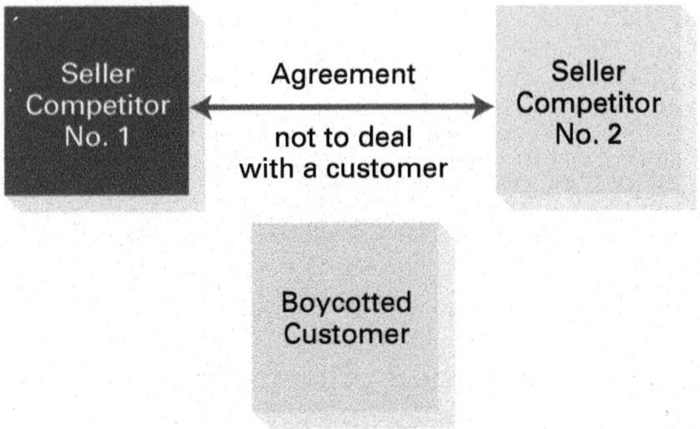

If a group of purchasers agrees not to purchase a product from a certain seller, they would be engaging in a **group boycott by purchasers**.

Example A group of rental car companies agrees not to purchase Ford automobiles for their fleets. This is a group boycott by purchasers (see **Exhibit 46.3**).

Exhibit 46.3 GROUP BOYCOTT BY PURCHASERS

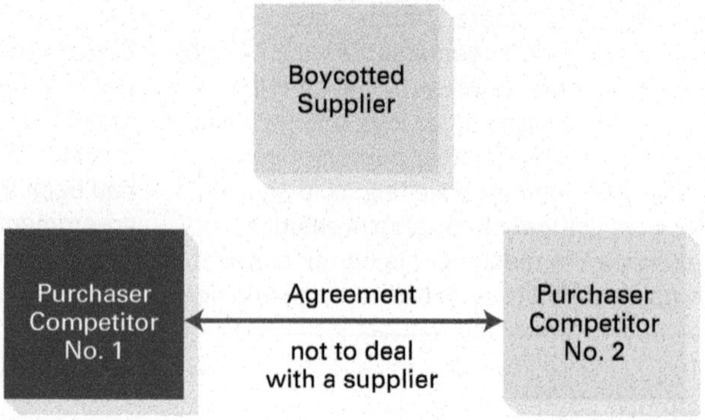

The courts have found that most group boycotts are *per se* illegal. If not found to be *per se* illegal, a group boycott will be examined using the rule of reason. Nevertheless, most group boycotts are found to be illegal.

Other Horizontal Agreements

Some horizontal agreements entered into by competitors at the same level of distribution—including trade association activities and rules, exchange of non-price information, participation in joint ventures, and the like—are examined using the rule of reason. Reasonable restraints are lawful; unreasonable restraints violate Section 1 of the Sherman Act.

Vertical Restraints of Trade

vertical restraint of trade
A restraint of trade that occurs when two or more parties on *different levels of distribution* enter into a contract, combination, or conspiracy to restrain trade.

A **vertical restraint of trade** occurs when two or more parties on *different levels of distribution* enter into a contract, combination, or conspiracy to restrain trade (see **Exhibit 46.4**). The Supreme Court has applied both the *per se* rule and the rule of reason in determining the legality of vertical restraints of trade under Section 1 of the Sherman Act. The most common forms of vertical restraint are discussed in the following paragraphs.

Exhibit 46.4 VERTICAL RESTRAINT OF TRADE

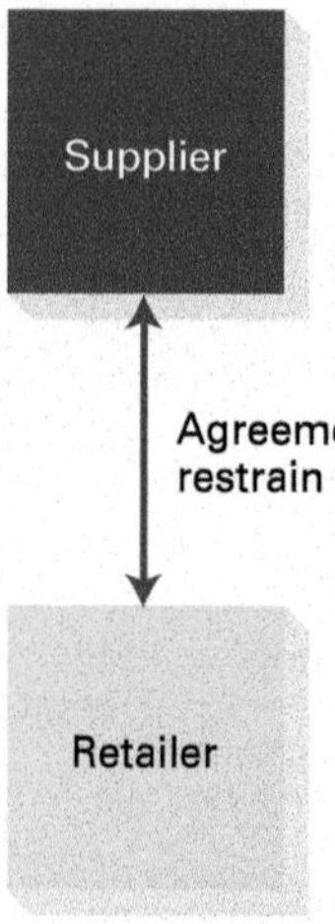

resale price maintenance (vertical price fixing)
A *per se* violation of Section 1 of the Sherman Act that occurs when a party at one level of distribution enters into an agreement with a party at another level to adhere to a price schedule that either sets or stabilizes prices.

Resale Price Maintenance

Resale price maintenance (or **vertical price fixing**) occurs when a party at one level of distribution enters an agreement with a party at another level to adhere to a price schedule that either sets or stabilizes prices.

The setting of a **minimum resale price** is a *per se* violation of Section 1.[12]

Example Prism Corporation manufactures a high-end digital camera and sets a *minimum* price below which the camera cannot be sold by retailers to consumers (e.g., the cameras cannot be sold for less than $10,000 to consumers by retailers). This constitutes *per se* illegal minimum resale price maintenance.

The setting of a **maximum resale price** is examined using the rule of reason to determine whether it violates Section 1.[13]

Example Binary Corporation produces a digital device on which it has a patent. Binary Corporation sets a *maximum* price above which the device cannot be sold by retailers to consumers (e.g., the device cannot be sold for more than $1,000 to consumers by retailers). This conduct will be examined using the rule of reason and most likely will be found to be lawful.

Nonprice Vertical Restraints

The legality of a **nonprice vertical restraint** of trade under Section 1 of the Sherman Act is examined by using the rule of reason. A nonprice vertical restraint is unlawful under this analysis if its anticompetitive effects outweigh its procompetitive effects. Nonprice vertical restraints include situations in which a manufacturer assigns exclusive territories to retail dealers or limits the number of dealers located in a territory.

nonprice vertical restraint A restraint of trade that is unlawful under Section 1 of the Sherman Act if its anticompetitive effects outweigh their procompetitive effects.

The following U.S. Supreme Court case considers the issue of whether federal antitrust law has been violated.

CASE 46.1 *U.S. SUPREME COURT CASE Section 1 of the Sherman Act*

Ohio v. American Express Company

138 S.Ct. 2274 (2018)
Supreme Court of the United States

"Vertical restraints can prevent retailers from free-loading."

—Clarence Thomas, Justice

Facts

American Express (Amex), Visa, and MasterCard are the dominant participants in the credit card market. Visa has 45 percent of the market, while Amex and MasterCard each have about 25 percent. An interrelated credit card network provides services to both cardholders and merchants. While Visa and MasterCard earn half of their revenue by collecting interest from their cardholders, Amex does not. Amex instead earns most of its revenue from merchant fees. To encourage cardholder spending, Amex provides better rewards than Visa or MasterCard. Due to its superior rewards, Amex tends to attract cardholders who are wealthier and spend more money. Merchants place a higher value on these cardholders.

Amex's business model sometimes causes friction with merchants. Merchants would prefer not to pay the higher fees. One way that merchants try to avoid them, while still enticing Amex's cardholders to shop at their stores, is by dissuading cardholders from using Amex at the point of sale. The practice is known as "steering." Amex prohibits steering by placing anti-steering provisions in its contracts with merchants. The United States and several states (collectively, plaintiffs) sued Amex, claiming that its anti-steering provisions violate Section 1 of the Sherman Act as an unreasonable restraint of trade.

The parties agreed that Amex's anti-steering provisions is vertical restraint that is subject to the rule of reason test. The district court held that Amex's anti-steering provisions violate Section 1 of the Sherman Act, but the court of appeals reversed. The plaintiffs appealed to the U.S. Supreme Court.

Issue

Do Amex's anti-steering provisions violate Section 1 of the Sherman Act?

Language of the U.S. Supreme Court

The plaintiffs did not offer any evidence that the price of credit card transaction was

(continued)

higher than the price one would expect to find in a competitive market. That Amex allocates prices between merchants and cardholders differently from Visa and MasterCard is simply not evidence that it wields market power to achieve anticompetitive ends. There is nothing inherently anticompetitive about Amex's anti-steering provisions. Vertical restraints can prevent retailers from free-loading.

Decision

The U.S. Supreme Court held that Amex had not violated federal antitrust law.

Ethics Questions

Do merchants act unethically when they try to steer Amex cardholders from using their Amex card? Is it unethical for Amex to use a different business model than Visa and MasterCard?

unilateral refusal to deal
A unilateral choice by one party not to deal with another party. This does not violate Section 1 of the Sherman Act because there is not concerted action.

conscious parallelism
A doctrine stating that, if two or more firms act the same but no concerted action is shown, there is no violation of Section 1 of the Sherman Act.

Unilateral Refusal to Deal

The U.S. Supreme Court has held that a firm can unilaterally choose not to deal with another party without being liable under Section 1 of the Sherman Act. A **unilateral refusal to deal** is not a violation of Section 1 because there is no concerted action with others. This rule was announced in *United States v. Colgate & Co.*[14] and is therefore often referred to as the ***Colgate* doctrine**.

Example If Louis Vuitton, a maker of expensive women's clothing, shoes, handbags, and accessories, refuses to sell its merchandise to Walmart stores, this is a lawful unilateral refusal to deal.

The following feature discusses conscious parallelism.

Business Environment

Conscious Parallelism

Sometimes two or more firms act the same but have done so individually. If two or more firms act the same but no concerted action is shown, there is no violation of Section 1 of the Sherman Act. This doctrine is often referred to as **conscious parallelism**. Thus, if two competing manufacturers of a similar product both separately reach an independent decision not to deal with a retailer, there is no violation of Section 1 of the Sherman Act. The key is that each of the manufacturers acted on its own.

Example If Louis Vuitton, Gucci, and Chanel, makers of expensive women's clothing, shoes, handbags, and accessories, each independently make a decision not to sell their products to Walmart, this is lawful conscious parallelism. There is no violation of Section 1 of the Sherman Act because the parties did not agree with one another in making their decisions.

Noerr Doctrine

Noerr doctrine
A doctrine stating that two or more persons can petition the executive, legislative, or judicial branch of the government or administrative agencies to enact laws or take other action without violating antitrust laws.

The ***Noerr* doctrine** holds that two or more persons may petition the executive, legislative, or judicial branch of the government or administrative agencies to enact laws or to take other action without violating antitrust laws. The rationale behind this doctrine is that the right to petition the government has precedence because it is guaranteed by the Bill of Rights.[15]

Example General Motors Company and Ford Motor Company, two large automobile manufacturers, collectively petition the U.S. Congress to pass a law that would limit the importation of foreign electric automobiles and vehicles to the United States so that they could dominate the domestic market for electric vehicles in the future. This is lawful activity under the *Noerr* doctrine.

Monopolization: Section 2 of the Sherman Act

46.3 Identify acts of monopolization that violate Section 2 of the Sherman Act

Monopolies affect the prices of goods and services. **Section 2 of the Sherman Act** was enacted in response to widespread concern about the power generated by this type of anticompetitive activity. Section 2 of the Sherman Act prohibits the act of monopolization. It states:

> *Every person who shall monopolize, or attempt to monopolize, or combine or conspire with any other person or persons, to monopolize any part of the trade or commerce among the several States, or with foreign nations, shall be deemed guilty of a felony.*[16]

Proving that a defendant is in violation of Section 2 means proving that the defendant (1) in a *relevant market* (2) possesses *monopoly power* and (3) engaged in a *willful act of monopolization* to acquire or to maintain that power. These three elements are discussed in the following paragraphs.

A monopoly granted either to an individual or to a trading company has the same effect as a secret in trade or manufacture. The monopolists, by keeping the market constantly understocked, by never fully supplying the effectual demand, sell their commodities much above the natural price, and raise their emoluments greatly above their natural rate.

Adam Smith
Wealth of Nations (1776)

1. Relevant Market

Identifying the **relevant market** for a Section 2 action requires defining the relevant product or service market and geographical market. The definition of the relevant market often determines whether the defendant has monopoly power. Consequently, this determination is often litigated.

Section 2 of the Sherman Act
A section that prohibits monopolization and attempts or conspiracies to monopolize trade.

The **relevant product or service market** generally includes substitute products or services that are reasonably interchangeable with the defendant's products or services. Defendants often try to make their market share seem smaller by arguing for a broad definition of the product or service market. Plaintiffs, on the other hand, usually argue for a narrow definition.

relevant product or service market
A relevant market that includes substitute products or services that are reasonably interchangeable with the defendant's products or services.

Example If the government sued Anheuser-Busch InBev, the largest beer producer in the United States, for violating Section 2 of the Sherman Act, the government would argue that the relevant product market is beer sales. Anheuser-Busch InBev, on the other hand, would argue that the relevant product market is sales of all alcoholic beverages or even of all drinkable beverages.

The **relevant geographical market** is usually defined as the area in which the defendant and its competitors sell the product or service. This may be a national, regional, state, or local area, depending on the circumstances.

relevant geographical market
An area in which the defendant and its competitors sell the product or service.

Examples If the government sued The Coca-Cola Company for violating Section 2 of the Sherman Act, the relevant geographical market would be the nation. If the owner of the largest automobile dealerships in south Florida were sued for violating Section 2, the geographical market would be the counties of south Florida.

2. Monopoly Power

For an antitrust action to be sustained, the defendant must possess **monopoly power** in the relevant market. Monopoly power is defined by the courts as the power to control prices or exclude competition. The courts generally apply the following guidelines: Market share above 70 percent is monopoly power; market share under 20 percent is not monopoly power. Otherwise, the courts generally prefer to examine the facts and circumstances of each case when determining monopoly power.

monopoly power
The power to control prices or exclude competition, measured by the market share the defendant possesses in the relevant market.

3. Willful Act of Monopolizing

Section 2 of the Sherman Act outlaws the **willful act of monopolizing**, not monopolies. Any act that otherwise violates any other antitrust law (e.g., illegal restraints of trade, in violation of Section 1 of the Sherman Act) is an act of monopolizing that violates Section 2. When coupled with monopoly power, certain otherwise lawful acts have been held to constitute acts of monopolizing.

willful act of monopolizing
An act that is required to find a violation of Section 2 of the Sherman Act. Possession of monopoly power without such act does not violate Section 2.

Predatory pricing—that is, pricing below average or marginal cost—that is intended to drive out competition has been held to violate Section 2.[17]

CONCEPT SUMMARY

MONOPOLIZATION: SECTION 2 OF THE SHERMAN ACT

Element	Description
1. Relevant market	*Relevant product or service market*: The market that includes substitute products or services that are reasonably interchangeable with the defendant's products or services. *Relevant geographical market*: The geographic area in which the defendant and its competitors sell the product or service.
2. Monopoly power	The power to control prices or exclude competition. If the defendant does not possess monopoly power, it cannot be held liable for monopolization. If the defendant possesses monopoly power, the court will determine whether the monopolist has engaged in an act of monopolizing.
3. Willful act of monopolization	The defendant's engagement in a willful act of monopolizing trade or commerce in the relevant market.

Attempts and Conspiracies to Monopolize

Firms that **attempt or conspire to monopolize** a relevant market may be found liable under Section 2 of the Sherman Act. A single firm may be found liable for monopolizing or attempting to monopolize. Two or more firms may be found liable for conspiring to monopolize.

Defenses to Monopolization

Only two narrow defenses to a charge of monopolizing have been recognized: (1) **innocent acquisition of a monopoly** (e.g., acquisition because of superior business acumen, skill, foresight, or industry) and (2) **natural monopoly** (e.g., a small market that can support only one competitor, such as a small-town newspaper). If a monopoly that fits into one of these categories exercises its power in a predatory or exclusionary way, the defense is lost.

CONCEPT SUMMARY

THE SHERMAN ACT

Section	Description
1	Prohibits contracts, combinations, and conspiracies in restraint of trade. To violate Section 1, the restraint must be found to be unreasonable under either of two tests: (1) rule of reason or (2) *per se* rule. A violation requires the concerted action of two or more parties.
2	Prohibits the act of monopolizing and attempts or conspiracies to monopolize. This act can be violated by the conduct of one firm.

Section 7 of the Clayton Act
A section stating that it is unlawful for a person or business to acquire the stock or assets of another "where in any line of commerce or in any activity affecting commerce in any section of the country, the effect of such acquisition may be substantially to lessen competition, or to tend to create a monopoly."

Mergers: Section 7 of the Clayton Act

46.4 Explain how the lawfulness of mergers is examined under Section 7 of the Clayton Act.

In 1914, Congress enacted **Section 7 of the Clayton Act**, which gave the federal government the power to prevent anticompetitive mergers. Originally, Section 7 of the Clayton Act applied only to stock mergers. The **Celler-Kefauver Act**, which was enacted in 1950, widened the scope of Section 7 to include asset acquisitions. Today, Section 7 applies to all methods of external expansion, including technical mergers, consolidations, purchases of assets, subsidiary operations, joint ventures, and other combinations.

Section 7 of the Clayton Act provides that it is unlawful for a person or business to acquire stock or assets of another "where in any line of commerce or in any activity affecting commerce in any section of the country, the effect of such acquisition may be substantially to lessen competition, or to tend to create a monopoly."[18]

In deciding whether a merger is lawful under Section 7 of the Clayton Act, the courts must (1) define the relevant *line of commerce*, (2) identify the *section of the country* affected by the merger, and (3) determine whether the merger or acquisition creates a reasonable *probability of the substantial lessening of competition* or *is likely to create a monopoly* in the market. These three elements are discussed in the following paragraphs.

1. Line of Commerce

Determining the **line of commerce** that will be affected by a merger involves defining the relevant *product or service market*. Traditionally, the courts have done this by applying the functional interchangeability test. Under this test, the relevant line of commerce includes products or services that consumers use as substitutes. If two products are substitutes for each other, they are considered part of the same line of commerce.

line of commerce
The products or services that will be affected by a merger, including those that consumers use as substitutes. If an increase in the price of one product or service leads consumers to purchase another product or service, the two products are substitutes for each other.

Example Suppose a price increase for regular coffee causes consumers to switch to tea. The two products are part of the same line of commerce because they are considered interchangeable.

2. Section of the Country

Defining the relevant **section of the country** consists of determining the relevant *geographical market*. The courts traditionally identify this market as the geographical area that will feel the direct and immediate effects of the merger. It may consist of a local, state, or regional market; the entire country; or some other geographical area.

section of the country
A division of the country that is based on the relevant geographical market; the geographical area that will feel the direct and immediate effects of a merger.

Example Anheuser-Busch InBev and MillerCoors are the two largest brewers of beer in the United States, and both sell beer nationally. If Anheuser-Busch and MillerCoors plan to merge, the relevant section of the country is the nation.

Example Anheuser-Busch InBev is a brewer that sells beer nationally. Yooper Brewery is a local brewery that sells beer only in the state of Michigan. If Anheuser-Busch intends to acquire Yooper Brewery, the relevant section of the country is the state of Michigan.

3. Probability of a Substantial Lessening of Competition or Likelihood of Creating a Monopoly

After the relevant product or service and geographical markets have been defined, the court must determine whether a merger or acquisition creates a reasonable **probability of a substantial lessening of competition or the likelihood of creating a monopoly**. If the court feels that a merger is likely to do either, it may prevent the merger. Section 7 tries to prevent potentially anticompetitive mergers before they occur. It deals in probabilities; actual proof of the lessening of competition is not required.

probability of a substantial lessening of competition or likelihood of creating a monopoly
The probability that a merger will substantially lessen competition or create a monopoly, in which case the court may prevent the merger, under Section 7 of the Clayton Act.

CONCEPT SUMMARY
MERGER: SECTION 7 OF THE CLAYTON ACT

Element	Description
1. Line of commerce	The market that will be affected by a merger. It includes products or services that consumers use as substitutes for those produced or sold by the merging firms.
2. Section of the country	The geographic market that will be affected by a merger.
3. Probability of a substantial lessening of competition	A probability of a substantial lessening of competition after a merger, in which case the merger may be prohibited. The statute deals with probabilities; actual proof of the lessening of competition is not required.

In applying Section 7, courts generally classify mergers as one of the following: *horizontal merger, vertical merger, market extension merger*, or *conglomerate merger*. These are discussed in the paragraphs that follow.

Horizontal Merger

horizontal merger
A merger between two or more companies that compete in the same business and geographical market.

A **horizontal merger** is a merger between two or more companies that compete in the same business and geographical market. The merger of two grocery store chains that serve the same geographical market fits this definition. Such mergers are subjected to strict review under Section 7 because they clearly result in an increase in concentration of the relevant market.

Example If Facebook and Twitter, two of the largest social media sites, merge, this would be a horizontal merger. This merger would most likely violate Section 7.

Vertical Merger

vertical merger
A merger that integrates the operations of a supplier and a customer.

A **vertical merger** is a merger between businesses that operate at different stages in the production and distribution of a product, such as a merger between a supplier and a customer.

Example When eBay, a prominent online auction and shopping website, merged with PayPal, a company that supports online payments and money transfers, this was a vertical merger in which both companies provided different services that supported each other.

There are the two types of vertical mergers, which are:

backward vertical merger (upstream vertical merger)
A vertical merger in which a customer acquires a supplier.

- **Backward vertical merger.** A **backward vertical merger**, also called an **upstream vertical merger**, is a when a company acquires a business that is one of its suppliers.

  Examples An automobile manufacturer acquires a tire manufacturer. Internet seller Amazon.com acquires the book publisher Simon & Schuster.

forward vertical merger (downstream vertical merger)
A vertical merger in which a supplier acquires a customer.

- **Forward vertical merger.** A **forward vertical merger**, also called a **downstream vertical merger**, is when a company acquires a business that is one of its customers.

  Examples An iron mining company acquires a steel factory. General Mills, Inc., a large food producer, acquires Kroger Company, a large grocery retailer.

Vertical mergers do not create an increase in market share because the merging firms serve different markets. They may, however, cause anticompetitive effects such as **foreclosing competition**—that is, foreclosing competitors from either selling goods or services to or buying them from the merged firm.

Example A large furniture manufacturer wants to acquire a large chain of retail furniture stores. The merger is likely unlawful if the merged firm will not buy furniture from other manufacturers or sell furniture to other retailers.

In examining the legality of vertical mergers, the courts usually consider factors such as the history of the firms, the trend toward concentration in the industries involved, the barriers to entry, the economic efficiencies of the merger, and the potential elimination of competition caused by the merger.

Market Extension Merger

A **market extension merger** is a merger between two companies in similar fields whose sales do not overlap. The merger may expand the acquiring firm's geographical or product market. The legality of market extension mergers is examined under Section 7 of the Clayton Act.

market extension merger
A merger between two companies in similar fields whose sales do not overlap.

Example A merger between two regional brewers that do not sell beer in the same geographical area is called a **geographical market extension merger**.

conglomerate merger
A merger that does not fit into any other category; a merger between firms in totally unrelated businesses.

Example A merger between sellers of similar products, such as a soft drink manufacturer and an orange juice producer, is called a **product market extension merger**.

The following feature discusses conglomerate mergers.

Business Environment

Conglomerate Merger

A **conglomerate merger** is a merger that does not fit into any other category. That is, they are mergers between firms in unrelated businesses.

Example If ExxonMobil, a large oil company, merged with Costco Wholesale Corporation, which operates a chain of warehouse-style stores, the result would be a conglomerate merger.

A conglomerate merger that would give one merging party an unfair advantage if it entered the other merging party's market can be prevented by the government under the **unfair advantage theory**. This could happen if a large company tried to acquire through merger a small company in a competitive market that has many rival companies. The acquisition would give the large company the advantage of being able to use its wealth and resources to overwhelm and drive out the competition in the market.

Example Walmart Stores, Inc. is a giant discount warehouse store and one of the largest and wealthiest companies in the world. The homebuilding industry is a fragmented market that is not dominated by a few large companies. Walmart may be prevented from acquiring Shea Homes, about the twentieth largest homebuilding company, under the unfair advantage theory. The court would be concerned that Walmart could bring its wealth to support and grow Shea Homes into an extremely large and monopolistic home builder.

Defenses to Section 7 Actions

There are two primary defenses to Section 7 actions. These defenses can be raised even if the merger would otherwise violate Section 7. The defenses are the following:

1. **Failing company doctrine.** According to the **failing company doctrine**, a competitor may merge with a failing company if (1) there is no other reasonable alternative for the failing company, (2) no other purchaser is available, and (3) the assets of the failing company would completely disappear from the market if the anticompetitive merger were not allowed to go through.
2. **Small company doctrine.** The courts have permitted two or more small companies to merge without liability under Section 7 if the merger allows them to compete more effectively with a large company. This is called the **small company doctrine**.

The following feature discusses premerger notification.

Business Environment

Premerger Notification

The **Hart-Scott-Rodino Antitrust Improvement Act (HSR Act)**[19] requires certain larger firms to notify the Federal Trade Commission (FTC) and the U.S. Department of Justice of any proposed merger and to provide information about the parties and the proposed transaction. On the date of filing, a 30-day waiting period begins (15 days for all-cash tender offers), during which time the government agencies may investigate the transaction. If the government agencies believe that the acquisition would have anticompetitive effects, they may extend the waiting period and request additional information from the parties. If the government sues within the waiting period, the suit is entitled to expedited treatment in the courts.

If the government does not challenge a proposed merger within 30 days, the merger may proceed. The parties may request that the waiting period be terminated early if the government agencies do not find anticompetitive effects. The sizes of the firms that are subject to the HSR Act are determined by complex rules concerning the size of the parties and the value of the transaction.

Hart-Scott-Rodino Antitrust Improvement Act (HSR Act)
An act that requires certain firms to notify the Federal Trade Commission and the Justice Department in advance of a proposed merger. Unless the government challenges a proposed merger within 30 days, the merger may proceed.

Section 3 of the Clayton Act
An act that prohibits tying arrangements involving sales and leases of goods.

tying arrangement
A restraint of trade in which a seller refuses to sell one product to a customer unless the customer agrees to purchase a second product from the seller.

Tying Arrangements: Section 3 of the Clayton Act

46.5 Describe tying arrangements that violate Section 3 of the Clayton Act.

Section 3 of the Clayton Act prohibits tying arrangements that involve sales and leases of goods (tangible personal property).[20] A **tying arrangement** is a vertical trade restraint that involves the seller's refusal to sell a product (the *tying item*) to a customer unless the customer purchases a second product (the *tied item*). Section 1 of the Sherman Act (restraints of trade) forbids tying arrangements involving goods, services, intangible property, and real property. The defendant must be shown to have had sufficient economic power in the tying product market to restrain competition in the tied product market.

Example A manufacturer makes one patented product and one unpatented product. An illegal tying arrangement occurs if the manufacturer refuses to sell the patented product to a buyer unless the buyer also purchases the unpatented product. The patented product is the tying product, and the unpatented product is the tied product.

A tying arrangement is lawful if there is some justifiable reason for it.

Example The protection of quality control coupled with a trade secret may make a tying arrangement lawful.

Section 2 of the Clayton Act (Robinson-Patman Act)
A federal statute that prohibits price discrimination in the sale of goods if certain requirements are met.

Section 2(a) of the Robinson-Patman Act
A section that prohibits direct and indirect price discrimination by sellers of a commodity of a like grade and quality, where the effect of such discrimination may be to substantially lessen competition or to tend to create a monopoly in any line of commerce.

Price Discrimination: Section 2 of the Clayton Act

46.6 List and describe the types of price discrimination that violate Section 2 of the Clayton Act.

Businesses in the U.S. economy survive by selling their goods at prices that allow them to make a profit. Sellers often offer favorable terms to their preferred customers. **Price discrimination** occurs if a seller does this without just cause. **Section 2 of the Clayton Act**, commonly referred to as the **Robinson-Patman Act**, prohibits price discrimination in the sale of goods if specified acts occur. **Section 2(a) of the Robinson-Patman Act** contains the following basic prohibition against price discrimination in the sale of goods:

> *It shall be unlawful for any person engaged in commerce, either directly or indirectly, to discriminate in price between different purchases of commodities of like grade and quality, where either or any of the purchases involved in such discrimination are in commerce, where the effect of such*

discrimination may be substantially to lessen competition or tend to create a monopoly in any line of commerce, or to injure, destroy, or prevent competition with any person who either grants or knowingly receives the benefit of such discrimination, or with customers of either of them.[21]

Section 2 does not apply to the sale of services, real estate, intangible property, securities, leases, consignments, or gifts. Mixed sales (i.e., sales involving both services and commodities) are controlled based on the dominant nature of the transaction.

Direct Price Discrimination

To prove a violation of Section 2(a) of the Robinson-Patman Act, the following elements of **direct price discrimination** must be shown:

direct price discrimination
Price discrimination in which (1) the defendant sold commodities of like grade and quality, (2) to two or more purchasers at different prices at approximately the same time, and (3) the plaintiff suffered injury because of the price discrimination.

- **Commodities of like grade and quality.** A Section 2(a) violation must involve goods of "like grade and quality." To avoid this rule, sellers sometimes try to differentiate identical or similar products by using brand names. Nevertheless, as one court stated, "Four Roses under any other name would still swill the same."[22]
- **Sales to two or more purchasers.** To violate Section 2(a), the price discrimination must involve sales to at least two different purchasers at approximately the same time. It is legal to make two or more sales of the same product to the same purchaser at different prices. The Robinson-Patman Act requires that the discrimination occur "in commerce."
- **Injury.** To recover damages, the plaintiff must have suffered actual injury because of the price discrimination. The injured party may be the purchaser who did not receive the favored price (*primary line injury*), that party's customers to whom the lower price could not be passed along (*secondary line injury*), and so on.

A plaintiff who has not suffered injury because of price discrimination cannot recover.

Example A wholesaler sells the same type of Michelin tires to one automobile repair and tire shop at a lower price than to another similar-size repair and tire shop. If the second tire shop cannot purchase the same type of Michelin tires at the same or a lower price, it has a good case of price discrimination against the wholesaler. If the second tire shop could have purchased comparable Michelin tires elsewhere at the lower price, it cannot recover for price discrimination.

The law directs itself not against conduct that is competitive, even severely so, but against conduct which unfairly tends to destroy competition itself.
Spectrum Sports, Inc. v. McQuillan
506 U.S. 447, 113 S.Ct. 884 (1993)
Byron White, Associate Justice
Supreme Court of the United States

Indirect Price Discrimination

Because direct forms of price discrimination are apparent, sellers of goods have devised sophisticated ways to provide discriminatory prices to favored customers. Favorable credit terms, freight charges, and so on, are examples of **indirect price discrimination** that violate the Robinson-Patman Act.

indirect price discrimination
A form of price discrimination (e.g., favorable credit terms) that is less readily apparent than direct forms of price discrimination.

Defenses to Price Discrimination

The Robinson-Patman Act establishes the following three statutory defenses to Section 2(a) liability:

1. **Cost justification.** Section 2(a) provides that a seller's price discrimination is not unlawful if the price differential is due to "differences in the cost of manufacture, sale, or delivery" of the product. This is called the **cost justification defense**. For example, quantity or volume discounts are lawful to the extent that they are supported by cost savings.

   Example If Procter & Gamble can prove that bulk shipping rates make it less costly to deliver 10,000 bottles of Tide than lesser quantities, it may charge purchasers accordingly.

cost justification defense
A defense in a Section 2(a) action providing that a seller's price discrimination is not unlawful if the price differential is due to "differences in the cost of manufacture, sale, or delivery" of the product.

2. **Changing conditions.** Price discrimination is not unlawful under Section 2(a) if it is in response to "changing conditions in the market for or the marketability of the goods." This is called the **changing conditions defense.**

changing conditions defense
A price discrimination defense that claims prices were lowered in response to changing conditions in the market for or the marketability of the goods.

   Examples The price of goods can be lowered to subsequent purchasers to reflect the deterioration of perishable goods (e.g., fish), obsolescence of seasonable goods (e.g., winter coats sold in the spring), a distress sale pursuant to court order, or discontinuance of a business.

3. **Meeting the competition.** The **meeting the competition defense** to price discrimination is stipulated in **Section 2(b) of the Robinson-Patman Act.**[23] This defense holds that a seller may lawfully engage in price discrimination to meet a competitor's price.

meeting the competition defense
A defense provided in Section 2(b) of the Robinson-Patman Act that says a seller may lawfully engage in price discrimination to meet a competitor's price.

   Example A manufacturer produces a specific product and sells it nationwide at $100. A regional manufacturer, which is located in Oregon, produces and sells a competing product in Oregon and Washington for $75. The nationwide seller can reduce the price of its product in Oregon and Washington to $75 to compete with the local manufacturer's price while still maintaining the $100 price elsewhere.

Federal Trade Commission Act

46.7 Describe antitrust acts and unfair methods of competition that violate Section 5 of the Federal Trade Commission Act.

Federal Trade Commission (FTC)
A federal government administrative agency that is empowered to enforce the Federal Trade Commission Act.

In 1914, Congress enacted the Federal Trade Commission Act (FTC Act) and created the **Federal Trade Commission (FTC). Section 5 of the Federal Trade Commission Act** prohibits **unfair methods of competition and unfair or deceptive acts or practices** in or affecting commerce.[24]

Section 5, which is broader than the other antitrust laws, covers conduct that (1) violates any provision of the Sherman Act or the Clayton Act, (2) violates the "spirit" of those acts, (3) fills the gaps of those acts, and (4) offends public policy; is immoral, oppressive, unscrupulous, or unethical; or causes substantial injury to competitors or consumers.

Section 5 of the Federal Trade Commission Act
A section that prohibits unfair methods of competition and unfair or deceptive acts or practices in or affecting commerce.

The FTC is exclusively empowered to enforce the FTC Act. It can issue interpretive rules, general statements of policy, trade regulation rules, and guidelines that define unfair or deceptive practices, and it can conduct investigations of suspected antitrust violations. It can also issue cease-and-desist orders against violators. These orders are appealable to federal court. The FTC Act provides for a private civil cause of action for injured parties. Treble damages are not available.

WEB EXERCISE
Visit the website of the Federal Trade Commission (FTC) at **www.ftc.gov**. Under "Tips and Advice," then click on "Competition Guidance." What does the FTC's Bureau of Competition do?

Exemptions from Antitrust Law

46.8 List and describe express and implied exemptions from antitrust laws.

Certain industries and businesses are exempt from federal antitrust laws. The three categories of exemptions are *statutory exemptions, implied exemptions*, and the *state action exemption*. These are discussed in the following paragraphs.

Statutory Exemptions

Certain statutes expressly exempt some forms of business and other activities from the reach of antitrust laws. **Statutory exemptions** include labor unions,[25] agricultural cooperatives,[26] export activities of American companies,[27] and insurance business that is regulated by a state.[28] Other federal statutes exempt railroad, utility, shipping, and securities industries from most antitrust laws.

statutory exemptions
Exemptions from antitrust laws that are expressly provided in statutes enacted by Congress.

Implied Exemptions

The federal courts have implied several exemptions from antitrust laws. Examples of **implied exemptions** include professional baseball (but not other professional sports) and airlines.[29] The implied exemption for airlines was granted because railroads and other forms of transportation were expressly exempt. The Supreme Court has held that professionals such as lawyers do not qualify for an implied exemption from antitrust laws.[30] The Supreme Court strictly construes these implied exemptions.

implied exemptions
Exemptions from antitrust laws that are implied by the federal courts.

State Action Exemption

Economic regulations mandated by state law are exempt from federal antitrust laws. The **state action exemption** extends to businesses that must comply with these regulations.

state action exemption
Business activities that are mandated by state law and are therefore exempt from federal antitrust laws.

Example States may set the rates that public utilities (e.g., gas, electric, cable television companies) charge their customers. The states that set these rates and the companies that must abide by them are not liable for price fixing that would be a violation of federal antitrust law.

State Antitrust Laws

46.9 Describe the scope of state antitrust laws.

Most states have enacted antitrust statutes. These statutes are usually patterned after federal antitrust statutes. They often contain the same language as well. **State antitrust laws** are used to attack anticompetitive activity that occurs in intrastate commerce. When federal antitrust laws are applied loosely, plaintiffs often bring lawsuits under state antitrust laws.

Key Terms and Concepts

Antitrust Division of the Department of Justice (804)
Antitrust injury (804)
Antitrust laws (803)
Attempt or conspire to monopolize (812)
Backward vertical merger (upstream vertical merger) (814)
Bureau of Competition of the Federal Trade Commission (804)
Celler-Kefauver Act (812)
Changing conditions defense (818)
Civil damages (804)
Clayton Antitrust Act (Clayton Act) (803)
Conglomerate merger (815)
Conscious parallelism (810)
Consent decree (804)
Cost justification defense (817)
Direct price discrimination (817)
Division of markets (market sharing) (807)
Failing company doctrine (815)
Federal antitrust statutes (803)
Federal Trade Commission (FTC) (818)
Federal Trade Commission Act (FTC Act) (803)
Foreclosing competition (814)
Forward vertical merger (downstream vertical merger) (814)
Geographical market extension merger (815)
Government action (804)
Government judgment (804)
Group boycott (refusal to deal) (807)
Group boycott by purchasers (807)
Group boycott by sellers (807)
Hart-Scott-Rodino Antitrust Improvement Act (HSR Act) (816)
Horizontal merger (814)
Horizontal restraint of trade (806)
Implied exemptions (819)
Indirect price discrimination (817)
Innocent acquisition of a monopoly (812)
Line of commerce (813)
Market extension merger (815)
Maximum resale price (809)
Meeting the competition defense (818)
Minimum resale price (808)
Monopoly power (811)
Natural monopoly (812)
Noerr doctrine (810)
Nolo contendere (804)
Nonprice vertical restraint (809)
Per se rule (805)
Predatory pricing (812)
Price discrimination (816)

Price fixing (806)
Private civil action (804)
Probability of a substantial lessening of competition or likelihood of creating a monopoly (813)
Product market extension merger (815)
Relevant geographical market (811)
Relevant market (811)
Relevant product or service market (811)
Resale price maintenance (vertical price fixing) (808)
Robinson-Patman Act (803, 816)
Rule of reason (805)
Section of the country (813)
Section 1 of the Sherman Act (804)
Section 2 of the Clayton Act (Robinson-Patman Act) (816)
Section 2 of the Sherman Act (811)
Section 2(a) of the Robinson-Patman Act (816)
Section 2(b) of the Robinson-Patman Act (818)
Section 3 of the Clayton Act (816)
Section 4 of the Clayton Act (804)
Section 5 of the Federal Trade Commission Act (818)
Section 7 of the Clayton Act (812)
Section 16 of the Clayton Act (804)
Sherman Antitrust Act (Sherman Act) (803)
Small company doctrine (815)
Standard Oil Company of New Jersey v. United States (805)
State action exemption (819)
State antitrust laws (819)
Statutory exemptions (818)
Treble damages (804)
Tying arrangement (816)
Unfair advantage theory (815)
Unfair methods of competition and unfair or deceptive acts or practices (818)
Unilateral refusal to deal (*Colgate* doctrine) (810)
Unreasonable restraint of trade (805)
Vertical merger (814)
Vertical restraint of trade (808)
Willful act of monopolizing (811)

Critical Legal Thinking Cases

46.1 Division of Markets Law school students, after they graduate from law school, must take and pass a bar exam before they can become a lawyer in a state. Most law students take a preparatory bar exam course before they take the bar exam. Harcourt Brace Jovanovich Legal (HBJ) was the nation's largest provider of bar review materials and preparatory services. HBJ began offering a Georgia bar review course in direct competition with BRG of Georgia, Inc. (BRG), which was the only other main provider of a bar review preparatory course in the state of Georgia. Subsequently, HBJ and BRG entered into an agreement whereby BRG was granted an exclusive license to market HBJ bar review materials in Georgia in exchange for paying HBJ $100 per student enrolled by BRG in the course. Thus, HBJ agreed not to compete with BRG in Georgia, and BRG agreed not to compete with HBJ outside Georgia. Immediately after the agreement was struck, the price of BRG's course in the state of Georgia was increased from $150 to $400. Jay Palmer and other law school graduates who took the BRG bar review course in preparation for the Georgia bar exam sued BRG and HBJ, alleging a geographical division of markets, in violation of Section 1 of the Sherman Act. Are BRG and HBJ liable for violating Section 1 of the Sherman Act? *Palmer v. BRG of Georgia, Inc.*, 498 U.S. 46, 111 S.Ct. 401, 1990 U.S. Lexis 5901 (Supreme Court of the United States, 1990)

46.2 Price Fixing Maricopa County Medical Society (Society) is a professional association that represents doctors of medicine, osteopathy, and podiatry in Maricopa County, Arizona. The society formed the Maricopa Foundation for Medical Care (Foundation), a nonprofit Arizona corporation. Approximately 70 percent of the doctors in the county belong to Foundation. Foundation acts as an insurance administrator between its member doctors and insurance companies that pay patients' medical bills.

Foundation established a maximum fee schedule for various medical services. The member doctors agreed to abide by this fee schedule when providing services to patients. The state of Arizona brought this action against Society and Foundation and its members, alleging price fixing, in violation of Section 1 of the Sherman Act. Who wins? *Arizona v. Maricopa County Medical Society*, 457 U.S. 332, 102 S.Ct. 2466, 1982 U.S. Lexis 5 (Supreme Court of the United States, 1982)

46.3 Tying Arrangement Mercedes-Benz of North America (MBNA) was the exclusive franchiser of Mercedes-Benz dealerships in the United States. MBNA's franchise agreements required each dealer to establish a customer service department for the repair of Mercedes-Benz automobiles and required dealers to purchase Mercedes-Benz replacement parts from MBNA. At least eight independent wholesale distributors, including Metrix Warehouse, Inc. (Metrix), sold replacement parts for Mercedes-Benz automobiles. Because they were precluded from selling parts to Mercedes-Benz dealers, these parts distributors sold their replacement parts to independent garages that specialized in the repair of Mercedes-Benz automobiles. Evidence showed that Metrix sold replacement parts for Mercedes-Benz automobiles of equal quality and at a lower price than those sold by MBNA. Metrix sued MBNA, alleging a tying arrangement, in violation of Section 1 of the Sherman Act. Who wins? *Metrix Warehouse, Inc. v. Mercedes-Benz of North America, Inc.*, 828 F.2d 1033, 1987 U.S. App. Lexis 12341 (United States Court of Appeals for the Fourth Circuit, 1987)

46.4 Merger Lipton Tea Co. (Lipton) was the second-largest U.S. producer of herbal teas, controlling 32 percent of the national market. Lipton announced that it would acquire Celestial Seasonings, the largest U.S. producer of herbal teas, which controlled 52 percent of the national market. R.C. Bigelow, Inc., the third-largest producer of herbal teas, with 13 percent of the national market, brought an action, alleging that the merger would violate Section 7 of the Clayton Act, and sought an injunction against the merger. What type of merger is proposed in this case? What is the relevant market? Should the merger be enjoined? *R. C. Bigelow, Inc., v. Unilever, N.V.*, 867 F.2d 102, 1989 U.S. App. Lexis 574 (United States Court of Appeals for the Second Circuit, 1989)

Ethics Case

46.5 Ethics Case Amazon.com, Inc. (Amazon) produces and sells the Kindle, a portable device that can hold digital copies of books (e-books). Amazon offered e-books, including new releases and best-selling books, at inexpensive prices. The multibillion-dollar book-publishing industry saw Amazon's e-books as a threat to their way of doing business.

Apple, Inc. created iBookstore on its iPad to sell and distribute e-books. Apple entered negotiations with the five largest publishing companies in the United States to distribute their e-books. Apple was not willing to do so at a retail price to compete with Amazon. The publishers saw colluding with Apple as a way of breaking Amazon's retail price and having both Apple and Amazon sell e-books at higher prices so that publishers and Apple could make a higher profit on their e-books. To put pressure on Amazon to raise prices, the publishers agreed to withhold books from Amazon.

In two months, Apple had orchestrated an arrangement whereby it had coerced the five publishers to enter the same agreement with Apple whereby the publishers had the authority to set prices of their books sold on Apple's iBookstore. The result was that Amazon was forced to give in and enter agreements with the publishers that raised the price of e-books sold on Amazon, which increased the profits that the publishers made on e-books. The price of new e-books increased by 24 percent, and the price of best-seller e-books increased by 40 percent.

The U.S. Department of Justice (DOJ) filed suit in U.S. district court against Apple and the five book publishers, alleging that Apple, by entering into the same agreement with the five publishers, had conspired with the defendant publishers to engage in a price-fixing scheme to raise prices in the e-book market. The DOJ argued that this hub-and-spoke agreement between Apple and the book publishers constituted price fixing that was a *per se* violation of Section 1 of the Sherman Act. Is Apple liable for price fixing in violation of Section 1 of the Sherman Act? Did Apple act ethically in this case? *United States v. Apple, Inc.*, 791 F.3d 290, 2015 U.S. App. Lexis 11271 (United States Court of Appeals for the Second Circuit, 2015)

Notes

1. *Federal Baseball Club v. National League*, 259 U.S. 200, 42 S.Ct. 465, 1922 U.S. Lexis 2475 (Supreme Court of the United States, 1922).
2. 15 U.S.C. Sections 1–7.
3. 15 U.S.C. Sections 12–27, 29 U.S.C. Sections 52–53.
4. 15 U.S.C. Sections 41–58.
5. 15 Section 13.
6. Antitrust Amendments Act of 1990, P.L. 101-588.
7. 15 U.S.C. Section 15.
8. 15 U.S.C. Section 26.
9. Justice Marshall, *United States v. Topco Associates, Inc.*, 405 U.S. 596, 92 S.Ct. 1126, 1972 U.S. Lexis 167 (Supreme Court of the United States).
10. 15 U.S.C. Section 1.
11. 221 U.S. 1, 31 S.Ct. 502, 1911 U.S. Lexis 1725 (Supreme Court of the United States). The Court found that Rockefeller's oil trust violated the Sherman Act and ordered the trust broken up into 30 separate companies.
12. *Dr. Miles Medical Co. v. John D. Park & Sons, Co.*, 220 U.S. 373, 31 S.Ct. 376, 1911 U.S. Lexis 1685 (Supreme Court of the United States).
13. *State Oil Company v. Khan*, 522 U.S. 3, 118 S.Ct. 275, 1997 U.S. Lexis 6705 (Supreme Court of the United States).
14. 250 U.S. 300, 39 S.Ct. 465, 1919 U.S. Lexis 1748 (Supreme Court of the United States).
15. *Eastern R.R. President's Conference v. Noerr Motor Freight, Inc.*, 365 U.S. 127, 81 S.Ct. 523, 1961 U.S. Lexis 2128 (Supreme Court of the United States).

16. 15 U.S.C. Section 2.
17. *William Inglis & Sons Baking Company v. ITT Continental Baking Company, Inc.*, 668 F.2d 1014, 1982 U.S. App. Lexis 21926 (United States Court of Appeals for the Ninth Circuit).
18. 15 U.S.C. Section 18.
19. 15 U.S.C. Section 18(a).
20. 15 U.S.C. Section 14.
21. 15 U.S.C. Section 13(a).
22. *Hartley & Parker, Inc. v. Florida Beverage Corp.*, 307 F.2d 916, 923, 1962 U.S. App. Lexis 4196 (United States Court of Appeals for the Fifth Circuit).
23. 15 U.S.C. Section 13(b).
24. 15 U.S.C. Section 45.
25. Section 6 of the Clayton Act, 15 U.S.C. Section 17; the Norris-LaGuardia Act of 1932, 29 U.S.C. Sections 101–155; and the National Labor Relations Act of 1935, 29 U.S.C. Sections 141 et seq.
26. Capper-Volstead Act of 1922, 7 U.S.C. Section 291; and Cooperative Marketing Act of 1926, 15 U.S.C. Section 521.
27. Webb-Pomerene Act, 15 U.S.C. Sections 61–65.
28. McCarran-Ferguson Act of 1945, 15 U.S.C. Sections 1011–1015.
29. *Community Communications Co., Inc. v. City of Boulder*, 455 U.S. 40, 102 S.Ct. 835, 1982 U.S. Lexis 65 (Supreme Court of the United States).
30. *Goldfarb v. Virginia State Bar*, 421 U.S. 773, 95 S.Ct. 2004, 1975 U.S. Lexis 13 (Supreme Court of the United States).

PART

X

Personal Property, Real Property, and Insurance

Henry R. Cheeseman

CHAPTER

47 Personal Property and Bailment

Flystock/Shutterstock

AUTOMOBILES

People own many articles of personal property, including automobiles, SUVs, trucks, and other vehicles. Other personal property includes jewelry, electronics, furniture and household goods, books, and photographs. Businesses own personal property such as computers, equipment, furniture, and vehicles. Personal property—sometimes referred to as goods or chattels—consists of everything that is not real property. Laws protect individual and business ownership interests in personal property.

Learning Objectives

After studying this chapter, you should be able to:

47.1 Define *personal property*.

47.2 Describe the methods for acquiring and transferring ownership in personal property.

47.3 Describe and apply rules regarding ownership rights in mislaid, lost, and abandoned property.

47.4 Define *bailment* and list and describe the elements for creating a bailment.

47.5 Describe an ordinary bailment and explain the liability of bailees for lost, damaged, or destroyed goods.

47.6 List and describe special forms of bailment.

"*Property and law are born and must die together.*"

—Jeremy Bentham (1748–1832)
Principles of the Civil Code, I Works 309

Introduction to Personal Property and Bailment

Private ownership of property forms the foundation of our economic system. Therefore, a comprehensive body of law has been developed to protect property rights. The law protects the rights of owners of personal property to use, sell, dispose of, control, and prevent others from trespassing on their rights.

Laws are always useful to persons of property, and hurtful to those who have none.
Jean-Jacques Rousseau
Du Contrat Social (1761)

Sometimes personal property is delivered to another party for transfer, safekeeping, or some other purpose. This is called a *bailment*. For example, goods are often entrusted to common carriers for transport and delivery. The bailee and bailor owe certain duties to each other.

This chapter discusses the kinds of personal property; methods of acquiring ownership in personal property; property rights in mislaid, lost, or abandoned property; and bailment.

Personal Property

47.1 Define *personal property*.

There are two kinds of property: *real property* and *personal property*. Real property includes land, buildings, mineral rights, and permanent fixtures. **Personal property** (sometimes referred to as *goods* or *chattels*) consists of everything that is not real property. Real property can become personal property if it is removed from the land.

personal property
Tangible property, such as automobiles, furniture, and equipment, and intangible property, such as securities, patents, and copyrights.

Example A tree that is part of a forest is real property; a tree that is cut down is personal property.

Personal property that is permanently affixed to land or buildings is called a **fixture**. Such property, which includes things like heating systems and storm windows, is categorized as real property. Unless otherwise agreed, fixtures remain with a building when it is sold. Personal property (e.g., furniture, pictures, other easily portable household items) may be removed by the seller prior to sale.

fixture
Personal property that is permanently affixed to land or buildings.

Personal property can be either tangible or intangible. **Tangible property** includes physically defined property, such as goods, animals, and minerals. **Intangible property** represents rights that cannot be reduced to physical form, such as stock certificates, certificates of deposit, bonds, and copyrights.

tangible property
All real property and physically defined personal property, such as buildings, goods, animals, and minerals.

intangible property
Rights that cannot be reduced to physical form, such as stock certificates, certificates of deposit, bonds, and copyrights.

Real and personal property may be owned by one person or by more than one person. If property is owned concurrently by two or more persons, there is *concurrent ownership*.

Ownership of Personal Property

47.2 Describe the methods for acquiring and transferring ownership in personal property.

Personal property can be acquired or transferred with a minimum of formality. Commerce would be severely curtailed if the transfer of such items were difficult.

The methods for acquiring ownership in personal property are *possession* or *capture; purchase; production; gift; accession; confusion; will, living trust*, or *inheritance*; and *divorce* or *annulment*. These methods for acquiring ownership in personal property are described as follows.

Possession or Capture

A person can acquire ownership in unowned personal property by taking **possession** of it, or **capturing** it. The most notable unowned objects are things in their natural state. This type of property acquisition was important when this country was being developed. In today's urbanized society, however, there are few unowned objects, and this method of acquiring ownership in personal property has become less important.

Example Someone who obtains the proper fishing license acquires ownership of all the fish he or she catches.

Purchase

The most common method of acquiring title to personal property is if a party **purchases** the property from its owner.

Example Urban Concrete owns a large piece of equipment. City Builders purchases the equipment from Urban Concrete for $100,000. Urban Concrete transfers title to the equipment to City Builders. City Builders is now the owner of the equipment.

Production

Production is a common method of acquiring ownership in personal property. A manufacturer that purchases raw materials and produces a finished product owns that product.

Example A soda manufacturer purchases carbonated water, high fructose corn syrup, phosphoric acid, coloring, and other ingredients and produces a brand of soda. The finished product is owned by the soda manufacturer.

Gift

gift
The voluntary transfer of title to property without payment of consideration by the donee. To be a valid gift, three elements must be shown: (1) donative intent, (2) delivery, and (3) acceptance.

donor
A person who gives a gift.

donee
A person who receives a gift.

A **gift** is a voluntary transfer of property without consideration. The lack of consideration is what distinguishes a gift from a purchase. The person making a gift is called the **donor**. The person who receives a gift is called the **donee**. There are three elements of a valid gift:

1. **Donative intent.** For a gift to be effective, the donor must have intended to make a gift. **Donative intent** can be inferred from the circumstances or language used by the donor. The courts also consider such factors as the relationship of the parties, the size of the gift, and the mental capacity of the donor.
2. **Delivery.** **Delivery** must occur for there to be a valid gift. Although **physical delivery** is the usual method of transferring personal property, it is sometimes impracticable. In such circumstances, **constructive delivery** (or *symbolic delivery*) is sufficient. For example, if the property being gifted is kept in a safe-deposit box, physically giving the key to the donee is enough to signal the gift. Most intangible property is transferred by written conveyance (e.g., conveying a stock certificate represents a transfer of ownership in a corporation).
3. **Acceptance.** **Acceptance** is usually not a problem because most donees readily accept gifts. In fact, the courts presume acceptance unless there is proof that the gift was refused. Nevertheless, a person cannot be forced to accept an unwanted gift.

gift *inter vivos*
A gift made during a person's lifetime that is an irrevocable transfer of ownership.

A gift can be classified as either a gift *inter vivos* or a gift *causa mortis*.

- **Gift *inter vivos*.** A gift made during a person's lifetime that is an irrevocable transfer of ownership is a **gift *inter vivos***.

Example A grandmother gives her diamond ring to her granddaughter. This is a gift *inter vivos*. The granddaughter now owns the ring.

- **Gift *causa mortis*.** A **gift *causa mortis*** is a gift made in contemplation of death. A gift *causa mortis* is established when (1) the donor makes a gift in anticipation of approaching death from some existing sickness or peril and (2) the donor dies from such sickness or peril without having revoked the gift. A gift *causa mortis* can be revoked by the donor up until the time he or she dies. A gift *causa mortis* takes precedence over a prior conflicting will.

gift *causa mortis*
A gift that is made in contemplation of death.

Example Salma is a patient in a hospital. She is to have a major operation from which she may not recover. Prior to going into surgery, Salma removes her diamond ring and gives it to her friend Paloma, stating, "In the event of my death, I want you to have this." This gift is a gift *causa mortis*. If Salma dies from the operation, the gift is effective, and Paloma owns the ring even if Salma has a prior executed will or living trust that leaves the ring to someone else. If Salma lives, the requisite condition for the gift (her death) has not occurred; therefore, the gift is not effective, and Salma can recover the ring from Paloma.

Uniform Gifts to Minors Act and Uniform Transfers to Minors Act

Many states have adopted in whole or part the **Uniform Gifts to Minors Act (UGMA)** or the **Uniform Transfers to Minors Act (UTMA)**. These acts were drafted by the National Conference of Commissioners on Uniform State Laws and do not become the law of a state until that state's legislature enacts the act as a statute. These laws establish procedures for adults to make irrevocable gifts of money and securities to minors. Gifts of money can be made by depositing the money in an account in a financial institution, with the donor or another trustee (e.g., another adult or bank) as custodian for the minor. Gifts of securities can be made by registering the securities in the name of a trustee as custodian for the minor.

Uniform Gifts to Minors Act (UGMA) and Uniform Transfers to Minors Act (UTMA)
Acts that establish procedures for adults to make gifts of money and securities to minors.

Accession

Accession occurs when the value of personal property increases because it is added to or improved by natural or manufactured means. Accession that occurs naturally belongs to the owner.

accession
An increase in the value of personal property because it is added to or improved by natural or manufactured means.

Example Jared owns a mare named Echo. Echo gives birth to a colt. Pursuant to accession, Jared owns the newborn colt.

If an improvement is made wrongfully, the owner acquires title to the improved property and does not have to pay the improver for the value of the improvements.

Example A thief steals a car and puts a new engine in it. The owner is entitled to recover the car as improved and does not have to pay the thief for the improvements.

If an improvement is mistakenly made by an improver and the improvement can be easily separated from the original article, the improver must remove the improvement and pay any damages caused by such removal.

Example A builder who puts the wrong door on a house must replace that door with the correct door at his own cost.

If an improvement is mistakenly made by an improver and the improvement cannot be removed from the original article, the owner owns title to the improved property and does not have to pay the improver for the improvement.

Example If a builder misreads blueprints and extends an addition to a building farther than the owner has contracted for, the owner of the building is entitled to keep the improvement at no extra cost.

Confusion

confusion
If fungible goods (goods that are exactly alike) are commingled, the owners share title to the commingled goods in proportion to the amount of goods contributed.

Confusion occurs if two or more persons commingle **fungible goods** (i.e., goods that are exactly alike, such as the same grade of oil, grain, or cattle). Title to goods can be acquired by confusion. The owners share ownership in the commingled goods in proportion to the amount of goods contributed by each owner. It does not matter whether the goods were commingled by agreement or accident. If goods are wrongfully or intentionally commingled without permission, the innocent party acquires title to them.

Example If three farmers voluntarily agree to store the same amount of Grade B winter wheat in a silo, each of them owns one-third. When the grain is sold, the profits are divided into three parts; if the silo burns to the ground, each farmer suffers one-third of the loss.

Will, Living Trust, or Inheritance

Title to personal property is frequently acquired by **will**, **living trust**, or **inheritance**. If a person dies with a valid will or living trust, the property is distributed to the *beneficiaries* named in the will or living trust, pursuant to the provisions of the will or living trust. If a person dies without having executed a will or living trust, the property is distributed to the *heirs* as provided in the state's inheritance statute.

Divorce or Annulment

Personal property has no locality.
Chief Justice Lord Loughborough
Sill v. Worswick, 1 H. Bl. 665, 690 (1791)

When a marriage is dissolved by **divorce** or **annulment**, the parties obtain certain rights in the property that composes the marital state. Often a settlement of property rights is reached. If not, the court must decide the property rights of the spouses.

Mislaid, Lost, and Abandoned Personal Property

47.3 Describe and apply rules regarding ownership rights in mislaid, lost, and abandoned property.

Often, people find other people's personal property. Ownership rights to found property differ, depending on whether the property was mislaid, lost, or abandoned. The following paragraphs discuss these legal rules.

Mislaid Property

mislaid property
Property that an owner voluntarily places somewhere and then inadvertently forgets.

Property is considered **mislaid property** when its owner voluntarily places the property somewhere and then inadvertently forgets it. It is likely that the owner will return for the property on realizing that it was misplaced.

The owner of the premises where the property is mislaid is entitled to take possession of the property against all except the rightful owner. This right is superior to the rights of the person who finds it. Such possession does not involve a change of title. Instead, the owner of the premises becomes an involuntary bailee of the property and owes a duty to take reasonable care of the property until it is reclaimed by the owner. (Bailments are discussed later in this chapter.)

Example Felicity is on a business trip and stays in a hotel during her trip. Felicity accidentally leaves her diamond engagement ring in the hotel room she has stayed in and checks out of the hotel. The engagement ring is mislaid property, and the hotel has a duty to return it to Felicity, its rightful owner.

Lost Property

Property is considered **lost property** when its owner negligently, carelessly, or inadvertently leaves it somewhere. The finder obtains title to such property against the whole world except the true owner. The lost property must be returned to its rightful owner, whether the finder discovers the loser's identity or the loser finds the finder. A finder who refuses to return the property to the loser is liable for the tort of conversion and the crime of larceny. Many states require the finder to conduct a reasonable search (e.g., to place advertisements in newspapers) to find the rightful owner.

lost property
Property that the owner leaves somewhere due to negligence, carelessness, or inadvertence.

Example If a commuter finds a smartphone on the floor of a subway station in New York City, the smartphone is considered lost property. The finder can claim title to the smartphone against the whole world except the true owner. If the true owner discovers that the finder has the smartphone, the owner may recover it from the finder. If there is identification of the owner on the smartphone (e.g., name, address, telephone number), the finder owes a duty to contact the rightful owner and give back the smartphone.

Abandoned Property

Property is classified as **abandoned property** if (1) an owner discards the property with the intent to relinquish rights in it or (2) an owner of mislaid or lost property gives up any further attempts to locate it. Anyone who finds abandoned property acquires title to it. The title is good against the whole world, including the original owner.

abandoned property
Property that an owner has discarded with the intent to relinquish his or her rights in it and mislaid or lost property that the owner has given up any further attempts to locate.

Example Property left at a garbage dump is abandoned property. It belongs to the first person who claims it.

In the following case, the court had to decide the rightful owner of personal property.

CASE 47.1 *STATE COURT CASE Mislaid or Abandoned Property*

Grande v. Jennings

278 P.3d 1287, 2012 Ariz. App. Lexis 86 (2012)
Court of Appeals of Arizona

"Although elementary school children like to say 'finders keepers'..."

—Maurice Portley, Judge

Facts

Robert A. Spann lived in his Paradise, Arizona, home until he passed away. Karen Spann Grande became the personal representative of the estate, and she and her sister Kim Spann took charge of the house. They knew that their father hid gold, cash, and other valuables in cans and other unusual places in the house. Over the course of seven years, they found stocks, bonds, and hundreds of military-style ammunition cans hidden throughout the house, some of which contained gold or cash.

Mr. Spann's daughters sold the house to Sarina Jennings and Clinton McCallum. Jennings and McCallum hired Randy Bueghly and his company, Trinidad Builders, Inc., to remodel the dilapidated house. Shortly after work began, Rafael Cuen, a Trinidad employee, discovered two ammunition cans full of cash in the kitchen wall and found two more cash-filled ammunition cans inside the framing of an upstairs bathroom. After Cuen reported the find to his boss, Bueghly took the ammo cans, which contained $500,000 cash, but did not tell the new owners of the find.

(continued)

Cuen eventually told the new owners of the discovery, and the police immediately took control of the cash. Bueghly claimed the money as the finder, Jennings/McCallum asserted that the cash had been abandoned and was therefore theirs, and Grande claimed that the cash was mislaid and therefore belonged to her father's estate. The trial court ruled that the cash was mislaid property and awarded it to Mr. Spann's estate. Jennings/McCallum appealed.

Issue

Was the $500,000 cash abandoned or mislaid property?

Language of the Court

Although elementary school children like to say "finders keepers . . ." a finder of mislaid property must turn the property over to the premises owner, who has a duty to safeguard the property for the true owner. Abandonment is a virtual throwing away of property without regard as to who may take over or carry on. In this connection, it has been said that people do not normally abandon their money. Here, the facts are undisputed that the estate did not intend to abandon the funds. As a result, and as the trial court found, the funds are, as a matter of law, mislaid funds that belong to the true owner, Spann's estate.

Decision

The court of appeals agreed with the trial court that the $500,000 cash was mislaid property that belonged to Spann's estate.

Critical Legal Thinking Questions

Did Bueghly act ethically? Did Jennings/McCallum have a rightful claim to the money? Do you think that Mr. Spann's daughters abandoned the money?

estray statute
A statute that permits a finder of mislaid or lost property to clear title to the property if certain prescribed legal formalities are met.

The following ethics feature discusses estray statutes that often apply to mislaid property and lost property.

Ethics

Estray Statutes Promote Honesty in Finders

Most states have enacted an **estray statute** that permits a finder of mislaid or lost property to clear title to the property if:

- The finder reports the found property to the appropriate government agency and then turns over possession of the property to this agency.
- Either the finder or the government agency posts notices and publishes advertisements describing the lost property.
- A specified time (usually a year or a number of years) has passed without the rightful owner reclaiming the property.

Many state estray statutes provide that the government receive a portion of the value of the property. Some statutes provide that title cannot be acquired in found property that is the result of illegal activity. For example, title has been denied to finders of property and money deemed to have been used for illegal drug purchases.

Ethics Questions

Do you think many people do not report to the government mislaid or lost property that they find? Do estray statutes encourage ethical behavior? Explain.

CONCEPT SUMMARY

MISLAID, LOST, AND ABANDONED PERSONAL PROPERTY

Type of Property	Ownership Rights
Mislaid property	The owner of the premises where property is mislaid is entitled to possession but does not acquire title. He or she holds the property as an involuntary bailee until the owner reclaims it.
Lost property	The finder acquires title to the property against the whole world except the true owner; the owner may reclaim the property from the finder.
Abandoned property	The finder acquires title to the property, even against its original owner.

Bailment

47.4 Define *bailment* and list and describe the elements for creating a bailment.

A **bailment** occurs when the owner of personal property delivers it to another person, either to be held, stored, or delivered or for some other purpose. In a bailment, the owner of the property is the **bailor**. The party to whom the property is delivered for safekeeping, storage, or delivery (e.g., warehouse, common carrier) is the **bailee** (see **Exhibit 47.1**). The law of bailment establishes the rights, duties, and liabilities of parties to a bailment.

bailment
A transaction in which an owner transfers his or her personal property to another to be held, stored, or delivered, or for some other purpose. Title to the property does not transfer.

Exhibit 47.1 BAILMENT

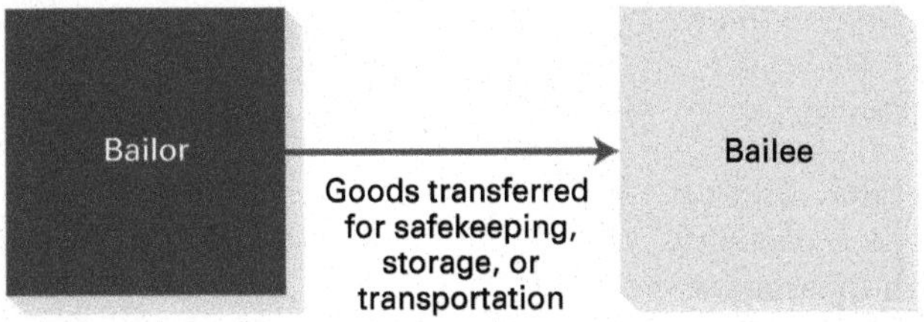

A bailment is different from a sale or a gift because title to the goods does not transfer to the bailee. Instead, the bailee must follow the bailor's directions concerning the goods.

bailor
The owner of property in a bailment.

bailee
A holder of goods who is not a seller or a buyer (e.g., warehouse, common carrier).

Example Hudson Corporation is relocating offices and hires American Van Lines to move its office furniture and equipment to the new location. American Van Lines (the bailee) must follow Hudson's (the bailor's) instructions regarding delivery.

Elements Necessary to Create a Bailment

Three elements are necessary to create a bailment:

1. **Bailment of personal property.** Only *personal property* can be bailed. This is called **bailment of personal property**. The property can be tangible (e.g., automobiles, jewelry, animals) or intangible (e.g., stocks, bonds, promissory notes).
2. **Delivery of possession. Delivery of possession** involves two elements: (1) The bailee must have exclusive control over the personal property, and (2) the bailee must knowingly accept the personal property.

   Examples No bailment is created if a patron goes into a restaurant and hangs her coat on an unattended coat rack because other patrons have access to the coat. However, a bailment is created if a patron checks her coat with a coatroom attendant because the restaurant has assumed exclusive control over the coat. If valuable property was left in the pocket of the coat, there would be no bailment of that property because the checkroom attendant did not knowingly accept it.

   Most bailments are created by *physical delivery*.

   Example A bailment is created if Great Lakes Shipping, Inc. delivers a vessel to Marina Repairs, Inc. for repairs.

3. **Bailment agreement.** The creation of a bailment does not require any formality. A bailment may be either express or implied. Most **express bailments** can be either written or oral. Under the Statute of Frauds, however, a **bailment agreement** must be in writing if it is for more than one year. An example of an **implied bailment** is the finding and safeguarding of lost property.

In the following case, the court had to decide whether a bailment had been created.

CASE 47.2 *STATE COURT CASE Bailment*

Ziva Jewelry, Inc. v. Car Wash Headquarters, Inc.

897 So.2d 1011, 2004 Ala. Lexis 238 (2004)
Supreme Court of Alabama

"Thus, Ziva Jewelry cannot claim that CWH knew or that it should have reasonably foreseen or expected that it was taking responsibility for over $850,000 worth of jewelry when it accepted Smith's vehicle for the purpose of washing it."

—Lyn Stuart, Judge

Facts

Ziva Jewelry, Inc. is a jewelry wholesaler. Stewart Smith was employed by Ziva Jewelry as a traveling sales representative. In connection with the employment, Smith drove his own vehicle to meet clients and attend trade shows. Smith's practice was to keep the jewelry in the trunk of his vehicle while he was traveling on business. He kept the trunk padlocked and kept the only key to the padlock on the key ring with his ignition key.

One day, when Smith was traveling from a jewelry trade show, he stopped at Rain Tunnel Car Wash, owned by Car Wash Headquarters, Inc. (CWH). At Rain Tunnel, the driver leaves a vehicle with employees of the car wash, and the vehicle is sent through a wash "tunnel." On completion of the car wash cycle, an employee drives the vehicle to another area of the car-wash premises to be hand dried. Once the vehicle is dried, the driver is signaled to retrieve the vehicle.

Smith left his car and the keys with a car-wash employee. Jewelry worth $850,000 was locked in the trunk of the vehicle. Smith watched the car as it went through the car-wash tunnel and as an employee dried the vehicle. As Smith was standing at the counter waiting to pay the cashier, he saw the employee wave a flag, indicating that the vehicle was ready for Smith. The employee then walked away from the vehicle. While Smith was standing at the cashier counter, someone jumped into Smith's vehicle and sped off. When the police recovered Smith's vehicle about 15 minutes later, the jewelry was gone.

Ziva Jewelry sued CWH to recover the value of the jewelry, alleging that a bailment had been created between Ziva and CWH and that CWH, as the bailee, was negligent in protecting the bailed goods. CWH defended, arguing that no bailment was created and therefore that it was not liable for the loss of Ziva's stolen jewelry. The trial court held that no bailment had been created and entered summary judgment for CWH. Ziva Jewelry appealed.

Issue

Was a bailment created between Ziva Jewelry and CWH?

Language of the Court

In this case, Ziva Jewelry cannot establish that CWH expressly or impliedly agreed to take responsibility for the jewelry hidden inside Smith's trunk. Ziva Jewelry acknowledges that the jewelry was not plainly visible; that its presence was not made known to the car-wash employees; and that there was no reason that the employees should have expected expensive jewelry to be in the trunk of Smith's vehicle. Thus, Ziva Jewelry cannot claim that CWH knew or that it should have reasonably foreseen or expected that it was taking responsibility for over $850,000 worth of jewelry when it accepted Smith's vehicle for the purpose of washing it.

Decision

The supreme court of Alabama held that no bailment had been created between Ziva Jewelry and CWH. The supreme court affirmed the trial court's ruling that granted summary judgment to CWH.

Critical Legal Thinking Questions

Did Ziva Jewelry have a good chance of winning this case? Why or why not? Do you think Smith was negligent in this case?

Ordinary Bailments

47.5 Describe an ordinary bailment and explain the liability of bailees for lost, damaged, or destroyed goods.

There are three types of **ordinary bailments**: *bailment for the sole benefit of the bailor, bailment for the sole benefit of the bailee*, and *mutual benefit bailment*. Each of these three types of bailments is discussed in the following paragraphs.

Bailment for the Sole Benefit of the Bailor

A **bailment for the sole benefit of the bailor** is a *gratuitous bailment* that benefits only the bailor. This ordinary bailment arises when the bailee is requested to care for the bailor's property as a favor. The bailee owes only a **duty of slight care** to protect the bailed property—that is, he or she owes a duty not to be grossly negligent in caring for the bailed goods.

bailment for the sole benefit of the bailor
A gratuitous bailment that benefits only the bailor. The bailee owes only a *duty of slight care* to protect the bailed property.

duty of slight care
Duty owed by a bailee not to be grossly negligent in caring for the bailed goods.

Example The O'Rourke family is going on vacation and asks the neighbors, the Smiths, to feed their dog, which is allowed to run free. The Smiths diligently feed the dog, but the dog runs away and does not return. The Smiths are not liable for the loss of the dog.

Bailment for the Sole Benefit of the Bailee

A **bailment for the sole benefit of the bailee** is a *gratuitous bailment* that solely benefits the bailee. This ordinary bailment arises when a bailee requests to use the bailor's property for personal reasons. In this situation, the bailee owes a **duty of great care** (or **duty of utmost care**) to protect the bailed property—that is, he or she owes a duty not to be slightly negligent in caring for the bailed goods.

bailment for the sole benefit of the bailee
A gratuitous bailment that benefits only the bailee. The bailee owes a *duty of utmost care* to protect the bailed property.

duty of great care (duty of utmost care)
Duty owed by a bailee not to be slightly negligent in caring for the bailed goods.

Example Mitch borrows Courtney's lawn mower (free of charge) to mow his own lawn. Mitch is the bailee, and Courtney is the bailor. This bailment is for the sole benefit of the bailee. Suppose Mitch, while mowing his lawn, leaves the lawn mower in his front yard while he goes into his house to answer the telephone. While he is gone, the lawn mower is stolen. Here, Mitch will be held liable to Courtney for the loss of the lawn mower because Mitch breached his duty of great care to protect the lawn mower.

Mutual Benefit Bailment

A **mutual benefit bailment** is a bailment that *benefits both parties*. The bailee owes a **duty of reasonable care** (or **duty of ordinary care**) to protect the bailed goods. This means that the bailee is liable for any goods that are lost, damaged, or destroyed because of his or her negligence.

mutual benefit bailment
A bailment for the mutual benefit of the bailor and bailee. The bailee owes a *duty of ordinary care* to protect the bailed property.

duty of reasonable care (duty of ordinary care)
Duty owed by a bailee not to be ordinarily negligent in caring for the bailed goods.

Example ABC Garment Co. delivers goods to Lowell, Inc., a commercial warehouser, for storage. A fee is charged for this service. ABC Garment Co. receives the benefit of having its goods stored, and Lowell, Inc. receives the benefit of being paid compensation for storing the goods. In this example, Lowell, Inc. (the bailee) owes a duty of ordinary care to protect the goods.

CONCEPT SUMMARY

ORDINARY BAILMENTS

Type of Bailment	Duty of Care Owed by Bailee	Bailee Liable to Bailor for
For the sole benefit of the bailor	Slight	Gross negligence
For the sole benefit of the bailee	Great	Slight negligence
For the mutual benefit of the bailor and bailee	Ordinary	Ordinary negligence

Duration and Termination of Bailments

A bailment generally expires at a specified time or when a certain purpose is accomplished. A **bailment for a fixed term** terminates at the end of the term or sooner, by mutual consent of the parties. A party who terminates a bailment in breach of the bailment agreement is liable to the innocent party for damages resulting from the breach.

bailment for a fixed term
A bailment that terminates at the end of the term or sooner, by mutual consent of the parties.

bailment at will
A bailment without a fixed term; can be terminated at any time by either party.

A bailment without a fixed term is called a **bailment at will**. A bailment at will can be terminated at any time by either party. Gratuitous bailees can generally

FREIGHTER
A bailment is created when the owner of personal property entrusts a common carrier, such as this freighter, to transport the property. The law of bailment establishes rules for liability if the property is damaged or lost during shipment.

Henry R. Cheeseman

terminate a fixed-term bailment prior to expiration of the term. On termination of a bailment, the bailee is legally obligated to do as the bailor directs with the property.

Special Bailments

47.6 List and describe special forms of bailment.

Several special forms of bailment require special procedures for formation and have their own special liability rules. **Special bailments** involve *warehouse companies, common carriers*, and *innkeepers*. These special types of bailments are discussed in the following paragraphs.

Warehouse Company

warehouser (warehouse company)
Warehouse companies and storage companies that engage in the business of storing property for compensation.

A **warehouser**, or **warehouse company**, is a bailee engaged in the business of storing personal property for compensation. Common warehousers are storage companies. The warehouse company is the bailee, and the party that stores the goods is the bailor.

Warehousers are subject to the rights, duties, and liability of an ordinary bailee. As such, they owe a duty of reasonable care (or duty of ordinary care) to protect the bailed property in their possession from harm or loss.[1] Warehousers are liable only for loss or damage to the bailed property caused by their own negligence. They are not liable for loss or damage caused to bailed goods by another person's negligence or conduct. Warehousers can limit the dollar amount of their liability if they offer the bailor the opportunity to increase the liability limit for the payment of an additional charge.

warehouse receipt
A document of title issued by a warehouse company stating that the bailor has title to the bailed goods.

The following feature discusses a warehouse receipt.

Business Environment

Warehouse Receipt

A **warehouse receipt** is a document of title issued by a company that is engaged in the business of storing goods for hire, such as a warehouse company or a storage company, that states that the bailor has title to the goods.[2]

A warehouse receipt that is issued to the bailor is often a preprinted form drafted by the warehouse company. A warehouse receipt includes the date of issue, a description of the goods or the packages containing the goods, the location of the warehouse where the goods are stored, and other terms related to the bailment.

A warehouse company has a **lien** on the goods in its possession for necessary expenses incurred in storing and handling the goods. If the charges are not paid, the warehouse company may sell the goods at a public or private auction and apply the proceeds to pay the charges. Any excess proceeds must be held for the persons who had the right to demand delivery of the goods.

Common Carrier

Common carriers offer transportation services to the general public. For example, commercial ships, commercial airlines, railroads, public trucking companies, and public pipeline companies are common carriers. The delivery of goods to a common carrier is a **consignment** that creates a mutual benefit bailment. The person shipping the goods is the **consignor** (the bailor). The transportation company is called the **common carrier** (the bailee). The person to whom the goods are to be delivered is called the **consignee** (see **Exhibit 47.2**).

consignor
A person shipping goods. The bailor.

common carrier
Common carriers are companies that offer transportation services to the public, such as airlines, railroads, and trucking firms.

Exhibit 47.2 COMMON CARRIER CONSIGNMENT

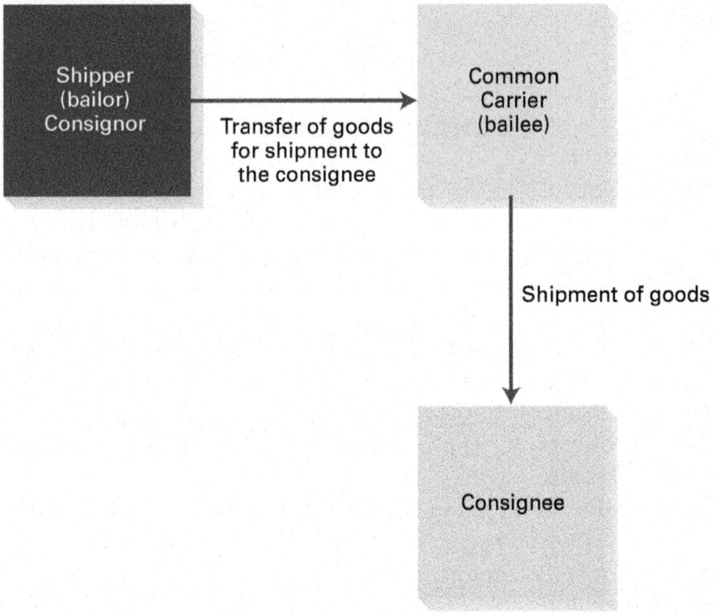

Common carriers are held to a **duty of strict liability**:[3] If the goods are lost, damaged, destroyed, or stolen, the common carrier is liable even if it was not at fault for the loss. Common carriers are not liable for the loss, damage, or destruction of goods caused by (1) an act of God (e.g., a tornado); (2) an act of a public enemy (e.g., a terrorist activity); (3) an order of the government (e.g., statutes, court decisions, government regulations); (4) an act of the shipper (e.g., improper packaging); or (5) the inherent nature of the goods (e.g., perishability).

Common carriers can limit their liability to a stated dollar amount by expressly stating that in the bailment agreement. Federal law requires common carriers who take advantage of such limitation to offer shippers the opportunity to pay a premium and declare a higher value for the goods.[4]

consignee
A person to whom bailed goods are to be delivered.

duty of strict liability
Duty owed by a common carrier whereby if the bailed goods are lost, damaged, destroyed, or stolen, the common carrier is liable even if the loss or damage was not its fault.

The following feature discusses a bill of lading.

Business Environment

Bill of Lading

A **bill of lading** is a document of title that is issued by a carrier-bailee to the bailor when goods are received for transportation. A carrier has a lien on the goods in its possession covered by a bill of lading for necessary charges and expenses. If the charges are not paid, the carrier can sell the goods at public or private sale and apply the proceeds to pay the charges. Any excess proceeds must be held for the person who had the right to demand delivery of the goods.[5]

In the following case, the court had to decide whether a shipping company was liable for a lost shipment.

CASE 47.3 *FEDERAL COURT CASE Common Carrier Shipment*

Exel, Inc. v. Southern Refrigerated Transport, Inc.

905 F.3d 455 (2018)
United States Court of Appeals for the Sixth Circuit

"A carrier cannot limit liability by implication."
—Ronald Gilman, Circuit Judge

Facts

Sandoz, Inc., a German company, manufactures pharmaceuticals. Sandoz hired Exel, Inc., a shipping broker, to make arrangements to have pharmaceuticals shipped from Pennsylvania to Tennessee. Exel entered into a contract with Southern Refrigerated Transport, Inc. (SRT), a motor transport company, to transport the pharmaceuticals. The bill of lading did not state the value of the goods being transported, nor did it limit SRT's liability for the loss of the shipment. While in transit, the SRT truck carrying the pharmaceuticals was stolen, and the goods were never recovered. Exel, on behalf of Sandoz, sued SRT to recover the value of the stolen goods. SRT alleged that the abbreviation "RVNX $2.40" in the bill of lading limited Exel's recovery to $56,766. SRT asserted that the abbreviation RVNX means "Released Value Not to Exceed." Thus, SRT alleged that $2.40 times the pounds of the goods shipped equals $56,766. The U.S. district court found that because the abbreviation RVNX was not defined in the bill of lading and was not in common usage in the trade, it was inapplicable. The district court awarded Exel $5.9 million, the replacement cost of the stolen pharmaceuticals. SRT appealed.

Issue

Were damages limited by the bill of lading?

Language of the Court

To overcome the default posture of full liability, the carrier must have a written agreement with the shipper that is sufficiently specific to manifest that the shipper in fact agreed to a limitation of liability. A carrier cannot limit liability by implication. There must be an absolute, deliberate, and well-informed choice by the shipper. SRT agreed with Exel to ship the goods at a rate not dependent on their value without inquiring into what that value was.

Decision

The U.S. court of appeals affirmed the decision of the district court.

Critical Legal Thinking Questions

Do you think that SRT should have inquired as to the value of the goods being shipped? Do you think that Exel should have inquired as to what the abbreviation RVNX meant? Why do you think that two sophisticated parties would fail to make these inquiries?

Innkeeper

bill of lading
A document of title issued by a common carrier stating that the bailor has title to the bailed goods.

An **innkeeper** is the owner of a facility (e.g., hotel, motel) that provides lodging to the public for compensation. Under the common law, innkeepers owe a duty of strict liability regarding loss caused to the personal property of transient guests. Under this rule, an innkeeper is liable for a guest's personal property that is lost or stolen from the innkeeper's premises even if the loss was not the innkeeper's fault.

Most states have enacted **innkeepers' statutes** that change the common law and limit the liability of innkeepers for the loss of goods by parties staying at their establishments. These statutes allow innkeepers to avoid liability for loss caused to guests' property if a safe is provided in which the guests' valuable property may be kept and the guests are aware of the safe's availability. State laws also allow innkeepers to limit the dollar amount of their liability by notifying their guests of this limit (e.g., by posting a notice on each guest room door).

innkeepers' statutes
State statutes that limit an innkeeper's common law liability. An innkeeper can avoid liability for loss caused to a guest's property if (1) a safe is provided in which the guest's valuable property may be kept and (2) the guest is notified of this fact.

Example Hospitality Hotel, Inc., operates a hotel located in a state that has an innkeepers' statute that (1) eliminates a hotel's liability for guests' property not placed in the safe located at the hotel's registration desk and (2) limits a hotel's liability to $500 for any guest's property stored in the hotel's safe. The hotel has proper notices posted at the registration counter and in guests' rooms, notifying them of these limitations on liability. Gion, a guest at the hotel, leaves expensive jewelry and cameras in his room when he temporarily leaves the hotel. When Gion returns, he finds that his jewelry and cameras have been stolen. Because of the innkeepers' statute, the hotel is not liable for Gion's loss. Suppose instead that Gion had taken items to the hotel's registration desk and had the hotel place the items in the hotel safe. If the items had been stolen from the hotel's safe, the innkeepers' statute would have limited the hotel's liability to $500.

CONCEPT SUMMARY
SPECIAL BAILMENTS

Type of Bailee	Liability	Limitation on Liability
Warehouse company	Ordinary negligence	May limit the dollar amount of liability by offering the bailor the right to declare a higher value for the bailed goods for an additional charge.
Common carrier	Strictly liable except for: 1. Act of God 2. Act of a public enemy 3. Order of the government 4. Act of the shipper 5. Inherent nature of the goods	May limit the dollar amount of liability by offering the bailor the right to declare a higher value for the bailed goods for an additional charge.
Innkeeper	Strictly liable	State innkeepers' statutes limit the liability of an innkeeper for others' negligence.

Key Terms and Concepts

Abandoned property (829)
Acceptance (826)
Accession (827)
Annulment (828)
Bailee (831)
Bailment (831)
Bailment agreement (831)
Bailment at will (833)
Bailment for a fixed term (833)
Bailment for the sole benefit of the bailee (833)
Bailment for the sole benefit of the bailor (833)
Bailment of personal property (831)
Bailor (831)
Bill of lading (836)
Capture (826)
Common carrier (835)
Confusion (828)
Consignee (835)
Consignment (835)
Consignor (835)
Constructive delivery (826)
Delivery (826)
Delivery of possession (831)
Divorce (828)
Donative intent (826)
Donee (826)
Donor (826)
Duty of great care (duty of utmost care) (833)
Duty of reasonable care (duty of ordinary care) (833)
Duty of slight care (833)
Duty of strict liability (835)
Estray statute (830)
Express bailment (831)
Fixture (825)
Fungible goods (828)
Gift (826)
Gift *causa mortis* (827)
Gift *inter vivos* (826)
Implied bailment (831)
Inheritance (828)
Innkeeper (836)
Innkeepers' statutes (837)
Intangible property (825)
Lien (835)
Living trust (828)
Lost property (829)

Mislaid property (828)
Mutual benefit bailment (833)
Ordinary bailments (832)
Personal property (825)
Physical delivery (826)
Possession (826)
Production (826)
Purchase (826)
Special bailments (834)
Tangible property (825)
Uniform Gifts to Minors Act (UGMA) (827)
Uniform Transfer to Minors Act (UTMA) (827)
Warehouser (warehouse company) (834)
Warehouse receipt (834)
Will (828)

Critical Legal Thinking Cases

47.1 Mislaid Property Alex Franks was a guest staying at a Comfort Inn in Searcy, Arkansas, while he was working on a highway project. Franks found a bundle of money in plain view in the left part of the left drawer in the dresser in his room. Franks notified the hotel manager, who notified the police. The police took custody of the money and discovered that the carefully wrapped bundle contained $14,200 in cash—46 $100 bills and 480 $20 bills. Franks sued to recover the cash. J.K. Kazi, the owner of the hotel, joined the lawsuit, also claiming the money. Franks argued that the money was lost property and therefore that he, as the finder, was entitled to it. Kazi argued that the money was mislaid property and that he, as the owner of the premises on which the money was found, was entitled to the money. The trial court held that the money had been mislaid and awarded the money to Kazi, the hotel owner. Franks appealed. Was the money mislaid or lost property? Who receives the property? *Franks v. Kazi*, 197 S.W.3d 5, 2004 Ark. App. Lexis 771 (Court of Appeals of Arkansas, 2004)

47.2 Bailment Sisters of Charity of the Incarnate Word, d.b.a. St. Elizabeth Hospital of Beaumont, operates a health and wellness center. Phil Meaux was a paying member of the health center. The rules of the center, which Meaux had been given, state, "The Health & Wellness Center is not responsible for lost or stolen items." A sign stating, "We cannot assure the safety of your valuables" was posted at the check-in desk. The wellness center furnished a lock and key to each member but had a master key to open lockers in case a member forgot or lost a key.

One day, Meaux went to the wellness center and placed his clothes, an expensive Rolex watch, and a money clip with $400 cash in the locker assigned him. On returning from swimming, Meaux discovered that his locker had been pried open and that his watch and money had been stolen by some unknown person. Meaux sued the Sisters of Charity, alleging that a bailment had been created between him and the Sisters and that the Sisters, as bailee, were negligent and therefore liable to him for the value of his stolen property. The trial court held in favor of Meaux and awarded him $19,500 as the value of the stolen property, plus interest and attorneys' fees. The Sisters of Charity appealed. Was a bailment created between Meaux and the Sisters of Charity? Who wins? *Sisters of Charity of the Incarnate Word v. Meaux*, 122 S.W.3d 428, 2003 Tex. App. Lexis 10189 (Court of Appeals of Texas, 2003)

47.3 Gift Victor Gruen was a successful architect. Victor purchased a painting titled *Schloss Kammer am Attersee II* by a noted Austrian modernist, Gustav Klimt, for $8,000. Four years after acquiring the painting, Victor wrote a letter to his son Michael, then an undergraduate student at Harvard University, giving the painting to Michael but reserving a life estate in the painting. The letter stated:

> *Dear Michael:*
> *The 21st birthday, being an important event in life, should be celebrated accordingly. I therefore wish to give you as a present the oil painting by Gustav Klimt of Schloss Kammer which now hangs in the New York living room.*
> *Happy birthday again.*
> *Love,*
> *[Signed] Victor*

Because Victor retained a life interest in the painting, Michael never took possession of it. Victor died 17 years later. The painting was appraised at $2.5 million. When Michael requested the painting from his stepmother, Kemija Gruen, she refused to turn it over to him. Michael sued to recover the painting. The trial court held in favor of the stepmother. The appellate division reversed and awarded the painting to Michael. The stepmother appealed. Did Victor Gruen make a valid gift *inter vivos* of the Klimt painting to his son Michael? *Gruen v. Gruen*, 68 N.Y.2d 48, 496 N.E.2d 869, 505 N.Y.S.2d 849, 1986 N.Y. Lexis 19366 (Court of Appeals of New York, 1986)

47.4 Bailment James D. Merritt leased a storage locker from Nationwide Warehouse Co., Ltd. (Nationwide), and agreed to pay a monthly fee to lease the locker. Merritt placed various items in the leased premises but never informed Nationwide as to the nature or quantity of articles stored therein. Merritt was free to store or remove whatever he wished without consultation with, permission from, or notice to Nationwide. Merritt locked the leased premises with his own lock and key. Nationwide was not furnished with a key. Subsequently, certain personal property belonging to Merritt disappeared from the storage space. Merritt sued Nationwide to recover damages of $5,275. Was a bailment created between Merritt and Nationwide? *Merritt v. Nationwide Warehouse Co., Ltd.*, 605 S.W.2d 250, 1980 Tenn. App. Lexis 338 (Court of Appeals of Tennessee, 1980)

47.5 Carrier Contract Billy Rykard allegedly shipped rare coins from Midland, Georgia, to Columbia Collectibles, LTD (Columbia) located in Patchogue, New York, by FedEx Ground Package System, Inc. (FedEx). The FedEx shipping contract stated that a shipper was prohibited from shipping money, cash, currency, or rare coins and that FedEx would not be liable for the loss of such items. The contract also stated that FedEx would not be liable for losses attributable to improper packaging, marking, and labeling of such shipments. Rykard had packaged and taped the shipment in a DHL box (DHL is a competitor shipper to FedEx) instead of a FedEx package and did not notify FedEx that the package contained rare coins. When the coins were not received by Columbia, Rykard sued FedEx in U.S. district court to recover damages. Is FedEx liable to Rykard for loss of the coins? *Rykard v. FedEx Ground Package System, Inc.*, 2010 U.S. Dist. Lexis 11097 (United States District Court for the Middle District of Georgia, 2010)

Ethics Cases

47.6 Ethics Case When Dr. Arthur M. Edwards died, leaving a will disposing of his property, he left the villa-type condominium in which he lived, its "contents," and $10,000 to his stepson, Ronald W. Souders. Edwards left the remainder of his estate to other named legatees. In administering the estate, certain stock certificates, passbook savings accounts, and other bank statements were found in Edwards's condominium. Souders claimed that these items belonged to him because they were "contents" of the condominium. The other legatees opposed Souders' claim, alleging that the disputed property was intangible personal property and not part of the contents of the condominium. The value of the property was as follows: condominium, $138,000; furniture in condominium, $4,000; stocks, $377,000; and passbook and other bank accounts, $124,000. Who is entitled to the stocks and bank accounts? Do you think Souders acted ethically in this case? *Souders v. Johnson*, 501 So.2d 745, 1987 Fla. App. Lexis 6579 (Court of Appeal of Florida, 1987)

47.7 Ethics Case Darryl Kulwin was employed by Nova Stylings, Inc. (Nova) as a jewelry salesperson. In that capacity, he traveled throughout the country, carrying with him jewelry owned and manufactured by Nova to show to prospective buyers. Kulwin was visiting Panoria Ruston, who was a guest registered with the Red Roof Inn in Overland Park, Kansas. Ruston and Kulwin met at the Red Roof Inn and later made plans to leave to go out for dinner. Kulwin asked Ruston to make arrangements with the desk clerk to leave his sample case in the office of the Red Roof Inn while they were at dinner. Ruston asked the clerk if she could leave the bag in the manager's office, and the clerk agreed. Ruston advised the clerk that the contents of the case were valuable but did not describe the contents of the bag. Kansas Statute Section 36-402(b) provides,

> *No hotel or motel keeper in this state shall be liable for the loss of, or damage to, merchandise for sale or samples belonging to a guest, lodger, or boarder unless the guest, lodger, or boarder upon entering the hotel or motel, shall give notice of having merchandise for sale or samples in his possession, together with an itemized list of such property, to the hotel or motel keeper, or his authorized agent or clerk in the registration office of the hotel or motel office.*
>
> *No hotel or motel keeper shall be liable for any loss of such property designated in this subsection (b), after notice of an itemized statement having been given and delivered as aforesaid, in an amount in excess of two hundred fifty dollars ($250), unless such hotel or motel keeper, by specific agreement in writing, individually, or by an authorized agent or clerk in charge of the registration office of the hotel or motel, shall voluntarily assume liability for a larger amount with reference to such property. The hotel or motel keeper shall not be compelled to receive such guests, lodgers, or boarders with merchandise for sale or samples.*

The inn posted the proper notice of the provisions of this act in all of the guests' rooms, including that of Ruston. An unidentified person obtained access to the manager's office and removed the case from the office. Nova sued Red Roof Inns for the alleged value of the jewelry, $650,000. Is Red Roof Inns liable? Did either party act unethically in this case? *Nova Stylings v. Red Roof Inns, Inc.*, 747 P.2d 107, 1987 Kan. Lexis 469 (Supreme Court of Kansas, 1987)

Notes

1. UCC 7-204(1), 7-403(1).
2. UCC 1-201(45).
3. UCC 7-301(1).
4. UCC 7-309(2).
5. UCC 7-308(1).

CHAPTER

48 Real Property

Korisbo/Shutterstock

HOUSE
A person's house is often his or her most valuable asset.

Learning Objectives

After studying this chapter, you should be able to:

48.1 List and describe the different types of real property.

48.2 Describe the different types of freehold estates.

48.3 Identify and describe the different types of concurrent ownership of real property.

48.4 Identify and describe the different types of future interests in real property.

48.5 Explain how ownership interests in real property can be transferred.

48.6 Define *marketable title* and describe the common methods of obtaining marketable title.

48.7 Describe and apply the doctrine of adverse possession.

48.8 List and describe the different types of express and implied easements.

48.9 Describe the liability of landowners to invitees, licensees, and trespassers.

48.10 Describe zoning laws and how they apply to real property.

> *"Without that sense of security which property gives, the land would still be uncultivated."*
>
> —François Quesnay (1694 – 1774)
> *Maximes, IV*

Introduction to Real Property and Land Use Regulation

Property and ownership rights in *real property* play an important part in the society and economy of the United States. Individuals and families own houses, farmers and ranchers own farmland and ranches, and businesses own commercial and office buildings. The concept of real property includes the legal rights to the property rather than the physical attributes of the tangible land. Thus, real property includes some items of personal property that are affixed to real property (e.g., fixtures) and other rights (e.g., minerals, air).

This chapter covers the law concerning the ownership and transfer of real property, adverse possession, easements, liability of landowners, and zoning laws.

A man complained that on his way home to dinner he had every day to pass through that long field of his neighbor's. I advised him to buy it, and it would never seem long again.
Ralph Waldo Emerson
(1803–1882)

Real Property

48.1 List and describe the different types of real property.

Property is usually classified as either real or personal property. **Real property** is immovable or attached to immovable land or buildings, whereas personal property is movable. The various types of real property are described in the following paragraphs.

real property
The land itself, as well as buildings, trees, soil, minerals, timber, plants, and other items permanently affixed to the land.

Land and Buildings

Land is the most common form of real property. A landowner usually purchases the **surface rights** to the land—that is, the right to occupy the land. The owner may use, enjoy, and develop the property as he or she sees fit, subject to any applicable government regulation.

A **building** that is constructed on land—a house, an apartment building, a manufacturing plant, an office building—is real property. Structures such as radio towers and bridges are usually considered real property as well.

Subsurface Rights

The owner of land possesses **subsurface rights**, or **mineral rights**, to the earth located beneath the surface of the land. These rights can be very valuable. Gold, uranium, oil, or natural gas may lie beneath the surface of the land. Theoretically, mineral rights extend to the center of the earth, although mines and oil wells usually only extend several miles into the earth. Subsurface rights may be sold separately from surface rights.

subsurface rights (mineral rights)
Rights to the earth located beneath the surface of the land.

Plant Life and Vegetation

Plant life and vegetation growing on the surface of land are considered real property. Such vegetation includes both natural plant life (e.g., trees) and cultivated plant life (e.g., crops). When land is sold, any plant life growing on the land is included in the sale, unless the parties agree otherwise. Plant life that is severed from the land is considered personal property.

plant life and vegetation
Plant life and vegetation growing on the surface of land are considered real property.

Fixtures

Certain personal property is so closely associated with real property that it becomes part of the realty. Such items are called **fixtures**. Kitchen cabinets, carpet, and doorknobs are fixtures, but throw rugs and furniture are personal

fixtures
Goods that are affixed to real estate and thus become part thereof.

property. Unless otherwise provided, if a building is sold, the fixtures are included in the sale. If the sale agreement is silent as to whether an item is a fixture, the courts make their determination on the basis of whether the item can be removed without causing substantial damage to the realty.

The following feature discusses air rights.

air rights
The owners of land may sell or lease air space parcels above their land.

Contemporary Environment

Air Rights

Owners of land may sell or lease **air rights** above their land if applicable legal requirements are met. An **air space parcel** is the air space above the surface of the earth of an owner's real property. Air space parcels are valuable property rights, particularly in densely populated metropolitan areas, where buildable property is scarce. Air rights are subject to Federal Aviation Administration (FAA) regulations and state and local laws.

Examples Railroads lease air rights over their railroad tracks. The Grand Central Terminal in New York City sold air rights over its railroad property for the construction of an office building next to Grand Central Terminal. Many other developments have been built in air space parcels in New York City and other cities in the United States. Fast-food restaurants and gas stations are often located on air rights over freeways.

Freehold Estates in Land

48.2 Describe the different types of freehold estates.

estate in land (estate)
Ownership rights in real property; the bundle of legal rights that the owner has to possess, use, and enjoy the property.

freehold estate
An estate in which the owner has a present possessory interest in the real property.

A person's ownership right in real property is called an **estate in land** (or **estate**). An estate is defined as the bundle of *legal rights* that the owner has to possess, use, and enjoy the property. The type of estate that an owner possesses is determined from the deed, will, or other document that transferred the ownership rights to him or her.

A **freehold estate** is an estate in which the owner has a **present possessory interest** in the real property; that is, the owner may use and enjoy the property as he or she sees fit, subject to applicable government regulation or private restraint. There are three types of freehold estates: *fee simple absolute* (or *fee simple*), *fee simple defeasible* (or *qualified fee*), and *life estate*. These are discussed in the following paragraphs.

Fee Simple Absolute (or Fee Simple)

fee simple absolute (fee simple)
A type of ownership of real property that grants the owner the fullest bundle of legal rights that a person can hold in real property.

A **fee simple absolute** (or **fee simple**) is an estate in fee that is the highest form of ownership of real property because it grants the owner the fullest bundle of legal rights that a person can hold in real property. It is the type of ownership most people connect with "owning" real property. A fee simple owner has the right to possess and use the property exclusively, to the extent that the owner has not transferred any interest in the property (e.g., by lease).

If a person owns real property in fee simple, that ownership is characterized as follows:

- It is infinite in duration (fee)
- It has no limitation on inheritability (simple)
- It does not end on the occurrence of any event (absolute)

Property and law are born and must die together.
Jeremy Bentham (1748–1832)
Principles of the Civil Code

Example Malai owns a fee simple absolute (or fee simple) in a piece of real property. This means that there are no limitations on her ownership rights. Malai owns this property while she is alive, with no conditions on her ownership rights, and she can transfer the property by will to a named beneficiary or beneficiaries when she dies.

Fee Simple Defeasible (or Qualified Fee)

A **fee simple defeasible** (or **qualified fee**) grants the owner all the rights of a fee simple absolute except that ownership may be taken away if a specified condition occurs or does not occur.

fee simple defeasible (qualified fee) A type of ownership of real property that grants the owner all the incidents of a fee simple absolute except that it may be taken away if a specified condition occurs or does not occur.

Example A conveyance of property to a church "as long as the land is used as a church or for church purposes" creates a qualified fee. The church has all the rights of a fee simple absolute owner except that its ownership rights are terminated if the property is no longer used for church purposes.

Life Estate

A **life estate** is an interest in real property that lasts for the life of a specified person, usually the grantee. The person who is given a life estate is called the **life tenant**. For example, an owner of real estate who makes a conveyance of real property "to Anna for her life" creates a life estate. Anna is the life tenant. A life estate may also be measured by the life of a third party, which is called ***estate pur autre vie*** (e.g., "To Anna for the life of Benjamin"). A life estate may be defeasible (e.g., "To Jalil for his life but only if he continues to occupy this residence"). On the death of the named person, the life estate terminates, and the property reverts to the grantor or the grantor's estate or to another designated person.

life estate An interest in real property for a person's lifetime; on that person's death, the interest is transferred to another party.

estate pur autre vie A life estate that is measured by the life of a third party.

A life tenant is treated as the owner of the property during the duration of the life estate. The life tenant has the right to possess and use the property except to the extent that it would cause permanent *waste* of the property.

CONCEPT SUMMARY

FREEHOLD ESTATES

Estate	Description
Fee simple absolute	The highest form of ownership of real property. Ownership (1) is infinite in duration, (2) has no limitation on inheritability, and (3) does not end on the occurrence or nonoccurrence of an event.
Fee simple defeasible	The owner has all the rights of a fee simple absolute except that ownership may be taken away if a specified condition occurs or does not occur.
Life estate	An interest in property that lasts for the life of a specified person. A life estate terminates on the death of the named person and reverts back to the grantor or his or her estate or to another designated person.

Concurrent Ownership

48.3 Identify and describe the different types of concurrent ownership of real property.

Two or more persons may own a piece of real property. This is called **concurrent ownership**, or **co-ownership**. The following forms of co-ownership of real property are recognized: *joint tenancy, tenancy in common, tenancy by the entirety, community property, condominiums*, and *cooperatives*.

concurrent ownership (co-ownership) A situation in which two or more persons own a piece of real property.

joint tenancy A form of co-ownership that includes the *right of survivorship*.

Joint Tenancy

Two or more parties can own real estate as **joint tenants**. To create a joint tenancy, words that clearly show a person's intent to create a joint tenancy must be used. Language such as "Marsha Leest and James Leest, as joint tenants" is usually sufficient.

The most distinguished feature of a **joint tenancy** is the co-owners' **right of survivorship of joint tenants**. This means that on the death of one of the co-owners (or joint tenants), the deceased person's interest in the property automatically

right of survivorship of joint tenants A legal rule providing that on the death of one joint tenant, the deceased person's interest in the real property automatically passes to the surviving joint tenant or joint tenants.

passes to the surviving joint tenant or joint tenants. Any contrary provision in the deceased's will is ineffective.

Example Ziyi, Heathcliff, Manuel, and Mohammad own a large commercial building as joint tenants. They are joint tenants with the right to survivorship. Heathcliff executes a will that leaves all of his property to his alma mater university. Heathcliff dies. The surviving joint tenants—Ziyi, Manuel, and Mohammad—and not the university acquire Heathcliff's ownership interest in the building. Ziyi, Manuel, and Mohammad are now joint tenants, each with a one-third interest in the building.

Laws are always useful to persons of property, and hurtful to those who have none.
Jean-Jacques Rousseau
Du Contrat Social (1761)

Each joint tenant has a right to sell or transfer his or her interest in the property, but such conveyance terminates the joint tenancy. The parties then become tenants in common.

Example Ziyi, Heathcliff, Manuel, and Mohammad own a large commercial building as joint tenants. They are joint tenants with the right to survivorship. Ziyi sells her one-quarter interest in the building to Wolfgang. At that time, the joint tenancy is broken, and the four owners—Wolfgang, Heathcliff, Manuel, and Mohammad—become tenants in common, with no right of survivorship. Wolfgang executes a will that leaves all of his property to his alma mater university. Wolfgang dies. Because the owners are not joint tenants, but are instead tenants in common, Wolfgang's quarter interest in the building goes to the university. The university is now a tenant in common with Heathcliff, Manuel, and Mohammad.

Tenancy in Common

tenancy in common
A form of co-ownership in which the interest of a surviving tenant in common passes to the deceased tenant's estate and not to the co-tenants.

In a **tenancy in common**, the interests of a surviving tenant in common pass to the deceased tenant's estate and not to the co-tenants. The parties to a tenancy in common are called **tenants in common**. A tenancy in common may be created by express words (e.g., "Ian Cespedes and Joy Park, as tenants in common"). Unless otherwise agreed, a tenant in common can sell, give, devise, or otherwise transfer his or her interest in the property without the consent of the other co-owners.

Example Alejandro, who is one of four tenants in common who own a piece of property, has a will that leaves all his property to his granddaughter. When Alejandro dies, the granddaughter receives his interest in the tenancy in common, and the granddaughter becomes a tenant in common with the other three owners.

Tenancy by the Entirety

tenancy by the entirety
A form of co-ownership of real property that can be used only by married couples.

community property
A form of ownership in which each spouse owns an equal one-half share of the income of both spouses and the assets acquired during the marriage.

Tenancy by the entirety is a form of co-ownership of real property that can be used only by married couples. This type of tenancy must be created by express words (e.g., "Atsa Yazzie and Natcha Yazzie, husband and wife, as tenants by the entirety"). A surviving spouse has the right of survivorship. Tenancy by the entirety is distinguished from joint tenancy in that neither spouse may sell or transfer an interest in the property without the other spouse's consent. Only about half of the states recognize tenancy by the entirety.

The following feature discusses community property.

Contemporary Environment

Community Property

Nine states—Arizona, California, Idaho, Louisiana, Nevada, New Mexico, Texas, Washington, and Wisconsin—recognize a form of co-ownership known as **community property**. This method of co-ownership applies only to married couples. It is based on the notion that a husband and wife should share equally in the fruits of the marital partnership. Under these laws, each spouse owns an equal one-half share of the *income* both spouses earned during the marriage and one-half of the *assets acquired by this income during the marriage*, regardless of who earns the income. Property that is acquired through gift or inheritance either before or during marriage remains **separate property**. Interest payments, dividends, and appreciation of separate property received or accrued during marriage are also separate property.

During the marriage, neither spouse can sell, transfer, or make a gift of community property without the consent of the other spouse. If the couple divorces, each spouse has a right to one-half of the community property. When a spouse dies, the surviving spouse automatically receives one-half of the community property. The other half passes to the heirs of the deceased spouse, as directed by will or by state *intestate statute* if there is no will.

The location of the real property determines whether community property law applies. If a married couple who lives in a noncommunity property state purchases real property located in a community property state, community property laws apply to that property.

Example Sasha and Brad live in a community property state. Sasha is a successful brain surgeon who makes $1 million per year. She meets and marries Brad, a struggling actor who makes $30,000 per year. When Sasha and Brad are married, she owns $1 million of real estate, which during the marriage she retains and maintains as her separate property. During the marriage, Sasha and Brad use joint income and purchase a parcel of real estate for $500,000—Sasha contributes $450,000 of the purchase price, and Brad contributes $50,000 of the purchase price. During the marriage, Sasha's real estate increases in value to $1.5 million, while the real estate they purchased together increases to $600,000. After three years, Sasha and Brad get a divorce. Upon divorce, Sasha keeps her separate real property worth $1.5 million. Sasha and Brad each receive $300,000 of the real estate they purchased with joint funds during the marriage.

CONCEPT SUMMARY

CONCURRENT OWNERSHIP

Form of Ownership	Right of Survivorship?	Tenant May Unilaterally Transfer His or Her Interest?
Joint tenancy	Yes, deceased tenant's interest automatically passes to co-tenants.	Yes, tenant may transfer his or her interest without the consent of co-tenants. Transfer severs joint tenancy.
Tenancy in common	No, deceased tenant's interest passes to his or her estate.	Yes, tenant may transfer his or her interest without the consent of co-tenants. Transfer does not sever tenancy in common.
Tenancy by the entirety	Yes, deceased tenant's interest automatically passes to his or her spouse.	No, neither spouse may transfer his or her interest without the other spouse's consent.
Community property	Yes, when a spouse dies, the surviving spouse automatically receives one-half of the community property. The other half passes to the heirs of the deceased spouse, as directed by a valid will or by state intestate statute if there is no will.	No, neither spouse may transfer his or her interest without the other spouse's consent.

Condominium

Condominiums are a common form of ownership in multiple-dwelling buildings. Purchasers of a condominium (1) have title to their individual unit and (2) own the common areas (e.g., hallways, elevators, parking areas, recreational facilities) as tenants in common with the other owners. Owners may sell or mortgage their units without the permission of the other owners. Owners are assessed monthly fees for the maintenance of common areas. In addition to being used for dwelling units, the condominium form of ownership is often used for office buildings, boat docks, and the like.

condominium
A common form of ownership in a multiple-dwelling building in which the purchaser has title to the individual unit and owns the common areas as a tenant in common with the other condominium owners.

Cooperative

A **cooperative** is a form of co-ownership of a multiple-dwelling building in which a corporation owns the building and the residents own shares in the corporation. Each cooperative owner leases a unit in the building from the

cooperative
A form of co-ownership of a multiple-dwelling building in which a corporation owns the building and the residents own shares in the corporation.

corporation under a renewable, long-term, proprietary lease. Individual residents may not secure loans for the units they occupy. The corporation can borrow money on a blanket mortgage, and each shareholder is jointly and severally liable on the loan. Usually, cooperative owners may not sell their shares or sublease their units without the approval of the other owners. Many coop buildings are located in major cities such as New York, Chicago, and Boston.

Future Interests

48.4 Identify and describe the different types of future interests in real property.

future interest
The interest that a grantor retains for him- or herself or a third party.

A person may be given the right to possess property in the *future* rather than in the present. This right is called a **future interest**. The two forms of future interests are *reversion* and *remainder*.

Reversion

reversion
A right of possession that returns to the grantor after the expiration of a limited or contingent estate.

A **reversion** is a right of possession that returns to the grantor after the expiration of a limited or contingent estate. Reversions do not have to be expressly stated because they arise automatically by law.

Example Gautam, an owner of real property, conveys his property "to Harriet Lawson for life." The grantor, Gautam, has retained a reversion in the property. That is, when Harriet dies, the property reverts to Gautam or, if he is not living, to his estate.

Remainder

remainder
A right of possession that returns to a third party on the expiration of a limited or contingent estate. A person who possesses this right is called a *remainder beneficiary*.

If the right of possession returns to a *third party* on the expiration of a limited or contingent estate, it is called a **remainder**. The person who is entitled to the future interest is called a **remainder beneficiary**.

Example Janice, an owner of real property, conveys her property "to Joe Jackson for life, remainder to Meredith Smith." This creates a vested remainder, with Meredith being the remainder beneficiary. The only contingency to Meredith's possessory interest is Joe's death. When Joe dies, Meredith obtains ownership of the property, or if she is not living, it goes to her estate.

CONCEPT SUMMARY

FUTURE INTERESTS

Future Interest	Description
Reversion	Right to possession of real property returns to the grantor after the expiration of a limited or contingent estate.
Remainder	Right to possession of real property goes to a third person on the expiration of a limited or contingent estate.

Transfer of Ownership of Real Property

48.5 Explain how ownership interests in real property can be transferred.

Ownership of real property can be transferred from one person to another. Title to real property can be transferred by sale; tax sale; gift, will, or inheritance; and adverse possession. The different methods of transfer provide different degrees of protection to the transferee.

Sale of Real Estate

A **sale**, or **conveyance**, is the most common method for transferring ownership rights in real property. An owner may offer real estate for sale either personally or by using a real estate broker. When a buyer has been located and the parties have negotiated the terms of the sale, a **real estate sales contract** is executed by the parties. The Statute of Frauds in most states requires this contract to be in writing.

sale (conveyance)
The passing of title from a seller to a buyer for a price.

The seller delivers a deed to the buyer, and the buyer pays the purchase price at the **closing**, or **settlement**. Unless otherwise agreed, it is implied that the seller is conveying fee simple absolute title to the buyer. If either party fails to perform, the other party may sue for breach of contract and obtain either monetary damages or specific performance.

Deeds

A **deed** is used to convey real property by sale or gift. The seller or donor is called the **grantor**. The buyer or recipient is called the **grantee**. A deed may be used to transfer a fee simple absolute interest in real property or any lesser estate (e.g., life estate). State laws recognize different types of deeds that provide different degrees of protection to grantees. The most common form of deeds are the (1) *general warranty deed*, (2) *special warranty deed*, and (3) *quitclaim deed*. These types of deeds are discussed in the following paragraphs.

deed
An instrument that describes a person's ownership interest in a piece of real property.

grantor
The party who transfers an ownership interest in real property.

grantee
The party to whom an interest in real property is transferred.

- **General Warranty Deed.** A **general warranty deed** (or **grant deed**) contains the greatest number of warranties and provides the highest level of protection to a grantee. General warranty deeds are usually used as a deed from a seller to a buyer of real property. In a general warranty deed, the seller warrants that he or she owns the property; that he or she has the legal right to sell it; that the property is not subject to encumbrances (e.g., mortgages), leases, or easements other than those that are disclosed; that his or her title is superior to any other claim of title to the property; that he or she will defend the grantee's title against all other claims; and that he or she will compensate the grantee for any losses suffered if the title proves faulty. The guarantee is not limited to the time that the grantor owned the property but extends back to the property's origins.

  Although the grantor is legally bound to compensate the grantee for losses caused by a breach of warranty, this guarantee is not helpful if the grantor is dead when the breach of warranty is discovered or if the grantor is financially unable to cover the losses.

general warranty deed (grant deed)
A deed that protects a grantee of real property from defects in title caused by the grantor and prior owners of the property.

  Example Before purchasing a vacant piece of property, Lawana checks the title to the property and finds no prior encumbrances or claims to the property. Unbeknownst to her, the sellers of the property had divorced, and one of the parties to the divorce did not sign the deed that purportedly transferred ownership of the property to Lawana. After several years, Lawana sells the property to Michael. After five years, Michael sells the property to Aileen using a general warranty deed. Subsequently, the divorced party who had not previously signed the deed claims his interest in the property. Here, even though the defect occurred before Michael purchased the property, he is liable to Aileen for any damages caused by the claim on the property.

  Often, a buyer of real estate will purchase title insurance to cover the warranties that they have made in general warranty deed.

- **Special Warranty Deed.** A **special warranty deed** (or **limited warranty deed**) protects a buyer only from defects in title that arose during the period of the seller's ownership of the property. Thus, under this type of deed, the seller is not liable for defects in title that existed before the seller obtained the property or for encumbrances that were present when the seller obtained the property.

special warranty deed (limited warranty deed)
A deed that protects a grantee of real property from defects in title caused by the grantor.

Example Before purchasing a home and property is a rural area, Ida checks the title to the property and finds no prior problems or claims to the property. Unbeknownst to her, a prior owner had obtained a loan on the property with the property being collateral for the loan. The loan has never been paid off. Five years after purchasing the property, Ida sells the property to Maximillian using a special warranty deed. Shortly thereafter, the prior lender claims her interest in the property. Because the defect in title occurred before Ida's purchase of the property, she is not liable to Maximillian for any damages caused by the prior claim on the property.

Often, a buyer of real estate will purchase title insurance to cover this risk inherent in special warranty deeds.

quitclaim deed
A deed in which the grantor of real property transfers whatever interest he or she has in the property to the grantee.

- **Quitclaim Deed.** A **quitclaim deed** is a deed in which the grantor transfers only whatever interest he or she has in the real property. In a quitclaim deed, the grantor does not guarantee that the title to the real estate is free of any claims or encumbrances. A quitclaim deed provides the least amount of protection to a grantee because only the grantor's interest in the property is conveyed. Quitclaim deeds are not usually used as a deed from a seller to a buyer. They are most often used when property is transferred between relatives by gift or in a divorce settlement where one party is awarded the property.

recording statute
A state statute that requires a mortgage or deed of trust to be recorded in the county recorder's office of the county in which the real property is located.

Example A husband and wife own a house, and in a divorce settlement the husband is to receive the house. Here, the wife signs a quitclaim deed to the husband that eliminates her interest in the property.

Because no guarantee or warranty is made regarding title in a quitclaim deed, title insurance cannot be obtained.

The following feature discusses recording statutes.

Contemporary Environment

Recording Statutes

Every state has a **recording statute** that provides that copies of deeds and other documents concerning interests in real property (e.g., mortgages, liens, easements) may be filed in a government office, where they become public records open to viewing by the public. Recording statutes are intended to prevent fraud and to establish certainty in the ownership and transfer of property. Instruments are usually filed in the **county recorder's office** of the county in which the property is located. A fee is charged to record an instrument.

Persons interested in purchasing property or lending on property should check these records to determine whether the grantor or borrower actually owns the property in question and whether any other parties (e.g., lienholders, mortgagees, easement holders) have an interest in the property. The recording of a deed is not required to pass title from the grantor to the grantee. Recording the deed gives **constructive notice** to the world of the owner's interest in the property.

Example City Bank makes a loan to Mary MacAlister to purchase a house, and the bank takes back a mortgage, making the house security for the repayment of the loan. At the time of making the loan, City Bank fails to record the mortgage in the proper county recorder's office. When Mary tries to borrow more money on the house from Country Bank, Country Bank checks the county recorder's office and finds no recorded mortgage. Country Bank makes the loan to Mary, takes back a mortgage on the house, and records the mortgage in the proper county recorder's office. If Mary defaults on these two loans, Country Bank has priority in foreclosing on the property to recover payment for its loan because it recorded its loan.

If the information on a deed that is recorded is incorrect, the owner may bring an action in court to have the deed rewritten to reflect the correct information. This is called the **reformation of a deed**.

Example A part of a very long deed should be written "... thence N 89-59-07 E 416.25 feet, to the line between Lots 14 & 15, said Plat; thence N 01-12-56 E 418.25 feet, parallel to said lot line ..." However, after the second place where the word "thence" appears in this portion of the recorded deed, the incorrect letter "N" appears instead of the correct letter "S." The owner may have the deed reformed to read correctly.

Tax Sale

If an owner of real property fails to pay property taxes, the government can obtain a lien on the property for the amount of the taxes. If the taxes remain unpaid for a statutory period of time, the government can sell the property at a **tax sale** to satisfy the lien. Any excess proceeds are paid to the taxpayer. The buyer receives title to the property. Many states provide a **period of redemption** after a tax sale during which the taxpayer can redeem the property by paying the unpaid taxes and penalties. In these states, the buyer at a tax sale does not receive title to the property until the period of redemption has passed.

period of redemption
The period of time during which a mortgagor may redeem real property after default and before foreclosure.

Gift or Inheritance

Ownership of real property can be transferred by **gift**. The gift is made when the deed to the property is delivered by the donor to the donee or to a third party to hold for the donee. No consideration is necessary.

Example A grandfather wants to give his farm to his granddaughter. To do so, he only has to execute a deed and give the deed to her or to someone to hold for her, such as her parents.

Real property can also be transferred by **will**, **trust**, or **inheritance**.

Example A person may leave a piece of real estate to his best friend by will when he dies. This transfer does not require the transfer of a deed during the testator's lifetime. A deed will be issued to the beneficiary when the will is probated. If a person dies without a valid will, the property is distributed to the heirs pursuant to the applicable state intestate statute. This statute specifies how the heirs of the deceased will inherit the deceased's property.

Marketable Title to Real Property

48.6 Define *marketable title* and describe the common methods of obtaining marketable title.

A grantor has the obligation to transfer **marketable title**, or **good title**, to the grantee. Marketable title means that the title is free from any encumbrances, defects of title, or other defects that are not disclosed but would affect the value of the property. The three common ways of best ensuring marketable title and protecting against losses caused by defects in title are (1) by purchasing *title insurance*, (2) by obtaining an *attorney's opinion*, and (3) by obtaining a *certificate of title* pursuant to a Torrens system. These three methods are discussed in the following paragraphs.

marketable title (good title)
Title to real property that is free from any encumbrances or other defects that are not disclosed but would affect the value of the property.

Title Insurance

The most effective and most often used way for a purchaser of real property to best be assured that they are acquiring marketable title to the property is to purchase **title insurance** from an insurance company. The title insurer does a thorough investigation of the property's title before issuing a title insurance policy. Lenders can buy title insurance for real property that is used as collateral for a loan that the bank makes. If the insured property increases in value, it is advisable to increase the amount of title insurance on the property. Each time a property is transferred or refinanced, a new title insurance policy should be obtained by the new buyer or collateral lender. Prior title insurance policies do not carry over to new buyers or lenders.

The title insurer must reimburse the insured for any losses caused by discovered defects in title that occurred prior to the purchase of the title insurance. Title insurance is the most common method for best ensuring marketable title and protecting against claims that cause a defect in the title to real property. Title insurance is available in most states.

title insurance
Insurance that purchasers of real estate, and lenders who make loans where real property is collateral for the loan, purchase to ensure that they will be paid for losses suffered by defects in the title to the property that occurred prior to the purchase or loan.

Example Kofi sells a piece of real estate to Nadia. Five years later, Nadia sells the real property to Louis, using a general warranty deed to transfer ownership. Louis purchases title insurance. Subsequently, a legitimate claim is asserted against the property that arose during the period when Kofi possessed the property, which causes a defect in the title of the property. Louis losses the property in a quiet title action brought by the claimant. The title insurance company must pay Louis for his monetary loss.

Attorney's Opinion

An attorney examines an **abstract of title**, which is a chronological history of the chain of title affecting the property, including recorded documents and public records relating prior ownership of the property, encumbrances, recorded easements, public claims of adverse possession, and other information affecting title to the property in the past. An attorney's opinion discloses only defects that are apparent from public records. If the attorney determines that clear title exists, he or she will render an **attorney's opinion** stating that the title to the property is clear as of the date of the opinion. If the opinion states that there are no defects to the title that appear in the public, but a defect later arises that could have been discovered in the public records, the attorney is liable for negligence and must pay for any losses incurred by the party who employed the attorney to render an opinion.

attorney's opinion
An opinion given by an attorney concerning the status of title to real property that is arrived at after examining a chronological history of the chain of title and encumbrances affecting the property.

Although an attorney's opinion discloses only defects that are apparent from public records, title insurance provides protection from defects that may occur in public records and also defects that do not appear in public records. Generally, title insurance provides greater title protection title defects than an attorney's opinion.

Certificate of Title

Several states recognize the **Torrens system** as a method of determining title to real property. Under this system, a person claiming ownership of land goes to a land court to register ownership. A judicial proceeding is held, at which others claiming an interest in the property can appear. After the evidence is heard, the court issues a **certificate of title** to the person who is determined to be the rightful owner. Mortgages, liens, or other interests in the land are listed on the certificate of title. The cost of registering the land funds an insurance pool that compensates parties whose interests in the land are omitted from certificates of title in error.

certificate of title
A certificate that is issued by a land court that determines the rightful owner of real property.

Quiet Title Action

A party who is concerned about his or her ownership rights in a parcel of real property can bring a **quiet title action**, which is a lawsuit to have a court determine the extent of those rights. Public notice of the hearing must be given so that anyone claiming an interest in the property can appear and be heard. After the hearing, the judge declares who has title to the property; that is, the court "quiets title" by its decision.

quiet title action
An action brought by a party, seeking an order of the court declaring who has title to disputed property. The court "quiets title" by its decision.

Adverse Possession

48.7 Describe and apply the doctrine of adverse possession.

In most states, a person who wrongfully possesses someone else's real property obtains title to that property if certain statutory requirements are met. This is called **adverse possession**. Property owned by federal, state, and local governments is not subject to adverse possession.

adverse possession
A situation in which a person who wrongfully possesses someone else's real property obtains title to that property if certain statutory requirements are met.

Under the doctrine of adverse possession, the transfer of the property is involuntary and does not require the delivery of a deed. To obtain title under adverse possession, most states require that the wrongful possession must be:

- **For a statutorily prescribed period of time.** The **statutorily prescribed period of time** varies from state to state but is usually between 5 and 20 years.

- **Open, visible, and notorious.** The adverse possessor must occupy the property so as to put the owner on notice of the possession.
- **Actual and exclusive.** The adverse possessor must physically occupy the premises. The planting of crops, grazing of animals, or building of a structure on the land constitutes physical occupancy.
- **Continuous and peaceful.** The occupancy must be continuous and uninterrupted for the required statutory period. Any break in normal occupancy terminates the adverse possession. This means that the adverse possessor may leave the property to go to work, to the store, on a vacation, and such. The adverse possessor cannot take the property by force from an owner.
- **Hostile and adverse.** The possessor must occupy the property without the express or implied permission of the owner. Thus, a lessee cannot claim title to property under adverse possession.

The disseisor must unfurl his flag on the land, and keep it flying, so that the owner may see, if he will, that an enemy has invaded his domains, and planted the standard of conquest.

Judge Ellington
Johnson v. Asfaw and Tanus
2005 Wash. App. Lexis 2167 (2005)

If the elements of adverse possession are met, the adverse possessor acquires clear title to the land. However, title is acquired only as to the property actually possessed and occupied during the statutory period, and not to the entire tract.

Example An adverse possessor who occupies one acre of a 50-acre parcel of property for the statutory period of time and meets the other elements for adverse possession acquires title only to the one acre.

Some states require that the adverse possessor have paid taxes on the claimed property during the statutorily prescribed period of time to acquire real property by adverse possession. Some real estate organizations have lobbied to eliminate the doctrine of adverse possession.

The best protection against losing property to an adverse possessor is for a landowner to check his or her property for adverse possessors. A landowner should have legal lots lines surveyed and staked so they know the bounds of their property and therefore can easily determine if any party is encroaching over the legal lot line. Owners of vacant property should periodically visit and check their property to make sure no one is squatting on or using the vacant property. If an encroachment is found, the landowner should take whatever legal action is necessary, including filing a quiet title action, to evict the encroaching party and clear title to the property.

WEB EXERCISE
Use Google or another internet search engine to find the statutory prescribed period for adverse possession in your state.

In the following case, the court had to decide whether adverse possession had occurred.

CASE 48.1 *STATE COURT CASE Adverse Possession*

Paine v. Sexton

37 N.E.3d 1103, 2015 Mass. App. Lexis 151 (2015)
Appeals Court of Massachusetts

"The determination whether a set of activities is sufficient to support a claim of adverse possession is inherently fact-specific."

—Frederick Brown, Justice

Facts

Robert Paine's parents operated a commercial campground beginning in approximately 1958. The campground, which is very large and can house up to 500 individuals, includes roads and cleared campsites while still maintaining the natural environment. It also features picnic tables, fire rings, toilet buildings, a volleyball pit, play areas, a parking lot, and an office building. A wall of railroad ties is set on the road frontage to the property but fencing and walls do not enclose the entirety of the campground. The campground is operated on a seasonal basis and charges a fee to customers, who are required to bring their own tents or campers.

(continued)

Robert Paine, on behalf of the persons who now own and operate the campground, filed a petition in Massachusetts Land Court to register by adverse possession 36 acres that the campground occupies but to which the owners of the campground do not own record title. For their claims of adverse possession, the plaintiffs assert non-permissive use of the disputed property for more than the statutorily required 20 years in a manner that was actual, open, notorious, exclusive, and adverse. David Sexton, as trustee for the defendant record owners of the 36 acres, contends that the plaintiffs cannot establish their claim of adverse possession because they have not enclosed the disputed property. The land court ruled that the plaintiffs had acquired the 36 acres through adverse possession. The defendants appealed.

Issue

Have the plaintiffs obtained the disputed property through adverse possession?

Language of the Court

The determination whether a set of activities is sufficient to support a claim of adverse possession is inherently fact-specific. In the circumstances of the present case, in which the plaintiffs operated the locus as a commercial campground advertised as such, improved the site by clearing campsites and constructing roadways, toilet buildings, and an office, and restricted access to paying customers, we are satisfied that the judge was correct in his assessment that the plaintiffs' use was sufficient to place the record owners on notice that the plaintiffs occupied the locus under a claim of right.

Decision

The appeals court affirmed the land court's decision finding that the plaintiffs had acquired the disputed 36 acres through adverse possession.

Critical Legal Thinking Questions

Should record holders of real property bear the burden of checking to discover whether someone else is using their property? Should adverse possession be abolished?

nonpossessory interest
A situation in which a person holds an interest in another party's real property without actually owning any part of the property.

easement
A given or required right to make limited use of someone else's real property without owning or leasing it.

express easements
Easements are created by words and must be in writing. Express easements include the following: (1) *easement appurtenant*, (2) *easement in gross*, (3) *easement by reservation*, and (4) *negative easement*.

easement appurtenant
An easement that is expressly created when the owner of one piece of real property purposefully grants an easement to the owner of an adjacent piece of real property to use his or her property in some specified way.

servient estate
The real property over which an easement appurtenant is granted.

dominant estate
The real property that benefits from an easement appurtenant.

Easements

48.8 List and describe the different types of express and implied easements.

A person can own a **nonpossessory interest** in another's real estate. Three nonpossessory interests—*easement, license*, and *profit*—are discussed in the following paragraphs.

The most prominent nonpossessory interest is an easement. An **easement** is an interest in land that gives the holder the right to make limited use of another's property without owning or leasing it.

Express Easements

Many easements are purposely granted by a landowner to another party. These are called **express easements**. Express easements are created by words and must be in writing. Express easements include: (1) *easement appurtenant*, (2) *easement in gross*, (3) *easement by reservation*, and (4) *negative easement*. These four express easements are discussed in the following paragraphs.

1. **Easement Appurtenant.** An **easement appurtenant** is an easement by grant that is *expressly* created when the owner of one piece of real property purposefully grants an easement to the owner of an adjacent piece of real property to use the first piece of property in some specified way. The land over which the easement is granted is called the **servient estate**. The land that benefits from the easement is called the **dominant estate**. An appurtenant easement runs with the land. If an owner sells the servient estate, the buyer who purchases the property cannot terminate the easement. If an owner sells the dominant estate, the new owner acquires the benefit of the easement.

   Example Two owners own adjacent pieces of real property. One owner grants the other owner the right to use a road that runs across her piece of property so that the owner of the other piece of property can more easily access his property. This is an easement appurtenant. The property upon which the easement runs is the servient estate, and the property that benefits from the easement is the dominant estate.

2. **Easement in Gross.** An **easement in gross** is an easement by grant that *expressly* authorizes a person who does not own adjacent real property the right to use the other party's nonadjacent real property in some specified way. An easement in gross is personal to the party who receives the benefit of the easement. There is no benefitted parcel of land. An easement in gross does not go with the land if the land is transferred. An easement in gross terminates if the owner of the land over which the easement is located or the holder of the easement transfers their property by sale, inheritance, or other means, or if either party to the easement dies. Commercial easements in gross, such as those held by utilities to run power, telephone, and cable television lines across a property, do transfer with the property.

   Example Ru Shi owns a piece of lakefront real estate that has a very nice beach. Edsel owns a piece of non-lakefront property several blocks from Ru Shi's property. Ru Shi grants Edsel the right to walk on a long path on her property to reach the beach. This is an easement in gross. If Ru Shi sells the property, Edsel's easement terminates.

easement in gross
An easement that expressly authorizes a person who does not own adjacent real property the right to use another party's nonadjacent real property in some specified way.

3. **Easement by Reservation.** An **easement by reservation** is an *express* easement that is created when an owner sells real property that he or she owns to another party but expressly reserves an easement on the sold property.

   Example A landowner owns a large parcel of land and decides to sell half of the land to another party. In the land transfer, the selling landowner expressly reserves the right to use a road that runs across the property that he is selling. This is an easement by reservation.

easement by reservation
An express easement that is created when an owner sells real property that he or she owns to another party but expressly reserves an easement on the sold property.

4. **Negative Easement.** A **negative easement** is an *express* easement whereby the owner of real property makes a promise to another owner of real property that he or she will not do something with or on his or her real property. The party who is granted a benefit by a negative easement usually pays the owner of the real property that is impacted by the easement.

   Example The owner of a piece of property promises not to build a structure that would block his neighbor's view.

negative easement
An express easement whereby the owner of real property makes a promise to another owner of real property that he or she will not do something with or on his or her real property.

CONCEPT SUMMARY

EXPRESS EASEMENTS

Express Easement	Description
Easement appurtenant	An easement that is expressly created when the owner of one piece of real property purposefully grants an easement to the owner of an adjacent piece of real property to use the first piece of property in some specified way.
Easement in gross	An easement that expressly authorizes a person who does not own adjacent real property the right to use another party's nonadjacent real property in some specified way.
Easement by reservation	An express easement that is created when an owner sells land that he or she owns to another party but expressly reserves an easement on the sold real property.
Negative easement	An express easement whereby the owner of real property makes a promise to another owner of real property that he or she will not do something with or on his or her real property.

Implied Easements

implied easements
Easements that are implied from the situation and circumstances. Implied easements include the following: (1) *easement by necessity*, (2) *easement by implication*, and (3) *easement by prescription*.

Some easements are not expressly provided for but are implied from the situation and circumstances. These are called **implied easements**. Implied easements include: (1) *easement by necessity*, (2) *easement by implication*, and (3) *easement by prescription*. These three implied easements are discussed in the following paragraphs.

easement by necessity
An implied easement that is created if two parcels of real property are so situated that an easement over one parcel is strictly necessary for the use and enjoyment of the other parcel.

1. **Easement by Necessity.** An **easement by necessity** is an *implied* easement that is created if two parcels of real property are so situated that an easement over one parcel is strictly necessary for the use and enjoyment of the other parcel. An easement by necessity is granted if there is no possible alternative way for a party to access their real property except by the creation of the easement.

   Example A parcel of land is "landlocked" and does not have ingress or egress to a public road. The courts will grant an implied easement by necessity across the adjoining piece of property to allow the owner of the landlocked property to reach and make use of his property.

easement by implication
An implied easement that is created when an owner subdivides a parcel of real property that has a beneficial appurtenant on it (e.g., a road, path, well) that serves the entire parcel, and the purchasers of the subdivided pieces of property automatically acquire an easement to use the beneficial appurtenant.

2. **Easement by Implication.** An **easement by implication** is an *implied easement* that is created when an owner subdivides a parcel of real property that has a beneficial appurtenant (e.g., a road or path) on it that serves the entire parcel, and the purchasers of the subdivided pieces of property automatically acquire an easement to use the beneficial appurtenant.

   Example A landowner subdivides a large piece of property into four pieces of property and sells them to different purchasers. A water well, which is the only source of water for the properties, is located on one of the subdivided parcels. An easement by implication will be granted to the owners of the other three subdivided lots so that they will have access to the water of the well.

easement by prescription
An implied easement whereby one party obtains the right to use a portion of another party's real property when the requirements for adverse possession are met.

3. **Easement by Prescription.** An **easement by prescription** is an *implied* easement whereby one party obtains the right to use a portion of another party's real property when the requirements for adverse possession are met. Thus, the use of another person's real property upon which an easement by prescription is created must have been open, visible, and notorious; must have been hostile and adverse; must have been actual and exclusive; must have been continuous and peaceful; and must have occurred for the statutory prescribed period of time.

   Example There are two large parcels of property located in a rural area. The owner of one parcel, on which there is a farm and farm house, has been using a long dirt road that runs across the other parcel, which is vacant undeveloped land, without that owner's knowledge or permission for longer than the statutory prescribed period of time for adverse possession. The farm owner has obtained an easement by prescription to continue using the dirt road even after his use is discovered by the owner of the vacant land.

CONCEPT SUMMARY
IMPLIED EASEMENTS

Implied Easement	Description
Easement by necessity	An implied easement that is created if two parcels of real property are so situated that an easement over one parcel is strictly necessary for the use and enjoyment of the other parcel.

Easement by implication	An implied easement that is created when an owner subdivides a parcel of real property that has a beneficial appurtenant on it that serves the entire parcel, and the purchasers of the subdivided pieces of property automatically acquire an easement to use the beneficial appurtenant.
Easement by prescription	An implied easement whereby one party obtains the right to use a portion of another party's real property when the requirements for adverse possession are met.

License

A **license of real property** grants a person the right to enter another's property for a specified and usually short period of time. The person granting the license is called the *licensor*; the person receiving the license is called the *licensee*.

license of real property
A document that grants a person the right to enter on another's property for a specified and usually short period of time.

Examples A ticket to a movie theater or sporting event that grants the holder the right to enter the premises for the performance is a common license. A license does not transfer any interest in the property. A license is a personal privilege that may be revoked by the **licensor** at any time.

Profit-à-Prendre

A ***profit-à-prendre*** (or **profit**) gives the holder the right to remove something from another's real property.

***profit-à-prendre* (profit)**
A document that grants a person the right to remove something from another's real property.

Examples The holder may remove gravel, minerals, grain, or timber from another person's property.

Liability of Landowners

48.9 Describe the liability of landowners to invitees, licensees, and trespassers.

Owners and renters of real property may, under certain circumstances, be held liable to visitors who are injured on their property. This is called **premises liability**. A landowner's or tenant's liability generally depends on the status of the visitor. Visitors fall into one of three categories: *invitee, licensee*, or *trespasser*.

premises liability
Liability that is imposed on landowners and tenants for breaching duties that they owe to visitors who are injured on their real property.

Invitee

An **invitee** is a person who has been expressly or impliedly invited to a landowner's or tenant's premises for the economic benefit of the landowner or tenant (e.g., diners at a restaurant, clients at an office, guests at a hotel, contractors working on your home's roof). A landowner or tenant owes a **duty of ordinary care** to invitees to make the premises safe from, or to warn of, dangerous conditions that pose an unreasonable risk of which the landowner or tenant has actual or constructive knowledge. A landowner or tenant is liable if he or she breaches this duty and the dangerous condition causes injury to an invitee.

invitee
A person who has been expressly or impliedly invited to a landowner's or tenant's premises for the economic benefit of the owner or tenant.

duty of ordinary care
A duty that a landowner or tenant owes to invitees to make the premises safe from, or to warn of, dangerous conditions that pose an unreasonable risk of which the landowner or tenant has actual or constructive knowledge.

Example A shopper enters a grocery store and slips on a grape on the floor and falls and injures himself. If the grape had only been on the floor for five minutes, the store is most likely not liable because this was not sufficient time for the store to have constructive notice that the grape was on the floor. However, if employees knew the grape was on the floor and did not pick it up, the store is liable. If the store did not have actual knowledge that the grape was on the floor, but the grape remained on the floor for two hours prior to the accident, the store would be held to have constructive notice of the danger and would be liable for the shopper's injuries.

mode-of-operation rule
A rule that states that when a business invitee is injured on a business's premises, the injured party is entitled to an inference of the business's negligence and is relived of the obligation of proving that the business owner had actual or constructive notice of the dangerous condition that caused the injury.

Some states apply the **mode-of-operation rule** when determining whether businesses are liable for negligence to business invitees. Under this rule, a business invitee who is injured on a business's premises is entitled to an inference of the business's negligence and is relieved of the obligation to prove that the business owner had actual or constructive notice of the dangerous condition that caused the injury. This rule applies to foreseeable risks incident to the business's operations. If the plaintiff is able to make such a showing, the burden is shifted to the defendant to prove that it exercised reasonable care under the circumstances. If the defendant has not exercised reasonable care, then it is liable to the plaintiff for negligence.

Example A shopper at a grocery store slips and falls on a liquid on the floor in the soda section of the store and is injured. This is a condition that would commonly arise while operating a grocery store. Under the mode-of-operation rule, the store would be liable for negligence unless it can prove that it exercised reasonable care under the circumstances.

Licensee

licensee
A person who is on someone's real property legally and with the express or implied permission of the landowner or tenant and is not there to convey an economic benefit to the landowner or tenant.

A **licensee** is a person who is on a landowner's or tenant's real property legally and with the express or implied permission of the landowner or tenant and is not there to convey an economic benefit to the landowner or tenant (e.g., post office letter carrier, a delivery person such as a FedEx driver, a person going door to door to solicit political support). An owner owes a *duty of ordinary care* to invitees to make the premises safe or warn the invitee of dangerous conditions posing an unreasonable risk of which the landowner has actual knowledge. An owner or tenant is liable if she breaches this duty and the dangerous condition causes injury to a licensee. A licensee cannot rely on constructive knowledge to prove her case.

Social guests such as a friend invited to visit or guests at a party are usually considered to be licensees.

Example An owner of a house invites a friend over for dinner. The homeowner leaves a garden hose across the walkway to the house. The walkway is not well lit, and the danger is not obvious. The invited friend trips on the garden house and is injured. The homeowner is liable for negligence.

Open and Obvious Danger

open and obvious danger
A rule that states that a possessor of real property is not liable to invitees who are injured by a danger that a reasonable person would have been able to observe, recognize, and perceive through casual inspection.

Although a landowner and tenant of real property owes a duty of ordinary care to invitees and licensees, the law recognizes an exception to this rule for an **open and obvious danger**. Thus, a possessor of real property is not liable to invitees and licensees who are injured by open and obvious dangers on the premises. A danger is open and obvious if a reasonable person would have been able to observe, recognize, and perceive the danger and risk through casual inspection. These hazards are so plain to see that any reasonable person would be aware of them and take care around them.

Examples A person is walking on a railroad track and is struck by a train. Walking on a railroad track is an open and obvious danger. A person who is texting and not looking where he is going trips on a crack in the sidewalk. There is an obvious danger in walking while distracted and without looking where one is going.

However, if the open and obvious condition is hidden from casual observation, or poses an unreasonable risk of danger that could harm an invitee despite it being open and obvious, the possessor owes a duty to take reasonable precautions to protect invitees from the risk. This could include posting warning signs, blocking off the dangerous area, or remedying the danger.

Example A person falls into an open trench that is hidden from view by bushes and that would not be expected to be seen by a reasonable person in the circumstances.

Some states have eliminated the open and obvious danger exception to premises liability of possessors of real property.

Trespasser

A **trespasser** is a person who is on a landowner's or tenant's real property but has no invitation, permission, or legal right to be there. Generally, a landowner or tenant does not owe a duty of ordinary care to a trespasser. A landowner or tenant has no duty to maintain the land or premises in a safe condition for strangers entering without permission or to warn trespassers of such conditions.

trespasser
A trespasser is a person who is on a landowner's or tenant's real property but has no invitation, permission, or legal right to be there.

Example A burglar trips and injures himself on a bicycle that a homeowner negligently left out on the property. The owner is not liable.

However, a landowner or tenant does owe a **duty not to willfully or wantonly injure a trespasser.**

Example A homeowner cannot purposely set traps to injure trespassers.

Landowners and tenants may use lawful force to protect themselves and others from being harmed by trespassers.

Several states have eliminated the invitee-licensee-trespasser distinction. These states hold that owners and renters owe a duty of ordinary care to all persons who enter upon the property, even trespassers.

Attractive Nuisance Doctrine. An exception to the general rule regarding trespassers applies to children. A landowner or possessor of land is subject to liability for physical harm to children caused by an artificial condition on the land if it is an attractive nuisance. The attractive nuisance doctrine applies to artificial conditions on land, and not to natural conditions of the land. In order for a plaintiff child trespasser to prevail under the **attractive nuisance doctrine**, he or she must prove the existence of the following five factors:

attractive nuisance doctrine
A special tort rule that imposes liability on a landowner or possessor of land to children who have trespassed onto the owner's or possessor's real property by an attractive nuisance with the intent to play and are injured or killed while doing so.

1. The defendant knew or should have known there was an artificial condition on the land and that children were likely to trespass.
2. The defendant knew or should have known the artificial condition posed an unreasonable risk of injury or death to children.
3. The child did not realize the risk involved because of his or her age.
4. The utility of the defendant maintaining the condition and the burden of eliminating the danger were slight compared to the risk to children.
5. The defendant's failure to exercise reasonable care to eliminate the danger or otherwise protect the child caused the child's injury.

Examples Examples of attractive nuisances would be a swimming pool that is unfenced or not safely fenced to prevent entry by children; discarded appliances such as refrigerators in which children can be trapped; construction sites with easy access to dangerous conditions such as unfinished floors of buildings; wells and open pits; and abandoned automobiles that can be set in motion and trap or pin children.

Property has its duties as well as its rights.
Benjamin Disraeli
Sybil, Book II, Chapter XI (1845)

Several states have abandoned the attractive nuisance doctrine.

In the following case, the court had to decide whether the attractive nuisance doctrine applied.

CASE 48.2 STATE COURT CASE Attractive Nuisance Doctrine

Hayes v. D.C.I. Properties-D Ky, LLC and The Nelson Stark Company

563 S.W.3d 619 (2018)
Supreme Court of Kentucky

"Kentucky law remains steadfast in its adherence to the traditional notion that duty is associated with the status of the injured party as invitee, licensee, or trespasser."

—Laurance VanMeter, Justice

Facts

One weekend evening, Alex Hayes, who was 16 years and 7 months old, and several of his friends entered a construction site owned by D.C.I. Properties-D Ky, LLC (DCI) without knowledge or permission. The site was being prepared for a residential development by the contractor, The Nelson Stark Company (NSC), whose employees had left several pieces of heavy equipment on the property. Alex and his friends spent several hours there, drinking whiskey and smoking marijuana. Alex, earlier in the evening, had removed the keys from a piece of machinery because he thought that a friend might get hurt if he started the machine.

As Alex and one of his friends started to leave, Alex climbed on a compactor owned by NSC, and despite his friend's protests, started it and began driving it up a floodwall. As Alex drove the compactor back down the floodwall, the compactor tipped over. Alex was thrown off the machine, and the compactor landed on his right leg, severely injuring it. Alex, through his parents, sued DCI and NSC, alleging negligence because the equipment constituted an attractive nuisance. The defendants asserted that Alex was a trespasser to whom they owed no duty except to not wantonly and willfully injure him, and that Alex was not a child, and therefore the attractive nuisance doctrine did not apply. The trial court granted the defendants' motion for summary judgment and dismissed the case. The court of appeals affirmed. Alex appealed.

Issue

Are the defendants liable to Alex under the attractive nuisance doctrine?

Language of the Court

Kentucky law remains steadfast in its adherence to the traditional notion that duty is associated with the status of the injured party as invitee, licensee, or trespasser. A possessor of land is subject to liability for physical harm to children trespassing thereon caused by an artificial condition upon the land if the possessor fails to exercise reasonable care to eliminate the danger or otherwise to protect children.

When a youth has grown beyond the protection humanely afforded to a child of tender years from his indiscretion and lack of capacity to appreciate peril, he is not entitled to the benefit of the attractive nuisance doctrine. The evidence in this case clearly demonstrates that Alex not only was capable of appreciating but also in fact did appreciate the risk of operating a piece of heavy machinery.

Decision

The Supreme Court of Kentucky affirmed the court of appeals' decision affirming the trial court's grant of summary judgment in favor of the defendants.

Critical Legal Thinking Questions

What is the attractive nuisance doctrine? Do you think it should have applied in this case? Up to what age should the attractive nuisance doctrine protect children?

Zoning

48.10 Describe zoning laws and how they apply to real property.

zoning ordinances
Local laws that are adopted by municipalities and local governments to regulate land use within their boundaries.

Most counties and municipalities have enacted **zoning ordinances** to regulate land use. **Zoning** generally (1) establishes land use districts within the municipality (i.e., areas are generally designated residential, commercial, or industrial); (2) restricts the height, size, and location of buildings on a building site; and (3) establishes aesthetic requirements or limitations for the exterior of buildings.

Example If a zoning ordinance designates an area as zoned for only single-family houses, no apartment buildings, commercial buildings, or other nonconforming structures can be built in this zoned area. If a zoning ordinance states that only apartment buildings up to four stories high can be built in a certain multifamily zoned area, buildings taller than four stories cannot be built in this area.

Example A landowner in an area zoned for traditional-style homes applies to build a geodesic dome made of glass and steel in this area. The zoning commission can rightfully turn down a building permit for this proposed house if it does not meet the aesthetic requirements established for the area.

A **zoning commission** usually formulates zoning ordinances, conducts public hearings, and makes recommendations to the city council, which must vote to enact an ordinance. Once a zoning ordinance is enacted, the zoning commission enforces it. If landowners believe that a zoning ordinance is illegal or that it has been unlawfully applied to them or their property, they may institute a court proceeding, seeking judicial review of the ordinance or its application.

An owner who wants to use his or her property for a use different from that permitted under a current zoning ordinance may seek relief from the ordinance by obtaining a **variance**. To obtain a variance, the landowner must prove that the ordinance causes an undue hardship by preventing him or her from making a reasonable return on the land as zoned. Variances are usually difficult to obtain.

variance
An exception that permits a type of building or use in an area that would not otherwise be allowed by a zoning ordinance.

Zoning laws act prospectively; that is, uses and buildings that already exist in the zoned area are permitted to continue even though they do not fit within new zoning ordinances. Such uses are called **nonconforming uses**. For example, if a new zoning ordinance making an area a residential zone is enacted, an existing funeral parlor is a nonconforming use.

nonconforming uses
Uses for real estate and buildings that already exist in a zoned area that are permitted to continue even though they do not fit within a new zoning use established for the area.

Key Terms and Concepts

Abstract of title (850)
Actual and exclusive (851)
Adverse possession (850)
Air rights (842)
Air space parcel (842)
Attorney's opinion (850)
Attractive nuisance doctrine (857)
Building (841)
Certificate of title (850)
Closing (settlement) (847)
Community property (844)
Concurrent ownership (co-ownership) (843)
Condominium (845)
Constructive notice (848)
Continuous and peaceful (851)
Cooperative (845)
County recorder's office (848)
Deed (847)
Dominant estate (852)
Duty not to willfully or wantonly injure a trespasser (857)
Duty of ordinary care (855)
Easement (852)
Easement appurtenant (852)
Easement by implication (854)
Easement by necessity (854)
Easement by prescription (854)
Easement by reservation (853)
Easement in gross (853)
Estate in land (estate) (842)
Estate pur autre vie (843)
Express easement (852)
Fee simple absolute (fee simple) (842)
Fee simple defeasible (qualified fee) (843)
Fixtures (841)
Freehold estate (842)
Future interest (846)
General warranty deed (grant deed) (847)
Gift (849)
Grantee (847)
Grantor (847)
Hostile and adverse (851)
Implied easement (854)
Inheritance (849)
Invitee (855)
Joint tenancy (843)
Joint tenants (843)
Land (841)
License of real property (855)
Licensee (856)
Licensor (855)
Life estate (843)
Life tenant (843)
Marketable title (good title) (849)
Mode-of-operation rule (856)
Negative easement (853)
Nonconforming use (859)
Nonpossessory interest (852)
Open and obvious danger (856)
Open, visible, and notorious (851)
Period of redemption (849)
Plant life and vegetation (841)
Premises liability (855)

Present possessory interest (842)
Profit-à-prendre (profit) (855)
Quiet title action (850)
Quitclaim deed (848)
Real estate sales contract (847)
Real property (841)
Recording statute (848)
Reformation of a deed (848)
Remainder (846)
Remainder beneficiary (846)
Reversion (846)
Right of survivorship of joint tenants (843)
Sale (conveyance) (847)
Separate property (845)
Servient estate (852)
Special warranty deed (limited warranty deed) (847)
Statutorily prescribed period of time (850)
Subsurface rights (mineral rights) (841)
Surface rights (841)
Tax sale (849)
Tenancy by the entirety (844)
Tenancy in common (844)
Tenants in common (844)
Title insurance (849)
Torrens system (850)
Trespasser (857)
Trust (849)
Variance (859)
Will (849)
Zoning (858)
Zoning commission (859)
Zoning ordinance (858)

Critical Legal Thinking Cases

48.1 Easement Herbert and Juanita Bogy (Bogy) and The Willows, LLC owned adjoining pieces of farmland in Jefferson County, Arkansas. Bogy cannot access a portion of his property because a Union Pacific railroad track bisects the property. For 39 years, Bogy and his farming tenants accessed that portion of the property by driving on a road that runs across The Willows' property. Bogy had never requested nor received permission from The Willows to use this road. After 36 years, The Willows blocked Bogy's access to the road. Bogy sued, alleging that there existed a prescriptive easement across The Willows' property. Has a prescriptive easement been created in favor of Bogy to use the road that runs across The Willows' property? *The Willows, LLC v. Bogy*, 2013 Ark. App. Lexis 66 (Court of Appeals of Arkansas, 2013)

48.2 Attractive Nuisance Doctrine Sixteen-year-old A.C. and his cousins decided to go "roofing"—climbing on roofs after dark. They climbed up onto the roof of a one-story building owned by Gateway Community Church (Gateway). Unbeknownst to A.C. and his cousins, and also unbeknownst to Gateway, the building contained an oval sign that was improperly wired. Due to the faulty wiring, the metal flashing on the roof had become electrified. When the boys decided to vacate the roof, the two cousins made it down safely. But on A.C.'s way down, his foot got caught on the metal flashing, and he was electrocuted for 10 to 15 seconds. A.C. died 10 days later from complications from the electrocution.

Lawrence and Sarah Jean Colosimo, A.C.'s parents and heirs, brought a wrongful death and survivor's lawsuit against Gateway to recover damages for negligence. The Colosimos alleged that Gateway was liable to their son under the attractive nuisance doctrine. Gateway moved for summary judgment, arguing that it owed A.C. no duty of ordinary care because he was a trespasser, and that the attractive nuisance doctrine did not apply because Gateway had no knowledge of the dangerous condition. Is Gateway liable for negligence to A.C.? *Colosimo v. Gateway Community Church*, 424 P.3d 866 (Supreme Court of Utah, 2018)

48.3 Adverse Possession In 2006, Allen and Michelle Loun (Loun) purchased real property in Kittitas County, Washington. In 2008, Michael and Lynn Whelan (Whelan) purchased adjacent real property south of Loun's property. A cinderblock and wood fence that had been in existence for more than 22 years separated the two properties. It was discovered that the fence was not situated on the legally described boundary line but was over the legal lot line by 12.25 feet on the Loun property, thus favoring the property owned by Whelan. In July 2008, Loun removed the fence. Whelan sued to quiet title in the 12.25-foot strip of land, alleging that they owned the disputed property by adverse possession. At trial, Haberman and Vasquez, the successive prior owners of Whelan's property since 1986, testified that they considered the fence the lot line. The statutorily prescribed period for adverse possession in Washington is 10 years. Did Whelan acquire the disputed property by adverse possession? *Whelan v. Loun*, 2011 Wash. App. Lexis 2768 (Court of Appeals of Washington, 2011)

48.4 Known and Obvious Danger Roland Critchfield went to Buffalo Wild Wings, a restaurant and sports bar, to meet a group of friends. The Buffalo Wild Wings was owned by Blazin Wings, Inc. (Blazin). Before joining his friends, Critchfield went to the restroom. The restroom featured two urinals and a toilet stall. As he entered, he saw a yellow sign on the floor by one urinal that said: "Caution: Wet Floor." Critchfield observed more water than you would expect to see on a public restroom floor, indicating that either a toilet had overflowed or cleaning had not been finished. There was a dry path to one urinal and to a toilet stall. Critchfield did not proceed along the dry path. Instead, he stepped in front of the caution sign and walked through a puddle of water to the nearest urinal. Upon finishing at the urinal, Critchfield headed back toward the sink, but before reaching the sink he slipped and fell, and was injured by the fall. Critchfield sued Blazin to recover damages for negligence. Blazin asserted that it owed no duty to Critchfield with respect to the known and obvious danger of the wet floor adjacent to the urinal Critchfield used. Is Blazin liable to Critchfield? *Critchfield v. Blazin Wings, Inc.*, No. 17-4100 (United States Court of Appeals for the Tenth Circuit, 2018)

Ethics Case

48.5 **Ethics Case** Ardell and Eileen Robenolt (Robenolt) owned 48 acres in Mahoning County, Ohio. J. Gary Zyznar contacted Robenolt about purchasing a 13-acre portion of the land with the intention of building a home on it. Robenolt agreed to sell the property but only if they would retain the mineral rights to the property. Zyznar agreed, and a sales contract was drawn up and signed by the parties wherein Robenolt would sell the property to Zyznar for $300,000 and Robenolt would retain the mineral rights to the property. The transaction closed, and a deed was filed with the county clerk. Subsequently, it was discovered that the deed did not reserve the mineral rights to Robenolt. When Zyznar refused to sign a corrective deed, Robenolt sued Zyznar seeking reformation of the deed based upon mutual mistake. Was there a mutual mistake that would warrant reformation of the deed? Did Zyznar act ethically in this case? *Robenolt v. Zyznar*, 2014 Ohio App. Lexis 2541 (Court of Appeals of Ohio, 2014)

CHAPTER

49 Landlord–Tenant Law and Land Use Regulation

APARTMENT BUILDING, NEW YORK CITY
Individuals often rent apartments. Businesses often rent office and commercial space.

Henry R. Cheeseman

Learning Objectives

After studying this chapter, you should be able to:

49.1 Define a *landlord–tenant relationship* and describe how it is created.

49.2 List and describe a landlord's duties to a tenant.

49.3 Define the legal doctrine *implied warranty of habitability*.

49.4 List and describe a tenant's duties to a landlord.

49.5 Explain how a landlord may transfer leased property.

49.6 Define *assignment* and *sublease* of a lease by a tenant.

49.7 Describe how the government regulates the landlord–tenant relationship.

49.8 List and describe the antidiscrimination laws that apply to real estate.

49.9 Describe the government's power of eminent domain in taking real property.

> "Good fences make good neighbors."
>
> —Robert Frost
> *"Mending Wall" (1914)*

Introduction to Landlord–Tenant Law and Land Use Regulation

Individuals and families rent houses and apartments, professionals and businesses lease office space, small businesses rent stores, and businesses lease commercial and manufacturing facilities. In these situations, a *landlord–tenant relationship* is created. The parties to a landlord–tenant relationship have certain legal rights and owe duties that are governed by a mixture of real estate and contract law.

Property has its duties as well as its rights.
Benjamin Disraeli
Sybil, Book II, Chapter XI (1845)

The ownership and possession of real estate in the United States is commonly a private affair. However, the ownership and leasing of real property is not free from government regulation. Federal, state, and local governments have enacted laws that regulate the ownership, possession, lease, and use of real property. These laws include antidiscrimination laws in leasing and selling real property. The government may also take private property for public use under its power of eminent domain, assuming that certain requirements are met and just compensation is paid to the owner.

This chapter covers the law concerning landlord–tenant relationships and government regulation of real estate.

Landlord–Tenant Relationship

49.1 Define a *landlord–tenant relationship* and describe how it is created.

A **landlord–tenant relationship** is created when the owner of a freehold estate in real estate (i.e., an estate in fee or a life estate) transfers a right to possess the owner's property exclusively and temporarily. The tenant receives a **nonfreehold estate** in the real property; that is, the tenant has a right to possession of the property but not title to the property.

The tenant's interest in the real property is called a **leasehold estate**, or **leasehold**. The owner who transfers the leasehold estate is called the **landlord**, or **lessor**. The party to whom the leasehold estate is transferred is called the **tenant**, or **lessee**. A landlord–tenant relationship is illustrated in **Exhibit 49.1**.

landlord–tenant relationship
A relationship that is created when the owner of a freehold estate transfers to another person the right to possess the owner's real property exclusively and temporarily.

nonfreehold estate
An estate where the tenant has a right to possess the real property but does not own title to the property.

leasehold estate (leasehold)
A tenant's interest in property.

landlord (lessor)
An owner who transfers a leasehold.

tenant (lessee)
The party to whom a leasehold is transferred.

Lease

A rental agreement between a landlord and a tenant is called a **lease**. Leases can generally be either oral or written, but most Statutes of Frauds require that leases for periods of time longer than one year be in writing. A lease must contain the essential terms of the parties' agreement. A lease is often a form contract that is prepared by the landlord and presented to the tenant. This practice is particularly true of residential leases. Other leases are often negotiated between the parties. For example, Bank of America's lease of a branch office would be negotiated with the owner of the building.

There are four types of *tenancies*: (1) *tenancy for years*, (2) *periodic tenancy*, (3) *tenancy at will*, and (4) *tenancy at sufferance*. They are described in the following paragraphs.

lease
A transfer of the right to the possession and use of real property for a set term in return for certain consideration; the rental agreement between a landlord and a tenant.

Tenancy for Years

A **tenancy for years** is created when a landlord and a tenant agree on a specific duration for the lease. Any lease for a stated period—no matter how long or short—is called a tenancy for years. A tenancy for years terminates automatically, without notice, on the expiration of the stated term.

tenancy for years
A tenancy created when a landlord and a tenant agree on a specific duration for a lease.

Exhibit 49.1 **LANDLORD–TENANT RELATIONSHIP**

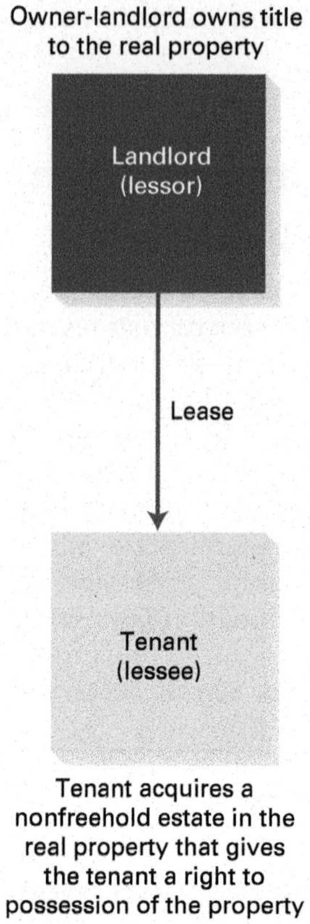
Owner-landlord owns title to the real property
Landlord (lessor)
Lease
Tenant (lessee)
Tenant acquires a nonfreehold estate in the real property that gives the tenant a right to possession of the property

Examples A business leases an office in a high-rise office building on a 10-year lease. This lease terminates after 10 years. A family leases a cabin for the month of July in the summer. This lease expires on July 31.

Periodic Tenancy

periodic tenancy
A tenancy created when a lease specifies intervals at which payments are due but does not specify how long the lease is for.

A **periodic tenancy** is created when a lease specifies intervals at which payments are due but does not specify the duration of the lease. A lease that states, "Rent is due on the first day of the month" establishes a periodic tenancy. Many such leases are created by implication. A periodic tenancy may be terminated by either party at the end of any payment interval, but adequate notice of the termination must be given. Under common law, the notice period equals the length of the payment period. That is, a **month-to-month tenancy** requires a one-month notice of termination.

Tenancy at Will

tenancy at will
A tenancy created by a lease that may be terminated at any time by either party.

A lease that may be terminated at any time by either party creates a **tenancy at will**. A tenancy at will may be created expressly (e.g., "to tenant so long as landlord wishes") but is more likely to be created by implication. Most states have enacted statutes requiring minimum advance notice for the termination of a tenancy at will. The death of either party terminates a tenancy at will.

Example A lessee and landlord agree to a lease that can be canceled at any time by either party. This is a tenancy at will.

Tenancy at Sufferance

tenancy at sufferance
A tenancy created when a tenant retains possession of property after the expiration of another tenancy or a life estate without the owner's consent.

A **tenancy at sufferance** is created when a tenant retains possession of property after the expiration of a tenancy or a life estate without the owner's consent. That is, the owner suffers the **wrongful possession** of his or her property by the holdover tenant. This is not a true tenancy but merely the possession of property without right. Technically, a tenant at sufferance is a trespasser. A tenant at sufferance is liable for the payment of rent during the period of sufferance. Most states require an owner to go through certain legal proceedings, called an **eviction proceeding** or **unlawful detainer action**, to evict a holdover tenant. A few states allow owners to use self-help to evict a holdover tenant, as long as force is not used.

eviction proceeding (unlawful detainer action) A legal process that a landlord must complete to evict a holdover tenant.

Example A landlord enters into a lease whereby she rents an apartment to a tenant for a one-year period, which expires on September 1, 2024. If the tenant remains longer than this date, it is a tenancy at sufferance.

CONCEPT SUMMARY

TYPES OF TENANCIES

Types of Tenancy	Description
Tenancy for years	Continues for the duration of the lease and terminates automatically on expiration of the stated term without requiring notice. It does not terminate on the death of either party.
Periodic tenancy	Continues from payment interval to payment interval. It may be terminated by either party with adequate notice. It does not terminate on the death of either party.
Tenancy at will	Continues at the will of the parties and may be terminated by either party at any time with adequate notice. It terminates on the death of either party.
Tenancy at sufferance	Arises when a tenant wrongfully occupies real property after the expiration of another tenancy or life estate. It continues until the owner either evicts the tenant or holds him or her over for another term. It terminates on the death of the tenant.

Landlord'S Duties to a Tenant

49.2 List and describe a landlord's duties to a tenant.

In a landlord–tenant relationship, the law imposes certain legal duties on the landlord. That is, the tenant has lawful rights that can be enforced against the landlord. The landlord owes the following duties to the tenant: (1) duty to deliver possession of the leased premises to the tenant, (2) duty not to interfere with the tenant's right of quiet enjoyment of the premises, and (3) duty to maintain the leased premises.

Duty to Deliver Possession

A landlord owes a **duty to deliver possession** of the leased premises to the lessee. A lease grants the tenant **exclusive possession** of the leased premises until (1) the term of the lease expires or (2) the tenant defaults on the obligations under the lease. The landlord is obligated to deliver possession of the leased premises to the tenant on the date the lease term begins. A landlord may not enter leased premises unless the right is specifically reserved in the lease.

Duty Not to Interfere with a Tenant's Right to Quiet Enjoyment

covenant of quiet enjoyment A covenant that says a landlord may not interfere with the tenant's quiet and peaceful possession, use, and enjoyment of the leased premises.

A landlord owes a **duty not to interfere with a tenant's right to quiet enjoyment** of the leased premises. The law implies a **covenant of quiet enjoyment** in all leases. Under this covenant, the landlord may not interfere with the tenant's quiet and peaceful possession, use, and enjoyment of the leased premises. The covenant is

Landlords grow rich in their sleep.
John Stuart Mill (1806–1873)

breached if the landlord, or anyone acting with the landlord's consent, interferes with the tenant's use and enjoyment of the property. This interference is called **wrongful eviction**, or **unlawful eviction**.

Examples If a landlord evicts a tenant by physically preventing the tenant from possessing or using the leased premises, this is wrongful eviction. If a landlord causes the leased premises to become unfit for the tenant's intended use (e.g., by failing to provide electricity) and the tenant leaves the premises, this is called **constructive eviction** and constitutes a wrongful eviction.

If the landlord refuses to cure a defect after a reasonable time, a tenant who has been *constructively evicted* may (1) sue for damages and possession of the premises or (2) treat the lease as terminated, vacate the premises, and cease paying rent. The landlord is not responsible for wrongful acts of third persons that were done without the landlord's authorization.

Duty to Maintain the Leased Premises

In common law, the doctrine of *caveat lessee* ("lessee beware") applied to leases. The landlord made no warranties about the quality of leased property and had no duty to repair it. The tenant took the property "as is." Modern real estate law, however, imposes certain statutory and judicially implied duties on landlords to repair and maintain leased premises. Thus, the landlord owes a **duty to maintain the leased premises** as provided in the lease, by express law, and as implied by law.

building codes (housing codes)
State and local statutes that impose specific standards on property owners to maintain and repair leased premises.

States and local municipalities have enacted statutes called **building codes**, or **housing codes**. These statutes impose specific standards on property owners to maintain and repair leased premises. They often provide certain minimum standards regarding heat, water, light, and other services. Depending on the statute, violators may be subject to fines by the government, loss of their claim for rent, and imprisonment for serious violations.

Implied Warranty of Habitability

49.3 Define the legal doctrine *implied warranty of habitability*.

implied warranty of habitability
A warranty that provides that leased premises must be fit, safe, and suitable for ordinary residential use.

The courts of many jurisdictions hold that an **implied warranty of habitability** applies to residential leases for their duration. This warranty provides that the leased premises must be fit, safe, and suitable for ordinary residential use.

Examples Unchecked rodent infestation, leaking roofs, unworkable bathroom facilities, and the like have been held to breach the implied warranty of habitability. On the other hand, a small crack in a wall or some paint peeling from a door does not breach this warranty.

Property is an instrument of humanity. Humanity is not an instrument of property.
Woodrow Wilson
(1856–1924)
Twenty-eighth President of the United States

State statutes and judicial decisions provide various remedies that can be used if a landlord's failure to maintain or repair leased premises affects the tenant's use or enjoyment of the premises. Generally, the tenant may (1) withhold from the rent the amount by which the defect reduced the value of the premises to the tenant, (2) repair the defect and deduct the cost of repairs from the rent due for the leased premises, (3) cancel the lease if the failure to repair constitutes constructive eviction, or (4) sue for damages in the amount by which the landlord's failure to repair the defect reduced the value of the leasehold.

In the following case, the court had to decide whether a landlord was liable to a tenant.

CASE 49.1 *STATE COURT CASE Landlord's Liability*

New Haverford Partnership v. Stroot

772 A.2d 792, 2001 Del. Lexis 2278 (2001)
Supreme Court of Delaware

"The presumption in Delaware is that a jury verdict is 'correct and just.'"

—Carolyn Berger, Justice

Facts

Elizabeth Stroot was a tenant at Haverford Place apartments, which was owned by New Haverford Partnership. Stroot was a 33-year-old graduate student. After moving into her apartment, Stroot noticed mold around the windows and in the bathroom. Although she attempted to remove the mold with bleach, the mold kept returning. There were also water leaks in the bathroom ceiling and in the kitchen and bathroom.

Stroot moved to another apartment at Haverford Place. Here, the bathroom ceiling leaked. Within a few months, the leaks caused holes in the drywall, and the edges of the holes were covered with a black substance. When Stroot showered, black water ran out of the holes. Stroot complained to the management, but nothing was done. One evening, Stroot's bathroom ceiling collapsed, and water flooded her floor. The exposed ceiling was covered with black, green, orange, and white mold. The room had a strong, nauseating odor. Stroot slept in the apartment that night. The next morning, she could not breathe. Stroot called an ambulance and was taken to the hospital. When she was released from the hospital, Stroot decided she could no longer live at Haverford Place.

Subsequently, Stroot was forced to go to the emergency room of the hospital seven times. She spent time as an inpatient at the hospital. Stroot sued New Haverford Partnership to recover damages for negligence for causing her medical problems because it permitted the water leaks and mold problem to persist in her apartments. Stroot incurred more than $28,000 in medical expenses. She alleged that she suffered asthma and allergies and cognitive deficits in the areas of attention, concentration, and executive functioning because of New Haverford's negligence.

The jury found the landlord liable for negligence and awarded Stroot $1 million. The landlord appealed the finding and made a motion for remittitur, asking the court that if it was held liable for negligence to reduce the amount of the award from $1 million to $250,000.

Issue

Was New Haverford Partnership liable, and if so, was the amount of the award of damages to Stroot appropriate?

Language of the Court

The presumption in Delaware is that a jury verdict is "correct and just." The jury may have chosen to accept testimony that Stroot's cognitive deficits in three areas—attention, concentration, and executive functioning—were proximately caused by her long-term exposure to microbial contamination at Haverford Place. Given the permanent nature of Plaintiff's injuries as well as the physical and emotional pain and suffering Stroot will have to endure for the remainder of her life, the Court does not find the $1,000,000 verdict to Stroot unreasonable, nor is its conscience shocked.

Decision

The supreme court of Delaware held that New Haverford Partnership was liable for negligence and that the award of damages to Stroot was supported by the evidence. The supreme court of Delaware affirmed the trial court's judgment in favor of Stroot.

Critical Legal Thinking Questions

Do you think the landlord was negligent in this case? Did New Haverford Partnership act ethically in this case? Do you think the award of damages in this case was appropriate?

Tenant's Duties to a Landlord

49.4 List and describe a tenant's duties to a landlord.

In a landlord–tenant relationship, the law imposes certain legal duties on the tenant. That is, the landlord has lawful rights that can be enforced against the tenant. The duties that a tenant owes to a landlord are discussed in the following paragraphs.

Duty to Pay Rent

A commercial or residential tenant owes a duty to pay the agreed-on amount of **rent** for the leased premises to the landlord at the agreed-on time and terms. This is referred to as the tenant's **duty to pay rent**. Generally, rent is payable in advance (e.g., on the first day of the month for use that month), although the lease may provide for other times and methods for payment. Reasonable late charges may be assessed on rent that is overdue.

gross lease
A lease in which the tenant pays a gross sum to the landlord and the landlord is responsible for paying the utilities, insurance, property taxes, and assessments on the property.

In a **gross lease**, the tenant pays a gross sum to the landlord. The landlord is responsible for paying the utilities, insurance, property taxes, and assessments on the property. If a tenant is responsible for paying rent and utilities, which is often the case in residential leases, it is called a **modified gross lease**.

Several of the most common commercial rental arrangements are the following:

net, net, net lease (triple net lease)
A lease where the tenant is responsible for paying the rent, utilities, insurance, and property taxes.

- **Net lease.** In a **net lease** arrangement, the tenant is responsible for paying rent and property taxes.
- **Double net lease.** In a **double net lease** arrangement, the tenant is responsible for paying rent, property taxes, and utilities.
- **Net, net, net lease (or triple net lease).** In a **net, net, net lease (triple net lease)** arrangement, the tenant is responsible for paying rent, property taxes, utilities, and insurance.

On nonpayment of rent, the landlord is entitled to recover possession of the leased premises from the tenant. This may require the landlord to *evict* the tenant. Most states provide a summary procedure called unlawful detainer action that a landlord can bring to evict a tenant. The landlord may also sue to recover the unpaid rent from the tenant. The more modern rule requires the landlord to make reasonable efforts to release the premises. This is called **mitigation of damages**.

CONCEPT SUMMARY

TENANT'S DUTY TO PAY RENT

Rental Agreement	Description
Gross lease	The tenant is responsible for paying rent.
Net lease	The tenant is responsible for paying rent and property taxes.
Double net lease	The tenant is responsible for paying rent, property taxes, and utilities.
Triple net lease	The tenant is responsible for paying rent, property taxes, utilities, and insurance.

Duty Not to Use Leased Premises for Illegal or Nonstipulated Purposes

A tenant may use leased property for any lawful purposes permitted by the lease. Leases often stipulate that the leased premises can be used only for specific purposes. The tenant owes a **duty not to use leased premises for illegal or**

nonstipulated purposes. If the tenant uses the leased premises for unlawful purposes (e.g., operating an illegal gambling casino) or nonstipulated purposes (e.g., operating a restaurant in a residence), the landlord may terminate the lease, evict the tenant, and sue for damages.

Duty Not to Commit Waste

A tenant is under a **duty not to commit waste** to the leasehold. Waste occurs when the tenant causes substantial and permanent damage to the leased premises that decreases the value of the property and the landlord's reversionary interest in it. Waste does not include ordinary wear and tear. The landlord can recover damages from the tenant for waste.

Example It would be waste if the floor of the premises buckled because a tenant permitted heavy equipment to be placed on the premises. It would not be waste if the paint chipped from the walls because of the passage of time.

Duty Not to Disturb Other Tenants

A tenant owes a **duty not to disturb other tenants** in the same building. A landlord may evict a tenant who interferes with other tenants' use and quiet enjoyment.

Example A tenant in an apartment building breaches the duty not to disturb other tenants if he or she disturbs the sleep of other tenants by playing loud music throughout the night.

Transfer of Leased Property by Landlords

49.5 Explain how a landlord may transfer leased property.

An owner-landlord can sell, gift, devise, or otherwise transfer ownership in property that is subject to leases. If complete title is transferred, the property is subject to the existing lease. The new owner-landlord cannot alter the terms of the lease (e.g., raise the rent) during the term of the lease unless the lease so provides.

A landlord can sell the right to receive rents. In such case, after proper notice, the tenants are to pay rent to the designated party. The landlord still owes normal duties to the tenants, however.

Assignment and Sublease of a Lease by Tenants

49.6 Define *assignment* and *sublease* of a lease by a tenant.

Unless otherwise restricted by the lease, a tenant may transfer a lease either by *assignment of the lease* or by *sublease* to another party. These transactions are discussed in the following paragraphs.

Assignment of a Lease by a Tenant

If a tenant transfers all of the interests under a lease, it is an **assignment of a lease**. The original tenant is the **assignor**, and the new tenant is the **assignee** (see **Exhibit 49.2**). Under an assignment, the assignee acquires all the rights that the assignor had under the lease. The assignee is obligated to perform the duties that the assignor had under the lease. That is, the assignee must pay the rent and perform other covenants contained in the original lease.

The assignor remains responsible for his or her obligations under the lease unless specifically released from doing so by the landlord. If the landlord recovers from the assignor, the assignor has a course of action to recover from the assignee. Many leases contain a provision that prohibits a lessee from assigning a lease without the lessor's consent.

assignment of a lease
A transfer by a tenant of his or her rights under a lease to another party.

assignor
A tenant who transfers rights under a lease.

assignee
A party to whom a tenant transfers rights under a lease.

Exhibit 49.2 ASSIGNMENT OF A LEASE

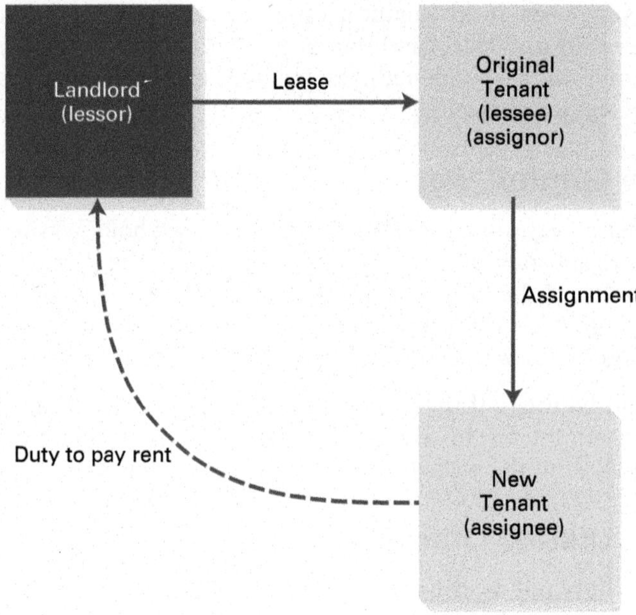

Sublease by a Tenant

sublease
An arrangement in which a tenant transfers some of his or her rights under a lease to another party.

sublessor
Original tenant who transfers some or all of his or her rights under a lease.

sublessee
The new tenant in a sublease arrangement.

If a tenant transfers only some rights under a lease, it is a **sublease**. The original tenant is the **sublessor**, and the new tenant is the **sublessee** (see **Exhibit 49.3**). The sublessor is not released from his or her obligations under the lease unless specifically released by the landlord.

Subleases differ from assignments in important ways. In a sublease, no legal relationship is formed between the landlord and the sublessee. Therefore, the sublessee does not acquire rights under the original lease. For example, a sublessee would not acquire the sublessor's option to renew a lease. Further, the landlord cannot sue the sublessee to recover rent payments or enforce duties under the original lease.

In most cases, tenants cannot sublease their leases without the landlord's consent. This right protects the landlord from the transfer of the leasehold to someone who might damage the property or not have the financial resources to pay the rent.

Exhibit 49.3 SUBLEASE

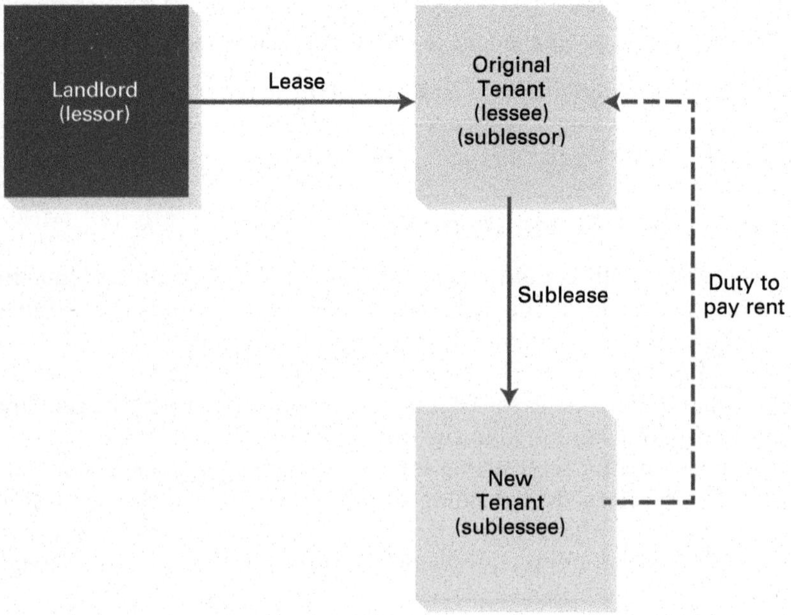

Government Regulation of Real Property

49.7 Describe how the government regulates the landlord–tenant relationship.

Although the United States has the most advanced private property system in the world, ownership and possession of real estate are not free from government regulation. Pursuant to constitutional authority, federal, state, and local governments have enacted laws that regulate the ownership, sale and transfer, possession, lease, and use of real property. These laws include zoning, rent control, antidiscrimination, and environmental laws. In addition, governments are provided the constitutional right to take private property for public use under certain conditions.

The following feature discusses rent control.

Contemporary Environment

Rent Control

Many local communities across the country have enacted rent-control ordinances. A **rent-control ordinance** is a law that stipulates the amount of rent that a landlord can charge for residential housing. Most of these ordinances fix the rent at a specific amount and provide for minor annual increases. Landlords, of course, oppose rent control, arguing that rent-control ordinances are merely a regulatory tax that transfers wealth from landlords to tenants. Tenants and proponents of rent control say that it is necessary to create affordable housing, particularly in high-rent urban areas.

Many cities have adopted rent control, including New York City; Santa Monica and San Francisco, California; Newark, New Jersey; and others. The U.S. Supreme Court has upheld the use of rent control.[1]

Antidiscrimination Laws and Real Property

49.8 List and describe the antidiscrimination laws that apply to real estate.

Federal and state governments have enacted statutes that prohibit discrimination in the sale and rental of real property. Several important federal statutes that prohibit discrimination in housing are the *Civil Rights Act of 1866*, the *Fair Housing Act of 1968*, and the *Americans with Disabilities Act of 1990*. These statutes are discussed in the following paragraphs.

Civil Rights Act of 1866

The **Civil Rights Act of 1866**[2] was passed at the end of the Civil War. This federal statute prohibits discrimination in the selling and renting of property based on race or color. It was designed to eliminate historically prevalent discrimination in housing. The law applies to all rentals of public and private property, property owners renting separate units within a dwelling in which they live, and persons renting space in their own homes.

The following feature discusses the Fair Housing Act.

Civil Rights Act of 1866
A federal statute that prohibits discrimination in the selling and renting of property based on race or color.

Fair Housing Act of 1968
A federal statute that makes it unlawful for a party to refuse to sell, rent, finance, or advertise housing to any person because of his or her race, color, national origin, sex, religion, disability, or family status, subject to several exceptions.

Landmark Law

Fair Housing Act

The **Fair Housing Act of 1968**,[3] as amended, is a federal statute that makes it unlawful for a party to refuse to sell, rent, finance, or advertise housing to any person because of race, color, national origin, sex, religion, disability, or family status (e.g., families with children under 18 years of age, pregnant women). These are called *protected classes*. The act applies to sellers, landlords, real estate brokers, banks and mortgage lenders, advertisers, and others involved in the housing market.

Examples Violations include refusing to rent or sell housing, setting different terms and conditions for the sale or rental of housing, falsely denying that housing is available for inspection, persuading owners to rent or sell only to persons who are not members of a protected class

(continued)

(blockbusting), refusing to make a mortgage loan, refusing to provide information regarding loans, imposing different terms or conditions on a loan (different interest rates or fees), discriminating in appraising property, discriminating against persons with a physical or mental disability, and threatening or intimidating anyone from exercising a fair housing right because of his or her protected class status.

The law does not apply to the following: (1) a person who owns a building of four or fewer units and occupies one of the units and leases the others and (2) a person who leases a single-family dwelling and does not own more than three single-family dwellings. To qualify for either exemption, the lessor cannot use a real estate broker or advertise in a discriminating manner.

The Fair Housing Act is administered by the **U.S. Department of Housing and Urban Development (HUD)**, a Cabinet-level department of the executive branch of the federal government. Complaints may be filed with HUD, which then conducts an investigation. If HUD determines that there is reasonable cause to believe that a discriminatory housing practice has occurred, it will hold an administrative hearing. However, either party has the right to elect to have the matter heard in federal court. The law provides for civil and criminal penalties.

Americans with Disabilities Act

The **Americans with Disabilities Act (ADA)**,[4] as amended by the **Americans with Disabilities Act Amendments Act (ADAAA)**,[5] is a federal statute that prohibits discrimination against disabled individuals in employment, public services, public accommodations and services, and telecommunications. **Title III of the Americans with Disabilities Act** prohibits discrimination because of a physical or mental disability in **places of public accommodation** operated by private entities.

Title III of the Americans with Disabilities Act
A section of a federal statute that prohibits discrimination on the basis of physical or mental disability in places of public accommodation operated by private entities.

Title III of the ADA applies to public accommodations and commercial facilities such as motels, hotels, restaurants, theaters, colleges and universities, department stores, retail stores, shopping malls, office buildings, doctor and lawyer offices, banks, recreation facilities, licensing centers, sports stadiums, convention centers, and transportation depots.

Title III requires covered facilities to be designed, constructed, and altered in compliance with specific accessibility requirements established by regulations issued pursuant to the ADA. This includes constructing ramps to accommodate wheelchairs, installing railings next to steps, placing signs written in Braille in elevators and at elevator call buttons, and so on.

New construction must be built in such a manner as to be readily accessible to and usable by disabled individuals. Any alterations made to existing buildings must be made so that the altered portions of the building are readily accessible to disabled individuals to the maximum extent feasible. With respect to existing buildings, architectural barriers must be removed if such removal is readily achievable. In determining when an action is readily achievable, the factors to be considered include the nature and cost of the action, the financial resources of the facility, and the type of operations of the facility.

Critical Legal Thinking Questions

Describe what each of the following federal acts do: (1) Civil Rights Act of 1866, (2) Fair Housing Act, and (3) Americans with Disabilities Act. What is the purpose of these acts? Why were these acts necessary?

The ADA provides for both private right of action and enforcement by the attorney general. Individuals may seek injunctive relief and monetary damages, while the attorney general may seek equitable relief and civil fines for any violation. Complaints are filed with the **U.S. Department of Justice (DOJ)**, which is a Cabinet-level department of the executive branch of the federal government. The DOJ will bring a lawsuit if it finds a pattern or practice of discrimination in violation of Title III or where an act of discrimination raises an issue of general public importance. Parties may also bring private lawsuits.

State and Local Fair Housing Laws

State and local governments may provide fair housing laws that prohibit discrimination in housing. State and local laws that are stricter than federal laws are permitted.

Government Taking of Real Property

49.9 Describe the government's power of eminent domain in taking real property.

At times, governments may need to acquire private property to be used for governmental purposes. For example, when the government needs property to build a new school or a firehouse, or to construct a road or freeway, it may need to acquire the necessary property from private landowners. The **Takings Clause** of the Fifth Amendment to the U.S. Constitution provides the government with this power. Private property can only be taken for *public use*.

Takings Clause
A clause of the U.S. Constitution that allows the government to take property for "public use."

The government obtains the property through a process called **eminent domain**. The government must provide due process and allow the owner of the property to make a case for keeping the property. Some landowners bring lawsuits to defend their right to keep their property. Where the government's need for the property is clearly proven, the government will be awarded the property.

eminent domain
The process by which the government can acquire private property for public use.

The **Just Compensation Clause** of the Fifth Amendment to the U.S. Constitution requires the government to compensate the property owner (and possibly others, such as lessees) when it exercises its power of eminent domain. Anyone who is not satisfied with the compensation offered by the government can bring an action to have the court determine the compensation to be paid.

Just Compensation Clause
A clause of the U.S. Constitution that requires the government to compensate the property owner, and possibly others, when the government takes property under its power of eminent domain.

Federal, state, and local governments may acquire public property for public use.

Example Henry owns a large piece of vacant beachfront property and intends to build his retirement home on the property at some future time. The city in which the property is located wants to build a new public boat dock on the property. The city can use its power of eminent domain to acquire the property for this public use. There has been a taking of property, and the government must pay Henry just compensation.

Government regulation usually does not arise to a taking.

Example A corporation owns a large piece of property with the intent of erecting a 10-story commercial building at some future time. Suppose the government enacts a zoning law that restricts buildings in the area to five stories. Although the corporation would suffer a substantial economic loss because of the zoning law, this is considered government regulation and would not constitute a taking that requires the payment of compensation.

Critical Legal Thinking Questions

What would be the consequences if the government did not have the power of eminent domain? Is it difficult to define "public use"?

The following feature discusses an important U.S. Supreme Court case regarding the government's power of eminent domain.

Critical Legal Thinking

Eminent Domain and the Taking of Real Property

"The concept of the public welfare is broad and exclusive. The values it represents are spiritual as well as physical, aesthetic as well as monetary."

—John Paul Stevens, Justice

The City of New London is located in southeastern Connecticut, at the junction of the Thames River and Long Island Sound. The city, including in the Fort Trumbull area, suffered decades of economic decline. The city's unemployment rate was nearly double the state's unemployment rate, and the city's population was declining.

To try to remedy the situation, state and local officials targeted the City of New London for economic revitalization. The government created the New London Development Corporation (NLDC) to assist the city in planning economic redevelopment. The NLDC finalized an integrated redevelopment plan for 90 acres in the Fort Trumbull area of the city. The redevelopment plan included a waterfront conference hotel, restaurants, stores, a marina, new residences, and office buildings. These projects were to be constructed and owned by private developers and parties selected by the city. The stated purposes were to make the city more attractive, create jobs, and increase tax revenue.

The city purchased most of the land needed for the redevelopment from private owners. However, Susette Kelo and several other homeowners in the redevelopment district (collectively, Kelo) refused to sell their properties. Their properties were well kept and were not blighted. A Connecticut state statute authorized the use of eminent domain to take property to promote economic development. Thus, the NLDC initiated eminent domain actions to take the properties. Kelo defended, arguing that the taking violated the "public use" requirement of the Fifth Amendment to the U.S. Constitution because the properties were being taken from one private party—Kelo and the other holdout homeowners—and were being transferred to other private owners—the developers. The state trial court and the supreme court of Connecticut held for Kelo.

The U.S. Supreme Court, in a 5-to-4 decision, held that the general benefit a community enjoys from economic growth qualifies as a permissible "public use" to support the taking of private property for redevelopment plans under the Takings Clause of the Fifth Amendment. Thus, Kelo's property could be taken by the redevelopment agency and transferred to another private party—the developers—who in turn would build and own commercial property where Kelo's house once stood. The Supreme Court's decision was widely criticized by members of the public who believed the decision violated private property rights. *Kelo v. City of New London, Connecticut*, 545 U.S. 469, 125 S.Ct. 2655, 2005 U.S. Lexis 5011 (Supreme Court of the United States, 2005).

Critical Legal Thinking Questions

What is the purpose of the Takings Clause in the U.S. Constitution? Did the U.S. Supreme Court properly apply the "public use" requirement for a government taking of private property?

Key Terms and Concepts

Americans with Disabilities Act (ADA) (872)
Americans with Disabilities Act Amendments Act (ADAAA) (872)
Assignee (869)
Assignment of a lease (869)
Assignor (869)
Building codes (housing codes) (866)
Civil Rights Act of 1866 (871)
Constructive eviction (866)
Covenant of quiet enjoyment (865)
Double net lease (868)
Duty not to commit waste (869)
Duty not to disturb other tenants (869)
Duty not to interfere with a tenant's right to quiet enjoyment (865)
Duty not to use leased premises for illegal or nonstipulated purposes (868)
Duty to deliver possession (865)
Duty to maintain the leased premises (866)
Duty to pay rent (868)
Eminent domain (873)
Eviction proceeding (unlawful detainer action) (865)
Exclusive possession (865)
Fair Housing Act of 1968 (871)
Gross lease (868)
Implied warranty of habitability (866)
Just Compensation Clause (873)
Landlord (lessor) (863)
Landlord–tenant relationship (863)
Lease (863)
Leasehold estate (leasehold) (863)
Mitigation of damages (868)
Modified gross lease (868)
Month-to-month tenancy (864)
Net lease (868)
Net, net, net lease (triple net lease) (868)
Nonfreehold estate (863)
Periodic tenancy (864)
Places of public accommodation (872)
Rent (868)
Rent-control ordinance (871)
Sublease (870)
Sublessee (870)
Sublessor (870)
Takings Clause (873)
Tenancy at sufferance (864)
Tenancy at will (864)
Tenancy for years (863)
Tenant (lessee) (863)
Title III of the Americans with Disabilities Act (872)
U.S. Department of Housing and Urban Development (HUD) (872)
U.S. Department of Justice (DOJ) (872)
Wrongful eviction (unlawful eviction) (866)
Wrongful possession (864)

Critical Legal Thinking Cases

49.1 Americans with Disabilities Act Title III of the Americans with Disabilities Act (ADA) requires that public accommodations must be "readily accessible to and usable by individuals with disabilities." The U.S. Department of Justice (DOJ) is empowered to adopt regulations to enforce the ADA. The DOJ adopted Standard 4.33.3 for movie theaters, which provides,

> *Wheelchair areas shall be an integral part of any fixed seating plan and shall be provided so as to provide people with physical disabilities a choice of admission prices and lines of sight comparable to those for members of the general public. They shall adjoin an accessible route that also serves as a means of egress in case of emergency. At least one companion fixed seat shall be provided next to each wheelchair seating area. When the seating capacity exceeds 300, wheelchair spaces shall be provided in more than one*

location. Readily removable seats may be installed in wheelchair spaces when the spaces are not required to accommodate wheelchair users.

Cinemark USA, Inc. owns and operates movie theaters throughout the United States. Cinemark has constructed stadium-style movie theaters with a stadium-style seating configuration, that is, rows of seats rising at a relatively steep grade to provide better sight lines for movie patrons. The stadium-style seating is inaccessible for wheelchair-using patrons. For wheelchair-using patrons, the theaters provide a flat area in front of the screen where these patrons do not have the same sight line to the screen as non-wheelchair-using patrons. The United States sued Cinemark, alleging that the seating arrangement in Cinemark stadium-style theaters violated Standard 4.33.3 and Title III of the ADA. Does Cinemark's wheelchair seating arrangement in its stadium-style theaters violate Standard 4.33.3 and Title III of the ADA? *United States of America v. Cinemark USA, Inc.*, 348 F.3d 569, 2003 U.S. App. Lexis 22757 (United States Court of Appeals for the Sixth Circuit, 2003)

49.2 Implied Warranty of Habitability The defendants are approximately 80 tenants of a 300-unit luxury apartment building on the upper east side of Manhattan. The monthly rents in the all-glass-enclosed building, which won several architectural awards, were very high. The landlord brought a summary proceeding against the tenants to recover rent when they engaged in a rent strike to protest what they viewed as deteriorating conditions and services. Among other things, the evidence showed that during the period in question, the elevator system made tenants and their guests wait interminable lengths of time, the elevators skipped floors and opened on the wrong floors, a stench emanated from garbage stored near the garage and mice appeared in that area, fixtures were missing in public areas, water seeped into mailboxes, the air conditioning in the lobby was inoperative, and air conditioners in individual units leaked. The defendant-tenants sought abatement of rent for breach of the implied warranty of habitability. Did the landlord breach the implied warranty of habitability? *Solow v. Wellner*, 150 Misc.2d 642, 569 N.Y.S.2d 882, 1991 N.Y. Misc. Lexis 169 (Civil Court of the City of New York, 1991)

Ethics Cases

49.3 Ethics Case Moe and Joe Rappaport (Tenants) leased space in a shopping mall owned by Bermuda Avenue Shopping Center Associates, L.P. (Landlord), to use as an indoor golf arcade. The lease was signed, and Tenants were given possession of the leased premises. Landlord did not tell Tenants about the extensive renovations planned for the mall. For one month, the golf arcade was busy and earned a net profit. However, at the end of the month, renovation of the mall began in front of the arcade. The tenants stated that their store sign was taken down, there was debris and dust in front of the store, the sidewalks and parking spaces in front of the store were taken away, and their business "died." Tenants closed their arcade approximately one month later and sued Landlord for damages. Landlord counterclaimed, seeking to recover lost rental income. Did Landlord act ethically in not explaining the planned renovations to Tenants? Did Tenants act ethically in terminating the lease? Were Tenants constructively evicted from the leased premise? Who wins? *Bermuda Avenue Shopping Center Associates v. Rappaport*, 565 So.2d 805, 1990 Fla. App. Lexis 5354 (Court of Appeal of Florida, 1990)

49.4 Ethics Case Middleton Tract consisted of approximately 560 acres of land located in the Santa Cruz Mountains in San Mateo County, California. The land, which had once been owned by William H. Middleton, had been subdivided into 80 parcels of various shapes and sizes that were owned by various parties. The original deeds of conveyance from Middleton to purchasers contained certain restrictive covenants. One covenant limited use of the land exclusively for "residential purposes." Most of the land consisted of thickly wooded forest with redwood and Douglas fir trees. The Holmeses, who owned parcels totaling 144 acres, proposed to engage in commercial logging activities on their land. The plaintiffs, who owned other parcels in the tract, sued the Holmeses, seeking an injunction against such commercial activities. Did the Holmeses act ethically in this case? Who wins? *Greater Middleton Assn. v. Holmes Lumber Co.*, 222 Cal. App.3d 980, 271 Cal. Rptr. 917, 1990 Cal. App. Lexis 816 (Court of Appeal of California, 1990)

Notes

1. *Yee v. City of Escondido, California*, 503 U.S. 519, 112 S.Ct. 1522, 1992 U.S. Lexis 2115 (Supreme Court of the United States).
2. 42 U.S.C. Section 1981.
3. 42 U.S.C. Sections 3601–3619.
4. 42 U.S.C. Section 12101 et seq.
5. Public Law 110-325.

CHAPTER

50 Insurance

AUTOMOBILE INSURANCE

All 50 states require owners and lessees of automobiles, SUVs, trucks, and other vehicles to prove financial responsibility in the event of an accident. This is often accomplished by purchasing a minimum amount of liability insurance set by state law. Many drivers purchase liability insurance that exceeds the minimum required amount.

Dmitry Kalinovsky/123RF

Learning Objectives

After studying this chapter, you should be able to:

50.1 Define *insurable interest* and describe an insurance policy.

50.2 List and describe the common clauses that are used in insurance policies.

50.3 Describe the parties to a life insurance policy and the various types of life insurance.

50.4 List and describe the various forms of health and disability insurance.

50.5 Identify the risks covered by a standard fire insurance and homeowners' policy.

50.6 Describe automobile insurance and explain no-fault insurance.

50.7 List and describe special forms of business insurance.

50.8 Identify the coverage provided by cyber insurance.

50.9 Describe the coverage provided by umbrella insurance.

> *"The underwriter knows nothing and the man who comes to him to ask him to insure knows everything."*
>
> —*Lord Justice Scrutton*
> *Rozanes v. Bowen (1928)*

Introduction to Insurance

Insurance is a means for persons and businesses to protect themselves against the risk of loss. For example, persons and business may purchase fire insurance to cover their buildings. If there is a fire and the property is damaged, the insurance company will pay for all or part of the loss, depending on the policy. Similarly, a person who purchases automobile insurance may be reimbursed by the insurer if his or her car is stolen. And a person may purchase life insurance that pays the named beneficiary or beneficiaries the insurance proceeds on his or her death. Insurance is crucial to personal, business, and estate planning.

This chapter covers the formation of an insurance contract, types of insurance, defenses of insurance companies to liability, and other topics of insurance law.

Insurance: An ingenious modern game of chance in which the player is permitted to enjoy the comfortable conviction that he is beating the man who keeps the table.
Ambrose Bierce (1842–1914)

Principles of Insurance

50.1 Define *insurable interest* and describe an insurance policy.

Insurance is a contract whereby one party undertakes to indemnify another against loss, damage, or liability arising from a contingent or unknown event. It is a means of transferring and distributing risk of loss. The risk of loss is *pooled* (i.e., spread) among all the parties (or **insureds**) who pay premiums to an insurance company. The insurance company—also called the **insurer**, or **underwriter**—is then obligated to pay insurance proceeds to those members of the pool who experience losses.

An insurance contract is called a *policy*. The money paid to the insurance company is called a **premium**. Premiums are based on an estimate of the number of parties within the pool who will suffer the risks insured against. The estimate is based on experience.

Insurance policies are often sold by insurance agents or brokers. An **insurance agent** usually works exclusively for one insurance company and is an agent of that company. An **insurance broker** is an independent contractor who represents several insurance companies. The broker is the agent of the insured. Some insurance is sold directly by the insurer to the insured (e.g., by direct mail, internet).

The following feature discusses insurable interest.

insurance
A means for persons and businesses to protect themselves against the risk of loss.

insured
A party who pays a premium to a particular insurance company for insurance coverage.

insurer (underwriter)
An insurance company that underwrites insurance coverage.

premium
Money paid to an insurance company.

insurable interest
A requirement that a person who purchases insurance have a personal interest in the insured item or person.

Contemporary Environment

Insurable Interest

Anyone who would suffer a pecuniary (monetary) loss from the destruction of real or personal property has an **insurable interest** in that property. If the insured does not have an insurable interest in the property being insured, the contract is treated as a wager and cannot be enforced.

Ownership creates an insurable interest. In addition, mortgagees, lienholders, and tenants have an insurable interest in property. The insurable interest in property must exist at the time of loss.

Examples A person purchases a house and borrows money from the bank to pay part of the purchase price. The lender takes back a security interest in the house whereby the house becomes collateral for the loan. If the borrower fails to make the payments on the loan, then the bank can foreclose and recover the property. Here, both the owner of the house and the bank have an insurable interest in the property and may purchase house insurance to protect their interest.

In the case of life insurance, a person must have a close family relationship or an economic benefit from the continued life of another to have an insurable interest in that person's life. Thus, spouses, parents, children, and sisters and

(continued)

brothers may insure each other's lives. Other more remote relationships (e.g., aunts, uncles, cousins) require additional proof of an economic interest (e.g., proof of support). The insurable interest must exist when the life insurance policy is issued but need not exist at the time of death.

A person may insure his or her own life and name anyone as the **beneficiary**. The named beneficiary or beneficiaries receive the proceeds from the life insurance policy when the insured dies. The beneficiary does not have to have an insurable interest in the insured's life.

---

beneficiary
A person who is to receive life insurance proceeds when the insured dies.

insurance policy
An insurance contract.

Insurance Policy

An insurance contract, called an **insurance policy**, is governed by the law of contracts. Most policies are prepared on standardized forms. Some states even make that a requirement. Often, state statutes mandate that specific language be included in different types of insurance contracts. These statutes concern coverage for certain losses, how limitations on coverage must be stated in the contract, and the like. The insurance coverage is in place once the insurance policy is issued.

If both the insurer and the insured agree, an insurance policy may be modified to add coverage, add an additional insured, change coverage, or restrict coverage. Modification is usually done by executing a document called an insurance **endorsement** or **rider**. The endorsement or rider becomes part of the insurance policy.

endorsement (rider)
A document that modifies an insurance policy and becomes part of the insurance policy.

In most instances, an insured can cancel an insurance policy at any time. An insurer may cancel an insurance policy for nonpayment of premiums. Many insurance policies provide a **grace period** during which an insured may pay an overdue premium. The insurance usually remains in effect during the grace period.

Duties of Insured and Insurer

The parties to an insurance contract are obligated to perform the duties imposed by the contract. The insured owes the following duties: (1) to pay the premiums stipulated by the policy, (2) to notify the insurer after the occurrence of an insured event within the time period stated in the policy or within a reasonable time, and (3) to cooperate with the insurer in investigating claims made against the insurer.

The insurer owes two primary duties. First, the insurer owes a **duty to defend** the insured against any lawsuit or legal proceeding brought against the insured that involves a claim within the coverage of the insurance policy. Thus, the insurer must provide and pay for the lawyers and court costs necessary to defend the lawsuit. Second, the insurer owes the **duty to pay** legitimate claims up to the policy limits. Insurers who wrongfully refuse to perform these duties are liable to the insured or a rightful beneficiary for damages.

duty to defend
Duty of the insurer to defend the insured against lawsuits or legal proceedings that involve a claim within the coverage of the insurance policy.

duty to pay
Duty of the insurer to pay legitimate claims up to the insurance policy limits.

Common Clauses in Insurance Policies

50.2 List and describe the common clauses that are used in insurance policies.

Certain clauses often appear in insurance policies. These include a *deductible clause, exclusions from coverage clause, coinsurance clause*, and an *incontestability clause*. These clauses are discussed in the following paragraphs.

Deductible Clause

deductible clause
A clause in an insurance policy that provides that insurance proceeds are payable only after the insured has paid a specified amount toward the damage or loss.

Many insurance policies, such as automobile insurance and medical insurance policies, contain deductible clauses. A **deductible clause** provides that insurance proceeds are payable only after the insured has paid a certain amount of the damage or loss. For example, typical deductibles for automotive collision insurance are $500 and $1,000.

Example Suppose that an insured has a $50,000 automobile collision policy with a $1,000 deductible and the insured's car suffers $10,000 in damages in an accident. The insured must pay the first $1,000; the insurer will pay the remaining $9,000.

Exclusions from Coverage Clause

Most insurance policies include certain **exclusions from coverage**. These are expressly stated risks that are not covered by the insurance policy.

exclusions from coverage clause
A clause in an insurance policy that expressly stipulates the risks that are not covered by the insurance policy.

Example Standard fire insurance policies often exclude coverage for damage caused by the storage of explosives or flammable liquids unless a special premium is paid for this coverage.

Coinsurance Clause

A **coinsurance clause**, or **copay clause**, requires an insured to pay part of the cost of an insured loss. Many coinsurance clauses require insureds to pay a percentage of the loss, while others require that insureds pay a fixed amount before the insurance pays the remainder.

coinsurance clause (copay clause)
A clause in an insurance policy that requires the insured to pay a percentage of an insured loss.

Example Some medical insurance policies require the insured to pay a stated percentage of medical costs. Thus, if a medical insurance policy has 10 percent coinsurance and an insured's medical bills are $50,000, the insurance company will pay $45,000, and the insured will have to pay $5,000.

incontestability clause
A clause that prevents insurers from contesting statements made by insureds in applications for insurance after the passage of a stipulated number of years.

The following feature discusses incontestability clauses.

Ethics

Incontestability Clauses

Insurance companies may require applicants to disclose certain information to help determine whether they will insure the risk and to calculate the premium. The insurer may avoid liability on a policy (1) if its decision is based on a material misrepresentation on the part of the applicant or (2) if the applicant concealed material information from the insurer. This rule applies whether the misrepresentation was intentional or unintentional.

Many states have enacted laws that require **incontestability clauses** be placed in insurance agreements. An incontestability clause prevents insurers from contesting statements made by insureds in applications for insurance after the passage of a stipulated number of years (typically two to five years).

Example An automobile insurance policy contains a two-year incontestability clause. An applicant, at the time of applying for an automobile insurance policy, had previously caused an automobile accident. He intentionally does not disclose this fact on his insurance application. The insurance company finds no record of this previous accident and issues an insurance policy to the insured. One year after the policy is issued, the insured negligently causes an automobile accident in which he injures several people and he himself is injured. If his insurance company discovers that he did not disclose his prior accident on the insurance application, the insurance company can deny his claim and the claims of his victims. However, if the accident happened three years after the policy was issued, the insurance company cannot deny the claim because the two-year incontestability period has been exceeded.

Ethics Questions
Why do some state laws require incontestability clauses be placed in insurance policies? Is it ethical for an applicant for insurance to fail to disclose relevant prior information?

Life Insurance

50.3 Describe the parties to a life insurance policy and the various types of life insurance.

life insurance
A form of insurance in which the insurer is obligated to pay a specific sum of money on the death of the insured.

Life insurance is really "death insurance" because the insurer is normally obligated to pay a specified sum of money on the death of the insured. The owner of the policy has the power to name the beneficiary of the insurance proceeds. Most life insurance contracts permit the owner to change beneficiaries. If no beneficiary is named, the proceeds go to the insured's estate.

Some life insurance policies provide for the payment of all or a portion of the proceeds to the insured before death if he or she is suffering from a terminal illness. This allows the insured to pay for medical and other costs associated with the illness.

Parties to a Life Insurance Contract

There are four parties to a life insurance contract:

1. The **insurance company** issues the policy.
2. The **owner** of the policy is the person who contracts with the insurance company and pays the premiums.
3. The insured is the person whose life is insured.
4. The beneficiary is the person who is to receive the insurance proceeds when the insured dies.

The owner of the policy has the power to name the beneficiary of the insurance proceeds. Most life insurance contracts permit the owner to change beneficiaries. If no beneficiary is named, the proceeds go to the insured's estate. Often, the owner and the insured are the same person. For example, an owner can take out an insurance policy on his or her own life.

A life insurance policy in which the insured takes out life insurance on his or her own life and names a beneficiary is illustrated in **Exhibit 50.1**.

Exhibit 50.1 LIFE INSURANCE

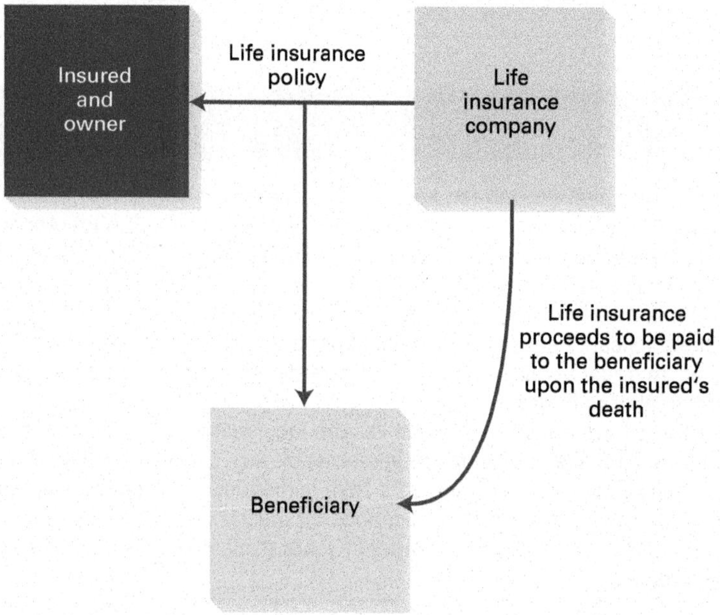

The most common forms of life insurance are described in **Exhibit 50.2**.

Suicide Clause

suicide clause
A clause in a life insurance contract that provides that if an insured commits suicide before a stipulated date, the insurance company does not have to pay the life insurance proceeds.

Many life insurance policies usually contain a **suicide clause**, which states that if the insured commits suicide within a certain period after taking out a life insurance policy on himself or herself, the insurance company does not have to pay the life insurance proceeds to the named beneficiary. The usual period for which a suicide clause is valid is two years.

If the insured commits suicide after the specified date, the insurance company must pay the life insurance proceeds to the insured's designated beneficiary or, if there is none, to the deceased insured's estate.

Exhibit 50.2 **TYPES OF LIFE INSURANCE**

Type	Description
Whole life insurance	Whole life insurance (also called ordinary life or straight life) provides coverage during the entire life of the insured. Premiums are paid during the life of the insured or until the insured reaches a certain age. Whole life insurance involves an element of savings. That is, premiums are set to cover both the death benefit and an additional amount for investment by the insurance company. This builds up a cash surrender value that may be borrowed against by the insured. Premiums for such insurance tend to be high.
Limited-payment life insurance	Limited-payment life insurance premiums are paid for a fixed number of years (e.g., 10 years) even though coverage is provided during the entire life of the insured. This form of insurance has cash surrender value. Premiums are higher than those for whole life insurance. Insurance companies have introduced single-premium life insurance where the insured pays the entire premium in a lump-sum payment.
Term life insurance	Term life insurance is issued for a limited period of time (e.g., five years), with premiums payable and coverage effective only during this term. Because term life insurance involves no savings feature, there is no cash surrender value. Because term life is "pure" insurance, premiums are less than for whole life or limited-payment life insurance. Term life policies usually provide for renewal or conversion to other forms of life insurance.
Universal life insurance	Universal life insurance combines features of both term and whole life insurance. The premium payment—called a contribution—is divided between the purchase of term insurance and an amount invested by the insurance company. The cash value grows at a variable interest rate rather than at a fixed rate.
Endorsement and annuity contracts	Endorsement and annuity contracts are forms of retirement and life insurance contracts. An endorsement contract is an agreement by an insurance company to pay an agreed-upon lump sum of money either to the insured when he or she reaches a certain age or to his or her beneficiary if he or she dies before that age. An annuity contract is an agreement by an insurance company to pay periodic payments (e.g., monthly) to the insured once he or she reaches a certain age.
Double indemnity	Double indemnity life insurance stipulates that the insurer will pay double the amount of the policy if death is caused by accident. Double indemnity insurance does not apply if the insured dies of a natural cause.

Example An insured purchases $1 million of life insurance and names his spouse as the beneficiary. The policy contains a two-year suicide clause. Twenty months after purchasing the insurance, the insured commits suicide. The beneficiary may not recover the insurance proceeds because the insured's suicide occurred within two years of issuance of the life insurance policy.

Health and Disability Insurance

50.4 List and describe the various forms of health and disability insurance.

An individual may require certain expenses to be covered if he or she becomes ill or disabled. The insurance industry provides two types of insurance—*health insurance* and *disability insurance*—that pay benefits for health-related costs during a person's lifetime.

Health Insurance

A person who is injured or sick may have to have medical treatment, surgery, or hospital care. **Health insurance** may be purchased to help cover the costs of such medical care. Health insurance usually covers only a portion of the costs. Many insurance companies also offer **dental insurance**. Many employers pay for health insurance coverage for their employees, but most require the employees to pay a portion of the health insurance premium.

health insurance
Insurance that is purchased to help cover the costs of medical treatment, surgery, or hospital care.

Example A manager works at a company that provides health insurance to its employees. The manager has pain in his hip and goes to see a doctor for a diagnosis. The doctor orders medical tests and determines that the patient needs hip replacement surgery. A surgeon conducts the hip replacement surgery. The health insurance will pay for the doctors, tests, and surgery (subject to the coinsurance and deductible clauses in the health insurance policy).

Disability Insurance

disability insurance
Insurance that provides a monthly income to an insured who is disabled and cannot work.

Disability insurance, which provides a monthly income to an insured who is disabled and cannot work, may be purchased to protect the insured against such an eventuality. The monthly benefits are usually based on the degree of disability. Many employers pay for disability insurance for their employees, but most require the employees to pay a portion of the disability insurance premium.

Example A person works at a company that provides disability insurance to its employees. While working on the job, a worker is injured and can no longer perform the job. The worker spends one year receiving medical treatment for the injury before he is able to return to work. During this one-year period, the injured worker will receive payments from the disability insurance to make up for all or a portion of the wages (as provided in the disability insurance policy) he lost by not working that year.

CONCEPT SUMMARY
HEALTH AND DISABILITY INSURANCE

Type	Description
Health	Insurance that covers the cost of medical treatment, surgery, and hospital care.
Dental	Insurance that covers the costs of dental care.
Disability	Insurance that provides monthly income to an insured who is disabled and cannot work. Benefits are based on the degree of disability.

Fire and Homeowners' Insurance

50.5 Identify the risks covered by a standard fire insurance and homeowners' policy.

Two major forms of insurance are available for residences: a *standard fire insurance policy* and a *homeowners' policy*. Such insurance is often required on real property that is mortgaged. Renters can also purchase insurance policies. These types of policies are discussed in the paragraphs that follow.

Standard Fire Insurance Policy

standard fire insurance
Insurance that protects the homeowner from loss caused by fire, lightning, smoke, and water damage.

A **standard fire insurance** policy protects real and personal property against loss resulting from fire and certain related perils. It does not, however, provide liability insurance for personal injury. Standard fire insurance protects the homeowner from loss caused by fire, lightning, smoke, and water damage. The coverage of a standard policy can be enlarged by adding riders or endorsements to the policy. Riders are often added to cover damage caused by windstorms, rainstorms, hail, explosions, theft, and liability. Additional coverage requires the payment of increased premiums.

replacement cost insurance
Insurance that pays the cost to replace the damaged or destroyed property up to the policy limits.

Most modern fire insurance policies provide **replacement cost insurance**. That is, the insurance will pay the cost to replace the damaged or destroyed property up to the policy limits (and subject to coinsurance). The insurer has the right to either pay the insured for the loss or pay to have the property restored or replaced.

Homeowners' Policy

homeowners' policy
A comprehensive insurance policy that includes coverage for the risks covered by a fire insurance policy as well as personal liability insurance.

A **homeowners' policy** is a comprehensive insurance policy that includes coverage for the real and personal risks covered by a fire insurance policy and also includes personal liability insurance. A homeowners' policy covers (1) the dwelling, (2) any appurtenant structures (e.g., garage, storage building), and

(3) personal property (e.g., furniture, clothing). A homeowners' policy also provides protection for losses caused by theft, whether the items are taken from the home or workplace or taken while traveling.

Personal liability coverage provides comprehensive *personal liability insurance* for the insured and members of his or her family. The insurer must pay property damage, personal injury, and medical expenses to persons injured on the insured's property (e.g., a guest slips on the sidewalk) and to persons injured by the insured or members of the insured's immediate family away from the insured's property (e.g., while golfing).

personal liability coverage
Insurance coverage that provides comprehensive *personal liability insurance* for the insured and members of his or her family.

In the following case, the court had to decide if insurance fraud had been committed.

CASE 50.1 *FEDERAL COURT CASE Insurance Fraud*

Neidenbach v. Amica Mutual Insurance Company

842 F.3d 560 (2016)
United States Court of Appeals for the Eighth Circuit

"The prejudice to the insurance company was obvious: the company was being asked to pay a fraudulent claim."

—Jane Kelly, Circuit Judge

Facts

Dale and Kim Neidenbach purchased a homeowners' insurance policy from Amica Mutual Insurance Company (Amica) that insured their home and personal property. The policy included a clause that stated, "We provide no coverage to insureds under this policy if, whether before or after a loss, an insured has: (1) intentionally concealed or misrepresented any material fact or circumstance; (2) engaged in fraudulent conduct; or (3) made false statements, relating to this insurance."

A fire caused substantial damage to Neidenbachs' house and personal property. They sought the limits of their insurance policy: $375,000 in damage to their house and garage and $262,500 in damage to their personal property. Approximately one year before the fire, the Neidenbachs had filed for personal bankruptcy and had declared that they had jointly owned only $7,000 worth of personal property. The Neidenbachs could not explain how their personal property had increased so substantially in value during the one year since they had declared bankruptcy.

Amica denied the Neidenbachs' insurance claim, alleging that they had committed fraud by filing inflated valuations of their property losses. The Neidenbachs sued Amica to recover on their homeowners' insurance policy. The U.S. district court found that the Neidenbachs had committed fraud and granted summary judgment in favor of Amica. The Neidenbachs appealed.

Issue

Was insurance coverage properly denied because of fraud?

Language of the Court

The only reasonable inference from the record before us is that the insureds intentionally made material misrepresentations in their proof of loss. The prejudice to the insurance company was obvious: the company was being asked to pay a fraudulent claim. Accordingly, we conclude as a matter of law that because the Neidenbachs intentionally made material misrepresentations, their entire insurance policy is void.

Decision

The U.S. court of appeals affirmed the decision.

Critical Legal Thinking Questions

Was the fraud obvious in this case? Do you think that fraudulent insurance claims are common?

Personal Articles Floater

An insured may wish to obtain insurance for specific valuable items (e.g., jewelry, works of art, furs). This is accomplished by adding a **personal articles floater**, or **personal effects floater**, to a homeowners' policy. The insured must submit a list of the items he or she wants covered, along with a statement of the value

personal articles floater (personal effects floater)
An addition to a homeowners' policy that covers specific valuable items.

of each item, to the insurance company. The insurance company will charge an increased premium based on the articles insured. A personal articles floater provides coverage for loss or damage to the articles while the insured is traveling.

Renters' Insurance

renters' insurance
Insurance that renters purchase to cover loss or damage to their possessions.

Renters may purchase insurance to cover loss or damage to their possessions. **Renters' insurance** covers a renter's possessions against the same perils as a homeowners' broad-form policy and provides personal liability coverage.

CONCEPT SUMMARY

FIRE AND HOMEOWNERS' INSURANCE

Type	Description
Standard fire insurance policy	Insurance that protects real and personal property against loss resulting from fire, lightning, smoke, water damage, and related perils. Most policies limit recovery to damage caused by *hostile fires* (e.g., fire caused by faulty electrical wiring) and not *friendly fires* (e.g., damage caused by a fire contained in a fireplace). No personal liability coverage is provided.
Homeowners' policy	A comprehensive insurance policy that includes coverage for the risks covered by a standard fire insurance policy as well as personal liability insurance. It includes coverage for property damage, personal injury, and medical expenses of persons injured on the insured's property.
Personal liability coverage	Insurance for the insured and members of his or her family. The insurer must pay property damage, personal injury, and medical expenses to persons injured on the insured's property (e.g., a guest slipping on the sidewalk) and to persons injured by the insured or members of the insured's immediate family away from the insured's property (e.g., while golfing).
Personal articles floater	Insurance that covers specific valuable items (e.g., jewelry, works of art, furs) that are usually excluded from standard fire and homeowners' policies.
Renters' insurance	Insurance that covers loss and damage to renters' possessions and provides personal liability coverage. Insures against the same perils as a homeowners' policy.

Title Insurance

title insurance
Insurance that owners of real property purchase to ensure that they have clear title to the property.

Owners of real property can purchase **title insurance** to ensure that they have clear title to the property. Mortgagees and other lienholders can purchase title insurance on property on which they have a lien.

Title insurance protects against defects in titles and liens or encumbrances that are not disclosed on the title insurance policy. An owner of real property or a mortgagee pays only one premium for title insurance, usually at closing. Each new owner or mortgagee who wants this coverage must purchase a new title insurance policy. Mortgagees sometimes require a debtor to purchase such a policy as a prerequisite for making a loan.

Automobile, Vehicle, and Vessel Insurance

50.6 Describe automobile insurance and explain no-fault insurance.

Several types of **automobile insurance** policies include both property and liability insurance. The term *automobile insurance* includes coverage of automobiles, SUVs, trucks, and other vehicles. Many states require proof of automobile insurance before license plates are issued. The basic types of automobile insurance policies are discussed in the paragraphs that follow.

Collision Insurance

An owner of an automobile may purchase **collision insurance** that insures his or her car against risk of loss or damage. This form of property insurance pays for damages caused if the car is struck by another car. The coverage is in effect whether the insured's car is moving or standing still.

collision insurance
Insurance that a car owner purchases to insure his or her car against risk of loss or damage.

Example A person obtains collision insurance to cover damage to his or her automobile. Another motorist negligently hits the insured's automobile in an accident. The collision insurance would pay for the damages caused to the insured's automobile.

Comprehensive Insurance

Comprehensive insurance is a form of insurance that insures an automobile from loss or damage due to causes other than collision, such as fire, theft, explosion, windstorm, hail, falling objects, earthquakes, floods, hurricanes, vandalism, and riot. Many insureds purchase both collision and comprehensive insurance when they insure their automobiles against damage.

comprehensive insurance
A form of property insurance that insures an automobile from loss or damage due to causes other than collision.

Automobile Liability Insurance

Automobile liability insurance covers damages that the insured causes to third parties, including both bodily injury and property damage. The limits of liability insurance are usually stated in three numbers, such as 100/300/25. This limits the insurer's obligation to pay insurance proceeds arising from an accident up to $100,000 for bodily injury to each injured person, up to $300,000 for total bodily injury to all persons injured, and up to $25,000 for property damage. States often require an insured to carry minimum liability insurance specified by statute. The minimum legal required liability insurance is usually quite low (e.g., $20,000).

automobile liability insurance
Automobile insurance that covers damages that the insured causes to third parties.

A basic automobile liability policy protects the insured when driving his or her own automobile. The owner, however, might want to expand coverage by adding (1) an **omnibus clause**, or **other-driver clause**, which protects the owner when someone else drives the car with permission, and (2) **drive-other coverage (D.O.C.)**, which protects the insured while he or she is driving other automobiles (e.g., rental cars). Some omnibus clauses extend coverage to third parties who drive automobiles with permission from a person to whom the owner gave permission to drive the car. Additional premiums are charged for this coverage.

WEB EXERCISE
Use **www.google.com** or other search engine and find out the minimum levels of automobile insurance your state requires.

In the following case, the court had to decide whether automobile insurance covered injuries suffered by a person whose automobile was hit by an insured drunk driver.

CASE 50.2 *FEDERAL COURT CASE Automobile Insurance*

Frederking v. Cincinnati Insurance Company

929 F.3d 195 (2019)
United States Court of Appeals for the Fifth Circuit

"Only an insurance company could come up with the policy interpretation advanced here."
—James Ho, Circuit Judge

Facts

Carlos Xavier Sanchez worked and drove a truck for his employer, Advanced Plumbing Services (Advanced). Advanced purchased automobile insurance, including liability coverage to compensate persons injured by Advanced employees, from Cincinnati Insurance Company (Cincinnati). The insurance policy exempted coverage for intentional conduct. One day when Sanchez was driving a truck for Advanced in Texas, he failed to yield a right of way, collided with a car, and injured Richard Brett Frederking. Sanchez was driving under the influence

(continued)

of alcohol at the time of the accident. Frederking sued Sanchez, Advanced, and Cincinnati. The jury awarded $207,000 in exemplary damages to Frederking. Under the Texas statute for at-fault insurance, Advanced's insurer, Cincinnati, would be liable. However, Cincinnati refused to pay the award, alleging that its policy only covered accidents, but that Sanchez intentionally chose to drink alcohol, so therefore there was no "accident" for which Cincinnati was liable to pay for Frederking's injuries. The U.S. district court agreed and granted summary judgment to Cincinnati. Frederking appealed.

Issue

Is an automobile accident caused by a drunk driver an "accident" covered by an automobile insurance liability policy?

Language of the Court

Only an insurance company could come up with the policy interpretation advanced here. This theory of interpretation conflicts with the plain meaning and the common usage of the word "accident"—and defies the understanding and expectation of everyone who drives a car. The term "accident" plainly includes the drunk driving collision that gave rise to this dispute.

Under Cincinnati's interpretation, it is not just drunk driving that would be excluded from coverage. A collision caused by texting while driving would also not be an accident. And a collision caused by eating while driving would not be an accident. In each of these scenarios, after all, a driver has made an intentional decision that contributes to an accident. But this is implausible on its face. Indeed, it would defeat the widely held expectations of the countless insureds who purchase automobile insurance precisely to protect against these kinds of "accidents."

Decision

The U.S. court of appeals reversed the decision of the district court and held that an accident had occurred and was covered by Cincinnati's insurance policy.

Critical Legal Thinking Questions

If you, while driving a vehicle, are struck by a drunk driver who has automobile insurance, do you think that your injuries would be covered? In this case, did Frederking and Advanced have the same interest in having Cincinnati be held accountable?

Medical Payment Insurance

Owners can obtain **medical payment insurance** that covers medical expenses incurred by themselves, other authorized drivers of the car, and passengers in the car who are injured in an automobile accident. Coverage includes payments for reasonable medical, surgical, and hospital services.

Uninsured Motorist Coverage

Usually, people injured in an automobile accident look to the insurer of the party at fault to recover for their personal injury. But what if the person who is at fault has no insurance? An owner of an automobile may purchase **uninsured motorist coverage**, which provides coverage to the driver and passengers who are injured by an uninsured motorist or a hit-and-run driver. Certain states require uninsured motorist coverage to be included in automobile insurance policies.

uninsured motorist coverage
Automobile insurance that provides coverage to a driver and passengers who are injured by an uninsured motorist or a hit-and-run driver.

no-fault insurance
An automobile insurance system used by some states in which the driver's insurance company pays for any injuries or death the driver suffers in an accident, no matter who caused the accident.

Example A person purchases uninsured motorist coverage. Another driver negligently causes an accident in which the insured and a passenger in the insured's car are injured. The driver who caused the accident has no liability insurance. Here, the insured's own insurance company is obligated to pay for his and his passenger's injuries.

The following feature discusses no-fault automobile liability insurance.

Contemporary Environment

No-Fault Automobile Liability Insurance

Until recently, most automobile insurance coverage in this country was based on the principle of "fault," whereby a party injured in an accident relied on the insurance of the at-fault party to pay for his or her injuries. This system led to substantial litigation, and many accident victims were unable to recover because the at-fault party had either inadequate insurance or no insurance at all.

To remedy this problem, more than half of the states have enacted legislation that mandates **no-fault insurance**. Under this system, a driver's insurance company pays for any injuries or death the driver suffered in an accident, no matter who caused the accident. No-fault insurance assures the insureds that coverage is available if they are injured in an automobile accident.

No-fault insurance policies provide coverage for medical expenses and lost wages. Pain and suffering are sometimes covered. No-fault insurance usually covers the insured, members of the insured's immediate family, authorized drivers of the automobile, and passengers.

CONCEPT SUMMARY

AUTOMOBILE INSURANCE

Type	Description
Collision	Property insurance that covers the insured's vehicle against risk of loss or damage when it is struck by another vehicle.
Comprehensive	Property insurance that covers the insured's vehicle against risk of loss or damage from causes other than collision, such as fire, theft, explosion, hail, windstorm, falling objects, earthquakes, floods, hurricanes, vandalism, and riots.
Liability	Insurance that covers damage and loss that the insured causes to third parties. This includes both bodily injury and property damage. States often require individuals to carry minimum liability insurance, specified by statute. Additional coverage may be purchased: Other-driver coverage is liability coverage that protects the owner of a vehicle when someone else drives his or her vehicle with his or her permission, and drive-other coverage is liability coverage that protects the insured while he or she is driving other vehicles.
Medical payment	Insurance that covers medical expenses incurred by the owner, passengers, and other authorized drivers of his or her car who are injured in an automobile accident.
Uninsured motorist	Insurance that provides coverage to the driver and passengers of a vehicle who are injured by an uninsured motorist or a hit-and-run driver.
No-fault	Insurance required in some states whereby the driver's insurance company pays for any injuries or death the driver suffers in an accident, no matter who caused the accident.

Marine Insurance

Owners of a vessel can purchase **marine insurance** to insure against loss or damage to the vessel and its cargo caused by perils on the water. Marine insurance is often comprehensive, covering property damage to the vessel or its cargo and liability insurance. Shippers can purchase marine insurance to cover the risk of loss to their goods during shipment. Marine insurance policies sometimes distinguish between *inland marine insurance* (for inland waters) and *ocean marine insurance* (for perils on the ocean).

marine insurance
Insurance that owners of a vessel can purchase to insure against loss or damage to the vessel and its cargo caused by perils on the water.

Business Insurance

50.7 List and describe special forms of business insurance.

Businesses usually purchase automobile insurance, property and casualty insurance, liability insurance, and other types of insurance previously discussed in this chapter. In addition, businesses often purchase insurance to cover risks uniquely applicable to conducting business. These special types of business insurance are discussed in the following paragraphs.

Business Interruption Insurance

When a business is severely damaged or destroyed by fire or some other peril, it usually takes time to repair or reconstruct the damaged property. During this time, the business loses money. A business can purchase a **business interruption insurance** policy that will reimburse it for any revenues lost during such a period.

business interruption insurance
Insurance that reimburses a business for loss of revenue incurred when the business has been damaged or destroyed by fire or some other peril.

Example A retail store that is covered by business interruption insurance is destroyed by fire, and it takes nine months to rebuild the store. During this nine-month period, the owner of the store will be paid the insurance proceeds provided in the business interruption insurance policy to cover the lost revenues the store would have made had it been open for business.

Workers' Compensation Insurance

Employees are sometimes injured while working within the scope of their employment. All states have enacted legislation that compensates employees for such injuries. Employers can purchase **workers' compensation insurance** to cover this risk. Many states require companies to purchase this form of insurance.

workers' compensation insurance
Insurance that compensates employees for work-related injuries.

Under a workers' compensation system, an injured worker submits a claim to the appropriate workers' compensation court or administrative agency for a determination of payment for loss. In most instances, the injured employee cannot sue the employer for liability because the workers' compensation award is the exclusive remedy.

Example Maribelle is injured while working on an assembly line of an automobile manufacturer and loses the use of one of her arms. Assume that the manufacturer has purchased appropriate workers' compensation insurance. In this case, Maribelle can pursue her claim and be awarded money for her injury from workers' compensation insurance. Maribelle cannot, however, sue her employer in court to recover tort damages in a normal court action.

Key-Person Life Insurance

In many small businesses, such as partnerships, limited liability companies, and close corporations, the death of one of the owners may cause a loss to the business. To compensate for such loss, the business often purchases **key-person life insurance** on owners and other important persons who work for the business. The business pays the premiums for the key-person life insurance policies. On the death of the insured person, the proceeds of the key-person life insurance are paid to the business.

key-person life insurance
Life insurance purchased and paid for by a business that insures against the death of owners and other key executives and employees of the business.

Sometimes key-person life insurance is used to fund buy–sell agreements among the owners of the business. Thus, if an insured owner dies, the insurance proceeds are paid to the deceased's beneficiaries, and the deceased's interest in the business then reverts to either the other owners or the business, according to the terms of the buy–sell agreement.

Directors' and Officers' Insurance

directors' and officers' liability insurance (D&O insurance)
Insurance that protects directors and officers of a corporation from liability for actions taken on behalf of the corporation.

Most large and medium-size corporations carry **directors' and officers' liability insurance (D&O insurance)** to protect directors and officers from liability for the actions they take on behalf of the corporation. Smaller companies tend to forgo this type of insurance because of the expense involved.

Example The iDot Computer Corporation has purchased D&O insurance. Assume that the shareholders of the corporation sue the board of directors, alleging that the directors were negligent in not catching a fraud perpetrated by management that caused a loss to the shareholders. If the court finds that the directors were negligent, the D&O insurance will pay the award and court costs.

Professional Malpractice Insurance

Professionals—such as attorneys, accountants, physicians, dentists, architects, and engineers—are liable for injuries resulting from their negligence in practicing their professions. These professionals can purchase **professional malpractice insurance** (or simply **malpractice insurance**) to insure against liability. Premiums for malpractice insurance are often quite high.

professional malpractice insurance (malpractice insurance)
Insurance that insures professionals against liability for injuries caused by their negligence.

Example Zach, a lawyer, purchases professional malpractice insurance. Zach represents a client in a lawsuit. Zach is negligent and fails to file legal documents with the court on time, and his negligence causes the client's case to be dismissed. The client successfully sues Zach for legal malpractice. In this case, the professional malpractice insurance will cover the client's award, up to its policy limits.

Product Liability Insurance

Manufacturers and sellers of products can be held liable for injuries caused by defective products. These businesses can purchase **product liability insurance** specifically to insure against this risk.

product liability insurance
Insurance that protects sellers and manufacturers against injuries caused by defective products.

Example Children's Toy Company purchases product liability insurance. The company produces a toy that is defectively designed and causes injury to a child using the toy. The child (through his or her parents) sues the company for product liability. The court finds the company liable and issues a judgment for monetary damages against the company. In this case, the company's product liability insurance would pay the judgment up to the policy limit of the insurance.

CONCEPT SUMMARY
TYPES OF BUSINESS INSURANCE

Type of Insurance	Description
Business interruption insurance	Reimburses business owners for loss of income caused when a fire or other peril interrupts their business during the time it takes to repair or reconstruct the damaged property.
Workers' compensation insurance	Insurance that pays compensation to employees who are injured on the job. In most cases, the employee cannot sue the employer for liability because the workers' compensation award is the exclusive remedy.
Key-person life insurance	Insurance that businesses purchase that covers the lives of owners and other important persons who work for the business. On the death of the insured person, the life insurance is paid to the business.
Directors' and officers' liability insurance (D&O insurance)	Insurance that protects directors and officers from liability for decisions and actions they take on behalf of the corporation.
Professional malpractice insurance	Professionals—such as attorneys, accountants, physicians, dentists, and architects—purchase malpractice liability insurance to cover injuries resulting from their negligence in practicing their professions.
Product liability insurance	The manufacturers and sellers of products can insure against liability caused by the sale of defective products.

Cyber Insurance

50.8 Identify the coverage provided by cyber insurance.

Companies face several dangers from cybercrimes. First, a company's own data might be compromised and stolen by cybercriminals. Second, companies that conduct business either through stores or online often electronically store sensitive customer data, such as credit card and other personal information. There is a risk that customer information will be obtained and used by cybercriminals, causing losses to the customers whose information has been stolen.

cyber insurance
Insurance that protects companies from losses and liability to customers caused by cyberattacks.

Companies can purchase **cyber insurance** to protect against losses caused to themselves by cyberattacks as well as from liability for the losses suffered by their customers whose data has been stolen. Cyber insurance is very expensive, however.

Examples Companies that have had data breaches where users' and customers' personal and financial information was stolen include Yahoo (3 billion user accounts), Zynga (218 million user accounts), Equifax (147 million customers), MySpace (360 million user accounts), and Marriot International (500 million customers). Cyber insurance covered many of the expenses and losses incurred by these data breaches.

Umbrella Insurance

50.9 Describe the coverage provided by umbrella insurance.

umbrella insurance
Additional insurance that provides coverage in excess of the basic policy limits of other insurance policies.

Liability coverage under most insurance policies, such as automobile and homeowners' insurance, is usually limited to a certain dollar amount. Insureds who want to increase their liability coverage beyond the original coverage can purchase **umbrella insurance**. Coverage under an umbrella policy is usually at least $1 million and often reaches $5 million. An umbrella policy pays only if the basic policy limits on other insurance policies have been exceeded. An insurer will issue an umbrella policy only if a stipulated minimum amount of basic coverage on other insurance policies has been purchased by the insured.

Example An insured purchases automobile liability insurance that pays up to $500,000 per accident and an umbrella policy with an additional $3 million of coverage. If the insured's negligence causes an automobile accident in which injuries to other persons total $2 million, the basic automobile policy will pay the first $500,000, and the umbrella policy will pay the remaining $1.5 million.

Key Terms and Concepts

Automobile insurance (884)
Automobile liability insurance (885)
Beneficiary (878)
Business interruption insurance (888)
Coinsurance clause (copay clause) (879)
Collision insurance (885)
Comprehensive insurance (885)
Cyber insurance (890)
Deductible clause (878)
Dental insurance (881)
Directors' and officers' liability insurance (D&O insurance) (888)
Disability insurance (882)
Drive-other coverage (D.O.C.) (885)
Duty to defend (878)
Duty to pay (878)
Endorsement (rider) (878)
Exclusions from coverage (879)
Grace period (878)
Health insurance (881)
Homeowners' policy (882)
Incontestability clause (879)
Insurable interest (877)
Insurance (877)
Insurance agent (877)
Insurance broker (877)
Insurance company (880)
Insurance policy (878)
Insured (877)
Insurer (underwriter) (877)
Key-person life insurance (888)
Life insurance (879)
Marine insurance (887)
Medical payment insurance (886)
No-fault insurance (887)
Omnibus clause (other-driver clause) (885)
Owner (880)

Personal articles floater (personal effects floater) (883)
Personal liability coverage (883)
Premium (877)
Product liability insurance (889)
Professional malpractice insurance (malpractice insurance) (889)
Renters' insurance (884)
Replacement cost insurance (882)
Standard fire insurance (882)
Suicide clause (880)
Title insurance (884)
Umbrella insurance (890)
Uninsured motorist coverage (886)
Workers' compensation insurance (888)

Critical Legal Thinking Cases

50.1 Exclusion from Insurance Coverage Joshua Green (Green), who was operating a boat, called his wife, Lindsey Green, at about 8:20 p.m. to say he was on his way home. When he did not arrive, she called the police. The U.S. Coast Guard found Green in his boat the next morning. Green died because of a head injury he sustained when his boat struck a concrete piling. The police report noted that Green had a blood alcohol concentration of .243, significantly above the state's limit of .08. There were empty beer bottles and cans in the boat. The official death certificate declared the death to be accidental and listed a skull fracture and contusion of the brain as the causes of death. The death certificate also listed acute alcohol intoxication as a significant factor contributing to Green's death.

Green had two life insurance policies with Life Insurance Company of North America (LINA). Lindsey Green, the beneficiary of the policies, filed to recover life insurance benefits from LINA. LINA denied payment because Green was legally intoxicated and the policies excluded recovery for any injury caused by operating a vehicle under the influence of alcohol or drugs. Lindsey Green filed suit in U.S. district court to recover the life insurance benefits. She alleged that a boat was not a vehicle, and therefore the exclusion did not apply. Does the exclusion for operating a vehicle while intoxicated prevent recovery of the life insurance benefits? *Green v. Life Insurance Company of North America*, 754 F.3d 324, 2014 U.S. App. Lexis 10875 (United States Court of Appeals for the Fifth Circuit, 2014)

50.2 Automobile Insurance Jowenna Surber owned a Mercedes-Benz automobile that she insured through an insurance broker, Mid-Century Insurance Company (Mid-Century). Mid-Century secured a policy for Surber with the Farmers Insurance Company (Farmers). Surber gave permission to her friend, Bruce Martin, to use the car. Martin held a valid California driver's license. Surber did not receive any compensation for allowing Martin to use the car. While driving the car, Martin was involved in a collision with another vehicle, driven by Loretta Haynes, who suffered severe injuries. Martin admitted that his negligence was the cause of the accident. Surber's policy stipulates that the policy covers "you or any family member or any person using your insured car." Is Farmers liable to Haynes? *Mid-Century Insurance Company v. Haynes*, 218 Cal. App.3d 737, 267 Cal. Rptr. 248, 1990 Cal. App. Lexis 219 (Court of Appeal of California, 1990)

50.3 Insurance Fraud Akiva Abraham's company 1st Call, LLC, acquired a property in Colonie, New York, on which stood an abandoned nightclub known as Saratoga Winners, for $1. On the same day, an entity called Parcel Road, LLC, was given a mortgage of $475,000 on the property, indicating that Parcel Road had loaned 1st Call that amount of money. And on the same day, Abraham took out fire insurance on the property for $475,000, the amount of the mortgage. Two weeks after the purchase, Saratoga Winners burned to the ground. Abraham reported the loss to his insurance company. He told the company that he did not know the cause of the fire.

Investigators found accelerants both inside and outside the building, the same as those contained in Tiki torch fuel, along with cinders of Duraflame fire logs. Investigators discovered that three days before the fire, Abraham had purchased four gallons of Tiki torch fuel and two 9-pack boxes of Duraflame fire logs at Home Depot. Police arrested Abraham, and a search of his premises revealed four empty gallon bottles of Tiki torch fuel and two empty Duraflame boxes. Further investigation revealed that Parcel Road, LLC, did not transfer any mortgage money to 1st Call, had $25 in its checking account, and was owned by Abraham's father. New York brought criminal charges for insurance fraud against Abraham. Is the defendant Abraham guilty of the crime of insurance fraud? *People v. Abraham*, 22 N.Y.3d 140, 978 N.Y.S.2d 723, 2013 N.Y. Lexis 321 (Court of Appeals of the State of New York, 2013)

50.4 Malpractice Insurance Donald Barker, a wealthy Oregon resident, went to the law firm Winokur, Schoenberg, Maier, Hamerman & Knudson to have his estate planned. An attorney at the firm repeatedly told Barker that he could convey half of his $20 million estate to his wife tax free under Oregon's marital deduction. Barker had his will made based on the law firm's advice. It was not until after Barker died three years later that Barker's family learned that Oregon does not recognize the marital deduction. As a result, the will's beneficiaries were subject to significant estate taxes. The beneficiaries sued the law firm for negligence, and the case was settled for $2 million.

At the time Barker was being advised by the law firm, it had a professional malpractice insurance policy with the Travelers Insurance Company (Travelers) that covered "all sums which the insured shall become legally obligated to pay as damages because of any act or omission of the insured arising out of the performance of professional services for others in the insured's capacity as a lawyer." The policy expired one year prior to Barker's death. Is Travelers liable for the $2 million settlement? *Travelers Insurance Company v. National Union Fire Insurance Company of Pittsburgh*, 207 Cal. App.3d 1390, 255 Cal. Rptr. 727, 1989 Cal. App. Lexis 130 (Court of Appeal of California, 1989)

50.5 Suicide Clause Terry Riggs worked for NuStar, LLC (NuStar). As part of his employment benefits, he was covered by a life insurance policy issued by Metropolitan Life Insurance Company (MetLife) in the amount of $261,000, which took effect on April 1, 2008. Argia Riggs, Terry's wife, was named as the beneficiary of the life insurance policy. The policy contained a two-year suicide clause. On November 17, 2009, Mr. Riggs was prescribed Abilify, an antipsychotic. Because Abilify made Mr. Riggs feel lethargic, on March 9, 2010, Mr. Riggs was prescribed Zyprexa for three days, but he told Ms. Riggs that he heard "uncontrollable thoughts and voices" and that "it made him feel like killing himself." On March 15, 2010, Mr. Riggs called his physician, who prescribed Cymbalta, an antidepressant. That evening, Mr. Riggs told a family friend that he had negative thoughts and "heard voices telling him to kill himself." At approximately 5:30 a.m. on March 17, 2010, Mr. Riggs shot himself in the head and died. The certificate of death issued by the state of New Jersey stated that the manner of death was suicide.

When Ms. Riggs applied to MetLife for the life insurance benefits, the company denied her claim because Mr. Riggs had died 16 days prior to the expiration of the two-year suicide exclusion. Ms. Riggs sued MetLife in U.S. district court, alleging that the hallucinations caused by the prescription medicine had caused Mr. Riggs to shoot himself and that he had not committed suicide because he could not have formed the intent to do so. MetLife filed a motion for summary judgment. Does the two-year suicide clause prevent Ms. Riggs from recovering life insurance benefits? *Riggs v. Metropolitan Life Insurance Company*, 940 F.Supp.2d 172, 2013 U.S. Dist. Lexis 55539 (United States District Court for the District of New Jersey, 2013)

Ethics Case

50.6 Ethics Case Gary and Ila Fedderson owned and operated Whiskey Flow, a restaurant and bowling alley located in Howard, South Dakota. After operating the business for some time, the Feddersons purchased a $1 million insurance policy from Columbia Insurance Group (Columbia) that covered damages to the business caused by fire. The policy included a "Concealment or Fraud Condition" that voided the insurance policy if "any insured" intentionally concealed or misrepresented a material fact or committed fraud or false swearing in connection with the insurance contract.

One month after the Feddersons took out the insurance, the Whiskey Flow was destroyed by fire. The Feddersons submitted a $1 million claim to Columbia. In their proof of loss statement, the Feddersons swore that an "unknown party started the fire." After investigation, Gary Fedderson was convicted of the crimes of conspiracy to commit arson and insurance fraud. Ila Fedderson was not involved in the arson and did not have knowledge of Gary Fedderson's involvement in the arson. Ila Fedderson sued Columbia to recover 50 percent of the insurance proceeds as an "innocent insured." Can Ila Fedderson collect half of the insurance proceeds? Did Gary Fedderson act ethically in this case? Did Ila Fedderson act unethically in trying to recover half of the insurance proceeds? *Fedderson v. Columbia Insurance Group*, 824 N.W.2d 793, 2012 S.D. Lexis 164 (2012).

PART XI

The Accounting Profession

Henry R. Cheeseman

CHAPTER 51

Accountants' Duties and Liability

Henry R. Cheeseman

WALL STREET

This is Wall Street, located in Manhattan, New York City. The street received its name because of the location of a wall built in the 1600s by the Dutch for protection. The wall was later taken down, but the name Wall Street was attached to the street located where the wall stood. Today, the name Wall Street is synonymous with securities trading. The New York Stock Exchange, NASDAQ, and other stock markets and exchanges are located on Wall Street and in the financial district surrounding Wall Street. Public accountants audit the firms listed on these exchanges.

Learning Objectives

After studying this chapter, you should be able to:

51.1 Describe public accounting and define the term *certified public accountant*.

51.2 Describe Generally Accepted Accounting Principles (GAAPs) and Generally Accepted Auditing Standards (GAASs).

51.3 Define *audit* and describe auditor's opinions.

51.4 Describe how accountants can be found liable to their clients.

51.5 Describe how accountants can be found liable to third parties, including under the *Ultramares* doctrine, Section 552 of the *Restatement (Second) of Torts*, and the foreseeability standard.

51.6 Describe how accountants can be held liable for violating securities laws.

51.7 Describe how accountants can be found criminally liable for their actions.

51.8 Describe the provisions of the Sarbanes-Oxley Act and how they apply to accountants.

51.9 Explain under what circumstances an accountant–client privilege applies.

> *"By certifying the public reports that collectively depict a corporation's financial status, the independent auditor assumes a public responsibility transcending any employment relationship with the client."*
>
> —Justice Warren Burger
> *United States v. Arthur Young & Co.*
> *465 U.S. 805, 104 S.Ct. 1495, 1984 U.S. Lexis 43 (1984)*

Introduction to Accountants' Duties and Liability

Although accountants provide a wide variety of services to corporations and other businesses, their primary functions are (1) auditing financial statements and (2) rendering opinions about audits. Accountants also prepare unaudited financial statements for clients, render tax advice, prepare tax forms, and provide consulting and other services to clients.

Audits generate the majority of litigation against accountants. Lawsuits against accountants are based on the common law (e.g., breach of contract, misrepresentation, negligence), or on violation of certain statutes (particularly federal securities laws). Accountants can be held liable both to clients and to third parties. This chapter examines the legal liability of accountants.

In our complex society the accountant's certificate and the lawyer's opinion can be instruments for inflicting pecuniary loss more potent than the chisel or the crowbar.

Justice Blackman
Dissenting Opinion,
Ernst & Ernst v. Hochfelder
425 U.S. 185, 96 S.Ct. 1375,
1976 U.S. Lexis 2 (1976)

Public Accounting

51.1 Describe public accounting and define the term *certified public accountant*.

The term **accountant** applies to persons who perform a variety of services, including bookkeepers and tax preparers. The term **certified public accountant (CPA)** applies to accountants who meet certain educational requirements, pass the CPA examination, and have a certain number of years of auditing experience. A person who is not certified is generally referred to as a **public accountant**.

certified public accountant (CPA)
An accountant who has met certain educational requirements, has passed the CPA examination, and has had a certain number of years of auditing experience.

Limited Liability Partnership (LLP)

Most public accounting firms are organized and operated as **limited liability partnerships (LLPs)**. In this form of partnership, all the partners are limited partners who may lose their capital contribution in the LLP if the LLP fails. The limited partners are not personally liable for the debts and obligations of the LLP (see Exhibit 51.1).

limited liability partnership (LLP)
A special form of partnership in which all partners are limited partners.

Exhibit 51.1 ACCOUNTING FIRM LLP

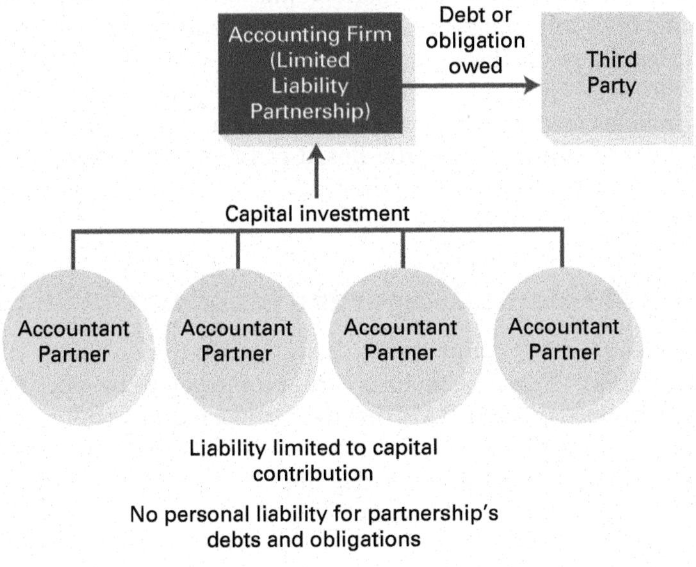

Example Four CPAs form an accounting firm as an LLP. The LLP leases office space in a building for a five-year period. After three years, the accounting firm dissolves and goes out of business while still owing two years of lease payments. None of the four partners are personally liable for the unpaid lease payments.

Operating as an LLP protects partners from personal liability for the accounting malpractice of another partner. The limited partner whose negligent or intentional conduct causes injury is personally liable for his or her own misconduct. Thus, if one partner commits accounting malpractice, the LLP is liable, and the partner who committed the malpractice is personally liable, but the other partners are not personally liable. They may lose their capital contribution in the LLP, but their personal assets are shielded. LLPs usually carry liability insurance to protect against malpractice liability.

Example Four CPAs form an accounting LLP. While working on an audit for a client company, one of the accountants commits accounting malpractice (negligence) by failing to detect accounting fraud at the company. Because of the fraud, the client goes bankrupt and its shareholders lose their entire investment. In this case, the shareholders can sue and most likely recover against the LLP and the negligent partner. However, the other three partners are not personally liable, though they could lose their capital investment in the firm.

Most accounting firms now operate as LLPs. Each of the "Big Four" accounting firms—Deloitte LLP; PricewaterhouseCoopers LLP; Ernst & Young LLP; and KPMG LLP—operate as LLPs.

Accounting Standards and Principles

51.2 Describe Generally Accepted Accounting Principles (GAAPs) and Generally Accepted Auditing Standards (GAASs).

CPAs must comply with two uniform standards of professional conduct: (1) *Generally Accepted Accounting Principles (GAAPs)* and (2) *Generally Accepted Auditing Standards (GAASs)*. Both are discussed in the following paragraphs.

Generally Accepted Accounting Principles (GAAPs)

Generally Accepted Accounting Principles (GAAPs) are standards for the preparation and presentation of financial statements.[1] These principles set forth rules for how companies and their accounting firms present their income, expenses, assets, and liabilities on the companies' financial statements. There are more than 150 "pronouncements" that compose these principles. GAAPs establish uniform principles for reporting financial statements and financial transactions. The Financial Accounting Standards Board (FASB), an organization created by the accounting profession, issues new GAAP rules and amends existing rules. GAAP applies mainly to U.S. companies.

Generally Accepted Accounting Principles (GAAPs)
Standards for the preparation and presentation of financial statements.

WEB EXERCISE
For a description of generally accepted accounting principles (GAAPs), go to **www.fasab.gov.**

International Financial Reporting Standards (IFRSs)

Most companies in other countries abide by **International Financial Reporting Standards (IFRSs)**. These principles are promulgated by the **International Accounting Standards Board (IASB)**, which is located in London, England. The IFRSs differ in some respects from GAAPs. As U.S. companies become more global, and as foreign companies increase their business in the United States, the IFRSs are replacing GAAPs.

Generally Accepted Auditing Standards (GAASs)

Generally Accepted Auditing Standards (GAASs) specify the methods and procedures that are to be used by public accountants when conducting external audits of company financial statements.[2] The standards are set by the **American Institute of Certified Public Accountants (AICPA)**. GAASs contain general standards of proficiency, independence, and professional care. They also establish standards for conducting fieldwork and require that sufficient evidence be obtained to afford a reasonable basis for issuing an opinion regarding the financial statements under audit. Compliance with audit standards provides a measure of audit quality.

Generally Accepted Auditing Standards (GAASs)
Standards for the methods and procedures that must be used to conduct audits.

Audit and Auditor's Opinions

51.3 Define *audit* and describe auditor's opinions.

An **audit** is a verification of a company's books and records. Pursuant to federal securities laws, state laws, and stock exchange rules, an audit must be performed by an independent CPA. The CPA must review the company's financial records, check their accuracy, and otherwise investigate the financial position of the company.

The auditor must also (1) conduct a sampling of inventory to verify the figures contained in the client's financial statements and (2) verify information from third parties (e.g., contracts, bank accounts, real estate, and accounts receivable). An accountant's failure to follow GAASs when conducting audits constitutes negligence.

audit
A verification of a company's books and records pursuant to federal securities laws, state laws, and stock exchange rules that must be performed by an independent CPA.

Auditor's Opinions

After an audit is complete, the auditor usually renders an *opinion* about how fairly the financial statements of the client company represent the company's financial position, results of operations, and change in cash flows. The **auditor's opinion** may be *unqualified, qualified*, or *adverse*. Alternatively, the auditor may offer a disclaimer of opinion. Most auditors give unqualified opinions. The various types of opinions are the following:

- **Unqualified opinion.** An **unqualified opinion** represents an auditor's finding that the company's financial statements fairly represent the company's financial position, the results of its operations, and the change in cash flows for the period under audit, in conformity with GAAPs. This is the most favorable opinion an auditor can give.
- **Qualified opinion.** A **qualified opinion** states that the financial statements are fairly represented except for, or subject to, a departure from GAAPs, a change in accounting principles, or a material uncertainty. The exception, departure, or uncertainty is noted in the auditor's opinion.
- **Adverse opinion.** An **adverse opinion** determines that the financial statements do not fairly represent the company's financial position, results of operations, or change in cash flows in conformity with GAAPs. This type of opinion is usually issued when an auditor determines that a company has materially misstated certain items on its financial statements.

auditor's opinion
An opinion of an auditor about how fairly the financial statements of the client company represent the company's financial position, results of operations, and change in cash flows.

unqualified opinion
An auditor's opinion that the company's financial statements fairly represent the company's financial position, the results of its operations, and the change in cash flows for the period under audit, in conformity with generally accepted accounting principles (GAAPs).

qualified opinion
An auditor's opinion that the financial statements are fairly represented except for, or subject to, a departure from GAAPs, a change in accounting principles, or a material uncertainty.

adverse opinion
An auditor's opinion that the financial statements do not fairly represent the company's financial position, results of operations, or change in cash flows in conformity with GAAPs.

Disclaimer of Opinion

A **disclaimer of opinion** expresses the auditor's inability to draw a conclusion about the accuracy of the company's financial records. This disclaimer is generally issued when the auditor lacks sufficient information about the financial records to issue an overall opinion.

The issuance of any opinion other than an *unqualified opinion* can have substantial adverse effects on the company undergoing the audit. A company that receives an opinion other than an unqualified opinion may not be able to

disclaimer of opinion
An auditor's opinion expressing the auditor's inability to draw a conclusion about the accuracy of the company's financial records.

sell its securities to the public, merge with another company, or obtain loans from banks. The Securities and Exchange Commission (SEC) has warned publicly held companies against "shopping" for accountants to obtain a favorable opinion.

Accountants' Liability to Their Clients

51.4 Describe how accountants can be found liable to their clients.

Accountants are employed by their clients to perform certain accounting services. Under the *common law*, accountants may be found liable to the clients who hire them under several legal theories, including breach of contract, fraud, and negligence.

Liability to Clients: Breach of Contract

engagement
A formal entrance into a contract between a client and an accountant.

The terms of an **engagement** are specified when an accountant and a client enter into a contract for the provision of accounting services by the accountant. An accountant who fails to perform may be sued for damages caused by the **breach of contract**. Generally, the courts consider damages to be the expenses the client incurs in securing another accountant to perform the needed services as well as any fines or penalties incurred by the client for missed deadlines, lost opportunities, and such.

Liability to Clients: Fraud

Rather fail with honor than succeed with fraud.
Sophocles (497–406 BCE)

Where an accountant has been found liable for **fraud (fraudulent misrepresentation)** the client may bring a civil lawsuit and recover any damages proximately caused by that fraud. Punitive damages may be awarded in cases of actual fraud. **Actual fraud** is defined as intentional misrepresentation or omission of a material fact that is relied on by the client and causes the client damage. Such cases are rare.

Constructive fraud occurs when an accountant acts with "reckless disregard" for the truth or the consequences of his or her actions. This type of fraud is sometimes categorized as **gross negligence**.

Liability to Clients: Accounting Malpractice (Negligence)

Accountants owe a duty to use *reasonable care, knowledge, skill*, and *judgment* when providing auditing and other accounting services to a client. In other words, an accountant's actions are measured against those of a "reasonable accountant" in similar circumstances. The development of GAAPs, GAASs, and other uniform accounting standards has generally made this a national standard. An accountant who fails to meet this standard may be sued for **negligence**, which is called **accounting malpractice**.

accounting malpractice (negligence)
Negligence where the accountant breaches the duty of reasonable care, knowledge, skill, and judgment that he or she owes to a client when providing auditing and other accounting services to the client.

Example An accountant does not comply with GAASs when conducting an audit and thereby fails to uncover a fraud or embezzlement by an employee of the company being audited. This accountant can be sued for damages arising from this negligence.

Violations of GAAPs or GAASs, or IFRSs if applicable, are *prima facie* evidence of negligence, although compliance does not automatically relieve the accountant of such liability. Accountants can also be held liable for their negligence in preparing **unaudited financial statements**. If an audit turns up a suspicious transaction or entry, the accountant is under a duty to investigate it and to inform the client of the results of the investigation.

In the following case, the court had to decide whether accountants were liable to their client.

CASE 51.1 *STATE COURT CASE Liability to a Client*

Yung v. Grant Thornton, LLP

563 S.W.3d 22 (2018)
Supreme Court of Kentucky

"In our view, these individual and cumulative acts place GT's behavior toward their clients at the high end of professional reprehensibility."

—Lisabeth Hughes, Justice

Facts

William J. Yung is an experienced business person who owns hotels and casinos in the Cayman Islands and the United States. Yung and a family trust also own hotels and casinos through two Cayman Island holding corporations, and they own 40 hotels in the United States through a corporation headquartered in Crestview Hills, Kentucky. The Yung family, the family trust, and their corporations (collectively, "Yung") follow a conservative tax strategy.

Grant Thornton, LLP (GT) is a large public accounting firm headquartered in Chicago, Illinois. For years, GT provided tax services and advice to Yung. In early 2000, GT created the Grant Thornton Leveraged Distribution Product (Lev301). Lev301 is a tax shelter that GT sells to clients with the stated purpose of reducing clients' tax liabilities. GT contacted Yung and promoted Lev301 to Yung. At the time GT began to develop Lev301, the U.S. Treasury Department was cracking down on products perceived to be abusive tax shelters. In December 1999, the federal Internal Revenue Service (IRS) warned that tax losses similar to those created by Lev301 were not allowable for federal income tax purposes and that the IRS could impose various tax penalties.

In July 2000, accountants and employees at GT introduced Lev301 to Yung. They did not disclose that the tax shelter benefits of Lev301 were questionable, or that GT believed that there was a 90 percent chance that the IRS would disallow the Lev301 tax benefits if Yung was audited by the IRS. GT stood to make $900,000 in fees if it could convince Yung to purchase the Lev301 product. The final engagement letter with Yung did not disclose that the IRS was likely to deem the Lev301 product to be an abusive tax shelter.

Based on GT's advice, Yung completed the Lev301 transaction. On October 1, 2001, GT prepared Yung's 2000 tax return and filed it with the IRS. The return did not report a $30 million distribution by Yung based on the Lev301 transaction. In early 2002, the IRS initiated an examination of GT and obtained the names of its Lev301 clients, including Yung. GT did not inform Yung of this fact. In the spring of 2004, the IRS audited Yung concerning Lev301. The IRS found it to be an abusive tax shelter and assessed back taxes and penalties. In February 2007, Yung and the IRS reached a settlement.

In August 2007, Yung filed a complaint against GT in a Kentucky circuit court alleging fraud, gross negligence, and breach of contract, and requested compensatory and punitive damages. After a bench trial, the judge found that GT had committed fraud and gross negligence in its scheme to sell Lev301 to Yung. The trial court awarded Yung compensatory damages consisting of the $900,000 engagement fee and the $19 million in taxes, interest, and penalties that Yung was forced to pay to the IRS.The court also awarded $80 million in punitive damages against GT. The Kentucky court of appeals affirmed the findings of the trial court, except it reduced the award of punitive damages to $20 million. GT appealed the finding of liability; Yung appealed the reduction in punitive damages.

Issue

Did Grant Thornton, LLP engage in fraud and gross negligence? Should the punitive damages be reinstated at $80 million?

Language of the Court

Here, Yung was definitely not part of the scheme to create an abusive tax shelter. Also, Yung was never put on notice that Lev301 was not a proper tax avoidance strategy and Yung did not know that GT's tax opinion was a sham. In this case, we conclude the trial court properly awarded taxes and interest as compensatory damages.

The court viewed GT's conduct as egregious and determined that a punitive damage award four times that of the compensatory damage award was needed to punish and deter like future behavior. GT's various misrepresentations and nondisclosures were made to save the $900,000 deal and to cover

(continued)

GT's negligent and fraudulent acts that accumulated over time. In our view, these individual and cumulative acts place GT's behavior toward their clients at the high end of professional reprehensibility. We reinstate the trial court's $80 million punitive damage award.

Decision

The Supreme Court of Kentucky affirmed the findings of fraud and gross negligence committed by GT, affirmed the award of compensatory damages, and reinstated the trial court's award of $80 million in punitive damages.

Critical Legal Thinking Questions

Do you agree with the court's finding that GT's conduct was reprehensible? Was the award of punitive damages warranted? Based on the facts of this case, was it likely that GT's fraud would be uncovered? Did the participating accountants at GT act ethically?

Accountants' Liability to Third Parties

51.5 Describe how accountants can be found liable to third parties, including under the *Ultramares* doctrine, Section 552 of the *Restatement (Second) of Torts*, and the foreseeability standard.

Many lawsuits against accountants involve liability of accountants to third parties. The plaintiffs are third parties (e.g., shareholders, bondholders, trade creditors, and banks) who relied on information supplied by the auditor. There are three major rules of liability that a state can adopt in determining whether an accountant is liable in negligence to third parties:

1. The *Ultramares* doctrine
2. Section 552 of the *Restatement (Second) of Torts*
3. The foreseeability standard

These rules are discussed in the paragraphs that follow.

Liability to Third Parties: *Ultramares* Doctrine

The landmark case that initially defined the liability of accountants for their negligence to third parties was ***Ultramares Corporation v. Touche.***[3] In that case, Touche Niven & Co. (Touche), a national firm of certified public accountants, was employed by Fred Stern & Co. (Stern) to conduct an audit of the company's financial statements. Touche was negligent in conducting the audit and did not uncover over $700,000 of accounts receivable that were based on fictitious sales and other suspicious activities. Touche rendered an unqualified opinion and provided 32 copies of the audited financial statements to Stern. Stern gave one copy to Ultramares Corporation (Ultramares). Ultramares made a loan to Stern on the basis of the information contained in the audited statements. When Stern failed to repay the loan, Ultramares brought a negligence action against Touche.

The court held that an accountant could not be held liable for negligence unless the plaintiff was in **privity of contract** or a **privity-like relationship** with the accountant. Privity of contract means that parties to a contract can sue one another for breach of the contract, but that third parties (with few exceptions) cannot sue for such breach because they are not parties to the contract. The court held that Touche was not liable to Ultramares because there was no privity-like relationship between them. This is now known as the ***Ultramares* doctrine.** In his now-famous opinion, Judge Benjamin Cardozo wrote,

Ultramares doctrine
A rule stating that an accountant is liable only for negligence to third parties who are in *privity of contract* or in a *privity-like relationship* with the accountant. It provides a narrow standard for holding accountants liable to third parties for negligence.

> *If liability for negligence exists, a thoughtless slip or blunder, the failure to detect a theft or forgery beneath the cover of deceptive entries may expose accountants to a liability in an indeterminate amount for an indeterminate*

time to an indeterminate class. The hazards of a business conducted on these terms are so extreme as to enkindle doubt whether a flaw may not exist in the implication of a duty that exposes to these consequences.

Under the *Ultramares* doctrine, a privity of contract relationship would occur in which a client employed an accountant to prepare financial statements to be used by a third party for a specific purpose. For example, if (1) a client employs an accountant to prepare audited financial statements to be used by the client to secure a bank loan and (2) the accountant is made aware of this special purpose, the accountant is liable for any damages incurred by the bank because of a negligently prepared report. The *Ultramares* doctrine provides a narrow standard for holding accountants liable to third parties. A minority of states apply the privity or near privity rules for finding accountants liable to third parties for their negligence.

In the following case, the court held that a privity-like relationship qualified to find accountants liable for negligence to third-party plaintiffs.

CASE 51.2 *STATE COURT CASE Privity-Like Relationship*

Credit Alliance Corporation v. Arthur Andersen & Company

65 N.Y.2d 536, 493 N.Y.S.2d 435, 1985 N.Y. Lexis 15157
Court of Appeals of New York

"The facts as alleged by plaintiffs fail to demonstrate the existence of a relationship between the parties sufficiently approaching privity."

—Matthew Jasen, Judge

Facts

L.B. Smith, Inc. (Smith) was a Virginia corporation engaged in the business of selling, leasing, and servicing heavy construction equipment. It was a capital-intensive business that regularly required debt financing. Arthur Andersen & Co. (Andersen), a large national firm of certified public accountants, was employed to audit Smith's financial statements. Andersen audited Smith's financial statements for two years. During that period, Andersen issued unqualified opinions concerning Smith's financial statements. Without Andersen's knowledge, Smith gave copies of its audited financial statements to Credit Alliance Corporation (Credit Alliance). Credit Alliance, relying on these financial statements, extended more than $15 million of credit to Smith to finance the purchase of capital equipment through installment sales and leasing arrangements.

The audited financial statements overstated Smith's assets, net worth, and general financial position. In performing the audits, Andersen was negligent and failed to conduct investigations in accordance with generally accepted auditing standards. Because of this negligence, Andersen failed to discover Smith's precarious financial condition. The next year, Smith filed a petition for bankruptcy. Smith defaulted on obligations owed Credit Alliance in an amount exceeding $8.8 million. Credit Alliance brought this action against Andersen for negligence. The trial court denied Andersen's motion to dismiss. The appellate division affirmed. Andersen appealed.

Issue

Is Andersen liable under the *Ultramares* doctrine?

Language of the Court

Upon examination of Ultramares, certain criteria may be gleaned. Before accountants may be held liable in negligence to noncontractual parties who rely to their detriment on inaccurate financial reports, certain prerequisites must be satisfied, (1) the accountants must have been aware that the financial reports were to be used for a particular purpose or purposes, (2) in the furtherance of which a known party or parties was intended to rely, and (3) there must have been some conduct on the part of the accountants linking them to that party or parties, which evinces the accountants' understanding of that party or parties' reliance. In the appeal we decide today, application of the foregoing principles presents little difficulty. The facts as alleged by plaintiffs fail to demonstrate the existence of a relationship between the parties sufficiently

(continued)

approaching privity. While the allegations in the complaint state that Smith sought to induce plaintiffs to extend credit, no claim is made that Andersen was being employed to prepare the reports with that particular purpose in mind.

Decision

In addition to privity, the court of appeals held that an accountant can be held liable for negligence to third parties who are in a "privity-like relationship" with the accountant. In applying this expanded rule, the court held that Arthur Andersen & Co., the accountants, were not liable to plaintiff third-party Credit Alliance Corporation. The court dismissed Credit Alliance's cause of action for negligence against defendant Andersen.

Note

In this case, the court went beyond the privity requirement established by *Ultramares* and extended the liability of accountants for negligence to parties who are in a privity-like arrangement with the accountant. Some states follow this expanded rule, while other states follow the strict *Ultramares* doctrine.

Critical Legal Thinking Questions

What does the *Ultramares* doctrine provide? Do you think that accountants favor the *Ultramares* doctrine? What rule was established by the *Credit Alliance* case? Did the accountants breach any ethical duty in this case?

Liability to Third Parties: Section 552 of the *Restatement (Second) of Torts*

Section 552 of the *Restatement (Second)* of Torts
A rule stating that an accountant is liable only for negligence to third parties who are members of a *limited class of intended users* of the client's financial statements. It provides a broader standard for holding accountants liable to third parties for negligence than does the *Ultramares* doctrine.

Section 552 of the *Restatement (Second)* *of Torts* provides a broader approach for holding accountants liable to third parties for negligence than does the privity of contract requirement of the *Ultramares* doctrine or the privity-like requirement of *Credit Alliance*.

Under the Section 552 *Restatement* standard, an accountant is liable for his or her negligence to any member of a **limited class of intended users** for whose benefit the accountant has been employed to prepare the client's financial statements or to whom the accountant knows the client will supply copies of the financial statements. In other words, the accountant does not have to know the specific name of the third party.

The majority of states have adopted this standard, which is worded as follows:

Section 552. Information Negligently Supplied for the Guidance of Others.

1. *One who, in the course of his business, profession or employment, or in any other transaction in which he has a pecuniary interest, supplies false information for the guidance of others in their business transactions, is subject to liability for pecuniary loss caused to them by their justifiable reliance upon the information, if he fails to exercise reasonable care or competence in obtaining or communicating the information.*
2. *Except as stated in Subsection (3), the liability stated in Subsection (1) is limited to loss suffered*
   a. *by the person or one of a limited group of persons for whose benefit and guidance he intends to supply the information or knows that the recipient intends to supply it; and*
   b. *through reliance upon it in a transaction that he intends the information to influence or knows that the recipient so intends or in a substantially similar transaction.*
3. *The liability of one who is under a public duty to give the information extends to loss suffered by any of the class of persons for whose benefit the duty is created, in any of the transactions in which it is intended to protect them.*

The intended users test has also been adopted by the *Restatement Third of Torts: Liability for Economic Harm*.

Example A client company needs an accountant to prepare audited financial statements to be used for the purpose of obtaining investors for the company. The company employs an accounting firm to conduct the audit and prepare the financial statements. The accountant is notified that the financial statements will be provided to potential investors. The accountant agrees to conduct the audit of the company and prepare financial statements to be used for this purpose. The accountant is negligent in conducting the audit and preparing the financial statements by not discovering that the company has significantly overstated its earnings. The company provides copies of the audited financial statements to potential investors, who rely on the financial statements and invest in the company. The company fails, and the investors lose their investments. In this example, the accountant is liable to the investors—a *limited class of intended users*—who relied on the information in the financial statements, purchased securities of the company, and were injured thereby. The accountant is liable even though the accountant does not know the specific identities of the investors.

In the following case, the court applied a Section 552 rule in deciding whether an accountant could be held liable for negligence to third-party nonclients.

CASE 51.3 *STATE COURT CASE Accountants' Liability to a Third Party*

Cast Art Industries, LLC v. KPMG LLP

36 A.3d 1049, 2012 N.J. Lexis 152 (2012)
Supreme Court of New Jersey

"KPMG was not told that a nonclient would be relying on its work."

—Dorothea Wefing, Judge

Facts

Papel Giftware produced and sold collectible figurines and giftware. KPMG LLP, certified public accountants, had audited Papel's financial statements for many years and produced audited financial statements with unqualified opinions. KPMG issued the financial statements for the year in question.

Cast Art Industries, LLC, was in the same line of business as Papel. Cast Art became interested in acquiring Papel and hired attorneys, investment bankers, and accountants to advise it in connection with the proposed transaction. Cast Art obtained copies of Papel's audited financial statements and had its accountants review the financial statements and KPMG's audit papers. Three months later, Cast Art decided to acquire Papel and obtained a $22 million loan from PNC Bank to fund the transaction. Major shareholders of Cast Art gave their personal guarantees to the bank for $3 million if the loan was not repaid.

Shortly after the merger was finalized, Cast Art began to experience difficulty in collecting some of Papel's accounts receivable. After conducting an investigation, Cast Art learned that the financial statements prepared by Papel were inaccurate in several ways. Papel recognized revenue from sales when goods were shipped and invoices sent, not when payment was received. In addition, Papel routinely booked revenue from goods that had not yet been shipped and would often not close its books for a month so that it could include revenue that was earned in the following month. Cast Art knew at the time of the merger that Papel was carrying a significant amount of debt. The surviving corporation from the merger was unable to generate sufficient revenue to carry its debt load and produce new goods, and it eventually failed.

Cast Art and its shareholders sued KPMG, alleging that KPMG had been negligent in auditing Papel's financial statements and that KPMG was therefore liable for their losses. KPMG asserted that it was not liable to the plaintiff nonclients based on the New Jersey Accountant Liability Act (Act), a state statute that adopted the rules of Section 552 of the *Restatement (Second) of Torts*. KPMG argued that, because Cast Art had not retained it to audit Papel, Cast Art was not its client, and KPMG did not know at the time it performed the audits that Papel and Cast Art were contemplating a merger or that Cast Art would be relying on KPMG's auditing work, and that therefore the plaintiffs' claims were barred by the act. KPMG asserted that the company's large debt and a decrease in sales caused its failure. The trial court held that KPMG was liable and

(continued)

awarded damages of $38 million to the plaintiffs. The appellate court upheld the verdict. KPMG appealed to the supreme court of New Jersey.

Issue

Is KPMG liable to the plaintiff-third parties for accounting malpractice?

Language of the Court

To forestall indeterminate liability, subsection (2) of Section 552 limits the scope of potential liability to those persons, or classes of persons, whom the accountant knows and intends will rely on his opinion, or whom he knows his client intends will so rely. Clearly, KPMG did not know, when it agreed to perform the audit, that its work could play a role in a subsequent merger. An auditor is entitled to know at the outset the scope of the work it is being requested to perform and the concomitant risk it is being asked to assume. KPMG was not told that a nonclient would be relying on its work. The statute requires agreement, not mere awareness, on the part of the accountant to the planned use of his work product. Because Cast Art failed to establish that KPMG knew at the time of the engagement by the client or thereafter agreed that Cast Art could rely on its work in proceeding with the merger, Cast Art failed to satisfy the requisite elements of the statute, and KPMG was entitled to judgment. In light of this conclusion, the remaining issues raised by the parties are moot and need not be addressed.

Decision

The supreme court of New Jersey held that KPMG was not liable to the nonclient third-party plaintiffs and ordered the case dismissed.

Critical Legal Thinking Questions

What does Section 552 of the *Restatement (Second) of Torts* require for an accountant to be held liable for negligence to nonclients? Is this a more reasonable rule than the *Ultramares* doctrine?

Liability to Third Parties: Foreseeability Standard

foreseeability standard
A rule stating that an accountant is liable for negligence to third parties who are members of a *foreseen class of users* of the client's financial statements. It provides the broadest standard for holding accountants liable to third parties for negligence.

A few states have adopted a broad rule known as the **foreseeability standard** for holding accountants liable to third parties for negligence. Under this standard, an accountant is liable to any member of a **foreseen class of users** of a client's financial statements. The accountant's liability does not depend on his or her knowledge of the identity of either the user or the intended class of users. Only a few states have adopted this rule.

Example A corporation makes a tender offer for the shares of a target corporation whose financial statements have been audited by a CPA. If the CPA prepared the financial statements negligently and the tender offeror relied on them to purchase the target corporation, the accountant is liable for injuries suffered by the tender offeror.

CONCEPT SUMMARY

ACCOUNTANTS' NEGLIGENCE LIABILITY TO THIRD PARTIES

Legal Theory	To Whom Liable?
Ultramares doctrine	Any person in *privity of contract* or a *privity-like relationship* with the accountant.
Section 552 of the *Restatement (Second) of Torts*	Any member of a *limited class of intended users* for whose benefit the accountant has been employed to prepare the client's financial statements or whom the accountant knows will be supplied copies of the client's financial statements.
Foreseeability standard	Any member of a *foreseen class of users* of the client's financial statements.

Liability to Third Parties: Fraud

If an accountant engages in *actual* or *constructive fraud*, a third party that relies on the accountant's fraud and is injured thereby may bring a tort action against the accountant to recover damages.

Example Salvo Retailers, Inc. (Salvo) applies for a bank loan, but the bank requires audited financial statements of the company before making the loan. Salvo hires a CPA to do the audit, and the CPA falsifies the financial position of the company. The bank extends the loan to Salvo, and the loan is not repaid. The bank can recover its losses from the CPA who committed fraud.

Liability to Third Parties: Breach of Contract

Third parties usually cannot sue accountants for breach of contract because the third parties are merely incidental beneficiaries who do not acquire any rights under the accountant–client contract. That is, they are not in privity of contract with the accountants.

Example An accountant contracts to perform an audit for Kim Manufacturing Company (Kim) but then fails to do so. A supplier to Kim cannot sue the accountant because the supplier is not in privity of contract with the accountant.

Securities Law Violations

51.6 Describe how accountants can be held liable for violating securities laws.

Accountants can be held liable for violating various federal and state securities laws. This section examines the civil and criminal liability of accountants under these statutes.

Section 11(a) of the Securities Act of 1933

Before a corporation or another business issues securities to the public in a registered public offering or as an emerging growth company, the Securities Act of 1933 requires that the issuer file a **registration statement** with the Securities and Exchange Commission (SEC). Accountants are employed to prepare and certify financial statements that are included in the registration statements filed with the SEC. Accountants are considered experts, and the financial statements they prepare are considered an **expertised portion** of the registration statement.

Section 11(a) of the Securities Act of 1933 imposes civil liability on accountants and others for (1) making misstatements or omissions of material facts in a registration statement or (2) failing to find such misstatements or omissions.[4] Accountants can be held liable for fraud or negligence under Section 11(a) if the financial statements they prepare for a registration statement contain such errors.

Accountants can, however, assert a **due diligence defense** to liability. An accountant avoids liability if he or she had, after reasonable investigation, reasonable grounds to believe and did believe, at the time the registration statement became effective, that the statements made therein were true and there was no omission of a material fact that would make the statements misleading.

Section 11(a) of the Securities Act of 1933
A section of the Securities Act of 1933 that imposes civil liability on accountants and others for (1) making misstatements or omissions of material facts in a registration statement or (2) failing to find such misstatements or omissions.

due diligence defense
A defense an accountant can assert that, if proven, avoids liability under Section 11(a).

Example While conducting an audit, accountants fail to detect a fraud in the financial statements. The accountants' unqualified opinion is included in the registration statement and prospectus for the offering. An investor purchases the securities and suffers a loss when the fraud is uncovered. The investor can sue the makers of the misrepresentations for fraud and the accountants for negligence.

The plaintiff may recover the difference between the price he or she paid for the security and the value of the security at the time of the lawsuit (or at the time the security was sold, if it was sold prior to the lawsuit). The plaintiff does not have to prove that he or she relied on the misstatement or omission. Privity of contract is irrelevant.

Section 10(b) of the Securities Exchange Act of 1934

Section 10(b) of the Securities Exchange Act of 1934
A section of the Securities Exchange Act of 1934 that prohibits any manipulative or deceptive practice in connection with the purchase or sale of a security.

Rule 10b-5
A rule adopted by the SEC to clarify the reach of Section 10(b) against deceptive and fraudulent activities in the purchase and sale of securities.

Section 10(b) of the Securities Exchange Act of 1934 prohibits any manipulative or deceptive practice in connection with the purchase or sale of any security.[5] Pursuant to its authority under Section 10(b), the SEC promulgated **Rule 10b-5**. This rule makes it unlawful for any person, by the use or means or instrumentality of interstate commerce, to employ any device or artifice to defraud; to make misstatements or omissions of material fact; or to engage in any act, practice, or course of conduct that would operate as a fraud or deceit on any person in connection with the purchase or sale of any security.[6]

The scope of these antifraud provisions is quite broad, and the courts have implied a civil private cause of action. Thus, plaintiffs injured by a violation of these provisions can sue the offending party for monetary damages. Only purchasers and sellers of securities can sue under Section 10(b) and Rule 10b-5. Privity of contract is irrelevant.

Accountants are often defendants in Section 10(b) and Rule 10b-5 actions. The U.S. Supreme Court has held that only intentional conduct and recklessness of accountants and others, but not ordinary negligence, violates Section 10(b) and Rule 10b-5.[7]

Section 18(a) of the Securities Exchange Act of 1934

Section 18(a) of the Securities Exchange Act of 1934
A section of the Securities Exchange Act of 1934 that imposes civil liability on any person who makes false or misleading statements in any application, report, or document filed with the SEC.

Section 18(a) of the Securities Exchange Act of 1934 imposes civil liability on any person who makes false or misleading statements of material fact in any application, report, or document filed with the SEC.[8] Accountants often file reports and other documents with the SEC on behalf of clients; they can be found liable for violating this section.

Like Section 10(b), Section 18(a) requires a showing of fraud or reckless conduct on the part of the defendant. Thus, the plaintiffs in a Section 18(a) action must prove that they relied on the misleading statement and that it affected the price of the security. Negligence is not actionable.

There are two ways an accountant or another defendant can defeat the imposition of liability under Section 18(a). First, the defendant can show that he or she acted in *good faith*. Second, he or she can show that the plaintiff had knowledge of the false or misleading statement when the securities were purchased or sold.

Private Securities Litigation Reform Act of 1995

Enacted in 1995, the **Private Securities Litigation Reform Act (PSLRA)**, a federal statute, changed the liability of accountants and other securities professionals in the following ways:

- The act imposes pleading and procedural requirements that make it more difficult for plaintiffs to bring class action securities lawsuits.
- The act replaces **joint and several liability** of defendants (where one party of several at-fault parties could be made to pay all of a judgment) with **proportionate liability**. This new rule limits a defendant's liability to his or her *proportionate* degree of fault. Thus, the act relieves accountants from being the "deep pocket" defendant except up to their degree of fault. The only exception to this rule—where joint and several liability is still imposed—is if the defendant acted knowingly.[9]

proportionate liability
A rule that limits a defendant's liability to his or her proportionate degree of fault.

Example Consider a case involving plaintiffs who are victims of a securities fraud perpetrated by a firm, and they suffer $1 million in damages. If the accountants for the firm are found to be 25 percent liable, the accountants are required to pay only their proportionate share in damages—$250,000. If the accountants knowingly participated in the fraud, however, they would be jointly and severally liable for the entire $1 million in damages.

Section 10A of the Securities Exchange Act of 1934
A law that imposes a duty on auditors to detect and report illegal acts committed by their clients.

The following ethics feature discusses an accountant's duty to report a client's illegal activity.

Ethics

Accountants' Duty to Report a Client's Illegal Activity

While conducting an audit of a client company's financial statements, an accountant could uncover information about the client's illegal activities. In 1995, Congress added **Section 10A of the Securities Exchange Act of 1934.**[10] Section 10A imposes duties on auditors to detect and report illegal acts committed by their clients. Under Section 10A, an *illegal act* is defined as an "act or omission that violates any law, or any rule or regulation having the force of law." Section 10A imposes the following reporting requirements on accountants:

- Unless an illegal act is "clearly inconsequential," the auditor must inform the client's management and audit committee of the illegal act.
- If management fails to take timely and appropriate remedial action, the auditor must report the illegal act to the client's full board of directors if (a) the illegal act will have a material effect on the client's financial statements and (b) the auditor expects to issue a nonstandard audit report or intends to resign from the audit engagement.
- Once the auditor reports the illegal act to the board of directors, the board of directors must inform the Securities and Exchange Commission (SEC) of the auditor's conclusion within one business day; if the client fails to do so, the auditor must notify the SEC the next business day.

Ethics Questions
What prompted Congress to add Section 10A to the Securities Exchange Act? Should accountants report the unethical conduct of their clients that is not considered illegal conduct? Why or why not?

Criminal Liability of Accountants

51.7 Describe how accountants can be found criminally liable for their actions.

Many statutes impose criminal penalties on accountants who violate their provisions. These criminal statutes are discussed in the following paragraphs.

Section 24 of the Securities Act of 1933
A section of the Securities Act of 1933 that makes it a criminal offense for any person to (1) willfully make any untrue statement of material fact in a registration statement filed with the SEC, (2) omit any material fact necessary to ensure that the statements made in the registration statement are not misleading, or (3) willfully violate any other provision of the Securities Act of 1933 or rule or regulation adopted thereunder.

Criminal Liability: Section 24 of the Securities Act of 1933

Section 24 of the Securities Act of 1933 makes it a criminal offense for any person to (1) willfully make any untrue statement of material fact in a registration statement filed with the SEC, (2) omit any material fact necessary to ensure that the statements made in the registration statement are not misleading, or (3) willfully violate any other provision of the Securities Act of 1933 or rule or regulation adopted thereunder. Because accountants prepare the financial reports included in the registration statements, they are subject to criminal liability for violating this section. Penalties for a violation of this statute include fines, imprisonment, or both.[11]

Section 32 of the Securities Exchange Act of 1934
A section of the Securities Exchange Act of 1934 that makes it a criminal offense for any person willfully and knowingly to make or cause to be made any false or misleading statement in any application, report, or other document required to be filed with the SEC pursuant to the Securities Exchange Act of 1934 or any rule or regulation adopted thereunder.

Criminal Liability: Section 32 of the Securities Exchange Act of 1934

Section 32 of the Securities Exchange Act of 1934 makes it a criminal offense for any person willfully and knowingly to make or cause to be made any false or misleading statement in any application, report, or other document required to be filed with the SEC pursuant to the Securities Exchange Act of 1934 or any rule or regulation adopted thereunder. Because accountants often file reports and documents with the SEC on behalf of clients, they are subject to this rule. Insider trading also falls within the parameters of this section.

On conviction under Section 32, an individual may be fined, imprisoned, or both. A corporation or another entity may be fined. A person cannot be imprisoned under Section 32 unless he or she had knowledge of the rule or regulation violated.[12]

If the SEC finds evidence of fraud or other willful violation of federal securities laws or other federal law (e.g., mail and wire fraud statutes), the matter may be referred to the U.S. Department of Justice, with a recommendation that the suspected offending party be criminally prosecuted. The Department of Justice determines whether criminal charges will be brought.

Criminal Liability: Tax Preparation

Tax Reform Act of 1976
An act that imposes criminal liability on accountants and others who prepare federal tax returns if they (1) willfully understate a client's tax liability, (2) negligently understate the tax liability, or (3) aid or assist in the preparation of a false tax return.

The **Tax Reform Act of 1976** imposes criminal liability on accountants and others who prepare federal tax returns and commit wrongdoing.[13] The act specifically imposes the following penalties: (1) fines for the willful understatement of a client's tax liability, (2) fines for the negligent understatement of a client's tax liability, and (3) fines and imprisonment for an individual and fines for a corporation for aiding and assisting in the preparation of a false tax return. Accountants who have violated these provisions can be enjoined from further federal income tax practice.

Criminal Liability: Racketeer Influenced and Corrupt Organizations Act

Racketeer Influenced and Corrupt Organizations Act (RICO)
A federal act that provides for both criminal and civil penalties for securities fraud.

Accountants and other professionals can be named as defendants in lawsuits that assert violations of the **Racketeer Influenced and Corrupt Organizations Act (RICO)**.[14] Securities fraud falls under the definition of racketeering activity, so the government often brings a RICO allegation in conjunction with a securities fraud allegation.

Persons injured by a RICO violation can bring a private *civil* action against the violator and recover treble (triple) damages. To bring a private civil RICO action based on securities fraud, the defendant must have been criminally convicted of the securities fraud.[15] A third-party independent contractor (e.g., an outside accountant) must have participated in the operation or management of the enterprise to be liable for civil RICO.[16]

Criminal Liability: State Securities Laws

Most states have enacted securities laws, many of which are patterned after federal securities laws. State securities laws provide for a variety of civil and criminal penalties for violations of these laws. Many states have enacted all or part of the **Uniform Securities Act**, a model act promulgated by the National Conference of Commissioners on Uniform State Laws. **Section 101 of the Uniform Securities Act** makes it a criminal offense for accountants and others to willfully falsify financial statements and other reports.

Sarbanes-Oxley Act

51.8 Describe the provisions of the Sarbanes-Oxley Act and how they apply to accountants.

During the late 1990s and early 2000s, many corporations in the United States engaged in fraudulent accounting in order to report inflated earnings or to conceal losses. Many public accounting firms that were hired to audit the financial statements of these companies failed to detect fraudulent accounting practices.

In response, Congress enacted the federal **Sarbanes-Oxley Act** (also called **SOX**).[17] SOX imposes new rules that affect public accountants. The goals of these rules are to improve financial reporting, eliminate conflicts of interest, and provide government oversight of accounting and audit services. Several major features of the act that apply to accountants are discussed in the following paragraphs.

The following feature discusses the Public Company Accounting Oversight Board.

Sarbanes-Oxley Act (SOX)
A federal act that imposes significant rules for the regulation of the accounting profession.

Business Environment

Public Company Accounting Oversight Board

The Sarbanes-Oxley Act creates the **Public Company Accounting Oversight Board (PCAOB)**, which consists of five financially literate members who are appointed by the SEC for five-year terms. Two of the members must be CPAs, and three must not be CPAs. The SEC has oversight and enforcement authority over the board. The board has the authority to adopt rules concerning auditing, accounting quality control, independence, and ethics of public companies and public accountants.

To audit a public company, a public accounting firm must register with the board. Registered accounting firms that audit more than 100 public companies annually are subject to inspection and review by the board once a year; all other public accounting firms must be audited by the board every three years. The board may discipline public accountants and accounting firms and order sanctions for intentional or reckless conduct, including suspending or revoking registration with the board, placing temporary limitations on activities, and assessing civil monetary penalties.

Audit and Nonaudit Services

The act makes it unlawful for a registered public accounting firm to simultaneously provide audit and certain nonaudit services to a public company. If a public accounting firm audits a public company, the accounting firm may not provide the following nonaudit services to the client: (1) bookkeeping services; (2) financial information systems; (3) appraisal or valuation services; (4) internal audit services; (5) management functions; (6) human resources services; (7) broker, dealer, or investment services; (8) investment banking services; (9) legal services; or (10) any other services determined by the board. A certified public accounting firm may provide tax services to audit clients if such tax services are preapproved by the audit committee of the client.

Public Company Accounting Oversight Board (PCAOB)
A board that reports to the Securities and Exchange Commission (SEC) that has the authority to adopt rules concerning auditing, accounting quality control, independence, and ethics of public companies and public accountants.

Audit Report Sign-Off

Each audit by a certified public accounting firm is assigned an audit partner of the firm to supervise the audit and approve the audit report. The act requires that a second partner of the accounting firm review and approve audit reports prepared by the firm. All audit papers must be retained for at least seven years. The lead audit partner and reviewing partner must rotate off an audit every five years.

WEB EXERCISE
Visit the website of the Public Company Accounting Oversight Board (PCAOB) at **www.pcaobus.org**. What is the mission of this board?

Certain Employment Prohibited

Any person who is employed by a public accounting firm that audits a client cannot be employed by that client as the chief executive officer (CEO), chief financial officer (CFO), controller, chief accounting officer, or equivalent position for a period of one year following the audit.

The following feature discusses the audit committee of the board of directors.

Business Environment

Audit Committee

The act requires that public corporations have an **audit committee** that is composed of independent members of the board of directors. These are outside board members who are not employed by the corporation and do not receive compensation other than for directors' duties from the corporation. The audit committee must have at least one member who is a financial expert by either education or experience who is able to understand generally accepted accounting principles, the preparation of financial statements, and audit committee functions.

The audit committee is responsible for the appointment of, payment of compensation for, and oversight of public accounting firms employed to audit the company. The audit committee must approve all audit and permissible nonaudit services to be performed by a public accounting firm. The audit committee has authority to employ independent legal counsel and other advisors.

The Sarbanes-Oxley Act requires public companies to establish and maintain adequate internal controls and procedures for financial reporting. The act requires a public company to prepare an assessment of the effectiveness of its internal controls at the end of each fiscal year. These internal audits are supervised by the audit committee.

CONCEPT SUMMARY

PROVISIONS OF THE SARBANES-OXLEY ACT

- Creates the Public Company Accounting Oversight Board (PCAOB)
- Requires public accounting firms to register with the PCAOB
- Separates audit services and certain nonaudit services provided by accountants to clients
- Requires an audit partner of the accounting firm to supervise an audit and approve an audit report prepared by the firm and requires a second partner of the accounting firm to review and approve the audit report
- Prohibits employment of an accountant by a previous audit client for certain positions for a period of one year following the audit
- Requires a public company to have an audit committee composed of independent members of the board of directors that employs and oversees a public accounting firm

Accountants' Privilege and Work Papers

51.9 Explain under what circumstances an accountant–client privilege applies.

audit committee
A committee of the board of directors that is composed of outside directors that is responsible for the oversight of the outside and internal audits of the corporation.

While conducting audits and providing other services to clients, accountants obtain information about their clients and prepare work papers. Sometimes clients are sued in court, and the court seeks information about the client from the accountant. The following paragraphs discuss the law that applies to these matters.

Accountant–Client Privilege

accountant–client privilege
A state law providing that an accountant cannot be called as a witness against a client in a court action.

Sometimes clients of accountants are sued in court. About 20 states have enacted statutes that create an **accountant–client privilege**. In these states, an accountant cannot be called as a witness against a client in a court action. The majority of the states follow the common law, which provides that an accountant may be called at court to testify against his or her client.

The U.S. Supreme Court has held that there is no accountant–client privilege under federal law.[18] Therefore an accountant could be called as a witness in cases involving federal securities laws, federal mail or wire fraud, federal RICO, or other federal criminal statutes.

Accountants' Work Papers

Accountants often generate substantial internal *work papers* as they perform their services. These papers often include plans for conducting audits, work assignments, notes regarding the collection of data, evidence about the testing of accounts, notes concerning the client's internal controls, notes reconciling the accountant's report and the client's records, research, comments, memorandums, explanations, opinions, and information regarding the affairs of the client.

Some state statutes provide **work product immunity**, which means an **accountant's work papers** cannot be discovered in a court case against the accountant's client. Most states do not provide this protection, and an accountant's work papers can be discovered. Federal law allows for discovery of an accountant's work papers in a federal case against the accountant's client.

work product immunity
A state law that provides that an accountant's work papers cannot be used against a client in a court action.

Key Terms and Concepts

Accountant (895)
Accountant–client privilege (910)
Accountant's work papers (911)
Accounting malpractice (negligence) (898)
Actual fraud (898)
Adverse opinion (897)
American Institute of Certified Public Accountants (AICPA) (897)
Audit (897)
Audit committee (910)
Auditor's opinion (897)
Breach of contract (898)
Certified public accountant (CPA) (895)
Constructive fraud (gross negligence) (898)
Disclaimer of opinion (897)
Due diligence defense (905)
Engagement (898)
Expertised portion (905)
Foreseeability standard (904)
Foreseen class of users (904)
Fraud (fraudulent misrepresentation) (898)
Generally Accepted Accounting Principles (GAAPs) (896)
Generally Accepted Auditing Standards (GAASs) (897)
Gross negligence (898)
International Accounting Standards Board (IASB) (896)
International Financial Reporting Standards (IFRSs) (896)
Joint and several liability (906)
Limited class of intended users (902)
Limited liability partnership (LLP) (895)
Private Securities Litigation Reform Act (PSLRA) (906)
Privity-like relationship (900)
Privity of contract (900)
Proportionate liability (906)
Public accountant (895)
Public Company Accounting Oversight Board (PCAOB) (909)
Qualified opinion (897)
Racketeer Influenced and Corrupt Organizations Act (RICO) (908)
Registration statement (905)
Rule 10b-5 (906)
Sarbanes-Oxley Act (SOX) (909)
Section 10A of the Securities Exchange Act of 1934 (907)
Section 10(b) of the Securities Exchange Act of 1934 (906)
Section 11(a) of the Securities Act of 1933 (905)
Section 18(a) of the Securities Exchange Act of 1934 (906)
Section 24 of the Securities Act of 1933 (907)
Section 32 of the Securities Exchange Act of 1934 (907)
Section 101 of the Uniform Securities Act (908)
Section 552 of the *Restatement (Second) of Torts* (902)
Tax Reform Act of 1976 (908)
Ultramares Corporation v. Touche (900)
Ultramares doctrine (900)
Unaudited financial statements (898)
Uniform Securities Act (908)
Unqualified opinion (897)
Work product immunity (911)

Critical Legal Thinking Cases

51.1 Accountant's Liability to Third Party Brandon Apparel Group, Inc. (Brandon) made and sold clothing and licensed the making and selling of clothing in exchange for a percentage of the licensees' sales revenues. Brandon began borrowing money from Johnson Bank and in two years owed the bank $10 million. George Korbakes & Company, LLP (GKCO) was the auditor of Brandon during the period at issue in this case. When Brandon was seeking an additional loan from the bank, Brandon instructed GKCO to give the bank the audit report that GKCO had just completed, which GKCO gave to Johnson Bank.

The audit report summarized Brandon's financial results for the year and revealed that Brandon had serious problems. But the audit report contained several errors. First, the audit report classified a $1 million lawsuit Brandon had brought against a third party as an asset, but it was in fact only a contingency that should not have been listed as an asset. Second, Brandon's sales were inflated by 50 percent because sales of a licensee were treated as if they were Brandon's sales. However, footnotes in the audit report indicated that Brandon might not prevail in the lawsuit and that Brandon's sales included those of a licensee.

After receiving the audit report, Johnson Bank made further loans to Brandon. Brandon did not repay Johnson Bank the new money it borrowed. Johnson Bank sued GKCO, alleging that GKCO committed the tort of negligent misrepresentation and was therefore liable for the money lost by the bank as a result of the errors in the audit report prepared by GKCO. Is GKCO, the auditor of Brandon, liable to Johnson Bank for negligent misrepresentation under Section 552 of the *Restatement (Second) of Torts*? *Johnson Bank v. George Korbakes & Company, LLP*, 472 F.3d 439, 2006 U.S. App. Lexis 31058 (United States Court of Appeals for the Seventh Circuit, 2006)

51.2 **Auditor's Liability to Third Party** Michael H. Clott was chairman and chief executive officer of First American Mortgage Company, Inc. (FAMCO), which originated loans and sold the loans to investors, including E. F. Hutton Mortgage Corp. (Hutton). FAMCO employed Ernst & Whinney, a national CPA firm, to conduct audits of its financial statements. Hutton received a copy of the financial statements with an unqualified certification by Ernst & Whinney. Hutton bought more than $100 million of loans from FAMCO. As a result of massive fraudulent activity by Clott, which was undetected by Ernst & Whinney during its audit, many of the loans purchased by Hutton proved to be worthless. Ernst & Whinney had no knowledge of Clott's activities. Hutton's own negligence contributed to most of the losses it suffered. Hutton sued Ernst & Whinney for fraud and negligence. Is Ernst & Whinney liable? *E. F. Hutton Mortgage Corporation v. Pappas*, 690 F.Supp. 1465, 1988 U.S. Dist. Lexis 6444 (United States District Court for the District of Maryland, 1988)

51.3 **Accountant's Liability to Third Party** Giant Stores Corporation (Giant) hired Touche Ross & Co. (Touche), a national CPA firm, to conduct audits of the company's financial statements for two years. Touche gave an unqualified opinion for both years. Touche was unaware of any specific use of the audited statements by Giant. After receiving copies of these audited financial statements from Giant, Harry and Barry Rosenblum (Rosenblums) sold their retail catalog showroom business to Giant in exchange for 80,000 shares of Giant stock.

One year later, a major fraud was uncovered at Giant that caused its bankruptcy. Because of the bankruptcy, the stock that the Rosenblums had received became worthless. In conducting Giant's audits, Touche had failed to uncover that Giant did not own certain assets that appeared on its financial statements and that Giant had omitted substantial amounts of accounts payable from its records. The Rosenblums sued Touche for accounting malpractice. Is Touche liable for accounting malpractice under any of the three negligence theories discussed in this chapter? *H. Rosenblum, Inc. v. Adler*, 461 A.2d 138, 1983 N.J. Lexis 2717 (Supreme Court of New Jersey, 1983)

51.4 **Accountant's Liability to Third Party** Texscan Corporation (Texscan) was a company located in Phoenix, Arizona. The company was audited by Coopers & Lybrand (Coopers), a national CPA firm that prepared audited financial statements for the company. The Lindner Fund, Inc. and the Lindner Dividend Fund, Inc. (Lindner Funds) were mutual funds that invested in securities of companies. After receiving and reviewing the audited financial statements of Texscan, Lindner Funds purchased securities in the company. Thereafter, Texscan suffered financial difficulties, and Lindner Funds suffered substantial losses on its investment. Lindner Funds sued Coopers, alleging that Coopers was negligent in conducting the audit and preparing Texscan's financial statements. Can Coopers be held liable to Lindner Funds for accounting malpractice under the *Ultramares* doctrine, Section 552 of the *Restatement (Second) of Torts*, or the foreseeability standard? *Lindner Fund v. Abney*, 770 S.W.2d 437, 1989 Mo. App. Lexis 490 (Court of Appeals of Missouri, 1989)

Ethics Cases

51.5 **Ethics Case** The archdiocese of Miami established a health and welfare plan to provide medical coverage for its employees. The archdiocese purchased a stop-loss insurance policy from Lloyd's of London (Lloyd's), which provided insurance against losses that exceeded the basic coverage of the plan. The archdiocese employed Coopers & Lybrand (Coopers), a national firm of CPAs, to audit the health plan every year for 12 years.

The audit program required Coopers to obtain a copy of the current stop-loss policy and record any changes. After two years, Coopers neither obtained a copy of the policy nor verified the existence of the Lloyd's insurance. Nevertheless, Coopers repeatedly represented to the trustees of the archdiocese that the Lloyd's insurance policy was in effect, but in fact it had been canceled. During this period of time, Dennis McGee, an employee of the archdiocese, had embezzled funds that were to be used to pay premiums on the Lloyd's policy. The archdiocese sued Coopers for accounting malpractice and sought to recover the funds stolen by McGee. Did Coopers act ethically in this case? Is Coopers liable? *Coopers & Lybrand v. Trustees of the Archdiocese of Miami*, 536 So.2d 278, 1988 Fla. App. Lexis 5348 (Court of Appeal of Florida, 1988)

51.6 Ethics Case Milton Mende purchased the Star Midas Mining Co., Inc., a Nevada corporation, for $6,500. This corporation was a shell corporation with no assets. Mende changed the name of the corporation to American Equities Corporation (American Equities) and hired Bernard Howard to prepare certain accounting reports so that the company could issue securities to the public. In preparing the financial accounts, Howard (1) made no examination of American Equities' books; (2) falsely included an asset of more than $700,000 on the books, which was a dormant mining company that had been through insolvency proceedings; (3) included in the profit and loss statement companies that Howard knew American Equities did not own; and (4) recklessly stated as facts things of which he was ignorant. Did Howard act unethically? The United States sued Howard for criminal conspiracy in violation of federal securities laws. Is Howard criminally liable? *United States v. Howard*, 328 F.2d 854, 1964 U.S. App. Lexis 6343 (United States Court of Appeals for the Second Circuit, 1964)

Notes

1. GAAPs are official standards promulgated by the Financial Accounting Standards Board (FASB) and predecessor accounting ruling bodies. GAAPs also include unofficial pronouncements, interpretations, research studies, and textbooks.
2. GAASs are issued by the Auditing Standards Committee of the American Institute of Certified Public Accountants (AICPA).
3. 255 N.Y. 170, 174 N.E. 441, 1931 N.Y. Lexis 660 (Court of Appeals of New York).
4. 15 U.S.C. Section 77k(a).
5. 15 U.S.C. Section 78j(b).
6. 17 C.F.R. Section 240.10b–5.
7. *Ernst & Ernst v. Hochfelder*, 425 U.S. 185, 96 S.Ct. 1375, 1976 U.S. Lexis 2 (Supreme Court of the United States).
8. 15 U.S.C. Section 78r(a).
9. 15 U.S.C. Section 78u-4(g).
10. 15 U.S.C. Section 78j-1.
11. 15 U.S.C. Section 77x.
12. 15 U.S.C. Section 78ff.
13. 26 U.S.C. Sections 7206(1), 7206(2).
14. 18 U.S.C. Sections 1961–1968.
15. Private Securities Litigation Reform Act of 1995.
16. *Reves v. Ernst & Young*, 507 U.S. 170, 113 S.Ct. 1163, 1993 U.S. Lexis 1940 (Supreme Court of the United States).
17. Public Law No. 107-204, 16 Statute 745, also known as the Public Company Accounting Reform and Investor Protection Act of 2002.
18. *Couch v. United States*, 409 U.S. 322, 93 S.Ct. 611, 1973 U.S. Lexis (Supreme Court of the United States).

PART

XII Personal Law

Henry R. Cheeseman

CHAPTER

52

Wills, Trusts, and Estates

Henry R. Cheeseman

VETERANS CEMETERY

The U.S. Congress enacted the National Holiday Act of 1971,[1] which made the last day in May Memorial Day, a national holiday. Memorial Day is a day of remembrance for veterans of the nation's military services. I miss my friend, Mark H. Dixon, with whom I served in the U.S. Army, who gave his life while saving a fellow soldier.

Learning Objectives

After studying this chapter, you should be able to:

52.1 List and describe the requirements for making a valid will.

52.2 Describe the process of probating a will.

52.3 Describe the different types of testamentary gifts.

52.4 Identify how property is distributed under intestacy statutes if a person dies without a will.

52.5 Define *irrevocable trust* and describe how an irrevocable trust works.

52.6 List and describe special forms of trusts.

52.7 Define a *living trust* and describe how a living trust works.

52.8 Describe how a will or trust may be found invalid under the doctrine of undue influence.

52.9 Define a *living will* and describe why a person would execute a living will and health care directive.

> *"When you have told someone you have left him a legacy, the only decent thing to do is to die at once."*
>
> —*Samuel Butler (1835–1902)*

Introduction to Wills, Trusts, and Estates

Wills and trusts are means of transferring property. *Wills* transfer property on a person's death. They permit people to state exactly where they want their property to go when they die. If a person dies *intestate*—that is, without a will—the deceased's property is distributed to relatives as provided in the state statute. The property escheats (goes) to the state if there are no relatives.

Trusts are used to transfer property that is to be held and managed for the benefit of another person or persons. A trust can be created to come into effect during one's lifetime. Trusts may also be created during one's lifetime and be worded to become effective only on the trustor's (or grantor's) death. A *living trust* is a special type of trust used for estate planning.

A living will and health care directive can be created by an individual. A *living will* sets forth a person's instructions regarding emergency medical treatment and whether that person should be kept alive on life support systems. A *health care directive* names an individual or individuals who can make health care decisions if the maker of the directive is unable to do so.

Disinherit: The prankish action of the ghosts in cutting the pockets out of trousers.

Frank McKinney Hubbard
The Roycroft Dictionary (1923)

Will

52.1 List and describe the requirements for making a valid will.

A **will** is a declaration of how a person wants his or her property to be distributed at death. It is a testamentary deposition of property. The person who makes a will is called a **testator** (if male) or **testatrix** (if female). Some states use the designation *testator* for both male and female persons. A person designated in the will to receive property of the testator is called a **beneficiary** (see Exhibit 52.1).

will
A declaration of how a person wants his or her property to be distributed on death.

testator or testatrix
A person who makes a will.

beneficiary of a will
A person or an organization designated in a will to receive all or a portion of the testator's property at the time of the testator's death.

Exhibit 52.1 PARTIES TO A WILL

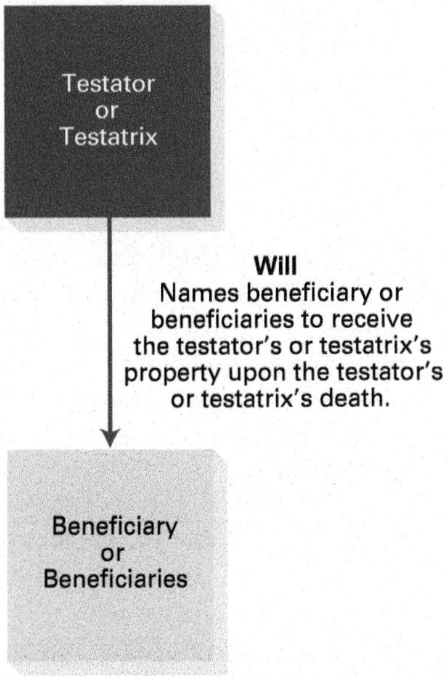
Testator
or
Testatrix
Will
Names beneficiary or beneficiaries to receive the testator's or testatrix's property upon the testator's or testatrix's death.
Beneficiary
or
Beneficiaries

Requirements for Making a Will

Statute of Wills
A state statute that establishes the requirements for making a valid will.

Every state has a **Statute of Wills** that establishes the requirements for making a valid will in that state. These requirements are the following:

- **Testamentary capacity.** The testator must have been of legal age and "sound mind" when the will was made. The courts determine **testamentary capacity** on a case-by-case basis. The legal age for executing a will is set by state statute.
- **Writing.** A **writing requirement** states that wills must be in writing to be valid (except for dying declarations, discussed later in this chapter). The writing may be formal or informal. Although most wills are typewritten and printed from a computer or other electronic device, they can be handwritten (see the later discussion of holographic wills). The writing may be on legal paper, letter paper, scratch paper, envelopes, napkins, or the like. A will may incorporate other documents by reference.
- **Testator's or testatrix's signature.** Wills must be signed. Most jurisdictions require the **testator's** or **testatrix's signature** to appear at the end of the will. This step is to prevent fraud that could occur if someone added provisions to the will below the testator's signature.

Say not you know another entirely till you have divided an inheritance with him.
Johann Kaspar Lavater (1741–1801)

Example Courts have held that initials (*R.K.H.*), a nickname (*Buffy*), a title (*mother*), and even an *X* is a valid signature on a will if it can be proven that the testator intended it to be his or her signature.

Attestation by Witnesses

attestation
The action of a will being witnessed by two or three objective and competent people.

Wills must be *attested* to by mentally competent witnesses. Although state law varies, most states require **attestation** by two or three witnesses. The witnesses do not have to reside in the jurisdiction in which the testator is domiciled. Most jurisdictions stipulate that interested parties (e.g., a beneficiary under the will, the testator's attorney) cannot be witnesses. If an interested party has attested to a will, state law either voids any clauses that benefit such person or voids the entire will. Witnesses usually sign a will following the signature of the testator. These signatures are called the **attestation clause**. Most jurisdictions require that each witness attest to the will in the presence of the other witnesses.

A will that meets the requirements of the Statute of Wills is called a **formal will**. Exhibit 52.2 contains a sample will.

Codicil

codicil
A separate document that must be executed to amend a will. It must be executed with the same formalities as a will.

A will cannot be amended by merely striking out existing provisions on the will and adding new provisions on the will itself. Preparing a **codicil** is the legal way to change an existing will. A codicil is a separate document that contains provisions that amend a will. The codicil must be executed with the same formalities as a will. In addition, it must incorporate by reference the will it is amending. The codicil and the will are then read as one instrument.

Revoking a Will

revocation
Termination of a will.

A will may be revoked by acts of the testator. **Revocation** of a will occurs if the testator intentionally tears, burns, obliterates, or otherwise destroys it. A properly executed **subsequent will** revokes a prior will.

Wills can also be revoked by operation of law. For example, divorce or annulment revokes disposition of property to the former spouse under a will. The remainder of the will is valid. The birth of a child after a will has been executed does not revoke the will but does entitle the child to receive a share of a parent's estate, as determined by state statute.

Last Will and Testament of Florence Winthorpe Blueblood

I, FLORENCE WINTHORPE BLUEBLOOD, presently residing at Boston, County of Suffolk, Massachusetts, being of sound and disposing mind and memory, hereby make, publish, and declare this to be my Last Will and Testament.

FIRST. I hereby revoke any and all Wills and Codicils previously made by me.

SECOND. I direct that my just debts and funeral expenses be paid out of my Estate as soon as practicable after my death.

THIRD. I am presently married to Theodore Hannah Blueblood III.

FOURTH. I hereby nominate and appoint my husband as the Personal Representative of this my Last Will and Testament. If he is unable to serve as Personal Representative, then I nominate and appoint Mildred Yardly Winthorpe as Personal Representative of this my Last Will and Testament. I direct that no bond or other security be required to be posted by my Personal Representative.

FIFTH. I hereby nominate and appoint my husband as Guardian of the person and property of my minor children. In the event that he is unable to serve as Guardian, then I nominate and appoint Mildred Yardly Winthorpe Guardian of the person and property of my minor children. I direct that no bond or other security be required to be posted by any Guardian herein.

SIXTH. I give my Personal Representative authority to exercise all the powers, rights, duties, and immunities conferred upon fiduciaries under law with full power to sell, mortgage, lease, invest, or reinvest all or any part of my Estate on such terms as he or she deems best.

SEVENTH. I hereby give, devise, and bequeath my entire estate to my husband, except for the following specific bequests:

I give my wedding ring to my daughter, Hillary Smythe Blueblood.

I give my baseball card collection to my son, Theodore Hannah Blueblood IV.

In the event that either my above-named daughter or son predeceases me, then and in that event, I give, devise, and bequeath my deceased daughter's or son's bequest to my husband.

EIGHTH. In the event that my husband shall predecease me, then and in that event, I give, devise and bequeath my entire estate, with the exception of the bequests in paragraph SEVENTH, to my beloved children or grandchildren surviving me, per stirpes.

NINTH. In the event I am not survived by my husband or any children or grandchildren, then and in that event, I give, devise, and bequeath my entire estate to Harvard University.

IN WITNESS WHEREOF, I, Florence Winthorpe Blueblood, the Testatrix, sign my name to this Last Will and Testament this 3rd day of January, 2020.

Florence Winthorpe Blueblood
(Signature)

Signed, sealed, published and declared by the above-named Testatrix, as and for her Last Will and Testament, in the presence of us, who at her request, in her presence, and in the presence of one another, have hereunto subscribed our names as attesting witnesses, the day and year last written above.

Witness	Address
Norm Peterson	100 Beacon Hill Rd Boston, Massachusetts
Clifford Claven	200 Minute Man Drive Boston, Massachusetts
Rebecca Howe	300 Charles River Place Boston, Massachusetts

Exhibit 52.2 WILL

Joint and Mutual Wills

If two or more testators execute the same instrument as their will, the document is called a **joint will**. Each party bequeaths property to the other person. A joint will includes a stipulation as to how the property is to be distributed when the second person dies. A joint will is an enforceable contract. The second party cannot change the will once the first person dies (e.g., disinherit the named beneficiaries or change beneficiaries). Both parties must agree to revoke a joint will.

joint will
A will that is executed by two or more testators.

Example Maude and Harry are married. They each have two children from prior marriages, but they do not have any children from their marriage. Maude and Harry are in agreement that all four children receive one-quarter of the property left after the last of Maude or Harry dies, so they sign a joint will whereby they each leave their property to the surviving spouse when one of them dies, and also agree that when the last of Maude or Harry dies she or he will leave the property to the four children equally. Maude dies first and leaves her property to Harry. Harry executes a new will leaving all of his property and the property he inherited from Maude to his two children, and leaving nothing to Maude's two children. Harry dies. Here, Maude's two children can have Harry's subsequent will declared void, and the court will enforce the joint will leaving the property equally to the four children.

mutual wills (reciprocal wills)
A situation in which two or more testators execute separate wills that leave their property to each other on the condition that the survivor leave the remaining property on his or her death as agreed by the testators.

Mutual wills, or **reciprocal wills**, arise where two or more testators execute separate wills that make testamentary dispositions of their property to each other on the condition that the survivor leave the remaining property at death as agreed by the testators. The wills are usually separate instruments with reciprocal terms. Because of their contractual nature, mutual wills cannot be unilaterally revoked after one of the parties has died. Valid mutual wills are enforceable. Mutual wills serve the same purpose as a joint will.

Special Types of Wills

The law recognizes several types of wills that do not meet all the requirements discussed previously. The special types of wills admitted by the courts include the following:

holographic will
A will that is entirely handwritten and signed by the testator.

nuncupative will (dying declaration or deathbed will)
An oral will that is made before a witness during the testator's last illness.

- **Holographic will.** A **holographic will** is entirely handwritten and signed by the testator. The writing may be in ink, pencil, crayon, or some other medium. Many states recognize the validity of such wills even though they are not witnessed.
- **Nuncupative will.** A **nuncupative will** is an oral will that is made before witnesses. Such wills are usually valid only if they are made during the testator's last illness and before he or she is about to die. They are sometimes called **dying declarations**, or **deathbed wills**.

Simultaneous Deaths

Uniform Simultaneous Death Act
An act that provides that if people who would inherit property from each other die simultaneously, each person's property is distributed as though he or she had survived.

Sometimes people who would inherit property from each other die simultaneously. If it is impossible to determine who died first, the question becomes one of inheritance. The **Uniform Simultaneous Death Act**, a model act adopted by many states, provides that each deceased person's property is distributed as though that person had survived.

Example A husband and wife make wills that leave their entire estate to each other. The husband and wife are killed simultaneously in an airplane crash. Here, the husband's property would go to his relatives, and the wife's property would go to her relatives.

Probate

52.2 Describe the process of probating a will.

probate (settlement of the estate)
The process of a deceased's property being collected, debts and taxes being paid, and the remainder of the estate being distributed.

probate court
A specialized state court that supervises the administration and settlement of estates.

When a person dies, his or her property must be collected, debts and taxes must be paid, and the remainder of the estate is then distributed to the beneficiaries of the will or the heirs under the state intestacy statute. This process is called **probate**, or **settlement of the estate**. The process and procedures for settling an estate are governed by state statute. A specialized state court, called the **probate court**, usually supervises the administration and settlement of estates.

A personal representative must be appointed to administer an estate during its settlement phase. If a testator's will designates a personal representative, that person is called an **executor (male) or executrix (female)**. If no one is named or if the decedent dies intestate, the court appoints an **administrator (male) or administratrix (female)**. Some states use the designations *executor* and *administrator* whether the representative is a man or a woman. This party is usually a relative of the deceased or a bank. An attorney is often appointed to help administer the estate and to complete the probate.

In the following case, the court addressed a novel question of inheritance.

CASE 52.1 *STATE COURT CASE Slayer's Statute*

Swain v. Estate of Tyre Ex Rel. Reilly

57 A.3d 283, 2012 R.I. Lexis 158 (2012)
Supreme Court of Rhode Island

"The clear intent of the Slayer's Act is to ensure that a slayer does not benefit from his or her wrongdoing."

—Gilbert Indeglia, Justice

Facts

Shelley Tyre, who married David Swain, executed a valid will that named David as the sole beneficiary of her estate. She named Jennifer and Jeremy Swain, David's adult children, as contingent beneficiaries who would inherit her estate if David predeceased her. Shelley drowned, which triggered the administration of her estate. David, who was named administrator of Shelley's estate, took $152,568 from the estate. Shelley's parents brought a wrongful death action against David, alleging that he had killed Shelley. The jury returned a verdict finding that David had intentionally killed Shelley. The jury awarded Shelley's parents $2,815,085 in compensatory damages and punitive damages of $2 million.

Rhode Island has a Slayer's Act that prohibits a slayer from in any way acquiring any property or receiving any benefit from causing the death of the decedent. The probate judge ordered David to return the $152,568 that he had wrongfully taken from the estate. Jennifer and Jeremy Swain, David's adult children, filed a lawsuit claiming that Shelley's estate belonged to them as contingent beneficiaries. David's parents alleged that the Slayer's Act prevented them from inheriting Shelley's estate because that would cause a benefit to David. The superior court held that the Slayer's Act barred Jennifer and Jeremy from inheriting under Shelley's will. Jennifer and Jeremy filed an appeal.

Issue

Does the Slayer's Act bar Jennifer and Jeremy from inheriting Shelley's estate?

Language of the Court

The inclusion of the language precluding a slayer from benefiting in any way, together with the broad construction required by the act, operates to bar plaintiffs from inheriting as contingent beneficiaries. The clear intent of the Slayer's Act is to ensure that a slayer does not benefit from his or her wrongdoing. Here, it is undisputed that David will benefit from murdering Shelley if Jennifer and Jeremy are allowed to inherit under her will.

Decision

The Supreme Court of Rhode Island held that the Slayer's Act bars Jennifer and Jeremy Swain from inheriting as contingent beneficiaries under Shelley's will.

Critical Legal Thinking Questions

What is the public policy for enacting the Slayer's Act? Should Jennifer and Jeremy, who did not do anything illegal, have been denied the inheritance?

Testamentary Gifts

52.3 Describe the different types of testamentary gifts.

A gift of real estate by will is called a **devise**. A gift of personal property by will is called a **bequest**, or **legacy**. Gifts in will can be *specific*, *general*, or *residuary*.

- **Specific gift.** A **specific gift** in a will is a gift of a specifically named piece of property.

devise
A gift of real estate by will.

bequest (legacy)
A gift of personal property by will.

specific gift
A gift of a specifically named piece of property.

Example A gift of a ring, a boat, or a piece of real estate in a will is a specific gift.

general gift
A gift that does not identify the specific property from which the gift is to be made.

- **General gift.** A **general gift** is a gift that does not identify the specific property from which the gift is to be made. These are gifts of an amount of money.

  Example A gift of $100,000 to a named beneficiary is an example of a general gift. The cash can come from any source in the decedent's estate.

residuary gift
A gift of an estate left after the debts, taxes, and specific and general gifts have been given.

- **Residuary gift.** A **residuary gift** is a gift that is established by a **residuary clause** in a will. This means that any portion of the estate left after the debts, taxes, and specific and general gifts have been paid belongs to the person or persons named in the residuary clause. Some wills contain only a residuary gift and do not contain specific or general gifts.

  Example A clause in a will that states, "I give my daughter the rest, remainder, and residual of my estate" is an example of a residuary gift.

A person who inherits property under a will or an intestacy statute takes the property subject to all the outstanding claims against it (e.g., liens, mortgages). A person can **renounce** an inheritance and often does where the liens or mortgages against the property exceed the value of the property.

Lineal Descendants

lineal descendants
Children, grandchildren, great-grandchildren, and other direct descendants of a testator.

A testator's will often states that property is to be left to **lineal descendants** (e.g., children, grandchildren, great-grandchildren) either *per stirpes* or *per capita*. The differences between these two methods are discussed in the following paragraphs.

Per Stirpes Distribution to Lineal Descendants

***per stirpes* distribution**
A distribution of an estate in which grandchildren and great-grandchildren of the deceased inherit by representation of their parent.

Pursuant to ***per stirpes* distribution**, the lineal descendants *inherit by representation of their parent*; that is, they split what their deceased parent would have received. If their parent is not deceased, they receive nothing.

Example Anne dies without a surviving spouse, and she had three children, Bart, Beth, and Bruce. Bart, who survives his mother, has no children. Beth has one child, Carla, and Carla has one child, Donovan, and they all survive Anne. Bruce, who predeceased his mother, had two children, Clayton and Cathy; and Cathy, who predeceased Anne, had two children, Deborah and Dominic, both of whom survive Anne. If Anne leaves her estate to her lineal descendants *per stirpes*, Bart and Beth each get one-third, Carla receives nothing because Beth is alive, Donovan receives nothing because both Beth and Carla are alive, Clayton gets one-sixth, and Deborah and Dominic each get one-twelfth. See Exhibit 52.3.

Per Capita Distribution to Lineal Descendants

***per capita* distribution**
A distribution of an estate in which each grandchild and great-grandchild of the deceased inherits equally with the children of the deceased.

Pursuant to ***per capita* distribution**, the lineal descendants *equally share the property of the estate*. That is, children of the testator share equally with grandchildren, great-grandchildren, and so forth.

Example Suppose the facts are the same as in the previous example, except that Anne leaves her estate to her lineal descendants *per capita*. In this case, all the surviving lineal descendants—Bart, Beth, Carla, Clayton, Donovan, Deborah, and Dominic—share equally in the estate. That is, they each get one-seventh of Anne's estate. See Exhibit 52.4.

Exhibit 52.3 ***PER STIRPES*** **DISTRIBUTION TO LINEAL DESCENDANTS**

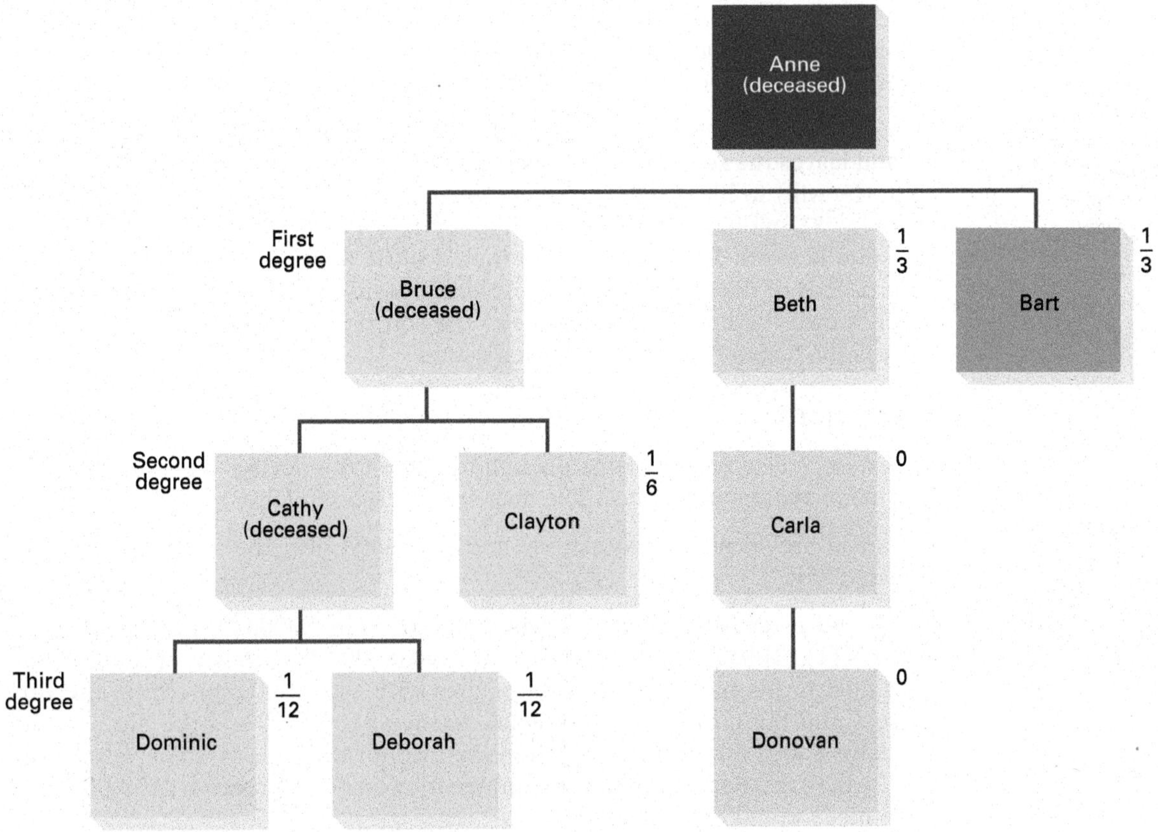

Exhibit 52.4 ***PER CAPITA*** **DISTRIBUTION TO LINEAL DESCENDANTS**

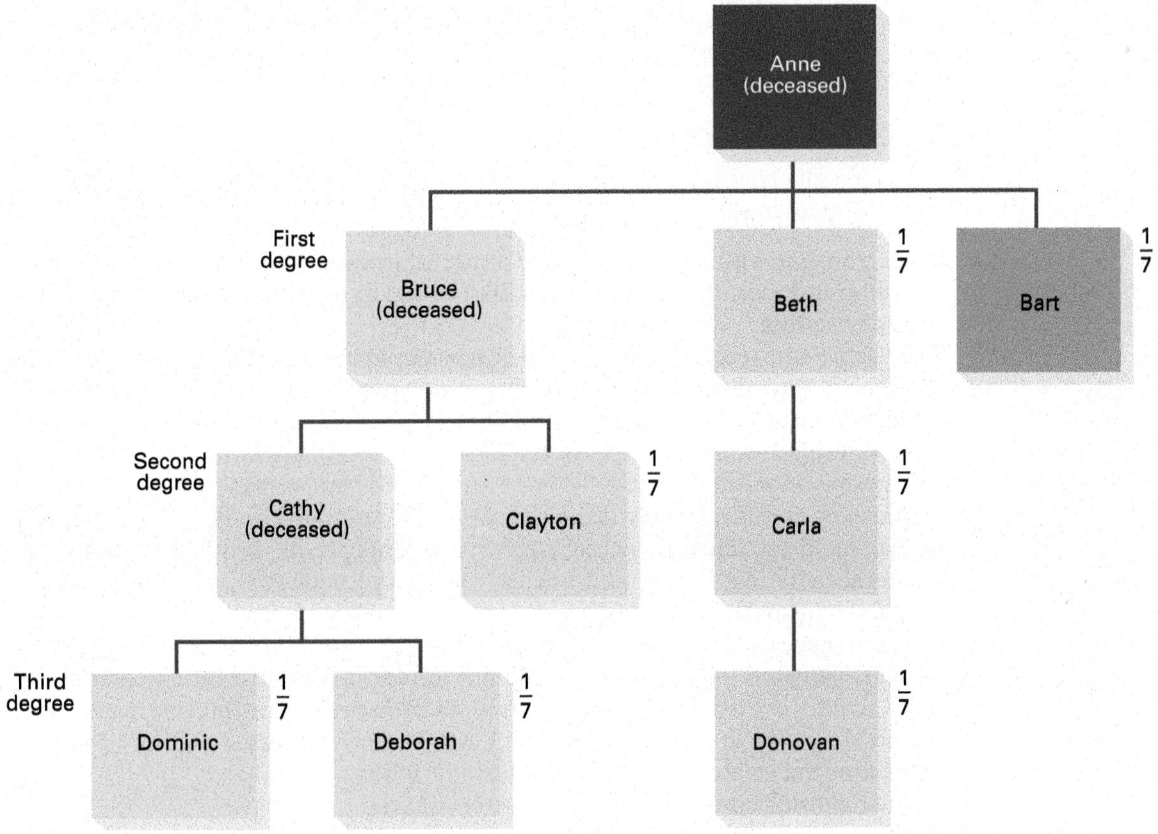

Ademption

If a testator leaves a specific gift of property to a beneficiary but the property is no longer in the estate of the testator when he or she dies, the beneficiary receives nothing. This doctrine is called the doctrine of **ademption**.

ademption
A principle that says if a testator leaves a specific devise of property to a beneficiary but the property is no longer in the estate when the testator dies, the beneficiary receives nothing.

Example A testator leaves his primary house, worth $1 million, to his son in his will and leaves the remainder of his estate (which is worth $1 million at the signing of the will) to his daughter. Several years before dying, the testator sells his house for $1 million and places the money in a bank. When the testator dies, his estate is worth $2 million, which includes the $1 million in the bank that is the proceeds of the sale of the house. Here, because of ademption—the testator does not own the house when he dies—the son receives nothing. The daughter receives the testator's entire $2 million estate.

Abatement

If a testator's estate is not large enough to pay all the devises and bequests, the doctrine of **abatement** applies. The doctrine works as follows:

abatement
A doctrine that says if the property a testator leaves is not sufficient to satisfy all the beneficiaries named in a will and there are both general and residuary bequests, the residuary bequest is abated first (i.e., paid last).

- If a will provides for both general and residuary gifts, the residuary gifts are abated first.

  Examples A testator executes a will when he owns $500,000 of property that leaves (1) $100,000 to the Red Cross, (2) $100,000 to a university, and (3) the residual to his niece. If the testator dies with this $500,000 estate, the Red Cross and the university would each receive $100,000, and the niece would receive $300,000. However, if when the testator dies, his estate is worth only $225,000, the Red Cross and the university would each receive $100,000, and the niece would receive $25,000.

- If a will provides only for general gifts, the reductions are proportionate.

  Examples A will bequests $200,000 to each of two beneficiaries. However, when the testator dies, his estate is worth only $100,000. Here, each beneficiary will receive $50,000.

Intestate Succession

52.4 Identify how property is distributed under intestacy statutes if a person dies without a will.

If a person dies without a will or trust—that is, **intestate**—or if a will or trust fails for some legal reason, the property is distributed to relatives pursuant to a state's **intestacy statute**.

intestate
The state of having died without leaving a will.

intestacy statute
A state statute that specifies how a deceased's property will be distributed if he or she dies without a will or if the last will is declared void and there is no prior valid will.

heir
The receiver of property under intestacy statutes.

A relative who receives property under intestacy statutes is called an **heir**. Although intestacy statutes differ from state to state, the general rule is that the deceased's real property is distributed according to the intestacy statute of the state where the real property is located, and the deceased's personal property is distributed according to the intestacy statute of the state where the deceased had permanent residence.

Intestacy statutes usually leave the deceased's property to heirs in this order: spouse, children, lineal heirs (e.g., grandchildren, parents, brothers and sisters), collateral heirs (e.g., aunts and uncles, nieces and nephews), and other next of kin (e.g., cousins).

If the deceased has no surviving relatives, then the deceased's property **escheats** (goes) to the state. In-laws do not inherit under most intestacy statutes.

WEB EXERCISE
Use **www.google.com** or another online search engine and find the intestacy statute for your state. What is the priority of distribution of assets under the statute?

To avoid the distribution of an estate as provided in an intestacy statute, a person should have a properly written, signed, and witnessed will or trust that distributes the estate property as the testator wishes.

The following case involves an intestacy statute.

CASE 52.2 *STATE COURT CASE Intestacy Statute*

Banner v. Vandeford

748 S.E.2d 927, 2013 Ga. Lexis 732 (2013)
Supreme Court of Georgia

"We find that the residue of Huscusson's estate passes through the laws of intestacy."

—Hugh Thompson, Chief Justice

Facts

John Huscusson had three adult daughters: Tina Banner, Deborah Vandeford, and Karen Nee. In a will executed in 2006, Huscusson stated that his three daughters were to share equally in his estate. In 2012, Huscusson executed a new will in which he stated that he was "extremely disappointed" in Vandeford and Nee and left them $10 each. Banner was not given a specific bequest, and the will did not contain a residuary clause. Banner was named executrix. When Huscusson died, Vandeford and Nee filed a declaratory judgment action asking the probate court to interpret the will. They argued that since there was no residuary clause, Huscusson died intestate other than for the $10 that he left each of them.

Under the intestacy statute, the three daughters would share equally in the remainder of the estate. Banner alleged that Huscusson wanted her to have the rest of the estate because he did not state that he was disappointed in her and by the fact that he made her the executrix of the estate. The probate court held that other than the $10 awarded each to Vandeford and Nee, Huscusson died intestate and that pursuant to the intestacy statute the three daughters would share equally in the remainder of their father's estate. Banner appealed.

Issue

Should the residue of Huscusson's estate be distributed pursuant to the intestacy statute?

Language of the Court

Construing the 2012 will, we must conclude, as did the probate court, that its terms are plain and unambiguous and must control. We find that the residue of Huscusson's estate passes through the laws of intestacy. Although it may be unusual for a testator to omit a residuary clause, this court cannot supply one. The plain language here involved cannot be changed by speculation.

Decision

The Supreme Court of Georgia held that the residue of Huscusson's estate was to be divided equally among his three daughters as provided by the intestacy statute.

Critical Legal Thinking Questions

What do you think Huscusson's intentions were when he executed the will? Could the lawyer who drafted the will be sued for alleged negligence?

CONCEPT SUMMARY

COMPARISON OF DYING WITH AND WITHOUT A VALID WILL

Situation	Parties Who Receive Deceased's Property
Deceased dies with a valid will	Beneficiaries named in the will.
Deceased dies without a valid will	Heirs set forth in the applicable state intestacy statute. If there are no heirs, the deceased's property escheats to the state.

Irrevocable Trusts

52.5 Define *irrevocable trust* and describe how an irrevocable trust works.

trust
A legal arrangement established when one person transfers title to property to another person to be held and used for the benefit of a third person.

A **trust** is a legal arrangement under which one person (the **trustor** or **settlor**) delivers and transfers legal title to property to another person, bank, or other entity (the **trustee**), to be held and used for the benefit of a third person or entity

trustor (settlor)
A person who creates a trust. Also known as a *transferor or grantor.*

trustee
A person or an entity that holds legal title to a trust corpus and manages the trust for the benefit of the beneficiary or beneficiaries.

trust corpus (trust res)
Property and assets held in trust.

(the beneficiary). The property and assets held in trust are called the **trust corpus**, or **trust res**. The trustee has legal title to the trust corpus, and the beneficiary has equitable title. Unlike wills, trusts are not public documents, so property can be transferred in privacy. An **express trust** is voluntarily created by the settlor. It is usually written, and the written agreement is called a **trust instrument**, or **trust agreement**. A trust is irrevocable unless the settlor reserves the right to revoke it. A trust that cannot be revoked is referred to as an **irrevocable trust**. Exhibit 52.5 shows the parties to a trust.

A trust can be created and become effective during a trustor's lifetime, or it can be created to become effective on the trustor's death. During the existence of a trust, the trustee collects money owed to the trust, pays taxes and necessary expenses of the trust, makes investment decisions, pays the income to the income beneficiary, and keeps necessary records of transactions.

Beneficiaries

income beneficiary
A person or an entity to be paid income from a trust.

remainder beneficiary
A person or an entity to receive the trust corpus on the termination of a trust.

Trusts often provide that any trust income is to be paid to a person or an entity called the **income beneficiary**. The person or entity to receive the trust corpus on the termination of the trust is called the **remainder beneficiary**. The income beneficiary and the remainder beneficiary can be the same person or different persons. The designated beneficiary can be any identifiable person, animal (e.g., a pet), charitable organization, or other institution or cause that the settlor chooses. There can be multiple income and remainder beneficiaries. An entire class of persons—for example, "my grandchildren"—can be named.

A trust can allow the trustee to invade (use) the trust corpus for certain purposes. These purposes can be named (e.g., "for the beneficiary's college education"). The trust agreement usually specifies how the receipts and expenses of the trust are to be divided between the income beneficiary and the remainder beneficiary.

Generally, the trustee has broad management powers over the trust property. Thus, the trustee can invest the trust property to preserve its capital and

Exhibit 52.5 **TRUST**

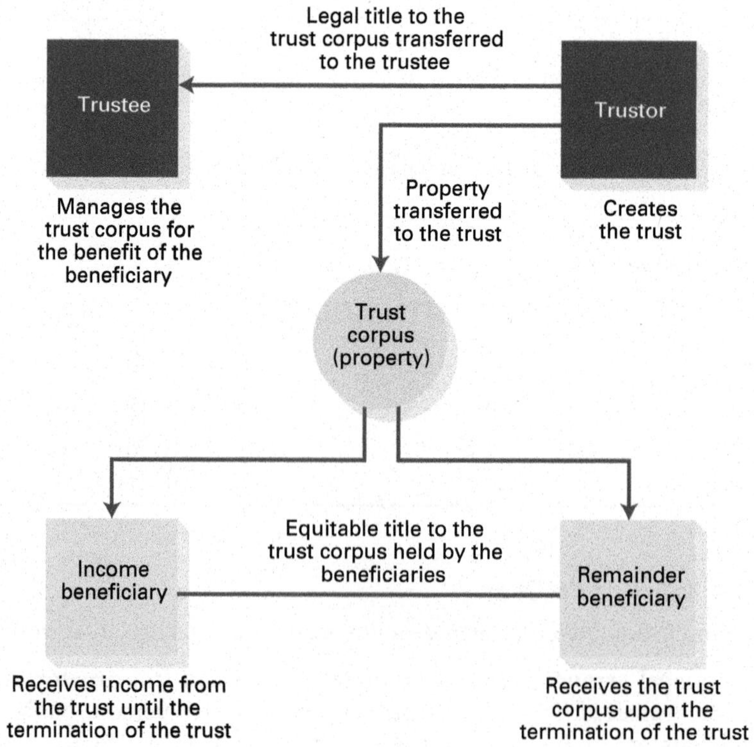

make it productive. The trustee must follow any restrictions on investments contained in the trust agreement or state statute.

Inter Vivos Trust

An ***inter vivos* trust** is created and its assets are distributed to the trust while the settlor is alive. The settlor transfers legal title of property to a named trustee to hold, administer, and manage for the benefit of named beneficiaries. The trust can be for a stated period of time (e.g., 10 years) or until some event happens (e.g., the settlor dies). The trust sometimes provides that an income beneficiary will receive income from the trust until the trust ends. The trust provides what will happen to the trust assets when the trust ends, such as being distributed to named beneficiaries.

***inter vivos* trust**
A trust that is created while the settlor is alive.

Examples Grandmother places cash, stock, bonds, and an apartment building in a trust while she is alive. She names a bank to administer the trust. Grandmother names her daughter as the income beneficiary of the trust; that is, the trust will pay the daughter interest income from bonds, dividends from stock, and profits from the apartment building while the daughter is alive. The trust provides that it will terminate on the death of the daughter. Three of Grandmother's grandchildren are named remainder beneficiaries of the trust with equal shares. If the daughter lives 20 years, the trust terminates at that time, and the assets of the trust are distributed to the grandchildren in equal shares. In this trust arrangement, when the grandmother dies is inconsequential.

Testamentary Trust

A **testamentary trust** is created by will. In other words, the trust comes into existence when the settlor dies.

testamentary trust
A trust created by will; the trust comes into existence when the settlor dies.

Examples Grandfather has a will that provides that when he dies, his estate will be placed in a testamentary trust. Grandfather names a bank to be trustee to administer the trust and invest its assets. The trust provides that when his grandson reaches the age of 25, the trust will terminate, and he will be given legal title to the assets. Grandfather dies when his grandson is age 10. The trust will exist for the next 15 years until the grandson reaches the age of 25. At that time, the trust terminates, and the grandson will receive possession and legal title to the assets.

Special Types of Trust

52.6 List and describe special forms of trusts.

There are several special types of trusts. These are described in the following paragraphs.

Constructive Trust

A **constructive trust** is an equitable trust that is implied by law to avoid fraud, unjust enrichment, and injustice. In constructive trust arrangements, the holder of the title to property (i.e., the trustee) holds the property in trust for its rightful owner. When a constructive trust is imposed, the party who is the implied trustee cannot sell or otherwise transfer ownership to the property or give a mortgage on the property.

constructive trust
An equitable trust that is implied by law to avoid fraud, unjust enrichment, and injustice.

Example Thaddeus and Kaye are partners. Kaye embezzles partnership funds and uses the stolen funds to purchase a piece of real estate. In this case, the court can impose a constructive trust whereby Kaye (who holds actual title to the land) is considered a trustee who is holding the property in trust for Thaddeus, its rightful owner.

Resulting Trust

resulting trust
A trust that is implied from the conduct of the parties.

A **resulting trust** is implied from the conduct of the parties.

Example Hashem is purchasing a piece of real estate but cannot attend the closing. He asks his sister, Amaya, to attend the closing and take title to the property until he can return. In this case, Amaya holds the title to the property as trustee for Hashem until he returns.

Charitable Trust

A **charitable trust** is created for the benefit of a segment of society or society in general.

Example A trust that is created for the construction and maintenance of a public park is an example of a charitable trust.

Spendthrift Trust

Man ... with all his wisdom, toils for heirs he knows not who.
Chief Justice Andrew Kirkpatrick
Nevison v. Taylor
18 N.J.L. 43 (1824)

A **spendthrift trust** is designed to prevent a beneficiary's personal creditors from reaching his or her trust interest. All control over the trust is removed from the beneficiary. Personal creditors still can go after trust income that is paid to the beneficiary, however.

Totten Trust

A **Totten trust** is created when a person deposits money in a bank account in his or her own name and holds it as a trustee for the benefit of another person. A Totten trust is a tentative trust because (1) the trustee can add or withdraw funds from the account and (2) the trust can be revoked at any time prior to the trustee's death or prior to completing delivery of the funds to the beneficiary.

Living Trust

52.7 Define a *living trust* and describe how a living trust works.

living trust (grantor's trust or revocable trust)
A method for holding property during a person's lifetime and distributing the property upon that person's death.

grantor (trustor)
A person who creates a living trust.

Living trusts have become a popular means of holding property during a person's lifetime and distributing the property on that person's death. A **living trust** works as follows. During life, a person establishes a living trust, which is a legal entity used for estate planning. A living trust is also referred to as a **grantor's trust**, or a **revocable trust**. The person who creates the trust is called the **grantor** (or the **trustor**).

Benefits of a Living Trust

The primary purpose of using a living trust is to avoid *probate* associated with using a will. If a person dies with a will, the will must be probated so that the deceased's assets can be properly distributed according to the will. A probate judge is named to oversee the probate process, and all documents, including the will, are public record. A living trust, on the other hand, is private. When the grantor dies, the assets are owned by the living trust and are therefore not subject to probate proceedings. In addition, if real property is owned in more than one state and a will is used, ancillary probate must be conducted in the other state. If a living trust is used, ancillary probate is avoided.

However, living trusts are often promoted for claimed benefits that do not exist. The true facts are that a living trust:

- Does not reduce estate taxes any more than a will.
- Does not reduce the grantor's income taxes. All the income earned by the trust is attributed to the grantor, who must pay income taxes on the earnings just as if the trust did not exist.

- Does not avoid creditors. Thus, creditors can obtain liens against property in the trust.
- Is subject to property division on divorce.
- Is usually not less expensive to create than a will. Both require payments to lawyers and usually to accountants and other professionals to draft and probate a will or to draft and manage a living trust.
- Does not avoid controversies on the grantor's death. Like wills, living trusts can be challenged for lack of capacity, undue influence, duress, and other legal grounds.

Funding and Operation of a Living Trust

To fund a living trust, the grantor transfers title to his or her property to the trust. This property is called the *trust corpus*. Bank accounts, stock certificates, real estate, personal property, intangible property, and other property owned by the grantor must be retitled to the trust's name. For example, the grantor must execute deeds transferring title to real estate to the trust. Once property is transferred to the trust, the trust is considered funded. A living trust is revocable during the grantor's lifetime. Thus, a grantor can later change his or her mind and undo the trust and retake title of the property in his or her own name.

A living trust names a **trustee** who is responsible for maintaining, investing, buying, or selling trust assets. The trustee is usually the grantor. Thus, the grantor who establishes the trust does not lose control of the property placed in the trust and may manage and invest trust assets during his or her lifetime. The trust should name a *successor trustee* to replace the grantor-trustee if the grantor becomes incapacitated or too ill to manage the trust.

trustee of a living trust
A person named in a living will to administer the trust assets. This is usually the grantor.

Beneficiaries

A living trust names a beneficiary or beneficiaries who are entitled to receive income from the living trust while it is in existence and to receive the property of the trust when the grantor dies. Usually the grantor is the **income beneficiary**, who receives the income from the trust during his or her lifetime. On the death of the grantor, assets of the trust are distributed to the **remainder beneficiary** or beneficiaries named in the trust. The designated trustee has the fiduciary duties of identifying assets, paying creditors, paying income and estate taxes, transferring assets to named beneficiaries, and rendering an accounting.

income beneficiary of a living trust
A person who receives the income from a living trust during his or her life. This is usually the grantor.

remainder beneficiary of a living trust
A person who receives the assets of a living trust on the death of the grantor.

Undue Influence

52.8 Describe how a will or trust may be found invalid under the doctrine of undue influence.

A will or trust may be found to be invalid if it was made because of **undue influence** on the testator. Undue influence can be inferred from the facts and circumstances surrounding the making of a will or trust.

undue influence
A situation in which one person takes advantage of another person's mental, emotional, or physical weakness and unduly persuades that person to make a will; the persuasion by the wrongdoer must overcome the free will of the testator.

Example If an 85-year-old woman leaves all her property to the lawyer who drafted her will and ignores her blood relatives, the court is likely to presume undue influence.

Undue influence is difficult to prove by direct evidence, but it may be proved by circumstantial evidence. The court considers elements such as the following to determine the presence of undue influence:

- The benefactor and beneficiary are involved in a relationship of confidence and trust.
- The will or trust contains substantial benefit to the beneficiary.

- The beneficiary caused or assisted in effecting execution of the will or trust.
- There was an opportunity to exert influence.
- The will or trust contains an unnatural disposition of the testator's property.
- The bequests constitute a change from a former will or trust.
- The testator or settlor was highly susceptible to undue influence.

In the following case, the court had to decide if there had been undue influence in a will contest.

CASE 52.3 *STATE COURT CASE Undue Influence*

In the Matter of the Estate of Barnes

367 P.3d 580, 185 Wash.2d 1 (2016)
Supreme Court of Washington

"The new will was executed on the heels of what appeared to be Wells's systematic manipulation of Barnes."

—Mary Yu, Justice

Facts

Eva Johanna Rova Barnes was born in Bellingham, Washington. She died at her home in Washington just a few weeks before her 95th birthday. At the time of Barnes's death, Vicki Rova, Karen Bow, Marsha Rova, and John Rova (the Rovas) were Barnes's closest relatives and lineal descendants. They grew up near Barnes, shared a close family relationship with her, and during Barnes's life spent a significant amount of time with her. Barnes's original will included the Rovas: first as alternative beneficiaries, then as primary beneficiaries following the death of Barnes's husband and daughter.

Michelle Wells became acquainted with Barnes as Barnes's rural mail carrier, and the two became friends after Barnes's husband and daughter passed away. After Barnes suffered a fall in her home, Wells became her caretaker. Barnes became increasingly dependent on Wells. Wells made numerous false statements to Barnes that caused Barnes to mistrust the Rovas. Wells accused John Rova of trying to "throw Ms. Barnes under the bus" and stated that the Rovas wanted to put Barnes in a nursing home—untrue statements that acted to further poison Barnes's relationship with the Rovas. Wells further isolated Barnes by changing her long-distance calling plan, making it difficult for family and friends to reach her by phone.

Barnes began writing checks to Wells and Wells's family members for various services and expenses. Barnes named Wells her attorney-in-fact with power to write checks from her bank accounts. Just previous to Barnes's death, Wells drove Barnes to a lawyer's office, where Barnes executed a new will. Barnes's new will completely disinherited the Rovas and left all of her estate to Wells and her husband. Just days before Barnes passed away, Wells paid her own mortgage with a check issued from Barnes's personal bank account.

When Barnes passed away, Wells submitted Barnes's last will for probate. The Rovas challenged the will, alleging that Wells had unduly influenced Barnes to change her will. The trial court held that there was a fiduciary relationship between Barnes and Wells, and therefore there was a presumption of undue influence that Wells had to overcome in order for Barnes's last will to be probated. The trial court invalidated the will, finding that it was the product of undue influence. The court of appeals reversed and remanded the case for a new trial. The Rovas appealed.

Issue

Did Wells unduly influence Barnes to make a new will that disinherited her relatives and left all of her property to Wells?

Language of the Court

Isolated from her family and friends, physically and mentally impaired, and totally dependent on Wells, it is undisputable that Barnes was highly vulnerable to undue influence. Wells exercised her power of attorney by signing checks on behalf of Barnes. These facts are sufficient to find that a fiduciary relationship existed. The new will was executed on the heels of what appeared to be Wells's systematic manipulation of Barnes. Barnes was elderly—nearly 95 when the will was executed—and extremely vulnerable to undue influence. The trial court properly found that the evidence presented by Wells was insufficient to overcome the presumption of undue influence in light of the totality of the evidence presented.

Decision

The Supreme Court of Washington reinstated the trial court's judgment invalidating the will as a product of undue influence. Barnes's prior will that left her property to the Rovas was to be probated.

Critical Legal Thinking Questions

Is it difficult to prove undue influence? Do you think that many cases of undue influence occur in drafting wills?

Living Will and Health Care Directive

52.9 Define a *living will* and describe why a person would execute a living will and health care directive.

Technological breakthroughs have greatly increased the life span of human beings. This same technology, however, permits life to be sustained long after a person is "brain dead." Some people say they have a right to refuse life-extending treatment. Others argue that human life must be preserved at all costs.

In 1990, in *Cruzan v. Director, Missouri Department of Health*,[2] the U.S. Supreme Court ruled that the right to refuse medical treatment is a personal liberty protected by the Due Process Clause of the U.S. Constitution. The Court stated that this interest must be expressed through clear and convincing proof that the patient did not want to be sustained by artificial means.

Living Will

The clear message of the Supreme Court's opinion in the *Cruzan* case is that people who do not want their life prolonged indefinitely by artificial means should sign a **living will** that stipulates their wishes before catastrophe strikes and they become unable to express themselves because of an illness or an accident. The living will should state which lifesaving measures the signor does and does not want. In addition, the signor can specify that any such treatments should be withdrawn if doctors determine that there is no hope of a meaningful recovery. A living will must provide clear and convincing proof of a patient's wishes with respect to medical treatment.

living will
A document that states which lifesaving measures the signor does and does not want; it can specify that he or she wants such treatments withdrawn if doctors determine that there is no hope of a meaningful recovery.

health care directive (health care proxy)
A document in which the maker names someone to be his or her health care agent to make all health care decisions in accordance with his or her wishes, as outlined in the living will.

Health Care Directive

Either in a living will or in a separate document, usually called a **health care directive**, also called a **health care proxy** or **advance directive**, the maker should name someone, such as a spouse or another relative or trusted party, to be the maker's **health care agent** to make all health care decisions in accordance with the wishes outlined in the living will. An alternative person should also be named in case the originally designated health care agent is unable or chooses not to serve in that capacity.

The following feature discusses the issue of aid in dying.

WEB EXERCISE
Use **www.google.com** or another online search engine and locate a living will and health care directive that is effective in your state.

Critical Legal Thinking

Medical Aid in Dying

One legal issue that is controversial is whether an individual has the right to choose to die when he or she is terminally ill and has less than a certain time to live. Today, many persons in the United States support this **right to die**, while others are against having such a law. The right to die involves a terminally ill person deciding to end his or her life.

Medical aid in dying, also called **physician-assisted death**, involves a physician who may provide a terminally ill person with the medical means to end his or her own life. State laws that permit medical aid in dying require that physicians (usually two physicians) make a diagnosis that a patient is terminally ill, that the person has less than an estimated period to live (e.g., six months), and that the decision to end his or her life is made by a person of sound mind. If these requirements are met, the terminally ill person is provided with, and self-administers, medications that will cause his or her loss of life. Several states, including California, Colorado, Hawaii, Maine, Montana, New Jersey, Oregon, Vermont, and Washington, permit medical aid in dying. No state permits euthanasia, that is, when a physician or another party administers a lethal dose of medications to the patient.

Today, some persons support medical aid in dying, while others do not. This issue will continue to be debated as states determine whether to enact right to die statutes.

Critical Legal Thinking Questions
What are the arguments in favor of permitting medical aid in dying laws? What are the arguments against permitting such laws? What is the difference between medical aid in dying and euthanasia?

Key Terms and Concepts

Critical Legal Thinking Cases

52.1 Ademption Ethel M. Ramchissel executed a will that made the following bequests: (1) one-half of the stock she owned in Pabst Brewing Company (Pabst) to Mary Lee Anderson, (2) the stock she owned in Houston Natural Gas Corporation (Houston Natural Gas) to Ethel Baker and others (Baker), and (3) the residual and remainder of her estate to Boysville, Inc.

Later, the following events happened. First, in response to an offer by G. Heilman Brewing Company to purchase Pabst, Ramchissel sold all of her Pabst stock and placed the cash proceeds in a bank account to which no other funds were added. Second, pursuant to a merger agreement between Internorth, Inc. and Houston Natural Gas, Ramchissel converted her Houston Natural Gas stock to cash and placed the cash in a bank account to which no other funds were added. When Ramchissel died about 3½ years after making her will, her will was admitted into probate. Anderson and Baker argued that they were entitled to the cash in the two bank accounts, respectively. Were the bequests to Anderson and Baker specific bequests that were adeemed when the stock was sold? *Opperman v. Anderson*, 782 S.W.2d 8, 1989 Tex. App. Lexis 3175 (Court of Appeals of Texas, 1989)

52.2 Will Martha Jansa executed a will naming her two sons as executors and leaving all her property to them. The will was properly signed and attested to by witnesses. Thereafter, Martha died. When Martha's safe-deposit box at a bank was opened, the original of this will was discovered, along with two other instruments that were dated after the will. One was a handwritten document that left her home to her grandson, with the remainder of her estate to her two sons; this document was not signed. The second document was a typed version of the handwritten one; this document was signed by Martha but was not attested to by witnesses. Which of the three documents should be admitted to probate? *In re Estate of Jansa*, 670 S.W.2d 767, 1984 Tex. App. Lexis 5503 (Court of Appeals of Texas, 1984)

52.3 Will During his first marriage to Miriam Talbot, Robert Mirkil Talbot executed a will in multiple originals that bequeathed his entire estate to Miriam, or if she should predecease him, to his friend J. Barker Killgore. After his first wife's death, Robert married Lois McClen Mills. After consulting a Louisiana intestacy chart, the Talbots determined that if Robert died, Lois would receive Robert's entire estate because he had no descendants, surviving parents, or siblings. However, Lois did have descendants. Lois wanted to leave Robert a portion of her estate. Robert and his new wife went to an attorney to execute the new wife's will. While there, the attorney took Robert aside and showed him his prior will that made Killgore the contingent beneficiary. The attorney asked Robert if he wanted to leave his estate to his new wife, and Robert answered "yes." Robert then tore the old will in half in the attorney's presence. After leaving the attorney's office, Robert and Lois went shopping for furnishings for their new house. That night, Robert became short of breath and was taken to a hospital, where he died. Killgore retrieved a multiple original of Robert's 1981 will and petitioned to have it probated. Lois opposed the petition. Who wins? *Succession of Talbot*, 530 So.2d 1132, 1988 La. Lexis 1597 (Supreme Court of Louisiana, 1988)

52.4 Intestacy Mr. and Mrs. Campbell were out in a small boat on Hyatt Lake near Ashland, Oregon. The boat capsized near the middle of the lake sometime in the afternoon. No one saw the capsizing or either of the Campbells in the water. The deputy sheriff was called to the lake about 5:00, after the Campbells' boat was found. Numerous people searched the shoreline and lake, but the Campbells were not located by nightfall. The body of Mrs. Campbell was found the next morning. The body of Mr. Campbell was found four days later. The pathologists who conducted the autopsies testified that both Mr. and Mrs. Campbell died of drowning but could not determine the exact time of death. Both parties died intestate. Mr. Campbell was survived by three sisters and a brother, and Mrs. Campbell was survived by a daughter and son from a prior marriage. Who inherits the Campbells' property? *In re Estate of Campbell*, 641 P.2d 610, 1982 Ore. App. Lexis 2448 (Court of Appeals of Oregon, 1982)

52.5 Murder Dr. Duncan R. Danforth, a 75-year-old man of substantial means, married 21-year-old Loretta Ollison. Immediately following the ceremony, the newlyweds went to a lawyer's office, where Danforth executed a newly prepared will, naming Ollison a principal beneficiary of his estate. Four days later, Danforth was murdered by Michael Stith, Ollison's lover. In a criminal trial, Ollison was convicted of conspiracy to commit murder and was sentenced to 10 years in prison. Can Ollison recover under the will or take her elective share of the estate under the state's intestacy statute? *In re the Estate of Danforth*, 705 S.W.2d 609, 1986 Mo. App. Lexis 3757 (Court of Appeals of Missouri, 1986)

Ethics Case

52.6 Ethics Case Homer and Edna Jones, husband and wife, executed a joint will that provided "We will and give to our survivor, whether it be Homer Jones or Edna Jones, all property and estate of which the first of us that dies may be seized and possessed. If we should both die in a common catastrophe, or on the death of our survivor, we will and give all property and estate then remaining to our children, Leonida Jones Eschman, daughter, Sylvia Marie Jones, daughter, and Grady V. Jones, son, share and share alike."

When Homer died 18 years later, Edna Jones received his entire estate under the will. Two years later, Edna executed a new will that left a substantially larger portion of the estate to her daughter Sylvia Marie Jones than to the other two children. Edna Jones died in 1982. Edna's daughter introduced her mother's will for probate. The other two children introduced the earlier joint will for probate. Did Edna act ethically in this case? Who wins? *Jones v. Jones*, 718 S.W.2d 416, 1986 Tex. App. Lexis 8929 (Court of Appeals of Texas, 1986)

Notes

1. Public Law 90-363.
2. 497 U.S. 261, 110 S.Ct. 2841, 1990 U.S. Lexis 3301 (Supreme Court of the United States).

CHAPTER

53 Family Law

FAMILY

Each member of a family has certain rights and adults have certain duties. The law provides important protections to all members of a family at all phases of family life.

Shutterstock

Learning Objectives

After studying this chapter, you should be able to:

53.1 Describe premarriage issues such as engagement.

53.2 Define *marriage* and enumerate the legal requirements of marriage.

53.3 Define *same-sex marriage* and describe the protections afforded same-sex marriage by the U.S. Constitution.

53.4 Explain parents' rights and duties for their children.

53.5 Describe marriage termination by annulment and divorce.

53.6 Describe a prenuptial agreement and what issues are usually addressed in a prenuptial agreement.

53.7 Describe how assets are divided upon divorce and annulment.

53.8 Explain the responsibilities for the payment of spousal and child support.

53.9 Explain child custody and visitation rights of parents.

"In family life, love is the oil that eases friction, the cement that binds closer together, and the music that brings harmony."

—Friedrich Nietzsche (1844–1900)

Introduction to Family Law

Family law and domestic relations is a broad area of the law, involving marriage, same-sex marriage, prenuptial agreements, dissolution of marriage, division of property on dissolution of marriage, spousal and child support, child custody, and other family law issues.

This chapter covers family law and domestic relations issues.

Premarriage Issues

53.1 Describe premarriage issues such as engagement.

Prior to marriage, several legal issues may arise. These include *promises to marry, engagement*, and *prenuptial agreements*.

Promise to Marry

In the 19th century, many courts recognized an action for breach of a **promise to marry**. This usually would occur if a person proposed marriage, the other person accepted, and then the person who proposed backed out before the marriage took place. The lawsuit was based on a breach-of-contract theory. Today, most courts do not recognize a breach of a promise-to-marry lawsuit. The denial of such lawsuits is based on current social norms.

Example Malia and Harold promise to marry each other, and to prove their commitment, they sign a written contract to marry each other one year from the signing of the contract. They get engaged. After six months, Malia calls off the engagement. Harold cannot enforce Malia's promise to marry him. Malia is free to leave Harold even though she has broken the contract.

If a person backs out close to the wedding date, after many of the items for the pending marriage have been purchased or contracted for (e.g., flowers, rental of a reception hall), he or she may be responsible for paying these costs, or a portion of them, if the other party has paid these costs.

Engagement

As a prelude to getting married, many couples go through a period known as **engagement**. The engagement usually begins when one person proposes marriage to another person. Often the proposing person gives an engagement ring (often a diamond ring) to the other person. Men can propose marriage to women, women can propose marriage to men, and persons of the same sex can propose marriage to members of the same sex. The engagement period runs until the wedding is held or the engagement is broken off. If the couple gets married, they often exchange wedding rings at the marriage ceremony. Some persons do not go through a formal engagement and do not exchange an engagement ring prior to marriage.

Sometimes the engagement is broken off prior to the wedding but after an engagement ring is purchased. Who gets the engagement ring if the engagement is broken off? Individual states abide by one of the two following rules:

- **Fault rule.** Some states follow a **fault rule**, which works as follows: If the person who gave the engagement ring breaks off the engagement, the other side gets to keep the engagement ring; if the person who has accepted an engagement ring breaks off the engagement, that person must return the engagement ring. The fault rule is sometimes difficult to apply because questions often arise as to who broke off the engagement, which then requires a trial to decide the issue.

- **Objective rule.** The modern rule and trend is to abandon the fault rule and adopt an **objective rule**. Under this rule, if the engagement is broken off, the person who was given the ring must return the engagement ring, regardless of who broke off the engagement. The objective rule is clear and usually avoids litigation unless the person who received the ring refuses to return it.

objective rule
A rule that states that if an engagement is broken off, the person who was given the engagement ring must return the ring, regardless of which party broke off the engagement.

Marriage

53.2 Define *marriage* and enumerate the legal requirements of marriage.

marriage
A legal union between spouses that confers certain legal rights and duties on the spouses and on the children born of the marriage.

Marriage confers certain legal rights and duties on the spouses, as well as on the children born of the marriage. A couple wishing to marry must meet the legal requirements established by the state in which they are to be married. The following paragraphs discuss marriage requirements and the legal rights and duties of spouses.

WEB EXERCISE
Use **www.google.com** or another online search engine and find the requirements to get married in your state.

Marriage Requirements

emancipation
A minor's act of legally separating from his or her parents and providing for him- or herself.

State law establishes certain requirements that must be met before two people can be married. The parties must be of a certain age (usually 18 or older). States will permit younger persons to be married if they have the consent of their parents or if they are emancipated from their parents. **Emancipation** means that the person is not supported by parents and provides for him- or herself.

All states provide that persons under a certain age cannot be married. Most states set the general age to be able to marry at 18. Many states permit exceptions where persons 16 or 17 years old may get married with parental consent or judicial declaration. Some states prohibit marriages between persons who are closely related, usually by blood.

Example Brothers and sisters are not allowed to marry each other. Cousins may marry in approximately half of the states.

Another requirement of marriage is that neither party can currently be married to someone else.

Marriage License

marriage license
A legal document issued by a state which certifies that two people are married.

For two people to be legally married, certain legal procedures must be followed. State law requires that the parties obtain a **marriage license** issued by the state. Marriage licenses are usually obtained at the county clerk's office.

Some states require that, in addition to a marriage license, there must be some sort of **marriage ceremony**. This ceremony usually is held in front of a justice of the peace or similar government officer or at a church, temple, synagogue, or mosque in front of a minister, priest, rabbi, or imam. At the ceremony, the parties exchange wedding vows, in which they make a public statement that they will take each other as spouses.

Marriage licenses are recorded, usually in the county recorder's office. In most states the marriage is a public record, but some states permit couples to designate that the marriage license not be made public.

Common Law Marriage

common law marriage
A type of marriage some states recognize in which a marriage license has not been issued but certain requirements are met.

Several states recognize a form of marriage called **common law marriage**. Common law marriage is one in which the parties have not obtained a valid marriage license, nor have they participated in a legal marriage ceremony.

Instead, common law marriage is recognized if the following requirements are met: (1) the parties are eligible to marry, (2) the parties voluntarily intend to be spouses, (3) the parties live together, and (4) the parties hold themselves out as spouses.

There are several misconceptions about common law marriages. First, cohabitation is not sufficient in and of itself to establish common law marriage. Second, the length of time that the parties live together is not sufficient to establish common law marriage. When a state recognizes common law marriage and the necessary requirements are met to establish one, the couple has a legal and formal marriage. All the rights and duties of a normal licensed marriage apply. A court decree of divorce or annulment must therefore be obtained to end common law marriage.

Same-Sex Marriage

53.3 Define *same-sex marriage* and describe the protections afforded same-sex marriage by the U.S. Constitution.

Same-sex partners had been fighting for decades to obtain the same right to marry that is enjoyed by opposite-sex partners. Many states, by legislation or constitutional provision, barred same-sex partners from marrying. Same-sex partners lobbied state legislatures and brought lawsuits in state and federal courts to change marriage laws to permit **same-sex marriage**. In these lawsuits, same-sex partners alleged that the state laws that permit opposite-sex but not same-sex partners to marry caused discrimination that violated the Due Process and Equal Protection clauses of state constitutions and the U.S. Constitution.

same-sex marriage
A marriage between two people of the same gender.

In 2015, the U.S. Supreme Court held that same-sex persons could marry. The case is described in the following feature.

Contemporary Environment

Same-Sex Marriage Is Protected by the U.S. Constitution

In 2015, the U.S. Supreme Court issued its landmark opinion in the case ***Obergefell v. Hodges***. In this case, same-sex partners challenged several states' laws that prohibited same-sex marriage. In a 5–4 decision, the Supreme Court held that state laws that prohibit same-sex marriage violate the Due Process Clause and the Equal Protection Clause of the Fourteenth Amendment to the U.S. Constitution. In its opinion, the Supreme Court stated,

> *The nature of marriage is that, through its enduring bond, two persons together can find other freedoms, such as expression, intimacy, and spirituality. This is true for all persons, whatever their sexual orientation. There is dignity in the bond between two men or two women who seek to marry and in their autonomy to make such profound choices. The right to marry thus dignifies couples who wish to define themselves by their commitment to each other. Same-sex couples have the same right as opposite-sex couples to enjoy intimate association.*
>
> *The Court now holds that same-sex couples may exercise the fundamental right to marry. No longer may this liberty be denied to them. The State laws challenged by Petitioners in these cases are now held invalid to the extent they exclude same-sex couples from civil marriage on the same terms and conditions as opposite-sex couples.*
>
> *The Court, in this decision, holds same-sex couples may exercise the fundamental right to marry in all States. It follows that the Court also must hold—and it now does hold—that there is no lawful basis for a State to refuse to recognize a lawful same-sex marriage performed in another State on the ground of its same-sex character.*
>
> *Petitioners ask for equal dignity in the eyes of the law. The Constitution grants them that right.*

Same-sex marriage provides partners with the same gender with the same rights, benefits, and responsibilities of parties to an opposite-sex marriage. *Obergefell v. Hodges*, 135 S.Ct. 2584, 2015 U.S. Lexis 4250 (Supreme Court of the United States, 2015).

Parents and Children

53.4 Explain parents' rights and duties for their children.

I think that I see something deeper, more infinite, more eternal than the ocean in the expression of the eyes of a little baby when it wakes in the morning and coos or laughs because it sees the sun shining on its cradle.
Vincent van Gogh (1853–1890)

In many instances, a major purpose of marriage is to have children. Couples who have children have certain legal rights and duties that develop from their parental status.

Parents' Rights and Duties

Parents have an obligation to provide food, shelter, clothing, medical care, and other necessities to their children until a child reaches age 18 or until emancipation. A child becomes emancipated if he or she leaves the parents and voluntarily lives on his or her own. The law imposes certain other duties on parents as well.

Examples A parent must see to it that the child attends school up until 16 or 18 years of age, depending on the state, unless the child is home schooled. Parents may be legally responsible for a child beyond the age of majority if the child has a disability.

Parents also have the right to control the behavior of their children. Parents have the right to select schools for their children and the religion they will practice.

child neglect
A parent's failure to provide a child with the necessities of life or other basic needs.

Child neglect occurs when a parent fails to provide a child with the necessities of life or other basic needs. The state may remove a child, either temporarily or permanently, from situations of child neglect. A parent's refusal to obtain medical care for a child can be punished as a crime.

Marriage Termination

53.5 Describe marriage termination by annulment and divorce.

Once a state has recognized the marital status of a couple, only the state can terminate this marital status. So long as they are married, the spouses continue to have certain legal rights and duties to one another. The law recognizes two methods for legally terminating a marriage: *annulment* and *divorce*.

Annulment

annulment
An order of the court that declares that a marriage did not exist.

An **annulment** is an order of the court declaring that a marriage did not exist. The order invalidates the marriage. Annulments are often difficult to obtain because certain grounds must be asserted and proved for a court to order an annulment. Most courts will annul a marriage if the marriage has lasted for a short time, such as one or two years, and a ground for annulment has been proven.

Examples Some of the grounds for annulment are that (1) one of the parties was a minor and had not obtained his or her parents' consent to marry, (2) one of the parties was mentally incapacitated at the time of marriage, (3) one of the parties was intoxicated at the time of the marriage, (4) the marriage was never consummated, (5) physical abuse occurred during the marriage, (6) one of the parties is an alcoholic or drug abuser, (7) there was bigamy (i.e., one of the parties was already married), or (8) there was duress or fraud leading to the marriage (e.g., one of the parties declared that he or she could conceive children when the person knew in fact that he or she could not).

When a marriage is annulled, issues of child support, child custody, spousal support, and property settlement must be agreed on by the couple or decided by the court. The law considers children born of a marriage that is annulled to be legitimate.

Divorce

The most common option used by married partners to terminate their marriage is divorce. **Divorce** is a legal proceeding whereby the court issues a decree that legally orders a marriage terminated.

divorce
A legal proceeding for the purpose of terminating a marriage.

All states currently recognize **no-fault divorce.** A spouse wishing to obtain a divorce must assert **irreconcilable differences** with his or her spouse. In a no-fault divorce, neither party is blamed for the divorce.

no-fault divorce
A divorce recognized by a state law whereby neither party is blamed for the divorce.

Some states allow a spouse to assert that the other party was at fault for causing the divorce. This is called an **at-fault divorce**. Such divorces are usually an option in states that consider fault when deciding how to divide marital assets and award spousal support. Grounds for granting an at-fault divorce are adultery, physical or emotional abuse, abandonment, alcohol or other substance abuse, or insanity.

Divorce Proceedings

A divorce proceeding is commenced by a spouse filing a **petition for divorce** with the proper state court. The petition must contain required information, such as the names of the spouses, date and place of marriage, names of minor children, and reason for the divorce. The petition must be served on the non-filing spouse. That spouse then has a certain time (usually 20 to 30 days) to file an answer to the petition.

petition for divorce
A document filed with the proper state court that commences a divorce proceeding.

If the spouses do not reach a settlement of the issues involved in the divorce—such as property division, custody of the children, and spousal and child support—the case will go to trial. The parties are permitted to conduct discovery, which includes taking depositions and producing documents. If the case goes to trial, each side is permitted to call witnesses, including expert witnesses (e.g., financial experts), to testify on his or her behalf. Both parties are also allowed to introduce evidence to support their claims.

Most states require a mandatory **waiting period** from the date that a petition for divorce is filed to the date that the court grants a divorce. The average waiting period is six months, but can be anywhere from the day of filing to one year later. The public policy for waiting periods is to give the parties time for reconciliation.

After the waiting period, a court will enter a **decree of divorce**, which is a court order that terminates the marriage. The decree of divorce may be granted even if the other issues concerning the divorce, such as the division of property or support payments, have not yet been settled or tried.

decree of divorce
A court order that terminates a marriage.

If there is a showing that one partner is likely to injure or harass the other spouse, a court may issue a **restraining order**. This places limitations on the ability of the dangerous partner to go near the other partner. Restraining orders may also be issued in nonmarital situations.

Once the parties are divorced, they are then free to marry again. Most states do not require a waiting period after a divorce for the parties to marry again.

Pro Se Divorce

In ***pro se* divorce**, the parties do not have to hire lawyers to represent them and may represent themselves in the divorce proceeding. Most states permit *pro se*—commonly called "do-it-yourself"—divorces. If there are substantial assets at stake in the divorce or if there are other complicated issues involving child custody, child support, or spousal support, the parties usually hire lawyers to represent them in the divorce proceeding.

***pro se* divorce**
A divorce proceeding in which the parties represent themselves in the divorce action.

Settlement Agreement

Approximately 90 percent of divorce cases are settled between the parties prior to trial. The parties often engage in negotiations to try to settle a divorce lawsuit to save the time and expense of a trial and to reach an agreement that is acceptable to each side. These negotiations are usually conducted between the parties with the assistance of their attorneys.

Some divorcing parties use **mediation** to try to reach a settlement of the issues involved in terminating their marriage. Some states require mediation before divorcing couples can use the court to try the case. In mediation, a neutral third party—often an attorney, a retired judge, or another party—acts as a **mediator** between the parties. A mediator is not empowered to make a decision, but instead acts as a go-between and facilitator to try to help the parties reach an acceptable settlement of the issues. Mediation is often successful because it forces the parties to consider all facets of the case, even the position of the opposing side.

settlement agreement
A written document signed by divorcing parties that evidences their agreement settling property rights and other issues of their divorce.

If a settlement is reached, a **settlement agreement** is drafted, usually by the attorneys. After being signed by the parties, the settlement agreement is presented to the court. The court accepts the terms of the settlement agreement if the judge believes that the settlement is fair and that the rights of the parties and minor children are properly taken care of. If a case is not settled, the case goes to trial.

Prenuptial Agreement

53.6 Describe a prenuptial agreement and what issues are usually addressed in a prenuptial agreement.

prenuptial agreement (premarital agreement)
A contract entered prior to marriage that specifies how property will be distributed upon the termination of the marriage by divorce or annulment, or the death of a spouse.

Many spouses sign prenuptial agreements in advance of their marriage. A **prenuptial agreement**—also called a **premarital agreement**—is a contract that specifies how property will be distributed on termination of the marriage by divorce or annulment, or the death of a spouse. To be enforced, a prenuptial agreement must be in writing.

Prenuptial agreements are often used where each party to a marriage has a career and has accumulated assets prior to the marriage or where one of the spouses has significant assets prior to the marriage. Prenuptial agreements are also often used where there are children from a prior marriage and the agreement guarantees that those children will receive a certain share of the assets of the remarrying spouse if that spouse dies or the marriage is terminated.

The following feature discusses topics often included in prenuptial agreements.

Contemporary Environment

Prenuptial Agreement

Prenuptial agreements usually address the following issues:

- **Separate property.** An agreement usually lists each party's separate property that is being brought into the marriage and includes a statement that the listed property shall remain separate property unless changed in writing during the marriage.
- **Income.** A common part of a prenuptial agreement is an agreement as to how income will be treated during the marriage. For example, a high-income earner may be awarded a certain percentage or dollar amount of his or her income earned during the marriage as separate property.
- **Valuation of a business.** If one partner owns a business prior to marriage, the agreement can value the business on the date of marriage, declare that value to be separate property, and provide for the distribution of the business on termination of the marriage and stipulate a formula for the division of the increase in value of the business that has occurred during the marriage (e.g., percentage).
- **Profession and license.** If a party is a professional, the prenuptial agreement can set forth the value or a formula for determining the value of the professional practice and license, and it can stipulate how much the professional will pay the other party on divorce.
- **Pension.** If one or both parties have contributed to a pension prior to marriage, this amount can be recognized as

separate property, and any contributions during marriage can either be designated as separate property or be divided on divorce, using some agreed-on formula.

- **Marital property.** A prenuptial agreement can address the division of marital property that has been acquired during marriage. For example, if one party is a high-income earner during marriage, a larger share of property acquired during marriage can be awarded to this partner on divorce.
- **Specific property.** A prenuptial agreement can set forth which party is to receive designated property on divorce. For example, the agreement may state that a designated party will receive the parties' primary residence on divorce. The award of other property, such as a second home, rental property, farm, investment property, securities, and other property, may also be agreed on.
- **Intellectual property and royalties.** If a party owns intellectual property, such as patents, copyrights, or trademarks, the value of the intellectual property and its income stream may be agreed on, and the parties can provide how this right and its income stream may be divided on divorce.
- **Personal items.** The agreement may allocate specifically identified personal items to designated parties. For example, furniture, jewelry, works of art, collectibles, china, and household items may be awarded to specifically named parties.
- **Alimony.** A prenuptial agreement can set forth the alimony that will be paid if the parties are divorced. For example, alimony may be set at a certain dollar amount for a stipulated time.
- **Child custody.** A prenuptial agreement can provide for child custody and visitation rights. For example, child custody may be awarded to one parent, with agreed-on visitation rights granted to the other parent.
- **Child support.** An agreement can provide for the payment of child support, often by the noncustodial parent. For example, child support may be set at a certain dollar amount for each child. The agreement may also provide for the payment of college and other expenses.
- **Other issues.** A prenuptial agreement can describe the treatment of other issues that can arise in a marriage and divorce.

For a prenuptial agreement to be enforceable, each party must make full disclosure of assets and liabilities, and each party should be represented by their own attorney. Prenuptial agreements must be voluntarily entered, without threats or undue pressure. They must provide for fair distribution of assets and must not be unconscionable. Generally, courts will enforce a properly negotiated prenuptial agreement even if the agreement provides for an unequal distribution of assets and eliminates financial support of a spouse when the marriage is terminated.

Sometimes the parties enter an agreement during the marriage, setting forth the distribution of property on the termination of the marriage or death of a spouse and settling other issues usually addressed in a prenuptial agreement. This is called a **postnuptial agreement**. With these agreements, the courts apply the same standards for enforceability as to prenuptial agreements.

In the following case, the court had to determine whether a prenuptial agreement was enforceable.

Critical Legal Thinking Questions

What purpose do prenuptial agreements serve? Would you want a prenuptial agreement to be signed prior to getting married?

CASE 53.1 *STATE COURT CASE Prenuptial Agreement*

Beyor v. Beyor

121 A.3d 734, 2015 Conn. App. 266 (2015)
Appellate Court of Connecticut

"Spouses may agree on an unequal distribution of assets at dissolution."

—Robert Beach, Justice

Facts

Carlton E. Beyor and Laura Pavano Beyor signed a prenuptial agreement four days prior to their wedding ceremony. In the agreement, each party waived any claim to the income or property of the other, and each party waived any ability to recover alimony or other support in the event of the dissolution of the marriage. Both sides were represented by attorneys, who had ample time to review the agreement. Full disclosure of assets, debts, and income were made by both parties.

At the time of the marriage, Laura was employed, earning approximately $30,000 per year. She owned a home, which she sold, netting $44,000 from the sale. At the time of marriage, Carlton had an income of approximately $250,000 per year and owned stock

(continued)

worth approximately $650,000. Following the marriage, Laura ceased working and moved into a house owned solely by Carlton.

After four years of marriage, Carlton filed for divorce and sought to enforce the prenuptial agreement. At that time, Carlton's net worth was approximately $4.5 million, and Laura's net worth was approximately $26,000. Laura claims that because of the disparity in assets owned by the parties at the time of divorce, the enforcement of the prenuptial agreement would be unconscionable. The trial court dissolved the marriage and enforced the prenuptial agreement. Laura appealed.

Issue

Was the prenuptial agreement unconscionable at the time of enforcement?

Language of the Court

The trial court found that the agreement was not forced upon the defendant. At the time of execution of the agreement, she was represented by legal counsel, and there had been full disclosure by the parties as to their respective financial situations. The defendant is not unemployable, medically disabled, not lacking skills that would permit her to be self-sufficient, although the financial quality of her life will undoubtedly diminish. Spouses may agree on an unequal distribution of assets at dissolution. The mere fact that hindsight may indicate the provisions of the agreement were improvident does not render the agreement unconscionable.

Decision

The appellate court affirmed the judgment of the trial court that enforced the prenuptial agreement.

Critical Legal Thinking Questions

Do you believe that the prenuptial agreement was unconscionable? Would you sign a prenuptial agreement if you were getting married?

In the following case, the court had to determine whether full disclosure was made by a party to a prenuptial agreement.

CASE 53.2 *STATE COURT CASE Prenuptial Agreement*

Dodson v. Dodson

779 S.E.2d 638, 2015 Ga. Lexis 874 (2015)
Supreme Court of Georgia

"In order to enforce a prenuptial agreement, the spouse seeking enforcement must show that the agreement contained full and fair disclosure of his or her material assets."

—Harold Melton, Justice

Facts

Prior to getting married, Ricky Dodson (Husband) and Kelly Dodson (Wife) signed a prenuptial agreement. In subsequent divorce proceedings, Wife filed a motion to deny enforcement of the prenuptial agreement on the basis that Husband failed to make full and fair disclosure of his financial position prior to the execution of the prenuptial agreement. Although the prenuptial agreement listed all of Husband's assets, it contained no values for these assets, including the values of Husband's bank accounts and two closely held businesses. In the divorce proceedings, the court was presented with evidence of the value of these assets and determined that these values were material facts that were necessary for a full and fair disclosure. The trial court found the prenuptial agreement unenforceable. Husband appealed.

Issue

Does the failure to disclose the value of Husband's assets make the prenuptial agreement unenforceable?

Language of the Court

In order to enforce a prenuptial agreement, the spouse seeking enforcement must show that the agreement contained full and fair disclosure of his or her material assets. Husband maintains that the law required only that he list all of his material assets, not that he apprise Wife as to their values. This is incorrect. The disclosure was neither full, because Wife had no real knowledge of the value of Husband's accounts, nor fair, because Husband never allowed Wife to have reasonable access to those accounts.

Decision

The Supreme Court of Georgia found that there had not been a full and fair disclosure by Husband of the value of his assets and held that the prenuptial agreement was unenforceable.

Critical Legal Thinking Questions

Why would a party not disclose the value of his or her assets in a prenuptial agreement? Did you learn a lesson from this case?

Division of Assets

53.7 Describe how assets are divided upon divorce and annulment.

On termination of a marriage, the parties may own certain assets, including property owned prior to marriage, gifts and inheritances received during marriage, and assets purchased with income earned during the marriage.

If the parties do not have an enforceable prenuptial agreement, the assets will be divided pursuant to a settlement agreement if one can be reached, or by a legal proceeding if an agreement cannot be reached. In most cases, the parties reach a settlement as to how the assets are divided. If no agreement is reached, the court determines how the assets will be divided.

Separate Property

In most states, on the termination of a marriage, each spouse is awarded his or her separate property. **Separate property** includes property owned by a spouse prior to the marriage as well as inheritances and gifts received during the marriage.

separate property
Property owned by a spouse prior to marriage, as well as inheritances and gifts received by a spouse during the marriage.

However, if separate property is commingled with marital property during the marriage or if the owner of the separate property changes title to the separate property by placing the other spouse's name on title to the property (e.g., real estate), the separate property is then considered a marital asset.

Example Robert and Frederick get married. At the time of marriage, Robert owns a $1 million house and has an investment account of $500,000. During their marriage, Robert makes Frederick a joint owner of the house and they commingle their income in Robert's investment account. Here, the house and investment account are no longer Robert's separate property but are now equally owned by Robert and Frederick.

Marital Property

Marital property consists of property acquired during the marriage, using income earned by the spouses during the marriage, and separate property that has been converted to marital property. There are two major legal theories that different states adhere to when dividing marital assets on the termination of a marriage. These are the theories of *equitable distribution* and *community property,* both of which are discussed in the following paragraphs.

marital property
Property acquired during the course of marriage, using income earned during the marriage, and separate property that has been converted to marital property.

Equitable Distribution of Marital Property

In states that follow the rule of **equitable distribution**, the court may order the *fair distribution* of marital property. The fair distribution of marital property does not necessarily mean the *equal* distribution of property. In determining the fair distribution of marital property, the court may consider factors such as:

equitable distribution
A law used by many states in which the court orders a fair distribution of marital property to the divorcing spouses.

- Length of the marriage
- Occupation of each spouse

- Standard of living during the marriage
- Wealth and income-earning ability of each spouse
- Which party is awarded custody of the children
- Health of the individuals
- Other factors relevant to the case

In most states, the house is often awarded to the parent who is granted custody of the children. A court also may order the house to be sold and the proceeds divided fairly between the individuals.

Community Property Distribution of Marital Property

community property
A law used by some states in which the court orders an equal division of marital property to the divorcing spouses.

Under the doctrine of **community property**, all property acquired during the marriage using income earned during the marriage is considered marital property. It does not matter which spouse earned the income or which spouse earned higher income. Money placed in pension funds, stock options, the value of businesses, the value of professional licenses, and so on is considered marital community property. In community property states the marital property is divided *equally* between the individuals.

Example Imelda and Cecilia are married. Imelda is a medical doctor who makes $1 million per year. Cecilia is a teacher who makes $100,000 per year. After five years of marriage, they have saved $4 million during their marriage. Under community property law, on divorce each would receive $2 million of the community property.

The law of community property does not necessarily mean that each piece of property is sold and the proceeds are divided equally between the individuals. Usually, each of the marital assets is valued using appraisers and expert witnesses. The court then awards the property to the spouses. If one spouse is awarded the house, the other spouse is awarded other property of equal value.

Currently they are nine community property states—Arizona, California, Idaho, Louisiana, Nevada, New Mexico, Texas, Washington, and Wisconsin.

CONCEPT SUMMARY

DIVISION OF MARITAL ASSETS

Law	Description
Equitable distribution	Marital property is fairly distributed. This does not necessarily mean equal distribution of the property.
Community property	Marital property is divided *equally* between the parties.

Division of Debts

Individuals often have debts that must be divided on termination of the marriage. How these debts are divided depends on the type of debt and on state law. In most states, each spouse is personally liable for his or her own premarital debts, and the other spouse is not liable for those debts. Student loans are a good example of these types of debts.

joint marital debts
Debts incurred during the marriage for joint needs.

Debts that are incurred during the marriage for necessities and other joint needs, including but not limited to shelter, clothing, automobiles, medical expenses, and the like, are **joint marital debts** and are the joint responsibility of the spouses. The court may distribute these debts to the spouses on termination of their marriage. However, if a debt is not paid by the spouse to whom the court has distributed the debt, a third-party creditor may recover payment of the debt from the other spouse. This individual's only recourse is to recover the amount paid from the former spouse. Spouses are jointly liable for taxes incurred during their marriage.

On the termination of a marriage, it is wise for the individuals to notify prior creditors that they will no longer be responsible for the other's debts. This is particularly true if the individuals have joint credit cards.

Spousal and Child Support

53.8 Explain the responsibilities for the payment of spousal and child support.

When a marriage is terminated, spousal support and child support may be awarded. These issues are discussed in the following paragraphs.

Spousal Support

In cases where a marriage is terminated, a court may award **spousal support**—also called **alimony**—to one of the divorced spouses. The other divorced spouse is usually ordered to pay the alimony in monthly payments. The parties may agree to the amount of alimony to be paid. If an agreement is not reached, the court determines whether the payment of alimony is warranted and, if so, the amount of alimony to be paid. Alimony may be awarded to either the female or the male spouse, depending on the circumstances.

spousal support (alimony)
Payments made by one divorced spouse to the other divorced spouse.

Alimony is usually awarded for a specific time. This is called **temporary alimony**, or **rehabilitation alimony**. This alimony is designed to provide the receiving individual with payment for a limited time during which the individual can obtain the education or job skills necessary to enter the workforce. Alimony is also awarded in cases where a parent, usually a woman, needs to care for a disabled child and must remain home to care for the child. The amount of alimony is based on the needs of the individual who will receive the alimony and the income and ability of the other individual to pay.

temporary alimony (rehabilitation alimony)
Alimony that is ordered by the court to be paid by one divorcing spouse to the other divorcing spouse for a limited period of time.

Spousal support payments usually terminate if the former spouse dies, remarries, or otherwise becomes self-sufficient. Spousal support awards can be modified by the court if circumstances change. This usually occurs if the paying individual loses a job or his or her income decreases or if the receiving individual's income increases. A party wishing to have a spousal support award changed must petition the court to *modify* the award of spousal support.

Permanent alimony—sometimes called **lifetime alimony**—is usually awarded only if the individual to receive the alimony is of an older age and if that individual has been a homemaker who has had little opportunity to obtain job skills. Permanent alimony must be paid until the individual receiving it dies or remarries.

permanent alimony (lifetime alimony)
Alimony that is ordered by the court to be paid by one divorcing spouse to the other divorcing spouse until the receiving spouse dies or remarries.

Child Support

The noncustodial parent is obligated to contribute to the financial support of biological and adopted children. This includes a child's costs for food, shelter, clothing, medical expenses, and other necessities of life. This payment is called **child support**. The custodial and noncustodial parents may agree to the amount of child support. If they do not, the court determines the amount of child support to be paid.

child support
Payments made by a noncustodial parent to help financially support his or her children.

In awarding child support, the court may consider several factors, including the number of children, the needs of the children, the net income of the parents, the standard of living of the children prior to termination of the marriage, special medical or other needs of the children, and other factors the court deems relevant. The duty to pay child support usually continues until a child reaches the age of majority, graduates from high school, or emancipates him- or herself by voluntarily choosing to live on his or her own.

To help in the determination of child support, about half of the states have adopted a formula for computing the amount. These formulas are usually based on a percentage of the noncustodial parent's income. A court is permitted to deviate from the formula if a child has special needs, such as a disability or a need for special educational assistance.

An award of child support may be modified if conditions change. For example, an award of child support may be decreased if the noncustodial parent loses a job. The amount of child support may be modified if the child's needs change, such as if the child needs special care because of a disability. The parent wishing to obtain modification of child support must petition the court to change the award.

Family Support Act
A federal statute that provides for the automatic wage withholding of child support payments from a noncustodial parent's income.

The following feature discusses the Family Support Act.

Landmark Law

Family Support Act

In the past, many noncustodial parents failed to pay child support when it was due. In many cases, the custodial parent had to initiate long and expensive legal procedures to obtain child support payments. To remedy this situation, the federal government enacted the **Family Support Act**.[1] This federal law, effective in 1994, provides that all original or modified child support orders require automatic wage withholding from a noncustodial parent's income. The Family Support Act was designed primarily to prevent noncustodial parents from failing to pay.

Assume that a court order requires a noncustodial parent to pay 25 percent of gross monthly income for child support. In this case, the court will order the noncustodial parent's employer to deduct this amount from that parent's income and send a check in that amount to the custodial parent. The noncustodial parent receives a check for the remainder of his or her income.

Child Custody

53.9 Explain child custody and visitation rights of parents.

When a couple terminates their marriage by divorce or annulment and they have children, the issue of who is legally and physically responsible for raising the children must be decided, either by settlement or by the court. The legal term *custody* is used to describe who has legal responsibility for raising a child. **Child custody** is one of the most litigated issues of divorcing couples.

child custody
The award of legal custody of a child to a parent in a divorce or annulment proceeding. This determination is made based on the best interests of the child.

Traditionally, the court usually granted custody of a child to the mother. Today, with fathers taking a more active role in childrearing, and with many mothers working, this is not always the case. In child custody disputes where both parents want custody of a child, the courts determine what is in the **best interests of the child** in awarding custody. Some of the factors that a court considers are the following:

- The ability of each parent to provide for the emotional needs of the child
- The ability of each parent to provide for other needs of the child, such as education
- The ability of each parent to provide a stable environment for the child
- The ability of each parent to provide for the special needs of a child if the child has a disability or requires special care
- The desire of each parent to provide for the needs of the child
- The religion of each parent
- Whether either parent abuses or has addictions to illegal drugs, prescription medicine, alcohol, or other factors that make them incapable of taking care of the physical and emotional needs of the child
- The wishes of the child (This factor is given more weight as the child gets older.)
- Other factors the court deems relevant

Sometimes the court determines that neither parent qualifies to be awarded custody of a child. In such cases, the court often awards custody to grandparents or other relatives who are willing to raise the child.

The **custodial parent** who is awarded custody has **legal custody** of the child. This usually includes physical custody. The custodial parent has the right to make day-to-day decisions and major decisions concerning the child's education, religion, and other such matters. The awarding of custody to a custodial parent is not permanent. Custody may be altered by the court if circumstances change.

custodial parent
The parent who is awarded custody of a child in a divorce or annulment proceeding.

Most states now permit joint custody of a child. **Joint custody** means that both parents are responsible for making major decisions concerning the child, such as education, religion, and other major matters.

joint custody
A custody arrangement that gives both parents responsibility for making major decisions concerning their child.

Parents are sometimes awarded **joint physical custody** of a child as well. This means that the child spends a certain portion of time being raised by each parent. For example, the child may spend every other week with each parent, or the child might spend the weekdays with one parent and the weekends with the other parent. These arrangements are awarded only if the child's best interests are served, such as the child being able to remain in the same school while in the physical custody of each parent.

joint physical custody
A custody arrangement whereby the child of divorcing parents spends a certain amount of time being raised by each parent.

The court does not award custody to a parent (and sometimes not to either parent) if it is in the child's best interest not to be with a parent, if there has been child abuse, or if there are other extenuating circumstances. In such cases, the court may award custody to other relatives, such as grandparents, or place the child in a foster home.

Visitation Rights

If the parents do not have joint custody of a child, the noncustodial parent is often awarded **visitation rights**. This means that the noncustodial parent is given the right to visit the child for limited periods of time, as determined by a settlement agreement or by the court.

visitation rights
Rights of a noncustodial parent to visit his or her child for limited periods of time.

If the court is concerned about the safety of a child, it may grant only supervised visitation rights to a noncustodial parent. This means that a court-appointed person must be present during the noncustodial parent's visitation with the child. This is usually done if there has been a history of child abuse or there is a strong possibility that the noncustodial parent might kidnap the child.

Key Terms and Concepts

Annulment (938)
At-fault divorce (939)
Best interests of the child (946)
Child custody (946)
Child neglect (938)
Child support (945)
Common law marriage (936)
Community property (944)
Custodial parent (947)
Decree of divorce (939)
Divorce (939)
Emancipation (936)
Engagement (935)
Equitable distribution (943)
Family Support Act (946)
Fault rule (935)
Irreconcilable differences (939)
Joint custody (947)
Joint marital debts (944)
Joint physical custody (947)
Legal custody (947)
Marital property (943)
Marriage (936)
Marriage ceremony (936)
Marriage license (936)
Mediation (940)
Mediator (940)
No-fault divorce (939)
Obergefell v. Hodges (937)
Objective rule (936)
Permanent alimony (lifetime alimony) (945)
Petition for divorce (939)
Postnuptial agreement (941)
Prenuptial agreement (premarital agreement) (940)
Pro se divorce (939)
Promise to marry (935)
Restraining order (939)
Same-sex marriage (937)
Separate property (943)
Settlement agreement (940)
Spousal support (alimony) (945)
Temporary alimony (rehabilitation alimony) (945)
Visitation rights (947)
Waiting period (939)

Critical Legal Thinking Cases

53.1 Marital Assets At the time George Neville and Tina Neville were married, George was 31 years old and a practicing attorney and Tina was a 23-year-old medical student. After seven years, Tina became a licensed physician. Soon after, George filed for divorce from Tina because she was having an adulterous affair with another doctor. At the time of the divorce, George was earning $55,000 per year practicing law; Tina was earning $165,000 per year as a physician.

The divorce was filed in Mississippi, where the couple lived. Mississippi follows the doctrine of equitable distribution. George sought that Tina's medical license and medical practice be valued as an ongoing business, and he claimed a portion of the value. The court refused George's request and instead applied the doctrine of equitable distribution and awarded him rehabilitative alimony of $1,400 per month for 120 months. The aggregate amount of the alimony was $168,000. George appealed this award, alleging on appeal that Tina's medical license and practice should be valued and that he should receive a portion of this value. Under the doctrine of equitable distribution, is the trial court's award fair, or should George win on appeal? *Neville v. Neville*, 734 So.2d 352, 1999 Miss. App. Lexis 68 (Court of Appeals of Mississippi, 1999)

53.2 Marital Assets Ronald R. and Edith Johnston were married and had three sons ranging in age from 12 to 16 when the parties separated. Edith filed for divorce the same year. The Johnstons owned a primary residence worth $186,000, with no mortgage on it. Ronald was a successful entrepreneur. He owned Depot Distributors, Inc., a business involved in selling and installing bathroom cabinets. He also owned several other businesses. In the four years leading up to the divorce, Ronald's income was $543,382, $820,439, $1,919,713, and $1,462,712. Ronald invested much of his income in commercial and residential real estate that was held in his name only. At the time of the divorce trial, the real estate was valued at $11,760,000 and was subject to mortgages of $4,966,343.

After their separation, Ronald engaged in certain transfers of property and distributions of property, in violation of the court's order, which obfuscated his income and net worth. The trial court judge therefore accepted Edith's appraisals of the value of the real estate. The trial court judge applied the equitable distribution doctrine of Massachusetts and awarded Edith real estate totaling $2,446,000, the family residence, and alimony of $1,200 per month. The trial court judge awarded Ronald real estate valued at $9,314,000 subject to mortgages of $4,966,343, for a net value of $4,347,657. The judge characterized this as a roughly 60–40 split of the real estate (i.e., 60 percent for Ronald and 40 percent for Edith). Ronald appealed the split of real estate and the award of alimony as violating the equitable distribution doctrine. Under the doctrine of equitable distribution, is the trial court's award fair, or should Ronald win on appeal? *Johnston v. Johnston*, 649 N.E.2d 799, 1995 Mass. App. Lexis 429 (Appeals Court of Massachusetts, 1995)

Ethics Case

53.3 Ethics Case Nagib Giha (Husband) filed a complaint for divorce from Nelly Giha (Wife), on the grounds of irreconcilable differences. On May 20, the parties reached an agreement for the disposition of their property, which provided that they would divide equally the net proceeds from the sale of their marital assets. There was a statutory waiting period before the divorce was final. On December 25, during the statutory waiting period, Husband learned that he had won $2.4 million in the Massachusetts MEGABUCKS state lottery. Husband kept this fact secret. After the waiting period was over, the family court entered its final judgment on April 27 of the following year, legally severing the parties' marriage. Six months later, Husband claimed his lottery prize. When Wife learned of the lottery winnings, she sued to recover her portion of the prize. She alleged that the lottery prize was a marital asset because Husband had won it before their divorce was final. Is the $2.4 million lottery prize a marital asset? Has Mr. Giha acted ethically in this case? *Giha v. Giha*, 609 A.2d 945, 1992 R.I. Lexus 133 (Supreme Court of Rhode Island, 1992)

Note

1. Public Law 100–485.

PART XIII

Global Environment

Henry R. Cheeseman

CHAPTER

54 International and World Trade Law

TIMBUKTU, MALI
Mali is a landlocked country in West Africa. The fabled city of Timbuktu was once a major trading and scholarly center of Africa.

Henry R. Cheeseman

Learning Objectives

After studying this chapter, you should be able to:

54.1 Describe the U.S. government's power under the Foreign Commerce Clause and Treaty Clause of the U.S. Constitution.

54.2 Describe the functions, governance, and organization of the United Nations.

54.3 Define *bilateral trade agreement* and *regional trade agreement* and describe the purpose of such agreements.

54.4 Describe the European Union (EU) and list the countries that belong to the EU.

54.5 Describe the United States–Mexico–Canada Agreement (USMCA) and the relevant provisions of the treaty.

54.6 Describe the trade organizations of Asia and the Indo-Pacific region.

54.7 Describe the Organization of the Petroleum Exporting Countries (OPEC) and list the countries that belong to OPEC.

54.8 Describe the trade organizations of South America, Central America, and the Caribbean.

54.9 Describe the trade organizations of Africa.

54.10 Describe the World Trade Organization (WTO) and explain how its dispute-resolution procedure works.

54.11 Describe the jurisdiction of U.S. courts over international disputes.

> "*International law, or the law that governs between nations, has at times, been like the common law within states, a twilight existence during which it is hardly distinguishable from morality or justice, till at length the imprimatur of a court attests its jural quality.*"
>
> —*Benjamin Cardozo, Justice*
> *New Jersey v. Delaware*
> *Supreme Court of the United States*
> *291 U.S. 361, 54 S.Ct. 407, 1934 U.S. Lexis 973 (1934)*

Introduction to International and World Trade Law

International law, important to both nations and businesses, has many unique features. First, there is no single legislative source of international law. All countries of the world and numerous international organizations are responsible for enacting international law. Second, there is no single world court that is responsible for interpreting international law. There are, however, several courts and tribunals that hear and decide international legal disputes of parties that agree to appear before them. Third, there is no world executive branch that can enforce international law. Thus, nations do not have to obey international law enacted by other countries or international organizations. Because of these uncertainties, some commentators question whether international law is *law*.

international law
Law that governs affairs between nations and that regulates transactions between individuals and businesses of different countries.

As technology and transportation bring nations closer together and as U.S. and foreign firms increase their global activities, international law will become even more important to governments and businesses. This chapter introduces the main concepts of international law and discusses the sources of international law and the organizations responsible for its administration.

The law of nations is founded on reason and justice.
Grover Cleveland (1837–1908)
Former president of the United States
Message to Congress (1893)

The United States and Foreign Affairs

54.1 Describe the U.S. government's power under the Foreign Commerce Clause and Treaty Clause of the U.S. Constitution.

The U.S. Constitution divides the power to regulate the internal affairs of this country between the federal and state governments. On the international level, however, the Constitution gives most of the power to the federal government. Two constitutional provisions establish this authority: the *Foreign Commerce Clause* and the *Treaty Clause*.

Foreign Commerce Clause

Article I, Section 8, Clause 3 of the U.S. Constitution—the **Foreign Commerce Clause**—vests Congress with the power "to regulate commerce with foreign nations." The Constitution does not vest exclusive power over foreign affairs in the federal government, but any state or local law that unduly burdens foreign commerce is unconstitutional, in violation of the Foreign Commerce Clause.

Foreign Commerce Clause
A clause of the U.S. Constitution that vests Congress with the power "to regulate commerce with foreign nations."

Example General Motors Company and Ford Motor Company, two U.S. automobile manufacturers, are headquartered in the state of Michigan. Michigan, in order to reduce the sales of foreign-made automobiles in the state, enacts a state law that imposes a 50 percent tax on foreign-made automobiles sold in the state but does not impose this tax on American-made automobiles sold in the state. This tax violates the Foreign Commerce Clause because it unduly burdens foreign commerce.

Example General Motors Company and Ford Motor Company, two U.S. automobile manufacturers, are headquartered in the state of Michigan. In order to protect the Great Lakes and the environment from pollution, Michigan enacts a 10 percent state tax on all automobile sales made in the state. This tax does not violate the Foreign Commerce Clause because it does not treat foreign commerce any differently than domestic commerce.

Treaty Clause

Treaty Clause
A clause of the U.S. Constitution stating that the president "shall have the power . . . to make treaties, provided two-thirds of the senators present concur."

Article II, Section 2, Clause 2 of the U.S. Constitution—the **Treaty Clause**—states that the president "shall have power, by and with the advice and consent of the Senate, to make treaties, provided two-thirds of the senators present concur."

Under the Treaty Clause, only the federal government can enter into treaties with foreign nations. Under the Supremacy Clause of the Constitution, treaties become part of the "law of the land," and conflicting state or local law is void. The president is the agent of the United States in dealing with foreign countries.

treaty
An agreement between two or more nations that is formally signed by an authorized representative of each nation and ratified by each nation.

bilateral treaty
A treaty between two nations.

multilateral treaty
A treaty involving more than two nations.

convention
A treaty that is sponsored by an international organization.

Treaties and *conventions* are the equivalents of legislation at the international level. A **treaty** is an agreement or a contract between two or more nations that is formally signed by an authorized representative and ratified by the supreme power of each nation. A **bilateral treaty** is a treaty between two nations; a **multilateral treaty** involves more than two nations. A **convention** is a treaty that is sponsored by an international organization, such as the United Nations. Conventions normally have many signatories.

Treaties and conventions address matters such as human rights, foreign aid, navigation, commerce, and the settlement of disputes. Most treaties are registered with and published by the United Nations.

Examples The federal government of the United States can enter into a treaty with China whereby the two countries agree to reduce trade barriers between them. However, the state of California cannot enter into a treaty with China that reduces trade barriers between California and China.

Henry R. Cheeseman

UNITED NATIONS, NEW YORK CITY
This is the United Nations headquarters located in New York City. Most countries are members of the United Nations.

United Nations

54.2 Describe the functions, governance, and organization of the United Nations.

One of the most important international organizations is the **United Nations (UN)**, which was created by a multilateral treaty on October 24, 1945.[1] Most countries are members of the UN. The goals of the UN, which is headquartered in New York City, are to maintain peace and security throughout the world, to promote economic and social cooperation, and to protect human rights (see Exhibit 54.1).

The UN is governed by the *General Assembly*, the *Security Council*, and the *Secretariat*, which are discussed in the following paragraphs.

United Nations (UN)
An international organization created by a multilateral treaty in 1945 to promote social and economic cooperation among nations and to protect human rights.

General Assembly

The **General Assembly** is composed of all UN member nations. As the legislative body of the UN, it adopts resolutions concerning human rights, trade, finance, and economics, as well as other matters within the scope of the UN Charter. Although resolutions have limited force, they are often enforced through persuasion and the use of economic and other sanctions.

General Assembly
The legislative body of the United Nations that is composed of all UN member nations.

Security Council

The UN **Security Council** is composed of 15 member nations, of which five (China, France, Russia, the United Kingdom, and the United States) are permanent members and 10 are countries selected by the members of the General Assembly to serve two-year terms. The Security Council is responsible primarily for maintaining international peace and security and has authority to use armed force.

Each of the five permanent members may exercise **veto power** to prevent the adoption of any substantive resolution of the UN. Thus, if any of the five permanent members vote "no" on a proposed resolution, then that resolution cannot be adopted by the UN. Critics claim that the use of the veto power has contributed to the UN's inability to address many issues, including war crimes, humanitarian crises, and breaches of the sovereignty of member nations.

Security Council
A council composed of 15 member nations of the United Nations, of which five are permanent members and 10 are countries chosen by the members of the General Assembly. The Security Council is responsible for maintaining international peace and security.

WEB EXERCISE
Use **www.google.com** to find what countries currently make up the Security Council.

Exhibit 54.1 SELECTED PROVISIONS FROM THE UNITED NATIONS CHARTER

Our respective Governments, through representatives assembled in the city of San Francisco, who have exhibited their full powers found to be in good and due form, have agreed to the present Charter of the United Nations and do hereby establish an international organization to be known as the United Nations.

Chapter 1. Purposes and Principles

Article 1 The Purposes of the United Nations are:

(1) To maintain international peace and security, and to that end: to take effective collective measures for the prevention and removal of threats to the peace, and for the suppression of acts of aggression or other breaches of the peace, and to bring about by peaceful means, and in conformity with the principles of justice and international law, adjustment or settlement of international disputes or situations which might lead to a breach of the peace;

(2) To develop friendly relations among nations based on respect for the principle of equal rights and self-determination of peoples, and to take other appropriate measures to strengthen universal peace;

(3) To achieve international co-operation in solving international problems of an economic, social, cultural, or humanitarian character, and in promoting and encouraging respect for human rights and for fundamental freedoms for all without distinction as to race, sex, language, or religion; and

(4) To be a centre for harmonizing the actions of nations in the attainment of these common ends.

Secretariat

Secretariat
A staff of persons that administers the day-to-day operations of the UN. It is headed by the *secretary-general.*

The **Secretariat** administers the day-to-day operations of the UN. It is headed by the **secretary-general**, who is elected by the General Assembly. The secretary-general may refer matters that threaten international peace and security to the Security Council and use his or her office to help solve international disputes.

United Nations Agencies

World Bank
An agency of the United Nations whose primary function is to provide money to developing countries to fund projects for humanitarian purposes and to relieve poverty.

The UN is composed of various autonomous agencies that deal with a wide range of economic and social problems. These include the United Nations Educational, Scientific, and Cultural Organization (UNESCO); the International Monetary Fund (IMF); the World Bank; the United Nations Children's Fund (UNICEF); and the International Fund for Agricultural Development (IFAD).

The following feature discusses the World Bank.

Global Law

World Bank

The **World Bank** is a United Nations agency that comprises more than 180 member nations. The World Bank is financed by contributions from developed countries, with the United States, the United Kingdom, Japan, and Germany being major contributors. The World Bank has employees located in its headquarters in Washington DC and in regional offices throughout the world.

The World Bank provides money to developing countries to fund projects for humanitarian purposes and to relieve poverty. It provides funds to build roads, construct dams and other water projects, establish hospitals and provide medical assistance, develop agriculture, and provide humanitarian aid. The World Bank provides outright grants of funds to developing countries for such projects and also makes long-term low-interest-rate loans to those countries. The bank routinely grants debt relief for these loans.

The following feature discusses the International Monetary Fund.

Global Law

International Monetary Fund

The **International Monetary Fund (IMF)**, an agency of the United Nations, was established by a treaty in 1945 to help promote the world economy following the Great Depression of the 1930s and the end of World War II in 1945. The IMF comprises more than 180 countries that are each represented on the board of directors, which makes the policy decisions of the IMF. The IMF is funded by monetary contributions of member nations, assessed based on the size of each nation's economy. The IMF's headquarters is in Washington DC.

The primary functions of the IMF are to promote sound monetary, fiscal, and macroeconomic policies worldwide and to provide assistance to poor countries. The IMF responds to financial crises around the globe. It does so by providing short-term loans to member countries to help them weather problems caused by unstable currencies, to balance payment problems, and to recover from the economic policies of past governments. The IMF examines a country's economy as a whole and its currency accounts, inflation, balance of payments with other countries, employment, consumer and business spending, and other factors to determine whether the country needs assistance. In return for the financial assistance, a country must agree to meet certain monetary, fiscal, employment, inflation, and other goals established by the IMF.

International Monetary Fund (IMF)
An agency of the United Nations whose primary function is to promote sound monetary, fiscal, and macroeconomic policies worldwide by providing assistance to poor countries.

United Nations Children's Fund (UNICEF)

The **United Nations Children's Fund (UNICEF)** is an agency of the United Nations whose goal is to provide humanitarian aid and assistance to children and mothers of children, primarily in developing countries. UNICEF provides vaccines, medicines, nutritional supplements, educational supplies, emergency shelter, and other assistance to promote the health and well-being of children. UNICEF operates in more than 190 countries and territories around the world and is funded by government and private donations.

International Court of Justice

The **International Court of Justice (ICJ)**, also called the **World Court**, is located in The Hague, the Netherlands. It is the judicial branch of the UN. Only nations, not individuals or businesses, can have cases decided by this court. The ICJ hears cases that nations refer to it as well as cases involving treaties and the UN Charter. A nation may seek redress on behalf of an individual or a business that has a claim against another country. The ICJ is composed of 15 judges who serve nine-year terms.

International Court of Justice (World Court)
The judicial branch of the United Nations, located in The Hague, the Netherlands.

Example The ICJ hears and decides cases where there have been alleged violations of human rights.

Bilateral and Regional Trade Agreements

54.3 Define *bilateral trade agreement* and *regional trade agreement* and describe the purpose of such agreements.

Countries often enter into trade agreements with one another whereby they agree to specific terms that govern trade between and among the participating nations. Such agreements include *bilateral trade agreements* and *regional trade agreements*. Each is discussed in the following paragraphs.

Bilateral Trade Agreements

A country may enter into a trade agreement with another country that facilitates trade between the countries. This is called a **bilateral trade agreement**. These trade agreements liberalize market access of goods and services, reduce tariffs, curb regulatory restrictions, allow for investment, and protect intellectual property rights. The detailed and complex agreements are usually reached after significant negotiations. The agreement may eliminate tariffs on some products, reduce tariffs on other products, allow for the provision of banking and other services, or promote other goals for either country. These agreements are not free trade agreements, but are limited trade agreements. Most agreements provide for the protection of some domestic markets of each country.

bilateral trade agreement
An agreement between two countries that facilitates trade between the countries.

Examples United States and Brazil, the Western Hemisphere's two largest economies, are parties to the Agreement on Trade and Economic Cooperation, which is a bilateral agreement on trade and investment. In 2019, the United States and Japan signed the U.S.–Japan Trade Agreement, a new trade treaty between the countries. The United States and China have entered into several trade agreements that address trade disputes between the two countries.

Regional Trade Agreements

A **regional trade agreement** is a treaty among multiple countries of a region that delineates terms of trade between the member countries. The signatory countries often agree to favorable trade terms among members that are not available to nonmember nations. Although the primary goal of these agreements is to facilitate trade, members oftentimes agree to work together to promote peace and security as well as economic, social, and cultural development.

regional trade agreement
An agreement among multiple countries of a region that delineates terms of trade between the member countries.

Examples Regional trade agreements include the United States–Mexico–Canada Agreement (USMCA), the European Union (EU), the Organization of the Petroleum Exporting Countries (OPEC), the Association of Southeast Asian

Nations (ASEAN), Mercosur (Southern Common Market), and the Common Market of Eastern and Southern Africa (COMESA). These and other regional trade agreements are discussed in this chapter.

There are many other regional trade agreements among countries of the world. Some individual countries have entered into trade agreements with international regional trade organizations, and some regional trade organizations have entered into trade agreements with other regional trade groups.

European Union

54.4 Describe the European Union (EU) and list the countries that belong to the EU.

European Union (EU)
A regional international organization that comprises many countries of Europe and was created to promote peace and security as well as economic, social, and cultural development.

One of the most important international regional organizations is the **European Union (EU)**, formerly called the *European Community*, or *Common Market*. The EU, which was created in 1957, is composed of many countries of Europe. Member nations include the following:

1. Austria
2. Belgium
3. Bulgaria
4. Croatia
5. Cyprus (the Greek part)
6. Czech Republic
7. Denmark
8. Estonia
9. Finland
10. France
11. Germany
12. Greece
13. Hungary
14. Ireland
15. Italy
16. Latvia
17. Lithuania
18. Luxembourg
19. Malta
20. Netherlands
21. Poland
22. Portugal
23. Romania
24. Slovakia
25. Slovenia
26. Spain
27. Sweden

A unanimous vote of existing EU members is needed to admit a new member country. Nonmember countries must apply for and be admitted as members of the EU, a process that takes many years. Countries that have been granted candidate status for future EU membership are Albania, Montenegro, North Macedonia, Serbia, and Turkey. Negotiations between the EU and these countries are currently being conducted. Bosnia-Herzegovina and Kosovo are potential candidates for future membership in the EU.

The EU treaty creates open borders for trade by providing for the free flow of capital, labor, goods, and services among member nations. Under the EU, customs duties have been eliminated among member nations, and common customs tariffs have been established for EU trade with the rest of the world. The EU represents more than 475 million people and has a gross community product that approximately equals that of the United States, Canada, and Mexico combined. A map of EU member countries is shown in Exhibit 54.2.

United Kingdom's Withdrawal from the European Union

The United Kingdom (UK) is composed of four countries: Britain, Wales, Scotland, and Northern Ireland. In 1973, the United Kingdom joined the European Community, which is now the EU. In 2016, the electorate of the United Kingdom voted to leave the EU. The reasons cited for doing so include restoring British sovereignty, freeing itself of EU laws, ending free movement

Exhibit 54.2 MAP OF THE EUROPEAN UNION (EU) COUNTRIES

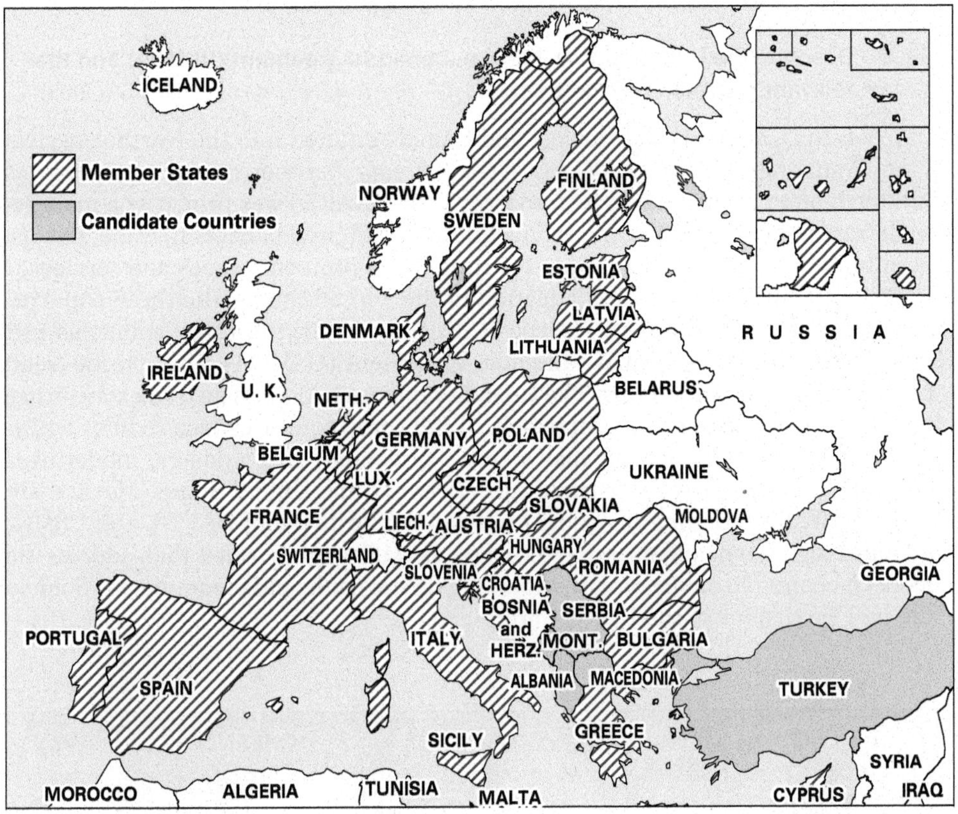

of EU workers into the UK, and regaining control over immigration. The United Kingdom officially separated from the EU and is no longer a member of the EU.

EU Administration

The EU's **Council of Ministers** is composed of representatives from each member country who meet periodically to coordinate efforts to fulfill the objectives of the treaty. The council votes on significant issues and changes to the treaty. Some matters require unanimity, whereas others require only a majority vote. The member nations have surrendered substantial sovereignty to the EU. The **European Union Commission**, which is independent of its member nations, is charged to act in the best interests of the union. The member nations have delegated substantial powers to the commission, including authority to enact legislation and to take enforcement actions to ensure member compliance with the treaty.

Euro

The European Union has introduced a single monetary unit, the **euro**. Many but not all EU countries have voted to use the euro. The countries that have voted to use the euro compose the **eurozone**, and the euro can be used in all countries of the eurozone. An EU central bank, equivalent to the U.S. Federal Reserve Board, has been established to set common monetary policy.

euro
A single monetary unit that has been adopted by many countries of the EU that compose the *eurozone*.

WEB EXERCISE
Use **www.google.com** to find the current exchange rate of the euro compared to the U.S. dollar.

United States–Mexico–Canada Agreement (USMCA)

54.5 Describe the United States–Mexico–Canada Agreement (USMCA) and the relevant provisions of the treaty.

In 1994, the United States, Mexico, and Canada entered into the **North American Free Trade Agreement (NAFTA)**, a trade treaty between the three countries. Although often referred to as a "free trade" pact, NAFTA was primarily a managed trade agreement that eliminated some duties, tariffs, and barriers to trade, but also permitted duties, tariffs, and trade restrictions on protected goods and services.

Beginning in 2018, at the instigation of the United States, the three countries entered into negotiations to replace NAFTA. In 2020, the three countries ratified the **United States–Mexico–Canada Agreement (USMCA)**, a new trade treaty between the member nations. The USMCA replaces NAFTA. The trade zone brings together more than 475 million people of the three countries (see Exhibit 54.3).

United States–Mexico–Canada Agreement (USMCA) A treaty that has removed or reduced tariffs, duties, quotas, and other trade barriers among the United States, Canada, and Mexico. The USMCA replaced the North American Free Trade Agreement (NAFTA) in 2020.

The USMCA is a comprehensive trade agreement that updates, modernizes, and rebalances cross-border trade rules between the United States, Mexico, and Canada. While retaining many features similar to those of NAFTA, the USMCA includes significant changes to prior law as well as new rules that address the modern economic environment, including digital trade and e-commerce. Some of the new provisions of the USMCA are:

Exhibit 54.3 MAP OF THE UNITED STATES–MEXICO–CANADA AGREEMENT (USMCA) MEMBER COUNTRIES

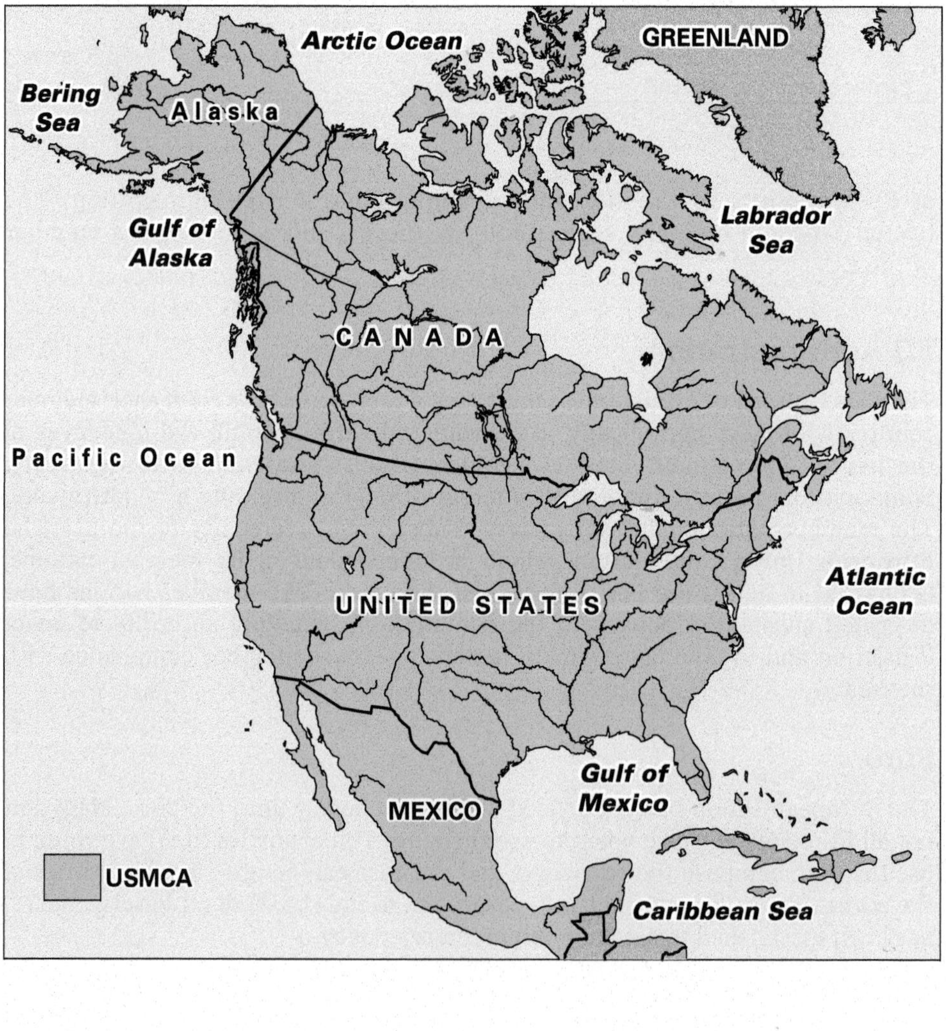

- **Digital trade.** When NAFTA was enacted, digital trade and e-commerce had not yet developed. The USMCA provides rules that govern digital trade and e-commerce between the three countries. These provisions include rules that ensure that data can be transferred across borders; prohibit duties on digital products distributed electronically, such as music, e-books, videos, software, and games; prohibit forced disclosure of proprietary computer source codes and algorithms; and prevent members from forcing companies to store data on in-country servers.
- **Intellectual property.** USMCA provides for increased protection of intellectual rights, including: increasing the term of copyright to 70 years beyond the life of the author or 75 years from date of publication (both up from 50 years); providing for criminal penalties for satellite and cable theft, stealing of trade secrets, and online piracy; providing patent extensions to remedy unreasonable patent and regulatory delays; and requiring customs officials to stop suspected counterfeit goods.
- **Labor provisions.** In order to join the agreement, Mexico had to adopt new labor laws that grant workers the right to strike and collectively bargain with employers, require secret voting concerning union matters, and prohibit violence against persons exercising their labor rights. The treaty provides for the monitoring and expedited arbitration and enforcement of labor rights in Mexico. The USMCA prohibits members from importing goods produced by child labor or forced labor.

Critical Legal Thinking Questions

What is the purpose of regional trade agreements? Do countries give up any sovereignty by joining such regional associations?

- **Automobiles and automotive parts.** To qualify for zero tariffs when crossing borders, a car or truck must have 75 percent (up from 62.5 percent) of its components manufactured in the United States, Canada, or Mexico. At least 70 percent of a producer's steel and aluminum purchases must originate in North America. The USMCA requires that 45 percent of automobile parts must be made by workers who earn at least $16 per hour, which is about three times higher than the average wage earned by Mexican auto workers at the time the USMCA went into effect.
- **Agricultural products.** The treaty requires Canada to open up its dairy market to U.S. farmers, eliminates discriminatory treatment of U.S. wine in grocery stores, eliminates discriminatory treatment regarding the sale and distribution of alcoholic beverages made in the United States, eliminates restrictions on the importation of U.S. cheese, and eliminates discretionary grading of U.S. wheat.
- **Energy.** The USMCA provides for the free flow of energy across borders in North America, and requires rules of origin certificates for energy products.
- **Textiles.** The USMCA reduces tariff levels imposed by Canada on the importation of textiles from the United States; requires the sourcing of thread, pocketing, and coated fabrics from within North America; and requires that uniforms and textile products for Transportation Security Administration (TSA) personnel must be made in the United States.
- **Financial services.** The USMCA requires member nations to permit cross-border provision of financial products, investment services, portfolio management, investment advice, and electronic payment services.
- **Non-market practices.** The USMCA addresses non-market practices that hinder cross-border trade. The USMCA prohibits unfair government subsidies to members' own producers and prohibits member nations from providing subsidies to their own state-owned enterprises (even if the government has a minority interest in the enterprise). Members may not require businesses to establish headquarters or other offices in order to conduct business in that country. The treaty requires Mexico and Canada to criminalize acts of corruption by domestic and foreign governments and to establish laws that criminalize bribery and embezzlement.

- **Currency manipulation.** NAFTA did not address currency issues. The USMCA requires member countries to maintain market-determined exchange rates, and prohibits currency manipulation, devaluations, and manipulation of exchange rates to gain a competitive advantage over other members.
- **Environment.** The USMCA includes the strongest, most advanced, and most comprehensive set of regulations of any U.S. trade agreement, and provides for enforceable dispute resolution of environmental violations. The treaty establishes a committee to monitor the members and ensure parties are meeting their environmental obligations.

The USMCA requires each member nation to publish online its laws, regulations, tariffs, duties, taxes, and government contact information. The treaty provides a mechanism whereby most disputes will be settled by arbitration, or eventually by a USMCA tribunal panel. The USMCA contains a 16-year sunset clause—meaning the terms of the agreement expire after 16 years. The agreement is subject to review every six years, at which point the United States, Mexico, and Canada can decide to extend the USMCA. The USMCA allows the three-country bloc to discriminate against outsiders and not provide them with benefits available under the USMCA.

Asian and Indo-Pacific Trade Organizations

54.6 Describe the trade organizations of Asia and the Indo-Pacific region.

There are several important regional economic organizations composed of countries of Asia and the Indo-Pacific region. These regional trade organizations are discussed in the following paragraphs.

Association of Southeast Asian Nations (ASEAN)

Association of Southeast Asian Nations (ASEAN)
An association of many countries of Southeast Asia that provides for economic and other coordination among member nations.

In 1967, **Association of Southeast Asian Nations (ASEAN)** was created. This is a cooperative regional association of diverse nations that work to promote economic, political, and cultural issues. The countries of Southeast Asia that belong to ASEAN are: Brunei, Cambodia, Indonesia, Laos, Malaysia, Myanmar, the Philippines, Singapore, Thailand, and Vietnam. The population of the ASEAN countries is more than 650 million.

ASEAN created a free trade zone for member countries. More than 90 percent of goods sold between members are traded with no tariffs. The bloc has prioritized eleven sectors for integration, including electronics, automotive, rubber-based products, textiles and apparels, agricultural products, and tourism. ASEAN is also designed to promote local manufacturing and attract investment capital.

Three of Asia's largest economies—China, Japan, and South Korea—are not members of ASEAN. A current association called **ASEAN Plus Three (APT)**—the "three" being China, Japan, and South Korea—does, however, discuss and coordinate regional economic, social, and political issues of mutual interest.

A map of Asia appears in Exhibit 54.4.

Regional Comprehensive Economic Partnership (RCEP)

Regional Comprehensive Economic Partnership (RCEP)
A regional trade agreement between 15 countries of Asia and the Indo-Pacific region that creates the world's largest regional trade zone.

The **Regional Comprehensive Economic Partnership (RCEP)** is a proposed free trade agreement involving 15 countries in the Asia-Pacific region. The countries include the ten members of ASEAN (Brunei, Cambodia, Indonesia, Laos, Malaysia, Myanmar, the Philippines, Singapore, Thailand, and Vietnam); the three associated members of ASEAN Plus Three—China, Japan, and South Korea; and Australia and New Zealand. The RCEP is a mega trade deal that accounts for 30 percent of the world's population and 30 percent of the world's gross domestic

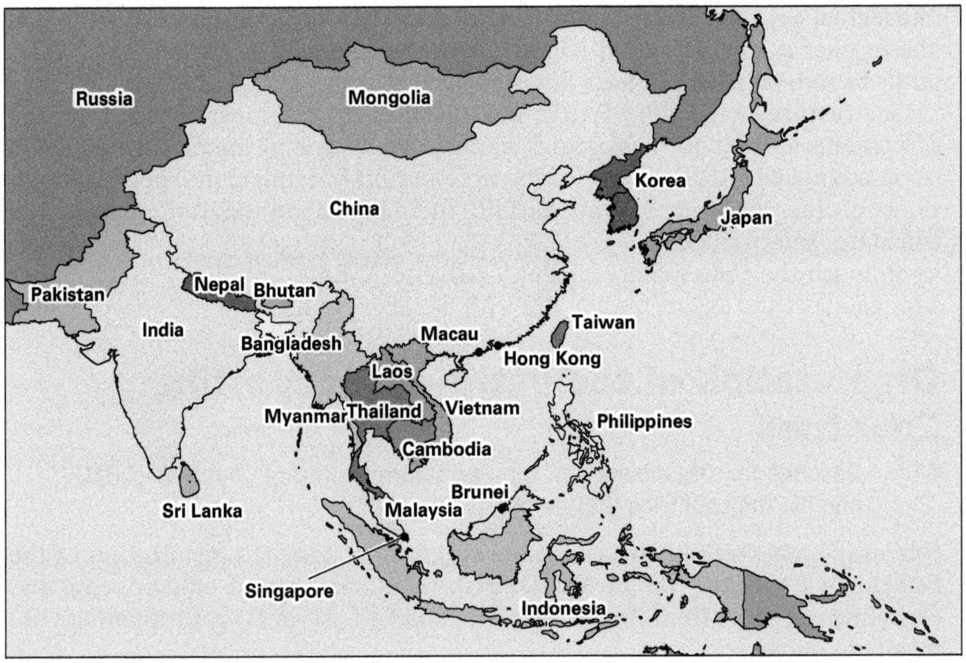

Exhibit 54.4 MAP OF ASIA

product, making it the largest regional trade zone in the world. China was a major force in forming the RCEP.

The major emphasis of the RCEP is reducing tariffs on a broad range of products. Tariff schedules were primarily negotiated bilaterally within the agreement, so tariff schedules are different based on which countries are involved. One of the most significant changes of the RCEP is the creation of a common rules of origin of products for the entire bloc. The RCEP countries will only require a single certificate of origin that will allow companies to ship products to all countries in the bloc without having to be concerned about individual country rules.

The RCEP is taking some steps to open up trade in services, investment, and e-commerce. The agreement does not include labor or environmental standards. Although the RCEP lacks the breadth and depth of some of the other major trade agreements, its massive scope will lead to a comprehensive integration of trade among Asian and Indo-Pacific countries.

The RCEP missed its planned start date of 2020. When it does begin operations, it may start with fewer than its originally proposed 15 members as countries focus on reviving their country's economy before joining the trade association. India was an original negotiating party to the RCEP, but dropped out during the negotiating process. India is a possible future member of the RCEP.

WEB EXERCISE
Use **www.google.com** to find out whether the Regional Comprehensive Economic Partnership (RCEP) has been established, and if so, what countries are current members.

Comprehensive and Progressive Agreement for Trans-Pacific Partnership (CPTPP)

The **Comprehensive and Progressive Agreement for Trans-Pacific Partnership (CPTPP)** is a free trade agreement between 11 countries located in the Indo-Pacific region. The CPTPP is a trading bloc representing 500 million people encompassing 13.5 percent of global gross domestic product. The CPTPP has been ratified by seven countries: Canada, Australia, Japan, Mexico, New Zealand, Singapore, and Vietnam. Four other signatory countries—Brunei, Chile, Malaysia, and Peru—have yet to ratify the trade agreement. The CPTPP entered into force in 2018.

Comprehensive and Progressive Agreement for Trans-Pacific Partnership (CPTPP)
A regional trade agreement between 11 countries of the Indo-Pacific region that eliminates tariffs across a broad range of products and services.

The CPTPP creates a free trade zone that provides comprehensive tariff elimination across a broad range of products and services, investment and financial services, telecommunications, digital trade and electronic commerce, and intellectual property sectors. Tariff reductions will be implemented in annual phases over a 15-year period. Once fully implemented, the CPTPP will reduce tariffs to zero on most products and services.

One feature of the CPTPP that distinguishes it from most other free trade agreements is that its basic rules apply equally among members, although some countries are allowed a longer time period to implement specific provisions of the agreement. The CPTPP includes labor, environmental, and consumer safety rules.

Although the United States is not a party to ASEAN, CPTPP, or RCEP, it has strong import and export trading ties with member countries of these trade pacts.

Organization of the Petroleum Exporting Countries

54.7 Describe the Organization of the Petroleum Exporting Countries (OPEC) and list the countries that belong to OPEC.

Organization of the Petroleum Exporting Countries (OPEC)
An association comprising many of the oil-producing and exporting countries of the world.

One of the most well-known economic organizations is the **Organization of the Petroleum Exporting Countries (OPEC)**. OPEC consists of oil-producing and exporting countries from Africa, Asia, the Middle East, and South America. The member nations are:

1. Algeria
2. Angola
3. Congo
4. Equatorial Guinea
5. Gabon
6. Iran
7. Iraq
8. Kuwait
9. Libya
10. Nigeria
11. Saudi Arabia
12. United Arab Emirates (UAE)
13. Venezuela

OPEC sets quotas on the output of oil production by member nations. OPEC members produce approximately 40 percent of the world's crude oil. OPEC member nations contain more than 80 percent of proven oil reserves. The population of the OPEC countries is more than 400 million.

South American, Central American, and Caribbean Trade Organizations

54.8 Describe the trade organizations of South America, Central America, and the Caribbean.

There are several major regional economic organizations in South America, Central America, and the Caribbean. These regional trading organizations are discussed in the following paragraphs.

Mercosur

Mercosur
A regional trading organization in South America composed of Argentina, Brazil, Paraguay, and Uruguay.

Mercosur, also called **Mercosul** or the **Southern Common Market**, is a regional trade bloc in South America composed of Argentina, Brazil, Paraguay, and Uruguay. Venezuela is a member of Mercosur, but has been suspended for several years. Bolivia is negotiating to become a member. The Common Market Council is the governing body, and the presidency rotates among its members.

Mercosur was formed to eliminate customs duties among its members and to provide for the free movement of goods, services, and factors of production between member nations. Trade among members is tariff-free except for certain protected sectors. The members of Mercosur impose a common external tariff on goods from outside Mercosur. Residents of the countries belonging to Mercosur are authorized to live and work in any of the member countries. Bolivia, Chile,

Colombia, Ecuador, Guyana, Peru, and Suriname are associate members who receive tariff reductions when trading with Mercosur's members, but they do not have voting rights.

Mercosur, which brings together more than 300 million people, is the largest regional economic organization in South America. Brazil is the largest member, with more than 230 million people, and Argentina is second, with more than 45 million people. Argentina and Brazil account for about 95 percent of the bloc's trade.

Andean Community of Nations

The **Andean Community of Nations**, also called the **Andean Community** or **CAN**, is a regional trading bloc in South America composed of Bolivia, Colombia, Ecuador, and Peru. It is the second largest regional economic organization in South America. The combined population of the countries of the Andean Community exceeds 120 million people. The countries of the Andean Community have established a common external tariff. Citizens of the four countries may reside and work for a period of two years in another member state and after two years may apply for permanent residency.

Andean Community of Nations
A regional trading organization in South America composed of Bolivia, Colombia, Ecuador, and Peru.

Central America–Dominican Republic Free Trade Agreement (CAFTA-DR).

The **Central America–Dominican Republic Free Trade Agreement (CAFTA-DR)** is a trade agreement that includes the United States and the Central American countries of Costa Rica, Dominican Republic, El Salvador, Guatemala, Honduras, and Nicaragua. This agreement provides for the removal of some tariffs, and the lowering of other tariffs, with a schedule of eliminating most tariffs over a 20-year period.

Central America–Dominican Republic Free Trade Agreement (CAFTA-DR)
An association of several Central American countries and the United States designed to reduce tariffs and trade barriers among member nations.

African Trade Organizations

54.9 Describe the trade organizations of Africa.

There are multiple regional trading blocs in Africa, many with overlapping country membership. Several of the primary regional economic communities of Africa are:

- **Common Market of Eastern and Southern Africa (COMESA)** The **Common Market of Eastern and Southern Africa (COMESA)** is a regional trade bloc of countries located in eastern and southern Africa. It is the most successful economic trade organization in Africa. COMESA is a trade area where member countries currently share preferential tariffs that are unavailable to nonmembers.
- **Economic Community of West African States (ECOWAS)** The **Economic Community of West African States (ECOWAS)** is a regional trade area of countries of West Africa that have a combined population of more than 350 million. ECOWAS is a common market for goods, services, labor, and capital for member nations. It enforces a fixed tariff for goods from nonmember countries. ECOWAS is composed of French-speaking, English-speaking, and Portuguese-speaking countries. Each of these groups has formed its own subgroup within ECOWAS.
- **East African Community (EAC)** The **East African Community (EAC)** is a regional intergovernmental organization of countries of East Africa. The EAC is a common market permitting the free movement of goods, services, labor, and capital among member nations. The EAC permits persons to establish residence within any of the member nations.

Common Market of Eastern and Southern Africa (COMESA)
A regional trading bloc of countries located in eastern and southern Africa.

Economic Community of West African States (ECOWAS)
A regional trading bloc of countries located in West Africa.

East African Community (EAC)
A regional trading bloc of countries located in East Africa.

African Union

African Union (AU)
An organization composed of the countries located on the African continent whose goal is to establish an integrated, politically united, and prosperous African continent based on the ideals of Pan-Africanism and Africa's Renaissance.

African Continental Free Trade Area (AfCFTA)
A regional trade agreement among the countries of Africa that would establish a single continental trade market for goods and services that would reduce tariffs, encourage investment, and promote job creation.

The **African Union (AU)** is an organization composed of the countries located on the African continent. The AU is primarily a political organization that seeks to establish an integrated, politically united, and prosperous African continent based on the ideals of Pan-Africanism and Africa's Renaissance. The African Union has launched the **African Continental Free Trade Area (AfCFTA)**. The goal is to establish a single market for goods and services across 54 countries comprising 1.3 billion people. The agreement would allow access to goods and services across the continent, remove tariffs from the majority of goods, encourage investment throughout the member nations, promote job creation, and allow for the free movement of travelers. Negotiations will be conducted to arrive at the final agreement.

World Trade Organization

54.10 Describe the World Trade Organization (WTO) and explain how its dispute-resolution procedure works.

World Trade Organization (WTO)
An international organization of more than 160 member nations created to promote and enforce trade agreements among member countries and customs territories.

In 1995, the **World Trade Organization (WTO)** was created. The WTO is an international organization headquartered in Geneva, Switzerland. Its main function is to ensure that trade flows as smoothly, predictably, and freely as possible. WTO members have entered into many trade agreements among themselves, covering goods, services, and intellectual property.

Through rounds of negotiations among its membership, the WTO aims to achieve major reform of the international trading system through the introduction of lower trade barriers and revised trade rules. A current objective of the WTO is to improve the trading prospects of developing countries.

The World Trade Organization has jurisdiction to enforce the most important and comprehensive trade agreements in the world among its more than 160 member nations and customs territories. The WTO is designed to peaceably solve trade disputes among member nations. Several nonmember countries are negotiating to join the WTO.

WTO Dispute Resolution

One of the primary functions of the WTO is to hear and decide trade disputes between or among member nations.

WTO panel
A body of three WTO judges that hears trade disputes between member nations and issues panel reports.

WTO dispute settlement body
A board composed of one representative from each WTO member nation that reviews panel reports.

WTO appellate body
A panel of seven judges selected from WTO member nations that hears and decides appeals from decisions of the dispute-settlement body.

A member nation that believes another member nation has breached one of the trade agreements can initiate a proceeding to have the WTO hear and decide the dispute. The dispute is first heard by a three-member **WTO panel**, which issues a panel report. The members of the panel are professional judges from member nations. The report, which is the decision of the panel, contains the panel's findings of fact and law, and it orders a remedy if a violation has been found. The report is then referred to the **WTO dispute settlement body**. This body is required to adopt the panel report unless the body, by consensus, agrees not to adopt it.

There is a **WTO appellate body** to which a party can appeal a decision of the dispute-settlement body. This appeals court is composed of seven professional justices selected from member nations. Appeals are limited to issues of law, not fact.

If a violation of a trade agreement is found, the panel report and appellate decision can order the offending nation to cease engaging in the violating practice and to pay damages to the other party. If the offending nation refuses to abide by the order, the WTO can order retaliatory trade sanctions (e.g., tariffs) by other member nations against the noncomplying nation.

Example In 2019, the WTO ruled that the European Union had given illegal government subsidies to Airbus SE, a European multinational aerospace corporation and airplane manufacturer. The government subsidies were provided so that the company could sell its airplanes at a lower price when competing with the large U.S. airplane manufacturer, the Boeing Company. The WTO ruled that the United States could impose $7.5 billion of tariffs annually on European goods imported to the United States. It is the largest WTO award to date.

Jurisdiction of U.S. Courts to Decide International Disputes

54.11 Describe the jurisdiction of U.S. courts over international disputes.

Most cases involving international law disputes are heard by **national courts** of individual nations. This is primarily the case for commercial disputes between private litigants that do not qualify to be heard by international courts. Some countries have specialized courts that hear international commercial disputes. Other countries permit such disputes to proceed through their regular court systems. In the United States, commercial disputes between U.S. companies and foreign governments or parties may be brought in U.S. district court.

national courts
The courts of individual nations.

Judicial Procedure

A party seeking judicial resolution of an international dispute faces several problems, including which nation's courts will hear the case and what law should be applied to the case. Jurisdiction is often a contested issue. Absent an agreement providing otherwise, a case involving an international dispute will be brought in the national court of the plaintiff's home country.

Many international contracts contain a **choice of forum clause** (or **forum-selection clause**) that designates which nation's court has jurisdiction to hear a case arising out of a contract. In addition, many contracts also include a **choice of law clause** that designates which nation's laws will be applied in deciding such a case.

choice of forum clause (forum-selection clause)
A clause in an international contract that designates which nation's court has jurisdiction to hear a case arising out of the contract.

choice of law clause
A clause in an international contract that designates which nation's laws will be applied in deciding a dispute arising out of the contract.

CONCEPT SUMMARY

INTERNATIONAL CONTRACT CLAUSES

Clause	Description
Forum-selection	A clause that designates the judicial or arbitral forum that will hear and decide a case.
Choice of law	A clause that designates the law to be applied by the court or arbitrator in deciding a case.

Act of State Doctrine

A general principle of international law is that a country has absolute authority over what transpires *within* its own territory. In furtherance of this principle, the **act of state doctrine** states that judges of one country cannot question the validity of an act committed by another country within that other country's own borders. In *United States v. Belmont*,[2] the U.S. Supreme Court declared, "Every sovereign state must recognize the independence of every other sovereign state; and the courts of one will not sit in judgment upon the acts of the government of another, done within its own territory." This restraint on jurisdiction is justified under the doctrine of separation of powers and permits the executive branch of the federal government to arrange affairs with foreign governments.

act of state doctrine
A doctrine stating that judges of one country cannot question the validity of an act committed by another country within that other country's borders. It is based on the principle that a country has absolute authority over what transpires within its own territory.

Example Suppose a foreign country changes its laws and outlaws the ownership of private property by individuals and businesses and confiscates all of the private property for the government. Milton, a person who is a citizen of, and living in, the United States, disagrees with the law and its consequences. Milton brings a lawsuit against the foreign country in a U.S. district court, arguing to the court that the foreign country's law should be declared illegal. The U.S. district court

Critical Legal Thinking Question

What would be the consequences if the act of state doctrine were not recognized?

will apply the act of state doctrine and dismiss Milton's lawsuit. The U.S. district court will rule that the foreign country's law is an act of that state (country) and that a U.S. court does not have authority to hear and decide Milton's case.

In the following case, the court was called on to apply the act of state doctrine.

CASE 54.1 ***FEDERAL COURT CASE Act of State Doctrine***

Glen v. Club Mediterranee, S.A.

450 F.3d 1251, 2006 U.S. App. Lexis 13400 (2006)
United States Court of Appeals for the Eleventh District

"The doctrine prevents any court in the United States from declaring that an official act of a foreign sovereign performed within its own territory is invalid."

—Emmett Cox, Circuit Judge

Facts

Prior to the communist revolution in Cuba, Elvira de la Vega Glen and her sister, Ana Maria de la Vega Glen, were Cuban citizens and residents who jointly owned beachfront property on the Peninsula de Hicacos in Varadero, Cuba. On or about January 1, 1959, in conjunction with Fidel Castro's communist revolution, the Cuban government expropriated the property without paying the Glens. That same year, the sisters fled Cuba. Ana Maria de la Vega Glen died and passed any interest she had in the Varadero beach property to her nephew, Robert M. Glen.

Approximately 40 years after the property was taken by Cuba, Club Mediterranee, S.A., and Club Mediterranee Group (Club Med) entered a joint venture with the Cuban government to develop the property. Club Med constructed and operated a five-star luxury hotel on the property that the Glens had owned. The Glens sued Club Med in a U.S. district court located in the state of Florida. The Glens alleged that the original expropriation of their property by the Cuban government was illegal and that Club Med had trespassed on their property and had been unduly enriched by its joint venture with the Cuban government to operate a hotel on their expropriated property. The Glens sought to recover the millions of dollars in profits earned by Club Med from its alleged wrongful occupation and use of the Glens' expropriated property. The U.S. district court held that the act of state doctrine barred recovery by the Glens and dismissed the Glens' claims against Club Med. The Glens appealed.

Issue

Does the act of state doctrine bar recovery by the Glens?

Language of the Court

The doctrine prevents any court in the United States from declaring that an official act of a foreign sovereign performed within its own territory is invalid. It requires that the acts of foreign sovereigns taken within their own jurisdictions shall be deemed valid. Because the act of state doctrine requires the courts deem valid the Cuban government's expropriation of the real property at issue in this case, the Glens cannot maintain their claims for trespass and unjust enrichment against Club Med.

Decision

The U.S. court of appeals applied the act of state doctrine and affirmed the judgment of the U.S. district court that dismissed the Glens' claim against Club Med.

Critical Legal Thinking Questions

Did the Cuban government act ethically when it expropriated the Glens' property? Did Club Med act ethically when it entered into a joint venture with the Cuban government to develop the property that had been expropriated from the Glens?

Doctrine of Sovereign Immunity

doctrine of sovereign immunity
A doctrine stating that countries are granted immunity from suits in courts of other countries.

One of the oldest principles of international law is the **doctrine of sovereign immunity**. Under this doctrine, *countries* are granted immunity from suits in courts in other countries. For example, a U.S. citizen who wanted to sue the government of China in a U.S. court could not (subject to certain exceptions).

Originally, the United States granted absolute immunity to foreign governments from suits in U.S. courts. In 1952, the United States switched to the principle of **qualified immunity**, or **restricted immunity**, which was eventually codified in the **Foreign Sovereign Immunities Act (FSIA)** of 1976.[3] This act now exclusively governs suits against foreign nations in the United States, whether in federal court or state court. Most Western nations have adopted the principle of restricted immunity. Other countries still follow the doctrine of absolute immunity.

Foreign Sovereign Immunities Act (FSIA)
An act that exclusively governs suits against foreign nations that are brought in federal or state courts in the United States. It codifies the principle of *qualified*, or *restricted, immunity*.

Exceptions to the FSIA

The FSIA provides that a foreign country is not immune to lawsuits in U.S. courts in the following situations:

- If the foreign country has waived its immunity, either explicitly or by implication.
- If the action is based on a commercial activity carried on in the United States by the foreign country or carried on outside the United States but causing a direct effect in the United States. This is called the **commercial activity exception**.

commercial activity exception
An exception stating that a foreign country is subject to lawsuit in the United States if it engages in commercial activity in the United States or if it carries on such activity outside the United States but causes a direct effect in the United States.

What constitutes "commercial activity" is the most litigated aspect of the FSIA. With commercial activity, the foreign sovereign is subject to suit in the United States; without it, the foreign sovereign is immune to suit in this country.

Example To raise money, the government of a foreign country sells 20-year bonds to investors in the United States. The bondholders are to be paid 10 percent interest annually, and the bonds are to be paid off at the end of 20 years. By selling bonds to investors in the United States, the foreign country is involved in commercial activity in the United States. If the country defaults and does not pay the U.S. investors the 10 percent interest on the bonds or the principal when due, the bondholders can sue the foreign country in U.S. district court under the commercial activity exception to the doctrine of sovereign immunity to recover the unpaid interest or principal.

Critical Legal Thinking Question
What would be the consequences if the doctrine of sovereign immunity were not recognized?

In the following case, the court had to decide whether the commercial activity exception to sovereign immunity applied.

CASE 54.2 FEDERAL COURT CASE Sovereign Immunity

Devengoechea v. Bolivarian Republic of Venezuela

889 F.3d 1213 (2018)
United States Court of Appeals for the Eleventh Circuit

"Nothing about this activity is uniquely or particularly sovereign in nature."
—Robin Rosenbaum, Circuit Judge

Facts

General Simón Bolívar was a contemporary of George Washington and was the founding father in South America and was instrumental in helping six countries obtain independence from Spain. Bolívar spent his last days at the home of his friend Joaquin de Mier, and de Mier obtained a treasure trove of Bolívar's possessions (Bolívar Collection). De Mier's ancestors passed down the Bolívar Collection from generation to generation until Ricardo Devengoechea inherited it. The collection is worth millions of dollars.

In 2006, officials of the Bolivarian Republic of Venezuela (Venezuela) traveled to the United States to meet with Devengoechea to negotiate the purchase of the Bolívar Collection. Devengoechea and the officials agreed that the officials would take the collection back to Venezuela for further inspection

(continued)

and that Venezuela would either purchase it or return it to Devengoechea. Five years later, despite Devengoechea's repeated inquiries, Venezuela had neither returned nor paid for the collection.

Devengoechea sued Venezuela in U.S. district court seeking payment for or return of the collection. Venezuela moved to dismiss the case, claiming sovereign immunity. Devengoechea asserted that the commercial activity exception applied. The U.S. district court held that the commercial activity exception applied and that Venezuela was subject to suit in U.S. district court. Venezuela appealed.

Issue

Does the commercial activity exception to sovereign immunity apply?

Language of the Court

Foreign Sovereign Immunities Act (FSIA) defines commercial activity as either a regular course of commercial conduct or a particular commercial transaction or act. Like a private buyer could do, Venezuela flew to the United States to meet with the seller, examined the collection, and negotiated to examine it further and return or purchase it. This is the type of activity that private persons and corporations regularly engage in. Nothing about this activity is uniquely or particularly sovereign in nature.

Decision

The U.S. court of appeals held that Venezuela is subject to suit in the United States.

Critical Legal Thinking Questions

What is the purpose of sovereign immunity? Why was the commercial activity exception adopted? Did Venezuela act ethically?

CONCEPT SUMMARY

ACT OF STATE AND SOVEREIGN IMMUNITY DOCTRINES COMPARED

Doctrine	Description
Act of state	A doctrine stating that an act of a government in its *own country* is not subject to suit in a foreign country's courts.
Sovereign immunity	A doctrine stating that an act of a government in a *foreign country* is not subject to suit in the foreign country. Some countries provide absolute immunity, and other countries (such as the United States) provide limited immunity.

Key Terms and Concepts

Act of state doctrine (965)
African Continental Free Trade Area (AfCFTA) (964)
African Union (AU) (964)
Andean Community of Nations (Andean Community or CAN) (963)
ASEAN Plus Three (APT) (960)
Association of Southeast Asian Nations (ASEAN) (960)
Bilateral trade agreement (955)
Bilateral treaty (952)
Central America–Dominican Republic Free Trade Agreement (CAFTA-DR) (963)
Choice of forum clause (forum-selection clause) (965)
Choice of law clause (965)
Commercial activity exception (967)
Common Market of Eastern and Southern Africa (COMESA) (963)
Comprehensive and Progressive Agreement for Trans-Pacific Partnership (CPTPP) (961)
Convention (952)
Council of Ministers (957)
Doctrine of sovereign immunity (966)
East African Community (EAC) (963)
Economic Community of West African States (ECOWAS) (963)
Euro (957)
European Union (EU) (956)

European Union Commission (957)
Eurozone (957)
Foreign Commerce Clause (951)
Foreign Sovereign Immunities Act (FSIA) (967)
General Assembly (953)
International Court of Justice (ICJ or World Court) (955)
International law (951)
International Monetary Fund (IMF) (954)
Mercosur (Mercosul or Southern Common Market) (962)
Multilateral treaty (952)
National courts (965)
North American Free Trade Agreement (NAFTA) (958)
Organization of the Petroleum Exporting Countries (OPEC) (962)
Qualified immunity (restricted immunity) (967)
Regional Comprehensive Economic Partnership (RCEP) (960)
Regional trade agreement (955)
Secretariat (954)
Secretary-general (954)
Security Council (953)
Treaty (952)
Treaty Clause (952)
United Nations (UN) (953)
United Nations Children's Fund (UNICEF) (954)
United States–Mexico–Canada Agreement (USMCA) (958)
Veto power (953)
World Bank (954)
World Trade Organization (WTO) (964)
WTO appellate body (964)
WTO dispute settlement body (964)
WTO panel (964)

Critical Legal Thinking Cases

54.1 Foreign Sovereign Immunity To stabilize its currency, Argentina and its central bank, Banco Central (collectively, Argentina), issued bonds called Bonods. The bonds, which were sold to investors worldwide, provided for repayment in U.S. dollars through transfers on the London, Frankfurt, Zurich, and New York markets at the bondholder's election. Argentina lacked sufficient foreign exchange to pay the bonds when they matured, so it unilaterally extended the time for payment and offered bondholders substitute instruments as a means of rescheduling the debts.

Two Panamanian corporations and a Swiss bank refused the rescheduling and insisted that full payment be made in New York. When Argentina did not pay, the Panamanian corporations brought a breach of contract action against Argentina in U.S. district court in New York. Argentina moved to dismiss, alleging that it was not subject to suit in U.S. courts, under the federal Foreign Sovereign Immunities Act (FSIA). The plaintiffs asserted that the commercial activity exception to the FSIA applied, which subjected Argentina to lawsuit in U.S. court. Is Argentina subject to the lawsuit in the United States? *Republic of Argentina v. Weltover, Inc.*, 504 U.S. 607, 112 S.Ct. 2160, 1992 U.S. Lexis 3542 (Supreme Court of the United States, 1992)

54.2 Commercial Activity Exception OBB Personenverkehr AG (OBB), which is wholly owned by the Austrian Federal Ministry of Transport, carries more than 200 million passengers each year on railway routes within Austria and to and from points outside of Austria. OBB and other railways throughout Europe are members of the Eurail Group, which sells Eurail passes to non-Europeans for unlimited travel on the railroads for a designated period of time. Eurail passes may be purchased directly from the Eurail Group or indirectly through a worldwide network of travel agents not owned by the Eurail Group. Carol Sachs, a resident of Berkeley, California, purchased a Eurail pass over the internet from The Rail Pass Experts, a Massachusetts-based travel agent. Sachs arrived at the Innsbruck, Austria, train station planning to use her Eurail pass to ride an OBB train to Prague, Czech Republic. As she attempted to board the train, Sachs fell from the platform onto the tracks. OBB's moving train crushed her legs, both of which had to be amputated above the knee.

Sachs sued OBB in the U.S. district court in California, asserting claims of negligence and strict liability for the design of the train and platform. OBB claimed sovereign immunity and moved to dismiss the suit for lack of subject matter jurisdiction. Sachs argued that her lawsuit fell under the commercial activity exception to sovereign immunity and that she should be permitted to pursue her lawsuit in federal court. Does the commercial activity exception to sovereign immunity apply to the facts of the case? *OBB Personenverkehr AG v. Sachs*, 136 S.Ct. 390, 2015 U.S. Lexis 7670 (Supreme Court of the United States, 2015)

54.3 Act of State Doctrine Banco Nacional de Costa Rica is a bank wholly owned by the government of Costa Rica. It is subject to the rules and regulations adopted by the minister of finance and the central bank of Costa Rica. The bank borrowed $40 million from a consortium of private banks located in the United Kingdom and the United States. The bank signed promissory notes, agreeing to repay the principal plus interest on the loan in four equal installments, due on July 30, August 30, September 30, and October 30 of the following year. The money was to be used to provide export financing of sugar and sugar products from Costa Rica. The loan agreements and promissory notes were signed in New York City, and the loan proceeds were tendered to the bank there.

The bank paid the first installment on the loan. The bank did not, however, make the other three installment payments and defaulted on the loan. The lending banks sued the bank in U.S. district court in New York to recover the unpaid principal and interest. The bank alleged in defense that the minister of finance and the central bank of Costa Rica had issued a decree forbidding the repayment of loans by the bank to private lenders, including the lending banks in this case. The action was taken because Costa Rica was having trouble servicing debts to foreign creditors. The bank alleged that the act of state doctrine prevented the plaintiffs from recovering on their loans to the bank. Who wins? *Libra Bank Limited v. Banco Nacional de Costa Rica*, 570 F.Supp. 870, 1983 U.S. Dist. Lexis 14677 (United States District Court for the Southern District of New York, 1983)

54.4 Forum-Selection Clause Zapata Off-Shore Company (Zapata) was a Houston, Texas–based U.S. corporation that engaged in drilling oil wells throughout the world. Unterweser Reederei, GMBH (Unterweser), was a German corporation that provided ocean shipping and towing services. Zapata requested bids from companies to tow its self-elevating drilling rig *Chaparral* from Louisiana to a point off Ravenna, Italy, in the Adriatic Sea, where Zapata had agreed to drill certain wells. Unterweser submitted the lowest bid and was requested to submit a proposed contract to Zapata, which it did. The contract submitted by Unterweser contained the following provision: "Any dispute arising must be treated before the London Court of Justice." Zapata executed the contract without deleting or modifying this provision.

Unterweser's deep sea tug *Bremen* departed Venice, Louisiana, with the *Chaparral* in tow, bound for Italy. While the flotilla was in international waters in the middle of the Gulf of Mexico, a severe storm arose. The sharp roll of the *Chaparral* in Gulf waters caused portions of it to break off and fall into the sea, seriously damaging the *Chaparral*. Zapata instructed the *Bremen* to tow the *Chaparral* to Tampa, Florida, the nearest port of refuge, which it did. Zapata filed suit against Unterweser and the *Bremen* in U.S. District Court in Florida, alleging negligent towing and breach of contract. The defendants asserted that suit could be brought only in the London Court of Justice. Who is correct? *M/S Bremen and Unterweser Reederei, GMBH v. Zapata Off-Shore Company*, 407 U.S. 1, 92 S.Ct. 1907, 1972 U.S. Lexis 114 (Supreme Court of the United States, 1972)

Ethics Case

54.5 Ethics Case While Nigeria, an African nation, was in the midst of a boom period due to oil exports, it entered into $1 billion of contracts with companies in various countries to purchase huge quantities of Portland cement from those companies. Nigeria was going to use the cement to build and improve the country's infrastructure. Several of the contracts were with U.S. companies, including Texas Trading & Milling Corporation (Texas Trading). Nigeria substantially overbought cement, and the country's docks and harbors became clogged with ships waiting to unload. Unable to accept delivery of the cement it had bought, Nigeria repudiated many of its contracts, including the one with Texas Trading. When Texas Trading sued Nigeria in U.S. district court to recover damages for breach of contract, Nigeria asserted in defense that the doctrine of sovereign immunity protected it from liability. Has Nigeria acted ethically in asserting that the doctrine of sovereign immunity relieves it of its contract liability? Who wins? *Texas Trading & Milling Corp. v. Federal Republic of Nigeria*, 647 F.2d 300, 1981 U.S. App. Lexis 14231 (United States Court of Appeals for the Second Circuit, 1981)

Notes

1. The Charter of the United Nations was entered October 24, 1945, and it was adopted by the United States on October 24, 1945 (59 Stat. 1031, T.S. 993, 3 Bevans 1153, 1976 Y.B.U.N. 1043).
2. 301 U.S. 324, 57 S.Ct. 758, 1937 U.S. Lexis 293 (Supreme Court of the United States).
3. 28 U.S.C. Sections 1602–1611.

APPENDIX A The Constitution of the United States of America

We the People of the United States, in Order to form a more perfect Union, establish Justice, insure domestic Tranquility, provide for the common defense, promote the general Welfare, and secure the Blessings of Liberty to ourselves and our Posterity, do ordain and establish this Constitution for the United States of America.

Article I

Section 1. All legislative Powers herein granted shall be vested in a Congress of the United States, which shall consist of a Senate and House of Representatives.

Section 2. The House of Representatives shall be composed of Members chosen every second Year by the People of the several States, and the Electors in each State shall have the Qualifications requisite for Electors of the most numerous Branch of the State Legislature.

No Person shall be a Representative who shall not have attained to the Age of twenty five Years, and been seven Years a Citizen of the United States, and who shall not, when elected, be an Inhabitant of that State in which he shall be chosen.

Representatives and direct Taxes shall be apportioned among the several States which may be included within this Union, according to their respective Numbers, which shall be determined by adding to the whole Number of free Persons, including those bound to Service for a Term of Years, and excluding Indians not taxed, three fifths of all other Persons. The actual Enumeration shall be made within three Years after the first Meeting of the Congress of the United States, and within every subsequent Term of ten Years, in such Manner as they shall by Law direct. The number of Representatives shall not exceed one for every thirty Thousand, but each State shall have at Least one Representative; and until such enumeration shall be made, the State of New Hampshire shall be entitled to chuse three, Massachusetts eight, Rhode Island and Providence Plantations one, Connecticut five, New York six, New Jersey four, Pennsylvania eight, Delaware one, Maryland six, Virginia ten, North Carolina five, South Carolina five, and Georgia three.

When vacancies happen in the Representation from any State, the Executive Authority thereof shall issue Writs of Election to fill such vacancies.

The House of Representatives shall chuse their Speaker and other Officers; and shall have the sole Power of Impeachment.

Section 3. The Senate of the United States shall be composed of two Senators from each State, chosen by the Legislature thereof, for six Years; and each Senator shall have one Vote.

Immediately after they shall be assembled in Consequence of the first Election, they shall be divided as equally as may be into three Classes. The Seats of the Senators of the first Class shall be vacated at the Expiration of the second Year, of the second Class at the Expiration of the fourth Year, and the third Class at the Expiration of the sixth Year, so that one third may be chosen every second Year; and if Vacancies happen by Resignation, or otherwise, during the Recess of the Legislature of any State, the Executive thereof may make temporary Appointments until the next meeting of the Legislature, which shall then fill such Vacancies.

No person shall be a Senator who shall not have attained to the Age of thirty Years, and been nine Years a Citizen of the United States, and who shall not, when elected, be an Inhabitant of that State for which he shall be chosen.

The Vice President of the United States shall be President of the Senate, but shall have no Vote, unless they be equally divided.

The Senate shall chuse their other Officers, and also a President pro tempore, in the Absence of the Vice President, or when he shall exercise the Office of President of the United States.

The Senate shall have the sole power to try all Impeachments. When sitting for that Purpose, they shall be an Oath or Affirmation. When the President of the United States is tried, the Chief Justice shall preside: And no Person shall be convicted without the Concurrence of two thirds of the Members present.

Judgment in Cases of Impeachment shall not extend further than to removal from Office, and disqualification to hold and enjoy any Office of honor, Trust or

Profit under the United States: but the Party convicted shall nevertheless be liable and subject to Indictment, Trial, Judgment and Punishment, according to Law.

Section 4. The Times, Places and Manner of holding Elections for Senators and Representatives, shall be prescribed in each State by the Legislature thereof: but the Congress may at any time by Law make or alter such Regulations, except as to the Places of chusing Senators.

The Congress shall assemble at least once in every Year, and such Meeting shall be on the first Monday in December, unless they shall by Law appoint a different day.

Section 5. Each House shall be the Judge of the Elections, Returns and Qualifications of its own Members, and a Majority of each shall constitute a Quorum to do Business; but a smaller Number may adjourn from day to day, and may be authorized to compel the Attendance of absent Members, in such Manner, and under such Penalties as each House may provide.

Each House may determine the Rules of its Proceedings, punish its Members for disorderly Behaviour, and, with the Concurrence of two thirds, expel a Member.

Each House shall keep a Journal of its Proceedings, and from time to time publish the same, excepting such Parts as may in their Judgment require Secrecy; and the Yeas and Nays of the Members of either House on any question shall, at the Desire of one fifth of those Present, be entered on the Journal.

Neither House, during the Session of Congress, shall, without the Consent of the other, adjourn for more than three days, nor to any other Place than that in which the two Houses shall be sitting.

Section 6. The Senators and Representatives shall receive a Compensation for their Services, to be ascertained by Law, and paid out of the Treasury of the United States. They shall in all Cases, except Treason, Felony and Breach of the Peace, be privileged from Arrest during their Attendance at the Session of their respective Houses, and in going to and returning from the same; and for any Speech or Debate in either House, they shall not be questioned in any other Place.

No Senator or Representative shall, during the Time for which he was elected, be appointed to any civil Office under the Authority of the United States, which shall have been created, or the Emoluments whereof shall have been increased during such time; and no Person holding any Office under the United States, shall be a Member of either House during his Continuance in Office.

Section 7. All Bills for raising Revenue shall originate in the House of Representatives; but the Senate may propose or concur with Amendments as on other Bills.

Every Bill which shall have passed the House of Representatives and the Senate, shall, before it become a Law, be presented to the President of the United States; If he approve he shall sign it, but if not he shall return it, with his Objections to that House in which it shall have originated, who shall enter the Objections at large on their Journal, and proceed to reconsider it. If after such Reconsideration two thirds of that House shall agree to pass the Bill, it shall be sent, together with the Objections, to the other House, by which it shall likewise be reconsidered, and if approved by two thirds of that House, it shall become a Law. But in all such Cases the Votes of both Houses shall be determined by Yeas and Nays, and the Names of the Persons voting for and against the Bill shall be entered on the Journal of each House respectively. If any Bill shall not be returned by the President within ten Days (Sundays excepted) after it shall have been presented to him, the Same shall be a Law, in like Manner as if he had signed it, unless the Congress by their Adjournment prevent its Return, in which Case it shall not be a Law.

Every Order, Resolution, or Vote to which the Concurrence of the Senate and House of Representatives may be necessary (except on a question of Adjournment) shall be presented to the President of the United States; and before the Same shall take Effect, shall be approved by him, or being disapproved by him, shall be repassed by two thirds of the Senate and House of Representatives, according to the Rules and Limitations prescribed in the Case of a Bill.

Section 8. The Congress shall have Power to lay and collect Taxes, Duties, Imposts and Excises, to pay the Debts and provide for the common Defence and general Welfare of the United States; but all Duties, Imposts and Excises shall be uniform throughout the United States;

To borrow Money on the credit of the United States;

To regulate Commerce with foreign Nations, and among the several States, and with the Indian Tribes;

To establish an uniform Rule of Naturalization, and uniform Laws on the subject of Bankruptcies throughout the United States;

To coin Money, regulate the Value thereof, and of foreign Coin, and fix the Standard of Weights and Measures;

To provide for the Punishment of counterfeiting the Securities and current Coin of the United States;

To establish Post Offices and post Roads;

To promote the Progress of Science and useful Arts, by securing for limited Times to Authors and Inventors the exclusive Right to their respective Writings and Discoveries;

To constitute Tribunals inferior to the supreme Court;

To define and punish Piracies and Felonies committed on the high Seas, and Offenses against the Law of Nations;

To declare War, grant Letters of Marque and Reprisal, and make Rules concerning Captures on Land and Water;

To raise and support Armies, but no Appropriation of Money to that Use shall be for a longer Term than two Years;

To provide and maintain a Navy;

To make Rules for the Government and Regulation of the land and naval Forces;

To provide for calling forth the Militia to execute the Laws of the Union, suppress Insurrections and repel Invasions;

To provide for organizing, arming, and disciplining, the Militia, and for governing such Part of them as may be employed in the Service of the United States, reserving to the States respectively, the Appointment of the Officers, and the Authority of training the Militia according to the discipline prescribed by Congress;

To exercise exclusive Legislation in all Cases whatsoever, over such District (not exceeding ten Miles square) as may, by Cession of particular States, and the Acceptance of Congress, become the Seat of the Government of the United States, and to exercise like Authority over all Places purchased by the Consent of the Legislature of the State in which the Same shall be, for the Erection of Forts, Magazines, Arsenals, dock-Yards, and other needful Buildings;—And

To make all Laws which shall be necessary and proper for carrying into Execution the foregoing Powers, and all other Powers vested by this Constitution in the Government of the United States, or in any Department or Officer thereof.

Section 9. The Migration or Importation of such Persons as any of the States now existing shall think proper to admit, shall not be prohibited by the Congress prior to the Year one thousand eight hundred and eight, but a Tax or Duty may be imposed on such Importation, not exceeding ten dollars for each Person.

The Privilege of the Writ of Habeas Corpus shall not be suspended, unless when in Cases of Rebellion or Invasion the public Safety may require it.

No Bill of Attainder or ex post facto Law shall be passed.

No Capitation, or other direct, Tax shall be laid, unless in Proportion to the Census or Enumeration herein before directed to be taken.

No Tax or Duty shall be laid on Articles exported from any State.

No Preference shall be given by any Regulation of Commerce or Revenue to the Ports of one State over those of another; nor shall Vessels bound to, or from, one State, be obliged to enter, clear, or pay Duties in another.

No Money shall be drawn from the Treasury, but in Consequence of Appropriations made by Laws; and a regular Statement and Account of the Receipts and Expenditures of all public Money shall be published from time to time.

No Title of Nobility shall be granted by the United States: And no Person holding any Office of Profit or Trust under them, shall, without the Consent of the Congress, accept of any present, Emolument, Office, or Title, of any kind whatever, from any King, Prince, or foreign State.

Section 10. No State shall enter into any Treaty, Alliance, or Confederation; grant Letters of Marque and Reprisal; coin Money; emit Bills of Credit; make any Thing but gold and silver Coin a Tender in Payment of Debts; pass any Bill of Attainder, ex post facto Law, or Law impairing the Obligation of Contracts, or grant any Title of Nobility.

No State shall, without the Consent of the Congress, lay any Imposts or Duties on Imports or Exports, except what may be absolutely necessary for executing its inspection Laws: and the net Produce of all Duties and Imposts, laid by any State on Imports or Exports, shall be for the Use of the Treasury of the United States; and all such Laws shall be subject to the Revision and Control of the Congress.

No State shall, without the Consent of Congress, lay any Duty of Tonnage, keep Troops, or Ships of War in time of Peace, enter into any Agreement or Compact with another State, or with a foreign Power, or engage in War, unless actually invaded, or in such imminent Danger as will not admit of delay.

Article II

Section 1. The executive Power shall be vested in a President of the United States of America. He shall hold his Office during the Term of four Years, and, together with the Vice President, chosen for the same Term, be elected, as follows:

Each State shall appoint, in such Manner as the Legislature thereof may direct, a Number of Electors, equal to the whole Number of Senators and Representatives to which the State may be entitled in the Congress: but no Senator or Representative, or Person holding an Office of Trust or Profit under the United States, shall be appointed an Elector.

The Electors shall meet in their respective States, and vote by Ballot for two Persons, of whom one at least shall not be an Inhabitant of the same State with themselves. And they shall make a list of all the Persons voted for, and of the Number of Votes for each; which List they shall sign and certify, and transmit sealed to the Seat of the Government of the United States, directed to the President of the Senate. The President of the Senate shall, in the presence of the

Senate and House of Representatives, open all the Certificates, and the Votes shall be counted. The Person having the greatest Number of Votes shall be the President, if such Number be a Majority of the whole Number of Electors appointed; and if there be more than one who have such Majority, and have an equal Number of Votes, then the House of Representatives shall immediately chuse by Ballot one of them for President; and if no Person have a Majority, then from the five highest on the List the said House shall in like Manner chuse the President. But in chusing the President, the Votes shall be taken by States, the Representation from each State having one Vote; A quorum for this Purpose shall consist of a Member or Members from two thirds of the States, and a Majority of all the States shall be necessary to a Choice. In every Case, after the Choice of the President, the Person having the greatest Number of Votes of the Electors shall be the Vice President. But if there should remain two or more who have equal Votes, the Senate shall chuse from them by Ballot the Vice President.

The Congress may determine the Time of Chusing the Electors, and the Day on which they shall give their Votes; which Day shall be the same throughout the United States.

No Person except a natural born Citizen, or a Citizen of the United States, at the time of the Adoption of this Constitution, shall be eligible to the Office of President; neither shall any Person be eligible to that Office who shall not have attained to the Age of thirty five Years, and been fourteen Years a Resident within the United States.

In Case of the Removal of the President from Office, or of his Death, Resignation, or Inability to discharge the Powers and Duties of the said Office, the Same shall devolve on the Vice President, and the Congress may by Law provide for the Case of Removal, Death, Resignation or Inability, both of the President and Vice President, declaring what Officer shall then act as President, and such Officer shall act accordingly, until the Disability be removed, or a President shall be elected.

The President shall, at stated Times, receive for his Services, a Compensation, which shall neither be increased nor diminished during the Period for which he shall have been elected, and he shall not receive within that Period any other Emolument from the United States, or any of them.

Before he enter on the Execution of his Office, he shall take the following Oath or Affirmation:—"I do solemnly swear (or affirm) that I will faithfully execute the Office of President of the United States, and will to the best of my Ability, preserve, protect and defend the Constitution of the United States."

Section 2. The President shall be Commander in Chief of the Army and Navy of the United States, and of the Militia of the several States, when called into the actual Service of the United States; he may require the Opinion, in writing, of the principal Officer in each of the executive Departments, upon any Subject relating to the Duties of their respective Offices, and he shall have Power to grant Reprieves and Pardons for Offences against the United States, except in Cases of Impeachment.

He shall have Power, by and with the Advice and Consent of the Senate, to make Treaties, provided two thirds of the Senators present concur; and he shall nominate, and by and with the Advice and Consent of the Senate, shall appoint Ambassadors, other public Ministers and Consuls, Judges of the supreme Court, and all other Officers of the United States, whose Appointments are not herein otherwise provided for, and which shall be established by Law: but the Congress may by Law vest the Appointment of such inferior Officers, as they think proper, in the President alone, in the Courts of Law, or in the Heads of Departments.

The President shall have Power to fill up all Vacancies that may happen during the Recess of the Senate, by granting Commissions which shall expire at the End of their next Session.

Section 3. He shall from time to time give to the Congress Information of the State of the Union, and recommend to their Consideration such Measures as he shall judge necessary and expedient; he may, on extraordinary Occasions, convene both Houses, or either of them, and in Case of Disagreement between them, with Respect to the Time of Adjournment, he may adjourn them to such Time as he shall think proper; he shall receive Ambassadors and other public Ministers; he shall take Care that the Laws be faithfully executed, and shall Commission all the Officers of the United States.

Section 4. The President, Vice President and all civil Officers of the United States, shall be removed from Office on Impeachment for, and Conviction of, Treason, Bribery, or other high Crimes and Misdemeanors.

Article III

Section 1. The judicial Power of the United States, shall be vested in one supreme Court, and in such inferior Courts as the Congress may from time to time ordain and establish. The Judges, both of the supreme and inferior Courts, shall hold their Offices during good Behaviour, and shall, at Times, receive for their Services, a Compensation, which shall not be diminished during their Continuance in Office.

Section 2. The judicial Power shall extend to all Cases, in Law and Equity, arising under this Constitution, the Laws of the United States, and Treaties made, or which shall be made, under their Authority;—to all Cases affecting Ambassadors, other public Ministers and Consuls;—to all Cases of admiralty and maritime Jurisdiction;—to Controversies to which the United States shall be a Party;—to Controversies between two or more States;—between a State and Citizens of another State;—between Citizens of different States;—between Citizens of the same State claiming Lands under Grants of different States, and between a State, or the Citizens thereof, and foreign States, Citizens or Subjects.

In all Cases affecting Ambassadors, other public Ministers and Consuls, and those in which a State shall be Party, the supreme Court shall have original Jurisdiction. In all the other Cases before mentioned, the supreme Court shall have appellate Jurisdiction, both as to Law and Fact, with such Exceptions, and under such Regulations as the Congress shall make.

The Trial of all Crimes, except in Cases of Impeachment, shall be by Jury; and such Trial shall be held in the State where the said Crimes shall have been committed; but when not committed within any State, the Trial shall be at such Place or Places as the Congress may by Law have directed.

Section 3. Treason against the United States, shall consist only in levying War against them, or in adhering to their Enemies, giving them Aid and Comfort. No Person shall be convicted of Treason unless on the Testimony of two Witnesses to the same overt Act, or on Confession in open Court.

The Congress shall have Power to declare the Punishment of Treason, but no Attainder of Treason shall work Corruption of Blood, or Forfeiture except during the Life of the Person attainted.

Article IV

Section 1. Full Faith and Credit shall be given in each State to the public Acts, Records, and judicial Proceedings of every other State. And the Congress may by general Laws prescribe the Manner in which such Arts, Records, and Proceedings shall be proved, and the Effect thereof.

Section 2. The Citizens of each State shall be entitled to all Privileges and Immunities of Citizens in the several States.

A person charged in any State with Treason, Felony, or other Crime, who shall flee from Justice, and be found in another State, shall on Demand of the executive Authority of the State from which he fled, be delivered up, to be removed to the State having Jurisdiction of the Crime.

No Person held to Service or Labour in one State, under the Laws thereof, escaping into another, shall, in Consequence of any Law or Regulation therein, be discharged from such Service or Labour, but shall be delivered up on Claim of the Party to whom such Service or Labour may be due.

Section 3. New States may be admitted by the Congress into this Union; but no new State shall be formed or erected within the Jurisdiction of any other State; nor any State be formed by the Junction of two or more States, or Parts of States, without the Consent of the Legislatures of the States concerned as well as of the Congress.

The Congress shall have Power to dispose of and make all needful Rules and Regulations respecting the Territory or other Property belonging to the United States; and nothing in this Constitution shall be so construed as to Prejudice any Claims of the United States, or of any particular State.

Section 4. The United States shall guarantee to every State in this Union a Republican Form of Government, and shall protect each of them against Invasion; and on Application of the Legislature, or of the Executive (when the Legislature cannot be convened) against domestic Violence.

Article V

The Congress, whenever two thirds of both Houses shall deem it necessary, shall propose Amendments to this Constitution, or, on the Application of the Legislatures of two thirds of the several States, shall call a Convention for proposing Amendments, which, in either Case, shall be valid to all Intents and Purposes, as Part of this Constitution, when ratified by the Legislatures of three fourths of the several States, or by Conventions in three fourths thereof, as the one or the other Mode of Ratification may be proposed by the Congress; Provided that no Amendment which may be made prior to the Year One thousand eight hundred and eight shall in any Manner affect the first and fourth Clauses in the Ninth Section of the first Article; and that no State, without its Consent, shall be deprived of its equal Suffrage in the Senate.

Article VI

All Debts contracted and Engagements entered into, before the Adoption of this Constitution, shall be as valid against the United States under this Constitution, as under the Confederation.

This Constitution, and the Laws of the United States which shall be made in Pursuance thereof; and all Treaties made, or which shall be made, under the Authority of the United States, shall be the supreme Law of the Land; and the Judges in every State shall be bound thereby, any Thing in the Constitution or Laws of any State to the Contrary notwithstanding.

The Senators and Representatives before mentioned, and the Members of the several State Legislatures, and all executive and judicial Officers, both of the United States and of the Several States, shall be bound by Oath or Affirmation, to support this Constitution; but no religious Test shall ever be required as a Qualification to any Office or public Trust under the United States.

Article VII

The Ratification of the Conventions of nine States, shall be sufficient for the Establishment of this Constitution between the States so ratifying the Same.

Amendment I [1791]

Congress shall make no law respecting an establishment of religion, or prohibiting the free exercise thereof; or abridging the freedom of speech, or the press; or the right of the people peaceably to assemble, and to petition the Government for a redress of grievances.

Amendment II [1791]

A well regulated Militia, being necessary to the security for a free State, the right of the people to keep and bear Arms, shall not be infringed.

Amendment III [1791]

No Soldier shall, in time of peace be quartered in any house, without the consent of the Owner, nor in time of war, but in a manner to be prescribed by law.

Amendment IV [1791]

The right of the people to be secure in their persons, houses, papers, and effects, against unreasonable searches and seizures, shall not be violated, and no Warrants shall issue, but upon probable cause, supported by Oath or Affirmation, and particularly describing the place to be searched, and the persons or things to be seized.

Amendment V [1791]

No person shall be held to answer for a capital, or otherwise infamous crime, unless on a presentment or indictment of a Grand Jury, except in cases arising in the land or naval forces, or in the Militia, when in actual service in time of War or public danger; nor shall any person be subject for the same offense to be twice put in jeopardy of life or limb; nor shall be compelled in any criminal case to be a witness against himself, nor be deprived of life, liberty, or property, without due process of law; nor shall private property be taken for public use, without just compensation.

Amendment VI [1791]

In all criminal prosecutions, the accused shall enjoy the right to a speedy and public trial, by an impartial jury of the State and district wherein the crime shall have been committed, which district shall have been previously ascertained by law, and to be informed of the nature and cause of the accusation; to be confronted with the Witnesses against him; to have compulsory process for obtaining witnesses in his favor, and to have the Assistance of counsel for his defence.

Amendment VII [1791]

In suits at common law, where the value in controversy shall exceed twenty dollars, the right of trial by jury shall be preserved, and no fact tried by a jury, shall be otherwise reexamined in any Court of the United States, than according to the rules of the common law.

Amendment VIII [1791]

Excessive bail shall not be required, nor excessive fines imposed, nor cruel and unusual punishments inflicted.

Amendment IX [1791]

The enumeration in the Constitution, of certain rights, shall not be construed to deny or disparage others retained by the people.

Amendment X [1791]

The powers not delegated to the United States by the Constitution, nor prohibited by it to the States, are reserved to the States respectively, or to the people.

Amendment XI [1795]

The judicial power of the United States shall not be construed to extend to any suit in law or equity, commenced or prosecuted against one of the United States by Citizens of another State, or by Citizens or Subjects of any Foreign State.

Amendment XII [1804]

The Electors shall meet in their respective States and vote by ballot for President and Vice President, one of whom, at least, shall not be an inhabitant of the same State with themselves; they shall name in their ballots the person voted for as President, and in distinct ballots the person voted for as Vice President, and they shall make distinct lists of all persons voted for as President, and of all persons voted for as Vice President, and of the number of votes for each, which lists they shall sign and certify, and transmit sealed to the seat of the government of the United States, directed to the President of the Senate;—The President of the Senate shall, in the presence of the Senate and House of Representatives, open all the certificates and the votes shall then be counted;—The person having the greatest number of votes for President, shall be the President, if such number be a majority of the whole number of Electors appointed; and if no person have such majority, then from the persons having the highest numbers not exceeding three on the list of those voted for as President, the House of Representatives shall choose immediately, by ballot, the President. But in choosing the President, the votes shall be taken by States, the representation from each State having one vote; a quorum for this purpose shall consist of a member or members from two-thirds of the States, and a majority of all the States shall be necessary to a choice. And if the House of Representatives shall not choose a President whenever the right of choice shall devolve upon them, before the fourth day of March next following, then the Vice President shall act as President, as in the case of the death or other constitutional disability of the President. The person having the greatest number of votes as Vice President, shall be the Vice President, if such number be a majority of the whole number of Electors appointed, and if no person have a majority, then from the two highest numbers on the list, the Senate shall choose the Vice President; a quorum for the purpose shall consist of two-thirds of the whole number of Senators, and a majority of the whole number shall be necessary to a choice. But no person constitutionally ineligible to the office of President shall be eligible to that of the Vice President of the United States.

Amendment XIII [1865]

Section 1. Neither slavery nor involuntary servitude, except as a punishment for crime whereof the party shall have been duly convicted, shall exist within the United States, or any place subject to their jurisdiction.

Section 2. Congress shall have power to enforce this article by appropriate legislation.

Amendment XIV [1868]

Section 1. All persons born or naturalized in the United States, and subject to the jurisdiction thereof, are citizens of the United States and of the State wherein they reside. No State shall make or enforce any law which shall abridge the privileges or immunities of citizens of the United States; nor shall any State deprive any person of life, liberty, or property, without due process of law; nor deny to any person within its jurisdiction the equal protection of the laws.

Section 2. Representatives shall be appointed among the several States according to their respective numbers, counting the whole number of persons in each State, excluding Indians not taxed. But when the right to vote at any election for the choice of electors for President and Vice President of the United States, Representatives in Congress, the Executive and Judicial officers of a State, or the members of the Legislature thereof, is denied to any of the male inhabitants of such State, being twenty-one years of age, and citizens of the United States, or in any way abridged, except for participation in rebellion, or other crime, the basis of representation therein shall be reduced in the proportion which the number of such male citizens shall bear to the whole number of male citizens twenty-one years of age in such State.

Section 3. No person shall be a Senator or Representative in Congress, or elector of President and Vice President, or hold any office, civil or military, under the United States, or under any State, who, having previously taken an oath, as a member of Congress, or as an officer of the United States, or as a member of any State legislature, or as an executive or judicial officer of any State, to support the Constitution of the United States, shall have engaged in insurrection or rebellion against the same, or given aid or comfort to the enemies thereof. But Congress may by a vote of two-thirds of each House, remove such disability.

Section 4. The validity of the public debt of the United States, authorized by law, including debts incurred for payment of pensions and bounties for services in suppressing insurrection or rebellion, shall not be questioned. But neither the United States nor any State shall assume or pay any debt or obligation incurred in aid of insurrection or rebellion against the United States, or any claim for the loss or emancipation of any slave; but all such debts, obligations and claims shall be held illegal and void.

Section 5. The Congress shall have power to enforce, by appropriate legislation, the provisions of this article.

Amendment XV [1870]

Section 1. The right of citizens of the United States to vote shall not be denied or abridged by the United

States or by any State on account of race, color, or previous condition of servitude.

Section 2. The Congress shall have power to enforce this article by appropriate legislation.

Amendment XVI [1913]

The Congress shall have power to lay and collect taxes on incomes, from whatever source derived, without apportionment among the several States, and without regard to any census or enumeration.

Amendment XVII [1913]

The Senate of the United States shall be composed of two Senators from each State, elected by the people thereof, for six years; and each Senator shall have one vote. The electors in each State shall have the qualifications requisite for electors of the most numerous branch of the State legislatures.

When vacancies happen in the representation of any State in the Senate, the executive authority of such State shall issue writs of election to fill such vacancies: *Provided,* That the legislature of any State may empower the executive thereof to make temporary appointments until the people fill the vacancies by election as the legislature may direct. This amendment shall not be so construed as to affect the election or term of any Senator chosen before it becomes valid as part of the Constitution.

Amendment XVIII [1919]

Section 1. After one year from the ratification of this article the manufacture, sale, or transportation of intoxicating liquors within, the importation thereof into, or the exportation thereof from the United States and all territory subject to the jurisdiction thereof for beverage purposes is hereby prohibited.

Section 2. The Congress and the several States shall have concurrent power to enforce this article by appropriate legislation.

Section 3. This article shall be inoperative unless it shall have been ratified as an amendment to the Constitution by the legislatures of the several States, as provided in the Constitution, within seven years from the date of the submission hereof to the States by the Congress.

Amendment XIX [1920]

The right of citizens of the United States to vote shall not be denied or abridged by the United States or by any State on account of sex.

Congress shall have power to enforce this article by appropriate legislation.

Amendment XX [1933]

Section 1. The terms of the President and Vice President shall end at noon on the 20th day of January, and the terms of Senators and Representatives at noon on the 3rd day of January, of the years in which such terms would have ended if this article had not been ratified; and the terms of their successors shall then begin.

Section 2. The Congress shall assemble at least once in every year, and such meeting shall begin at noon on the 3rd day of January, unless they shall by law appoint a different day.

Section 3. If, at the time fixed for the beginning of the term of the President, the President elect shall have died, the Vice President elect shall become President. If a President shall not have been chosen before the time fixed for the beginning of his term, or if the President elect shall have failed to qualify, then the Vice President elect shall act as President until a President shall have qualified; and the Congress may by law provide for the case wherein neither a President elect nor a Vice President elect shall have qualified, declaring who shall then act as President, or the manner in which one who is to act shall be selected, and such person shall act accordingly until a President or Vice President shall have qualified.

Section 4. The Congress may by law provide for the case of the death of any of the persons from whom the House of Representatives may choose a President whenever the right of choice shall have devolved upon them, and for the case of the death of any of the persons from whom the Senate may choose a Vice President whenever the right of choice shall have devolved upon them.

Section 5. Sections 1 and 2 shall take effect on the 15th day of October following the ratification of this article.

Section 6. This article shall be inoperative unless it shall have been ratified as an amendment to the Constitution by the legislatures of three-fourths of the several States within seven years from the date of its submission.

Amendment XXI [1933]

Section 1. The eighteenth article of amendment to the Constitution of the United States is hereby repealed.

Section 2. The transportation or importation into any State, Territory, or possession of the United States for delivery or use therein of intoxicating liquors, in violation of the laws thereof, is hereby prohibited.

Section 3. This article shall be inoperative unless it shall have been ratified as an amendment to the Constitution by conventions in the several States, as provided in the Constitution, within seven years from the date of the submission hereof to the States by the Congress.

Amendment XXII [1951]

Section 1. No person shall be elected to the office of the President more than twice, and no person who has held the office of President, or acted as President, for more than two years of a term to which some other person was elected President shall be elected to the office of the President more than once. But this Article shall not apply to any person holding the office of President when this article was proposed by the Congress, and shall not prevent any person who may be holding the office of President, or acting as President, during the term within which this Article becomes operative from holding the office of President, or acting as President during the remainder of such term.

Section 2. This article shall be inoperative unless it shall have been ratified as an amendment to the Constitution by the legislatures of three-fourths of the several States within seven years from the date of its submission to the States by the Congress.

Amendment XXIII [1961]

Section 1. The District constituting the seat of Government of the United States shall appoint in such manner as the Congress may direct:

A number of electors of President and Vice President equal to the whole number of Senators and Representatives in Congress to which the District would be entitled if it were a State, but in no event more than the least populous State; they shall be in addition to those appointed by the States, but they shall be considered, for the purposes of the election of President and Vice President, to be electors appointed by a State; and they shall meet in the District and perform such duties as provided by the twelfth article of amendment.

Section 2. The Congress shall have power to enforce this article by appropriate legislation.

Amendment XXIV [1964]

Section 1. The right of citizens of the United States to vote in any primary or other election for President or Vice President, for electors for President or Vice President, or for Senator or Representative in Congress, shall not be denied or abridged by the United States or any State by reason of failure to pay any poll tax or other tax.

Section 2. The Congress shall have power to enforce this article by appropriate legislation.

Amendment XXV [1967]

Section 1. In case of the removal of the President from office or of his death or resignation, the Vice President shall become President.

Section 2. Whenever there is a vacancy in the office of the Vice President, the President shall nominate a Vice President who shall take office upon confirmation by a majority vote of both Houses of Congress.

Section 3. Whenever the President transmits to the President pro tempore of the Senate and the Speaker of the House of Representatives his written declaration that he is unable to discharge the powers and duties of his office, and until he transmits to them a written declaration to the contrary, such powers and duties shall be discharged by the Vice President as Acting President.

Section 4. Whenever the Vice President and a majority of either the principal officers of the executive departments or of such other body as Congress may by law provide, transmit to the President pro tempore of the Senate and the Speaker of the House of Representatives their written declaration that the President is unable to discharge the powers and duties of his office, the Vice President shall immediately assume the powers and duties of the office as Acting President.

Thereafter, when the President transmits to the President pro tempore of the Senate and the Speaker of the House of Representatives his written declaration that no inability exists, he shall resume the powers and duties of his office unless the Vice President and a majority of either the principal officers of the executive department or of such other body as Congress may by law provide, transmit within four days to the President pro tempore of the Senate and the Speaker of the House of Representatives their written declaration that the President is unable to discharge the powers and duties of his office. Thereupon Congress shall decide the issue, assembling within forty-eight hours for that purpose if not in session. If the Congress, within twenty-one days after receipt of the latter written declaration, or, if Congress is not in session, within twenty-one days after Congress is required to assemble, determines by two-thirds vote of both Houses that the President is unable to discharge the powers and duties of his office, the Vice President shall continue to discharge the same as Acting President; otherwise, the President shall resume the powers and duties of his office.

Amendment XXVI [1971]

Section 1. The right of citizens of the United States, who are 18 years of age or older, to vote, shall not be denied or abridged by the United States or any State on account of age.

Section 2. The Congress shall have the power to enforce this article by appropriate legislation.

Amendment XXVII [1992]

No law, varying the compensation for the services of the Senators and Representatives, shall take effect, until an election of Representatives shall have intervened.

GLOSSARY

2010 Amendments to Revised Article 9 Amendments to Revised Article 9 that address modern commercial issues and expand the use of electronic methods in secured transactions.
.biz A top-level domain that represents the word *business* and is a used by businesses.
.club A top-level domain that is a generic term used by people and organizations, such as tennis clubs, chess clubs, fan clubs, prominent individuals, and others.
.com A top-level domain that represents the word *commercial* and is mainly used by businesses.
.coop A top-level domain that is used by cooperatives.
.edu A top-level domain that is used by educational institutions.
.info A top-level domain that represents the word *information* but does not prescribe any particular theme.
.int A top-level domain reserved for international treaty-based organizations and United Nations agencies and organizations.
.mil A top-level domain used by the U.S. Department of Defense and its subsidiary and affiliated organizations.
.mobi A top-level domain that is reserved for websites that are viewable on mobile devices.
.museum A top-level domain that is used by museums.
.name A top-level domain for individuals.
.net A top-level domain that represents the word *network* and is highly used by businesses involved in the infrastructure of the internet.
.org A top-level domain that represents the word *organization* and is primarily used by nonprofit and trade organizations.
.pro A top-level domain that represents the word *professional* and is used by certified professionals.
.us A country code top-level domain (ccTLD) for the country of the United States of America. It is open to registrations by citizens, residents, and businesses with a presence in the United States.
.xyz A top-level domain that is a generic term that can be used for any general purpose.
© A symbol that provides notification that the work to which it is attached is copyrighted. The symbol should be accompanied by the author's name and the year of publication.
® A symbol that designates marks that have been registered with the U.S. Patent and Trademark Office.
abandoned property Personal property that an owner has discarded with the intent to relinquish rights in it, or mislaid or lost property that an owner has given up any further attempts to locate.
abandonment of a mark The nonuse of a trademark, service mark, or other mark in commerce for three consecutive years.
abatement A rule that says if the property a testator leaves is not sufficient to satisfy all the beneficiaries named in a will and there are both general and residuary bequests, the residuary bequest is abated first (i.e., paid last).
abnormal misuse A defense that relieves a seller of product liability if the user *abnormally* misused the product.
abnormally dangerous activities Dangerous activities for which strict liability is imposed.
abstract of title (attorney's opinion) A chronological history of the chain of title and encumbrances affecting real property that an attorney examines in order to render an *opinion* concerning the status of the title.
abusive homestead exemption A bankruptcy rule that stipulates that a debtor may not exempt more than a specified dollar amount as a homestead exemption.
acceleration clause A clause in an instrument that allows the payee or holder to accelerate the payment of the principal amount of an instrument, plus accrued interest, upon the occurrence of an event (e.g., default).
acceptance A manifestation of assent by the offeree to the terms of the offer in a manner invited or required by the offer as measured by the objective theory of contracts; A manifestation of assent required for a gift to be effective.
acceptance method A method whereby the court confirms a plan of reorganization if the creditors accept the plan and if other requirements are met.
acceptance-upon-dispatch rule (mailbox rule or posting rule) A rule that states that an acceptance is effective when it is dispatched, even if it is lost in transmission; also known as the *mailbox rule*.
accession An increase in the value of personal property because it is added to or improved by natural or manufactured means.
accessions Goods that are physically united with other goods in such a manner that the identity of the original goods is not lost.
accommodation A shipment of goods that is offered to a buyer as a replacement for the original shipment when the original shipment cannot be filled.
accommodation indorser An accommodation party who signs an instrument guaranteeing collection of the instrument.
accommodation maker An accommodation party who signs an instrument guaranteeing payment of the instrument and who is primarily liable on the instrument.
accommodation party A party who signs an instrument and lends his or her name (and credit) to another party to the instrument.
accord An agreement whereby the parties agree to accept something different in satisfaction of the original contract.
accord and satisfaction (compromise) The settlement of a contract dispute.
accountant A term that denotes persons who perform a variety of services, including bookkeepers, tax preparers, and so on.
accountant–client privilege A state law that provides that an accountant cannot be called as a witness against a client in a court action. Federal courts do not recognize this privilege.
accountant's work papers Internal work papers generated by accountants while performing services for their clients. These papers often include notes regarding the collection of data, evidence about the testing of accounts, memorandums, opinions, information regarding the affairs of the client, and so on.
accounting malpractice (negligence) Negligence in which the accountant breaches the duty of reasonable care, knowledge, skill, and judgment that he or she owes to a client when providing auditing and other accounting services to the client.
accounts Intangible personal property that includes the right to payment of monetary obligations for personal or real property sold or leased, services rendered, and policies of insurance.
accredited investor A person, a corporation, a company, an institution, or an organization that meets the net worth, income, asset, position, and other requirements established by the Securities and Exchange Commission (SEC) to qualify as an *accredited investor*.
act of state doctrine A doctrine that states that judges of one country cannot question the validity of an act committed by another country within that other country's borders. It is based on the principle that a country has absolute authority over what transpires within its own territory.
action for an accounting A formal judicial proceeding in which the court is authorized to review the partnership and the partners' transactions and award each partner his or her share of the partnership assets.
actual and exclusive A requirement that must be proven by a person to obtain real property by adverse possession. It requires that the adverse possessor has physically occupied the premises.
actual authority Authority that a general partner has to enter into contracts and obligations on behalf of a general partnership.
actual cause The actual cause of negligence. A person who commits a negligent act is not liable unless actual cause can be proven; also called *causation in fact*.
actual contract A contract that is either *express* or *implied-in-fact*.
actual fraud An intentional misrepresentation or omission of a material fact that is relied on by the client and causes the client damage.

actual notice Giving an express notice in writing, verbally, or by phone, text, electronic record, or other means of communication.
actus reus "Guilty act"—the actual performance of a criminal act.
additional terms Additional terms that an offeree can include in his or her acceptance of a sales contract where the acceptance, including the additional terms, acts as an acceptance rather than a counteroffer.
ademption A rule that says if a testator leaves a specific devise of property to a beneficiary but the property is no longer in the estate when the testator dies, the beneficiary receives nothing.
adequate assurance of performance Adequate assurance of performance from the other party if there is an indication that a contract will be breached by that party.
adjudicated mentally incompetent A situation in which a court or administrative agency has declared a person to be mentally incompetent. Contracts entered into by the person are *void*.
administrative agencies Agencies that the legislative and executive branches of federal and state governments establish.
administrative dissolution Involuntary dissolution of a corporation that is ordered by the secretary of state if a corporation has failed to comply with certain procedures required by law.
administrative employee exemption An exemption from federal minimum wage and overtime pay requirements that applies to employees who are compensated on a salary or fee basis, whose primary duty is the performance of office or nonmanual work, and whose work includes the exercise of discretion and independent judgment with respect to matters of significance.
administrative law Substantive and procedural law that governs the operation of administrative agencies.
administrative law judge (ALJ) A judge who presides over administrative proceedings and decides questions of law and fact concerning a case.
administrative order A decision made by an administrative law judge.
Administrative Procedure Act (APA) A federal statute that establishes certain administrative procedures that federal administrative agencies must follow in conducting their affairs.
administrative rules and regulations Directives issued by federal and state administrative agencies that interpret the statutes that the agency is authorized to enforce.
administrative search A search of businesses or other premises conducted by an administrative agency.
administrative subpoena A subpoena issued to an administrative agency to conduct a search of business or other premises.
administrator (male) or administratrix (female) A person who is appointed by the probate court to administer the estate of a testator's or testatrix's will if no one is named in the will or if the decedent dies intestate without a will.
adulterated food Food that consists in whole or in part of any filthy, putrid, or decomposed substance or is otherwise unfit for food.
adverse opinion An auditor's opinion that states that a company's financial statements do not fairly represent the company's financial position, results of operations, or change in cash flows, in conformity with generally accepted accounting principles (GAAPs).
adverse possession A situation in which a person who wrongfully possesses someone else's real property obtains title to that property if certain statutory requirements are met.
advertisement An invitation to make an offer, or an actual offer.
affirmative action A policy that provides that certain job preferences will be given to minority or other protected-class applicants when an employer makes an employment decision.
affirmative action plan A plan adopted by an employer that provides that certain job preferences will be given to members of minority racial and ethnic groups, women, and other protected-class applicants when an employer makes an employment decision.
affirmative defense A defense that is asserted in a defendant's answer to allegations contained in a plaintiff's complaint; A defense that an employer may raise against a charge of sexual, racial, or other harassment.
AFL-CIO A labor organization formed in 1955 by the combination of the American Federation of Labor (AFL) and the Congress of Industrial Organizations (CIO).
African Continental Free Trade Area (AfCFTA) A regional trade agreement among the countries of Africa that would establish a single continental trade market for goods and services that would reduce tariffs, encourage investment, and promote job creation.
African Union (AU) An organization composed of the countries located on the African continent whose goal is to establish an integrated, politically united, and prosperous African continent based on the ideals of Pan-Africanism and Africa's Renaissance.
after-acquired property Property that a debtor acquires after a security agreement is executed.
age discrimination Discrimination in employment based on a person's age. Federal law prohibits age discrimination against employees who are 40 and older. State and local laws can establish younger ages for protection against age discrimination.
Age Discrimination in Employment Act (ADEA) A federal statute that prohibits age discrimination practices against employees who are 40 and older.
age of majority The legal age, as set by state law, for a person to have the capacity to enter into a contract. The most prevalent age of majority is 18 years for both men and women.
agency A fiduciary relationship that results from the manifestation of consent by one person to act on behalf of another person, with that person's consent.
agency by ratification An agency that occurs when (1) a person misrepresents himself or herself as another's agent when in fact he or she is not and (2) the purported principal ratifies the unauthorized act.
agency law The large body of common law that governs agency; a mixture of contract law and tort law.
agency shop A workplace where an employer may hire anyone, whether he belongs to a union or not. After an employee has been hired, he does not have to join an existing labor union, but if he does not join the union, he must pay an agency fee to the union.
agent A party who agrees to act on behalf of another; a general partner of a general partnership; a general partner of a limited partnership.
agents' contract Real estate agents' contracts to sell real property for another party, which are covered by the Statute of Frauds and must be in writing to be enforceable.
agent's signature An agent's signature on a contract entered into on the principal's behalf determines the agent's status and his or her liability on the contract.
agreement The manifestation by two or more persons of the substance of a contract.
aiders and abettors Individuals who knowingly provide assistance to parties who have committed securities fraud.
air pollution Pollution caused by factories, homes, vehicles, and the like that affects the air.
air quality control regions (AQCRs) Regions of each state that the Environmental Protection Agency (EPA) has designated to measure compliance with air quality standards.
air rights The owners of land own air rights above the real property they own.
air space parcel Property rights owned by the owner of real property above the land they own. The owners of air space parcels often sell or lease them to other parties.
algorithmic discrimination (Weblining) The use of social network users' personal information to place discriminatory advertising online in violation of antidiscrimination laws.
alien corporation A corporation that is incorporated in another country.
alimony (spousal support) Payments made by one divorced spouse to the other divorced spouse.
allonge A separate piece of paper attached to an instrument on which an indorsement is written.
alter ego doctrine (piercing the corporate veil) A doctrine that says if a shareholder dominates a corporation and uses it for improper purposes, a court of equity can disregard the corporate entity and hold the shareholder personally liable for the corporation's debts and obligations.
altered check A check that has been altered without authorization and thus modifies the legal obligation of a party.
alternative dispute resolution (ADR) Methods of resolving disputes other than litigation.
amendments to the U.S. Constitution Changes or clarifications that have been added to the U.S. Constitution.
American Federation of Labor (AFL) A labor organization that was formed in 1886, to which only skilled craft workers such as silversmiths and artisans were allowed to belong.
American Institute of Certified Public Accountants (AICPA) An organization that has promulgated the *generally accepted auditing standards (GAASs)*.

American rule A rule that stipulates that where there have been successive assignments of the same contract right, the first assignment in time prevails regardless of when notice was given to the obligor; also known as the *New York Rule*.
Americans with Disabilities Act (ADA) A federal statute that imposes obligations on employers and providers of public transportation, telecommunications, and public accommodations to accommodate individuals with disabilities.
Americans with Disabilities Act Amendments Act (ADAAA) A federal statute that amends the Americans with Disabilities Act of 1990 (ADA) by expanding the definition of disability, requiring that the definition of disability be broadly construed, and requiring commonsense assessments in applying certain provisions of the ADA.
Analytical School A school of jurisprudential thought that maintains that law is shaped by logic.
Andean Community of Nations (Andean Community or CAN) A regional trading organization in South America composed of the countries of Bolivia, Columbia, Ecuador, and Peru.
annual percentage rate (APR) The annual interest rate that a debtor will pay on a debt, which includes in its calculation many of the fees charged by the lender.
annual report (Form 10-K) A report that must be filed on an annual basis with the Securities and Exchange Commission (SEC) by reporting companies that sets forth their financial condition.
annual shareholders' meeting A meeting of the shareholders of a corporation that must be held by the corporation to elect directors and to vote on other matters.
annulment A court order that declares that a marriage did not exist.
answer The defendant's written response to a plaintiff's complaint that is filed with the court and served on the plaintiff.
antecedent debt Existing debt of a partnership when a new partner joins the partnership.
anti-assignment clause A clause that prohibits the assignment of rights under the contract.
anticipatory breach (anticipatory repudiation) A breach that occurs when one contracting party informs the other that he or she will not perform his or her contractual duties when they are due.
Anticybersquatting Consumer Protection Act (ACPA) A federal statute that permits trademark owners and famous persons to recover domain names that use their names where the domain name has been registered by another person or business in bad faith.
anti-deficiency statute A statute that prohibits deficiency judgments regarding certain types of mortgages, such as those on residential property.
anti-delegation clause A clause that prohibits the delegation of duties under the contract.
antifraud provision Section 14(a) of the Securities Exchange Act of 1934, which prohibits misrepresentations or omissions of a material fact in the proxy materials.
antitakeover statute A statute that is enacted by a state legislature that protects against the hostile takeover of corporations incorporated in or doing business in the state.
Antitrust Division of the Department of Justice A division within the U.S. Department of Justice that is authorized to investigate suspected antitrust violations and to prosecute criminal antitrust lawsuits on behalf of the federal government.
antitrust injury Injury suffered by a person or business to his or her "business or property" caused by an antitrust violation.
antitrust laws A series of laws enacted to limit anticompetitive behavior in almost all industries, businesses, and professions operating in the United States.
apparent agency (agency by estoppel) (1) Agency that arises when a principal creates the appearance of an agency that in actuality does not exist. Also known as *agency by estoppel*. (2) In a franchise arrangement, an agency that arises when a franchisor creates the appearance that a franchisee is its agent when in fact an actual agency does not exist.
apparent authority Authority that an agent possesses by implication beyond the express authority granted to the agent by a principal, partnership, corporation, limited liability company, or other entity.
appeal The act of asking an appellate court to overturn a decision after the trial court's final judgment has been entered.
appellant The appealing party in an appeal; also known as the *petitioner*.
appellee The responding party in an appeal; also known as the *respondent*.
applicant A buyer of goods in an international sales transaction that purchases a letter of credit from an issuing bank.
appropriate bargaining unit A group of employees that a union seeks to represent; also referred to as a *bargaining unit*.
approval clause A clause that permits the assignment of a contract only upon receipt of an obligor's approval.
arbitration A form of alternative dispute resolution in which the parties choose an impartial third party to hear and decide their dispute.
arbitration agreement An agreement that requires disputes arising out of the contract to be submitted to arbitration.
arbitration clause A clause in a contract that requires disputes arising out of the contract to be submitted to arbitration.
arbitrator A neutral third party who hears and decides a dispute in arbitration.
area franchise (area development franchise or master franchise) A franchise in which a franchisor authorizes a franchisee to negotiate and sell franchises on its behalf in designated areas. The area franchisee is called a *subfranchisor*.
arraignment A hearing during which the accused is brought before a court and is (1) informed of the charges against him or her and (2) asked to enter a plea.
arrearages The amount of unpaid cumulative dividends.
arrest A situation in which a person is taken into custody for the alleged commission of a crime.
arrest warrant A document for a person's detainment based on a showing of probable cause that the person committed a crime.
arson The willful or malicious burning of a building.
Article I of the U.S. Constitution The part of the U.S. Constitution that establishes the legislative branch of the federal government.
Article I, Section 8 of the U.S. Constitution The part of the U.S. Constitution that lists express powers granted to the U.S. Congress. It also grants Congress the power to enact laws that are necessary and proper to implement its express powers.
Article I, Section 8, Clause 4 of the U.S. Constitution The part of the U.S. Constitution that provides that "The Congress shall have the power . . . to establish . . . uniform laws on the subject of bankruptcies throughout the United States."
Article II of the U.S. Constitution The part of the U.S. Constitution that establishes the executive branch of the federal government.
Article III of the U.S. Constitution The part of the U.S. Constitution that establishes the judicial branch of the federal government.
Article 2 (Sales) of the Uniform Commercial Code An article of the Uniform Commercial Code (UCC) that governs sales of goods.
Article 2A (Leases) of the Uniform Commercial Code An article of the Uniform Commercial Code (UCC) that governs leases of goods.
Article 3 (Commercial Paper) of the Uniform Commercial Code A model act promulgated in 1952 that established rules for the creation of, transfer of, enforcement of, and liability on negotiable instruments.
Article 4 (Bank Deposits and Collections) of the Uniform Commercial Code An article of the Uniform Commercial Code (UCC) that establishes the rules and principles that regulate bank deposits and collection procedures.
Article 4A (Funds Transfers) of the Uniform Commercial Code An article of the Uniform Commercial Code (UCC) that establishes rules regulating the creation and collection of and liability for commercial wire transfers.
Article 5 (Letters of Credit) of the Uniform Commercial Code An article of the Uniform Commercial Code (UCC) that governs letters of credit.
Article 9 (Secured Transactions) of the Uniform Commercial Code An article of the Uniform Commercial Code (UCC) that governs secured transactions in personal property.
articles of amendment A document filed with the secretary of state's office that amends to the articles of incorporation of a corporation, the articles of organization of a limited liability company (LLC), or the articles of limited liability partnership of a limited liability partnership.
Articles of Confederation A document adopted in 1777 that created a federal Congress composed of representatives of the 13 new states.
articles of dissolution A document that must be filed with the secretary of state that makes the voluntary dissolution of a corporation effective.

articles of incorporation (corporate charter) The basic governing documents of a corporation. They must be filed with the secretary of state of the state of incorporation.
articles of limited liability partnership The formal documents that must be filed at the secretary of state's office of the state of organization of a limited liability partnership (LLP) to form the LLP.
articles of merger A document that must be filed with the secretary of state by the surviving corporation of a merger.
articles of organization (certificate of organization) A document that must be filed at the secretary of state's office of the state of organization of a limited liability company (LLC) to form an LLC.
articles of share exchange A document that must be filed with the secretary of state by the surviving corporation after a share exchange.
articles of termination A document that is filed with the secretary of state to terminate a limited liability company (LLC) as of the date of filing or upon a later effective date specified in the articles.
artisan's lien (super-priority lien) A statutory lien given to workers on personal property to which they furnish services or materials in the ordinary course of business, which usually prevails over all other security interests in the goods.
"as is" disclaimer A term that makes it clear to the buyer of a good that no implied warranties attach to the sale of the good.
ASEAN Plus Three (APT) An agreement among the member nations of the Association of Southeast Asian Nations (ASEAN) plus China, Japan, and South Korea to meet regularly to discuss regional issues.
assault (1) The threat of immediate harm or offensive contact. (2) Any action that arouses reasonable apprehension of imminent harm. Actual physical contact is unnecessary.
assessment fee A fee paid by a franchisee to a franchisor for advertising, promotional campaigns, administrative costs, and the like.
assignee A party to whom a right to receive performance under a contract has been transferred; The new tenant to whom a tenant has transferred all of his or her interests under a lease by assignment.
assignment (assignment of a right) The transfer of rights under a contract; A transfer by a tenant of his or her rights under a lease to another party.
assignment and delegation The transfer of contractual rights by the obligee to another party. The transfer of rights under a contract. A transfer by a tenant of his or her rights under a lease to another.
assignor A party who transfers the right to receive performance under a contract; A tenant who transfers all of his or her interests under a lease to a new tenant by assignment.
associate justices of the U.S. Supreme Court Justices of the U.S. Supreme Court other than the chief justice.
Association of Southeast Asian Nations (ASEAN) An agreement among nations of Southeast Asia that reduces tariffs on products traded among the signatory counties and provides economic and other coordination among member nations.
assumption of duties A situation in which a delegation of duties contains the term *assumption*, the phrase *I assume the duties*, or other similar language. In such a case, the delegatee is legally liable to the obligee for nonperformance.
assumption of the risk A defense a defendant can use against a plaintiff who knowingly and voluntarily enters into or participates in a risky activity that results in injury.
at-fault divorce A divorce recognized by some states whereby one or both parties to a marriage is blamed for causing the divorce (e.g., through adultery, physical or emotional abuse, abandonment, alcohol or other substance abuse, or insanity).
at-will employee An employee who does not have a term employment contract. An at-will employee may be terminated by an employer without cause.
at-will limited liability company A limited liability company (LLC) that has no specified term of duration.
attachment A prejudgment court order that permits the seizure of a debtor's property while the lawsuit is pending; A situation in which a creditor has an enforceable security interest against a debtor and can satisfy the debt out of the designated collateral.
attempt or conspire to monopolize Firms that attempt or conspire to monopolize a relevant market violate Section 2 of the Sherman Act.
attestation The action of a will being witnessed by two or three objective and competent people.
attestation clause A clause in a will that usually follows the signature of the testator or testatrix in which the witnesses sign certifying that they have witnessed the signing of the will by the testator or testatrix.
attorney certification A certification that an attorney who represents a client in bankruptcy must file certifying the accuracy of the information contained in the bankruptcy petition and the debtor's schedules, under penalty of perjury.
attorney–client privilege A rule that says a client can tell his or her lawyer anything about the case without fear that the attorney will be called as a witness against the client.
attorney-in-fact The agent named in a power of attorney. This agent does not have to be a lawyer.
attorney's opinion An opinion given by an attorney concerning the status of title to real property that is arrived at after examining a chronological history of the chain of title and encumbrances affecting the property.
attractive nuisance doctrine A special tort rule that imposes liability on a landowner or possessor of land to children who have trespassed onto the owner's or possessor's real property by an attractive nuisance with the intent to play and are injured or killed while doing so.
auction A sale in which a seller of goods offers goods for sale through an auctioneer.
auction with reserve An auction in which the seller retains the right to refuse the highest bid and withdraw the goods from sale. Unless expressly stated otherwise, an auction is an auction with reserve.
auction without reserve An auction in which the seller expressly gives up his or her right to withdraw the goods from sale and must accept the highest bid.
audit A verification of a company's books and records, pursuant to federal securities laws, state laws, and stock exchange rules that must be performed by an independent CPA.
audit committee A committee of the board of directors of a corporation that oversees the integrity of financial statements, public audits of the company by certified public accountants, internal audits of the company, and compliance with legal and regulatory requirements. The audit committee must be composed of independent members of the board of directors.
auditor's opinion An opinion of an auditor about how fairly the financial statements of the client company represent the company's financial position, results of operations, and changes in cash flow.
authenticate The act of signing a document or adopting or accepting an electronic record by electronic signature (electronic symbol, sound, or process).
authorized means of communication A rule that states that an offeree must accept an offer by means expressly specified in the offer, or if there is no such requirement, then by any means customary in similar transactions, usage of trade, or prior dealings between the parties.
authorized shares The number of shares provided for in a corporation's articles of incorporation.
automated teller machine (ATM) An electronic machine that is located either on a bank's premises or at some other location that is connected online to the bank's computers and permits the withdrawal of funds, the deposit of funds, and the conduct of other banking transactions.
automatic stay The suspension of certain legal actions by creditors against a debtor or the debtor's property.
automobile insurance A type of insurance that covers automobiles and other vehicles.
automobile liability insurance Automobile insurance that covers damages that the insured causes to third parties.
B Lab A nonprofit corporation that certifies that a corporation is a certified benefit corporation if the corporation attains certain general or specific public benefit goals.
B-1 visa A visa issued to persons seeking temporary entry to the United States for business purposes.
B-2 visa A visa issued to persons seeking temporary entry to the United States for tourism and non-business purposes.
backward vertical merger (upstream vertical merger) A vertical merger in which a customer acquires a supplier.
bail An amount of money established by a court that a person who has been arrested may post with the court in order to be released from custody, usually jail, pending the trial of his or her case.
bail bond An instrument that is purchased from a bail bondsperson by a person who

has been arrested and ordered to post a bond with the court in order to be released from custody, usually jail, pending the trial of his or her case. The bail bondsperson submits the bail bond to the court in substitution for the bail that the arrested person would be required to post.
bailee A holder of goods who is not a seller or a buyer (e.g., warehouse, common carrier).
bailment A transaction in which an owner transfers his or her personal property to another to be held, stored, or delivered, or for some other purpose. Title to the property does not transfer.
bailment agreement An agreement that creates a bailment. The agreement must be in writing if it is for more than one year.
bailment at will A bailment without a fixed term; can be terminated at any time by either party.
bailment for a fixed term A bailment that terminates at the end of the term or sooner, by mutual consent of the parties.
bailment for the sole benefit of the bailee A gratuitous bailment that benefits only the bailee. The bailee owes a *duty of utmost care* to protect the bailed property.
bailment for the sole benefit of the bailor A gratuitous bailment that benefits only the bailor. The bailee owes only a *duty of slight care* to protect the bailed property.
bailment of personal property The bailment of personal property includes the bailment of tangible (e.g. automobiles, equipment, jewelry) and intangible property (e.g., stocks, bonds, notes).
bailor The owner of property in a bailment.
bank check A certified check or a cashier's check, the payment for which a bank is solely or primarily liable.
Bank Secrecy Act A federal statute that requires financial institutions and other covered entities to file Currency Transaction Reports (CTR) with the Internal Revenue Service (IRS) reporting certain cash and other cash-like transactions.
Bankruptcy Abuse Prevention and Consumer Protection Act of 2005 A federal statute that substantially amended federal bankruptcy law. This act makes it more difficult for debtors to file for bankruptcy and have their unpaid debts discharged.
Bankruptcy Code The name given to federal bankruptcy law, as amended.
bankruptcy estate The debtor's property and earnings that compose the estate in a bankruptcy proceeding.
bankruptcy law Federal law that establishes procedures for filing for bankruptcy, resolving creditors' claims, and protecting debtors' rights.
Bankruptcy Reform Act of 1978 A federal statute that substantially changed federal bankruptcy law. The act made it easier for debtors to file for bankruptcy and have their unpaid debts discharged. This act was considered debtor-friendly.
bankruptcy trustee The legal representative of a debtor's estate that is appointed in a Chapter 7 (liquidation), Chapter 12 (family farmer or family fisherman), or Chapter 13 (adjustment of debts) bankruptcy case. May be appointed in a Chapter 11 (reorganization) case upon a showing of cause.
bargained-for exchange Exchange that parties engage in that leads to an enforceable contract.
battery Unauthorized and harmful or offensive direct or indirect physical contact with another person that causes injury.
battle of the forms A UCC rule that states that if both parties are merchants, then additional terms contained in the acceptance become part of the sales contract *unless* (1) the offer expressly limits the acceptance to the terms of the offer, (2) the additional terms materially alter the original contract, or (3) the offeror notifies the offeree that he or she objects to the additional terms within a reasonable time after receiving the offeree's modified acceptance. There is no contract if the additional terms so materially alter the terms of the original offer that the parties cannot agree on the contract.
bearer A person who is in possession of an instrument that is payable to anyone in physical possession of the instrument.
bearer instrument (bearer paper) An instrument that is payable to anyone in physical possession of the instrument who presents it for payment when it is due. The person in possession of the instrument is called the *bearer*. Bearer paper results when the drawer or maker does not make the instrument payable to a specific payee. An instrument that is negotiated by delivery; indorsement is not necessary.
beneficiary The lender-creditor of a three-party deed of trust in a real estate financing arrangement; A person or party designated in a will to receive all or a portion of the testator's property at the time of the testator's death; A person or party for whose benefit a trust is created; A person or party who is to receive the life insurance proceeds when the insured dies; A party who is designated to be paid funds by an issuing bank of a letter of credit.
benefit corporation (B corporation or B corp) A corporation that requires directors and officers to make decisions to accomplish general-public benefits and stipulated specific public benefit purposes stated in the articles of incorporation and to consider stakeholders other than shareholders, such as employees, customers, suppliers, and the community, when making corporate decisions.
benefit report An annual report that a benefit corporation must deliver to its shareholders that assesses its social and environment performance.
bequest (legacy) A gift of personal property by will.
Berne Convention An international copyright treaty.
best-efforts contract A contract that contains a clause that requires one or both of the parties to use their *best efforts* to achieve the objective of the contract.
best interests of the child A standard applied by courts in determining which parent should receive custody of children of divorcing parents.
beyond a reasonable doubt A doctrine that requires that the government prove that the accused is guilty beyond a reasonable doubt in order to be found guilty of a crime.
bicameral Being composed of two chambers. The legislative branch of the federal government is composed of the U.S. Senate and the U.S. House of Representatives.
bilateral contract A contract entered into by way of exchange of promises of the parties; "a promise for a promise."
bilateral trade agreement An agreement between two countries that facilitates trade between the countries.
bilateral treaty A treaty between two nations.
bill A document introduced in the U.S. Congress that begins the process whereby a bill can become a statute.
bill of lading A document of title issued by a common carrier that states that the bailor has title to the bailed goods.
Bill of Rights The first 10 amendments to the U.S. Constitution that were added in 1791.
binding arbitration An agreement between the parties to a dispute whereby they agree that the decision and award of the arbitrator cannot be appealed to the courts.
bioengineered or BE Terms used in federal statutes to designate that plants and animals have been modified by laboratory techniques such as genetic engineering and biotechnology.
blank indorsement An indorsement that does not specify a particular indorsee. It creates bearer paper.
blue-sky laws State laws that regulate the issuance and trading of securities.
blurring A situation that occurs when a party uses another party's famous mark to designate a product or service in another market so that the unique significance of the famous mark is weakened.
board of directors A panel of persons who are elected by the shareholders that makes policy decisions concerning the operation of a corporation.
bona fide occupational qualification (BFOQ) A true job qualification. Employment discrimination based on a protected class (other than race or color) is lawful if it is *job related* and a *business necessity*. This exception is narrowly interpreted by the courts.
bond A long-term debt security that is secured by some form of collateral (e.g., real estate, personal property).
booking An administrative procedure that occurs at a police station after a person is arrested whereby the arrest is recorded, the suspect is fingerprinted, and a photograph is taken of the suspect.
borrower (debtor) A party who borrows money or other assets in a credit transaction.
BP oil spill An oil spill that occurred in the Gulf of Mexico from an oil rig owned by BP p.l.c. (formerly British Petroleum) that spilled 5 million barrels of oil over a 5,000-mile area of the Gulf of Mexico, killing thousands of marine animals, birds, fish and aquatic species, and causing extensive damage to hundreds of miles of coastline, particularly in Louisiana, Florida, and Mississippi. This was the largest oil spill in U.S. history.
breach A contracting party's failure to perform an absolute duty owed under a contract.

breach of confidentiality Disclosure of confidential information (e.g., trade secrets, formulas, customer lists) that agents, general partners, officers, directors and employees of corporations, employees of businesses, and others that is obtained from their principal to third parties other than their principal.
breach of contract A contracting party's failure to perform an absolute duty owed under a contract.
breach of the duty of care A failure to exercise care or to act as a reasonable person would act.
bribery (kickback, payoff) A crime in which one person gives another person money, property, favors, or anything else of value for a favor in return. A bribe is often referred to as a *payoff* or *kickback*.
Brown v. Board of Education A U.S. Supreme Court case decided in 1954 that held that the "separate but equal" doctrine for schools that was established by an earlier U.S. Supreme Court decision violated the Equal Protection Clause of the Fourteenth Amendment to the Constitution and was unconstitutional.
building A structure constructed on land.
building codes (housing codes) State and local statutes that impose specific standards on property owners to maintain and repair leased premises.
burden of proof A burden a plaintiff bears in a civil or criminal trial to persuade the trier of fact of the merits of his or her case.
Bureau of Competition of the Federal Trade Commission A bureau within the Federal Trade Commission (FTC) that is authorized to investigate suspected antitrust violations and bring civil actions on behalf of the federal government.
burglary The taking of personal property from another's home, office, or commercial or other type of building.
business interruption insurance Insurance that reimburses a business for loss of revenue incurred when the business has been damaged or destroyed by some peril.
business judgment rule A rule that protects the decisions of a board of directors of a corporation where the board has acted on an informed basis, in good faith, and in the honest belief that the action taken was in the best interests of the corporation and its shareholders.
buy-and-sell agreement An agreement among shareholders of a corporation that requires a selling shareholder who is a signatory to the agreement to sell his or her shares to the other shareholders or to the corporation at the price specified in the agreement.
buyer in the ordinary course of business A person who, in good faith and without knowledge of another's ownership or security interest in goods, buys the goods in the ordinary course of business from a person in the business of selling goods of that kind.
buyout The purchase of a dissociating partner's interest in a general partnership.
bylaws A detailed set of rules adopted by the board of directors after a corporation is incorporated that contains provisions for managing the business and the affairs of the corporation.
C corporation A corporation that does not qualify for or has not elected to be taxed as an S corporation. Where there is a C corporation, there is double taxation—that is, a C corporation pays taxes at the corporate level, and shareholders pay taxes on dividends paid by the corporation.
C.&F. (cost and freight) A pricing term that means the price of goods includes the cost of the goods and the cost of freight.
cabinet-level departments Highest-level federal departments that advise the president and are responsible for enforcing specific laws enacted by Congress.
cancellation Cancellation of a negotiable instrument that can be accomplished by (1) any manner apparent on the face of the instrument or the indorsement (e.g., writing *canceled* on the instrument) or (2) destruction or mutilation of a negotiable instrument with the intent of eliminating the obligation.
capital murder A murder for which the defendant could be executed if found guilty of committing the murder.
capture The right of a buyer or lessee to purchase or rent substitute goods if the seller or lessor fails to make delivery of the goods or repudiates the contract or if the buyer or lessee rightfully rejects the goods or justifiably revokes their acceptance.
cashier's check A check issued by a bank for which the customer has paid the bank the amount of the check and a fee. The bank guarantees payment of the check.
caveat emptor "Let the buyer beware," the traditional guideline of sales transactions.
Celler-Kefauver Act A federal statute, enacted in 1950, that widened Section 7 of the Clayton Act's scope to include asset acquisitions (previously only applied to stock mergers).
Central America–Dominican Republic Free Trade Agreement (CAFTA–DR) An association of several Central American countries and the United States designed to reduce tariffs and trade barriers among member nations.
centralized management The board of directors and the officers of a corporation manage the affairs of the corporation. The board of directors make policy decisions, and the officers run the corporation's day-to-day operations.
CEO and CFO certification A certification that the Sarbanes-Oxley Act requires, which the chief executive officer (CEO) and chief financial officer (CFO) of a public company file with each annual and quarterly report of the company.
certificate of authority A formal document that must be issued by the secretary of state before a foreign corporation, foreign limited liability company (LLC), foreign limited partnership, foreign limited liability partnership (LLP), or foreign limited liability limited partnership (LLLP) may conduct business in that state.
certificate of deposit (CD) A two-party negotiable instrument that is a special form of note created when a depositor deposits money at a financial institution in exchange for the institution's promise to pay back the amount of the deposit plus an agreed upon rate of interest upon the expiration of a set time period agreed upon by the parties. The financial institution is the borrower (the *maker* of a certificate of deposit), and the depositor is the lender (the *payee* of a certificate of deposit).
certificate of dissolution A document issued by the secretary of state that dissolves a corporation.
certificate of interest A document that evidences a member's ownership interest in a limited liability company (LLC).
certificate of limited liability limited partnership A document that two or more persons must sign and file with the secretary of state of the state organization to form a limited liability limited partnership.
certificate of limited partnership A document that two or more persons must sign and file with the secretary of state of the state organization to form a limited partnership.
certificate of partnership (statement of partnership) A written document that a general partnership may file with the secretary of state that records that it is a general partnership.
certificate of title A document that evidences ownership of motor vehicles, trailers, mobile homes, boats, farm tractors, and the like; A certificate that is issued by a land court that determines the rightful owner of real property.
certificate of title statute A state statute that provides for filing of certificates of title for motor vehicles, trailers, mobile homes, boats, farm tractors, or the like, and that may specify security interests held in the property.
certification mark A mark that certifies that a seller of a product or service has met certain geographical location requirements, quality standards, material standards, or mode of manufacturing standards established by the owner of the mark.
certified benefit corporation A corporation that has been certified by B Lab as meeting certain general and specific public benefit goals.
certified check A type of check for which a bank agrees in advance (*certifies*) to accept the check when it is presented for payment.
certified public accountant (CPA) An accountant who has met certain educational requirements, has passed the CPA examination, and has had a certain number of years of auditing experience.
chain of distribution The chain of manufacturers, distributors, wholesalers, retailers, lessors, subcomponent manufacturers, and others who distribute a defective product.
chain-style franchise A situation in which a franchisor licenses a franchisee to make and sell its products or distribute its services to the public from a retail outlet serving an exclusive territory.
chamber A portion of the legislative branch of government; refers to either the U.S. House of Representatives or the U.S. Senate.
change of venue Movement of a trial to a venue where a more impartial jury can be found in cases where pretrial publicity or

other reason may prejudice jurors located in the proper venue.
changing conditions defense A defense to a Robinson-Patman Act Section 2(a) price discrimination action in which prices were lowered in response to changing conditions in the market for the goods.
Chapter 7 discharge The termination of the legal duty of an individual debtor to pay unsecured debts that remain unpaid upon the completion of a Chapter 7 proceeding.
Chapter 7—Liquidation A form of bankruptcy in which the debtor's nonexempt property is sold for cash, the cash is distributed to the creditors, and any unpaid debts are discharged; also referred to as *straight bankruptcy*.
Chapter 11 plan of reorganization A plan that sets forth a proposed new capital structure for a debtor to assume when it emerges from Chapter 11 reorganization bankruptcy.
Chapter 11—Reorganization A bankruptcy method that allows the reorganization of the debtor's financial affairs under the supervision of the bankruptcy court.
Chapter 12—Adjustment of Debts of a Family Farmer or Fisherman with Regular Income A special form of bankruptcy that provides for the reorganization bankruptcy of family farmers and fisherman.
Chapter 13—Adjustment of Debts of an Individual with Regular Income A rehabilitation form of bankruptcy that permits bankruptcy courts to supervise the debtor's plan for the payment of unpaid debts in installments over the plan period.
Chapter 13 discharge A discharge in a Chapter 13 case that is granted to the debtor after the debtor's plan of payment is completed (which could be up to three or up to five years).
Chapter 13 plan of payment A plan set forth by a debtor in a Chapter 13—Adjustment of Debts of an Individual with Regular Income bankruptcy proceeding that lays out the debtor's plan for paying his or her disposable income to prepetition creditors during the plan period.
characteristics of a corporation Characteristics of a corporation include legal existence, free transferability of shares, perpetual existence, centralized management, and limited liability of shareholders.
charitable trust A trust that is created for the benefit of a segment of society or society in general.
chattel paper A record that evidences both a monetary obligation and a security interest in specific goods.
check A distinct form of draft that is an order by a drawer (i.e., checking account holder) to the drawer's financial institution (the drawee) to pay a specified sum of money from the drawer's checking account to the named payee (or holder).
checks and balances A system built into the U.S. Constitution to prevent any one of the three branches of the government from becoming too powerful.
Chief Justice of the U.S. Supreme Court The justice who is responsible for the administration of the Supreme Court.
child custody The award of legal custody of a child to a parent in a divorce or annulment proceeding. This determination is made based on the best interests of the child.
child labor The use of children to work is restricted and regulated by the Fair Labor Standards Act (FLSA).
child neglect A parent's failure to provide a child with the necessities of life or other basic needs.
child support Payments made by a noncustodial parent to help financially support his or her children.
choice of forum clause (forum-selection clause) A clause in an international contract that designates which nation's court has jurisdiction to hear a case arising out of the contract; also known as a *forum-selection clause*.
choice of law clause A contract provision that designates a certain state's law or country's law that will be applied in any dispute concerning nonperformance of the contract.
C.I.F. (cost, insurance, and freight) A pricing term that means the price of goods includes the cost of the goods and the costs of insurance and freight.
circuit The geographical area served by a U.S. circuit court of appeals.
civil action A lawsuit brought by a party to recover monetary damages or other remedies from a defendant.
civil damages Damages awarded for violations of antitrust laws, including treble damages.
civil law Law based on codes or statutes. In civil law, the adjudication of a case is based on the application of the code or statutes to a particular set of facts.
civil penalty A penalty that the Securities and Exchange Commission (SEC) can obtain against a defendant of up to three times (*treble damages*) the illegal profits gained or losses avoided on insider trading.
civil RICO A federal statute that permits a civil lawsuit to be brought by persons injured by a pattern of racketeering to recover treble damages from the racketeer for injury caused to the plaintiff's business or property.
Civil Rights Act of 1866 A federal statute enacted after the Civil War that says all persons "have the same right . . . to make and enforce contracts . . . as is enjoyed by white persons." It prohibits racial and color discrimination.
Civil Rights Act of 1964 A federal statute that makes it illegal to discriminate in employment, housing, transportation, and public accommodations based on race, national origin, color, gender, or religion.
Civil Service Reform Act A federal statute that permits federal government employees to voluntarily choose to join a union or choose not to join a union.
Clarifying Lawful Overseas Use of Data Act (CLOUD Act) A federal statute that provides a streamlined process by which law enforcement agencies may obtain user information from internet, media, and tech companies.
class action A situation in which a group of plaintiffs collectively bring a lawsuit against a defendant.
Class Action Fairness Act (CAFA) A federal statute that requires certain class action lawsuits to be brought in or transferred to federal courts.
class action waiver A clause in an arbitration agreement whereby a party agrees not to join a class action to pursue a defendant in an arbitration proceeding.
Clayton Antirust Act (Clayton Act) A federal statute, enacted in 1914, that regulates mergers and prohibits certain exclusive dealing arrangements.
Clean Air Act (CAA) A federal statute that provides comprehensive regulation of air quality in the United States.
Clean Air Act Amendments Amendments to the Clean Air Act that increase the protection of air quality.
Clean Water Act (CWA) A federal statute that establishes water quality standards and regulates water pollution.
close corporation A small corporation that has met specified requirements and may choose this designation under state law. As such, the corporation may dispense with some corporate formalities and operate without a board of directors, without bylaws, and without keeping minutes of meetings.
closed shop A business in which an employer hires only employees who are already members of a labor union and cannot hire employees who are not members of a union. Closed shops are illegal in the United States.
closely held corporation (privately held corporation) A corporation owned by one or a few shareholders.
closing (settlement) The finalization of a real estate sales transaction that passes title to the property from the seller to the buyer.
closing argument (closing statement) Statements made by each party's attorney to the jury at the close of a trial.
code books Books that contain statutes enacted by the U.S. Congress and state legislatures and ordinances enacted by municipalities.
code of ethics A code adopted by a company wherein the company sets forth rules of ethics for the company's managers and employees to follow when dealing with customers, employees, suppliers, and others.
codicil A separate document that must be executed to amend a will. It must be executed with the same formalities as a will.
codified law Statutes enacted by Congress and state legislatures and ordinances passed by municipalities and local government bodies.
coinsurance clause (copay clause) A clause in an insurance policy that requires the insured to pay a percentage of an insured loss.
collateral Security against repayment of a debt that lenders sometimes require; can be a car, a house, or other property. The property is subject to a security interest.
collateral note A note that is secured by personal property.
collecting bank The depository bank and other banks in the collection process (other than the payer bank).
collection process The process of collecting checks that are drawn on other banks.
collection remedies Procedures that can be used by plaintiffs to recover damages against defendants.

collective bargaining The process of negotiating contract terms between an employer and the members of a union.
collective bargaining agreement The contract that results from a collective bargaining procedure.
collective membership mark A mark that indicates that a person has met the standards set by an organization and is a member of that organization.
collision insurance Insurance that a car owner purchases to insure his or her car against risk of loss or damage.
color discrimination Employment discrimination against a person because of his or her color, for example, where a light-skinned person of a race discriminates against a dark-skinned person of the same race.
coming and going rule (going and coming rule) A rule that says a principal is generally not liable for injuries caused by its agents and employees while they are on their way to or from work. Also known as the *going and coming rule*.
Command School A school of jurisprudential thought that postulates that law is a set of rules developed, communicated, and enforced by the ruling party.
Commerce Clause A clause of the U.S. Constitution that grants Congress the power "to regulate commerce with foreign nations, and among the several states, and with Indian tribes."
commercial activity exception An exception that states that a foreign country is subject to lawsuits in the United States if it engages in commercial activity in the United States or if it carries on such activity outside the United States but causes a direct effect in the United States.
commercial electronic funds transfer An electronic transfer of funds from a bank to another party that is subject to Article 4A of the Uniform Commercial Code (UCC).
commercial paper Short-term notes issued by corporations that do not exceed nine months.
commercial reasonableness A term used in the Uniform Commercial Code that applies to merchants in the performance of their duties under sales and lease contracts.
commercial speech Speech used by businesses, such as for advertising. It is subject to time, place, and manner restrictions.
commercial wire transfer (wholesale wire transfer) An electronic transfer of funds from a bank to another party that is often used to transfer funds between businesses and financial institutions.
committee A special group composed of members of the U.S. House of Representatives or the U.S. Senate to which a bill that has been introduced in the U.S. Congress is referred for review.
committees of the board of directors Committees created by a corporation's board of directors composed of board members who are granted special powers as authorized by the board.
Committee on Foreign Investment in the United States (CFIUS) A federal interagency committee that has been delegated executive power to review and reject foreign acquisitions and investments that violate federal laws administered by the committee.
common carrier A company that offers transportation services to the public, such as an airline, a railroad, or a trucking firm; the *bailee* in a bailment situation.
common crime Ordinary crimes that are committed against persons and property.
common law marriage A type of marriage some states recognize in which a marriage license has not been issued but certain requirements are met.
common law of contracts Contract law developed primarily by state courts.
Common Market of Eastern and Southern Africa (COMESA) A regional trading block of countries located in eastern and southern Africa.
common securities Interests or instruments that are commonly known as securities, such as common stock, preferred stock, bonds, debentures, and warrants.
common stock A type of equity security that represents the *residual* value of a corporation.
common stock certificate A document that represents a common shareholder's investment in the corporation.
common stockholder A person who owns common stock.
Communications Decency Act A federal statute that states that internet service providers (ISPs) are not liable for the content transmitted over their networks by email users and websites.
community property A form of ownership in which each spouse owns an equal one-half share of the income of both spouses and the assets acquired during the marriage.
comparative negligence (comparative fault) A doctrine under which damages are apportioned according to fault.
compensation committee A committee of the board of directors of a corporation that is responsible for human resources policies and procedures, employee benefit plans, and executive and employee compensation.
compensatory damages An award of money intended to compensate a nonbreaching party for the loss of a bargain. Compensatory damages place the nonbreaching party in the same position as if the contract had been fully performed by restoring the "benefit of the bargain."
competing with the corporation A situation that occurs when a director or officer of a corporation engages in undisclosed and unauthorized competition with the corporation that has employed him or her.
competing with the partnership A situation that occurs when a general partner of a partnership engages in undisclosed and unauthorized competition with the partnership of which he or she is a partner.
competing with the principal A situation that occurs when an agent, a general partner, a director or officer of a corporation, a partner in a limited liability partnership, certain members of a limited liability company, and anyone else who owes a fiduciary duty to a principal engages in undisclosed and unauthorized competition with their principal.
complaint A document a plaintiff files with the court and serves on the defendant to initiate a lawsuit.
complete integration A concept that a written contract is a complete and final statement of the parties' agreement.
complete performance (strict performance) A situation in which a party to a contract renders performance exactly as required by the contract. Complete performance discharges that party's obligations under the contract.
composition An agreement that provides for the reduction of a debtor's debts.
Comprehensive Environmental Response, Compensation, and Liability Act (CERCLA or Superfund) A federal statute that authorizes the federal government to deal with hazardous wastes. The act creates a monetary fund to finance the cleanup of hazardous waste sites.
comprehensive insurance A form of property insurance that insures an automobile from loss or damage due to causes other than collision.
Comprehensive and Progressive Agreement for Trans-Pacific Partnership (CPTPP) A regional trade agreement between 11 countries of the Indo-Pacific region that eliminates tariffs across a broad range of products and services.
compulsory subjects Subjects of collective bargaining that must be negotiated by an employer with a labor union, such as issues concerning wages, hours, and other terms and conditions of employment.
computer employee exemption An exemption from federal minimum wage and overtime pay requirements that applies to employees compensated either on a salary or fee basis; are employed as computer systems analysts, computer programmers, software engineers, or in similarly skilled occupations in the computer field; and are engaged in the design, development, documentation, analysis, creation, testing, or modification of computer systems or programs.
concurrent conditions Conditions that exists when the parties to a contract must render performance simultaneously; each party's absolute duty to perform is conditioned on the other party's absolute duty to perform.
concurrent jurisdiction Jurisdiction shared by two or more courts.
concurrent ownership (co-ownership) A situation in which two or more persons own a piece of real property. The following forms of co-ownership of real property are recognized: joint tenancy, tenancy in common, tenancy by the entirety, community property, condominiums, and cooperatives.
concurring opinion An opinion written by a justice who agrees with the outcome of a case reached by other justices but not the reason proffered by them, wherein the justice sets forth his or her reasons for deciding the case.
condition A qualification of a promise that becomes a covenant if it is met. There are three types of conditions: conditions precedent, conditions subsequent, and concurrent conditions.
condition precedent A condition that requires the occurrence of an event before a party is obligated to perform a duty under a contract.

condition subsequent A condition in which the occurrence or nonoccurrence of a specific event automatically excuses the performance of an existing contractual duty to perform.
conditional A promise or an order that is conditional on another promise or event.
conditional promise (qualified promise) A situation in which a promisor's duty to perform or not perform a contract arises only if a condition does or does not occur.
conditional sale A sale of goods that is subject to a condition of sale.
condominium A common form of ownership in a multiple-dwelling building where the purchaser has title to the individual unit and owns the common areas as a tenant in common with the other condominium owners.
conference committee A special group composed of members of both the U.S. House of Representatives and the U.S. Senate whose task is to try to reconcile the differences in bills passed by each chamber.
confidential draft registration statement A confidential draft of a proposed registration statement that may be filed by an emerging growth company (EGC) for review by the staff of the Securities and Exchange Commission (SEC) that the EGC may withdraw if it chooses to do so after such review.
confidentiality agreement (nondisclosure agreement or NDA) An agreement whereby an employee, independent consultant, and others who are privy to a company's secret or proprietary information agrees not to disclose such information to any other party.
confirmation of a Chapter 11 plan of reorganization The bankruptcy court's approval of a plan of reorganization for a Chapter 11 bankruptcy.
confusion A situation in which fungible goods (i.e., goods that are exactly alike) are commingled and the owners share title to the commingled goods in proportion to the quantity of goods contributed.
conglomerate merger A merger that does not fit into any other category; a merger between firms in totally unrelated businesses.
Congress of Industrial Organizations (CIO) A labor organization formed in 1935 that permitted semiskilled and unskilled workers to become members.
conscious parallelism A situation in which if two or more firms act the same but no concerted action is shown, there is no violation of Section 1 of the Sherman Act.
consent decree A plea entered by a civil defendant who has been sued by the government whereby the accused agrees to the imposition of a penalty but does not admit liability.
consent election An election to establish a labor union that is not contested by the employer and may be held without National Labor Relations Board (NLRB) supervision.
consequential damages (special damages) Foreseeable damages that arise from circumstances outside a contract. To be liable for these damages, the breaching party must know or have reason to know that the breach will cause special damages to the other party.
consideration Something of legal value given in exchange for a promise.
consignee The party to whom a seller (the *consignor*) delivers goods to be sold on the seller's behalf. In a common carrier bailment arrangement, the person to whom the bailed goods are to be delivered.
consignment An arrangement in which a seller (the consignor) delivers goods to a buyer (the consignee) to sell; The delivery of goods by a consigner (shipper, bailor) to a common carrier (bailee) for delivery of the goods to another party (consignee).
consignor The party who delivers goods to a buyer (the *consignee*) to sell on his or her behalf. In a common carrier bailment arrangement, the person who is shipping goods; the *bailor*.
consolidated corporation A new corporation that is formed by the consolidation of two corporations.
Consolidated Omnibus Budget Reconciliation Act (COBRA) A federal statute that permits employees and their beneficiaries to continue their group health insurance after an employee's employment has ended.
consolidation The act of a court to combine two or more separate lawsuits into one lawsuit; The combination of two corporations in which a new corporation is created and the two merging corporations cease to exist.
conspicuous disclaimer A written disclaimer of an implied warranty associated with the sale of goods that must be noticeable to a reasonable person.
Constitution of the United States of America The fundamental law of the United States of America. It was ratified by the states in 1788 and is the supreme law of the United States.
Constitutional Convention A meeting convened by delegates of many states in 1787 with the primary purpose of strengthening the federal government.
construction lien (mechanic's lien) A contractor's, laborer's, and material person's statutory lien that makes the real property to which services or materials have been provided security for the payment of the services and materials.
constructive delivery A method used on some occasions in making gifts of personal property where the donor makes a symbolic delivery of the property to the donee instead of making a physical delivery of the property.
constructive eviction A wrongful eviction that occurs if a landlord causes the leased premises to become unfit for the tenant's intended use (e.g., by failing to provide electricity) and the tenant leaves the premises.
constructive fraud (gross negligence) Fraud that occurs when an accountant acts with "reckless disregard" for the truth or the consequences of his or her actions.
constructive notice Notice given by publishing the information in a newspaper of general circulation; Recording of a deed, mortgage, lien, or other document pertaining to an interest in real property gives constructive notice to the world of the owner's or other recorder's interest in the real property; Notice given by a general partnership by filing a statement of dissociation of a partner; Notice given by a general partnership by filing a statement of dissolution of a partner.
constructive trust An equitable trust that is implied by law to avoid fraud, unjust enrichment, and injustice.
consulting fee A fee paid by franchisees and other parties to obtain the services of experts in an area.
consumer credit Credit that is extended to natural persons for personal, family, or household purposes.
consumer debt For bankruptcy purposes, debts incurred by an individual for personal, family, or household purposes.
consumer expectation test A test to determine whether a product's design or warnings are defective that requires a showing that the product is more dangerous than the ordinary reasonable consumer would expect. A test to determine the merchantability of food and drink products based on what the average consumer would expect to find or not find in food and drink products.
consumer financial protection A set of government laws that protect consumer-debtors in credit transactions.
Consumer Financial Protection Act A federal statute that requires increased disclosure of credit information and terms to consumers and regulates consumer credit providers and others.
Consumer Financial Protection Bureau (CFPB) A federal regulatory agency that has broad authority to regulate consumer financial products and services.
consumer goods Goods that are purchased by consumers, such as furniture, television sets, home appliances, and other goods used primarily for personal, family, or household purposes.
Consumer Leasing Act (CLA) An amendment to the Truth-in-Lending Act (TILA) that extends the TILA's coverage to lease terms in consumer leases.
Consumer Product Safety Act (CPSA) A federal statute that regulates potentially dangerous consumer products and that created the Consumer Product Safety Commission.
Consumer Product Safety Commission (CPSC) A federal administrative agency empowered to adopt rules and regulations to interpret and enforce the Consumer Product Safety Act.
Consumer Product Safety Improvement Act (CPSIA) A federal statute that mandates that toys and products that are to be sold for use by children 12 and under must be tested and certified as meeting Consumer Product Safety Commission children's safety standards.
consumer products Products that are sold to consumers.
consumer protection laws Federal and state statutes and regulations that promote product safety and prohibit abusive, unfair, and deceptive business practices.
contested election An election to establish a labor union that is opposed and contested by the employer and must be supervised by the National Labor Relations Board (NLRB).

contingency fee A fee arrangement between a lawyer and client whereby the lawyer is paid a percentage of damages won through trial judgment or by settlement.
continuation agreement An agreement among the surviving or remaining general partners of a general partnership, limited partnership, or limited liability partnership, or members of a limited liability company, to continue a business after the disassociation of a partner or member or the dissolution of the partnership or company.
continuation statement A document that can be filed by a secured creditor up to six months prior to the expiration of a financing statement's term to continue the creditor's perfected interest in the collateral designated in the financing statement.
continuous and peaceful A requirement that must be proven by a person to obtain real property by adverse possession. It requires that the adverse possessor has occupied the property continuously and uninterrupted for the required statutory period. Any break in normal occupancy terminates the adverse possession.
contract An agreement that is enforceable by a court of law or equity. "A contract is a promise or a set of promises for the breach of which the law gives a remedy or the performance of which the law in some way recognizes a duty" (*Restatement [Second] of Contracts*).
contract contrary to law A contract to perform activities that are prohibited by law.
contract contrary to public policy A contract to perform activities that have a negative impact on society or interfere with the public's safety and welfare. This constitutes an illegal contract.
contract in restraint of trade A contract that unreasonably restrains trade.
contract liability Liability of principals and agents for contracts entered into with third parties.
contract of adhesion A preprinted contract prepared by a provider of goods or services in which the contract terms are set and the consumer or other party cannot negotiate the contract terms and must accept the terms of the contract in order to obtain the product or service.
contractual capacity The necessary capacity of parties to enter into the contract.
contributory negligence A doctrine that says a plaintiff who is partially at fault for his or her own injury cannot recover against a negligent defendant.
Controlling the Assault of Non-Solicited Pornography and Marketing Act (CAN-SPAM Act) A federal statute that places certain restrictions on persons and businesses that send unsolicited commercial advertising (spam) to email accounts, prohibits falsified headers, prohibits deceptive subject lines, and requires spammers to label sexually oriented email as such.
convention A treaty that is sponsored by an international organization.
convertible preferred stock Stock that permits the preferred stockholders to convert their shares into common stock.
cooling-off period A mandatory 60 days' notice before a strike can commence.
cooperative A form of co-ownership of a multiple-dwelling building in which a corporation owns the building and the residents own shares in the corporation.
co-ownership A requirement for the formation of a general partnership that requires that the partners co-own the partnership business.
copyright A legal right that gives the author of qualifying subject matter, and who meets other requirements established by copyright law, the exclusive right to publish, produce, sell, license, and distribute the work.
copyright infringement An infringement that occurs when a party copies a substantial and material part of a plaintiff's copyrighted work without permission. A copyright holder may recover damages and other remedies against the infringer.
copyright registration certificate A certificate that is issued to a copyright holder who has properly registered his or her copyright with the U.S. Copyright Office.
Copyright Revision Act A federal statute that (1) establishes the requirements for obtaining a copyright and (2) protects copyrighted works from infringement.
Copyright Term Extension Act A federal statute that established the time periods for copyright protection.
corporate citizenship A theory of social responsibility that says a business has a responsibility to do good.
corporate criminal liability Criminal liability of corporations for actions of their officers, employees, or agents.
corporate electronic communications (corporate e-communications) The use of electronic communications (e-communication) by corporations to communicate with shareholders, among directors, with regulatory agencies, and with others.
corporate governance and nominating committee A committee of the board of directors of a corporation that examines the eligibility of nominees for the board of directors, reviews corporate governance principles and practices, and recommends board members' compensation.
corporate management Together, the directors and the officers of a corporation.
corporate officers Employees of a corporation who are appointed by the board of directors to manage the day-to-day operations of the corporation.
corporate seal A design containing the name of the corporation and the date of incorporation that is imprinted by the corporate secretary using a metal stamp on certain legal documents.
corporation A fictitious legal entity that is created according to statutory requirements.
corporation codes State statutes that regulates the formation, operation, and dissolution of corporations.
cost–benefit analysis The examination of relevant factors to determine whether to bring or settle a lawsuit.
cost justification defense A defense to a Robinson-Patman Act Section 2(a) price discrimination action that provides that a seller's price discrimination is not unlawful if the price differential is due to "differences in the cost of manufacture, sale, or delivery" of the product.
cost of supplies Payments made by a franchisee to the franchisor for supplies purchased from the franchisor.
Council of Ministers A council of the European Union (EU) that is composed of representatives from each member country who meet periodically to coordinate efforts to fulfill the objectives of the European Union.
Counterfeit Access Device and Computer Fraud and Abuse Act (CFAA) A federal statute that makes it a federal crime to access a computer knowingly to obtain (1) restricted federal government information, (2) financial records of financial institutions, or (3) consumer reports of consumer reporting agencies.
counteroffer A response by an offeree that contains terms and conditions different from or in addition to those of the offer. A counteroffer terminates an offer.
country code top-level domain (ccTLD) A top-level domain that is assigned to a country, territory, or sovereign state.
county recorder's office An office where deeds, mortgages, and other documents pertaining to real property located in the county are recorded and security interests in personal property are often recorded.
coupon settlement A settlement of a lawsuit in which the plaintiffs are given coupons to purchase the defendant's merchandise instead of being paid cash.
course of dealing The conduct of contracting parties in prior transactions and contracts.
course of performance Previous conduct of contracting parties concerning the contract in question.
court of chancery Court that grants relief based on fairness, which is also called an *equity court*; A special court of Delaware that hears and decides business cases.
covenant An unconditional promise to perform.
covenant not to compete (noncompete agreement) A contract that provides that a seller of a business, an employee, or another covered party will not engage in a similar business or occupation within a specified geographical area for a specified time following the sale of the business or termination of employment.
covenant of good faith and fair dealing An implied covenant under which the parties to a contract not only are held to the express terms of the contract but are also required to act in "good faith" and deal fairly in all respects in obtaining the objective of the contract.
covenant of quiet enjoyment An implied covenant that says a landlord may not interfere with the tenant's quiet and peaceful possession, use, and enjoyment of the leased premises.
cover The right of a buyer or lessee to purchase or lease substitute goods if a seller or lessor fails to make delivery of the goods or repudiates the contract or if the buyer or lessee rightfully rejects the goods or justifiably revokes their acceptance.

coworker An employee who is not a supervisor or manager.
cram-down provision A provision in bankruptcy law whereby the court can confirm a plan of reorganization over an objecting class of creditors if certain requirements are met.
crashworthiness doctrine A doctrine that says automobile manufacturers are under a duty to design automobiles so they take into account the possibility of harm from a person's body striking something inside the automobile in the case of a car accident.
creative employee exemption An exemption from federal minimum wage and overtime pay requirements that applies to employees compensated on a salary or fee basis, who perform work that requires invention, imagination, originality, or talent in a recognized field of artistic or creative endeavor.
credit A situation in which one party makes a loan to another party.
Credit Card Accountability Responsibility and Disclosure Act (Credit CARD Act) A federal statute that requires disclosures to consumers, adds transparency to the creditor–debtor relationship, and eliminates many of the abusive practices of credit card issuers.
credit report Information about a person's credit history that can be secured from a credit bureau.
creditor (lender) The lender in a credit transaction.
creditor beneficiary An original creditor who becomes a beneficiary under the debtor's new contract with another party.
creditor beneficiary contract A contract that arises in the following situation: (1) A debtor borrows money, (2) the debtor signs an agreement to pay back the money plus interest, (3) the debtor sells the item to a third party before the loan is paid off, and (4) the third party promises the debtor that he or she will pay the remainder of the loan to the original creditor.
creditor–debtor relationship A relationship that is created when a customer deposits its money into a bank; the customer is the creditor, and the bank is the debtor.
creditors' committee A committee of unsecured creditors that is appointed by the court to represent the class of unsecured claims. The court can also appoint committees for secured creditors and for equity holders.
crime A violation of a statute for which the government imposes a punishment.
criminal conspiracy A crime in which two or more persons enter into an agreement to commit a crime, and an overt act is taken to further the crime.
criminal fraud (false pretenses, deceit) A crime that involves obtaining title to property through deception or trickery.
criminal intent The requisite state of mind when an act was performed for an accused to be found guilty of an intent crime. Also called *mens rea* ("evil intent").
criminal law Laws that prohibit certain conduct and provide an incentive for persons to act reasonably in society and impose penalties on persons who violate them.
criminal RICO A federal statute that makes it a crime to acquire or maintain an interest in, use income from, or conduct or participate in the affairs of an enterprise through a pattern of racketeering activity.
Critical Legal Studies School A school of jurisprudential thought that maintains that legal rules are unnecessary and that legal disputes should be solved by applying arbitrary rules based on fairness.
critical legal thinking The process of investigating, analyzing, evaluating, and interpreting information to solve legal issues or cases.
cross-border IPO An initial public offering made in the United States by a company based in a foreign country.
cross-complainant A defendant who files a cross-complaint against a plaintiff.
cross-complaint A document filed by a defendant against a plaintiff to seek damages or some other remedy.
cross-defendant A plaintiff against whom a cross-complaint is filed by the defendant.
cross-examination Examination of the plaintiff's witnesses by the defendant and examination of the defendant's witnesses by the plaintiff.
crossover workers Individual members of a labor union that is on strike who choose not to strike and who remain working or return to work after joining the strikers for a time.
crowdfunding A funding mechanism that allows entrepreneurs and small business to raise up to $1 million in capital from public investors during a 12-month period by using an internet website funding portal.
crown jewel A valuable asset of a target corporation that the tender offeror particularly wants to acquire in a tender offer.
cruel and unusual punishment A clause of the Eighth Amendment to the U.S. Constitution that protects criminal defendants from torture and other cruel and abusive punishment.
cryptocurrency A digital currency or virtual currency that is a decentralized form of online currency that uses cryptography for security.
cumulative preferred stock Stock for which any missed dividend payments must be paid in the future to the preferred shareholders before the common shareholders can receive any dividends.
cumulative voting A system of shareholder voting for the board of directors of a corporation whereby each shareholder can *accumulate* all of his or her votes (determined by the number of directors to be elected multiplied by the number of shares the shareholder owns) and vote them all for a single candidate or split them among several candidates.
cure The legal right of a seller or lessor who has delivered defective or nonconforming goods to repair or replace the defective or nonconforming goods if the time for performance has not expired and the seller or lessor notifies the buyer or lessee of his or her intention to make a conforming delivery within the contract time.
Currency Transaction Report (CTR) A form that must be filed with the Internal Revenue Service (IRS) by financial institutions and other entities regarding certain cash transactions and suspected criminal activities.
custodial parent The parent who is awarded custody of a child in a divorce or annulment proceeding.
cyber insurance Insurance that protects an insured against liability for losses suffered by themselves or by their customers whose data has been stolen because of a cyberattack or hacking.
cybercrime Crimes that are committed using computers, email, the internet, and other electronic means.
cybersquatting A situation that occurs when a party registers a domain name that is the same as another party's trademarked name or a famous person's name.
d.b.a. (doing business as) A designation for a business that is operating under a trade name.
damages Money a buyer or lessee recovers from a seller or lessor who fails to deliver the goods or repudiates the contract. Damages are measured as the difference between the contract price (or original rent) and the market price (or rent) at the time the buyer or lessee learned of the breach.
debenture A long-term (often 30 years or more) unsecured debt instrument that is based on a corporation's general credit standing.
debit card A card that is issued to a bank customer that can be used to purchase goods and services. No credit is extended. Instead, the customer's bank account is immediately debited for the amount of a purchase.
debt collector An agent who collects debts for other parties.
debt securities (fixed income securities) Securities that establish a debtor–creditor relationship in which the corporation borrows money from the investor to whom a debt security is issued.
debtor (borrower) The borrower in a credit transaction.
debtor-in-possession A debtor who is left in place to operate the business during the reorganization proceeding.
decertification election An election to decertify a labor union that is held if some employees no longer want to be represented by a union. Decertification elections must be supervised by the NLRB.
declaration of duties If the delegatee has not assumed the duties under a contract, the delegatee is not legally liable to the oblige for nonperformance.
Declaration of Independence A document that declared the independence of the American colonies from England.
decree of dissolution An order issued by a court when it judicially dissolves a partnership, corporation, or other business entity.
decree of divorce A court order that terminates a marriage.
deductible clause A clause in an insurance policy that provides that insurance proceeds are payable only after the insured has paid a specified amount toward the damage or loss.

deed A document that describes a person's ownership interest in a piece of real property.

deed of trust An instrument that gives a creditor a security interest in the debtor's property that is pledged as collateral.

defamation of character False statement(s) made by one person about another. In court, the plaintiff must prove that (1) the defendant made an untrue statement of fact about the plaintiff and (2) the statement was intentionally or accidentally published to a third party.

default A situation that occurs when a debtor does not make the required payments on a debt.

default judgment A judgment that is entered against a defendant if he or she does not answer a plaintiff's complaint.

defect in design A defect that occurs when a product is improperly designed.

defect in manufacture A defect that occurs when a manufacturer fails to (1) properly assemble a product, (2) properly test a product, or (3) adequately check the quality of the product.

defect in packaging A defect that occurs when a product has been placed in packaging that is insufficiently tamper-proof.

defective formation A situation that occurs when a certificate of limited partnership of a limited partnership, articles of organization of a limited liability company, certificate of limited liability partnership of a limited liability partnership, or articles of incorporation of a corporation are not properly filed with the secretary of state or other required government agency, or there are defects in the document that is filed, or some other statutory requirement for the creation of the entity is not met.

Defend Trade Secrets Act (DTSA) A federal statute that allows an owner of a trade secret to bring a civil lawsuit in federal court against a defendant for the misappropriation of a trade secret.

defendant A party who is being sued.

defendant's case The part of a trial that occurs after the plaintiff has put on his or her case, when the defendant calls and examines witnesses and introduces evidence supporting his or her case.

defense attorney The lawyer who represents the accused defendant in a criminal trial.

deferred posting rule A rule that allows banks to fix an afternoon hour of 2:00 P.M. or later as a cutoff hour for the purpose of processing bank instruments.

deficiency judgment A judgment of a court that permits a secured lender to recover other property or income from a defaulting debtor if the collateral is insufficient to repay the unpaid loan.

degree of control A crucial factor in determining whether someone is an independent contractor or an employee is the *degree of control* that the principal has over that party.

Delaware Court of Chancery A Delaware state court that hears and decides cases involving business and corporate matters.

Delaware General Corporation Law A state statute that was enacted by the legislature of the state of Delaware that governs the formation, operation, and dissolution of corporations incorporated in the state of Delaware.

delegate To transfer a contractual duty by an obligor to another party for performance.

delegatee A party to whom a duty of performance has been transferred by a delegator.

delegation doctrine A doctrine that says that when an administrative agency is created, it is delegated certain powers; the agency can use only those legislative, judicial, and executive powers that are delegated to it.

delegation of a duty (delegation) A transfer of contractual duty by an obligor to another party for performance.

delegator An obligor who has transferred his or her duty of performance to another to complete.

delivery A donor of a gift must deliver the property to the donee.

delivery of possession An element for the creation of a bailment that requires that the bailee must have exclusive control over the personal property, and that the bailee must knowingly accept the personal property.

demand draft A draft payable on sight; also called a *sight draft*.

demand instrument An instrument that is payable on demand.

demand note A note payable on demand.

dental insurance Insurance that may be purchased to help cover the costs of dental care.

deponent A party who gives his or her deposition.

deposit The placement of funds by a customer into his or her checking or savings account at a bank or other financial institution.

deposit account Intangible personal property that includes demand, time, savings, passbook, or similar accounts maintained at a bank or financial institution.

deposition Oral testimony given by a party or witness prior to trial. The testimony is given under oath and is transcribed.

depository bank The bank where a payee or holder has an account.

derivative lawsuit (derivative action) A lawsuit a shareholder brings against an offending party on behalf of a corporation when the corporation fails to bring the lawsuit.

design patent A patent that may be obtained for the ornamental nonfunctional design of an item.

destination contract A contract that requires the seller to deliver the goods either to the buyer's place of business or to another destination specified in the sales contract.

devise A gift of real estate by will.

Digital Millennium Copyright Act (DMCA) A federal statute that prohibits unauthorized access to copyrighted digital works by circumventing encryption technology or the manufacture and distribution of technologies designed for the purpose of circumventing encryption protection of digital works.

dilution The lessening of the capacity of a famous mark to identify and distinguish its holder's goods and services. The two most common forms of dilution are *blurring* and *tarnishment*.

direct examination Examination of the plaintiff's witness by the plaintiff.

direct notice Express notice of the termination of an agency that needs to be given to all persons with whom the agent dealt.

direct price discrimination Price discrimination in which (1) the defendant sold commodities of like grade and quality, (2) to two or more purchasers at different prices at approximately the same time, and (3) the plaintiff suffered injury because of the price discrimination.

direct public offering (DPO) A security offering in which a company sells its securities directly to the public without using underwriters, investment banks, broker-dealers, or other intermediaries.

direct sex discrimination Discrimination by an employer who refuses to hire a qualified job applicant or to promote a qualified employee because of his or her gender.

directors' and officers' liability insurance (D&O insurance) Insurance that protects directors and officers of a corporation from liability for actions taken on behalf of the corporation.

disability insurance Insurance that provides a monthly income to an insured person who is disabled and cannot work.

disaffirm The act of a minor to rescind a contract under the infancy doctrine. Disaffirmance may be accomplished orally, in writing, or by the minor's conduct.

discharge Discharge from liability on negotiable instruments.

discharge by agreement Discharge of contractual duties under a contract by mutual assent of the parties.

discharge in bankruptcy A bankruptcy court order that relieves a debtor of the legal liability to pay his or her unpaid debts that were not required to be paid and remain unpaid in the bankruptcy proceeding.

disclaimer of consequential damages A contract provision that states that a breaching party is not responsible to pay consequential damages.

disclaimer of opinion A disclaimer issued by an auditor that states the auditor's inability to draw a conclusion about the accuracy of a company's financial records.

disclaimer of the implied warranty of fitness for a particular purpose The disclaimer of an implied warranty for particular purpose by language such as "as is" or general language that is in writing.

disclaimer of the implied warranty of merchantability The disclaimer of an implied warranty of merchantability by language such as "as is" or language that expressly mentions the term *merchantability*.

discovery A legal process during which each party engages in various activities to discover facts of the case from the other party and witnesses prior to trial.

discrimination Acts by employers, universities, public accommodations, and others that treat a person or a class of persons differently because of their race, color, national origin, gender, religion, age, disability, or other classes protected by law.

dishonored instrument An instrument that is presented for payment, and payment is refused.

disparagement (trade libel, product disparagement, or slander of title) False statements about a competitor's products, services, property, or business reputation. Also known as *trade libel, product disparagement*, and *slander of title*.

disparate-impact discrimination A form of discrimination that occurs when an employer discriminates against an entire protected class. An example would be discrimination in which a racially neutral employment practice or rule causes an adverse impact on a protected class.

disparate-treatment discrimination A form of discrimination that occurs when an employer discriminates against a specific individual because of his or her race, color, national origin, sex, or religion.

disposable income For bankruptcy purposes, income that is determined by taking the debtor's actual income and subtracting expenses for a typical family the same size as the debtor's family, as determined by government tables.

disposition of collateral A secured creditor's repossession of collateral upon a debtor's default and selling, leasing, or otherwise disposing of it in a commercially reasonable manner.

dissenting opinion An opinion written by a justice who does not agree with a decision of the majority of the justices wherein the justice sets forth the reasons for his or her dissent.

dissenting shareholder appraisal rights (appraisal rights) The rights of shareholders who object to a proposed merger, share exchange, or sale or lease of all or substantially all of the property of a corporation to have their shares valued by the court and receive cash payment of this value from the corporation.

dissociation The change in the relation of partners caused by any general partner ceasing to be associated in the carrying on of partnership business that does not cause dissolution of a general or limited partnership; the change in relation of members caused by a member ceasing to be associated with a limited liability company.

dissolution The change in the relation of partners caused by any general partner ceasing to be associated in the carrying on of the business of a general or limited partnership, or limited liability partnership, that causes dissolution of the partnership; The process of ending a limited liability company's existence or a corporation's existence.

distinctive A word or a design that is unique and therefore qualifies as a trademark.

distributional interest A member's ownership interest in a limited liability company (LLC) that entitles the member to receive distributions of money and property from the LLC.

distributorship franchise A business in which a franchisor manufactures a product and licenses a franchisee to distribute the product to the public.

district The area served by a U.S. district court.

diversity of citizenship A means for bringing a lawsuit in federal court that involves a nonfederal question but where the parties are (1) citizens of different states or (2) a citizen of a state and a citizen or subject of a foreign country.

dividend A distribution of profits of a corporation to shareholders.

dividend preference The right to receive a fixed dividend at stipulated periods during the year (e.g., quarterly).

division of markets (market sharing) A restraint of trade in which competitors agree that each will serve only a designated portion of the market. This is a *per se* violation of Section 1 of the Sherman Act as an unreasonable restraint of trade.

divorce A court order that terminates a marriage.

doctrine of sovereign immunity A doctrine that states that countries are granted immunity from suits in courts of other countries.

document of title A document, such as a warehouse receipt or bill of lading, that is required in some transactions of pickup and delivery.

Dodd-Frank Wall Street Reform and Consumer Protection Act (Dodd-Frank Act) A federal statute that reorganizes the federal government's supervision of the banking system, corrects abuses in the banking system, regulates previous unregulated financial products and institutions, ends abusive practices in the securities industry, establishes new federal consumer-debtor financial protection laws, and adds a new federal consumer protection agency to protect consumers from abusive lending practices.

domain name A unique internet name that identifies an individual's or a company's website.

domestic corporation A corporation in the state in which it is organized.

domestic limited liability company A limited liability company (LLC) in the state in which it is organized.

domestic limited liability partnership A limited liability partnership (LLP) in the state in which it is organized.

domestic limited partnership A limited partnership in the state in which it is organized.

dominant estate The real property that benefits from an easement appurtenant.

dominant party A person who has a dominant position over another person, taking advantage of the other person's mental, emotional, or physical weakness to unduly influence that person to enter into a contract.

donative intent The intent of a donor to make a gift.

donee A person who receives a gift.

donee beneficiary A third party on whom a benefit is to be conferred under a donee-beneficiary contract.

donee beneficiary contract A contract entered into with the intent to confer a benefit or gift on an intended third party.

donor A person who gives a gift.

Dormant Commerce Clause A name given to a situation that occurs when the federal government has chosen not to regulate an area of interstate commerce that it has the power to regulate under its Commerce Clause powers.

Do-Not-Call Implementation Act A federal statute that authorized the Federal Trade Commission (FTC) to create a registry on which consumers can place their names and personal mobile or residential telephone numbers to prevent most unsolicited commercial telephone calls.

Double Jeopardy Clause A clause of the Fifth Amendment to the U.S. Constitution that protects persons from being tried twice for the same crime.

double net lease A lease arrangement in which the tenant is responsible for paying rent, property taxes, and utilities.

double taxation Taxation that occurs where there is a C corporation because one tax is paid at the corporate level and another tax is paid on dividends received by shareholders on their personal income tax forms.

draft A three-party instrument that is an unconditional written order by one party (drawer) that orders a second party (drawee) to pay money to a third party (payee).

drawee of a check The financial institution where the drawer of a check has his or her account and who has been ordered to pay the check to a payee.

drawee of a draft The party who must pay the money stated in the draft; also called the *acceptor of a draft*.

drawer of a check The checking account holder and writer of a check.

drawer of a draft The party who writes the order for a draft.

drive-other coverage (D.O.C.) A clause that can be added to automobile insurance that protects the insured while driving other automobiles (e.g., rental cars).

Drug Efficacy Amendment An amendment to the Food, Drug, and Cosmetic Act (FDCA) that gives the Food and Drug Administration (FDA) broad powers to license new drugs in the United States.

dual agency A situation that occurs when an agent acts for two or more different principals in the same transaction. This practice is generally prohibited unless all the parties involved in the transaction agree to it.

dual-purpose mission An errand or another act that a principal requests of an agent to perform while the agent is on his or her own personal business.

due diligence defense A defense that accountants, lawyers, directors, managers, and others can assert, which, if proven, avoids liability under Section 11(a) of the Securities Act of 1933.

Due Process Clause A clause in the U.S. Constitution that provides that no person shall be deprived of "life, liberty, or property" without due process of the law.

dues checkoff A situation in which, upon proper notification by a labor union, employers are required to deduct union dues or agency fees from labor union employees' wages and forward these dues to the union.

durable power of attorney A power of attorney that remains effective even though the principal becomes incapacitated.

duress A situation in which one party threatens to do a wrongful act unless the other party enters into a contract.

duty not to commit waste A duty of a tenant not to commit waste to leased premises that causes substantial and permanent damage to the leased premises. Waste does not include ordinary wear and tear.

duty not to disturb other tenants A duty of a tenant not to disturb other tenants in the building. A landlord may evict a tenant who interferes with the use and quiet enjoyment of other tenants.

duty not to interfere with a tenant's right to quiet enjoyment A duty that a landlord owes to a tenant not to interfere with a tenant's right to quiet enjoyment of the leased premises.

duty not to use leased premises for illegal or nonstipulated purposes A duty of a tenant not to use leased premises for unlawful purposes (e.g., illegal gambling casino) or nonstipulated purposes (e.g., operating a restaurant in a residence).

duty not to willfully or wantonly injure a trespasser A duty that a landowner or tenant owes to a trespasser not to intentionally harm the trespasser beyond using lawful force to protect themselves and others from being harmed by the trespasser.

duty of care of corporate officers and directors A duty of corporate directors and officers to use care and diligence when acting on behalf of the corporation.

duty of care of individuals The obligation people owe each other not to cause any unreasonable harm or risk of harm.

duty of great care (duty of utmost care) A duty owed by a bailee in a *gratuitous* bailment for the sole benefit of the bailee not to be slightly negligent in caring for the bailed goods.

duty of limited care A fiduciary duty imposed on general partners of a general partnership and general partners of a limited partnership whereby a general partner owes a duty not to engage in the following conduct that would injure the partnership or other partners: (1) a known violation of law, (2) intentional conduct, (3) reckless conduct, or (4) grossly negligent conduct. A partner who commits an ordinarily negligent act is not liable to the partnership or other partners.

duty of loyalty A duty that directors and officers of a corporation owe not to act adversely to the interests of the corporation and to subordinate their personal interests to those of the corporation and its shareholders; A duty that a partner owes not to act adversely to the interests of the limited liability partnership; A duty owed by a member of a member-managed LLC and a manager of a manager-managed LLC to be honest in his or her dealings with the LLC and not act adversely to the interests of the LLC.

duty of loyalty of agents A fiduciary duty owed by an agent not to act adversely to the interests of the principal; A duty that a general partner of a general partnership and a general partner of a limited partnership owe not to act adversely to the interests of the partnership.

duty of obedience A duty that requires partners to adhere to the provisions of the partnership agreement and the decisions of the partnership; A duty that directors and officers owe to their corporation to act within the authority conferred upon them by state corporation codes, the articles of incorporation, the corporate bylaws, and the resolutions adopted by the board of directors.

duty of ordinary care A duty that a landowner or tenant owes to invitees and licensees to make the premises safe from, or to warn of, dangerous conditions posing an unreasonable risk of which the landowner or tenant has actual or constructive knowledge.

duty of reasonable care (duty of ordinary care) A duty owed by a bailee in a mutual benefit bailment for benefit both parties. This means that the bailee is liable for any goods that are lost, damaged, or destroyed because of his or her negligence.

duty of restitution A duty of an adult when a minor has disaffirmed a contract to return any money, property, or other valuables received from the minor, or if the consideration has been sold or has depreciated in value, then to pay the minor the cash equivalent; a minor owes a duty of restitution if the minor's intentional, reckless, or grossly negligent conduct caused the loss of value to the adult's property or if the minor misrepresented his or her age when entering into a contract.

duty of restoration A duty of a minor who has disaffirmed a contract to return the goods or property he or she has received from the other party in the condition it is in at the time of disaffirmance.

duty of slight care A duty owed by a bailee in a *gratuitous* bailment for the sole benefit of the bailor not to be grossly negligent in caring for the bailed goods.

duty of strict liability In a common carrier bailment arrangement, the duty owed by a common carrier whereby if the bailed goods are lost, damaged, destroyed, or stolen, the common carrier is liable even if the loss or damage was not due to its fault; In a situation involving an innkeeper, a common law rule that makes innkeepers strictly liable to guests for personal property that is lost or stolen from the innkeeper's premises even if the loss was not due to the innkeeper's fault.

duty to account (duty of accountability) A duty that an agent owes to maintain an accurate accounting of all transactions undertaken on the principal's behalf; also known as the *duty of accountability*; a duty owed by a general partner of a general partnership and a general partner of a limited partnership to account to the partnership of any property, profit, benefit derived by the partner in the conduct of partnership business or derived from the use of partnership property, including the appropriation of partnership property.

duty to compensate A duty that a principal owes to pay an agreed-upon amount to the agent either upon the completion of the agency or at some other mutually agreeable time.

duty to cooperate Unless otherwise agreed, the duty of a principal to cooperate with and assist the agent in the performance of the agent's duties and the accomplishment of the agency.

duty to defend A duty of the insurer to defend the insured against lawsuits or legal proceedings that involve a claim within the coverage of the insurance policy.

duty to deliver possession A duty a landlord owes to deliver possession of the leased premises to the lessee.

duty to indemnify A duty of a principal to indemnify the agent for any losses the agent suffers because of the principal's conduct.

duty to inform A duty a general partner owes to inform co-partners of all the information he or she possesses that is relevant to the affairs of the partnership.

duty to maintain the leased premises A duty of a landlord to maintain the leased premises as provided in the lease, by express law, and as implied by law.

duty to notify A duty of an agent to notify the principal of important information concerning the agency.

duty to notify laws State laws that require persons who see someone in peril to immediately report the incident to the proper authorities so that legal, fire, or medical help may respond.

duty to pay A duty of an insurer to pay legitimate claims up to the insurance policy limits.

duty to pay rent A duty of a commercial or residential tenant to pay the agreed-upon amount of rent for the leased premises to the landlord at the agreed-upon time and place.

duty to perform An agent's duty to a principal that includes (1) performing the lawful duties expressed in the contract and (2) meeting the standards of reasonable care, skill, and diligence implicit in all contracts.

duty to reimburse Unless otherwise agreed, the duty of a principal to reimburse the agent for expenses incurred by the agent if the expenses were (1) authorized by the principal, (2) within the scope of the agency, and (3) necessary to discharge the agent's duties in carrying out the agency.

duty to rescue laws State laws that require persons to render reasonable assistance to rescue others in peril if certain requirements are met and to do so would not endanger the rescuer.

e-proxy rule A rule of the Securities and Exchange Commission (SEC) that permits corporations subject to SEC jurisdiction to post proxy materials electronically on a designated website.

E-Verify A U.S. Citizenship and Immigration Services (USCIS) internet-based system to verify the employment eligibility of employees.

EAP exemptions (white-collar exemptions) Exemptions from federal overtime pay rules for white-collar workers who are paid a salary above a certain dollar amount and/or perform certain job duties.

easement A given or required right to make limited use of someone else's real property without owning or leasing it.

easement appurtenant An easement that is expressly created when the owner of one piece of real property purposefully grants an easement to the owner of an adjacent piece of real property to use the first piece of property in some specified way.

easement by implication An implied easement that is created when an owner subdivides a parcel of real property that has a beneficial appurtenant on it (e.g., road, path, well) that serves the entire parcel, and the purchasers of the subdivided pieces of property automatically acquire an easement to use the beneficial appurtenant.

easement by necessity An implied easement that is created if two parcels of real property are so situated that an easement over one parcel is strictly necessary for the use and enjoyment of the other parcel. Easements of necessity are often granted so that owners can reach "landlocked" property.
easement by prescription An implied easement whereby one party obtains the right to use a portion of another party's real property when the requirements for adverse possession are met.
easement by reservation An express easement that occurs where an owner sells real property that he or she owns to another party but reserves an easement on the sold property.
easement in gross An easement that expressly authorizes a person who does not own adjacent real property the right to use another party's nonadjacent real property in some specified way.
East African Community (EAC) A regional trading bloc of countries located in East Africa.
EB-1 Extraordinary Ability visa (EB-1 visa) A visa issued by the U.S. government that allows U.S. employers to employ foreign nationals in the United States who possess extraordinary ability for certain types of employment, such as having extraordinary ability in the sciences, arts, education, business, or athletics; who are outstanding professors and researchers; or who are multinational managers or executives employed by a firm outside the United States and who seek to continue to work for that firm in the United States.
EB-5 Investor visa (EB-5 visa) A visa that permits persons who invest a required amount of money in a commercial enterprise located in the United States, and who meet other established requirements, to immigrate to the United States.
economic adulteration The adulterating of food by adding a substance to increase the food's bulk or weight, to reduce its quality or strength, or to make it appear more valuable than it is.
Economic Community of West African States (ECOWAS) A regional trading bloc of countries located in West Africa.
Economic Espionage Act (EEA) A federal statute that makes it a crime for any person to convert a trade secret for his or her own or another's benefit, knowing or intending to cause injury to the owners of the trade secret.
economic injury Injury that is economic in nature that is usually compensated by monetary damages.
EDGAR The electronic data and record system of the Securities and Exchange Commission (SEC).
effect of illegality A doctrine that states that the courts will refuse to enforce or rescind an illegal contract and will leave the parties where it finds them.
effective date The date on which a registration of securities filed with the Securities and Exchange Commission (SEC) becomes effective.
effects on interstate commerce test A test developed by the U.S. Supreme Court to determine whether commerce is interstate commerce that can be regulated by the federal government.
Eighth Amendment An amendment to the U.S. Constitution that protects criminal defendants from *cruel and unusual punishment*.
Electoral College A group of persons composed of representatives appointed by state delegations to vote for a presidential candidate.
electronic Relating to technology having electrical, digital, magnetic, wireless, optical, electromagnetic, or similar capabilities.
electronic agent A computer program or an electronic or other automated means used independently to initiate an action or respond to electronic records or performances in whole or in part, without review or action by an individual.
electronic arbitration (e-arbitration) The arbitration of a dispute using online arbitration services.
electronic chattel paper Chattel paper evidenced in a record or records consisting of information stored in an electronic medium.
electronic commerce (e-commerce) The sale of goods and services or the licensing of intellectual property by computer over the internet.
Electronic Communications Privacy Act (ECPA) A federal statute that makes it a crime to intercept an electronic communication at the point of transmission, while in transit, when stored by a router or server or after receipt by the intended recipient. There are some exceptions to this law.
electronic contract (e-contract) A contract that is entered into electronically.
electronic contract law (e-contract law) Contract law that is based on electronic contracts (e-contracts) and electronic licenses (e-licenses).
electronic court (e-court or virtual court) A court that either mandates or permits the electronic filing of pleadings, briefs, and other documents related to a lawsuit; also called a *virtual courthouse*.
electronic discovery (e-discovery) A process whereby relevant electronic documents are discovered, exchanged, collected, preserved, and processed during a lawsuit.
electronic dispute resolution (e-dispute resolution) Use of online alternative dispute resolution services to resolve a dispute.
electronic filing (e-filing) The electronic filing of pleadings, briefs, and other documents related to a lawsuit.
electronic financing statement (e-financing statement) A financing statement in personal property that is electronic.
Electronic Fund Transfer Act (EFTA) A federal statute that regulates consumer electronic funds transfers.
electronic funds transfer system (EFTS) Computer and electronic technology that makes it possible for banks to offer electronic payment and collection systems to bank customers.
electronic initial public offering (e-public offering or e-IPO) The process of an issuer selling shares of stock to the public over the internet.
electronic lease contract (e-lease contract) A contract for the lease of goods that is in electronic form.
electronic license (e-license) A contract whereby the owner of software or a digital application grants limited rights to the owner of a computer or digital device to use the software or digital application for a limited period and under specified conditions.
electronic licensee (e-licensee) The owner of a computer or digital device to whom an electronic license (e-license) is granted to use another's software program or digital application.
electronic licensor (e-licensor) The owner of a software program or digital application that grants a license to someone to use the software program or digital application.
electronic mail (email) Electronic written communication between individuals and businesses using computers connected to the internet.
electronic mail contract (email contract) Contracts that are formed using email.
electronic mediation (e-mediation) The mediation of a dispute using online mediation services.
electronic record (e-record) A record that is created, generated, sent, communicated, received, or stored by electronic means.
electronic sales contract (e-sales contract) A contract for the sale of goods that is in electronic form.
electronic secured transaction (e-secured transaction) A secured transaction that is created electronically.
electronic securities transactions (e-securities transactions) The issuing of securities, trading in securities, disseminating information to investors, managing securities accounts online, and other securities activities being conducted electronically.
electronic signature (e-signature or digital signature) A signature that is inscribed using an electronic means.
Electronic Signatures in Global and National Commerce Act (E-Sign Act) A federal statute that (1) recognizes electronic contracts as meeting the writing requirement of the Statute of Frauds and (2) recognizes and gives electronic signatures—e-signatures—the same force and effect as pen-inscribed signatures on paper.
electronically stored information (ESI) Electronic and digital information that includes Microsoft Word documents, Excel spreadsheets, emails, instant messages, text messages, cloud storage, phone records, pdfs of key files, PowerPoint slides, photographs, audio and visual files, social media posts, website captures, metadata, and other digital information.
email spam Unsolicited commercial email.
emancipation A minor's act of legally separating from his or her parents and providing for himself or herself.
embezzlement The fraudulent conversion of property by a person to whom that property was entrusted.
Emergency Planning and Community Right-to-Know Act (EPCRA) A federal statute that is designed to help communities prepare for chemical emergencies.

emerging growth company (EGC) A class of public company used by entrepreneurs and high-tech companies that meet certain requirements who then can sell securities to the public without having to meet many of the issuer requirements of the Securities and Exchange Commission (SEC) that would be applicable to larger companies.
eminent domain The government's power to take private property for public use, provided that just compensation is paid to the private property holder.
Employee Retirement Income Security Act (ERISA) A federal statute designed to prevent fraud and other abuses associated with private pension funds.
employee stock ownership plan (ESOP) A plan that places a certain percentage of a corporation's securities in the plan for distribution to employees of the corporation.
employer–employee relationship A relationship that results when an employer hires an employee to perform some task or service but the employee has not been authorized to enter into contracts on behalf of his or her employer.
employer lockout An act of an employer to prevent employees from entering the work premises when the employer reasonably anticipates a strike.
employment discrimination Discrimination by an employer against an employee or a prospective employee based on race, national origin, color, gender, religion, age, disability, veteran status, and other protected classes.
employment-related injury A requirement that employees who are awarded workers' compensation benefits have suffered from injuries that have arisen out of and in the course of their employment.
***en banc* review** The review of a decision of a three-judge panel by the all of the justices of a U.S. court of appeals.
encryption technology Technology and software that protect copyrighted works from unauthorized access.
Endangered Species Act (ESA) A federal statute that protects endangered and threatened species of wildlife.
endorsement (rider) A document that modifies an insurance policy and becomes part of the insurance policy.
engagement Occurs when an accountant and client enter into a contract for the provision of accounting services by the accountant; A period of time that begins when a person proposes marriage to another person, the other person accepts, and the person who proposed gives the other person an engagement ring (usually a diamond ring); the engagement period ends when the parties are married or if one or both of the parties terminate the engagement.
English common law Law developed by judges who issued their opinions when deciding a case. The principles announced in these cases became precedent for deciding similar cases in the future.
English rule A rule that stipulates that where there have been successive assignments of the same contract right, the first person to give notice to the obligor prevails.
entrepreneur A person who forms and operates a new business either by himself or herself or with others.
entrustment rule A rule that states that if the owner of goods entrusts the possession of these goods to a merchant who deals in goods of that kind (e.g., for repair or consignment), the merchant has the power to transfer all rights (including title) in the goods to a buyer in the ordinary course of business. The real owner cannot reclaim the goods from this buyer.
enumerated powers Certain powers delegated to the federal government.
environmental impact statement (EIS) A document that must be prepared for any proposed legislation or major federal action that significantly affects the quality of the human environment.
environmental protection Actions and laws that protect the nation's and world's air and water from pollution, reduce the harm from hazardous wastes, and protect wildlife.
Environmental Protection Agency (EPA) A federal administrative agency created by Congress to coordinate the implementation and enforcement of the federal environmental protection laws.
environmental protection laws Laws enacted by federal and state governments to protect air and water from pollution, reduce the harm from hazardous wastes, and protect wildlife.
Equal Access to Justice Act A federal statute that protects persons from harassment by federal administrative agencies and provides monetary penalties.
Equal Credit Opportunity Act (ECOA) A federal statute that prohibits discrimination in the extension of credit based on sex, marital status, race, color, national origin, religion, age, or receipt of income from public assistance programs.
equal dignity rule A rule that says that real estate agents' contracts to sell the real property of another are covered by the Statute of Frauds and must be in writing to be enforceable.
Equal Employment Opportunity Commission (EEOC) A federal administrative agency that is responsible for enforcing most federal antidiscrimination laws.
equal opportunity in employment The right of all employees and job applicants (1) to be treated without discrimination and (2) to be able to sue employers if they are discriminated against.
Equal Pay Act A federal statute that protects both sexes from pay discrimination based on sex. It extends to jobs that require equal skill, equal effort, equal responsibility, and similar working conditions.
Equal Protection Clause A clause that provides that a state cannot "deny to any person within its jurisdiction the equal protection of the laws."
equipment Tangible personal property such as trucks, cranes, assembly line equipment, and other equipment.
equitable distribution A law used by many states by which the court orders a fair distribution of marital property to the divorcing spouses.
equitable remedies A remedy that is available if there has been a breach of contract that cannot be adequately compensated through a legal remedy or to prevent unjust enrichment.
equity A doctrine that permits judges to make decisions based on fairness, equality, moral rights, and natural law.
equity securities (stocks) Representation of ownership rights to a corporation; also called *stocks*.
equivocal response An offeree's response to an offer that is not clear, is not unambiguous, or has more than one possible meaning. An offeree's equivocal response to an offer does not create a contract.
error of law Error regarding law decisions made by a court during a trial.
escheat A rule of state law that provides that if the deceased dies intestate without a will or trust and there are no surviving relatives, then the deceased's property belongs to the state.
Establishment Clause A clause of the First Amendment to the U.S. Constitution that prohibits the government from either establishing a state religion or promoting one religion over another.
estate in land (estate) Ownership rights in real property; the bundle of legal rights that the owner has to possess, use, and enjoy the property; also known as *estate*.
estate *pur autre vie* A life estate that is measured by the life of a third party.
estop A doctrine that prevents a promisor from revoking his or her promise even though there is lack of consideration.
estopped A doctrine that states that when an apparent agency has been established the principal is prevented from denying the agency relationship.
estray statute A statute that permits a finder of mislaid or lost property to clear title to the property if certain prescribed legal formalities are met.
ethical fundamentalism A theory of ethics that says a person looks to an outside source for ethical rules or commands.
ethical relativism A theory of ethics that holds that individuals must decide what is ethical, based on their own feelings about what is right and wrong.
ethics A set of moral principles or values that governs the conduct of an individual or a group.
ethics and the law The relationship between ethics and the law. Sometimes the rule of law and the rule of ethics demand the same response by a person confronted with a problem, while in other situations the law may permit an act that is ethically wrong.
euro A single monetary unit that has been adopted by many countries of the EU that compose the *eurozone*.
European Union (EU) A regional international organization that comprises many countries of Western and Eastern Europe and was created to promote peace and security as well as economic, social, and cultural development.
European Union Commission A commission that is independent of its member nations, that has been delegated substantial powers, including authority to enact legislation and to take enforcement actions to ensure member nations' compliance with the European Union treaty.
eurozone Countries of the European Union that use the euro as their currency.

eviction proceeding (unlawful detainer action) A legal process that a landlord must complete to *evict* a holdover tenant.
exclusionary rule A rule that says evidence obtained from an unreasonable search and seizure can generally be prohibited from introduction at a trial or an administrative proceeding against the person searched.
exclusions from coverage A clause in an insurance policy that expressly stipulates the risks that are not covered by the insurance policy.
exclusive agency contract A contract a principal and an agent enter into that says the principal cannot employ any agent other than the exclusive agent.
exclusive jurisdiction Sole jurisdiction of a federal court to hear and decide cases involving specified subject matters.
exclusive license A license in which, for the specified duration of the license, the licensor will not grant to any other person rights to the same information.
exclusive possession A lessee's exclusive right to leased premises for the term of the lease or until the tenant defaults on the obligations under the lease.
exclusive remedy A sole remedy for employees who are covered by workers' compensation and have been injured on the job. Thus, workers have given up their right to sue their employer for damages. There are several exceptions to this rule.
exclusive territory A geographical area assigned by a franchisor for a franchisee to serve that is exclusive to the franchisee; the franchisor cannot grant other franchises in this territory.
exculpatory agreement (release of liability agreement) An agreement that relieves one (or both) of the parties to a contract from tort liability for ordinary negligence.
executed contract A contract that has been fully performed on both sides; a completed contract.
execution A post-judgment court order that permits the seizure of the debtor's property that is in the possession of the debtor.
executive branch The part of the government that consists of the president and vice president.
executive committee A committee of the board of directors of a corporation, usually consisting of the chairman of the board, chief executive officer, and other key directors and officers, that has the power to act as the full board in case of emergencies.
executive employee exemption An exemption from federal minimum wage and overtime pay requirements that applies to executives who are compensated on a salary basis, who engage in management, who have authority to hire employees, and who regularly direct two or more employees.
executive order An order issued by a member of the executive branch of the government.
executive power The power of an administrative agency to investigate and prosecute possible violations of statutes, administrative rules, and administrative orders.
executor (male) or executrix (female) A personal representative who is named in a testator's or testatrix's will who is appointed to administer the estate during the probate of a will.
executory agreement (executory contract) A contract that has not been fully performed by either or both sides.
executory contract In bankruptcy law, a contract that has not been fully performed. With the bankruptcy court's approval, a debtor may reject executory contracts in bankruptcy.
exempt property Property that may be retained by a debtor pursuant to federal or state law that does not become part of the bankruptcy estate.
exempt securities Securities that are exempt from registration with the Securities and Exchange Commission (SEC).
exempt transactions Transactions in which securities are issued but are exempt from registration with the Securities and Exchange Commission (SEC) because they meet specified requirements. The most widely used exempt transactions include the *non-issuer exemption, intrastate offering exemption, private placement exemption*, and *small offering exemption*.
Exon-Florio Foreign Investment Provision A federal law that mandates that the president of the United States suspend, prohibit, or dismantle the acquisition of a U.S. business by foreign investors if there is credible evidence that the foreign investor might take action that threatens to impair national security.
expertised portion A portion of a registration statement that is filed with the Securities and Exchange Commission (SEC) that is prepared by accountants and other experts.
exporter The seller in an international sales contract that is located in one country and that is selling goods to a buyer located in another country.
express agency An agency that occurs when a principal and an agent expressly agree to enter into an agency agreement with each other.
express authorization A means of communication for accepting an offer to enter into a contract that is specified in the offer (e.g., registered mail).
express bailment A bailment that is either written or oral.
express condition A condition in a contract that the parties have agreed on.
express contract An agreement that is expressed in written or oral words.
express easements Easements that are created by words and must be in writing. Express easements include the following: (1) *easement appurtenant*, (2) *easement in gross*, (3) *easement by reservation*, and (4) *negative easement*.
express powers Powers given to a corporation by (1) the U.S. Constitution, (2) state constitutions, (3) federal statutes and state statutes, (4) corporation codes, (5) articles of incorporation, (6) bylaws, and (7) resolutions of the board of directors.
express terms Terms in offers and contracts that expressly identify the parties, the subject matter of the offer or contract, the consideration to be paid by the parties, and the time of performance, as well as other terms of the offer and contract.
express trust A trust created voluntarily by the settlor.
express warranty A warranty that is created when a seller or lessor makes an affirmation that the goods he or she is selling or leasing meet certain standards of quality, description, performance, or condition.
ex-ship (from the carrying vessel) A shipping term that requires the seller to bear the expense and risk of loss until the goods are unloaded from the ship at its port of destination.
extension A provision that allows a debtor a longer period of time to pay his or her debts.
extension clause A clause in an instrument that allows the date of maturity of an instrument to be extended to sometime in the future.
extension of credit Occurs where a lender loans money to a borrower.
extortion (blackmail) A threat to expose something about another person unless that other person gives money or property; often referred to as *blackmail*.
extortion under color of official right Extortion of a public official.
F-1 visa A visa issued to foreign nationals to study at colleges and universities and English language programs in the United States.
F-2 visa A visa issued to spouses and unmarried children under the age of 21 of a foreign national who has been granted an F-1 visa to study at colleges and universities and English language programs in the United States.
failing company doctrine A doctrine that permits a competitor to merge with another competitor that is a failing company if there is no other reasonable alternative for the failing company.
failure to provide adequate instructions A defect that occurs when a manufacturer does not provide detailed directions for safe assembly and use of a product.
failure to warn A defect that occurs when a manufacturer or seller of a product fails to place an adequate warning on the packaging on the product that could cause injury if the danger is unknown.
Fair and Accurate Credit Transactions Act (FACTA) A federal statute that gives consumers the right to obtain one free credit report each year from credit reporting agencies, permits consumers to purchase their credit score, and allows consumers to place fraud alerts in their credit files.
Fair Credit and Charge Card Disclosure Act An amendment to the Truth-in-Lending Act (TILA) that requires disclosure of certain credit terms on credit- and charge-card solicitations and applications.
Fair Credit Billing Act (FCBA) A federal statute that regulates billing errors involving consumer credit and requires that creditors promptly acknowledge in writing consumer billing complaints and investigate billing errors.
Fair Credit Reporting Act (FCRA) An amendment to the Truth-in-Lending Act (TILA) that protects customers who are subjects of a credit report by setting out guidelines for credit bureaus.
Fair Debt Collection Practices Act (FDCPA) A federal statute that protects consumer debtors from abusive, deceptive, and unfair practices used by debt collectors.

Fair Employment Practice Agency (FEPA) A state agency that some states have where a complainant may file his or her employment discrimination claim instead of with the federal Equal Employment Opportunity Commission (EEOC).
Fair Housing Act of 1968 A federal statute that makes it unlawful for a party to refuse to rent or sell a dwelling to any person because of his or her race, color, national origin, sex, or religion.
Fair Labor Standards Act (FLSA) A federal statute enacted to protect workers. It prohibits child labor and sets minimum wage and overtime pay requirements.
fair price rule (best price rule) A rule that says any increase in price paid for shares tendered must be offered to all shareholders, even those who have previously tendered their shares.
fair use doctrine A doctrine that permits certain limited use of a copyright by someone other than the copyright holder without the permission of the copyright holder.
false and deceptive advertising Advertising that contains misinformation or omits important information that is likely to mislead a reasonable consumer or that makes unsubstantiated claims.
false and misleading labeling or packaging Labeling that contains misinformation or omits important information that is likely to mislead a reasonable consumer or that makes unsubstantiated claims. The Food, Drug, and Cosmetic Act (FDCA) prohibits false and misleading labeling of food products.
false and misleading statements Statements made on labels of meat and poultry products that are false and misleading.
false imprisonment The intentional confinement or restraint of another person without authority or justification and without that person's consent.
Family and Medical Leave Act (FMLA) A federal statute that guarantees workers up to 12 weeks of unpaid leave in a 12-month period to attend to family and medical emergencies and other specified situations.
family limited partnership (FLP) A limited partnership that is formed to own family businesses or investments.
Family Smoking Prevention and Tobacco Control Act (Tobacco Control Act) A federal statute that authorizes the Food and Drug Administration (FDA) to place restrictions on distribution, advertising, and marketing tobacco products to children.
Family Support Act A federal statute that provides for the automatic wage withholding of child support payments from a noncustodial parent's income.
F.A.S. (free alongside ship) port of shipment or F.A.S. (vessel) port of shipment A shipping term that requires the seller to deliver and tender the goods alongside the named vessel or on the dock designated and provided by the buyer.
farm products Tangible personal property such as crops, livestock, aquatic goods, and supplies produced in farming operations.
fault rule In an engagement situation, a rule that states that if the person who gave the engagement ring breaks off the engagement, the other side gets to keep the engagement ring; if the person who has accepted an engagement ring breaks off the engagement, that person must return the engagement ring.
federal administrative agencies Administrative agencies that are created by the executive or legislative branch of federal government.
federal antitrust statutes Federal statutes that regulate anticompetitive behavior and monopoly business practices.
Federal Arbitration Act (FAA) A federal statute that provides for the enforcement of most arbitration agreements.
Federal Communications Commission (FCC) A federal administrative agency that is empowered to enforce the Telephone Consumer Protection Act (TCPA) and adopt rules and regulations to implement the law.
Federal Deposit Insurance Corporation (FDIC) A government agency that insures deposits at most banks and savings institutions ("insured banks") in the United States.
federal government The government of the United States of America.
Federal Insecticide, Fungicide, and Rodenticide Act (FIFRA) A federal statute that requires pesticides, herbicides, fungicides, and rodenticides to be registered with the EPA; the EPA may deny, suspend, or cancel registration.
Federal Insurance Contributions Act (FICA) A federal statute that requires certain employees to make contributions (pay taxes) into the Social Security fund.
federal minimum wage A requirement of the Fair Labor Standards Act (FLSA), a federal statute, that workers be paid a minimum wage. The federal minimum wage is set by Congress and can be changed. States and local governments may set minimum wages that are higher than the federal minimum wage.
Federal Motor Vehicle Safety Standards (FMVSS) Safety regulations that have been issued by the National Highway Traffic Safety Administration (NHTSA) to reduce the number of fatalities and injuries caused by automobiles and other vehicles.
Federal Patent Statute A federal statute that establishes the requirements for obtaining a patent and protects patented inventions from infringement.
federal question case A means for bringing a lawsuit in federal court because it arises under the U.S. Constitution, treaties, federal statutes, federal regulations, or executive orders.
Federal Register A public register in which federal administrative agencies must publish agency procedures, rules, regulations, interpretations, and other such information.
Federal Reserve System (Federal Reserve, the Fed) A system of 12 regional Federal Reserve banks that assist other banks in the collection of checks.
federal securities statutes Federal statutes that regulate the issuance of and trading in securities.
federal statutes Statutes enacted by the U.S. Congress.
Federal Trade Commission (FTC) A federal administrative agency that is empowered to enforce the Federal Trade Commission Act (FTC Act), the Do-Not-Call Implementation Act, and other federal consumer protection statutes.
Federal Trade Commission Act (FTC Act) A federal statute, enacted in 1914, that creates certain consumer protections, regulates business conduct, prohibits unfair and deceptive practices, and grants certain antitrust powers to the Federal Trade Commission (FTC).
Federal Trademark Dilution Act (FTDA) A federal statute that protects famous marks from dilution, erosion, blurring, or tarnishing.
Federal Unemployment Tax Act (FUTA) A federal statute that requires employers to pay unemployment taxes; unemployment compensation is paid to workers who are temporarily unemployed.
Federal Water Pollution Control Act (FWPCA) A federal statute that regulates water pollution.
federalism The U.S. form of government in which the federal government and the 50 state governments share powers.
fee simple absolute (fee simple) A type of ownership of real property that grants the owner the full bundle of legal rights that a person can hold in real property.
fee simple defeasible (qualified fee) A type of ownership of real property that grants the owner all the incidents of a fee simple absolute except that it may be taken away if a specified condition occurs or does not occur.
felony The most serious type of crime; inherently evil crime. Most crimes against persons and some business-related crimes are felonies.
felony murder rule A rule that stipulates that if a murder is committed during the commission of another crime, even though the perpetrator did not originally intend to commit murder, the perpetrator is liable for the crime of murder.
fictitious business name statement (certificate of trade name) A document that is filed with the state that designates a trade name of the business, the name and address of the applicant, and the address of the business.
fictitious payee rule A rule that states that a drawer or maker is liable on a forged or unauthorized indorsement of a fictitious payee.
Fifth Amendment An amendment to the U.S. Constitution that provides that no person "shall be compelled in any criminal case to be a witness against himself." Thus, a person cannot be compelled to give testimony against himself. The right is referred to as the *privilege against self-incrimination*. The Fifth Amendment also contains the *Double Jeopardy Clause,* which protects persons from being tried twice for the same crime.
final judgment Judgment of a trial court entered after all post-trial motions are decided.
final prospectus A document that must be made available either in writing or electronically by the issuer of securities to purchasers of issued securities before or at the time of the purchase of the securities.
finance lease A three-party lease transaction of goods consisting of a lessor, a lessee, and a supplier.

financing statement A document filed by a secured creditor with the appropriate government office that constructively notifies the world of his or her security interest in personal property.
finding of fact A decision regarding the facts of a case made by a jury, or if there is no jury, then by the judge.
firm offer rule A UCC rule that says that a merchant who (1) makes an offer to buy, sell, or lease goods and (2) assures the other party in a separate writing that the offer will be held open cannot revoke the offer for the time stated or, if no time is stated, for a reasonable time.
First Amendment An amendment to the U.S. Constitution that guarantees freedom of speech, freedom to assemble, freedom of the press, and freedom of religion.
first purchase money mortgage A mortgage (or deed of trust and note) taken out to purchase a house.
first-degree murder The intentional unlawful killing of a human being by another person with premeditation, malice aforethought, and willful act.
first-to-file rule A rule that stipulates that the first person to file a patent on an invention receives the patent even though some other party was the first to invent the invention. This rule superseded the *first-to-invent rule*.
first-to-invent rule A rule that stipulates that the first person to invent an item or a process is given patent protection over a later inventor who was first to file a patent application. This rule has been superseded by the *first-to-file rule*.
FISA warrant A warrant issued by the Foreign Intelligence Surveillance Court (FISA Court) that permits physical and electronic surveillance of Americans or foreigners in the United States who are deemed a threat to national security.
fixed amount of money A requirement that a negotiable instrument contain a promise or an order to pay a fixed amount of money. A requirement of a negotiable instrument that ensures that the value of the instrument can be determined with certainty.
fixed dividend A preferred dividend that is paid at set periods during the year (e.g., quarterly).
fixture Personal property that is permanently affixed to land or buildings.
flip-in rights plan A defensive plan of a corporation that provides that existing shareholders of the corporation may convert their shares for a greater number (e.g., twice the value) of debt instruments of the corporation once a specified percentage of its shares have been acquired by an acquiring corporation.
flip-over rights plan A defensive plan of a corporation that provides that existing shareholders of the corporation may convert their shares for a greater number (e.g., twice the value) of shares of an acquiring corporation once a specified percentage of its shares have been acquired by the acquiring corporation.
floating lien A security interest in property that was not in the possession of the debtor when the security agreement was executed.
flow-through taxation A tax rule that provides that the income and losses of a sole proprietorship, general partnership, limited partnership, limited liability company, limited liability partnership, limited liability limited partnership, and S corporation are reported on the owner's personal income tax return.
F.O.B. (free on board) place of destination A shipping term that requires the seller to bear the expense and risk of loss of goods until the goods are tendered to the buyer at the place of destination.
F.O.B. (free on board) point of shipment A shipping term that requires the seller to arrange to ship the goods and put the goods in the carrier's possession.
Food and Drug Administration (FDA) A federal administrative agency that administers and enforces the federal Food, Drug, and Cosmetic Act and other federal consumer protection laws.
Food, Drug, and Cosmetic Act (FDCA or FDC Act) A federal statute that provides the basis for the regulation of much of the testing, manufacture, distribution, and sale of food, drugs, cosmetics, and medicinal products.
food label claims Claims made on food labels regarding calories, cholesterol, fat, sugar, and other information. The Food and Drug Administration (FDA) has established legal definitions for most commonly used food label claims.
***force majeure* clause** A clause in a contract in which the parties specify certain events that will excuse nonperformance.
foreclosing competition A situation that occurs in a vertical merger if competitors of the merged firms are prevented (foreclosed) from either selling goods or services to, or buying goods or services from, the merged firm.
foreclosure sale A legal procedure by which a secured creditor causes the judicial sale of the secured real estate to pay a defaulted loan.
Foreign Commerce Clause A clause of the U.S. Constitution that vests Congress with the power "to regulate commerce with foreign nations."
foreign corporation A corporation in any state other than the one in which it is organized.
Foreign Corrupt Practices Act (FCPA) A federal statute that makes it illegal for a U.S. citizen or resident or U.S. companies or their officers, directors, agents, shareholders, employees, partners, or intermediaries to bribe a foreign official, a foreign political party official, a candidate for foreign political office, or an official of a public international organization, where the bribe is intended to influence the official's act or decision such that the bribing party obtains or retains business or secures an improper advantage.
foreign guest worker A person from a foreign country who is permitted to work in the United States pursuant to a visa issued by the U.S. government.
Foreign Investment Risk Review Modernization Act (FIRRMA) A federal statute that prohibits foreign companies, persons, and enterprises owned by foreign governments or agencies from acquiring sensitively located real estate; non-controlling interests in U.S. businesses involved in critical technologies, critical infrastructure, or sensitive personal data of U.S. citizens; and joint ventures that involve the transfer of U.S.-origin technology.
foreign limited liability company A limited liability company (LLC) in any state other than the one in which it is organized.
foreign limited liability partnership A limited liability partnership (LLP) in any state other than the one in which it is organized.
foreign limited partnership A limited partnership in any state other than the one in which it is organized.
foreign registration statement A statement that must be filed by a foreign corporation with the secretary of state of a state other than the state of its own jurisdiction before conducting business in the other state.
Foreign Sovereign Immunities Act (FSIA) A federal statute that exclusively governs suits against foreign nations that are brought in federal or state courts in the United States. It codifies the principle of *qualified, or restricted, immunity*.
foreign substance test A test to determine merchantability based on foreign objects found in food.
foreseeability standard A rule that says that an accountant is liable for negligence to third parties who are members of a foreseen class of users of the client's financial statements. It provides the broadest standard for holding accountants liable to third parties for negligence.
foreseen class of users Users of financial statements of a business that are prepared by an accountant who are foreseeable users of the financial statements. The accountant's liability does not depend on his or her knowledge of the identity of either the user or the intended class of users.
forged indorsement The forged signature of a payee or holder on a negotiable instrument.
forged instrument A check with a forged drawer's signature on it.
forgery The fraudulent making or alteration of a written document that affects the legal liability of another person.
form Contract law that requires that certain contracts must be in a certain form to be enforceable.
Form C A form that must be filed with the Securities and Exchange Commission (SEC) before an offeror may raise funds pursuant to the SEC Crowdfunding Regulation.
Form D A form that must be filed with the Securities and Exchange Commission (SEC) by a company within 15 days after the sale of securities pursuant to the small offering exemption.
Form 1040 A personal income tax form that is filed by a sole proprietor with the federal government that reports his or her personal income.
Form 2553 A form that is filed with the Internal Revenue Service (IRS) to elect Subchapter S federal income tax status for a qualifying corporation.
Form I-9, Employment Eligibility Verification A form that employers must obtain from every prospective employee, regardless of citizenship or national origin, with supporting documents, that demonstrates whether the prospective employee is either a U.S. citizen

or otherwise authorized to work in the country (e.g., has a proper work visa).
Form S-1 A registration statement that must be filed with the Securities and Exchange Commission (SEC) by companies who intend to issue securities to the public in a public offering. It must include information about the company, its business, the company's financial statements, and other relevant information.
formal contract A contract that requires a special form, words, or method of creation.
formal rulemaking Rulemaking by an administrative agency that involves conducting a trial-like hearing at which parties may present evidence, engage in cross-examination, and present rebuttal evidence before the agency decides whether to adopt the proposed rule.
formal will A document that contains a declaration of how a person wants his or her property to be distributed upon his or her death.
Formerly Incarcerated Reenter Society Transformed Safely Transitioning Every Person Act (First Step Act) A federal act that reforms sentencing laws, steers federal prisons toward rehabilitation rather than just punishment, reduces recidivism, and provides nonviolent offenders the opportunity to reenter society as productive citizens.
for-profit corporation (profit corporation) A corporation created to conduct a business for profit that can distribute profits to shareholders in the form of dividends.
forum shopping A party's looking for a favorable court in which to bring a lawsuit without a valid reason for being in that court.
forum-selection clause (choice-of-forum clause) A clause in a contract that designates that a certain court has jurisdiction to hear and decide a case arising out of the contract. Also called a *choice of forum clause*.
forward vertical merger (downstream vertical merger) A vertical merger in which a supplier acquires a customer.
Fourteenth Amendment An 1868 amendment added to the U.S. Constitution that contains the Due Process, Equal Protection, and Privileges and Immunities clauses.
Fourth Amendment An amendment to the U.S. Constitution that protects the right of the people to be free from *unreasonable search and seizure* by the government.
franchise An arrangement that is established when one party (the *franchisor*) licenses another party (the *franchisee*) to use the franchisor's trade name, trademarks, commercial symbols, patents, copyrights, and other property in the distribution and selling of goods and services.
franchise agreement An agreement that a franchisor and franchisee enter into that sets forth the terms and conditions of a franchise.
franchise application An application filed by a prospective franchisee to obtain a franchise from a franchisor. The application includes detailed financial and other information about the applicant.
franchisee (licensee) A party who is granted a franchise and license by a franchisor in a franchise arrangement.
franchisor (licensor) A party who grants a franchise and license to a franchisee in a franchise arrangement.
Frank R. Lautenberg Chemical Safety for the 21st Century Act (Lautenberg Chemical Safety Act) A federal statute that requires the Environmental Protection Agency (EPA) to evaluate the safety of existing chemicals used in commerce and to make an affirmative determination on proposed new chemicals before they can be manufactured and distributed in commerce.
fraud (fraudulent misrepresentation) An event that occurs when one person consciously decides to induce another person to rely and act on a misrepresentation.
fraud by concealment Fraud that occurs when one party takes specific action to conceal a material fact from another party.
fraud in the inception (fraud in the factum) Fraud that occurs if a person is deceived as to the nature of his or her act and does not know what he or she is signing.
fraud in the inducement Fraud that occurs when the party knows what he or she is signing but has been fraudulently induced to enter into the contract.
fraudulent transfer A transfer of a debtor's property or an obligation incurred by a debtor within two years of the filing of a petition, where (1) the debtor had actual intent to hinder, delay, or defraud a creditor or (2) the debtor received less than a reasonable equivalent in value.
Free Exercise Clause A clause of the First Amendment to the U.S. Constitution that prohibits the government from interfering with the free exercise of religion in the United States.
Freedom of Information Act (FOIA) A federal statute that gives the public the ability to obtain access to most documents in the possession of federal administrative agencies. Some documents are protected from disclosure because of national security and other reasons.
freedom of religion A right established in the First Amendment to the U.S. Constitution.
freedom of speech The right to engage in oral, written, and symbolic speech that is protected by the First Amendment to the U.S. Constitution.
freehold estate An estate in which the owner has a present possessory interest in the real property. There are three types of freehold estates: *fee simple absolute* (or *fee simple*), *fee simple defeasible* (or *qualified fee*), and *life estate*.
freely transferrable Unless otherwise agreed, the shares of a corporation are freely transferable by a shareholder by sale, assignment, pledge, or gift.
French Civil Code of 1804 (Napoleonic Code) A civil law based on a code of laws.
fresh start The goal of federal bankruptcy law to grant a debtor relief from some of his or her burdensome debts while protecting creditors by requiring the debtor to pay more of his or her debts than would otherwise have been required prior to the 2005 act.
frolic and detour A situation in which an agent does something during the course of his or her employment to further his or her own interests rather than the principal's.
FTC franchise notice A statement required by the Federal Trade Commission (FTC) to appear in at least 12-point boldface type on the cover of a franchisor's required disclosure statement to prospective franchisees.
FTC franchise rule A rule set out by the Federal Trade Commission (FTC) that requires franchisors to make full presale disclosures to prospective franchisees.
FTC HDC rule A rule adopted by the Federal Trade Commission (FTC) that eliminates holder in due course (HDC) status with regard to negotiable instruments arising out of certain *consumer* credit transactions. This subjects the HDC of a consumer credit instrument to *all* the defenses and claims of the consumer.
Full Faith and Credit Clause A clause in the U.S. Constitution (Article IV, Section 1) that states that a judgment of a court of one state must be given "full faith and credit" by the courts of another state.
full warranty An express warranty made by a seller or lessor of goods that guarantees free repair or replacement of a defective product.
fully disclosed agency An agency in which a contracting third party knows (1) that the agent is acting for a principal and (2) the identity of the principal.
fully disclosed principal The principal in a fully disclosed agency.
fully protected speech Speech that the government cannot prohibit or regulate.
fundamental changes Major changes to a corporation's structure, including proxy contests, mergers, sales of assets, hostile tender offers, and such.
fundamental rights Rights (e.g., *voting*) that are protected by the strict scrutiny test of the Equal Protection Clause of the Fourth Amendment to the U.S. Constitution.
funding portal (web platform) An internet website through which an issuer may issue securities to the public in a crowdfunding offering.
fungible goods Goods that are exactly alike, such as the same grade of oil, grain, or cattle.
futility exception A rule that excuses a shareholder from making a demand on the board of directors to sue a third party prior to the shareholder bringing a derivative lawsuit on behalf of the corporation if such demand would be futile to make.
future advances Funds advanced to a debtor in the future as prearranged in a security agreement.
future goods Goods that are not yet in existence (e.g., ungrown crops, unborn stock animals).
future interest The interest in real property that a grantor retains for himself or herself or a third party. Two forms of future interests are *reversion* and *remainder*.
future right A currently nonexistent right that a person is expected to have in the future.
gambling statutes Statutes that make certain forms of gambling illegal.
gap-filling rule A rule that says an open term can be "read into" a sales or lease contract.

garnishee The third party in a garnishment situation who possesses property of the debtor who is subject to garnishment.
garnishment A post judgment court order that permits the seizure of a debtor's property that is in the possession of third parties.
garnishor The creditor in a garnishment situation whose property in the hands of a third party is being garnished.
gender identity A term that refers to an individual's internal sense of being a man, a woman, neither, or both.
gender identity discrimination Employment discrimination based on a person's personal experience of one's own gender, which can correlate with an assigned sex at birth or differ from it.
General Assembly The legislative body of the United Nations that is composed of all member nations.
general corporation statutes State statutes that permit corporations to be formed without the separate approval of the legislature.
general duty standard An Occupational Safety and Health Administration (OSHA) standard that requires an employer to provide a work environment free from recognized hazards that are causing or are likely to cause death or serious physical harm to employees.
general gift A gift in a will that does not identify the specific property from which the gift is to be made (e.g., a gift of a certain amount of money).
general government regulation Laws that regulate businesses and industries collectively; most of the industries and businesses in the United States are subject to these laws (e.g., antidiscrimination laws).
general intangible Defined by the Uniform Commercial Code (UCC) as being personal property other than accounts, chattel paper, deposit accounts, documents, goods, instruments, investment property, letters of credit, money, and oil, gas, or other minerals prior to extraction.
general intent crime A crime that requires that the perpetrator either knew or should have known that his or her actions would lead to harmful results.
general jurisdiction (all-purpose jurisdiction) The jurisdiction in which a defendant can be sued, regardless of where the underlying action prompting the lawsuit occurred.
general partner (ordinary partner or partner) Partners of general and limited partnerships who invest capital, manage the business, and are personally liable for the partnership's debts.
general partnership (ordinary partnership or partnership) An association of two or more persons to carry on as co-owners of a business for profit; also known as an *ordinary partnership*.
general partnership agreement (articles of general partnership or articles of partnership) An agreement between partners of a general partnership that sets forth the terms and conditions of their relationship as partners.
general power of attorney A power of attorney in which a principal confers broad powers on the agent to act in any matters on the principal's behalf.
general public benefits Benefits, such as the advancement of social issues, that are taken into consideration by directors and officers of benefit corporations when making corporate decisions.
general warranty deed (grant deed) A deed to real property that contains the greatest number of warranties and provides the highest level of protection to a grantee. The seller warrants that he or she owns the property, that he or she has the legal right to sell it, and that the property is not subject to encumbrances other than those that are disclosed.
general-jurisdiction trial court (court of record) Courts that hear cases of a general nature that are not within the jurisdiction of limited-jurisdiction trial courts; often referred to as *courts of record*.
Generally Accepted Accounting Principles (GAAPs) Standards for the preparation and presentation of financial statements.
Generally Accepted Auditing Standards (GAASs) Standards promulgated by the American Institute of Certified Public Accountants (AICPA) that establish methods and procedures to be used in conducting audits.
generally known danger A defense that acknowledges that certain products are inherently dangerous and are known to the general population to be so.
general-purpose clause A clause that can be included in the articles of incorporation that permits the corporation to engage in any activity permitted by law.
generic name A term for a mark that has become a common term for a product line or type of service and therefore has lost its trademark protection.
generic top-level domain (gTLD) A domain that is not restricted to any geographic or country designation.
genetic information discrimination Employment discrimination based on a person's propensity to be stricken by diseases.
Genetic Information Nondiscrimination Act (GINA) A federal statute that makes it illegal for an employer to discriminate against job applicants and employees based on genetic information.
genetically modified organisms (G.M.O.s or GMOs) Plants and animals modified by laboratory techniques such as genetic engineering and biotechnology. Also referred to as *living modified organisms* (*L.M.O.s* or *LMOs*).
genuineness of assent The requirement that a party's assent to a contract be genuine and not have been obtained by duress, undue influence, or fraud.
geographical market extension merger A market extension merger between two firms that sell the same products or services but do not sell their products or services in the same geographical areas.
German Civil Code of 1896 A civil law based on a code of laws.
gift The voluntary transfer of title to property without payment of consideration by the donee. To be a valid gift, three elements must be shown: (1) donative intent, (2) delivery, and (3) acceptance.
gift *causa mortis* A gift that is made in contemplation of death.
gift *inter vivos* A gift made during a person's lifetime that is an irrevocable present transfer of ownership.
gift promise (gratuitous promise) A promise that is unenforceable because it lacks consideration.
glossary A section in many contracts that defines many of the words and terms used in the contract.
going public A situation that occurs when a company sells securities to the public for the first time.
good faith Honesty in the conduct or transaction concerned; An obligation of good faith that every contract or duty within the UCC imposes in its performance or enforcement.
good faith purchaser for value A person to whom good title can be transferred from a person with voidable title. The real owner cannot reclaim goods from a good faith purchaser for value.
good faith subsequent lessee A person to whom a lease interest can be transferred from a person with voidable title. The real owner cannot reclaim the goods from the subsequent lessee until the lease expires.
Good Samaritan laws Statutes that relieves medical professionals from liability for ordinary negligence when they stop and render aid to victims in emergency situations.
goods Tangible things that are movable at the time of their identification to a contract.
government The governing body of a nation, state, county, or city.
government action An action brought by the federal government to enforce federal antitrust laws.
government contractor defense A defense that says a contractor who was provided specifications by the government is not liable for any defect in the product that occurs as a result of those specifications.
Government in the Sunshine Act A federal statute that requires most federal administrative agency meetings to be open to the public. There are some exceptions to this rule.
government judgment A government judgment obtained against a defendant for an antitrust violation may be used as *prima facie* evidence of liability in a private, civil, treble damages action.
government license A grant issued by an administrative agency that permits a person to enter a certain type of business (e.g., banks, television and radio stations) or profession (e.g., doctors, lawyers, contractors).
government-owned corporation (public corporation) A corporation that is formed by a government entity to meet specific government or political purposes.
grace period A period of time granted in an insurance policy during which an insured may pay an overdue premium. The insurance usually remains in effect during the grace period.
grand jury A special jury that hears evidence of serious crimes (e.g., murder) against an accused person, evaluates the evidence presented, and determines whether there is sufficient evidence to hold the accused for trial. The grand jury does not determine guilt. If the grand jury issues an *indictment*, the accused will be held for later trial.

grantee The party to whom an interest in real property is transferred.
grantor The party who transfers an ownership interest in real property; A person who creates a living trust, who is also called a *trustor*.
greenmail The purchase by a target corporation of its stock from an actual or perceived tender offeror at a premium.
Greenman v. Yuba Power Products, Inc. A landmark case in which the court adopted the doctrine of strict liability in tort as a basis for product liability actions.
gross lease A lease in which the tenant pays a gross sum to the landlord, and the landlord is responsible for paying the utilities, property taxes, and assessments on the property.
gross negligence A finding that a person has engaged in willful misconduct or reckless behavior that caused injury or death to another person.
group boycott (refusal to deal) A restraint of trade in which two or more competitors at one level of distribution agree not to deal with others at another level of distribution; also known as *refusal to deal*.
group boycott by purchasers A restraint of trade in which two or more purchasers at the same level of distribution agree not to purchase a product from a specified seller.
group boycott by sellers A restraint of trade in which two or more sellers at the same level of distribution agree not to sell their product to a specified purchaser.
guarantee of collection A form of accommodation in which the accommodation party guarantees *collection* of a negotiable instrument; the accommodation party is *secondarily liable* on the instrument.
guarantee of payment A form of accommodation in which the accommodation party guarantees *payment* of a negotiable instrument; the accommodation party is *primarily liable* on the instrument.
guarantor A person who agrees to pay a debt if the primary debtor does not; a third person who agrees to be liable in a guaranty arrangement. The guarantor is *secondarily liable* on the debt.
guaranty agreement (guaranty contract) A promise in which one person agrees to answer for the debts or duties of another person. It is a contract between the guarantor and the original creditor.
guaranty arrangement (guaranty contract) An arrangement in which a third party promises to be *secondarily liable* for the payment of another's debt.
guilty A plea that may be entered by an accused at his or her arraignment whereby the accused states that he or she committed the crime that he or she is charged with.
H-1B Foreign Guest Worker visa (H-1B visa) A visa issued by the U.S. government that allows U.S. employers to employ foreign nationals in the United States who are skilled in specialty occupations.
H-2A Temporary Agricultural Worker visa (H-2A visa) A visa issued by the U.S. government that allows U.S. employers to employ foreign nationals in the United States to perform temporary and seasonal agricultural work.
H-2B Temporary Non-Agricultural Worker visa (H-2B visa) A visa issued by the U.S. government that allows U.S. employers to employ foreign nationals in the United States to perform nonagricultural work on a one-time, seasonal, peak-load, or intermittent basis.
H4 visa A visa issued by the U.S. government that allows immediate family members (i.e., spouse and children under 21) into the United States as dependents of workers issued H-1B work visas.
harassment Conduct by supervisors, employees, and coworkers that is offensive to employees or job applicants because it is sexually, racially, ethnically, religiously, or otherwise charged. Harassment that is so severe or frequent that it creates a hostile work environment in violation of Title VII of the Civil Rights Act of 1964.
Hart-Scott-Rodino Antitrust Improvement Act (HSR Act) A federal statute that requires certain firms to notify the Federal Trade Commission (FTC) and the U.S. Department of Justice in advance of a proposed merger. Unless the government challenges a proposed merger within 30 days, the merger may proceed.
hazardous wastes Wastes that may cause or significantly contribute to an increase in mortality or serious illness, or pose a hazard to human health or the environment if improperly managed.
health care agent A person named in a *health care directive* to make all health care decisions in accordance with the wishes outlined in the maker's living will.
health care directive (health care proxy or advance directive) A document in which the maker names someone to be his or her health care agent to make all health care decisions in accordance with his or her wishes, as outlined in the living will.
health insurance Insurance that is purchased to help cover the costs of medical treatment, surgery, or hospital care.
heir A person who receives property from a person who dies intestate, that is, without a will or trust. State intestacy statutes determine how the deceased person's property is distributed to heirs.
highest state court The highest court in a state court system, which hears appeals from intermediate appellate state courts and certain trial courts; often called the *state supreme court*.
highly compensated employee exemption An exemption from federal minimum wage and overtime pay requirements that applies to employees who are compensated on a salary basis, perform office or nonmanual work, and regularly perform at least one of the duties of an exempt executive, administrative, or professional employee.
Historical School A school of jurisprudential thought that postulates that law is an aggregate of social traditions and customs.
holder A person who is in possession of a negotiable instrument that is drawn, issued, or indorsed to him or his order, or to bearer, or in blank.
holder in due course (HDC) A holder who takes a negotiable instrument for value, in good faith, and without notice that it is defective or is overdue.
holding company A corporation that owns and operates a variety of other corporations and entities as subsidiaries.
holographic will A will that is entirely handwritten and signed by the testator.
Homeland Security Act (HSA) A federal statute that created the cabinet-level U.S. Department of Homeland Security (DHS) and enacted laws to prevent domestic terrorist attacks and related criminal activities.
homeowners' policy A comprehensive insurance policy that includes coverage for the risks covered by a fire insurance policy as well as personal liability insurance.
homestead exemption Equity in a debtor's home that the debtor is permitted to retain in bankruptcy.
honor To pay a drawer's properly drawn check.
horizontal merger A merger between two or more companies that compete in the same business and geographical market.
horizontal restraint of trade A restraint of trade that occurs when two or more competitors at the same level of distribution enter into a contract, combination, or conspiracy to restrain trade.
hostile and adverse A requirement that must be proven by a person to obtain real property by adverse possession. It requires that the adverse possessor has occupied the property without the express or implied permission of the owner.
hostile tender offer A tender offer that is made without the permission of the target company's management.
hostile work environment A work environment that involves sexual or racial harassment or harassment against other protected classes that creates a physically threatening or humiliating workplace, creates a workplace that negatively impacts an employee's ability to go to work, or unreasonably interferes with an employee's work performance. Such conduct violates equal opportunity in employment laws.
***Howey* test** A test that states that an arrangement is an investment contract if there is an investment of money by an investor in a common enterprise and the investor expects to make profits based on the sole or substantial efforts of the promoter or others.
hung jury A jury that cannot come to a unanimous decision about the defendant's guilt. In the case of a hung jury, the government may choose to retry the case.
identification of goods Distinguishing the goods named in a contract from the seller's or lessor's other goods.
identity theft (ID theft) A theft in which someone steals information about another person, poses as that person, and takes the innocent person's money or property to purchase goods and services using the victim's credit information. Identity theft is a crime.
Identity Theft and Assumption Deterrence Act A federal statute that makes it a federal crime to knowingly transfer or use, without authority, the identity of another person with the intent to commit any unlawful activity as defined by federal law and state and local felony laws.

Identity Theft Enforcement and Restitution Act A federal statute that makes it easier to prosecute identity theft cases and permits identity theft cases to be brought in federal court even if the cybercriminal and the victim live in the same state.
illegal consideration A promise to refrain from doing an illegal act. Such a promise will not support a contract.
illegal contract A contract that has an illegal object. Such contracts are *void*.
illegal strike Strikes by employees that are illegal and not protected by federal labor law.
illegal subjects Subjects of collective bargaining that cannot be discussed by management and labor unions and cannot be included in a collective bargaining agreement (e.g., discrimination).
illusory promise (illusory contract) A contract into which both parties enter but one or both of the parties can choose not to perform their contractual obligations. Thus, the contract lacks consideration.
Immigration Act of 1990 A federal statute that regulates immigration, the employment of immigrants in the United States, and naturalization and citizenship.
Immigration Reform and Control Act of 1986 A federal statute that requires employers to attest to their employees' immigration status and makes it unlawful for employers to knowingly recruit illegal immigrants.
immoral contract A contract whose objective is the commission of an act that society considers immoral. Immoral contracts may be found to be illegal as against public policy.
immunity from prosecution The government's agreement with a person not to use any evidence given by that person against that person.
impairment of the right of recourse A situation in which certain parties (i.e., holders, indorsers, accommodation parties) are discharged from liability on an instrument if the holder (1) releases an obligor from liability or (2) surrenders collateral without the consent of the parties who would benefit by it.
impanel The act of being sworn in as a juror to hear a case.
implied agency An agency that occurs when a principal and an agent do not expressly create an agency but one is inferred from the conduct of the parties.
implied authorization A means of communication for accepting an offer to enter into a contract that is inferred from what is customary in similar transactions, usage of trade, or prior dealings between the parties.
implied bailment A bailment that occurs when someone finds and safeguards lost property.
implied by law A characteristic of warranties that are not expressly stated in a sales or lease contract.
implied easements Easements that are implied from the situation and circumstances. Implied easements include the following: (1) *easement by necessity*, (2) *easement by implication*, and (3) *easement by prescription*.
implied exemptions Exemptions from antitrust laws that are implied by the federal courts.
implied integration A doctrine that permits the formation of a contract if several documents are somehow physically attached to each other (e.g., in an envelope). The contract that is created consists of the terms of the separate documents.
implied powers Powers beyond express powers that allow a corporation to accomplish its corporate purpose.
implied term A missing term that is not expressly stated in an offer or a contract that can reasonably be supplied by the courts if a reasonable term can be implied from other sources.
implied warranties Certain warranties that the law implies on transferors of negotiable instruments. There are two types of implied warranties: transfer and presentment warranties.
implied warranty (sale or lease) A warranty that is not expressly stated in the sales or lease contract but instead is implied by law.
implied warranty of authority A warranty of an agent who enters into a contract on behalf of another party that he or she has the authority to represent.
implied warranty of fitness for a particular purpose A warranty that arises where a seller or lessor warrants that the goods will meet the buyer's or lessee's expressed needs.
implied warranty of fitness for human consumption A warranty that applies to food or drink consumed on or off the premises of restaurants, grocery stores, fast-food outlets, coffee shops, bars, vending machines, and other purveyors of food and drink.
implied warranty of habitability A implied warranty that provides that leased premises must be fit, safe, and suitable for ordinary residential use.
implied warranty of merchantability Unless properly disclosed, a warranty that is implied that sold or leased goods are fit for the ordinary purpose for which they are sold or leased, as well as other assurances.
implied-in-fact condition A condition that can be implied from the circumstances surrounding a contract and the parties' conduct.
implied-in-fact contract A contract in which agreement between parties has been inferred from their conduct.
implied-in-law contract (quasi contract) An equitable doctrine whereby a court may award monetary damages to a plaintiff for providing work or services to a defendant even though no actual contract existed. The doctrine is intended to prevent unjust enrichment and unjust detriment.
importer The buyer in an international sales contract that is located in one country and that is buying goods from a seller located in another country.
impossibility of performance (objective impossibility) A legal rule that states that a contract terminates if a situation arises that makes its fulfillment impossible; A legal rule that states that an agency terminates if a situation arises that makes its fulfillment impossible.
imposter rule A rule that states that if an imposter forges the indorsement of the named payee, the drawer or maker is liable on the instrument and bears the loss.
imputed knowledge Information that is learned by an agent that is attributed to the principal; Information that is learned by a general partner that is attributed to the general partnership.
in pari delicto A situation in which both parties are equally at fault in an illegal contract.
***in personam* jurisdiction (personal jurisdiction)** A court's jurisdiction over a party to a lawsuit. Also called *personal jurisdiction*.
***in rem* jurisdiction** Jurisdiction of a court to hear and decide a case because the property of the lawsuit is located in that state.
inaccessibility exception A rule that permits employees and union officials to engage in union solicitation on company property if the employees are beyond reach of reasonable union efforts to communicate with them.
incidental beneficiary A third party who is unintentionally benefited by other people's contracts.
incidental damages When goods are resold or released, damages that are reasonable expenses incurred in stopping delivery, transportation charges, storage charges, sales commissions, and so on.
income beneficiary A person or an entity to be paid income from a trust.
incoming partner A person or an entity that is admitted as a partner of an existing general partnership.
incomplete check A check from which certain information has been omitted, such as the amount of the check or the payee's name, either on purpose or by mistake.
incontestability clause A clause that prevents insurers from contesting statements made by insureds in applications for insurance after the passage of a stipulated number of years.
incorporating a corporation To form a corporation the organizers must follow the requirements set forth by the corporation code of the state in which the corporation is to be incorporated.
incorporation by reference Integration made by express reference in one document that refers to and incorporates another document within it.
incorporation doctrine A doctrine applied by the U.S. Supreme Court that holds that most of the fundamental guarantees contained in the Bill of Rights are not only applicable to federal government action but are also applicable to state and local government action.
incorporator The person or persons, partnerships, or corporations that are responsible for incorporation of a corporation.
incoterms Specific terms set forth in the Uniform Customs and Practice for Documentary Credits (UCP) that govern international letters of credit.
incumbent director A current member of the board of directors of a corporation.
indemnification The right of an agent of a principal, partner of a partnership, member

of a limited liability company, and an officer or employee of a corporation or other business entity to be reimbursed for expenditures incurred on behalf of the principal or organization.

indenture agreement (indenture) A contract between a corporation and a holder that contains the terms of a debt security; also known as an *indenture*.

independent contractor A person who contracts with another to do something for him who is not controlled by the other nor subject to the other's right to control with respect to his physical conduct in the performance of the undertaking.

Indian Gaming Regulatory Act (IGRA) A federal statute that sets the requirements for establishing casino gambling and other gaming activities on tribal land.

indictment The charge of having committed a crime (usually a felony), based on the judgment of a grand jury.

indirect price discrimination A form of price discrimination (e.g., favorable credit terms) that is less readily apparent than direct forms of price discrimination.

individual with regular income An individual whose income is sufficiently stable and regular to enable the individual to make payments under a Chapter 13 plan.

indoor air pollution (sick building syndrome) Air pollution that occurs inside some buildings.

indorsee The person to whom a negotiable instrument is indorsed. The party to whom a check is indorsed.

indorsement The signature of a signer (other than as a maker, a drawer, or an acceptor) that is placed on an instrument to negotiate it to another person. The signature (and other directions) written by or on behalf of the holder somewhere on an instrument.

indorsement for deposit or collection A restrictive indorsement that makes the indorsee the indorser's collecting agent (e.g., "for deposit only").

indorsements in trust A restrictive indorsement that states that it is for the benefit or use of the indorser or another person; also known as *agency indorsement*.

indorser The person who indorses a negotiable instrument; the payee who indorses a check to another party.

infancy doctrine A doctrine that allows minors to disaffirm (cancel) most contracts they have entered into with adults.

inferior performance A situation in which a party fails to perform express or implied contractual obligations and impairs or destroys the essence of a contract; there is a *material breach*.

informal contract (simple contract) A contract that is not formal. Valid informal contracts are fully enforceable and may be sued upon if breached.

informal rulemaking Rulemaking by an administrative agency where it notifies the public of a proposed rule, permits interested persons to comment on the proposed rule, and possibly holds an informal hearing before deciding on whether to adopt the proposed rule.

Information Infrastructure Protection Act (IIP Act) A federal statute that makes it a federal crime for anyone to intentionally access and acquire information from a protected computer without authorization.

information return A document that is filed by general and limited partnerships with the government disclosing how much income was earned or the amount of losses incurred by the partnership.

information statement The charge of having committed a crime (usually a misdemeanor), based on the judgment of a judge (magistrate) or prosecutor.

inherently dangerous activity Activities (e.g., use of explosives, clearing of land by fire) for which a principal is liable for the negligence of an independent contractor whom the principal has hired.

inheritance Occurs when a person dies without having a valid will or living trust and the deceased's property is distributed to the heirs of the deceased as provided in the state's inheritance statute.

initial coin offering (ICO) The issuance of a cryptocurrency coins or tokens by an issuer to investors.

initial license fee A lump-sum payment paid by a franchisee to a franchisor for the privilege of being granted a franchise.

initial public offering (IPO) A situation in which a company or other issuer sells securities to the public for the first time.

injunction A court order that prohibits a person or business from doing a certain act.

injury A plaintiff's personal injury or damage to his or her property that enables him or her to recover monetary damages for the defendant's negligence.

innkeeper The owner of a facility that provides lodging to the public for compensation (e.g., hotel, motel).

innkeepers' statutes State statutes that limit an innkeeper's common law liability. An innkeeper can avoid liability for loss caused to a guest's property if (1) a safe is provided in which the guest's valuable property may be kept and (2) the guest is notified of this fact.

innocent acquisition of a monopoly The acquisition of a monopoly through innocent means, such as by superior business acumen, skill, foresight, or industry. This is a defense to a charge of committing an act of monopolization.

innocent misrepresentation Fraud that occurs when a person makes a statement of fact that he or she honestly and reasonably believes to be true even though it is not.

inside director A member of the board of directors of a corporation who is also an officer of the corporation.

insider trading A situation in which an insider makes a profit by personally purchasing shares of the corporation prior to public release of favorable information or by selling shares of the corporation prior to the public disclosure of unfavorable information.

Insider Trading Sanctions Act A federal statute that permits the Securities and Exchange Commission (SEC) to obtain a civil penalty of up to three times (*treble damages*) the illegal benefits received from insider trading.

installment contract A contract that requires or authorizes goods to be delivered and accepted in separate lots.

installment note A note that is paid in installments.

instrument Intangible personal property such as checks, notes, stocks, bonds, and other investment securities; A special form of contract that satisfies the requirements established by Article 3 of the UCC; also called *negotiable instrument* or *commercial paper*.

insufficient funds A situation that occurs when a drawer does not have enough money in his or her checking account when a properly payable check is presented for payment.

insurable interest A requirement that a person who purchases insurance have a personal interest in the insured goods, property, or person.

insurance A means for persons and businesses to protect themselves against the risk of loss.

insurance agent An agent who sells insurance who usually works exclusively for one insurance company.

insurance broker A person who sells insurance who is an independent contractor who represents a number of insurance companies.

insurance company A company that sells various types of insurance to persons and businesses.

insurance policy An insurance contract.

insured A party who pays a premium to a particular insurance company for insurance coverage.

insurer (underwriter) An insurance company that underwrites insurance coverage.

insurgent director A person who is a shareholder who proposes to replace an incumbent director of the board of directors of a corporation.

intangible collateral Personal property that has no physical substance and cannot be touched or held that is specified as security in a security agreement.

intangible personal property Nonphysical personal property to which a security interest can attach, which includes negotiable instruments, securities, accounts, chattel paper, deposit accounts, patents, copyrights, trademarks, royalties, and the like.

integration The combination of several writings to form a single contract.

intellectual property Patents, copyrights, trademarks, and trade secrets. Federal and state laws protect intellectual property rights from misappropriation and infringement.

intended third-party beneficiary A third party who is not in privity of contract but who has rights under the contract and can enforce the contract against the promisor.

intent crime A crime that requires the defendant to be found guilty of committing a criminal act (*actus reus*) with criminal intent (*mens rea*).

intent to deceive An element of fraud that occurs when a person makes a misrepresentation of a material fact with knowledge that the representation is false or makes it without sufficient knowledge of the truth. This is called *scienter* ("guilty mind").

intentional infliction of emotional distress (tort of outrage) A tort that says a person whose extreme and outrageous conduct intentionally or recklessly causes severe emotional distress to another person is liable for that emotional distress; also known as the *tort of outrage*.
intentional interference with contractual relations A tort that arises when a third party induces a contracting party to breach the contract with another party.
intentional misrepresentation (fraudulent misrepresentation or fraud or deceit) An event that occurs when one person consciously decides to induce another person to rely and act on an intentional misrepresentation. When fraud has occurred, an injured plaintiff can bring a *civil fraud* lawsuit against the defendant to recover economic damages that he or she suffered because of the fraud. Also, when fraud has been committed, the government may bring *criminal fraud* charges against the defendant to seek criminal penalties such as jail time and/or fines.
intentional tort A category of torts that requires that the defendant possessed the intent to do the act that caused the plaintiff's injuries. Occurs when a person has intentionally committed a wrong against (1) another person or his or her character, or (2) another person's property.
***inter vivos* trust** A trust that is created while the settlor is alive.
intermediary bank A bank in the collection process that is not the depository bank or the payer bank.
intermediate appellate court (appellate court or court of appeal) A court that hears appeals from trial courts.
intermediate scrutiny test A test that is applied to determine the constitutionality of classifications by the government based on a protected class (e.g., gender).
internal union rules Rules adopted by a labor union that regulate the operation of the union.
International Accounting Standards Board (IASB) An organization located in London, England, that has promulgated the International Financial Reporting Standards (IFRS).
international branch office An office opened by a multinational corporation to conduct business in another country. A branch office is not a separate legal entity but merely an office of the corporation.
International Court of Justice (ICJ or World Court) The judicial branch of the United Nations that is located in The Hague, the Netherlands; also called the *World Court*.
International Financial Reporting Standards (IFRS) Accounting principles that are promulgated by the International Accounting Standards Board (IASB), which are used by foreign companies, and some U.S. companies, in place of generally accepted accounting principles (GAAPs).
international law Law that governs affairs between nations and that regulates transactions between individuals and businesses of different countries.
International Monetary Fund (IMF) An agency of the United Nations whose primary function is to promote sound monetary, fiscal, and macroeconomic policies worldwide by providing assistance to needy countries.
International Shoe Company v. State of Washington A U.S. Supreme Court decision that established the "minimum contacts" and "traditional notions of fair play and substantial justice" tests to determine whether a defendant is subject to the jurisdiction of a court.
international subsidiary corporation A corporation owned by a multinational corporation that conducts business in another country. This subsidiary corporation is a separate legal entity from the parent *corporation*.
internet A collection of millions of computers that provide a network of electronic connections between computers.
Internet Corporation for Assigned Names and Numbers (ICANN) The organization that oversees the registration and regulation of domain names.
internet service provider (ISP) A company that operates servers on which websites and web pages are stored.
interpretive rule A rule adopted by an administrative agency that interprets existing statutory language.
interrogatories Written questions submitted by one party to another party. The questions must be answered in writing within a stipulated time.
interstate commerce Commerce that moves between states or that affects commerce between states.
intervention The act of others to join as parties to an existing lawsuit.
intestacy statute A state statute that specifies how a deceased's property will be distributed if he or she dies without a will or trust or if the last will is declared void and there is no prior valid will.
intestate The state of having died without leaving a will or trust. The persons who receive the property as determined by state intestacy statutes are called *heirs*.
intoxicated person A person who is under contractual incapacity because of ingestion of alcohol or drugs to the point of incompetence.
intrastate commerce Commerce within a state.
intrastate offering exemption An exemption from registration that permits local businesses to raise capital from local investors without the need to register with the Securities and Exchange Commission. There are two intrastate offering exemptions, one provided under SEC Rule 147 and another under SEC Rule 147A.
invasion of the right to privacy The unwarranted and undesired publicity of a private fact about a person. The fact does not have to be untrue.
inventory Tangible personal property held for sale or lease, including work in progress and materials.
investment banker Independent securities companies that sell issuer's securities to the public and perform other securities-related functions.
investment contract A flexible standard for defining a *security*. An arrangement where there is an investment of money by an investor in a common enterprise in which the investor expects to make profits based on the sole or substantial efforts of the promoter or others.
investment property A security, whether certificated or uncertificated, securities account, security entitlement, or commodity contract or account, such as stocks, bonds, and commodities future contracts.
invitation to make an offer A general rule that states that an advertisement for the sale of goods, even at a specific price, is treated as an invitation to make an offer and not an offer.
invitee A person who has been expressly or impliedly invited to a landowner's or tenant's premises for the economic benefit of the landowner or tenant.
involuntary manslaughter A nonintent crime that occurs when the death of a person results from the reckless or grossly negligent conduct of another person.
involuntary petition A petition filed by creditors of a debtor to begin an involuntary bankruptcy proceeding against the debtor.
IPO on-ramp Refers to the use by an emerging growth company (EGC) of an internet website crowdfunding portal to issue shares to the public in an initial public offering (IPO).
IRAC method A critical legal thinking method for analyzing court cases. The acronym IRAC stands for issue, rule, application, and conclusion.
irreconcilable differences A situation that exists between married persons that a married person may assert as a reason for getting a divorce where no-fault divorces are recognized.
irrevocable trust A trust that cannot be revoked by the trustor or settler who created the trust.
issued shares Authorized shares that have been sold by a corporation.
issuing bank The bank that issues a letter of credit on behalf of a buyer in an international sales transaction.
issuer A business or party selling securities to the public.
joint and several liability A form of liability of general partners whereby a plaintiff may sue all of the partners (jointly) or some or one of the partners (individually) to recover payment of a judgment against a partnership that has not been satisfied in whole or in part from partnership assets.
joint custody A custody arrangement that gives both parents responsibility for making major decisions concerning the child.
joint liability A form of liability of general partners whereby a plaintiff must name the partnership and all of the partners (jointly) in a single lawsuit to recover payment from partners of a judgment against a partnership that has not been satisfied in whole or in part from partnership assets.
joint marital debts Debts incurred during the marriage for joint needs.
joint physical custody A custody arrangement whereby the child of divorcing parents spends a certain amount of time being raised by each parent.

joint tenancy A form of co-ownership of real property that includes the *right of survivorship*.
joint tenants Parties who co-own real property in a joint tenancy arrangement.
joint venture An arrangement in which two or more business entities combine their resources to pursue a single project or transaction.
joint venture corporation A corporation owned by two or more joint venturers that is created to operate a joint venture.
joint venture partnership A partnership owned by two or more joint venturers that is formed to operate a joint venture.
joint venturer The parties to a joint venture.
joint will A will that is executed by two or more testators.
judgment The decision of the judge in a trial usually based on the verdict of the jury; the judge may enter a judgment if there is no jury.
judgment notwithstanding the verdict (judgment N.O.V., J.N.O.V.) A judgment issued by a judge that overturns the verdict of the jury if the judge finds jury bias or misconduct.
judgment proof A situation in which a defendant does not have the money to pay a civil judgment.
judicial authority The power of an administrative agency to adjudicate cases through an administrative proceeding often conducted by an administrative law judge (ALJ).
judicial branch (courts) The branch of state and federal governments that is composed of courts of the relevant jurisdiction; Federal courts are authorized by Article III of the U.S. Constitution.
judicial decision A decision in a lawsuit made by a federal or state court.
judicial dissolution Dissolution of a corporation through a court proceeding instituted by the state.
judicial review of administrative agency actions The power of federal and state courts to review the actions of federal and state administrative agencies that are subject to their jurisdiction.
jumbo certificate of deposit (jumbo CD) A certificate of deposit that is commonly $100,000 or more.
Jumpstart Our Business Startups Act (JOBS Act) A federal statute that makes it easier for start-up companies to raise capital from the public through small initial public offerings of securities.
jurisprudence The philosophy or science of law.
jury deliberation A process whereby a jury retires to the jury room to consider the evidence.
jury instructions Instructions given by a judge to the jury to inform them of the law to be applied in the case.
jury trial A lawsuit decided by a jury.
Just Compensation Clause A clause of the U.S. Constitution that requires the government to compensate the property owner, and possibly others, when the government takes property under its power of eminent domain.
Kantian ethics (duty ethics or deontological ethics) A theory of ethics that says that people owe moral duties that are based on universal rules, such as the categorical imperative "Do unto others as you would have them do unto you."
key-person life insurance Life insurance purchased and paid for by a business that insures against the death of owners and other key executives and employees of the business.
labor law The statutes, rules, and regulations adopted by administrative agencies, and court decisions interpreting and applying the statutes and rules and regulations, that regulate labor relations.
Labor Management Relations Act (Taft-Hartley Act) A federal statute enacted in 1947 that expanded the activities labor unions could engage in.
Labor Management Reporting and Disclosure Act (Landrum-Griffin Act) A federal statute enacted in 1959 that regulates internal union affairs and establishes the rights of union members.
labor union exception A rule that restricts an employer's ability to discharge an at-will employee who is a member of a labor union. Certain procedures must be followed to seek the discharge of a union-represented employee.
land The most common form of real property; includes the land and buildings and other structures permanently attached to the land.
land pollution Pollution of the land that is generally caused by hazardous waste being disposed of in an improper manner.
land sale contract (land contract) An arrangement in which the owner of real property sells property to a purchaser and extends credit to the purchaser.
landlord (lessor) An owner of real property who transfers a leasehold.
landlord–tenant relationship A relationship that is created when the owner of a freehold estate transfers to another person the right to exclusively and temporarily possess the owner's real property.
Lanham Trademark Act (Lanham Act) A federal statute that (1) establishes the requirements for obtaining a federal mark and (2) protects marks from infringement. Also called the *Lanham Act*.
lapse of time A stated time period after which an offer terminates. If no time is stated, an offer terminates after a reasonable time.
larceny The taking of another's personal property other than from his or her person or building.
law That which must be obeyed and followed by citizens, subject to sanctions or legal consequences; a body of rules of action or conduct prescribed by controlling authority and having binding legal force.
Law and Economics School A school of jurisprudential thought that postulates that promoting market efficiency should be the central concern of legal decision making.
law courts A court that developed and administered a uniform set of laws decreed by the kings and queens after William the Conqueror; legal procedure was emphasized over merits at this time.
Law Merchant Rules developed in England to solve commercial disputes that were based on common trade practices and usage.
lawful contract A contract whose object is lawful.
lawful object An element of a contract that is met where the object of a contract is not illegal.
Leahy-Smith America Invents Act (AIA) A federal statute that established the first-to-file rule of patent law.
learned professional employee exemption An exemption from federal minimum wage and overtime pay requirements that applies to employees compensated on a salary or fee basis who perform work that is predominantly intellectual in character, who possess advanced knowledge in a field of science or learning, and whose advanced knowledge was acquired through a prolonged course of specialized intellectual instruction.
lease A term that is used to indicate a contract for the lease of goods and a contract for the rental of real property; The transfer of the right to use real property for a specified period of time. The rental agreement between a landlord and a tenant is called a *lease*.
lease contract A contract for the lease of goods that is subject to Article 2A (Leases) of the Uniform Commercial Code (UCC).
lease fee Rent payments paid by a franchisee to a franchisor for land and premises leased from the franchisor.
leasehold estate (leasehold) A tenant's interest in property.
legal custody Custody that is given a custodial parent who is awarded custody of the child. This usually includes physical custody of the child and the right to make day-to-day decisions and major decisions concerning the child's education, religion, and other such matters.
legal entity (legal person) An artificial person, such as a corporation, a limited liability company (LLC), a general partnership, a limited partnership, and a limited liability partnership (LLP), that can own property, sue and be sued, enter into and enforce contracts, and such.
legal value Support for a contract when either (1) the promisee suffers a legal detriment or (2) the promisor receives a legal benefit.
legally enforceable contract A contract in which if one party fails to perform as promised, the other party can use the court system to enforce the contract and recover damages or other remedy.
legislative branch The branch of the federal government that consists of the U.S. Congress (the U.S. Senate and the U.S. House of Representatives). The U.S. Congress enacts federal statutes.
lender A party who lends money or another asset and is the creditor in a credit transaction.
lessee of goods A person who acquires the right to possession and use of goods under a lease of goods.
lessor of goods A person who transfers the right of possession and use of goods under a lease of goods.

letter of credit (documentary credit) A document that is issued by a bank on behalf of a buyer who purchases goods from a seller that guarantees that the bank will pay the seller.
LGBTQ (lesbian, gay, bisexual, transgender, and queer or questioning) An initialism that generally refers to an individuals' sexual orientation or gender identity.
LGBTQ+ An initialism that is used to ensure inclusion of all spectrums of sexuality and gender.
liability of a general partnership A rule that states that a general partnership is liable for loss or injury caused to a person, or for a penalty incurred, as a result of a wrongful act or omission, or other actionable conduct, of a partner acting in the ordinary course of business of the partnership or with authority of the partnership.
liability of a limited liability company A rule that states that a limited liability company is liable for loss or injury caused to a person, or for a penalty incurred, as a result of a wrongful act or omission, or other actionable conduct, of a member acting in the ordinary course of business of the company or with authority of the company.
liability of a limited liability partnership A rule that states that a limited liability partnership is liable for loss or injury caused to a person, or for a penalty incurred, as a result of a wrongful act or omission, or other actionable conduct, of a partner acting in the ordinary course of business of the partnership or with authority of the partnership.
liability of a limited partnership A rule that states that a limited partnership is liable for loss or injury caused to a person, or for a penalty incurred, as a result of a wrongful act or omission, or other actionable conduct, of a general partner acting in the ordinary course of activities of the limited partnership or with authority of the partnership.
liability without fault Liability that is imposed on a party even though he or she has exercised all possible care and has not been at fault for the injuries suffered by the plaintiff; also known as *strict liability*.
libel A false statement that appears in a letter, newspaper, magazine, book, photograph, movie, video, and so on.
license In a licensing arrangement, a contract that permits one party (the *licensee*) to use the trademarks, service marks, trade names, and other intellectual property of another party (the *licensor*) in the distribution of goods and services.
license of real property A contract that grants a person the right to enter upon another's property for a specified and usually short period of time.
licensee The party to whom a license is granted; A person who is on landowner's or tenant's real property legally and with the express or implied permission of the landowner or tenant and is not there to convey an economic benefit to the landowner or tenant.
licensing A business arrangement that occurs when the owner of intellectual property (the *licensor*) contracts to permit another party (the *licensee*) to use the intellectual property.
licensing agreement A detailed and comprehensive written agreement between a licensor and a licensee that sets forth the express terms of their agreement.
licensing statute A statute that requires a person or business to obtain a license from the government prior to engaging in a specified occupation or activity.
licensor The party who grants a license.
lien A legal right given to a warehouse company in the bailor's goods in its possession for necessary expenses incurred in storing and handling the goods.
lien release (release of lien) A written document signed by a contractor, subcontractor, laborer, or material person, waiving his or her statutory lien against real property; also known as *release of lien*.
life estate An interest in real property for a person's lifetime; upon that person's death, the interest will be transferred to another party.
life insurance A form of insurance in which the insurer is obligated to pay a specific sum of money upon the death of the insured.
life tenant A person who is given a life estate.
Lilly Ledbetter Fair Pay Act A federal statute that permits a complainant to file an employment discrimination claim against an employer within 180 days of the most recent paycheck violation and to recover back pay for up to two years preceding the filing of the claim if similar violations had occurred during the two-year period.
limited class of intended users Users of financial statements for whose benefit an accountant has been employed to prepare a client's financial statements or to whom the accountant knows the client will supply copies of the financial statements.
limited duty of care A fiduciary duty that a partner of a partnership and member of a limited liability company owes not to engage in: (1) known violation of the law, (2) intentional misconduct, (3) reckless conduct, or (4) grossly negligent conduct that injures the partnership or other partners. This duty does not include liability for ordinary negligence.
limited liability company (LLC) An unincorporated business entity that combines the most favorable attributes of general partnerships, limited partnerships, and corporations.
limited liability company codes (limited liability company acts) State statutes that regulate the formation, operation, and dissolution of limited liability companies (LLCs).
limited liability company operating agreement An agreement that regulates the affairs of a limited liability company and the conduct of its business and governs relations among the members, managers, and the company.
limited liability limited partnership (LLLP) A special type of limited partnership that has both general partners and limited partners where both the general and limited partners have limited liability and are not personally liable for the debts of the LLLP.
limited liability of limited partners The liability of limited partners of a limited partnership is limited to their capital contributions to the limited partnership; limited partners are not personally liable for the debts and obligations of the limited partnership.
limited liability of members of limited liability companies The liability of the members of a limited liability company (LLC) for the LLC's debts, obligations, and liabilities is limited to the extent of their capital contributions. Members of LLCs are not personally liable for the LLC's debts, obligations, and liabilities.
limited liability of partners of limited liability partnerships The liability of partners of a limited liability partnership (LLP) for the LLP's debts, obligations, and liabilities is limited only to the extent of their capital contributions. Partners of an LLP are not personally liable for the LLP's debts, obligations, and liabilities.
limited liability of shareholders A general rule of corporate law that provides that generally shareholders are liable only to the extent of their capital contributions for the debts and obligations of their corporation and are not personally liable for the debts and obligations of the corporation.
limited liability partnership (LLP) A special form of partnership in which all partners have limited liability. Partners are not personally liable for the partnership's debts and obligations.
limited liability partnership agreement An agreement that regulates the affairs of a limited liability partnership and the conduct of its business and governs relations among the partners and the partnership.
limited liability partnership codes (limited liability partnership acts) State statutes that regulate the formation, operation, and dissolution of limited liability partnerships (LLPs).
limited partner A partner in a limited partnership who invests capital but does not participate in management and is not personally liable for partnership debts beyond his or her capital contributions; A partner in a limited liability partnership (LLP) who invests capital, participates in management, and who is not personally liable for partnership debts beyond his or her capital contributions.
limited partnership (LP) A type of partnership that has two types of partners: (1) general partners and (2) limited partners.
limited partnership agreement (articles of limited partnership) A document that sets forth the rights and duties of general and limited partners; the terms and conditions regarding the operation, termination, and dissolution of a partnership, and so on.
limited protected speech Speech that is subject to time, place, and manner restrictions.
limited public offering A securities offering made by an issuer pursuant to Securities and Exchange Commission Regulation A.
limited warranty An express warranty made by a seller or lessor of goods that restricts or limits the remedy for the sale or lease of a defective product.
limited-jurisdiction trial court (inferior trial court) A court that hears matters of a specialized or limited nature.
limited-purpose clause A clause that can be included in the articles of incorporation

that stipulates the activities that a corporation can engage in. The corporation can engage in no other purposes or activities.
line of commerce The products or services that will be affected by a merger, including those that consumers use as substitutes. If an increase in the price of one product or service leads consumers to purchase another product or service, the two products are substitutes for each other.
lineal descendants Children, grandchildren, great-grandchildren, and so on of a testator.
liquidated damages Damages that parties to a contract agree in advance should be paid if the contract is breached.
liquidated damages clause A clause in a contract that provides that agreed-upon liquidated damages will be paid upon the breach of the contract.
liquidation preference The right to be paid a stated dollar amount if a corporation is dissolved and liquidated.
litigation The process of bringing, maintaining, and defending a lawsuit.
living modified organisms (L.M.O.s or LMOs) Plants and animals modified by laboratory techniques such as genetic engineering and biotechnology. Also referred to as *genetically modified organisms* (*G.M.O.s* or *GMOs*).
living trust (grantor's trust or revocable trust) A method for holding property during a person's lifetime and distributing the property upon that person's death.
living wage laws Local laws that set minimum wage rates that are usually higher than the federal minimum wage.
living will A document that states which lifesaving measures the signor does and does not want; it can specify that he or she wants such treatments withdrawn if doctors determine that there is no hope of a meaningful recovery.
local administrative agencies Administrative agencies created by cities, municipalities, and counties to administer local regulatory laws.
local consumer protection laws Laws enacted by cities and counties that regulate the safety of restaurant food, prohibit deceptive and false advertising, and the like.
long-arm statute A statute that extends a state's jurisdiction to nonresidents who were not served a summons within the state.
lost property Property that the owner leaves somewhere due to negligence, carelessness, or inadvertence. The finder obtains title to such property against the whole world except the true owner.
lost volume seller A seller who could have produced more of an item and sold it to a new buyer can sue a defaulting buyer to recover the profit it would have made from the defaulting buyer.
magistrate judge A judge who hears evidence of lesser crimes against an accused person, evaluates the evidence presented, and determines whether there is sufficient evidence to hold the accused for trial. The magistrate does not determine guilt. If the magistrate issues an *information statement*, the accused will be held for later trial.
Magnuson-Moss Warranty Act A federal statute that regulates written warranties on consumer products.
mail fraud The use of mail to defraud another person.
main purpose exception (leading object exception) An exception to the Statute of Frauds that states that if the main purpose of a transaction and an oral collateral contract is to provide pecuniary benefit to the guarantor, the collateral contract does not have to be in writing to be enforced.
majority decision A decision of the court in which a majority of the justices agree as to the outcome and reasoning used to decide a case. The decision becomes precedent.
maker of a certificate of deposit The financial institution that issues a certificate of deposit (borrower).
maker of a note The party who makes a promise to pay (borrower).
mala in se Crimes that are inherently evil.
mala prohibita Crimes that are not inherently evil but are prohibited by society.
malicious prosecution A lawsuit in which the original defendant sues the original plaintiff. In the second lawsuit, the defendant becomes the plaintiff and vice versa.
manager-managed limited liability company A limited liability company (LLC) that has designated in its articles of organization that it is a manager-managed LLC; the nonmanager members give their management rights over to designated managers. The managers have authority to bind the LLC to contracts, but nonmanager members cannot bind the LLC to contracts. Managers of a manager-managed LLC owe a duty of loyalty to the LLC; nonmanager members of a manager-managed LLC do not owe a duty of loyalty to the LLC. A manager of a manager-managed LLC owes a duty of care not to engage in intentional, reckless, or grossly negligent conduct that injures the LLC.
marine insurance Insurance that owners of vessels purchase to insure against loss or damage to the vessel and its cargo caused by perils at sea.
Marine Protection, Research, and Sanctuaries Act (MPRSA or Ocean Dumping Act) A federal statute that extends limited environmental protection to the oceans.
marital property Property acquired during the course of marriage using income earned during the marriage, and separate property that has been converted to marital property.
mark Any trade name, symbol, word, logo, design, or device used to identify and distinguish goods of a manufacturer or seller or services of a provider from those of other manufacturers, sellers, or providers. Collectively refers to trademarks, service marks, certification marks, and collective marks.
market extension merger A merger between two companies in similar fields whose sales do not overlap.
marketable title (good title) Title to real property that is free from any encumbrances or other defects that are not disclosed but would affect the value of the property.
marriage A legal union between two adults that confers certain legal rights and duties upon the spouses and upon the children born of the marriage.
marriage ceremony A ceremony usually held in front of a justice of the peace or similar government officer, or at a church, temple, synagogue, or mosque, in front of a minister, priest, rabbi, or imam. At the ceremony, the parties make a public statement that they will take each other as spouses.
marriage license A legal document issued by a state that certifies that two people are married.
mass layoff As defined in the Worker Adjustment and Retraining Notification (WARN) Act, the reduction of 33 percent of the employees or at least 50 employees during any 30-day period.
master limited partnership (MLP) (publicly traded partnership [PTP]) A limited partnership that is listed on a stock exchange and has units that are publicly traded.
material alteration A partial defense against enforcement of a negotiable instrument by a holder in due course (HDC). An HDC can enforce an altered instrument in the original amount for which the drawer wrote the check.
material breach A breach that occurs when a party renders inferior performance of his or her contractual duties.
material fact A fact that is important to the subject matter of a contract.
Matter of Cady, Roberts & Company A decision wherein the Securities and Exchange Commission (SEC) announced the duty of an insider who possesses material nonpublic information to abstain from trading in the securities of the company or disclosing the information to the person on the other side of the transaction.
maximum resale price A manufacturer's requirement that a retailer not sell a good it produces for more than a designated price. This arrangement is examined under the rule of reason to determine if it violates Section 1 of the Sherman Act as an unreasonable restraint of trade.
maximize profits A theory of social responsibility that says a corporation owes a duty to take actions that maximize profits for shareholders.
means test A bankruptcy rule that applies to a debtor who has a median family income that exceeds the state's median family income for families the same size as the debtor's family. A debtor in this category qualifies for Chapter 7 bankruptcy if he has disposable income below an amount determined by bankruptcy law, but does not qualify for Chapter 7 bankruptcy if he has disposable income above an amount determined by bankruptcy law.
median income test A bankruptcy rule that states that if a debtor's median family income is at or below the state's median family income for a family the same size as the debtor's family, the debtor can receive Chapter 7 relief.
mediation A form of alternative dispute resolution in which the parties use a mediator to assist in reaching a settlement of their dispute.
mediator A neutral third party that presides at a mediation proceeding.
medical aid in dying (physician-assisted death) Occurs when a patient who has

been diagnosed with a fatal disease and has less than an estimated period to live (e.g., six months) is prescribed a lethal dose of medicine that the patient self-administers to end his or her life.

Medical Device Amendments Amendments to the Food, Drug, and Cosmetic Act (FDCA) that give the Food and Drug Administration (FDA) authority to regulate medical devices and equipment (e.g., heart pacemakers, surgical equipment).

medical payment insurance Insurance that covers medical expenses incurred by the insured, other authorized drivers of the car, and passengers in the car who are injured in an automobile accident.

meeting of the creditors (first meeting of the creditors) A meeting of the creditors in a bankruptcy case that must occur within a reasonable time after an order for relief. The debtor must appear at this meeting. Also referred to as the *first meeting of the creditors*.

meeting the competition defense A defense to a Robinson-Patman Act Section 2(a) price discrimination action that provides that a seller's price discrimination is not unlawful if a seller lawfully engaged in the price discrimination to meet a competitor's price.

member An owner of a limited liability company (LLC).

member-managed limited liability company A limited liability company (LLC) that has not designated that it is a manager-managed LLC in its articles of organization and is managed by its members. All members have agency authority to bind the LLC to contracts. A member of a member-managed LLC owes a duty of loyalty to the LLC. A member of a member-managed LLC owes a duty of care to the LLC not to engage in intentional, reckless, or grossly negligent conduct that injures the LLC.

***mens rea* (criminal intent, evil intent)** The possession of the requisite state of mind to commit a prohibited act.

mental or psychological disorders Under the Americans with Disabilities Act, as amended, a disability, such as intellectual disability (i.e., mental retardation), organic brain syndrome, emotional or mental illness, and specific learning disabilities.

mentally incompetent but not adjudicated mentally incompetent A situation in which a person is mentally incompetent but a court or administrative agency has not declared that person to be mentally incompetent. Contracts and negotiable instruments entered into by the person are *voidable*.

Menu Labeling Rule A federal regulation that requires restaurants and retail food establishments with 20 or more locations and vending machine operators who own or operate 20 or more vending machines to disclose calorie counts of their food items.

merchant A person who (1) deals in the goods of the kind involved in a transaction or (2) by his or her occupation holds himself or herself out as having knowledge or skill peculiar to the goods involved in the transaction.

Merchant Court A court in England that solved commercial disputes by applying common trade practices and usage.

merchant protection statute (shopkeeper's privilege) Statute that permits merchants to stop, detain, and investigate suspected shoplifters without being held liable for false imprisonment if (1) there are reasonable grounds for the suspicion, (2) suspects are detained for only a reasonable time, and (3) investigations are conducted in a reasonable manner.

Mercosur (Mercosul or Southern Common Market) A regional trading organization in South America composed of the countries of Argentina, Brazil, Paraguay, and Uruguay.

merged corporation The corporation that is absorbed in a merger and ceases to exist after the merger.

merger A situation in which one corporation is absorbed into another corporation and ceases to exist.

merger clause (integration clause) A clause in a contract that stipulates that it is a complete integration and the exclusive expression of the parties' agreement.

midnight deadline The midnight of the next banking day following the banking day on which the bank received an "on them" check for collection.

Miller v. California A U.S. Supreme Court decision that set forth the elements for determining when speech is obscene speech.

minimum contact An amount of contact that a defendant must have with a state in order for that state's courts to have jurisdiction over that person or business.

minimum resale price A manufacturer's requirement that a retailer not sell a good it produces for less than a designated price. This is a *per se* violation of Section 1 of the Sherman Act as an unreasonable restraint of trade.

minor A person who has not reached the age of majority.

minor breach A breach that occurs when a party renders substantial performance of his or her contractual duties.

minutes Written record of actions taken by the board of directors at their meetings.

***Miranda* rights** Rights that a suspect must be informed of before being interrogated so that the suspect will not unwittingly give up his or her Fifth Amendment rights.

mirror image rule A rule that states that for an acceptance of a contract to exist, the offeree must accept the terms as stated in the offer.

misappropriation of a trade secret The unlawful misappropriation of another's trade secret.

misappropriation of the right to publicity (tort of appropriation) An attempt by a person to appropriate another person's name or identity for commercial purposes. Also known as the *tort of appropriation*.

misappropriation theory A rule that imposes liability under Section 10(b) of the Securities Exchange Act of 1934 and SEC Rule 10b-5 on an *outsider* who misappropriates information about a company in violation of his or her fiduciary duty and then trades in the securities of that company.

misdemeanor A less-serious crime; not inherently evil but prohibited by society. Many crimes against property are misdemeanors.

mislaid property Property that an owner voluntarily places somewhere and then inadvertently forgets. The owner of the premises where the property is mislaid is entitled to take possession of the property against all except the rightful owner.

misrepresentation of a material fact An element of fraud that occurs when a wrongdoer makes a false representation of material fact to another person.

misrepresentation of law A type of fraud that occurs when one party misrepresents the law to another party. Usually not actionable as fraud unless a professional who knows what the law is intentionally misrepresents the law to a less sophisticated contracting party.

mistake A situation that occurs when one or both of the parties to a contract have an erroneous belief about the subject matter, value, or some other aspect of the contract.

misuse of confidential information A duty of agents, general partners, officers, directors and employees of corporations, employees of businesses, and others not to disclose or misuse confidential information (e.g., trade secrets, formulas, customer lists) of the principal either during or after the course of the agency.

misuse of property A duty of agents, general partners, officers, directors and employees of corporations, employees of businesses, and others not to misuse the property of their principal for their own personal use.

mitigation of damages A nonbreaching party's legal duty to avoid or reduce damages caused by a breach of contract.

mixed sale A sale that involves the provision of a service and a good in the same transaction.

mobile payment app An app on an electronic device such as a smartphone, tablet, or smartwatch that is used for the payment of goods or services.

mobile sources of air pollution Sources of air pollution such as automobiles, trucks, buses, motorcycles, and airplanes.

Model Benefit Corporation Legislation (MBCL) A model act that provides for the creation and operation of benefit corporations.

Model Business Corporation Act (MBCA) A model act, drafted in 1950, that was intended to provide a uniform law for the formation, operation, and termination of corporations.

Model Business Corporation Act (2016) (MBCA) A free-standing model business corporation act that provides modern and comprehensive law for the formation, operation, and dissolution of corporations.

Model Nonprofit Corporation Act (MNCA) A model act that provides comprehensive and modern law for the formation, operation, and dissolution of nonprofit corporations.

mode-of-operation rule A rule that states that when a business invitee is injured on a business's premises the injured party is entitled to an inference of the business's negligence and is relieved of the obligation of proving that the business owner had actual or constructive notice of the dangerous condition that caused the injury.

modified gross lease A lease in which the tenant pays rent and utilities and the landlord is responsible for paying the property taxes and assessments on the property.
monetary damages (dollar damages) Monetary damages that are awarded for breach of contract.
money A medium of exchange authorized or adopted by a domestic or foreign government as part of its currency.
money laundering The crime of running illegally obtained money through legitimate businesses to "wash" the money and make it look as though it was earned legitimately.
Money Laundering Control Act A federal statute that makes it a crime to (1) knowingly engage in a money transaction through a financial institution involving property from an unlawful activity worth more than $10,000 and (2) knowingly engage in a financial transaction involving the proceeds of an unlawful activity.
monopoly power The power to control prices or exclude competition, measured by the market share the defendant possesses in the relevant market.
monthly report (current report) (Form 8-K) A report that must be filed with the Securities and Exchange Commission (SEC) by a reporting company within 10 days of the end of the month in which a material event such as a merger occurs.
month-to-month tenancy A periodic tenancy of real property where length of the tenancy is one month.
moral minimum A theory of social responsibility that says a corporation's duty is to make a profit while avoiding causing harm to others.
moral theory of law A school of thought that emphasizes that law should be based on morality and ethics.
mortgage An interest in real property given to a lender as security for the repayment of a loan.
mortgage note A note that is secured by real estate.
Mortgage Reform and Anti-Predatory Lending Act A federal statute that is designed to eliminate many abusive mortgage loan practices and that mandates new duties and disclosure requirements on mortgage lenders and others.
mortgagee (creditor) The lender or creditor in a mortgage transaction.
mortgagor (owner-debtor) The borrowers or owner-debtor in a mortgage transaction.
motion for judgment on the pleadings A motion that alleges that if all the facts presented in the pleadings are taken as true, the party making the motion would win the lawsuit when the proper law is applied to these asserted facts.
motion for summary judgment A motion that asserts that there are no factual disputes to be decided by the jury and that the judge can apply the proper law to the undisputed facts and decide the case without a jury. These motions are supported by affidavits, documents, and deposition testimony.
motivation test A test that determines whether an agent's motivation in committing an intentional tort is to promote the principal's business; if so, the principal is liable for any injury caused by the tort.
multilateral treaty A treaty involving more than two nations.
multinational corporation (transnational corporation) A corporation that operates in more than one country.
municipal corporation A local government-owned corporation, such as a city.
murder The unlawful killing of a human being by another person without justification.
Music Modernization Act (MMA) A federal statute that provides for the creation of a music database and permits digital services to obtain a blanket license to stream and permit the downloading of the music.
mutual assent (meeting of the minds) An assent by the parties—a "meeting of the minds"—to perform current or future contractual duties.
mutual benefit bailment A bailment for the mutual benefit of the bailor and bailee. The bailee owes a *duty of ordinary care* to protect the bailed property.
mutual fund An investment fund that sells shares to the public and invests in stocks and bonds for the long term and is restricted from investing in risky investments.
mutual mistake of a material fact A mistake made by both parties concerning a material fact that is important to the subject matter of a contract.
mutual mistake of value A mistake that occurs if both parties know the object of the contract but are mistaken as to its value.
mutual rescission Mutual termination of a contract that occurs when the parties to a contract enter into a second contract that expressly terminates the first one.
mutual wills (reciprocal wills) A situation in which two or more testators execute separate wills that leave their property to each other on the condition that the survivor leave the remaining property on his or her death as agreed by the testators.
national ambient air quality standards (NAAQS) Standards for certain pollutants set by the EPA that protect (1) human beings (primary level) and (2) vegetation, climate, visibility, and economic values (secondary level).
National Association of Securities Dealers Automated Quotation System (NASDAQ) An electronic stock market where more than 3,000 companies' stocks are traded.
National Bioengineered Food Disclosure Law A federal statute that requires the U.S. Department of Agriculture (USDA) to adopt standards whereby foods that have been genetically modified must contain a label disclosing this information.
National Bioengineered Food Disclosure Standard (NBSDS or Standard) A standard issued by the U.S. Department of Agriculture (USDA) that requires that foods that have been genetically modified contain a label disclosing this information.
national courts The courts of individual nations.
National Do-Not-Call Registry A federal registry on which consumers can place their names and personal wireless or wire-connected telephone numbers to prevent unsolicited telemarketing and commercial telephone calls and texts.
National Environmental Policy Act (NEPA) A federal statute that mandates that the federal government consider the adverse impact a federal government action would have on the environment before the action is implemented.
National Highway Traffic Safety Administration (NHTSA) A federal administrative agency that is part of the U.S. Department of Transportation. It administers and issues regulations to enforce the National Traffic and Motor Vehicle Safety Act.
National Labor Relations Act (NLRA) (Wagner Act) A federal statute enacted in 1935 that established the right of employees to form and join labor organizations, to bargain collectively with employers, and to engage in concerted activity to promote these rights.
National Labor Relations Board (NLRB) A federal administrative agency that oversees union elections, prevents employers and unions from engaging in illegal and unfair labor practices, and enforces and interprets certain federal labor laws.
national origin The country or section of the world of a person's ancestors; physical, linguistic, or cultural characteristics; or heritage.
national origin discrimination Employment discrimination against a person because of his or her heritage, cultural characteristics, or the country of the person's ancestors.
national origin harassment Lewd remarks, intimidation, or derogatory conduct about a person's national origin or ethnicity that occurs on the job that creates a hostile work environment.
National Traffic and Motor Vehicle Safety Act A federal statute that regulates the safety of automobiles, SUVs, vans, trucks, electric powered vehicles, self-driving vehicles, school buses, and motorcycles.
Natural Law School A school of jurisprudential thought that postulates that law is based on what is "correct." It emphasizes a moral theory of law—that is, law should be based on morality and ethics.
natural monopoly A monopoly that exists because of the nature of the market (e.g., a small market that can support only one competitor, such as a small-town newspaper). This is a defense to a charge of committing an act of monopolization.
necessaries of life Food, clothing, shelter, medical care, and other items considered necessary to the maintenance of life. Minors must pay the reasonable value of necessaries of life for which they contract.
Necessary and Proper Clause (elastic clause) A clause of the U.S. Constitution that grants the U.S. Congress the power to make federal laws that are necessary and proper to implement its express powers.
negative easement An express easement whereby the owner of real property makes a promise to another owner of real property that he or she will not do something with or on his or her real property.
negligence (unintentional tort or ordinary negligence) The failure to do something that a reasonable person would do or doing

something that a reasonable person would not do, in like or similar circumstances.
negligence *per se* A tort in which the violation of a statute or an ordinance constitutes the breach of the duty of care.
negligent infliction of emotional distress A tort that permits a person to recover for emotional distress caused by the defendant's negligent conduct.
negotiable instrument (commercial paper) A special form of contract that satisfies the requirements established by Article 3 of the UCC.
negotiation A procedure whereby the parties to a dispute engage in discussions and bargaining to try to reach a voluntary settlement of their dispute; A term that describes the transfer of negotiable instruments to subsequent transferees.
net lease A lease arrangement in which the tenant is responsible for paying rent and property taxes.
net, net, net lease (triple net lease) A lease arrangement in which the tenant is responsible for paying the rent, property taxes, utilities, and insurance.
New York Stock Exchange (NYSE) A primary stock exchange that lists the stocks and securities of approximately 3,000 of the world's largest companies for trading.
New York Times Co. v. Sullivan U.S. Supreme Court decision that held that *public officials* cannot recover for defamation unless they can prove that the defendant acted with "actual malice."
No Electronic Theft Act (NET Act) A federal statute that makes it a crime for a person to willfully infringe on a copyright.
no par value shares Common stock on which the corporation has not set the lowest price at which the shares may be issued by the corporation.
no-arrival, no-sale contract A shipping term that requires the seller of goods to bear the expense and risk of loss of the goods during transportation.
***Noerr* doctrine** A doctrine that says that two or more persons can petition the executive, legislative, or judicial branch of the government or administrative agencies to enact laws or take other action without violating antitrust laws.
no-fault automobile insurance An automobile insurance system used by some states in which the driver's insurance company pays for any injuries or death the driver suffers in an accident, no matter who caused the accident.
no-fault divorce A divorce recognized by the law of a state whereby neither party is blamed for the divorce.
nolo contendere A plea entered by a criminal defendant who has been sued by the government whereby the accused agrees to the imposition of a penalty but does not admit guilt.
nominal damages Damages awarded when the nonbreaching party sues the breaching party even though no financial loss has resulted from the breach. Nominal damages are usually $1 or some other small amount.
nominated bank (accepting bank) The bank that accepts a letter of credit on behalf of a seller in an international sales transaction.
nonaccredited investor An investor who does not meet the net worth, income, asset, position, and other requirements established by the Securities and Exchange Commission (SEC) to qualify as an *accredited investor*.
nonattainment area A geographical area that does not meet government-established air quality standards.
nonbinding arbitration An agreement between the parties to a dispute whereby they agree that the decision and award of the arbitrator can be appealed to the courts.
nonconforming use Uses and buildings that already exist in a zoned area that are permitted to continue even though they do not fit within new zoning ordinances.
nonconvertible preferred stock Preferred stock that does not permit preferred stockholders to convert their shares into common stock.
noncumulative preferred stock Preferred stock that has no right of accumulation; that is, the corporation does not have to pay previously missed preferred stock dividends before common shareholders can be paid dividends.
nonexempt property Property of a debtor that is not exempt from the bankruptcy estate that is distributed to the debtor's secured and unsecured creditors pursuant to statutory priority established by the Bankruptcy Code.
nonfreehold estate An estate where the tenant has a right to possess the real property but does not own title to the property.
nonintent crime A crime that imposes criminal liability without a finding of *mens rea* (intent).
nonissuer exemption An exemption that says that securities transactions not performed by an issuer, an underwriter, or a dealer do not have to be registered with the Securities and Exchange Commission (SEC) (e.g., normal purchases of securities by investors).
nonjudicial dispute resolution An arrangement in which disputes are resolved outside of the court judicial system. This is often referred to as *alternative dispute resolution (ADR)*.
nonnegotiable contract A contract that fails to meet the requirements of a negotiable instrument and, therefore, is not subject to the provisions of Revised Article 3 (Negotiable Instruments) of the Uniform Commercial Code (UCC). A nonnegotiable contract can be enforced under normal contract law.
nonobvious A patent requirement that an invention is nonobvious; if it is obvious, then it does not qualify for a patent.
nonparticipating preferred stock Preferred stock that does not give a preferred stockholder a right to participate in the profits of the corporation beyond the fixed dividend rate of the preferred stock.
nonpossessory interest A situation in which a person holds an interest in another party's real property without actually owning any part of the property. Three types of nonpossessory interests are *easements, licenses*, and *profits*.
nonprice vertical restraint Restraints of trade that are unlawful under Section 1 of the Sherman Act if their anticompetitive effects outweigh their precompetitive effects.
nonrecordation of a mortgage A situation that occurs if a mortgage or deed of trust is not recorded in the county recorder's office in the county in which the real property is located.
nonredeemable preferred stock Preferred stock that does not permit a corporation to buy back the preferred stock at some future date.
nonrestrictive indorsement An indorsement that has no instructions or conditions attached to the payment of the funds.
non-solicitation agreement An agreement in which an employee agrees that they will not solicit the clients or customers of the employer for their own benefit or for the benefit of a competitor of the employer after their employment ends.
Norris-LaGuardia Act A federal statute enacted in 1932 that made it lawful for employees to organize labor unions.
North American Free Trade Agreement (NAFTA) A treaty that removed or reduced tariffs, duties, quotas, and other trade barriers between the United States, Canada, and Mexico. NAFTA was replaced by the United States–Mexico–Canada Agreement (USMCA) in 2020.
no-strike clause A clause in a collective bargaining agreement between an employer and a labor union whereby the union agrees to not strike during a particular period of time.
not guilty A plea that may be entered by an accused at his or her arraignment whereby the accused states that he or she did not commit the crime that he or she is charged with.
note An instrument that evidences the borrower's debt to the lender; A debt security with a maturity of five years or less; An instrument that evidences a borrower's debt to a lender where a deed of trust and note is used for the purchase of real property on credit. Notes can be either unsecured or secured.
not-for-profit corporation (nonprofit corporation) A corporation formed to operate charitable institutions, colleges, universities, and other not-for-profit entities. These corporations have no shareholders.
notice of appeal A document filed by a party within a prescribed time after judgment is entered to appeal the decision of a court.
notice of assignment Notice given by an assignee to an obligor under a contract that an assignment of the obligor's duty of performance has been made and that his or her performance must be rendered to the assignee.
notice of dishonor The formal act of letting the party with secondary liability to pay a negotiable instrument know that the instrument has been dishonored.
notice of lien Notice filed by a lienholder with the county recorder's office in the county in which real property is located stating that a mechanic's lien has been filed against the property.
notice of termination of an agency A notice that must be given by a principal that notifies third parties that a person is no longer his or her agent. Failure to give such notice may make the principal liable for the prior agent's acts under the doctrine of apparent agency.

novation agreement (novation) An agreement that substitutes a new party for one of the original contracting parties and relieves the exiting party of liability on the contract.
novel A patent requirement that an invention is new and has not been invented and used in the past.
Nuclear Regulatory Commission (NRC) A federal administrative agency that licenses the construction and opening of commercial nuclear power plants.
Nuclear Waste Policy Act (NWPA) A federal statute that mandates that the federal government select permanent sites for the disposal of nuclear wastes.
nuclear wastes Consist of pollution from nuclear power plants and emissions from uranium mines and mills.
nuncupative will (dying declaration or deathbed will) An oral will that is made before a witness during the testator's last illness.
Nutrition Facts Label A label required by federal law that must appear on certain food and beverage items. It discloses calorie nutrition information that is easily visible to consumers.
Nutrition Labeling and Education Act (NLEA) A federal statute that requires food manufacturers to place on food labels that disclose nutritional information about the food.
NYSE Euronext The organization that operates the New York Stock Exchange (NYSE) and Euronext electronic stock exchange.
Oath of Citizenship An oath that foreign nationals who qualify and have met the necessary requirements must take to become a citizen of the United States.
Obergefell v. Hodges A U.S. Supreme Court decision that held that same-sex partners have the right to marry.
objective rule In an engagement situation, a rule that states that if the engagement is broken off, the person who was given the ring must return the engagement ring, regardless of who broke off the engagement.
objective theory of contracts A theory that says the intent to contract is judged by the reasonable person standard and not by the subjective intent of the parties.
obligee The party who is owed a right under a contract.
obligor The party who owes a duty of performance under a contract.
obscene speech Speech that (1) appeals to the prurient interest, (2) depicts sexual conduct in a patently offensive way, and (3) lacks serious literary, artistic, political, or scientific value.
Occupational Safety and Health Act A federal statute that promotes safety in the workplace.
Occupational Safety and Health Administration (OSHA) A federal administrative agency that is empowered to enforce the Occupational Safety and Health Act.
offensive speech Speech that is offensive to many members of society. It is subject to time, place, and manner restrictions.
offer The manifestation of willingness to enter into a bargain, so made as to justify another person in understanding that his assent to that bargain is invited and will conclude it.
offeree The party to whom an offer to enter into a contract is made.
offering circular A document that must be provided by an issuer of securities to investors who are purchasing securities issued pursuant to Regulation A of the Securities Act of 1933.
offering statement A document that must be filed by an issuer with the Securities and Exchange Commission (SEC) prior to selling most securities pursuant to Regulation A of the Securities Act of 1933.
offeror The party who makes an offer to enter into a contract.
offshoring The practice of a U.S. company relocating a business function to another country, retaining ownership of the division of unit, and hiring foreign workers to do the work.
Oil Pollution Act (OPA) A federal statute that requires the oil industry to take measures to prevent oil spills and to readily respond to and clean up oil spills.
Older Workers Benefit Protection Act (OWBPA) A federal statute that prohibits age discrimination in regard to employee benefits.
omnibus clause (other-driver clause) A clause that can be added to automobile insurance that protects the owner of the vehicle when someone else drives the car with his or her permission.
"on them" item A check presented for payment by a payee or holder where the depository bank and the payer bank are not the same bank.
"on us" item A check presented for payment where the depository bank is also the payer bank. That is, the drawer and payee or holder have accounts at the same bank.
one-year rule A rule that states that an executory contract that cannot be performed on its own terms within one year of its formation must be in writing; A rule that stipulates that if a drawer fails to report a forged or altered check to the bank within one year of receiving the bank statement and canceled checks containing it, the bank is relieved of any liability for paying the instrument.
online banking A system in which bank customers can check their bank statements online, pay bills from their bank accounts, transfer funds between accounts, and conduct other banking services using the internet.
open and obvious danger A rule that states that a possessor of real property is not liable to invitees who are injured by a danger that a reasonable person would have been able to observe, recognize, and perceive through casual inspection.
open assortment term A term in a sales contract that says that if the assortment of goods to a sales contract is left open, the buyer is given the option of choosing those goods but must make the selection in good faith and within limits set by commercial reasonableness.
open delivery term A term in a sales contract that says that if the parties do not agree to the time, place, and manner of delivery of the goods, the place for delivery is the seller's place of business. If the seller does not have a place of business, delivery is to be made at the seller's residence.
open payment term A term in a sales contract that says that if the parties do not agree as to the time and place of payment, then payment is due at the time and place at which the buyer is to receive the goods.
open price term A term in a sales contract that says that if the contract does not contain a specific price then a "reasonable price" is implied at the time of delivery.
open shop A place of employment where a worker is not required to join or financially support a union.
open terms Terms left open in a sales or lease contract that are permitted to be "read into" the sales or lease contract.
open time term A term in a sales contract that says that if the parties do not set a specific time of performance for any obligation under the contract, the contract must be performed within a reasonable time.
open, visible, and notorious A requirement that must be proven by a person to obtain real property by adverse possession. It requires that the adverse possessor has occupied the property so as to put the owner on notice of the possession.
opening brief A written document prepared by an appellant and filed with an appellate court that sets forth legal research and other information that supports the appellant's contentions on appeal.
opening statement Statements made by each party's attorney to the jury at the beginning of a trial.
option contract A contract that is created when an offeree pays an offeror compensation to keep an offer open for an agreed-upon period of time. An option contract prevents the offeror from revoking his or her offer during the option period.
Optional Practical Training (OPT) A program that allows F-1 visa holders to temporarily work in the United States to get practical training after graduation or completion of at least nine months of an academic program.
order A decision of an administrative law judge (ALJ) that is issued in the form of an administrative order.
order for relief An order that occurs upon the filing of either a voluntary petition or an unchallenged involuntary petition, or an order that is granted after a trial of a challenged involuntary petition.
order instrument (order paper) An instrument that is payable (1) to the order of an identified person or (2) to an identified person or order. An instrument that is negotiated by (1) delivery and (2) indorsement.
order to pay A drawer's unconditional order to a drawee to pay a draft or check to a payee.
ordinance Law enacted by local government bodies, such as cities and municipalities, counties, school districts, and water districts.
ordinary bailments Bailments such as a bailment for the sole benefit of the bailor, a bailment for the sole benefit of the bailee, and a mutual benefit bailment.
ordinary check An order by a drawer to a drawee bank to pay a specified sum of

money from the drawer's checking account to the named payee (or holder).
ordinary lease Under the Uniform Commercial Code (UCC), a lease of goods by a lessor to a lessee.
ordinary negligence (unintentional tort or negligence) The failure to do something that a reasonable person would do or doing something that a reasonable person would not do, in like or similar circumstances.
Organic Foods Production Act (OFPA) A federal statute that establishes a program for producers and handlers of agricultural foods produced using organic methods to be certified as organic.
Organization of the Petroleum Exporting Countries (OPEC) An association composed of many of the oil-producing countries of the world.
organizational meeting A meeting that must be held by the initial directors of a corporation after the articles of incorporation are filed.
original contract (primary contract) In a guarantee situation, the contract between the debtor and the creditor, which the guarantor has guaranteed to pay.
original tenor The original amount for which the drawer wrote a check.
outgoing partner A partner who leaves a partnership.
output contract A contract in which a seller agrees to sell all of its production to a single buyer.
outside director (independent director) A member of a board of directors of a corporation who is not an officer of the corporation.
outside sales representative exemption An exemption from federal minimum wage and overtime pay requirements that applies to employees whose primary duty is making sales or obtaining orders or contracts for services, who are customarily and regularly engaged away from the employer's place of business, and who will be paid by the client or customer.
outsourcing The practice of a U.S. company hiring an independent third-party company in another country to produce a good or service.
outstanding shares Shares that are in shareholder hands, whether originally issued shares or shares that have been repurchased by the corporation and reissued. Only outstanding shares have the right to vote.
overdraft The amount of money a drawer owes a bank after it has paid a check despite the drawer's account having insufficient funds.
overdue time instrument A time instrument that has not been paid on its expressed due date; it becomes overdue the next day.
oversecured creditor A secured creditor in a bankruptcy proceeding where the value of the collateral securing the secured loan exceeds the creditor's secured interest.
overtime pay A requirement of the Fair Labor Standards Act (FLSA), a federal statute, that workers be paid overtime pay of one-and-a-half times their regular pay for each hour worked in excess of 40 hours per week, with each week being treated separately.
owner A person who contracts with the insurance company for life insurance coverage.
own recognizance (OR) The grant of a suspect's release pending trial for less serious charges and if the suspect is not a flight risk, based on the suspect's promise to return for future court proceedings. No bail money need be paid to the court, and no bond is necessary.
ownership interest The interest that a partner owns of a partnership.
Palsgraf v. The Long Island Railroad Company A landmark case that established the doctrine of proximate cause.
par value shares Common stock on which the corporation has set the lowest price at which the shares may be issued by the corporation.
parent corporation A multinational corporation that owns the shares of a subsidiary corporation located in another country; A corporation that owns the shares of a subsidiary corporation in a share exchange.
parent–child privilege A privilege granted to an accused through the Fifth Amendment to the U.S. Constitution to keep his or her child or his or her parent from testifying against him or her; a child or parent may testify against his or her parent or child where the accused is charged with harming his or her child or parent.
parol evidence Any oral or written words outside the four corners of a written contract.
parol evidence rule A rule that says if a written contract is a complete and final statement of the parties' agreement, any prior or contemporaneous oral or written statements that alter, contradict, or are in addition to the terms of the written contract are inadmissible in court regarding a dispute over the contract. There are several exceptions to this rule.
part performance An equitable doctrine that allows the court to order an oral contract for the sale of land or transfer of another interest in real property to be specifically performed if it has been partially performed and performance is necessary to avoid injustice.
partial comparative negligence (modified comparative negligence) A rule that provides that a plaintiff must be less than 50 percent responsible for causing his or her own injuries to recover under comparative negligence; otherwise, contributory negligence applies.
partial strike (intermittent strike) A labor strike in which the striking employees strike part of the day or workweek and work the other part. Such strikes are illegal because they deny the employer's statutory right to continue its operations during a strike; also known as *intermittent strike*.
partially disclosed agency An agency in which a contracting third party knows that the agent is acting for a principal but does not know the identity of the principal.
partially disclosed principal The principal in a partially disclosed agency.
participating preferred stock Stock that allows the preferred stockholder to participate in the profits of the corporation along with the common stockholders.
partnership at will (at-will partnership) A partnership with no fixed duration.
partnership for a term (term partnership) A partnership with a fixed duration or stated purpose.
passage of title Precise rules in Article 2 of the Uniform Commercial Code (UCC) for determining how title passes in sales contracts.
past consideration A prior act or performance. Past consideration (e.g., prior acts) will not support a new contract. New consideration must be given.
patent A grant by the federal government upon the inventor of an invention for the exclusive right to use, sell, or license the patent for a limited amount of time.
patent application An application that is filed with the U.S. Patent and Trademark Office (PTO) that must contain a written description of the invention sought to be patented.
patent infringement Unauthorized use of another's patent. A patent holder may recover damages and other remedies against a patent infringer.
patent number A number that is assigned to a patent if a patent is granted.
patent pending A designation that an applicant can use on an article if a patent application has been filed but a patent has not yet been issued.
Patent Trial and Appeal Board (PTAB) A government body within the U.S. Patent and Trademark Office that reviews adverse decisions by patent examiners, reviews reexaminations, conducts post-grant reviews, and conducts other patent challenge proceedings.
payable at a definite time (time instrument) An instrument that is payable at a designated future date.
payable in foreign currency A provision of Revised Article 3 (Negotiable Instruments) of the Uniform Commercial Code (UCC) that an instrument may state that it is payable in a foreign currency.
payable in money A requirement that a negotiable instrument be payable in a fixed amount of *money* defined as a medium of exchange authorized or adopted by a domestic or foreign government as part of its currency.
payable in the alternative An instrument that is payable to two or more payees or indorsees because it uses the word *or*; either person's indorsement signature alone is sufficient to negotiate the instrument.
payable jointly An instrument that is payable to two or more payees or indorsees because it uses the word *and*; both persons' indorsements are necessary to negotiate the instrument.
payable on demand A requirement that a negotiable instrument be payable either on demand or at a definite time.
payable to bearer A designation on a negotiable instrument that makes it payable to anyone who is in possession of the instrument who presents it for payment when it is due.
payable to order A designation on a negotiable instrument that makes it payable to an identified person or order.
payee of a certificate of deposit A depositor who lends a financial institution money and is issued a certificate of deposit (borrower).

payee of a check A party to whom a check is written.
payee of a draft A party who receives the money from a draft.
payee of a note A party to whom a promise to pay is made (lender).
payer bank A bank where a drawer has a checking account and on which a check is drawn.
payment Unless the parties agree otherwise, payment is due from a buyer when and where the goods or property is delivered.
penal code A collection of criminal statutes.
penalty A fine that is imposed if liquidated damages are excessive or unconscionable or if actual damages are clearly determinable in advance and make the liquidated damage clause unenforceable.
***per capita* distribution** A distribution of an estate in which each grandchild and great-grandchild of the deceased inherits equally with the children of the deceased.
***per se* rule** A rule that is applicable to restraints of trade considered inherently anticompetitive (e.g., price fixing). Once this determination is made about a restraint of trade, the court will not permit any defenses or justifications to save it.
***per stirpes* distribution** A distribution of an estate in which grandchildren and great-grandchildren of the deceased inherit by representation of their parent.
peremptory challenge (peremptory strike) A rule that permits each party to a lawsuit to dismiss a limited number of proposed jurors from becoming jurors without having to show that the dismissed individuals were biased.
perfect tender rule A rule that says if the goods or tender of a delivery fail in any respect to conform to the contract, the buyer may opt either (1) to reject the whole shipment, (2) to accept the whole shipment, or (3) to reject part and accept part of the shipment.
perfection by a purchase money security interest in consumer goods A creditor who extends credit to a consumer to purchase a consumer good under a written security agreement obtains a security interest in the consumer good that automatically perfects the creditor's security interest at the time of the sale. Also known as *perfection by attachment* or the *automatic perfection rule*.
perfection by attachment (automatic perfection rule) A rule that stipulates that a creditor who extends credit to a consumer to purchase a consumer good under a written security agreement has an automatically perfected security interest in the goods at the time of the sale without having to file a financing statement.
perfection by filing a financing statement In a secured transaction, perfecting a creditor's security interest in collateral by filing a financing statement in the appropriate government office.
perfection by possession of collateral A rule that says if a secured creditor has physical possession of the collateral, no financing statement has to be filed; the creditor's possession is sufficient to put other potential creditors on notice of the creditor's secured interest in the property.
perfection of a security interest A process that establishes the right of a secured creditor against other creditors who claim an interest in the collateral.
period of minority The period below the statutory age of majority, as set by state law for a person to have the capacity to enter into contracts.
period of redemption The period of time during which a mortgagor may redeem real property after default and before foreclosure.
periodic tenancy A tenancy of real property created when a lease specifies intervals at which payments are due but does not specify how long the lease is for.
permanency requirement A requirement that a negotiable instrument be in a permanent state, such as written on paper.
permanent alimony (lifetime alimony) Alimony that is ordered by the court to be paid by one divorcing spouse to the other divorcing spouse until the receiving spouse dies or remarries.
permissive subjects Subjects of collective bargaining that are not compulsory subjects of bargaining but are employment issues that the company and union agree to bargain over.
perpetuity Corporations may exist in perpetuity unless a specific duration is stated in the corporation's articles of corporation.
personal articles floater (personal effects floater) An addition to a homeowners' policy that covers specific valuable items. An insured usually purchases a personal liability floater to obtain insurance for specific valuable items (e.g., jewelry, works of art, furs).
personal defenses Defenses that can be raised against enforcement of a negotiable instrument by an ordinary holder but not against a holder in due course (HDC).
personal guarantee A guarantee given by an individual, a limited partner of a limited partnership, a partner of a limited liability partnership, a member of a limited liability company, a shareholder of a corporation, and others whereby they guaranty that if another party does not repay a loan or debt or obligation, then they will pay the unpaid amount.
personal liability Liability imposed on individuals whereby they are personally liable for their own debts, and are sometimes held liable for another party's debts and obligations, such as being a guarantor of another person's debt or a general partner of a general or limited partnership.
personal property Tangible property such as equipment, vehicles, furniture, and jewelry, as well as intangible property such as securities, patents, trademarks, and copyrights.
personal representative A person who is named in a testator's or testatrix's will who is appointed to administer the estate during the probate of a will. Also called an *executor* (male) or *executrix* (female).
personal satisfaction test A subjective test that is used to determine if contracts involving personal taste and comfort meet a condition precedent.
personal service contract A contract for the provision of personal services.
petition for bankruptcy A document filed with a bankruptcy court that starts a bankruptcy proceeding.
petition for certiorari A petition asking the Supreme Court to hear a case.
petition for divorce A document filed with the proper state court that commences a divorce proceeding.
petitioner The party appealing the decision of an administrative agency.
physical delivery The usual method of transferring personal property.
physical or mental examination A court-ordered examination of a party to a lawsuit before trial to determine the extent of the alleged injuries.
physiological impairments Under the Americans with Disabilities Act, as amended, a disability such as a physical disorder or condition, cosmetic disfigurement, or anatomical loss affecting one or more of the following body systems: neurological, musculoskeletal, special sense organs, respiratory, cardiovascular, reproductive, digestive, genitourinary, hemic and lymphatic, skin, and endocrine.
picketing The action of strikers walking in front of an employer's premises, carrying signs announcing their strike.
piercing the corporate veil (alter ego doctrine) A doctrine that says if a shareholder dominates a corporation and uses it for improper purposes, a court of equity can disregard the corporate entity and hold the shareholder personally liable for the corporation's debts and obligations; also called the *alter ego doctrine*.
place of delivery The place where goods subject to a sales or lease contract are to be delivered to the buyer or lessee.
places of public accommodation Places such as motels, hotels, restaurants, movie theaters, and such.
plaintiff The party who files a complaint that initiates a lawsuit.
plaintiff's case The case presented by the plaintiff, who bears the burden of proof and therefore proceeds before the defendant in calling and examining witnesses and introducing evidence supporting his or her case.
plant closing As defined in the Worker Adjustment and Retraining Notification (WARN) Act, the permanent or temporary shutdown of a single site that results in a loss of employment of 50 or more employees during any 30-day period.
plant life and vegetation Plant life and vegetation that is growing on the surface of land and is considered part of the real property.
plea An accused's statement as to whether he or she is *guilty* or *not guilty* of the crime charged at his or her arraignment.
plea bargain Negotiations between an accused and the government with the intent of reaching an agreement between the parties to avoid a trial.
plea bargain agreement An agreement in which the accused admits to a lesser crime than charged. In return, the government agrees to impose a lesser sentence than might have been obtained had the case gone to trial.

pleadings The paperwork that is filed with the court to initiate and respond to a lawsuit.
plurality decision A decision of the court in which a majority of the justices agree as to the outcome of a case but not as to the reasoning for reaching the outcome. A plurality decision settles the case but is not precedent for later cases.
point sources of water pollution Sources of water pollution such as mines, manufacturing plants, electric utility plants, paper mills, and sewage plants.
poison pill Defensive strategies built into a corporation's articles of incorporation, corporate bylaws, or the corporation's contracts and leases that prevent the takeover of the corporation.
police power Power that permits states and local governments to enact laws to protect or promote the public health, safety, morals, and general welfare.
portability requirement A requirement that a negotiable instrument must be able to be easily transported.
possession Acquiring ownership to unowned personal property by taking possession of it, or capturing it. The most notable unowned objects are things in their natural state (e.g., hunting game).
possession of tangible token rule A rule that stipulates that where there have been successive assignments of a contract right that is represented by a tangible token (e.g., stock certificate, savings account passbook), the first assignee who receives delivery of the tangible token prevails over subsequent assignees.
post judgment court order An order of a court that permits the seizure of a debtor's property that is in the debtor's possession or in the possession of third parties after a creditor has won a judgment against a debtor.
postdated check A check that a drawer does not want cashed until sometime in the future.
postnuptial agreement An agreement entered into by spouses during the marriage that sets forth the distribution of property upon termination of the marriage, and addresses other issues (e.g., alimony).
postpetition counseling Personal financial counseling that a debtor must receive before he or she receives a discharge in a Chapter 7 or Chapter 13 bankruptcy.
power of attorney An express agency agreement that is often used to give an agent the power to sign legal documents on behalf of the principal.
power of sale A power stated in a mortgage or deed that permits foreclosure without court proceedings and sale of the property through an auction.
precedent A rule of law established in a court decision. Lower courts must follow the precedent established by higher courts.
predatory pricing Pricing of a product or service below average or marginal cost that is intended to drive out competition.
preemption doctrine A doctrine that provides that federal law takes precedence over state or local law.
preemptive rights Rights that give existing shareholders of a corporation the option to purchase new shares issued by the corporation in proportion to their current ownership interests.
preexisting duty Something a person is already under an obligation to do. A promise lacks consideration if a person promises to perform a preexisting duty.
preferred stock A type of equity security that is given certain preferences and rights over common stock.
preferred stock certificate A document that represents a preferred shareholder's investment in the corporation.
preferred stockholder A person who owns preferred stock.
Pregnancy Discrimination Act A federal statute that forbids employment discrimination because of pregnancy, childbirth, or related medical conditions.
prejudgment court order An order of a court that permits the seizure of a debtor's property that is in the debtor's possession while a lawsuit against the debtor is pending.
preliminary prospectus A written disclosure document that must be submitted by an issuer of securities to the Securities and Exchange Commission (SEC) with the registration statement and is provided to potential investors to enable them to evaluate the financial risk of an investment.
premises liability Liability that is imposed on landowners and tenants for breaching duties that they owe to visitors who are injured on their real property.
premium Money paid to an insurance company by an insured to purchase insurance.
prenuptial agreement (premarital agreement) A contract entered into prior to marriage that specifies how property will be distributed upon the termination of the marriage or death of a spouse.
prepayment clause A clause in an instrument that permits the maker to pay the amount due prior to the due date of the instrument.
prepetition counseling Counseling that a debtor must receive within 180 days prior to filing his or her petition for bankruptcy.
present possessory interest A principle that states that an owner of real property may use and enjoy the property as he or she sees fit, subject to any applicable government regulation or private restraint.
presentment A demand for acceptance or payment of an instrument made upon the maker, acceptor, drawee, or other payer by or on behalf of the holder.
presentment across the counter A depositor's physically presenting a check for payment at the payor bank instead of depositing an "on them" check for collection.
presentment warranties Three warranties that a person who presents a draft or check for payment or acceptance makes to a drawee or an acceptor who pays or accepts the instrument in good faith: (1) The presenter has good title to the instrument or is authorized to obtain payment or acceptance of the person who has good title; (2) the instrument has not been materially altered; and (3) the presenter has no knowledge that the signature of the maker or drawer is unauthorized.
presumed innocent until proven guilty A legal rule that provides that a person charged with a crime in the United States is presumed innocent until proven guilty.
pretrial motions A motion a party can make to try to dispose of all or part of a lawsuit prior to trial.
price discrimination Discrimination that occurs when a seller sells goods of like grade and quality to different buyers at different prices contemporaneously in time. There are several exceptions to this rule.
price fixing A restraint of trade that occurs when competitors in the same line of business agree to set the price of the goods or services they sell, raising, depressing, fixing, pegging, or stabilizing the price of a commodity or service. This is a *per se* violation of Section 1 of the Sherman Act as an unreasonable restraint of trade.
priest/rabbi/minister/imam–penitent privilege A privilege granted to an accused through the Fifth Amendment to the U.S. Constitution to keep his or her priest/rabbi/minister/imam from testifying against him or her. There are exceptions to this privilege.
primarily liable Liability of a surety (co-debtor, co-signor) where the surety has co-signed another's person's debt and promises to be liable for paying the debt.
primary liability Absolute liability to pay a negotiable instrument, subject to certain universal (real) defenses. Makers of promissory notes and certificates of deposit have primary liability for paying the instrument.
principal A party who employs another person to act on his or her behalf.
principal–agent relationship A relationship formed when an employer hires an employee and gives that employee authority to act and enter into contracts on his or her behalf; A relationship that is created if a bank customer writes a check against his or her account or deposits a check that the bank must collect. The customer is the principal, and the bank is the agent.
principal–independent contractor relationship The relationship between a principal and an independent contractor who is not an employee of the principal but has been employed by the principal to perform a certain task on behalf of the principal.
prior art A reference, description, or event in the past that demonstrates that an invention is not new and therefore does not qualify to be patented.
priority of claims The order in which conflicting claims of creditors to the same collateral are solved.
Privacy Act A federal statute that stipulates that federal administrative agencies can only maintain information about an individual that is relevant and necessary to accomplish a legitimate agency purpose. The act permits persons to have access to their records and to correct information.
private civil action A lawsuit that any person who suffers antitrust injury in his or her "business or property" may bring against offenders to recover monetary damages caused by the violation, including treble damages.
private placement exemptions Exemptions from registration with the Securities and Exchange Commission of an issue of securities that do not involve a public offering. There are two private placement exemptions, one

provided under SEC Rule 506(b) and another under SEC Rule 506(c).
privilege against self-incrimination A provision of the Fifth Amendment to the U.S. Constitution that provides that a person need not be a witness against himself or herself in any criminal case.
Privileges and Immunities Clause A clause in Article IV of the U.S. Constitution which provides that "The Citizens of each State shall be entitled to all Privileges and Immunities of Citizens in the several states."
Privileges and Immunities Clauses A term that is sometimes used to collectively refer to both the Privileges and Immunities Clause and the Privileges or Immunities Clause. These constitutional provisions prohibit states from enacting laws that unduly discriminate in favor of their residents.
Privileges or Immunities Clause A clause in the Fourteenth Amendment to the U.S. Constitution which provides that "No State shall make or enforce any law that shall abridge the privileges or immunities of the citizens of the United States."
privity of contract The state of two specified parties being in a contract. Parties to a contract can sue one another for breach of the contract, but third parties (with few exceptions) cannot sue for such breach because they are not parties to the contract.
privity-like relationship The state where a relationship is almost one of privity of contract.
pro rata rule A rule that says shares must be purchased on a pro rata basis if too many shares are tendered.
***pro se* divorce** A divorce proceeding in which the parties represent themselves in the divorce action.
probability of a substantial lessening of competition or likelihood of creating a monopoly A test that is used in determining a violation of Section 7 of the Clayton Act when examining the legality of mergers.
probable cause Evidence of the substantial likelihood that a person either committed or is about to commit a crime.
probate The process of a deceased's property being collected, debts and taxes being paid, and the remainder of the estate being distributed; also called *settlement of the estate*.
probate court A specialized state court that supervises the administration and settlement of estates.
procedural administrative law Law that establishes the procedures that must be followed by administrative agencies while enforcing substantive laws.
procedural due process A category of due process that requires that the government give a person proper notice and hearing of the legal action before that person is deprived of his or her life, liberty, or property.
processing plant franchise A franchise arrangement in which a franchisor provides a secret formula or process to a franchisee, and the franchisee manufactures the product and distributes it to retail dealers.
product defect Something wrong, inadequate, or improper in the manufacture, design, packaging, warning, or instructions about a product.
product liability The liability of manufacturers, sellers, and others for the injuries caused by defective products.
product liability insurance Insurance that protects sellers and manufacturers against injuries caused by defective products.
product market extension merger A market extension merger between two firms that sell similar but not the same products in the same geographical area (e.g., a soft drink manufacturer and an orange juice producer).
product safety standards Safety standards issued by the Consumer Product Safety Commission (CPSC) for consumer products that pose unreasonable risk of injury.
production A common method of acquiring ownership in personal property. A manufacturer that purchases raw materials and produces a finished product owns that product.
production of documents A request by one party to another party to produce all documents relevant to the case prior to the trial.
professional corporation A corporation formed by lawyers, doctors, or other professionals.
professional limited liability company (PLLC) A type of limited liability company that can be formed and operated by professionals such as accountants, lawyers, doctors, and other designated professionals that have the benefits and attributes of an LLC.
professional malpractice The liability of a professional who breaches his or her duty of ordinary care.
professional malpractice insurance (malpractice insurance) Insurance that insures professionals against liability for injuries caused by their negligence.
profit motive A requirement for the formation of a general partnership that requires that the business is formed with the intent to make a profit.
profit-a-prendre A document that grants a person the right to remove something from another's real property; also known as *profit*.
promise to marry A promise of a person to marry another person.
promise to pay A maker's (borrower's) unconditional and affirmative undertaking to repay a debt to a payee (lender).
promisee A contracting party who directs that the benefit of his or her contract with another be conferred on a third party.
promisor A contracting party who agrees to confer the performance of his or her contract with another to a third party.
promissory estoppel (detrimental reliance) An equity doctrine that permits a court to order enforcement of a contract that lacks consideration.
promissory estoppel (equitable estoppel) An equity doctrine that permits enforcement of oral contracts that should have been in writing. It is applied to avoid injustice.
promissory note (note) A two-party negotiable instrument that is an unconditional written promise by one party (maker) to pay money to another party (payee).
promoter A person or persons who organize and start a corporation, negotiate and enter into contracts in advance of its formation, find the initial investors to finance the corporation, and so forth.
promoters' contracts A collective term for such things as leases, sales contracts, contracts to purchase property, and employment contracts entered into by promoters on behalf of the proposed corporation prior to its actual incorporation.
promoters' liability The liability of a person for the debts and obligations he or she has entered into on behalf of a proposed corporation prior to the formation of the corporation.
proof of claim A document required to be filed by a creditor that states the amount of his or her claim against the debtor.
proof of interest A document required to be filed by an equity security holder that states the amount of his or her interest against the debtor.
properly dispatched An acceptance of an offer being properly addressed, packaged, and posted.
proportionate liability A rule that limits a defendant's liability to its proportionate degree of fault.
proposed additions Additions to a sales contract proposed by an offeree where one or both parties are nonmerchants. If the offeree's proposed additions are accepted by the offeror they become part of the contract; If they are not accepted, the sales contract is formed on the basis of the terms of the original offer.
prosecutor (prosecuting attorney) The lawyer who represents the government in a criminal trial. Also called *prosecuting attorney*.
protected class A class of individuals (e.g., *women, people of color*) that is protected by the intermediate scrutiny test of the Equal Protection Clause of the Fourth Amendment to the U.S. Constitution.
provisional application An application that an inventor may file with the Patent and Trademark Office that gives the inventor three months to prepare a final patent application.
proximate cause (legal cause) A point along a chain of events caused by a negligent party after which that party is no longer legally responsible for the consequences of his or her actions; also called *legal cause*.
proxy A person who is granted authority to vote the shares of a shareholder; A written or electronic document signed by a shareholder that authorizes another person to vote the shareholder's shares.
proxy contest A contest in which opposing factions of shareholders and managers solicit proxies from other shareholders; the side that receives the greatest number of votes wins the proxy contest.
proxy statement A document that fully describes (1) the matter for which a proxy is being solicited, (2) who is soliciting the proxy, and (3) any other pertinent information.
psychiatrist/psychologist–patient privilege A privilege granted to an accused through the Fifth Amendment to the U.S. Constitution to keep his or her psychiatrist or psychologist from testifying against him or her. There are exceptions to this privilege.

public accountant A term that denotes persons who perform a variety of accounting services, including bookkeepers, tax preparers, and so on who are not certified as a certified public accountant (CPA).
Public Company Accounting Oversight Board (PCAOB) A board created by the Sarbanes-Oxley Act of 2002 that has the authority to adopt rules concerning auditing, accounting quality control, independence, and ethics of public companies and public accountants.
public defender A government or government-paid attorney who represents the accused defendant in a criminal trial if the accused cannot afford a private defense lawyer.
public domain The point in time when anyone can produce and sell a prior patented invention, copyrighted material, or trademark, after a patent period or copyright period runs out, or trademark is not renewed, or the patent, copyright, or trademark is abandoned.
public figure Plaintiffs such as movie stars, sports personalities, and other celebrities who cannot recover for defamation unless they can prove that the defendant acted with "actual malice."
public organic record A record that is available to the public for inspection that is the correct source of the debtor's name that appears on a financing statement.
public policy exception A law that states that employees, including at-will employees, cannot be discharged by an employer if such discharge violates public policy.
publicly held corporation A corporation that has many shareholders and whose securities are often traded on national stock exchanges.
punitive damages Damages that are awarded to punish the defendant, to deter the defendant from similar conduct in the future, and to set an example for others.
purchase The most common method of acquiring title to personal property is by *purchasing* the property from its owner.
purchase money security interest An interest a creditor automatically obtains when he or she extends credit to a consumer to purchase consumer goods.
qualified immunity (restricted immunity) A doctrine that states that foreign governments have qualified immunity from suits in U.S. courts, and are therefore subject to prosecution in U.S. courts under certain circumstances; also known as *restricted immunity*.
qualified individual with a disability A person who has a physical or mental impairment that substantially limits a major life activity who, with or without reasonable accommodation, can perform the essential functions of the job he or she desires or holds.
qualified indorsement An indorsement that includes the notation "without recourse" or similar language that disclaims liability of the indorser.
qualified indorser A party who disclaims liability and is not secondarily liable on negotiable instruments they endorse. A qualified indorser does not guarantee payment of the instrument if the maker, drawer, or acceptor defaults on it.
qualified opinion An auditor's opinion that states that a company's financial statements are fairly represented except for, or subject to, a departure from generally accepted accounting principles (GAAPs), a change in accounting principles, or a material uncertainty.
quality-control standards Standards that are set forth in a franchise agreement that require a franchisee to meet certain quality standards established by the franchisor.
quarterly report (Form 10-Q) A report that must be filed quarterly with the Securities and Exchange Commission (SEC) by reporting companies that sets forth their financial condition.
***quasi in rem* jurisdiction (attachment jurisdiction)** Jurisdiction that allows a plaintiff who obtains a judgment in one state to try to collect the judgment by attaching property of the defendant located in another state. Also called *attachment jurisdiction*.
quasi-contract An equitable doctrine whereby a court may award monetary damages to a plaintiff for providing work or services to a defendant even though no actual contract existed. The doctrine is intended to prevent unjust enrichment and unjust detriment. Also called *implied-in-law contract*.
quid pro quo sex discrimination Gender discrimination in employment that occurs when sexual favors are requested in order to obtain a job or be promoted. This violates Title VII of the Civil Rights Act.
quiet title action An action brought by a party, seeking an order of the court declaring who has title to disputed property. The court "quiets title" by its decision.
quitclaim deed A deed that provides the least amount of protection to the grantee because the grantor transfers only the interest he or she has in the property.
quorum The number of directors necessary to hold a board meeting or committee meeting in order to transact business of the board; the number of shares needed to be represented at a shareholders' meeting, in person or by proxy, before a shareholders' meeting can be held.
race discrimination Employment discrimination against a person because of his or her race, which includes African Americans, Asians, Caucasians, Native Americans, and Pacific Islanders.
racial harassment Lewd remarks, intimidation, or derogatory conduct about a person's race that occurs on the job that creates a hostile work environment.
Racketeer Influenced and Corrupt Organizations Act (RICO) A federal act that provides for both criminal and civil penalties for racketeering.
radiation pollution Emissions from radioactive wastes that can cause injury and death to humans and other life and can cause severe damage to the environment.
Railway Labor Act A federal statute enacted in 1926 and amended in 1934 that regulates labor organizing by employees of railroads and airlines.
ratification The act of a person after he or she has reached the age of majority by which he or she accepts a contract entered into when he or she was a minor.
ratification of a contract A situation in which a principal accepts an agent's unauthorized contract.
rational basis test A test that is applied to determine the constitutionality of classifications by the government that are not based on a suspect class, a fundamental right, or a protected class (e.g., age, government regulation).
Rawls's social justice theory (social contract theory) A theory of ethics that asserts that fairness is the essence of justice. The theory proffers that each person is presumed to have entered into a social contract with all others in society to obey moral rules that are necessary for people to live in peace and harmony.
reaffirmation agreement An agreement entered into by a debtor with a creditor prior to discharge, whereby the debtor agrees to pay the creditor a debt that would otherwise be discharged in bankruptcy. Certain requirements must be met for a reaffirmation agreement to be enforced.
real estate sales contract A contract for the sale of real property.
real property The land itself, as well as buildings, trees, soil, minerals, timber, plants, crops, fixtures, and other things permanently affixed to the land or buildings.
reasonable accommodation Under Title I of the Americans with Disabilities Act, assistance an employer is under an obligation to give to accommodate an individual's disability if doing so does not cause an undue hardship to the employer; Under Title VII of the Civil Rights Act of 1964, assistance an employer is under an obligation to give for the religious observances, practices, or beliefs of its employees if doing so does not cause an undue hardship to the employer.
reasonable person standard How an objective, careful, and conscientious person would have acted in the same circumstances. In a negligence action, the defendant's conduct is measured against that standard.
reasonable person test An objective test that is used to determine whether commercial contracts and contracts involving mechanical fitness meet a condition precedent.
reasonable professional standard How an objective, careful, and conscientious equivalent professional would have acted in the same circumstances. In a negligence action, the defendant professional's conduct is measured against that standard.
reasonable search and seizure Searches and seizures that are based on *probable cause* and do not violate the Fourth Amendment to the U.S. Constitution.
reasonable woman standard A standard that is applied in determining whether sexual discrimination or sexual harassment has occurred that allows a case to be analyzed from the perspective of the female complainant and not of the defendant.
reasonableness A word used throughout the UCC to establish the duties of performance by the parties to sales and lease contracts.
reasonably foreseeable misuse A misuse of a product that is foreseeable, and the

product could easily and reasonably be designed to prevent injury from the misuse.
rebuttal A process whereby after the defendant's attorney has finished calling witnesses, the plaintiff's attorney can call additional witnesses and put forth evidence to rebut the defendant's case.
receiving stolen property To (1) knowingly receive stolen property and (2) intend to deprive the rightful owner of that property.
recognizance A formal contract in which a party acknowledges in court that he or she will pay a specified sum of money if a certain event occurs.
reconveyance (satisfaction of a mortgage) A written document filed by a lender or trustee with the county recorder's office, which is proof that a mortgage or note secured by real property has been paid.
record Information about a trial such as the trial transcript, evidence introduced at trial, and the court's written memorandum; As defined by the Uniform Commercial Code, information that is inscribed on a tangible medium or that is stored in an electronic or other medium and is retrievable in perceivable form.
record date A date specified in corporate bylaws that determines whether a shareholder may vote at a shareholders' meeting.
recording statute A state statute that requires a mortgage or deed of trust to be recorded in the county recorder's office of the county in which the real property is located.
record-keeping device Negotiable instruments often serve as record-keeping devices.
redeemable preferred stock (callable preferred stock) Preferred stock that permits a corporation to buy back the preferred stock at some future date; also known as *callable preferred stock*.
re-direct examination Examination of the plaintiff's witness by the plaintiff after the defendant has examined the plaintiff's witness on cross-examination.
reformation An equitable doctrine that permits the court to rewrite a contract to express the parties' true intentions.
reformation of a deed The correction of inaccurate information in a real estate deed by action of a court.
Regional Comprehensive Economic Partnership (RCEP) A regional trade agreement between 15 countries of Asia and Pacific region that creates the world's largest regional trade zone.
regional trade agreement An agreement among multiple countries of a region that delineates terms of trade between the member countries.
registered Occurs when a business files a registration statement and prospectus with the Securities and Exchange Commission (SEC) registering its intent to issue securities to the public.
registered agent A person or corporation that is empowered to accept service of process on behalf of a corporation.
registered office An office designated in the articles of incorporation of a corporation that specifies where service of process on the corporation must be delivered.
registered organization An organization that is formed under the laws of a state or the United States, such as a corporation, limited liability company, limited partnership, general partnership, sole proprietorship, business trust, and such.
registration statement A document that an issuer of securities files with the Securities and Exchange Commission (SEC) that contains required information about the issuer, the securities to be issued, and other relevant information.
regular meeting of a board of directors A meeting held by the board of directors at the time and place established in the bylaws.
Regulation E A regulation adopted by the Federal Reserve Board that enforces and interprets the Electronic Funds Transfer Act.
Regulation Z A regulation that sets forth detailed rules for compliance with the TILA.
regulatory crime Violations of regulatory statutes that include securities, antitrust, environmental, consumer, employment, credit, bankruptcy, intellectual property, and other statutes.
regulatory licensing statutes Statutes that are enacted to protect the public that require certain persons or businesses to obtain a license from the government before being able to practice certain professions or engage in certain types of businesses.
regulatory statutes Statutes such as environmental laws, securities laws, and antitrust laws that provide for criminal violations and penalties.
rejection of an offer Express words or conduct by the offeree that rejects an offer. Rejection terminates the offer.
rejoinder A process whereby a defendant's attorney can call additional witnesses and introduce other evidence to counter the plaintiff's rebuttal.
relevant geographical market A relevant market that is defined as the area in which the defendant and its competitors sell the product or service.
relevant market The market required to be defined for a Sherman Act Section 2 charge of monopolization; includes defining the relevant product or service market and the geographical market.
relevant product or service market A relevant market that includes substitute products or services that are reasonably interchangeable with the defendant's products or services.
reliance on a misrepresentation An element of fraud that occurs when the innocent party to whom a misrepresentation of a material fact has been made justifiably relies on the misrepresentation and acts on it.
religious discrimination Discrimination against a person solely because of his or her religion or religious practices.
remainder A right of possession to real property that returns to a third party upon the expiration of a limited or contingent estate (e.g., life estate).
remainder beneficiary A person who possesses the right of remainder to real property upon the expiration of a limited or contingent estate (e.g., life estate); A person or an entity who receives the trust corpus upon the termination of a trust.
remittitur An action of a judge that reduces the amount of monetary damages awarded by the jury where the judge finds that the jury was biased, emotional, or inflamed in awarding damages.
renounce The action by a person who has been left an inheritance that rejects an inheritance.
rent The amount of money that a commercial or residential tenant has agreed to pay a landlord for the leased premises.
rent-control ordinances Local laws that stipulate the amount of rent a landlord can charge for residential housing.
renters' insurance Insurance that renters purchase to cover loss or damage to their possessions.
reorganization bankruptcy A form of bankruptcy in which a debtor reorganizes its capital structure, receives a partial discharge of unpaid debts, and takes other actions to emerge from bankruptcy as a viable concern.
replacement cost insurance Insurance that pays the cost to replace the damaged or destroyed property up to the policy limits.
replacement workers Workers who are hired by a company to take the place of striking employees. Replacement workers do not have to be dismissed when the strike is over.
replevin The right of a buyer or lessee to recover goods from a seller or lessor who is wrongfully withholding the goods.
reply A document filed by the original plaintiff to answer the defendant's cross complaint.
reporting company A company whose shares are traded on a national securities exchange, an issuer who has made a registered offering under the Securities Act of 1933, and a company with assets of at least $10 million that has at least 500 unaccredited shareholders or 2,000 total shareholders.
repossession A right granted to a secured creditor to take possession of the collateral upon default by the debtor.
representative's signature An authorized signature of a designated agent on a written document that is made on behalf of the agent's principal.
requirements contract A contract in which a buyer contracts to purchase all of its requirements for an item from one seller.
res ipsa loquitur A tort in which the presumption of negligence arises because (1) the defendant was in exclusive control of the situation and (2) the plaintiff would not have suffered injury but for someone's negligence. The burden switches to the defendant to prove that he or she was not negligent.
resale price maintenance (vertical price fixing) A *per se* violation of Section 1 of the Sherman Act that occurs when a party at one level of distribution enters into an agreement with a party at another level to adhere to a price schedule that either sets or stabilizes prices; also called *vertical price fixing*.
rescind An act that cancels a contract.
rescission An action to *rescind* (undo) a contract. Rescission is available if there has been a material breach of contract, fraud, duress, undue influence, or mistake.
reserved powers Powers that are not specifically delegated to the federal government

in the U.S. Constitution are reserved to the state governments.
residuary clause A clause in a will that leaves the remainder of an estate that remains after specific and general gifts are made and debts, taxes, and other costs are paid, to a beneficiary.
residuary gift A gift of an estate left after the debts, taxes, and specific and general gifts have been paid.
resolution Actions taken by the board of directors of a corporation, usually at a board meeting (e.g., authorizing the corporation to enter into contracts or mergers, or to employ corporate officers). Corporate resolutions are recorded in minutes of the board of directors' meetings and specify the decisions that were made by the board during their meetings.
Resource Conservation and Recovery Act (RCRA) A federal statute that authorizes the Environmental Protection Agency (EPA) to regulate facilities that generate, treat, store, transport, and dispose of hazardous wastes.
respondeat superior A rule that says an employer or a principal is liable for the tortious conduct of its employees or agents while they are acting within the scope of its authority.
responding brief A written document prepared by an appellee and filed with an appellate court that sets forth legal research and other information that supports the appellee's position on appeal.
Restatement of the Law of Contracts A compilation of model contract law principles drafted by legal scholars. The *Restatement* is not law.
Restatement (Second) of Agency The second edition of a compilation of model agency law principles drafted by legal scholars. The *Restatement* is not law.
Restatement (Second) of Contracts The second edition of the *Restatement of the Law of Contracts*. The *Restatement* is not law.
restitution The return of goods or property received from the other party to rescind a contract. If the actual goods or property are not available, a cash equivalent must be made.
restraining order An order that a court may issue if there is a showing that one person is likely to injure or harass another person; this order places limitations on the ability of the dangerous person to go near the person who has obtained the restraining order.
restrictive agreements Agreements in business and employment contracts that protect businesses and employers from employees, past employees, and others from using secret or proprietary knowledge about the company to harm the company.
restrictive indorsement An indorsement that contains some sort of instruction from the indorser.
retainer An amount of money deposited by a client with an attorney prior to the attorney agreeing to represent the client, from which fees are taken as the attorney provides services to the client.
resulting trust A trust that is implied from the conduct of the parties.
retaliation An action taken by an employer against an employee for filing a charge of discrimination or participating in a discrimination proceeding against the employer (e.g., dismissal or demotion). Retaliation violates antidiscrimination laws.
retention of collateral A secured creditor's repossession of collateral upon a debtor's default and proposal to retain the collateral in satisfaction of the debtor's obligation.
revenue-raising statute A licensing statute whose primary purpose is raising revenue for the government.
reverse discrimination Discrimination against a group that is usually thought of as a majority.
reverse engineering Taking apart and examining a rival's product or re-creating a secret recipe.
reverse tender offer A tender offer that is made by a target corporation to purchase the shares of the corporation that is making the tender offer on the target corporation.
reversion The right of possession that returns to the grantor of real property after the expiration of a limited or contingent estate (e.g., life estate).
Revised Article 3 (Negotiable Instruments) of the Uniform Commercial Code A comprehensive revision of the Uniform Commercial Code law of negotiable instruments that reflects modern commercial practices for the creation of, transfer of, enforcement of, and liability on negotiable instruments.
Revised Article 9 (Secured Transactions) of the Uniform Commercial Code An article of the Uniform Commercial Code that governs secured transactions in personal property.
Revised Model Business Corporation Act (RMBCA) A revision of the Model Business Corporation Act of 1950 that arranges the provisions of the act more logically, revises the language to be more consistent, and makes substantial changes in the provisions. A model act that is intended to provide a uniform law for the formation, operation, and termination of corporations.
Revised Uniform Limited Liability Company Act (RULLCA or Re-ULLCA or Uniform Limited Liability Company Act [2006]) A revision of the Uniform Limited Liability Company Act (ULLCA) that provides a more modern, comprehensive law for the formation, operation, and dissolution of limited liability companies.
Revised Uniform Limited Partnership Act (RULPA) A revision of the Uniform Limited Partnership Act (ULPA) that provides a modern, comprehensive law for the formation, operation, and dissolution of limited partnerships.
Revised Uniform Partnership Act (RUPA) A revision of the Uniform Partnership Act (UPA) that provides a more modern, comprehensive law for the formation, operation, and dissolution of general partnerships.
revocation Reversal of acceptance; Withdrawal of an offer by the offeror prior to its acceptance by the offeree, which terminates the offer; A situation that occurs when a testator or testatrix intentionally tears, burns, obliterates, or otherwise destroys his or her will.
reward An award given for performance of some service or attainment. To collect a reward, the offeree must (1) have knowledge of the reward offer prior to completing the requested act and (2) perform the requested act.
right of first refusal An agreement among shareholders of a corporation that requires a selling shareholder who is a signatory to the agreement to offer his or her shares for sale to the other parties to the agreement before selling them to anyone else.
right of redemption The right of a mortgagor to recover real property that is collateral for a mortgage after the debtor's default and before foreclosure by paying the mortgagee the full amount of the debt plus costs; The right of a debtor to recover personal property that is collateral for a secured transaction after the debtor's default and before the creditor has disposed of the property by paying the secured creditor the full amount of the debt plus costs.
right of survivorship of joint tenants A legal rule that provides upon the death of one joint tenant, the deceased person's interest in the real property automatically passes to the surviving joint tenant or joint tenants.
right to a public jury trial A right contained in the Sixth Amendment to the U.S. Constitution that guarantees a criminal defendant the right to a public jury trial.
right to cancel a contract The right of a buyer or lessee of goods if a seller or lessor fails to deliver conforming goods or repudiates the contract; The right of a seller or lessor of goods if the buyer or lessee breaches the contract by rejecting or revoking acceptance of the goods, failing to pay for the goods, or repudiating all or any part of the contract.
right to cover The right of a buyer or lessee to purchase or lease substitute goods if a seller or lessor fails to make delivery of the goods or repudiates the contract or if the buyer or lessee rightfully rejects the goods or justifiably revokes their acceptance.
right to cure The legal right of a seller or lessor who has delivered defective or nonconforming goods to repair or replace the defective or nonconforming goods if the time for performance has not expired and the seller or lessor notifies the buyer or lessee of his or her intention to make a conforming delivery within the contract time.
right to die The right of a terminally ill person to make a decision to end his or her life by assisted suicide. Assisted suicide takes place when a physician provides a terminally ill person with the means to end his or her own life. Only a few states permit assisted suicide.
right to dispose of goods The right to dispose of goods in a good faith and commercially reasonable manner. A seller or lessor who is in possession of goods at the time the buyer or lessee breaches or repudiates a contract may in good faith resell, release, or otherwise dispose of the goods in a commercially reasonable manner and recover damages, including incidental damages, from the buyer or lessee.
right to information The right of each partner of a general partnership to demand true and full information from any other partner of all things affecting the partnership.

right to inspect The right of a buyer or lessee of goods to inspect goods that are tendered, delivered, or identified in a sales or lease contract prior to accepting or paying for them.

right to obtain specific performance The right of a buyer or lessee of goods to obtain the goods from a seller or lessor if the goods are unique.

right to participate in management A situation in which, unless otherwise agreed, each general partner of a general or limited partnership, each partner of a limited liability partnership, and each nonmanager member of a limited liability company has a right to participate in the management of the business and has an equal vote on entity matters.

right to reclaim goods The right of a seller or lessor to demand the return of goods from the buyer or lessee under specified situations.

right to recover damages for accepted nonconforming goods The right of a buyer or lessee of goods who has accepted nonconforming goods to recover damages from the breaching seller or lessor.

right to recover damages for breach of contract A seller's or lessor's right to recover damages measured as the difference between the contract price (or rent) and the market price (or rent) at the time and place the goods were to be delivered, plus incidental damages, from a buyer or lessee who repudiates the contract or wrongfully rejects tendered goods.

right to recover damages for nondelivery or repudiation The right of the buyer or lessee of goods to recover damages if a seller or lessor fails to deliver the goods or repudiates the sales or lease contract.

right to recover goods from the insolvent seller or lessor The right of a buyer or lessee who has wholly or partially paid for goods before they are received to recover the goods from a seller or lessor who becomes insolvent within 10 days after receiving the first payment; the buyer or lessee must tender the remaining purchase price or rent due under the contract.

right to recover lost profits The right of a seller to sue a defaulting buyer to recover the profit it would have made from the defaulting buyer in a situation where the seller sold the goods to a new buyer but could have produced more of an item for sale.

right to recover the purchase price or rent A seller's or lessor's right to recover the contracted-for purchase price or rent from the buyer or lessee (1) if the buyer or lessee fails to pay for accepted goods, (2) if the buyer or lessee breaches the contract and the seller or lessor cannot dispose of the goods, or (3) if the goods are damaged or lost after the risk of loss passes to the buyer or lessee.

right to reject nonconforming goods or improperly tendered goods A situation in which a buyer or lessee rejects goods that do not conform to the contract. If the goods or the seller's or lessor's tender of delivery fails to conform to the contract, the buyer or lessee may (1) reject the whole, (2) accept the whole, or (3) accept any commercial unit and reject the rest.

right to replevy (recover) goods The right of a buyer or lessee to recover goods from a seller or lessor who is wrongfully withholding the goods.

right to share in profits A situation in which, unless otherwise agreed, each partner has a right to an equal share in the partnership's profits; losses are treated similarly.

right to stop delivery of goods in transit The right of a seller or lessor to stop delivery of goods in transit if he or she learns of the buyer's or lessee's insolvency or if the buyer or lessee repudiates the contract, fails to make payment when due, or gives the seller or lessor some other right to withhold the goods.

right to sue The right of each partner of a general partnership to sue the partnership or other partners at law for breach of the partnership agreement, for nonadherence to the decisions of the partnership, or for breach of duty.

right to sue letter A letter that is issued by EEOC if it chooses not to bring an action against an employer that authorizes a complainant to sue the employer for employment discrimination.

right to withhold delivery A seller's or lessor's right to refuse to deliver goods to a buyer or lessee upon breach of a sales or lease contract by the buyer or lessee or the insolvency of the buyer or lessee.

right-to-work laws Laws enacted by some states that provide that an individual employee cannot be forced to join a union or pay union dues and fees even though a labor union has been elected by other employees.

risk of loss Under the common law of contracts, the risk of loss of goods is placed on the party who holds title to the goods; The UCC's detailed rules as to who bears the risk of loss in destination and shipment contracts.

risk of loss in a destination contract A situation in which the seller bears the risk of loss during transportation.

risk of loss in a shipment contract A situation in which the buyer bears the risk of loss during transportation.

risk–utility test A test to determine whether a product's design or warnings are defective that requires a court to consider the gravity of the danger posed by the design, the likelihood that injury will occur, the availability and cost of producing a safer alternative design, the social utility of the product, and other factors.

robbery The taking of personal property from another person by the use of fear or force.

Robinson-Patman Act A federal statute, enacted in 1930, that prohibits price discrimination in the sale of goods if certain requirements are met.

Romano-Germanic civil law system A civil law system based on a code of laws, which dates to 450 BCE, when Rome adopted the Twelve Tables, a code of laws applicable to the Romans.

royalty fee A fee paid by a franchisee to a franchisor for the continued use of the franchisor's trade name, property, and assistance, which is often computed as a percentage of the franchisee's gross sales and is paid on a regular basis.

Rule 10b-5 A rule of the Securities and Exchange Commission (SEC) that helps define the prohibitions of Section 10(b) of the Securities and Exchange Act of 1934 against deceptive and fraudulent activities in the purchase and sale of securities.

rule of four A rule that requires the votes of four justices to grant an appeal and schedule an oral argument before the U.S. Supreme Court.

rule of reason A rule that holds that only unreasonable restraints of trade violate Section 1 of the Sherman Act. The court must examine the pro- and anticompetitive effects of a challenged restraint.

rulemaking A process whereby administrative agencies adopt rules and regulations.

rules and regulations Laws adopted by administrative agencies to enforce and interpret statutes.

S corporation A corporation that has met certain requirements and has elected to be taxed as an S corporation for federal income tax purposes. An S corporation pays no federal income tax at the corporate level. The S corporation's income or loss flows to the shareholders and must be reported on the shareholders' individual income tax returns.

Safe Drinking Water Act (SDWA) A federal statute that authorizes the EPA to establish national primary drinking water standards.

sale (conveyance) The passing of title to real property from a seller to a buyer; also called a *conveyance*.

sale of goods The passing of title of goods from a seller to a buyer for a price; also called a *conveyance*.

sale on approval A type of sale in which there is no actual sale unless and until the buyer accepts the goods.

sale or return A contract in which the seller delivers goods to a buyer with the understanding that the buyer may return them if they are not used or resold within a stated or reasonable period of time.

sale proceeds The resulting assets from the sale, exchange, or disposal of collateral subject to a security agreement.

sales contract A contract for the sale of goods that is subject to Article 2 (Sales) of the Uniform Commercial Code (UCC).

same-sex marriage A marriage between two people of the same gender.

same-sex harassment Harassment in the workplace against an employee by another employee of the same sex that constitutes actionable sexual harassment.

Sarbanes-Oxley Act (SOX) A federal statute enacted by Congress to improve corporate governance, bring more transparency to securities markets, eliminate conflicts of interest that previously existed in the securities industry, promote business ethics, and impose civil and criminal penalties for violations of the act.

satisfaction The performance of an accord.

Schedule C (Profit or Loss from Business) A federal income tax form that is attached to a sole proprietor's federal personal income tax form that shows the income or loss from his or her sole proprietorship.

schedules Documents filed by a debtor upon filing a voluntary petition for bankruptcy that name secured and unsecured creditors and that describe property owned by the debtor, the debtor's income, and other financial information.
scienter (guilty mind) Knowledge that a representation is false or that it was made without sufficient knowledge of the truth. Intent to deceive.
scope of employment The scope of an agent's or employee's duties while conducting work for his or her principal or employer.
SCOR form (Form U-7) A question-and-answer disclosure form that must be completed by a company and made available to potential investors when a company sells securities pursuant to a Small Company Offering Registration (SCOR).
search warrant A warrant issued by a court that authorizes the police to search a designated place for specified contraband, articles, items, or documents. A search warrant must be based on probable cause.
SEC Regulation A+ An exemption from full registration or emerging growth company registration that allows entrepreneurs, mature startups, and midsize companies to raise equity or debt capital from the public and to publicly and electronically advertise their offerings.
SEC Regulation Crowdfunding (Regulation CF) A regulation of the Securities and Exchange Commission (SEC) that permits securities of an issuer to be sold to the public exclusively using an intermediary's internet-based funding portal or web platform.
SEC Rule 10b-5 A rule of the Securities and Exchange Commission (SEC) that helps define the prohibitions of Section 10(b) of the Securities and Exchange Act of 1934 against deceptive and fraudulent activities in the purchase and sale of securities.
SEC Rule 10b5-1 A rule of the Securities and Exchange Commission (SEC) that prohibits outsiders from trading in the security of any issuer on the basis of material nonpublic information that is obtained by a breach of duty of trust or confidence owed to the person who is the source of the information.
SEC Rule 147 A rule of the Securities and Exchange Commission (SEC) that permits an offeror to sell securities to purchasers who are residents of the state of which the issuer is a resident and in which the issuer has its principal place of business and is doing business. Offers and sales may not be made to out-of-state residents.
SEC Rule 147A A rule of the Securities and Exchange Commission (SEC) that permits an offeror to sell securities to purchasers who are residents of the state in which the issuer has its principal place of business and is doing business. The offeror does not have to be a resident of the state and may use general solicitation and advertising, including by electronic communications. Sales may not be made to out-of-state residents.
SEC Rule 504 A rule of the Securities and Exchange Commission (SEC) that exempts from registration the sale of securities not exceeding $1 million during a 12-month period. Called the *small offering exemption.*
SEC Rule 506(b) A rule of the Securities and Exchange Commission (SEC) that permits issuers to raise any amount of capital from an unlimited number of accredited investors and no more than 35 nonaccredited investors without having to register the offering with the SEC. General solicitation of or advertising of the offering to the public is not permitted.
SEC Rule 506(c) A rule of the Securities and Exchange Commission (SEC) that permits issuers to raise any amount of capital from an unlimited number of accredited investors without having to register the offering with the SEC. General solicitation and advertising of the offering to the public, including using the internet, is permitted.
secondarily liable Liability of a guarantor in which the guarantor agrees to pay the principal debtor's debt if the principal fails to pay the debt when it is due.
secondary boycott picketing A type of picketing in which a union tries to bring pressure against an employer by picketing the employer's suppliers or customers.
secondary liability Liability on a negotiable instrument that is imposed on a party only when the party primarily liable on the instrument defaults and fails to pay the instrument when due. Drawers of checks and drafts and unqualified indorsers of negotiable instruments have secondary liability on the instruments.
secondary meaning Consists of the use of ordinary words or symbols by a party to the extent that they have acquired a secondary meaning and qualify for trademark or service mark status under federal trademark law.
second-degree murder The intentional unlawful killing of a human being by another person that is not premeditated or planned in advance but involves some deliberation.
secret profit Profits that occur where an agent, a general partner, a director or an officer of a corporation, a partner in a limited liability partnership, certain members of a limited liability company, or someone else who owes a fiduciary duty to a principal makes a secret profit during the course of their employment by their principal.
Secretariat A staff of persons that administers the day-to-day operations of the United Nations. It is headed by the *secretary-general.*
secretary-general The person who heads the Secretariat of the United Nations. The secretary-general is elected by the General Assembly of the United Nations.
section of the country A division of the country that is based on the relevant geographical market; the geographical area that will feel the direct and immediate effects of a merger.
Section 1 of the Sherman Act A section of a federal statute that prohibits contracts, combinations, and conspiracies in restraint of trade.
Section 2 of the Clayton Act (Robinson-Patman Act) A section of a federal statute that prohibits price discrimination in the sale of goods if certain requirements are met.
Section 2 of the Sherman Act A section of a federal statute that prohibits monopolization and attempts or conspiracies to monopolize trade.
Section 2(a) of the Robinson-Patman Act A section of a federal statute that prohibits price discrimination in the sale of commodities of like grade and quality in sales to two or more purchasers contemporaneously in time that causes actual injury to the plaintiff.
Section 2(b) of the Robinson-Patman Act A section of a federal statute that establishes the meeting the competition defense to price discrimination.
Section 2-201(1) of the Uniform Commercial Code A section of the Uniform Commercial Code (UCC) that states that sales contracts for the sale of goods costing $500 or more must be in writing. Revised Article 2 raises this amount to $5,000.
Section 2A-201(1) of the Uniform Commercial Code A section of the Uniform Commercial Code (UCC) that states that lease contracts involving payments of $1,000 or more must be in writing. Revised Article 2A raises this amount to $20,000.
Section 3 of the Clayton Act A section of a federal statute that prohibits tying arrangements involving sales and leases of goods.
Section 4 of the Clayton Act A section of a federal statute that provides that anyone injured in his or her business or property by the defendant's violation of any federal antitrust law (except the Federal Trade Commission Act) may bring a private civil action and recover from the defendant treble damages plus reasonable costs and attorneys' fees.
Section 5 of the Federal Trade Commission Act A section of a federal statute that prohibits unfair methods of competition and unfair or deceptive acts or practices in or affecting commerce.
Section 5 of the Securities Act of 1933 A section of a federal statute that requires an issuer to register its securities with the Securities and Exchange Commission (SEC) prior to selling them to the public.
Section 7 of the Clayton Act A section of a federal statute that provides that it is unlawful for a person or business to acquire the stock or assets of another "where in any line of commerce or in any activity affecting commerce in any section of the country, the effect of such acquisition may be substantially to lessen competition, or to tend to create a monopoly."
Section 7 of the NLRA A section of a federal statute that provides that employees shall have the right to self-organize; to form, join, or assist labor organizations; to bargain collectively with employers through representatives of their own choosing; and to engage in other concerted activities in support of union organization and collective bargaining.
Section 8(a) of the NLRA A section of a federal statute that makes it an unfair labor practice for an employer to interfere with, coerce, or restrain employees from exercising their statutory right to form and join unions.
Section 8(b) of the NLRA A section of a federal statute that makes it an unfair labor practice for a labor union to interfere with, coerce, or restrain employees from exercising their statutory right to form and join unions.

Section 10A of the Securities Exchange Act of 1934 A section of a federal statute that imposes a duty on auditors to detect and report illegal acts committed by their clients.
Section 10(b) of the Securities Exchange Act of 1934 A section of a federal statute that prohibits any manipulative or deceptive practice in connection with the purchase or sale of a security.
Section 10(b) insider Parties include (1) officers, directors, and employees at all levels of a company; (2) lawyers, accountants, consultants, and agents and representatives who are hired by the company on a temporary and nonemployee basis to provide services or work to the company; and (3) others who owe a fiduciary duty to the company.
Section 11 of the Securities Act of 1933 A section of a federal statute that imposes civil liability on persons who intentionally defraud investors by making misrepresentations or omissions of material facts in the registration statement or who are negligent for not discovering the fraud.
Section 11(a) of the Securities Act of 1933 A section of a federal statute that imposes civil liability on accountants and others for (1) making misstatements or omissions of material facts in a registration statement or (2) failing to find such misstatements or omissions.
Section 12 of the Securities Act of 1933 A section of a federal statute that imposes civil liability on any person who violates the provisions of Section 5 of the act.
Section 13(d) of the Securities Exchange Act of 1934 A section of a federal statute that requires any party that acquires 5 percent or more of an equity security of a company registered with the Securities and Exchange Commission (SEC) to report the acquisition to the SEC and disclose its intentions regarding the acquisition.
Section 14(a) of the Securities Exchange Act of 1934 A section of a federal statute that gives the Securities and Exchange Commission (SEC) the authority to regulate the solicitation of proxies.
Section 14(e) of the Williams Act A section of the Williams Act that prohibits fraudulent, deceptive, and manipulative practices in connection with a tender offer.
Section 16 of the Clayton Act A section of a federal statute that permits the government or a private plaintiff to obtain an injunction against anticompetitive behavior that violates antitrust laws.
Section 16 statutory insider Any person who is an executive officer, a director, or a 10 percent shareholder of an equity security of a reporting company.
Section 16(a) of the Securities Exchange Act of 1934 A section of a federal statute that defines any person who is an executive officer, a director, or a 10 percent shareholder of an equity security of a reporting company as a statutory insider for Section 16 purposes.
Section 16(b) of the Securities Exchange Act of 1934 A section of a federal statute that requires that any profits made by a statutory insider on transactions involving *short-swing profits* belong to the corporation.
Section 18(a) of the Securities Exchange Act of 1934 A section of a federal statute that imposes civil liability on any person who makes false or misleading statements in any application, report, or document filed with the SEC.
Section 24 of the Securities Act of 1933 A section of a federal statute that imposes criminal liability on any person who willfully violates the Securities Act of 1933 or the rules or regulations adopted thereunder.
Section 32 of the Securities Exchange Act of 1934 A section of a federal statute that imposes criminal liability on any person who willfully violates the Securities Exchange Act of 1934 or the rules or regulations adopted thereunder, or who willfully and knowingly makes or causes to be made any false or misleading statement in any application, report, or other document required to be filed with the Securities and Exchange Commission (SEC) pursuant to the act or any rule or regulation adopted thereunder.
Section 43 of the Lanham Act A section of a federal statute that allows a competitor to sue another competitor for engaging in unfair competition, including false advertising and misleading labeling.
Section 101 of the Uniform Securities Act A section of a model act that makes it a criminal offense for accountants and others to willfully falsify financial statements and other reports.
Section 406 of the Sarbanes-Oxley Act A section of a federal statute that requires a public company to disclose whether it has adopted a *code of ethics* for senior financial officers, including its principal financial officer and principal accounting officer.
Section 552 of the *Restatement (Second) of Torts* A rule that says that an accountant is liable only for negligence to third parties who are *members of a limited class of intended users* of the client's financial statements.
Section 1981 of the Civil Rights Act of 1866 A section of a federal statute enacted after the Civil War that says all persons "have the same right . . . to make and enforce contracts . . . as is enjoyed by white persons." It prohibits racial and color discrimination.
secured credit Credit that requires security (collateral) to secure payment of the loan.
secured creditor (secured party) A creditor who has a security interest in collateral.
secured party The seller, lender, or other party who has a security interest in personal property.
secured transaction A transaction that is created when a creditor makes a loan to a debtor in exchange for the debtor's pledge of personal property as security.
Securities Act of 1933 A federal statute that primarily regulates the issuance of securities by corporations, limited partnerships, and associations.
Securities and Exchange Commission (SEC) A federal administrative agency that is empowered to administer federal securities laws. The Securities and Exchange Commission (SEC) can adopt rules and regulations to interpret and implement federal securities laws.
Securities Exchange Act of 1934 A federal statute that primarily regulates the trading in securities.
securities law Federal and state laws that regulate the issuance and trading of securities.
security (1) An interest or instrument that is common stock, preferred stock, a bond, a debenture, or a warrant; (2) an interest or instrument that is expressly mentioned in securities acts; and (3) an investment contract.
security agreement A written document signed by a debtor that creates a security interest in personal property.
Security Council A council of the United Nations that is composed of 15 member nations, five of which are permanent members and 10 of which are chosen by the members of the General Assembly, and which is responsible for maintaining international peace and security.
security interest An interest that is created when a party borrows money from a lender and pledges personal property as security for repayment of the loan; An interest in real property that arises if an owner of real property borrows money from a lender and pledges the real property as security for repayment of the loan.
security token Tokens that are issued pursuant to a security token offering (STO), which is an investment that can be sold or traded on cryptocurrency markets.
security token offering (STO) The issuance of tokenized digital securities by an issuer to investors.
self-dealing A situation that occurs when an agent, a general partner, a director or an officer of a corporation, a partner in a limited liability partnership, certain members of a limited liability company, or anyone else who owes a fiduciary duty to a principal engages in undisclosed self-dealing with their principal, such as undisclosed purchasing, selling, or leasing of property with their principal.
Self-Employment Contributions Act A federal statute that requires certain self-employed persons to contribute (pay taxes) to the Social Security fund.
self-incrimination A provision of the Fifth Amendment to the U.S. Constitution that no person shall be compelled in any criminal case to be a witness against himself or herself.
separate property Property owned by a spouse prior to marriage, as well as inheritances and gifts received by a spouse during the marriage.
sequester A process in which jurors are separated from family and others during jury deliberation.
series of forgeries or alterations A rule that stipulates that if the same wrongdoer engages in a series of forgeries or alterations on the same account, the customer must report that to the payer bank within a reasonable period of time, not exceeding 30 days from the date that the bank statement was made available to the customer.

service mark A mark that distinguishes the services of the holder from those of its competitors.
service of process The process of serving a summons on a defendant to obtain personal jurisdiction over him or her.
servient estate The real property over which an easement appurtenant is granted.
servient party A person who is subject to the influence of a dominant person who takes advantage of the servient person's mental, emotional, or physical weakness and unduly influences the servient person to enter into a contract.
settlement agreement An agreement voluntarily entered into by the parties to a lawsuit whereby they agree to settle their dispute; In a divorce proceeding, a written document signed by divorcing parties that evidences their agreement settling property rights and other issues of their divorce.
settlement conference (pretrial hearing) A hearing before a trial in order to facilitate the settlement of a case.
sex discrimination (gender discrimination) Discrimination against a person because of his or her sex.
sex-plus discrimination A form of gender discrimination in which an employer does not discriminate against a class as a whole but treats a subset of the class differently (e.g., does not discriminate against women in general, but does discriminate against married women or women with children).
sexual harassment (gender harassment) Lewd remarks, touching, intimidation, posting of indecent materials, or other verbal or physical conduct of a sexual nature that occurs on the job that creates a hostile work environment.
sexual orientation A term that refers to an individual's romantic or sexual attraction to persons of the opposite sex or gender, the same sex or gender, both sexes or more than one gender, or lack of sexual attraction to others.
sexual orientation discrimination Employment discrimination based on a person's romantic or sexual attraction to persons of the opposite sex or gender, the same sex or gender, both sexes or more than one gender, or lack of sexual attraction to others.
share exchange (stock-for-stock merger) A situation in which one corporation acquires all the shares of another corporation, and both corporations retain their separate legal existence.
shareholder Owners of a corporation who elect the board of directors and vote on fundamental changes in the corporation.
shareholder agreement An agreement that shareholders may enter into for the operation of a corporation regarding the board of directors, management of the corporation, allocating voting rights, and such.
shareholder resolution (shareholder proposal) A resolution that a shareholder who meets certain ownership requirements may submit to other shareholders for a vote. Many shareholder resolutions concern social issues.
shareholder voting agreement An agreement between two or more shareholders of a corporation that stipulates how they will vote their shares for the election of directors or other matters that require a shareholder vote.
shareholders' list A list that contains the names and addresses of the shareholders of a corporation as of the record date and the class and number of shares owned by each shareholder.
shareholders' meeting Meetings of the shareholders of a corporation that are held to elect directors, choose an independent auditor, and take other actions.
shelf registration A securities registration that permits a well-known seasoned investor (WKSI) to file a registration statement with the Securities and Exchange Commission (SEC) and issue securities pursuant to the registration for a three-year period.
shelter principle A rule that says that a holder who does not qualify as a holder in due course in his or her own right becomes a holder in due course if he or she acquires the instrument through a holder in due course.
Sherman Antitrust Act (Sherman Act) A federal statute, enacted in 1890, that makes certain restraints of trade and monopolistic acts illegal.
shipment contract A contract that requires a seller to ship the goods to the buyer via a common carrier.
shipping terms Terms in sales contracts that establish duties and assess risk of loss when goods are shipped by a common carrier such as a trucking company, a ship, or a railroad.
short-form merger A merger between a parent corporation and a subsidiary corporation that does not require the approval of the shareholders of either corporation or the approval of the board of directors of the subsidiary corporation.
short-swing profits Profits that are made by statutory insiders on trades involving equity securities of their corporation that occur within six months of each other.
sight draft (demand draft) A draft payable on sight.
signature Any name or word, mark, or symbol used in lieu of a written signature, that may be handwritten, typed, printed, stamped, or made in almost any other manner that is executed or adopted by a party to authenticate a writing.
signature liability (contract liability) A liability rule that holds that a person cannot be held contractually liable on a negotiable instrument unless his or her signature appears on the instrument.
signature requirement A requirement that a negotiable instrument must be signed by the drawer or maker. Any symbol executed or adopted by a party with a present intent to authenticate the writing qualifies as his or her signature.
signer A person who signs an instrument in the capacity of (1) a maker of notes or certificates of deposit, (2) a drawer of drafts or checks, (3) a drawee who certifies or accepts checks or drafts, (4) an indorser who indorses an instrument, (5) an agent who signs on behalf of others, or (6) an accommodation party.
sit-down strike A labor strike in which the striking employees continue to occupy the employer's premises. Such strikes are illegal because they deny the employer's statutory right to continue its operations during a strike.
Sixth Amendment An amendment to the U.S. Constitution that guarantees that a criminal defendant has the right to a public jury trial, the right to have a speedy trial, the right to examine witnesses, and other trial-related rights.
slander Oral defamation of character.
SM A symbol that designates an owner's legal claim to an unregistered mark that is associated with a service.
small business bankruptcy A bankruptcy proceeding that provides an efficient and cost-saving method for small businesses to reorganize under Chapter 11 reorganization bankruptcy.
small certificate of deposit (small CD) A certificate of deposit that is commonly under $100,000.
small claims court A court that hears civil cases involving small dollar amounts.
small company doctrine A doctrine that permits two or more small competing companies to merge without violating antitrust law if the merger would allow the merged firm to compete more effectively with a large company.
Small Company Offering Registration (SCOR) A method for small companies to sell up to $1 million of securities to the public by using a question-and-answer disclosure SCOR Form U-7.
small offering exemption An exemption from registration that permits the sale of securities not exceeding $1 million during a 12-month period.
social responsibility committee A committee of the board of directors of a corporation that oversees corporate efforts to address social and environmental concerns.
social responsibility of business A requirement that corporations and businesses act with awareness of the consequences and impact that their decisions will have on others.
Social Security A federal system that provides government benefits to covered persons and their dependents, including (1) retirement benefits, (2) survivors' benefits to family members of deceased workers, (3) disability benefits, and (4) medical and hospitalization benefits.
Social Security Administration A federal agency that administers the Social Security system.
Sociological School A school of jurisprudential thought that asserts that law is a means of achieving and advancing certain sociological goals.
Socratic method A question and answer method used by law professors in class to stimulate class discussions and debate.
sole proprietor The owner of a sole proprietorship.
sole proprietorship A form of business in which the owner is actually the business; the business is not a separate legal entity.
special bailments Bailments that involve warehouse companies, common carriers, and innkeepers.
special federal courts Federal courts that hear matters of specialized or limited jurisdiction.

special indorsement An indorsement that contains the signature of the indorser and specifies the person (indorsee) to whom the indorser intends the instrument to be payable. It creates *order paper*.
special meeting of a board of directors A meeting convened by a board of directors to consider important topics such as the issuance of new shares, merger proposals, hostile takeover attempts, and so forth.
special power of attorney (limited power of attorney) A power of attorney in which a principal confers powers on an agent to act in specified matters on the principal's behalf.
special shareholders' meeting Meetings of shareholders that may be called to consider and vote on important or emergency issues, such as a proposed merger or amending the articles of incorporation.
special warranty deed (limited warranty deed) A deed to real property that protects a buyer from defects in title that were caused by the seller. The seller is not liable for defects in title or for encumbrances that existed before the seller obtained the property.
specially manufactured goods Goods that buyers and lessees order that are to be manufactured to the buyer's or lessee's unique specifications.
specific duty standards Occupational Safety and Health Administration (OSHA) standards that address safety problems of a specific nature (e.g., a requirement for a safety guard on a particular type of equipment).
specific gift A gift of a specifically named piece of property in a will.
specific government regulation Laws that regulate specific industries (e.g., banking).
specific intent crime A crime that requires that the perpetrator intended to achieve a specific result from his or her illegal act.
specific jurisdiction (case specific jurisdiction) The jurisdiction in which a defendant can be sued because of the defendant's contacts with that jurisdiction.
specific performance A remedy that orders the breaching party to perform the acts promised in the contract. Specific performance is usually awarded in cases in which the subject matter is unique, such as in contracts involving land, heirlooms, and paintings.
specific public benefits Benefits, such as reducing the company's carbon footprint, engaging in sustainability efforts, promoting economic opportunities for low-income individuals or communities, improving human health, promoting the arts or sciences, giving a percentage of its profits to charity, and such, that are taken into consideration by directors and officers of benefit corporations when making corporate decisions.
Speedy Trial Act A federal statute that requires that a criminal defendant in a federal case be brought to trial within 70 days after indictment.
spendthrift trust A trust that is designed to prevent a beneficiary's personal creditors from reaching his or her trust interest. All control over the trust is removed from the beneficiary.
spousal support (alimony) Payments made by one divorced spouse to the other divorced spouse.
spouse–spouse privilege A privilege granted to an accused through the Fifth Amendment to the U.S. Constitution to keep his or her spouse from testifying against him or her; a spouse may testify against his or her spouse where the accused spouse is charged with harming his or her spouse.
staggered terms A situation in which a board of directors of a corporation is divided into classes that are elected to serve two or three years on the board of directors.
stakeholder interest A theory of social responsibility that says a corporation must consider the effects its actions have on persons other than its stockholders.
stale check A check that has been outstanding for more than six months.
standard fire insurance Insurance that protects a homeowner from loss caused by fire, lightning, smoke, and water damage.
Standard Oil Company of New Jersey v. United States A U.S. Supreme Court decision that found Standard Oil Company guilty of monopolizing the petroleum industry through abusive and anticompetitive practices and as a remedy broke up Standard Oil into 30 competing firms. The Supreme Court adopted the *rule of reason* standard for analyzing Section 1 of the Sherman Act antitrust cases.
standards of interpretation Rules applied by courts in defining ordinary words, technical words, specific terms, and other words used in contracts.
standby letter of credit A letter of credit whereby a bank guarantees that if a buyer does not pay for the goods purchased from a seller, then the bank will pay the seller.
standing to sue A requirement that a plaintiff have some stake in the outcome of a lawsuit in order to bring a lawsuit.
standstill agreement An agreement entered into by a target company with a tender offeror whereby the tender offeror who receives a payment of greenmail agrees to abandon its tender offer and not purchase any additional stock of the target company for an agreed-upon period of time.
stare decisis A doctrine that requires adherence to precedent. *Stare decisis* is Latin for "to stand by the decision."
state action exemption Business activities that are mandated by state law and are therefore exempt from federal antitrust laws.
state administrative agencies Administrative agencies that states create to enforce and interpret state law.
state antitrust laws State statutes that regulate anticompetitive behavior and monopoly business practices.
state constitution Constitutions that are adopted by states. State constitutions are often patterned after the U.S. Constitution, although many are more detailed.
state consumer protection laws Laws enacted by states that prohibit fraudulent, deceptive, and unfair trade practices that harm consumers.
state courts Courts established by states.
state implementation plan (SIP) A plan that must be submitted by each state that sets forth how the state plans to meet federal ambient air quality standards.
state median income For a family of any size, income for which half of the state's families of this size have incomes more than this figure and half of the state's families of this size have incomes less than this figure.
state minimum wage A minimum wage set by a state that is usually higher than the federal minimum wage.
state securities laws State laws that regulate the issuance and trading of securities; often referred to as *blue-sky laws*.
state statute Statutes enacted by state legislatures.
state supreme court The name often given to a state's highest court.
statement of dissociation A statement filed by a partnership or a partner with the appropriate state agency stating the name of the partnership and name of the partner who has dissociated from the partnership.
statement of dissolution A statement filed by a partnership or a partner with the appropriate state agency stating the name of the partnership and that the partnership has dissolved and is winding up its business.
statement of opinion (puffing) A commendation of goods, made by a seller or lessor, that does not create an express warranty.
statement of partnership authority A statement filed by a general partnership with the appropriate state agency that states the authority, or limitations on the authority, of some or all of the partners to enter into certain transactions on behalf of the partnership.
statement of policy A statement issued by an administrative agency that announces a proposed course of action that an agency intends to follow in the future.
stationary sources of air pollution Sources of air pollution such as industrial plants, oil refineries, petrochemical plants, and public utilities.
statute Written law enacted by the legislative branch of the federal and state governments that establishes certain courses of conduct that must be adhered to by covered parties.
Statute of Frauds A state statute that requires certain types of contracts to be in writing.
statute of limitations A statute that establishes the period during which a plaintiff must bring a lawsuit against a defendant.
statute of repose A statute that limits the seller's liability to a certain number of years from the date the product was first sold.
Statute of Wills A state statute that establishes the requirements for making a valid will.
statutorily defined securities Interests or instruments that are expressly defined as *securities*, including interests in oil, gas, and mineral rights; preorganization subscription agreements; and deposit receipts for foreign securities.
statutorily prescribed period of time The required statutory period during which a person must wrongfully possess another party's real property to obtain title to that property through adverse possession.

statutory exception A law that prohibits employers from refusing to hire, not promoting, or discharging at-will or term employees in violation of federal and state statutes. Employees cannot be discharged because of their race, national origin, color, gender, religion, age, or disabilities, or for being a member of other protected classes.
statutory exemptions Exemptions from antitrust laws that are expressly provided in statutes enacted by Congress.
statutory period of redemption The specified period of time during which a state allows a mortgagor to redeem real property after foreclosure on the property because of default on a loan.
statutory priority of unsecured claims A rule of bankruptcy law that stipulates the priority of unsecured claims that are to be satisfied out of the bankruptcy estate.
stock dividend Additional shares of stock distributed as a dividend.
stop-payment order An order by a drawer of a check to the payer bank not to pay or certify a check.
Stored Communications Act (SCA) A federal statute that makes it a crime for a third party to intentionally review the contents of the files of a subscriber stored by a third-party internet service provider (ISP), including records such as a subscriber's name, billing records, or IP address.
straight voting (noncumulative voting) A system of shareholder voting for the board of directors of a corporation whereby each shareholder votes the number of shares he or she owns for his or her choices from the candidates running for the board of director positions that must be filed.
strategic alliance An arrangement between two or more companies whereby they agree to ally themselves and work together to accomplish a designated objective.
strict liability Liability without fault.
strict liability crime A crime that imposes criminal liability for the commission of a prohibited act without requiring proof of intent, recklessness, or grossly negligent conduct.
strict scrutiny test A test that is applied to determine the constitutionality of classifications by the government based on a suspect class (e.g., race, national origin, religion, citizenship) or a fundamental right (e.g., voting, access to courts).
strike A cessation of work by union members in order to obtain economic benefits or to correct an unfair labor practice.
student loan Under bankruptcy law, educational loans made by or guaranteed by governmental units or nongovernmental commercial institutions such as banks, as well as funds for scholarships, benefits, or stipends granted by educational institutions.
Subchapter S Revision Act A federal statute that allows shareholders of qualifying corporations to avoid double taxation by electing S corporation status.
subcommittee A special group composed of members of a committee of the U.S. House of Representatives or the U.S. Senate.
subfranchisor An area franchisee who has been granted an area franchise for a designated geographical area and who has the authority to negotiate and sell franchises on behalf of the franchisor in that area.
sublease An arrangement in which a tenant transfers some of his or her rights under a lease to another party.
sublessee The new tenant in a sublease arrangement.
sublessor An original tenant who transfers some or all of his rights under a lease by sublease.
submission agreement An agreement entered into by parties to a dispute where there is no arbitration agreement to have their dispute arbitrated.
subsequent assignee (subassignee) A party to whom an assignee has transferred a right to receive performance under a contract.
subsequent will A will that is executed after a previous will that revokes the prior will.
subsidiary corporation A corporation that is owned by the parent corporation.
substantial performance Performance by a contracting party that deviates only slightly from complete performance; there is a *minor breach*.
substantive administrative law Law that administrative agencies enforce.
substantive due process A category of due process that requires that government statutes, ordinances, regulations, or other laws be clear on their face and not overly broad in scope.
substantive rule Government regulation that has the force of law and must be adhered to by covered persons and businesses.
substitute for money Certain forms of negotiable instruments—such as checks—serve as substitutes for money.
substituted contract A contract that contracting parties enter into that revokes and discharges an existing contract and is a substitute for the first contract.
subsurface rights (mineral rights) Rights to the earth located beneath the surface of the land.
successor trustee A trustee who replaces the grantor-trustee if the grantor becomes incapacitated or too ill to manage the trust.
suicide clause A clause in a life insurance contract that provides that if an insured commits suicide before a stipulated date, the insurance company does not have to pay the life insurance proceeds.
summons A court order directing the defendant to appear in court and answer the complaint.
superseding, or intervening, event In tort law, an event for which a defendant is not responsible. The defendant is not liable for injuries caused by the superseding or intervening event.
supervening event An alteration or a modification of a product by a party in the chain of distribution that absolves all prior sellers from strict liability.
supervening illegality The enactment of a statute, regulation, or court decision that makes the object of an offer illegal. This action terminates the offer.
supervisor For Title VII purposes, a supervisor is a person who is empowered by an employer to take tangible employment actions against a person, such as hiring, firing, promoting, demoting, reassigning, or making significant changes in employment benefits.
supplier The party in a three-party finance lease transaction that sells the goods to a lessor, who leases the goods to a lessee.
supramajority voting requirement (supermajority voting requirement) A rule established by a corporation that stipulates that more than a majority of shares (the percentage as set by corporation code or corporate document) are needed to constitute a quorum for a vote of the shareholders.
Supremacy Clause A clause of the U.S. Constitution that establishes that the U.S. Constitution and federal treaties, laws, and regulations are the supreme law of the land.
Supreme Court of the United States The highest court of the federal court system. It hears appeals from the U.S. courts of appeals and, in some instances, from special federal courts, U.S. district courts, and the highest state courts. Also called the *U.S. Supreme Court*.
surety (co-debtor, accommodation party, or co-signor) A party in a surety arrangement who promises to be liable for the payment of another person's debt. A surety is *primarily liable* on the debt, thus being equally liable on the debt with the borrower.
surety arrangement An arrangement in which a third party promises to be *primarily liable* with the borrower for the payment of the borrower's debt.
surface rights The right to occupy the land. The owner may use, enjoy, and develop the property as he or she sees fit, subject to any applicable government laws and regulations.
surviving corporation The corporation that continues to exist after a merger.
suspect class A class of individuals (e.g., *race, national origin*, and *citizenship*) that is protected by the strict scrutiny test of the Equal Protection Clause of the Fourth Amendment to the U.S. Constitution.
taking for value A requirement that says a holder must give value for a negotiable instrument in order to qualify as a holder in due course (HDC).
taking in good faith A requirement that says a holder must take the instrument in good faith in order to qualify as a holder in due course (HDC).
taking possession of the collateral A situation that occurs when a creditor takes possession of collateral when a secured loan is in default.
taking where there is no evidence of forgery, alteration, or irregularity A requirement that says a holder does not qualify as a holder in due course (HDC) if at the time the instrument was issued or negotiated by the holder it bore evidence of forgery or alteration or was otherwise so irregular or incomplete as to call attention to its authenticity.
taking without notice of defect A requirement that says a person cannot qualify as a holder in due course (HDC) if he or she has notice that the instrument is defective in certain ways.
Takings Clause A clause of the Fifth Amendment to the U.S. Constitution that provides that the government may take private property from property owners for

public use. The government must pay the owner of the property just compensation for the taking.
tangible chattel paper Chattel paper that is evidenced by a record or records consisting of information that is inscribed on a tangible medium (writing).
tangible collateral Personal property that can be touched and can be moved from one place to another that is specified as security in a security agreement.
tangible personal property All things that are movable when a security interest attaches such as goods, equipment, vehicles, inventory, furniture, computers, clothing, and jewelry.
tangible property All real property and buildings, and personal property such as goods, equipment, vehicles, farm products, furniture, computers, clothing, jewelry. animals, and minerals.
tangible writings Writings that can be physically seen, which are subject to copyright registration and protection.
target corporation A corporation that is proposed to be acquired in a tender offer situation.
tarnishment A situation that occurs when a famous mark is linked to products of inferior quality or is portrayed in an unflattering, immoral, or reprehensible context likely to evoke negative beliefs about the mark's owner.
Tax Reform Act of 1976 A federal statute that imposes criminal liability on accountants and others who prepare federal tax returns if they (1) willfully understate a client's tax liability, (2) negligently understate the tax liability, or (3) aid or assist in the preparation of a false tax return.
tax sale A government sale of property belonging to an owner of real property who fails to pay property taxes in order to raise the amount of the taxes. If the taxes remain unpaid for a statutory period of time, the government can sell the property at a tax sale to satisfy the lien.
teacher exemption An exemption from federal minimum wage and overtime pay requirements that applies to employees who have a primary duty of teaching, tutoring, instructing, or lecturing in an activity of imparting knowledge, and who do so in an educational establishment.
Telephone Consumer Protection Act (TCPA) A federal statute that curbs abusive telemarking calls, texts, and faxes.
Telephone Robocall Abuse Criminal Enforcement and Deterrence Act (TRACED Act) A federal statute that provides protections against illegal robocalls, spam calls and texts, and caller ID spoofing.
temporary alimony (rehabilitation alimony) Alimony that is ordered by the court to be paid by one divorcing spouse to the other divorcing spouse for a limited period of time.
tenancy at sufferance A tenancy created when a tenant retains possession of property after the expiration of another tenancy or a life estate without the owner's consent.
tenancy at will A tenancy created by a lease of real property that may be terminated at any time by either party.
tenancy by the entirety A form of co-ownership of real property that can be used only by married couples.
tenancy for years A tenancy for real property created when a landlord and a tenant agree on a specific duration for a lease.
tenancy in common A form of co-ownership in which the interest of a deceased tenant in common passes to the deceased tenant's estate and not to the co-tenants.
tenant (lessee) The party to whom a leasehold is transferred.
tenant in common Parties who co-own real property in a tenancy in common arrangement.
tender of delivery The obligation of a seller to transfer and deliver goods to the buyer or lessee in accordance with a sales or lease contract.
tender of performance (tender) An unconditional and absolute offer by a contracting party to perform his or her obligations under a contract.
tender offer An offer that an acquirer makes directly to a target corporation's shareholders in an effort to acquire the target corporation.
tender offeror A party who makes a tender offer.
term employee An employee who has an employment contract with an employer for a stated time.
term limited liability company A limited liability company (LLC) that has a specified term of duration.
termination of a corporation An act that occurs after the winding up of the corporation's affairs, the liquidation of its assets, and the distribution of the proceeds to the claimants.
termination of an agency by an act of the parties A situation in which the parties to an agency contract terminate their contract by mutual agreement or when a previously agreed upon event occurs.
termination of an agency by an unusual change of circumstances A situation in which an agency terminates because an unusual change in circumstances has occurred that would lead the agent to believe that the principal's original instructions should no longer be valid.
termination of an agency by impossibility of performance A situation in which an agency terminates because a situation arises that makes the fulfillment of the agency impossible.
termination of an agency by operation of law A situation in which an agency terminates because of the occurrence of legally specified events.
termination of an offer by act of the parties The termination of an offer when one party takes an action that indicates that he is not interested in forming a contract under the terms of the offer, including (1) rejection of an offer by the offeree, (2) counteroffer by the offeree, and (3) revocation of an offer by the offeror.
termination of an offer by operation of law The termination of an offer by the operation of law, including (1) the destruction of the subject matter, (2) the death or incompetency of the offeror or the offeree, (3) a supervening illegality, and (4) lapse of time of the offer.
termination statement A document filed by a secured party that ends a secured interest because the debt has been paid.
termination-at-will clause A clause in a franchise agreement that permits a franchisor to terminate a franchise without cause; these clauses are generally held to be void.
territory A geographical area assigned by a franchisor for a franchisee to serve; often the geographical territory is granted exclusively to the franchisee.
test the waters The ability of companies to communicate with institutional accredited investors to determine if there is enough interest in company's proposed initial public offering to go through with it.
testamentary capacity The requirement that a testator or testatrix be of legal age and "sound mind" when a will was executed.
testamentary trust A trust created by will; the trust comes into existence when the settlor dies.
testator (male) or testatrix (female) A person who makes a will.
testator's or testatrix's signature The signature of a person who makes a will.
text contract A contract entered into by the parties by use of text messaging.
text messaging (texting) Composing and sending electronic messages between users of mobile devices.
theft A crime that does not distinguish among and includes the crimes of robbery, burglary, and larceny.
thermal pollution Heated water or material discharged into waterways that upsets the ecological balance and decreases the oxygen content.
third-party beneficiary A third party who benefits by the performance by others of the others' contracts.
third-party lender A party from whom a buyer obtains financing to purchase goods from a seller in which the lender takes a security interest in the goods.
three-party secured transaction A transaction that occurs when a seller sells goods to a buyer who has obtained financing from a third-party lender who takes a security interest in the goods sold.
tie decision A decision in which appellate or supreme court justices reach a tie (equal) vote. The lower court's decision stands. The decision is not precedent.
tier 1 An SEC Regulation A+ offering exemption that permits an issuer to raise up to $20 million in a 12-month period.
tier 2 An SEC Regulation A+ offering exemption that permits an issuer to raise up to $50 million in a 12-month period.
time draft A draft payable at a designated future date.
time instrument An instrument that specifies a designated future date for payment of the instrument.
time is of the essence A condition used in contracts that designates that the performance of the contract by a stated time is an express condition and that there is a breach of contract if the contracting party does not perform by the stated date.
time note A note payable at a specific time.
tippee A person who receives material nonpublic information from a tipper.
tipper A person who discloses material nonpublic information to another person.
tipper-tippee liability Liability that occurs when a tipper discloses material nonpublic

information to a tippee that the tippee knows or has reason to know is inside information, and the tippee trades securities based on this information.
title Legal, tangible evidence of ownership of goods, real property, or other property.
Title I of the Americans with Disabilities Act A title of a federal statute that prohibits employment discrimination against qualified individuals with disabilities in regard to job application procedures, hiring, compensation, training, promotion, and termination.
Title I of the Landrum-Griffin Act (labor's bill of rights) Labor's "bill of rights," which gives each union member equal rights and privileges to nominate candidates for union office, vote in elections, and participate in membership meetings.
Title II of the Genetic Information Nondiscrimination Act A title of a federal statute that makes it illegal for an employer to discriminate against job applicants and employees based on genetic information (e.g., propensity to be stricken by diseases).
Title III of the Americans with Disabilities Act A title of a federal statute that prohibits discrimination on the basis of disability in places of public accommodation operated by private entities.
Title III of the Consumer Credit Protection Act A title of a federal statute that allows debtors who are subject to a writ of garnishment to retain the greater of (1) 75 percent of their weekly disposable earnings (after taxes) or (2) an amount equal to 30 hours of work paid at federal minimum wage.
Title VII of the Civil Rights Act of 1964 A title of a federal statute enacted to eliminate job discrimination based on five protected classes: *race, color, religion, sex*, and *national origin*. Also known as the *Fair Employment Practices Act*.
Title IX of the Education Amendments of 1972 (Patsy Mink Equal Opportunity in Education Act) A federal law that prohibits gender discrimination at colleges, universities, secondary schools, and elementary schools that receive federal government financial assistance.
title insurance Insurance that purchasers of real property, and lenders who make loans where real property is collateral for the loan, purchase to ensure that they will be paid for losses suffered by defects in the title to the property that occurred prior to the purchase or loan.
TM A symbol that designates an owner's legal claim to an unregistered mark that is associated with a product.
top-level domain (TLD) A domain extension at the highest level in the hierarchical domain name system of the internet.
Torrens system A method of determining title to real property in a judicial proceeding at which everyone claiming an interest in the property can appear and be heard. After the evidence is heard, the court issues a *certificate of title* to the person who is determined to be the rightful owner.
tort A wrong. There are three categories of torts: (1) intentional torts, (2) unintentional torts (negligence), and (3) strict liability.
tort of bad faith Breach of the implied covenant of good faith and fair dealing.
tort liability Liability of a person that arises by the violation of the legal doctrines of intentional tort, negligence, or strict liability.
tortious conduct An act that is a tort (wrong).
Totten trust A trust that is created when a person deposits money in a bank account in his or her own name and holds it as a trustee for the benefit of another person.
toxic air pollutants Toxic chemicals such as asbestos, mercury, vinyl chloride, benzene, beryllium, and radionuclides.
toxic substances Chemicals used by agriculture, industry, business, mining, and households that cause injury to humans, birds, animals, fish, and vegetation.
Toxic Substances Control Act (TSCA) A federal statute that authorizes the Environmental Protection Agency to regulate toxic substances.
trade acceptance (bill of exchange) A sight draft that arises when credit is extended (by a seller to a buyer) with the sale of goods. The seller is both the drawer and the payee, and the buyer is the drawee.
trade name A name under which a sole proprietor, partnership, corporation, limited liability company, or other business entity may operate a business.
trade secret A product formula, pattern, design, compilation of data, customer list, or other business secret.
trademark A distinctive mark, symbol, name, word, motto, or device that identifies the goods of a particular business.
Trademark Dilution Revision Act A federal statute that provides that a dilution plaintiff does not need to show that it has suffered actual harm to prevail in its dilution lawsuit, but instead only show that there would be the *likelihood of dilution*.
Trademark Electronic Application System (TEAS) A system that permits the electronic filing of trademark applications with the U.S. Patent and Trademark Office (PTO).
trademark infringement Unauthorized use of another's mark. The holder may recover damages and other remedies from the infringer.
traditional contract law Contract law that is based on the common law of contracts.
transfer Any passage of an instrument other than its issuance and presentment for payment.
transfer warranties Any of the following five implied warranties: (1) the transferor has good title to the instrument or is authorized to obtain payment or acceptance on behalf of one who does have good title; (2) all signatures are genuine or authorized; (3) the instrument has not been materially altered; (4) no defenses of any party are good against the transferor; and (5) the transferor has no knowledge of any insolvency proceeding against the maker, the acceptor, or the drawer of an unaccepted instrument.
transferred intent doctrine A doctrine under which the law transfers the perpetrator's intent from the target to the actual victim of the act.
treasury shares Issued shares that have been repurchased by the corporation. Treasury shares may not be voted by the corporation. Treasury shares may be resold by the corporation.
treaty An agreement between two or more nations that is formally signed by an authorized representative of each nation and ratified by each nation.
Treaty Clause A clause of the U.S. Constitution that states that the president "shall have the power . . . to make treaties, provided two-thirds of the senators present concur."
treble damages Damages that may be awarded in a successful civil antitrust lawsuit, which is an amount that is triple the amount of actual damages.
trespasser A person who is on a landowner's or tenant's real property but has no invitation, permission, or legal right to be there.
trial brief Documents submitted by the parties' attorneys to the judge that contain legal support for their side of the case.
trier of fact The jury in a jury trial; the judge where there is no jury trial.
trust A legal arrangement established when one person transfers title to property to another person to be held and used for the benefit of a third person.
trust corpus (trust res) Property and assets held in trust.
trust instrument (trust agreement) A written agreement that creates a trust.
trustee A party who holds legal title to real property where a deed of trust and note are used to obtain credit for the purchase of real property until the amount borrowed has been paid; A party who holds legal title to the trust corpus and manages the trust for the benefit of the beneficiary or beneficiaries.
trustor (owner-debtor) The owner-debtor where a deed of trust and note are used to obtain credit for the purchase of real property.
trustor (settlor) A person who creates a trust.
Truth-in-Lending Act (TILA) A federal statute that requires creditors to make certain disclosures to debtors in consumer transactions and real estate loans on the debtor's principal dwelling.
two-party secured transaction A transaction that occurs when a seller sells goods to a buyer on credit and retains a security interest in the goods.
tying arrangement A restraint of trade in which a seller refuses to sell one product to a customer unless the customer agrees to purchase a second product from the seller. Types of sales in which the seller entrusts possession of goods to a buyer on a trial basis.
U.S. Army Corps of Engineers (USACE) A federal agency that is authorized to issue permits for discharge of dredged or fill material into navigable waters and qualified wetlands in the United States.
U.S. bankruptcy courts Federal courts that decide cases that involve federal bankruptcy laws.
U.S. Citizenship and Immigration Services (USCIS) A federal agency that is part of the U.S. Department of Homeland Security and that processes immigrant visa and naturalization petitions and has other duties involving immigration.

U.S. Congress (Congress) The name of the U.S. Senate and the U.S. House of Representatives jointly.
U.S. Constitution The fundamental and supreme law of the United States of America. It was ratified by the required number of states in 1788.
U.S. Copyright Office A federal government agency with which copyrights for published and unpublished works may be registered.
U.S. Court of Appeals for the Armed Forces A federal court that decides cases involving members of the armed forces.
U.S. Court of Appeals for the Federal Circuit A court of appeals located in Washington DC, that has special appellate jurisdiction to review the decisions of the U.S. Court of Federal Claims, the U.S. Patent and Trademark Office, and the U.S. Court of International Trade.
U.S. Court of Appeals for Veterans Claims A federal court that decides cases involving veterans of the armed forces.
U.S. Court of Federal Claims A federal court that decides cases brought against the United States.
U.S. Court of International Trade A federal court that decides cases involving tariffs and international trade disputes.
U.S. courts of appeals Federal intermediate appellate courts that decide appeals from U.S. district courts, several other federal courts, and some federal administrative agencies.
U.S. Department of Agriculture (USDA) A federal cabinet-level department that is primarily responsible for regulating meat, poultry, and other food products.
U.S. Department of Homeland Security (DHS) A federal cabinet-level department that enforces laws to prevent domestic terrorist attacks and related criminal activities, reduce vulnerability to terrorist attacks, and assist in recovery in the event of a terrorist attack.
U.S. Department of Housing and Urban Development (HUD) A federal cabinet-level department that enforces the Fair Housing Act and other federal statutes and provides other government housing services.
U.S. Department of Justice (Justice Department or DOJ) A federal cabinet-level department that is responsible for the enforcement of federal laws.
U.S. Department of Labor A federal cabinet-level department that is empowered to enforce specific federal employment laws.
U.S. district courts Federal trial courts of general jurisdiction that decide cases not within the jurisdiction of specialized federal courts.
U.S. District of Columbia Circuit A federal intermediate appellate court located in Washington DC.
U.S. Foreign Intelligence Surveillance Court (FISA Court) A special federal court that hears requests from federal intelligence agencies to issue warrants to conduct physical and electronic surveillance of Americans or foreigners in the United States who are deemed a threat to national security.
U.S. Foreign Intelligence Surveillance Court of Review (FISCR) A special federal court to which the U.S. government may appeal a decision of the U.S. Foreign Intelligence Surveillance Court (FISA Court) when it denies a government application for a FISA warrant.
U.S. House of Representatives One of the two legislative bodies that make up the bicameral legislative system of the U.S. government. The number of representatives in the U.S. House of Representatives is determined according to the population of each state.
U.S. Patent and Trademark Office (PTO) A federal government agency where applications for patents and trademarks are filed and decisions regarding these applications are made.
U.S. Senate One of the two legislative bodies that make up the bicameral legislative system of the U.S. government. The U.S. Senate is composed of two senators from each state.
U.S. Supreme Court (Supreme Court of the United States) The highest court of the federal court system. It hearsappeals from the U.S. courts of appeals and, in some instances, from special federal courts, U.S. district courts, and the highest state courts.
U.S. Tax Court A federal court that decides cases involving federal tax laws.
U.S. territorial courts Federal trial courts located on Guam, the Mariana Islands, and the U.S. Virgin Islands.
U.S. Trustee A federal government official who is responsible for handling and supervising many of the administrative tasks of a bankruptcy case.
UCC Financing Statement (Form UCC1) A uniform financing statement form that is used in all states to perfect a security interest in personal property.
UCC Statute of Frauds A rule that requires all contracts for the sale of goods priced at $500 or more and lease contracts requiring payments of $1,000 or more to be in writing.
UCC statute of limitations A rule that provides that an action for breach of any written or oral sales or lease contract must commence within four years after the cause of action accrues. The parties may agree to reduce the limitations period to one year.
***ultra vires* act** An act by a corporation that is beyond its express or implied powers.
Ultramares Corporation v. Touche A famous court decision by Judge Cardozo that established the *Ultramares* doctrine for finding accountants liable to third parties.
***Ultramares* doctrine** A rule that says that an accountant is liable only for negligence to third parties who are in *privity of contract* or in a *privity-like relationship* with the accountant. This is a narrow standard for holding accountants liable to third parties for negligence.
umbrella insurance Liability insurance coverage that exceeds the basic liability insurance on individual places or possessions (e.g., home, automobile, land, etc.). An umbrella policy pays only if the basic policy limits on other liability insurance policies have been exceeded.
unanimous decision A decision of the court in which all of the justices agree as to the outcome and reasoning used to decide a case and the decision becomes precedent; A decision in a criminal trial in which the jury members unanimously find the defendant guilty or not guilty of a crime.
unaudited financial statements Financial statements of a company that have not been audited by an accountant.
unauthorized signature A signature made by a purported agent without authority from the purported principal.
unconditional A requirement that a negotiable instrument must contain either an *unconditional promise to pay* (note or CD) or an *unconditional order to pay* (draft or check).
unconditional promise or order to pay requirement A requirement that a negotiable instrument must contain either an *unconditional promise to pay* (note or CD) or an *unconditional order to pay* (draft or check).
unconscionability A doctrine contained in the Uniform Commercial Code (UCC) that permits a judge to find a sales or lease contract to be unconscionable because the contract or lease is oppressive or manifestly unfair or unjust.
unconscionable contract A contract that courts refuse to enforce in part or at all because it is so oppressive or manifestly unfair as to be unjust.
undersecured creditor A secured creditor in a bankruptcy proceeding where the value of the collateral securing the secured loan is less than the creditor's secured interest.
undisclosed agency An agency in which a contracting third party does not know of either the existence of the agency or the principal's identity.
undisclosed principal The principal in an undisclosed agency.
undue hardship A reason or cost that is so great as to excuse an employer from having to accommodate an employee's disability or religious observances, practices, or beliefs.
undue hardship in bankruptcy A bankruptcy test that stipulates that student loans cannot be discharged in any form of bankruptcy unless the nondischarge would cause an undue hardship to the debtor and his or her dependents. Whether undue hardship exists is construed strictly.
undue influence A situation in which one person takes advantage of another person's mental, emotional, or physical weakness and unduly persuades that person to enter into a contract or make a will; the persuasion by the wrongdoer must overcome the free will of the innocent party.
unduly burdening interstate commerce A concept that says states may enact laws that protect or promote the public health, safety, morals, and general welfare, as long as the laws do not unduly burden interstate commerce.
unemployment compensation Compensation that is paid by the government to workers who are temporarily unemployed.
unenforceable contract A contract in which the essential elements to create a valid contract are met but there is some legal defense to the enforcement of the contract.
unequivocal acceptance An offeree's acceptance of an offer that is clear, unambiguous, and has only one possible meaning.
unexpired lease In bankruptcy law, a lease that has not been fully performed. With the

bankruptcy court's approval, a debtor may reject unexpired leases in bankruptcy.

unfair advantage theory A theory that holds that a merger may not give the acquiring firm an unfair advantage over its competitors in finance, marketing, or expertise.

unfair labor practice A practice that occurs when an employer or a labor union interferes with, coerces, or restrains employees from exercising their statutory right to form and join labor unions.

unfair methods of competition and unfair or deceptive acts or practices Unfair methods of competition and deceptive practices used by businesses that are prohibited by Section 5 of the Federal Trade Commission Act (FTC Act), including such conduct as false and deceptive advertising, bait-and-switch operations, overly aggressive sales tactics, and the like.

unexpired lease A lease that has not been fully performed.

unfinished goods Goods subject to a sales or lease contract that are not completed.

Unified Contract Law (UCL) A statute of China that establishes contract law that provides for the formation of contracts and the enforcement of contracts, and sets forth remedies for the breach of contracts.

Uniform Arbitration Act A uniform law that many states have adopted that promotes the arbitration of disputes at the state level.

Uniform Commercial Code (UCC) A comprehensive statutory scheme that includes laws that cover aspects of commercial transactions.

Uniform Customs and Practice for Documentary Credits (UCP) A set of rules promulgated by the International Chamber of Commerce (ICC) that establishes specific terms (called Incoterms) that are used to govern international letters of credit.

Uniform Franchise Offering Circular (UFOC) A uniform disclosure document that requires a franchisor to make specific presale disclosures to prospective franchisees.

Uniform Gifts to Minors Act (UGMA) An act that establishes procedures for adults to make gifts of money and other assets to minors.

Uniform Limited Liability Company Act (ULLCA) A model act that provides comprehensive and uniform laws for the formation, operation, and dissolution of LLCs.

Uniform Limited Liability Partnership Amendments (ULLPA) Amendments to the Revised Uniform Partnership Act (RUPA) that provide for the formation, operation, and termination of limited liability partnerships.

Uniform Limited Partnership Act (ULPA) A model act that provides comprehensive and uniform laws for the formation, operation, and dissolution of limited partnerships.

Uniform Limited Partnership Act (2001) (ULPA [2001] or re-RULPA) A model act that provides comprehensive and uniform laws for the formation, operation, and dissolution of limited partnerships, and provides for the formation of a limited liability limited partnership (LLLP).

Uniform Partnership Act (UPA) A model act that provides a comprehensive law for the formation, operation, and dissolution of general partnerships.

Uniform Sales Act A uniform law that was promulgated in the United States in 1906 to govern the sales of goods.

Uniform Securities Act An act that was drafted to coordinate state securities laws with federal securities laws; it has been adopted by many states.

Uniform Simultaneous Death Act An act that provides that if people who would inherit property from each other die simultaneously, each person's property is distributed as though he or she had survived.

Uniform Trade Secrets Act A uniform law that many states have adopted that gives statutory protection to trade secrets.

Uniform Transfers to Minors Act (UTMA) An act that establishes procedures for adults to make gifts of money and other assets to minors.

Uniformed Services Employment and Reemployment Rights Act (USERRA) A federal statute that protects and grants employment benefits to persons who serve or have served in the U.S. military services (Air Force, Army, Coast Guard, Marines, and Navy), or who are or have been members of the Reserves or National Guard.

unilateral contract A contract in which the offeror's offer can be accepted only by the performance of an act by the offeree; a "promise for an act."

unilateral mistake A mistake in which only one party is mistaken about a material fact regarding the subject matter of a contract.

unilateral refusal to deal (*Colgate* doctrine) A unilateral choice by one party not to deal with another party. This does not violate Section 1 of the Sherman Act because there is not concerted action.

unilateral rescission An attempt by one party to a contract to terminate the contract without the other party's consent; unilateral rescission is not effective and constitutes a breach of the contract.

uninsured motorist coverage Automobile insurance that provides coverage to a driver and passengers who are injured by an uninsured motorist or a hit-and-run driver.

unintentional negligence (unintentional tort or negligence) The failure to do something that a reasonable person would do or doing something that a reasonable person would not do, in like or similar circumstances.

union security agreement An agreement between an employer and a union that provides some form of security for union workers, such as a union shop or an agency shop agreement.

union shop A workplace where an employee must join the union within a certain number of days after being hired.

unissued shares Authorized shares that a corporation has available to issue, including shares that the corporation has not issued and shares that were originally issued by the corporation but that have been repurchased by the corporation and not yet reissued.

unit (limited partnership unit) An ownership interest in a master limited partnership that is traded on an organized securities exchange.

unitholder A limited partner who owns an ownership unit of a master limited partnership.

United Nations (UN) An international organization created by a multilateral treaty in 1945 to promote social and economic cooperation among nations and to protect human rights.

United Nations Children's Fund (UNICEF) An agency of the United Nations whose goal is to provide humanitarian aid and assistance to children and mothers of children, primarily in developing countries.

United Nations Convention Against Corruption (UNCAC) An international treaty that requires signatory countries to adopt anti-corruption laws, to cooperate in criminal matters and assist each other in investigating and prosecuting violators, and to return proceeds from corruption.

United Nations Convention on Contracts for the International Sale of Goods (CISG) A model act for international sales contracts that provides legal rules that govern the formation, performance, and enforcement of international sales contracts entered into between businesses located in different countries that are signatories of the CISG, and to sales contracts not otherwise subject to the CISG if the parties select in their contract to be governed by the CISG.

United States–Mexico–Canada Agreement (USMCA) A treaty that removes or reduces tariffs, duties, quotas, and other trade barriers between the United States, Canada, and Mexico. The USMCA replaced the North American Free Trade Agreement (NAFTA) in 2020.

universal default rule A rule that permits all credit card companies with whom a card holder has a credit card to raise the interest on their card if the card holder is late in making a payment to any credit card company.

universal defense (real defense) A defense against payment of an instrument that can be raised against both holders and holders in due course (HDCs).

universal demand rule A rule that requires a shareholder to make a demand on the directors of a corporation to bring a legal action against a party for allegedly injuring the corporation before the shareholder can bring a derivative lawsuit (derivative action) on behalf of the corporation.

unlimited personal liability A situation in which a person is personally liable for the debts and obligations of certain business entities, such as sole proprietors of sole proprietorships, and general partners of general and limited partnerships.

unprotected speech Speech that is not protected by the First Amendment and may be forbidden by the government.

unqualified indorsement An indorsement whereby the indorser promises to pay the holder or any subsequent indorser the amount of the instrument if the maker, drawer, or acceptor defaults on it.

unqualified indorser An indorser who signs an unqualified indorsement to an instrument. This person has secondary liability on negotiable instruments.

unqualified opinion An auditor's opinion that states that the company's financial statements fairly represent the company's financial position, the results of its operations, and the change in cash flows for the period under audit, in conformity with generally accepted accounting principles (GAAPs).

unreasonable restraint of trade Restraints of trade that are found to be unreasonable violate Section 1 of the Sherman Antitrust Act.
unreasonable search and seizure A search and seizure of persons, or their houses, papers, and effects, by the government without probable cause, which violates the Fourth Amendment to the U.S. Constitution.
unregistered securities Securities that under the law were required to be registered with the Securities and Exchange Commission (SEC) before being issued but were not registered when they were sold to the public.
unsecured credit Credit that does not require any security (collateral) to protect the payment of the debt.
unsecured creditor The creditor in a credit transaction in which the debtor does not give security (collateral) to protect the payment of the debt.
usage of trade Any practice or method of dealing that is regularly observed or adhered to in a place, a vocation, a trade, a profession, or an industry.
useful A patent requirement that an invention has some practical purpose.
usurping an opportunity A situation that occurs when an agent, a general partner, a director or an officer of a corporation, a partner in a limited liability partnership, certain members of a limited liability company, and anyone else who owes a fiduciary duty to a principal personally takes (usurps) an opportunity that belongs to their principal.
usury law A law that sets an upper limit on the interest rate that can be charged on certain types of loans.
utilitarianism A theory of ethics that dictates that people must choose the action or follow the rule that provides the greatest good to society.
utility patent A patent that protects the functionality of the invention.
utility tokens (utility coins) Tokens or coins that are issued pursuant to an initial coin offering (ICO), which are then used to purchase goods or services or held for investment.
valid contract A contract that meets all the essential elements to establish a contract; a contract that is enforceable by at least one of the parties.
variance An exception to a zoning ordinance that permits a type of building or use in an area that would not otherwise be allowed there.
venue The geographical location of the state court (county) or federal court (district) that will hear a law case.
verdict A decision reached by a jury.
vertical merger A merger that integrates the operations of a supplier and a customer.
vertical restraint of trade A restraint of trade that occurs when two or more parties on different levels of distribution enter into a contract, combination, or conspiracy to restrain trade.
vesting A situation that occurs when an employee has a nonforfeitable right to receive pension benefits.
Veterans' Benefits Act of 2010 A federal statute that protects and grants employment benefits to persons who serve or have served in the U.S. military services (Air Force, Army, Coast Guard, Marines, and Navy), or who are or have been members of the Reserves or National Guard.
veto power The power of each of the five permanent members of the Security Council of the United Nations to prevent the adoption of any substantive resolution of the United Nations.
vicarious liability Liability without fault that occurs when a principal is liable for an agent's tortious conduct because of the employment contract between the principal and agent, not because the principal was personally at fault.
violation A crime that is neither a felony nor a misdemeanor, which is usually punishable by a fine.
violent strike A labor strike in which the striking employees cause substantial damage to property of the employer or a third party. Violent strikes are illegal.
virgule A slash mark (/). If an instrument is payable to two or more payees or indorsees by using a slash mark (/)—called a virgule—to separate their names, then the instrument is *payable in the alternative*—that is, the instrument is treated as if the / is an "or." In such case, either person may individually negotiate the instrument.
Visa Waiver Program (VWP) A program that allows citizens or nationals of designated countries to come to the United States for business or travel without a visa for stays of not more than 90 days.
visitation rights Rights of a noncustodial parent to visit his or her child for limited periods of time.
void contract A contract that has no legal effect; a nullity.
void leasehold interest An invalid leasehold interest. In a case in which a lessee leases goods from a thief who has stolen them, the lessee does not acquire any leasehold interest in the goods. The lessee has a *void leasehold interest*, and the real owner can reclaim the goods from the lessee.
void title An invalid title. In a case in which a buyer purchases goods from a thief who has stolen them, the purchaser does not acquire title to the goods. The buyer has *void title,* and the real owner can reclaim the goods from the purchaser.
voidable contract A contract in which one or both parties have the option to void their contractual obligations. If a contract is voided, both parties are released from their contractual obligations.
voidable leasehold interest An interest in goods that a lessee acquires if he leases the goods through fraud, a check that is later dishonored, or impersonation of another person. A person with a voidable leasehold interest in goods can transfer a valid leasehold interest to a *good faith subsequent lessee*.
voidable title A title to goods that a purchaser acquires if he acquires the goods through fraud, a check that is later dishonored, or impersonation of another person. A person with voidable title to goods can transfer good title to a *good faith purchaser for value*.
voir dire A process whereby prospective jurors are asked questions by the judge and attorneys to determine whether they would be biased in their decisions.
voluntary association A requirement for the formation of a general partnership that requires that partners voluntarily agree to form the partnership to carry on as co-owners of the business.
voluntary dissolution Dissolution of a corporation that has begun business or issued shares, upon recommendation of the board of directors and a majority vote of the shares entitled to vote.
voluntary manslaughter The intentional unlawful killing of a human being by another person that is not premeditated or planned in advance but that occurs under circumstances that would cause a person to become emotionally upset. Sometimes referred to as *third-degree murder*.
voluntary petition A petition voluntarily filed by a debtor to begin a bankruptcy proceeding.
voting trust An arrangement in which the shareholders transfer their stock certificates to a trustee who is empowered to vote the shares. Legal title to these shares is held in the name of the trustee.
voting trust certificate Documents that are issued to shareholders that evidence their ownership interests in a voting trust.
waiting period The period of time from the date that a petition for divorce is filed to the date that the court grants the divorce.
warehouse receipt A document of title issued by a warehouse company stating that the bailor has title to the bailed goods.
warehouser Companies that engage in the business of storing property for compensation; also known as *warehouse company*.
warrantless arrest An arrest that is made without an arrest warrant. The arrest must be based on probable cause and have viable proof that it was not feasible to obtain an arrest warrant prior to the arrest.
warrantless search A search that is made without a search warrant. Warrantless searches are constitutional if they are based on *probable cause* and are made (1) incident to arrest, (2) where evidence is in "plain view," or (3) where it is likely that evidence will be destroyed.
warranty A seller's or lessor's express or implied assurance to a buyer or lessee that the goods sold or leased meet certain quality standards.
warranty against infringements An automatic warranty that a seller or lessor of goods who is a merchant regularly dealing in goods of the kind being sold or leased makes that warrants that the goods are delivered free of any third-party patent, trademark, or copyright claim.
warranty disclaimer A statement that negates implied warranties and sometimes express warranties if certain requirements are met.
warranty liability Liability that is imposed on transferors of instruments for breaching certain *implied warranties* when negotiating instruments. Warranty liability is imposed whether or not the transferor signed the instrument.
warranty of good title A warranty that is made by a seller of goods that warrants that the seller has valid title to the goods he or she is selling and that the transfer of title is rightful.
warranty of no interference (warranty of quiet possession) A warranty made by the lessor of goods that no person holds a claim

or an interest in the goods that will interfere with the lessee's enjoyment of his or her leasehold interest.
warranty of no security interests An automatic warranty that sellers of goods make that warrants that the goods they are selling are free from any third-party security interests, liens, or encumbrances that are unknown to the buyer.
water pollution Pollution of lakes, rivers, oceans, and other bodies of water.
web contract Contracts entered into with internet sellers, lessors, and licensors who use web addresses to sell and lease goods and services and license software and other intellectual property over the internet.
website Internet address used by persons and businesses to sell and lease goods, license software, or otherwise communicate information.
well-known seasoned investor (WKSI) An issuer whose size and presence in the market permits it to provide information in addition to that contained in a preliminary prospectus, such as forward-looking information, electronic communications, and other factual information, to investors prior to its securities being sold to the public.
wetlands Areas that are inundated or saturated by surface water or ground water and support vegetation typically adapted for life in such conditions.
whistleblower bounty program A program that allows the government to pay an informant 10 to 30 percent of money collected in a successful Securities and Exchange Commission (SEC) action against a defendant based on the information provided by the informant.
white knight merger A merger of a target company of a tender offer with a friendly party that usually leaves the target corporation and/or its management intact.
white-collar crime Crimes that are prone to being committed by businesspersons.
Wickard, Secretary of Agriculture v. Filburn U.S. Supreme Court decision that upheld a federal government statute as constitutionally regulating interstate commerce.
wildcat strike A labor strike in which the striking employee union members go on strike without proper authorization from the union. Such a strike is illegal but becomes lawful if it is quickly ratified by the union.
will A document that stipulates how a person wants his or her property distributed upon death.
willful act of monopolizing An act that is required for there to be a violation of Section 2 of the Sherman Act. Possession of monopoly power without such act does not violate Section 2.
Williams Act A federal act that amended the Securities Exchange Act of 1934 that specifically regulates tender offers.
winding up The process of liquidating the assets of corporations, general partnerships, limited liability companies, limited partnerships, limited liability partnerships, special partnerships or other business, and distributing the proceeds to satisfy claims against the business.
wire fraud The use of a telephone, smartphone, radio, television, computer, or internet communication to defraud another person.
Wiretap Act A federal statute that makes it a crime for a third party to use an electronic, mechanical, or other device to intentionally intercept, disclose, or use the contents of any oral, wire, or electronic communication of another party at the point of transmission, while in transit, and after receipt by the intended recipient.
work product immunity A law that provides that an accountant's work papers cannot be used against a client in a court action. Some states follow this rule, but the federal government does not.
Worker Adjustment and Retraining Notification Act (WARN Act or Plant Closing Act) A federal statute that requires employers with 100 or more employees to give their employees 60 days' notice before engaging in certain plant closings and layoffs.
workers' compensation Compensation paid to workers and their families when workers are injured in connection with their jobs.
workers' compensation acts Acts that compensate workers and their families if workers are injured in connection with their jobs.
workers' compensation board (workers' compensation commission) A government agency that determines the legitimacy of workers' claims for workers' compensation benefits.
workers' compensation insurance Insurance that compensates employees for work-related injuries.
work-related test A test that determines whether an agent committed an intentional tort within a work-related time or space; if so, the principal is liable for any injury caused by the agent's intentional tort.
World Bank An agency of the United Nations whose primary function is to provide money to developing countries to fund projects for humanitarian purposes and to relieve poverty.
World Trade Organization (WTO) An international organization of 153 member nations created to promote and enforce trade agreements among member countries and customs territories.
writ of attachment A prejudgment court order that permits the seizure of a debtor's property while a lawsuit is pending.
writ of certiorari An official notice that the Supreme Court will review a case.
writ of execution A post judgment court order that permits the seizure of the debtor's property that is in the possession of the debtor.
writ of garnishment A post judgment court order that permits the seizure of a debtor's property that is in the possession of third parties.
writing requirement A situation in which a contract must be in writing to be enforceable; A requirement that a will must be in writing to be valid. There are limited exceptions to this rule; A requirement that a negotiable instrument be in writing.
written confirmation rule A UCC rule that provides that if both parties to an oral sales or lease contract are merchants, the Statute of Frauds writing requirement can be satisfied if (1) one of the parties to an oral agreement sends a written confirmation of the sale or lease within a reasonable time after contracting and (2) the other merchant does not give written notice of an objection to the contract within ten days after receiving the confirmation.
written memorandum A memorandum issued by a trial court that sets forth the reasons for the judgment.
wrongful discharge The termination of an employee subject to a term employment contract by an employer without cause during the stated period of the employment contract.
wrongful dishonor A situation in which there are sufficient funds in a drawer's account to pay a properly payable check, but the bank does not pay the check.
wrongful dissociation A situation in which a general partner dissociates from a general partnership or limited partnership, a partner dissociates from a limited liability partnership, or a member dissociates from a limited liability company, without having the right to do so at that time.
wrongful dissolution A situation in which a general partner's act causes the dissolution of a general partnership or limited partnership without the partner having the right to cause dissolution at that time.
wrongful eviction (unlawful eviction) A situation that occurs when a landlord, or anyone acting with the landlord's consent, interferes with the tenant's use and enjoyment of the property. A violation of the covenant of quiet enjoyment.
wrongful possession A situation that occurs when a tenant retains possession of property after the expiration of a tenancy or a life estate without the owner's consent.
wrongful termination The termination of an agency contract, in violation of the terms of the agency contract. In this situation, the nonbreaching party may recover damages from the breaching party; A situation that occurs if a franchisor terminates a franchise agreement without just cause. The franchisee may recover damages from the franchisor.
WTO appellate body A panel of seven judges selected from World Trade Organization member nations that hears and decides appeals from decisions of the dispute settlement body.
WTO dispute settlement body A board composed of one representative from each World Trade Organization member nation that reviews panel reports.
WTO panel A body of three World Trade Organization judges that hears trade disputes between member nations and issues a panel report.
Zippo Manufacturing Company v. Zippo Dot Com, Inc. A seminal case that established rules for determining the jurisdiction of courts over parties that sell goods over the internet.
zoning Government regulation that establishes land use districts (i.e., areas are generally designated residential, commercial, or industrial); restricts the height, size, and location of buildings; and establishes aesthetic requirements or other limitations for the exterior of buildings.
zoning commission A local administrative body that formulates zoning ordinances, conducts public hearings, and makes recommendations to the city council.
zoning ordinance Local laws that are adopted by municipalities and local governments to regulate land use within their boundaries.

CASE INDEX

Cases cited or discussed are in roman type. Principal cases are in **bold type**.

SUBJECT INDEX

S